Commonly Used Notation

b	Retention or plowback ratio
C	Call option value
CF	Cash flow
D	Duration
E	Exchange rate
$E(x)$	Expected value of random variable x
F	Futures price
e	2.718, the base for the natural logarithm, used for continuous compounding
e_{it}	The firm-specific return, also called the residual return, of security i in period t
f	Forward rate of interest
g	Growth rate of dividends
H	Hedge ratio for an option, sometimes called the option's delta
i	Inflation rate
k	Market capitalization rate, the required rate of return on a firm's stock
$\ln$	Natural logarithm function
M	The market portfolio
$N(d)$	Cumulative normal function, the probability that a standard normal random variable will have value less than d
p	Probability
P	Put value
PV	Present value
P/E	Price-to-earnings multiple
r	Rate of return on a security; for fixed-income securities, r may denote the rate of interest for a particular period

r_f	The risk-free rate of interest
r_M	The rate of return on the market portfolio
ROE	Return on equity, incremental economic earnings per dollar reinvested in the firm
S_p	Reward-to-volatility ratio of a portfolio, also called Sharpe's measure; the excess expected return divided by the standard deviation
t	Time
T_p	Treynor's measure for a portfolio, excess expected return divided by beta
V	Intrinsic value of a firm, the present value of future dividends per share
X	Exercise price of an option
y	Yield to maturity
α	Rate of return beyond the value that would be forecast from the market's return and the systematic risk of the security
β	Systematic or market risk of a security
ρ_{ij}	Correlation coefficient between returns on securities i and j
σ	Standard deviation
σ^2	Variance
$Cov(r_i, r_j)$	Covariance between returns on securities i and j

With the purchase of a New Book*

You Can Access the Real Financial Data that the Experts Use!

*Access is available to purchasers of new books only. If you purchased a used book, the site ID may have expired.

This card entitles the purchaser of a new textbook to a semester of access to the Educational Version of Standard & Poor's Market Insight®, a rich online resource featuring hundreds of the most often researched companies in the Market Insight database.

For 1,000 companies, this website provides you:

- Access to six years' worth of fundamental financial data from the renowned Standard & Poor's COMPUSTAT® database
- 12 Excel Analytics Reports, including balance sheets, income statements, ratio reports and cash flow statements; adjusted prices reports, and profitability; forecasted values and monthly valuation data reports
- Access to Financial Highlights Reports including key ratios
- S & P Stock Reports that offer fundamental, quantitative and technical analysis
- EDGAR reports updated throughout the day
- Industry Surveys, written by S & P's Equity analysts
- News feeds (updated hourly) for companies and industries.

See other side for your unique site ID access code.

Welcome to the Educational Version of Market Insight!

www.mhhe.com/edumarketinsight

Check out your textbook's website for details on how this special offer enhances the value of your purchase!

1. To get started, use your web browser to go to **www.mhhe.com/edumarketinsight**

2. Enter your site ID exactly as it appears below.

3. You may be prompted to enter the site ID for future use—please keep this card.

Your site ID is:

ap178381

STANDARD &POOR'S

ISBN	**978-0-07-724605-1**
MHID	**0-07-724605-5**

McGraw-Hill Irwin

*If you purchased a used book, this site ID may have expired.

Essentials *of* Investments

The McGraw-Hill/Irwin Series in Finance, Insurance, and Real Estate

Stephen A. Ross
Franco Modigliani Professor of Finance
and Economics
Sloan School of Management
Massachusetts Institute of Technology
Consulting Editor

FINANCIAL MANAGEMENT

Adair
Excel Applications for Corporate Finance
First Edition
Block, Hirt, and Danielsen
Foundations of Financial Management
Thirteenth Edition
Brealey, Myers, and Allen
Principles of Corporate Finance
Ninth Edition
Brealey, Myers, and Allen
Principles of Corporate Finance, Concise
First Edition
Brealey, Myers, and Marcus
Fundamentals of Corporate Finance
Sixth Edition
Brooks
FinGame Online 5.0
Bruner
Case Studies in Finance: Managing for Corporate Value Creation
Sixth Edition
Chew
The New Corporate Finance: Where Theory Meets Practice
Third Edition
Cornett, Adair, and Nofsinger
Finance: Applications and Theory
First Edition
DeMello
Cases in Finance
Second Edition
Grinblatt (editor)
Stephen A. Ross, Mentor: Influence through Generations
Grinblatt and Titman
Financial Markets and Corporate Strategy
Second Edition
Higgins
Analysis for Financial Management
Ninth Edition
Kellison
Theory of Interest
Third Edition
Kester, Ruback, and Tufano
Case Problems in Finance
Twelfth Edition

Ross, Westerfield, and Jaffe
Corporate Finance
Ninth Edition
Ross, Westerfield, Jaffe, and Jordan
Corporate Finance: Core Principles and Applications
Second Edition
Ross, Westerfield, and Jordan
Essentials of Corporate Finance
Sixth Edition
Ross, Westerfield, and Jordan
Fundamentals of Corporate Finance
Ninth Edition
Shefrin
Behavioral Corporate Finance: Decisions that Create Value
First Edition
White
Financial Analysis with an Electronic Calculator
Sixth Edition

INVESTMENTS

Bodie, Kane, and Marcus
Essentials of Investments
Eighth Edition
Bodie, Kane, and Marcus
Investments
Eighth Edition
Hirt and Block
Fundamentals of Investment Management
Ninth Edition
Hirschey and Nofsinger
Investments: Analysis and Behavior
Second Edition
Jordan and Miller
Fundamentals of Investments: Valuation and Management
Fifth Edition

FINANCIAL INSTITUTIONS AND MARKETS

Rose and Hudgins
Bank Management and Financial Services
Eighth Edition
Rose and Marquis
Money and Capital Markets: Financial Institutions and Instruments in a Global Marketplace
Tenth Edition
Saunders and Cornett
Financial Institutions Management: A Risk Management Approach
Sixth Edition
Saunders and Cornett
Financial Markets and Institutions
Fourth Edition

INTERNATIONAL FINANCE

Eun and Resnick
International Financial Management
Fifth Edition
Kuemmerle
Case Studies in International Entrepreneurship: Managing and Financing Ventures in the Global Economy
First Edition

REAL ESTATE

Brueggeman and Fisher
Real Estate Finance and Investments
Thirteenth Edition
Ling and Archer
Real Estate Principles: A Value Approach
Third Edition

FINANCIAL PLANNING AND INSURANCE

Allen, Melone, Rosenbloom, and Mahoney
Retirement Plans: 401(k)s, IRAs, and Other Deferred Compensation Approaches
Tenth Edition
Altfest
Personal Financial Planning
First Edition
Harrington and Niehaus
Risk Management and Insurance
Second Edition
Kapoor, Dlabay, and Hughes
Focus on Personal Finance: An Active Approach to Help You Develop Successful Financial Skills
Third Edition
Kapoor, Dlabay, and Hughes
Personal Finance
Ninth Edition

Essentials *of* Investments

Eighth Edition

ZVI BODIE

Boston University

ALEX KANE

University of California, San Diego

ALAN J. MARCUS

Boston College

ISBN 978-0-07-338240-1
MHID 0-07-338240-X

Vice president and editor-in-chief: *Brent Gordon*
Publisher: *Douglas Reiner*
Executive editor: *Michele Janicek*
Director of development: *Ann Torbert*
Senior development editor: *Christina Kouvelis*
Vice president and director of marketing: *Robin J. Zwettler*
Marketing director: *Rhonda Seelinger*
Senior marketing manager: *Melissa S. Caughlin*
Vice president of editing, design, and production: *Sesha Bolisetty*
Managing editor: *Lori Koetters*
Lead production supervisor: *Michael R. McCormick*
Interior design: *BrainWorx Studio Inc.*
Senior media project manager: *Greg Bates*
Cover design: *BrainWorx Studio Inc.*
Cover image: *F. Smyth; AdStock Images*
Typeface: *10/12 Times Roman*
Compositor: *Laserwords Private Limited*
Printer: *World Color USA*

Library of Congress Cataloging-in-Publication Data

Bodie, Zvi.
     Essentials of investments/Zvi Bodie, Alex Kane, Alan J. Marcus.—8th ed.
       p. cm.
     Includes index.
     ISBN-13: 978-0-07-338240-1 (alk. paper)
     ISBN-10: 0-07-338240-X (alk. paper)
     1. Investments. I. Kane, Alex. II. Marcus, Alan J. III. Title.
HG4521.B563 2010
332.6—dc22

                                        2009020016

To our wives and eight wonderful daughters

About the Authors

Zvi Bodie
Boston University

Zvi Bodie is Professor of Finance and Economics at Boston University School of Management. He holds a PhD from the Massachusetts Institute of Technology and has served on the finance faculty at Harvard Business School and MIT's Sloan School of Management. Professor Bodie has published widely on pension finance and investment strategy in leading professional journals. His books include *Foundations of Pension Finance, Pensions in the U.S. Economy, Issues in Pension Economics,* and *Financial Aspects of the U.S. Pension System.* Professor Bodie is a member of the Pension Research Council of the Wharton School, University of Pennsylvania. His latest book is *Worry-Free Investing: A Safe Approach to Achieving Your Lifetime Financial Goals.*

Alex Kane
University of California, San Diego

Alex Kane is Professor of Finance and Economics at the Graduate School of International Relations and Pacific Studies at the University of California, San Diego. He holds a PhD from the Stern School of Business of New York University and has been Visiting Professor at the Faculty of Economics, University of Tokyo; Graduate School of Business, Harvard; Kennedy School of Government, Harvard; and Research Associate, National Bureau of Economic Research. An author of many articles in finance and management journals, Professor Kane's research is mainly in corporate finance, portfolio management, and capital markets.

Alan J. Marcus
Boston College

Alan Marcus is Professor of Finance in the Wallace E. Carroll School of Management at Boston College. He received his PhD from MIT, has been a Visiting Professor at MIT's Sloan School of Management and Athens Laboratory of Business Administration, and has served as a Research Fellow at the National Bureau of Economic Research, where he participated in both the Pension Economics and the Financial Markets and Monetary Economics Groups. Professor Marcus also spent two years at the Federal Home Loan Mortgage Corporation (Freddie Mac), where he helped to develop mortgage pricing and credit risk models. Professor Marcus has published widely in the fields of capital markets and portfolio theory. He currently serves on the Research Foundation Advisory Board of the CFA Institute.

Brief Contents

Contents

The end of 2008 capped three decades of rapid and profound change in the investment industry with a financial crisis of historic magnitude. The vast expansion of financial markets over recent decades was due in part to innovations in securitization and credit enhancement that gave birth to new trading strategies. These strategies were in turn made feasible by developments in information technology, as well as by advancements in the theory of investments.

The crisis can be traced in part to macroeconomic imbalances in global trading patterns. Huge savings in exporting countries fed low interest rates and historically high leverage in business and investment portfolios around the world. Yet the crisis was rooted in cracks of the financial system. The innovation-driven, massive capacity of the system to facilitate highly leveraged investments was coupled with, and indeed enhanced by, relaxation of regulation as well as incentive schemes that reduced transparency and masked the overvaluation of investment assets.

These developments highlight the importance of two innovations that were coincidentally emerging in the theory of investments, namely, the centrality of liquidity in asset valuation and the importance of investor behaviors that contribute to herding and at times low-quality, wildly optimistic forecasts. Broadly speaking, asset liquidity is often hard to measure—and investors may at times become overly optimistic or pessimistic—but these are just additional factors in the assessment and incorporation of overall market risk in asset valuation, a central theme of this text which we have updated in this eighth edition. Still, the idea that *security markets are nearly efficient*, meaning that most securities are usually priced appropriately given their risk and return attributes, nevertheless remains a justifiably powerful approach to security valuation. While the degree of market efficiency is and will always be a matter of debate, this first principle of valuation, specifically that in the absence of private information prices are the best guide to value, is still valid. Greater emphasis on risk analysis is the lesson we have weaved into the text.

This text also continues to emphasize *asset allocation* more than most other books. We prefer this emphasis for two important reasons. First, it corresponds to the procedure that most individuals actually follow when building an investment portfolio. Typically, you start with all of your money in a bank account, only then considering how much to invest in something riskier that might offer a higher expected return. The logical step at this point is to consider other risky asset classes, such as stock, bonds, or real estate. This is an asset allocation decision. Second, in most cases the asset allocation choice is far more important than specific security-selection decisions in determining overall investment performance. Asset allocation is the primary determinant of the risk-return profile of the investment portfolio, and so it deserves primary attention in a study of investment policy.

Our book also focuses on investment analysis, which allows us to present the practical applications of investment theory, and to convey insights of practical value. In this edition of the text, we have continued to expand a systematic collection of Excel spreadsheets that give you tools to explore concepts more deeply than was previously possible. These spreadsheets are available on the text's Web site (**www.mhhe.com/bkm**), and provide a taste of the sophisticated analytic tools available to professional investors.

In our efforts to link theory to practice, we also have attempted to make our approach consistent with that of the CFA Institute. The Institute administers an education and certification program to candidates for the title of Chartered Financial Analyst (CFA). The CFA curriculum represents the consensus of a committee of distinguished scholars and practitioners regarding the core of knowledge required by the investment professional.

This text will introduce you to the major issues of concern to all investors. It can give you the skills to conduct a sophisticated assessment of current issues and debates covered by both the popular media and more specialized finance journals. Whether you plan to become an investment professional, or simply a sophisticated individual investor, you will find these skills essential.

Zvi Bodie
Alex Kane
Alan J. Marcus

Organization of the Eighth Edition

Essentials of Investments, Eighth Edition, is intended as a textbook on investment analysis most applicable for a student's first course in investments. The chapters are written in a modular format to give instructors the flexibility to either omit certain chapters or rearrange their order. The highlights in the margins describe updates for this edition.

This part lays out the general framework for the investment process in a nontechnical manner. We discuss the major players in the financial markets and provide an overview of security types and trading mechanisms. These chapters make it possible for instructors to assign term projects analyzing securities early in the course.

Updated to reflect market developments during the credit crisis, such as the demise of the investment banks, new restrictions on short-selling, and turmoil in the markets for short-term instruments and money market funds.

Includes excerpts from the "Code of Ethics and Standards of Professional Conduct" of the CFA Institute.

This part contains the core of modern portfolio theory. For courses emphasizing security analysis, this part may be skipped without loss of continuity.

All data are updated and available on the Web through our Online Learning Center at **www.mhhe.com/bkm**. The data are used in new treatments of risk management and Value at Risk.

Introduces simple in-chapter spreadsheets that can be used to compute investment opportunity sets and the index model.

Includes greater focus on the use of factor and index models as a means to understand and measure various risk exposures.

Contains new discussion of asset price bubbles in the context of market efficiency.

Contains extensive treatment of behavioral finance and provides an introduction to technical analysis.

This is the first of three parts on security valuation.

Includes considerable new material on credit default swaps and systemic risk.

Contains spreadsheet material on duration and convexity.

This part is presented in a "top-down" manner, starting with the broad macroeconomic environment before moving to more specific analysis.

Discusses how international political developments have had major impacts on economic prospects.

Contains free cash flow equity valuation models as well as a discussion of corporate earnings management strategies.

Contains new coverage of the debate over mark-to-market accounting and its ramifications for the market crash of 2008.

This part highlights how these markets have become crucial and integral to the financial universe and are major sources of innovation.

Offers thorough introduction to option payoffs, strategies, and securities with embedded options.

Includes in-chapter spreadsheet material on the Black-Scholes model and estimation of implied volatility.

This part unifies material on active management and is ideal for a closing-semester unit on applying theory to actual portfolio management.

Fully revised development of performance evaluation methods.

Provides evidence on international correlation and the benefits of diversification.

New! Introduces hedge fund strategies, problems in evaluating hedge fund performance, the exposure of hedge funds to "black swans," and hedge fund fees.

Employs extensive spreadsheet analysis of the interaction of taxes and inflation on long-term financial strategies.

Modeled after the CFA Institute curriculum, also includes guidelines on "How to Become a Chartered Financial Analyst."

Pedagogical Features

Chapter Objectives

Each chapter begins with a summary of the chapter objectives, providing students with an overview of the concepts they should understand after reading the chapter. A chapter overview follows.

After Studying This Chapter You Should Be Able To:

- Define an investment.
- Distinguish between real assets and financial assets.
- Describe the major steps in the construction of an investment portfolio.
- Identify major participants in financial markets.
- Identify types of financial markets and recent trends in those markets.

Chapter Overview

Each chapter begins with a brief narrative to explain the concepts that will be covered in more depth. Relevant Web sites related to chapter material can be found on the book Web site at **www.mhhe.com/bkm.** These sites make it easy for students to research topics further and retrieve financial data and information.

What constitutes a satisfactory investment portfolio? Until the early 1970s, a reasonable answer would have been a Federally insured bank savings account (a risk-free asset) plus a risky portfolio of U.S. stocks. Nowadays, investors have access to a vastly wider array of assets and may contemplate complex portfolio strategies that may include foreign stocks and bonds, real estate, precious metals, and collectibles. Even more complex strategies may expected return and the risk of the entire portfolio. To guide us in forming reasonable expectations for portfolio performance, we will start this chapter with an examination of various conventions for measuring and reporting rates of return. Given these measures, we turn to the historical performance of several broadly diversified investment portfolios. In doing so, we use a risk-free portfolio of Treasury bills as a benchmark to evaluate the historical performance of diversified stock and bond

Key Terms in the Margin

Key terms are indicated in color and defined in the margin the first time the term is used. A glossary is available on the book Web site at **www.mhhe.com/bkm.**

Therefore, investors interested in larger trades face an *effective* spread greater than the nominal one since they cannot execute their entire trades at the inside price quotes.

Until 2001, when U.S. markets adopted decimal pricing, the minimum possible spread was "one tick," which on the New York Stock Exchange was $\frac{1}{8}$ until 1997 and $\frac{1}{16}$ thereafter. With decimal pricing, the spread can be far lower. The average quoted bid–ask spread on the NYSE is less than 5 cents.

stop order
Trade is not to be executed unless stock hits a price limit.

Stop orders are similar to limit orders in that the trade is not to be executed unless the stock hits a price limit. For *stop-loss orders*, the stock is to be *sold* if its price falls *below* a stipulated level. As the name suggests, the order lets the stock be sold to stop further losses from accumulating. Similarly, *stop-buy orders* specify that a stock should be bought when its price rises above a limit. These trades often accompany *short sales* (sales of securities you don't own but have borrowed from your broker) and are used to limit potential losses from the short position. Short sales are discussed in greater detail later in this chapter. Figure 3.5 organizes these types of trades in a convenient matrix.

Numbered Equations

Key equations are called out in the text and identified by equation numbers. Equations that are frequently used are also featured on the text's end sheets for convenient reference.

be necessary to provide an after-tax return equal to that of municipals. To derive this value, we set after-tax yields equal and solve for the *equivalent taxable yield* of the tax-exempt bond. This is the rate a taxable bond would need to offer in order to match the after-tax yield on the tax-free municipal.

$$r(1 - t) = r_m \qquad \text{(2.1)}$$

or

$$r = \frac{r_m}{1 - t} \qquad \text{(2.2)}$$

Thus, the equivalent taxable yield is simply the tax-free rate divided by $1 - t$. Table 2.3 presents equivalent taxable yields for several municipal yields and tax rates.

On the MARKET FRONT

MONEY MARKET FUNDS AND THE CREDIT CRISIS OF 2008

Money market funds are mutual funds that invest in the short-term debt instruments that comprise the money market. In 2008, these funds had investments totaling about $3.4 trillion. They are required to hold only short-maturity debt of the highest quality: the average maturity of their holdings must be maintained at less than three months. Their biggest investments tend to be in commercial paper, but they also hold sizable fractions of their portfolios in certificates of deposit, repurchase agreements, and Treasury securities. Because of this very conservative investment profile, money market funds typically experience extremely low price risk. Investors for their part usually acquire check-writing privileges with their funds and often use them as a close substitute for a bank account. This is feasible because the funds almost always maintain share value at $1.00 and pass along all investment earnings to their investors as interest.

Until 2008, only one fund had "broken the buck," that is, suffered losses large enough to force value per share below $1. But when Lehman Brothers filed for bankruptcy protection on September 15, 2008, several funds that had invested heavily in its commercial paper suffered large losses. The next day, Reserve Primary Fund, the oldest money market fund, broke the buck when its value per share fell to only $.97.

The realization that money market funds were at risk in the credit crisis led to a wave of investor redemptions similar to a run on a bank. Only three days after the Lehman bankruptcy, Putman's Prime Money Market Fund announced that it was liquidating due to heavy redemptions. Fearing further outflows, the U.S. Treasury announced that it would make federal insurance available to money market funds willing to pay an insurance fee. This program would thus be similar to FDIC bank insurance. With the federal insurance in place, the outflows were quelled.

However, the turmoil in Wall Street's money market funds had already spilled over into "Main Street." Fearing further investor redemptions, money market funds had become afraid to commit funds even over short periods, and their demand for commercial paper had effectively dried up. Firms that had been able to borrow at 2% interest rates in previous weeks now had to pay up to 8%, and the commercial paper market was on the edge of freezing up altogether. Firms throughout the economy had come to depend on those markets as a major source of short-term finance to fund expenditures ranging from salaries to inventories. Further breakdown in the money markets would have had an immediate crippling effect on the broad economy. Within days, the Federal government put forth its first plan to spend $700 billion to stabilize the credit markets.

On the Market Front Boxes

Current articles from financial publications such as *The Wall Street Journal* are featured as boxed readings. Each box is referred to within the narrative of the text, and its real-world relevance to the chapter material is clearly defined.

Computer networks have made it much cheaper and easier for small investors to trade for their own accounts and perform their own security analysis. What will be the likely effect on financial intermediation?

CONCEPT *check* **1.2**

Concept Checks

These self-test questions in the body of the chapter enable students to determine whether the preceding material has been understood and then reinforce understanding before students read further. Detailed Solutions to the Concept Checks are found at the end of each chapter.

EXAMPLE 1.1

Carl Icahn's proxy fight with Yahoo!

In February 2008, Microsoft offered to buy Yahoo by paying its current shareholders $31 for each of their shares, a considerable premium to its closing price of $19.18 on the day before the offer. Yahoo's management rejected that offer and a better one at $33 a share; Yahoo!'s CEO Jerry Yang held out for $37 per share, a price that Yahoo! had not reached in over two years. Billionaire investor Carl Icahn was outraged, arguing that management was protecting its own position at the expense of shareholder value. Icahn notified Yahoo! that he had been asked to "lead a proxy fight to attempt to remove the current board and to establish a new board which would attempt to negotiate a successful merger with Microsoft."[3] To that end, he had purchased approximately 59 million shares of Yahoo! and formed a 10-person slate to stand for election against the current board. Despite this challenge, Yahoo!'s management held firm in its refusal of Microsoft's offer, and with the support of the board, Yang managed to fend off both Microsoft and Icahn. In July, Icahn agreed to end the proxy fight in return for three seats on the board to be held by his allies. But the 11-person board was still dominated by current Yahoo! management. Yahoo!'s share price, which had risen to $29 a share during the Microsoft negotiations, fell back to around $21 a share. Given the difficulty that a well-known billionaire faced in defeating a determined and entrenched management, it is no wonder that proxy

Numbered Examples

Numbered and titled examples are integrated in each chapter. Using the worked-out solutions to these examples as models, students can learn how to solve specific problems step-by-step as well as gain insight into general principles by seeing how they are applied to answer concrete questions.

Excel Integration

Excel Applications

Since many courses now require students to perform analyses in spreadsheet format, Excel has been integrated throughout the book once again. It is used in examples as well as in this chapter feature which shows students how to create and manipulate spreadsheets to solve specific problems. This feature starts with an example presented in the chapter, briefly discusses how a spreadsheet can be valuable for investigating the topic, shows a sample spreadsheet, and then directs the student to the Web to work with an interactive version of the spreadsheet. The student can obtain the actual spreadsheet from the book's Web site (**www.mhhe.com/bkm**); available spreadsheets are denoted by an icon. As extra guidance, the spreadsheets include a comment feature that documents both inputs and outputs. Solutions for these exercises are located on the password-protected instructor site only, so instructors can assign these exercises either for homework or just for practice.

Excel application spreadsheets are available for the following:

Spreadsheet exhibit templates are also available for the following:

EXCEL APPLICATIONS

Performance Measures

The Excel model "Performance Measures" calculates all of the performance measures discussed in this chapter. The model available on our Web site is built to allow you to compare eight different portfolios and to rank them on all measures discussed in this chapter.

eXcel

Please visit us at
www.mhhe.com/bkm

	A	B	C	D	E	F	G	H	I	J	K
1					Performance Measurement						
2											
3											
4											
5		Average	Standard	Beta	Unsystematic	Sharpe	Treynor	Jensen	M²	T²	Appraisal
6	Fund	Return	Deviation	Coefficient	Risk	Ratio	Measure	Alpha	Measure	Measure	Ratio
7	Alpha	.2800	.2700	1.7000	.0500	0.8148	.1294	-.0180	-.0015	-.0106	-0.3600
8	Omega	.3100	.2600	1.6200	.0600	0.9615	.1543	.0232	.0235	.0143	0.3867
9	Omicron	.2200	.2100	0.8500	.0200	0.7619	.1882	.0410	-.0105	.0482	2.0500
10	Millennium	.4000	.3300	2.5000	.2700	1.0303	.1360	-.0100	.0352	-.0040	-0.0370
11	Big Value	.1500	.1300	0.9000	.0300	0.6923	.1000	-.0360	-.0223	-.0400	-1.2000
12	Momentum Watcher	.2900	.2400	1.4000	.1600	0.9583	.1643	.0340	.0229	.0243	0.2125
13	Big Potential	.1500	.1100	0.5500	.0150	0.8182	.1636	.0130	-.0009	.0236	0.8667
14	S&P Index Return	.2000	.1700	1.0000	.0000	0.8235	.1400	.0000	.0000	.0000	0.0000
15	T-Bill Return	.06		0							
16											
17	Ranking by Sharpe										
18		Return	S.D.	Beta	Unsy. Risk	Sharpe	Treynor	Jensen	M²	T²	Appraisal
19	Millennium	.4000	.3300	2.5000	.2700	1.0303	.1360	-.0100	.0352	-.0040	-0.0370
20	Omega	.3100	.2600	1.6200	.0600	0.9615	.1543	.0232	.0235	.0143	0.3867
21	Momentum Watcher	.2900	.2400	1.4000	.1600	0.9583	.1643	.0340	.0229	.0243	0.2125
22	S&P Index Return	.2000	.1700	1.0000	.0000	0.8235	.1400	.0000	.0000	.0000	0.0000
23	Big Potential	.1500	.1100	0.5500	.0150	0.8182	.1636	.0130	-.0009	.0236	0.8667
24	Alpha	.2800	.2700	1.7000	.0500	0.8148	.1294	-.0180	-.0015	-.0106	-0.3600
25	Omicron	.2200	.2100	0.8500	.0200	0.7619	.1882	.0410	-.0105	.0482	2.0500
26	Big Value	.1500	.1300	0.9000	.0300	0.6923	.1000	-.0360	-.0223	-.0400	-1.2000
27											
28	Ranking by Treynor										

End-of-Chapter Features

PROBLEM SETS

connect
Select problems are available in McGraw-Hill Connect. Please see the packaging options of the preface for more information.

Quiz
1. What are the differences between equity and fixed-income securities?
2. What is the difference between a primary asset and a derivative asset?
3. What is the difference between asset allocation and security selection?

For Problems 20–22, download the Spreadsheet of Table 5.3: Rates of return, 1926–2008, from www.mhhe.com/bkm.

20. Calculate the same subperiod means and standard deviations for small stocks as Table 5.5 of the text provides for large stocks.
   a. Have small stocks provided better reward-to-volatility ratios than large stocks?
   b. Do small stocks show a similar higher standard deviation in the earliest subperiod as Table 5.5 documents for large stocks?
21. Convert the nominal returns on both large and small stocks to real rates. Reproduce Table 5.5 using real rates instead of excess returns. Compare the results to those of Table 5.5.
22. Repeat the previous problem for small stocks and compare with the results for nominal rates.

eXcel
Please visit us at
www.mhhe.com/bkm

eXcel
Please visit us at
www.mhhe.com/bkm

eXcel

Problem Sets
We strongly believe that practice in solving problems is a critical part of learning investments, so we provide a good variety. New to this edition, we separated the questions by level of difficulty: Basic, Intermediate, and Challenge.

Excel Problems
Select end-of-chapter questions require the use of Excel. These problems are denoted with an icon. A template is available at the book Web site **www.mhhe.com/bkm.**

CFA Problems
1. A portfolio of nondividend-paying stocks earned a geometric mean return of 5.0% between January 1, 2003, and December 31, 2009. The arithmetic mean return for the same period was 6.0%. If the market value of the portfolio at the beginning of 2003 was $100,000, what was the market value of the portfolio at the end of 2009?
2. Which of the following statements about the standard deviation is/are *true*? A standard deviation:
   a. Is the square root of the variance.
   b. Is denominated in the same units as the original data.
   c. Can be a positive or a negative number.

CFA® PROBLEMS

CFA Problems
We provide several questions from recent CFA exams in applicable chapters. These questions represent the kinds of questions that professionals in the field believe are relevant to the practicing money manager. Appendix B, at the back of the book, lists each CFA question and the level and year of the CFA Exam it was included in, for easy reference when studying for the exam.

Use data from the Standard & Poor's Market Insight Database at www.mhhe.com/edumarketinsight to answer the following questions.

1. Select the Company tab and enter ticker symbol RRD. Click on the Company Profile in the Compustat Reports section. What kind of firm is Donnelley & Sons?
2. Open the S&P Stock Report for Donnelley. How many shares of the company's stock are outstanding? How many stockholders are there? Is Insider Activity rated as unfavorable, neutral, or favorable?
3. Open the most recently available Proxy Statement for Donnelley (under the EDGAR heading). Locate the section that describes the stock ownership. How many total shares are held by directors and officers? Approximately what percentage is this of the total number of shares outstanding?
4. Look at the Executive Compensation section, which lists data for executives' salaries and other benefits. How much of each executive's compensation is in the form of stock awards? How much is in the form of option awards? Compare these numbers with the executives' salaries.
5. Scroll down further in the Proxy Statement to see what other kinds of benefits executives received. What types of benefits are listed in this section?

STANDARD & POOR'S

S&P Problems
Relevant chapters contain several problems directly related to Standard & Poor's Educational Version of Market Insight. Because of our unique relationship with S&P, students have access to this remarkable database. Problems are based on market data provided by 1,000 real companies to gain better understanding of practical business situations. The site is updated daily to ensure the most current information is available.

WEB master **MUTUAL FUND REPORT**

Go to **www.morningstar.com.** In the Morningstar Tools section, click on the link for the Mutual Fund Screener. Set the criteria you desire, then click on the Show Results tab. If you get no funds that meet all of your criteria, choose the criterion that is least important to you and relax that constraint. Continue the process until you have several funds to compare.

1. Examine all of the views available in the drop-down box menu (Snapshot, Performance, Portfolio, and Nuts and Bolts) to answer the following questions:
   • Which fund has the best expense ratio?
   • Which funds have the lowest Morningstar Risk rating?

   • Which fund has the lowest turnover ratio? Which has the highest?
   • Which fund has the longest manager tenure? Which has the shortest?
   • Do you need to eliminate any of the funds from consideration due to a minimum initial investment that is higher than you are capable of making?
2. Based on what you know about the funds, which one do you think would be the best one for your investment?
3. Select up to five funds that are of the most interest to you. Click on the button that says Score These Results. Customize the criteria listed by indicating their importance to you. Examine

WebMaster Exercises
A great way to allow students to test their skills on the Internet. Each exercise consists of an activity related to practical problems and real-world scenarios.

Supplements

FOR THE INSTRUCTOR

Instructor's Resource CD
ISBN-13: 9780077245993   ISBN-10: 0077245997

This comprehensive CD contains all of the following instructor supplements. We have compiled them in electronic format for easier access and convenience. Print copies are available through your McGraw-Hill representative.

Instructor's Manual

Prepared by Tim Manuel, University of Montana, this instructional tool provides an integrated learning approach revised for this edition. Each chapter includes a Chapter Overview, Learning Objectives, and Presentation of Material that outlines and organizes the material around the PowerPoint Presentation.

Test Bank

Prepared by Edward Zajicek, Winston-Salem State University, the Test Bank contains more than 1,200 questions and includes over 300 new questions. Each question is ranked by level of difficulty (easy, medium, hard), which allows greater flexibility in creating a test. A computerized format for Windows is also available.

Computerized Test Bank

A comprehensive bank of test questions is provided within a computerized test bank powered by McGraw-Hill's flexible electronic testing program, EZ Test Online (**www.eztestonline. com**). You can select questions from multiple McGraw-Hill test banks or write your own, and then either print the test for paper distribution or give it online. This user-friendly program allows you to sort questions by format, edit existing questions or add new ones, and scramble questions for multiple versions of the same test. You can export your tests for use in WebCT, Blackboard, PageOut, and Apple's iQuiz. Sharing tests with colleagues, adjuncts, and TAs is easy! Instant scoring and feedback is provided and EZ Test's grade book is designed to easily export to your grade book.

PowerPoint Presentation System

These presentation slides, also developed by Tim Manuel, contain figures and tables from the text, key points, and summaries in a visually stimulating collection of slides. These slides follow the order of the chapters, but if you have PowerPoint software, you may customize the program to fit your lecture.

Solutions Manual

Matthew Will, University of Indianapolis, prepared detailed solutions to the end-of-chapter problems.

FOR THE STUDENT

Solutions Manual
ISBN-13: 9780077246013   ISBN-10: 0077246012

Revised by Matthew Will, University of Indianapolis, this manual provides detailed solutions to the end-of-chapter problems. There is consistency between the solution approaches in the examples featured within the text and those presented in the manual.

Student Problem Manual
ISBN-13: 9780077246020   ISBN-10: 0077246020

Prepared by Maryellen Epplin, University of Central Oklahoma, this useful supplement contains problems created to specifically relate to the concepts discussed in each chapter. Solutions are provided at the end of each chapter in the manual. Perfect for additional practice in working through problems!

ONLINE SUPPORT

Online Learning Center
www.mhhe.com/bkm

Find a wealth of information online! At this book's Web site instructors have access to teaching supports such as electronic files of the ancillary materials. Students have access to study materials created specifically for this text, and much more. All Excel spreadsheets, denoted by an icon in the text, are located at this site. Links to the following support material, as described below, are also included.

Related Web Sites

A list of suggested Web sites is provided for each chapter. To keep them up-to-date, the suggested sites as well as their links are now provided online. Each chapter contains specific sites of particular use.

Excel Templates

There are templates for selected spreadsheets featured within the text, as well as the ones featured among the Excel Applications boxes. Select end-of-chapter problems have also been designated as Excel problems, in which there is a template available for students to solve the problem and gain experience using spreadsheets. Each template can also be found at the book's Web site and is denoted by an icon.

Standard & Poor's Educational Version of Market Insight

McGraw-Hill/Irwin has partnered exclusively with Standard and Poor's to bring you the Educational Version of Market Insight. This rich online resource provides six years of financial data for 1,000 companies in the renowned COMPUSTAT ® database. S&P problems can be found at the end of relevant chapters of the text.

Wall Street Survivor

Students receive free access to this Web-based portfolio simulation with a hypothetical $100,000 brokerage account to buy and sell stocks and mutual funds. Students can use the real data found at this site in conjunction with the chapters on investments. They can also compete against students around the United States. This site is powered by Stock-Trak, the leading provider of investment simulation services to the academic community.

MCGRAW-HILL CONNECT FINANCE

Less Managing. More Teaching. Greater Learning.

McGraw-Hill *Connect Finance* is an online assignment and assessment solution that connects students with the tools and resources they'll need to achieve success.

McGraw-Hill *Connect Finance* helps prepare students for their future by enabling faster learning, more efficient studying, and higher retention of knowledge.

McGraw-Hill Connect Finance features

Connect Finance offers a number of powerful tools and features to make managing assignments easier, so faculty can spend more time teaching. With *Connect Finance,* students can engage with their coursework anytime and anywhere, making the learning process more accessible and efficient. *Connect Finance* offers you the features described below.

Simple assignment management

With *Connect Finance* creating assignments is easier than ever, so you can spend more time teaching and less time managing. The assignment management function enables you to:

- Create and deliver assignments easily with selectable end-of-chapter questions and test bank items.
- Streamline lesson planning, student progress reporting, and assignment grading to make classroom management more efficient than ever.
- Go paperless with the eBook and online submission and grading of student assignments.

Smart grading

When it comes to studying, time is precious. *Connect Finance* helps students learn more efficiently by providing feedback and practice material when they need it, where they need it. When it comes to teaching, your time also is precious. The grading function enables you to:

- Have assignments scored automatically, giving students immediate feedback on their work and side-by-side comparisons with correct answers.
- Access and review each response; manually change grades or leave comments for students to review.
- Reinforce classroom concepts with practice tests and instant quizzes.

Instructor library

The *Connect Finance* Instructor Library is your repository for additional resources to improve student engagement in and out of class. You can select and use any asset that enhances your lecture.

Student study center

The *Connect Finance* Student Study Center is the place for students to access additional resources. The Student Study Center:

- Offers students quick access to lectures, practice materials, eBooks, and more.
- Provides instant practice material and study questions, easily accessible on the go.
- Gives students access to the Personal Learning Plan described on the next page.

Personal Learning Plan

The Personal Learning Plan (PLP) connects each student to the learning resources needed for success in the course. For each chapter, students:

- Take a practice test to initiate the Personal Learning Plan.
- Immediately upon completing the practice test, see how their performance compares to the chapter objectives to be achieved within each section of the chapters.
- Receive a Personal Learning Plan that recommends specific readings from the text, supplemental study material, and practice work that will improve their understanding and mastery of each learning objective.

Student progress tracking

Connect Finance keeps instructors informed about how each student, section, and class is performing, allowing for more productive use of lecture and office hours. The progress-tracking function enables you to:

- View scored work immediately and track individual or group performance with assignment and grade reports.
- Access an instant view of student or class performance relative to learning objectives.

Lecture capture through Tegrity Campus

For an additional charge Lecture Capture offers new ways for students to focus on the in-class discussion, knowing they can revisit important topics later. This can be delivered through Connect or separately. See the next page for more details.

MCGRAW-HILL *CONNECT PLUS FINANCE*

McGraw-Hill reinvents the textbook learning experience for the modern student with *Connect Plus Finance*. A seamless integration of an eBook and *Connect Finance, Connect Plus Finance* provides all of the *Connect Finance* features plus the following:

- An integrated eBook, allowing for anytime, anywhere access to the textbook.
- Dynamic links between the problems or questions you assign to your students and the location in the eBook where that problem or question is covered.
- A powerful search function to pinpoint and connect key concepts in a snap.

In short, *Connect Finance* offers you and your students powerful tools and features that optimize your time and energies, enabling you to focus on course content, teaching, and student learning. *Connect Finance* also offers a wealth of content resources for both instructors and students. This state-of-the-art, thoroughly tested system supports you in preparing students for the world that awaits.

For more information about Connect, go to **www.mcgrawhillconnect.com** or contact your local McGraw-Hill sales representative.

TEGRITY CAMPUS: LECTURES 24/7

Tegrity Campus is a service that makes class time available 24/7 by automatically capturing every lecture in a searchable format for students to review when they study and complete assignments. With a simple one-click start-and-stop process, you capture all computer screens and corresponding audio. Students can replay any part of any class with easy-to-use browser-based viewing on a PC or Mac.

Educators know that the more students can see, hear, and experience class resources, the better they learn. In fact, studies prove it. With Tegrity Campus, students quickly recall key moments by using Tegrity Campus's unique search feature. This search helps students efficiently find what they need, when they need it, across an entire semester of class recordings. Help turn all your students' study time into learning moments immediately supported by your lecture.

To learn more about Tegrity watch a 2-minute Flash demo at **http://tegritycampus. mhhe.com**.

McGraw-Hill Customer Care Contact Information

At McGraw-Hill, we understand that getting the most from new technology can be challenging. That's why our services don't stop after you purchase our products. You can e-mail our Product Specialists 24 hours a day to get product-training online. Or you can search our knowledge bank of Frequently Asked Questions on our support website. For Customer Support, call **800-331-5094,** e-mail **hmsupport@mcgraw-hill.com,** or visit **www.mhhe. com/support**. One of our Technical Support Analysts will be able to assist you in a timely fashion.

Acknowledgments

We received help from many people as we prepared this book. An insightful group of reviewers commented on this and previous editions of this text. Their comments and suggestions improved the exposition of the material considerably. These reviewers all deserve special thanks for their contributions.

Sandro C. Andrade   *University of Miami*

Bala Arshanapalli   *Indiana University Northwest*

Randall S. Billingsley   *Virginia Polytechnic Institute and State University*

Howard Bohnen   *St. Cloud State University*

Paul Bolster   *Northeastern University*

Lyle Bowlin   *University of Northern Iowa*

Thor W. Bruce   *University of Miami*

Alyce R. Campbell   *University of Oregon*

Mark Castelino   *Rutgers University*

Greg Chaudoin   *Loyola University*

Ji Chen   *University of Colorado, Denver*

Joseph Chen   *University of California, Davis*

Mustafa Chowdhury   *Louisiana State University*

Ron Christner   *Loyola University, New Orleans*

Shane Corwin   *University of Notre Dame*

Brent Dalrymple   *University of Central Florida*

Diane Del Guercio   *University of Oregon*

David C. Distad   *University of California at Berkeley*

Gary R. Dokes   *University of San Diego*

John Earl   *University of Richmond*

Jeff Edwards   *Portland Community College*

Peter D. Ekman   *Kansas State University*

James Falter   *Franklin University*

Philip Fanara   *Howard University*

Joseph Farinella   *University of North Carolina, Wilmington*

James F. Feller   *Middle Tennessee State University*

James Forjan   *York College*

Beverly Frickel   *University of Nebraska, Kearney*

Ken Froewiss   *New York University*

Phillip Ghazanfari   *California State University, Pomona*

Eric Girard   *Siena College*

Richard A. Grayson   *University of Georgia*

Richard D. Gritta   *University of Portland*

Deborah Gunthorpe   *University of Tennessee*

Weiyu Guo   *University of Nebraska, Omaha*

Pamela Hall   *Western Washington University*

Thomas Hamilton   *St. Mary's University*

Bing Han   *Ohio State University*

Yvette Harman   *Miami University of Ohio*

Gay Hatfield   *University of Mississippi*

Larry C. Holland   *Oklahoma State University*

Harris Hordon   *New Jersey City University*

Stephen Huffman   *University of Wisconsin, Oshkosh*

Ron E. Hutchins   *Eastern Michigan University*

David Ikenberry   *University of Illinois, Urbana-Champaign*

A. Can (John) Inci   *Florida State University*

Victoria Javine   *University of Southern Alabama*

Nancy Jay   *Mercer University*

Richard Johnson   *Colorado State University*

Douglas Kahl   *University of Akron*

Richard J. Kish   *Lehigh University*

Tom Krueger   *University of Wisconsin, La Crosse*

Donald Kummer   *University of Missouri, St. Louis*

Merouane Lakehal-Ayat   *St. John Fisher College*

Reinhold P. Lamb   *University of North Florida*

Angeline Lavin   *University of South Dakota*

Hongbok Lee   *Western Illinois University*

Kartono Liano   *Mississippi State University*

Jim Locke   *Northern Virginia Community College*

John Loughlin   *St. Louis University*

David Louton   *Bryant College*

David Loy   *Illinois State University*

Christian Lundblad   *Indiana University*

Robert A. Lutz   *University of Utah*

Laurian Casson Lytle   *University of Wisconsin, Whitewater*

Leo Mahoney   *Bryant College*

Herman Manakyan   *Salisbury State University*

Steven V. Mann   *University of South Carolina*

Jeffrey A. Manzi   *Ohio University*

James Marchand   *Westminster College*

Robert J. Martel   *Bentley College*

Linda J. Martin   *Arizona State University*

Stanley A. Martin   *University of Colorado, Boulder*

Edward Miller   *University of New Orleans*

Rosemary Minyard   *Pfeiffer University*

Walter Morales   *Louisiana State University*

Mbodja Mougoue   *Wayne State University*

Majed Muhtaseb   *California State Polytechnic University*

Deborah Murphy   *University of Tennessee, Knoxville*

Mike Murray   *Winona State University*

C. R. Narayanaswamy   *Georgia Institute of Technology*

Karyn Neuhauser   *SUNY, Plattsburgh*

Mike Nugent   *SUNY Stonybrook*

Raj Padmaraj   *Bowling Green University*

Elisabeta Pana   *Illinois Wesleyan University*

John C. Park   *Frostburg State University*

Percy Poon   *University of Nevada, Las Vegas*

Robert B. Porter   *University of Florida*

Dev Prasad   *University of Massachusetts, Lowell*

Rose Prasad   *Central Michigan University*

Elias A. Raad   *Ithaca College*

Murli Rajan   *University of Scranton*

Rathin Rathinasamy   *Ball State University*

Craig Rennie   *University of Arkansas*

Cecilia Ricci   *Montclair University*

Craig Ruff   *Georgia State University*

Tom Sanders   *University of Miami*

David Schirm   *John Carroll University*

Ravi Shukla   *Syracuse University*

Allen B. Snively, Jr.   *Indiana University*

Andrew Spieler   *Hofstra University*

Edwin Stuart   *Southeastern Oklahoma State University*

George S. Swales   *Southwest Missouri State University*

Paul Swanson   *University of Cincinnati*

Bruce Swensen   *Adelphi University*

Glenn Tanner   *University of Hawaii*

John L. Teall   *Pace University*

Anne Macy Terry   *West Texas A&M University*

Donald J. Thompson   *Georgia State University*

Steven Thorley   *Brigham Young University*

James Tipton   *Baylor University*

Steven Todd   *DePaul University*

William Trainor   *Western Kentucky University*

Michael Toyne   *Northeastern State University*

Cevdet Uruk   *University of Memphis*

Joseph Vu   *DePaul University*

Jessica Wachter   *New York University*

Richard Warr   *North Carolina State University*

Joe Walker   *University of Alabama at Birmingham*

William Welch   *Florida International University*

Russel Wermers   *University of Maryland*

Andrew L. Whitaker   *North Central College*

Howard Whitney   *Franklin University*

Michael E. Williams   *University of Texas at Austin*

Michael Willoughby   *University of California, San Diego*

Tony Wingler   *University of North Carolina*

Annie Wong   *Western Connecticut State University*

David Wright   *University of Wisconsin, Parkside*

Richard H. Yanow   *North Adams State College*

Tarek Zaher   *Indiana State University*

Allan Zebedee   *San Diego State University*

Zhong-guo Zhou   *California State University, Northridge*

Thomas J. Zwirlein   *University of Colorado, Colorado Springs*

For granting us permission to include many of their examination questions in the text, we are grateful to the CFA Institute.

Much credit is also due to the development and production team of McGraw-Hill/Irwin: Michele Janicek, Executive Editor; Christina Kouvelis, Senior Developmental Editor; Lori Koetters, Managing Editor; Melissa Caughlin, Senior Marketing Manager; Jennifer Jelinski, Marketing Specialist; Michael McCormick, Lead Production Supervisor; Laurie Entringer, Designer; and Greg Bates, Lead Media Project Manager.

Finally, once again, our most important debts are to Judy, Hava, and Sheryl for their unflagging support.

Zvi Bodie
Alex Kane
Alan J. Marcus

Elements of Investments

Even a cursory glance at *The Wall Street Journal* reveals a bewildering collection of securities, markets, and financial institutions. But although it may appear so, the financial environment is not chaotic: There is rhyme and reason behind the vast array of financial instruments and the markets in which they trade.

These introductory chapters provide a bird's-eye view of the investing environment. We will give you a tour of the major types of markets in which securities trade, the trading process, and the major players in these arenas. You will see that both markets and securities have evolved to meet the changing and complex needs of different participants in the financial system.

Markets innovate and compete with each other for traders' business just as vigorously as competitors in other industries. The competition between the National Association of Securities Dealers Automatic Quotation System (NASDAQ), the New York Stock Exchange (NYSE), and a number of electronic and non-U.S. exchanges is fierce and public.

Trading practices can mean big money to investors. The explosive growth of online trading has saved them many millions of dollars in trading costs. Even more dramatically, new electronic communication networks promise to allow investors to trade directly without a broker. These advances will change the face of the investments industry, and Wall Street firms are scrambling to formulate strategies that respond to these changes.

These chapters will give you a good foundation with which to understand the basic types of securities and financial markets as well as how trading in those markets is conducted.

Investments: Background and Issues

After Studying This Chapter You Should Be Able To:

- Define an investment.
- Distinguish between real assets and financial assets.
- Describe the major steps in the construction of an investment portfolio.
- Identify major participants in financial markets.
- Identify types of financial markets and recent trends in those markets.

investment

Commitment of current resources in the expectation of deriving greater resources in the future.

An **investment** is the *current* commitment of money or other resources in the expectation of reaping *future* benefits. For example, an individual might purchase shares of stock anticipating that the future proceeds from the shares will justify both the time that her money is tied up as well as the risk of the investment. The time you will spend studying this text (not to mention its cost) also is an investment. You are forgoing either current leisure or the income you could be earning at a job in the expectation that your future career will be sufficiently enhanced to justify this commitment of time and effort. While these two investments differ in many ways, they share one key attribute that is central to all investments: You sacrifice something of value now, expecting to benefit from that sacrifice later.

This text can help you become an informed practitioner of investments. We will focus on investments in securities such as stocks, bonds, or options and futures contracts, but much of what we discuss will be useful in the analysis of any type of investment. The text will provide you with background in the organization of various securities markets, will survey the valuation and risk-management principles useful in particular markets, such as those for bonds or stocks, and will introduce you to the principles of portfolio construction.

Broadly speaking, this chapter addresses three topics that will provide a useful perspective for the material that is to come later. First, before delving into the topic of "investments," we consider the role of financial assets in the economy. We discuss the relationship between securities and the "real" assets that actually produce goods and services for consumers, and we consider why financial assets are important to the functioning of a developed economy. Given this background, we then take a first look at the types of decisions that confront investors as they assemble a portfolio of assets. These investment decisions are made in an environment where higher returns usually can be obtained only at the price of greater risk and in which it is rare to find assets that are so mispriced as to be obvious bargains. These themes—the risk-return trade-off and the efficient pricing of financial assets—are central to the investment process, so it is worth

pausing for a brief discussion of their implications as we begin the text. These implications will be fleshed out in much greater detail in later chapters.

Finally, we conclude with an introduction to the organization of security markets, the various players that participate in those markets, and a brief overview of some of the more important changes in those markets in recent years. Together, these various topics should give you a feel for who the major participants are in the securities markets as well as the setting in which they act. We close the chapter with an overview of the remainder of the text.

Related Web sites for this chapter are available at www.mhhe.com/bkm.

1.1 Real Assets versus Financial Assets

The material wealth of a society is ultimately determined by the productive capacity of its economy, that is, the goods and services its members can create. This capacity is a function of the **real assets** of the economy: the land, buildings, equipment, and knowledge that can be used to produce goods and services.

real assets

Assets used to produce goods and services.

In contrast to such real assets are **financial assets** such as stocks and bonds. Such securities are no more than sheets of paper or, more likely, computer entries and do not contribute directly to the productive capacity of the economy. Instead, these assets are the means by which individuals in well-developed economies hold their claims on real assets. Financial assets are claims to the income generated by real assets (or claims on income from the government). If we cannot own our own auto plant (a real asset), we can still buy shares in Honda or Toyota (financial assets) and, thereby, share in the income derived from the production of automobiles.

financial assets

Claims on real assets or the income generated by them.

While real assets generate net income to the economy, financial assets simply define the allocation of income or wealth among investors. Individuals can choose between consuming their wealth today or investing for the future. If they choose to invest, they may place their wealth in financial assets by purchasing various securities. When investors buy these securities from companies, the firms use the money so raised to pay for real assets, such as plant, equipment, technology, or inventory. So investors' returns on securities ultimately come from the income produced by the real assets that were financed by the issuance of those securities.

The distinction between real and financial assets is apparent when we compare the balance sheet of U.S. households, shown in Table 1.1, with the composition of national wealth in the United States, shown in Table 1.2. Household wealth includes financial assets such as bank accounts, corporate stock, or bonds. However, these securities, which are financial assets of households, are *liabilities* of the issuers of the securities. For example, a bond that you treat as an asset because it gives you a claim on interest income and repayment of principal from Toyota is a liability of Toyota, which is obligated to make these payments to you. Your asset is Toyota's liability. Therefore, when we aggregate over all balance sheets, these claims cancel out, leaving only real assets as the net wealth of the economy. National wealth consists of structures, equipment, inventories of goods, and land.[1]

[1]You might wonder why real assets held by households in Table 1.1 amount to $26,395 billion, while total real assets in the domestic economy (Table 1.2) are far larger, at $40,925 billion. One major reason is that real assets held by firms, for example, property, plant, and equipment, are included as *financial* assets of the household sector, specifically through the value of corporate equity and other stock market investments. Another reason is that equity and stock investments in Table 1.1 are measured by market value, whereas plant and equipment in Table 1.2 are valued at replacement cost.

TABLE 1.1

Balance sheet of U.S. households, 2008

Assets	$ Billion	% Total	Liabilities and Net Worth	$ Billion	% Total
Real assets					
Real estate	$22,070	31.3%	Mortgages	$10,864	15.4%
Consumer durables	4,082	5.8	Consumer credit	2,543	3.6
Other	243	0.3	Bank and other loans	247	0.4
Total real assets	$26,395	37.5%	Security credit	363	0.5
			Other	479	0.7
			Total liabilities	$14,496	20.6%
Financial assets					
Deposits	$ 7,588	10.8%			
Life insurance reserves	1,184	1.7			
Pension reserves	12,163	17.3			
Corporate equity	4,898	7.0			
Equity in noncorp. business	7,935	11.3			
Mutual fund shares	4,736	6.7			
Debt securities	3,895	5.5			
Other	1,672	2.4			
Total financial assets	44,071	62.5	Net worth	55,970	79.4
Total	$70,466	100.0%		$70,466	100.0%

Note: Column sums may differ from totals because of rounding error.

Source: *Flow of Funds Accounts of the United States,* Board of Governors of the Federal Reserve System, June 2008.

TABLE 1.2

Domestic net worth

Assets	$ Billion
Nonresidential real estate	$ 9,001
Residential real estate	22,070
Equipment and software	3,923
Inventories	1,849
Consumer durables	4,082
Total	$40,925

Note: Column sum may differ from total because of rounding error.

Source: *Flow of Funds Accounts of the United States,* Board of Governors of the Federal Reserve System, June 2008.

We will focus almost exclusively on financial assets. But you shouldn't lose sight of the fact that the successes or failures of the financial assets we choose to purchase ultimately depend on the performance of the underlying real assets.

CONCEPT *check* **1.1**

Are the following assets real or financial?
a. Patents   b. Lease obligations   c. Customer goodwill
d. A college education   e. A $5 bill

1.2 · A Taxonomy of Financial Assets

It is common to distinguish among three broad types of financial assets: debt, equity, and derivatives. **Fixed-income** or **debt securities** promise either a fixed stream of income or a stream of income that is determined according to a specified formula. For example, a corporate bond typically would promise that the bondholder will receive a fixed amount of interest each year. Other so-called floating-rate bonds promise payments that depend on current interest rates. For example, a bond may pay an interest rate that is fixed at two percentage points above the rate paid on U.S. Treasury bills. Unless the borrower is declared bankrupt, the payments on these securities are either fixed or determined by formula. For this reason, the investment performance of debt securities typically is least closely tied to the financial condition of the issuer.

fixed-income (debt) securities

Pay a specified cash flow over a specific period.

Nevertheless, debt securities come in a tremendous variety of maturities and payment provisions. At one extreme, the *money market* refers to fixed-income securities that are short term, highly marketable, and generally of very low risk. Examples of money market securities are U.S. Treasury bills or bank certificates of deposit (CDs). In contrast, the fixed-income *capital market* includes long-term securities such as Treasury bonds, as well as bonds issued by federal agencies, state and local municipalities, and corporations. These bonds range from very safe in terms of default risk (for example, Treasury securities) to relatively risky (for example, high yield or "junk" bonds). They also are designed with extremely diverse provisions regarding payments provided to the investor and protection against the bankruptcy of the issuer. We will take a first look at these securities in Chapter 2 and undertake a more detailed analysis of the fixed-income market in Part Three.

Unlike debt securities, common stock, or **equity,** in a firm represents an ownership share in the corporation. Equityholders are not promised any particular payment. They receive any dividends the firm may pay and have prorated ownership in the real assets of the firm. If the firm is successful, the value of equity will increase; if not, it will decrease. The performance of equity investments, therefore, is tied directly to the success of the firm and its real assets. For this reason, equity investments tend to be riskier than investments in debt securities. Equity markets and equity valuation are the topics of Part Four.

equity

An ownership share in a corporation.

Finally, **derivative securities** such as options and futures contracts provide payoffs that are determined by the prices of *other* assets such as bond or stock prices. For example, a call option on a share of Intel stock might turn out to be worthless if Intel's share price remains below a threshold or "exercise" price such as $20 a share, but it can be quite valuable if the stock price rises above that level.[2] Derivative securities are so named because their values derive from the prices of other assets. For example, the value of the call option will depend on the price of Intel stock. Other important derivative securities are futures and swap contracts. We will treat these in Part Five.

derivative securities

Securities providing payoffs that depend on the values of other assets.

Derivatives have become an integral part of the investment environment. One use of derivatives, perhaps the primary use, is to hedge risks or transfer them to other parties. This is done successfully every day, and the use of these securities for risk management is so commonplace that the multitrillion-dollar market in derivative assets is routinely taken for granted. Derivatives also can be used to take highly speculative positions, however. Every so often, one of these positions blows up, resulting in well-publicized losses of hundreds of millions of dollars. While these losses attract considerable attention, they do not negate the potential use of such securities as risk management tools. Derivatives will continue to play an important role in portfolio construction and the financial system. We will return to this topic later in the text.

---

[2] A call option is the right to buy a share of stock at a given exercise price on or before the option's expiration date. If the market price of Intel remains below $20 a share, the right to buy for $20 will turn out to be valueless. If the share price rises above $20 before the option expires, however, the option can be exercised to obtain the share for only $20.

In addition to these financial assets, individuals might invest directly in some real assets. For example, real estate or commodities such as precious metals or agricultural products are real assets that might form part of an investment portfolio.

1.3 | Financial Markets and The Economy

We stated earlier that real assets determine the wealth of an economy, while financial assets merely represent claims on real assets. Nevertheless, financial assets and the markets in which they trade play several crucial roles in developed economies. Financial assets allow us to make the most of the economy's real assets.

The Informational Role of Financial Markets

In a capitalist system, financial markets play a central role in the allocation of capital resources. Investors in the stock market ultimately decide which companies will live and which will die. If a corporation seems to have good prospects for future profitability, investors will bid up its stock price. The company's management will find it easy to issue new shares or borrow funds to finance research and development, build new production facilities, and expand its operations. If, on the other hand, a company's prospects seem poor, investors will bid down its stock price. The company will have to downsize and may eventually disappear.

The process by which capital is allocated through the stock market sometimes seems wasteful. Some companies can be "hot" for a short period of time, attract a large flow of investor capital, and then fail after only a few years. But that is an unavoidable aspect of economic uncertainty. It is impossible to predict with absolute precision which ventures will succeed and which will fail. The stock market encourages allocation of capital to those firms that appear *at the time* to have the best prospects. Many smart, well-trained, and well-paid professionals analyze the prospects of firms whose shares trade on the stock market. Stock prices reflect their collective judgment.

Consumption Timing

Some individuals in an economy are earning more than they currently wish to spend. Others, for example, retirees, spend more than they currently earn. How can you shift your purchasing power from high-earnings periods to low-earnings periods of life? One way is to "store" your wealth in financial assets. In high-earnings periods, you can invest your savings in financial assets such as stocks and bonds. In low-earnings periods, you can sell these assets to provide funds for your consumption needs. By so doing, you can "shift" your consumption over the course of your lifetime, thereby allocating your consumption to periods that provide the greatest satisfaction. Thus, financial markets allow individuals to separate decisions concerning current consumption from constraints that otherwise would be imposed by current earnings.

Allocation of Risk

Virtually all real assets involve some risk. When Toyota builds its auto plants, for example, it cannot know for sure what cash flows those plants will generate. Financial markets and the diverse financial instruments traded in those markets allow investors with the greatest taste for risk to bear that risk, while other, less risk-tolerant individuals can, to a greater extent, stay on the sidelines. For example, if Toyota raises the funds to build its auto plant by selling both stocks and bonds to the public, the more optimistic or risk-tolerant investors can buy shares of stock in Toyota, while the more conservative ones can buy Toyota bonds. Because the bonds promise to provide a fixed payment, the stockholders bear most of the business risk but reap potentially higher rewards. Thus, capital markets allow the risk that is inherent to all investments to be borne by the investors most willing to bear that risk.

This allocation of risk also benefits the firms that need to raise capital to finance their investments. When investors are able to select security types with the risk-return characteristics that best suit their preferences, each security can be sold for the best possible price. This facilitates the process of building the economy's stock of real assets.

Separation of Ownership and Management

Many businesses are owned and managed by the same individual. This simple organization is well suited to small businesses and, in fact, was the most common form of business organization before the Industrial Revolution. Today, however, with global markets and large-scale production, the size and capital requirements of firms have skyrocketed. For example, in 2008 General Electric listed on its balance sheet about $80 billion of property, plant, and equipment, and total assets in excess of $840 billion. Corporations of such size simply cannot exist as owner-operated firms. GE actually has about 650,000 stockholders with an ownership stake in the firm proportional to their holdings of shares.

Such a large group of individuals obviously cannot actively participate in the day-to-day management of the firm. Instead, they elect a board of directors that in turn hires and supervises the management of the firm. This structure means that the owners and managers of the firm are different parties. This gives the firm a stability that the owner-managed firm cannot achieve. For example, if some stockholders decide they no longer wish to hold shares in the firm, they can sell their shares to other investors, with no impact on the management of the firm. Thus, financial assets and the ability to buy and sell those assets in the financial markets allow for easy separation of ownership and management.

How can all of the disparate owners of the firm, ranging from large pension funds holding hundreds of thousands of shares to small investors who may hold only a single share, agree on the objectives of the firm? Again, the financial markets provide some guidance. All may agree that the firm's management should pursue strategies that enhance the value of their shares. Such policies will make all shareholders wealthier and allow them all to better pursue their personal goals, whatever those goals might be.

Do managers really attempt to maximize firm value? It is easy to see how they might be tempted to engage in activities not in the best interest of shareholders. For example, they might engage in empire building or avoid risky projects to protect their own jobs or overconsume luxuries such as corporate jets, reasoning that the cost of such perquisites is largely borne by the shareholders. These potential conflicts of interest are called **agency problems** because managers, who are hired as agents of the shareholders, may pursue their own interests instead.

Several mechanisms have evolved to mitigate potential agency problems. First, compensation plans tie the income of managers to the success of the firm. A major part of the total compensation of top executives is typically in the form of stock options, which means that the managers will not do well unless the stock price increases, benefiting shareholders. (Of course, we've learned more recently that overuse of options can create its own agency problem. Options can create an incentive for managers to manipulate information to prop up a stock price temporarily, giving them a chance to cash out before the price returns to a level reflective of the firm's true prospects. More on this shortly.) Second, while boards of directors are sometimes portrayed as defenders of top management, they can, and in recent years increasingly do, force out management teams that are underperforming. Third, outsiders such as security analysts and large institutional investors such as pension funds monitor the firm closely and make the life of poor performers at the least uncomfortable.

Finally, bad performers are subject to the threat of takeover. If the board of directors is lax in monitoring management, unhappy shareholders in principle can elect a different board. They can do this by launching a *proxy contest* in which they seek to obtain enough proxies (i.e., rights to vote the shares of other shareholders) to take control of the firm and vote in another board. However, this threat is usually minimal. Shareholders who attempt such a fight have to use their own funds, while management can defend itself using corporate coffers. Most proxy fights fail. The real takeover threat is from other firms. If one firm observes another underperforming, it can acquire the underperforming business and replace management with its own team. The stock price should rise to reflect the prospects of improved performance, which provides incentive for firms to engage in such takeover activity.

agency problems

Conflicts of interest between managers and stockholders.

EXAMPLE 1.1

*Carl Icahn's proxy
fight with Yahoo!*

In February 2008, Microsoft offered to buy Yahoo! by paying its current shareholders $31 for each of their shares, a considerable premium to its closing price of $19.18 on the day before the offer. Yahoo's management rejected that offer and a better one at $33 a share; Yahoo!'s CEO Jerry Yang held out for $37 per share, a price that Yahoo! had not reached in over two years. Billionaire investor Carl Icahn was outraged, arguing that management was protecting its own position at the expense of shareholder value. Icahn notified Yahoo! that he had been asked to "lead a proxy fight to attempt to remove the current board and to establish a new board which would attempt to negotiate a successful merger with Microsoft."[3] To that end, he had purchased approximately 59 million shares of Yahoo! and formed a 10-person slate to stand for election against the current board. Despite this challenge, Yahoo!'s management held firm in its refusal of Microsoft's offer, and with the support of the board, Yang managed to fend off both Microsoft and Icahn. In July, Icahn agreed to end the proxy fight in return for three seats on the board to be held by his allies. But the 11-person board was still dominated by current Yahoo! management. Yahoo!'s share price, which had risen to $29 a share during the Microsoft negotiations, fell back to around $21 a share. Given the difficulty that a well-known billionaire faced in defeating a determined and entrenched management, it is no wonder that proxy contests are rare. Historically, about three of four proxy fights go down to defeat.

Corporate Governance and Corporate Ethics

We've argued that securities markets can play an important role in facilitating the deployment of capital resources to their most productive uses. But for markets to effectively serve this purpose, there must be enough transparency for investors to make well-informed decisions. If firms can mislead the public about their prospects, then much can go wrong.

Despite the many mechanisms to align incentives of shareholders and managers, the three years between 2000 and 2002 were filled with a seemingly unending series of scandals that collectively signaled a crisis in corporate governance and ethics. For example, the telecom firm WorldCom overstated its profits by at least $3.8 billion by improperly classifying expenses as investments. When the true picture emerged, it resulted in the largest bankruptcy in U.S. history. The second-largest U.S. bankruptcy was Enron, which used its now notorious "special purpose entities" to move debt off its own books and similarly present a misleading picture of its financial status. Unfortunately, these firms had plenty of company. Other firms such as Rite Aid, HealthSouth, Global Crossing, and Qwest Communications also manipulated and misstated their accounts to the tune of billions of dollars. And the scandals were hardly limited to the U.S. Parmalat, the Italian dairy firm, claimed to have a $4.8 billion bank account that turned out not to exist. These episodes suggest that agency and incentive problems are far from solved.

Other scandals of that period included systematically misleading and overly optimistic research reports put out by stock market analysts (their favorable analysis was traded for the promise of future investment banking business, and analysts were commonly compensated not for their accuracy or insight, but for their role in garnering investment banking business for their firms) and allocations of initial public offerings to corporate executives as a quid pro quo for personal favors or the promise to direct future business back to the manager of the IPO.

What about the auditors who were supposed to be the watchdogs of the firms? Here too, incentives were skewed. Recent changes in business practice made the consulting businesses of these firms more lucrative than the auditing function. For example, Enron's (now defunct) auditor Arthur Andersen earned more money consulting for Enron than auditing it; given its incentive to protect its consulting profits, it should not be surprising that it, and other auditors, were overly lenient in their auditing work.

In 2002, in response to the spate of ethics scandals, Congress passed the Sarbanes-Oxley Act to tighten the rules of corporate governance. For example, the Act requires corporations

---

[3]Open letter from Carl Icahn to Board of Directors of Yahoo!, May 15, 2008, published in press release from ICAHN CAPITAL LP.

to have more independent directors, that is, more directors who are not themselves managers (or affiliated with managers). The Act also requires each CFO to personally vouch for the corporation's accounting statements, creates a new oversight board to oversee the auditing of public companies, and prohibits auditors from providing various other services to clients.

Wall Street and its regulators have learned (admittedly belatedly) that markets require trust to function. In the wake of the scandals, the value of reputation and straightforward incentive structures has increased. As one Wall Street insider put it, "This is an industry of trust; it's one of its key assets. . . . [Wall Street] is going to have to invest in getting [that trust] back . . . without that trust, there's nothing."[4] Ultimately, a firm's reputation for integrity is key to building long-term relationships with its customers and is therefore one of its most valuable assets. Indeed, the motto of the London Stock Exchange is "My word is my bond." Every so often firms forget this lesson, but in the end, investments in reputation are in fact good business practice.

1.4 The Investment Process

An investor's *portfolio* is simply his collection of investment assets. Once the portfolio is established, it is updated or "rebalanced" by selling existing securities and using the proceeds to buy new securities, by investing additional funds to increase the overall size of the portfolio, or by selling securities to decrease the size of the portfolio.

Investment assets can be categorized into broad asset classes, such as stocks, bonds, real estate, commodities, and so on. Investors make two types of decisions in constructing their portfolios. The **asset allocation** decision is the choice among these broad asset classes, while the **security selection** decision is the choice of which particular securities to hold *within* each asset class.

"Top-down" portfolio construction starts with asset allocation. For example, an individual who currently holds all of his money in a bank account would first decide what proportion of the overall portfolio ought to be moved into stocks, bonds, and so on. In this way, the broad features of the portfolio are established. For example, while the average annual return on the common stock of large firms since 1926 has been about 12% per year, the average return on U.S. Treasury bills has been less than 4%. On the other hand, stocks are far riskier, with annual returns (as measured by the Standard & Poor's 500 Index) that have ranged as low as −46% and as high as 55%. In contrast, T-bill returns are effectively risk-free: you know what interest rate you will earn when you buy the bills. Therefore, the decision to allocate your investments to the stock market or to the money market where Treasury bills are traded will have great ramifications for both the risk and the return of your portfolio. A top-down investor first makes this and other crucial asset allocation decisions before turning to the decision of the particular securities to be held in each asset class.

Security analysis involves the valuation of particular securities that might be included in the portfolio. For example, an investor might ask whether Merck or Pfizer is more attractively priced. Both bonds and stocks must be evaluated for investment attractiveness, but valuation is far more difficult for stocks because a stock's performance usually is far more sensitive to the condition of the issuing firm.

In contrast to top-down portfolio management is the "bottom-up" strategy. In this process, the portfolio is constructed from the securities that seem attractively priced without as much concern for the resultant asset allocation. Such a technique can result in unintended bets on one or another sector of the economy. For example, it might turn out that the portfolio ends up with a very heavy representation of firms in one industry, from one part of the country, or with exposure to one source of uncertainty. However, a bottom-up strategy does focus the portfolio on the assets that seem to offer the most attractive investment opportunities.

asset allocation

Allocation of an investment portfolio across broad asset classes.

security selection

Choice of specific securities within each asset class.

security analysis

Analysis of the value of securities.

---

[4]*BusinessWeek,* "How Corrupt Is Wall Street?" May 13, 2002.

1.5 Markets Are Competitive

Financial markets are highly competitive. Thousands of well-backed analysts constantly scour securities markets searching for the best buys. This competition means that we should expect to find few, if any, "free lunches," securities that are so underpriced that they represent obvious bargains. There are several implications of this no-free-lunch proposition. Let's examine two.

The Risk-Return Trade-Off

Investors invest for anticipated future returns, but those returns rarely can be predicted precisely. There will almost always be risk associated with investments. Actual or realized returns will almost always deviate from the expected return anticipated at the start of the investment period. For example, in 1931 (the worst calendar year for the market since 1926), the stock market lost 46% of its value. In 1933 (the best year), the stock market gained 55%. You can be sure that investors did not anticipate such extreme performance at the start of either of these years.

Naturally, if all else could be held equal, investors would prefer investments with the highest expected return.[5] However, the no-free-lunch rule tells us that all else cannot be held equal. If you want higher expected returns, you will have to pay a price in terms of accepting higher investment risk. If higher expected return can be achieved without bearing extra risk, there will be a rush to buy the high-return assets, with the result that their prices will be driven up. Individuals considering investing in the asset at the now-higher price will find the investment less attractive: If you buy at a higher price, your expected rate of return (that is, profit per dollar invested) is lower. The asset will be considered attractive and its price will continue to rise until its expected return is no more than commensurate with risk. At this point, investors can anticipate a "fair" return relative to the asset's risk, but no more. Similarly, if returns were independent of risk, there would be a rush to sell high-risk assets. Their prices would fall (and their expected future rates of return rise) until they eventually were attractive enough to be included again in investor portfolios. We conclude that there should be a **risk-return trade-off** in the securities markets, with higher-risk assets priced to offer higher expected returns than lower-risk assets.

risk-return trade-off

Assets with higher expected returns entail greater risk.

Of course, this discussion leaves several important questions unanswered. How should one measure the risk of an asset? What should be the quantitative trade-off between risk (properly measured) and expected return? One would think that risk would have something to do with the volatility of an asset's returns, but this guess turns out to be only partly correct. When we mix assets into diversified portfolios, we need to consider the interplay among assets and the effect of diversification on the risk of the entire portfolio. *Diversification* means that many assets are held in the portfolio so that the exposure to any particular asset is limited. The effect of diversification on portfolio risk, the implications for the proper measurement of risk, and the risk-return relationship are the topics of Part Two. These topics are the subject of what has come to be known as *modern portfolio theory*. The development of this theory brought two of its pioneers, Harry Markowitz and William Sharpe, Nobel Prizes.

Efficient Markets

Another implication of the no-free-lunch proposition is that we should rarely expect to find bargains in the security markets. We will spend all of Chapter 8 examining the theory and evidence concerning the hypothesis that financial markets process all relevant information about securities quickly and efficiently, that is, that the security price usually reflects all the information available to investors concerning the value of the security. According to this hypothesis, as new information about a security becomes available, the price of the security

---

[5]The "expected" return is not the return investors believe they necessarily will earn, or even their most likely return. It is instead the result of averaging across all possible outcomes, recognizing that some outcomes are more likely than others. It is the average rate of return across possible economic scenarios.

quickly adjusts so that at any time, the security price equals the market consensus estimate of the value of the security. If this were so, there would be neither underpriced nor overpriced securities.

One interesting implication of this "efficient market hypothesis" concerns the choice between active and passive investment-management strategies. **Passive management** calls for holding highly diversified portfolios without spending effort or other resources attempting to improve investment performance through security analysis. **Active management** is the attempt to improve performance either by identifying mispriced securities or by timing the performance of broad asset classes—for example, increasing one's commitment to stocks when one is bullish on the stock market. If markets are efficient and prices reflect all relevant information, perhaps it is better to follow passive strategies instead of spending resources in a futile attempt to outguess your competitors in the financial markets.

If the efficient market hypothesis were taken to the extreme, there would be no point in active security analysis; only fools would commit resources to actively analyze securities. Without ongoing security analysis, however, prices eventually would depart from "correct" values, creating new incentives for experts to move in. Therefore, in Chapter 9, we examine challenges to the efficient market hypothesis. Even in environments as competitive as the financial markets, we may observe only *near*-efficiency, and profit opportunities may exist for especially diligent and creative investors. This motivates our discussion of active portfolio management in Part Six. More importantly, our discussions of security analysis and portfolio construction generally must account for the likelihood of nearly efficient markets.

passive management

Buying and holding a diversified portfolio without attempting to identify mispriced securities.

active management

Attempting to identify mispriced securities or to forecast broad market trends.

1.6 The Players

From a bird's-eye view, there would appear to be three major players in the financial markets:

1. Firms are net borrowers. They raise capital now to pay for investments in plant and equipment. The income generated by those real assets provides the returns to investors who purchase the securities issued by the firm.
2. Households typically are net savers. They purchase the securities issued by firms that need to raise funds.
3. Governments can be borrowers or lenders, depending on the relationship between tax revenue and government expenditures. Since World War II, the U.S. government typically has run budget deficits, meaning that its tax receipts have been less than its expenditures. The government, therefore, has had to borrow funds to cover its budget deficit. Issuance of Treasury bills, notes, and bonds is the major way that the government borrows funds from the public. In contrast, in the latter part of the 1990s, the government enjoyed a budget surplus and was able to retire some outstanding debt.

Corporations and governments do not sell all or even most of their securities directly to individuals. For example, about half of all stock is held by large financial institutions such as pension funds, mutual funds, insurance companies, and banks. These financial institutions stand between the security issuer (the firm) and the ultimate owner of the security (the individual investor). For this reason, they are called *financial intermediaries*. Similarly, corporations do not directly market their securities to the public. Instead, they hire agents, called investment bankers, to represent them to the investing public. Let's examine the roles of these intermediaries.

Financial Intermediaries

Households want desirable investments for their savings, yet the small (financial) size of most households makes direct investment difficult. A small investor seeking to lend money to businesses that need to finance investments doesn't advertise in the local newspaper to find a willing and desirable borrower. Moreover, an individual lender would not be able to diversify across borrowers to reduce risk. Finally, an individual lender is not equipped to assess and monitor the credit risk of borrowers.

financial intermediaries

Institutions that "connect" borrowers and lenders by accepting funds from lenders and loaning funds to borrowers.

For these reasons, **financial intermediaries** have evolved to bring lenders and borrowers together. These financial intermediaries include banks, investment companies, insurance companies, and credit unions. Financial intermediaries issue their own securities to raise funds to purchase the securities of other corporations.

For example, a bank raises funds by borrowing (taking deposits) and lending that money to other borrowers. The spread between the interest rates paid to depositors and the rates charged to borrowers is the source of the bank's profit. In this way, lenders and borrowers do not need to contact each other directly. Instead, each goes to the bank, which acts as an intermediary between the two. The problem of matching lenders with borrowers is solved when each comes independently to the common intermediary.

Financial intermediaries are distinguished from other businesses in that both their assets and their liabilities are overwhelmingly financial. Table 1.3 presents the aggregated balance sheet of commercial banks, one of the largest sectors of financial intermediaries. Notice that the balance sheet includes only very small amounts of real assets. Compare Table 1.3 to the aggregated balance sheet of the nonfinancial corporate sector in Table 1.4 for which real assets are about half of all assets. The contrast arises because intermediaries simply move funds from one sector to another. In fact, the primary social function of such intermediaries is to channel household savings to the business sector.

Other examples of financial intermediaries are investment companies, insurance companies, and credit unions. All these firms offer similar advantages in their intermediary role. First, by pooling the resources of many small investors, they are able to lend considerable sums to large borrowers. Second, by lending to many borrowers, intermediaries achieve significant diversification, so they can accept loans that individually might be too risky. Third, intermediaries build expertise through the volume of business they do and can use economies of scale and scope to assess and monitor risk.

TABLE 1.3

Balance sheet of commercial banks, 2008

Assets	$ Billion	% Total	Liabilities and Net Worth	$ Billion	% Total
Real assets			Liabilities		
Equipment and premises	$ 106.9	0.9%	Deposits	$ 7,422.7	65.0%
Other real estate	14.3	0.1	Borrowed funds	2,016.6	17.6
Total real assets	$ 121.2	1.1%	Federal funds and repurchase agreements	831.5	7.3
			Total liabilities	$10,270.8	89.9%
Financial assets					
Cash	$ 519.1	4.5%			
Investment securities	2,356.9	20.6			
Loans and leases	6,562.9	57.4			
Other financial assets	884.5	7.7			
Total financial assets	$10,323.4	90.3			
Other assets					
Intangible assets	$ 439.3	3.8%			
Other	542.3	4.7			
Total other assets	981.6	8.6	Net worth	1,155.4	10.1
Total	$11,426.2	100.0%		$11,426.2	100.0%

Note: Column sums may differ from totals because of rounding error.

Source: Federal Deposit Insurance Corporation, **www.fdic.gov,** September 2008.

Assets	$ Billion	% Total	Liabilities and Net Worth	$ Billion	% Total
Real assets			Liabilities		
Equipment and software	$ 3,923	13.8%	Bonds and mortgages	$ 4,583	16.1%
Real estate	9,001	31.6	Bank loans	701	2.5
Inventories	1,849	6.5	Other loans	846	3.0
			Trade debt	2,036	7.1
Total real assets	$14,773	51.8%	Other	4,396	15.4
			Total liabilities	$12,561	44.1%
Financial assets					
Deposits and cash	$ 571	2.0%			
Marketable securities	992	3.5			
Trade and consumer credit	2,468	8.7			
Other	9,704	34.0			
Total financial assets	13,734	48.2	Net worth	15,946	55.9
Total	$28,507	100.0%		$28,507	100.0%

Note: Column sums may differ from totals because of rounding error.

Source: *Flow of Funds Accounts of the United States,* Board of Governors of the Federal Reserve System, June 2008.

Investment companies, which pool and manage the money of many investors, also arise out of economies of scale. Here, the problem is that most household portfolios are not large enough to be spread among a wide variety of securities. It is very expensive in terms of brokerage fees and research costs to purchase one or two shares of many different firms. Mutual funds have the advantage of large-scale trading and portfolio management, while participating investors are assigned a prorated share of the total funds according to the size of their investment. This system gives small investors advantages they are willing to pay for via a management fee to the mutual fund operator.

Investment companies also can design portfolios specifically for large investors with particular goals. In contrast, mutual funds are sold in the retail market, and their investment philosophies are differentiated mainly by strategies that are likely to attract a large number of clients.

Economies of scale also explain the proliferation of analytic services available to investors. Newsletters, databases, and brokerage house research services all engage in research to be sold to a large client base. This setup arises naturally. Investors clearly want information, but with small portfolios to manage, they do not find it economical to personally gather all of it. Hence, a profit opportunity emerges: A firm can perform this service for many clients and charge for it.

investment companies

Firms managing funds for investors. An investment company may manage several mutual funds.

Computer networks have made it much cheaper and easier for small investors to trade for their own accounts and perform their own security analysis. What will be the likely effect on financial intermediation?

CONCEPT **1.2**
c h e c k

Investment Bankers

Just as economies of scale and specialization create profit opportunities for financial intermediaries, so too do these economies create niches for firms that perform specialized services for businesses. Firms raise much of their capital by selling securities such as stocks and bonds to the public. Because these firms do not do so frequently, however, **investment bankers** that specialize in such activities can offer their services at a cost below that of maintaining an in-house security issuance division.

investment bankers

Firms specializing in the sale of new securities to the public, typically by underwriting the issue.

THE END OF THE STAND-ALONE INVESTMENT BANKING INDUSTRY

Until 1999, the Glass-Steagall Act had prohibited banks from both accepting deposits and underwriting securities. In other words, it forced a separation of the investment and commercial banking industries. But when Glass-Steagall was repealed, many large commercial banks began to transform themselves into "universal banks" that could offer a full range of commercial and investment banking services. In some cases, commercial banks started their own investment banking divisions from scratch, but more commonly they expanded through merger. For example, Chase Manhattan acquired J. P. Morgan to form JPMorgan Chase. Similarly, Citigroup acquired Salomon Smith Barney to offer wealth management, brokerage, investment banking, and asset management services to its clients. Most of Europe had never forced the separation of commercial and investment banking, so their giant banks such as Credit Suisse, Deutsche Bank, HSBC, and UBS had long been universal banks. Until 2008, however, the stand-alone investment banking sector in the U.S. remained large and apparently vibrant, including such storied names as Goldman, Sachs, Morgan Stanley, Merrill Lynch, and Lehman Brothers.

But the industry was shaken to its core in 2008, when several investment banks were beset by enormous losses on their holdings of mortgage-backed securities. In March, on the verge of insolvency, Bear Stearns was merged into JPMorgan Chase. On September 14, Merrill Lynch, also suffering steep mortgage-related losses, negotiated an agreement to be acquired by Bank of America. The next day, Lehman Brothers entered into the largest bankruptcy in U.S. history, having failed to find an acquirer who was able and willing to rescue it from its steep losses. The next week, the only two remaining major independent investment banks, Goldman, Sachs and Morgan Stanley, decided to convert from investment banks to traditional bank holding companies. In so doing, they became subject to the supervision of national bank regulators such as the Federal Reserve and the far tighter rules for capital adequacy that govern commercial banks.[6] The firms decided that the greater stability they would enjoy as commercial banks, particularly the ability to fund their operations through bank deposits and access to emergency borrowing from the Fed, justified the conversion. These mergers and conversions marked the effective end of the independent investment banking industry—but not of investment banking. Those services now will be supplied by the large universal banks.

---

primary market

A market in which new issues of securities are offered to the public.

secondary market

Previously issued securities are traded among investors.

Investment bankers advise an issuing corporation on the prices it can charge for the securities issued, appropriate interest rates, and so forth. Ultimately, the investment banking firm handles the marketing of the security in the **primary market,** where new issues of securities are offered to the public. In this role, the banks are called underwriters. Later, investors can trade previously issued securities among themselves in the so-called **secondary market.**

For most of the last century, investment banks and commercial banks in the U.S. were separated by law. While those regulations were effectively eliminated in 1999, until 2008 the industry known as "Wall Street" still comprised large, independent investment banks such as Goldman, Sachs, Merrill Lynch, or Lehman Brothers. But that stand-alone model came to an abrupt end in September 2008, when all the remaining major U.S. investment banks were absorbed into commercial banks, declared bankruptcy, or reorganized as commercial banks. The nearby box presents a brief introduction to these events.

1.7 | Recent Trends

Four important trends have changed the contemporary investment environment: (1) globalization, (2) securitization, (3) financial engineering, and (4) information and computer networks.

Globalization

globalization

Tendency toward a worldwide investment environment, and the integration of international capital markets.

If a wider range of investment choices can benefit investors, why should we limit ourselves to purely domestic assets? Increasingly efficient communication technology and the dismantling of regulatory constraints have encouraged **globalization** in recent years.

U.S. investors commonly can participate in foreign investment opportunities in several ways: (1) purchase foreign securities using American Depository Receipts (ADRs), which are domestically traded securities that represent claims to shares of foreign stocks; (2) purchase

---

[6]For example, a typical leverage ratio (total assets divided by bank capital) at commercial bank in 2008 was about 10 to 1. In contrast, leverage at investment banks reached 30 to 1. Such leverage increased profits when times were good, but provided an inadequate buffer agaisnt losses and left the banks exposed to failure when their investment portfolios were shaken by large losses.

foreign securities that are offered in dollars; (3) buy mutual funds that invest internationally; and (4) buy derivative securities with payoffs that depend on prices in foreign security markets.

Brokers who act as intermediaries for ADRs purchase an inventory of stock from some foreign issuer. The broker then issues an ADR that represents a claim to some number of those foreign shares held in inventory. The ADR is denominated in dollars and can be traded on U.S. stock exchanges but is in essence no more than a claim on a foreign stock. Thus, from the investor's point of view, there is no more difference between buying a British versus a U.S. stock than there is in holding a Massachusetts-based company compared with a California-based one. Of course, the investment implications may differ: ADRs still expose investors to exchange-rate risk.

World Equity Benchmark Shares (WEBS) are a variation on ADRs. WEBS use the same depository structure to allow investors to trade *portfolios* of foreign stocks in a selected country. Each WEBS security tracks the performance of an index of share returns for a particular country. WEBS can be traded by investors just like any other security and thus enable U.S. investors to obtain diversified portfolios of foreign stocks in one fell swoop.

A giant step toward globalization took place in 1999 when 11 European countries replaced their existing currencies with a new currency called the *euro*.[7] The idea behind the euro is that a common currency facilitates trade and encourages integration of markets across national boundaries. (In early 2009, the euro was worth about $1.35; the symbol for the euro is €.)

Securitization

In 1970, mortgage **pass-through securities** were introduced by the Government National Mortgage Association (GNMA, or Ginnie Mae). These securities aggregate individual home mortgages into relatively homogeneous pools. Each pool acts as backing for a GNMA pass-through security. Investors who buy GNMA securities receive prorated shares of all the principal and interest payments made on the underlying mortgage pool.

For example, the pool might total $100 million of 6%, 30-year conventional mortgages. The banks that originated the mortgages continue to service them (receiving fee-for-service), but they no longer own the mortgage investment; they pass the cash flows from the underlying mortgages through to the GNMA security holders.

Pass-through securities were a tremendous innovation in mortgage finance. **Securitization** meant that mortgages could be traded just like any other security. Moreover, with investors from all over the world able to buy mortgage-backed securities, the availability of funds no longer depended on local credit conditions, but instead could flow from any region (literally worldwide) to wherever demand was greatest.

Securitization also expanded the menu of choices for the investors. Whereas it would have been impossible before 1970 for investors to hold mortgages directly, they can now purchase mortgage-backed securities or invest in mutual funds that offer portfolios of such securities.

While Ginnie Mae bought government-guaranteed mortgages issued primarily through the Federal Housing administration and other federal agencies, Fannie Mae (FNMA, or Federal National Mortgage Association) and Freddie Mac (FHLMC, or Federal Home Loan Mortgage Corporation) created pass-throughs for mortgages originated through lenders such as banks or mortgage brokers. Originally created as government agencies, they were eventually sold via the stock market to private investors—Fannie in 1968 and Freddie 20 years later. Fannie and Freddie became the behemoths of the mortgage market, between them buying around half of all mortgages originated by the private sector and selling massive amounts of mortgage-backed securities to the investing public. By 2008, about $4.6 trillion of mortgage-backed securities were outstanding, making this market larger than that for corporate bonds.

However, in 2007 and 2008, housing prices began falling and default rates on home loans began climbing. Because Fannie and Freddie guarantee the performance of the home loans pooled to create the mortgage-backed securities they issue, they suffered large and rapidly increasing losses on their mortgage guarantees. Faced with their imminent failure,

pass-through securities

Pools of loans (such as home mortgage loans) sold in one package. Owners of pass-throughs receive all of the principal and interest payments made by the borrowers.

securitization

Pooling loans into standardized securities backed by those loans, which can then be traded like any other security.

[7]The original 11 countries are Belgium, Germany, Spain, France, Ireland, Italy, Luxembourg, The Netherlands, Austria, Portugal, and Finland. Greece joined the common currency in 2001, Slovenia was admitted in 2007, and Cyprus and Malta joined in 2008.

THE DEMISE OF FREDDIE MAC AND FANNIE MAE

Fannie Mae was created in 1938 to provide funds to and enhance the liquidity of the mortgage market. It initially operated by issuing large amounts of its own debt to raise funds, using those funds to buy mortgages from their originators, and holding them in its own portfolio. The originator would typically continue to service the mortgage (keep track of monthly payments, taxes, and insurance) for a fee. Often, the originator did not have an independent source of funds. These mortgage brokers, as they are called, do not take deposits. They simply originate loans to sell to Fannie, Freddie, and other buyers.

Freddie Mac was created in 1970 to create a secondary market where conventional mortgages could be traded. At the time, most mortgages were issued and held by local savings and loan associations, which were largely restricted to taking deposits and making mortgage loans. However, interest rate ceilings on deposits and laws against interstate banking made it difficult for the savings and loan industry to provide sufficient funds for the housing market. Freddie pioneered the mortgage pass-through security. This created a national mortgage market, alleviating regional imbalances in the supply and demand for mortgage credit. Mortgage-backed securities traded like other securities, and the funds used to purchase them became another large source of financing for homebuyers. Ultimately, both Fannie and Freddie mimicked each other's policies; both issued many mortgage-backed securities and both held many mortgages on their own balance sheets, financed by issuing their own debt.

Freddie and Fannie bore the credit risk of the mortgages they purchased as well as the mortgages they bundled and sold as pass-throughs. This is because mortgage pass-through securities were sold with guarantees that if the homeowner defaulted on the loans, the agencies would in effect buy the loans back from the investor. Fannie and Freddie charged a guarantee fee for this credit insurance, priced at what appeared at the time to provide a generous profit margin. Because the agencies were presumably in a better position to evaluate the risk of the loans than were outside investors, it made sense for them to monitor credit risk and charge an appropriate fee for bearing it.

Until the last decade, the vast majority of mortgages held or guaranteed by the agencies were low-risk "conforming" mortgages, meaning that the loans couldn't be too big and homeowners had to meet criteria establishing their ability to repay the loan. But several developments in recent years all worked to put the companies at risk. First, an enormous market developed in the securitization of subprime mortgages. These loans did not conform to usual underwriting standards for borrower creditworthiness, and the down payments were far lower than the standard 20% that the agencies traditionally required. These riskier loans were packaged by so-called "private-label" originators, and, unlike agency pass-throughs, did not provide investors with protection against defaults on the underlying loans. While Freddie and Fannie were prohibited from buying subprime loans directly, they were encouraged by Congress and the Department of Housing and Urban Development (HUD) to purchase subprime pass-through securities as a way of channeling funds to the subprime market, thus supporting affordable housing goals; they also chose to purchase these loans as a way of maintaining growth and market share. Second, a severe downturn in home prices starting in 2006 meant that default rates on even apparently safe conforming loans spiked. With heavy default rates, particularly on the subprime pass-throughs held in their portfolios, the agencies experienced large losses. Finally, despite the clearly increasing risks these companies were assuming, they failed to raise more capital as a buffer against potential losses. For example, at the end of 2007, they were reported to have only $83.2 billion of capital to support $5.2 trillion of debt and guarantees. This was not a sufficient cushion when trouble hit. Fearing the fallout from their imminent collapse, the U.S. Treasury decided in September 2008 to place the firms into conservatorship. The government promised to make good on the bonds previously issued by the agencies, but the investors in both common and preferred stock of the companies were largely wiped out.

in September 2008 the government took them into consevatorship.[8] The nearby box discusses their path to insolvency.

Despite these troubles, few believe that securitization itself will cease, although it is highly likely that practices in this market will be far more conservative than in previous years, particularly with respect to the credit standards that must be met by the ultimate borrower. Indeed, securitization has become an increasingly common staple of many credit markets. For example, it is now common for car loans, student loans, home equity loans, credit card loans, and even debt of private firms to be bundled into pass-through securities that can be traded in the capital market. Figure 1.1 documents the rapid growth of non-mortgage asset–backed securities since 1995.

Financial Engineering

bundling, unbundling
Creation of new securities either by combining primitive and derivative securities into one composite hybrid or by separating returns on an asset into classes.

Financial engineering refers to the creation of new securities by **unbundling**—breaking up and allocating the cash flows from one security to create several new securities—or by **bundling**—combining more than one security into a composite security. Such creative

---

[8]The companies did not go through a normal bankruptcy. Fearing the damage that their insolvency would wreak on capital and housing markets, the federal government instead put the agencies into "conservatorship," meaning that they could continue to operate, but would be run by the Federal Housing Finance Agency until they could be restructured. However, at this time, no one knows precisely how Freddie and Fannie will be reorganized.

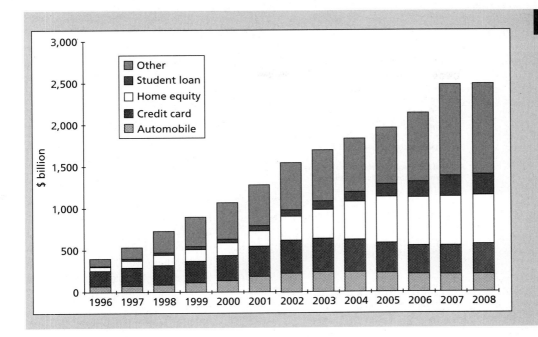

FIGURE 1.1

Asset-backed securities outstanding

Source: Securities Industry and Financial Markets Association. Data from Thomson Reuters and Bloomberg, **www.sifma.org.**

engineering of new investment products allows one to design securities with custom-tailored risk attributes. An example of bundling appears in Figure 1.2.

financial engineering

The process of creating and designing securities with custom-tailored characteristics.

Boise Cascade, with the assistance of Goldman, Sachs and other underwriters, has issued a hybrid security with features of preferred stock combined with various call and put option contracts. The security is structured as preferred stock for four years, at which time it is converted into common stock of the company. However, the number of shares of common stock into which the security can be converted depends on the price of the stock in four years, which means that the security holders are exposed to risk similar to the risk they would bear if they held option positions on the firm.

Often, creating a security that appears to be attractive requires the unbundling of an asset. An example is given in Figure 1.3. There, a mortgage pass-through certificate is unbundled into classes. Class 1 receives only principal payments from the mortgage pool, whereas Class 2 receives only interest payments.

The process of bundling and unbundling is called **financial engineering,** which refers to the creation and design of securities with

$172,500,000

Boise Cascade Corporation

7.50% Adjustable Conversion-rate Equity Security Unit

———

Price $50 Per Unit

———

Upon request, a copy of the Prospectus Supplement and the related Prospectus describing these securities and the business of the Company may be obtained within any State from any Underwriter who may legally distribute it within such State. The securities are offered only by means of the Prospectus Supplement and the related Prospectus and this announcement is neither an offer to sell nor a solicitation of any offer to buy.

Goldman, Sachs & Co.
    ABN AMRO Rothschild LLC
        Banc of America Securities LLC
        JPMorgan
            Wachovia Securities

December 19, 2001

FIGURE 1.2

Bundling creates a complex security

Source: *The Wall Street Journal,* December 19, 2001. Reprinted by permission of *The Wall Street Journal,* Copyright © 2001 Dow Jones & Company, Inc. All Rights Reserved Worldwide.

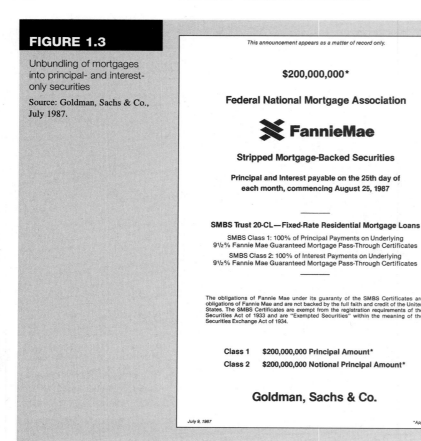

custom-tailored characteristics, often regarding exposures to various sources of risk. Financial engineers view securities as bundles of (possible risky) cash flows that may be carved up and rearranged according to the needs or desires of traders in the security markets.

Computer Networks

The Internet and other advances in computer networking have transformed many sectors of the economy, and few more so than the financial sector. These advances will be treated in greater detail in Chapter 3, but for now we can mention a few important innovations: online trading, online information dissemination, and automated trade crossing.

Online trading connects a customer directly to a brokerage firm. Online brokerage firms can process trades more cheaply and therefore can charge lower commissions. The average commission for an online trade is below $20, compared to more than $100 at full-service brokers.

The Internet has also allowed vast amounts of information to be made cheaply and widely available to the public. Individual investors today can obtain data, investment tools, and even analyst reports that just a decade ago would have been available only to professionals.

Electronic communication networks that allow direct trading among investors have exploded in recent years. These networks allow members to post buy or sell orders and to have those orders automatically matched up or "crossed" with orders of other traders in the system without benefit of an intermediary such as a securities dealer.

CONCEPT *check* **1.3**

Some observers argue that the excessive risk-taking on Wall Street ultimately leading to the collapse of 2008 was an attempt to maintain profits in the face of a business model severely challenged by the new technology of the last few decades. How did the rise of computer networks impair the profitability of Wall Street firms?

1.8 Outline of The Text

The text has six parts, which are fairly independent and may be studied in a variety of sequences. Part One is an introduction to financial markets, instruments, and trading of securities. This part also describes the mutual fund industry.

Part Two is a fairly detailed presentation of "modern portfolio theory." This part of the text treats the effect of diversification on portfolio risk, the efficient diversification of investor portfolios, the choice of portfolios that strike an attractive balance between risk and return, and the trade-off between risk and expected return. This part also treats the efficient market hypothesis as well as behavioral critiques of theories based on investor rationality.

Parts Three through Five cover security analysis and valuation. Part Three is devoted to debt markets and Part Four to equity markets. Part Five covers derivative assets, such as options and futures contracts.

Part Six is an introduction to active investment management. It shows how different investors' objectives and constraints can lead to a variety of investment policies. This part discusses the role of active management in nearly efficient markets, considers how one should evaluate the performance of managers who pursue active strategies, and takes a close look at hedge funds. It also shows how the principles of portfolio construction can be extended to the international setting.

SUMMARY

- Real assets create wealth. Financial assets represent claims to parts or all of that wealth. Financial assets determine how the ownership of real assets is distributed among investors.
- Financial assets can be categorized as fixed-income (debt), equity, or derivative instruments. Top-down portfolio construction techniques start with the asset allocation decision—the allocation of funds across broad asset classes—and then progress to more specific security-selection decisions.
- Competition in financial markets leads to a risk-return trade-off, in which securities that offer higher expected rates of return also impose greater risks on investors. The presence of risk, however, implies that actual returns can differ considerably from expected returns at the beginning of the investment period. Competition among security analysts also results in financial markets that are nearly informationally efficient, meaning that prices reflect all available information concerning the value of the security. Passive investment strategies may make sense in nearly efficient markets.
- Financial intermediaries pool investor funds and invest them. Their services are in demand because small investors cannot efficiently gather information, diversify, and monitor portfolios. The financial intermediary, in contrast, is a large investor that can take advantage of scale economies.
- Investment banking brings efficiency to corporate fund raising. Investment bankers develop expertise in pricing new issues and in marketing them to investors. By the end of 2008, all the major stand-alone U.S. investment banks had been absorbed into commercial banks or had reorganized themselves into bank holding companies. In Europe, where universal banking had never been prohibited, large banks had long maintained both commercial and investment banking divisions.
- Recent trends in financial markets include globalization, securitization, financial engineering of assets, and growth of information and computer networks.

KEY TERMS

active management, 11
agency problems, 7
asset allocation, 9
bundling, 16
derivative securities, 5
equity, 5
financial assets, 3
financial engineering, 17
financial intermediaries, 12

fixed-income (debt)
  securities, 5
globalization, 14
investment, 2
investment bankers, 13
investment companies, 13
passive management, 11
pass-through
  securities, 15

primary market, 14
real assets, 3
risk-return trade-off, 10
secondary market, 14
securitization, 15
security analysis, 9
security selection, 9
unbundling, 16

PROBLEM SETS

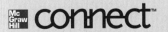 Select problems are available in McGraw-Hill Connect. Please see the packaging options of the preface for more information.

Basic

1. What are the differences between equity and fixed-income securities?
2. What is the difference between a primary asset and a derivative asset?
3. What is the difference between asset allocation and security selection?
4. What are agency problems? What are some approaches to solving them?

www.mhhe.com/bkm

5. What are the differences between real and financial assets?

6. How does investment banking differ from commercial banking?

Intermediate

7. For each transaction, identify the real and/or financial assets that trade hands. Are any financial assets created or destroyed in the transaction?
   a. Toyota takes out a bank loan to finance the construction of a new factory.
   b. Toyota pays off its loan.
   c. Toyota uses $10 million of cash on hand to purchase additional inventory of spare auto parts.

8. Suppose that in a wave of pessimism, housing prices fall by 10% across the entire economy.
   a. Has the stock of real assets of the economy changed?
   b. Are individuals less wealthy?
   c. Can you reconcile your answers to (a) and (b)?

9. Lanni Products is a start-up computer software development firm. It currently owns computer equipment worth $30,000 and has cash on hand of $20,000 contributed by Lanni's owners. For each of the following transactions, identify the real and/or financial assets that trade hands. Are any financial assets created or destroyed in the transaction?
   a. Lanni takes out a bank loan. It receives $50,000 in cash and signs a note promising to pay back the loan over three years.
   b. Lanni uses the cash from the bank plus $20,000 of its own funds to finance the development of new financial planning software.
   c. Lanni sells the software product to Microsoft, which will market it to the public under the Microsoft name. Lanni accepts payment in the form of 5,000 shares of Microsoft stock.
   d. Lanni sells the shares of stock for $25 per share and uses part of the proceeds to pay off the bank loan.

10. Reconsider Lanni Products from the previous problem.
    a. Prepare its balance sheet just after it gets the bank loan. What is the ratio of real assets to total assets?
    b. Prepare the balance sheet after Lanni spends the $70,000 to develop its software product. What is the ratio of real assets to total assets?
    c. Prepare the balance sheet after Lanni accepts the payment of shares from Microsoft. What is the ratio of real assets to total assets?

11. Financial engineering has been disparaged as nothing more than paper shuffling. Critics argue that resources used for *rearranging* wealth (that is, bundling and unbundling financial assets) might be better spent on *creating* wealth (that is, creating real assets). Evaluate this criticism. Are any benefits realized by creating an array of derivative securities from various primary securities?

12. Examine the balance sheet of commercial banks in Table 1.3. What is the ratio of real assets to total assets? What is that ratio for nonfinancial firms (Table 1.4)? Why should this difference be expected?

13. Why do financial assets show up as a component of household wealth, but not of national wealth? Why do financial assets still matter for the material well-being an economy?

14. Discuss the advantages and disadvantages of the following forms of managerial compensation in terms of mitigating agency problems, that is, potential conflicts of interest between managers and shareholders.
    a. A fixed salary.
    b. Stock in the firm that must be held for five years.
    c. A salary linked to the firm's profits.

15. We noted that oversight by large institutional investors or creditors is one mechanism to reduce agency problems. Why don't individual investors in the firm have the same incentive to keep an eye on management?

16. Wall Street firms have traditionally compensated their traders with a share of the trading profits that they generated. How might this practice have affected traders' willingness to assume risk? What is the agency problem this practice engendered?

17. Why would you expect securitization to take place only in highly developed capital markets?

18. What is the relationship between securitization and the role of financial intermediaries in the economy? What happens to financial intermediaries as securitization progresses?

19. Give an example of three financial intermediaries and explain how they act as a bridge between small investors and large capital markets or corporations.

20. Firms raise capital from investors by issuing shares in the primary markets. Does this imply that corporate financial managers can ignore trading of previously issued shares in the secondary market?

21. The average rate of return on investments in large stocks has outpaced that on investments in Treasury bills by over 7% since 1926. Why, then, does anyone invest in Treasury bills?

22. You see an advertisement for a book that claims to show how you can make $1 million with no risk and with no money down. Will you buy the book?

Use data from the Standard & Poor's Market Insight Database at www.mhhe.com/edumarketinsight to answer the following questions.

STANDARD
&POOR'S

1. Select the Company tab and enter ticker symbol RRD. Click on the Company Profile in the Compustat Reports section. What kind of firm is Donnelley & Sons?

2. Open the S&P Stock Report for Donnelley. How many shares of the company's stock are outstanding? How many stockholders are there? Is Insider Activity rated as unfavorable, neutral, or favorable?

3. Open the most recently available Proxy Statement for Donnelley (under the EDGAR heading). Locate the section that describes the stock ownership. How many total shares are held by directors and officers? Approximately what percentage is this of the total number of shares outstanding?

4. Look at the Executive Compensation section, which lists data for executives' salaries and other benefits. How much of each executive's compensation is in the form of stock awards? How much is in the form of option awards? Compare these numbers with the executives' salaries.

5. Scroll down further in the Proxy Statement to see what other kinds of benefits executives received. What types of benefits are listed in this section?

6. How might stock awards, option awards, and other benefits affect Donnelley's agency costs?

WEB *master* **MARKET REGULATORS**

1. Visit the Web site of the Securities and Exchange Commission, **www.sec.gov.** What is the mission of the SEC? What information and advice does the SEC offer to beginning investors?

2. Now visit the Web site of the NASD, **www.finra.org.** What is its mission? What information and advice does it offer to beginners?

3. Now visit the Web site of the IOSCO, **www.iosco.org.** What is its mission? What information and advice does it offer to beginners?

1.1. *a.* Real

   b. Financial

   c. Real

   d. Real

   e. Financial

1.2. If the new technology enables investors to trade and perform research for themselves, the need for financial intermediaries will decline. Part of the service intermediaries now offer is a lower-cost method for individuals to participate in securities markets. This part of the intermediaries' service would be less sought after.

1.3. Wall Street traditionally had made money through brokerage services, including buying and selling securities on behalf of clients, as well as providing clients with advice. When the prices of these services fell in response to competition from low-cost online providers, profit margins suffered. Another important source of profits had been bid–ask spreads on securities that Wall Street firms held available for sale to or purchase from investors. (These spreads are essentially markups or markdowns on security prices that provide compensation to the firm for making a market in the security.) The new electronic networks cut into this market as well, reducing the spreads that could be charged by security dealers.

Chapter 2

Asset Classes and Financial Instruments

After Studying This Chapter You Should Be Able To:

- Distinguish among the major assets that trade in money markets and in capital markets.

- Describe the construction of stock market indexes.

- Calculate the profit or loss on investments in options and futures contracts.

You learned in Chapter 1 that the process of building an investment portfolio usually begins by deciding how much money to allocate to broad classes of assets, such as safe money-market securities or bank accounts, longer-term bonds, stocks, or even asset classes such as real estate or precious metals. This process is called *asset allocation*. Within each class the investor then selects specific assets from a more detailed menu. This is called *security selection*.

Each broad asset class contains many specific security types, and the many variations on a theme can be overwhelming. Our goal in this chapter is to introduce you to the important features of broad classes of securities. Toward this end, we organize our tour of financial instruments according to asset class.

Financial markets are traditionally segmented into money markets and capital markets. Money market instruments include short-term, marketable, liquid, low-risk debt securities. Money market instruments sometimes are called *cash equivalents,* or just *cash* for short. Capital markets, in contrast, include longer-term and riskier securities. Securities in the capital market are much more diverse than those found within the money market. For this reason, we will subdivide the capital market into three segments: longer-term debt markets, equity markets, and derivative markets in which options and futures trade.

We first describe money market instruments. We then move on to debt and equity securities. We explain the structure of various stock market indexes in this chapter because market benchmark portfolios play an important role in portfolio construction and evaluation. Finally, we survey the derivative security markets for options and futures contracts. A selection of the markets, instruments, and indexes covered in this chapter appears in Table 2.1.

Related Web sites for this chapter are available at www.mhhe.com/bkm.

2.1 | The Money Market

money markets

Include short-term, highly liquid, and relatively low-risk debt instruments.

The **money market** is a subsector of the debt market. It consists of very short-term debt securities that are highly marketable. Many of these securities trade in large denominations and so are out of the reach of individual investors. Money market mutual funds, however, are easily accessible to small investors. These mutual funds pool the resources of many investors and purchase a wide variety of money market securities on their behalf.

Figure 2.1 is an excerpt of a money rates listing from *The Wall Street Journal.* It includes the various instruments of the money market that we describe in detail below. Table 2.2 lists outstanding volume of the major instruments of the money market.

Treasury Bills

Treasury bills

Short-term government securities issued at a discount from face value and returning the face amount at maturity.

U.S. **Treasury bills** (T-bills, or just bills, for short) are the most marketable of all money market instruments. T-bills represent the simplest form of borrowing. The government raises money by selling bills to the public. Investors buy the bills at a discount from the stated maturity value. At the bill's maturity, the holder receives from the government a payment equal to the face value of the bill. The difference between the purchase price and the ultimate maturity value represents the investor's earnings.

T-bills are issued with initial maturities of 4, 13, 26, or 52 weeks. Individuals can purchase T-bills directly from the Treasury or on the secondary market from a government securities dealer. T-bills are highly liquid; that is, they are easily converted to cash and sold at low transaction cost and with little price risk. Unlike most other money market instruments, which sell in minimum denominations of $100,000, T-bills sell in minimum denominations of only $100, although $10,000 denominations are more common. While the income earned on T-bills is taxable at the federal level, it is exempt from all state and local taxes, another characteristic distinguishing T-bills from other money market instruments.

Figure 2.2 is a partial listing of T-bills from *The Wall Street Journal Online* (look for Market Data Center). Rather than providing prices of each bill, the financial press reports yields based on those prices. You will see yields corresponding to both bid and asked prices. The *asked price* is the price you would have to pay to buy a T-bill from a securities dealer. The *bid price* is the slightly lower price you would receive if you wanted to sell a bill to a dealer. The *bid–asked spread* is the difference in these prices, which is the dealer's source of profit.

The first two yields in Figure 2.2 are reported using the *bank-discount method.* This means that the bill's discount from par value is "annualized" based on a 360-day year, and then reported as a percentage of par value. For example, for the highlighted bill maturing

TABLE 2.1 Financial markets and indexes	**The money market**	**The bond market**
	Treasury bills	Treasury bonds and notes
	Certificates of deposit	Federal agency debt
	Commercial paper	Municipal bonds
	Bankers' acceptances	Corporate bonds
	Eurodollars	Mortgage-backed securities
	Repos and reverses	**Equity markets**
	Federal funds	Common stocks
	Brokers' calls	Preferred stocks
	Indexes	**Derivative markets**
	Dow Jones averages	Options
	Standard & Poor's indexes	Futures and forwards
	Bond market indicators	Swaps
	International indexes	

Money Rates

January 5, 2009

International rates

Prime rates	Latest	Week ago	—52-WEEK— High	Low
U.S.	3.25	3.25	7.25	3.25
Canada	3.50	3.50	6.00	3.50
Euro zone	2.50	2.50	4.25	2.50
Japan	1.675	1.675	1.875	1.675
Switzerland	0.52	2.03	4.56	0.52
Britain	2.00	2.00	5.50	2.00
Australia	4.25	4.25	7.25	4.25
Hong Kong	5.00	5.00	7.00	5.00

Overnight repurchase	Latest	Week ago	High	Low
U.S.	0.10	0.10	4.17	0.08
U.K. (BBA)	1.925	1.858	5.742	1.483
Euro zone	2.14	2.17	4.50	2.13

U.S. government rates

Federal funds	Latest	Week ago	High	Low
Effective rate	0.15	0.15	4.28	0.12
High	0.5000	0.5000	10.0000	0.5000
Low	0.0300	0.0400	4.1875	0.0000
Bid	0.0625	0.0625	4.7500	0.0000
Offer	0.2500	0.1250	7.0000	0.0500

Treasury bill auction	Latest	Week ago	High	Low
4 weeks	0.030	0.000	3.240	0.000
13 weeks	0.150	0.050	3.180	0.005
26 weeks	0.320	0.250	3.170	0.250

Secondary market

Freddie Mac

30-year mortgage yields	Latest	Week ago	High	Low
30 days	4.25	4.44	6.49	4.09
60 days	4.46	4.61	6.56	4.37
One-year RNY	3.375	3.375	3.375	3.375

Fannie Mae

30-year mortgage yields	Latest	Week ago	High	Low
30 days	4.652	4.470	6.566	4.099
60 days	4.809	4.583	6.618	4.186

Bankers acceptances	Latest	Week ago	High	Low
30 days	0.50	0.68	5.13	0.50
60 days	0.88	0.88	5.13	0.88
90 days	1.25	1.13	5.00	1.13
120 days	1.50	1.50	5.00	1.50
150 days	1.50	1.50	5.00	1.50
180 days	1.75	1.88	5.00	1.75

Commercial paper	Latest	Week ago	High	Low
30 to 97 days	n.q.	...	...	...
98 to 119 days	0.15	...	...	...
120 to 149 days	0.20	...	...	...
150 to 165 days	0.30	...	...	...
166 to 180 days	0.35	...	...	...
181 to 270 days	n.q.	...	...	...

Dealer commercial paper	Latest	Week ago	High	Low
30 days	0.84	0.74	5.95	0.52
60 days	0.94	0.94	5.95	0.94
90 days	1.14	1.14	5.95	1.12

Euro commercial paper	Latest	Week ago	High	Low
30 day	2.27	2.37	4.75	2.27
Two month	2.50	2.50	4.80	2.48
Three month	2.60	2.59	5.00	2.58
Four month	2.64	2.86	5.00	2.64
Five month	2.65	2.89	5.02	2.65
Six month	2.68	2.91	5.07	2.68

London interbank offered rate, or Libor

	Latest	Week ago	High	Low
One month	0.42875	0.46125	4.58750	0.42875
Three month	1.42125	1.45875	4.81875	1.41250
Six month	1.79375	1.81125	4.39375	1.75000
One year	2.09250	2.07750	4.23375	2.00375

Libor Swaps (USD)

	Latest	Week ago	High	Low
Two year	1.579	1.461	3.978	1.431
Three year	1.892	1.714	4.325	1.692
Five year	2.319	2.076	4.661	1.996
Ten year	2.856	2.477	4.968	2.304
20 year	3.164	2.736	5.200	2.438
30 year	3.177	2.713	5.248	2.365

Euro interbank offered rate (Euribor)

	Latest	Week ago	High	Low
One month	2.543	2.692	5.197	2.543
Three month	2.822	2.973	5.393	2.822
Six month	2.913	3.037	5.448	2.913
One year	2.995	3.126	5.526	2.995

Asian dollars

	Latest	Week ago	High	Low
One month	0.432	0.468	4.588	0.430
Three month	1.422	1.462	4.780	1.415
Six month	1.754	1.818	4.438	1.754
One year	2.018	2.076	5.408	2.018

	LATEST Offer	Bid	Week ago	52-WEEK High	Low
Eurodollars (mid rates)					
One month	0.50	1.00	1.00	6.25	0.63
Two month	0.75	1.25	1.25	5.50	0.88
Three month	1.00	1.75	1.50	5.75	1.00
Four month	1.25	2.00	1.75	5.25	1.25
Five month	1.25	2.00	1.75	5.25	1.50
Six month	1.50	2.25	2.00	5.25	1.75

FIGURE 2.1

Rates on money market securities

Source: From *The Wall Street Journal,* January 6, 2009. Reprinted by permission of *The Wall Street Journal* © 2009 Dow Jones & Company, Inc. All Rights Reserved Worldwide.

TABLE 2.2		**$ Billion**
Major components of the money market	Repurchase agreements	$ 944.4
	Savings deposits and small-denomination time deposits*	5,411.8
	Large-denomination time deposits*	2,413.3
	Treasury bills	1,003.9
	Commercial paper	1,748.0
	Money market mutual funds	3,343.2

*Small denominations are less than $100,000.

Sources: *Economic Report of the President,* U.S. Government Printing Office, 2008; *Flow of Funds Accounts of the United States,* Board of Governors of the Federal Reserve System, September 2008.

FIGURE 2.2

Treasury bill listings

Source: *The Wall Street Journal Online,* September 25, 2008. Reprinted by permission of *The Wall Street Journal,* Copyright © 2008 Dow Jones & Company, Inc. All Rights Reserved Worldwide.

Treasury Bills

MATURITY	DAYS TO MAT	BID	ASKED	CHG	ASK YLD
Nov 20 08	56	0.205	0.185	−0.25	0.188
Dec 04 08	70	0.240	0.220	−0.18	0.223
Jan 02 08	99	0.510	0.490	−0.52	0.497
Jan 29 09	126	0.600	0.585	−0.15	0.594
Feb 26 09	154	1.200	1.175	−0.02	1.197
Mar 05 09	161	1.200	1.190	−0.14	1.213
Mar 12 09	168	1.190	1.175	0	1.198
Mar 26 09	182	1.435	1.430	−0.18	1.460

on March 5, days to maturity are 161 and the yield under the column labeled ASKED is given as 1.19%. This means that a dealer was willing to sell the bill at a discount from par value of $1.19\% \times (161/360) = .532\%$. So a bill with $10,000 par value could be purchased for $10,000 \times (1 − .00532) = \$9,946.80$. Similarly, on the basis of the bid yield of 1.20%, a dealer would be willing to *purchase* the bill for $10,000 \times [1 − .0120 \times (161/360)] = \$9,946.33$. Notice that prices and yields are inversely related, so the higher bid *yield* reported in Figure 2.2 implies a lower bid *price.*

The bank discount method for computing yields has a long tradition, but it is flawed for at least two reasons. First, it assumes that the year has only 360 days. Second, it computes the yield as a fraction of par value rather than of the price the investor paid to acquire the bill.[1] An investor who buys the bill for the asked price and holds it until maturity will see her investment grow over 161 days by a multiple of $10,000/$9,946.80 = 1.00535, or .535%. Annualizing this return using a 365-day year results in a yield of .535% × 365/161 = 1.213%, which is the value reported in the last column under "asked yield." This last value is called the Treasury bill's *bond-equivalent yield.*

Certificates of Deposit

certificate of deposit

A bank time deposit.

A **certificate of deposit** (CD) is a time deposit with a bank. Time deposits may not be withdrawn on demand. The bank pays interest and principal to the depositor only at the end of the fixed term of the CD. CDs issued in denominations larger than $100,000 are usually negotiable, however; that is, they can be sold to another investor if the owner needs to cash in the certificate before its maturity date. Short-term CDs are highly marketable, although the market significantly thins out for maturities of three months or more. CDs are treated as bank deposits by the Federal Deposit Insurance Corporation, so they are insured for up to $100,000 in the event of a bank insolvency. (In October 2008, FDIC deposit insurance temporarily increased from $100,000 to $250,000 per depositor through December 31, 2009.)

Commercial Paper

The typical corporation is a net borrower of both long-term funds (for capital investments) and short-term funds (for working capital). Large, well-known companies often issue their own

---

[1] Both of these "errors" were dictated by computational simplicity in the days before computers. It is easier to compute percentage discounts from a round number such as par value rather than from purchase price. It is also easier to annualize using a 360-day year, since 360 is an even multiple of so many numbers.

short-term unsecured debt notes directly to the public, rather than borrowing from banks. These notes are called **commercial paper** (CP). Sometimes, CP is backed by a bank line of credit, which gives the borrower access to cash that can be used if needed to pay off the paper at maturity.

CP maturities range up to 270 days; longer maturities require registration with the Securities and Exchange Commission and so are almost never issued. CP most commonly is issued with maturities of less than one or two months in denominations of multiples of $100,000. Therefore, small investors can invest in commercial paper only indirectly, through money market mutual funds.

CP is considered to be a fairly safe asset, given that a firm's condition presumably can be monitored and predicted over a term as short as one month. CP trades in secondary markets and so is quite liquid. Most issues are rated by at least one agency such as Standard & Poor's. The yield on CP depends on its time to maturity and credit rating.

While most CP historically was issued by nonfinancial firms, in recent years there was a sharp increase in so-called *asset-backed commercial paper* issued by financial firms such as banks. This short-term CP typically was used to raise funds for the institution to invest in other assets. These assets in turn were used as collateral for the CP—hence the label "asset-backed." This practice led to many difficulties starting in the summer of 2007 when the subprime mortgages in which the banks often invested performed poorly as default rates spiked. The banks found themselves unable to issue new CP to refinance their positions as the old paper matured.

commercial paper
Short-term unsecured debt issued by large corporations.

Bankers' Acceptances

A **bankers' acceptance** starts as an order to a bank by a bank's customer to pay a sum of money at a future date, typically within six months. At this stage, it is like a postdated check. When the bank endorses the order for payment as "accepted," it assumes responsibility for ultimate payment to the holder of the acceptance. At this point, the acceptance may be traded in secondary markets much like any other claim on the bank. Bankers' acceptances are considered very safe assets, as they allow traders to substitute the bank's credit standing for their own. They are used widely in foreign trade where the creditworthiness of one trader is unknown to the trading partner. Acceptances sell at a discount from the face value of the payment order, just as T-bills sell at a discount from par value.

bankers' acceptance
An order to a bank by a customer to pay a sum of money at a future date.

Eurodollars

Eurodollars are dollar-denominated deposits at foreign banks or foreign branches of American banks. By locating outside the United States, these banks escape regulation by the Federal Reserve Board. Despite the tag "Euro," these accounts need not be in European banks, although that is where the practice of accepting dollar-denominated deposits outside the United States began.

Most Eurodollar deposits are for large sums, and most are time deposits of less than six months' maturity. A variation on the Eurodollar time deposit is the Eurodollar certificate of deposit. A Eurodollar CD resembles a domestic bank CD except it is the liability of a non-U.S. branch of a bank, typically a London branch. The advantage of Eurodollar CDs over Eurodollar time deposits is that the holder can sell the asset to realize its cash value before maturity. Eurodollar CDs are considered less liquid and riskier than domestic CDs, however, and so offer higher yields. Firms also issue Eurodollar bonds, that is, dollar-denominated bonds outside the U.S., although such bonds are not a money market investment by virtue of their long maturities.

Eurodollars
Dollar-denominated deposits at foreign banks or foreign branches of American banks.

Repos and Reverses

Dealers in government securities use **repurchase agreements,** also called repos, or RPs, as a form of short-term, usually overnight, borrowing. The dealer sells securities to an investor on an overnight basis, with an agreement to buy back those securities the next day at a slightly higher price. The increase in the price is the overnight interest. The dealer thus takes out a one-day loan from the investor. The securities serve as collateral for the loan.

repurchase agreements (repos)
Short-term sales of government securities with an agreement to repurchase the securities at a higher price.

A *term repo* is essentially an identical transaction, except the term of the implicit loan can be 30 days or more. Repos are considered very safe in terms of credit risk because the loans are backed by the government securities. A *reverse repo* is the mirror image of a repo. Here, the dealer finds an investor holding government securities and buys them with an agreement to resell them at a specified higher price on a future date.

Brokers' Calls

Individuals who buy stocks on margin borrow part of the funds to pay for the stocks from their broker. The broker in turn may borrow the funds from a bank, agreeing to repay the bank immediately (on call) if the bank requests it. The rate paid on such loans is usually about one percentage point higher than the rate on short-term T-bills.

Federal Funds

Federal funds

Funds in the accounts of commercial banks at the Federal Reserve Bank.

Just as most of us maintain deposits at banks, banks maintain deposits of their own at the Federal Reserve Bank, or the Fed. Each member bank of the Federal Reserve System is required to maintain a minimum balance in a reserve account with the Fed. The required balance depends on the total deposits of the bank's customers. Funds in the bank's reserve account are called **Federal funds** or *Fed funds*. At any time, some banks have more funds than required at the Fed. Other banks, primarily big New York and other financial center banks, tend to have a shortage of Federal funds. In the Federal funds market, banks with excess funds lend to those with a shortage. These loans, which are usually overnight transactions, are arranged at a rate of interest called the Federal funds rate.

Although the Fed funds market arose primarily as a way for banks to transfer balances to meet reserve requirements, today the market has evolved to the point that many large banks use Federal funds in a straightforward way as one component of their total sources of funding. Therefore, the Fed funds rate is simply the rate of interest on very short-term loans among financial institutions. While most investors cannot participate in this market, the Fed funds rate commands great interest as a key barometer of monetary policy.

The LIBOR Market

LIBOR

Lending rate among banks in the London market.

The **London Interbank Offer Rate (LIBOR)** is the rate at which large banks in London are willing to lend money among themselves. This rate has become the premier short-term interest rate quoted in the European money market and serves as a reference rate for a wide range of transactions. A corporation might borrow at a rate equal to LIBOR plus two percentage points, for example. Like the Fed funds rate, LIBOR is a statistic widely followed by investors.

LIBOR interest rates may be tied to currencies other than the U.S. dollar. For example, LIBOR rates are widely quoted for transactions denominated in British pounds, yen, euros, and so on. There is also a similar rate called EURIBOR (European Interbank Offer Rate) at which banks in the euro zone are willing to lend euros among themselves.

Yields on Money Market Instruments

Although most money market securities are of low risk, they are not risk-free. The securities of the money market promise yields greater than those on default-free T-bills, at least in part because of their greater relative risk. Investors who require more liquidity also will accept lower yields on securities, such as T-bills, that can be more quickly and cheaply sold for cash. Figure 2.3 shows that bank CDs, for example, consistently have paid a risk premium over T-bills. Moreover, as Figure 2.3 shows, that premium increases with economic crises such as the energy price shocks associated with the Organization of Petroleum Exporting Countries

MONEY MARKET FUNDS
AND THE CREDIT CRISIS OF 2008

Money market funds are mutual funds that invest in the short-term debt instruments that comprise the money market. In 2008, these funds had investments totaling about $3.4 trillion. They are required to hold only short-maturity debt of the highest quality: the average maturity of their holdings must be maintained at less than three months. Their biggest investments tend to be in commercial paper, but they also hold sizable fractions of their portfolios in certificates of deposit, repurchase agreements, and Treasury securities. Because of this very conservative investment profile, money market funds typically experience extremely low price risk. Investors for their part usually acquire check-writing privileges with their funds and often use them as a close substitute for a bank account. This is feasible because the funds almost always maintain share value at $1.00 and pass along all investment earnings to their investors as interest.

Until 2008, only one fund had "broken the buck," that is, suffered losses large enough to force value per share below $1. But when Lehman Brothers filed for bankruptcy protection on September 15, 2008, several funds that had invested heavily in its commercial paper suffered large losses. The next day, Reserve Primary Fund, the oldest money market fund, broke the buck when its value per share fell to only $.97.

The realization that money market funds were at risk in the credit crisis led to a wave of investor redemptions similar to a run on a bank. Only three days after the Lehman bankruptcy, Putman's Prime Money Market Fund announced that it was liquidating due to heavy redemptions. Fearing further outflows, the U.S. Treasury announced that it would make federal insurance available to money market funds willing to pay an insurance fee. This program would thus be similar to FDIC bank insurance. With the federal insurance in place, the outflows were quelled.

However, the turmoil in Wall Street's money market funds had already spilled over into "Main Street." Fearing further investor redemptions, money market funds had become afraid to commit funds even over short periods, and their demand for commercial paper had effectively dried up. Firms that had been able to borrow at 2% interest rates in previous weeks now had to pay up to 8%, and the commercial paper market was on the edge of freezing up altogether. Firms throughout the economy had come to depend on those markets as a major source of short-term finance to fund expenditures ranging from salaries to inventories. Further breakdown in the money markets would have had an immediate crippling effect on the broad economy. Within days, the Federal government put forth its first plan to spend $700 billion to stabilize the credit markets.

(OPEC) disturbances, the failure of Penn Square Bank, the stock market crash in 1987, the collapse of Long Term Capital Management in 1998, and the credit crisis resulting from the breakdown of the subprime mortgage market beginning in 2007.

Money market funds are mutual funds that invest in money market instruments and have become major sources of funding to that sector. The nearby box discusses the fallout of the credit crisis of 2008 on those funds.

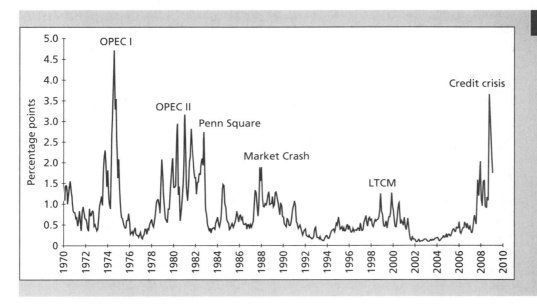

FIGURE 2.3

Spread between three-month CD and T-bill rates

2.2 | The Bond Market

The bond market is composed of longer-term borrowing or debt instruments than those that trade in the money market. This market includes Treasury notes and bonds, corporate bonds, municipal bonds, mortgage securities, and federal agency debt.

These instruments are sometimes said to comprise the *fixed-income capital market,* because most of them promise either a fixed stream of income or stream of income that is determined according to a specified formula. In practice, these formulas can result in a flow of income that is far from fixed. Therefore, the term "fixed income" is probably not fully appropriate. It is simpler and more straightforward to call these securities either debt instruments or bonds.

Treasury Notes and Bonds

Treasury notes or bonds

Debt obligations of the federal government with original maturities of one year or more.

The U.S. government borrows funds in large part by selling **Treasury notes** and **bonds.** T-notes are issued with original maturities ranging up to 10 years, while T-bonds are issued with maturities ranging from 10 to 30 years. Both bonds and notes may be issued in increments of $100, but far more commonly trade in denominations of $1,000. Both bonds and notes make semiannual interest payments called *coupon payments,* so named because in precomputer days, investors would literally clip a coupon attached to the bond and present it to receive the interest payment.

Figure 2.4 is an excerpt from a listing of Treasury issues in *The Wall Street Journal Online.* The highlighted bond matures in February 2015. The coupon income or interest paid by the bond is 4% of par value, meaning that for a $1,000 face value bond, $40 in annual interest payments will be made in two semiannual installments of $20 each. The numbers to the right of the colon in the bid and ask prices represent units of $1/32$ of a point.

The bid price of the highlighted bond is $105^{20}/_{32}$, or 105.625. The asked price is $105^{22}/_{32}$, or 105.6875. Although bonds are typically traded in denominations of $1,000 par value, the prices are quoted as a percentage of par value. Thus, the asked price of 105.6875 should be interpreted as 105.6875% of par or $1,056.875 for the $1,000 par value bond. Similarly, the bond could be sold to a dealer for $1,056.25. The +29 change means the closing price on this day rose $^{29}/_{32}$ (as a percentage of par value) from the previous day's closing price. Finally, the yield to maturity on the bond based on the ask price is 3.017%.

The yield to maturity reported in the last column is a measure of the annualized rate of return to an investor who buys the bond and holds it until maturity. It accounts for both coupon income as well as the difference between the purchase price of the bond and its final value of $1,000 at maturity. We discuss the yield to maturity in detail in Chapter 10.

FIGURE 2.4

Listing of Treasury issues

Source: Compiled from data from *The Wall Street Journal Online,* September 25, 2008. Reprinted by permission of Dow Jones & Company, Inc. © 2008 Dow Jones & Company, Inc. All Rights Reserved Worldwide.

MATURITY	COUPON	BID	ASKED	CHG	YLD TO MATURITY
2009 Feb 15	4.5	101:06	101:06	−2	1.401
2012 Feb 15	4.875	107:26	107:27	22	2.448
2013 Feb 15	3.875	104:18	104:19	24	2.756
2015 Feb 15	4	105:20	105:22	29	3.017
2015 Jan 15 i	1.625	98:26	98:27	15	1.820
2017 Feb 15	4.625	106:26	106:27	17	3.671
2020 Feb 15	8.5	139:14	139:15	29	4.122
2026 Feb 15	6	119:02	119:03	23	4.416
2026 Jan 15 i	2	94:07	94:08	9	2.408
2036 Feb 15	4.5	101:06	101:07	26	4.423
2038 Feb 15	4.5	101:31	102:01	28	4.378

CONCEPT *check* **2.1**   What were the bid price, asked price, and yield to maturity of the 4½% February 2036 Treasury bond displayed in Figure 2.4? What was its asked price the previous day?

Inflation-Protected Treasury Bonds

The best place to start building an investment portfolio is at the least risky end of the spectrum. Around the world, governments of many countries, including the U.S., have issued bonds that are linked to an index of the cost of living in order to provide their citizens with an effective way to hedge inflation risk.

In the United States, inflation-protected Treasury bonds are called TIPS (Treasury Inflation Protected Securities). The principal amount on these bonds is adjusted in proportion to increases in the Consumer Price Index. Therefore, they provide a constant stream of income in real (inflation-adjusted) dollars, and the real interest rates you earn on these securities are risk-free if you hold them to maturity. An *i* following the bond's maturity date in Figure 2.4 denotes that the bond is an inflation-indexed TIPS bond, and you will see that the reported yields on these bonds are lower than those on surrounding conventional Treasuries. Compare, for example, the reported yield on the January 2015*i* bond, 1.820%, to the 3.017% yield on the February 2015 bond that precedes it. The yields on TIPS bonds should be interpreted as real or inflation-adjusted interest rates. We return to TIPS bonds in more detail in Chapter 10.

Federal Agency Debt

Some government agencies issue their own securities to finance their activities. These agencies usually are formed for public policy reasons to channel credit to a particular sector of the economy that Congress believes is not receiving adequate credit through normal private sources.

The major mortgage-related agencies are the Federal Home Loan Bank (FHLB), the Federal National Mortgage Association (FNMA, or Fannie Mae), the Government National Mortgage Association (GNMA, or Ginnie Mae), and the Federal Home Loan Mortgage Corporation (FHLMC, or Freddie Mac).

Although the debt of federal agencies is not explicitly insured by the federal government, it has long been assumed that the government would assist an agency nearing default. Those beliefs were validated when Fannie Mae and Freddie Mac actually encountered severe financial distress in September 2008. With both firms on the brink of insolvency, the government stepped in and put them both into conservatorship, assigned the Federal Housing Finance Agency to run the firms, but did in fact agree to make good on the firm's bonds. (Turn back to Chapter 1 for more discussion of the Fannie and Freddie failures.)

International Bonds

Many firms borrow abroad and many investors buy bonds from foreign issuers. In addition to national capital markets, there is a thriving international capital market, largely centered in London.

A *Eurobond* is a bond denominated in a currency other than that of the country in which it is issued. For example, a dollar-denominated bond sold in Britain would be called a Euro-dollar bond. Similarly, investors might speak of Euroyen bonds, yen-denominated bonds sold outside Japan. Since the new European currency is called the euro, the term Eurobond may be confusing. It is best to think of them simply as international bonds.

In contrast to bonds that are issued in foreign currencies, many firms issue bonds in foreign countries but in the currency of the investor. For example, a Yankee bond is a dollar-denominated bond sold in the U.S. by a non-U.S. issuer. Similarly, Samurai bonds are yen-denominated bonds sold in Japan by non-Japanese issuers.

Municipal Bonds

municipal bonds

Tax-exempt bonds issued by
state and local governments.

Municipal bonds ("munis") are issued by state and local governments. They are similar to Treasury and corporate bonds, except their interest income is exempt from federal income taxation. The interest income also is exempt from state and local taxation in the issuing state. Capital gains taxes, however, must be paid on munis if the bonds mature or are sold for more than the investor's purchase price.

There are basically two types of municipal bonds. *General obligation bonds* are backed by the "full faith and credit" (i.e., the taxing power) of the issuer, while *revenue bonds* are issued to finance particular projects and are backed either by the revenues from that project or by the municipal agency operating the project. Typical issuers of revenue bonds are airports, hospitals, and turnpike or port authorities. Revenue bonds are riskier in terms of default than general obligation bonds.

An *industrial development bond* is a revenue bond that is issued to finance commercial enterprises, such as the construction of a factory that can be operated by a private firm. In effect, this device gives the firm access to the municipality's ability to borrow at tax-exempt rates, and the federal government limits the amount of these bonds that may be issued.[2] Figure 2.5 plots outstanding amounts of industrial revenue bonds as well as general obligation municipal bonds.

Like Treasury bonds, municipal bonds vary widely in maturity. A good deal of the debt issued is in the form of short-term *tax anticipation notes* that raise funds to pay for expenses before actual collection of taxes. Other municipal debt may be long term and used to fund large capital investments. Maturities range up to 30 years.

The key feature of municipal bonds is their tax-exempt status. Because investors pay neither federal nor state taxes on the interest proceeds, they are willing to accept lower yields on these securities.

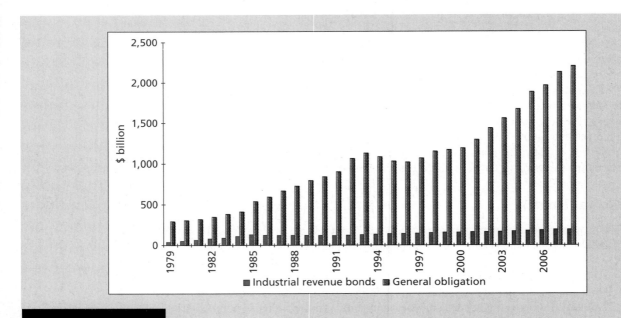

FIGURE 2.5

Outstanding tax-exempt debt

Source: *Flow of Funds Accounts of the U.S.*, Board of Governors of the Federal Reserve System, 2008.

[2]A warning, however. Although interest on industrial development bonds usually is exempt from federal tax, it can be subject to the alternative minimum tax if the bonds are used to finance projects of for-profit companies.

An investor choosing between taxable and tax-exempt bonds needs to compare after-tax returns on each bond. An exact comparison requires the computation of after-tax rates of return with explicit recognition of taxes on income and realized capital gains. In practice, there is a simpler rule of thumb. If we let t denote the investor's combined federal plus local marginal tax rate and r denote the total before-tax rate of return available on taxable bonds, then $r(1 - t)$ is the after-tax rate available on those securities.[3] If this value exceeds the rate on municipal bonds, r_m, the investor does better holding the taxable bonds. Otherwise, the tax-exempt municipals provide higher after-tax returns.

One way of comparing bonds is to determine the interest rate on taxable bonds that would be necessary to provide an after-tax return equal to that of municipals. To derive this value, we set after-tax yields equal and solve for the *equivalent taxable yield* of the tax-exempt bond. This is the rate a taxable bond would need to offer in order to match the after-tax yield on the tax-free municipal.

$$r(1 - t) = r_m \qquad \text{(2.1)}$$

or

$$r = \frac{r_m}{1 - t} \qquad \text{(2.2)}$$

Thus, the equivalent taxable yield is simply the tax-free rate divided by $1 - t$. Table 2.3 presents equivalent taxable yields for several municipal yields and tax rates.

This table frequently appears in the marketing literature for tax-exempt mutual bond funds because it demonstrates to high tax-bracket investors that municipal bonds offer highly attractive equivalent taxable yields. Each entry is calculated from Equation 2.2. If the equivalent taxable yield exceeds the actual yields offered on taxable bonds, after taxes the investor is better off holding municipal bonds. The equivalent taxable interest rate increases with the investor's tax bracket; the higher the bracket, the more valuable the tax-exempt feature of municipals. Thus, high-bracket individuals tend to hold municipals.

We also can use Equation 2.1 or 2.2 to find the tax bracket at which investors are indifferent between taxable and tax-exempt bonds. The cutoff tax bracket is given by solving Equation 2.1 for the tax bracket at which after-tax yields are equal. Doing so, we find

$$t = 1 - \frac{r_m}{r} \qquad \text{(2.3)}$$

TABLE 2.3

Equivalent taxable yields corresponding to various tax-exempt yields

Marginal Tax Rate	Tax-Exempt Yield				
	1%	2%	3%	4%	5%
20%	1.25%	2.50%	3.75%	5.00%	6.25%
30	1.43	2.86	4.29	5.71	7.14
40	1.67	3.33	5.00	6.67	8.33
50	2.00	4.00	6.00	8.00	10.00

[3]An approximation to the combined federal plus local tax rate is just the sum of the two rates. For example, if your federal tax rate is 28% and your state rate is 5%, your combined tax rate would be approximately 33%. A more precise approach would recognize that state taxes are deductible at the federal level. You owe federal taxes only on income net of state taxes. Therefore, for every dollar of income, your after-tax proceeds would be $(1 - t_{federal}) \times (1 - t_{state})$. In our example, your after-tax proceeds on each dollar earned would be $(1 - .28) \times (1 - .05) = .684$, which implies a combined tax rate of $1 - .684 = .316$ or 31.6%.

FIGURE 2.6

Ratio of yields on tax-exempt to taxable bonds

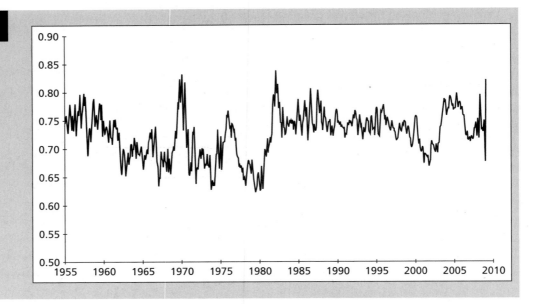

Thus, the yield ratio r_m/r is a key determinant of the attractiveness of municipal bonds. The higher the yield ratio, the lower the cutoff tax bracket, and the more individuals will prefer to hold municipal debt. Figure 2.6 graphs the yield ratio since 1955.

EXAMPLE 2.1

Taxable versus Tax-Exempt Yields

Figure 2.6 shows that for most of the last 30 years, the ratio of tax-exempt to taxable yields fluctuated around .75. What does this imply about the cutoff tax bracket above which tax-exempt bonds provide higher after-tax yields? Equation 2.3 shows that an investor whose combined tax bracket (federal plus local) exceeds $1 - .75 = .25$, or 25%, will derive a greater after-tax yield from municipals. Note, however, that it is difficult to control precisely for differences in the risks of these bonds, so the cutoff tax bracket must be taken as approximate.

CONCEPT check 2.2

Suppose your tax bracket is 28%. Would you prefer to earn a 6% taxable return or a 4% tax-free yield? What is the equivalent taxable yield of the 4% tax-free yield?

Corporate Bonds

corporate bonds

Long-term debt issued by private corporations typically paying semi-annual coupons and returning the face value of the bond at maturity.

Corporate bonds are the means by which private firms borrow money directly from the public. These bonds are structured much like Treasury issues in that they typically pay semiannual coupons over their lives and return the face value to the bondholder at maturity. Where they differ most importantly from Treasury bonds is in risk.

Default risk is a real consideration in the purchase of corporate bonds. We treat this issue in considerable detail in Chapter 10. For now, we distinguish only among secured bonds, which have specific collateral backing them in the event of firm bankruptcy; unsecured bonds, called *debentures,* which have no collateral; and subordinated debentures, which have a lower priority claim to the firm's assets in the event of bankruptcy.

Corporate bonds sometimes come with options attached. *Callable bonds* give the firm the option to repurchase the bond from the holder at a stipulated call price. *Convertible bonds* give the bondholder the option to convert each bond into a stipulated number of shares of stock. These options are treated in more detail in Part Three.

Mortgages and Mortgage-Backed Securities

Forty years ago, your investments text probably would not have included a section on mortgage loans, for investors could not invest in these loans. Now, because of the explosion in mortgage-backed securities, almost anyone can invest in a portfolio of mortgage loans, and these securities have become a major component of the fixed-income market.

Until the 1970s, almost all home mortgages were written for a long term (15- to 30-year maturity), with a fixed interest rate over the life of the loan, and with equal, fixed monthly payments. These so-called conventional mortgages are still the most popular, but a diverse set of alternative mortgage designs have appeared.

Fixed-rate mortgages can create considerable difficulties for banks in years of increasing interest rates. Because banks commonly issue short-term liabilities (the deposits of their customers) and hold long-term assets, such as fixed-rate mortgages, they suffer losses when interest rates increase. The rates they pay on deposits increase, while their mortgage income remains fixed.

The adjustable-rate mortgage was a response to this problem. These mortgages require the borrower to pay an interest rate that varies with some measure of the current market interest rate. The interest rate, for example, might be set at two points above the current rate on one-year Treasury bills and might be adjusted once a year. The adjustable-rate contract shifts the risk of fluctuations in interest rates from the bank to the borrower. Because the borrower bears interest rate risk, lenders are willing to offer lower rates on adjustable-rate mortgages than on conventional fixed-rate mortgages.

As described in Chapter 1, a *mortgage-backed security* is either an ownership claim in a pool of mortgages or an obligation that is secured by such a pool. These claims represent securitization of mortgage loans. Mortgage lenders originate loans and then sell packages of these loans in the secondary market. Specifically, they sell their claim to the cash inflows from the mortgages as those loans are paid off. The mortgage originator continues to service the loan, collecting principal and interest payments, and passes these payments along to the purchaser of the mortgage. For this reason, these mortgage-backed securities are called *pass-throughs.* Investors can buy and sell securitized mortgages like any other bond.

Until very recently, the great majority of mortgage-backed securities were issued by FNMA (Fannie Mae) and FHLMC (Freddie Mac). By 2008, over $4.7 trillion of outstanding mortgages were securitized into Freddie or Fannie mortgage-backed securities, making the mortgage-backed securities market larger than the $3.7 trillion corporate bond market and nearly the size of the $5.1 trillion market in Treasury securities. Figure 2.7 illustrates the explosive growth of these securities since 1979.

Most pass-throughs traditionally comprised *conforming mortgages,* which meant that the loans had to satisfy certain underwriting guidelines (standards for the creditworthiness of the borrower) before they could be purchased by Fannie Mae or Freddie Mac. In the years leading up to 2008, however, a large amount of *subprime mortgages,* that is, riskier loans made to

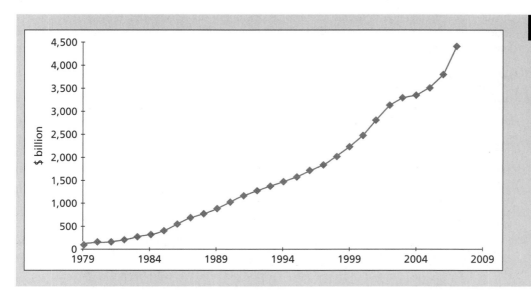

FIGURE 2.7

Mortgage-backed securities outstanding

Source: *Flow of Funds Accounts of the U.S.,* Board of Governors of the Federal Reserve System, September 2008.

financially weaker borrowers, were bundled and sold by "private label" issuers. In an effort to make housing more affordable to low-income households, the agencies were allowed and encouraged to buy these subprime securities. These loans turned out to be disastrous, with trillion-dollar losses spread among banks, hedge funds and other investors, and Freddie and Fannie, which lost billions of dollars on the subprime mortgages they had purchased.

Notwithstanding these recent travails, the growth of mortgage-backed pass-throughs has encouraged the introduction of pass-through securities backed by other assets. These "asset-backed" securities have grown rapidly, from a level of about $316 billion in 1995 to $2,480 billion in 2008.

2.3 Equity Securities

Common Stock as Ownership Shares

common stocks

Ownership shares in a publicly held corporation. Shareholders have voting rights and may receive dividends.

Common stocks, also known as equity securities, or equities, represent ownership shares in a corporation. Each share of common stock entitles its owners to one vote on any matters of corporate governance put to a vote at the corporation's annual meeting and to a share in the financial benefits of ownership (e.g., the right to any dividends that the corporation may choose to distribute).[4]

A corporation is controlled by a board of directors elected by the shareholders.[5] The board, which meets only a few times each year, selects managers who run the corporation on a day-to-day basis. Managers have the authority to make most business decisions without the board's approval. The board's mandate is to oversee management to ensure that it acts in the best interests of shareholders.

The members of the board are elected at the annual meeting. Shareholders who do not attend the annual meeting can vote by proxy, empowering another party to vote in their name. Management usually solicits the proxies of shareholders and normally gets a vast majority of these proxy votes. Thus, management usually has considerable discretion to run the firm as it sees fit, without daily oversight from the equityholders who actually own the firm.

We noted in Chapter 1 that such separation of ownership and control can give rise to "agency problems," in which managers pursue goals not in the best interests of shareholders. However, there are several mechanisms designed to alleviate these agency problems. Among these are compensation schemes that link the success of the manager to that of the firm; over-sight by the board of directors as well as outsiders such as security analysts, creditors, or large institutional investors; the threat of a proxy contest in which unhappy shareholders attempt to replace the current management team; or the threat of a takeover by another firm.

The common stock of most large corporations can be bought or sold freely on one or more of the stock markets. A corporation whose stock is not publicly traded is said to be *closely held*. In most closely held corporations, the owners of the firm also take an active role in its management. Takeovers generally are not an issue.

Characteristics of Common Stock

The two most important characteristics of common stock as an investment are its residual claim and its limited liability features.

Residual claim means stockholders are the last in line of all those who have a claim on the assets and income of the corporation. In a liquidation of the firm's assets, the shareholders have claim to what is left after paying all other claimants, such as the tax authorities, employees,

---

[4]Sometimes a corporation issues two classes of common stock, one bearing the right to vote, the other not. Because of their restricted rights, the nonvoting stocks sell for a lower price, reflecting the value of control.

[5]The voting system specified in the corporate articles determines the chances of affecting the elections to specific directorship seats. In a majority voting system, each shareholder can cast one vote per share for each seat. A cumulative voting system allows shareholders to concentrate all their votes in one seat, enabling minority shareholders to gain representation.

suppliers, bondholders, and other creditors. In a going concern, shareholders have claim to the part of operating income left after interest and income taxes have been paid. Management either can pay this residual as cash dividends to shareholders or reinvest it in the business to increase the value of the shares.

Limited liability means that the most shareholders can lose in event of the failure of the corporation is their original investment. Shareholders are not like owners of unincorporated businesses, whose creditors can lay claim to the personal assets of the owner—such as houses, cars, and furniture. In the event of the firm's bankruptcy, corporate stockholders at worst have worthless stock. They are not personally liable for the firm's obligations: Their liability is limited.

a. If you buy 100 shares of IBM common stock, to what are you entitled? b. What is the most money you can make over the next year? c. If you pay $95 per share, what is the most money you could lose over the year?	**CONCEPT** *check* **2.3**

Stock Market Listings

Figure 2.8 presents key trading data for a small sample of stocks traded on the New York Stock Exchange. The NYSE is one of several markets in which investors may buy or sell shares of stock. We will examine issues of trading in these markets in the next chapter.

To interpret Figure 2.8, consider the highlighted listing for General Electric. The table provides the ticker symbol (GE), the closing price of the stock ($25.25), and its change (−$.43) from the previous trading day. Over 44 million shares of GE traded on this day. The table also provides the highest and lowest price at which GE has traded in the last 52 weeks. The 1.24 value in the DIV column means that the last quarterly dividend payment was $.31 per share, which is consistent with annual dividend payments of $.31 × 4 = $1.24. This corresponds to a dividend yield (i.e., annual dividend per dollar paid for the stock) of 1.24/25.25 = .049 or 4.9%.

The dividend yield is only part of the return on a stock investment. It ignores prospective *capital gains* (i.e., price increases) or losses. Shares in low dividend firms presumably offer greater prospects for capital gains, or investors would not be willing to hold these stocks in their portfolios. If you scan Figure 2.8, you will see that dividend yields vary widely across companies.

The P/E ratio, or price-to-earnings ratio, is the ratio of the current stock price to last year's earnings. The P/E ratio tells us how much stock purchasers must pay per dollar of earnings the firm generates for each share. For GE, the ratio of price to earnings is 12. The P/E ratio also varies widely across firms. Where the dividend yield and P/E ratio are not reported in Figure 2.8, the firms have zero dividends, or zero or negative earnings. We shall have much to say about P/E ratios in Part Four. Finally, we see that GE's stock price has declined by 31.9% since the beginning of the year.

FIGURE 2.8

NAME	SYMBOL	CLOSE	CHG	VOLUME	52 WK HIGH	52 WK LOW	DIV	P/E	YIELD	YTD% CHG
Gencorp	GY	7.09	−0.37	375,381	13.10	6.87	....	21	....	−39.2
Genentech	DNA	91.19	−0.56	2,395,127	99.14	65.35	....	34	....	36.0
General Cable	BGC	38.74	−1.08	1,256,777	83.50	32.96	....	9	....	−47.1
General Dynamics	GD	74.92	−1.82	5,947,222	95.13	74.01	1.40	13	1.9	−15.8
General Electric	GE	25.25	−0.43	44,302,631	42.15	22.16	1.24	12	4.9	−31.9
General Mills Inc	GIS	69.61	0.76	2,322,562	72.01	51.00	1.72	19	2.5	22.1
General Motors	GM	9.76	−0.27	20,601,043	43.20	8.81	....	dd	....	−60.8
Genesco	GCO	35.44	0.08	430,115	43.86	16.97	....	7	....	3.6
Genesee & Wyoming	GWR	38.97	−1.19	376,189	47.41	21.96	....	26	....	61.2
Genesis Lease ADS	GLS	10.00	−0.04	239,532	25.38	9.12	1.88	....	....	−46.7
Genuine Parts	GPC	41.62	0.15	564,795	50.97	36.94	1.56	14	3.7	−10.1
Genworth Financial	GNW	8.14	−2.44	4,820,039	32.33	3.51	0.40	7	4.9	−68.0
Georgia Gulf	GGC	3.25	−0.15	146,290	14.33	1.96	....	dd	....	−50.9
Gerber Scientific	GRB	8.99	....	74,475	12.64	7.96	....	17	....	−16.8

Listing of stocks traded on the New York Stock Exchange

Source: Compiled from data from *The Wall Street Journal Online*, September 29, 2008. Reprinted by permission of Dow Jones & Company, Inc. © 2008 Dow Jones & Company, Inc. All Rights Reserved Worldwide.

Note: dd means that P/E cannot be computed because earnings were negative.

Preferred Stock

preferred stock

Nonvoting shares in a corporation, usually paying a fixed stream of dividends.

tax-deductible expenses)
의 차이점

Preferred stock has features similar to both equity and debt. Like a bond, it promises to pay to its holder a fixed stream of income each year. In this sense, preferred stock is similar to an infinite-maturity bond, that is, a perpetuity. It also resembles a bond in that it does not give the holder voting power regarding the firm's management.

Preferred stock is an equity investment, however. The firm retains discretion to make the dividend payments to the preferred stockholders: It has no contractual obligation to pay those dividends. Instead, preferred dividends are usually *cumulative;* that is, unpaid dividends cumulate and must be paid in full before any dividends may be paid to holders of common stock. In contrast, the firm does have a contractual obligation to make timely interest payments on the debt. Failure to make these payments sets off corporate bankruptcy proceedings.

Preferred stock also differs from bonds in terms of its tax treatment for the firm. Because preferred stock payments are treated as dividends rather than as interest on debt, they are not tax-deductible expenses for the firm. This disadvantage is largely offset by the fact that corporations may exclude 70% of dividends received from domestic corporations in the computation of their taxable income. Preferred stocks, therefore, make desirable fixed-income investments for some corporations.

Even though preferred stock ranks after bonds in terms of the priority of its claim to the assets of the firm in the event of corporate bankruptcy, preferred stock often sells at lower yields than corporate bonds. Presumably this reflects the value of the dividend exclusion, because the higher risk of preferred stock would tend to result in higher yields than those offered by bonds. Individual investors, who cannot use the 70% exclusion, generally will find preferred stock yields unattractive relative to those on other available assets.

Corporations issue preferred stock in variations similar to those of corporate bonds. Preferred stock can be callable by the issuing firm, in which case it is said to be *redeemable*. It also can be convertible into common stock at some specified conversion ratio. A relatively recent innovation is adjustable-rate preferred stock, which, like adjustable-rate bonds, ties the dividend rate to current market interest rates.

Depository Receipts

American Depository Receipts, or ADRs, are certificates traded in U.S. markets that represent ownership in shares of a foreign company. Each ADR may correspond to ownership of a fraction of a foreign share, one share, or several shares of the foreign corporation. ADRs were created to make it easier for foreign firms to satisfy U.S. security registration requirements. They are the most common way for U.S. investors to invest in and trade the shares of foreign corporations. In Figure 2.8, the letters ADS denote American Depository Shares, an alternative terminology for ADRs. See, for example, the listing for Genesis Lease.

2.4   Stock and Bond Market Indexes

Stock Market Indexes

The daily performance of the Dow Jones Industrial Average is a staple portion of the evening news report. While the Dow is the best-known measure of the performance of the stock market, it is only one of several indicators. Other more broadly based indexes are computed and published daily. In addition, several indexes of bond market performance are widely available.

The ever-increasing role of international trade and investments has made indexes of foreign financial markets part of the general news. Thus, foreign stock exchange indexes such as the Nikkei Average of Tokyo or the *Financial Times* index of London have become household names.

Dow Jones Averages

The Dow Jones Industrial Average (DJIA) of 30 large, "blue-chip" corporations has been computed since 1896. Its long history probably accounts for its preeminence in the public mind. (The average covered only 20 stocks until 1928.)

Originally, the DJIA was calculated as the simple average of the stocks included in the index. So, if there were 30 stocks in the index, one would add up the value of the 30 stocks and divide by 30. The percentage change in the DJIA would then be the percentage change in the average price of the 30 shares.

This procedure means that the percentage change in the DJIA measures the return (excluding any dividends paid) on a portfolio that invests one share in each of the 30 stocks in the index. The value of such a portfolio (holding one share of each stock in the index) is the sum of the 30 prices. Because the percentage change in the *average* of the 30 prices is the same as the percentage change in the *sum* of the 30 prices, the index and the portfolio have the same percentage change each day.

The Dow measures the return (excluding dividends) on a portfolio that holds one share of each stock. The amount of money invested in each company in that portfolio is therefore proportional to the company's share price, so the Dow is called a **price-weighted average.**

price-weighted average

An average computed by adding the prices of the stocks and dividing by a "divisor."

Consider the data in Table 2.4 for a hypothetical two-stock version of the Dow Jones Average. Let's compare the changes in the value of the portfolio holding one share of each firm and the price-weighted index. Stock ABC starts at $25 a share and increases to $30. Stock XYZ starts at $100, but falls to $90.

EXAMPLE 2.2

Price-Weighted Average

Portfolio:
    Initial value = $25 + $100 = $125
    Final value = $30 + $90 = $120
    Percentage change in portfolio value = −5/125 = −.04 = −4%

Index:
    Initial index value = (25 + 100)/2 = 62.5
    Final index value = (30 + 90)/2 = 60
    Percentage change in index = −2.5/62.5 = −.04 = −4%

The portfolio and the index have identical 4% declines in value.

Notice that price-weighted averages give higher-priced shares more weight in determining the performance of the index. For example, although ABC increased by 20% while XYZ fell by only 10%, the index dropped in value. This is because the 20% increase in ABC represented a smaller dollar price gain ($5 per share) than the 10% decrease in XYZ ($10 per share). The "Dow portfolio" has four times as much invested in XYZ as in ABC because XYZ's price is four times that of ABC. Therefore, XYZ dominates the average. We conclude that a high-price stock can dominate a price-weighted average.

You might wonder why the DJIA is now (in mid-2009) at a level of about 8,500 if it is supposed to be the average price of the 30 stocks in the index. The DJIA no longer equals the

---

TABLE 2.4

Data to construct stock price indexes

Stock	Initial Price	Final Price	Shares (millions)	Initial Value of Outstanding Stock ($ million)	Final Value of Outstanding Stock ($ million)
ABC	$ 25	$30	20	$500	$600
XYZ	100	90	1	100	90
Total				$600	$690

TABLE 2.5

Data to construct stock price indexes after a stock split

Stock	Initial Price	Final Price	Shares (millions)	Initial Value of Outstanding Stock ($ million)	Final Value of Outstanding Stock ($ million)
ABC	$25	$30	20	$500	$600
XYZ	50	45	2	100	90
Total				$600	$690

average price of the 30 stocks because the averaging procedure is adjusted whenever a stock splits, pays a stock dividend of more than 10%, or when one company in the group of 30 industrial firms is replaced by another. When these events occur, the divisor used to compute the "average price" is adjusted so as to leave the index unaffected by the event.

EXAMPLE 2.3

Splits and Price-Weighted Averages

Suppose firm XYZ from Example 2.2 were to split two for one so that its share price fell to $50. We would not want the average to fall, as that would incorrectly indicate a fall in the general level of market prices. Following a split, the divisor must be reduced to a value that leaves the average unaffected. Table 2.5 illustrates this point. The initial share price of XYZ, which was $100 in Table 2.4, falls to $50 if the stock splits at the beginning of the period. Notice that the number of shares outstanding doubles, leaving the market value of the total shares unaffected.

We find the new divisor as follows. The index value before the stock split was 125/2 = 62.5. We must find a new divisor, d, that leaves the index unchanged after XYZ splits and its price falls to $50. Therefore we solve for d in the following equation:

$$\frac{\text{Price of ABC} + \text{Price of XYZ}}{d} = \frac{25 + 50}{d} = 62.5$$

which implies that the divisor must fall from its original value of 2.0 to a new value of 1.20.

Because the split changes the price of stock XYZ, it also changes the relative weights of the two stocks in the price-weighted average. Therefore, the return of the index is affected by the split.

At period-end, ABC will sell for $30, while XYZ will sell for $45, representing the same negative 10% return it was assumed to earn in Table 2.4. The new value of the price-weighted average is (30 + 45)/1.20 = 62.5. The index is unchanged, so the rate of return is zero, greater than the −4% return that would have resulted in the absence of a split. The relative weight of XYZ, which is the poorer-performing stock, is reduced by a split because its price is lower; so the performance of the average is higher. This example illustrates that the implicit weighting scheme of a price-weighted average is somewhat arbitrary, being determined by the prices rather than by the outstanding market values (price per share times number of shares) of the shares in the average.

In the same way that the divisor is updated for stock splits, if one firm is dropped from the average and another firm with a different price is added, the divisor has to be updated to leave the average unchanged by the substitution. By mid-2009, the divisor for the Dow Jones Industrial Average had fallen to a value of about .132.

Because the Dow Jones averages are based on small numbers of firms, care must be taken to ensure that they are representative of the broad market. As a result, the composition of the average is changed every so often to reflect changes in the economy. Table 2.6 presents the composition of the Dow industrials in 1928 as well as its composition today, in 2009. The table presents striking evidence of the changes in the U.S. economy in the last 80 years. Many of the "bluest of the blue chip" companies in 1928 no longer exist, and the industries that were the backbone of the economy in 1928 have given way to ones that could not have been imagined at the time.

TABLE 2.6

Companies included in the Dow Jones Industrial Average: 1928 and 2009

Dow Industrials in 1928	Current Dow Companies	Ticker Symbol	Industry	Year Added to Index
Wright Aeronautical	3M	MMM	Diversified industrials	1976
Allied Chemical	Alcoa	AA	Aluminum	1959
North American	American Express	AXP	Consumer finance	1982
Victor Talking Machine	AT&T	T	Telecommunications	1999
International Nickel	Bank of America	BAC	Banking	2008
International Harvester	Boeing	BA	Aerospace & defense	1987
Westinghouse	Caterpillar	CAT	Construction	1991
Texas Gulf Sulphur	Chevron	CVX	Oil and gas	2008
American Sugar	Travelers	TRV	Insurance	2009
American Tobacco	Coca-Cola	KO	Beverages	1987
Texas Corp	DuPont	DD	Chemicals	1935
Standard Oil (NJ)	ExxonMobil	XOM	Oil & gas	1928
Sears Roebuck	General Electric	GE	Diversified industrials	1907
General Electric	Cisco Systems	CSCO	Computer equipment	2009
General Motors	Hewlett-Packard	HPQ	Computers	1997
Chrysler	Home Depot	HD	Home improvement retailers	1999
Atlantic Refining	Intel	INTC	Semiconductors	1999
Paramount Publix	IBM	IBM	Computer services	1979
Bethlehem Steel	Johnson & Johnson	JNJ	Pharmaceuticals	1997
General Railway Signal	JPMorgan Chase	JPM	Banking	1991
Mack Trucks	Kraft Foods	KFT	Food processing	2008
Union Carbide	McDonald's	MCD	Restaurants	1985
American Smelting	Merck	MRK	Pharmaceuticals	1979
American Can	Microsoft	MSFT	Software	1999
Postum Inc	Pfizer	PFE	Pharmaceuticals	2004
Nash Motors	Procter & Gamble	PG	Household products	1932
Goodrich	United Technologies	UTX	Aerospace	1939
Radio Corp	Verizon	VZ	Telecommunications	2004
Woolworth	Wal-Mart	WMT	Retailers	1997
U.S. Steel	Walt Disney	DIS	Broadcasting & entertainment	1991

CONCEPT *check* **2.4**

Suppose XYZ's final price in Table 2.4 increases in price to $110, while ABC falls to $20. Find the percentage change in the price-weighted average of these two stocks. Compare that to the percentage return of a portfolio that holds one share in each company.

Dow Jones & Company also computes a Transportation Average of 20 airline, trucking, and railroad stocks; a Public Utility Average of 15 electric and natural gas utilities; and a Composite Average combining the 65 firms of the three separate averages. Each is a price-weighted average and thus overweights the performance of high-priced stocks.

Standard & Poor's Indexes

The Standard & Poor's Composite 500 (S&P 500) stock index represents an improvement over the Dow Jones averages in two ways. First, it is a more broadly based index of 500 firms.

**market value–
weighted index**

Computed by calculating
a weighted average of the
returns of each security in the
index, with weights proportional to outstanding market
value.

Second, it is a **market value–weighted index.** In the case of the firms XYZ and ABC in
Example 2.2, the S&P 500 would give ABC five times the weight given to XYZ because the
market value of its outstanding equity is five times larger, $500 million versus $100 million.

The S&P 500 is computed by calculating the total market value of the 500 firms in the
index and the total market value of those firms on the previous day of trading.[6] The percentage
increase in the total market value from one day to the next represents the increase in the index.
The rate of return of the index equals the rate of return that would be earned by an investor
holding a portfolio of all 500 firms in the index in proportion to their market value, except that
the index does not reflect cash dividends paid by those firms.

EXAMPLE   2.4

*Value-Weighted
Indexes*

To illustrate how value-weighted indexes are computed, look again at Table 2.4. The final value
of all outstanding stock in our two-stock universe is $690 million. The initial value was $600 million. Therefore, if the initial level of a market value–weighted index of stocks ABC and XYZ were
set equal to an arbitrarily chosen starting value such as 100, the index value at year-end would be
$100 \times (690/600) = 115$. The increase in the index would reflect the 15% return earned on a portfolio
consisting of those two stocks held in proportion to outstanding market values.

Unlike the price-weighted index, the value-weighted index gives more weight to ABC. Whereas
the price-weighted index fell because it was dominated by higher-price XYZ, the value-weighted
index rose because it gave more weight to ABC, the stock with the higher total market value.

Note also from Tables 2.4 and 2.5 that market value–weighted indexes are unaffected by stock
splits. The total market value of the outstanding XYZ stock increases from $100 million to $110
million regardless of the stock split, thereby rendering the split irrelevant to the performance of
the index.

A nice feature of both market value–weighted and price-weighted indexes is that they
reflect the returns to straightforward portfolio strategies. If one were to buy each share in the
index in proportion to its outstanding market value, the value-weighted index would perfectly
track capital gains on the underlying portfolio. Similarly, a price-weighted index tracks the
returns on a portfolio comprised of equal shares of each firm.

Investors today can easily buy market indexes for their portfolios. One way is to purchase
shares in mutual funds that hold shares in proportion to their representation in the S&P 500
as well as other stock indexes. These *index funds* yield a return equal to that of the particular
index and so provide a low-cost passive investment strategy for equity investors. Another
approach is to purchase an *exchange-traded fund* or ETF, which is a portfolio of shares that
can be bought or sold as a unit, just as a single share would be traded. Available ETFs range
from portfolios that track extremely broad global market indexes all the way to narrow industry indexes. We discuss both mutual funds and ETFs in detail in Chapter 4.

Standard & Poor's also publishes a 400-stock Industrial Index, a 20-stock Transportation
Index, a 40-stock Utility Index, and a 40-stock Financial Index.

CONCEPT
check **2.5**

Reconsider companies XYZ and ABC from Concept Check Question 2.4. Calculate the percentage change in the market value–weighted index. Compare that to the rate of return of a
portfolio that holds $500 of ABC stock for every $100 of XYZ stock (i.e., an index portfolio).

Other U.S. Market Value Indexes

The New York Stock Exchange publishes a market value–weighted composite index of all
NYSE-listed stocks, in addition to subindexes for industrial, utility, transportation, and financial stocks. These indexes are even more broadly based than the S&P 500. The National

---

[6]Actually, most indexes today use a modified version of market-value weights. Rather than weighting by total market
value, they weight by the market value of "free float," that is, by the value of shares that are freely tradable among
investors. For example, this procedure does not count shares held by founding families or governments, which are
effectively not available for investors to purchase. The distinction is more important in Japan and Europe, where a
higher fraction of shares are held in such nontraded portfolios.

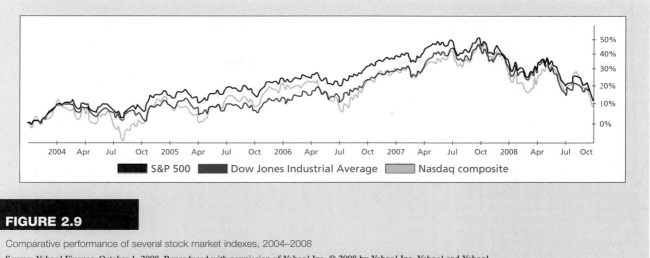

FIGURE 2.9

Comparative performance of several stock market indexes, 2004–2008

Source: Yahoo! Finance, October 1, 2008. Reproduced with permission of Yahoo! Inc. © 2008 by Yahoo! Inc. Yahoo! and Yahoo! Logo are trademarks of Yahoo! Inc.

Association of Securities Dealers publishes an index of more than 3,000 firms traded on the NASDAQ market.

The ultimate U.S. equity index so far computed is the Wilshire 5000 Index of the market value of essentially all actively traded stocks in the U.S. Despite its name, the index actually includes about 6,000 stocks. The performance of many of these indexes appears daily in *The Wall Street Journal*.

Figure 2.9 shows the performance of the S&P 500, Dow Jones Industrial Average, and NASDAQ composite over the five-year period ending in late 2008. Usually, the indexes move closely together. Occasionally though, they diverge. For example, during the Internet boom and bust of 1999–2002, the NASDAQ index, which is dominated by the technology sector, first greatly outperformed, and then underperformed, the S&P 500.

Equally Weighted Indexes

Market performance is sometimes measured by an equally weighted average of the returns of each stock in an index. Such an averaging technique, by placing equal weight on each return, corresponds to a portfolio strategy that places equal dollar values in each stock. This is in contrast to both price weighting, which requires equal numbers of shares of each stock, and market value weighting, which requires investments in proportion to outstanding value.

Unlike price- or market value–weighted indexes, **equally weighted indexes** do not correspond to buy-and-hold portfolio strategies. Suppose you start with equal dollar investments in the two stocks of Table 2.4, ABC and XYZ. Because ABC increases in value by 20% over the year, while XYZ decreases by 10%, your portfolio is no longer equally weighted but is now more heavily invested in ABC. To reset the portfolio to equal weights, you would need to rebalance: Either sell some ABC stock and/or purchase more XYZ stock. Such rebalancing would be necessary to align the return on your portfolio with that on the equally weighted index.

equally weighted index

An index computed from a simple average of returns.

Foreign and International Stock Market Indexes

Development in financial markets worldwide includes the construction of indexes for these markets. Among these are the Nikkei (Japan), FTSE (U.K., pronounced "footsie"), DAX (Germany), Hang Seng (Hong Kong), and TSX (Toronto). A leader in the construction of international indexes has been MSCI (Morgan Stanley Capital International), which computes over 50 country indexes and several regional indexes. Table 2.7 presents many of the indexes computed by MCSI.

TABLE 2.7

Sample of MSCI stock indexes

Regional Indexes		Countries	
Developed Markets	**Emerging Markets**	**Developed Markets**	**Emerging Markets**
EAFE (Europe, Australia, Far East)	Emerging Markets (EM)	Australia	Argentina
EASEA (EAFE excluding Japan)	EM Asia	Austria	Brazil
Europe	EM Far East	Belgium	Chile
EMU	EM Latin America	Canada	China
Far East	Emerging Markets Free (EMF)	Denmark	Colombia
Kokusai (World excluding Japan)	EMF Asia	Finland	Czech Republic
Nordic Countries	EMF Eastern Europe	France	Egypt
North America	EMF Europe	Germany	Hungary
Pacific	EMF Europe & Middle East	Greece	India
The World Index	EMF Far East	Hong Kong	Indonesia
G7 countries	EMF Latin America	Ireland	Israel
World excluding U.S.		Italy	Jordan
		Japan	Korea
		Netherlands	Malaysia
		New Zealand	Mexico
		Norway	Morocco
		Portugal	Pakistan
		Singapore	Peru
		Spain	Philippines
		Sweden	Poland
		Switzerland	Russia
		U.K.	South Africa
		U.S.	Sri Lanka
			Taiwan
			Thailand
			Turkey
			Venezuela

Source: MSCI, **www.mscibarra.com**. Reprinted by permission.

TABLE 2.8

The U.S. bond market

Sector	Size ($ billion)	% of Market
Treasury	$ 5,055.7	23.2%
Gov't sponsored enterprise	3,104.0	14.3
Corporate	3,685.3	16.9
Tax-exempt*	2,661.5	12.2
Mortgage-backed	4,761.5	21.9
Asset-backed	2,480.3	11.4
Total	$21,748.3	100.0%

*Includes private purpose tax-exempt debt.

Source: *Flow of Funds Accounts of the United States: Flows and Outstandings,* Board of Governors of the Federal Reserve System, September 2008.

Bond Market Indicators

Just as stock market indexes provide guidance concerning the performance of the overall stock market, several bond market indicators measure the performance of various categories of bonds. The three most well-known groups of indexes are those of Merrill Lynch, Barclays (formerly Lehman Brothers), and Salomon Smith Barney (now part of Citigroup). Table 2.8 lists the components of the bond market in 2008.

The major problem with these indexes is that true rates of return on many bonds are difficult to compute because bonds trade infrequently, which makes it hard to get reliable, up-to-date prices. In practice, some prices must be estimated from bond-valuation models. These so-called matrix prices may differ from true market values.

2.5 Derivative Markets

A significant development in financial markets in recent years has been the growth of futures and options markets. Futures and options provide payoffs that depend on the values of other assets, such as commodity prices, bond and stock prices, or market index values. For this reason, these instruments sometimes are called **derivative assets** or **contingent claims.** Their values derive from or are contingent on the values of other assets. We discuss derivative assets in detail in Part Five.

derivative asset or contingent claim

A security with a payoff that depends on the prices of other securities.

Options

A **call option** gives its holder the right to purchase an asset for a specified price, called the *exercise* or *strike price,* on or before some specified expiration date. An October call option on Apple stock with exercise price $110, for example, entitles its owner to purchase Apple stock for a price of $110 at any time up to and including the option's expiration date in October. Each option contract is for the purchase of 100 shares, with quotations made on a per share basis. The holder of the call need not exercise the option; it will make sense to exercise only if the market value of the asset that may be purchased exceeds the exercise price.

When the market price exceeds the exercise price, the option holder may "call away" the asset for the exercise price and reap a benefit equal to the difference between the stock price and the exercise price. Otherwise, the option will be left unexercised. If not exercised before the expiration date, the option expires and no longer has value. Calls, therefore, provide greater profits when stock prices increase and so represent bullish investment vehicles.

In contrast, a **put option** gives its holder the right to sell an asset for a specified exercise price on or before a specified expiration date. An October put on Apple with exercise price $110 entitles its owner to sell Apple stock to the put writer at a price of $110 at any time before expiration in October even if the market price of Apple is lower than $110. Whereas profits on call options increase when the asset increases in value, profits on put options increase when the asset value falls. The put is exercised only if its holder can deliver an asset worth less than the exercise price in return for the exercise price.

call option

The right to buy an asset at a specified price on or before a specified expiration date.

put option

The right to sell an asset at a specified exercise price on or before a specified expiration date.

Figure 2.10 is an excerpt of the option quotations for Apple from the *The Wall Street Journal Online.* The price of Apple shares on that date was $110.35. The first two columns give the expiration month and exercise (equivalently, strike) price of each option. Thus, we see listings for call and put options on Apple with exercise prices ranging from $100 to $115, and with expiration dates in October and November 2008 and January and April 2009.

The next columns provide the closing prices, trading volume, and open interest (outstanding contracts) of each option. For example, 9,335 call contracts traded on the October 2008 expiration call with an exercise price of $110. The last trade was at $7.45, meaning that an option to purchase one share of Apple at an exercise price of $110 sold for $7.45. Each option *contract* (on 100 shares of stock), therefore, costs $7.45 × 100 = $745.

Notice that the prices of call options decrease as the exercise price increases. For example, the October 2008 expiration call with exercise price $115 costs only $5.30. This makes sense, as the right to purchase a share at a higher exercise price is less valuable. Conversely, put prices increase with the exercise price. The right to sell a share of Apple in October at a price of $110 costs $8.10 while the right to sell at $115 costs $11.00.

Option prices also increase with time until expiration. Clearly, one would rather have the right to buy Apple for $110 at any time until April 2009 than at any time until October 2008. Not surprisingly, this shows up in a higher price for the more-distant expiration options. For example, the call with exercise price $110 expiring in April 2009 sells for $20.40, compared to only $7.45 for the October 2008 call.

FIGURE 2.10

Stock options on Apple

Source: From *The Wall Street Journal Online*, October 2, 2008. Reprinted by permission of Dow Jones & Company, Inc. © 2008 Dow Jones & Company, Inc. All Rights Reserved Worldwide.

Prices at close October 1, 2008

Apple (AAPL) — Underlying stock price: 110.35

Expiration	Strike	Call			Put		
		Last	Volume	Open Interest	Last	Volume	Open Interest
Oct	100	13.45	2387	2938	4.04	7431	13848
Nov	100	18.20	390	730	8.63	1596	4228
Jan	100	21.65	1427	11505	11.35	1541	48586
Apr	100	25.10	58	838	14.50	146	1786
Oct	105	10.35	7025	2894	5.90	14166	12871
Nov	105	15.50	1236	584	10.68	680	4029
Jan	105	19.00	358	720	13.70	40	1243
Apr	105	22.40	230	630	16.20	86	893
Oct	110	7.45	9335	17361	8.10	11790	16832
Nov	110	12.93	3693	2866	13.23	839	5898
Jan	110	16.30	313	7430	16.00	578	48552
Apr	110	20.40	375	2123	19.24	244	1565
Oct	115	5.30	12833	6681	11.00	6082	22068
Nov	115	10.65	1549	1995	15.80	654	5108
Jan	115	14.20	1936	5733	18.75	89	27947
Apr	115	18.00	44	530	22.20	48	891

CONCEPT check 2.6

What would be the profit or loss per share of stock to an investor who bought the October 2008 expiration Apple call option with exercise price $110, if the stock price at the expiration of the option is $120? What about a purchaser of the put option with the same exercise price and expiration?

Futures Contracts

futures contract

Obliges traders to purchase or sell an asset at an agreed-upon price at a specified future date.

A **futures contract** calls for delivery of an asset (or in some cases, its cash value) at a specified delivery or maturity date, for an agreed-upon price, called the *futures price,* to be paid at contract maturity. The long position is held by the trader who commits to purchasing the commodity on the delivery date. The trader who takes the short position commits to delivering the commodity at contract maturity.

Figure 2.11 illustrates the listing of the corn futures contract on the Chicago Board of Trade for October 2, 2008. Each contract calls for delivery of 5,000 bushels of corn. Each row details prices for contracts expiring on various dates. The first row is for the nearest term or "front" contract, with maturity in December 2008. The most recent price was $4.555 per bushel. (The numbers after the apostrophe denote eighths of a cent.) That price is down $.285 from yesterday's close. The next columns show the contract's opening price that day as well as the high and low price over each contract's life. Volume is the number of contracts trading that day; open interest is the number of outstanding contracts.

The trader holding the long position profits from price increases. Suppose that at expiration, corn is selling for $4.575 per bushel. The long position trader who entered the contract at the futures price of $4.555 on October 2 would pay the previously agreed-upon $4.555 for each bushel of corn, which at contract maturity would be worth $4.575.

Because each contract calls for delivery of 5,000 bushels, the profit to the long position, ignoring brokerage fees, would equal $5{,}000 \times (\$4.575 - \$4.555) = \$1{,}000$. Conversely, the short position must deliver 5,000 bushels for the previously agreed-upon futures price. The short position's loss equals the long position's profit.

The distinction between the *right* to purchase and the *obligation* to purchase the asset is the difference between a call option and a long position in a futures contract. A futures

MATURITY	LAST	CHG	OPEN	HIGH	LOW	VOLUME	OPEN INT
Dec '08	455'4	−28'4	485'4	488'0	454'6	103193	517447
Mar '09	474'6	−28'2	504'6	506'4	473'4	17005	200555
May '09	486'0	−29'0	517'6	517'6	486'0	2571	47010
Jul '09	498'0	−27'6	527'4	529'2	497'2	4894	96555
Sep '09	505'4	−26'4	534'0	535'0	504'2	779	19780
Dec '09	511'6	−25'2	538'6	539'6	509'2	8727	114099
Mar '10	526'0	−20'0	546'0	546'0	525'0	1365	6691
May '10	533'6	−17'2	533'0	546'2	533'0	43	277
Jul '10	542'4	−13'0	535'4	542'4	535'4	78	1941
Dec '10	503'0	−27'0	532'0	532'0	503'0	313	27991
Dec '11	511'0	−19'0	530'0	530'0	511'0	21	501

FIGURE 2.11

Corn futures prices in the Chicago Board of Trade, October 2, 2008

Source: Data from *The Wall Street Journal Online*, October 2, 2008. Reprinted by permission of Dow Jones & Company, Inc. © 2008 Dow Jones & Company, Inc. All Rights Reserved Worldwide.

contract *obliges* the long position to purchase the asset at the futures price; the call option merely *conveys the right* to purchase the asset at the exercise price. The purchase will be made only if it yields a profit.

Clearly, the holder of a call has a better position than the holder of a long position on a futures contract with a futures price equal to the option's exercise price. This advantage, of course, comes only at a price. Call options must be purchased; futures investments are contracts only. The purchase price of an option is called the *premium*. It represents the compensation the purchaser of the call must pay for the ability to exercise the option only when it is profitable to do so. Similarly, the difference between a put option and a short futures position is the right, as opposed to the obligation, to sell an asset at an agreed-upon price.

SUMMARY

- Money market securities are very short-term debt obligations. They are usually highly marketable and have relatively low credit risk. Their low maturities and low credit risk ensure minimal capital gains or losses. These securities often trade in large denominations, but they may be purchased indirectly through money market funds.
- Much of U.S. government borrowing is in the form of Treasury bonds and notes. These are coupon-paying bonds usually issued at or near par value. Treasury bonds are similar in design to coupon-paying corporate bonds.
- Municipal bonds are distinguished largely by their tax-exempt status. Interest payments (but not capital gains) on these securities are exempt from income taxes.
- Mortgage pass-through securities are pools of mortgages sold in one package. Owners of pass-throughs receive all principal and interest payments made by the borrower. The firm that originally issued the mortgage merely services the mortgage, simply "passing through" the payments to the purchasers of the mortgage. Payment of interest and principal on government agency pass-through securities are guaranteed, but payments on private-label mortgage pools are not.
- Common stock is an ownership share in a corporation. Each share entitles its owner to one vote on matters of corporate governance and to a prorated share of the dividends paid to shareholders. Stock, or equity, owners are the residual claimants on the income earned by the firm.
- Preferred stock usually pays a fixed stream of dividends for the life of the firm: It is a perpetuity. A firm's failure to pay the dividend due on preferred stock, however, does not set off corporate bankruptcy. Instead, unpaid dividends simply cumulate. Varieties of preferred stock include convertible and adjustable-rate issues.

www.mhhe.com/bkm

- Many stock market indexes measure the performance of the overall market. The Dow Jones averages, the oldest and best-known indicators, are price-weighted indexes. Today, many broad-based, market value–weighted indexes are computed daily. These include the Standard & Poor's composite 500 stock index, the NYSE, the NASDAQ index, the Wilshire 5000 Index, and several international indexes, including the Nikkei, FTSE, and DAX.
- A call option is a right to purchase an asset at a stipulated exercise price on or before an expiration date. A put option is the right to sell an asset at some exercise price. Calls increase in value, while puts decrease in value, as the price of the underlying asset increases.
- A futures contract is an obligation to buy or sell an asset at a stipulated futures price on a maturity date. The long position, which commits to purchasing, gains if the asset value increases, while the short position, which commits to delivering the asset, loses.

KEY TERMS

bankers' acceptance, 27	equally weighted index, 43	municipal bonds, 32
call option, 45	Eurodollars, 27	preferred stock, 38
certificate of deposit, 26	Federal funds, 28	price-weighted average, 39
commercial paper, 27	futures contract, 46	put option, 45
common stocks, 36	LIBOR, 28	repurchase agreements, 27
corporate bonds, 34	market value–weighted	Treasury bills, 24
derivative asset/contingent	index, 42	Treasury bonds, 30
claim, 45	money markets, 24	Treasury notes, 30

PROBLEM SETS

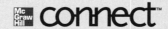

Select problems are available in McGraw-Hill Connect. Please see the packaging options of the preface for more information.

Basic

1. What are the key differences between common stock, preferred stock, and corporate bonds?
2. Why do most professionals consider the Wilshire 5000 a better index of the performance of the broad stock market than the Dow Jones Industrial Average?
3. What features of money market securities distinguish them from other fixed-income securities?
4. What are the major components of the money market?
5. Describe alternative ways that an investor may add positions in international equity to his or her portfolio.
6. Why are high-tax-bracket investors more inclined to invest in municipal bonds than are low-bracket investors?
7. What is meant by the LIBOR rate? The Federal funds rate?
8. How does a municipal revenue bond differ from a general obligation bond? Which would you expect to have a lower yield to maturity?
9. Why are corporations more apt to hold preferred stock than are other potential investors?
10. What is meant by limited liability?

Intermediate

11. Why are money market securities sometimes referred to as "cash equivalents"?
12. A municipal bond carries a coupon rate of 6¾% and is trading at par. What would be the equivalent taxable yield of this bond to a taxpayer in a 35% tax bracket?

13. Suppose that short-term municipal bonds currently offer yields of 4%, while comparable taxable bonds pay 5%. Which gives you the higher after-tax yield if your tax bracket is:
    a. Zero
    b. 10%
    c. 20%
    d. 30%

14. An investor is in a 30% combined federal plus state tax bracket. If corporate bonds offer 9% yields, what must municipals offer for the investor to prefer them to corporate bonds?

15. Find the equivalent taxable yield of the municipal bond in Problem 13 for tax brackets of zero, 10%, 20%, and 30%.

16. Turn back to Figure 2.4 and look at the Treasury bond maturing in February 2012.
    a. How much would you have to pay to purchase one of these bonds?
    b. What is its coupon rate?
    c. What is the current yield (i.e., coupon income as a fraction of bond price) of the bond?

17. Turn to Figure 2.8 and look at the listing for General Dynamics.
    a. What was the firm's closing price *yesterday*?
    b. How many shares could you buy for $5,000?
    c. What would be your annual dividend income from those shares?
    d. What must be its earnings per share?

18. Consider the three stocks in the following table. P_t represents price at time t, and Q_t represents shares outstanding at time t. Stock C splits two-for-one in the last period.

	P_0	Q_0	P_1	Q_1	P_2	Q_2
A	90	100	95	100	95	100
B	50	200	45	200	45	200
C	100	200	110	200	55	400

    a. Calculate the rate of return on a price-weighted index of the three stocks for the first period ($t = 0$ to $t = 1$).
    b. What must happen to the divisor for the price-weighted index in year 2?
    c. Calculate the rate of return of the price-weighted index for the second period ($t = 1$ to $t = 2$).

19. Using the data in the previous problem, calculate the first period rates of return on the following indexes of the three stocks:
    a. a market value–weighted index.
    b. an equally weighted index.

20. What problems would confront a mutual fund trying to create an index fund tied to an equally weighted index of a broad stock market?

21. What would happen to the divisor of the Dow Jones Industrial Average if FedEx, with a current price of around $60 per share, replaced General Motors (with a current value of about $3 per share)?

22. A T-bill with face value $10,000 and 87 days to maturity is selling at a bank discount ask yield of 3.4%. What is the price of the bill? What is its bond equivalent yield?

23. Which security should sell at a greater price?
    a. A 10-year Treasury bond with a 9% coupon rate or a 10-year T-bond with a 10% coupon.
    b. A three-month expiration call option with an exercise price of $40 or a three-month call on the same stock with an exercise price of $35.
    c. A put option on a stock selling at $50 or a put option on another stock selling at $60. (All other relevant features of the stocks and options are assumed to be identical.)

24. Look at the futures listings for corn in Figure 2.11.
    a. Suppose you buy one contract for December 2009 delivery. If the contract closes in December at a price of $5.25 per bushel, what will be your profit or loss?
    b. How many December 2009 maturity contracts are outstanding?

25. Turn back to Figure 2.10 and look at the Apple options. Suppose you buy an April expiration call option with exercise price 105.
    a. If the stock price in April is $111, will you exercise your call? What are the profit and rate of return on your position?
    b. What if you had bought the April call with exercise price 100?
    c. What if you had bought an April put with exercise price 105?

26. What options position is associated with:
    a. The right to buy an asset at a specified price?
    b. The right to sell an asset at a specified price?
    c. The obligation to buy an asset at a specified price?
    d. The obligation to sell an asset at a specified price?

27. Why do call options with exercise prices higher than the price of the underlying stock sell for positive prices?

28. Both a call and a put currently are traded on stock XYZ; both have strike prices of $50 and maturities of six months. What will be the profit to an investor who buys the call for $4 in the following scenarios for stock prices in six months? (*a*) $40; (*b*) $45; (*c*) $50; (*d*) $55; (*e*) $60. What will be the profit in each scenario to an investor who buys the put for $6?

29. What would you expect to happen to the spread between yields on commercial paper and Treasury bills if the economy were to enter a steep recession?

30. Examine the stocks listed in Figure 2.8. For how many of these stocks is the 52-week high price at least 50% greater than the 52-week low price? What do you conclude about the volatility of prices on individual stocks?

31. Find the after-tax return to a corporation that buys a share of preferred stock at $40, sells it at year-end at $40, and receives a $4 year-end dividend. The firm is in the 30% tax bracket.

Challenge

32. Explain the difference between a put option and a short position in a futures contract.

33. Explain the difference between a call option and a long position in a futures contract.

CFA Problems

1. Preferred stock yields often are lower than yields on bonds of the same quality because of
    a. Marketability
    b. Risk
    c. Taxation
    d. Call protection

STANDARD &POOR'S

Use data from the Standard & Poor's Market Insight Database at www.mhhe.com/edumarketinsight to answer the following questions.

Select the Company tab and enter ticket symbol DIS. Click on the EDGAR section and find the link for Disney's most recent annual report (10-K).

Locate the company's Consolidated Balance Sheets and answer these questions:

1. How much preferred stock is Disney authorized to issue? How much has been issued?

2. How much common stock is Disney authorized to issue? How many shares are currently outstanding?

Search for the term "Financing Activities."

3. What is the total amount of borrowing listed for Disney? How much of this is medium-term notes?

4. What other types of debt does Disney have outstanding?

WEB *master* **STOCK MARKET INDEX**

Not all stock market indexes are created equal. Different methods are used to calculate various indexes, and different indexes will yield different assessments of "market performance." Using one of the following data sources, retrieve the stock price for five different firms on the first and last trading days of the previous month.

www.nasdaq.com—Get a quote, then select Charts and specify one month. When the chart appears, click on a data point to display the underlying data.

www.bloomberg.com—Get a quote, then plot the chart; next, use the moving line to see the closing price today and one month ago.

finance.yahoo.com—Get a quote, then click on Historical Data and specify a date range.

1. Compute the monthly return on a price-weighted index of the five stocks.
2. Compute the monthly return on a value-weighted index of the five stocks.
3. Compare the two returns and explain their differences. Explain how you would interpret each measure.

SOLUTIONS TO CONCEPT *checks*

2.1. The bond sells for 101:06 bid which is a price of 101.1875% of par or $1,011.875 and 101:07 ask, or $1,012.1875. This ask price corresponds to a yield of 4.423%. The ask price rose 26/32 from its level yesterday, so the ask price then must have been 100:13 or $1,004.0625.

2.2. A 6% taxable return is equivalent to an after-tax return of $6(1 - .28) = 4.32\%$. Therefore, you would be better off in the taxable bond. The equivalent taxable yield of the tax-free bond is $4/(1 - .28) = 5.55\%$. So a taxable bond would have to pay a 5.55% yield to provide the same after-tax return as a tax-free bond offering a 4% yield.

2.3. *a.* You are entitled to a prorated share of IBM's dividend payments and to vote in any of IBM's stockholder meetings.

   b. Your potential gain is unlimited because IBM's stock price has no upper bound.

   c. Your outlay was $95 \times 100 = \$9,500$. Because of limited liability, this is the most you can lose.

2.4. The price-weighted index increases from $62.50[=(100 + 25)/2]$ to $65[=(110 + 20)/2]$, a gain of 4%. An investment of one share in each company requires an outlay of $125 that would increase in value to $130, for a return of 4% $(=5/125)$, which equals the return to the price-weighted index.

2.5. The market value–weighted index return is calculated by computing the increase in value of the stock portfolio. The portfolio of the two stocks starts with an initial value of $100 million + $500 million = $600 million and falls in value to $110 million + $400 million = $510 million, a loss of 90/600 = .15, or 15%. The index portfolio return is a weighted average of the returns on each stock with weights of ⅙ on XYZ and ⅚ on ABC (weights proportional to relative investments). Because the return on XYZ is 10%, while that on ABC is −20%, the index portfolio return is (⅙) 10 +(⅚) (−20) = −15%, equal to the return on the market value–weighted index.

2.6. The payoff to the call option is $120 − $110 = $10. The call cost $7.45. The profit is $10 − $7.45 = $2.55 per share. The put will pay off zero—it expires worthless since the stock price exceeds the exercise price. The loss is the cost of the put, $8.10.

3 Chapter

Securities Markets

After Studying This Chapter You Should Be Able To:

- Describe the role of investment bankers in primary issues.

- Identify the various security markets.

- Compare trading practices in stock exchanges with those in dealer markets.

- Describe the role of brokers.

- Compare the mechanics and investment implications of buying on margin and short-selling.

his chapter will provide you with a broad introduction to the many venues and procedures available for trading securities in the United States and international markets. We will see that trading mechanisms range from direct negotiation among market participants to fully automated computer crossing of trade orders.

The first time a security trades is when it is issued to the public. Therefore, we begin with a look at how securities are first marketed to the public by investment bankers, the midwives of securities. We turn next to a broad survey of how already-issued securities may be traded among investors, focusing on the differences between dealer markets, electronic markets, and specialist markets.

With this background, we then turn to specific trading arenas such as the New York Stock Exchange, NASDAQ, and several foreign security markets, examining the competition among these markets for the patronage of security traders. We consider the costs of trading in these markets, the quality of trade execution, and the ongoing quest for cross-market integration of trading.

We then turn to the essentials of some specific types of transactions, such as buying on margin and short-selling stocks. We close the chapter with a look at some important aspects of the regulations governing security trading, including insider trading laws, circuit breakers, and the role of security markets as self-regulating organizations.

3.1 How Firms Issue Securities

When firms need to raise capital they may choose to sell or *float* securities. These new issues of stocks, bonds, or other securities typically are marketed to the public by investment bankers in what is called the **primary market.** Trading of already-issued securities among investors occurs in the **secondary market.** Trading in secondary markets does not affect the outstanding amount of securities; ownership is simply transferred from one investor to another.

There are two types of primary market issues of common stock. **Initial public offerings,** or **IPOs,** are stocks issued by a formerly privately owned company that is going public, that is, selling stock to the public for the first time. *Seasoned equity offerings* are offered by companies that already have floated equity. For example, a sale by IBM of new shares of stock would constitute a seasoned new issue.

In the case of bonds, we also distinguish between two types of primary market issues, a *public offering* and a *private placement.* The former refers to an issue of bonds sold to the general investing public that can then be traded on the secondary market. The latter refers to an issue that usually is sold to one or a few institutional investors and is generally held to maturity.

Investment Banking

Public offerings of both stocks and bonds typically are marketed by investment bankers who in this role are called **underwriters.** More than one investment banker usually markets the securities. A lead firm forms an underwriting syndicate of other investment bankers to share the responsibility for the stock issue.

Investment bankers advise the firm regarding the terms on which it should attempt to sell the securities. A preliminary registration statement must be filed with the Securities and Exchange Commission (SEC), describing the issue and the prospects of the company. This preliminary prospectus is known as a *red herring* because it includes a statement printed in red, stating that the company is not attempting to sell the security before the registration is approved. When the statement is in final form, and approved by the SEC, it is called the **prospectus.** At this point, the price at which the securities will be offered to the public is announced.

In a typical underwriting arrangement, the investment bankers purchase the securities from the issuing company and then resell them to the public. The issuing firm sells the securities to the underwriting syndicate for the public offering price less a spread that serves as compensation to the underwriters. This procedure is called a *firm commitment.* In addition to the spread, the investment banker also may receive shares of common stock or other securities of the firm. Figure 3.1 depicts the relationships among the firm issuing the security, the lead underwriter, the underwriting syndicate, and the public.

primary market

Market for new issues of securities.

secondary market

Market for already-existing securities.

initial public offering (IPO)

First sale of stock by a formerly private company.

underwriters

Underwriters purchase securities from the issuing company and resell them.

prospectus

A description of the firm and the security it is issuing.

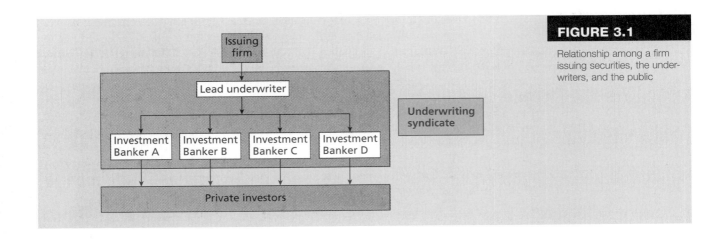

FIGURE 3.1

Relationship among a firm issuing securities, the underwriters, and the public

Shelf Registration

An important innovation in the issuing of securities was introduced in 1982 when the SEC approved Rule 415, which allows firms to register securities and gradually sell them to the public for two years following the initial registration. Because the securities are already registered, they can be sold on short notice, with little additional paperwork. Moreover, they can be sold in small amounts without incurring substantial flotation costs. The securities are "on the shelf," ready to be issued, which has given rise to the term *shelf registration.*

CONCEPT *check* **3.1**   Why does it make sense for shelf registration to be limited in time?

Private Placements

private placement

Primary offerings in which shares are sold directly to a small group of institutional or wealthy investors.

Primary offerings also can be sold in a **private placement** rather than a public offering. In this case, the firm (using an investment banker) sells shares directly to a small group of institutional or wealthy investors. Private placements can be far cheaper than public offerings. This is because Rule 144A of the SEC allows corporations to make these placements without preparing the extensive and costly registration statements required of a public offering. On the other hand, because private placements are not made available to the general public, they generally will be less suited for very large offerings. Moreover, private placements do not trade in secondary markets like stock exchanges. This greatly reduces their liquidity and presumably reduces the prices that investors will pay for the issue.

Initial Public Offerings

Investment bankers manage the issuance of new securities to the public. Once the SEC has commented on the registration statement and a preliminary prospectus has been distributed to interested investors, the investment bankers organize *road shows* in which they travel around the country to publicize the imminent offering. These road shows serve two purposes. First, they generate interest among potential investors and provide information about the offering. Second, they provide information to the issuing firm and its underwriters about the price at which they will be able to market the securities. Large investors communicate their interest in purchasing shares of the IPO to the underwriters; these indications of interest are called a *book* and the process of polling potential investors is called *bookbuilding*. These indications of interest provide valuable information to the issuing firm because institutional investors often will have useful insights about both the market demand for the security as well as the prospects of the firm and its competitors. It is common for investment bankers to revise both their initial estimates of the offering price of a security and the number of shares offered based on feedback from the investing community.

Why do investors truthfully reveal their interest in an offering to the investment banker? Might they be better off expressing little interest, in the hope that this will drive down the offering price? Truth is the better policy in this case because truth telling is rewarded. Shares of IPOs are allocated across investors in part based on the strength of each investor's expressed interest in the offering. If a firm wishes to get a large allocation when it is optimistic about the security, it needs to reveal its optimism. In turn, the underwriter needs to offer the security at a bargain price to these investors to induce them to participate in bookbuilding and share their information. Thus, IPOs commonly are underpriced compared to the price at which they could be marketed. Such underpricing is reflected in price jumps that occur on the date when the shares are first traded in public security markets. The most dramatic case of underpricing occurred in December 1999 when shares in VA Linux were sold in an IPO at $30 a share and closed on the first day of trading at $239.25, a 698% one-day return.[1]

---

[1]It is worth noting, however, that by December 2000, shares in VA Linux (now renamed VA Software) were selling for less than $9 a share, and by 2002, for less than $1. This example is extreme, but consistent with the generally poor long-term investment performance of IPOs.

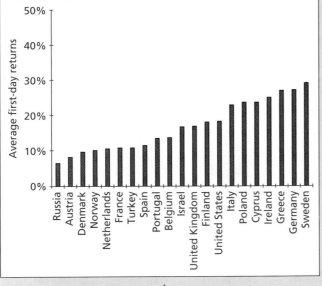
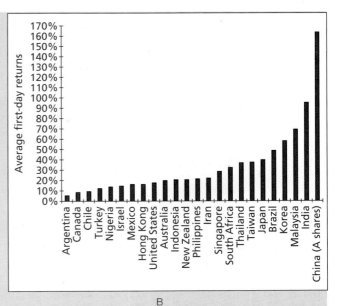

A   B

FIGURE 3.2

Average initial returns for (A) European and (B) Non-European IPOs

Source: Provided by Professor J. Ritter of the University of Florida, 2008. This is an updated version of the information contained in T. Loughran, J. Ritter, and K. Rydqvist, "Initial Public Offerings," *Pacific-Basin Finance Journal* 2 (1994), pp. 165–199. Copyright 1994 with permission from Elsevier Science.

While the explicit costs of an IPO tend to be around 7% of the funds raised, such underpricing should be viewed as another cost of the issue. For example, if VA Linux had sold its shares for the $239 that investors obviously were willing to pay for them, its IPO would have raised 8 times as much as it actually did. The money "left on the table" in this case far exceeded the explicit cost of the stock issue. This degree of underpricing is far more dramatic than is common, but underpricing seems to be a universal phenomenon.

Figure 3.2 presents average first-day returns on IPOs of stocks across the world. The results consistently indicate that IPOs are marketed to investors at attractive prices. Underpricing of IPOs makes them appealing to all investors, yet institutional investors are allocated the bulk of a typical new issue. Some view this as unfair discrimination against small investors. However, our analysis suggests that the apparent discounts on IPOs may be in part payments for a valuable service, specifically, the information contributed by the institutional investors. The right to allocate shares in this way may contribute to efficiency by promoting the collection and dissemination of such information.[2]

Both views of IPO allocations probably contain some truth. IPO allocations to institutions do serve a valid economic purpose as an information-gathering tool. Nevertheless, the system can be—and has been—abused. Part of the Wall Street scandals of 2000–2002 centered on the allocation of shares in IPOs. In a practice known as "spinning," some investment bankers used IPO allocations to corporate insiders to curry favors, in effect as implicit kickback schemes. These underwriters would award generous IPO allocations to executives of particular firms in return for the firm's future investment banking business.

Pricing of IPOs is not trivial and not all IPOs turn out to be underpriced. Some do poorly after issue. The 2006 IPO of Vonage was a notable disappointment. The stock lost about 30% of its value in its first seven days of trading. Other IPOs cannot even be fully sold to the market. Underwriters left with unmarketable securities are forced to sell them at a loss on the secondary market. Therefore, the investment banker bears the price risk of an underwritten issue.

[2]Benveniste and Wilhelm (1997) provide an elaboration of this point and a more complete discussion of the bookbuilding process.

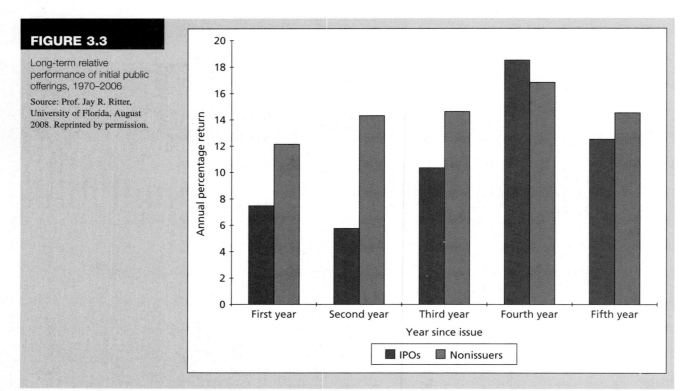

FIGURE 3.3

Long-term relative
performance of initial public
offerings, 1970–2006

Source: Prof. Jay R. Ritter,
University of Florida, August
2008. Reprinted by permission.

Interestingly, despite their dramatic initial investment performance, IPOs have been poor long-term investments. Figure 3.3 compares the stock price performance of IPOs with shares of other firms of the same size for each of the five years after issue of the IPO. The year-by-year underperformance of the IPOs is dramatic, suggesting that, on average, the investing public may be too optimistic about the prospects of these firms. Such long-lived systematic errors on the part of investors would be surprising. An interesting study by Brav, Geczy, and Gompers (2000), however, suggests that apparent IPO underperformance may be illusory. When they carefully match firms based on size and ratios of book values to market values, they find that IPO returns are actually similar to those of comparison firms.

3.2 How Securities are Traded

Financial markets develop to meet the needs of particular traders. Consider what would happen if organized markets did not exist. Any household wishing to invest in some type of financial asset would have to find others wishing to sell. Soon, venues where interested traders could meet would become popular. Eventually, financial markets would emerge from these meeting places. Thus, a pub in old London called Lloyd's launched the maritime insurance industry. A Manhattan curb on Wall Street became synonymous with the financial world.

Types of Markets

We can differentiate four types of markets: direct search markets, brokered markets, dealer markets, and auction markets.

Direct search markets A *direct search market* is the least organized market. Buyers and sellers must seek each other out directly. An example of a transaction in such a market is the sale of a used refrigerator where the seller advertises for buyers on Craigslist. Such markets are characterized by sporadic participation and low-priced and nonstandard goods. It would not pay for most people or firms to specialize in such markets.

Brokered markets   The next level of organization is a *brokered market.* In markets where trading in a good is active, brokers find it profitable to offer search services to buyers and sellers. A good example is the real estate market, where economies of scale in searches for available homes and for prospective buyers make it worthwhile for participants to pay brokers to conduct the searches. Brokers in particular markets develop specialized knowledge on valuing assets traded in that market.

An important brokered investment market is the *primary market,* where new issues of securities are offered to the public. In the primary market, investment bankers who market a firm's securities to the public act as brokers; they seek investors to purchase securities directly from the issuing corporation.

Another brokered market is that for large block transactions, in which very large blocks of stock are bought or sold. These blocks are so large (technically more than 10,000 shares but usually much larger) that brokers or "block houses" often are engaged to search directly for other large traders, rather than bring the trade directly to the markets where relatively smaller investors trade.

Dealer markets   When trading activity in a particular type of asset increases, **dealer markets** arise. Dealers specialize in various assets, purchase these assets for their own accounts, and later sell them for a profit from their inventory. The spreads between dealers' buy (or "bid") prices and sell (or "ask") prices are a source of profit. Dealer markets save traders on search costs because market participants can easily look up the prices at which they can buy from or sell to dealers. A fair amount of market activity is required before dealing in a market is an attractive source of income. The over-the-counter (OTC) securities market is one example of a dealer market.

dealer markets

Markets in which traders specializing in particular assets buy and sell for their own accounts.

Auction markets   The most integrated market is an **auction market,** in which all traders converge at one place (either physically or "electronically") to buy or sell an asset. The New York Stock Exchange (NYSE) is an example of an auction market. An advantage of auction markets over dealer markets is that one need not search across dealers to find the best price for a good. If all participants converge, they can arrive at mutually agreeable prices and save the bid–ask spread.

Continuous auction markets (as opposed to periodic auctions, such as in the art world) require very heavy and frequent trading to cover the expense of maintaining the market. For this reason, the NYSE and other exchanges set up listing requirements, which limit the stocks traded on the exchange to those of firms in which sufficient trading interest is likely to exist.

The organized stock exchanges are also secondary markets. They are organized for investors to trade existing securities among themselves.

auction market

A market where all traders meet at one place to buy or sell an asset.

Many assets trade in more than one type of market. What types of markets do the following trade in?
  a. Used cars
  b. Paintings
  c. Rare coins

CONCEPT *check* **3.2**

Types of Orders

Before comparing alternative trading practices and competing security markets, it is helpful to begin with an overview of the types of trades an investor might wish to have executed in these markets. Broadly speaking, there are two types of orders: market orders and orders contingent on price.

bid price

The price at which a dealer or other trader is willing to purchase a security.

Market orders   Market orders are buy or sell orders that are to be executed immediately at current market prices. For example, our investor might call her broker and ask for the market price of IBM. The broker might report back that the best **bid price** is $90 and the best **ask price** is $90.05, meaning that the investor would need to pay $90.05 to purchase a share,

ask price

The price at which a dealer or other trader will sell a security.

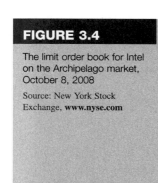

FIGURE 3.4

The limit order book for Intel on the Archipelago market, October 8, 2008

Source: New York Stock Exchange, **www.nyse.com**

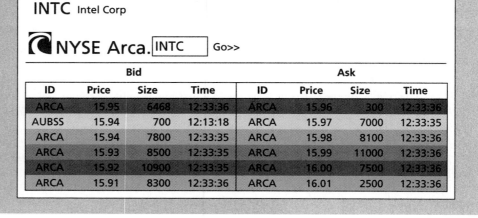

INTC Intel Corp

NYSE Arca. | INTC | Go>>

	Bid				Ask		
ID	**Price**	**Size**	**Time**	**ID**	**Price**	**Size**	**Time**
ARCA	15.95	6468	12:33:36	ARCA	15.96	300	12:33:36
AUBSS	15.94	700	12:13:18	ARCA	15.97	7000	12:33:35
ARCA	15.94	7800	12:33:35	ARCA	15.98	8100	12:33:36
ARCA	15.93	8500	12:33:35	ARCA	15.99	11000	12:33:36
ARCA	15.92	10900	12:33:35	ARCA	16.00	7500	12:33:36
ARCA	15.91	8300	12:33:36	ARCA	16.01	2500	12:33:36

bid–ask spread

The difference between a dealer's bid and asked price.

and could receive $90 a share if she wished to sell some of her own holdings of IBM. The **bid–ask spread** in this case is $.05. So an order to buy 100 shares "at market" would result in purchase at $90.05, and an order to "sell at market" would be executed at $90.

This simple scenario is subject to a few potential complications. First, posted price quotes actually represent commitments to trade up to a specified number of shares. If the market order is for more than this number of shares, the order may be filled at multiple prices. For example, if the asked price is good for orders up to 1,000 shares, and the investor wishes to purchase 1,500 shares, it may be necessary to pay a slightly higher price for the last 500 shares. Second, another trader may beat our investor to the quote, meaning that her order would then be executed at a worse price. Finally, the best price quote may change before her order arrives, again causing execution at a different price than the one at the moment of the order.

Price-contingent orders   Investors also may place orders specifying prices at which they are willing to buy or sell a security. A **limit buy order** may instruct the broker to buy some number of shares if and when IBM may be obtained at or below a stipulated price. Conversely, a **limit sell** instructs the broker to sell if and when the stock price rises *above* a specified limit. A collection of limit orders waiting to be executed is called a *limit order book.*

limit buy (sell) order

An order specifying a price at which an investor is willing to buy or sell a security.

Figure 3.4 is a portion of the limit order book for shares in Intel taken from the Archipelago exchange (one of several electronic exchanges; more on these shortly) on one day in 2008. Notice that the best orders are at the top of the list: the offers to buy at the highest price and to sell at the lowest price. The buy and sell orders at the top of the list—$15.95 and $15.96—are called the *inside quotes;* they are the highest buy and lowest sell orders. For Intel, the inside spread is only 1 cent. Note, however, that order sizes at the inside quotes are often fairly small. Therefore, investors interested in larger trades face an *effective* spread greater than the nominal one since they cannot execute their entire trades at the inside price quotes.

Until 2001, when U.S. markets adopted decimal pricing, the minimum possible spread was "one tick," which on the New York Stock Exchange was $\frac{1}{8}$ until 1997 and $\frac{1}{16}$ thereafter. With decimal pricing, the spread can be far lower. The average quoted bid–ask spread on the NYSE is less than 5 cents.

stop order

Trade is not to be executed unless stock hits a price limit.

Stop orders are similar to limit orders in that the trade is not to be executed unless the stock hits a price limit. For *stop-loss orders,* the stock is to be *sold* if its price falls *below* a stipulated level. As the name suggests, the order lets the stock be sold to stop further losses from accumulating. Similarly, *stop-buy orders* specify that a stock should be bought when its price rises above a limit. These trades often accompany *short sales* (sales of securities you don't own but have borrowed from your broker) and are used to limit potential losses from the short position. Short sales are discussed in greater detail later in this chapter. Figure 3.5 organizes these types of trades in a convenient matrix.

CONCEPT check 3.3

What type of trading order might you give to your broker in each of the following circumstances?

a. You want to buy shares of Intel to diversify your portfolio. You believe the share price is approximately at the "fair" value, and you want the trade done quickly and cheaply.

b. You want to buy shares of Intel, but believe that the current stock price is too high given the firm's prospects. If the shares could be obtained at a price 5% lower than the current value, you would like to purchase shares for your portfolio.

c. You plan to purchase a condominium sometime in the next month or so and will sell your shares of Intel to provide the funds for your down payment. While you believe that Intel share price is going to rise over the next few weeks, if you are wrong and the share price drops suddenly, you will not be able to afford the purchase. Therefore, you want to hold on to the shares for as long as possible, but still protect yourself against the risk of a big loss.

Trading Mechanisms

Broadly speaking, there are three trading systems employed in the United States: over-the-counter dealer markets, electronic communication networks, and formal exchanges. The best-known markets such as NASDAQ or the New York Stock Exchange actually use a variety of trading procedures, so before delving into these markets, it is useful to understand the basic operation of each type of trading system.

FIGURE 3.5

Price-contingent orders

Action	Condition: Price falls below the limit	Condition: Price rises above the limit
Buy	Limit buy order	Stop-buy order
Sell	Stop-loss order	Limit sell order

Dealer markets Roughly 35,000 securities trade on the **over-the-counter** or **OTC market.** Thousands of brokers register with the SEC as security dealers. Dealers quote prices at which they are willing to buy or sell securities. A broker then executes a trade by contacting a dealer listing an attractive quote.

over-the-counter (OTC) market

An informal network of brokers and dealers who negotiate sales of securities.

Before 1971, all OTC quotations were recorded manually and published daily on so-called pink sheets. In 1971, the National Association of Securities Dealers Automatic Quotations System, or NASDAQ, was developed to link brokers and dealers in a computer network where price quotes could be displayed and revised. Dealers could use the network to display the bid price at which they were willing to purchase a security and the ask price at which they were willing to sell. The difference in these prices, the bid–ask spread, was the source of the dealer's profit. Brokers representing clients could examine quotes over the computer network, contact the dealer with the best quote, and execute a trade.

As originally organized, NASDAQ was more of a price quotation system than a trading system. While brokers could survey bid and ask prices across the network of dealers in the search for the best trading opportunity, actual trades required direct negotiation (often over the phone) between the investor's broker and the dealer in the security. However, as we will see shortly, NASDAQ has progressed far beyond a pure price quotation system. While dealers still post bid and ask prices over the network, NASDAQ now allows for electronic execution of trades at quoted prices without the need for direct negotiation, and the vast majority of trades are executed electronically.

Electronic communication networks (ECNs) **Electronic communication networks** allow participants to post market and limit orders over computer networks. The limit order book is available to all participants. An example of such an order book from Archipelago, one of the leading ECNs, appeared in Figure 3.4. Orders that can be "crossed,"

ECNs

Computer networks that allow direct trading without the need for market makers.

that is, matched against another order, are done so automatically without requiring the intervention of a broker. For example, an order to buy a share at a price of $50 or lower will be immediately executed if there is an outstanding asked price of $50. Therefore, ECNs are true trading systems, not merely price quotation systems.

ECNs offer several attractions. Direct crossing of trades without using a broker-dealer system eliminates the bid–ask spread that otherwise would be incurred. Instead, trades are automatically crossed at a modest cost, typically less than a penny per share. ECNs are attractive as well because of the speed with which a trade can be executed. Finally, these systems offer investors considerable anonymity in their trades.

Specialist markets   In formal exchanges such as the New York Stock Exchange, trading in each security is managed by a **specialist** assigned responsibility for that security. Brokers who wish to buy or sell shares on behalf of their clients must direct the trade to the specialist's post on the floor of the exchange.

specialist

A trader who makes a market in the shares of one or more firms and who maintains a "fair and orderly market" by dealing personally in the market.

Each security is assigned to one specialist, but each specialist firm—currently there are fewer than 10 on the NYSE—makes a market in many securities. This task may require the specialist to act as either a broker or a dealer. The specialist's role as a broker is simply to execute the orders of other brokers. Specialists also may buy or sell shares of stock for their own portfolios, in this role acting as a dealer in the stock. When no other trader can be found to take the other side of a trade, specialists will do so even if it means they must buy for or sell from their own accounts. Specialist firms earn income both from commissions for managing orders (as implicit brokers) and from the spreads at which they buy and sell securities (as implicit dealers).

Part of the specialist's job as a broker is simply clerical. The specialist maintains a limit order book of all outstanding unexecuted limit orders entered by brokers on behalf of clients. When limit orders can be executed at market prices, the specialist executes, or "crosses," the trade.

The specialist is required to use the highest outstanding offered purchase price and the lowest outstanding offered selling price when matching trades. Therefore, the specialist system results in an auction market, meaning all buy and all sell orders come to one location, and the best orders "win" the trades. In this role, the specialist acts merely as a facilitator.

The more interesting function of the specialist is to maintain a "fair and orderly market" by acting as a dealer in the stock. In return for the exclusive right to make the market in a specific stock on the exchange, the specialist is required by the exchange to maintain an orderly market by buying and selling shares from inventory. Specialists maintain their own portfolios of stock and quoted bid and ask prices at which they are obligated to meet at least a limited amount of market orders.

Ordinarily, in an active market, specialists can match buy and sell orders without using their own accounts. That is, the specialist's own inventory of securities need not be the primary means of order execution. Sometimes, however, the specialist's bid and ask prices are better than those offered by any other market participant. Therefore, at any point, the effective ask price in the market is the lower of either the specialist's ask price or the lowest of the unfilled limit-sell orders. Similarly, the effective bid price is the highest of the unfilled limit buy orders or the specialist's bid. These procedures ensure that the specialist provides liquidity to the market. In practice, specialists participate in approximately one-quarter of the transactions on the NYSE.

Specialists strive to maintain a narrow bid–ask spread for at least two reasons. First, one source of the specialist's income is frequent trading at the bid and ask prices, with the spread as a trading profit. A too-large spread would make the specialist's quotes uncompetitive with the limit orders placed by other traders. If the specialist's bid and asked quotes are consistently worse than those of public traders, the specialist will not participate in any trades and will lose the ability to profit from the bid–ask spread.

An equally important reason for narrow specialist spreads is that they are obligated to provide *price continuity* to the market. To illustrate price continuity, suppose the highest limit buy order for a stock is $30, while the lowest limit sell order is $32. When a market buy order comes in, it is matched to the best limit sell at $32. A market sell order would be matched to the best limit buy at $30. As market buys and sells come to the floor randomly, the stock price would fluctuate between $30 and $32. The exchange authorities would consider this excessive volatility, and the specialist would be expected to step in with bid and/or ask prices between these values to reduce the bid–ask spread to an acceptable level, typically below $.05 for large firms. When a firm is newly listed on an exchange, specialist firms vigorously compete to be awarded the rights to maintain the market in those shares. Since specialists are evaluated in part on their past performance in maintaining price continuity, they have considerable incentive to maintain tight spreads.

3.3 U.S. Securities Markets

We have briefly sketched the three major trading mechanisms used in the United States: over-the-counter dealer markets, exchange trading managed by specialists, and direct trading among brokers or investors over electronic networks. The NASDAQ market historically was the most important dealer market in the United States, and the New York Stock Exchange the most important formal equity exchange. As we will see, however, these markets have evolved in response to new information technology and both have dramatically increased their commitment to automated electronic trading.

NASDAQ

While any security can be traded in the over-the-counter network of security brokers and dealers, not all securities were included in the original National Association of Security Dealers Automated Quotations System. That system, now called the **NASDAQ Stock Market,** lists about 3,200 firms and offers three listing options. The NASDAQ Global Select Market is for the largest, most actively traded firms, the NASDAQ Global Market is for the next tier of firms, and the NASDAQ Capital Market is the third tier of listed firms. Some of the requirements for initial listing are presented in Table 3.1. For even smaller firms that may not be eligible for listing or that wish to avoid disclosure requirements associated with listing on regulated markets, Pink Sheets LLC offers real-time stock quotes on **www.pinksheets.com,** as well as Pink Link, an electronic messaging and trade negotiation service.

NASDAQ Stock Market

The computer-linked priced quotation system for the OTC market.

Because the NASDAQ system does not use a specialist, OTC trades do not require a centralized trading floor as do exchange-listed stocks. Dealers can be located anywhere they can communicate effectively with other buyers and sellers.

NASDAQ has three levels of subscribers. The highest, level 3 subscribers, are for firms dealing, or "making markets," in OTC securities. These market makers maintain inventories of a security and constantly stand ready to buy or sell these shares from or to the public at the quoted bid and ask prices. They earn profits from the spread between the bid and ask prices. Level 3 subscribers may enter the bid and ask prices at which they are willing to buy or sell stocks into the computer network and may update these quotes as desired.

Level 2 subscribers receive all bid and ask quotes, but they cannot enter their own quotes. These subscribers tend to be brokerage firms that execute trades for clients but do not actively deal in the stocks on their own account. Brokers buying or selling shares trade with the market maker (a level 3 subscriber) displaying the best price quote.

TABLE 3.1	NASDAQ Global Market	NASDAQ Capital Market
Partial requirements for initial listing on NASDAQ markets		
Shareholders' equity	$15 million	$5 million
Shares in public hands	1.1 million	1 million
Market value of publicly traded shares	$8 million	$5 million
Minimum price of stock	$5	$4
Pretax income	$1 million	$750,000
Shareholders	400	300

Source: The NASDAQ Stock Market, **www.nasdaq.com**, October 2008.

Level 1 subscribers receive only the inside quotes (i.e., the highest bid and lowest ask prices on each stock). Level 1 subscribers tend to be investors who are not actively buying and selling securities but want information on current prices.

As noted, NASDAQ was originally more a price quotation system than a trading system. But that has changed. Investors today (through their brokers) typically access bids and offers electronically without human interaction. NASDAQ has steadily introduced ever-more sophisticated electronic trading platforms, which today handle the great majority of its trades. The latest version, called the NASDAQ Market Center, was introduced in 2004 and consolidates all of NASDAQ's previous electronic markets into one integrated system.

Market Center is NASDAQ's competitive response to the growing popularity of ECNs, which have captured a large share of order flow. By enabling automatic trade execution, Market Center allows NASDAQ to function much like an ECN. In addition, NASDAQ purchased Instinet, which operates the major electronic communications network INET in order to capture a greater share of the electronic trading market. Nevertheless, larger orders may still be negotiated among brokers and dealers, so NASDAQ retains some features of a pure dealer market.

The New York Stock Exchange

stock exchanges

Secondary markets where already-issued securities are bought and sold by members.

The New York Stock Exchange is by far the largest **stock exchange** in the United States. Shares of about 2,800 firms trade there, with a combined market capitalization in early 2008 of around $14 trillion. Daily trading on the NYSE regularly exceeded 3 billion shares in 2008, with a dollar value of approximately $150 billion.

An investor who wishes to trade shares on the NYSE places an order with a brokerage firm, which either sends the order to the floor of the exchange via computer network or contacts its broker on the floor of the exchange to "work" the order. Smaller orders are almost always sent electronically for automatic execution, while larger orders that may require negotiation or judgment are more prone to be sent to a floor broker. A floor broker sent a trade order takes the order to the specialist's post. At the post is a monitor called the Display Book that presents current offers from interested traders to buy or sell given numbers of shares at various prices. The specialist can cross the trade with that of another broker if that is feasible, or match the trade using its own inventory of shares. Brokers might also seek out traders willing to take the other side of a trade at a price better than those currently appearing in the Display Book. If they can do so, they will bring the agreed-upon trade to the specialist for final execution.

Brokers must purchase the right to trade on the floor of the NYSE. Originally, the NYSE was organized as a not-for-profit company owned by its members or "seat holders." For example, in 2005 there were 1,366 seat-holding members of the NYSE. Each seat entitled its owner to place a broker on the floor of the exchange, where he or she could execute trades. Member firms could charge investors for executing trades on their behalf, which made a seat a valuable asset. The commissions that members might earn by trading on behalf of clients determined the market value of seat, which were bought and sold like any other asset. Seat prices fluctuated widely, ranging from as low as $4,000 (in 1878) to as high as $4 million (in 2005).

More recently, most exchanges have switched from a mutual form of organization, in which seat-holders are joint owners, to publicly traded corporations owned by shareholders. In 2006, the NYSE merged with the Archipelago Exchange to form a publicly held company called the NYSE Group. (In 2007, the NYSE Group merged with Euronext to form NYSE-Euronext.) As a publicly traded corporation, its share price rather than the price of a seat on the exchange has become the best indicator of its financial health. Each seat on the exchange has been replaced by an annual license permitting traders to conduct business on the exchange floor.

The move toward public listing of exchanges is widespread. Other exchanges that have recently gone public include the Chicago Mercantile Exchange (derivatives trading, 2002), the International Securities Exchange (options, 2005), and the Chicago Board of Trade (derivatives, 2005), which has since merged with the CME. The Chicago Board Options Exchange reportedly also is considering going public.

Table 3.2 gives some of the initial listing requirements for the NYSE. These requirements ensure that a firm is of significant trading interest before the NYSE will allocate facilities for

TABLE 3.2	Minimum annual pretax income in previous two years	$ 2,000,000
Some initial listing requirements for the NYSE	Revenue	$100,000,000
	Market value of publicly held stock	$100,000,000
	Shares publicly held	1,100,000
	Number of holders of 100 shares or more	2,200

Source: Data from the New York Stock Exchange–Euronext, **www.nyse.com**, October 2008.

it to be traded on the floor of the exchange. If a listed company suffers a decline and fails to meet the criteria in Table 3.2, it may be delisted.

Regional exchanges also sponsor trading of some firms that are traded on national exchanges. This dual listing enables local brokerage firms to trade in shares of large firms without purchasing a membership on the NYSE.

About 75% of the share volume transacted in NYSE-listed securities actually is executed on the NYSE. The NYSE's market share measured by trades rather than share volume is considerably lower, as smaller retail orders are far more likely to be executed off the exchange. Nevertheless, the NYSE remains the venue of choice for large trades.

Block sales Institutional investors frequently trade tens of thousands of shares of stock. Larger **block transactions** (technically transactions exceeding 10,000 shares, but often much larger) are often too large for specialists to handle, as they do not wish to hold such large amounts of stock in their inventory.

block transactions

Large transactions in which at least 10,000 shares of stock are bought or sold.

"Block houses" have evolved to aid in the placement of larger block trades. Block houses are brokerage firms that specialize in matching block buyers and sellers. Once a buyer and a seller have been matched, the block is sent to the exchange floor where specialists execute the trade. If a buyer cannot be found, the block house might purchase all or part of a block sale for its own account. The block house then can resell the shares to the public.

You can observe in Table 3.3 that the share of block trading peaked in the mid-1990s, but has since declined sharply. This reflects changing trading practices since the advent of electronic markets. Large trades are now much more likely to be split up into multiple small trades and executed electronically. The lack of depth on the electronic exchanges reinforces this pattern: Because the inside quote on these exchanges is valid only for small trades, it generally is preferable to buy or sell a large stock position in a series of smaller transactions.

TABLE 3.3	Year	Shares (millions)	% Reported Volume	Average Number of Block Transactions per Day
Block transactions on the New York Stock Exchange	1965	48	03.1%	9
	1970	451	15.4	68
	1975	779	16.6	136
	1980	3,311	29.2	528
	1985	14,222	51.7	2,139
	1990	19,682	49.6	3,333
	1995	49,737	57.0	7,793
	2000	135,772	51.7	21,941
	2002	161,075	44.4	25,300
	2004	116,926	31.9	17,000
	2005	112,027	27.7	17,445
	2006	97,576	21.3	14,360
	2007	57,079	10.7	7,332

Source: Data from the New York Stock Exchange–Euronext, **www.nyse.com,** October 2008.

program trade

Coordinated sale or purchase of a portfolio of stocks.

Electronic trading on the NYSE   The NYSE has recently stepped up its commitment to electronic trading. Its SuperDot is an electronic order-routing system that enables brokerage firms to send market and limit orders directly to the specialist over computer lines. SuperDot is especially useful to program traders. A **program trade** is a coordinated purchase or sale of an entire portfolio of stocks.

While SuperDot simply transmits orders to the specialist's post electronically, the NYSE also has instituted a fully automated trade-execution system called DirectPlus or Direct+. It matches orders against the inside bid or ask price with execution times of a small fraction of a second. Direct+ has captured an ever-larger share of trades on the NYSE. Today, the vast majority of all orders are submitted electronically, but these tend to be smaller orders. Larger orders are still more likely to go through a specialist.

Settlement   Orders executed on the exchange must be settled within three working days. This requirement is often called T + 3, for trade date plus three days. The purchaser must deliver the cash, and the seller must deliver the stock to the broker, who in turn delivers it to the buyer's broker. Frequently, a firm's clients keep their securities in *street name,* which means the broker holds the shares registered in the firm's own name on behalf of the client. This convention can speed security transfer. T + 3 settlement has made such arrangements more important: It can be quite difficult for a seller of a security to complete delivery to the purchaser within the three-day period if the stock is kept in a safe deposit box.

Settlement is simplified further by the existence of a clearinghouse. The trades of all exchange members are recorded each day, with members' transactions netted out, so that each member need transfer or receive only the net number of shares sold or bought that day. A brokerage firm then settles with the clearinghouse instead of individually with every firm with which it made trades.

Electronic Communication Networks

ECNs are private computer networks that directly link buyers with sellers. As an order is received, the system determines whether there is a matching order, and if so, the trade is executed immediately. Brokers that have an affiliation with an ECN have computer access and can enter orders in the limit order book. Moreover, these brokers may make their terminals (or Internet access) available directly to individual traders who then can enter their own orders into the system. The two biggest ECNs by far are INET, formed by a merger of Island and Instinet, and Archipelago.

As noted, the NYSE and Archipelago merged in 2006. In principle, the merged firm can fill simple orders quickly without human interaction through ArcaEx (the Archipelago Exchange), and large complex orders using human traders on the floor of the NYSE. At the same time, NASDAQ purchased the other leading ECN, Instinet, which operates INET. Thus, the securities markets appear to be consolidating and it seems that each market will, at least for a time, offer multiple trading platforms. But the trend toward electronic trading continues unabated.

The National Market System

The Securities Act Amendments of 1975 directed the Securities and Exchange Commission to implement a national competitive securities market. Such a market would entail centralized reporting of transactions and a centralized quotation system, with the aim of enhanced competition among market makers.

In 1975, Consolidated Tape began reporting trades on the NYSE, Amex, and major regional exchanges, as well as trades of NASDAQ-listed stocks. In 1977, the Consolidated Quotations Service began providing online bid and ask quotes for NYSE securities also traded on various other exchanges. In 1978, the Intermarket Trading System (ITS) was implemented. ITS currently links nine exchanges by computer: NYSE, Amex, Boston, National (formerly Cincinnati), Pacific, Philadelphia, Chicago, NASDAQ, and the Chicago Board Options Exchange. The system allows brokers and market makers to display and view quotes for all markets and to execute cross-market trades when the Consolidated Quotation System shows better prices in other markets. However, the ITS has been only a limited success. Orders need to be directed to alternative markets by participants who might find it inconvenient or unprofitable to do so.

However, the growth of automated electronic trading has made market integration more feasible. The SEC reaffirmed its *trade-through rule* in 2005. Its Regulation NMS requires that investors' orders be filled at the best price that can be executed immediately, even if that price is available in a different market.

The trade-through rule is meant to improve speed of execution and enhance integration of competing stock markets. Linking markets electronically through a unified book displaying all limit orders would be a logical extension of the ITS, enabling trade execution across markets. But this degree of integration has not yet been realized. Regulation NMS requires only that the inside quotes of each market be publicly shared. Because the inside or best quote is typically available only for a small number of shares, there is still no guarantee that an investor will receive the best available prices for an entire trade, especially for larger trades.

Bond Trading

In 2006, the NYSE obtained regulatory approval to expand its bond trading system to include the debt issues of any NYSE-listed firm. In the past, each bond needed to be registered before listing; such a requirement was too onerous to justify listing most bonds. In conjunction with these new listings, the NYSE has expanded its electronic bond-trading platform, which is now called NYSE Bonds, and is the largest centralized bond market of any U.S. exchange.

Nevertheless, the vast majority of bond trading occurs in the OTC market among bond dealers, even for bonds that are actually listed on the NYSE. This market is a network of bond dealers such as Merrill Lynch (now part of Bank of America), Salomon Smith Barney (a division of Citigroup), or Goldman, Sachs that is linked by a computer quotation system. However, because these dealers do not carry extensive inventories of the wide range of bonds that have been issued to the public, they cannot necessarily offer to sell bonds from their inventory to clients or even buy bonds for their own inventory. They may instead work to locate an investor who wishes to take the opposite side of a trade. In practice, however, the corporate bond market often is quite "thin," in that there may be few investors interested in trading a bond at any particular time. As a result, the bond market is subject to a type of liquidity risk, for it can be difficult to sell one's holdings quickly if the need arises.

3.4 Market Structure in Other Countries

The structure of security markets varies considerably from one country to another. A full cross-country comparison is far beyond the scope of this text. Therefore, we will instead briefly review three of the biggest non-U.S. stock markets: the London, Euronext, and Tokyo exchanges. Figure 3.6 shows the market capitalization of firms trading in the major stock markets.

London

The London Stock Exchange uses an electronic trading system dubbed SETS (Stock Exchange Electronic Trading Service). This is an electronic clearing system similar to ECNs in which buy and sell orders are submitted via computer networks and any buy and sell orders that can be crossed are executed automatically. However, less liquid shares are traded in a more traditional dealer market called the SEAQ (Stock Exchange Automated Quotations) system in which market makers enter bid and ask prices at which they are willing to transact. These trades may entail direct communication between brokers and market makers. The major stock index for London is the FTSE (Financial Times Stock Exchange; pronounced "footsie") 100 Index.

Euronext

Euronext was formed in 2000 by a merger of the Paris, Amsterdam, and Brussels exchanges, and itself merged with the NYSE Group in 2007. Euronext, like most European exchanges, uses an electronic trading system. Its system, called NSC (for Nouveau Système de Cotation,

FIGURE 3.6

Market capitalization of major world stock exchanges, 2008

Source: New York Stock Exchange, **www.nyse.com,** January 20, 2009.

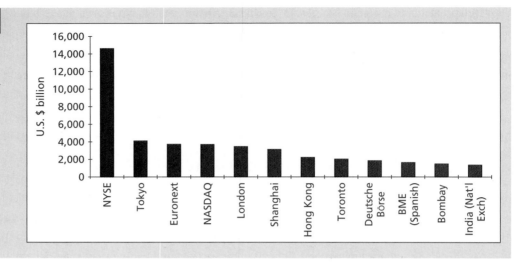

or New Quotation System), has fully automated order routing and execution. In fact, investors can enter their orders directly without contacting their brokers. An order submitted to the system is executed immediately if it can be crossed against an order in the public limit order book; if it cannot be executed, it is entered into the limit order book.

Euronext has established cross-trading agreements with several other European exchanges such as Helsinki or Luxembourg. In 2002, it also purchased LIFFE, the London International Financial Futures and Options Exchange.

Tokyo

The Tokyo Stock Exchange (TSE) is among the largest in the world, measured either by trading volume or the market capitalization of its roughly 2,400 listed firms. Its exemplifies many of the general trends that we have seen affecting stock markets throughout the world. In 1999, it closed its trading floor and switched to all-electronic trading. It switched from a membership form of organization to a corporate form in 2001.

The TSE maintains three "sections." The First section is for large companies, the Second is for midsized firms, and the "Mothers" section is for emerging and high-growth stocks. About three-quarters of all listed firms trade on the First section, and about 200 trade in the Mothers section.

The two major stock market indexes for the TSE are the Nikkei 225 index, which is a price-weighted average of 225 top-tier Japanese firms, and the TOPIX index, which is a value-weighted index of the First section companies.[3]

Globalization and Consolidation of Stock Markets

All stock markets have come under increasing pressure in recent years to make international alliances or mergers. Much of this pressure is due to the impact of electronic trading. To a growing extent, traders view stock markets as networks that link them to other traders, and there are increasingly fewer limits on the securities around the world that they can trade. Against this background, it becomes more important for exchanges to provide the cheapest and most efficient mechanism by which trades can be executed and cleared. This argues for global alliances that can facilitate the nuts and bolts of cross-border trading and can benefit from economies of scale. Moreover, in the face of competition from electronic networks,

---

[3]As we noted in Chapter 2, most value-weighted indexes today are based on *free float* (the value of shares freely tradable among investors) rather than total shares. Free float excludes shares held by founding families or governments. This is true of the TOPIX as well.

established exchanges feel that they eventually need to offer 24-hour global markets. Finally, companies want to be able to go beyond national borders when they wish to raise capital.

These pressures have resulted in a broad trend toward market consolidation. In the last decade, most of the mergers were "local," that is, involving exchanges operating in the same continent. In the U.S., the NYSE merged with the Archipelago ECN in 2006, and in 2008 acquired the American Stock Exchange. NASDAQ acquired Instinet (which operated the other major ECN, INET) in 2005 and the Boston Stock Exchange in 2007. In the derivatives market, the Chicago Mercantile Exchange acquired the Chicago Board of Trade in 2007. In Europe, Euronext was formed by the merger of the Paris, Brussels, Lisbon, and Amsterdam exchanges and shortly thereafter purchased LIFFE, the derivatives exchange based in London. The LSE merged in 2007 with Borsa Italiana, which operates the Milan exchange.

There has also been a wave of intercontinental consolidation. The NYSE Group and Euronext merged in 2007. The NYSE has purchased 5% of India's National Stock Exchange and has entered a cooperation agreement with the Tokyo Stock Exchange. In March 2006, NASDAQ made an offer to acquire the London Stock Exchange, but the LSE rejected that proposal. However, NASDAQ finally acquired a foothold in Europe in 2007, when it joined forces with Börse Dubai to acquire the Swedish exchange OMX. In 2007, Eurex acquired International Securities Exchange Holdings, and ISE announced that it would launch a new derivatives market in partnership with the Toronto Stock Exchange.

3.5 Trading Costs

Part of the cost of trading a security is obvious and explicit. Your broker must be paid a commission. Individuals may choose from two kinds of brokers: full-service or discount brokers. Full-service brokers who provide a variety of services often are referred to as account executives or financial consultants.

Besides carrying out the basic services of executing orders, holding securities for safekeeping, extending margin loans, and facilitating short sales, brokers routinely provide information and advice relating to investment alternatives.

Full-service brokers usually depend on a research staff that prepares analyses and forecasts of general economic as well as industry and company conditions and often makes specific buy or sell recommendations. Some customers take the ultimate leap of faith and allow a full-service broker to make buy and sell decisions for them by establishing a *discretionary account*. In this account, the broker can buy and sell prespecified securities whenever deemed fit. (The broker cannot withdraw any funds, though.) This action requires an unusual degree of trust on the part of the customer, for an unscrupulous broker can "churn" an account, that is, trade securities excessively with the sole purpose of generating commissions.

Discount brokers, on the other hand, provide "no-frills" services. They buy and sell securities, hold them for safekeeping, offer margin loans, facilitate short sales, and that is all. The only information they provide about the securities they handle is price quotations. Discount brokerage services have become increasingly available in recent years. Many banks, thrift institutions, and mutual fund management companies now offer such services to the investing public as part of a general trend toward the creation of one-stop "financial supermarkets." Stock trading fees have fallen steadily over the last decade, and discount brokerage firms such as Schwab, E*Trade, or Ameritrade now offer commissions below $15, or even below $10 for preferred customers.

In addition to the explicit part of trading costs—the broker's commission—there is an implicit part—the dealer's bid–ask spread. Sometimes the broker is a dealer in the security being traded and charges no commission but instead collects the fee entirely in the form of the bid–ask spread. Another implicit cost of trading that some observers would distinguish is the price concession an investor may be forced to make for trading in quantities greater than those associated with the posted bid or asked prices.

An ongoing controversy between the NYSE and its competitors is the extent to which better execution on the NYSE offsets the generally lower explicit costs of trading in other markets. The NYSE believes that many investors focus too intently on the costs they can see, despite the fact that "quality of execution" may be far more important to their total trading costs. Part of the quality execution refers to the ability of a large exchange like the NYSE to accomodate big trades without encountering a large impact on security price. Another part is the size of the effective bid–ask spread. Finally, the NYSE emphasizes the possibility of "price improvement" in a market. This refers to the possibility of trades being crossed "inside the quoted spread." To illustrate, suppose IBM is trading at $98.03 bid, $98.07 asked. A broker who has received a market buy order can meet a broker with a market sell order, and agree to a price of $98.05. By meeting in the middle of the quoted spread, both buyer and seller obtain "price improvement," that is, transaction prices better than the best quoted prices. Such "meetings" of brokers are more than accidental. Because all trading takes place at the specialist's post, floor brokers know where to look for counterparties to a trade.

3.6   Buying on Margin

When purchasing securities, investors have easy access to a source of debt financing called *broker's call loans*. The act of taking advantage of broker's call loans is called *buying on margin*.

margin

Describes securities purchased with money borrowed in part from a broker. The margin is the net worth of the investor's account.

Purchasing stocks on margin means the investor borrows part of the purchase price of the stock from a broker. The **margin** in the account is the portion of the purchase price contributed by the investor; the remainder is borrowed from the broker. The brokers in turn borrow money from banks at the call money rate to finance these purchases; they then charge their clients that rate (defined in Chapter 2), plus a service charge for the loan. All securities purchased on margin must be maintained with the brokerage firm in street name, for the securities are collateral for the loan.

The Board of Governors of the Federal Reserve System limits the extent to which stock purchases can be financed using margin loans. The current initial margin requirement is 50%, meaning that at least 50% of the purchase price must be paid for in cash, with the rest borrowed.

EXAMPLE   3.1

Margin

The percentage margin is defined as the ratio of the net worth, or the "equity value," of the account to the market value of the securities. To demonstrate, suppose an investor initially pays $6,000 toward the purchase of $10,000 worth of stock (100 shares at $100 per share), borrowing the remaining $4,000 from a broker. The initial balance sheet looks like this:

Assets		Liabilities and Owners' Equity	
Value of stock	$10,000	Loan from broker	$4,000
		Equity	$6,000

The initial percentage margin is

$$\text{Margin} = \frac{\text{Equity in account}}{\text{Value of stock}} = \frac{\$6,000}{\$10,000} = .60, \text{ or } 60\%$$

If the price declines to $70 per share, the account balance becomes:

Assets		Liabilities and Owners' Equity	
Value of stock	$7,000	Loan from broker	$4,000
		Equity	$3,000

The assets in the account fall by the full decrease in the stock value, as does the equity. The percentage margin is now

$$\text{Margin} = \frac{\text{Equity in account}}{\text{Value of stock}} = \frac{\$3,000}{\$7,000} = .43, \text{ or } 43\%$$

If the stock value in Example 3.1 were to fall below $4,000, owners' equity would become negative, meaning the value of the stock is no longer sufficient collateral to cover the loan from the broker. To guard against this possibility, the broker sets a *maintenance margin.* If the percentage margin falls below the maintenance level, the broker will issue a *margin call,* which requires the investor to add new cash or securities to the margin account. If the investor does not act, the broker may sell securities from the account to pay off enough of the loan to restore the percentage margin to an acceptable level.

Suppose the maintenance margin is 30%. How far could the stock price fall before the investor would get a margin call?

Let P be the price of the stock. The value of the investor's 100 shares is then $100P$, and the equity in the account is $100P - \$4,000$. The percentage margin is $(100P - \$4,000)/100P$. The price at which the percentage margin equals the maintenance margin of .3 is found by solving the equation

$$\frac{100P - 4,000}{100P} = .3$$

which implies that $P = \$57.14$. If the price of the stock were to fall below $57.14 per share, the investor would get a margin call.

EXAMPLE 3.2

Maintenance Margin

Suppose the maintenance margin in Example 3.2 is 40%. How far can the stock price fall before the investor gets a margin call?

CONCEPT *check* **3.4**

Why do investors buy securities on margin? They do so when they wish to invest an amount greater than their own money allows. Thus, they can achieve greater upside potential, but they also expose themselves to greater downside risk.

To see how, let's suppose an investor is bullish on IBM stock, which is selling for $100 per share. An investor with $10,000 to invest expects IBM to go up in price by 30% during the next year. Ignoring any dividends, the expected rate of return would be 30% if the investor invested $10,000 to buy 100 shares.

But now assume the investor borrows another $10,000 from the broker and invests it in IBM, too. The total investment in IBM would be $20,000 (for 200 shares). Assuming an interest rate on the margin loan of 9% per year, what will the investor's rate of return be now (again ignoring dividends) if IBM stock goes up 30% by year's end?

The 200 shares will be worth $26,000. Paying off $10,900 of principal and interest on the margin loan leaves $15,100 (i.e., $26,000 − $10,900). The rate of return in this case will be

$$\frac{\$15,100 - \$10,000}{\$10,000} = 51\%$$

The investor has parlayed a 30% rise in the stock's price into a 51% rate of return on the $10,000 investment.

Doing so, however, magnifies the downside risk. Suppose that, instead of going up by 30%, the price of IBM stock goes down by 30% to $70 per share. In that case, the 200 shares will be worth $14,000, and the investor is left with $3,100 after paying off the $10,900 of principal and interest on the loan. The result is a disastrous return of

$$\frac{\$3,100 - \$10,000}{\$10,000} = -69\%$$

Table 3.4 summarizes the possible results of these hypothetical transactions. If there is no change in IBM's stock price, the investor loses 9%, the cost of the loan.

EXCEL
APPLICATIONS

Buying on Margin

eXcel

**Please visit us at
www.mhhe.com/bkm**

The Excel spreadsheet model below makes it easy to analyze the impacts of different margin levels and the volatility of stock prices. It also allows you to compare return on investment for a margin trade with a trade using no borrowed funds.

	A	B	C	D	E	F	G	H
1								
2			Action or Formula	Ending	Return on		Ending	Return with
3			for Column B	St Price	Investment		St Price	No Margin
4	Initial Equity Investment	$10,000.00	Enter data		−42.00%			−19.00%
5	Amount Borrowed	$10,000.00	(B4/B10)−B4	$20.00	−122.00%		$20.00	−59.00%
6	Initial Stock Price	$50.00	Enter data	25.00	−102.00%		25.00	−49.00%
7	Shares Purchased	400	(B4/B10)/B6	30.00	−82.00%		30.00	−39.00%
8	Ending Stock Price	$40.00	Enter data	35.00	−62.00%		35.00	−29.00%
9	Cash Dividends During Hold Per.	$0.50	Enter data	40.00	−42.00%		40.00	−19.00%
10	Initial Margin Percentage	50.00%	Enter data	45.00	−22.00%		45.00	−9.00%
11	Maintenance Margin Percentage	30.00%	Enter data	50.00	−2.00%		50.00	1.00%
12				55.00	18.00%		55.00	11.00%
13	Rate on Margin Loan	8.00%	Enter data	60.00	38.00%		60.00	21.00%
14	Holding Period in Months	6	Enter data	65.00	58.00%		65.00	31.00%
15				70.00	78.00%		70.00	41.00%
16	**Return on Investment**			75.00	98.00%		75.00	51.00%
17	Capital Gain on Stock	−$4,000.00	B7*(B8−B6)	80.00	118.00%		80.00	61.00%
18	Dividends	$200.00	B7*B9					
19	Interest on Margin Loan	$400.00	B5*(B14/12)*B13					
20	Net Income	−$4,200.00	B17+B18−B19			LEGEND:		
21	Initial Investment	$10,000.00	B4			Enter data		
22	Return on Investment	−42.00%	B20/B21			Value calculated		

TABLE 3.4		End-of-Year	Repayment of	
Illustration of buying stock on margin	Change in Stock Price	Value of Shares	Principal and Interest*	Investor's Rate of Return
	30% increase	$26,000	$10,900	51%
	No change	20,000	10,900	−9
	30% decrease	14,000	10,900	−69

*Assuming the investor buys $20,000 worth of stock by borrowing $10,000 at an interest rate of 9% per year.

CONCEPT
check   **3.5**   Suppose that in the IBM example above, the investor borrows only $5,000 at the same interest rate of 9% per year. What will the rate of return be if the price of IBM goes up by 30%? If it goes down by 30%? If it remains unchanged?

3.7 | Short Sales

short sale

The sale of shares not owned by the investor but borrowed through a broker and later purchased to replace the loan.

Normally, an investor would first buy a stock and later sell it. With a short sale, the order is reversed. First, you sell and then you buy the shares. In both cases, you begin and end with no shares.

A **short sale** allows investors to profit from a decline in a security's price. An investor borrows a share of stock from a broker and sells it. Later, the short-seller must purchase a share of the same stock in order to replace the share that was borrowed.[4] This is called *covering the short position.* Table 3.5 compares stock purchases to short sales.

The short-seller anticipates the stock price will fall, so that the share can be purchased later at a lower price than it initially sold for; if so, the short-seller will reap a profit. Short-sellers must not only replace the shares but also pay the lender of the security any dividends paid during the short sale.

In practice, the shares loaned out for a short sale are typically provided by the short-seller's brokerage firm, which holds a wide variety of securities of its other investors in street name (i.e., the broker holds the shares registered in its own name on behalf of the client). The owner of the shares need not know that the shares have been lent to the short-seller. If the owner wishes to sell the shares, the brokerage firm will simply borrow shares from another investor. Therefore, the short sale may have an indefinite term. However, if the brokerage firm cannot locate new shares to replace the ones sold, the short-seller will need to repay the loan immediately by purchasing shares in the market and turning them over to the brokerage house to close out the loan.

Finally, exchange rules require that proceeds from a short sale must be kept on account with the broker. The short-seller cannot invest these funds to generate income, although large or institutional investors typically will receive some income from the proceeds of a short sale being held with the broker. Short-sellers also are required to post margin (cash or collateral) with the broker to cover losses should the stock price rise during the short sale.

EXAMPLE 3.3

Short Sales

To illustrate the mechanics of short-selling, suppose you are bearish (pessimistic) on Dot Bomb stock, and its market price is $100 per share. You tell your broker to sell short 1,000 shares. The broker borrows 1,000 shares either from another customer's account or from another broker.

The $100,000 cash proceeds from the short sale are credited to your account. Suppose the broker has a 50% margin requirement on short sales. This means you must have other cash or securities in your account worth at least $50,000 that can serve as margin on the short sale.

Let's say that you have $50,000 in Treasury bills. Your account with the broker after the short sale will then be:

Assets		Liabilities and Owners' Equity	
Cash	$100,000	Short position in Dot Bomb stock (1,000 shares owed)	$100,000
T-bills	50,000	Equity	50,000

Your initial percentage margin is the ratio of the equity in the account, $50,000, to the current value of the shares you have borrowed and eventually must return, $100,000:

$$\text{Percentage margin} = \frac{\text{Equity}}{\text{Value of stock owed}} = \frac{\$50,000}{\$100,000} = .50$$

Suppose you are right and Dot Bomb falls to $70 per share. You can now close out your position at a profit. To cover the short sale, you buy 1,000 shares to replace the ones you borrowed. Because the shares now sell for $70, the purchase costs only $70,000.[5] Because your account was credited for $100,000 when the shares were borrowed and sold, your profit is $30,000: The profit equals the decline in the share price times the number of shares sold short.

---

[4]*Naked short-selling* is a variant on conventional short-selling. In a naked short, a trader sells shares that have not yet been borrowed, assuming that the shares can be acquired and delivered whenever the short sale needs to be closed out.

[5]Notice that when buying on margin, you borrow a given amount of dollars from your broker, so the amount of the loan is independent of the share price. In contrast, when short-selling you borrow a given number of *shares,* which must be returned. Therefore, when the price of the shares changes, the value of the loan also changes.

TABLE 3.5

Cash flows from purchasing versus short-selling shares of stock

Purchase of Stock

Time	Action	Cash Flow*
0	Buy share	−Initial price
1	Receive dividend, sell share	Ending price + Dividend

Profit = (Ending price + Dividend) − Initial price

Short Sale of Stock

Time	Action	Cash Flow*
0	Borrow share; sell it	+Initial price
1	Repay dividend and buy share to replace the share originally borrowed	−(Ending price + Dividend)

Profit = Initial price − (Ending price + Dividend)

*Note: A negative cash flow implies a cash *outflow*.

Like investors who purchase stock on margin, a short-seller must be concerned about margin calls. If the stock price rises, the margin in the account will fall; if margin falls to the maintenance level, the short-seller will receive a margin call.

EXAMPLE 3.4

Margin Calls on Short Positions

Suppose the broker has a maintenance margin of 30% on short sales. This means the equity in your account must be at least 30% of the value of your short position at all times. How much can the price of Dot Bomb stock rise before you get a margin call?

Let P be the price of Dot Bomb stock. Then the value of the shares you must pay back is $1,000P$, and the equity in your account is $\$150,000 - 1,000P$. Your short position margin ratio is equity/value of stock = $(150,000 - 1,000P)/1,000P$. The critical value of P is thus

$$\frac{\text{Equity}}{\text{Value of shares owed}} = \frac{150,000 - 1,000P}{1,000P} = .3$$

which implies that $P = \$115.38$ per share. If Dot Bomb stock should *rise* above $\$115.38$ per share, you will get a margin call, and you will either have to put up additional cash or cover your short position by buying shares to replace the ones borrowed.

CONCEPT check 3.6

a. Construct the balance sheet if Dot Bomb goes up to $110.
b. If the short position maintenance margin in Example 3.4 is 40%, how far can the stock price rise before the investor gets a margin call?

You can see now why stop-buy orders often accompany short sales. Imagine that you short-sell Dot Bomb when it is selling at $100 per share. If the share price falls, you will profit from the short sale. On the other hand, if the share price rises, let's say to $130, you will lose $30 per share. But suppose that when you initiate the short sale, you also enter a stop-buy order at $120. The stop-buy will be executed if the share price surpasses $120, thereby limiting your losses to $20 per share. (If the stock price drops, the stop-buy will never be executed.) The stop-buy order thus provides protection to the short-seller if the share price moves up.

Short-selling periodically comes under attack, particularly during times of financial stress when share prices fall. The last few years have been no exception to this rule, and the nearby box examines the controversy surrounding short sales in greater detail.

SHORT-SELLING COMES UNDER FIRE—AGAIN

Short-selling has long been viewed with suspicion, if not outright hostility. England banned short sales for a good part of the eighteenth century. Napoleon called short sellers enemies of the state. In the U.S., short-selling was widely viewed as contributing to the market crash of 1929, and in 2008, short sellers were blamed for the collapse of the investment banks Bear Stearns and Lehman Brothers. With share prices of other financial firms collapsing in September 2008, the SEC instituted a temporary ban on short-selling about 800 of those firms. Similarly, the Financial Services Authority, the financial regulator in the U.K., prohibited short sales on about 30 financial companies, and Australia banned shorting altogether.

The motivation for these bans is that short sales put downward pressure on share prices that in some cases may be unwarranted: rumors abound of investors who first put on a short sale and then spread negative rumors about the firm to drive down its price. More often, however, shorting is an innocent bet that a share price is too high and is due to fall. Nevertheless, during the market stresses of late 2008, the widespread feeling was that even if short positions were legitimate, regulators should do what they could to prop up the affected institutions.

Hostility to short-selling may well stem from confusion between bad news and the bearer of that news. Short-selling allows investors whose analysis indicates a firm is overpriced to take action on that belief—and to profit if they are correct. Rather than *causing* the stock price to fall, shorts may simply be *anticipating* a decline in the stock price. Their sales simply force the market to reflect the deteriorating prospects of troubled firms sooner than it might have otherwise. In other words, short-selling is part of the process by which the full range of information and opinion—pessimistic as well as optimistic—is brought to bear on stock prices.

For example, short-sellers took large (negative) positions in firms such as WorldCom, Enron, and Tyco even before these firms were exposed by regulators. In fact, one might argue that these emerging short positions helped regulators identify the previously undetected scandals. And in the end, Lehman and Bear Stearns were brought down by their very real losses on their mortgage-related investments—not by unfounded rumors.

Academic research supports the conjecture that short sales contribute to efficient "price discovery." For example, the greater the demand for shorting a stock, the lower its future returns tend to be; moreover, firms that attack short-sellers with threats of legal action or bad publicity tend to have especially poor future returns.[6] Short sale bans may in the end be nothing more than an understandable, but nevertheless misguided, impulse to "shoot the messenger."

3.8 Regulation of Securities Markets

Trading in securities markets in the United States is regulated by a myriad of laws. The major governing legislation includes the Securities Act of 1933 and the Securities Exchange Act of 1934. The 1933 Act requires full disclosure of relevant information relating to the issue of new securities. This is the act that requires registration of new securities and issuance of a prospectus that details the financial prospects of the firm. SEC approval of a prospectus or financial report is not an endorsement of the security as a good investment. The SEC cares only that the relevant facts are disclosed; investors must make their own evaluation of the security's value.

The 1934 Act established the Securities and Exchange Commission to administer the provisions of the 1933 Act. It also extended the disclosure principle of the 1933 Act by requiring periodic disclosure of relevant financial information by firms with already-issued securities on secondary exchanges.

The 1934 Act also empowers the SEC to register and regulate securities exchanges, OTC trading, brokers, and dealers. While the SEC is the administrative agency responsible for broad oversight of the securities markets, it shares responsibility with other regulatory agencies. The Commodity Futures Trading Commission (CFTC) regulates trading in futures markets, while the Federal Reserve has broad responsibility for the health of the U.S. financial system. In this role, the Fed sets margin requirements on stocks and stock options and regulates bank lending to securities markets participants.

The Securities Investor Protection Act of 1970 established the Securities Investor Protection Corporation (SIPC) to protect investors from losses if their brokerage firms fail. Just

---

[6]See, for example, C. Jones and O. A. Lamont, "Short Sale Constraints and Stock Returns," *Journal of Financial Economics*, November 2002, pp. 207–39 or O. A. Lamont, "Go Down Fighting: Short Sellers vs. Firms," *Yale ICF Working Paper No. 04-20*, July 2004.

EXCEL
APPLICATIONS

Short Sale

**Please visit us at
www.mhhe.com/bkm**

This Excel spreadsheet model was built using the text example for Dot Bomb. The model allows you to analyze the effects of returns, margin calls, and different levels of initial and maintenance margins. The model also includes a sensitivity analysis for ending stock price and return on investment.

	A	B	C	D	E
1					
2			**Action or Formula**	**Ending**	**Return on**
3			**for Column B**	**St Price**	**Investment**
4	Initial Investment	$50,000.00	Enter data		60.00%
5	Initial Stock Price	$100.00	Enter data	$170.00	−140.00%
6	Number of Shares Sold Short	1,000	(B4/B9)/B5	160.00	−120.00%
7	Ending Stock Price	$70.00	Enter data	150.00	−100.00%
8	Cash Dividends Per Share	$0.00	Enter data	140.00	−80.00%
9	Initial Margin Percentage	50.00%	Enter data	130.00	−60.00%
10	Maintenance Margin Percentage	30.00%	Enter data	120.00	−40.00%
11				110.00	−20.00%
12	**Return on Short Sale**			100.00	0.00%
13	Capital Gain on Stock	$30,000.00	B6*(B5−B7)	90.00	20.00%
14	Dividends Paid	$0.00	B8*B6	80.00	40.00%
15	Net Income	$30,000.00	B13−B14	70.00	60.00%
16	Initial Investment	$50,000.00	B4	60.00	80.00%
17	Return on Investment	60.00%	B15/B16	50.00	100.00%
18				40.00	120.00%
19	**Margin Positions**			30.00	140.00%
20	Margin Based on Ending Price	114.29%	(B4+(B5*B6)−B14−(B6*B7))/(B6*B7)	20.00	160.00%
21				10.00	180.00%
22	Price for Margin Call	$115.38	(B4+(B5*B6)−B14)/(B6*(1+B10))		
23					**LEGEND:**
24					**Enter data**
25					**Value calculated**

as the Federal Deposit Insurance Corporation provides depositors with federal protection against bank failure, the SIPC ensures that investors will receive securities held for their account in street name by a failed brokerage firm up to a limit of $500,000 per customer. The SIPC is financed by levying an "insurance premium" on its participating, or member, brokerage firms.

In addition to federal regulations, security trading is subject to state laws, known generally as *blue sky laws* because they are intended to give investors a clearer view of investment prospects. State laws to outlaw fraud in security sales existed before the Securities Act of 1933. Varying state laws were somewhat unified when many states adopted portions of the Uniform Securities Act, which was enacted in 1956.

Self-Regulation

In addition to government regulation, there is considerable self-regulation of the securities market. The most important overseer in this regard is the Financial Industry Regulatory Authority (FINRA), which is the largest nongovernmental regulator of all securities firms in the United States. FINRA was formed in 2007 through the consolidation of the National Association of Securities Dealers (NASD) with the self-regulatory arm of the New York Stock Exchange. It describes its broad mission as the fostering of investor protection and market integrity. It examines securities firms, writes and enforces rules concerning trading practices, and administers a dispute resolution forum for investors and registered firms.

There is also self-regulation among the community of investment professionals. For example, the CFA Institute has developed standards of professional conduct that govern the behavior of members with the Chartered Financial Analysts designation, commonly referred to as CFAs. The nearby box presents a brief outline of those principles.

EXCERPTS FROM CFA INSTITUTE STANDARDS OF PROFESSIONAL CONDUCT

I. Professionalism
- Knowledge of law. Members must understand knowledge of and comply with all applicable laws, rules, and regulations including the Code of Ethics and Standards of Professional Conduct.
- Independence and objectivity. Members shall maintain independence and objectivity in their professional activities.
- Misrepresentation. Members must not knowingly misrepresent investment analysis, recommendations, or other professional activities.

II. Integrity of Capital Markets
- Non-public information. Members must not exploit material non-public information.
- Market manipulation. Members shall not attempt to distort prices or trading volume with the intent to mislead market participants.

III. Duties to Clients
- Loyalty, prudence, and care. Members must place their clients' interests before their own and act with reasonable care on their behalf.
- Fair dealing. Members shall deal fairly and objectively with clients when making investment recommendations or taking actions.
- Suitability. Members shall make a reasonable inquiry into a client's financial situation, investment experience, and investment objectives prior to making appropriate investment recommendations.
- Performance presentation. Members shall attempt to ensure that investment performance is presented fairly, accurately, and completely.
- Confidentiality. Members must keep information about clients confidential unless the client permits disclosure.

IV. Duties to Employers
- Loyalty. Members must act for the benefit of their employer.
- Compensation. Members must not accept compensation from sources that would create a conflict of interest with their employer's interests without written consent from all involved parties.
- Supervisors. Members must make reasonable efforts to detect and prevent violation of applicable laws and regulations by anyone subject to their supervision.

V. Investment Analysis and Recommendations
- Diligence. Members must exercise diligence and have reasonable basis for investment analysis, recommendations, or actions.
- Communication. Members must distinguish fact from opinion in their presentation of analysis and disclose general principles of investment processes used in analysis.

VI. Conflicts of Interest
- Disclosure of conflicts. Members must disclose all matters that reasonably could be expected to impair their objectivity or interfere with their other duties.
- Priority of transactions. Transactions for clients and employers must have priority over transactions for the benefit of a member.

VII. Responsibilities as Member of CFA institute
- Conduct. Members must not engage in conduct that compromises the reputation or integrity of the CFA Institute or CFA designation.

SOURCE: Excerpts from the CFA Institute Standards of Professional Conduct.

Regulatory Responses to Recent Scandals

The scandals of 2000–2002 centered largely on three broad practices: allocations of shares in initial public offerings, tainted securities research and recommendations put out to the public, and probably most important, misleading financial statements and accounting practices. The regulatory response to these issues is still evolving, but some initiatives have been put in place. Many of these are contained in the Sarbanes-Oxley Act passed by Congress in 2002. Among the key reforms are:

- Creation of a Public Company Accounting Oversight Board to oversee the auditing of public companies.
- Rules requiring independent financial experts to serve on audit committees of a firm's board of directors.
- CEOs and CFOs must now personally certify that their firms' financial reports "fairly represent, in all material respects, the operations and financial condition of the company," and are subject to personal penalties if those reports turn out to be misleading. Following the letter of GAAP rules may still be necessary, but it is no longer sufficient accounting practice.

- Auditors may no longer provide several other services to their clients. This is intended to prevent potential profits on consulting work from influencing the quality of their audit.
- The Board of Directors must be composed of independent directors and hold regular meetings of Directors in which company management is not present (and therefore cannot impede or influence the discussion).

More recently, there has been a fair amount of push-back on Sarbanes-Oxley. Many observers believe that the compliance costs associated with the law are too onerous, especially for smaller firms, and that heavy-handed regulatory oversight is giving foreign locales an undue advantage over the United States when firms decide where to list their securities. Moreover, the efficacy of single-country regulation is being tested in the face of increasing globalization and the ease with which funds can move across national borders.

One of the most contentious issues in regulation has to do with "rules" versus "principles." Rules-based regulation attempts to lay out specifically what practices are or are not allowed. This has generally been the American approach, particularly at the SEC. In contrast, principles-based regulation relies on a less explicitly defined set of understandings about risk taking, the goals of regulation, and the sorts of financial practices considered allowable. This has been the dominant approach in the U.K., and seems to be the more popular model for regulators throughout the world.

Insider Trading

inside information

Nonpublic knowledge about a corporation possessed by corporate officers, major owners, or other individuals with privileged access to information about the firm.

Regulations also prohibit insider trading. It is illegal for anyone to transact in securities to profit from **inside information,** that is, private information held by officers, directors, or major stockholders that has not yet been divulged to the public. But the definition of insiders can be ambiguous. While it is obvious that the chief financial officer of a firm is an insider, it is less clear whether the firm's biggest supplier can be considered an insider. Yet a supplier may deduce the firm's near-term prospects from significant changes in orders. This gives the supplier a unique form of private information, yet the supplier is not technically an insider. These ambiguities plague security analysts, whose job is to uncover as much information as possible concerning the firm's expected prospects. The distinction between legal private information and illegal inside information can be fuzzy.

The SEC requires officers, directors, and major stockholders to report all transactions in their firm's stock. A compendium of insider trades is published monthly in the SEC's *Official Summary of Securities Transactions and Holdings.* The idea is to inform the public of any implicit vote of confidence or no confidence made by insiders.

Insiders *do* exploit their knowledge. Three forms of evidence support this conclusion. First, there have been well-publicized convictions of principals in insider trading schemes.

Second, there is considerable evidence of "leakage" of useful information to some traders before any public announcement of that information. For example, share prices of firms announcing dividend increases (which the market interprets as good news concerning the firm's prospects) commonly increase in value a few days *before* the public announcement of the increase. Clearly, some investors are acting on the good news before it is released to the public. Share prices still rise substantially on the day of the public release of good news, however, indicating that insiders, or their associates, have not fully bid up the price of the stock to the level commensurate with the news.

A third form of evidence on insider trading has to do with returns earned on trades by insiders. Researchers have examined the SEC's summary of insider trading to measure the performance of insiders. In one of the best known of these studies, Jaffe (1974) examined the abnormal return of stocks over the months following purchases or sales by insiders. For months in which insider purchasers of a stock exceeded insider sellers of the stock by three or more, the stock had an abnormal return in the following eight months of about 5%. Moreover, when insider sellers exceeded insider buyers, the stock tended to perform poorly.

- Firms issue securities to raise the capital necessary to finance their investments. Investment bankers market these securities to the public on the primary market. Investment bankers generally act as underwriters who purchase the securities from the firm and resell them to the public at a markup. Before the securities may be sold to the public, the firm must publish an SEC-approved prospectus that provides information on the firm's prospects.
- Already-issued securities are traded on the secondary market, that is, in organized stock markets; the over-the-counter market; and for large trades, through direct negotiation. Only license holders of exchanges may trade on the exchange. Brokerage firms holding licenses on the exchange sell their services to individuals, charging commissions for executing trades on their behalf.
- Trading may take place in dealer markets, via electronic communication networks, or in specialist markets. In dealer markets, security dealers post bid and ask prices at which they are willing to trade. Brokers for individuals execute trades at the best available prices. In electronic markets, the existing book of limit orders provides the terms at which trades can be executed. Mutually agreeable offers to buy or sell securities are automatically crossed by the computer system operating the market. In specialist markets, the specialist acts to maintain an orderly market with price continuity. Specialists maintain a limit order book, but also sell from or buy for their own inventories of stock. Thus, liquidity in specialist markets comes from both the limit order book and the specialist's inventory.
- NASDAQ was traditionally a dealer market in which a network of dealers negotiated directly over sales of securities. The NYSE was traditionally a specialist market. In recent years, however, both exchanges dramatically increased their commitment to electronic and automated trading. Most trades today are electronic.
- Trading costs include explicit commissions as well as the bid–ask spread. An ongoing controversy among markets concerns overall trading costs including the effect of spreads. The NYSE argues that it is often the cheapest trading venue when quality of execution (including price impact and the possibility of price improvement) is recognized.
- Buying on margin means borrowing money from a broker in order to buy more securities than can be purchased with one's own money alone. By buying securities on a margin, an investor magnifies both the upside potential and the downside risk. If the equity in a margin account falls below the required maintenance level, the investor will get a margin call from the broker.
- Short-selling is the practice of selling securities that the seller does not own. The short-seller borrows the securities sold through a broker and may be required to cover the short position at any time on demand. The cash proceeds of a short sale are kept in escrow by the broker, and the broker usually requires that the short-seller deposit additional cash or securities to serve as margin (collateral) for the short sale.
- Securities trading is regulated by the Securities and Exchange Commission, by other government agencies, and through self-regulation of the exchanges. Many of the important regulations have to do with full disclosure of relevant information concerning the securities in question. Insider trading rules also prohibit traders from attempting to profit from inside information.

ask price, 57
auction market, 57
bid–ask spread, 58
bid price, 57
block transactions, 63
dealer markets, 57
electronic communication
   networks (ECNs), 59

initial public offering
   (IPO), 53
inside information, 76
limit buy (sell) order, 58
margin, 68
NASDAQ Stock Market, 61
over-the-counter (OTC)
   market, 59
primary market, 53

private placement, 54
program trade, 64
prospectus, 53
secondary market, 53
short sale, 70
specialist, 60
stock exchanges, 62
stop order, 58
underwriters, 53

PROBLEM SETS

Basic

1. What is the difference between an IPO (initial public offering) and an SEO (seasoned equity offering)?

2. What are some different components of the effective costs of buying or selling shares of stock?

3. What is the difference between a primary and secondary market?

4. How do specialist firms earn their profits?

5. In what circumstances are private placements more likely to be used than public offerings?

6. What are the differences between a stop-loss order, a limit sell order, and a market order?

7. What is a block order, and why has the proportion of trades done in block orders declined in recent years?

8. What is the role of an underwriter? A prospectus?

9. How do margin trades magnify both the upside potential and downside risk of an investment portfolio?

Intermediate

10. Suppose you short sell 100 shares of IBM, now selling at $120 per share.
    a. What is your maximum possible loss?
    b. What happens to the maximum loss if you simultaneously place a stop-buy order at $128?

11. Call one full-service broker and one discount broker and find out the transaction costs of implementing the following strategies:
    a. Buying 100 shares of IBM now and selling them six months from now.
    b. Investing an equivalent amount in six-month at-the-money call options on IBM stock now and selling them six months from now.

12. DRK, Inc., has just sold 100,000 shares in an initial public offering. The underwriter's explicit fees were $60,000. The offering price for the shares was $40, but immediately upon issue, the share price jumped to $44.
    a. What is your best guess as to the total cost to DRK of the equity issue?
    b. Is the entire cost of the underwriting a source of profit to the underwriters?

13. Dée Trader opens a brokerage account, and purchases 300 shares of Internet Dreams at $40 per share. She borrows $4,000 from her broker to help pay for the purchase. The interest rate on the loan is 8%.
    a. What is the margin in Dée's account when she first purchases the stock?
    b. If the share price falls to $30 per share by the end of the year, what is the remaining margin in her account? If the maintenance margin requirement is 30%, will she receive a margin call?
    c. What is the rate of return on her investment?

14. Old Economy Traders opened an account to short-sell 1,000 shares of Internet Dreams from the previous question. The initial margin requirement was 50%. (The margin account pays no interest.) A year later, the price of Internet Dreams has risen from $40 to $50, and the stock has paid a dividend of $2 per share.
    a. What is the remaining margin in the account?
    b. If the maintenance margin requirement is 30%, will Old Economy receive a margin call?
    c. What is the rate of return on the investment?

15. Consider the following limit order book of a specialist. The last trade in the stock occurred at a price of $50.

Limit Buy Orders		Limit Sell Orders	
Price	**Shares**	**Price**	**Shares**
$49.75	500	$50.25	100
49.50	800	51.50	100
49.25	500	54.75	300
49.00	200	58.25	100
48.50	600		

   a. If a market buy order for 100 shares comes in, at what price will it be filled?
   b. At what price would the next market buy order be filled?
   c. If you were the specialist, would you want to increase or decrease your inventory of this stock?

16. You are bullish on Telecom stock. The current market price is $50 per share, and you have $5,000 of your own to invest. You borrow an additional $5,000 from your broker at an interest rate of 8% per year and invest $10,000 in the stock.
   a. What will be your rate of return if the price of Telecom stock goes up by 10% during the next year? (Ignore the expected dividend.)
   b. How far does the price of Telecom stock have to fall for you to get a margin call if the maintenance margin is 30%? Assume the price fall happens immediately.

Please visit us at www.mhhe.com/bkm

17. You are bearish on Telecom and decide to sell short 100 shares at the current market price of $50 per share.
   a. How much in cash or securities must you put into your brokerage account if the broker's initial margin requirement is 50% of the value of the short position?
   b. How high can the price of the stock go before you get a margin call if the maintenance margin is 30% of the value of the short position?

Please visit us at www.mhhe.com/bkm

18. Here is some price information on Marriott:

	Bid	Asked
Marriott	19.95	20.05

   You have placed a stop-loss order to sell at $20. What are you telling your broker? Given market prices, will your order be executed?

19. Here is some price information on Fincorp stock. Suppose first that Fincorp trades in a dealer market.

Bid	Asked
55.25	55.50

   a. Suppose you have submitted an order to your broker to buy at market. At what price will your trade be executed?
   b. Suppose you have submitted an order to sell at market. At what price will your trade be executed?
   c. Suppose you have submitted a limit order to sell at $55.62. What will happen?
   d. Suppose you have submitted a limit order to buy at $55.37. What will happen?

20. Now reconsider the previous problem assuming that Fincorp sells in an exchange market like the NYSE.
   a. Is there any chance for price improvement in the market orders considered in parts (*a*) and (*b*)?
   b. Is there any chance of an immediate trade at $55.37 for the limit buy order in part (*d*)?

21. You've borrowed $20,000 on margin to buy shares in Disney, which is now selling at $40 per share. Your account starts at the initial margin requirement of 50%. The maintenance margin is 35%. Two days later, the stock price falls to $35 per share.

    a. Will you receive a margin call?

    b. How low can the price of Disney shares fall before you receive a margin call?

22. On January 1, you sold short one round lot (that is, 100 shares) of Lowe's stock at $21 per share. On March 1, a dividend of $3 per share was paid. On April 1, you covered the short sale by buying the stock at a price of $15 per share. You paid 50 cents per share in commissions for each transaction. What is the value of your account on April 1?

Challenge

Please visit us at www.mhhe.com/bkm

23. Suppose that Intel currently is selling at $40 per share. You buy 500 shares using $15,000 of your own money, borrowing the remainder of the purchase price from your broker. The rate on the margin loan is 8%.

    a. What is the percentage increase in the net worth of your brokerage account if the price of Intel *immediately* changes to: (i) $44; (ii) $40; (iii) $36? What is the relationship between your percentage return and the percentage change in the price of Intel?

    b. If the maintenance margin is 25%, how low can Intel's price fall before you get a margin call?

    c. How would your answer to (b) change if you had financed the initial purchase with only $10,000 of your own money?

    d. What is the rate of return on your margined position (assuming again that you invest $15,000 of your own money) if Intel is selling *after one year* at: (i) $44; (ii) $40; (iii) $36? What is the relationship between your percentage return and the percentage change in the price of Intel? Assume that Intel pays no dividends.

    e. Continue to assume that a year has passed. How low can Intel's price fall before you get a margin call?

Please visit us at www.mhhe.com/bkm

24. Suppose that you sell short 500 shares of Intel, currently selling for $40 per share, and give your broker $15,000 to establish your margin account.

    a. If you earn no interest on the funds in your margin account, what will be your rate of return after one year if Intel stock is selling at: (i) $44; (ii) $40; (iii) $36? Assume that Intel pays no dividends.

    b. If the maintenance margin is 25%, how high can Intel's price rise before you get a margin call?

    c. Redo parts (a) and (b), but now assume that Intel also has paid a year-end dividend of $1 per share. The prices in part (a) should be interpreted as ex-dividend, that is, prices after the dividend has been paid.

CFA Problems

CFA® PROBLEMS

1. If you place a stop-loss order to sell 100 shares of stock at $55 when the current price is $62, how much will you receive for each share if the price drops to $50?

    a. $50.

    b. $55.

    c. $54.87.

    d. Cannot tell from the information given.

2. You wish to sell short 100 shares of XYZ Corporation stock. If the last two transactions were at $34.12 followed by $34.25, you can sell short on the next transaction only at a price of

    a. 34.12 or higher

    b. 34.25 or higher

    c. 34.25 or lower

    d. 34.12 or lower

3. Specialists on the New York Stock Exchange do all of the following *except:*
   a. Act as dealers for their own accounts.
   b. Execute limit orders.
   c. Help provide liquidity to the marketplace.
   d. Act as odd-lot dealers.

Use data from the Standard & Poor's Market Insight Database at www.mhhe.com/edumarketinsight to answer the following questions.

1. Select the Company tab and enter ticker symbol "T" and click GO. AT&T should appear. Click on the Compustat Reports section and find the link for the company's profile. Where is the company's headquarters located? On what exchange does the company's stock primarily trade?

2. Back to the Compustat Reports, click on the Ticker History. Briefly summarize what you find out about the company's history with regard to its name and its ticker symbol.

3. Link to the Financial Highlights section of the Compustat Reports. Who is the primary auditor of the firm's financial statements? Is the auditor's opinion qualified in any way?

4. Repeat this process for GM and compare the Auditor's Opinion of the two firms.

WEB *master* CHOOSING A BROKER

There are several factors that should be considered when you are choosing which brokerage firm(s) to use to execute your trades. There are also a wide range of services that claim to objectively recommend brokerage firms. Many are actually sponsored by the brokerage firms themselves.

Go to the website **www.consumersearch.com/online-brokers/reviews** and read the information provided under "Our Sources." Then follow the link for the Barron's ratings. Here you can read the Barron's annual broker survey and download the "How The Brokers Stack Up" report, which contains a list of fees. Suppose that you have $3,000 to invest and want to put it in a non-IRA account.

1. Are all of the brokerage firms suitable if you want to open a cash account? Are they all suitable if you want a margin account?

2. Choose two of the firms listed. Assume that you want to buy 200 shares of LLY stock using a market order. If the order is filled at $42 per share, how much will the commission be for the two firms if you place an online order?

3. Are there any maintenance fees associated with the account at either brokerage firm?

4. Now assume that you have a margin account and the balance is $3,000. Calculate the interest rate you would pay if you borrowed money to buy stock.

SOLUTIONS TO CONCEPT *checks*

3.1. Limited-time shelf registration was introduced because of its favorable trade-off of saving issue costs versus providing disclosure. Allowing unlimited shelf registration would circumvent "blue sky" laws that ensure proper disclosure as the financial circumstances of the firm change over time.

3.2. *a.* Used cars trade in dealer markets (used-car lots or auto dealerships) and in direct search markets when individuals advertise in local newspapers or Internet listings.

    b. Paintings trade in broker markets when clients commission brokers to buy or sell art for them, in dealer markets at art galleries, and in auction markets.

    c. Rare coins trade in dealer markets, for example, in coin shops or shows, but they also trade in auctions and in direct search markets when individuals advertise they want to buy or sell coins.

3.3. *a.* You should give your broker a market order. It will be executed immediately and is the cheapest type of order in terms of brokerage fees.

    b. You should give your broker a limit buy order, which will be executed only if the shares can be obtained at a price about 5% below the current price.

    c. You should give your broker a stop-loss order, which will be executed if the share price starts falling. The limit or stop price should be close to the current price to avoid the possibility of large losses.

3.4. Solving

$$\frac{100P - \$4,000}{100P} = .4$$

yields $P = \$66.67$ per share.

3.5. The investor will purchase 150 shares, with a rate of return as follows:

Year-End Change in Price	Year-End Value of Shares	Repayment of Principal and Interest	Investor's Rate of Return
30%	$19,500	$5,450	40.5%
No change	15,000	5,450	−4.5
−30%	10,500	5,450	−49.5

3.6. *a.* Once Dot Bomb stock goes up to $110, your balance sheet will be:

Assets		Liabilities and Owner's Equity	
Cash	$100,000	Short position in Dot Bomb	$110,000
T-bills	50,000	Equity	40,000

b. Solving

$$\frac{\$150,000 - 1,000P}{1,000P} = .4$$

yields $P = \$107.14$ per share.

Chapter 4

Mutual Funds and Other Investment Companies

After Studying This Chapter You Should Be Able To:

- Cite advantages and disadvantages of investing with an investment company rather than buying securities directly.

- Contrast open-end mutual funds with closed-end funds and unit investment trusts.

- Define net asset value and measure the rate of return on a mutual fund.

- Classify mutual funds according to investment style.

- Demonstrate the impact of expenses and turnover on mutual fund investment performance.

The previous chapter provided an introduction to the mechanics of trading securities and the structure of the markets in which securities trade. Increasingly, however, individual investors are choosing not to trade securities directly for their own accounts. Instead, they direct their funds to investment companies that purchase securities on their behalf. The most important of these financial intermediaries are mutual funds, which are currently owned by about one-half of U.S. households. Other types of investment companies, such as unit investment trusts and closed-end funds, also merit distinction.

We begin the chapter by describing and comparing the various types of investment companies available to investors—unit investment trusts, closed-end investment companies, and open-end investment companies, more commonly known as mutual funds. We devote most of our attention to mutual funds, examining the functions of such funds, their investment styles and policies, and the costs of investing in these funds.

Next, we take a first look at the investment performance of these funds. We consider the impact of expenses and turnover on net performance and examine the extent to which

Related Web sites for this chapter are available at www.mhhe.com/bkm.

performance is consistent from one period to the next. In other words, will the mutual funds that were the best past performers be the best *future* performers? Finally, we discuss sources of information on mutual funds and consider in detail the information provided in the most comprehensive guide, Morningstar's *Mutual Fund Sourcebook*.

4.1 Investment Companies

investment companies

Financial intermediaries that invest the funds of individual investors in securities or other assets.

Investment companies are financial intermediaries that collect funds from individual investors and invest those funds in a potentially wide range of securities or other assets. Pooling of assets is the key idea behind investment companies. Each investor has a claim to the portfolio established by the investment company in proportion to the amount invested. These companies thus provide a mechanism for small investors to "team up" to obtain the benefits of large-scale investing.

Investment companies perform several important functions for their investors:

1. *Record keeping and administration.* Investment companies issue periodic status reports, keeping track of capital gains distributions, dividends, investments, and redemptions, and they may reinvest dividend and interest income for shareholders.

2. *Diversification and divisibility.* By pooling their money, investment companies enable investors to hold fractional shares of many different securities. They can act as large investors even if any individual shareholder cannot.

3. *Professional management.* Most, but not all, investment companies have full-time staffs of security analysts and portfolio managers who attempt to achieve superior investment results for their investors.

4. *Lower transaction costs.* Because they trade large blocks of securities, investment companies can achieve substantial savings on brokerage fees and commissions.

While all investment companies pool the assets of individual investors, they also need to divide claims to those assets among those investors. Investors buy shares in investment companies, and ownership is proportional to the number of shares purchased. The value of each share is called the **net asset value,** or **NAV.** Net asset value equals assets minus liabilities expressed on a per-share basis:

net asset value (NAV)

Assets minus liabilities expressed on a per-share basis.

$$\text{Net asset value} = \frac{\text{Market value of assets minus liabilities}}{\text{Shares outstanding}}$$

Consider a mutual fund that manages a portfolio of securities worth $120 million. Suppose the fund owes $4 million to its investment advisers and owes another $1 million for rent, wages due, and miscellaneous expenses. The fund has 5 million shares. Then

$$\text{Net asset value} = \frac{\$120 \text{ million} - \$5 \text{ million}}{5 \text{ million shares}} = \$23 \text{ per share}$$

CONCEPT check 4.1

Consider these data from the January 2008 balance sheet of the Growth and Income mutual fund sponsored by the Vanguard Group. (All values are in millions.) What was the net asset value of the portfolio?

Assets:	$4,517.0
Liabilities:	$ 11.1
Shares:	154.8

4.2 | Types of Investment Companies

In the United States, investment companies are classified by the Investment Company Act of 1940 as either unit investment trusts or managed investment companies. The portfolios of unit investment trusts are essentially fixed and thus are called "unmanaged." In contrast, managed companies are so named because securities in their investment portfolios continually are bought and sold: The portfolios are managed. Managed companies are further classified as either closed-end or open-end. Open-end companies are what we commonly call mutual funds.

Unit Investment Trusts

Unit investment trusts are pools of money invested in a portfolio that is fixed for the life of the fund. To form a unit investment trust, a sponsor, typically a brokerage firm, buys a portfolio of securities which are deposited into a trust. It then sells to the public shares, or "units," in the trust, called *redeemable trust certificates*. All income and payments of principal from the portfolio are paid out by the fund's trustees (a bank or trust company) to the shareholders.

There is little active management of a unit investment trust because once established, the portfolio composition is fixed; hence these trusts are referred to as *unmanaged*. Trusts tend to invest in relatively uniform types of assets; for example, one trust may invest in municipal bonds, another in corporate bonds. The uniformity of the portfolio is consistent with the lack of active management. The trusts provide investors a vehicle to purchase a pool of one particular type of asset, which can be included in an overall portfolio as desired. The lack of active management of the portfolio implies that management fees can be lower than those of managed funds.

Sponsors of unit investment trusts earn their profit by selling shares in the trust at a premium to the cost of acquiring the underlying assets. For example, a trust that has purchased $5 million of assets may sell 5,000 shares to the public at a price of $1,030 per share, which (assuming the trust has no liabilities) represents a 3% premium over the net asset value of the securities held by the trust. The 3% premium is the trustee's fee for establishing the trust.

Investors who wish to liquidate their holdings of a unit investment trust may sell the shares back to the trustee for net asset value. The trustees can either sell enough securities from the asset portfolio to obtain the cash necessary to pay the investor, or they may instead sell the shares to a new investor (again at a slight premium to net asset value).

Unit investment trusts have steadily lost market share to mutual funds in recent years. Assets in such trusts declined from $105 billion in 1990 to only $53 billion in 2007.

Managed Investment Companies

There are two types of managed companies: closed-end and open-end. In both cases, the fund's board of directors, which is elected by shareholders, hires a management company to manage the portfolio for an annual fee that typically ranges from .2% to 1.5% of assets. In many cases the management company is the firm that organized the fund. For example, Fidelity Management and Research Corporation sponsors many Fidelity mutual funds and is responsible for managing the portfolios. It assesses a management fee on each Fidelity fund. In other cases, a mutual fund will hire an outside portfolio manager. For example, Vanguard has hired Wellington Management as the investment adviser for its Wellington Fund. Most management companies have contracts to manage several funds.

Open-end funds stand ready to redeem or issue shares at their net asset value (although both purchases and redemptions may involve sales charges). When investors in open-end funds wish to "cash out" their shares, they sell them back to the fund at NAV. In contrast, **closed-end funds** do not redeem or issue shares. Investors in closed-end funds who wish to cash out must sell their shares to other investors. Shares of closed-end funds are traded on organized exchanges and can be purchased through brokers just like other common stock; their prices therefore can differ from NAV.

unit investment trusts

Money pooled from many investors that is invested in a portfolio fixed for the life of the fund.

open-end fund

A fund that issues or redeems its shares at net asset value.

closed-end fund

Shares may not be redeemed, but instead are traded at prices that can differ from net asset value.

CLOSED-END FUNDS

FUND	NAV	MKT PRICE	PREM/DISC	52 WEEK RETURN %	FUND	NAV	MKT PRICE	PREM/DISC	52 WEEK RETURN %
Adams Express Company (ADX)	12.11	10.34	−14.62	−27.45	Dreman/Claymore Div&Inc (DCS)	6.06	4.81	20.63	−74.05
Advent/Clay Enhcd G & I (LCM)	12.59	10.05	−20.17	−37.41	DWS Dreman Val Inc Edge (DHG)	9.40	7.37	−21.60	−45.99
BlackRock Div Achvrs (BDV)	11.64	9.92	−14.78	−24.59	Eaton Vance Tax Div Inc (EVT)	18.76	15.06	−19.72	−43.69
BlackRock Str Div Achvr (BDT)	12.04	9.95	−17.36	−22.56	Gabelli Div & Inc Tr (GDV)	16.19	13.42	−17.11	−33.17
Blue Chip Value Fund (BLU)	3.78	3.30	−12.70	−41.20	Gabelli Equity Trust (GAB)	5.60	6.11	9.11	−29.22
Cornerstone Prog Return (CFP)	9.23	10.14	9.86	−32.86	General Amer Investors (GAM)	27.17	23.36	−14.02	−34.89

Figure 4.1 is a listing of closed-end funds from *The Wall Street Journal Online*. The first column gives the fund's name and ticker symbol. The next two columns give the fund's most recent net asset value and closing share price. The premium or discount is the percentage difference between price and NAV: (Price − NAV)/NAV. Notice that there are more funds selling at discounts to NAV (indicated by negative differences) than premiums. Finally, the 52-week return based on the percentage change in share price plus dividend income is presented in the last column.

The common divergence of price from net asset value, often by wide margins, is a puzzle that has yet to be fully explained. To see why this is a puzzle, consider a closed-end fund that is selling at a discount from net asset value. If the fund were to sell all the assets in the portfolio, it would realize proceeds equal to net asset value. The difference between the market price of the fund and the fund's NAV would represent the per-share increase in the wealth of the fund's investors. Despite this apparent profit opportunity, sizable discounts seem to persist for long periods of time.

Moreover, several studies (e.g., Thompson, 1978) have shown that on average, fund premiums or discounts tend to dissipate over time, so funds selling at a discount receive a boost to their rate of return as the discount shrinks. Pontiff (1995) estimates that a fund selling at a 20% discount would have an expected 12-month return more than 6% greater than funds selling at net asset value.

Interestingly, while many closed-end funds sell at a discount from net asset value, the prices of these funds when originally issued are often above NAV. This is a further puzzle, as it is hard to explain why investors would purchase these newly issued funds at a premium to NAV when the shares tend to fall to a discount shortly after issue.

In contrast to closed-end funds, the price of open-end funds cannot fall below NAV, because these funds stand ready to redeem shares at NAV. The offering price will exceed NAV, however, if the fund carries a **load**. A load is, in effect, a sales charge, which is paid to the seller. Load funds are sold by securities brokers and directly by mutual fund groups.

load

A sales commission charged on a mutual fund.

Unlike closed-end funds, open-end mutual funds do not trade on organized exchanges. Instead, investors simply buy shares from and liquidate through the investment company at net asset value. Thus, the number of outstanding shares of these funds changes daily. In mid-2008, about $280 billion of assets were held in closed-end funds.

Other Investment Organizations

There are intermediaries not formally organized or regulated as investment companies that nevertheless serve functions similar to investment companies. Among the more important are commingled funds, real estate investment trusts, and hedge funds.

Commingled funds Commingled funds are partnerships of investors that pool their funds. The management firm that organizes the partnership, for example, a bank or insurance company, manages the funds for a fee. Typical partners in a commingled fund might be trust or retirement accounts that have portfolios much larger than those of most individual investors but are still too small to warrant managing on a separate basis.

Commingled funds are similar in form to open-end mutual funds. Instead of shares, though, the fund offers *units,* which are bought and sold at net asset value. A bank or insurance company may offer an array of different commingled funds, for example, a money market fund, a bond fund, and a common stock fund.

Real Estate Investment Trusts (REITs) A REIT is similar to a closed-end fund. REITs invest in real estate or loans secured by real estate. Besides issuing shares, they raise capital by borrowing from banks and issuing bonds or mortgages. Most of them are highly leveraged, with a typical debt ratio of 70%.

There are two principal kinds of REITs. *Equity trusts* invest in real estate directly, whereas *mortgage trusts* invest primarily in mortgage and construction loans. REITs generally are established by banks, insurance companies, or mortgage companies, which then serve as investment managers to earn a fee.

Hedge funds Like mutual funds, **hedge funds** are vehicles that allow private investors to pool assets to be invested by a fund manager. Unlike mutual funds, however, hedge funds are commonly structured as private partnerships and thus are not subject to many SEC regulations. Typically they are open only to wealthy or institutional investors. Many require investors to agree to initial "lock-ups," that is, periods as long as several years in which investments cannot be withdrawn. Lock-ups allow hedge funds to invest in illiquid assets without worrying about meeting demands for redemption of funds. Moreover, since hedge funds are only lightly regulated, their managers can pursue other investment strategies that are not open to mutual fund managers, for example, heavy use of derivatives, short sales, and leverage.

Hedge funds by design are empowered to invest in a wide range of investments, with various funds focusing on derivatives, distressed firms, currency speculation, convertible bonds, emerging markets, merger arbitrage, and so on. Other funds may jump from one asset class to another as perceived investment opportunities shift.

Hedge funds enjoyed great growth in the last several years, with assets under management ballooning from about $50 billion in 1990 to nearly $2 trillion in 2008, before contracting in the face of the credit crisis beginning in mid-2008. Because of their recent prominence, we devote all of Chapter 20 to these funds.

hedge fund

A private investment pool, open to wealthy or institutional investors, that is exempt from SEC regulation and can therefore pursue more speculative policies than mutual funds.

4.3 Mutual Funds

Mutual fund is the common name for an open-end investment company. This is the dominant investment company in the U.S. today, accounting for more than 90% of investment company assets. Assets under management in the U.S. mutual fund industry were a bit above $9 trillion in early 2009. Roughly another $10 trillion were invested in mutual funds of non-U.S. sponsors.

Investment Policies

Each mutual fund has a specified investment policy, which is described in the fund's prospectus. For example, money market mutual funds hold the short-term, low-risk instruments of the money market (see Chapter 2 for a review of these securities), while bond funds hold fixed-income securities. Some funds have even more narrowly defined mandates. For example, some bond funds will hold primarily Treasury bonds, others primarily mortgage-backed securities.

Management companies manage a family, or "complex," of mutual funds. They organize an entire collection of funds and then collect a management fee for operating them. By managing a collection of funds under one umbrella, these companies make it easy for investors to allocate assets across market sectors and to switch assets across funds while still benefiting from centralized record keeping. Some of the most well-known management companies are Fidelity, Vanguard, Putnam, and Dreyfus. Each offers an array of open-end mutual funds with different investment policies. In early 2008, there were over 8,000 mutual funds in the United States, which were offered by fewer than 500 fund complexes.

Some of the more important fund types, classified by investment policy, are discussed next.

Money market funds   These funds invest in money market securities such as commercial paper, repurchase agreements, or certificates of deposit. The average maturity of these assets tends to be a bit more than one month. They usually offer check-writing features, and net asset value is fixed at $1 per share,[1] so that there are no tax implications such as capital gains or losses associated with redemption of shares.

Equity funds   Equity funds invest primarily in stock, although they may, at the portfolio manager's discretion, also hold fixed-income or other types of securities. Funds commonly will hold about 5% of total assets in money market securities to provide the liquidity necessary to meet potential redemption of shares.

It is traditional to classify stock funds according to their emphasis on capital appreciation versus current income. Thus *income funds* tend to hold shares of firms with high dividend yields that provide high current income. *Growth funds* are willing to forgo current income, focusing instead on prospects for capital gains. While the classification of these funds is couched in terms of income versus capital gains, it is worth noting that in practice the more relevant distinction concerns the level of risk these funds assume. Growth stocks—and therefore growth funds—are typically riskier and respond far more dramatically to changes in economic conditions than do income funds.

Specialized sector funds   Some equity funds, called *sector funds,* concentrate on a particular industry. For example, Fidelity markets dozens of "select funds," each of which invests in a specific industry such as biotechnology, utilities, precious metals, or telecommunications. Other funds specialize in securities of particular countries.

Bond funds   As the name suggests, these funds specialize in the fixed-income sector. Within that sector, however, there is considerable room for specialization. For example, various funds will concentrate on corporate bonds, Treasury bonds, mortgage-backed securities, or municipal (tax-free) bonds. Indeed, some of the municipal bond funds will invest only in bonds of a particular state (or even city!) in order to satisfy the investment desires of residents of that state who wish to avoid local as well as federal taxes on the interest paid on the bonds. Many funds also will specialize by the maturity of the securities, ranging from short-term to intermediate to long-term, or by the credit risk of the issuer, ranging from very safe to high-yield or "junk" bonds.

International funds   Many funds have international focus. *Global funds* invest in securities worldwide, including the United States. In contrast, *international funds* invest in securities of firms located outside the U.S. *Regional funds* concentrate on a particular part of the world, and *emerging market funds* invest in companies of developing nations.

Balanced funds   Some funds are designed to be candidates for an individual's entire investment portfolio. These *balanced funds* hold both equities and fixed-income securities in relatively stable proportions. *Life-cycle funds* are balanced funds in which the asset mix can range from aggressive (primarily marketed to younger investors) to conservative (directed at older investors). Static allocation life-cycle funds maintain a stable mix across stocks and bonds, while *targeted-maturity funds* gradually become more conservative as the investor ages.

---

[1]The box in Chapter 2 noted that money market funds are able to maintain NAV at $1.00 because they invest in short-maturity debt of the highest quality with minimal price risk. In rare circumstances, funds have experienced losses sufficient to drive NAV below $1.00. In September 2008, Reserve Primary Fund, the nation's oldest money market fund, broke the buck when it suffered losses on its holding of Lehman Brothers commercial paper, and its NAV fell to $.97.

Asset allocation and flexible funds   These funds are similar to balanced funds in that they hold both stocks and bonds. However, asset allocation funds may dramatically vary the proportions allocated to each market in accord with the portfolio manager's forecast of the relative performance of each sector. Hence, these funds are engaged in market timing and are not designed to be low-risk investment vehicles.

Index funds   An index fund tries to match the performance of a broad market index. The fund buys shares in securities included in a particular index in proportion to the security's representation in that index. For example, the Vanguard 500 Index Fund is a mutual fund that replicates the composition of the Standard & Poor's 500 stock price index. Because the S&P 500 is a value-weighted index, the fund buys shares in each S&P 500 company in proportion to the market value of that company's outstanding equity. Investment in an index fund is a low-cost way for small investors to pursue a passive investment strategy—that is, to invest without engaging in security analysis. Of course, index funds can be tied to nonequity indexes as well. For example, Vanguard offers a bond index fund and a real estate index fund.

Table 4.1 breaks down the number of mutual funds by investment orientation. Often the fund name describes its investment policy. For example, Vanguard's GNMA fund invests in mortgage-backed securities, the Municipal Intermediate fund invests in intermediate-term municipal bonds, and the High-Yield Corporate bond fund invests in large part in speculative grade, or "junk," bonds with high yields. However, names of common stock funds frequently reflect little or nothing about their investment policies. Examples are Vanguard's Windsor and Wellington funds.

TABLE 4.1

U.S. mutual funds by investment classification

	Assets ($ billion)	Percent of Total Assets	Number of Funds
Equity funds			
Capital appreciation focus	$ 2,911.8	24.2%	3,037
World/international	1,659.5	13.8	968
Total return focus	1,950.2	16.2	762
Total equity funds	$ 6,521.4	54.3%	4,767
Bond funds			
Corporate	$ 301.1	2.5%	293
High yield	156.7	1.3	206
World	84.0	0.7	122
Government	203.2	1.7	301
Strategic income	560.3	4.7	370
Single-state municipal	155.8	1.3	451
National municipal	218.0	1.8	224
Total bond funds	$ 1,679.0	14.0%	1,967
Hybrid (bond/stock) funds	$ 713.4	5.9%	488
Money market funds			
Taxable	$ 2,642.1	22.0%	548
Tax-exempt	465.1	3.9	259
Total money market fund	$ 3,107.2	25.8%	807
Total	$12,021.0	100.0%	8,029

Note: Column sums subject to rounding error.

Source: Investment Company Institute, *2008 Investment Company Fact Book*. Copyright © 2008 by the Investment Company Institute.

How Funds Are Sold

Most mutual funds have an underwriter that has exclusive rights to distribute shares to investors. Mutual funds are generally marketed to the public either directly by the fund underwriter or indirectly through brokers acting on behalf of the underwriter. Direct-marketed funds are sold through the mail, various offices of the fund, over the phone, and, increasingly, over the Internet. Investors contact the fund directly to purchase shares. For example, if you look at the financial pages of your local newspaper, you will see several advertisements for funds, along with toll-free phone numbers that you can call to receive a fund's prospectus and an application to open an account.

About half of fund sales today are distributed through a sales force. Brokers or financial advisers receive a commission for selling shares to investors. (Ultimately, the commission is paid by the investor. More on this shortly.) In some cases, funds use a "captive" sales force that sells only shares in funds of the mutual fund group they represent.

Investors who rely on their broker's advice to select their mutual funds should be aware that brokers may have a conflict of interest with regard to fund selection. This arises from a practice called *revenue sharing,* in which fund companies pay the brokerage firm for preferential treatment when making investment recommendations. The payment sometimes comes in the form of direct payments, computed either as a one-time payment based on sales of the mutual fund or as an ongoing payment based on fund assets held by the brokerage's clients.

Revenue-sharing arrangements pose potential conflicts of interest if they induce brokers to recommend mutual funds based on criteria other than the best interests of their clients. In addition, the mutual fund may be violating its obligation to its investors if it uses fund assets to obtain favored status in new sales.

Revenue sharing is not illegal as long as the investor is informed about the arrangement and the potential conflict of interest. Disclosure in practice, however, typically has been oblique at best. The SEC has devised new rules that would require brokerage firms to explicitly reveal any compensation or other incentives they receive to sell a particular fund. This disclosure would be required both at the time of sale and in the trade confirmation.

Many funds also are sold through "financial supermarkets" that can sell shares in funds of many complexes. This approach was made popular by the OneSource program of Charles Schwab & Co. These programs allow customers to buy funds from many different fund groups. Instead of charging customers a sales commission, the supermarket splits management fees with the mutual fund company. Another advantage is unified record keeping for all funds purchased from the supermarket, even if the funds are offered by different complexes. On the other hand, many contend that these supermarkets result in higher expense ratios because mutual funds pass along the costs of participating in these programs in the form of higher management fees.

4.4   Costs of Investing in Mutual Funds

Fee Structure

An individual investor choosing a mutual fund should consider not only the fund's stated investment policy and past performance, but also its management fees and other expenses. Comparative data on virtually all important aspects of mutual funds are available in the annual reports prepared by CDA/Wiesenberger or in Morningstar's *Mutual Fund Sourcebook,* which can be found in many academic and public libraries. You should be aware of four general classes of fees.

Operating expenses   Operating expenses are the costs incurred by the mutual fund in operating the portfolio, including administrative expenses and advisory fees paid to the investment manager. These expenses, usually expressed as a percentage of total assets under management, may range from 0.2% to 2%. Shareholders do not receive an explicit bill for these operating expenses; however, the expenses periodically are deducted from the assets of the fund. Shareholders pay for these expenses through the reduced value of the portfolio.

In addition to operating expenses, most funds assess fees to pay for marketing and distribution costs. These charges are used primarily to pay the brokers or financial advisors who sell the funds to the public. Investors can avoid these expenses by buying shares directly from the fund sponsor, but many investors are willing to incur these distribution fees in return for the advice they may receive from their broker.

Front-end load A front-end load is a commission or sales charge paid when you purchase the shares. These charges, which are used primarily to pay the brokers who sell the funds, may not exceed 8.5%, but in practice they are rarely higher than 6%. *Low-load funds* have loads that range up to 3% of invested funds. *No-load funds* have no front-end sales charges. About half of all funds today (measured by assets) are no load. Loads effectively reduce the amount of money invested. For example, each $1,000 paid for a fund with a 6% load results in a sales charge of $60 and fund investment of only $940. You need cumulative returns of 6.4% of your net investment (60/940 = .064) just to break even.

Back-end load A back-end load is a redemption, or "exit," fee incurred when you sell your shares. Typically, funds that impose back-end loads start them at 5% or 6% and reduce them by one percentage point for every year the funds are left invested. Thus, an exit fee that starts at 6% would fall to 4% by the start of your third year. These charges are known more formally as "contingent deferred sales charges."

12b-1 charges The Securities and Exchange Commission allows the managers of so-called 12b-1 funds to use fund assets to pay for distribution costs such as advertising, promotional literature including annual reports and prospectuses, and, most important, commissions paid to brokers who sell the fund to investors. These **12b-1 fees** are named after the SEC rule that permits use of these plans. Funds may use annual 12b-1 charges instead of, or in addition to, front-end loads to generate the fees with which to pay brokers. As with operating expenses, investors are not explicitly billed for 12b-1 charges. Instead, the fees are deducted from the assets of the fund. Therefore, 12b-1 fees (if any) must be added to operating expenses to obtain the true annual expense ratio of the fund. The SEC now requires that all funds include in the prospectus a consolidated expense table that summarizes all relevant fees. The 12b-1 fees are limited to 1% of a fund's average net assets per year.[2]

> **12b-1 fees**
> Annual fees charged by a mutual fund to pay for marketing and distribution costs.

Many funds offer "classes" which represent ownership in the same portfolio of securities, but with different combinations of fees. Typical Class A shares have front-end loads and a small 12b-1 fee, often around .25%. Class B shares rely on larger 12b-1 fees, commonly 1%, and often charge a modest back-end load. If an investor holds Class B shares for a long enough duration, typically 6–8 years, the shares often will convert into Class A shares which have lower 12b-1 fees. Class C shares generally rely on 12b-1 fees and back-end loads. These shares usually will not convert to Class A shares.

EXAMPLE 4.1

Fees for Various Classes (Dreyfus Founders Growth Fund)

Here are fees for different classes of the Dreyfus Founders Equity Growth Fund as of late 2008. Notice the trade-off between the front-end loads versus 12b-1 charges.

	Class A	Class B	Class C	Class T
Front-end load	0–5.75%[a]	0	0	0–4.50%[a]
Back-end load	0	0–4%[b]	0–1%[b]	0
12b-1 fees[c]	.25%	1.0	1.0	.50%
Expense ratio	1.05%	1.42%	1.05%	1.71%

Notes:
[a]Depending on size of investment.
[b]Depending on years until holdings are sold.
[c]Including service fee of .25%.

---

[2] The maximum 12b-1 charge for the sale of the fund is .75%. However, an additional service fee of .25% of the fund's assets also is allowed for personal service and/or maintenance of shareholder accounts.

Each investor must choose the best combination of fees. Obviously, pure no-load no-fee funds distributed directly by the mutual fund group are the cheapest alternative, and these will often make the most sense for knowledgeable investors. But as we noted earlier, many investors are willing to pay for financial advice, and the commissions paid to advisers who sell these funds are the most common form of payment. Alternatively, investors may choose to hire a fee-only financial manager who charges directly for services and does not accept commissions. These advisers can help investors select portfolios of low- or no-load funds (as well as provide other financial advice). Independent financial planners have become increasingly important distribution channels for funds in recent years.

If you do buy a fund through a broker, the choice between paying a load and paying 12b-1 fees will depend primarily on your expected time horizon. Loads are paid only once for each purchase, whereas 12b-1 fees are paid annually. Thus, if you plan to hold your fund for a long time, a one-time load may be preferable to recurring 12b-1 charges.

Fees and Mutual Fund Returns

The rate of return on an investment in a mutual fund is measured as the increase or decrease in net asset value plus income distributions such as dividends or distributions of capital gains expressed as a fraction of net asset value at the beginning of the investment period. If we denote the net asset value at the start and end of the period as NAV_0 and NAV_1, respectively, then

$$\text{Rate of return} = \frac{NAV_1 - NAV_0 + \text{Income and capital gain distributions}}{NAV_0}$$

For example, if a fund has an initial NAV of $20 at the start of the month, makes income distributions of $.15 and capital gain distributions of $.05, and ends the month with NAV of $20.10, the monthly rate of return is computed as

$$\text{Rate of return} = \frac{\$20.10 - \$20.00 + \$.15 + \$.05}{\$20.00} = .015, \text{ or } 1.5\%$$

Notice that this measure of the rate of return ignores any commissions such as front-end loads paid to purchase the fund.

On the other hand, the rate of return is affected by the fund's expenses and 12b-1 fees. This is because such charges are periodically deducted from the portfolio, which reduces net asset value. Thus the rate of return on the fund equals the gross return on the underlying portfolio minus the total expense ratio.

EXAMPLE 4.2
Expenses and Rates of Return

To see how expenses can affect rate of return, consider a fund with $100 million in assets at the start of the year and with 10 million shares outstanding. The fund invests in a portfolio of stocks that provides no income but increases in value by 10%. The expense ratio, including 12b-1 fees, is 1%. What is the rate of return for an investor in the fund?

The initial NAV equals $100 million/10 million shares = $10 per share. In the absence of expenses, fund assets would grow to $110 million and NAV would grow to $11 per share, for a 10% rate of return. However, the expense ratio of the fund is 1%. Therefore, $1 million will be deducted from the fund to pay these fees, leaving the portfolio worth only $109 million, and NAV equal to $10.90. The rate of return on the fund is only 9%, which equals the gross return on the underlying portfolio minus the total expense ratio.

Fees can have a big effect on performance. Table 4.2 considers an investor who starts with $10,000 and can choose between three funds that all earn an annual 12% return on investment before fees but have different fee structures. The table shows the cumulative amount in each fund after several investment horizons. Fund A has total operating expenses of .5%, no load, and no 12b-1 charges. This might represent a low-cost producer like Vanguard. Fund B has no load but has 1% management expenses and .5% in 12b-1 fees. This level of charges is fairly

TABLE 4.2 Impact of costs on investment performance		Cumulative Proceeds (all dividends reinvested)		
		Fund A	Fund B	Fund C
	Initial investment*	$10,000	$10,000	$ 9,200
	5 years	17,234	16,474	15,502
	10 years	29,699	27,141	26,123
	15 years	51,183	44,713	44,018
	20 years	88,206	73,662	74,173

Notes: Fund A is no-load with .5% expense ratio, Fund B is no-load with 1.5% total expense ratio, and Fund C has an 8% load on purchases and a 1% expense ratio. Gross return on all funds is 12% per year before expenses.

*After front-end load, if any.

typical of actively managed equity funds. Finally, Fund C has 1% in management expenses, no 12b-1 charges, but assesses an 8% front-end load on purchases.

Note the substantial return advantage of low-cost Fund A. Moreover, that differential is greater for longer investment horizons.

CONCEPT *check* **4.2**

The Equity Fund sells Class A shares with a front-end load of 4% and Class B shares with 12b-1 fees of .5% annually as well as back-end load fees that start at 5% and fall by 1% for each full year the investor holds the portfolio (until the fifth year). Assume the rate of return on the fund portfolio net of operating expenses is 10% annually. What will be the value of a $10,000 investment in Class A and Class B shares if the shares are sold after (a) 1 year, (b) 4 years, (c) 10 years? Which fee structure provides higher net proceeds at the end of each investment horizon?

Although expenses can have a big impact on net investment performance, it is sometimes difficult for the investor in a mutual fund to measure true expenses accurately. This is because of the common practice of paying for some expenses in **soft dollars.** A portfolio manager earns soft-dollar credits with a brokerage firm by directing the fund's trades to that broker. Based on those credits, the broker will pay for some of the mutual fund's expenses, such as databases, computer hardware, or stock-quotation systems. The soft-dollar arrangement means that the stockbroker effectively returns part of the trading commission to the fund. Purchases made with soft dollars are not included in the fund's expenses, so funds with extensive soft-dollar arrangements may report artificially low expense ratios to the public. However, the fund will have paid its brokers needlessly high commissions to obtain its soft-dollar "rebates." The impact of the higher trading commissions shows up in net investment performance rather than the reported expense ratio.

The SEC allows soft-dollar arrangements as long as the proceeds are used for research that may ultimately benefit the mutual fund shareholder. About half of such funds have been used to purchase stock research reports. There have certainly been cases in which soft dollars were used for purposes other than the welfare of shareholders, however, and the Investment Company Institute, the mutual fund industry trade group, has proposed that their use be curtailed. Moreover, amid the growing consensus that these arrangements make it difficult for investors to compare fund expenses, the SEC is currently considering requirements for more prominent disclosure of all brokerage commissions paid by the fund.

soft dollars

The value of research services brokerage houses provide "free of charge" in exchange for the investment manager's business.

Late Trading and Market Timing

Mutual funds calculate net asset value (NAV) at the end of each trading day. All buy or sell orders arriving during the day are executed at that NAV following the market close at 4:00 P.M. New York time. Allowing some favored investors to buy shares below NAV or sell above NAV would impose costs on all other investors. Yet, that is precisely what many mutual funds did until these practices were exposed in 2003.

Late trading refers to the practice of accepting buy or sell orders after the market closes and NAV is determined. Suppose that based on market closing prices at 4:00, a fund's NAV equals $100, but at 4:30, some positive economic news is announced. While NAV already has been fixed, it is clear that the fair market value of each share now exceeds $100. If they are able to submit a late order, investors can buy shares at the now-stale NAV and redeem them the next day after prices and NAV have adjusted to reflect the news.[3] Late traders therefore can buy shares in the fund at a price below what NAV would be if it reflected up-to-date information. This transfers value from the other shareholders to the privileged traders and shows up as a reduction in the rate of return of the mutual fund.

Market timing also exploits stale prices. Consider the hypothetical "Pacific Basin Mutual Fund," which specializes in Japanese stocks. Because of time-zone differences, the Japanese market closes several hours before trading ends in New York. NAV is set based on the closing price of the Japanese shares. If the U.S. market jumps significantly while the Japanese market is closed, however, it is likely that Japanese prices will rise when the market opens in Japan the next day. A market timer will buy the Pacific Basin fund in the U.S. today at its now-stale NAV, planning to redeem those shares the next day for a likely profit. While such activity often is characterized as rapid in-and-out trading, the more salient issue is that the market timer is allowed to transact at a stale price.

While late trading clearly violates securities laws, market timing does not. However, many funds that claimed to prohibit or discourage such trading actually allowed it, at least for some customers. And some funds even had illicit arrangements with privileged customers to allow late trading. Why did they engage in practices that reduced the rate of return to most shareholders? The answer is the management fee. Market timers and late traders in essence paid for their access to such practices by investing large amounts in the funds on which the fund manager charged its management fee. Of course, the traders possibly earned far more than those fees through their trading activity, but those costs were borne by the other shareholders, not the fund sponsor.

By mid-2004, mutual fund sponsors had paid more than $1.65 billion in penalties to settle allegations of improper trading. In addition, new rules have been implemented and others proposed to eliminate these illicit practices. These include:

- *4:00 P.M. hard cutoff.* Strict policies that a trade order must arrive at the mutual fund (not merely an intermediary such as a broker) by 4:00 to be executed. Orders arriving after 4:00 are deferred until the close of the next trading day.
- *Fair value pricing.* When computing fund NAV, prices of securities in closed markets are adjusted to reflect the likely impact of big price changes in open markets.
- *Redemption fees.* A redemption fee of 2% or more to be charged on mutual funds shares sold within seven days of purchase. These fees would be paid not to the management company, but directly into the fund to compensate other investors for potential losses due to the rapid trading.

4.5 Taxation of Mutual Fund Income

Investment returns of mutual funds are granted "pass-through status" under the U.S. tax code, meaning that taxes are paid only by the investor in the mutual fund, not by the fund itself. The income is treated as passed through to the investor as long as the fund meets several requirements, most notably that the fund be sufficiently diversified and that virtually all income is distributed to shareholders.

---

[3]Late trading can be difficult to monitor. Intermediaries such as brokerage firms or administrators of retirement plans that receive trade orders before 4:00 may legitimately send them on to the fund after 4:00 for execution at that day's NAV. This practice makes it difficult to trace late trading if a cooperative intermediary is willing to batch orders received after 4:00 with legitimate orders received before 4:00.

A fund's short-term capital gains, long-term capital gains, and dividends are passed through to investors as though the investor earned the income directly.[4] The pass-through of investment income has one important disadvantage for individual investors. If you manage your own portfolio, you decide when to realize capital gains and losses on any security; therefore, you can time those realizations to efficiently manage your tax liabilities. When you invest through a mutual fund, however, the timing of the sale of securities from the portfolio is out of your control, which reduces your ability to engage in tax management. Of course, if the mutual fund is held in a tax-deferred retirement account such as an IRA or 401(k) account, these tax management issues are irrelevant.

A fund with a high portfolio turnover rate can be particularly "tax inefficient." **Turnover** is the ratio of the trading activity of a portfolio to the assets of the portfolio. It measures the fraction of the portfolio that is "replaced" each year. For example, a $100 million portfolio with $50 million in sales of some securities with purchases of other securities would have a turnover rate of 50%. High turnover means that capital gains or losses are being realized constantly, and therefore that the investor cannot time the realizations to manage his or her overall tax obligation. Turnover rates in equity funds in the last decade have typically been around 60% when weighted by assets under management. By contrast, a low-turnover fund such as an index fund may have turnover as low as 2%, which is both tax efficient and economical with respect to trading costs.

SEC rules require funds to disclose the tax impact of port-folio turnover. Funds must include in their prospectus after-tax returns for the past 1-, 5-, and 10-year periods. Marketing literature that includes performance data also must include after-tax results. The after-tax returns are computed accounting for the impact of the taxable distributions of income and capital gains passed through to the investor, assuming the investor is in the maximum federal tax bracket.

turnover

The ratio of the trading activity of a portfolio to the assets of the portfolio.

An investor's portfolio currently is worth $1 million. During the year, the investor sells 1,000 shares of FedEx at a price of $80 per share and 4,000 shares of Cisco Systems at a price of $20 per share. The proceeds are used to buy 1,600 shares of IBM at $100 per share.
a. What was the portfolio turnover rate?
b. If the shares in FedEx originally were purchased for $70 each and those in Cisco were purchased for $17.50, and if the investor's tax rate on capital gains income is 20%, how much extra will the investor owe on this year's taxes as a result of these transactions?

CONCEPT *check* **4.3**

4.6 Exchange-Traded Funds

Exchange-traded funds (ETFs) are offshoots of mutual funds first introduced in 1993 that allow investors to trade index portfolios just as they do shares of stock. The first ETF was the "Spider," a nickname for SPDR or Standard & Poor's Depository Receipt, which is a unit investment trust holding a portfolio matching the S&P 500 index. Unlike mutual funds, which can be bought or sold only at the end of the day when NAV is calculated, investors could trade Spiders throughout the day, just like any other share of stock. Spiders gave rise to many similar products such as "Diamonds" (based on the Dow Jones Industrial Average, ticker DIA), Qubes (pronounced cubes, based on the NASDAQ 100 Index, ticker QQQQ), and WEBS (World Equity Benchmark Shares, which are shares in portfolios of foreign stock market indexes). By early 2008, about $600 billion was invested in over 600 ETFs in four general

exchange-traded funds

Offshoots of mutual funds that allow investors to trade index portfolios.

---

[4]An interesting problem that an investor needs to be aware of derives from the fact that capital gains and dividends on mutual funds are typically paid out to shareholders once or twice a year. This means that an investor who has just purchased shares in a mutual fund can receive a capital gain distribution (and be taxed on that distribution) on transactions that occurred long before he or she purchased shares in the fund. This is particularly a concern late in the year when such distributions typically are made.

TABLE 4.3
ETF sponsors and products

A. ETF Sponsors

Sponsor	Product Name
Barclays Global Investors	i-Shares
Merrill Lynch	HOLDRS (Holding Company Depository Receipts: "Holders")
StateStreet/Merrill Lynch	Select Sector SPDRs (S&P Depository Receipts: "Spiders")
Vanguard	Vanguard ETFs.

B. Sample of ETF Products

Name	Ticker	Index Tracked
Broad U.S. Indexes		
Spiders	SPY	S&P 500
Diamonds	DIA	Dow Jones Industrials
Qubes	QQQQ	NASDAQ 100
iShares Russell 2000	IWM	Russell 2000
Total Stock Market (Vanguard)	VTI	Wilshire 5000
Industry Indexes		
Energy Select Spider	XLE	S&P 500 energy companies
iShares Energy Sector	IYE	Dow Jones energy companies
Oil Service HOLDRS	OIH	Portfolio of oil service firms
Financial Sector Spider	XLF	S&P 500 financial companies
iShares Financial Sector	IYF	Dow Jones financial companies
Vanguard Financials ETF	VFH	MSCI financials index
International Indexes		
WEBS United Kingdom	EWU	MCSI U.K. Index
WEBS France	EWQ	MCSI France Index
WEBS Japan	EWJ	MCSI Japan Index

classes: broad U.S. market indexes, narrow industry or "sector" portfolios, international indexes, and bond portfolios. Table 4.3, Panel A, presents some of the sponsors of ETFs; Panel B is a small sample of ETFs, which we include to give you a flavor of the sort of products available.

Barclay's Global Investors is the market leader in the ETF market, using the product name iShares. Barclay's sponsors ETFs for several dozen equity index funds, including many broad U.S. equity indexes, broad international and single-country funds, and U.S. and global industry sector funds. Barclay's also offers several bond ETFs, and a few commodity funds such as ones for gold and silver. For more information on these funds, go to **www.iShares.com.**

Figure 4.2 shows the growth of ETFs by type since 1998. The figure documents the rapid growth of global and international funds starting in 2000 and the more recent growth of commodity and bond funds.

ETFs offer several advantages over conventional mutual funds. First, as we just noted, a mutual fund's net asset value is quoted—and therefore, investors can buy or sell their shares in the fund—only once a day. In contrast, ETFs trade continuously. Moreover, like other shares, but unlike mutual funds, ETFs can be sold short or purchased on margin.

ETFs also offer a potential tax advantage over mutual funds. When large numbers of mutual fund investors redeem their shares, the fund must sell securities to meet the redemptions. The sale can trigger capital gains taxes, which are passed through to and must be paid by the remaining

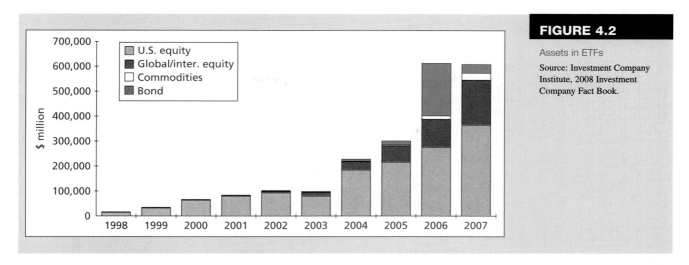

FIGURE 4.2

Assets in ETFs

Source: Investment Company Institute, 2008 Investment Company Fact Book.

shareholders. In contrast, when small investors wish to redeem their position in an ETF they simply sell their shares to other traders, with no need for the fund to sell any of the underlying portfolio. Moreover, when large traders wish to redeem their position in the ETF, redemptions are satisfied with shares of stock in the underlying portfolio. Again, a redemption does not trigger a stock sale by the fund sponsor.

The ability of large investors to redeem ETFs for a portfolio of stocks comprising the index, or to exchange a portfolio of stocks for shares in the corresponding ETF, ensures that the price of an ETF cannot depart significantly from the NAV of that portfolio. Any meaningful discrepancy would offer arbitrage trading opportunities for these large traders, which would quickly eliminate the disparity.

ETFs are also cheaper than mutual funds. Investors who buy ETFs do so through brokers, rather than buying directly from the fund. Therefore, the fund saves the cost of marketing itself directly to small investors. This reduction in expenses translates into lower management fees.

There are some disadvantages to ETFs, however. Because they trade as securities, there is the possibility that their prices can depart by small amounts from NAV. As noted, this discrepancy cannot be too large without giving rise to arbitrage opportunities for large traders, but even small discrepancies can easily swamp the cost advantage of ETFs over mutual funds. Second, while mutual funds can be bought for NAV with no expense from no-load funds, ETFs must be purchased from brokers for a fee. Investors also incur a bid–ask spread when purchasing an ETF.

4.7 | Mutual Fund Investment Performance: A First Look

We noted earlier that one of the benefits of mutual funds for the individual investor is the ability to delegate management of the portfolio to investment professionals. The investor retains control over the broad features of the overall portfolio through the asset allocation decision: Each individual chooses the percentages of the portfolio to invest in bond funds versus equity funds versus money market funds, and so forth, but can leave the specific security selection decisions within each investment class to the managers of each fund. Shareholders hope that these portfolio managers can achieve better investment performance than they could obtain on their own.

What is the investment record of the mutual fund industry? This seemingly straightforward question is deceptively difficult to answer because we need a standard against which to evaluate performance. For example, we clearly would not want to compare the investment performance of an equity fund to the rate of return available in the money market. The vast differences in the risk of these two markets dictate that year-by-year as well as average performance will differ considerably. We would expect to find that equity funds outperform money market funds (on average) as compensation to investors for the extra risk incurred in equity markets. How can we determine whether mutual fund portfolio managers are performing up to par *given* the level of risk they incur? In other words, what is the proper benchmark against which investment performance ought to be evaluated?

Measuring portfolio risk properly and using such measures to choose an appropriate benchmark is an extremely difficult task. We devote all of Parts Two and Three of the text to issues surrounding the proper measurement of portfolio risk and the trade-off between risk and return. In this chapter, therefore, we will satisfy ourselves with a first look at the question of fund performance by using only very simple performance benchmarks and ignoring the more subtle issues of risk differences across funds. However, we will return to this topic in Chapter 8, where we take a closer look at mutual fund performance after adjusting for differences in the exposure of portfolios to various sources of risk.

Here, we will use as a benchmark for the performance of equity fund managers the rate of return on the Wilshire 5000 Index. Recall from Chapter 2 that this is a value-weighted index of around 6,000 stocks that trade on the NYSE, NASDAQ, and Amex stock markets. It is the most inclusive index of the performance of U.S. equities. The performance of the Wilshire 5000 is a useful benchmark with which to evaluate professional managers because it corresponds to a simple passive investment strategy: Buy all the shares in the index in proportion to their outstanding market value. Moreover, this is a feasible strategy for even small investors, because the Vanguard Group offers an index fund (its Total Stock Market Index Fund) designed to replicate the performance of the Wilshire 5000 Index. Using the Wilshire 5000 Index as a benchmark, we may pose the problem of evaluating the performance of mutual fund portfolio managers this way: How does the typical performance of actively managed equity mutual funds compare to the performance of a passively managed portfolio that simply replicates the composition of a broad index of the stock market?

Casual comparisons of the performance of the Wilshire 5000 Index versus that of professionally managed mutual fund portfolios show disappointing results for most fund managers. Figure 4.3 shows that the average returns on diversified equity funds was below the return on the Wilshire 5000 Index in 23 of the 38 years from 1971 to 2008. The average return on the index was 11.4%, which was 1% greater than that of the average mutual fund.[5]

This result may seem surprising. After all, it would not seem unreasonable to expect that professional money managers should be able to outperform a very simple rule such as "hold an indexed portfolio." As it turns out, however, there may be good reasons to expect such a result. We will explore them in detail in Chapter 8, where we discuss the efficient market hypothesis.

Of course, one might argue that there are good managers and bad managers, and that good managers can, in fact, consistently outperform the index. To test this notion, we examine whether managers with good performance in one year are likely to repeat that performance in a following year. Is superior performance in any particular year due to luck, and therefore random, or due to skill, and therefore consistent from year to year?

To answer this question, we can examine the performance of a large sample of equity mutual fund portfolios, divide the funds into two groups based on total investment return, and ask: "Do funds with investment returns in the top half of the sample in one period continue to perform well in the subsequent period?"

Table 4.4 presents such an analysis from a study by Malkiel (1995). The table shows the fraction of "winners" (i.e., top-half performers) in each year that turn out to be winners or

---

[5]Of course, actual funds incur trading costs while indexes do not, so a fair comparison between the returns on actively managed funds versus those on a passive index would first reduce the return on the Wilshire 5000 by an estimate of such costs. Vanguard's Total Stock Market Index portfolio, which tracks the Wilshire 5000, charges an expense ratio of .19%, and, because it engages in little trading, incurs low trading costs. Therefore, it would be reasonable to reduce the returns on the index by about .30%. This reduction would not erase the difference in average performance.

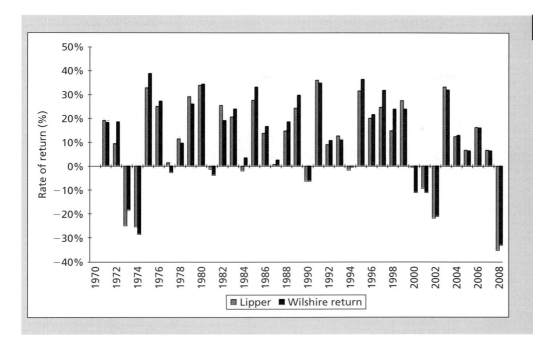

FIGURE 4.3

Diversified equity funds versus Wilshire 5000 Index

Source: **www.wilshire.com**, Dow Jones Wilshire, The Dow Jones Wilshire IndexesSM are calculated, distributed, and marketed by Dow Jones & Company, Inc. pursuant to an agreement between Dow Jones and Wilshire Associates Incorporated and have been licensed for use. All content of the Dow Jones Wilshire IndexesSM © 2008 Dow Jones & Company, Inc. & Wilshire Associates Incorporated.

TABLE 4.4		**Successive Period Performance**	
Consistency of investment results	**Initial Period Performance**	**Top Half**	**Bottom Half**
	A. Malkiel study, 1970s		
	Top half	65.1%	34.9%
	Bottom half	35.5%	64.5%
	B. Malkiel study, 1980s		
	Top half	51.7%	48.3%
	Bottom half	47.5%	52.5%

Source: "Returns from Investing in Equity Mutual Funds 1971–1991," by Burton G. Malkiel, *Journal of Finance* 50 (June 1995), pp. 549–72. Reprinted by permission of Blackwell Science, U.K.

losers in the following year. If performance were purely random from one period to the next, there would be entries of 50% in each cell of the table, as top- or bottom-half performers would be equally likely to perform in either the top or bottom half of the sample in the following period. On the other hand, if performance were due entirely to skill, with no randomness, we would expect to see entries of 100% on the diagonals and entries of 0% on the off-diagonals: Top-half performers would all remain in the top half while bottom-half performers similarly would all remain in the bottom half. In fact, Panel A shows that 65.1% of initial top-half performers in the 1970s fall in the top half of the sample in the following period, while 64.5% of initial bottom-half performers fall in the bottom half in the following period. This evidence is consistent with the notion that at least part of a fund's performance is a function of skill as opposed to luck, so that relative performance tends to persist from one period to the next.[6]

On the other hand, this relationship does not seem stable across different sample periods. While initial-year performance predicts subsequent-year performance in the 1970s (see Panel A), the pattern of persistence in performance virtually disappears in the 1980s (Panel B).

[6]Another possibility is that performance consistency is due to variation in fee structure across funds. We return to this possibility in Chapter 8.

Other studies suggest that bad performance is more likely to persist than good performance. This makes some sense: It is easy to identify fund characteristics that will predictably lead to consistently poor investment performance, notably, high expense ratios and high turnover ratios with associated trading costs. It is far harder to identify the secrets of successful stock picking. (If it were easy, we would all be rich!) Thus the consistency we do observe in fund performance may be due in large part to the poor performers. This suggests that the real value of past performance data is to avoid truly poor funds, even if identifying the future top performers is still a daunting task.

CONCEPT
check **4.4**

Suppose you observe the investment performance of 400 portfolio managers and rank them by investment returns during the year. Twenty percent of all managers are truly skilled, and therefore always fall in the top half, but the others fall in the top half purely because of good luck. What fraction of these top-half managers would you expect to be top-half performers next year? Assume skilled managers always are top-half performers.

4.8   Information on Mutual Funds

The first place to find information on a mutual fund is in its prospectus. The Securities and Exchange Commission requires that the prospectus describe the fund's investment objectives and policies in a concise "Statement of Investment Objectives" as well as in lengthy discussions of investment policies and risks. The fund's investment adviser and its portfolio manager also are described. The prospectus also presents the costs associated with purchasing shares in the fund in a fee table. Sales charges such as front-end and back-end loads as well as annual operating expenses such as management fees and 12b-1 fees are detailed in the fee table.

Funds provide information about themselves in two other sources. The Statement of Additional Information, or SAI, also known as Part B of the prospectus, includes a list of the securities in the portfolio at the end of the fiscal year, audited financial statements, a list of the directors and officers of the fund as well as their personal investments in the fund, and data on brokerage commissions paid by the fund. Unlike the fund prospectus, however, investors do not receive the SAI unless they specifically request it; one industry joke is that SAI stands for "something always ignored." The fund's annual report also includes portfolio composition and financial statements, as well as a discussion of the factors that influenced fund performance over the last reporting period.

With more than 8,000 mutual funds to choose from, it can be difficult to find and select the fund that is best suited for a particular need. Several publications now offer "encyclopedias" of mutual fund information to help in the search process. Two prominent sources are Wiesenberger's *Investment Companies* and Morningstar's *Mutual Fund Sourcebook.* Morningstar's Web site **www.morningstar.com** is another excellent source of information, as is Yahoo!'s site, **finance.yahoo.com/funds**. The Investment Company Institute—the national association of mutual funds, closed-end funds, and unit investment trusts—publishes an annual *Directory of Mutual Funds* that includes information on fees as well as phone numbers to contact funds. To illustrate the range of information available about funds, we consider Morningstar's report on Fidelity's Magellan fund, reproduced in Figure 4.4.

Some of Morningstar's analysis is qualitative. The top box on the left-hand side of the page of the report reproduced in the figure provides a short description of fund strategy, in particular the types of securities in which the fund manager tends to invest. The bottom box on the left ("Morningstar's Take") is a more detailed discussion of the fund's income strategy. The short statement of the fund's investment policy is in the top right-hand corner: Magellan is a "large growth" fund, meaning that it tends to invest in large firms, with an emphasis on growth over value stocks.

The table on the left in the figure labeled "Performance" reports on the fund's quarterly returns over the last few years and then over longer periods up to 15 years. Comparisons of

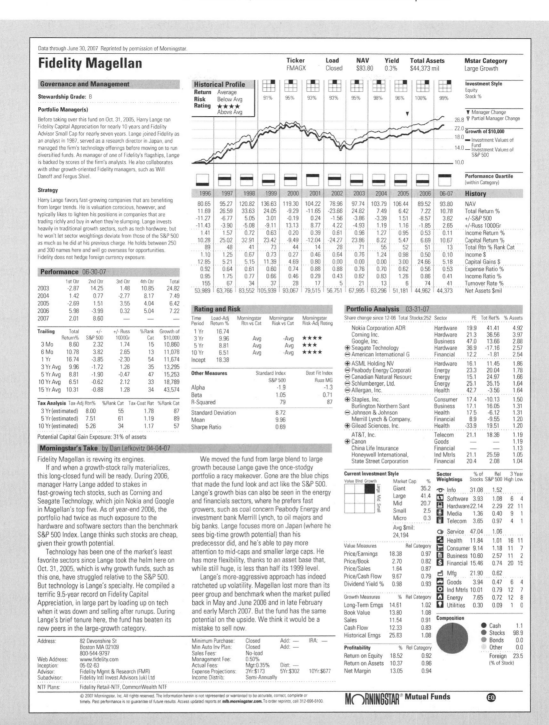

FIGURE 4.4

Morningstar report

Source: Morningstar Mutual Funds. © 2007 Morningstar, Inc. All rights reserved. Used with permission.

returns to relevant indexes, in this case, the S&P 500 and the Russell 1000 indexes, are provided to serve as benchmarks in evaluating the performance of the fund. The values under these columns give the performance of the fund relative to the index. The returns reported for the fund are calculated net of expenses, 12b-1 fees, and any other fees automatically deducted from fund assets, but they do not account for any sales charges such as front-end loads or back-end charges. Next appear the percentile ranks of the fund compared to all other funds with the same investment objective (see column headed by %Rank Cat). A rank of 1 means the fund is a top performer. A rank of 80 would mean that it was beaten by 80% of funds in the comparison group. Finally, growth of $10,000 invested in the fund over various periods ranging from the past three months to the past 15 years is given in the last column.

More data on the performance of the fund are provided in the graph near the top of the figure. The line graph compares the growth of $10,000 invested in the fund and the S&P 500 over the last 10 years. Below the graph are boxes for each year that depict the relative performance of the fund for that year. The shaded area on the box shows the quartile in which the fund's performance falls relative to other funds with the same objective. If the shaded band is at the top of the box, the firm was a top quartile performer in that period, and so on. The table below the bar charts presents historical data on characteristics of the fund such as return data and expense ratios.

The table on the right entitled Portfolio Analysis presents the 20 largest holdings of the portfolio, showing the price–earnings ratio and year-to-date return of each of those securities. Investors can thus get a quick look at the manager's biggest bets.

Below the portfolio analysis table is a box labeled Current Investment Style. In this box, Morningstar evaluates style along two dimensions: One dimension is the size of the firms held in the portfolio as measured by the market value of outstanding equity; the other dimension is a value/growth measure. Morningstar defines *value stocks* as those with low ratios of market price per share to various measures of value. It puts stocks on a growth-value continuum based on the ratios of stock price to the firm's earnings, book value, sales, cash flow, and dividends. Value stocks are those with a low price relative to these measures of value. In contrast, *growth stocks* have high ratios, suggesting that investors in these firms must believe that the firm will experience rapid growth to justify the prices at which the stocks sell. The shaded box for Magellan shows that the portfolio tends to hold larger firms (top row) and growth stocks (right column). A year-by-year history of Magellan's investment style is presented in the sequence of such boxes at the top of Figure 4.4.

The center of the figure, labeled Rating and Risk, is one of the more complicated but interesting facets of Morningstar's analysis. The column labeled Load-Adj Return rates a fund's return compared to other funds with the same investment policy. Returns for periods ranging from 1 to 10 years are calculated with all loads and back-end fees applicable to that investment period subtracted from total income. The return is then compared to the average return for the comparison group of funds to obtain the Morningstar Return vs. Category. Similarly, risk measures compared to category are computed and reported in the next column.

The last column presents Morningstar's risk-adjusted rating, ranging from one to five stars. The rating is based on the fund's return score minus risk score compared to other funds with similar investment styles. To allow funds to be compared to other funds with similar investment styles, Morningstar employs a large number of categories; there are now 48 separate stock and bond fund categories. Of course, we are accustomed to the disclaimer that "past performance is not a reliable measure of future results," and this is true as well of the coveted Morningstar 5-star rating. The nearby box discusses the predictive value of the Morningstar ranking.

The tax analysis box shown on the left in Figure 4.4 provides some evidence on the tax efficiency of the fund. The after-tax return, given in the first column, is computed based on the dividends paid to the portfolio as well as realized capital gains, assuming the investor is in the maximum federal tax bracket at the time of the distribution. State and local taxes are ignored. The tax efficiency of the fund is measured by the "Tax-Cost Ratio," which is an estimate of the impact of taxes on the investor's after-tax return. Morningstar ranks each fund compared to its category for both tax-adjusted return and tax-cost ratio.

MUTUAL-FUND RATINGS COME UNDER FIRE

Two methods for rating mutual funds, including the widely used Morningstar system, have come under fire.

A new study concludes that mutual funds given high ratings by Morningstar and Value Line—both used by investors to choose among funds—don't necessarily perform better than those with middling ratings.

The ratings are widely trumpeted in mutual funds' advertisements, and many people rely on them to make key investment decisions, such as where to put their retirement savings. Last year, for example, stock funds with coveted four- and five-star ratings from Morningstar took in nearly $80 billion, compared with the more than $108 billion that was withdrawn from lower-rated funds, according to Nov. 30 [2002] data from Financial Research Corp.

"Mutual-fund ratings services can't really predict winners," says the study's author, finance professor Matthew R. Morey of New York's Pace University.

To test ratings' predictive abilities, Prof. Morey sifted the fund market for diversified stock funds that had at least three years of history at the end of 1994. He then tracked the performance of these funds over the next six years to see how funds with high ratings from Morningstar and Value Line compared with those with lower ratings.

Prof. Morey found that, from 1995 through 2000, lower-rated funds kept slumping to some extent. But highly rated funds, which draw heavy promotion and sales, didn't tend to perform any better than funds with middle-of-the-pack ratings.

Morningstar previously compared funds in four categories: U.S. stock, foreign stock, taxable bond and municipal bond. But this past summer the firm began comparing funds in 48 narrower stock- and bond-fund categories. The narrower categories keep one group from ending up with a disproportionate percentage of the top ratings, such as when 90% of rated tech funds had five stars at the end of 1999.

So, how should investors use fund ratings? Cautiously.

The best approach is to research how a rating is derived and, if you're comfortable with its criteria, only use it as a first cut to winnow the vast field of options. A ratings screen will leave you with a more manageable pack of funds to study closely and shoe-horn into a well-diversified portfolio.

The bottom of the page in Figure 4.4 provides information on the expenses and loads associated with investments in the fund, as well as information on the fund's investment adviser. Thus, Morningstar provides a considerable amount of the information you would need to decide among several competing funds.

SUMMARY

- Unit investment trusts, closed-end management companies, and open-end management companies are all classified and regulated as investment companies. Unit investment trusts are essentially unmanaged in the sense that the portfolio, once established, is fixed. Managed investment companies, in contrast, may change the composition of the portfolio as deemed fit by the portfolio manager. Closed-end funds are traded like other securities; they do not redeem shares for their investors. Open-end funds will redeem shares for net asset value at the request of the investor.

- Net asset value equals the market value of assets held by a fund minus the liabilities of the fund divided by the shares outstanding.

- Mutual funds free the individual from many of the administrative burdens of owning individual securities and offer professional management of the portfolio. They also offer advantages that are available only to large-scale investors, such as lower trading costs. On the other hand, funds are assessed management fees and incur other expenses, which reduce the investor's rate of return. Funds also eliminate some of the individual's control over the timing of capital gains realizations.

- Mutual funds often are categorized by investment policy. Major policy groups include money market funds; equity funds, which are further grouped according to emphasis on income versus growth; fixed-income funds; balanced and income funds; asset allocation funds; index funds; and specialized sector funds.

- Costs of investing in mutual funds include front-end loads, which are sales charges; back-end loads, which are redemption fees or, more formally, contingent-deferred sales charges; fund operating expenses; and 12b-1 charges, which are recurring fees used to pay for the expenses of marketing the fund to the public.

- Income earned on mutual fund portfolios is not taxed at the level of the fund. Instead, as long as the fund meets certain requirements for pass-through status, the income is treated as being earned by the investors in the fund.
- The average rate of return of the average equity mutual fund in the last 25 years has been below that of a passive index fund holding a portfolio to replicate a broad-based index like the S&P 500 or Wilshire 5000. Some of the reasons for this disappointing record are the costs incurred by actively managed funds, such as the expense of conducting the research to guide stock-picking activities, and trading costs due to higher portfolio turnover. The record on the consistency of fund performance is mixed. In some sample periods, the better-performing funds continue to perform well in the following periods; in other sample periods they do not.

KEY TERMS

closed-end fund, 85	load, 86	12b-1 fees, 91
exchange-traded funds, 95	net asset value (NAV), 84	turnover, 95
hedge fund, 87	open-end fund, 85	unit investment trust, 85
investment company, 84	soft dollars, 93	

PROBLEM SETS

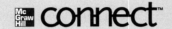

Select problems are available in McGraw-Hill Connect. Please see the packaging options section of the preface for more information.

Basic

1. What are the benefits to small investors of investing via mutual funds? What are the costs?
2. Why can closed-end funds sell at prices that differ from net value while open-end funds do not?
3. What is a 12b-1 fee?
4. What are some differences between a unit investment trust and a closed-end fund?
5. What are the advantages and disadvantages of exchange-traded funds versus mutual funds?
6. What are some differences between hedge funds and mutual funds?
7. Would you expect a typical open-end fixed-income mutual fund to have higher or lower operating expenses than a fixed-income unit investment trust? Why?
8. Balanced funds and asset allocation funds invest in both the stock and bond markets. What is the difference between these types of funds?
9. What are some comparative advantages of investing your assets in the following:
   a. Unit investment trusts.
   b. Open-end mutual funds.
   c. Individual stocks and bonds that you choose for yourself.
10. Open-end equity mutual funds find it necessary to keep a significant percentage of total investments, typically around 5% of the portfolio, in very liquid money market assets. Closed-end funds do not have to maintain such a position in "cash-equivalent" securities. What difference between open-end and closed-end funds might account for their differing policies?.

Intermediate

11. An open-end fund has a net asset value of $10.70 per share. It is sold with a front-end load of 6%. What is the offering price?
12. If the offering price of an open-end fund is $12.30 per share and the fund is sold with a front-end load of 5%, what is its net asset value?

13. The composition of the Fingroup Fund portfolio is as follows:

Stock	Shares	Price
A	200,000	$35
B	300,000	40
C	400,000	20
D	600,000	25

The fund has not borrowed any funds, but its accrued management fee with the portfolio manager currently totals $30,000. There are 4 million shares outstanding. What is the net asset value of the fund?

14. Reconsider the Fingroup Fund in the previous problem. If during the year the portfolio manager sells all of the holdings of stock D and replaces it with 200,000 shares of stock E at $50 per share and 200,000 shares of stock F at $25 per share, what is the portfolio turnover rate?

15. The Closed Fund is a closed-end investment company with a portfolio currently worth $200 million. It has liabilities of $3 million and 5 million shares outstanding.
    a. What is the NAV of the fund?
    b. If the fund sells for $36 per share, what is its premium or discount as a percent of NAV?

16. Corporate Fund started the year with a net asset value of $12.50. By year-end, its NAV equaled $12.10. The fund paid year-end distributions of income and capital gains of $1.50. What was the rate of return to an investor in the fund?

17. A closed-end fund starts the year with a net asset value of $12.00. By year-end, NAV equals $12.10. At the beginning of the year, the fund is selling at a 2% premium to NAV. By the end of the year, the fund is selling at a 7% discount to NAV. The fund paid year-end distributions of income and capital gains of $1.50.
    a. What is the rate of return to an investor in the fund during the year?
    b. What would have been the rate of return to an investor who held the same securities as the fund manager during the year?

18. Loaded-Up Fund charges a 12b-1 fee of 1.0% and maintains an expense ratio of .75%. Economy Fund charges a front-end load of 2%, but has no 12b-1 fee and an expense ratio of .25%. Assume the rate of return on both funds' portfolios (before any fees) is 6% per year. How much will an investment in each fund grow to after:
    a. 1 year
    b. 3 years
    c. 10 years

19. City Street Fund has a portfolio of $450 million, and liabilities of $10 million.
    a. If there are 44 million shares outstanding, what is net asset value?
    b. If a large investor redeems 1 million shares, what happens to the portfolio value, to shares outstanding, and to NAV?

20. a. Impressive Fund had excellent investment performance last year, with portfolio returns that placed it in the top 10% of all funds with the same investment policy. Do you expect it to be a top performer next year? Why or why not?
    b. Suppose instead that the fund was among the poorest performers in its comparison group. Would you be more or less likely to believe its relative performance will persist into the following year? Why?

21. Consider a mutual fund with $200 million in assets at the start of the year and with 10 million shares outstanding. The fund invests in a portfolio of stocks that provides dividend income at the end of the year of $2 million. The stocks included in the fund's portfolio increase in price by 8%, but no securities are sold, and there are no capital gains distributions. The fund charges 12b-1 fees of 1%, which are deducted from

portfolio assets at year-end. What is net asset value at the start and end of the year? What is the rate of return for an investor in the fund?

22. The New Fund had average daily assets of $2.2 billion in the past year. The fund sold $400 million and purchased $500 million worth of stock during the year. What was its turnover ratio?

23. If New Fund's expense ratio was 1.1% and the management fee was .7%, what were the total fees paid to the fund's investment managers during the year? What were the other administrative expenses?

24. You purchased 1,000 shares of the New Fund at a price of $20 per share at the beginning of the year. You paid a front-end load of 4%. The securities in which the fund invests increase in value by 12% during the year. The fund's expense ratio is 1.2%. What is your rate of return on the fund if you sell your shares at the end of the year?

25. The Investments Fund sells Class A shares with a front-end load of 6% and Class B shares with 12b-1 fees of .5% annually as well as back-end load fees that start at 5% and fall by 1% for each full year the investor holds the portfolio (until the fifth year). Assume the portfolio rate of return net of operating expenses is 10% annually. If you plan to sell the fund after four years, are Class A or Class B shares the better choice for you? What if you plan to sell after 15 years?

26. You are considering an investment in a mutual fund with a 4% load and an expense ratio of .5%. You can invest instead in a bank CD paying 6% interest.
    a. If you plan to invest for two years, what annual rate of return must the fund portfolio earn for you to be better off in the fund than in the CD? Assume annual compounding of returns.
    b. How does your answer change if you plan to invest for six years? Why does your answer change?
    c. Now suppose that instead of a front-end load the fund assesses a 12b-1 fee of .75% per year. What annual rate of return must the fund portfolio earn for you to be better off in the fund than in the CD? Does your answer in this case depend on your time horizon?

27. Suppose that every time a fund manager trades stock, transaction costs such as commissions and bid–ask spreads amount to .4% of the value of the trade. If the portfolio turnover rate is 50%, by how much is the total return of the portfolio reduced by trading costs?

28. You expect a tax-free municipal bond portfolio to provide a rate of return of 4%. Management fees of the fund are .6%. What fraction of portfolio income is given up to fees? If the management fees for an equity fund also are .6%, but you expect a portfolio return of 12%, what fraction of portfolio income is given up to fees? Why might management fees be a bigger factor in your investment decision for bond funds than for stock funds? Can your conclusion help explain why unmanaged unit investment trusts tend to focus on the fixed-income market?

Challenge

29. Suppose you observe the investment performance of 350 portfolio managers for five years and rank them by investment returns during each year. After five years, you find that 11 of the funds have investment returns that place the fund in the top half of the sample in each and every year of your sample. Such consistency of performance indicates to you that these must be the funds whose managers are in fact skilled, and you invest your money in these funds. Is your conclusion warranted?

Go to **www.morningstar.com.** In the Morningstar Tools section, click on the link for the Mutual Fund Screener. Set the criteria you desire, then click on the Show Results tab. If you get no funds that meet all of your criteria, choose the criterion that is least important to you and relax that constraint. Continue the process until you have several funds to compare.

1. Examine all of the views available in the drop-down box menu (Snapshot, Performance, Portfolio, and Nuts and Bolts) to answer the following questions:

   - Which fund has the best expense ratio?
   - Which funds have the lowest Morningstar Risk rating?
   - Which fund has the best 3-year return? Which has the best 10-year return?

- Which fund has the lowest turnover ratio? Which has the highest?
- Which fund has the longest manager tenure? Which has the shortest?
- Do you need to eliminate any of the funds from consideration due to a minimum initial investment that is higher than you are capable of making?

2. Based on what you know about the funds, which one do you think would be the best one for your investment?

3. Select up to five funds that are of the most interest to you. Click on the button that says Score These Results. Customize the criteria listed by indicating their importance to you. Examine the Score Results. Does the fund with the highest score match the choice you made in Part 2?

SOLUTIONS TO CONCEPT *checks*

4.1. $\text{NAV} = (\$4,517.0 - \$11.1)/154.8 = \$29.11$

4.2. The net investment in the Class A shares after the 4% commission is \$9,600. If the fund earns a 10% return, the investment will grow after n years to $\$9,600 \times (1.10)^n$. The Class B shares have no front-end load. However, the net return to the investor after 12b-1 fees will be only 9.5%. In addition, there is a back-end load that reduces the sales proceeds by a percentage equal to $(5 - \text{years until sale})$ until the fifth year, when the back-end load expires.

Horizon	Class A Shares $\$9,600 \times (1.10)^n$	Class B Shares $\$10,000 \times (1.095)^n \times (1 - \text{percentage exit fee})$
1 year	\$10,560.00	$\$10,000 \times (1.095) \times (1 - .04) = \$10,512.00$
4 years	\$14,055.36	$\$10,000 \times (1.095)^4 \times (1 - .01) = \$14,232.89$
10 years	\$24,899.93	$\$10,000 \times (1.095)^{10} \quad = \$24,782.28$

For a very short horizon such as one year, the Class A shares are the better choice. The front-end and back-end loads are equal, but the Class A shares don't have to pay the 12b-1 fees. For moderate horizons such as four years, the Class B shares dominate because the front-end load of the Class A shares is more costly than the 12b-1 fees and the now-smaller exit fee. For long horizons of 10 years or more, Class A again dominates. In this case, the one-time front-end load is less expensive than the continuing 12b-1 fees.

4.3. *a.* Turnover = \$160,000 in trades per \$1 million of portfolio value = 16%.

b. Realized capital gains are $\$10 \times 1,000 = \$10,000$ on FedEx and $\$2.50 \times 4,000 = \$10,000$ on Cisco. The tax owed on the capital gains is therefore $.20 \times \$20,000 = \$4,000$.

4.4. Twenty percent of the managers are skilled, which accounts for $.2 \times 400 = 80$ of those managers who appear in the top half. There are 120 slots left in the top half, and 320 other managers, so the probability of an unskilled manager "lucking into" the top half in any year is 120/320, or .375. Therefore, of the 120 lucky managers in the first year, we would expect $.375 \times 120 = 45$ to repeat as top-half performers next year. Thus, we should expect a total of $80 + 45 = 125$, or 62.5%, of the better initial performers to repeat their top-half performance.

PART 2

Portfolio Theory

The last 80 years witnessed the Great Depression, seven additional recessions of varying severity, and the deep recession that began in 2008. Yet even with these downturns, a dollar invested in a broad portfolio of stocks over this period still grew to a value about 80 times greater than a dollar invested (and reinvested) in safe assets. Why then would anyone invest in a safe asset? Because investors are risk averse, and risk is as important to them as the mean value of returns. Chapter 5, the first of five in Part Two, provides the tools needed to interpret the history of rates of return, and the lessons that history offers for how investors might go about constructing portfolios using safe as well as risky assets.

Deciding the proportion an investor desires to put at risk must be augmented by a decision of how to construct an efficient portfolio of risky assets. Chapter 6 lays out modern portfolio theory (MPT), which involves the construction of the risky portfolio. It aims to accomplish efficient diversification across asset classes like bonds and stocks, and across individual securities within these asset classes.

This analysis quickly leads to other questions. For example, how should one measure the risk of an individual asset held as part of a diversified portfolio? You will probably be surprised at the answer. Once we have an acceptable measure of risk, what precisely should be the relation between risk and return? And what is the minimally acceptable rate of return for an investment to be considered attractive? These questions also are addressed in this part of the text. Chapter 7 introduces the Capital Asset Pricing Model (CAPM), Arbitrage Pricing Theory (APT), as well as index and multi-index models, the mainstays of applied financial economics. These models link risk, properly measured, with the return investors can reasonably expect on various securities.

Next, we come to one of the most controversial topics in investment management, the question of whether portfolio managers—amateur or professional—can outperform simple investment strategies such as "buy a market index fund." The evidence in Chapter 8 will at least make you pause before pursuing active strategies. You will come to appreciate how good active managers must be to outperform their passive counterparts. Finally, Chapter 9 on behavioral finance is concerned with lessons from psychology that have been proposed to explain how irrational investor behavior can explain observed anomalies in patterns of asset returns.

Risk and Return: Past and Prologue

After Studying This Chapter You Should Be Able To:

- Use data on the past performance of stocks and bonds to characterize the risk and return features of these investments.

- Determine the expected return and risk of portfolios that are constructed by combining risky assets with risk-free investments in Treasury bills.

- Evaluate the performance of a passive strategy.

What constitutes a satisfactory investment portfolio? Until the early 1970s, a reasonable answer would have been a Federally insured bank savings account (a risk-free asset) plus a risky portfolio of U.S. stocks. Nowadays, investors have access to a vastly wider array of assets and may contemplate complex portfolio strategies that may include foreign stocks and bonds, real estate, precious metals, and collectibles. Even more complex strategies may include futures, options, and other derivatives to insure portfolios against unacceptable losses. How might such portfolios be constructed?

Clearly every individual security must be judged on its contributions to both the expected return and the risk of the entire portfolio. To guide us in forming reasonable expectations for portfolio performance, we will start this chapter with an examination of various conventions for measuring and reporting rates of return. Given these measures, we turn to the historical performance of several broadly diversified investment portfolios. In doing so, we use a risk-free portfolio of Treasury bills as a benchmark to evaluate the historical performance of diversified stock and bond portfolios.

We then proceed to consider the trade-offs investors face when they practice the simplest form of risk control, capital allocation: choosing the fraction of the portfolio invested in virtually risk-free money market securities versus risky

Related Web sites for this chapter are available at www.mhhe.com/bkm.

securities such as stocks. We show how to calculate the performance one may reasonably expect from various allocations between a risk-free asset and a risky portfolio and discuss the considerations that determine the mix that would best suit different investors. With this background, we can evaluate a passive strategy that will serve as a benchmark for the active strategies considered in the next chapter.

5.1 Rates of Return

holding-period return

Rate of return over a given investment period.

A key measure of investors' success is the rate at which their funds have grown during the investment period. The total **holding-period return (HPR)** of a share of stock depends on the increase (or decrease) in the price of the share over the investment period as well as on any dividend income the share has provided. The rate of return is defined as dollars earned over the investment period (price appreciation as well as dividends) per dollar invested:

$$\text{HPR} = \frac{\text{Ending price} - \text{Beginning price} + \text{Cash dividend}}{\text{Beginning price}} \qquad (5.1)$$

This definition of the HPR assumes that the dividend is paid at the end of the holding period. To the extent that dividends are received earlier, the definition ignores reinvestment income between the receipt of the dividend and the end of the holding period. Recall also that the percentage return from dividends is called the dividend yield, and so the dividend yield, cash dividend/beginning price, plus the capital gains yield equals the HPR.

This definition of holding return is easy to modify for other types of investments. For example, the HPR on a bond would be calculated using the same formula, except that the bond's interest or coupon payments would take the place of the stock's dividend payments.

EXAMPLE 5.1

Holding-Period Return

Suppose you are considering investing some of your money, now all invested in a bank account, in a stock market index fund. The price of a share in the fund is currently $100, and your time horizon is one year. You expect the cash dividend during the year to be $4, so your expected dividend yield is 4%.

Your HPR will depend on the price one year from now. Suppose your best guess is that it will be $110 per share. Then your *capital gain* will be $10, so your capital gains yield is $10/$100 = .10, or 10%. The total holding-period rate of return is the sum of the dividend yield plus the capital gain yield, 4% + 10% = 14%.

$$\text{HPR} = \frac{\$110 - \$100 + \$4}{\$100} = .14, \text{ or } 14\%$$

Measuring Investment Returns over Multiple Periods

The holding-period return is a simple and unambiguous measure of investment return over a single period. But often you will be interested in average returns over longer periods of time. For example, you might want to measure how well a mutual fund has performed over the preceding five-year period. In this case, return measurement is more ambiguous.

Consider, for example, a fund that starts with $1 million under management at the beginning of the year. The fund receives additional funds to invest from new and existing shareholders, and also receives requests for redemptions from existing shareholders. Its net cash inflow can be positive or negative. Suppose its quarterly results are as given in Table 5.1 with negative numbers reported in parentheses.

The story behind these numbers is that when the firm does well (i.e., reports a good HPR), it attracts new funds; otherwise it may suffer a net outflow. For example, the 10% return in the first quarter by itself increased assets under management by 0.10 × $1 million = $100,000;

TABLE 5.1		1st Quarter	2nd Quarter	3rd Quarter	4th Quarter
Quarterly cash flows and rates of return of a mutual fund	Assets under management at start of quarter ($ million)	1.0	1.2	2.0	0.8
	Holding-period return (%)	10.0	25.0	(20.0)	25.0
	Total assets before net inflows	1.1	1.5	1.6	1.0
	Net inflow ($ million)*	0.1	0.5	(0.8)	0.0
	Assets under management at end of quarter ($ million)	1.2	2.0	0.8	1.0

*New investment less redemptions and distributions, all assumed to occur at the end of each quarter.

it also elicited new investments of $100,000, thus bringing assets under management to $1.2 million by the end of the quarter. An even better HPR in the second quarter elicited a larger net inflow, and the second quarter ended with $2 million under management. However, HPR in the third quarter was negative, and net inflows were negative.

How would we characterize fund performance over the year, given that the fund experienced both cash inflows and outflows? There are several candidate measures of performance, each with its own advantages and shortcomings. These are the *arithmetic average*, the *geometric average*, and the *dollar-weighted return*. These measures may vary considerably, so it is important to understand their differences.

Arithmetic average   The arithmetic average of the quarterly returns is just the sum of the quarterly returns divided by the number of quarters; in the above example: $(10 + 25 - 20 + 25)/4 = 10\%$. Since this statistic ignores compounding, it does not represent an equivalent, single quarterly rate for the year. The arithmetic average is useful, though, because it is the best forecast of performance for the next quarter, using this particular sample of historic returns. (Whether the sample is large enough or representative enough to make accurate forecasts is, of course, another question.)

arithmetic average

The sum of returns in each period divided by the number of periods.

Geometric average   The geometric average of the quarterly returns is equal to the single per-period return that would give the same cumulative performance as the sequence of actual returns. We calculate the geometric average by compounding the actual period-by-period returns and then finding the equivalent single per-period return. In this case, the geometric average quarterly return, r_G, is defined by:

$$(1 + .10) \times (1 + .25) \times (1 - .20) \times (1 + .25) = (1 + r_G)^4$$

The left-hand side of this equation is the compounded year-end value of a $1 investment earning the four quarterly returns used in our example. The right-hand side is the compounded value of a $1 investment earning r_G each quarter. We solve for r_G:

$$r_G = [(1 + .10) \times (1 + .25) \times (1 - .20) \times (1 + .25)]^{1/4} - 1 = .0829, \text{ or } 8.29\% \quad \textbf{(5.2)}$$

geometric average

The single per-period return that gives the same cumulative performance as the sequence of actual returns.

The geometric return is also called a *time-weighted average return* because it ignores the quarter-to-quarter variation in funds under management. In fact, an investor will obtain a larger cumulative return if high returns are earned in those periods when additional sums have been invested, while lower returns are realized when less money is at risk. In Table 5.1, the highest returns (25%) were achieved in quarters 2 and 4, when the fund managed $1,200,000 and $800,000, respectively. The worst returns (−20% and 10%) occurred when the fund managed $2,000,000 and $1,000,000, respectively. In this case, better returns were earned when *less* money was under management—an unfavorable combination.

The appeal of the time-weighted return is that in some cases we *wish* to ignore variation in money under management. For example, published data on past returns earned by mutual funds actually are *required* to be time-weighted returns. The rationale for this practice is that since the fund manager does not have full control over the amount of assets under management, we should not weight returns in one period more heavily than those in other periods when assessing "typical" past performance. Another reason to use the time-weighted average is that over time individual investors will add to or subtract from the amounts they have invested in the mutual fund. The total assets under management will not track the investment positions of any particular investor, and so we prefer a return measure that abstracts from funds under management.

Dollar-weighted return When we wish to account for the varying amounts under management, we treat the fund cash flows to investors as we would a capital budgeting problem in corporate finance. The initial value of $1 million and the net cash inflows are treated as the cash flows associated with an investment "project." The year-end "liquidation value" of the portfolio is the final cash flow of the project. In this case, therefore, investor net cash flows are as follows:

	Quarter				
	0	**1**	**2**	**3**	**4**
Net cash flow ($ million)	−1.0	−.1	−.5	.8	1.0

The entry for time 0 reflects the starting contribution of $1 million, while the entries for times 1, 2, and 3 represent net inflows at the end of the first three quarters. Finally, the entry for time 4 represents the value of the portfolio at the end of the fourth quarter. This is the value for which the portfolio could have been liquidated by year-end based on the initial investment and net additional investments earlier in the year.

dollar-weighted average return

The internal rate of return on an investment.

The **dollar-weighted average return** is the internal rate of return (IRR) of the project, which is 4.17%. The IRR is the interest rate that sets the present value of the cash flows realized on the portfolio (including the $1 million for which the portfolio can be liquidated at the end of the year) equal to the initial cost of establishing the portfolio. It therefore is the interest rate that satisfies the following equation:

$$1.0 = \frac{-.1}{1 + \text{IRR}} + \frac{-.5}{(1 + \text{IRR})^2} + \frac{.8}{(1 + \text{IRR})^3} + \frac{1.0}{(1 + \text{IRR})^4} \qquad \textbf{(5.3)}$$

The dollar-weighted return in this example is less than the time-weighted return of 8.29% because, as we noted, the portfolio returns were higher when less money was under management. The difference between the dollar- and time-weighted average return in this case is quite large.

CONCEPT **5.1**
check

A fund begins with $10 million and reports the following three-month results (with negative figures in parentheses):

	Month		
	1	**2**	**3**
Net inflows (end of month, $ million)	3	5	0
HPR (%)	2	8	(4)

Compute the arithmetic, time-weighted, and dollar-weighted average returns.

Conventions for Quoting Rates of Return

We've seen that there are several ways to compute average rates of return. There also is some variation in how the mutual fund in our example might annualize its quarterly returns.

Returns on assets with regular cash flows, such as mortgages (with monthly payments) and bonds (with semiannual coupons), usually are quoted as annual percentage rates, or APRs, which annualize per-period rates using a simple interest approach, ignoring compound interest. The APR can be translated to an effective annual rate (EAR) by remembering that

$$APR = \text{Per-period rate} \times \text{Periods per year}$$

Therefore, to obtain the EAR if there are n compounding periods in the year, we first recover the rate per period as APR/n and then compound that rate for the number of periods in a year. (For example, $n = 12$ for mortgages and $n = 2$ for bonds making payments semiannually.)

$$1 + EAR = (1 + \text{Rate per period})^n = \left(1 + \frac{APR}{n}\right)^n \qquad \textbf{(5.4)}$$

The formula assumes that you can earn the APR each period. Therefore, after one year (when n periods have passed), your cumulative return would be $(1 + APR/n)^n$. Note that one needs to know the holding period when given an APR in order to convert it to an effective rate.

Rearranging Equation 5.4, we can also find APR given EAR:

$$APR = [(1 + EAR)^{1/n} - 1] \times n$$

The EAR diverges by greater amounts from the APR as n becomes larger (that is, as we compound cash flows more frequently). In the limit, we can envision continuous compounding when n becomes extremely large in Equation 5.4. With continuous compounding, the relationship between the APR and EAR becomes

$$1 + EAR = e^{APR} \qquad \textbf{(5.5)}$$

or, equivalently,

$$APR = \ln(1 + EAR)$$

EXAMPLE 5.2

Annualizing Treasury-Bill Returns

Suppose you buy a $10,000 face value Treasury bill maturing in one month for $9,900. On the bill's maturity date, you collect the face value. Since there are no other interest payments, the holding-period return for this one-month investment is:

$$HPR = \frac{\text{Cash income} + \text{Price change}}{\text{Initial price}} = \frac{\$100}{\$9,900} = .0101 = 1.01\%$$

The APR on this investment is therefore 1.01% $\times$ 12 = 12.12%. The effective annual rate is higher:

$$1 + EAR = (1.0101)^{12} = 1.1282$$

which implies that EAR = .1282 = 12.82%

A warning: Terminology can be loose. Occasionally, "annual percentage yield" or APY (but not APR!) may be used interchangeably with effective annual rate, and this can lead to confusion. To avoid error, you must be alert to context.

The difficulties in interpreting rates of return over time do not end here. Two thorny issues remain: the uncertainty surrounding the investment in question and the effect of inflation.

5.2 Risk and Risk Premiums

Any investment involves some degree of uncertainty about future holding-period returns, and in many cases that uncertainty is considerable. Sources of investment risk range from macroeconomic fluctuations, to the changing fortunes of various industries, to asset-specific unexpected developments. Analysis of these multiple sources of risk is presented in Part Four on Security Analysis.

Scenario Analysis and Probability Distributions

When we attempt to quantify risk, we begin with the question: What HPRs are possible, and how likely are they? A good way to approach this question is to devise a list of possible economic outcomes, or *scenarios,* and specify both the likelihood (i.e., the probability) of each scenario and the HPR the asset will realize in that scenario. Therefore, this approach is called **scenario analysis.** The list of possible HPRs with associated probabilities is called the **probability distribution** of HPRs. Consider an investment in a broad portfolio of stocks, say, an index fund, which we will refer to as the "stock market." A very simple scenario analysis for the stock market (assuming only four possible scenarios) is illustrated in Spreadsheet 5.1.

The probability distribution lets us derive measurements for both the reward and the risk of the investment. The reward from the investment is its **expected return,** which you can think of as the average HPR you would earn if you were to repeat an investment in the asset many times. The expected return also is called the mean of the distribution of HPRs and often is referred to as the *mean return.*

To compute the expected return from the data provided, we label scenarios by s and denote the HPR in each scenario as $r(s)$, with probability $p(s)$. The expected return, denoted $E(r)$, is then the weighted average of returns in all possible scenarios, $s = 1, \ldots, S$, with weights equal to the probability of that particular scenario.

$$E(r) = \sum_{s=1}^{S} p(s)\,r(s) \tag{5.6}$$

Each entry in column D of Spreadsheet 5.1 corresponds to one of the terms in the summation in Equation 5.6. The value in cell D7, which is the sum of each of these terms, is therefore the expected return. Therefore, $E(r) = 10\%$.

Of course, there is risk to the investment, and the actual return may be more or less than 10%. If a "boom" materializes, the return will be better, 30%, but in a severe recession, the return will be a disappointing −37%. How can we quantify the uncertainty of the investment?

The "surprise" return on the investment in any scenario is the difference between the actual return and the expected return. For example, in a boom (scenario 4) the surprise is 20%: $r(4) - E(r) = 30\% - 10\% = 20\%$. In a severe recession (scenario 1), the surprise is −47%: $r(1) - E(r) = -37\% - 10\% = -47\%$.

Uncertainty surrounding the investment is a function of the magnitudes of the possible surprises. To summarize risk with a single number we first define the **variance** as the expected value of the *squared* deviation from the mean (i.e., the expected value of the squared "surprise" across scenarios).

$$\mathrm{Var}(r) \equiv \sigma^2 = \sum_{s=1}^{S} p(s)[\,r(s) - E(r)\,]^2 \tag{5.7}$$

scenario analysis

Process of devising a list of possible economic scenarios and specifying the likelihood of each one, as well as the HPR that will be realized in each case.

probability distribution

List of possible outcomes with associated probabilities.

expected return

The mean value of the distribution of HPR.

variance

The expected value of the squared deviation from the mean.

SPREADSHEET 5.1

Scenario analysis for the stock market

**Please visit us at
www.mhhe.com/bkm**

	A	B	C	D	E	F
1				Column B x Column C	Deviation from Mean Return	Column B x Squared Deviation
2	**Scenario**	**Probability**	**HPR (%)**			
3	1. Severe recession	.05	−37	−1.85	−47.00	110.45
4	2. Mild recession	.25	−11	−2.75	−21.00	110.25
5	3. Normal growth	.40	14	5.60	4.00	6.40
6	4. Boom	.30	30	9.00	20.00	120.00
7	Column sums:		Expected return =	10.00	Variance =	347.10
8			Square root of variance = Standard deviation (%) =			18.63

We square the deviations because negative deviations would offset positive deviations otherwise, with the result that the expected deviation from the mean return would necessarily be zero. Squared deviations are necessarily positive. Squaring (a nonlinear transformation) exaggerates large (positive or negative) deviations and relatively deemphasizes small deviations.

Another result of squaring deviations is that the variance has a dimension of percent squared. To give the measure of risk the same dimension as expected return (%), we use the **standard deviation,** defined as the square root of the variance:

$$SD(r) \equiv \sigma = \sqrt{\text{Var}(r)} \tag{5.8}$$

standard deviation

The square root of the variance.

EXAMPLE   5.3

Expected Return and Standard Deviation

Applying Equation 5.6 to the data in Spreadsheet 5.1, we find that the expected rate of return on the stock index fund is

$$E(r) = .05 \times (-37) + .25 \times (-11) + .40 \times 14 + .30 \times 30 = 10\%$$

We use Equation 5.7 to find the variance. First we take the difference between the holding-period return in each scenario and the mean return, then we square that difference, and finally we multiply by the probability of each scenario. The sum of the probability-weighted squared deviations is the variance.

$$\sigma^2 = .05(-37 - 10)^2 + .25(-11 - 10)^2 + .40(14 - 10)^2 + .30(30 - 10)^2 = 347.10$$

and so the standard deviation is

$$\sigma = \sqrt{347.10} = 18.63\%$$

Column F of Spreadsheet 5.1 replicates these calculations. Each entry in that column is the squared deviation from the mean multiplied by the probability of that scenario. The sum of the probability-weighted squared deviations that appears in cell F7 is the variance, and the square root of that value is the standard deviation (in cell F8).

The Normal Distribution

The normal distribution is central to the theory *and* practice of investments. Its familiar bell-shaped plot is symmetric, with identical values for all three standard measures of "typical" results: the mean (the expected value discussed earlier), the median (the value above and below which we expect 50% of the observations), and the mode (the most likely value).

Figure 5.1 illustrates a normal distribution with a mean of 10% and standard deviation (SD) of 20%. Notice that the probabilities are highest for outcomes near the mean and are significantly lower for outcomes far from the mean. But what do we mean by an outcome "far" from the mean? A return 15% below the mean would hardly be noteworthy if typical volatility were high, for example, if the standard deviation of returns were 20%, but that same outcome would be highly unusual if the standard deviation were only 5%. For this reason, it is often useful to think about deviations from the mean in terms of how many standard deviations they represent. If the standard deviation is 20%, that 15% negative surprise would be only three-fourths of a standard deviation, unfortunate perhaps, but not so uncommon. But if the standard deviation were only 5%, a 15% deviation would be a "3-sigma event," and very unusual.

We can transform any normally distributed return, r_i, into a "standard deviation score," by first subtracting its mean (to obtain distance from the mean), and then dividing by the standard deviation (which enables us to measure distance from the mean in units of standard deviations).

$$sr_i = \frac{r_i - E(r_i)}{\sigma_i} \tag{5.9A}$$

This standardized return, which we have denoted sr_i, is normally distributed with a mean of zero and a standard deviation of 1. We therefore say that sr_i is a "standard normal" variable.

FIGURE 5.1

The normal distribution with
mean return 10% and
standard deviation 20%

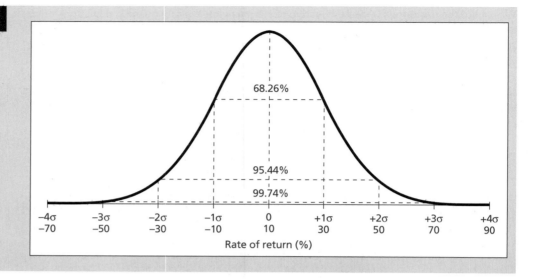

Conversely, we can start with a standard normal return, sr_i, and recover the original return by multiplying by the standard deviation and adding back the mean return:

$$r_i = E(r_i) + sr_i \times \sigma_i \qquad \text{(5.9B)}$$

In fact, this is how we drew Figure 5.1. Start with a standard normal (mean = 0 and SD = 1); next, multiply the distance from the mean by the assumed standard deviation of 20%; finally, recenter the mean away from zero by adding 10%. This gives us a normal variable with mean 10% and standard deviation 20%.

Figure 5.1 shows that if returns are normally distributed, then roughly two-thirds (more precisely, 68.26%) of the observations fall within one standard deviation of the mean, that is, the probability that any observation in a sample of returns would be no more than one standard deviation away from the mean is quite high at 68.26%. Deviations from the mean of more than two SDs are even rarer: 95.44% of the observations are expected to lie within this range. Finally, only 2.6 out of 1,000 observations are expected to deviate from the mean by three or more SDs.

The special shape of the normal distribution leads to two critical theoretical and practical simplifications of investment management:

1. The return on a portfolio comprising two or more assets whose returns are normally distributed also will be normally distributed.

2. The normal distribution is completely described by its mean and standard deviation. No other statistic is needed to learn about the behavior of normally distributed returns.

These two properties in turn imply this far-reaching conclusion:

3. The standard deviation is the appropriate measure of risk for a portfolio of assets with normally distributed returns. In this case, no other statistic can improve the risk assessment conveyed by the standard deviation of a portfolio.

Suppose you are worried about the magnitude of your possible investment losses. You may try to think about worst-case scenarios for your portfolio. For example, you might ask: "If I were to rank order possible outcomes from worst to best, how much would I lose in a fairly extreme outcome, for example, if my return were in the fifth percentile of the distribution?" We would expect our investment experience to be worse than this value only 5% of the time and better than this value in the great majority of cases, specifically 95% of the time. In investments parlance, this cutoff is called the **value at risk** (denoted by **VaR,** to distinguish it from Var, the common notation for variance). A highly loss-averse investor might seek the portfolio with the most conservative VaR, that is, the least loss corresponding to a given probability of 5%.

Value at risk (VaR)

Measure of downside risk. Loss that will be suffered given an extreme, adverse, price change.

We can obtain the VaR by finding the standard deviation value that corresponds to any percentile of the distribution using either a table of the standard normal distribution or an equivalent Excel function. For example, the function =NORMINV(.05,0,1) computes the fifth percentile of a normal distribution with a mean of zero and a variance of 1, which turns out to be −1.64485. In other words, a value that is 1.64485 standard deviations below the mean would correspond to the fifth percentile of the distribution.

To find the portfolio's 5% value at risk expressed as a rate of return, we can subtract 1.64485 standard deviations from its mean return as follows:

$$VaR = E(r) + (-1.64485)\sigma \tag{5.10}$$

We also can obtain this value directly from Excel as =NORMINV(.05, $E(r)$, σ).

Notice that VaR for a normal distribution is proportional to standard deviation; for example, expressed in terms of deviation from the mean, the 5% VaR is just −1.64485σ. Because it is proportional, VaR adds no information about risk beyond what is already conveyed by the standard deviation. Nevertheless, VaR is commonly used as a measure of downside exposure, and when returns are *not* normally distributed, it does in fact convey information beyond the standard deviation. A central question in investments research, risk management, and portfolio choice is, therefore, whether investment assets are actually (at least approximately) normally distributed. We will examine the empirical evidence shortly.

CONCEPT *check* **5.2**

e**X**cel

Please visit us at www.mhhe.com/bkm

The current value of a stock portfolio is $23 million. A financial analyst summarizes the uncertainty about next year's holding-period return using the scenario analysis in the following spreadsheet. What are the annual holding-period returns of the portfolio in each scenario? Calculate the expected holding-period return, the standard deviation of returns, and the 5% VaR. What is the VaR of a portfolio with normally distributed returns with the same mean and standard deviation as this stock? The spreadsheet is available at the Online Learning Center (go to **www.mhhe.com/bkm**, link to the Chapter 5 material).

	A	B	C	D	E
1	Business Conditions	Scenario, s	Probability, p	End-of-Year Value ($ million)	Annual Dividend ($ million)
2	High growth	1	.30	35	4.40
3	Normal growth	2	.45	27	4.00
4	No growth	3	.20	15	4.00
5	Recession	4	.05	8	2.00

Deviation from Normality and Value at Risk

The scenario analysis of Spreadsheet 5.1 offers insight about the issue of normality in practice. While a four-scenario analysis is quite simplistic, this simple example can nevertheless shed light on how practical analysis might take shape.

Figure 5.2 superimposes the distribution of the four-scenario analysis on a normal distribution with an identical mean (10%) and standard deviation (18.63%). As the number of scenarios in an alternative analysis grows, the probability assigned to any particular scenario falls and the distribution begins to approach a continuous one. Still, there is no guarantee that it will approach the normal.

In the scenario analysis laid out in Spreadsheet 5.1, the rate of return in a severe recession (−37%, similar to the market return in 2008) has a probability of .05; therefore, the projected 5% VaR is −37%. In this scenario, the deviation from the mean return is −37% −10% = −47%. For the normal distribution with the same mean and standard deviation, the fifth percentile outcome falls below the mean by −1.64485 × 18.63 = 30.64%, therefore, with a mean return of 10%, the VaR is 10% − 30.64% = −20.64%. Thus, from the standpoint of

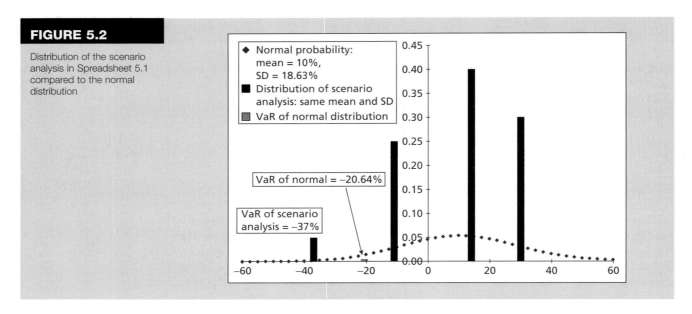

FIGURE 5.2

Distribution of the scenario analysis in Spreadsheet 5.1 compared to the normal distribution

downside risk, the departure from normality of the scenario analysis is extreme, as reflected by its much larger VaR (−37% compared with −20.64%). For such nonnormal distributions, the rationale for augmenting the standard deviation with the VaR as an additional risk measure is compelling.[1]

Because risk is largely driven by the likelihood of extreme negative returns, two statistics are used to indicate whether a portfolio's probability distribution differs significantly from normality with respect to potential extreme values. The first is **kurtosis,** which compares the frequency of extreme values to that of the normal distribution. The kurtosis of the normal distribution is zero, so positive values indicate higher frequency of extreme values than this benchmark. A negative value suggests that extreme values are less frequent than with the normal distribution. Kurtosis sometimes is called "fat tail risk," as plots of probability distributions with higher likelihood of extreme events will be higher than the normal distribution at both ends or "tails" of the distribution; in other words, the distributions exhibit "fat tails." Similarly, exposure to extreme events is often called tail risk, because these are outcomes in the far reaches or "tail" of the probability distribution.

The second statistic is the **skew,** which measures the asymmetry of the distribution. Skew takes on a value of zero if, like the normal, the distribution is symmetric. Negative skew suggests that extreme negative values are more frequent than extreme positive ones. Nonzero values for kurtosis and skew indicate that special attention should be paid to the VaR, in addition to the use of standard deviation as measure of portfolio risk.

kurtosis

Measure of the fatness of the tails of a probability distribution. Indicates likelihood of extreme outcomes.

skew

Measure of the asymmetry of a probability distribution.

Using Time Series of Return

Scenario analysis postulates a probability distribution of future returns. But where do the probabilities and rates of return come from? In large part, they come from observing a sample history of returns. Suppose we observe a 10-year time series of monthly returns on a diversified portfolio of stocks. We can interpret each of the 120 observations as one potential "scenario" offered to us by history. Adding judgment to this history, we can develop a scenario analysis of future returns.

As a first step, we estimate the expected return, standard deviation, and VaR for the sample history. We assume that each of the 120 returns represents one independent draw from the historical probability distribution. Hence, each return is assigned an equal probability

[1]The financial crisis of 2008 has demonstrated that bank portfolio returns are far from normally distributed, with exposure to unlikely but catastrophic returns in extreme market meltdowns. The international Basel accord on bank regulation requires banks to monitor portfolio VaR to better control risk.

of $1/120 = .0083$. When you use a fixed probability in Equation 5.6, you obtain the simple average of the observations and this is often used to estimate the mean return.

The same principle applies to the VaR. We sort the returns from high to low. The bottom six observations comprise the lower 5% of the distribution. The sixth observation from the bottom is just at the fifth percentile, and so would be the 5% VaR for the historical sample.

Estimating variance from Equation 5.7 requires a minor correction. Remember that variance is the expected value of squared deviations from the mean return. But the true mean is not observable; we *estimate* it using the sample average. If we compute variance as the average of squared deviations from the sample average, we will slightly underestimate it because this procedure ignores the fact that the average necessarily includes some estimation error. The necessary correction turns out to be simple: with a sample of n observations, we divide the sum of the squared deviations from the sample average by $n - 1$ instead of n. Thus, the estimates of variance and standard deviation from a time series of returns, r_t, are as follows:

$$\text{Var}(r_t) = \frac{1}{n-1}\Sigma(r_t - \bar{r}_t)^2 \quad \text{SD}(r_t) = \sqrt{\text{Var}(r_t)} \quad \bar{r}_t = \frac{1}{n}\Sigma r_t \qquad \textbf{(5.11)}$$

To illustrate how to calculate average returns and standard deviations from historical data, let's compute these statistics for the returns on the S&P 500 portfolio using five years of data from the following table. The average return over this period is 16.7%, computed by dividing the sum of column (1), below, by the number of observations. In column (2), we take the deviation of each year's return from the 16.7% average return. In column (3), we calculate the squared deviation. The variance is, from Equation 5.12, the sum of the five squared deviations divided by (5 − 1). The standard deviation is the square root of the variance. If you input the column of rates into a spreadsheet, the AVERAGE and STDEV functions will give you the statistics directly.

Year	(1) Rate of Return	(2) Deviation from Average Return	(3) Squared Deviation
1	16.9%	0.2%	0.0
2	31.3	14.6	213.2
3	−3.2	−19.9	396.0
4	30.7	14.0	196.0
5	7.7	−9.0	81.0
Total	83.4%		886.2

Average rate of return = 83.4/5 = 16.7

$$\text{Variance} = \frac{1}{5-1} \times 886.2 = 221.6$$

Standard deviation = $\sqrt{221.6}$ = 14.9%

EXAMPLE 5.4

Historical Means and Standard Deviations

Risk Premiums and Risk Aversion

How much, if anything, would you invest in an index stock fund such as the one described in Spreadsheet 5.1? First, you must ask how much of an expected reward is offered to compensate for the risk involved in investing in stocks.

We measure the "reward" as the difference between the expected HPR on the index stock fund and the **risk-free rate,** that is, the rate you can earn by leaving money in risk-free assets such as Treasury bills, money market funds, or the bank. We call this difference the **risk premium** on common stocks. For example, if the risk-free rate in the example is 4% per year, and the expected index fund return is 10%, then the risk premium on stocks is 6% per year.

risk-free rate

The rate of return that can be earned with certainty.

risk premium

An expected return in excess of that on risk-free securities.

excess return

Rate of return in excess of
the risk-free rate.

risk aversion

Reluctance to accept risk.

The rate of return on Treasury bills also varies over time. However, we know the rate of return we will earn on T-bills *at the beginning* of the holding period, while we can't know the return we will earn on risky assets until the end of the holding period. Therefore, to study the risk premium available on risky assets we compile a series of **excess returns,** that is, returns in excess of the T-bill rate in each period. One reasonable forecast of the risk premium of any asset is the average of its historical excess returns.

The degree to which investors are willing to commit funds to stocks depends on **risk aversion.** It seems obvious that investors are risk averse in the sense that, if the risk premium were zero, people would not be willing to invest any money in stocks. In theory then, there must always be a positive risk premium on all risky assets in order to induce risk-averse investors to hold the existing supply of these assets instead of placing all their money in a risk-free asset.

In fact, the risk premium is what distinguishes gambling from speculation. Investors who are willing to take on risk because they expect to earn a risk premium are speculating. Speculation is undertaken *despite* the risk because the speculator sees a favorable risk-return trade-off. In contrast, gambling is the assumption of risk for no purpose beyond the enjoyment of the risk itself. Gamblers take on risk even without the prospect of a risk premium.[2]

It occasionally will be useful to quantify an investor's degree of risk aversion. To do so, suppose that investors choose portfolios based on both expected return, $E(r_P)$, and the volatility of returns as measured by the variance. If we denote the risk-free rate on Treasury bills as r_f, then the risk premium of a portfolio is $E(r_P) - r_f$. Risk-averse investors will demand higher risk premiums to place their wealth in portfolios with higher volatility; that risk premium will be greater the greater is their risk aversion. Therefore, if we quantify the degree of risk aversion with the parameter A, it makes sense to assert that the risk premium an investor demands of a portfolio will be dependent on both risk aversion, A, and the risk of the portfolio.

Therefore, we will assume that the risk premium that an investor demands to hold a risky portfolio rather than placing all funds in safe T-bills offering the risk-free rate is proportional to the product of risk aversion, A, and the variance of the risky portfolio's rate of return:[3]

$$E(r_P) - r_f = \tfrac{1}{2} A \sigma_P^2 \tag{5.12}$$

As a benchmark, notice that Equation 5.12 implies that investors would not demand a risk premium to hold a risk-free portfolio (for which $\sigma_P^2 = 0$). But for any positive variance, the required risk premium is positive and is greater for more risk-averse investors (who have higher values of A). Not surprisingly, when a risky portfolio offers a greater risk premium relative to risk, investors will place a higher fraction of their overall portfolios in it, and place a correspondingly lower fraction in the risk-free asset. Conversely, if a portfolio is riskier, investors will shy away from it.

In fact, we can make this conclusion about capital allocation more precise. If investors behave according to Equation 5.12, then one can show that their optimal allocation to the risky portfolio will be

$$w_P = \frac{E(r_P) - r_f}{A\sigma_P^2} \tag{5.13}$$

The equation tells us that the allocation to the risky asset is directly proportional to its risk premium and inversely proportional to both investors' aversion to bearing risk as well as the portfolio's volatility (measured by variance).

Now consider the total market portfolio, which is the aggregation of the holdings of all investors and therefore may be viewed as representative of a "typical" investor's portfolio.[4]

---

[2]Sometimes a gamble might *seem* like speculation to the participants. If two investors differ in their forecasts of the future, they might take opposite positions in a security, and both may have an expectation of earning a positive risk premium. In such cases, only one party can, in fact, be correct.

[3]The factor of ½ on the right-hand side of Equation 5.12 is merely a scale factor. It is widely used by convention, but has no bearing on the analysis. Note also that to use this equation, all rates of return must be expressed as decimals rather than percentages.

[4]In practice, a broad market index such as the S&P 500 often is taken as representative of the entire market.

By examining the risk-return trade-off offered by this representative portfolio (and willingly held by the representative investor) we should be able to infer something about the typical investor's risk aversion. If we recognize that the representative investor must hold the representative market portfolio, then we may set w_P in Equation 5.13 equal to 1, and rearrange to infer average risk aversion from the characteristics of the market portfolio, M, as follows:

$$A = \frac{E(r_M) - r_f}{\sigma_M^2} \qquad \textbf{(5.14)}$$

Equation 5.14 quantifies the reasonable proposition that investors' risk aversion will be reflected in the risk premium they demand per unit of portfolio risk. A higher market risk premium (per unit of risk) must indicate that investors are more risk averse. For example, if the risk premium is 8%, and the standard deviation is 20%, then we would infer risk aversion as $A = .08/.20^2 = 2$. Notice that we must express returns as decimals to use Equation 5.14.

In practice, of course, we cannot observe the risk premium investors *expect* to earn. We can observe only actual returns after the fact. Moreover, different investors may have different expectations about the risk and return of various assets. Finally, Equations 5.12 and 5.14 apply only to the variance of an investor's overall portfolio, not to individual assets held in that portfolio. While the exact relationship between risk and return in capital markets therefore cannot be known exactly, many studies conclude that investors' risk aversion is likely in the range of 2–4. This implies that to accept an increase of .01 in portfolio variance, investors would require an increase in the risk premium of between .01 and .02 (i.e., 1%–2%).

The Sharpe (Reward-to-Volatility) Measure

Risk aversion implies that investors will accept a lower reward (as measured by their portfolio expected return) in exchange for a sufficient reduction in risk (as measured by the standard deviation of their portfolio return). A statistic commonly used to rank portfolios in terms of this risk-return trade-off is the **Sharpe (or reward-to-volatility) measure**, defined as

$$S = \frac{\text{Portfolio risk premium}}{\text{Standard deviation of portfolio excess return}} = \frac{E(r_P) - r_f}{\sigma_P} \qquad \textbf{(5.15)}$$

Sharpe (or reward-to-volatility) measure
Ratio of portfolio risk premium to standard deviation.

A risk-free asset would have a risk premium of zero and a standard deviation of zero. Therefore, the reward-to-volatility measure of a risky portfolio quantifies the incremental reward (in terms of the increase in expected excess return compared to the risk-free position) for each increase of 1% in the standard deviation of that portfolio. For example, the Sharpe measure of a portfolio with an annual risk premium of 8% and standard deviation of 20% is $8/20 = 0.4$. A higher Sharpe measure indicates a better reward per unit of volatility, in other words, a more efficient portfolio. Portfolio analysis in terms of mean and standard deviation (or variance) of excess returns is called **mean-variance analysis.**

mean-variance analysis
Ranking portfolios by their Sharpe measures.

A warning: We will see in the next chapter that while standard deviation and VaR of returns are useful risk measures for diversified portfolios, these are not useful ways to think about the risk of individual securities. Therefore, the Sharpe measure is a valid statistic only for ranking portfolios; it is *not* valid for individual assets. For now, therefore, let's examine the historical reward-to-volatility ratios of broadly diversified portfolios that reflect the performance of some important asset classes.

CONCEPT check 5.3

a. A respected analyst forecasts that the return of the S&P 500 Index portfolio over the coming year will be 10%. The one-year T-bill rate is 5%. Examination of recent returns of the S&P 500 Index suggest that the standard deviation of returns will be 18%. What does this information suggest about the degree of risk aversion of the average investor, assuming that the average portfolio resembles the S&P 500?

b. What is the Sharpe measure of the portfolio in (a)?

5.3 | The Historical Record

World and U.S. Risky Stock and Bond Portfolios

We begin our examination of risk with an analysis of a long sample of return history (83 years) for five risky asset classes. These include three well-diversified stock portfolios: World large stocks, U.S. large stocks, and U.S. small stocks, as well as two long-term bond portfolios: World and U.S. Treasury bonds. The 83 annual observations for each of the five time series of returns span the period 1926–2008.

The "World Portfolio" of stocks is diversified across large capitalization stocks of 16 developed countries (including the U.S., Europe, and Japan). Until 1968, country portfolio shares in this index were determined by the relative size of gross domestic product, measured in U.S. dollars. Since 1967, shares have been determined by the relative capitalization of each market, again measured in U.S. dollars. "Large Stocks" is the Standard & Poor's market value–weighted portfolio of 500 U.S. common stocks selected from the largest market capitalization stocks. "Small U.S. Stocks" are the smallest 20% of all stocks trading on the NYSE, NASDAQ, and Amex.

The World Portfolio of bonds was constructed from the same set of countries as the World Portfolio of stocks, using long-term bonds from each of the 16 countries. Until 1996, "Long-Term T-Bonds" were represented by U.S. government bonds with at least a 20-year maturity and approximately current-level coupon rate.[5] Since 1996, this bond series has been measured by the Barclay's (formerly the Lehman Brothers) Long-Term Treasury Bond Index. Excess returns in Table 5.2 are annual returns on each asset class in excess of the annual rate of return one would have earned by investing in one-month Treasury bills, "rolling over" the bills each month as they matured.

Look first at Figure 5.3, which shows histograms of total (not excess) returns of the five risky portfolios and of Treasury bills. Notice the hierarchy of risk: small stocks are the most risky, followed by large stocks and then long-term bonds. At the same time, the higher average return offered by riskier assets is evident, consistent with investor risk aversion. T-bill returns are by far the least volatile. In fact, despite the variability in their returns, bills are actually riskless, since you know the return you will earn at the beginning of the holding period. The small dispersion in these returns reflects the variation in interest rates over time.

Figure 5.4 provides another view of the hierarchy of risk. Here we plot the year-by-year returns on U.S. large stock, long-term U.S. Treasury bond portfolios, and T-bills. Risk is reflected by wider swings of returns from year to year.

Table 5.2 presents statistics of the return history of the five portfolios over the full 83-year period, 1926–2008, as well as for three subperiods.[6] The first 30-year subperiod, 1926–1955, includes the Great Depression (1929–1939), World War II, the postwar boom, and a subsequent recession. The second subperiod (1956–1985) includes four recessions (1957–1958, 1960–1961, 1973–1975, and 1980–1982) and a period of "stagflation" (poor growth combined with high inflation (1974–1980). Finally, the most recent 23-year subperiod (1986–2008) included two recessions (1990–1991, 2001–2003) bracketing the so-called high-tech bubble of the 1990s, and a severe recession that started in December 2007 and is projected to last into 2010. Let us compare capital asset returns in these three subperiods.

We start with the geometric averages of total returns in the top panel of the table. This is the average annual *compounded* rate of return that an investor would have earned over the period. In contrast, the simple arithmetic average of a return series ignores compounding and, hence, is not useful in computing cumulative returns. Nevertheless, it provides the best estimate for next year's single-period return, at least assuming that past experience is a good guide to the probability distribution of future returns.

---

[5]The importance of the coupon rate when comparing returns on bonds is discussed in Part Three.
[6]Year-by-year returns are available on the Online Learning Center. Go to **www.mhhe.com/bkm,** and link to material for Chapter 5.

TABLE 5.2

Annual rates of return statistics for diversified portfolios for 1926–2008, and three subperiods (%)

	World Portfolio		U.S. Market		
	Equity Return in U.S. Dollars	Bond Return in U.S. Dollars	Small Stocks	Large Stocks	Long-Term T-Bonds
Total Return—Geometric Average					
1926–2008	9.20	5.56	11.43	9.34	5.31
1926–1955	8.31	2.54	11.32	9.66	3.46
1956–1984	10.53	5.94	13.81	9.52	4.64
1985–2008	8.66	9.11	8.56	8.68	8.67
Total Real Return—Geometric Average					
1926–2008	6.00	2.46	8.17	6.13	2.22
1926–1955	6.86	1.16	9.82	8.18	2.07
1956–1984	5.47	1.09	8.60	4.51	−0.15
1985–2008	5.58	6.03	5.49	5.60	5.59
Excess Return Statistics					
Arithmetic average					
1926–2008	7.25	2.17	13.51	7.68	1.85
1926–1955	9.30	1.75	20.02	11.67	2.43
1956–1984	5.85	0.38	12.18	5.01	−0.87
1985–2008	6.40	5.05	6.77	5.95	4.63
Standard deviation					
1926–2008	19.50	8.88	37.81	20.88	7.81
1926–1955	21.50	8.10	49.25	25.40	4.12
1956–1984	16.68	8.42	32.31	17.58	8.29
1985–2008	20.76	10.04	25.44	18.23	9.79
Minimum (lowest excess return)					
1926–2008	−45.55	−18.50	−55.34	−46.65	−13.43
1926–1955	−41.03	−13.86	−55.34	−46.65	−6.40
1956–1984	−33.49	−18.50	−45.26	−34.41	−13.09
1985–2008	−45.55	−10.29	−36.52	−40.04	−13.43
Maximum (highest excess return)					
1926–2008	70.51	28.96	152.88	54.26	26.07
1926–1955	70.51	28.96	152.88	54.26	10.94
1956–1984	35.25	26.40	99.94	42.25	24.96
1985–2008	38.94	24.40	73.73	32.11	26.07
Deviation from the Normal Distribution					
Kurtosis					
1926–2008	1.03	1.10	1.60	−0.10	0.85
1926–1955	1.80	4.03	0.53	−0.33	−0.24
1956–1984	−0.22	2.28	0.56	−0.28	1.90
1985–2008	0.46	−0.94	0.93	0.35	−0.24
Skew					
1926–2008	−0.16	0.77	0.81	−0.26	0.51
1926–1955	0.27	1.11	0.61	−0.42	−0.12
1956–1984	−0.34	0.72	0.42	−0.19	1.06
1985–2008	−0.82	0.47	0.57	−0.73	0.06
Performance Statistics					
Sharpe ratio					
1926–2008	0.37	0.24	0.36	0.37	0.24
1926–1955	0.43	0.22	0.41	0.46	0.59
1956–1984	0.35	0.05	0.38	0.28	−0.11
1985–2008	0.31	0.50	0.27	0.33	0.47
VaR					
1926–2008	−21.89	−6.54	−46.25	−29.79	−7.61
1926–1955	−31.94	−12.55	−53.71	−40.40	−4.35
1956–1984	−22.32	−8.44	−35.81	−22.25	−6.56
1985–2008	−22.32	−8.44	−35.81	−22.25	−6.56
VaR of a normal with same mean and SD					
1926–2008	−21.07	−8.69	−44.93	−22.92	−7.25
1926–1955	−24.97	−10.47	−59.91	−29.02	−3.24
1956–1984	−15.76	−7.63	−35.13	−18.07	−8.67
1985–2008	−23.26	−6.97	−30.59	−19.54	−6.99

Sources: Inflation data: Bureau of Labor Statistics. T-bill and U.S. small stock returns: Web site of Prof. Kenneth French, **http://mba. tuck.dartmouth.edu/pages/faculty/ken.french/data_library.html**. Large U.S. stocks: S&P 500, Center for Research in Security Prices (CRSP). Long-term U.S. Treasury bonds: 1926–2003, return on 20-year T-bonds Bonds (CRSP); 2004–2008 Barclay's (Lehman Brothers) long-term Treasury index. World portfolio of large stocks: Datastream. World portfolio of Treasury bonds: 1926–2003 Dimson, Elroy, and Marsh (2001); 2004–2008, Datastream.

Please visit us at www.mhhe.com/bkm

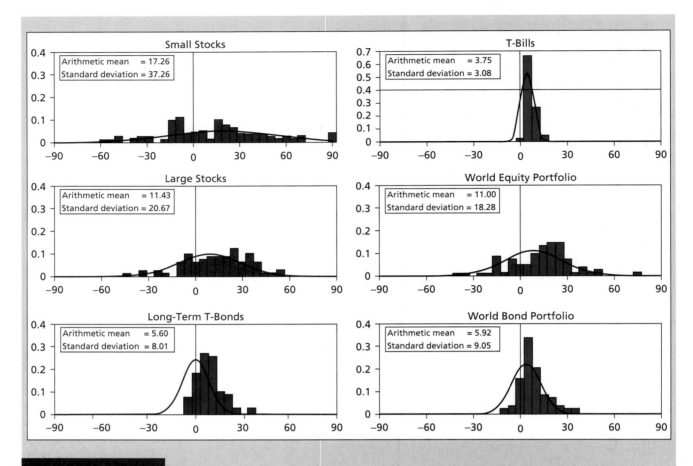

FIGURE 5.3

Frequency distribution of annual HPRs, 1926–2008

Source: Prepared from data used in Table 5.2.

FIGURE 5.4

Rates of return on stocks, bonds, and bills, 1926–2008

Source: Prepared from data used in Table 5.2.

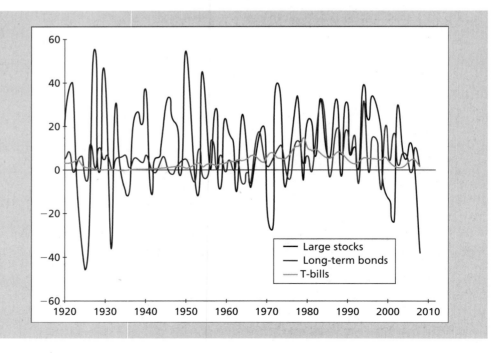

The geometric average is always less than the arithmetic average. For a normal distribution, the difference is exactly half the variance of the return (with returns measured as decimals, not percentages). Here are the arithmetic averages (from Figure 5.3) and geometric averages (from Table 5.2) for the three stock portfolios over the period (1926–2008), the differences between the two averages, as well as half the variance computed from the respective standard deviations in Table 5.2.

	Portfolio		
	World Stocks	**U.S. Small Stocks**	**U.S. Large Stocks**
Arithmetic average	.1100	.1726	.1143
Geometric average	.0920	.1143	.0934
Difference	.0180	.0583	.0209
Half historical variance	.0186	.0694	.0214

You can see immediately that the differences between the geometric and arithmetic averages are consequential. The difference between them is close to one-half the variance of returns for large stocks (World and U.S.), suggesting that these distributions may be approximately normal, but there is a greater discrepancy for small stocks; therefore, VaR will certainly be an important risk measure, beyond standard deviation, at least for this asset class.

We have suggested that the geometric average is the correct measure of cumulative return over some historical holding period. But investors presumably are concerned about their inflation-adjusted or *real* rates of return, not the paper profits indicated by the nominal (dollar) return. The real geometric averages for the overall period suggest that the real cost of equity capital for large corporations has been about 6%, and about 8% for small ones. The real rate on long-term debt has been only about 2%, suggesting that the risk premium of stocks over bonds is substantial.

In the previous section we discussed the importance of risk and risk premiums. Let us now turn to the excess-return panel of Table 5.2 to see what can be learned about these portfolios along these lines. Having discussed the real rate, it should be noted that excess returns do not need to be adjusted for inflation because they are returns over and above the nominal risk-free rate, which already includes an inflation premium. Moreover, bond portfolios are not really candidates for an investor's sole-investment vehicle, because they are not sufficiently diversified. We have included them simply to compare the historical experience of these important asset classes.

The first thing we notice is the large variability across subperiods in average excess return, which is our estimate of the risk premium, as well as in standard deviation, our basic measure of risk; this despite the fact that the stock portfolios are well diversified. The volatility is large enough to have caused average returns to have differed significantly across subperiods, even if the initially expected returns were the same in all of them. The large volatility of capital asset returns, in addition to posing large risks, also implies that attempts to estimate expected returns and risk premiums also are subject to considerable estimation error.

For another manifestation of volatility, notice the extreme returns (minimum and maximum). As extreme as they appear, if you calculate the ratio of the maximum to the average or of the average to the minimum, you will find an average ratio of a little over 2, not so different from what you would expect from a normal distribution. This means that in every generation, you can expect a very bad year, as well as a very good one. Incidentally, in two of the five portfolios, both the highest and lowest returns over the 83 years occurred in the 1930s, during the Great Depression.

EXAMPLE 5.5

The Risk Premium and Growth of Wealth

The potential import of the risk premium can be illustrated with a simple example. Consider two investors with $1 million as of December 31, 2000. One invests in the small-stock portfolio, and the other in T-bills. Suppose both investors reinvest all income from their portfolios and liquidate their investments eight years later, on December 31, 2008. We can find the annual rates of return for this period from the spreadsheet of returns at the Online Learning Center. (Go to **www.mhhe.com/bkm**. Look for the link to Chapter 5 material.) We compute a "wealth index" for each investment

(continued)

by compounding wealth at the end of each year by the return earned in the following year. For example, we calculate the value of the wealth index for small stocks as of 2003 by multiplying the value as of 2002 (1.1404) by one plus the rate of return earned in 2003 (measured in decimals), that is, by 1 + .7475, to obtain 1.9928.

	Small Stocks		Treasury Bills	
Year	Return (%)	Wealth Index	Return (%)	Wealth Index
2000		1		1
2001	29.25%	1.2925	3.86%	1.0386
2002	−11.77	1.1404	1.63	1.0555
2003	74.75	1.9928	1.02	1.0663
2004	14.36	2.2790	1.19	1.0790
2005	3.26	2.3533	2.98	1.1111
2006	17.69	2.7696	4.81	1.1646
2007	−8.26	2.5408	4.67	1.2190
2008	−34.97	1.6523	1.55	1.2379

The final value of each portfolio as of December 31, 2008, equals its initial value ($1 million) multiplied by the wealth index at the end of the period:

	Small Stocks	T-Bills
December 31, 2000	$1,000,000	$1,000,000
December 31, 2008	1,652,300	1,237,900

The difference in total return is dramatic. Even with its devasting 2008 return, the value of the small-stock portfolio after eight years is 33% more than that of the T-bill portfolio.

We can also calculate the geometric average return of each portfolio over this period. For T-bills, the geometric average over the five-year period is computed from:

$$(1 + r_G)^8 = 1.2379$$

$$1 + r_G = 1.2379^{1/8} = 1.0310$$

$$r_G = 2.70\%$$

Similarly, the geometric average for small stocks is 6.48%. The difference in geometric average reflects the difference in cumulative wealth provided by the small-stock portfolio over this period.

Notice, however, how imprecise our estimate of the risk premium can be. For example, at the end of 2007, the wealth index for small stocks was more than double that of bills. Only one year later, the difference had fallen to 33%.

Are these portfolios normally distributed? The next section of the table shows the kurtosis and skew of the distributions. Because these measures derive from higher exponents of deviations from the mean (the cubed deviation for skew and the fourth power of the deviation for kurtosis), these measures are highly sensitive to rare but extreme outliers; therefore, we can rely on these measures only in very large samples that allow for sufficient observations to be taken as exhibiting a "representative" number of such events. You can see that these measures also vary considerably across subperiods. The numbers suggest that kurtosis risk is present in U.S. small stocks, as well as in foreign stocks and bonds. In contrast, U.S. large stocks generally exhibit small but negative kurtosis, as well as negative skew. We will look for further evidence concerning normality in the difference between these portfolios' VaR relative to what would be expected from similar normal distributions.

The last section in Table 5.3 presents performance statistics, Sharpe ratios, and value at risk. Notice first the Sharpe ratios of the bond portfolios. Except for the recent subperiod when falling interest rates favored these portfolios, their Sharpe ratios were far inferior to

TABLE 5.3 Size-decile portfolios of the NYSE/AMEX/ NASDAQ Summary Statistics of Annual Returns, 1927–2006	Decile	Geometric Average	Arithmetic Average	Standard Deviation
	1 Largest	9.6%	11.4%	19.1%
	2	10.9	13.2	21.6
	3	11.4	13.8	22.9
	4	11.9	14.8	25.2
	5	12.0	15.2	26.6
	6	12.1	15.6	27.6
	7	12.4	16.3	30.0
	8	12.5	17.0	32.5
	9	12.2	17.5	35.3
	10 Smallest	13.8	20.4	40.9
	Total Value Weighted Index	10.1%	12.1%	20.2%

Source: Web site of Professor Kenneth R. French, **http://mba.tuck.dartmouth.edu/pages/faculty/ken.french/data_library.html**.

those of stocks. This confirms our assertion that bond portfolios would be inadequate as a sole investment. For the various stock portfolios, it is perhaps surprising to find that the best subperiod was consistently the one that included the Great Depression and WWII. It suggests that investors required—and received—a higher risk premium relative to risk in hard times. Notice also that despite the consistently higher risk premium of small stocks, they underperformed on a volatility-adjusted basis (i.e., in terms of their Sharpe ratios) in two of the three subperiods.

Finally, compare the VaR from the sample returns to what we would expect from normal distributions with means and volatilities matching the sample averages and standard deviations. Surprisingly, only large U.S. stock's returns exhibited a consistently worse VaR than the normal. This reflects their consistently negative skew. Investors would want to be aware of this property.

Both the average return and standard deviation of the small-stock portfolio documented in Table 5.2 are striking. Table 5.3 shows average returns and standard deviations for NYSE portfolios of U.S. stocks arranged by firm size, as measured by the market value of outstanding equity. Firms are then assigned to one of 10 deciles, from the largest 10% of all firms (decile 1) to the smallest 10% (decile 10). Average returns generally are higher as firm size declines. The data clearly suggest that small firms have earned a substantial risk premium and therefore that firm size seems to be an important proxy for risk. In later chapters we will further explore this phenomenon and will see that the size effect can be further related to other attributes of the firm.

Investing internationally is no longer considered exotic, and Table 5.2 also provides some information on the historical results from international investments. Over the 1926–2008 period, the world stock portfolio offered lower average returns, but also lower volatility, than large U.S. stocks. On the other hand, world bonds provided higher average returns but more volatility than long-term U.S. bonds. These patterns also are consistent with a risk-return trade-off. Foreign stocks offer U.S. investors opportunities for diversification, however, and we therefore devote Chapter 19 to international investing.

Compute the average excess return on large company stocks (over the T-bill rate) and the standard deviation for the years 1926–1934. You will need to obtain data from the spreadsheet available at the Online Learning Center at **www.mhhe.com/bkm**. Look for Chapter 5 material.

5.4 Inflation and Real Rates of Return

A 10% annual rate of return means that your investment was worth 10% more at the end of the year than it was at the beginning of the year. This does not necessarily mean, however, that you could have bought 10% more goods and services with that money, for it is possible that in the course of the year prices of goods also increased. If prices have changed, the increase in your purchasing power will not equal the increase in your dollar wealth.

inflation rate

The rate at which prices are rising, measured as the rate of increase of the CPI.

At any time, the prices of some goods may rise while the prices of other goods may fall; the *general* trend in prices is measured by examining changes in the consumer price index, or CPI. The CPI measures the cost of purchasing a bundle of goods that is considered representative of the "consumption basket" of a typical urban family of four. Increases in the cost of this standardized consumption basket are indicative of a general trend toward higher prices. The **inflation rate,** or the rate at which prices are rising, is measured as the rate of increase of the CPI.

Suppose the rate of inflation (the percentage change in the CPI, denoted by i) for the last year amounted to $i = 6\%$. This tells you the purchasing power of money is reduced by 6% a year. The value of each dollar depreciates by 6% a year in terms of the goods it can buy. Therefore, part of your investment earnings are offset by the reduction in the purchasing power of the dollars you will receive at the end of the year. With a 10% interest rate, for example, after you net out the 6% reduction in the purchasing power of money, you are left with a net increase in purchasing power of about 4%. Thus, we need to distinguish between a **nominal interest rate**—the growth rate of your money—and a **real interest rate**—the growth rate of your purchasing power. If we call R the nominal rate, r the real rate, and i the inflation rate, then we conclude

nominal interest rate

The interest rate in terms of nominal (not adjusted for purchasing power) dollars.

real interest rate

The excess of the interest rate over the inflation rate. The growth rate of purchasing power derived from an investment.

$$r \approx R - i \qquad \text{(5.16)}$$

In words, the real rate of interest is the nominal rate reduced by the loss of purchasing power resulting from inflation.

In fact, the exact relationship between the real and nominal interest rate is given by

$$1 + r = \frac{1 + R}{1 + i} \qquad \text{(5.17)}$$

In words, the growth factor of your purchasing power, $1 + r$, equals the growth factor of your money, $1 + R$, divided by the new price level that is $1 + i$ times its value in the previous period. The exact relationship can be rearranged to

$$r = \frac{R - i}{1 + i} \qquad \text{(5.18)}$$

which shows that the approximate rule overstates the real rate by the factor $1 + i$.

EXAMPLE 5.6

Real versus Nominal Rates

If the interest rate on a one-year CD is 8%, and you expect inflation to be 5% over the coming year, then using the approximation given in Equation 5.16, you expect the real rate to be $r = 8\% - 5\% = 3\%$. Using the exact formula given in Equation 5.18, the real rate is $r = \dfrac{.08 - .05}{1 + .05} = .0286$, or 2.86%. Therefore, the approximation rule overstates the expected real rate by only .14 percentage points. The approximation rule is more accurate for small inflation rates and is perfectly exact for continuously compounded rates.

The Equilibrium Nominal Rate of Interest

We've seen that the real rate of return on an asset is approximately equal to the nominal rate minus the inflation rate. Because investors should be concerned with their real returns—the increase in their purchasing power—we would expect that as inflation increases, investors will demand higher nominal rates of return on their investments. This higher rate is necessary to maintain the expected real return offered by an investment.

Irving Fisher (1930) argued that the nominal rate ought to increase one-for-one with increases in the expected inflation rate. If we use the notation $E(i)$ to denote the current expectation of the inflation rate that will prevail over the coming period, then we can state the so-called Fisher equation formally as

$$R = r + E(i) \qquad \text{(5.19)}$$

Suppose the real rate of interest is 2%, and the inflation rate is 4%, so that the nominal interest rate is about 6%. If the expected inflation rate rises to 5%, the nominal interest rate should climb to roughly 7%. The increase in the nominal rate offsets the increase in expected inflation, giving investors an unchanged growth of purchasing power at a 2% real rate.

a. Suppose the real interest rate is 3% per year, and the expected inflation rate is 8%. What is the nominal interest rate?
b. Suppose the expected inflation rate rises to 10%, but the real rate is unchanged. What happens to the nominal interest rate?

CONCEPT *check* **5.5**

U.S. History of Interest Rates, Inflation, and Real Interest Rates

Figure 5.5 plots nominal interest rates, real rates, and inflation rates in the U.S. between 1926 and 2008. Since the mid-1950s, nominal rates have increased roughly in tandem with inflation, generally consistent with the Fisher equation. In the 1930s and 1940s, however, it appears that very volatile levels of unexpected inflation played havoc with realized *real* rates of return. The lesson is that while the return on a U.S. T-bill usually is considered riskless, strictly speaking, this is true only with regard to its nominal rate. To infer the *real* expected return on a T-bill, you must subtract your expectation for inflation from the nominal rate.

Table 5.4 quantifies what we see in Figure 5.5. The geometric average real rate of return on T-bills is small (.66%) and quite variable over time, with average values ranging across the subperiods from −.27% to 1.52%. Moreover, the correlation between the nominal rate and inflation rate, while positive, is actually fairly low; even in the most recent period it is only .53. By itself, the low correlation does not imply that Fisher's theory is wrong, or that inflation is unpredictable; nevertheless, other evidence suggests that the Fisher hypothesis, if correct, is not very tight.

Inflation-indexed bonds called Treasury Inflation-Protected Securities (TIPS) were introduced in the U.S. in 1997. These are bonds of 5- to 20-year original maturities with coupons and principal that increase at the rate of inflation. (We discuss these bonds in more detail in Chapter 10.) The difference between nominal rates on conventional T-bonds and the rates on equal-maturity TIPS provide a measure of expected inflation (often called break-even inflation) over that maturity. The history of these bonds is still too short to examine the accuracy of these implied forecasts.

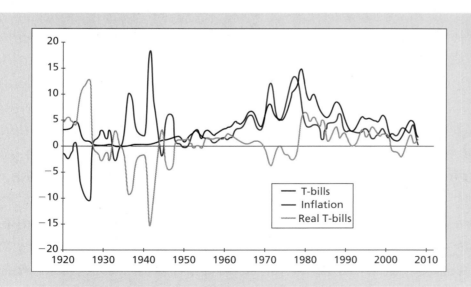

FIGURE 5.5

Interest rates, inflation, and real interest rates, 1926–2008

Source: T-bills: Prof. Kenneth French, **http://mba.tuck.dartmouth.edu/pages/faculty/ken.french/data_library.html**; Inflation: Bureau of Labor Statistics, **www.bls.gov**; Real rate: authors' calculations.

TABLE 5.4

Annual rates of return statistics for U.S. T-bills, inflation, and real interest rates, 1926–2008 and three subperiods

	U.S. Market		
	T-Bills (%)	Inflation (%)	Real T-Bills
Geometric average			
1926–2008	3.71	3.02	0.66
1926–1955	1.09	1.36	−0.27
1956–1984	5.79	4.80	0.95
1985–2008	4.47	2.91	1.52
Arithmetic average			
1926–2008	3.75	3.11	0.74
1926–1955	1.10	1.51	−0.11
1956–1984	5.84	4.85	0.98
1985–2008	4.49	2.92	1.53
Standard deviation			
1926–2008	3.08	4.21	3.91
1926–1955	1.22	5.55	5.84
1956–1984	3.19	3.50	2.39
1985–2008	1.97	1.31	1.66
Correlation of inflation with T-bills			
1926–2008		0.41	
1926–1955		−0.30	
1956–1984		0.72	
1985–2008		0.53	
Minimum (lowest rate)			
1926–2008*	−0.04	−10.27	−15.04
1926–1955	−0.04	−10.27	−15.04
1956–1984	1.53	0.67	−3.65
1985–2008	1.02	0.10	−2.08
Maximum (highest rate)			
1926–2008	14.72	18.13	12.50
1926–1955	4.74	18.13	12.50
1956–1984	14.72	13.26	6.45
1985–2008	8.38	6.26	4.91

*Two slightly negative rates were encountered in the 1930s, before modern T-bills were introduced. In those years, the Treasury instead guaranteed short-term bonds. In highly uncertain times, great demand for these bonds could push up their prices considerably above face value, resulting in a negative rate of return.

Source: T-bill returns: Web site of Prof. Kenneth French: **http://mba.tuck.dartmouth.edu/pages/faculty/ken.french/data library. html**.

5.5 | Asset Allocation Across Risky and Risk-free Portfolios

History shows us that long-term bonds have been riskier investments than investments in Treasury bills and that stock investments have been riskier still. On the other hand, the riskier investments have offered higher average returns. Investors, of course, do not make all-or-nothing choices from these investment classes. They can and do construct their portfolios using securities from all asset classes. Some of the portfolio may be in risk-free Treasury bills and some in high-risk stocks.

asset allocation

Portfolio choice among broad investment classes.

The most straightforward way to control the risk of a portfolio is through the fraction of the portfolio invested in Treasury bills and other safe money market securities versus risky assets. This is an example of an **asset allocation** choice—a choice among broad investment classes, rather than among the specific securities within each asset class. Most investment professionals consider asset allocation the most important part of portfolio construction. Consider this statement by John Bogle, made when he was the chairman of the Vanguard Group of Investment Companies:

> The most fundamental decision of investing is the allocation of your assets: How much should you own in stock? How much should you own in bonds? How much should you own in cash reserves? . . . That decision [has been shown to account] for an astonishing 94% of the differences in total returns achieved by institutionally managed pension funds. . . . There is no reason to believe that the same relationship does not also hold true for individual investors.[7]

Therefore, we start our discussion of the risk-return trade-off available to investors by examining the most basic asset allocation choice: the choice of how much of the portfolio to place in risk-free money market securities versus other risky asset classes.

We will denote the investor's portfolio of risky assets as *P*, and the risk-free asset as *F*. We will assume for the sake of illustration that the risky component of the investor's overall portfolio comprises two mutual funds: one invested in stocks and the other invested in long-term bonds. For now, we take the composition of the risky portfolio as given and focus only on the allocation between it and risk-free securities. In the next chapter, we turn to security selection for the risky portfolio.

The Risky Asset

When we shift wealth from the risky portfolio (*P*) to the risk-free asset, we do not change the relative proportions of the various securities within the risky portfolio. Rather, we reduce the relative weight of the risky portfolio as a whole in favor of risk-free assets.

A simple example demonstrates the procedure. Assume the total market value of an investor's portfolio is $300,000. Of that, $90,000 is invested in shares of the Ready Assets money market fund, a risk-free asset. The remaining $210,000 is in risky securities, say, $113,400 in shares of Vanguard's S&P 500 Index Fund and $96,600 in shares of Fidelity's Investment Grade Bond Fund.

The Vanguard fund (*V*) is a passive equity fund that replicates the S&P 500 portfolio. The Fidelity Investment Grade Bond Fund (*IG*) invests primarily in corporate bonds with high safety ratings and also in Treasury bonds. We choose these two funds for the risky portfolio in the spirit of a low-cost, well-diversified portfolio. While in the next chapter we discuss portfolio optimization, here we simply assume the investor considers the given weighting of *V* and *IG* to be optimal.

The holdings of the Vanguard and Fidelity shares make up the risky portfolio, with 54% in *V* and 46% in *IG*.

$$w_V = 113,400/210,000 = 0.54 \text{ (Vanguard)}$$
$$w_{IG} = 96,600/210,000 = 0.46 \text{ (Fidelity)}$$

The weight of the risky portfolio, *P*, in the **complete portfolio,** *including* risk-free as well as risky investments, is denoted by *y*, and so the weight of the money market fund is $1 - y$.

complete portfolio

The entire portfolio including risky and risk-free assets.

$$y = 210,000/300,000 = 0.7 \text{ (risky assets, portfolio } P)$$
$$1 - y = 90,000/300,000 = 0.3 \text{ (risk-free assets)}$$

The weights of the individual assets in the *complete* portfolio (*C*) are:

Vanguard	$113,400/300,000$	$= 0.378$
Fidelity	$96,600/300,000$	$= 0.322$
Portfolio *P*	$210,000/300,000$	$= 0.700$
Ready Assets *F*	$90,000/300,000$	$= 0.300$
Portfolio *C*	$300,000/300,000$	$= 1.000$

[7]John C. Bogle, *Bogle on Mutual Funds* (Burr Ridge, IL: Irwin Professional Publishing, 1994), p. 235.

Suppose the investor decides to decrease risk by reducing the exposure to the risky portfolio from $y = .7$ to $y = .56$. The risky portfolio would total only $.56 \times 300,000 = \$168,000$, requiring the sale of $42,000 of the original $210,000 risky holdings, with the proceeds used to purchase more shares in Ready Assets. Total holdings in the risk-free asset will increase to $300,000(1 - .56) = \$132,000$ (the original holdings plus the new contribution to the money market fund: $90,000 + $42,000 = $132,000).

The key point is that we leave the proportion of each asset in the risky portfolio unchanged. Because the weights of Vanguard and Fidelity in the risky portfolio are .54 and .46, respectively, we sell $.54 \times 42,000 = \$22,680$ of Vanguard shares and $.46 \times 42,000 = \$19,320$ of Fidelity shares. After the sale, the proportions of each fund in the risky portfolio are unchanged.

$$w_V = \frac{113,400 - 22,680}{210,000 - 42,000} = .54 \text{ (Vanguard)}$$

$$w_{IG} = \frac{96,600 - 19,320}{210,000 - 42,000} = .46 \text{ (Fidelity)}$$

This procedure shows that rather than thinking of our risky holdings as Vanguard and Fidelity separately, we may view our holdings as if they are in a single fund holding Vanguard and Fidelity in fixed proportions. In this sense, we may treat the collection of securities in our risky fund as a single risky asset. As we shift in and out of safe assets, we simply alter our holdings of that risky fund commensurately.

With this simplification, we now can turn to the desirability of reducing risk by changing the risky/risk-free asset mix, that is, reducing risk by decreasing the proportion y. Because we do not alter the weights of each asset within the risky portfolio, the probability distribution of the rate of return on the *risky portfolio* remains unchanged by the asset reallocation. What will change is the probability distribution of the rate of return on the *complete portfolio* of both risky and risk-free assets.

CONCEPT *check* **5.6** What will be the dollar value of your position in Vanguard and its proportion in your complete portfolio if you decide to hold 50% of your investment budget in Ready Assets?

The Risk-Free Asset

The power to tax and to control the money supply lets the government, and only the government, issue default-free (Treasury) bonds. The default-free guarantee by itself is not sufficient to make the bonds risk-free in real terms, since inflation affects the purchasing power of the proceeds from the bonds. The only risk-free asset in real terms would be a price-indexed government bond. Even then, a default-free, perfectly indexed bond offers a guaranteed real rate to an investor only if the maturity of the bond is identical to the investor's desired holding period.

These qualifications notwithstanding, it is common to view Treasury bills as *the* risk-free asset. Because they are short-term investments, their prices are relatively insensitive to interest rate fluctuations. An investor can lock in a short-term nominal return by buying a bill and holding it to maturity. Any inflation uncertainty over the course of a few weeks, or even months, is negligible compared to the uncertainty of stock market returns.

In practice, most investors treat a broader range of money market instruments as effectively risk-free assets. All the money market instruments are virtually immune to interest rate risk (unexpected fluctuations in the price of a bond due to changes in market interest rates) because of their short maturities, and all are fairly safe in terms of default or credit risk.

Money market mutual funds hold, for the most part, three types of securities: Treasury bills, bank certificates of deposit (CDs), and commercial paper. The instruments differ slightly in their default risk. The yields to maturity on CDs and commercial paper, for identical maturities, are always slightly higher than those of T-bills. A history of this yield spread for 90-day CDs is shown in Figure 2.3 in Chapter 2.

Money market funds have changed their relative holdings of these securities over time, but by and large, T-bills have tended to make up only about 15% of their portfolios. Nevertheless, the risk of such blue-chip, short-term investments as CDs and commercial paper is minuscule compared to that of most other assets, such as long-term corporate bonds, common stocks, or real estate. Hence, we treat money market funds as representing the most easily accessible risk-free asset for most investors.

Portfolio Expected Return and Risk

Now that we have specified the risky portfolio and the risk-free asset, we can examine the risk-return combinations that result from various investment allocations between these two assets. Finding the available combinations of risk and return is the "technical" part of asset allocation; it deals only with the opportunities available to investors given the features of the asset markets in which they can invest. In the next section, we address the "personal" part of the problem, the specific individual's choice of the best risk-return combination from the set of feasible combinations, given his or her level of risk aversion.

Since we assume the composition of the optimal risky portfolio (P) already has been determined, the concern here is with the proportion of the investment budget (y) to be allocated to it. The remaining proportion ($1 - y$) is to be invested in the risk-free asset (F).

We denote the *actual* risky rate of return by r_P, the *expected* rate of return on P by $E(r_P)$, and its standard deviation by σ_P. The rate of return on the risk-free asset is denoted as r_f. In the numerical example, $E(r_P) = 15\%$, $\sigma_P = 22\%$, and $r_f = 7\%$. Thus, the risk premium on the risky asset is $E(r_P) - r_f = 8\%$.

Let's start with two extreme cases. If you invest all of your funds in the risky asset, that is, if you choose $y = 1.0$, the expected return on your complete portfolio will be 15% and the standard deviation will be 22%. This combination of risk and return is plotted as point P in Figure 5.6. At the other extreme, you might put all of your funds into the risk-free asset, that is, you choose $y = 0$. In this case, your portfolio would behave just as the risk-free asset, and you would earn a riskless return of 7%. (This choice is plotted as point F in Figure 5.6.)

Now consider more moderate choices. For example, if you allocate equal amounts of your overall or *complete portfolio, C,* to the risky and risk-free assets, that is, if you choose $y = .5$, the expected return on the complete portfolio will be an average of the expected return on portfolios F and P. Therefore, $E(r_C) = .5 \times 7\% + .5 \times 15\% = 11\%$. The risk premium of

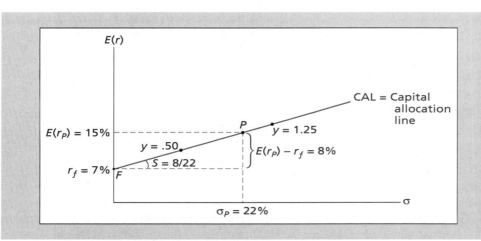

FIGURE 5.6

The investment opportunity set with a risky asset and a risk-free asset the complete portfolio is therefore $11\% - 7\% = 4\%$, which is half of the risk premium of P. The standard deviation of the portfolio also is one-half of P's, that is, 11%. When you reduce the fraction of the complete portfolio allocated to the risky asset by half, you reduce both the risk and risk premium by half.

To generalize, the risk premium of the complete portfolio, C, will equal the risk premium of the risky asset times the fraction of the portfolio invested in the risky asset.

$$E(r_C) - r_f = y[E(r_P) - r_f] \qquad \text{(5.20)}$$

The standard deviation of the complete portfolio will equal the standard deviation of the risky asset times the fraction of the portfolio invested in the risky asset.

$$\sigma_C = y\sigma_P \qquad \text{(5.21)}$$

In sum, both the risk premium and the standard deviation of the complete portfolio increase in proportion to the investment in the risky portfolio. Therefore, the points that describe the risk and return of the complete portfolio for various asset allocations, that is, for various choices of y, all plot on the straight line connecting F and P, as shown in Figure 5.6, with an intercept of r_f and slope (rise/run) of

$$S = \frac{E(r_P) - r_f}{\sigma_P} = \frac{15 - 7}{22} = .36 \qquad \text{(5.22)}$$

CONCEPT check 5.7

What are the expected return, risk premium, standard deviation, and ratio of risk premium to standard deviation for a complete portfolio with $y = .75$?

The Capital Allocation Line

The line plotted in Figure 5.6 depicts the risk-return combinations available by varying asset allocation, that is, by choosing different values of y. For this reason, it is called the **capital allocation line, or CAL.** The slope, S, of the CAL equals the increase in expected return that an investor can obtain per unit of additional standard deviation. In other words, it shows extra return per extra risk. For this reason, as we noted above, the slope also is called the *reward-to-volatility ratio,* or Sharpe measure, after William Sharpe who first suggested its use.

capital allocation line

Plot of risk-return combinations available by varying portfolio allocation between a risk-free asset and a risky portfolio.

Notice that the reward-to-volatility ratio is the same for risky portfolio P and the complete portfolio that was formed by mixing P and the risk-free asset in equal proportions.

	Expected Return	Risk Premium	Standard Deviation	Reward-to-Volatility Ratio
Portfolio P:	15%	8%	22%	$\frac{8}{22} = 0.36$
Portfolio C:	11%	4%	11%	$\frac{4}{11} = 0.36$

In fact, the reward-to-volatility ratio is the same for all complete portfolios that plot on the capital allocation line. While the risk-return combinations differ, the *ratio* of reward to risk is constant.

What about points on the line to the right of portfolio P in the investment opportunity set? If investors can borrow at the (risk-free) rate of $r_f = 7\%$, they can construct complete portfolios that plot on the CAL to the right of P. They simply choose values of y greater than 1.0.

EXAMPLE 5.7

Levered Complete Portfolios

Suppose the investment budget is $300,000, and our investor borrows an additional $120,000, investing the $420,000 in the risky asset. This is a levered position in the risky asset, which is financed in part by borrowing. In that case

$$y = \frac{420,000}{300,000} = 1.4$$

and $1 - y = 1 - 1.4 = -.4$, reflecting a short position in the risk-free asset, or a borrowing position. Rather than lending at a 7% interest rate, the investor borrows at 7%. The portfolio rate of return is

$$E(r_c) = 7 + (1.4 \times 8) = 18.2$$

Another way to find this portfolio rate of return is as follows. Your income statement will show that you expect to earn $63,000 (15% of $420,000) and pay $8,400 (7% of $120,000) in interest on the loan. Simple subtraction yields an expected profit of $54,600, which is 18.2% of your investment budget of $300,000. Therefore, $E(r_c) = 18.2\%$.

Your portfolio still exhibits the same reward-to-volatility ratio:

$$\sigma_c = 1.4 \times 22 = 30.8$$

$$S = \frac{E(r_c) - r_f}{\sigma_c} = \frac{11.2}{30.8} = .36$$

As you might have expected, the levered portfolio has both a higher expected return and a higher standard deviation than an unlevered position in the risky asset.

Risk Tolerance and Asset Allocation

We have developed the CAL, the graph of all feasible risk-return combinations available from allocating the complete portfolio between a risky portfolio and a risk-free asset. The investor confronting the CAL now must choose one optimal combination from the set of feasible choices. This choice entails a trade-off between risk and return. Individual investors with different levels of risk aversion, given an identical capital allocation line, will choose different positions in the risky asset. Specifically, the more risk-averse investors will choose to hold *less* of the risky asset and *more* of the risk-free asset.

Graphically, more risk-averse investors will choose portfolios near point F on the capital allocation line plotted in Figure 5.6. More risk-tolerant investors will choose points closer to P, with higher expected return and higher risk. The most risk-tolerant investors will choose portfolios to the right of point P. These levered portfolios provide even higher expected returns, but even greater risk.

The investor's asset allocation choice also will depend on the trade-off between risk and return. If the reward-to-volatility ratio increases, then investors might well decide to take on riskier positions. For example, suppose an investor reevaluates the probability distribution of the risky portfolio and now perceives a greater expected return without an accompanying increase in the standard deviation. This amounts to an increase in the reward-to-volatility ratio or, equivalently, an increase in the slope of the CAL. As a result, this investor will choose a higher *y*, that is, a greater position in the risky portfolio.

One role of a professional financial adviser is to present investment opportunity alternatives to clients, obtain an assessment of the client's risk tolerance, and help determine the appropriate complete portfolio.[8]

5.6 Passive Strategies and The Capital Market Line

The capital allocation line shows the risk-return trade-offs available by mixing risk-free assets with the investor's risky portfolio. Investors can choose the assets included in the risky portfolio using either passive or active strategies. A **passive strategy** is based on the premise that

passive strategy

Investment policy that avoids security analysis.

---

[8]"Risk tolerance" is simply the flip side of "risk aversion." Either term is a reasonable way to describe attitudes toward risk. We generally find it easier to talk about risk *aversion,* but practitioners often use the term risk *tolerance.*

securities are fairly priced and it avoids the costs involved in undertaking security analysis. Such a strategy might at first blush appear to be naive. However, we will see in Chapter 8 that intense competition among professional money managers might indeed force security prices to levels at which further security analysis is unlikely to turn up significant profit opportunities. Passive investment strategies may make sense for many investors.

To avoid the costs of acquiring information on any individual stock or group of stocks, we may follow a "neutral" diversification approach. A natural strategy is to select a diversified portfolio of common stocks that mirrors the corporate sector of the broad economy. This results in a value-weighted portfolio, which, for example, invests a proportion in GM stock that equals the ratio of GM's market value to the market value of all listed stocks.

capital market line

The capital allocation line using the market index portfolio as the risky asset.

Such strategies are called *indexing.* The investor chooses a portfolio with all the stocks in a broad market index such as the Standard & Poor's 500 Index. The rate of return on the portfolio then replicates the return on the index. Indexing has become an extremely popular strategy for passive investors. We call the capital allocation line provided by one-month T-bills and a broad index of common stocks the **capital market line** (CML). That is, a passive strategy based on stocks and bills generates an investment opportunity set that is represented by the CML.

Historical Evidence on the Capital Market Line

Can we use past data to help forecast the risk-return trade-off offered by the CML? The notion that one can use historical returns to forecast the future seems straightforward but actually is somewhat problematic. On one hand, you wish to use all available data to obtain a large sample. But when using long time series, old data may no longer be representative of future circumstances. Another reason for weeding out subperiods is that some past events simply may be too improbable to be given equal weight with results from other periods. Do the data we have pose this problem?

Table 5.5 breaks the 83-year period 1926–2008 into three subperiods and shows the risk premium, standard deviation, and reward-to-volatility ratio for large U.S. stocks in each subperiod. That ratio is the slope of the CML based on the subperiod data. Indeed, the differences across subperiods are quite striking.

The most plausible explanation for the variation in subperiod returns is based on the observation that the standard deviation of returns is quite large in all subperiods. If we take the 83-year standard deviation of 20.88% as representative and assume that returns in one year are nearly uncorrelated with those in other years (the evidence suggests that any correlation across years is small), then the standard deviation of our estimate of the mean return in any of our 30-year subperiods will be $20.88/\sqrt{30} = 3.81\%$, which is fairly large. This means that in approximately one out of three cases, a 30-year average will deviate by 3.81% or more from the true mean. Applying this insight to the data in Table 5.5 tells us that we cannot reject with any confidence the possibility that the true mean is similar in all subperiods! In other words, the "noise" in the data is so large that we simply cannot make reliable inferences from average

TABLE 5.5	Excess Return (%)		
Average excess rate of return, standard deviation, and the reward-to-volatility ratio of large U.S. common stocks over one-month bills over 1926–2008 and various subperiods	**Average**	**Standard Deviation**	**Sharpe Ratio**
1926–2008	7.68	20.88	0.37
1926–1955	11.67	25.40	0.46
1956–1984	5.01	17.58	0.28
1985–2008	5.95	18.23	0.33

Source: Data in Table 5.2.

TRIUMPH OF THE OPTIMISTS

As a whole, the last eight decades have been very kind to U.S. equity investors. Even accounting for miserable 2008 returns, stock investments have outperformed investments in safe Treasury bills by more than 7% per year. The real rate of return averaged more than 6%, implying an expected doubling of the real value of the investment portfolio about every 12 years!

Is this experience representative? A book by three professors at the London Business School, Elroy Dimson, Paul Marsh, and Mike Staunton, extends the U.S. evidence to other countries and to longer time periods. Their conclusion is given in the book's title, *Triumph of the Optimists**: In every country in their study (which included markets in North America, Europe, Asia, and Africa), the investment optimists—those who bet on the economy by investing in stocks rather than bonds or bills—were vindicated. Over the long haul, stocks beat bonds everywhere.

On the other hand, the equity risk premium is probably not as large as the post-1926 evidence from Table 5.3 would seem to indicate. First, results from the first 25 years of the last century (which included the first World War) were less favorable to stocks. Second, U.S. returns have been better than those of most other countries, and so a more representative value for the historical risk premium may be lower than the U.S. experience. Finally, the sample that is amenable to historical analysis suffers from a self-selection problem. Only those markets that have survived to be studied can be included in the analysis. This leaves out countries such as Russia or China, whose markets were shut down during communist rule, and whose results if included would surely bring down the average historical performance of equity investments. Nevertheless, there is powerful evidence of a risk premium that shows its force everywhere the authors looked.

*Elroy Dimson, Paul Marsh, Mike Staunton, *Triumph of the Optimists: 101 Years of Global Investment Returns* (Princeton, NJ: Princeton University Press, 2002).

---

returns in any subperiod. The differences in returns across subperiods may simply reflect statistical variation, and we have to reconcile ourselves to the fact that the market return and the reward-to-volatility ratio for passive (as well as active!) strategies is simply very hard to predict.

The instability of average excess return on stocks over the 30-year subperiods in Table 5.5 also calls into question the precision of the 83-year average excess return (7.68%) as an estimate of the risk premium on stocks looking into the future. In fact, there has been considerable recent debate among financial economists about the "true" equity risk premium, with an emerging consensus that the historical average may be an unrealistically high estimate of the future risk premium. This argument is based on several factors: the use of longer time periods in which equity returns are examined; a broad range of countries rather than just the U.S. in which excess returns are computed (Dimson, Marsh, and Staunton, 2001); direct surveys of financial executives about their expectations for stock market returns (Graham and Harvey, 2001); and inferences from stock market data about investor expectations (Jagannathan, McGrattan, and Scherbina, 2000; Fama and French, 2002). The nearby box discusses some of this evidence.

Costs and Benefits of Passive Investing

How reasonable is it for an investor to pursue a passive strategy? We cannot answer such a question definitively without comparing passive strategy results to the costs and benefits accruing to an active portfolio strategy. Some issues are worth considering, however.

First, the alternative active strategy entails costs. Whether you choose to invest your own valuable time to acquire the information needed to generate an optimal active portfolio of risky assets or whether you delegate the task to a professional who will charge a fee, constructing an active portfolio is more expensive than constructing a passive one. The passive portfolio requires only small commissions on purchases of U.S. T-bills (or zero commissions if you purchase bills directly from the government) and management fees to a mutual fund company that offers a market index fund to the public. An index fund has the lowest operating expenses of all mutual stock funds because it requires the least effort.

A second argument supporting a passive strategy is the free-rider benefit. If you assume there are many active, knowledgeable investors who quickly bid up prices of undervalued assets and offer down overvalued assets (by selling), you have to conclude that most of the time most assets will be fairly priced. Therefore, a well-diversified portfolio of common stock will be a reasonably fair buy, and the passive strategy may not be inferior to that of the average active investor. We will expand on this insight and provide a more comprehensive analysis of the relative success of passive strategies in Chapter 8.

To summarize, a passive strategy involves investment in two passive portfolios: virtually risk-free short-term T-bills (or a money market fund) and a fund of common stocks that mimics a broad market index. Recall that the capital allocation line representing such a strategy is called the *capital market line*. Using Table 5.5, we see that using 1926 to 2008 data, the passive risky portfolio has offered an average excess return of 7.68% with a standard deviation of 20.88%, resulting in a reward-to-volatility ratio of .37.

SUMMARY

- Investors face a trade-off between risk and expected return. Historical data confirm our intuition that assets with low degrees of risk should provide lower returns on average than do those of higher risk.
- Shifting funds from the risky portfolio to the risk-free asset is the simplest way to reduce risk. Another method involves diversification of the risky portfolio. We take up diversification in later chapters.
- U.S. T-bills provide a perfectly risk-free asset in nominal terms only. Nevertheless, the standard deviation of real rates on short-term T-bills is small compared to that of assets such as long-term bonds and common stocks, so for the purpose of our analysis, we consider T-bills the risk-free asset. Besides T-bills, money market funds hold short-term, safe obligations such as commercial paper and CDs. These entail some default risk but relatively little compared to most other risky assets. For convenience, we often refer to money market funds as risk-free assets.
- A risky investment portfolio (referred to here as the risky asset) can be characterized by its reward-to-volatility ratio. This ratio is the slope of the capital allocation line (CAL), the line connecting the risk-free asset to the risky asset. All combinations of the risky and risk-free asset lie on this line. Investors would prefer a steeper sloping CAL, because that means higher expected returns for any level of risk.
- An investor's preferred choice among the portfolios on the capital allocation line will depend on risk aversion. Risk-averse investors will weight their complete portfolios more heavily toward Treasury bills. Risk-tolerant investors will hold higher proportions of their complete portfolios in the risky asset.
- The capital market line is the capital allocation line that results from using a passive investment strategy that treats a market index portfolio, such as the Standard & Poor's 500, as the risky asset. Passive strategies are low-cost ways of obtaining well-diversified portfolios with performance that will reflect that of the broad stock market.

KEY TERMS

arithmetic average, 111
asset allocation, 130
capital allocation line, 134
capital market line, 136
complete portfolio, 131
dollar-weighted average return, 112
excess return, 120
expected return, 114
geometric average, 111

holding-period return, 110
inflation rate, 128
kurtosis, 118
mean-variance analysis, 121
nominal interest rate, 128
passive strategy, 135
probability distribution, 114
real interest rate, 128
risk aversion, 120

risk-free rate, 119
risk premium, 119
scenario analysis, 114
Sharpe (or reward-to-volatility) measure, 121
skew, 118
standard deviation, 115
value at risk, 116
variance, 114

www.mhhe.com/bkm

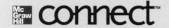 **CONNECT™**   Select problems are available in McGraw-Hill
Connect. Please see the packaging options
section of the preface for more information.

PROBLEM SETS

Basic

1. Suppose you've estimated that the fifth-percentile value at risk of a portfolio is -30%.
   Now you wish to estimate the portfolio's first-percentile VaR (the value below which lie
   1% of the returns). Will the 1% VaR be greater or less than -30%?

2. To estimate the Sharpe ratio of a portfolio from a history of asset returns, we use the
   difference between the simple (arithmetic) average rate of return and the T-bill rate.
   Why not use the geometric average?

3. When estimating a Sharpe ratio, would it make sense to use the average excess real
   return that accounts for inflation?

4. You've just decided upon your capital allocation for the next year, when you realize that
   you've underestimated both the expected return and the standard deviation of your risky
   portfolio by 4%. Will you increase, decrease, or leave unchanged your allocation to
   risk-free T-bills?

Intermediate

5. Suppose your expectations regarding the stock market are as follows:

State of the Economy	Probability	HPR
Boom	0.3	44%
Normal growth	0.4	14
Recession	0.3	−16

   Use Equations 5.6−5.8 to compute the mean and standard deviation of the HPR on stocks.

6. The stock of Business Adventures sells for $40 a share. Its likely dividend payout and
   end-of-year price depend on the state of the economy by the end of the year as follows:

	Dividend	Stock Price
Boom	$2.00	$50
Normal economy	1.00	43
Recession	.50	34

   a. Calculate the expected holding-period return and standard deviation of the holding-
      period return. All three scenarios are equally likely.
   b. Calculate the expected return and standard deviation of a portfolio invested half in
      Business Adventures and half in Treasury bills. The return on bills is 4%.

7. XYZ stock price and dividend history are as follows:

Year	Beginning-of-Year Price	Dividend Paid at Year-End
2007	$100	$4
2008	$110	$4
2009	$ 90	$4
2010	$ 95	$4

   An investor buys three shares of XYZ at the beginning of 2007, buys another two shares
   at the beginning of 2008, sells one share at the beginning of 2009, and sells all four
   remaining shares at the beginning of 2010.
   a. What are the arithmetic and geometric average time-weighted rates of return for the
      investor?

b. What is the dollar-weighted rate of return? (*Hint:* Carefully prepare a chart of cash flows for the *four* dates corresponding to the turns of the year for January 1, 2007, to January 1, 2010. If your calculator cannot calculate internal rate of return, you will have to use a spreadsheet or trial and error.)

8. a. Suppose you forecast that the standard deviation of the market return will be 20% in the coming year. If the measure of risk aversion in Equation 5.14 is $A = 4$, what would be a reasonable guess for the expected market risk premium?

   b. What value of A is consistent with a risk premium of 9%?

   c. What will happen to the risk premium if investors become more risk tolerant?

9. Using the historical risk premiums as your guide, what is your estimate of the expected annual HPR on the S&P 500 stock portfolio if the current risk-free interest rate is 5%?

10. What has been the historical average *real* rate of return on stocks, Treasury bonds, and Treasury bills?

11. Consider a risky portfolio. The end-of-year cash flow derived from the portfolio will be either $50,000 or $150,000, with equal probabilities of 0.5. The alternative riskless investment in T-bills pays 5%.

    a. If you require a risk premium of 10%, how much will you be willing to pay for the portfolio?

    b. Suppose the portfolio can be purchased for the amount you found in (a). What will the expected rate of return on the portfolio be?

    c. Now suppose you require a risk premium of 15%. What is the price you will be willing to pay now?

    d. Comparing your answers to (a) and (c), what do you conclude about the relationship between the required risk premium on a portfolio and the price at which the portfolio will sell?

For Problems 12–16, assume that you manage a risky portfolio with an expected rate of return of 17% and a standard deviation of 27%. The T-bill rate is 7%.

12. a. Your client chooses to invest 70% of a portfolio in your fund and 30% in a T-bill money market fund. What is the expected return and standard deviation of your client's portfolio?

    b. Suppose your risky portfolio includes the following investments in the given proportions:

Stock A	27%
Stock B	33%
Stock C	40%

    What are the investment proportions of your client's overall portfolio, including the position in T-bills?

    c. What is the reward-to-volatility ratio (S) of your risky portfolio and your client's overall portfolio?

    d. Draw the CAL of your portfolio on an expected return/standard deviation diagram. What is the slope of the CAL? Show the position of your client on your fund's CAL.

13. Suppose the same client in the previous problem decides to invest in your risky portfolio a proportion (y) of his total investment budget so that his overall portfolio will have an expected rate of return of 15%.

    a. What is the proportion y?

    b. What are your client's investment proportions in your three stocks and the T-bill fund?

    c. What is the standard deviation of the rate of return on your client's portfolio?

14. Suppose the same client as in the previous problem prefers to invest in your portfolio a proportion (y) that maximizes the expected return on the overall portfolio subject to the constraint that the overall portfolio's standard deviation will not exceed 20%.

    a. What is the investment proportion, y?

    b. What is the expected rate of return on the overall portfolio?

15. You estimate that a passive portfolio invested to mimic the S&P 500 stock index yields an expected rate of return of 13% with a standard deviation of 25%. Draw the CML and your fund's CAL on an expected return/standard deviation diagram.
    a. What is the slope of the CML?
    b. Characterize in one short paragraph the advantage of your fund over the passive fund.

16. Your client (see previous problem) wonders whether to switch the 70% that is invested in your fund to the passive portfolio.
    a. Explain to your client the disadvantage of the switch.
    b. Show your client the maximum fee you could charge (as a percent of the investment in your fund deducted at the end of the year) that would still leave him at least as well off investing in your fund as in the passive one. (*Hint:* The fee will lower the slope of your client's CAL by reducing the expected return net of the fee.)

17. What do you think would happen to the expected return on stocks if investors perceived an increase in the volatility of stocks?

18. You manage an equity fund with an expected risk premium of 10% and an expected standard deviation of 14%. The rate on Treasury bills is 6%. Your client chooses to invest $60,000 of her portfolio in your equity fund and $40,000 in a T-bill money market fund. What is the expected return and standard deviation of return on your client's portfolio?

19. What is the reward-to-volatility ratio for the *equity fund* in the previous problem?

For Problems 20–22, download the Spreadsheet containing the data for Table 5.2: Rates of return, 1926–2008, from www.mhhe.com/bkm.

20. Calculate the same subperiod means and standard deviations for small stocks as Table 5.5 of the text provides for large stocks.
    a. Have small stocks provided better reward-to-volatility ratios than large stocks?
    b. Do small stocks show a similar higher standard deviation in the earliest subperiod as Table 5.5 documents for large stocks?

Please visit us at www.mhhe.com/bkm

21. Convert the nominal returns on both large and small stocks to real rates. Reproduce Table 5.5 using real rates instead of excess returns. Compare the results to those of Table 5.5.

Please visit us at www.mhhe.com/bkm

22. Repeat the previous problem for small stocks and compare with the results for nominal rates.

Please visit us at www.mhhe.com/bkm

Challenge

23. Download the annual returns on the combined NYSE/NASDAQ/AMEX markets as well as the S&P 500 from the Online Learning Center at **www.mhhe.com/bkm**. For both indexes, calculate:
    a. Average return.
    b. Standard deviation of return.
    c. Skew of return.
    d. Kurtosis of return.
    e. The 5% value at risk.
    f. Based on your results to parts (b)–(e), compare the risk of the two indices.

CFA Problems

1. A portfolio of nondividend-paying stocks earned a geometric mean return of 5.0% between January 1, 2003, and December 31, 2009. The arithmetic mean return for the same period was 6.0%. If the market value of the portfolio at the beginning of 2003 was $100,000, what was the market value of the portfolio at the end of 2009?

2. Which of the following statements about the standard deviation is/are *true*? A standard deviation:
    a. Is the square root of the variance.
    b. Is denominated in the same units as the original data.
    c. Can be a positive or a negative number.

3. Which of the following statements reflects the importance of the asset allocation decision to the investment process? The asset allocation decision:
   a. Helps the investor decide on realistic investment goals.
   b. Identifies the specific securities to include in a portfolio.
   c. Determines most of the portfolio's returns and volatility over time.
   d. Creates a standard by which to establish an appropriate investment time horizon.

Use the following data in answering CFA Questions 4–6.

Utility Formula Data		
Investment	Expected Return, $E(r)$	Standard Deviation, σ
1	.12	.30
2	.15	.50
3	.21	.16
4	.24	.21

$$\text{Required risk premium} = \tfrac{1}{2}A\sigma^2 \text{ where } A = 4$$

4. Based on the formula for required risk premium above, which investment would you select if you were risk averse with $A = 4$?
5. Based on the formula above, which investment would you select if you were risk neutral?
6. The variable (A) in the utility formula represents the:
   a. Investor's return requirement.
   b. Investor's aversion to risk.
   c. Certainty equivalent rate of the portfolio.
   d. Preference for one unit of return per four units of risk.

Use the following scenario analysis for Stocks X and Y to answer CFA Questions 7 through 9.

	Bear Market	Normal Market	Bull Market
Probability	.2	.5	.3
Stock X	−20%	18%	50%
Stock Y	−15%	20%	10%

7. What are the expected returns for Stocks X and Y?
8. What are the standard deviations of returns on Stocks X and Y?
9. Assume that of your $10,000 portfolio, you invest $9,000 in Stock X and $1,000 in Stock Y. What is the expected return on your portfolio?
10. Probabilities for three states of the economy and probabilities for the returns on a particular stock in each state are shown in the table below.

State of Economy	Probability of Economic State	Stock Performance	Probability of Stock Performance in Given Economic State
Good	.3	Good	.6
		Neutral	.3
		Poor	.1
Neutral	.5	Good	.4
		Neutral	.3
		Poor	.3
Poor	.2	Good	.2
		Neutral	.3
		Poor	.5

What is the probability that the economy will be neutral *and* the stock will experience poor performance?

11. An analyst estimates that a stock has the following probabilities of return depending on the state of the economy. What is the expected return of the stock?

State of Economy	Probability	Return
Good	.1	15%
Normal	.6	13
Poor	.3	7

Use data from the Standard & Poor's Market Insight Database at www.mhhe.com/edumarketinsight to answer the following questions.

1. Select the Company tab and enter the ticker symbol ADBE. Click on the Stock Report link in the S&P Stock Reports section to view the report for Adobe Systems.

2. What is the latest price reported in the "Key Stock Statistics" section? What is the 12-month target price? Calculate the expected holding-period return based on these prices.

3. In the Key Stock Statistics section, find the answer to the question "How much would I have today if I invested $10,000 in ADBE five years ago?" Using this information, calculate the five-year holding-period return on Adobe's stock.

4. What is Adobe's volatility rating (high, average, low)? Look for this in the Quantitative Evaluations section of the report.

5. What is S&P's fair value calculation for the price of Adobe stock today? By how much, in dollars and as a percent, does the stock's S&P fair value differ from its current price?

WEB *master* INFLATION AND INTEREST RATES

Calculating the real rate of return is an important part of evaluating an investment's performance. To do this, you need to know the nominal yield on your investment and the rate of inflation during the corresponding period. To estimate the expected real rate of return before you make an investment, you can use the promised yield and the expected inflation rate.

1. Go to **www.bankrate.com** and click on the CDs and Investments tab. Using Compare CDs & Investment Rates box, find the average 1-year CD rate from banks across the nation (these will be nominal rates).

2. Use the St. Louis Federal Reserve's Web site at **research. stlouisfed.org/fred2** as a source for data about expected inflation. Search for "MICH inflation," which will provide you with the University of Michigan Inflation Expectation data series (MICH). Click on the View Data link and find the latest available data point. What is the expected inflation rate for the next year?

3. On the basis of your answers to parts 1 and 2, calculate the expected real rate of return on a 1-year CD investment.

4. What does the result tell you about real interest retes? Are they positive or negative, and what does this mean?

5.1. *a.* The arithmetic average is $(2 + 8 - 4)/3 = 2\%$ per month.

b. The time-weighted (geometric) average is
$$[(1 + .02) \times (1 + .08) \times (1 - .04)]^{1/3} - 1 = .0188 = 1.88\% \text{ per month.}$$

c. We compute the dollar-weighted average (IRR) from the cash flow sequence (in $ millions):

	Month		
	1	**2**	**3**
Assets under management at beginning of month	10.0	13.2	19.256
Investment profits during month (HPR × Assets)	0.2	1.056	(0.77)
Net inflows during month	3.0	5.0	0.0
Assets under management at end of month	13.2	19.256	18.486

www.mhhe.com/bkm

	Time			
	0	**1**	**2**	**3**
Net cash flow*	−10	−3.0	−5.0	+18.486

*Time 0 is today. Time 1 is the end of the first month. Time 3 is the end of the third month, when net cash flow equals the ending value (potential liquidation value) of the portfolio.

The IRR of the sequence of net cash flows is 1.17% per month.

The dollar-weighted average is less than the time-weighted average because the negative return was realized when the fund had the most money under management.

5.2. Computing the HPR for each scenario, we convert the price and dividend data to rate of return data:

Scenario	Prob	Ending Value ($ million)	Dividend ($ million)	HPR	HPR x Prob	Deviation: HPR-mean	Prob x dev'n squared
1	.30	$35	$4.40	.713	.214	.406	.049
2	.45	27	4.00	.348	.157	.040	.001
3	.20	15	4.00	−.174	−.035	−.481	.046
4	.05	8	2.00	−.565	−.028	−.873	.038
Sum:					.307		.135

Expected HPR = .307 = 30.7%.

Variance = .135.

Standard deviation = $\sqrt{.135}$ = .367 = 36.7%.

5% VaR = −56.5%.

For the corresponding normal distribution, VaR would be 30.7% − 1.64485 × 36.7% = −29.67%.

5.3. a. If the average investor chooses the S&P 500 portfolio, then the implied degree of risk aversion is given by Equation 5.14:

$$A = \frac{.10 - .05}{½ \times .18^2} = 3.09$$

b. $S = \dfrac{10 - 5}{18} = .28$

5.4. The mean excess return for the period 1926–1934 is 3.56% (below the historical average), and the standard deviation (using $n - 1$ degrees of freedom) is 32.55% (above the historical average). These results reflect the severe downturn of the great crash and the unusually high volatility of stock returns in this period.

5.5. a. Solving

$$1 + R = (1 + r)(1 + i) = (1.03)(1.08) = 1.1124$$
$$R = 11.24\%$$

b. Solving

$$1 + R = (1.03)(1.10) = 1.133$$
$$R = 13.3\%$$

5.6. Holding 50% of your invested capital in Ready Assets means your investment proportion in the risky portfolio is reduced from 70% to 50%.

Your risky portfolio is constructed to invest 54% in Vanguard and 46% in Fidelity. Thus, the proportion of Vanguard in your overall portfolio is .5 × 54% = 27%, and the dollar value of your position in Vanguard is 300,000 × .27 = $81,000.

5.7. $E(r) = 7 + .75 \times 8\% = 13\%$

$\sigma = .75 \times 22\% = 16.5\%$

Risk premium = 13 − 7 = 6%

$\dfrac{\text{Risk premium}}{\text{Standard deviation}} = \dfrac{13 - 7}{16.5} = .36$

Efficient Diversification

After Studying This Chapter You Should Be Able To:

- Show how covariance and correlation affect the power of diversification to reduce portfolio risk.

- Construct efficient portfolios.

- Calculate the composition of the optimal risky portfolio.

- Use index models to analyze the risk characteristics of securities and portfolios.

In this chapter we describe how investors can construct the best possible risky portfolio. The key concept is efficient diversification.

The notion of diversification is age-old. The adage "don't put all your eggs in one basket" obviously predates formal economic theory. However, a rigorous model showing how to make the most of the power of diversification was not devised until 1952, a feat for which Harry Markowitz eventually won the Nobel Prize in Economics. This chapter is largely developed from his work, as well as from later insights that built on his work.

We start with a bird's-eye view of how diversification reduces the variability of portfolio returns. We then turn to the construction of optimal risky portfolios. We follow a top-down approach, starting with asset allocation across a small set of broad asset classes, such as stocks, bonds, and money market securities. Then we show how the principles of optimal asset allocation can easily be generalized to solve the problem of security selection among many risky assets. We discuss the efficient set of risky portfolios and show how it leads us to the best attainable capital allocation. Finally, we show how index models of security returns can simplify the search for efficient portfolios and the interpretation of the risk characteristics of individual securities.

The last section examines the common fallacy that long-term investment horizons mitigate the impact of asset risk. We argue that the common belief in "time diversification" is in fact an illusion and is not real diversification.

Related Web sites for this chapter are available at www.mhhe.com/bkm.

6.1 | Diversification and Portfolio Risk

Suppose you have in your risky portfolio only one stock, say, Dell Computer Corporation. What are the sources of risk affecting this "portfolio"?

We can identify two broad sources of uncertainty. The first is the risk that has to do with general economic conditions, such as the business cycle, the inflation rate, interest rates, exchange rates, and so forth. None of these macroeconomic factors can be predicted with certainty, and all affect the rate of return Dell stock eventually will provide. Then you must add to these macro factors firm-specific influences, such as Dell's success in research and development, its management style and philosophy, and so on. Firm-specific factors are those that affect Dell without noticeably affecting other firms.

Now consider a naive diversification strategy, adding another security to the risky portfolio. If you invest half of your risky portfolio in ExxonMobil, leaving the other half in Dell, what happens to portfolio risk? Because the firm-specific influences on the two stocks differ (statistically speaking, the influences are independent), this strategy should reduce portfolio risk. For example, when oil prices fall, hurting ExxonMobil, computer prices might rise, helping Dell. The two effects are offsetting, which stabilizes portfolio return.

But why stop at only two stocks? Diversifying into many more securities continues to reduce exposure to firm-specific factors, so portfolio volatility should continue to fall. Ultimately, however, even with a large number of risky securities in a portfolio, there is no way to avoid all risk. To the extent that virtually all securities are affected by common (risky) macroeconomic factors, we cannot eliminate our exposure to general economic risk, no matter how many stocks we hold.

Figure 6.1 illustrates these concepts. When all risk is firm-specific, as in Figure 6.1A, diversification can reduce risk to low levels. With all risk sources independent, and with investment spread across many securities, exposure to any particular source of risk is negligible. This is just an application of the law of averages. The reduction of risk to very low levels because of independent risk sources is sometimes called the *insurance principle*.

When common sources of risk affect all firms, however, even extensive diversification cannot fully eliminate risk. In Figure 6.1B, portfolio standard deviation falls as the number of securities increases, but it is not reduced to zero. The risk that remains even after diversification is called **market risk,** risk that is attributable to marketwide risk sources. Other terms are **systematic risk** or **nondiversifiable risk.** The risk that *can* be eliminated by diversification is called **unique risk, firm-specific risk, nonsystematic risk,** or **diversifiable risk.**

This analysis is borne out by empirical studies. Figure 6.2 shows the effect of portfolio diversification, using data on NYSE stocks. The figure shows the average standard deviations

market risk, systematic risk, nondiversifiable risk

Risk factors common to the whole economy.

unique risk, firm-specific risk, nonsystematic risk, diversifiable risk

Risk that can be eliminated by diversification.

FIGURE 6.1

Portfolio risk as a function of the number of stocks in the portfolio

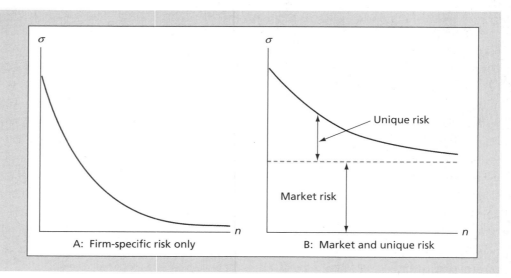

DANGER: HIGH LEVELS OF COMPANY STOCK

Q: I'm 48 years old and have about 90% of my 401(k) invested in my company's stock and the rest in an international equity fund. I want to diversify further, but don't know where to turn. Any suggestions?

A: Diversify further? That's an understatement. You, my friend, need a total 401(k) portfolio makeover.

The glaring trouble spot, of course, is your huge concentration of company stock. Generally, I recommend that, to the extent you own your employer's stock at all in your 401(k), you limit it to 10% or so of your account's value.

The problem is that once you get beyond a small holding of company stock—or the shares of any one company for that matter—you dramatically increase the riskiness of your portfolio in two ways.

First, you expose yourself to the possibility that your company may simply implode, decimating the stock's value (and your

401(k)'s balance along with it) virtually overnight. But even if that doesn't happen, there's another risk: heightened volatility. A single stock is typically two to three times more volatile than a diversified portfolio. And when you load up your 401(k) with the stock of one company, it subjects your account value to the possibility of much wider swings.

In short, the payoff you'll likely get from investing in company stock doesn't adequately compensate you for the risk you're taking.

So, about that further diversification. Basically, you need to rebuild your portfolio from the ground up so that you not only own a broad range of stocks, but bonds as well. As for which investments you should choose from your 401(k)'s lineup, I'd recommend sticking as much as possible to low-cost funds and particularly index funds to the extent they're available.

SOURCE: Walter Updegrave, "Danger: High Levels of Company Stock," **http://money.cnn.com**, January 19, 2009. Copyright © CNNMoney. All Rights Reserved.

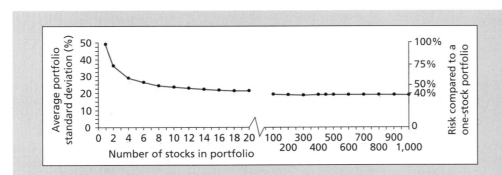

FIGURE 6.2

Portfolio risk decreases as diversification increases

Source: Meir Statman, "How Many Stocks Make a Diversified Portfolio?" *Journal of Financial and Quantitative Analysis* 22, September 1987.

of equally weighted portfolios constructed by selecting stocks at random as a function of the number of stocks in the portfolio. On average, portfolio risk does fall with diversification, but the power of diversification to reduce risk is limited by common sources of risk. The nearby box "Danger: High Levels of Company Stock" highlights the dangers of neglecting diversification.

In light of this discussion, it is worth pointing out that general macroeconomic conditions in the U.S. do not move in lockstep with those in other countries. International diversification may further reduce portfolio risk, but here too, global economic and political factors affecting all countries to various degrees will limit the extent of risk reduction.

6.2 Asset Allocation with Two Risky Assets

In the last chapter we examined the simplest asset allocation decision, that involving the choice of how much of the portfolio to place in risk-free money market securities versus in a risky portfolio. We simply assumed that the risky portfolio comprised a stock and a bond fund in given proportions. Of course, investors need to decide on the proportion of their portfolios to allocate to the stock versus the bond market. This, too, is an asset allocation decision. As the other nearby box "First Take Care of Asset Allocation Needs" emphasizes, most investment professionals recognize that the asset allocation decision must take precedence over the choice of particular stocks.

FIRST TAKE CARE OF ASSET ALLOCATION NEEDS

If you want to build a top-performing mutual-fund portfolio, you should start by hunting for top-performing funds, right?

Wrong.

Too many investors gamely set out to find top-notch funds without first settling on an overall portfolio strategy. Result? These investors wind up with a mishmash of funds that don't add up to a decent portfolio.

So what should you do? With thousands of stock, bond, and money-market funds to choose from, you couldn't possibly analyze all the funds available. Instead, to make sense of the bewildering array of funds available, you should start by deciding what basic mix of stock, bond, and money-market funds you want to hold. This is what experts call your "asset allocation."

This asset allocation has a major influence on your portfolio's performance. The more you have in stocks, the higher your likely long-run return.

But with the higher potential return from stocks come sharper short-term swings in a portfolio's value. As a result, you may want to include a healthy dose of bond and money-market funds, especially if you are a conservative investor or you will need to tap your portfolio for cash in the near future.

Once you have settled on your asset allocation mix, decide what sort of stock, bond, and money-market funds you want to own. This is particularly critical for the stock portion of your portfolio. One way to damp the price swings in your stock portfolio is to spread your money among large, small, and foreign stocks.

You could diversify even further by making sure that, when investing in U.S. large- and small-company stocks, you own both growth stocks with rapidly increasing sales or earnings and also beaten-down value stocks that are inexpensive compared with corporate assets or earnings.

Similarly, among foreign stocks, you could get additional diversification by investing in both developed foreign markets such as France, Germany, and Japan, and also emerging markets like Argentina, Brazil, and Malaysia.

We examined capital allocation between risky and risk-free assets in the last chapter. We turn now to asset allocation between two risky assets, which we will continue to assume are two mutual funds, one a bond fund and the other a stock fund. After we understand the properties of portfolios formed by mixing two risky assets, we will reintroduce the choice of the third, risk-free portfolio. This will allow us to complete the basic problem of asset allocation across the three key asset classes: stocks, bonds, and risk-free money market securities. Once you understand this case, it will be easy to see how portfolios of many risky securities might best be constructed.

Covariance and Correlation

Because we now envision forming a risky portfolio from two risky assets, we need to understand how the uncertainties of asset returns interact. It turns out that the key determinant of portfolio risk is the extent to which the returns on the two assets tend to vary either in tandem or in opposition. Portfolio risk depends on the *correlation* between the returns of the assets in the portfolio. We can see why using a simple scenario analysis.

Suppose there are four possible scenarios for the economy: a severe recession, a mild recession, normal growth, and a boom. The performance of stock funds tends to follow the performance of the broad economy. So suppose that in a normal growth period stocks will return 14% and in a boom, 30%. Conversely, in a severe recession, stocks will return −37% and in a mild recession, −11%. In contrast, a mild recession with falling interest rates will benefit the bond fund, which will return 15%, but in a severe recession, the bond fund will suffer from some corporate defaults and return −9%. Notice that bonds outperform stocks in both the mild and severe recession scenarios. In a normal growth period, the bond fund will return 8%, while in a boom period characterized by accelerating inflation, increases in interest rates will reduce the bond fund return to −5%. In both normal growth and boom scenarios, stocks outperform bonds. These assumptions and the probability of each scenario are summarized in Spreadsheet 6.1.

SPREADSHEET 6.1

Capital market expectations for the stock and bond funds

Please visit us at www.mhhe.com/bkm

	A	B	C	D	E	F
1			Stock Fund		Bond Fund	
2	Scenario	Probability	Rate of Return	Col B x Col C	Rate of Return	Col B x Col E
3	Severe recession	.05	−37	−1.9	−9	−0.45
4	Mild recession	.25	−11	−2.8	15	3.8
5	Normal growth	.40	14	5.6	8	3.2
6	Boom	.30	30	9.0	−5	−1.5
7	Expected or Mean Return:		SUM:	10.0	SUM:	5.0

The expected return on each fund equals the probability-weighted average of the outcomes in the four scenarios. The last row of Spreadsheet 6.1 shows that the expected return of the stock fund is 10%, and that of the bond fund is 5%. As we discussed in the last chapter, the variance is the probability-weighted average across all scenarios of the squared deviation between the actual return of the fund and its expected return; the standard deviation is the square root of the variance. These values are computed in Spreadsheet 6.2.

What about the risk and return characteristics of a portfolio made up from the stock and bond funds? The portfolio return is the weighted average of the returns on each fund with weights equal to the proportion of the portfolio invested in each fund. Suppose we form a portfolio with 40% invested in the stock fund and 60% in the bond fund. Then the portfolio return in each scenario is the weighted average of the returns on the two funds. For example

$$\text{Portfolio return in mild recession} = .40 \times (-11\%) + .60 \times 15\% = 4.6\%$$

which appears in cell C6 of Spreadsheet 6.3.

SPREADSHEET 6.2

Variance of returns

Please visit us at www.mhhe.com/bkm

	A	B	C	D	E	F	G	H	I	J
1			Stock Fund				Bond Fund			
2				Deviation				Deviation		
3			Rate	from		Column B	Rate	from		Column B
4			of	Expected	Squared	×	of	Expected	Squared	×
5	Scenario	Prob.	Return	Return	Deviation	Column E	Return	Return	Deviation	Column I
6	Severe recession	.05	−37	−47	2209	110.45	−9	−14	196	9.80
7	Mild recession	.25	−11	−21	441	110.25	15	10	100	25.00
8	Normal growth	.40	14	4	16	6.40	8	3	9	3.60
9	Boom	.30	30	20	400	120.00	−5	−10	100	30.00
10				Variance = SUM		347.10			Variance:	68.40
11			Standard deviation = SQRT(Variance)			18.63			Std. Dev.:	8.27

SPREADSHEET 6.3

Performance of a portfolio invested in the stock and bond funds

Please visit us at www.mhhe.com/bkm

	A	B	C	D	E	F	G
1			Portfolio invested 40% in stock fund and 60% in bond fund				
2			Rate	Column B	Deviation from		Column B
3			of	×	Expected	Squared	×
4	Scenario	Probability	Return	Column C	Return	Deviation	Column F
5	Severe recession	.05	−20.2	−1.01	−27.2	739.84	36.99
6	Mild recession	.25	4.6	1.15	−2.4	5.76	1.44
7	Normal growth	.40	10.4	4.16	3.4	11.56	4.62
8	Boom	.30	9.0	2.70	2.0	4.00	1.20
9		Expected return:		7.00		Variance:	44.26
10						Standard deviation:	6.65

Spreadsheet 6.3 shows the rate of return of the portfolio in each scenario. Notice that both funds suffer in a severe downturn and, therefore, the portfolio also experiences a substantial loss of 20.2%. This is a manifestation of systematic risk affecting a broad spectrum of securities, as discussed in Section 6.1. Declines of more than 25% in the S&P 500 Index have occurred five times in the past 83 years (1930, 1931, 1937, 1974, and 2008), roughly once every 16 years. Avoiding losses in these extreme outcomes would require one to devote a large allocation of the portfolio to risk-free (money market) investments or (expensive) portfolio insurance (which we will discuss in Chapter 16). Extreme events such as a severe recession make for the large standard deviation of stocks, 18.63%, and even of bonds, 8.27%. Still, diversification mitigates the worst-case return, which for stocks is −37% but for the portfolio is a far milder −20.2%; the overall standard deviation of the diversified portfolio, 6.65%, is considerably smaller than that of stocks and even smaller than that of bonds.

The low risk of the portfolio is due to the inverse relationship between the performances of the stock and bond funds. For example, in a mild recession, stocks fare poorly, but this is offset by the large positive return of the bond fund. Conversely, in the boom scenario, bond prices fall, but stocks do very well. Notice that while the portfolio's expected return is just the weighted average of the expected return of the two assets, *the portfolio standard deviation is actually less than that of either component fund.*

Portfolio risk is reduced most when the returns of the two assets most reliably offset each other. The natural question investors should ask, therefore, is how one can measure the tendency of the returns on two assets to vary either in tandem or in opposition to each other. The statistics that provide this measure are the covariance and the correlation coefficient.

The covariance is calculated in a manner similar to the variance. Instead of measuring the typical difference of an asset return from its expected value, however, we wish to measure the extent to which the variation in the returns on the two assets tend to reinforce or offset each other.

We start in Spreadsheet 6.4 with the deviation of the return on each fund from its expected or mean value. For each scenario, we multiply the deviation of the stock fund return from its mean by the deviation of the bond fund return from its mean. The product will be positive if both asset returns exceed their respective means in that scenario or if both fall short of their respective means. The product will be negative if one asset exceeds its mean return, while the other falls short of its mean return. For example, Spreadsheet 6.4 shows that the stock fund return in a mild recession falls short of its expected value by 21%, while the bond fund return exceeds its mean by 10%. Therefore, the product of the two deviations in the recession is −21 × 10 = −210, as reported in column E. The product of deviations is negative if one asset performs well when the other is performing poorly. It is positive if both assets perform well or poorly in the same scenarios.

If we compute the probability-weighted average of the products across all scenarios, we obtain a measure of the *average* tendency of the asset returns to vary in tandem. Since this is a measure of the extent to which the returns tend to vary with each other, that is, to co-vary, it is called the *covariance*. Therefore, the formula for the covariance of the returns on the stock and bond portfolios is given in the following equation. Each particular scenario in this equation is labeled or "indexed" by i. In general, i ranges from scenario 1 to S (the total number of

---

SPREADSHEET 6.4

Covariance between the returns of the stock and bond funds

Please visit us at www.mhhe.com/bkm

	A	B	C	D	E	F
1			Deviation from Mean Return		Covariance	
2	Scenario	Probability	Stock Fund	Bond Fund	Product of Dev	Col B × Col E
3	Severe recession	.05	−47	−14	658	32.9
4	Mild recession	.25	−21	10	−210	−52.5
5	Normal growth	.40	4	3	12	4.8
6	Boom	.30	20	−10	−200	−60.0
7					Covariance = SUM:	−74.8
8	Correlation coefficient = Covariance/(StdDev(stocks)*StdDev(bonds)) =					−0.49

scenarios). In this example, $S = 4$, the four possible scenarios being severe recession, mild recession, normal growth, and boom conditions. The probability of each scenario is denoted $p(i)$.

$$\text{Cov}(r_S, r_B) = \sum_{i=1}^{S} p(i)[r_S(i) - \bar{r}_S][r_B(i) - \bar{r}_B] \qquad \textbf{(6.1)}$$

The covariance of the stock and bond funds is computed in the next-to-last line of Spreadsheet 6.4 using Equation 6.1. The negative value for the covariance indicates that the two assets vary inversely, that is, when one asset performs well, the other tends to perform poorly.

Unfortunately, it is difficult to interpret the magnitude of the covariance. For instance, does the covariance of -74.8 in cell F7 indicate that the inverse relationship between the returns on stock and bond funds is strong or weak? It's hard to say. An easier statistic to interpret is the *correlation coefficient,* which is simply the covariance divided by the product of the standard deviations of the returns on each fund. We denote the correlation coefficient by the Greek letter rho, ρ.

$$\text{Correlation coefficient} = \rho_{SB} = \frac{\text{Cov}(r_S, r_B)}{\sigma_S \sigma_B} = \frac{-74.8}{18.63 \times 8.27} = -.49 \qquad \textbf{(6.2)}$$

Correlations can range from values of -1 to $+1$. Values of -1 indicate perfect negative correlation, that is, the strongest possible tendency for two returns to vary inversely. Values of $+1$ indicate perfect positive correlation. Correlations of zero indicate that the returns on the two assets are unrelated to each other. The correlation coefficient of $-.49$ confirms the significant tendency of the returns on the stock and bond funds to vary inversely in this particular scenario analysis.

Here is another reason that the correlation coefficient is a useful statistic. Like the variance, the dimension of covariance is percent squared. However, a square root of the covariance is not available because the covariance can be negative. Instead, it is customary to refer to the correlation coefficient, which because it is a pure, scaled number between -1 and $+1$, is more telling. Equation 6.2 shows that whenever the covariance is called for in a calculation we can replace it with the following expression using the correlation coefficient:

$$\text{Cov}(r_S, r_B) = \rho_{SB} \sigma_S \sigma_B \qquad \textbf{(6.3)}$$

We are now in a position to derive the risk and return features of portfolios of risky assets.

Suppose the rates of return of the bond portfolio in the four scenarios of Spreadsheet 6.1 are -10% in a severe recession, 10% in a mild recession, 7% in a normal period, and 2% in a boom. The stock returns in the four scenarios are -37%, -11%, 14%, and 30%. What are the covariance and correlation coefficient between the rates of return on the two portfolios?

CONCEPT *check* **6.1**

Using Historical Data

We've seen that portfolio risk and return depend on the means and variances of the component securities, as well as on the covariance between their returns. One way to obtain these inputs is a scenario analysis as in Spreadsheets 6.1–6.4. As we noted in Chapter 5, however, a common alternative approach to produce these inputs is to make use of historical data. The idea is that variability and covariability change slowly over time. Thus, if we estimate these statistics from a recent data sample, our estimates will provide useful predictions for the near future—perhaps next month or next quarter.

In this approach, we use realized returns to estimate mean returns and volatility as well as the tendency for security returns to co-vary. The estimate of the mean return for each security is its average value in the sample period; the estimate of variance is the average value of the squared deviations around the sample average; the estimate of the covariance is the average value of the cross-product of deviations.

Notice that, as in scenario analysis, the focus for risk and return analysis is on average returns and the deviations of returns from their average value. Instead of using mean returns based on the scenario analysis, however, we use average returns during the sample period. We can illustrate this approach with a simple example.

EXAMPLE   6.1

Using Historical Data to Estimate Means, Standard Deviations, Covariance, and Correlation.

Consider the 10 years of returns for the two mutual funds presented in the following spreadsheet. While these are far less data than most analysts would use, for the sake of illustration we will pretend that they are adequate to estimate mean returns and relevant risk statistics. In practice, analysts would use higher-frequency data (e.g., monthly or even daily data) to estimate risk coefficients, and would as well supplement historical data with fundamental analysis to forecast future returns.

The spreadsheet starts with the raw return data in columns B and C. We use standard Excel functions to obtain average returns, standard deviation, covariance, and correlation (see rows 18–21). We also confirm (in cell F14) that covariance is the average value of the product of each asset's deviation from its mean return.

The average returns and standard deviations in this spreadsheet are similar to those of our previous scenario analysis. However, the correlation between stock and bond returns in this example is low but positive, which is more consistent with historical experience than the strongly negative correlation of −.49 implied by our scenario analysis.

	A	B	C	D	E	F
1		**Rates of Return**		**Deviations from Average Returns**		Products of
2	**Year**	Stock Fund	Bond Fund	Stock Fund	Bond Fund	Deviations
3	2006	30.17	5.08	20.17	0.08	1.53
4	2007	32.97	7.52	22.97	2.52	57.78
5	2008	21.04	−8.82	11.04	−13.82	−152.56
6	2009	−8.10	5.27	−18.10	0.27	−4.82
7	2010	−12.89	12.20	−22.89	7.20	−164.75
8	2011	−28.53	−7.79	−38.53	−12.79	493.00
9	2012	22.49	6.38	12.49	1.38	17.18
10	2013	12.58	12.40	2.58	7.40	19.05
11	2014	14.81	17.29	4.81	12.29	59.05
12	2015	15.50	0.51	5.50	−4.49	−24.70
13						
14	Average	10.00	5.00	Covariance = average product of deviations:		30.08
15	SD	19.00	8.00	Correlation = Covariance/(SD stocks*SD bonds):		0.20
16						
17	**Excel formulas**					
18	Average	=average(B3:B12)				
19	Std deviation	=stdevp(B3:B12)				
20	Covariance	=covar(B3:B12,C3:C12)				
21	Correlation	=correl(B3:B12,C3:C12)				
22						
23						

Two comments on Example 6.1 are in order. First is a small point that you may recall from a statistics class (or from Chapter 5). When variance is estimated from a sample of n observed returns, it is common to divide the squared deviations by $n − 1$ rather than by n. This is because we take deviations from an estimated average return rather than the true (but unknown) expected return; this procedure is said to adjust for a "lost degree of freedom." In Excel, the function STDEVP computes standard deviation dividing by n while the function STDEV uses $n − 1$. Excel's covariance and correlation functions both use n. In Example 6.1, we ignored this fine point, and divided by n throughout. In any event, the correction for the lost degree of freedom is negligible when there are plentiful observations. For example with 60 returns (e.g., five years of monthly data), the difference between dividing by 60 or 59 will affect variance or covariance by a factor of only 1.017.

The more important comment on Example 6.1 has to do with the statistical reliability of historical estimates. Estimates of variance and covariance constructed from past data are generally considered reliable forecasts of these statistics (at least for the short term). However, averages of past returns typically provide highly noisy (i.e., imprecise) forecasts of future expected returns. In this discussion we freely use past averages computed from small samples of data, because our objective here is to demonstrate the methodology. In practice, professional investors spend most of their resources on macroeconomic and security analysis to improve their estimates of mean returns.

The following tables present returns on various pairs of stocks in several periods. In part A, we show you a scatter diagram of the returns on the first pair of stocks. Draw (or prepare in Excel) similar scatter diagrams for cases B through E. Match up your diagrams (A–E) to the following list of correlation coefficients by choosing the correlation that best describes the relationship between the returns on the two stocks: $\rho = -1, 0, .2, .5, 1.0$.

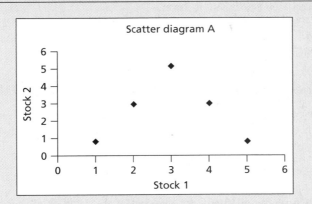

A.

% Return	
Stock 1	**Stock 2**
5	1
1	1
4	3
2	3
3	5

B.

% Return	
Stock 1	**Stock 2**
1	1
2	2
3	3
4	4
5	5

C.

% Return	
Stock 1	**Stock 2**
1	5
2	4
3	3
4	2
5	1

D.

% Return	
Stock 1	**Stock 2**
5	5
1	3
4	3
2	0
3	5

E.

% Return	
Stock 1	**Stock 2**
5	4
1	3
4	1
2	0
3	5

The Three Rules of Two-Risky-Assets Portfolios

Suppose a proportion denoted by w_B is invested in the bond fund, and the remainder $1 - w_B$, denoted by w_S, is invested in the stock fund. The properties of the portfolio are determined by the following three rules, which apply the rules of statistics governing combinations of random variables:

> *Rule 1: The rate of return on the portfolio is a weighted average of the returns on the component securities, with the investment proportions as weights.*

$$r_P = w_B r_B + w_S r_S \qquad \text{(6.4)}$$

> *Rule 2: The expected rate of return on the portfolio is a weighted average of the expected returns on the component securities, with the same portfolio proportions as weights. In symbols, the expectation of Equation 6.4 is*

$$E(r_P) = w_B E(r_B) + w_S E(r_S) \qquad \text{(6.5)}$$

The first two rules are simple linear expressions. This is not so in the case of the portfolio variance, as the third rule shows.

> *Rule 3: The variance of the rate of return on the two-risky-asset portfolio is*

$$\sigma_P^2 = (w_B \sigma_B)^2 + (w_S \sigma_S)^2 + 2(w_B \sigma_B)(w_S \sigma_S)\rho_{BS} \qquad \text{(6.6)}$$

> *where ρ_{BS} is the correlation coefficient between the returns on the stock and bond funds. Notice that using Equation 6.3, we may replace the last term in Equation 6.6 with $2w_B w_S Cov(r_B, r_S)$.*

The variance of the portfolio is a *sum* of the contributions of the component security variances *plus* a term that involves the correlation coefficient (and hence, covariance) between the returns on the component securities. We know from the last section why this last term arises. If the correlation between the component securities is small or negative, then there will be a greater tendency for the variability in the returns on the two assets to offset each other. This will reduce portfolio risk. Notice in Equation 6.6 that portfolio variance is lower when the correlation coefficient is lower.

The formula describing portfolio variance is more complicated than that describing portfolio return. This complication has a virtue, however: namely, the tremendous potential for gains from diversification.

The Risk-Return Trade-Off with Two-Risky-Assets Portfolios

We can assess the benefit from diversification by using Rules 2 and 3 to compare the risk and expected return of a better-diversified portfolio to a less-diversified benchmark. Suppose an investor estimates the following input data:

$$E(r_B) = 5\% \quad \sigma_B = 8\% \quad E(r_S) = 10\% \quad \sigma_S = 19\% \quad \rho_{BS} = .2$$

Currently, all funds are invested in the bond fund, but the invester ponders a portfolio invested 40% in stock and 60% in bonds. Using Rule 2, the expected return of this portfolio is

$$E(r_P) = .4 \times 10\% + .6 \times 5\% = 7\%$$

which represents a gain of 2% compared to a bond-only investment. Using Rule 3, the portfolio standard deviation is

$$\sigma = \sqrt{(.4 \times 19)^2 + (.6 \times 8)^2 + 2(.4 \times 19) \times (.6 \times 8) \times .2} = 9.76\%$$

Had we mistakenly computed the portfolio standard deviation as the weighted average of the component standard deviations, we would have concluded that it is $.4 \times 19 + .6 \times 8 = 12.40\%$, rather than the correct value of 9.76%. The difference of 2.64% reflects the benefits of diversification. This benefit is cost-free in the sense that diversification allows us to experience the full contribution of the stock's higher expected return, while keeping the portfolio standard deviation below the average of the component standard deviations.

EXAMPLE 6.2	Suppose we invest 85% in bonds and only 15% in stocks. We can construct a portfolio with an expected return higher than bonds (.85 × 5) + (.15 × 10) = 5.75% and, at the same time, a standard deviation less than bonds. Using Equation 6.6 again, we find that the portfolio variance is
Benefits from Diversification	$$(.85 \times 8)^2 + (.15 \times 19)^2 + 2(.85 \times 8)(.15 \times 19) \times .2 = 62.1$$

and, accordingly, the portfolio standard deviation is $\sqrt{62.1} = 7.88\%$, which is less than the standard deviation of either bonds or stocks alone. Taking on a more volatile asset (stocks) actually reduces portfolio risk! Such is the power of diversification.

We can find investment proportions that will reduce portfolio risk even further. The risk-minimizing proportions are 90.7% in bonds and 9.3% in stocks.[1] With these proportions,

---

[1] The minimum-variance portfolio minimizes the variance (and hence standard deviation) of returns, regardless of the expected return. The formula for the weight in bonds is $w_B = \dfrac{\sigma_S^2 - \sigma_B \sigma_S \rho_{BS}}{\sigma_S^2 + \sigma_B^2 - 2\sigma_B \sigma_S \rho_{BS}}$, and the weight in stocks is $w_S = 1 - w_B$. Notice that when correlation is zero, the variance-minimizing weight simplifies to the ratio of stock variance to the sum of the variances of stocks and bonds: $w_B = \dfrac{\sigma_S^2}{\sigma_S^2 + \sigma_B^2}$.

SPREADSHEET 6.5

The investment opportunity set with the stock and bond funds

	A	B	C	D	E
1			Input Data		
2	$E(r_S)$	$E(r_B)$	σ_S	σ_B	ρ_{BS}
3	10	5	19	8	0.2
4	Portfolio Weights		Expected Return, $E(r_p)$		Std Dev
5	$w_S = 1 - w_B$	w_B	Col A*A3 + Col B*B3		(Equation 6.6)
6	−0.2	1.2	4.0		9.59
7	−0.1	1.1	4.5		8.62
8	0.0	1.0	5.0		8.00
9	0.0932	0.9068	5.5		7.804
10	0.1	0.9	5.5		7.81
11	0.2	0.8	6.0		8.07
12	0.3	0.7	6.5		8.75
13	0.4	0.6	7.0		9.77
14	0.5	0.5	7.5		11.02
15	0.6	0.4	8.0		12.44
16	0.7	0.3	8.5		13.98
17	0.8	0.2	9.0		15.60
18	0.9	0.1	9.5		17.28
19	1.0	0.0	10.0		19.00
20	1.1	−0.1	10.5		20.75
21	1.2	−0.2	11.0		22.53
22	Notes:				
23	1. Negative weights indicate short positions.				
24	2. The weights of the minimum-variance portfolio are computed using the formula in Footnote 1.				

eXcel

**Please visit us at
www.mhhe.com/bkm**

the portfolio standard deviation will be 7.80%, and the portfolio's expected return will be 5.47%.

Is this portfolio preferable to the one considered in Example 6.2, with 15% in the stock fund? That depends on investor preferences, because the portfolio with the lower variance also has a lower expected return.

What the analyst can and must do, however, is to show investors the entire **investment opportunity set.** This is the set of all attainable combinations of risk and return offered by portfolios formed using the available assets in differing proportions. We find the investment opportunity set using Spreadsheet 6.5. Columns A and B set out several different proportions for investments in the stock and bond funds. The next columns present the portfolio expected return and standard deviation corresponding to each allocation. These risk-return combinations are plotted in Figure 6.3.

investment opportunity set

Set of available portfolio risk-return combinations.

The Mean-Variance Criterion

Investors desire portfolios that lie to the "northwest" in Figure 6.3. These are portfolios with high expected returns (toward the "north" of the figure) and low volatility (to the "west"). These preferences mean that we can compare portfolios using a *mean-variance criterion* in the following way. Portfolio A is said to dominate portfolio B if all investors prefer A over B. This will be the case if it has higher mean return and lower variance or standard deviation:

$$E(r_A) \geq E(r_B) \quad \text{and} \quad \sigma_A \leq \sigma_B$$

Graphically, if the expected return and standard deviation combination of each portfolio were plotted in Figure 6.3, portfolio A would lie to the northwest of B. Given a choice between portfolios A and B, *all* investors would choose A. For example, the stock fund in Figure 6.3 dominates portfolio Z; the stock fund has higher expected return and lower volatility.

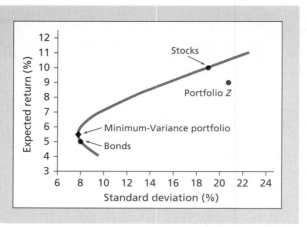

Portfolios that lie below the minimum-variance portfolio in the figure can therefore be rejected out of hand as inefficient. Any portfolio on the downward sloping portion of the curve (including the bond fund) is "dominated" by the portfolio that lies directly above it on the upward-sloping portion of the curve since that portfolio has higher expected return and equal standard deviation. The best choice among the portfolios on the upward-sloping portion of the curve is not as obvious, because in this region higher expected return is accompanied by greater risk. We will discuss the best choice when we introduce the risk-free asset to the portfolio decision.

So far we have assumed a correlation of .2 between stock and bond returns. We know that low correlations aid diversification and that a higher correlation coefficient results in a reduced effect of diversification. What are the implications of perfect positive correlation between bonds and stocks?

A correlation coefficient of 1.0 simplifies Equation 6.6 for portfolio variance. Looking at it again, you will see that substitution of $\rho_{BS} = 1$ in Equation 6.6 allows us to "complete the square" of the quantities $w_B\sigma_B$ and $w_S\sigma_S$ to obtain

$$\sigma_P^2 = w_B^2\sigma_B^2 + w_S^2\sigma_S^2 + 2w_B\sigma_B w_S\sigma_S = (w_B\sigma_B + w_S\sigma_S)^2$$

$$\sigma_P = w_B\sigma_B + w_S\sigma_S$$

The portfolio standard deviation is a weighted average of the component security standard deviations only in the special case of perfect positive correlation. In this circumstance, there are no gains to be had from diversification. Whatever the proportions of stocks and bonds, both the portfolio mean and the standard deviation are simple weighted averages. Figure 6.4 shows the opportunity set with perfect positive correlation—a straight line through the component securities. No portfolio can be discarded as inefficient in this case, and the choice among portfolios depends only on risk aversion. Diversification in the case of perfect positive correlation is not effective.

Perfect positive correlation is the *only* case in which there is no benefit from diversification. Whenever $\rho < 1$, the portfolio standard deviation is less than the weighted average of the standard deviations of the component securities. Therefore, *there are benefits to diversification whenever asset returns are less than perfectly positively correlated.*

Our analysis has ranged from very attractive diversification benefits ($\rho_{BS} < 0$) to no benefits at all ($\rho_{BS} = 1.0$). For ρ_{BS} within this range, the benefits will be somewhere in between. As Figure 6.4 illustrates, $\rho_{BS} = .5$ is a lot better for diversification than perfect positive correlation and quite a bit worse than zero correlation.

A realistic correlation coefficient between stocks and bonds based on historical experience is actually around .20.

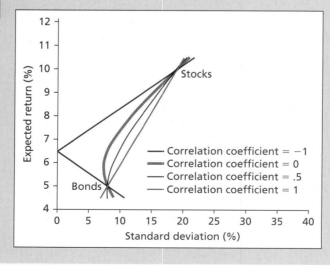

SPREADSHEET 6.6

Investment opportunity set for stocks and bonds with various correlation coefficients

	A	B	C	D	E	F	G
1		Input Data					
2	$E(r_S)$	$E(r_B)$	σ_S	σ_B			
3	10	5	19	8			
4							
5	Weights in Stocks	Portfolio Expected Return	Portfolio Standard Deviation[1] for Given Correlation, ρ				
6	w_S	$E(r_P) = $ Col A*A3 + (1 − Col A)*B3	−1	0	0.2	0.5	1
7	−0.1	4.5	10.70	9.00	8.62	8.02	6.90
8	0.0	5.0	8.00	8.00	8.00	8.00	8.00
9	0.1	5.5	5.30	7.45	7.81	8.31	9.10
10	0.2	6.0	2.60	7.44	8.07	8.93	10.20
11	0.3	6.5	0.10	7.99	8.75	9.79	11.30
12	0.4	7.0	2.80	8.99	9.77	10.83	12.40
13	0.6	8.0	8.20	11.84	12.44	13.29	14.60
14	0.8	9.0	13.60	15.28	15.60	16.06	16.80
15	1.0	10.0	19.00	19.00	19.00	19.00	19.00
16	1.1	10.5	21.70	20.92	20.75	20.51	20.10
17			Minimum-Variance Portfolio[2,3,4,5]				
18	w_S(min) = $(\sigma_B{}^2 - \sigma_B\sigma_S\rho)/(\sigma_S{}^2 + \sigma_B{}^2 - 2{*}\sigma_B\sigma_S\rho)$ =		0.2963	0.1506	0.0923	−0.0440	−0.7273
19	$E(r_P) = w_S$(min)*A3 + (1 − w_S(min))*B3 =		6.48	5.75	5.46	4.78	1.36
20		σ_P =	0.00	7.37	7.80	7.97	0.00

Notes:

1. $\sigma_P = $ SQRT[(Col A*C3)^2 + ((1 − Col A)*D3)^2 + 2*Col A*C3*(1 − Col A)*D3*ρ]

2. The standard deviation is calculated from Equation 6.6 using the weights of the miniumum-variance portfolio:

$$\sigma_P = \text{SQRT}[(w_s(\text{min})*\text{C3})^{\wedge}2 + ((1 - w_s(\text{min}))*\text{D3})^{\wedge}2 + 2*w_s(\text{min})*\text{C3}*(1 - w_s(\text{min}))*\text{D3}*\rho]$$

3. As the correlation coefficient grows, the minimum variance portfolio requires a smaller position in stocks (even a negative position for higher correlations), and the performance of this portfolio becomes less attractive.

4. Notice that with correlation of .5 or higher, minimum variance is achieved with a short position in stocks. The standard deviation is lower than that of bonds, but the mean is lower as well.

5. With perfect positive correlation (column G), you can drive the standard deviation to zero by taking a large, short position in stocks. The mean return is then as low as 1.36%.

eXcel

Please visit us at www.mhhe.com/bkm

The expected returns and standard deviations that we have so far assumed also reflect historical experience, which is why we include a graph for $\rho_{BS} = .2$ in Figure 6.4. Spreadsheet 6.6 enumerates some of the points on the various opportunity sets in Figure 6.4.

Negative correlation between a pair of assets is also possible. When correlation is negative, there will be even greater diversification benefits. Again, let us start with an extreme. With perfect negative correlation, we substitute $\rho_{BS} = -1.0$ in Equation 6.6 and simplify it in the same way as with positive perfect correlation. Here, too, we can complete the square, this time, however, with different results

$$\sigma_P^2 = (w_B\sigma_B - w_S\sigma_S)^2$$

and, therefore,

$$\sigma_P = \text{ABS}[w_B\sigma_B - w_S\sigma_S] \tag{6.7}$$

The right-hand side of Equation 6.7 denotes the absolute value of $w_B\sigma_B - w_S\sigma_S$. The solution involves the absolute value because standard deviation is never negative.

With perfect negative correlation, the benefits from diversification stretch to the limit. Equation 6.7 points to the proportions that will reduce the portfolio standard deviation all the way to zero.[2] With our data, this will happen when $w_B = 70.37\%$. While exposing us to zero risk, investing 29.63% in stocks (rather than placing all funds in bonds) will still increase

[2]The proportion in bonds that will drive the standard deviation to zero when $\rho = -1$ is

$$w_B = \frac{\sigma_S}{\sigma_B + \sigma_S}$$

Compare this formula to the formula in footnote 1 for the variance-minimizing proportions when $\rho = 0$.

the portfolio expected return from 5% to 6.48%. Of course, we can hardly expect results this attractive in reality.

Suppose that for some reason you are *required* to invest 50% of your portfolio in bonds and 50% in stocks. Use the data on mean returns and standard deviations in Spreadsheet 6.5 to answer the following questions.
  a. If the standard deviation of your portfolio is 10%, what must be the correlation coefficient between stock and bond returns?
  b. What is the expected rate of return on your portfolio?
  c. Now suppose that the correlation between stock and bond returns is .22 instead of the value you found in part (a), but that you are free to choose whatever portfolio proportions you desire. Are you likely to be better or worse off than you were in part (a)?

6.3 | The Optimal Risky Portfolio with a Risk-free Asset

Now we can expand the asset allocation problem to include a risk-free asset. Let us continue to use the input data from Spreadsheet 6.5. Suppose then that we are still confined to the risky bond and stock funds, but now can also invest in risk-free T-bills yielding 3%. When we add the risk-free asset to a stock-plus-bond risky portfolio, the resulting opportunity set is the straight line that we called the CAL (capital allocation line) in Chapter 5. We now consider various CALs constructed from risk-free bills and a variety of possible risky portfolios, each formed by combining the stock and bond funds in alternative proportions.

We start in Figure 6.5 with the opportunity set of risky assets constructed only from the bond and stock funds. The lowest-variance risky portfolio is labeled MIN (denoting the *minimum-variance portfolio*). CAL$_{MIN}$ is drawn through it and shows the risk-return trade-off with various positions in T-bills and portfolio MIN. It is immediately evident from the figure that we could do better (i.e., obtain a higher Sharpe ratio) by using portfolio A instead of MIN as the risky portfolio. CAL$_A$ dominates CAL$_{MIN}$, offering a higher expected return for any level of volatility. Spreadsheet 6.6 (see bottom panel of column E) shows that portfolio MIN's expected return is 5.46%, and its standard deviation (SD) is 7.80%. Portfolio A (row 10 in Spreadsheet 6.6) offers an expected return of 6% with an SD of 8.07%.

The slope of the CAL is the Sharpe ratio of the risky portfolio, that is, the ratio of excess return to standard deviation:

$$S_P = \frac{E(r_P) - r_f}{\sigma_P} \qquad (6.8)$$

FIGURE 6.5

The opportunity set of stocks, bonds, and a risk-free asset with two capital allocation lines

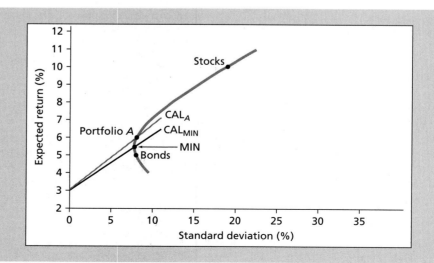

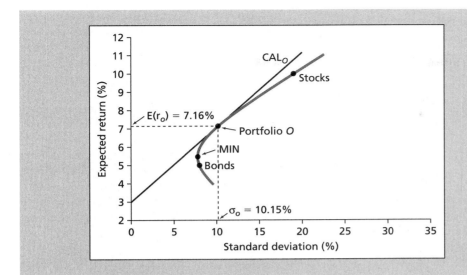

FIGURE 6.6

The optimal capital allocation line with bonds, stocks, and T-bills.

This is the rate at which the investor can increase expected return by accepting higher portfolio volatility. With a T-bill rate of 3% we obtain the Sharpe ratio of the two portfolios:

$$S_{MIN} = \frac{5.46 - 3}{7.80} = .32 \qquad S_A = \frac{6 - 3}{8.07} = .37 \qquad \textbf{(6.9)}$$

The higher ratio for portfolio A compared to MIN measures the improvement it offers in the risk-return trade-off.

But why stop at portfolio A? We can continue to ratchet the CAL upward until it reaches the ultimate point of tangency with the investment opportunity set. This must yield the CAL with the highest feasible reward-to-volatility ratio. Therefore, the tangency portfolio (O) in Figure 6.6 is the **optimal risky portfolio** to mix with T-bills, which may be defined as the risky portfolio resulting in the highest possible CAL.

Figure 6.6 clearly shows the improvement in the risk-return trade-off obtained with CAL_O. For any portfolio standard deviation, CAL_O offers a higher expected return than would be attainable using portfolios constructed only from the stock or bond fund (i.e., from the opportunity set constructed only from the two risky portfolios).

To find the composition of the optimal risky portfolio, O, we search for weights in the stock and bond funds that maximize the portfolio's Sharpe ratio. With only two risky assets, we can solve for the optimal portfolio weights using the following formula:

optimal risky portfolio

The best combination of risky assets to be mixed with safe assets to form the complete portfolio.

$$w_B = \frac{[E(r_B) - r_f]\sigma_S^2 - [E(r_S) - r_f]\sigma_B \sigma_S \rho_{BS}}{[E(r_B) - r_f]\sigma_S^2 + [E(r_S) - r_f]\sigma_B^2 - [E(r_B) - r_f + E(r_S) - r_f]\sigma_B \sigma_S \rho_{BS}}$$

$$w_S = 1 - w_B \qquad \textbf{(6.10)}$$

Using the risk premiums (expected excess return over the risk-free rate) of the stock and bond funds, their standard deviations, as well as the correlation between their returns in Equation 6.10, we find that the weights of the optimal portfolio are $w_B(O) = .568$ and $w_S(O) = .432$. Using these weights, Equations 6.5, 6.6, and 6.8 imply that $E(r_O) = 7.16\%$, $\sigma_O = 10.15\%$ and therefore, that the Sharpe ratio of the optimal portfolio (the slope of its CAL) is

$$S_O = \frac{E(r_O) - r_f}{\sigma_O} = \frac{7.16 - 3}{10.15} = .41$$

This Sharpe ratio is significantly higher than those provided by either the bond or stock portfolios alone.

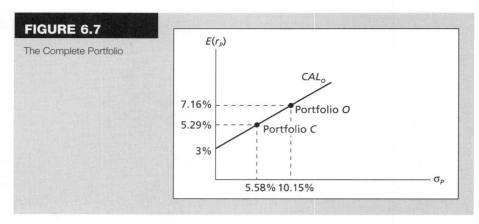

In the last chapter we saw that the preferred *complete* portfolio formed from a risky portfolio and a risk-free asset depends on the investor's risk aversion. More risk-averse investors prefer low-risk portfolios despite the lower expected return, while more risk-tolerant investors choose higher-risk, higher-return portfolios. Both investors, however, will choose portfolio *O* as their risky portfolio since that portfolio results in the highest return per unit of risk, that is, the steepest capital allocation line. Investors will differ only in their allocation of investment funds between portfolio *O* and the risk-free asset.

Figure 6.7 shows one possible choice for the preferred complete portfolio, *C*. The investor places 55% of wealth in portfolio *O* and 45% in Treasury bills. The rate of return and volatility of the portfolio are

$$E(r_C) = 3 + .55 \times (7.16 - 3) = 5.29\%$$
$$\sigma_C = .55 \times 10.15 = 5.58\%$$

We found above that the optimal risky portfolio *O* is formed by mixing the bond fund and stock fund with weights of 56.8% and 43.2%. Therefore, the overall asset allocation of the *complete* portfolio is as follows:

Weight in risk-free asset		45.00%
Weight in bond fund	.568 × 55% =	31.24
Weight in stock fund	.432 × 55% =	23.76
Total		100.00%

Figure 6.8 depicts the overall asset allocation. The allocation reflects considerations of both efficient diversification (the construction of the optimal risky portfolio, *O*) and risk aversion (the allocation of funds between the risk-free asset and the risky portfolio *O* to form the complete portfolio, *C*).

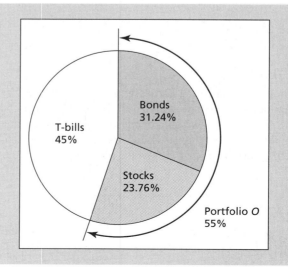

A universe of securities includes a risky stock (X), a stock index fund (M), and T-bills. The data for the universe are:

	Expected Return	Standard Deviation
X	15%	50%
M	10	20
T-bills	5	0

The correlation coefficient between X and M is $-.2$.

a. Draw the opportunity set of securities X and M.
b. Find the optimal risky portfolio (O), its expected return, standard deviation, and Sharpe ratio. Compare with the Sharpe ratio of X and M.
c. Find the slope of the CAL generated by T-bills and portfolio O.
d. Suppose an investor places 2/9 (i.e., 22.22%) of the complete portfolio in the risky portfolio O and the remainder in T-bills. Calculate the composition of the complete portfolio, its expected return, SD, and Sharpe ratio.

6.4 Efficient Diversification With Many Risky Assets

We can extend the two-risky-assets portfolio construction methodology to cover the case of many risky assets and a risk-free asset. First, we offer an overview. As in the two-risky-assets example, the problem has three separate steps. To begin, we identify the best possible or most *efficient* risk-return combinations available from the universe of risky assets. Next we determine the optimal portfolio of risky assets by finding the portfolio that supports the steepest CAL (i.e., maximizes its Sharpe ratio). Finally, we choose an appropriate complete portfolio on CAL_O based on the investor's risk aversion by mixing the risk-free asset with the optimal risky portfolio.

The Efficient Frontier of Risky Assets

To get a sense of how additional risky assets can improve the investor's investment opportunities, look at Figure 6.9. Points *A, B,* and *C* represent the expected returns and standard deviations of three stocks. The curve passing through *A* and *B* shows the risk-return combinations of all the portfolios that can be formed by combining those two stocks. Similarly, the curve passing through *B* and *C* shows all the portfolios that can be formed from those two stocks. Now observe point *E* on the *AB* curve and point *F* on the *BC* curve. These points represent two portfolios chosen from the set of *AB* combinations and *BC* combinations. The curve that passes through *E* and *F* in turn represents all the portfolios that can be constructed from portfolios *E* and *F*. Since *E* and *F* are themselves constructed from *A, B,* and *C,* this curve also may be viewed as depicting some of the portfolios that can be constructed from these *three* securities. Notice that curve *EF* extends the investment opportunity set to the northwest, which is the desired direction.

Now we can continue to take other points (each

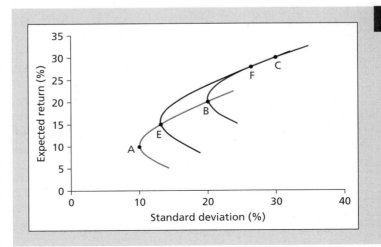

representing portfolios) from these three curves and further combine them into new portfolios, thus shifting the opportunity set even farther to the northwest. You can see that this process would work even better with more stocks. Moreover, the efficient frontier, the boundary or "envelope" of all the curves thus developed, will lie quite away from the individual stocks in the northwesterly direction, as shown in Figure 6.10.

The analytical technique to derive the efficient frontier of risky assets was developed by Harry Markowitz at the University of Chicago in 1951 and ultimately earned him the Nobel Prize in Economics. We will sketch his approach here.

First, we determine the risk-return opportunity set. The aim is to construct the northwestern-most portfolios in terms of expected return and standard deviation from the universe of securities. The inputs are the expected returns and standard deviations of each asset in the universe, along with the correlation coefficients between each pair of assets. These data come from security analysis, to be discussed in Part Four. The graph that connects all the northwesternmost portfolios is called the **efficient frontier** of risky assets. It represents the set of portfolios that offers the highest possible expected rate of return for each level of portfolio standard deviation. These portfolios may be viewed as efficiently diversified. One such frontier is shown in Figure 6.10.

efficient frontier

Graph representing a set of portfolios that maximizes expected return at each level of portfolio risk.

Any *individual* asset ends up inside the efficient frontier, because single-asset portfolios are inefficient—they are not efficiently diversified.

When we choose among portfolios on the efficient frontier, we can immediately discard portfolios below the minimum-variance portfolio. These are dominated by portfolios on the upper half of the frontier with equal risk but higher expected returns. Therefore, the real choice is among portfolios on the efficient frontier above the minimum-variance portfolio.

Various constraints may preclude a particular investor from choosing portfolios on the efficient frontier, however. If an institution is prohibited by law from taking short positions in any asset, for example, the portfolio manager must add constraints to the computer-optimization program that rule out negative (short) positions.

Short sale restrictions are only one possible constraint. Some clients may want to assure a minimum level of expected dividend yield. In this case, input data must include a set of expected dividend yields. The optimization program is made to include a constraint to ensure that the expected *portfolio* dividend yield will equal or exceed the desired level. Another common constraint forbids investments in companies engaged in "undesirable social activity." This constraint implies that portfolio weights in these companies must equal zero.

In principle, portfolio managers can tailor an efficient frontier to meet any particular objective. Of course, satisfying constraints carries a price tag. An efficient frontier subject to a number of constraints will offer a lower reward-to-volatility (Sharpe) ratio than a less constrained one. Clients should be aware of this cost and may want to think twice about constraints that are not mandated by law.

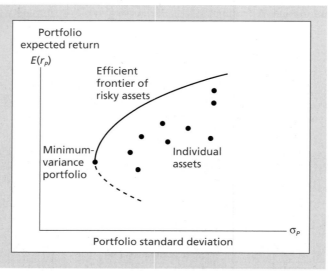

FIGURE 6.10

The efficient frontier of risky assets and individual assets

Portfolio expected return $E(r_P)$

Efficient frontier of risky assets

Minimum-variance portfolio

Individual assets

Portfolio standard deviation σ_P

Deriving the efficient frontier and graphing it with any number of assets and any set of constraints is quite straightforward. For a not-too-large number of assets, the efficient frontier can be computed and graphed even with a spreadsheet program.

The spreadsheet program, available at **www.mhhe.com/ bkm**, can easily incorporate restrictions against short sales, which is a constraint imposed on some portfolio managers. To impose this restriction, the program simply requires that each weight in the optimal portfolio be greater than or equal to zero.

Efficient Frontier For Many Stocks

Excel spreadsheets can be used to construct an efficient frontier for a group of individual securities or a group of portfolios of securities. The Excel model "Efficient Portfolio" is built using a sample of actual returns on stocks that make up a part of the Dow Jones Industrial Average Index. The efficient frontier is graphed, similar to Figure 6.10, using various possible target returns. The model is built for eight securities and can be easily modified for any group of eight assets.

Please visit us at
www.mhhe.com/bkm

	A	B	C	D	E	F	G	H	I
3	TKR SYM	Return	S.D.						
4	C	46.6	34.8						
5	GE	37.3	25.0						
6	HD	41.8	31.4						
7	INTC	46.0	45.9						
8	JNJ	24.6	26.2						
9	MRK	32.6	31.0						
10	SBC	19.0	28.1						
11	WMT	41.2	31.4						
12									
13				Correlation Matrix					
14									
15		C	GE	HD	INTC	JNJ	MRK	SBC	WMT
16	C	1.00	0.54	0.26	0.26	0.35	0.29	0.25	0.40
17	GE	0.54	1.00	0.58	0.26	0.29	0.20	0.34	0.52
18	HD	0.26	0.58	1.00	-0.09	-0.02	-0.12	0.15	0.58
19	INTC	0.26	0.26	-0.09	1.00	0.09	0.11	-0.05	-0.02
20	JNJ	0.35	0.29	-0.02	0.09	1.00	0.58	0.28	0.28
21	MRK	0.29	0.20	-0.12	0.11	0.58	1.00	0.37	0.12
22	SBC	0.25	0.34	0.15	-0.05	0.28	0.37	1.00	0.16
23	WMT	0.40	0.52	0.58	-0.02	0.28	0.12	0.16	1.00
24									
25				Covariance Matrix					
26		C	GE	HD	INTC	JNJ	MRK	SBC	WMT
27	C	1211.55	468.81	282.30	419.81	320.52	308.52	239.86	440.95
28	GE	468.81	627.47	451.99	299.86	189.64	158.28	240.96	409.29
29	HD	282.30	451.99	983.39	-133.54	-17.19	-117.25	133.28	566.72
30	INTC	419.81	299.86	-133.54	2106.34	113.73	151.78	-63.77	-34.46
31	JNJ	320.52	189.64	-17.19	113.73	686.88	473.15	203.37	229.77
32	MRK	308.52	158.28	-117.25	151.78	473.15	961.63	324.53	119.16
33	SBC	239.86	240.96	133.28	-63.77	203.37	324.53	790.22	140.90
34	WMT	440.95	409.29	566.72	-34.46	229.77	119.16	140.90	987.13

One way to see whether the short-sale constraint actually matters is to find the efficient portfolio without it. If one or more of the weights in the optimal portfolio turn out negative, we know the short-sale restrictions will result in a different efficient frontier with a less attractive risk-return trade-off.

Choosing the Optimal Risky Portfolio

The second step of the optimization plan involves the risk-free asset. Using the current risk-free rate, we search for the capital allocation line with the highest Sharpe ratio (the steepest slope), as shown in Figures 6.5 and 6.6.

The CAL formed from the optimal risky portfolio (*O*) will be tangent to the efficient frontier of risky assets discussed above. This CAL dominates all feasible CALs. Portfolio *O*, therefore, is the optimal risky portfolio. This step is also within the capability of a spreadsheet program.

The Preferred Complete Portfolio and the Separation Property

Finally, in the third step, the investor chooses the appropriate mix between the optimal risky portfolio (*O*) and T-bills, exactly as in Figure 6.7.

A portfolio manager will offer the same risky portfolio (*O*) to all clients, no matter what their degrees of risk aversion. Risk aversion comes into play only when clients select their desired point on the CAL. More risk-averse clients will invest more in the risk-free asset and less in the optimal risky portfolio *O* than less risk-averse clients, but both will use portfolio *O* as the optimal risky investment vehicle.

This result is called a **separation property,** introduced by James Tobin (1958), the 1983 Nobel Laureate for Economics: It implies that portfolio choice can be separated into two

separation property

The property that implies portfolio choice can be separated into two independent tasks: (1) determination of the optimal risky portfolio, which is a purely technical problem, and (2) the personal choice of the best mix of the risky portfolio and the risk-free asset.

independent tasks. The first task, which includes steps one and two, determination of the optimal risky portfolio (O), is purely technical. Given the particular input data, the best risky portfolio is the same for all clients regardless of risk aversion. The second task, construction of the complete portfolio from bills and portfolio O, however, depends on personal preference. Here the client is the decision maker.

Of course, the optimal risky portfolio for different clients may vary because of portfolio constraints such as dividend yield requirements, tax considerations, or other client preferences. Our analysis, though, suggests that a few portfolios may be sufficient to serve the demands of a wide range of investors. We see here the theoretical basis of the mutual fund industry.

If the optimal portfolio is the same for all clients, professional management is more efficient and less costly. One management firm can serve a number of clients with relatively small incremental administrative costs.

The (computerized) optimization technique is the easiest part of portfolio construction. If different managers use different input data to develop different efficient frontiers, they will offer different "optimal" portfolios. Therefore, the real arena of the competition among portfolio managers is in the sophisticated security analysis that underlies their choices. The rule of GIGO (garbage in–garbage out) applies fully to portfolio selection. If the quality of the security analysis is poor, a passive portfolio such as a market index fund can yield better results than an active portfolio tilted toward *seemingly* favorable securities.

Constructing the Optimal Risky Portfolio: An Illustration

To illustrate how the optimal risky portfolio might be constructed, suppose an analyst wished to construct an efficiently diversified global portfolio using the stock market indices of seven countries. The top panel of Table 6.1 shows the input list for the construction of the optimal portfolio. These inputs are estimated from recent historical data. Examination of the column presenting each country's risk premium (expected excess return), standard deviation, and Sharpe ratio shows the U.S. index portfolio has the highest Sharpe ratio. Given these data, one might be tempted to conclude (incorrectly) that, perhaps, U.S. investors would not benefit from international diversification during this period. The correlation coefficients between pairs of country returns are quite high, ranging from .43 (for Japan-U.S. and Japan-Germany), to .96 (France-Germany). In particular, with the exception of Japan, correlations of U.S. index returns with the other six countries are all at least .79. This casts further doubt on the value of international diversification to U.S. investors. But even in this sample period, we will see that diversification is beneficial.

Panel B presents 12 points on the efficient frontier, each found by choosing a target risk premium (line 1) and using Excel to find the minimum possible standard deviation consistent with that return. (In this panel, we allow short positions, i.e., negative weights in particular indices.) Each of the 10 numbered points corresponds to one portfolio on the efficient frontier, with portfolio weights also given in Panel B. In addition, the panel presents both the minimum-variance portfolio (labeled Min-Var), which is found by minimizing the portfolio volatility regardless of risk premium, and the optimal risky portfolio (labeled Optimal), which is constructed by maximizing the Sharpe ratio regardless of both risk premium and variance.

The first three lines of Panel B show the risk premium, standard deviation, and Sharpe ratio of each frontier portfolio. The Sharpe ratio initially increases as we consider frontier portfolios with higher risk premiums, ultimately peaking at the optimal portfolio. Beyond that point, the Sharpe ratio declines. Despite the apparent superiority of the U.S. market-index portfolio, efficiently mixing it with portfolios representing the other six countries allows us to increase the Sharpe ratio from .40 to .41.

Notice the portfolio weights shown in Panel B. The weight of the U.S. index in the optimal portfolio is 70.2%, while the weights on the indices of France (-9.3%) and Canada ($-.9\%$) are negative. The standard deviation of the minimum-variance portfolio, 11.32%, is considerably lower than any country's index. Despite the fact that the U.S. index has the smallest standard deviation among countries, its weight in the minimum-variance portfolio (61.1%) is smaller than its weight in the optimal portfolio. The minimum-variance portfolio entails a greater number of and more extreme short positions, for example, in France (-21%), Germany (-51%), and Canada (-4%).

The CAL using this frontier is shown in Panel C. Each point is the risk premium-standard deviation pair corresponding to a position mixing T-bills with the optimal risky portfolio in

TABLE 6.1
Efficient frontiers and a CAL for international diversification with and without short sales

A. Input list

Excess Returns

	Mean	SD	Sharpe Ratio
U.S.	0.0600	0.1495	0.4013
U.K.	0.0530	0.1493	0.3551
France	0.0700	0.2008	0.3485
Germany	0.0800	0.2270	0.3525
Australia	0.0580	0.1617	0.3587
Japan	0.0450	0.1878	0.2397
Canada	0.0590	0.1727	0.3417

Correlation Matrix

	U.S.	U.K.	France	Germany	Australia	Japan	Canada
U.S.	1						
U.K.	0.83	1					
France	0.83	0.92	1				
Germany	0.85	0.88	0.96	1			
Australia	0.81	0.84	0.80	0.82	1		
Japan	0.43	0.44	0.47	0.43	0.49	1	
Canada	0.79	0.80	0.79	0.78	0.84	0.49	1

B. Efficient frontier—short sales allowed

Portfolio:	(1)	(2)	Min-Var	(3)	(4)	(5)	(6)	Optimal	(7)	(8)	(9)	(10)
Risk premium	0.0350	0.0375	0.0383	0.0400	0.0450	0.0500	0.0550	0.0564	0.0575	0.0600	0.0700	0.0800
Std Dev	0.1141	0.1133	0.1132	0.1135	0.1168	0.1238	0.1340	0.1374	0.1401	0.1466	0.1771	0.2119
Slope (Sharpe)	0.3066	0.3310	0.3386	0.3525	0.3853	0.4037	0.4104	0.4107	0.4106	0.4092	0.3953	0.3774
Portfolio weights												
U.S.	0.5944	0.6070	0.6112	0.6195	0.6446	0.6696	0.6947	0.7018	0.7073	0.7198	0.7699	0.8201
U.K.	1.0175	0.9129	0.8778	0.8083	0.5992	0.3900	0.1809	0.1214	0.0758	−0.0283	−0.4465	−0.8648
France	−0.2365	−0.2197	−0.2140	−0.2029	−0.1693	−0.1357	−0.1021	−0.0928	−0.0852	−0.0685	−0.0014	0.0658
Germany	−0.6077	−0.5344	−0.5097	−0.4610	−0.3144	−0.1679	−0.0213	0.0205	0.0524	0.1253	0.4185	0.7117
Australia	0.0588	0.0668	0.0695	0.0748	0.0907	0.1067	0.1226	0.1271	0.1306	0.1385	0.1704	0.2023
Japan	0.2192	0.2090	0.2055	0.1987	0.1781	0.1575	0.1369	0.1311	0.1266	0.1164	0.0752	0.0341
Canada	−0.0459	−0.0416	−0.0402	−0.0374	−0.0288	−0.0203	−0.0118	−0.0093	−0.0075	−0.0032	0.0139	0.0309

C. Capital allocation line (CAL)

| Risk premium | 0.0000 | 0.0465 | 0.0465 | 0.0466 | 0.0480 | 0.0509 | 0.0550 | 0.0564 | 0.0575 | 0.0602 | 0.0727 | 0.0871 |
| Std Dev | 0.0000 | 0.1133 | 0.1132 | 0.1135 | 0.1168 | 0.1238 | 0.1340 | 0.1374 | 0.1401 | 0.1466 | 0.1771 | 0.2199 |

D. Efficient frontier—no short sales

			Min-Var					Optimal				
Risk premium	0.0450	0.0475	0.0500	0.0525	0.0536	0.0550	0.0564	0.0575	0.0600	0.0700	0.0700	0.0800
Std Dev	0.1878	0.1555	0.1396	0.1355	0.1351	0.1358	0.1378	0.1401	0.1467	0.1813	0.1813	0.2270
Slope (Sharpe)	0.2397	0.3055	0.3582	0.3875	0.3965	0.4049	0.4094	0.4104	0.4089	0.3862	0.3862	0.3525
Portfolio weights												
U.S.	0.0000	0.0000	0.0115	0.2692	0.3785	0.5122	0.6157	0.6948	0.6932	0.5000	0.5000	0.0000
U.K.	0.0000	0.3125	0.6034	0.4328	0.3604	0.2551	0.1366	0.0459	0.0000	0.0000	0.0000	0.0000
France	0.0000	0.0000	0.0000	0.0000	0.0000	0.0000	0.0000	0.0000	0.0000	0.0000	0.0000	0.0000
Germany	0.0000	0.0000	0.0000	0.0000	0.0000	0.0000	0.0000	0.0000	0.0885	0.5000	0.5000	1.0000
Australia	0.0000	0.0000	0.0000	0.0000	0.0000	0.0211	0.0842	0.1326	0.1158	0.0000	0.0000	0.0000
Japan	1.0000	0.6875	0.3851	0.2980	0.2611	0.2115	0.1635	0.1268	0.1026	0.0000	0.0000	0.0000
Canada	0.0000	0.0000	0.0000	0.0000	0.0000	0.0000	0.0000	0.0000	0.0000	0.0000	0.0000	0.0000

FIGURE 6.11

Efficient frontiers and
CAL from Table 6.1

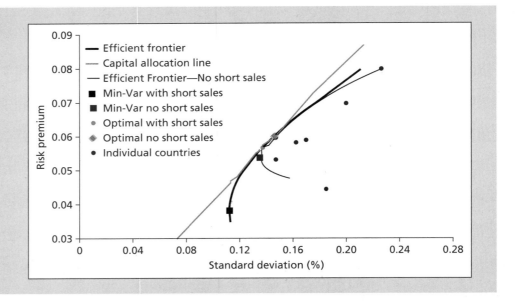

various proportions. We show risk-return pairs for the standard deviations corresponding to the 12 portfolios in Panel B.[3] The CAL is tangent to the efficient frontier at the optimal portfolio, and so has the same risk premium. But for any other standard deviation, the CAL lies *above* the efficient frontier, providing a higher risk premium for any standard deviation.

Panel D repeats this analysis, but with the additional constraint that no portfolio weights may be negative, that is, ruling out short sales. The extra constraint is costly, in that the efficient frontier constructed without short sales lies below and to the right of the unconstrained frontier. For any risk premium, it entails higher volatility. For example, compare the standard deviation of the minimum-variance portfolio in Panel D, 13.5%, to the value obtained in Panel B where short positions were allowed, 11.3%. The weight in the U.S. in this portfolio is 38%, considerably lower than its weight in the unconstrained minimum-variance portfolio from Panel B, and four country indexes are eliminated (that is, they receive zero weights in the portfolio). Despite this, short-sale restrictions do not greatly affect the performance of the optimal portfolio in this particular example, largely because of the dominant role of the U.S. index in the optimal risky portfolio. The weight in the U.S. index in the no-short-sale optimal portfolio, 69.3%, is almost identical to its weight in the unconstrained optimal portfolio, 70.2%.

Figure 6.11 shows this analysis graphically. The black circles are the standard deviation-risk premium pairs for each individual country index. The individual country portfolios (although each well diversified within that country), lie well inside the frontier and therefore offer inferior risk-return combinations. Even in this unusual case, where one asset (the U.S. index) offers a far better risk-return trade-off than any other individual country index, further diversification still improves performance. Observe that while the presence or absence of short-sale constraints results in large differences in frontiers, the tangency points in this period result in surprisingly similar optimal portfolios and CALs. This would not be expected as a general outcome. Finally, notice that an efficient frontier disallowing short sales starts with the security with the lowest risk premium and ends with the asset with the highest risk premium.

CONCEPT
check   **6.5**

Two portfolio managers work for competing investment management houses. Each employs security analysts to prepare input data for the construction of the optimal portfolio. When all is completed, the efficient frontier obtained by manager *A* dominates that of manager *B* in that *A*'s optimal risky portfolio lies northwest of *B*'s. Is the more attractive efficient frontier asserted by manager *A* evidence that she really employs better security analysts?

[3]Portfolio (1) is on the inefficient portion of the frontier. We replace it in Panel C with a point corresponding to risk-free T-bills. Notice that the risk premium corresponding to a standard deviation of zero is also zero. This would correspond to a portfolio invested fully in bills. The portfolio would earn the risk-free rate or, equivalently, a risk premium of zero.

6.5 | A Single-Index Asset Market

We started this chapter with the distinction between systematic and firm-specific risk. Systematic risk is largely macroeconomic, affecting all securities, while firm-specific risk factors affect only one particular firm or, perhaps, its industry. **Index models** are statistical models designed to estimate these two components of risk for a particular security or portfolio. The first to use an index model to explain the benefits of diversification was another Nobel Prize winner, William F. Sharpe (1963). We will introduce his major work (the capital asset pricing model) in the next chapter.

The popularity of index models is due to their practicality. To construct the efficient frontier from a universe of 100 securities, we would need to estimate 100 expected returns, 100 variances, and $100 \times 99/2 = 4,950$ covariances. And a universe of 100 securities is actually quite small. A universe of 1,000 securities would require estimates of $1,000 \times 999/2 = 499,500$ covariances, as well as 1,000 expected returns and variances. Assuming that one common factor is responsible for all the covariability of stock returns, with all other variability due to firm-specific factors, dramatically simplifies the analysis.

Let us use R_i to denote the **excess return** on a security, that is, the rate of return in excess of the risk-free rate: $R_i = r_i - r_f$. Then we can express the distinction between macroeconomic and firm-specific factors by decomposing this excess return in some holding period into three components:[4]

$$R_i = \beta_i R_M + e_i + \alpha_i \qquad \text{(6.11)}$$

The first two terms on the right-hand side of Equation 6.11 reflect the impact of two sources of uncertainty. R_M is the excess return on a broad market index (the S&P 500 is commonly used for this purpose), so variation in this term reflects the influence of economy wide or macroeconomic events that generally affect all stocks to greater or lesser degrees. The security's **beta,** β_i, is the typical response of that particular stock's excess return to changes in the market index's excess return. As such, beta measures a stock's comparative sensitivity to macroeconomic news. A value greater than 1 would indicate a stock with greater sensitivity to the economy than the average stock in the market. These are known as cyclical stocks. Betas less than 1 indicate below-average sensitivity and therefore are known as defensive stocks. Recall that the risk attributable to the stock's exposure to uncertain market returns is called market or *systematic* risk, because it relates to the uncertainty that pervades the whole economic system.

The second source of uncertainty, represented by the term e_i in Equation 6.11, is the impact of unanticipated firm-specific events, sometimes called **firm-specific risk** or **residual risk.** The expected value of e_i is zero, as the impact of unanticipated events must average out to zero. Firm-specific and systematic risk each contribute to the total volatility of returns.

The last term in Equation 6.11 is not a risk measure. Instead, α_i represents the expected return on the stock *beyond* any return induced by movements in the market index. This term is called the security **alpha.** A positive alpha is attractive to investors and suggests an underpriced security: Among securities with identical sensitivity (beta) to the market index, securities with higher alpha values will offer higher expected returns. Conversely, stocks with negative alphas are apparently overpriced; for any value of beta, they offer lower expected returns.

In sum, the index model separates the realized rate of return on a security into macro (systematic) and micro (firm-specific) components. The excess rate of return on each security is the sum of three components:

---

index model

Model that relates stock returns to returns on both a broad market index as well as firm-specific influences.

excess return

Rate of return in excess of the risk-free rate.

beta

The sensitivity of a security's returns to the systematic or market factor.

firm-specific or residual risk

Component of return variability that is independent of broad market movements.

alpha

A stock's expected return beyond that induced by the broad market; its expected excess return when the market's excess return is zero.

---

[4]Equation 6.11 is surprisingly simple and would appear to require very strong assumptions about security market equilibrium. But, in fact, if rates of return are normally distributed, then returns will be linear in one or more indexes. Statistics theory tells us that, when rates of return on a set of securities are *joint-normally* distributed, then the rate of return on each asset is linear in one identical index as in Equation 6.11. When rates of return exhibit a multivariate normal distribution, we can use a multi-index generalization of Equation 6.11. Practitioners employ index models such as 6.11 extensively because of the ease of use as we just noted, but they would not do so unless empirical evidence supported them. We emphasize that the usefulness of these index models is independent of the particular models of risk and return discussed in the next chapter. Hence, it is logical to introduce factor models in this chapter prior to a discussion of equilibrating forces and their potential impact on expected returns of various securities.

	Symbol
1. The component of return due to movements in the overall market (as represented by the index R_M); β_i is the security's responsiveness to the market.	$\beta_i R_M$
2. The component attributable to unexpected events that are relevant only to this security (firm-specific).	e_i
3. The stock's expected excess return if the market factor is neutral, that is, if the market's excess return is zero.	α_i

Equation 6.11 specifies two sources of security risk: market or systematic risk ($\beta_i R_M$), attributable to the security's sensitivity (as measured by beta) to movements in the overall market, and firm-specific risk (e_i), which is the part of uncertainty independent of the market factor. Because the firm-specific component of the firm's return is uncorrelated with the market return, we can write the variance of the excess return of the stock as[5]

$$
\begin{aligned}
\text{Variance } (R_i) &= \text{Variance } (\alpha_i + \beta_i R_M + e_i) \\
&= \text{Variance } (\beta_i R_M) + \text{Variance } (e_i) \\
&= \beta_i^2 \sigma_M^2 \qquad\qquad + \sigma^2(e_i) \\
&= \text{Systematic risk} + \text{Firm-specific risk}
\end{aligned}
\tag{6.12}
$$

Therefore, the total variability of the rate of return of each security depends on two components:

1. The variance attributable to the uncertainty common to the entire market. This systematic risk is attributable to the uncertainty in R_M. Notice that the systematic risk of each stock depends on both the volatility in R_M (that is, σ_M^2) *and* the sensitivity of the stock to fluctuations in R_M. That sensitivity is measured by β_i.

2. The variance attributable to firm-specific risk factors, the effects of which are measured by e_i. This is the variance in the part of the stock's return that is independent of market performance.

This single-index model is convenient. It relates security returns to a market index that investors follow. Moreover, as we soon shall see, its usefulness goes beyond mere convenience.

Statistical and Graphical Representation of the Single-Index Model

Equation 6.11, $R_i = \alpha_i + \beta_i R_M + e_i$, may be interpreted as a single-variable *regression equation* of R_i on the market excess return R_M. The excess return on the security (R_i) is the dependent variable that is to be explained by the regression. On the right-hand side of the equation are the intercept α_i; the regression (or slope) coefficient beta, β_i, multiplying the independent (or explanatory) variable R_M; and the security residual (unexplained) return, e_i. We can plot this regression relationship as in Figure 6.12, which shows a possible scatter diagram for Dell's excess return against the excess return of the market index.

The horizontal axis of the scatter diagram measures the explanatory variable, here the market excess return, R_M. The vertical axis measures the dependent variable, here Dell's excess return, R_D. Each point on the scatter diagram represents a sample pair of returns (R_M, R_D) that might be observed for a particular holding period. Point T, for instance, describes a holding period when the excess return was 17% on the market index and 27% on Dell.

Regression analysis lets us use the sample of historical returns to estimate a relationship between the dependent variable and the explanatory variable. The regression line in Figure 6.12 is drawn so as to minimize the sum of all the squared deviations around it. Hence, we say the regression line "best fits" the data in the scatter diagram. The line is called the **security characteristic line,** or SCL.

The regression intercept (α_D) is measured from the origin to the intersection of the regression line with the vertical axis. Any point on the vertical axis represents zero market excess return, so the intercept gives us the *expected excess* return on Dell during the sample period when

security characteristic line

Plot of a security's excess return as a function of the excess return of the market.

---

[5]Notice that because α_i is a constant, it has no bearing on the variance of R_i.

market performance was neutral. The intercept in Figure 6.12 is about 4.5%.

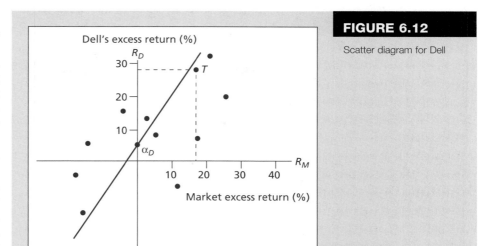

FIGURE 6.12

Scatter diagram for Dell

The slope of the regression line can be measured by dividing the rise of the line by its run. It also is called the regression coefficient or the slope coefficient or simply the beta. In Figure 6.12, Dell's beta is 1.4. The regression beta is a natural measure of systematic risk since it predicts the typical response of the security return to market fluctuations. In particular, it measures the extra return the security will typically exhibit for each extra 1% return on the market index.

The regression line does not represent the *actual* returns; that is, the points on the scatter diagram almost never lie on the regression line, although the actual returns are used to calculate the regression coefficients. Rather, the line represents average tendencies; it shows the effect of the index return on our *expectation* of R_D. The algebraic representation of the regression line is

$$E(R_D | R_M) = \alpha_D + \beta_D R_M \qquad \text{(6.13)}$$

which reads: The expectation of R_D *given* a value of R_M equals the intercept plus the slope coefficient times the given value of R_M.

Because the regression line represents expectations, and because these expectations may not be realized in any or all of the *actual* returns (as the scatter diagram shows), the *actual* security returns also include a residual, the firm-specific surprise, e_i. This surprise (at point *T*, for example) is measured by the vertical distance between the point of the scatter diagram and the regression line. For example, the expected return on Dell, given a market return of 17%, would have been 4.5% + 1.4 × 17% = 28.3%. The actual return was only 27%, so point *T* falls below the regression line by 1.3%.

Equation 6.12 shows that the greater the beta of a security, that is, the greater the slope of the regression, the greater the security's systematic risk, as well as its total variance. The *average security* has a slope coefficient (beta) of 1.0: Because the market is composed of all securities, the typical response to a market movement must be one for one. An "aggressive" investment will have a beta higher than 1.0; that is, the security has above-average market risk.[6] Conversely, securities with betas lower than 1.0 are called defensive.

A security may have a negative beta. Its regression line will then slope downward, meaning that, for more favorable macro events (higher R_M), we would expect a *lower* return, and vice versa. The latter means that when the macro economy goes bad (negative R_M) and securities with positive beta are expected to have negative excess returns, the negative-beta security will shine. The result is that a negative-beta security has *negative* systematic risk, that is, it provides a hedge against systematic risk.

The dispersion of the scatter of actual returns about the regression line is determined by the residual variance $\alpha^2(e_D)$, which measures the effects of firm-specific events. The magnitude of firm-specific risk varies across securities. One way to measure the relative importance of systematic risk is to measure the ratio of systematic variance to total variance.

[6]Note that the average beta of all securities will be 1.0 only when we compute a *weighted* average of betas (using market values as weights), since the stock market index is value weighted. We know from Chapter 5 that the distribution of securities by market value is not symmetric: There are relatively few large corporations and many more smaller ones. Thus, if you were to take a randomly selected sample of stocks, you should expect smaller companies to dominate. As a result, the simple average of the betas of individual securities, when computed against a value-weighted index such as the S&P 500, will be greater than 1.0, pushed up by the tendency for stocks of low-capitalization companies to have betas greater than 1.0.

FIGURE 6.13

Various scatter diagrams

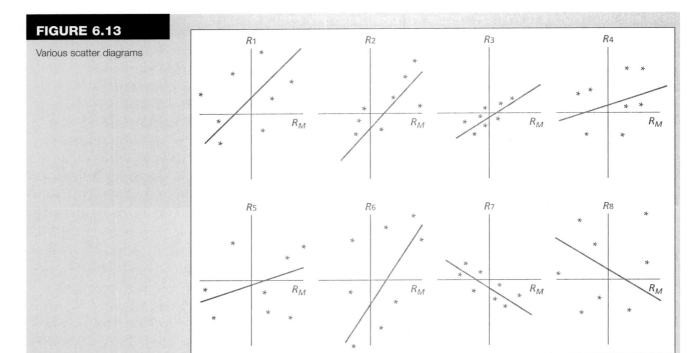

$$\rho^2 = \frac{\text{Systematic (or explained) variance}}{\text{Total variance}}$$
$$= \frac{\beta_D^2 \sigma_M^2}{\sigma_D^2} = \frac{\beta_D^2 \sigma_M^2}{\beta_D^2 \sigma_M^2 + \sigma^2(e_D)} \tag{6.14}$$

where ρ is the correlation coefficient between R_D and R_M. Its square measures the ratio of explained variance to total variance, that is, the proportion of total variance that can be attributed to market fluctuations. But if beta is negative, so is the correlation coefficient, an indication that the explanatory and dependent variables are expected to move in opposite directions.

At the extreme, when the correlation coefficient is either 1.0 or −1.0, the security return is fully explained by the market return, that is, there are no firm-specific effects. All the points of the scatter diagram will lie exactly on the line. This is called perfect correlation (either positive or negative); the return on the security is perfectly predictable from the market return. A large correlation coefficient (in absolute value terms) means systematic variance dominates the total variance; that is, firm-specific variance is relatively unimportant. When the correlation coefficient is small (in absolute value terms), the market factor plays a relatively unimportant part in explaining the variance of the asset, and firm-specific factors dominate.

CONCEPT
c.h.e.c.k **6.6**

Interpret the eight scatter diagrams of Figure 6.13 in terms of systematic risk, diversifiable risk, and the intercept.

Example 6.3 on the following page illustrates how you can use a spreadsheet to estimate the single-index model from historical data.

Diversification in a Single-Index Security Market

Imagine a portfolio that is divided equally among securities whose returns are given by the single-index model in Equation 6.11. What are the systematic and nonsystematic (firm-specific) variances of this portfolio?

The beta of the portfolio is the simple average of the individual security betas, which we denote β. Hence, the systematic variance equals $\beta_P^2 \sigma_M^2$. This is the level of market risk in Figure 6.1B. The market variance (σ_M^2) and the market sensitivity of the portfolio (β_P) determine the market risk of the portfolio.

The systematic component of each security return, $\beta_i R_M$, is fully determined by the market factor and therefore is perfectly correlated with the systematic part of any other security's return. Hence, there are no diversification effects on systematic risk no matter how many securities are involved. As far as *market risk* goes, a single-security portfolio with a small beta will result in a low market-risk portfolio. The number of securities makes no difference.

EXAMPLE 6.3

Estimating the Index Model Using Historical Data

The direct way to calculate the slope and intercept of the characteristic lines for ABC and XYZ is from the variances and covariances. Here, we use the Data Analysis menu of Excel to obtain the covariance matrix in the following spreadsheet.

The slope coefficient for ABC is given by the formula

$$\beta_{ABC} = \frac{Cov(R_{ABC}, R_{Market})}{Var(R_{Market})} = \frac{773.31}{669.01} = 1.156$$

The intercept for ABC is

$$\alpha_{ABC} = Average(R_{ABC}) - \beta_{ABC} \times Average(R_{Market})$$
$$= 15.20 - 1.156 \times 9.40 = 4.33$$

Therefore, the security characteristic line of ABC is given by

$$R_{ABC} = 4.33 + 1.156 R_{Market}$$

This result also can be obtained by using the "Regression" command from Excel's Data Analysis menu, as we show at the bottom of the spreadsheet. The minor differences between the direct regression output and our calculations above are due to rounding error.

	A	B	C	D	E	F	G	H	I
2			**Annualized Rates of Return**					**Excess Returns**	
3	Week	ABC	XYZ	Mkt. Index	Risk free		ABC	XYZ	Market
4	1	65.13	-22.55	64.40	5.23		59.90	-27.78	59.17
5	2	51.84	31.44	24.00	4.76		47.08	26.68	19.24
6	3	-30.82	-6.45	9.15	6.22		-37.04	-12.67	2.93
7	4	-15.13	-51.14	-35.57	3.78		-18.91	-54.92	-39.35
8	5	70.63	33.78	11.59	4.43		66.20	29.35	7.16
9	6	107.82	32.95	23.13	3.78		104.04	29.17	19.35
10	7	-25.16	70.19	8.54	3.87		-29.03	66.32	4.67
11	8	50.48	27.63	25.87	4.15		46.33	23.48	21.72
12	9	-36.41	-48.79	-13.15	3.99		-40.40	-52.78	-17.14
13	10	-42.20	52.63	20.21	4.01		-46.21	48.62	16.20
14	**Average:**						**15.20**	**7.55**	**9.40**
15									
16	**COVARIANCE MATRIX**								
17		ABC	XYZ	Market					
18	ABC	3020.933							
19	XYZ	442.114	1766.923						
20	Market	773.306	396.789	669.010					
21									
22	**SUMMARY OUTPUT OF EXCEL REGRESSION**								
23									
24	Regression Statistics								
25	Multiple R	0.544							
26	R-Square	0.296							
27	Adj. R-Square	0.208							
28	Standard Error	48.918							
29	Observations	10.000							
30									
31									
32		Coefficients	Std. Error	t-Stat	p-value				
33	Intercept	4.336	16.564	0.262	0.800				
34	Market return	1.156	0.630	1.834	0.104				
35									

Note: This is the output provided by the Data Analysis tool in Excel. As a technical aside, we should point out that the covariance matrix produced by Excel does not adjust for degrees of freedom. In other words, it divides total squared deviations from the sample average (for variance) or total cross product of deviations from sample averages (for covariance) by total observations, despite the fact that sample averages are estimated parameters. This procedure does not affect regression coefficients, however, because in the formula for beta, both the numerator (i.e., the covariance) and denominator (i.e., the variance) are affected equally.

It is quite different with firm-specific or unique risk. If you choose securities with small residual variances for a portfolio, it, too, will have low unique risk. But you can do even better simply by holding more securities, even if each has a large residual variance. Because the firm-specific effects are independent of each other, their risk effects are offsetting. This is the insurance principle applied to the firm-specific component of risk. The portfolio ends up with a negligible level of nonsystematic risk.

In sum, when we control the systematic risk of the portfolio by manipulating the average beta of the component securities, the number of securities is of no consequence. But for *nonsystematic* risk, the number of securities involved is more important than the firm-specific variance of the securities. Sufficient diversification can virtually eliminate firm-specific risk. Understanding this distinction is essential to understanding the role of diversification in portfolio construction.

We have just seen that when forming highly diversified portfolios, firm-specific risk becomes *irrelevant*. Only systematic risk remains. We conclude that in measuring security risk for diversified investors, we should focus our attention on the security's systematic risk. This means that for diversified investors, the relevant risk measure for a security will be the security's beta, β, since firms with higher β have greater sensitivity to broad market disturbances. As Equation 6.12 makes clear, systematic risk will be determined both by market volatility, σ_M^2, and the firm's sensitivity to the market, β.

CONCEPT
check **6.7**

a. What is the characteristic line of XYZ in Example 6.3?
b. Does ABC or XYZ have greater systematic risk?
c. What proportion of the variance of XYZ is firm-specific risk?

Using Security Analysis with the Index Model

Imagine that you are a portfolio manager in charge of the endowment of a small charity. Absent the resources to engage in security analysis, you would choose a passive portfolio comprising one or more index funds. Denote this portfolio as M. You estimate its standard deviation as σ_M and acquire a forecast of its risk premium as R_M. Now you find that you have sufficient resources to perform fundamental analysis on one stock, say Google. You forecast Google's risk premium as R_G, and estimate its beta (β_G) and residual SD, $\sigma(e_G)$, against the benchmark portfolio M. How should you proceed?

Since you do not know the efficient frontier of all risky assets, all you can do is compute the efficient frontier that can be constructed using the benchmark passive portfolio and Google, and then construct the optimal portfolio (with the highest Sharpe ratio) using the methodology developed in Section 6.1. You know that the variance of Google is $\sigma_G^2 = \beta_G^2 \sigma_M^2 + \sigma^2(e_G)$, and using the variance of M and the risk premiums of M and G you can use Equation 6.10 to accomplish the task. But it turns out that you can more easily use the index model for the same purpose.

Notice that your forecast of R_G implies that $\alpha_G = R_G - \beta_G R_M$. It turns out that there are two key statistics to obtain the optimal portfolio, specifically, R_M/σ_M^2 and $\alpha_G/\sigma^2(e_G)$. When we compute

$$w_G^0 = \frac{\alpha_G/\sigma^2(e_G)}{R_M/\sigma_M^2} \qquad (6.15)$$

the weights of Google and the benchmark portfolio M in the optimal risky portfolio, O, are

$$w_G^* = \frac{w_G^0}{1 + w_G^0(1 - \beta_G)} \qquad w_M^* = 1 - w_G^* \qquad (6.16)$$

The Sharpe measure of this portfolio exceeds that of the passive portfolio M, S_M, according to

$$S_O^2 - S_M^2 = \left(\frac{\alpha_G}{\sigma(e_G)}\right)^2 \qquad (6.17)$$

We see that the improvement over the passive benchmark is determined by the ratio $\alpha_G/\sigma(e_G)$, which is called Google's **information ratio.** Using the index model in this way is called the Treynor-Black model, after Fischer Black and Jack Treynor who first proposed this approach in 1973.

The value of the Treynor-Black model becomes dramatic when you analyze more than one stock. To compute the optimal portfolio comprising the benchmark portfolio and two or more stocks (therefore, three or more risky assets), you would need to use the involved Markowitz methodology of Section 6.3. But with the Treynor-Black model, the task is quite straightforward. You can view Google in the previous discussion as your **active portfolio.** Now if instead of Google alone you had analyzed several stocks, a portfolio of these stocks would make up your active portfolio, which then would be mixed with the passive index. You would then use the alpha, beta, and residual SD of the active portfolio in Equations 6.15–6.17 to obtain the weights of the optimal portfolio, O, and its Sharpe ratio. Thus, the only task left is to determine the exact composition of the active portfolio, as well as its alpha, beta, and residual standard deviation.

Now suppose that in addition to your analysis for Google, you also analyze Dell's stock (D) and estimate its alpha, beta, and residual variance. You calculate the ratio for Google $\alpha_G/\sigma^2(e_G)$, the corresponding ratio for Dell, and the sum of these ratios for all stocks in the active portfolio. In this example, with two stocks,

$$\sum_i \alpha_i/\sigma^2(e_i) = \alpha_G/\sigma^2(e_G) + \alpha_D/\sigma^2(e_D)$$

Treynor and Black showed that the optimal weight of each security in the active portfolio should be

$$w_G(\text{active}) = \frac{\alpha_G/\sigma^2(e_G)}{\sum_i \alpha_i/\sigma^2(e_i)} \qquad w_D(\text{active}) = \frac{\alpha_D/\sigma^2(e_D)}{\sum_i \alpha_i/\sigma^2(e_i)} \qquad \textbf{(6.18)}$$

Notice that the active portfolio entails two offsetting considerations. On the one hand, a stock with a higher alpha value calls for a high weight to take advantage of its attractive expected return. On the other hand, a high residual variance leads us to temper our position in the stock to avoid bearing firm-specific risk.

The alpha and beta of the active portfolio are weighted averages of each component stock's alpha and beta, and the residual variance is the weighted sum of each stock's residual variance, using the squared portfolio weights:

$$\alpha_A = w_{GA}\alpha_{GA} + w_{DA}\alpha_{DA} \qquad \beta_A = w_{GA}\beta_{GA} + w_{DA}\beta_{DA}$$
$$\sigma^2(e_A) = w_{GA}^2\sigma^2(e_G) + w_{DA}^2\sigma^2(e_D) \qquad \textbf{(6.19)}$$

Given these parameters, we can now use Equations 6.15–6.17 to determine the weight of the active portfolio in the optimal portfolio, and the Sharpe ratio it achieves.

information ratio

Ratio of alpha to standard deviation of residual return.

active portfolio

The portfolio formed by optimally combining analyzed stocks with perceived non-zero alpha values.

EXAMPLE 6.5

The Treynor-Black Model

Suppose your benchmark portfolio is the S&P 500 Index. The input list in Panel A of Table 6.2 includes the data for the passive index as well as the two stocks, Google and Dell. Both stocks have positive alpha values, so you would expect the optimal portfolio to be tilted toward these stocks. However, the tilt will be limited to avoid excessive exposure to otherwise-diversifiable firm-specific risk. The optimal trade-off maximizes the Sharpe ratio. We use the Treynor-Black model to accomplish this task.

We begin in Panel B assuming that the *active portfolio* comprises solely Google, which has an information ratio of .115. This "portfolio" is then combined with the passive index to form the optimal risky portfolio as in Equations 6.15–6.17. The calculations in Table 6.2 show that the optimal portfolio achieves a Sharpe ratio of .20, compared with .16 for the passive benchmark. This optimal portfolio is invested 43.64% in Google and 56.36% in the benchmark.

In Panel C, we add Dell to the list of actively analyzed stocks. The optimal weights of each stock in the active portfolio are 55.53% in Google and 44.47% in Dell. This gives the active portfolio an information ratio of .14, which improves the Sharpe ratio of the optimal portfolio to .24. The optimal portfolio invests 91.73% in the active portfolio and 8.27% in the index. This large tilt is acceptable because the residual standard deviation of the active portfolio (6.28%) is far less than that of either stock. Finally, the optimal portfolio weight in Google is 50.94% and in Dell, 40.79%. Notice that the weight in Google is now *larger* than its weight without Dell! This, too, is a result of diversification within the active position that allows a larger tilt toward Google's large alpha.

TABLE 6.2

Construction of optimal portfolios using the index model

Input List

		Active Portfolio	
	Benchmark Portfolio (S&P 500)	Google	Dell
A. Input data			
Risk premium	0.7	2.20	1.74
Standard deviation	4.31	11.39	10.49
Sharpe ratio	0.16	not applicable	
Alpha		1.04	0.75
Beta		1.65	1.41
Residual standard deviation		9.01	8.55
Information ratio = alpha/residual SD		0.1154	0.0877
Alpha/residual variance		0.0128	0.0103

Portfolio Construction

B. Optimal portfolio with Google only in active portfolio

Performance data			
Sharpe ratio = SQRT (index Sharpe^2 + Google information ratio^2)	0.20		
Composition of optimal portfolio			
w^0 = (alpha/residual SD)/(index risk premium/ index variance)		0.3400	
$w^* = w^0/(1 + w^0(1 - beta))$	0.5636	0.4364	

C. Optimal portfolio with Google and Dell in the active portfolio

		Google	Dell	Active Portfolio (sum)
Composition of the active portfolio				
w^0 of stock (Equation 6.15)		0.3400	0.2723	0.6122
w^0/Sum w^0 of analyzed stocks		0.5553	0.4447	1.0000
Performance of the active portfolio				
alpha = weight in active portfolio × stock alpha		0.58	0.33	0.91
beta = weight in active portfolio × stock beta		0.92	0.63	1.54
Residual variance = square weight × stock residual variance		25.03	14.46	39.49
Residual SD = SQRT (active portfolio residual variance)				6.28
Information ratio = active portfolio alpha/ residual SD				0.14
Performance of the optimal portfolio				
Sharpe ratio	0.24			

	Index	Active		
Composition of optimal portfolio				
w^0		0.6122		
w^*	0.0827	0.9173		

		Google	Dell
Weight of active portfolio × weight of stock in active portfolio		0.5094	0.4079

Please visit us at
www.mhhe.com/bkm

6.6 Risk of Long-term Investments

So far we have envisioned portfolio investment for one period. We have not made any explicit assumptions about the duration of that period, so one might take it to be of any length, and thus our analysis would seem to apply as well to long-term investments. Yet investors are frequently advised that stock investments for the long run are not as risky as it might appear from the statistics presented in this chapter and the previous one. To understand this widespread misconception, we must first understand how the argument goes.

Are Stock Returns Less Risky in the Long Run?

Advocates of the notion that investment risk is lower over longer horizons apply the logic of diversification across many risky *assets* to an investment in a risky portfolio over many *years*. Because stock returns in successive years are almost uncorrelated, they conclude that (1) the annual standard deviation of an investment in stocks falls with the investment horizon and, hence, (2) investment risk in a stock portfolio declines with the investment horizon.

To be concrete, consider a two-year investment for which the rate of return in each year is normally distributed with an identical standard deviation of σ, and for which the returns in different years are uncorrelated with each other, so that $Cov(r_1, r_2) = 0$. The total rate of return over the two years[7] is: $r(2 \text{ years}) = r_1 + r_2$. The variance of the total return over the two years equals

$$
\begin{aligned}
\text{Var(2-year total return)} &= \text{Var}(r_1 + r_2) \\
&= \text{Var}(r_1) + \text{Var}(r_2) + 2\,\text{Cov}(r_1, r_2) \\
&= \sigma^2 \quad + \quad \sigma^2 \quad + \quad 0 \\
&= 2\sigma^2 \tag{6.20}
\end{aligned}
$$

The standard deviation is the square root of the variance, so

$$
\text{Standard deviation(2-year total return)} = \sigma\sqrt{2}
$$

Thus, the variance of the total two-year return is double that of the one-year return, and the standard deviation is higher by a multiple of $\sqrt{2}$. Generalizing to an investment horizon of n years, the variance and standard deviation of the total return over n years will grow to:

$$
\text{Var}(n\text{-year total return}) = n\sigma^2
$$

$$
\text{Standard deviation}(n\text{-year total return}) = \sigma\sqrt{n} \tag{6.21}
$$

To put the standard deviation of *total* return on a per-year or annualized basis, we divide the standard deviation by the number of years, n, to obtain:

$$
\sigma(\text{annualized for an } n\text{-year investment}) = \frac{1}{n}\sigma\sqrt{n} = \frac{\sigma}{\sqrt{n}} \tag{6.22}
$$

In fact, this result seems identical to the annual standard deviation of an equally weighted portfolio diversified across n uncorrelated stocks, all with a common standard deviation, σ.

[7]To account for compounding of rates over the years, these rates must be viewed as continuously compounded returns, as explained in Chapter 5.

To illustrate, consider a portfolio of two identical, uncorrelated stocks. Since the stocks are identical, the efficient portfolio will be equally weighted. Applying Equation 6.6 with weights of $w_A = w_B = \frac{1}{2}$,

$$\sigma_P^2 = (\tfrac{1}{2})^2\sigma_A^2 + (\tfrac{1}{2})^2\sigma_B^2 + 2[\tfrac{1}{2}\,\sigma_A][\tfrac{1}{2}\,\sigma_B]\rho_{AB} \tag{6.23}$$

If each stock has identical standard deviation, then $\sigma_A = \sigma_B = \sigma$, and if they are uncorrelated, then $\rho_{AB} = 0$. In this case, therefore,

$$\sigma_P^2 = 2 \times (\tfrac{1}{2})^2\sigma^2 = \tfrac{1}{2}\sigma^2$$

$$\sigma_P = \sigma\sqrt{\tfrac{1}{2}}$$

Similarly for n stocks, with portfolio weights of $1/n$ in each stock,

$$\sigma_P = \frac{\sigma}{\sqrt{n}} \tag{6.24}$$

In fact, we used Equation 6.24 to draw Figure 6.1A illustrating diversification with uncorrelated stocks. Since the annual standard deviation of a portfolio diversified across n identical, uncorrelated stocks in Equation 6.24 is similar to the annualized standard deviation of a stock portfolio invested over n years (Equation 6.22), there is a temptation (to which many financial advisers have succumbed) to interpret the latter as evidence of "time diversification" and conclude that risk over the long haul declines with investment horizon. By this reasoning, Figure 6.1A would seem to apply to time diversification as well, if you replace the number of stocks on the horizontal axis with the number of years. If this were true, time diversification would be very comforting to the many long-term investors who should, by this logic, replace safe investments with risky investments in stocks. Unfortunately, however, the logic is flawed.

The Fly in the "Time Diversification" Ointment (or More Accurately, the Snake Oil)

The flaw in the logic is the use of the annualized standard deviation to gauge the risk of a long-term investment. Annualized standard deviation is an appropriate measure of risk *only* for annual horizon portfolios! It cannot serve to measure risk when comparing investments of different horizons and different scales.

To illustrate with a simple example, suppose that investors can invest in safe bonds, and that the rate of return on all bonds is zero. The value of a stock portfolio in any year will either double or fall by one-half with equal probability. Our investor considers two strategies:

A. Short-term risky strategy:

Invest the entire budget in stocks for one year, then liquidate and invest the proceeds in a safe bond for the second year.

B. Long-term risky strategy:

Invest the entire budget in stocks for two years. The possible outcomes to this strategy are: quadrupling of value (doubling in each year), unchanged value (doubling in one year and halving in the other), or value falling by a factor of ¼ (halving in each year).

The following table compares the probability distributions of final outcomes of the two investments.

A. One Year in Stocks		B. Two Years in Stocks	
Possible Outcome	**Probability**	**Possible Outcome**	**Probability**
Value doubles	.5	Value quadruples	.25
Value falls by half	.5	Value unchanged	.5
		Value falls by 75%	.25

Since risk aversion makes investors concerned with downside risk, you can see that the two strategies cannot be compared on the basis of standard deviation of annualized returns. Surely a risk-averse investor will consider the two-year investment (for which value can decline by 75%) riskier and will reject outright the notion that the two-year stock investment is less risky. Time diversification advocates will say: "But the probability of a loss is smaller, only 25%." This argument implies that, somehow, *probability* of loss is a valid measure of risk. The fact of the matter is that probability of loss alone is not a legitimate measure of risk any more than is the size of the loss alone.

The correct comparison is based on risk of the total (end of horizon) return, which accounts for both magnitudes as well as probabilities of possible losses. The variance of the total rate of return, which accounts for both, grows in direct proportion to the number of years, and the standard deviation grows in proportion to $\sqrt{n}$, as in Equation 6.21. While the average risk per year may be smaller with longer horizons as in Equation 6.22, that risk compounds for a greater number of years, which certainly makes your cumulative investment outcome riskier, as Equation 6.21 makes clear.

Empirical evidence on this debate is provided by the actual cost of portfolio insurance. Such insurance is common and we can observe the actual cost of insurance for various horizons and loss coverage. Suppose that for the two-year stock portfolio in our example, we purchase portfolio insurance against an investment loss that exceeds 50%. Such a policy will pay us 25¢ per dollar invested if the portfolio value falls by 75%, thereby equating the maximum possible loss of the two strategies. The expected loss to the insurer, per dollar of coverage, is: .25 × 25 = 6.25¢. But we observe that in capital markets, such insurance costs much more for longer horizons, which contradicts any notion that the long-term risky investment is safer than shorter-term one. Time diversification advocates consistently ignore this unshakable fact.

SUMMARY

- The expected rate of return of a portfolio is the weighted average of the component asset expected returns with the investment proportions as weights.
- The variance of a portfolio is a sum of the contributions of the component-security variances *plus* terms involving the covariance among assets.
- Even if correlations are positive, the portfolio standard deviation will be less than the weighted average of the component standard deviations, as long as the assets are not *perfectly* positively correlated. Thus, portfolio diversification is of value as long as assets are less than perfectly correlated.
- The contribution of an asset to portfolio variance depends on its correlation with the other assets in the portfolio, as well as on its own variance. An asset that is perfectly negatively correlated with a portfolio can be used to reduce the portfolio variance to zero. Thus, it can serve as a perfect hedge.
- The efficient frontier of risky assets is the graphical representation of the set of portfolios that maximizes portfolio expected return for a given level of portfolio standard deviation. Rational investors will choose a portfolio on the efficient frontier.
- A portfolio manager identifies the efficient frontier by first establishing estimates for the expected returns and standard deviations and determining the correlations among them. The input data are then fed into an optimization program that produces the investment proportions, expected returns, and standard deviations of the portfolios on the efficient frontier.

- In general, portfolio managers will identify different efficient portfolios because of differences in the methods and quality of security analysis. Managers compete on the quality of their security analysis relative to their management fees.
- If a risk-free asset is available and input data are identical, all investors will choose the same portfolio on the efficient frontier, the one that is tangent to the CAL. All investors with identical input data will hold the identical risky portfolio, differing only in how much each allocates to this optimal portfolio and to the risk-free asset. This result is characterized as the separation principle of portfolio selection.
- The single-index model expresses the excess return on a security as a function of the market excess return: $R_i = \alpha_i + \beta_i R_M + e_i$. This equation also can be interpreted as a regression of the security excess return on the market-index excess return. The regression line has intercept α_i and slope β_i and is called the security characteristic line.
- In a single-index model, the variance of the rate of return on a security or portfolio can be decomposed into systematic and firm-specific risk. The systematic component of variance equals β^2 times the variance of the market excess return. The firm-specific component is the variance of the residual term in the index model equation.
- The beta of a portfolio is the weighted average of the betas of the component securities. A security with negative beta reduces the portfolio beta, thereby reducing exposure to market volatility. The unique risk of a portfolio approaches zero as the portfolio becomes more highly diversified.

KEY TERMS

active portfolio, 173	index model, 167	optimal risky portfolio, 159
alpha, 167	information ratio, 173	residual risk, 167
beta, 167	investment opportunity	security characteristic
diversifiable risk, 146	set, 155	line, 168
efficient frontier, 162	market risk, 146	separation property, 163
excess return, 167	nondiversifiable risk, 146	systematic risk, 146
firm-specific risk, 147	nonsystematic risk, 146	unique risk, 146

PROBLEM SETS

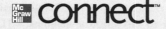

Select problems are available in McGraw-Hill Connect. Please see the packaging options section of the preface for more information.

Basic

1. In forming a portfolio of two risky assets, what must be true of the correlation coefficient between their returns if there are to be gains from diversification? Explain.

2. When adding a risky asset to a portfolio of many risky assets, which property of the asset is more important, its standard deviation or its covariance with the other assets? Explain.

3. A portfolio's expected return is 12%, its standard deviation is 20%, and the risk-free rate is 4%. Which of the following would make for the greatest increase in the portfolio's Sharpe ratio?
   a. An increase of 1% in expected return.
   b. A decrease of 1% in the risk-free rate.
   c. A decrease of 1% in its standard deviation.

4. An investor ponders various allocations to the optimal risky portfolio and risk-free T-bills to construct his complete portfolio. How would the Sharpe ratio of the complete portfolio be affected by this choice?

Intermediate

5. The standard deviation of the market index portfolio is 20%. Stock *A* has a beta of 1.5 and a residual standard deviation of 30%.
   a. What would make for a larger increase in the stock's variance: an increase of .15 in its beta or an increase of 3% in its residual standard deviation?
   b. An investor who currently holds the market-index portfolio decides to reduce the portfolio allocation to the market index to 90%, and to invest 10% in stock *A*. Which of the changes in (*a*) will have a greater impact on the portfolio's standard deviation?

6. Suppose that the returns on the stock fund presented in Spreadsheet 6.1 were −40%, −14%, 17%, and +33% in the four scenarios.
   a. Would you expect the mean return and variance of the stock fund to be more than, less than, or equal to the values computed in Spreadsheet 6.2? Why?
   b. Calculate the new values of mean return and variance for the stock fund using a format similar to Spreadsheet 6.2. Confirm your intuition from part (*a*).
   c. Calculate the new value of the covariance between the stock and bond funds using a format similar to Spreadsheet 6.4. Explain intuitively the change in the covariance.

7. Use the rate of return data for the stock and bond funds presented in Spreadsheet 6.1, but now assume that the probability of each scenario is: Severe recession: .10; Mild recession: .20; Normal growth: .35; Boom: .35.
   a. Would you expect the mean return and variance of the stock fund to be more than, less than, or equal to the values computed in Spreadsheet 6.2? Why?
   b. Calculate the new values of mean return and variance for the stock fund using a format similar to Spreadsheet 6.2. Confirm your intuition from part (*a*).
   c. Calculate the new value of the covariance between the stock and bond funds using a format similar to Spreadsheet 6.4. Explain intuitively why the absolute value of the covariance has changed.

The following data apply to Problems 8–12.

A pension fund manager is considering three mutual funds. The first is a stock fund, the second is a long-term government and corporate bond fund, and the third is a T-bill money market fund that yields a sure rate of 5.5%. The probability distributions of the risky funds are:

	Expected Return	Standard Deviation
Stock fund (S)	15%	32%
Bond fund (B)	9	23

The correlation between the fund returns is .15.

8. Tabulate and draw the investment opportunity set of the two risky funds. Use investment proportions for the stock fund of 0 to 100% in increments of 20%. What expected return and standard deviation does your graph show for the minimum-variance portfolio?

9. Draw a tangent from the risk-free rate to the opportunity set. What does your graph show for the expected return and standard deviation of the optimal risky portfolio?

10. What is the reward-to-volatility ratio of the best feasible CAL?

11. Suppose now that your portfolio must yield an expected return of 12% and be efficient, that is, on the best feasible CAL.
    a. What is the standard deviation of your portfolio?
    b. What is the proportion invested in the T-bill fund and each of the two risky funds?

12. If you were to use only the two risky funds and still require an expected return of 12%, what would be the investment proportions of your portfolio? Compare its standard deviation to that of the optimal portfolio in the previous problem. What do you conclude?

13. Stocks offer an expected rate of return of 10% with a standard deviation of 20%, and gold offers an expected return of 5% with a standard deviation of 25%.

    a. In light of the apparent inferiority of gold to stocks with respect to both mean return and volatility, would anyone hold gold? If so, demonstrate graphically why one would do so.

    b. How would you answer (a) if the correlation coefficient between gold and stocks were 1.0? Draw a graph illustrating why one would or would not hold gold. Could these expected returns, standard deviations, and correlation represent an equilibrium for the security market?

14. Suppose that many stocks are traded in the market and that it is possible to borrow at the risk-free rate, r_f. The characteristics of two of the stocks are as follows:

Stock	Expected Return	Standard Deviation
A	8%	40%
B	13	60
Correlation = −1		

Could the equilibrium r_f be greater than 10%? (*Hint:* Can a particular stock portfolio be substituted for the risk-free asset?)

Please visit us at www.mhhe.com/bkm

15. You can find a spreadsheet containing the historic returns presented in Table 5.2 on the text's Web site at **www.mhhe.com/bkm.** (Look for the link to Chapter 5 material.) Copy the data for the last 20 years into a new spreadsheet. Analyze the risk-return trade-off that would have characterized portfolios constructed from large stocks and long-term Treasury bonds over the last 20 years. What was the average rate of return and standard deviation of each asset? What was the correlation coefficient of their annual returns? What would have been the average return and standard deviation of portfolios with differing weights in the two assets? For example, consider weights in stocks starting at zero and incrementing by .10 up to a weight of 1.0. What was the average return and standard deviation of the minimum-variance combination of stocks and bonds?

16. Assume expected returns and standard deviations for all securities, as well as the risk-free rate for lending and borrowing, are known. Will investors arrive at the same optimal risky portfolio? Explain.

17. Your assistant gives you the following diagram as the efficient frontier of the group of stocks you asked him to analyze. The diagram looks a bit odd, but your assistant insists he double-checked his analysis. Would you trust him? Is it possible to get such a diagram?

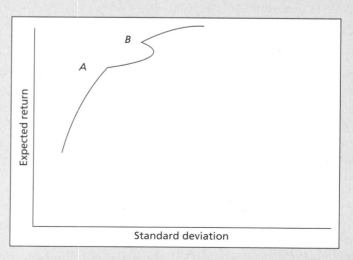

18. What is the relationship of the portfolio standard deviation to the weighted average of the standard deviations of the component assets?

19. A project has a .7 chance of doubling your investment in a year and a .3 chance of halving your investment in a year. What is the standard deviation of the rate of return on this investment?

20. Investors expect the market rate of return this year to be 10%. The expected rate of return on a stock with a beta of 1.2 is currently 12%. If the market return this year turns out to be 8%, how would you revise your expectation of the rate of return on the stock?

21. The following figure shows plots of monthly rates of return and the stock market for two stocks.
    a. Which stock is riskier to an investor currently holding her portfolio in a diversified portfolio of common stock?
    b. Which stock is riskier to an undiversified investor who puts all of his funds in only one of these stocks?

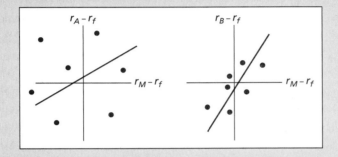

22. Go to **www.mhhe.com/bkm** and link to the material for Chapter 6, where you will find a spreadsheet containing monthly rates of return for GM, the S&P 500, and T-bills over a recent five-year period. Set up a spreadsheet just like that of Example 6.3 and find the beta of GM.

23. Here are rates of return for six months for Generic Risk, Inc. What is Generic's beta? (*Hint:* Find the answer by plotting the scatter diagram.)

Month	Market Return	Generic Return
1	0%	+2%
2	0	0
3	−1	0
4	−1	−2
5	+1	+4
6	+1	+2

Challenge

24. Go to the Online Learning Center at **www.mhhe.com/bkm**, where you will find rate of return data over 60 months for Google, the T-bill rate, and the S&P 500, which we will use as the market index portfolio.
    a. Use these data and Excel's regression function to compute Google's excess return each period as well as its alpha, beta, and residual standard deviation, $\sigma(e)$.
    b. What was the Sharpe ratio of the S&P 500 over this period?
    c. What was Google's information ratio over this period?
    d. If someone whose risky portfolio is currently invested in an index portfolio such as the S&P 500 wishes to take a position in Google based on the estimates from parts (a)–(c), what would be the optimal fraction of the risky portfolio to invest in Google? Use Equations 6.15 and 6.16.
    e. Based on Equation 6.17 and your answer to part (d), by how much would the Sharpe ratio of the optimal risky portfolio increase given the incremental position in Google?

CFA Problems

1. A three-asset portfolio has the following characteristics:

Asset	Expected Return	Standard Deviation	Weight
X	15%	22%	0.50
Y	10	8	0.40
Z	6	3	0.10

   What is the expected return on this three-asset portfolio?

2. George Stephenson's current portfolio of $2.0 million is invested as follows:

Summary of Stephenson's Current Portfolio				
	Value	Percent of Total	Expected Annual Return	Annual Standard Deviation
Short-term bonds	$ 200,000	10%	4.6%	1.6%
Domestic large-cap equities	600,000	30	12.4	19.5
Domestic small-cap equities	1,200,000	60	16.0	29.9
Total portfolio	$2,000,000	100%	13.8%	23.1%

   Stephenson soon expects to receive an additional $2.0 million and plans to invest the entire amount in an index fund that best complements the current portfolio. Stephanie Coppa, CFA, is evaluating the four index funds shown in the following table for their ability to produce a portfolio that will meet two criteria relative to the current portfolio: (1) maintain or enhance expected return and (2) maintain or reduce volatility.

   Each fund is invested in an asset class that is not substantially represented in the current portfolio.

Index Fund Characteristics			
Index Fund	Expected Annual Return	Expected Annual Standard Deviation	Correlation of Returns with Current Portfolio
Fund A	15%	25%	+0.80
Fund B	11	22	+0.60
Fund C	16	25	+0.90
Fund D	14	22	+0.65

   State which fund Coppa should recommend to Stephenson. Justify your choice by describing how your chosen fund *best* meets both of Stephenson's criteria. No calculations are required.

3. Abigail Grace has a $900,000 fully diversified portfolio. She subsequently inherits ABC Company common stock worth $100,000. Her financial adviser provided her with the following estimates:

Risk and Return Characteristics		
	Expected Monthly Returns	Standard Deviation of Monthly Returns
Original Portfolio	0.67%	2.37%
ABC Company	1.25	2.95

The correlation coefficient of ABC stock returns with the original portfolio returns is .40.

a. The inheritance changes Grace's overall portfolio and she is deciding whether to keep the ABC stock. Assuming Grace keeps the ABC stock, calculate the:

    i. Expected return of her new portfolio which includes the ABC stock.

    ii. Covariance of ABC stock returns with the original portfolio returns.

    iii. Standard deviation of her new portfolio which includes the ABC stock.

b. If Grace sells the ABC stock, she will invest the proceeds in risk-free government securities yielding .42% monthly. Assuming Grace sells the ABC stock and replaces it with the government securities, calculate the:

    i. Expected return of her new portfolio which includes the government securities.

    ii. Covariance of the government security returns with the original portfolio returns.

    iii. Standard deviation of her new portfolio which includes the government securities.

c. Determine whether the beta of her new portfolio, which includes the government securities, will be higher or lower than the beta of her original portfolio.

d. Based on conversations with her husband, Grace is considering selling the $100,000 of ABC stock and acquiring $100,000 of XYZ Company common stock instead. XYZ stock has the same expected return and standard deviation as ABC stock. Her husband comments, "It doesn't matter whether you keep all of the ABC stock or replace it with $100,000 of XYZ stock." State whether her husband's comment is correct or incorrect. Justify your response.

e. In a recent discussion with her financial adviser, Grace commented, "If I just don't lose money in my portfolio, I will be satisfied." She went on to say, "I am more afraid of losing money than I am concerned about achieving high returns." Describe *one* weakness of using standard deviation of returns as a risk measure for Grace.

The following data apply to CFA Problems 4–6:

    Hennessy & Associates manages a $30 million equity portfolio for the multimanager Wilstead Pension Fund. Jason Jones, financial vice president of Wilstead, noted that Hennessy had rather consistently achieved the best record among the Wilstead's six equity managers. Performance of the Hennessy portfolio had been clearly superior to that of the S&P 500 in four of the past five years. In the one less favorable year, the shortfall was trivial.

    Hennessy is a "bottom-up" manager. The firm largely avoids any attempt to "time the market." It also focuses on selection of individual stocks, rather than the weighting of favored industries.

    There is no apparent conformity of style among the six equity managers. The five managers, other than Hennessy, manage portfolios aggregating $250 million, made up of more than 150 individual issues.

    Jones is convinced that Hennessy is able to apply superior skill to stock selection, but the favorable results are limited by the high degree of diversification in the portfolio. Over the years, the portfolio generally held 40–50 stocks, with about 2% to 3% of total funds committed to each issue. The reason Hennessy seemed to do well most years was that the firm was able to identify each year 10 or 12 issues that registered particularly large gains.

    Based on this overview, Jones outlined the following plan to the Wilstead pension committee:

Let's tell Hennessy to limit the portfolio to no more than 20 stocks. Hennessy will double the commitments to the stocks that it really favors and eliminate the remainder. Except for this one new restriction, Hennessy should be free to manage the portfolio exactly as before.

    All the members of the pension committee generally supported Jones's proposal, because all agreed that Hennessy had seemed to demonstrate superior skill in selecting stocks. Yet, the proposal was a considerable departure from previous practice, and several committee members raised questions.

4. Answer the following:
   a. Will the limitation of 20 stocks likely increase or decrease the risk of the portfolio? Explain.
   b. Is there any way Hennessy could reduce the number of issues from 40 to 20 without significantly affecting risk? Explain.

5. One committee member was particularly enthusiastic concerning Jones's proposal. He suggested that Hennessy's performance might benefit further from reduction in the number of issues to 10. If the reduction to 20 could be expected to be advantageous, explain why reduction to 10 might be less likely to be advantageous. (Assume that Wilstead will evaluate the Hennessy portfolio independently of the other portfolios in the fund.)

6. Another committee member suggested that, rather than evaluate each managed portfolio independently of other portfolios, it might be better to consider the effects of a change in the Hennessy portfolio on the total fund. Explain how this broader point of view could affect the committee decision to limit the holdings in the Hennessy portfolio to either 10 or 20 issues.

7. Dudley Trudy, CFA, recently met with one of his clients. Trudy typically invests in a master list of 30 equities drawn from several industries. As the meeting concluded, the client made the following statement: "I trust your stock-picking ability and believe that you should invest my funds in your five best ideas. Why invest in 30 companies when you obviously have stronger opinions on a few of them?" Trudy plans to respond to his client within the context of Modern Portfolio Theory.
   a. Contrast the concepts of systematic risk and firm-specific risk, and give an example of each type of risk.
   b. Critique the client's suggestion. Discuss how both systematic and firm-specific risk change as the number of securities in a portfolio is increased.

STANDARD &POOR'S

Use data from the Standard & Poor's Market Insight Database at www.mhhe.com/edumarketinsight to answer the following questions.

1. Use data from Market Insight to plot the characteristic lines for Alcoa and Eli Lilly & Company. First locate the Market Insight page for Alcoa by clicking on the "Company" tab. (If you don't know the stock symbol, use the "Lookup" feature to find it.) Find the one-month total returns of Alcoa and the S&P 500 in the Monthly Adjusted Prices Report in the Excel Analytics, Market Data section. Download the data into Excel, and then plot the Alcoa returns vs. the S&P 500 returns. Use an XY Scatter Plot chart type, with no line joining the points. Select one of the data points, then right-click your mouse to get a shortcut menu which allows you to add a trend line. This is the characteristic line for Alcoa. Repeat the process for Eli Lilly & Company. What conclusions can you draw about Alcoa and Eli Lilly & Company based on their characteristic lines?

2. Use data from Market Insight to calculate the beta of Staples, Inc. Start by finding the monthly price changes of Staples and the S&P 500 in Monthly Adjusted Prices Report in the Excel Analytics, Market Data section. Copy the data into Excel and confirm the monthly rates of return (based on closing prices) for each series. Using the entire period for which data are available, estimate a regression with Staples' return as the dependent (Y) variable and the S&P 500 return as the independent (X) variable. Now repeat the procedure using only the most recent two years of data. Estimate a third regression using only the earliest two years of data. How stable is the beta estimate? Finally, compare your three results to the beta listed in Staples' S&P Stock Report (in the S&P Stock Reports section). Do any of your results match the S&P Report's beta? What factors might explain any differences?

3. The S&P Report gives information about the company's operations and opinions about its expected performance. Enter the symbol for Gap, Inc., and follow the link to S&P's Stock Report on the company. What companies does Gap operate? What is its weight in the S&P 500? What is the trend in Gap's earnings? What is the trend in its dividend payout ratio? Use the current price listed to calculate the holding-period return on the

stock assuming that you purchased it at the 52-week low price and that you received the specified dividends for the year. Repeat the calculation using the 52-week high price.

4. In the Excel Analytics section, find the monthly returns in the Monthly Adjusted Prices report for the following firms: Genzyme Corporation, Sony, Cardinal Health, Inc., Black & Decker Corporation, and Kellogg Company. Copy the returns from these five firms into a single Excel workbook, with the returns for each company properly aligned. Use the full range of available data. Then do the following:

   a. Using the Excel functions for average (AVERAGE) and sample standard deviation (STDEV), calculate the average and the standard deviation of the returns for each of the firms.

   b. Using Excel's correlation function (CORREL), construct the correlation matrix for the five stocks based on their monthly returns for the entire period. What are the lowest and the highest individual pairs of correlation coefficients? (*Alternative:* You may use Excel's Data Analysis Tool to generate the correlation matrix.)

WEB *master* MINIMUM VARIANCE PORTFOLIOS

There are some free online tools that will calculate the optimal asset weights and draw the efficient frontier for the assets that you specify. One of the sites is **www.investorcraft.com/PortfolioTools/EfficientFrontier.aspx.**

Go to this site and enter at least eight assets in the selection box. You can search for the companies by name or by symbol. Click on the "Next Step" button and select one of the time spans offered. Specify an appropriate risk-free rate, a minimum allowable asset weight of 0, and a maximum allowable asset weight of 100. Click on "Calculate" to get your results.

1. What are the expected return and the standard deviation of the portfolio based on adjusted weights?

2. How do they compare to those for the optimal portfolio and the minimum variance portfolio?

3. Of the three portfolios shown, with which one would you feel most comfortable as an investor?

SOLUTIONS TO CONCEPT *checks*

6.1. Recalculation of Spreadsheet 6.1, and 6.4 shows that the covariance is now −5.80 and the correlation coefficient is −.07.

	A	B	C	D	E	F
1			Stock Fund		Bond Fund	
2	Scenario	Probability	Rate of Return	Col B × Col C	Rate of Return	Col B × Col E
3	Severe recession	.05	−37.0	−1.9	−10	−0.5
4	Mild recession	.25	−11.0	−2.8	10	2.5
5	Normal growth	.40	14.0	5.6	7	2.8
6	Boom	.30	30.0	9.0	2	0.6
7	Expected or Mean Return:		SUM:	10.0	SUM:	5.4
8						
9			Deviation from Mean Return		Covariance	
10	Scenario	Probability	Stock Fund	Bond Fund	Product of Dev	Col B × Col E
11	Severe recession	.05	−47.0	−15.4	723.8	36.19
12	Mild recession	.25	−21.0	4.6	−96.6	−24.15
13	Normal growth	.40	4.0	1.6	6.4	2.56
14	Boom	.30	20.0	−3.4	−68.0	−20.40
15		SD =	18.63	4.65	Covariance =	−5.80
16		Correlation coefficient = Covariance/(StdDev(stocks)*StdDev(bonds)) =				−0.07

6.2. The scatter diagrams for pairs B–E are shown below. Scatter diagram A (presented with the Concept Check) shows an exact conflict between the pattern of points 1,2,3 versus 3,4,5. Therefore, the correlation coefficient is zero. Scatter diagram B shows perfect positive correlation (1.0). Similarly, C shows perfect negative correlation (−1.0). Now compare the scatters of D and E.

Both show a general positive correlation, but scatter D is tighter. Therefore, D is associated with a correlation of about .5 (use a spreadsheet to show that the exact correlation is .54), and E is associated with a correlation of about .2 (show that the exact correlation coefficient is .23).

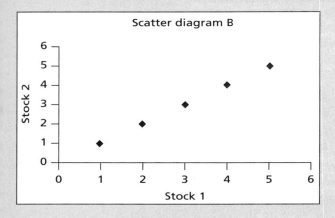

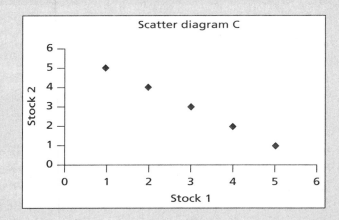

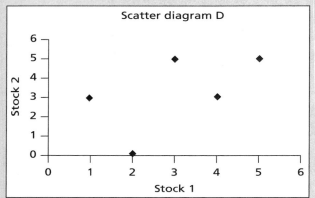

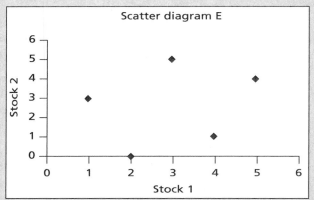

6.3. *a.* Using Equation 6.6 with the data: $\sigma_B = 8$; $\sigma_S = 19$; $w_B = .5$; and $w_S = 1 - w_B = .5$, we obtain the equation

$$\sigma_P^2 = 10^2 = (w_B\sigma_B)^2 + (w_S\sigma_S)^2 + 2(w_B\sigma_B)(w_S\sigma_S)\rho_{BS}$$
$$= (.5 \times 8)^2 + (.5 \times 19)^2 + 2(.5 \times 8)(.5 \times 19)\rho_{BS}$$

which yields $\rho = .1728$.

b. Using Equation 6.5 and the additional data: $E(r_B) = 5\%$; $E(r_S) = 10\%$, we obtain

$$E(r_P) = w_B E(r_B) + w_S E(r_S) = (.5 \times 5) + (.5 \times 10) = 7.5\%$$

c. On the one hand, you should be happier with a correlation of .17 than with .22 since the lower correlation implies greater benefits from diversification and means that, for any level of expected return, there will be lower risk. On the other hand, the constraint that you must hold 50% of the portfolio in bonds represents a cost to you since it prevents you from choosing the risk-return trade-off most suited to your tastes. Unless you would choose to hold about 50% of the portfolio in bonds anyway, you are better off with the slightly higher correlation but with the ability to choose your own portfolio weights.

6.4. *a.* Implementing Equations 6.5 and 6.6, we generate data for the graph. See Spreadsheet 6.7 and Figure 6.14 on the following pages.

b. Implementing the formulas indicated in Spreadsheet 6.6, we generate the optimal risky portfolio (*O*) and the minimum-variance portfolio.

c. The slope of the CAL is equal to the risk premium of the optimal risky portfolio divided by its standard deviation, $(11.28 - 5)/17.59 = .357$.

d. The mean of the complete portfolio is $.2222 \times 11.28 + .7778 \times 5 = 6.395\%$, and its standard deviation is $.2222 \times 17.58 = 3.91\%$. Sharpe ratio $= (6.395 - 5)/3.91 = .357$.

SPREADSHEET 6.7

For Concept Check 4. Mean and standard deviation for various portfolio applications

	A	B	C	D	E	F	G
5		Data	X	M	T-Bills		
6		Mean (%)	15	10	5		
7		Std. Dev. (%)	50	20	0		
8		Corr. Coeff. X and S		-0.20			
9		Portfolio Opportunity set					
10		Weight in X	Weight in S	Pf Mean (%)	Pf Std Dev (%)		
11		-1.00	2.00	5.00	70.00		
12		-0.90	1.90	5.50	64.44		
13		-0.80	1.80	6.00	58.92		
14		-0.70	1.70	6.50	53.45	=B13*$C$6+C13*$D$6	
15		-0.60	1.60	7.00	48.04		
16		-0.50	1.50	7.50	42.72		
17		-0.40	1.40	8.00	37.52		
18		-0.30	1.30	8.50	32.51	=(B15^2*$C$7^2	
19		-0.20	1.20	9.00	27.78	+C15^2*$D$7^2	
20		-0.10	1.10	9.50	23.52	+2*B15*C15	
21		0.00	1.00	10.00	20.00	*$C$7*$D$7*$D$8)^0.5	
22		0.10	0.90	10.50	17.69		
23		0.20	0.80	11.00	17.09		
24		0.30	0.70	11.50	18.36		
25		0.40	0.60	12.00	21.17		
26		0.50	0.50	12.50	25.00		
27		0.60	0.40	13.00	29.46		
28		0.70	0.30	13.50	34.31		
29		0.80	0.20	14.00	39.40		
30		0.90	0.10	14.50	44.64		
31		1.00	0.00	15.00	50.00		
32		1.10	-0.10	15.50	55.43		
33		1.20	-0.20	16.00	60.93		
34		1.30	-0.30	16.50	66.46		
35		1.40	-0.40	17.00	72.03		
36		1.50	-0.50	17.50	77.62		
37		1.60	-0.60	18.00	83.23		
38		1.70	-0.70	18.50	88.87		
39		1.80	-0.80	19.00	94.51		
40		1.90	-0.90	19.50	100.16		
41		2.00	-1.00	20.00	105.83		
42	Min. Var Pf	0.18	0.82	10.91	17.06		
43	Optimal Pf	0.26	0.74	11.28	17.59		
44							
45							
46		=((C6-E6)*D7^2-(D6-E6)*C7*D7*D8)/					
47		((C6-E6)*D7^2+(D6-E6)*C7^2-(C6-E6+D6-E6)*C7*D7*D8)					
48							
49							

The composition of the complete portfolio is

$.2222 \times .26 = .06$ (i.e., 6%) in X

$.2222 \times .74 = .16$ (i.e., 16%) in M

and 78% in T-bills.

6.5. Efficient frontiers derived by portfolio managers depend on forecasts of the rates of return on various securities and estimates of risk, that is, standard deviations and correlation coefficients. The forecasts themselves do not control outcomes. Thus, to prefer a manager with a rosier forecast (northwesterly frontier) is tantamount to rewarding the bearers of good news and punishing the bearers of bad news. What the investor wants is to reward bearers of *accurate* news. Investors should monitor forecasts of portfolio managers on a regular basis to develop a track record of their forecasting accuracy. Portfolio choices of the more accurate forecasters will, in the long run, outperform the field.

6.6. *a.* Beta, the slope coefficient of the security on the factor: Securities R_1–R_6 have a positive beta. These securities move, on average, in the same direction as the market (R_M). R_1, R_2, R_6 have large betas, so they are "aggressive" in that they carry more systematic risk than R_3, R_4, R_5, which are "defensive." R_7 and R_8 have a negative beta. These are hedge assets that carry negative systematic risk.

FIGURE 6.14

For Concept Check 4. Plot of mean return versus standard deviation using data from spreadsheet.

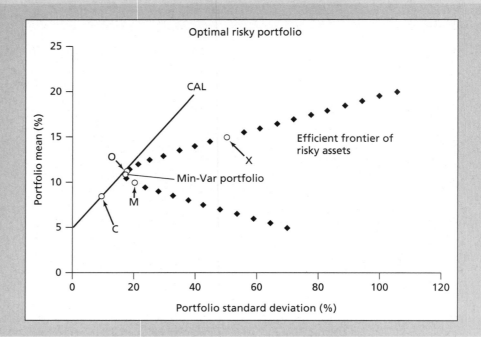

b. Intercept, the expected return when the market is neutral: The estimates show that R_1, R_4, R_8 have a positive intercept, while R_2, R_3, R_5, R_6, R_7 have negative intercepts. To the extent that one believes these intercepts will persist, a positive value is preferred.

c. Residual variance, the nonsystematic risk: R_2, R_3, R_7 have a relatively low residual variance. With sufficient diversification, residual risk eventually will be eliminated, and, hence, the difference in the residual variance is of little economic significance.

d. Total variance, the sum of systematic and nonsystematic risk: R_3 has a low beta and low residual variance, so its total variance will be low. R_1, R_6 have high betas and high residual variance, so their total variance will be high. But R_4 has a low beta and high residual variance, while R_2 has a high beta with a low residual variance. In sum, total variance often will misrepresent systematic risk, which is the part that matters.

6.7. a. To obtain the characteristic line of XYZ, we continue the spreadsheet of Example 6.3 and run a regression of the excess return of XYZ on the excess return of the market index fund.

Summary Output	
Regression Statistics	
Multiple R	0.363
R-square	0.132
Adjusted R-square	0.023
Standard error	41.839
Observations	10

	Coefficients	Standard Error	t-Stat	p-Value	Lower 95%	Upper 95%
Intercept	3.930	14.98	0.262	0.800	−30.62	38.48
Market	0.582	0.528	1.103	0.302	−0.635	1.798

The regression output shows that the slope coefficient of XYZ is .582 and the intercept is 3.93%, hence the characteristic line is: $R_{XYZ} = 3.93 + .582R_{Market}$.

b. The beta coefficient of ABC is 1.156, greater than XYZ's .582, implying that ABC has greater systematic risk.

c. The regression of XYZ on the market index shows an R-square of .132. Hence the proportion of unexplained variance (nonsystematic risk) is .868, or 86.8%.

Capital Asset Pricing and Arbitrage Pricing Theory

After Studying This Chapter You Should Be Able To:

- Use the implications of capital market theory to estimate security risk premiums.

- Construct and use the security market line.

- Specify and use a multifactor security market line.

- Take advantage of an arbitrage opportunity with a portfolio that includes mispriced securities.

- Use arbitrage pricing theory with more than one factor to identify mispriced securities.

The capital asset pricing model, almost always referred to as the CAPM, is a centerpiece of modern financial economics. It was first proposed by William F. Sharpe, who was awarded the 1990 Nobel Prize in Economics.

The CAPM provides a precise prediction of the relationship we should observe between the risk of an asset and its expected return. This relationship serves two vital functions.

First, it provides a benchmark rate of return for evaluating possible investments. For example, a security analyst might want to know whether the expected return she forecasts for a stock is more or less than its

"fair" return given its risk. Second, the model helps us make an educated guess as to the expected return on assets that have not yet been traded in the marketplace. For example, how do we price an initial public offering of stock? How will a major new investment project affect the return investors require on a company's stock? Although the CAPM does not fully withstand empirical tests, it is widely used because of the insight it offers and because its accuracy suffices for many important applications.

Once you understand the intuition behind the CAPM, it becomes clear that the model may be improved by generalizing it to allow for multiple sources of risk. Therefore, we turn next to multifactor models of risk and return, and show how these result in richer descriptions of the risk-return relationship.

Finally, we consider an alternative derivation of the risk-return relationship known as Arbitrage Pricing Theory, or APT. Arbitrage is the exploitation of security mispricing to earn risk-free economic profits. The most basic principle of capital market theory is that prices ought to be aligned to eliminate risk-free profit opportunities. If actual prices allowed for such arbitrage, the resulting opportunities for profitable trading would lead to strong pressure on security prices that would persist until equilibrium was restored and the opportunities were eliminated. We will see that this no-arbitrage principle leads to a risk-return relationship like that of the CAPM. Like the generalized version of the CAPM, the simple APT is easily extended to accommodate multiple sources of systematic risk.

Related Web sites for this chapter are available at www.mhhe.com/bkm.

7.1 | The Capital Asset Pricing Model

capital asset pricing model (CAPM)

A model that relates the required rate of return for a security to its risk as measured by beta.

The **capital asset pricing model,** or **CAPM,** was developed by Treynor, Sharpe, Lintner, and Mossin in the early 1960s, and further refined later. The model predicts the relationship between the risk and equilibrium expected returns on risky assets. We will approach the CAPM in a simplified setting. Thinking about an admittedly unrealistic world allows a relatively easy leap to the solution. With this accomplished, we can add complexity to the environment, one step at a time, and see how the theory must be amended. This process allows us to develop a reasonably realistic and comprehensible model.

A number of simplifying assumptions lead to the basic version of the CAPM. The fundamental idea is that individuals are alike, with the notable exceptions of initial wealth and risk aversion. The list of assumptions that describes the necessary conformity of investors follows:

1. Investors cannot affect prices by their individual trades. This means that there are many investors, each with an endowment of wealth that is small compared with the total endowment of all investors. This assumption is analogous to the perfect competition assumption of microeconomics.
2. All investors plan for one identical holding period.
3. Investors form portfolios from a common universe of publicly traded financial assets, such as stocks and bonds, and have access to unlimited risk-free borrowing or lending opportunities.
4. Investors pay neither taxes on returns nor transaction costs (commissions and service charges) on trades in securities. In such a simple world, investors will not care about the difference between returns from capital gains and those from dividends.
5. All investors attempt to construct efficient frontier portfolios; that is, they are rational mean-variance optimizers.
6. All investors analyze securities in the same way and share the same economic view of the world. Hence, they all end with identical estimates of the probability distribution of future cash flows from investing in the available securities. This means that, given a set of security prices and the risk-free interest rate, all investors use the same expected returns, standard deviations, and correlations to generate the efficient frontier and the unique optimal risky portfolio. This assumption is called *homogeneous expectations.*

Obviously, these assumptions ignore many real-world complexities. However, they lead to some powerful insights into the nature of equilibrium in security markets.

Given these assumptions, we summarize the equilibrium that will prevail in this hypothetical world of securities and investors. We elaborate on these implications in the following sections.

1. All investors will choose to hold the **market portfolio (M),** which includes all assets of the security universe. For simplicity, we shall refer to all assets as stocks. The proportion of each stock in the market portfolio equals the market value of the stock (price per share times the number of shares outstanding) divided by the total market value of all stocks.

2. The market portfolio will be on the efficient frontier. Moreover, it will be the optimal risky portfolio, the tangency point of the capital allocation line (CAL) to the efficient frontier. As a result, the capital market line (CML), the line from the risk-free rate through the market portfolio, *M,* is also the best attainable capital allocation line. All investors hold *M* as their optimal risky portfolio, differing only in the amount invested in it as compared to investment in the risk-free asset.

3. The risk premium on the market portfolio will be proportional to the variance of the market portfolio and investors' typical degree of risk aversion. Mathematically,

$$E(r_M) - r_f = A^* \sigma_M^2 \qquad \textbf{(7.1)}$$

where σ_M is the standard deviation of the return on the market portfolio and A^* is a scale factor representing the degree of risk aversion of the average investor.

4. The risk premium on individual assets will be proportional to the risk premium on the market portfolio (*M*) and to the *beta coefficient* of the security on the market portfolio. This implies that the rate of return on the market portfolio is the single systematic risk factor of the security market. The beta measures the extent to which returns on the stock respond to the returns of the market portfolio. Formally, beta is the regression (slope) coefficient of the security return on the market return, representing the sensitivity of the stock return to fluctuations in the overall security market.

market portfolio

The portfolio for which each security is held in proportion to its market value.

Why All Investors Would Hold the Market Portfolio

Given all our assumptions, it is easy to see why all investors hold identical risky portfolios. If all investors use identical mean-variance analysis (assumption 5), apply it to the same universe of securities (assumption 3), with an identical time horizon (assumption 2), use the same security analysis (assumption 6), and experience identical tax consequences (assumption 4), they all must arrive at the same determination of the optimal risky portfolio. That is, they all derive identical efficient frontiers and find the same tangency portfolio for the capital allocation line (CAL) from T-bills (the risk-free rate, with zero standard deviation) to that frontier, as in Figure 7.1.

With everyone choosing to hold the same risky portfolio, stocks will be represented in the aggregate risky portfolio in the same proportion as they are in each investor's (common) risky portfolio. If Google represents 1% in each common risky portfolio, Google will be 1% of the aggregate risky portfolio. This in fact is the market portfolio since the market is no more than the aggregate of all individual portfolios. Because each investor uses the market portfolio for the optimal risky portfolio, the CAL in this case is called the capital market line, or CML, as in Figure 7.1.

Suppose the optimal portfolio of our investors does not include the stock of some company, say, Southwest Air

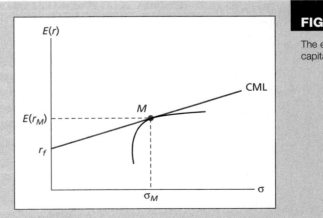

FIGURE 7.1

The efficient frontier and the capital market line

Lines. When no investor is willing to hold Southwest stock, the demand is zero, and the stock price will take a free fall. As Southwest stock gets progressively cheaper, it begins to look more attractive, while all other stocks look (relatively) less attractive. Ultimately, Southwest will reach a price at which it is desirable to include it in the optimal stock portfolio, and investors will buy.

This price adjustment process guarantees that all stocks will be included in the optimal portfolio. The only issue is the price. At a given price level, investors will be willing to buy a stock; at another price, they will not. The bottom line is this: If all investors hold an *identical* risky portfolio, this portfolio must be the *market* portfolio.

The Passive Strategy Is Efficient

The CAPM implies that a passive strategy, using the CML as the optimal CAL, is a powerful alternative to an active strategy. The market portfolio proportions are a result of profit-oriented "buy" and "sell" orders that cease only when there is no more profit to be made. And in the simple world of the CAPM, all investors use precious resources in security analysis. A passive investor who takes a free ride by simply investing in the market portfolio benefits from the efficiency of that portfolio. In fact, an active investor who chooses any other portfolio will end on a CAL that is less efficient than the CML used by passive investors.

mutual fund theorem

States that all investors desire the same portfolio of risky assets and can be satisfied by a single mutual fund composed of that portfolio.

We sometimes call this result a **mutual fund theorem** because it implies that only one mutual fund of risky assets—the market portfolio—is sufficient to satisfy the investment demands of all investors. The mutual fund theorem is another incarnation of the separation property discussed in Chapter 6. Assuming all investors choose to hold a market index mutual fund, we can separate portfolio selection into two components: (1) a technical side, in which an efficient mutual fund is created by professional management; and (2) a personal side, in which an investor's risk aversion determines the allocation of the complete portfolio between the mutual fund and the risk-free asset. Here, all investors agree that the mutual fund they would like to hold is the market portfolio.

While different investment managers do create risky portfolios that differ from the market index, we attribute this in part to the use of different estimates of risk and expected return. Still, a passive investor may view the market index as a reasonable first approximation to an efficient risky portfolio.

The logical inconsistency of the CAPM is this: If a passive strategy is costless *and* efficient, why would anyone follow an active strategy? But if no one does any security analysis, what brings about the efficiency of the market portfolio?

We have acknowledged from the outset that the CAPM simplifies the real world in its search for a tractable solution. Its applicability to the real world depends on whether its predictions are accurate enough. The model's use is some indication that its predictions are reasonable. We discuss this issue in Section 7.3 and in greater depth in Chapter 8.

CONCEPT
check **7.1**

If only some investors perform security analysis while all others hold the market portfolio (*M*), would the CML still be the efficient CAL for investors who do not engage in security analysis? Explain.

The Risk Premium of the Market Portfolio

In Chapters 5 and 6 we showed how individual investors decide how much to invest in the risky portfolio when they can include a risk-free asset in the investment budget. Returning now to the decision of how much to invest in the market portfolio *M* and how much in the risk-free asset, what can we deduce about the equilibrium risk premium of portfolio *M*?

We asserted earlier that the equilibrium risk premium of the market portfolio, $E(r_M) - r_f$, will be proportional to the degree of risk aversion of the average investor and to the risk of the market portfolio, σ_M^2. Now we can explain this result.

When investors purchase stocks, their demand drives up prices, thereby lowering expected rates of return and risk premiums. But if risk premiums fall, then relatively more risk-averse investors will pull their funds out of the risky market portfolio, placing them instead in the risk-free asset. In equilibrium, of course, the risk premium on the market portfolio must be just high enough to induce investors to hold the available supply of stocks. If the risk premium is too high compared to the average degree of risk aversion, there will be excess demand for securities, and prices will rise; if it is too low, investors will not hold enough stock to absorb the supply, and prices will fall. The *equilibrium* risk premium of the market portfolio is therefore proportional to both the risk of the market, as measured by the variance of its returns, and to the degree of risk aversion of the average investor, denoted by A^* in Equation 7.1.

Suppose the risk-free rate is 5%, the average investor has a risk-aversion coefficient of $A^* = 2$, and the standard deviation of the market portfolio is 20%. Then, from Equation 7.1, we estimate the equilibrium value of the market risk premium[1] as $2 \times .20^2 = .08$. So the expected rate of return on the market must be

$$E(r_M) = r_f + \text{Equilibrium risk premium}$$
$$= .05 + .08 = .13 = 13\%$$

If investors were more risk averse, it would take a higher risk premium to induce them to hold shares. For example, if the average degree of risk aversion were 3, the market risk premium would be $3 \times .20^2 = .12$, or 12%, and the expected return would be 17%.

EXAMPLE 7.1

Market Risk, the Risk Premium, and Risk Aversion

Historical data for the S&P 500 Index show an average excess return over Treasury bills of about 7.5% with standard deviation of about 20%. To the extent that these averages approximate investor expectations for the sample period, what must have been the coefficient of risk aversion of the average investor? If the coefficient of risk aversion were 3.5, what risk premium would have been consistent with the market's historical standard deviation?

CONCEPT *check* **7.2**

Expected Returns on Individual Securities

The CAPM is built on the insight that the appropriate risk premium on an asset will be determined by its contribution to the risk of investors' overall portfolios. Portfolio risk is what matters to investors, and portfolio risk is what governs the risk premiums they demand.

We know that nonsystematic risk can be reduced to an arbitrarily low level through diversification (Chapter 6); therefore, investors do not require a risk premium as compensation for bearing nonsystematic risk. They need to be compensated only for bearing systematic risk, which cannot be diversified. We know also that the contribution of a single security to the risk of a large diversified portfolio depends only on the systematic risk of the security as measured by its beta, as we saw in Chapter 6, Section 6.5. Therefore, it should not be surprising that the risk premium of an asset is proportional to its beta; for example, if you double a security's systematic risk, you must double its risk premium for investors still to be willing to hold the security. Thus, the ratio of risk premium to beta should be the same for any two securities or portfolios.

For example, if we were to compare the ratio of risk premium to systematic risk for the market portfolio, which has a beta of 1, with the corresponding ratio for Dell stock, we would conclude that

$$\frac{E(r_M) - r_f}{1} = \frac{E(r_D) - r_f}{\beta_D}$$

Rearranging this relationship results in the CAPM's **expected return–beta relationship**

expected return–beta relationship

Implication of the CAPM that security risk premiums (expected excess returns) will be proportional to beta.

---

[1]To use Equation 7.1, we must express returns in decimal form rather than as percentages.

$$E(r_D) = r_f + \beta_D[E(r_M) - r_f] \tag{7.2}$$

In words, the rate of return on any asset exceeds the risk-free rate by a risk premium equal to the asset's systematic risk measure (its beta) times the risk premium of the (benchmark) market portfolio. This expected return–beta relationship is the most familiar expression of the CAPM.

The expected return–beta relationship of the CAPM makes a powerful economic statement. It implies, for example, that a security with a high variance but a relatively low beta of .5 will carry one-third the risk premium of a low-variance security with a beta of 1.5. Thus, Equation 7.2 quantifies the conclusion we reached in Chapter 6 that only systematic risk matters to investors who can diversify and that systematic risk is measured by the beta of the security.

EXAMPLE 7.2	Suppose the risk premium of the market portfolio is 9%, and we estimate the beta of Dell as $\beta_D = 1.3$. The risk premium predicted for the stock is therefore 1.3 times the market risk premium, or $1.3 \times 9\% = 11.7\%$. The expected rate of return on Dell is the risk-free rate plus the risk premium. For example, if the T-bill rate were 5%, the expected rate of return would be $5\% + 11.7\% = 16.7\%$ or, using Equation 7.2 directly,
Expected Returns and Risk Premiums	

$$E(r_D) = r_f + \beta_D[\text{Market risk premium}]$$
$$= 5\% + 1.3 \times 9\% = 16.7\%$$

If the estimate of the beta of Dell were only 1.2, the required risk premium for Dell would fall to 10.8%. Similarly, if the market risk premium were only 8% and $\beta_D = 1.3$, Dell's risk premium would be only 10.4%.

The fact that few real-life investors actually hold the market portfolio does not necessarily invalidate the CAPM. Recall from Chapter 6 that reasonably well-diversified portfolios shed (for practical purposes) firm-specific risk and are subject only to systematic or market risk. Even if one does not hold the precise market portfolio, a well-diversified portfolio will be so highly correlated with the market that a stock's beta relative to the market still will be a useful risk measure.

In fact, several researchers have shown that modified versions of the CAPM will hold despite differences among individuals that may cause them to hold different portfolios. A study by Brennan (1970) examines the impact of differences in investors' personal tax rates on market equilibrium. Another study by Mayers (1972) looks at the impact of nontraded assets such as human capital (earning power). Both find that while the market portfolio is no longer each investor's optimal risky portfolio, a modified version of the expected return–beta relationship still holds.

If the expected return–beta relationship holds for any individual asset, it must hold for any combination of assets. The beta of a portfolio is simply the weighted average of the betas of the stocks in the portfolio, using as weights the portfolio proportions. Thus, beta also predicts the portfolio's risk premium in accordance with Equation 7.2.

EXAMPLE 7.3	Consider the following portfolio:
Portfolio Beta and Risk Premium	

Asset	Beta	Risk Premium	Portfolio Weight
Microsoft	1.2	9.0%	0.5
American Electric Power	0.8	6.0	0.3
Gold	0.0	0.0	0.2
Portfolio	0.84	?	1.0

If the market risk premium is 7.5%, the CAPM predicts that the risk premium on each stock is its beta times 7.5%, and the risk premium on the portfolio is $.84 \times 7.5\% = 6.3\%$. This is the same result that is obtained by taking the weighted average of the risk premiums of the individual stocks. (Verify this for yourself.)

A word of caution: We often hear that well-managed firms will provide high rates of return. We agree this is true if one measures the *firm's* return on investments in plant and equipment. The CAPM, however, predicts returns on investments in the *securities* of the firm that trade in capital markets.

Say that everyone knows a firm is well run. Its stock price should, therefore, be bid up, and returns to stockholders who buy at those high prices will not be extreme. Security *prices* reflect public information about a firm's prospects, but only the risk of the company (as measured by beta in the context of the CAPM) should affect *expected returns*. In a rational market, investors receive high expected returns only if they are willing to bear risk.

CONCEPT *check* **7.3**

Suppose the risk premium on the market portfolio is estimated at 8% with a standard deviation of 22%. What is the risk premium on a portfolio invested 25% in GE with a beta of 1.15 and 75% in Dell with a beta of 1.25?

The Security Market Line

We can view the expected return–beta relationship as a reward-risk equation. The beta of a security is the appropriate measure of its risk because beta is proportional to the risk the security contributes to the optimal risky portfolio.

Risk-averse investors measure the risk of the optimal risky portfolio by its standard deviation. In this world, we would expect the reward, or the risk premium on individual assets, to depend on the risk an individual asset contributes to the overall portfolio. Because the beta of a stock measures the stock's contribution to the standard deviation of the market portfolio, we expect the required risk premium to be a function of beta. The CAPM confirms this intuition, stating further that the security's risk premium is directly proportional to both the beta and the risk premium of the market portfolio; that is, the risk premium equals $\beta[E(r_M) - r_f]$.

The expected return–beta relationship is graphed as the **security market line (SML)** in Figure 7.2. Its slope is the risk premium of the market portfolio. At the point where $\beta = 1.0$ (which is the beta of the market portfolio) on the horizontal axis, we can read off the vertical axis the expected return on the market portfolio.

It is useful to compare the security market line to the capital market line. The CML graphs the risk premiums of efficient portfolios (that is, complete portfolios made up of the risky market portfolio and the risk-free asset) as a function of portfolio standard deviation. This is appropriate because standard deviation is a valid measure of risk for portfolios that are candidates for an investor's complete (overall) portfolio.

The SML, in contrast, graphs *individual asset* risk premiums as a function of asset risk. The relevant measure of risk for an individual asset (which is held as part of a well-diversified portfolio) is not the asset's standard deviation; it is, instead, the contribution of the asset to the portfolio standard deviation as measured by the asset's beta. The SML is valid both for portfolios and individual assets.

The security market line provides a benchmark for evaluation of investment performance. Given the risk of an investment as measured by its beta, the SML provides the required rate of return that will compensate investors for the risk of that investment, as well as for the time value of money.

Because the security market line is the graphical representation of the expected return–beta relationship, "fairly priced" assets plot exactly on the SML. The expected returns of such assets are commensurate with their risk. Whenever the CAPM holds, all securities must lie on the SML in

security market line (SML)

Graphical representation of the expected return–beta relationship of the CAPM.

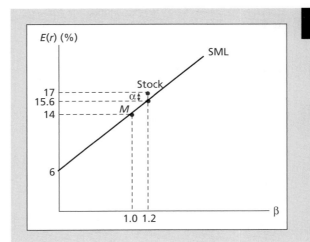

FIGURE 7.2

The security market line and a positive-alpha stock

alpha

The abnormal rate of return on a security in excess of what would be predicted by an equilibrium model such as the CAPM.

market equilibrium. Underpriced stocks plot above the SML: Given their betas, their expected returns are greater than is indicated by the CAPM. Overpriced stocks plot below the SML. The difference between the fair and actually expected rate of return on a stock is called the stock's **alpha,** denoted α. The expected return on such a mispriced security is given by $E(r_s) = \alpha_s + r_f + \beta_s[E(r_M) - r_f]$.

EXAMPLE 7.4

The Alpha of a Security

Suppose the return on the market is expected to be 14%, a stock has a beta of 1.2, and the T-bill rate is 6%. The SML would predict an expected return on the stock of

$$E(r) = r_f + \beta[E(r_M) - r_f]$$
$$= 6 + 1.2(14 - 6) = 15.6\%$$

If one believes the stock will provide instead a return of 17%, its implied alpha would be 1.4%, as shown in Figure 7.2.

Applications of the CAPM

One place the CAPM may be used is in the investment management industry. Suppose the SML is taken as a benchmark to assess the *fair* expected return on a risky asset. Then an analyst calculates the return she actually expects. Notice that we depart here from the simple CAPM world in that some investors apply their own analysis to derive an "input list" that may differ from their competitors'. If a stock is perceived to be a good buy, or underpriced, it will provide a positive alpha, that is, an expected return in excess of the fair return stipulated by the SML.

The CAPM is also useful in capital budgeting decisions. If a firm is considering a new project, the CAPM can provide the return the project needs to yield to be acceptable to investors. Managers can use the CAPM to obtain this cutoff internal rate of return (IRR) or "hurdle rate" for the project.

EXAMPLE 7.5

The CAPM and Capital Budgeting

Suppose Silverado Springs Inc. is considering a new spring-water bottling plant. The business plan forecasts an internal rate of return of 14% on the investment. Research shows the beta of similar products is 1.3. Thus, if the risk-free rate is 4%, and the market risk premium is estimated at 8%, the hurdle rate for the project should be 4 + 1.3 × 8 = 14.4%. Because the IRR is less than the risk-adjusted discount or hurdle rate, the project has a negative net present value and ought to be rejected.

Yet another use of the CAPM is in utility rate-making cases. Here the issue is the rate of return a regulated utility should be allowed to earn on its investment in plant and equipment.

EXAMPLE 7.6

The CAPM and Regulation

Suppose equityholders' investment in the firm is $100 million, and the beta of the equity is .6. If the T-bill rate is 6%, and the market risk premium is 8%, then a fair annual profit will be 6 + (.6 × 8) = 10.8% of $100 million, or $10.8 million. Since regulators accept the CAPM, they will allow the utility to set prices at a level expected to generate these profits.

CONCEPT
check **7.4**

a. Stock *XYZ* has an expected return of 12% and risk of $\beta = 1.0$. Stock *ABC* is expected to return 13% with a beta of 1.5. The market's expected return is 11% and $r_f = 5\%$. According to the CAPM, which stock is a better buy? What is the alpha of each stock? Plot the SML and the two stocks and show the alphas of each on the graph.

b. The risk-free rate is 8% and the expected return on the market portfolio is 16%. A firm considers a project with an estimated beta of 1.3. What is the required rate of return on the project? If the IRR of the project is 19%, what is the project alpha?

7.2 The CAPM and Index Models

The CAPM has two limitations: It relies on the theoretical market portfolio, which includes *all* assets (such as real estate, foreign stocks, etc.), and it deals with *expected* as opposed to actual returns. To implement the CAPM, we cast it in the form of an *index model* and use realized, not expected, returns.

An index model uses actual portfolios, such as the S&P 500, rather than the theoretical market portfolio to represent the relevant systematic factors in the economy. The important advantage of index models is that the composition and rate of return of the index is unambiguous and easily measured.

In contrast to an index model, the CAPM revolves around the "market portfolio." However, because many assets are not traded, investors would not have full access to the market portfolio even if they could exactly identify it. Thus, the theory behind the CAPM rests on a shaky real-world foundation. But, as in all science, a theory may be viewed as legitimate if its predictions approximate real-world outcomes with a sufficient degree of accuracy. In particular, the reliance on the market portfolio shouldn't faze us if we can verify that the predictions of the CAPM are sufficiently accurate when the index portfolio is substituted for the market.

We can start with one central prediction of the CAPM: The market portfolio is mean-variance efficient. An index model can be used to test this hypothesis by verifying that an index chosen to be representative of the full market is a mean-variance efficient portfolio.

Another aspect of the CAPM is that it predicts relationships among *expected* returns, while all we can observe are realized (historical) holding-period returns; actual returns in a particular holding period seldom, if ever, match our initial expectations. For example, the S&P 500 returned −39% in 2008. Could this possibly have been the previously expected return? Consider that investors may always invest in risk-free Treasury bills with a positive return and zero risk. Surely, then, they would not have accepted the risk inherent in a stock market investment if they had expected a negative return at the outset of the year. In fact, this logic implies that any stock-index return less than the return available from T-bills must entail a negative departure from expectations. Conversely, of course, stock returns must exceed their expected value in other periods.

To test the mean-variance efficiency of an index portfolio, we would have to show that the reward-to-volatility ratio of the index is not surpassed by any other portfolio. We will examine this question in the next chapter.

The Index Model, Realized Returns, and the Expected Return–Beta Relationship

To move from a model cast in expectations to a realized-return framework, we start with a form of the single-index equation in realized excess returns, similar to that of Equation 6.11 in Chapter 6. Notice that this equation may be interpreted as a regression relationship

$$r_{it} - r_{ft} = \alpha_i + \beta_i(r_{Mt} - r_{ft}) + e_{it} \tag{7.3}$$

where r_{it} is the holding-period return (HPR) on asset i in period t, and α_i and β_i are the intercept and slope of the line that relates asset i's realized excess return to the realized excess return of the index. We denote the index return by r_M to emphasize that the index portfolio is proxying for the market. The e_{it} measures firm-specific effects during holding period t; it is the deviation in that period of security i's realized HPR from the regression line, that is, the deviation from the forecast that accounts for the index's actual HPR. We set the relationship in terms of *excess* returns (over the risk-free rate in that period, r_{ft}), for consistency with the CAPM's logic of risk premiums.

Given that the CAPM is a statement about the expectation of asset returns, we look at the expected return of security i predicted by Equation 7.3. Recall that the expectation of e_{it} is zero (the firm-specific surprise is expected to average zero over time), so the relationship expressed in terms of expectations is

$$E(r_{it}) - r_{ft} = \alpha_i + \beta_i[E(r_{Mt}) - r_{ft}] \tag{7.4}$$

ALPHA BETTING

IT HAS never been easier to pay less to invest. No fewer than 136 exchange-traded funds (ETFs) were launched in the first half of 2006, more than in the whole of 2005.

For those who believe in efficient markets, this represents a triumph. ETFs are quoted securities that track a particular index, for a fee that is normally just a fraction of a percentage point. They enable investors to assemble a low-cost portfolio covering a wide range of assets from international equities, through government and corporate bonds, to commodities.

But as fast as the assets of ETFs and index-tracking mutual funds are growing, another section of the industry seems to be flourishing even faster. Watson Wyatt, a firm of actuaries, estimates that "alternative asset investment" (ranging from hedge funds through private equity to property) grew by around 20% in 2005, to $1.26 trillion. Investors who take this route pay much higher fees in the hope of better performance. One of the fastest-growing assets, funds of hedge funds, charge some of the highest fees of all.

Why are people paying up? In part, because investors have learned to distinguish between the market return, dubbed beta, and managers' outperformance, known as alpha. "Why wouldn't you buy beta and alpha separately?" asks Arno Kitts of Henderson Global Investors, a fund-management firm. "Beta is a commodity and alpha is about skill."

Clients have become convinced that no one firm can produce good performance in every asset class. That has led to a "core and satellite" model, in which part of the portfolio is invested in index trackers with the rest in the hands of specialists. But this creates its own problems. Relations with a single balanced manager are simple. It is much harder to research and monitor the performance of specialists. That has encouraged the middlemen—managers of managers (in the traditional institutional business) and funds-of-funds (in the hedge-fund world), which are usually even more expensive.

That their fees endure might suggest investors can identify outperforming fund managers in advance. However, studies suggest this is extremely hard. And even where you can spot talent, much of the extra performance may be siphoned off into higher fees. "A disproportionate amount of the benefits of alpha go to the manager, not the client," says Alan Brown at Schroders, an asset manager.

In any event, investors will probably keep pursuing alpha, even though the cheaper alternatives of ETFs and tracking funds are available. Craig Baker of Watson Wyatt says that, although above-market returns may not be available to all, clients who can identify them have a "first mover" advantage. As long as that belief exists, managers can charge high fees.

Comparing this relationship to the expected return–beta relationship of the CAPM (Equation 7.2) reveals that the CAPM predicts $\alpha_i = 0$. Thus, we have converted the CAPM prediction about unobserved expectations of security returns relative to an unobserved market portfolio into a prediction about the intercept in a regression of observed variables: realized excess returns of a security relative to those of a specified index.

Operationalizing the CAPM in the form of an index model has a drawback, however. If intercepts of regressions of returns on an index differ substantially from zero, you will not be able to tell whether it is because you chose a bad index to proxy for the market or because the theory is not useful.

In actuality, few instances of persistent, positive significant alpha values have been identified; these will be discussed in Chapter 8. Among these are: (1) small versus large stocks; (2) stocks of companies that have recently announced unexpectedly good earnings; (3) stocks with high ratios of book value to market value; and (4) stocks with "momentum" that have experienced recent advances in price. In general, however, future alphas are practically impossible to predict from past values. The result is that index models are widely used to operationalize capital asset pricing theory (see the nearby box).

Estimating the Index Model

To illustrate how to estimate the index model, we will use actual data and apply the model to the stock of Google (G), in a manner similar to that followed by practitioners. Let us rewrite Equation 7.3 for Google, denoting Google's excess return as R_G (i.e., $R_G = r_G - r_f$) and denoting any particular month using the subscript t. Then the index model may be expressed as

$$R_{Gt} = \alpha_G + \beta_G R_{Mt} + e_{Gt}$$

As noted, this relationship may be viewed as a regression equation. The dependent variable in this case is Google's excess return in each month. It is a straight-line function of the excess return on the market index in that month, R_{Mt}, with intercept α_G and slope β_G.

In addition to the influence of the market, the excess return of Google is also affected by firm-specific factors, the net effect of which is captured by the last term in the equation, e_{Gt}. This term is called a residual, as it captures the variation in Google's monthly return that remains after taking account of the impact of the market. The residual is the difference between Google's actual return and the return that would be predicted from the regression line describing the usual relationship between the returns of Google and the market:

$$\text{Residual} = \text{Actual return} - \text{Predicted return for Google based on market return}$$
$$e_{Gt} = R_{Gt} - (\alpha_G + \beta_G R_{Mt})$$

We are interested in estimating the intercept α_G and Google's systematic (i.e., market) risk as measured by the slope coefficient, β_G. We would also like an estimate of the magnitude of Google's firm-specific risk. This can be measured by *residual standard deviation,* which is just the standard deviation of the residual terms, *e*. Because residuals are the part of excess returns not explained by the market index, that is, firm-specific effects, their standard deviation gives a guide as to the typical magnitude of those effects.

We conduct the analysis in three steps: Collect and process relevant data; feed the data into a statistical program (here we will use Excel) to estimate and interpret the regression Equation 7.3; and use the results to answer questions about Google's stock. For example, we will consider (*a*) what we have learned about the behavior of Google's returns, (*b*) what required rate of return is appropriate for investments with the same risk as Google's equity, and (*c*) how we might assess the performance of a portfolio manager who invested heavily in Google stock during this period.

Collecting and processing data   We start with the monthly series of Google stock prices and the S&P 500 Index, adjusted for stock splits and dividends over the period January 2006–December 2008.[2] From these series we computed monthly holding-period returns on Google and the market index for this three-year period.

For the same period we compiled monthly rates of return on one-month T-bills, which will serve as the risk-free rate.[3] With these three series of returns we generate monthly excess return on Google's stock and the market index. Some statistics for these returns are shown in Table 7.1.

The period of January 2006–December 2008 includes the late stage of recovery from the mild 2001 recession, as well as the severe recession that officially began in December 2007. Contrary to typical patterns, the stock market index did not lead the real economy in this period; instead, it began declining in tandem with the real economy, around December 2007. The average market return of –.64%/month indicates that investor expectations were not realized over this three-year period.   The market excess return compared to the positive average rate on T-bills was, of course, even lower, –.93%/month. Its cumulative three-year return was –23.44%, implying a geometric average return of –.74%/month. Its standard deviation was 4.31%/month.

Google's average excess return was better than the market's, with a negative value of "only" –.50%/month, but Google's standard deviation was considerably higher, 11.39%/month. The much larger SD of Google is responsible for the fact that while its arithmetic return was higher than the index, its geometric average (–.83%/month) and cumulative return were lower.[4] Notice that the monthly variation in the T-bill return reported in Table 7.1 does not reflect risk, as investors knew the return on bills at the beginning of each month.

---

[2]Five-year samples are more common, but we use a shorter period here to avoid clutter in some figures. Returns are available from several Web sources. Market Insight (**www.mhhe.com/edumarketinsight**), which comes with this text, is a good source of returns. You can also find returns at sites such as **finance.yahoo.com.** We need to use the price series adjusted for dividends and splits in order to obtain holding-period returns (HPRs). The unadjusted price series would tell us about capital gains alone rather than total returns.

[3]We downloaded these rates from Professor Kenneth French's Web site: **mba.tuck.dartmouth.edu/pages/faculty/ ken.french/data_library.html.**

[4]When returns are normally distributed, the relation between the arithmetic average return, r_A, and the geometric average return, r_G (expressed as decimals, not percentages), is: arithmetic average = geometric average plus one-half variance of returns. This relation holds approximately when returns are not precisely normally distributed.

TABLE 7.1			
Monthly return statistics: T-bills, S&P 500, and Google, January 2006–December 2008			
Statistic (%)	**T-bills**	**S&P 500**	**Google**
Average rate of return	0.29	−0.64	−0.21
Average excess return	–	−0.93	−0.50
Standard deviation*	0.14	4.31	11.39
Cumulative total 3-year return	10.99	−23.44	−25.84
Geometric average	0.29	−0.74	−0.83
Gain in 2008	1.37	−36.79	−55.51

* The standard deviation of the T-bill return reflects variation over time in the risk-free rate, not risk concerning the return on bills in any period.

Figure 7.3 Panel A shows the monthly return on the securities during the sample period. The significantly higher volatility of Google is evident, and the graph suggests that its beta is greater than 1.0: When the market moves, Google tends to move in the same direction, but by greater amounts. It does appear, however, that Google's return relative to the index is more highly magnified when the market is up than when it is down.

Figure 7.3 Panel B shows the evolution of cumulative returns. It illustrates the positive index returns in the early years of the sample, and the steep decline since the onset of the recession.

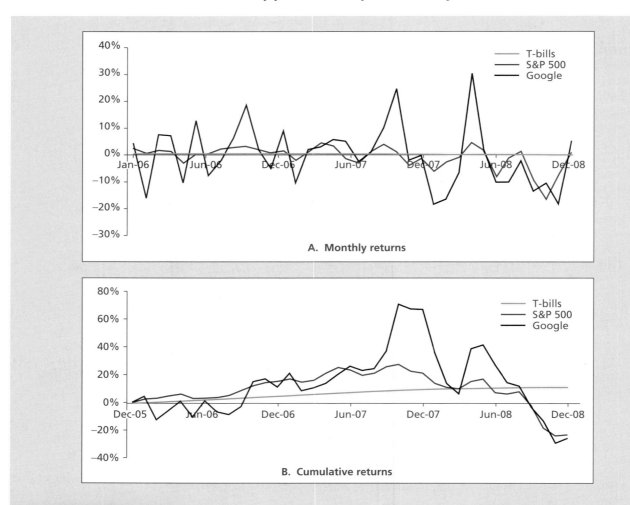

FIGURE 7.3

Returns for T-bills, S&P 500 Index, and Google stock. *Panel A*: monthly returns; *Panel B*: cumulative returns.

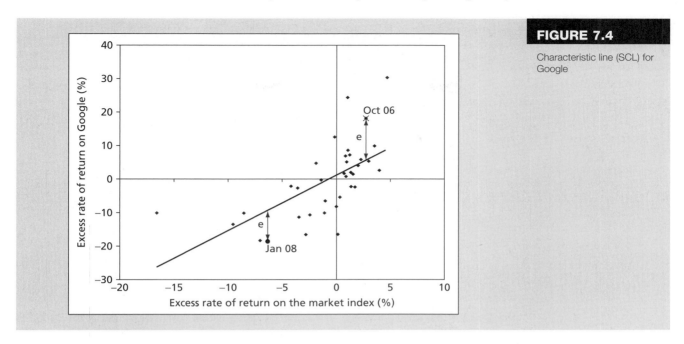

FIGURE 7.4

Characteristic line (SCL) for Google

Despite the large initial positive swing of Google, its evidently high beta landed it lower than the index for the full period with a lower geometric average return. Overall, T-bills outperform both securities by a large margin over the period, highlighting the worse-than-expected realizations in the capital market.

Estimation results We regressed Google's excess returns against those of the index using the Regression command from the Data Analysis menu of Excel. The scatter diagram in Figure 7.4 shows the data points for each month as well as the regression line that best fits the data. As noted in the previous chapter, this is called the **security characteristic line (SCL)**, because it can be used to describe the relevant characteristics of the stock. Figure 7.4 allows us to view the residuals, the deviation of Google's return each month from the prediction of the regression equation. By construction, these residuals *average* to zero, but in any particular month, the residual may be positive or negative.

For example, the residuals for October 2006 (12.55%) and January 2008 (−9.28%) are labeled explicitly. The October 2006 point lies above the regression line, indicating that in this month, Google's return was better than one would have predicted from knowledge of the market return. The spread between the point and the regression line is Google's firm-specific return, which is the residual for October.

The standard deviation of the residuals indicates the accuracy of predictions from the regression line. If there is a lot of firm-specific risk, for example, there will be a wide scatter of points around the line (a high residual standard deviation), indicating that knowledge of the market return will not enable a precise forecast of Google's return.

Table 7.2 is the regression output from Excel. The first line shows that the correlation coefficient between the excess returns of Google and the index was 0.626. The more relevant statistic, however, is the *adjusted R-square* (.374). It is the square of the correlation coefficient, adjusted downward for the number of coefficients or "degrees of freedom" used to estimate the regression line.[5] The adjusted R-square tells us that 37.42% of the variation in Google's

security characteristic line (SCL)

A plot of a security's expected excess return over the risk-free rate as a function of the excess return on the market.

---

[5]The relationship between the adjusted R-square (R_A^2) and the unadjusted (R^2) with n observations and k independent

variables (plus intercept) is: $1 - R_A^2 = (1 - R^2)\dfrac{n - 1}{n - k - 1}$, and thus a greater k will result in a larger downward

adjustment to R_A^2. While R^2 cannot fall when you add an additional independent variable to a regression, R_A^2 can actually fall, indicating that the explanatory power of the added variable is not enough to compensate for the extra degree of freedom it uses. The more "parsimonious" model (without the added variable) would be considered statistically superior.

TABLE 7.2

Security characteristic line (SCL) for Google

Regression Statistics

Multiple R	0.6261
R-square	0.3920
Adjusted R-square	0.3742
Standard error	9.0077
Observations	36

ANOVA

	df	SS	MS	F	Significance F
Regression	1	1779.01	1779.01	21.93	0.00004
Residual	34	2758.73	81.14		
Total	35	4537.74			

	Coefficients	Std Error	t-statistic	p-value	Lower 95%	Upper 95%
Intercept	1.0426	1.5369	0.6784	0.5021	−2.0807	4.1659
S&P 500	1.6547	0.3534	4.6825	0.0000	0.9365	2.3729

excess returns is explained by the variation in the excess returns of the index, and hence the remainder, or 62.58%, of the variation is firm specific, or unexplained by market movements. The dominant contribution of firm-specific factors to variation in Google's returns is typical of individual stocks, reminding us why diversification can greatly reduce risk.

The standard deviation of the residuals is referred to in the output (below the adjusted R-square) as the "standard error" of the regression (9.01%). In roughly two-thirds of the months, the firm-specific component of Google's excess return was between ±9.01%. This wide spread is more evidence of Google's considerable firm-specific volatility.

The middle panel of Table 7.2, labeled ANOVA (for analysis of variance), analyzes the sources of variability in Google returns, those two sources being variation in market returns and variation due to firm-specific factors. For the most part, these statistics are not essential for our analysis. You can, however, use the total sum of squares, labeled *SS,* to find Google's variance over this period. Divide the total *SS,* or 4,537, by the degrees of freedom, *df,* or 35, and you will find that variance of excess returns was 129.65, implying a monthly standard deviation of 11.39%.

Finally, the bottom panel of the table shows the estimates of the regression intercept and slope (alpha = 1.04% and beta = 1.65). The positive alpha means that, measured by *realized* returns, Google stock was above the security market line (SML) for this period. But the next column shows that the imprecision of this estimate as measured by its standard error is quite large, considerably larger than the estimate itself. The *t*-statistic (the ratio of the estimate of alpha to its standard error) is only .678, indicating low statistical significance. This is reflected in the large *p*-value in the next column, .502, which indicates that the probability is 50.2% that an estimate of alpha this large could have resulted from pure chance even if the true alpha were zero. The low *t*-statistic and correspondingly high *p*-value indicate that the estimate of alpha is not significantly different from zero. The last two columns give the upper and lower bounds of the 95% confidence interval around the coefficient estimate. This confidence interval tells us that, with a probability of .95, the true alpha lies in the wide interval from −2.03 to +4.11%. Thus, we cannot conclude from this particular sample, with any degree of confidence, that Google's true alpha was not zero, which would be the prediction of the CAPM.

The second line in the panel gives the estimate of Google's beta, which is 1.65. The standard error of this estimate is .35, resulting in a *t*-statistic of 4.68, and a practically zero *p*-value for the hypothesis that the true beta is in fact zero. In other words, the probability of observing an estimate this large if the true beta were zero is negligible. But still, we should not be too satisfied with these results, as the estimate of beta is also not so precise. The standard error of the beta estimate is fairly large and the 95% confidence interval for beta ranges from .95 to 2.36.

What we learn from this regression   The regression analysis reveals much about Google, but we must temper our conclusions by acknowledging that the tremendous volatility in stock market returns makes it difficult to derive strong statistical conclusions about the parameters of the index model, at least for individual stocks. With such noisy variables we must expect imprecise estimates; such is the reality of capital markets.

Despite these qualifications, we can safely say that Google is a strongly cyclical stock, that is, its returns vary significantly more than the overall market, as its beta is significantly higher than the average value of 1.0. Thus, we would expect Google's excess return to vary, on average, more than one-for-one with the market index. Absent additional information, if we had to forecast the volatility of a portfolio that includes Google, we would use the beta estimate of 1.65 to compute the contribution of Google to portfolio variance.

Moreover, if we had to advise Google's management of the appropriate discount rate for a project that is similar in risk to its equity,[6] we would use this beta estimate in conjunction with the prevailing risk-free rate and our forecast of the expected excess return on the market index. Suppose the current T-bill rate is 2.75%, and our forecast for the market excess return is 5.5%. Then the required rate of return for an investment with the same risk as Google's equity would be:

$$\text{Required rate} = \text{Risk-free rate} + \beta \times \text{Expected excess return of index}$$
$$= r_f + \beta(r_M - r_f) = 2.75 + 1.65 \times 5.5 = 11.83\%.$$

However, in light of the imprecision of Google's beta estimate, we would try to bring more information to bear about the true beta. For example, we would compute the betas of other firms in the industry, which ought to be similar to Google's, to sharpen our estimate of Google's systematic risk.

Finally, suppose we were asked to determine whether, given Google's positive alpha, a portfolio manager was correct in loading up a managed portfolio with Google stock over the period 2006–2008.

To answer this question, let's find the optimal position in Google that would have been prescribed by a portfolio optimization program such as those discussed in the last chapter. Let us assume that the manager had an accurate estimate of Google's alpha and beta, as well as its residual standard deviation and correlation with the index (from Tables 7.1 and 7.2). We still need information about the manager's forecast for the index, since we know it was *not* the actual (negative) return. Suppose the manager assumed a market-index risk premium of .7%/month (near the historical average), and correctly estimated the index standard deviation of 4.31%/month. Thus, the manager's input list would have included:

Security	Risk Premium (%)	Standard Deviation (%)	Correlation
Index	.7%	4.31%	
Google	$1.04 + 1.65 \times .7 = 2.195$	11.39	.62

[6]We need to be careful here. First, remember that as a general rule, equity beta is greater than asset beta, because leverage increases the exposure of equity to business risk. The required rate of return on Google's *stock* would be appropriate for an investment with the same risk as Google's *equity*. In this instance, Google has virtually no debt so this issue may be moot, but this is not generally the case. Second, it appears that Google exhibits some asymmetry in its risk characteristics, with an attractive pattern of greater sensitivity to up markets than down markets. This suggests a beta of 1.65 may exaggerate the risk of Google and the resultant cost of capital.

We can apply the lessons of Chapter 6 and compute the optimal portfolio constructed of the index portfolio (*M*) and Google (G).[7]

Using Equation 6.10 we calculate for the optimized portfolio (*P*):

$$w_M = .5636 \qquad w_G = .4364 \qquad E(R_P) = 1.35\% \qquad \sigma_P = 6.79\%$$

Thus, it appears the manager would have been quite right to tilt the portfolio heavily toward Google during this period. This reflects its large positive alpha over the sample period.

We can also measure the improvement in portfolio performance. Using Equation 6.8, the Sharpe ratio of the index and the optimized portfolios based on expected returns are

$$S_M = 0.16 \qquad S_P = 0.20$$

So the position in Google substantially increased the Sharpe ratio.

How did this portfolio actually perform relative to the passive index given the realized (rather than expected) returns for the period? Because realizations generally do not match expectations, it is possible for the incremental position in Google to have hurt or helped performance. As it turns out, the actual performance statistics were as follows:

Portfolio	Average Excess Return (%)	Standard Deviation (%)	Sharpe Ratio
Index	−.93%	4.31%	−.22
Google + index	−.54	10.57	−.05

We conclude that if the security analysis of individual assets is valid, the optimized portfolio will likely outperform the index even if the forecast of the index return is flawed, as the portfolio still maintains a tilt toward positive-alpha stocks.

On the other hand, recall that the estimate of Google's alpha was not even close to achieving statistical significance. Thus, this superior performance might well be explained away as pure luck. Note that this is a harsh conclusion. It means that the decision to forgo full diversification by choosing a Google-heavy portfolio actually may have been an imprudent bet that just happened to pay off. If we accept this explanation, then there is no violation of the CAPM here. To the extent that some managers do beat the index as in the foregoing example, then the question becomes whether such a feat is common. As we will see in the next chapter, however, this apparently is not the case: Managers consistently exhibiting such performance are exceedingly rare.

How realistic is this example? The procedure we followed is almost identical to those used in the industry. One difference is that we used only three years of data. While practitioners use various periods to estimate betas, five years is the most common choice. It is driven by the fact that security betas change over time due to the changing nature of the firm's underlying business. A period of five years provides a reasonable number of observations, yet the period is not so long as to be contaminated by old and possibly no-longer-relevant returns. Using daily returns to obtain a large number of observations over a short estimation period would create new problems: (1) relevant information about the various securities does not flow to the market at a uniform rate, so daily returns may not reflect significant longer-term correlations between securities, and (2) if some stocks do not trade frequently enough, the precise time of the last trade of a day may not be synchronized across securities, and so returns measured from the last recorded daily price may be somewhat misaligned. The intermediate choice of weekly returns is also reasonable. For example, Value Line (a popular and respected investment service company) uses weekly returns from the most recent year to produce beta estimates; but most services opt for monthly data.

As we have seen, important inferences and decisions are routinely made from estimates of betas. The procedure illustrated here does deviate from that of some practitioners in one

[7]You may recall that we solved this very problem in Example 6.6 using the index model method. Google's alpha, beta, and the residual standard deviation from the regression results in Table 7.2 were used in that example.

respect. They may make more sophisticated efforts to account for changing betas over time, as we explain in the next section.

Predicting Betas

Even if a single-index model representation is not fully consistent with the CAPM, the concept of systematic versus diversifiable risk is still useful. Systematic risk is approximated well by the regression equation beta and nonsystematic risk by the residual variance of the regression.

Often, we estimate betas in order to forecast the rate of return of an asset. The beta from the regression equation is an estimate based on past history; it will not reveal possible changes in future beta. As an empirical rule, it appears that betas exhibit a statistical property called "regression toward the mean." This means that high β (that is, $\beta > 1$) securities in one period tend to exhibit a lower β in the future, while low β (that is, $\beta < 1$) securities exhibit a higher β in future periods. Researchers who desire predictions of future betas often adjust beta estimates derived from historical data to account for regression toward the mean. For this reason, it is necessary to verify whether the estimates are already "adjusted betas."

A simple way to account for the tendency of future betas to "regress" toward the average value of 1.0 is to use as your forecast of beta a weighted average of the sample estimate with the value 1.0.

Suppose that past data yield a beta estimate of .65. A common weighting scheme is $2/3$ on the sample estimate and $1/3$ on the value 1.0. Thus, the adjusted forecast of beta will be $$\text{Adjusted beta} = \tfrac{2}{3} \times .65 + \tfrac{1}{3} \times 1.0 = .77$$ The final forecast of beta is in fact closer to 1.0 than the sample estimate.	**EXAMPLE 7.7** *Forecast of Beta*

A more sophisticated technique would base the weight assigned to the sample estimate of beta on its statistical reliability. That is, if we have a more precise estimate of beta from historical data, we increase the weight placed on the sample estimate.

However, obtaining a precise statistical estimate of beta from past data on individual stocks is a formidable task, because the volatility of rates of return is so large. In other words, there is a lot of "noise" in the data due to the impact of firm-specific events. The problem is less severe with diversified portfolios because diversification reduces the effect of firm-specific events.

One might hope that more precise estimates of beta could be obtained by using more data, that is, by using a long time series of the returns on the stock. Unfortunately, this is not a solution, because regression analysis presumes that the regression coefficient (the beta) is constant over the sample period. If betas change over time, old data could provide a misleading guide to current betas.

Two methods can help improve forecasts of beta. The first is an application of a technique that goes by the name of ARCH[8] models. ARCH models better predict variance and covariance using historical data, by optimally weighting recent experience more heavily than more distant observations. The second method involves an additional step where beta estimates from time series regressions are augmented by other information about the firm, for example, P/E ratios.

7.3 The CAPM and the Real World

In limited ways, portfolio theory and the CAPM have become accepted tools in the practitioner community. Many investment professionals think about the distinction between firm-specific and systematic risk and are comfortable with the use of beta to measure systematic risk. Still, the nuances of the CAPM are not nearly as well established in the community. For

---

[8]ARCH stands for autoregressive conditional heteroskedasticity. (The model was developed by Robert F. Engle, who received the 2003 Nobel Prize in Economics.) This is a fancy way of saying that the volatility (and covariance) of stocks change over time in ways that can be at least partially predicted from their past levels.

example, the compensation of portfolio managers is not based on appropriate risk-adjusted performance measures (see Chapter 18). What can we make of this?

New ways of thinking about the world (that is, new models or theories) displace old ones when the old models become either intolerably inconsistent with data or when the new model is demonstrably more consistent with available data. For example, when Copernicus over-threw the age-old belief that Earth is fixed in the center of the Universe and that the stars orbit about it in circular motions, it took many years before astronomers and navigators replaced old astronomical tables with superior ones based on his theory. The old tools fit the data available from astronomical observation with sufficient precision to suffice for the needs of the time. To some extent, the slowness with which the CAPM has permeated daily practice in the money management industry also has to do with its precision in fitting data, that is, in pre-cisely explaining variation in rates of return across assets. Let's review some of the evidence on this score.

The CAPM was first published by Sharpe in the *Journal of Finance* (the journal of the American Finance Association) in 1964 and took the world of finance by storm. Early tests by Black, Jensen, and Scholes (1972) and Fama and MacBeth (1973) were only partially sup-portive of the CAPM: average returns were higher for higher-beta portfolios, but the reward for beta risk was less than the predictions of the simple theory.

While this sort of evidence against the CAPM remained largely within the ivory towers of academia, Roll's (1977) paper "A Critique of Capital Asset Pricing Tests" shook the practitio-ner world as well. Roll argued that since the true market portfolio can never be observed, the CAPM is *necessarily* untestable.

The publicity given the now classic "Roll's critique" resulted in popular articles such as "Is Beta Dead?" that effectively slowed the permeation of portfolio theory through the world of finance.[9] This is quite ironic since, although Roll is absolutely correct on theoretical grounds, some tests suggest that the error introduced by using a broad market index as proxy for the true, unobserved market portfolio is perhaps not the greatest of the problems involved in test-ing the CAPM.

Fama and French (1992) published a study that dealt the CAPM an even harsher blow. They claimed that once you control for a set of widely followed characteristics of the firm, such as the size of the firm and its ratio of market value to book value, the firm's beta (that is, its systematic risk) does not contribute much to the prediction of future returns.

Fama and French and several others have published many follow-up studies of this topic. We will review some of this literature later in the chapter, and the nearby box discusses controversies about the risk-return relationship that have been reinforced in the wake of the financial crisis of 2008. However, it seems clear from these studies that beta does not tell the whole story of risk. There seem to be risk factors that affect security returns beyond beta's one-dimensional measurement of market sensitivity. In fact, in the next section of this chapter, we will introduce a theory of risk premiums that explicitly allows for multiple risk factors.

Liquidity, a different kind of risk factor, was ignored for a long time. Although first ana-lyzed by Amihud and Mendelson as early as 1986, it is yet to be accurately measured and incorporated in portfolio management. Measuring liquidity and the premium commensurate with illiquidity is part of a larger field in financial economics, namely, market structure. We now know that trading mechanisms on stock exchanges can affect the liquidity of assets traded on these exchanges and thus significantly affect their market value.

Despite all these issues, beta is not dead. More recent research shows that when we use a more inclusive proxy for the market portfolio than the S&P 500 (specifically, an index that includes human capital) and allow for the fact that beta changes over time, the perfor-mance of beta in explaining security returns is considerably enhanced (Jagannathan and Wang, 1996). We know that the CAPM is not a perfect model and that ultimately it will be far from the last word on security pricing. Still, the logic of the model is compelling, and more sophisticated models of security pricing all rely on the key distinction between

---

[9]A. Wallace, "Is Beta Dead?" *Institutional Investor* 14 (July 1980), pp. 22–30.

TAKING STOCK

Since the stock market bubble of the late 1990s burst, investors have had ample time to ponder where to put the remains of their money. Economists and analysts too have been revisiting old ideas. None has been dearer to them than the capital asset pricing model (CAPM), a formula linking movements in a single share price to those of the market as a whole. The key statistic here is "beta."

Many investors and managers have given up on beta, however. Although it is useful for working out overall correlation with the market, it tells you little about share-price performance in absolute terms. In fact, the CAPM's obituary was already being written more than a decade ago when a paper by Eugene Fama and Kenneth French showed that the shares of small companies and "value stocks" (shares with low price–earnings ratios or high ratios of book value to market value) do much better over time than their betas would predict.

Another paper, by John Campbell and Tuomo Vuolteenaho of Harvard University, tries to resuscitate beta by splitting it into two.* The authors start from first principles. In essence, the value of a company depends on two things: its expected profits and the interest rate used to discount these profits. Changes in share prices therefore stem from changes in one of these factors.

From this observation, these authors propose two types of beta: one to gauge shares' responses to changes in profits; the other to pick up the effects of changes in the interest rate. Allowing for separate cash flow versus interest rate betas helps better explain the performance of small and value companies. Shares of such companies are more sensitive than the average to news about profits, in part because they are bets on future growth. Shares with high price–earnings ratios

vary more with the discount rate. In all cases, above-average returns compensate investors for above-average risks.

EQUITY'S ALLURE

Beta is a tool for comparing shares with each other. Recently, however, investors have been worried about equity as an asset class. The crash left investors asking what became of the fabled equity premium, the amount by which they can expect returns on shares to exceed those from government bonds.

History says that shareholders have a lot to be optimistic about. Over the past 100 years, investors in American shares have enjoyed a premium, relative to Treasury bonds, of around seven percentage points. Similar effects have been seen in other countries. Some studies have reached less optimistic conclusions, suggesting a premium of four or five points. But even this premium seems generous.

Many answers have been put forward to explain the premium. One is that workers cannot hedge against many risks, such as losing their jobs, which tend to hit at the same time as stock market crashes; this means that buying shares would increase the volatility of their income, so that investors require a premium to be persuaded to hold them. Another is that shares, especially in small companies, are much less liquid than government debt. It is also sometimes argued that in extreme times—in depression or war, or after bubbles—equities fare much worse than bonds, so that equity investors demand higher returns to compensate them for the risk of catastrophe.

Yes, over long periods equities have done better than bonds. But the equity "premium" is unpredictable. Searching for a consistent, God-given premium is a fool's errand.

---

*John Campbell and Tuomo Vuolteenaho, "Bad Beta, Good Beta," *American Economic Review* 94 (December 2004), pp. 1249–1275.

---

systematic versus diversifiable risk. The CAPM therefore provides a useful framework for thinking rigorously about the relationship between security risk and return. This is as much as Copernicus had when he was shown the prepublication version of his book just before he passed away.

7.4 | Multifactor Models and the CAPM

The index model introduced earlier in the chapter gave us a way of decomposing stock variability into market or systematic risk, due largely to macroeconomic factors, versus firm-specific effects that can be diversified in large portfolios. In the index model, the return on the market portfolio summarized the aggregate impact of macro factors. In reality, however, systematic risk is not due to one source, but instead derives from uncertainty in many economywide factors such as business-cycle risk, interest or inflation rate risk, energy price risk, and so on. It stands to reason that a more explicit representation of systematic risk, allowing for the possibility that different stocks exhibit different sensitivities to its various facets, would constitute a useful refinement of the single-factor model. It is easy to see that models that allow for several systematic factors—**multifactor models**—can provide better descriptions of security returns.

Let's illustrate with a two-factor model. Suppose the two most important macroeconomic sources of risk are uncertainties surrounding the state of the business cycle, news of which

multifactor models

Models of security returns positing that returns respond to several systematic factors.

207

we again assume is reflected in the rate of return on a broad market index such as the S&P 500, and unanticipated changes in interest rates, which may be captured by the return on a Treasury-bond portfolio. The return on any stock will respond to both sources of macro risk as well as to its own firm-specific influences. Therefore, we can expand the single-index model, Equation 7.3, describing the excess rate of return on stock i in some time period t as follows:

$$R_{it} = \alpha_i + \beta_{iM} R_{Mt} + \beta_{iTB} R_{TBt} + e_{it} \qquad \text{(7.5)}$$

where β_{iTB} is the sensitivity of the stock's excess return to that of the T-bond portfolio, and R_{TBt} is the excess return of the T-bond portfolio in month t.

The two indexes on the right-hand side of the equation capture the effect of the two systematic factors in the economy. As in the single-index model, the coefficients of each index in Equation 7.5 measure the sensitivity of share returns to that source of systematic risk. As before, e_{it} reflects firm-specific influences in period t.

How will the security market line of the CAPM generalize once we recognize the presence of multiple sources of systematic risk? Not surprisingly, a multifactor index model gives rise to a multifactor security market line in which the risk premium is determined by the exposure to *each* systematic risk factor and by a risk premium associated with each of those factors. Such a multifactor CAPM was first presented by Merton (1973).

For example, in a two-factor economy in which risk exposures can be measured by Equation 7.5, the expected rate of return on a security would be the sum of three terms:

1. The risk-free rate of return.
2. The sensitivity to the market index (i.e., the market beta, β_{iM}) times the risk premium of the index, $[E(r_M) - r_f]$.
3. The sensitivity to interest rate risk (i.e., the T-bond beta, β_{iTB}) times the risk premium of the T-bond portfolio, $[E(r_{TB}) - r_f]$.

This assertion is expressed mathematically as a two-factor security market line for security i:

$$E(r_i) = r_f + \beta_{iM}[E(r_M) - r_f] + \beta_{iTB}[E(r_{TB}) - r_f] \qquad \text{(7.6)}$$

Equation 7.6 is an expansion of the simple security market line. In the usual SML, the benchmark risk premium is given by the risk premium of the market portfolio, $E(r_M) - r_f$, but once we generalize to multiple risk sources, each with its own risk premium, we see that the insights are highly similar.

EXAMPLE   7.8

A Two-Factor SML

Northeast Airlines has a market beta of 1.2 and a T-bond beta of .7. Suppose the risk premium of the market index is 6%, while that of the T-bond portfolio is 3%. Then the overall risk premium on Northeast stock is the sum of the risk premiums required as compensation for each source of systematic risk.

The risk premium attributable to market risk is the stock's exposure to that risk, 1.2, multiplied by the corresponding risk premium, 6%, or $1.2 \times 6\% = 7.2\%$. Similarly, the risk premium attributable to interest rate risk is $.7 \times 3\% = 2.1\%$. The total risk premium is $7.2 + 2.1 = 9.3\%$. Therefore, if the risk-free rate is 4%, the expected return on the portfolio should be

4.0%	Risk-free rate
+ 7.2	+ Risk premium for exposure to market risk
+ 2.1	+ Risk premium for exposure to interest-rate risk
13.3%	Total expected return

More concisely,

$$E(r) = 4\% + 1.2 \times 6\% + .7 \times 3\% = 13.3\%$$

Suppose the risk premiums in Example 7.8 were $E(r_M) - r_f = 4\%$ and $E(r_{TB}) - r_f = 2\%$. What would be the equilibrium expected rate of return on Northeast Airlines?

CONCEPT *check* **7.5**

The multifactor model clearly gives us a much richer way to think about risk exposures and compensation for those exposures than the single-index model or the CAPM. But what are the relevant additional systematic factors?

One approach to selecting additional factors is to identify major systematic risks facing investors. Each source of risk would carry its own risk premium, as we just saw in Example 7.8. The challenge here is to identify the empirically important factors.

An alternative approach is to search for characteristics that seem on *empirical* grounds to proxy for exposure to systematic risk. The factors are chosen as variables that on past evidence seem to predict high average returns and therefore may be capturing risk premiums. We start with this approach.

The Fama-French Three-Factor Model

Fama and French (1996) proposed a three-factor model that has become a standard tool for empirical studies of asset returns. Fama and French add firm size and book-to-market ratio to the market index to explain average returns. These additional factors are motivated by the observations that average returns on stocks of small firms and on stocks of firms with a high ratio of book value of equity to market value of equity have historically been higher than predicted by the security market line of the CAPM. This observation suggests that size or the book-to-market (B/M) ratio may be *proxies* for exposures to sources of systematic risk not captured by the CAPM beta, and thus result in return premiums. For example, Fama and French point out that firms with high ratios of book-to-market value are more likely to be in financial distress and that small stocks may be more sensitive to changes in business conditions. Thus, these variables may capture sensitivity to macroeconomic risk factors.

While the high book-to-market group includes many firms in financial distress, which depresses market value relative to book value, for the most part this group includes relatively mature firms. The latter derive a larger share of their market value from assets already in place, rather than growth opportunities. This group often is called "value" stocks. In contrast, low B/M companies are viewed as "growth firms" whose market values derive from anticipated future cash flows, rather than from assets already in place. Considerable evidence (which we will review in the following chapter) suggests that value stocks trade at lower prices than growth stocks (or equivalently, have offered a higher expected rate of return); the differential is known as the value premium.

While a value premium may be appropriate compensation for risk for a firm whose high B/M ratio reflects potential financial distress, it would seem paradoxical for firms whose high B/M ratio reflects maturity and thus more predictable future cash flows. It implies that, other things equal, the required rate for growth stocks is lower than that of more mature value firms. This is a puzzle; one explanation is that mature firms with large amounts of installed capital confront higher adjustment costs in adapting to shocks in the product markets in which they operate.

How can we make the Fama-French (FF) model operational? To illustrate, we will follow the same general approach that we applied for Google earlier, but now using the more general model.

Collecting and processing data To create portfolios that track the size and B/M factors, one can sort industrial firms by size (market capitalization or market "cap") and by B/M ratio. The size premium is constructed as the difference in returns between small and large firms and is denoted by SMB ("small minus big"). Similarly, the B/M premium is calculated as the difference in returns between firms with a high versus low B/M ratio, and is denoted HML ("high minus low" ratio).

TABLE 7.3
Statistics for monthly rates of return January 2006–December 2008

Security	Average (%)	SD (%)	Geometric Average (%)	Cumulative Return%*
T-bill	0.31%	0.12%	0.32%	11.77%
Broad index excess return	−0.99	4.77	−2.02	−51.06
SMB return	−0.11	2.16	−1.02	−30.20
HML return	0.11	2.10	−0.86	−26.10
Google excess return	−0.65	11.51	−1.84	−47.85

*Total (not excess) return.

Taking the difference in returns between two portfolios has an economic interpretation. The SMB return, for example, equals the return from a long position in small stocks, financed with a short position in the large stocks. Note that this is a portfolio that entails no *net* investment.[10]

Summary statistics for these portfolios in our sample period are reported in Table 7.3. We use a broad market index, the value-weighted return on all stocks traded on U.S. national exchanges (NYSE, Amex, and NASDAQ) to compute the excess return on the market portfolio.

The SMB portfolio returned a negative average of −.11% per month, with a standard deviation of 2.16%. The HML portfolio lived up to its reputation for better-than-average returns. A long position in higher B/M stocks, financed by a short position in low B/M stocks, shows a positive average return of .11%, compared with −.99% on the broad market index. The HML return also is less volatile, with a standard deviation of 2.10%.

The "returns" of the SMB and HML portfolios require careful interpretation, however. As noted above, these portfolios do not by themselves represent investment portfolios, as they entail zero net investment. Rather, they represent the additional returns to investors who add positions in these portfolios to the rest of their portfolios. The role of these positions is to identify the average rewards earned for exposures to the sources of risk for which they proxy.

To apply the FF three-factor portfolio to Google, we need to estimate Google's beta on each factor. To do so, we generalize the regression Equation 7.3 of the single-index model and fit a multivariate regression:[11]

$$r_G - r_f = \alpha_G + \beta_M (r_M - r_f) + \beta_{HML} r_{HML} + \beta_{SMB} r_{SMB} + e_G \qquad (7.7)$$

To the extent that returns on the size (SMB) and book-to-market (HML) portfolios proxy for risk that is not fully captured by the market index, the beta coefficients on these portfolios represent exposure to systematic risks beyond the market-index beta.[12]

---

[10]Interpreting the returns on the SMB and HML portfolios is a bit subtle because both portfolios are zero net investments, and therefore one cannot compute profit per dollar invested. For example in the SMB portfolio, for every dollar held in small capitalization stocks, there is an offsetting short position in large capitalization stocks. The "return" for this portfolio is actually the profit on the overall position per dollar invested in the small-cap firms (or equivalently, per dollar shorted in the large-cap firms).

[11]These data are available from Kenneth French's Web site: **mba.tuck.dartmouth.edu/pages/faculty/ken.french/data_library.html.**

[12]Here is a subtle point. When we estimate Equation 7.7, we subtract the risk-free return from the market portfolio, but not from the returns on the SMB or HML portfolios. The total rate of return on the market index represents compensation for *both* the time value of money (the risk-free rate) and investment risk. Therefore, only the excess of its return above the risk-free rate represents a premium or reward for bearing risk. In contrast, the SMB or HML portfolios are zero net investment positions. As a result, there is no compensation required for time value, only for risk, and the total "return" therefore may be interpreted as a risk premium.

TABLE 7.4			
Regression statistics for Google using the single-index and the FF three-factor models			

	Single-Index Regression		FF 3-Factor Model
	S&P 500	**Broad Market Index**	**FF 3-Factor Model**
Correlation coefficient	0.62	0.64	0.66
Adjusted *R*-square	0.37	0.39	0.39
Regression standard error	9.14	9.02	9.02
Intercept (alpha)	0.97	0.87	1.04
Market beta	1.64	1.53	1.61
SMB beta	–	–	−0.15
HML beta	–	–	−1.01

Estimation results   We summarize in Table 7.4 the estimation results from both the single-index model (estimated alternatively employing the S&P 500 Index and the broad market index) and the FF three-factor model.

First, notice that the broad market index includes more than 4,000 stocks, while the S&P 500 includes only 500 of the largest U.S. stocks, in which list Google ranked twenty-fourth in January 2009.[13] Second, keep in mind that these regressions use only 35 observations, significantly less than the standard practice of 60 observations or more. This limits the accuracy of the coefficient estimates (hence their standard errors are not shown) as well as the adjusted *R*-square.

Google's SMB beta is negative, −.15, consistent with its large size. We tend to observe large negative SMB coefficients only for the largest stocks. Google's HML beta of −1.01 indicates that despite its size, investors still view it as a growth firm. Google's market beta of 1.61 is consistent with Figure 7.3, and indicates high systematic risk.[14]

Finally, the correlation coefficients, adjusted *R*-square, and regression standard error indicate a slightly better ability of the FF model to explain patterns of returns. The superior explanatory power of the FF model is far clearer when applied to longer samples or portfolios rather than to individual securities.

What we learn from this regression   The FF three-factor model offers a richer and more accurate description of asset returns. The estimate suggests that, in addition to the cyclicality of Google, it is sensitive to the returns on the size (SMB) and value (HML) portfolios. Applying this model requires two more forecasts of future returns, namely, for the SMB and HML portfolios. We have so far in this section been using a T-bill rate of 2.75% and a market risk premium of 5.5%. If we add to these values a forecast of 2.5% for SMB and 4% for HML, the required rate for an investment with the same risk as Google's equity would be

$$E(r_{\mathrm{G}}) = r_f + \beta_M[E(r_M) - r_f] + \beta_{\mathrm{SMB}}E(r_{\mathrm{SMB}}) + \beta_{\mathrm{HML}}E(r_{\mathrm{HML}})$$
$$= 2.75 + 1.61 \times 5.5 - .15 \times 2.5 - 1.01 \times 4 = 7.19\%$$

which is considerably lower than the rate derived from cyclical considerations alone (i.e., single-beta models). Notice from this example that to obtain expected rates of return, the

[13]You may ask, "Why switch to another market index?" In Table 7.2 we were concerned with typical industry practice. When using the more sophisticated FF model, it is important to use a more representative index than the S&P 500, specifically one with greater representation of smaller and younger firms.

[14]It is worth noting that most practitioners use a single-index regression, employing the S&P 500 as the market index. The FF regressions use a broader index not so heavily concentrated in large stocks to measure systematic risk, and allow the SMB factor to capture some of the size effect. For large stocks like Google, the single-index model may give the appearance of higher beta (and therefore systematic risk) because size is not explicitly controlled for, and a large stock may have tighter correlation with an index composed solely of large firms.

FF model requires, in addition to a forecast of the market index return, a forecast of the returns of the SMB and HML portfolios, making the model much more difficult to apply. This can be a critical issue. If such forecasts are difficult to devise, the single-factor model may be preferred even if it is less successful in explaining *past* returns.

Another reason a multi-index model is more difficult to implement is that currently it would be difficult to hold the prescribed optimal portfolio. As of yet, there are no vehicles (index funds or ETFs) to directly invest in SMB and HML.

Passive investors would have to invest in a suitable small-stock portfolio and short a large-stock portfolio to substitute for SMB. Similarly, they would have to buy value stocks and short growth stocks to substitute for HML. This is no small feat. Even for professional managers, investing in SMB and HML would be challenging. It is no wonder that while the FF model (and its successors with even additional factors) has largely superseded the single-index CAPM for the purpose of benchmarking investment performance, the single-index model still dominates the investments industry.

Factor Models with Macroeconomic Variables

The alternative to the Fama-French approach, which selects factors based on past empirical association with high average returns, is to select risk factors that capture uncertainties that might concern a large segment of investors. We choose factors that concern investors sufficiently that they will demand meaningful risk premiums to bear exposure to those sources of risk. These are said to be *priced* risk factors.[15]

An early and still influential foray into multivariate models with economic variables was made by Chen, Roll, and Ross (1986), who used an extensive list of economic variables to proxy for various systematic factors affecting returns: change in industrial production, change in expected inflation, unanticipated inflation, the excess return of long-term government bonds over short-term government bonds, and the excess return on long-term corporate bonds over long-term government bonds.

Industrial production is a proxy for overall economic activity. The rate of inflation affects many economic variables that bear on stock prices. Changes in the expected rate of inflation and transitory changes in that rate may affect stock prices in different ways and so are considered separately. The difference between the yields to maturity (YTM) on long- and short-term default-free (government) bonds is called the *term premium* and measures term structure risk. Finally, the difference between the YTM on long-term corporate bonds that are subject to default risk and the YTM on equal maturity default-free (government) bonds—called the *default premium*—reflects probabilities of bankruptcy in the corporate sector and hence helps measure business-cycle conditions.

Multifactor Models and the Validity of the CAPM

The single-index CAPM fails empirical tests because the single-market index used to test these models fails to fully explain returns on too many securities. In short, too many statistically significant values of alpha (which the CAPM implies should be zero) show up in regressions of the type we have demonstrated. Despite this failure, it is still used widely in the industry.

Multifactor models such as the FF model may also be tested by the prevalence of significant alpha values. The three-factor model shows a material improvement over the single-index model in that regard. But the use of such models comes at a price: In many applications, they require forecasts of the additional factor returns. If forecasts of those additional factors are

---

[15]Some factors might help to explain returns but still might not carry a risk premium. For example, securities of firms in the same industry may be highly correlated. If we were to run a regression of the returns on one such security on the returns of the market index and a portfolio of the other securities in the industry, we would expect to find a significant coefficient on the industry portfolio. However, if this industry is a small part of the broad market, the industry risk can be diversified away. Thus, although an industry coefficient measures sensitivity to the industry factor, it does not necessarily represent exposure to systematic risk and will not result in a risk premium. We say that such factors *are not priced*, i.e., they do not carry a risk premium.

less accurate than forecasts of the market index, these models will be less accurate than the theoretically inferior single-index model. Nevertheless, multifactor models have a definite appeal, since it is clear that real-world risk is multifaceted.

Merton (1973) first showed that the CAPM could be extended to allow for multiple sources of systematic risk. His model results in a multifactor security market line like that of Equation 7.8, but with risk factors that relate to the extra-market sources of risk that investors wish to hedge. In this light, the correct interpretation of multivariate index models such as FF or Chen, Roll, and Ross is that they constitute an application of the multifactor CAPM, rather than a rejection of the underlying logic of the simple model.

7.5 Factor Models and The Arbitrage Pricing Theory

One reason for skepticism about the validity of the CAPM is the unrealistic nature of the assumptions needed to derive it. For this reason, as well as for the important economic insights it offers, the arbitrage pricing theory (APT) is of great interest. This model also provides an SML relating risk and return. To understand this theory we begin with the concept of *arbitrage*.

Arbitrage is the act of exploiting the mispricing of two or more securities to achieve risk-free profits. As a trivial example, consider a security that is priced differently in two markets. A long position in the cheaper market financed by a short position in the more expensive one will lead to a sure profit. As investors avidly pursue this strategy, prices are forced back into alignment, so arbitrage opportunities vanish almost as quickly as they materialize.

arbitrage

Creation of riskless profits made possible by relative mispricing among securities.

The first to apply this concept to equilibrium security returns was Ross (1976), who developed the arbitrage pricing theory (APT). The APT depends on the assumption that well-functioning capital markets preclude arbitrage opportunities. A violation of the APT's pricing relationships will cause extremely strong pressure to restore them even if only a limited number of investors become aware of the disequilibrium. Ross's accomplishment is to derive the equilibrium rates of return and risk premiums that would prevail in a market where prices are in alignment to the extent that arbitrage opportunities have been eliminated. The APT thus arrives at a model of risk and return without the more objectionable assumptions of the CAPM, specifically, the assumptions concerning how individual investors form their portfolios.

Well-Diversified Portfolios and Arbitrage Pricing Theory

The APT uses factor models to describe individual security returns, but its central insight emerges by considering highly diversified portfolios for which residual risk may be effectively ignored. We will see that fairly straightforward no-arbitrage restrictions apply to these portfolios, and these considerations quickly lead to a risk-return relationship. Therefore, this path to a security market line is called **arbitrage pricing theory.**

In its simple form, just like the CAPM, the APT posits a single-factor security market. Thus, the excess rate of return on each security, $R_i = r_i - r_f$, can be represented by

$$R_i = \alpha_i + \beta_i R_M + e_i \qquad (7.8)$$

arbitrage pricing theory (APT)

A theory of risk-return relationships derived from no-arbitrage considerations in large capital markets.

where alpha, α_i, and beta, β_i, are known, and where we treat R_M as the single factor.

Suppose now that we construct a highly diversified portfolio with a given beta. If we use enough securities to form the portfolio, the resulting diversification will strip the portfolio of nonsystematic risk. Because such a **well-diversified portfolio** has for all practical purposes zero firm-specific risk, we can write its returns as

$$R_P = \alpha_P + \beta_P R_M \qquad (7.9)$$

well-diversified portfolio

A portfolio sufficiently diversified that nonsystematic risk is negligible.

(This portfolio is risky, however, because the excess return on the index, R_M, is random.)

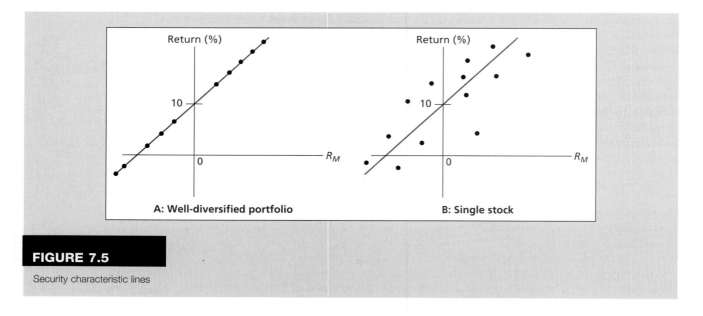

FIGURE 7.5

Security characteristic lines

Figure 7.5 illustrates the difference between a single security with a beta of 1.0 and a well-diversified portfolio with the same beta. For the portfolio (Panel A), all the returns plot exactly on the security characteristic line. There is no dispersion around the line, as in Panel B, because the effects of firm-specific events are eliminated by diversification. Therefore, in Equation 7.9, there is no residual term, e.

Notice that Equation 7.9 implies that if the portfolio beta is zero, then $R_P = \alpha_P$. This implies a riskless rate of return: There is no firm-specific risk because of diversification and no factor risk because beta is zero. Remember, however, that R denotes excess returns. So the equation implies that a portfolio with a beta of zero has a riskless *excess* return of α_P, that is, a return higher than the risk-free rate by the amount α_P. But this implies that α_P must equal zero, or else an immediate arbitrage opportunity opens up. For example, if α_P is greater than zero, you can borrow at the risk-free rate and use the proceeds to buy the well-diversified zero-beta portfolio. You borrow risklessly at rate r_f and invest risklessly at rate $r_f + \alpha_P$, clearing the riskless differential of α_P.

EXAMPLE | 7.9

Arbitrage with a Zero-Beta Portfolio

Suppose that the risk-free rate is 6%, and a well-diversified zero-beta portfolio earns (a sure) rate of return of 7%, that is, an excess return of 1%. Then borrow at 6% and invest in the zero-beta portfolio to earn 7%. You will earn a sure profit of 1% of the invested funds without putting up any of your own money. If the zero-beta portfolio earns 5%, then you can sell it short and lend at 6% with the same result.

In fact, we can go further and show that the alpha of *any* well-diversified portfolio in Equation 7.9 must be zero, even if the beta is not zero. The proof is similar to the easy zero-beta case. If the alphas were not zero, then we could combine two of these portfolios into a zero-beta riskless portfolio with a rate of return not equal to the risk-free rate. But this, as we have just seen, would be an arbitrage opportunity.

To see how the arbitrage strategy would work, suppose that portfolio V has a beta of β_v and an alpha of α_v. Similarly, suppose portfolio U has a beta of β_u and an alpha of α_u.

Taking advantage of any arbitrage opportunity involves buying and selling assets in proportions that create a risk-free profit on a costless position. To eliminate risk, we buy portfolio V and sell portfolio U in proportions chosen so that the combination portfolio $(V + U)$ will have a beta of zero. The portfolio weights that satisfy this condition are

$$w_v = \frac{-\beta_u}{\beta_v - \beta_u} \qquad w_u = \frac{\beta_v}{\beta_v - \beta_u}$$

Note that w_v plus w_u add up to 1.0 and that the beta of the combination is in fact zero:

$$\text{Beta}(V + U) = \beta_v \frac{-\beta_u}{\beta_v - \beta_u} + \beta_u \frac{\beta_v}{\beta_v - \beta_u} = 0$$

Therefore, the portfolio is riskless: It has no sensitivity to the factor. But the excess return of the portfolio is not zero unless α_v and α_u equal zero:

$$R(V + U) = \alpha_v \frac{-\beta_u}{\beta_v - \beta_u} + \alpha_u \frac{\beta_v}{\beta_v - \beta_u} \neq 0$$

Therefore, unless α_v and α_u equal zero, the zero-beta portfolio has a certain rate of return that differs from the risk-free rate (its excess return is different from zero). We have seen that this gives rise to an arbitrage opportunity.

Suppose that the risk-free rate is 7% and a well-diversified portfolio, *V*, with beta of 1.3 has an alpha of 2% and another well-diversified portfolio, *U*, with beta of .8 has an alpha of 1%. We go long on *V* and short on *U* with proportions

$$w_v = \frac{-.8}{1.3 - .8} = -1.6 \qquad w_u = \frac{1.3}{1.3 - .8} = 2.6$$

These proportions add up to 1.0 and result in a portfolio with beta = $-1.6 \times 1.3 + 2.6 \times .8 = 0$. The alpha of the portfolio is: $-1.6 \times 2\% + 2.6 \times 1\% = -.6\%$. This means that the riskless portfolio will earn a rate of return that is less than the risk-free rate by .6%. We now complete the arbitrage by selling (or going short on) the combination portfolio and investing the proceeds at 7%, risklessly profiting by the 60 basis-point differential in returns.

EXAMPLE 7.10

Arbitrage with Mispriced Portfolios

We conclude that the only value for alpha that rules out arbitrage opportunities is zero. Therefore, rewrite Equation 7.9 setting alpha equal to zero:

$$R_P = \beta_P R_M$$
$$r_P - r_f = \beta_P (r_M - r_f)$$
$$E(r_P) = r_f + \beta_P [E(r_M) - r_f]$$

Hence, we arrive at the same expected return–beta relationship as the CAPM without requiring assumptions about either investor preferences or access to the all-inclusive (and elusive) market portfolio.

The APT and the CAPM

Why did we need so many restrictive assumptions to derive the CAPM when the APT seems to arrive at the expected return–beta relationship with seemingly fewer and less objectionable assumptions? The answer is simple: The APT applies only to well-diversified portfolios. Absence of riskless arbitrage alone cannot guarantee that, in equilibrium, the expected return–beta relationship will hold for any and all assets.

With additional effort, however, one can use the APT to show that the relationship must hold approximately even for individual assets. The essence of the proof is that if the expected return–beta relationship were violated by many individual securities, it would be virtually impossible for all well-diversified portfolios to satisfy the relationship. So the relationship must *almost* surely hold true for individual securities.

We say "almost" because, according to the APT, there is no guarantee that all individual assets will lie on the SML. If only a few securities violated the SML, their effect on well-diversified portfolios could conceivably be negligible. In this sense, it is possible that the SML relationship is violated for some securities. If many securities violate the expected return–beta relationship, however, the relationship will no longer hold for well-diversified portfolios comprising these securities, and arbitrage opportunities will be available.

The APT serves many of the same functions as the CAPM. It gives us a benchmark for fair rates of return that can be used for capital budgeting, security evaluation, or investment performance evaluation. Moreover, the APT highlights the crucial distinction between nondiversifiable risk (systematic or factor risk) that requires a reward in the form of a risk premium and diversifiable risk that does not.

The bottom line is that neither of these theories dominates the other. The APT is more general in that it gets us to the expected return–beta relationship without requiring many of the unrealistic assumptions of the CAPM, particularly the reliance on the market portfolio. The latter improves the prospects for testing the APT. But the CAPM is more general in that it applies to all assets without reservation. The good news is that both theories agree on the expected return–beta relationship.

It is worth noting that because past tests of the expected return–beta relationship examined the rates of return on highly diversified portfolios, they actually came closer to testing the APT than the CAPM. Thus, it appears that econometric concerns, too, favor the APT.

Multifactor Generalization of the APT and CAPM

So far, we've examined the APT in a one-factor world. As we noted earlier in the chapter, this is too simplistic. In reality, there are several sources of systematic risk such as uncertainty in the business cycle, interest rates, energy prices, and so on. Presumably, exposure to any of these factors singly or together will affect a stock's perceived riskiness and appropriate expected rate of return. We can use a multifactor version of the APT to accommodate these multiple sources of risk.

Suppose we generalize the single-factor model expressed in Equation 7.8 to a two-factor model:

$$R_i = \alpha_i + \beta_{i1}R_{M1} + \beta_{i2}R_{M2} + e_i \qquad (7.10)$$

where R_{M1} and R_{M2} are the excess returns on portfolios that represent the two systematic factors. Factor 1 might be, for example, unanticipated changes in industrial production, while factor 2 might represent unanticipated changes in short-term interest rates. We assume again that there are many securities available with any combination of betas. This implies that we can form well-diversified **factor portfolios,** that is, portfolios that have a beta of 1.0 on one factor and a beta of zero on all others. Thus, a factor portfolio with a beta of 1.0 on the first factor will have a rate of return of R_{M1}; a factor portfolio with a beta of 1.0 on the second factor will have a rate of return of R_{M2}; and so on. Factor portfolios can serve as the benchmark portfolios for a multifactor generalization of the security market line relationship.

factor portfolio

A well-diversified portfolio constructed to have a beta of 1.0 on one factor and a beta of zero on any other factor.

EXAMPLE 7.11

Multifactor APT

Suppose the two-factor portfolios, here called portfolios 1 and 2, have expected returns $E(r_1) = 10\%$ and $E(r_2) = 12\%$. Suppose further that the risk-free rate is 4%. The risk premium on the first factor portfolio is therefore 6%, while that on the second factor portfolio is 8%.

Now consider an arbitrary well-diversified portfolio (*A*), with beta on the first factor, $\beta_{A1} = .5$, and on the second factor, $\beta_{A2} = .75$. The multifactor APT states that the portfolio risk premium must equal the sum of the risk premiums required as compensation to investors for each source of systematic risk. The risk premium attributable to risk factor 1 is the portfolio's exposure to factor 1, β_{A1}, times the risk premium earned on the first factor portfolio, $E(r_1) - r_f$. Therefore, the portion of portfolio A's risk premium that is compensation for its exposure to the first risk factor is $\beta_{A1}[E(r_1) - r_f] = .5(10\% - 4\%) = 3\%$, while the risk premium attributable to risk factor 2 is $\beta_{A2}[E(r_2) - r_f] = .75(12\% - 4\%) = 6\%$. The total risk premium on the portfolio, therefore, should be 3 + 6 = 9%, and the total return on the portfolio should be 13%.

4%	Risk-free rate
+ 3%	Risk premium for exposure to factor 1
+ 6%	Risk premium for exposure to factor 2
13%	Total expected return

The spreadsheet below contains monthly returns for a small sample of stocks. A related workbook (also available at **www.mhhe.com/bkm**) contains spreadsheets that show raw returns, risk premiums, and beta coefficients for the stocks in the Dow Jones Industrial Average. The security characteristic lines are estimated with five years of monthly returns.

eXcel
Please visit us at
www.mhhe.com/bkm

Rates of Return					
Month	Ford	GM	Toyota	S&P 500	T-bills
Dec-08	-18.34	23.02	-2.95	-8.31	0.09
Nov-08	-14.87	-25.44	3.71	0.97	0.02
Oct-08	22.83	-26.04	-17.07	-7.04	0.08
Sep-08	-57.88	-13.77	-11.32	-16.67	0.15
Aug-08	16.59	-29.61	-4.23	-9.54	0.12
Jul-08	-7.08	-4.92	4.11	1.40	0.15
Jun-08	-0.21	-11.01	-8.46	-1.07	0.17

To generalize the argument in Example 7.11, note that the factor exposure of any portfolio P is given by its betas, β_{P1} and β_{P2}. A competing portfolio, Q, can be formed from factor portfolios with the following weights: β_{P1} in the first factor portfolio; β_{P2} in the second factor portfolio; and $1 - \beta_{P2} - \beta_{P2}$ in T-bills. By construction, Q will have betas equal to those of portfolio P and an expected return of

$$E(r_Q) = \beta_{P1}E(r_1) + \beta_{P2}E(r_2) + (1 - \beta_{P1} - \beta_{P2})r_f$$
$$= r_f + \beta_{P1}[E(r_1) - r_f] + \beta_{P2}[E(r_2) - r_f] \qquad \textbf{(7.11)}$$

Using the numbers in Example 7.11,

$$E(r_Q) = 4 + .5 \times (10 - 4) + .75 \times (12 - 4) = 13\%$$

Because portfolio Q has precisely the same exposures as portfolio A to the two sources of risk, their expected returns also ought to be equal. So portfolio A also ought to have an expected return of 13%.

Suppose, however, that the expected return on portfolio A is 12% rather than 13%. This return would give rise to an arbitrage opportunity. Form a portfolio from the factor portfolios with the same betas as portfolio A. This requires weights of .5 on the first factor portfolio, .75 on the second portfolio, and −.25 on the risk-free asset. This portfolio has exactly the same factor betas as portfolio A: a beta of .5 on the first factor because of its .5 weight on the first factor portfolio and a beta of .75 on the second factor.

Now invest $1 in portfolio Q and sell (short) $1 in portfolio A. Your net investment is zero, but your expected dollar profit is positive and equal to

$$\$1 \times E(r_Q) - \$1 \times E(r_A) = \$1 \times .13 - \$1 \times .12 = \$.01$$

Moreover, your net position is riskless. Your exposure to each risk factor cancels out because you are long $1 in portfolio Q and short $1 in portfolio A, and both of these well-diversified portfolios have exactly the same factor betas. Thus, if portfolio A's expected return differs from that of portfolio Q's, you can earn positive risk-free profits on a zero net investment position. This is an arbitrage opportunity.

Hence, any well-diversified portfolio with betas β_{P1} and β_{P2} must have the return given in Equation 7.11 if arbitrage opportunities are to be ruled out. A comparison of Equations 7.2

and 7.11 shows that 7.11 is simply a generalization of the one-factor SML. In fact, if you compare Equation 7.11 to Equation 7.6, you will see that they are nearly identical. Equation 7.6 is simply more specific about the identities of the relevant factor portfolios. We conclude that the multifactor generalizations of the security market line of the APT and the CAPM are effectively equivalent.

Finally, extension of the multifactor SML of Equation 7.11 to individual assets is precisely the same as for the one-factor APT. Equation 7.11 cannot be satisfied by every well-diversified portfolio unless it is satisfied by virtually every security taken individually. Equation 7.11 thus represents the multifactor SML for an economy with multiple sources of risk.

The generalized APT must be qualified with respect to individual assets just as in the single-factor case. A multifactor CAPM would, at the cost of additional assumptions, apply to any and all individual assets. As we have seen, the result will be a security market equation (a multidimensional SML) that is identical to that of the multifactor APT.

CONCEPT
check **7.6**

Using the factor portfolios of Example 7.11, find the fair rate of return on a security with $\beta_1 = .2$ and $\beta_2 = 1.4$.

SUMMARY

- The CAPM assumes investors are rational, single-period planners who agree on a common input list from security analysis and seek mean-variance optimal portfolios.
- The CAPM assumes ideal security markets in the sense that: (*a*) markets are large and investors are price takers, (*b*) there are no taxes or transaction costs, (*c*) all risky assets are publicly traded, and (*d*) any amount can be borrowed and lent at a fixed, risk-free rate. These assumptions mean that all investors will hold identical risky portfolios. The CAPM implies that, in equilibrium, the market portfolio is the unique mean-variance efficient tangency portfolio, which indicates that a passive strategy is efficient.
- The market portfolio is a value-weighted portfolio. Each security is held in a proportion equal to its market value divided by the total market value of all securities. The risk premium on the market portfolio is proportional to its variance, σ_M^2, and to the risk aversion of the average investor.
- The CAPM implies that the risk premium on any individual asset or portfolio is the product of the risk premium of the market portfolio and the asset's beta. The security market line shows the return demanded by investors as a function of the beta of their investment. This expected return is a benchmark for evaluating investment performance.
- In a single-index security market, once an index is specified, a security beta can be estimated from a regression of the security's excess return on the index's excess return. This regression line is called the security characteristic line (SCL). The intercept of the SCL, called alpha, represents the average excess return on the security when the index excess return is zero. The CAPM implies that alphas should be zero.
- The CAPM and the security market line can be used to establish benchmarks for evaluation of investment performance or to determine appropriate discount rates for capital budgeting applications. They are also used in regulatory proceedings concerning the "fair" rate of return for regulated industries.
- The CAPM is usually implemented as a single-factor model, with all systematic risk summarized by the return on a broad market index. However, multifactor generalizations of the basic model may be specified to accommodate multiple sources of systematic risk. In such multifactor extensions of the CAPM, the risk premium of any security is determined by its sensitivity to each systematic risk factor as well as the risk premium associated with that source of risk.
- There are two general approaches to finding extra-market systematic risk factors. One is characteristics based and looks for factors that are empirically associated with high

average returns and so may be proxies for relevant measures of systematic risk. The other focuses on factors that are plausibly important sources of risk to wide segments of investors and may thus command risk premiums.

- An arbitrage opportunity arises when the disparity between two or more security prices enables investors to construct a zero net investment portfolio that will yield a sure profit. The presence of arbitrage opportunities and the resulting volume of trades will create pressure on security prices that will persist until prices reach levels that preclude arbitrage. Only a few investors need to become aware of arbitrage opportunities to trigger this process because of the large volume of trades in which they will engage.

- When securities are priced so that there are no arbitrage opportunities, the market satisfies the no-arbitrage condition. Price relationships that satisfy the no-arbitrage condition are important because we expect them to hold in real-world markets.

- Portfolios are called *well diversified* if they include a large number of securities in such proportions that the residual or diversifiable risk of the portfolio is negligible.

- In a single-factor security market, all well-diversified portfolios must satisfy the expected return–beta relationship of the SML in order to satisfy the no-arbitrage condition. If all well-diversified portfolios satisfy the expected return–beta relationship, then all but a small number of securities also must satisfy this relationship.

- The APT implies the same expected return–beta relationship as the CAPM, yet does not require that all investors be mean-variance optimizers. The price of this generality is that the APT does not guarantee this relationship for all securities at all times.

- A multifactor APT generalizes the single-factor model to accommodate several sources of systematic risk.

alpha, 196	expected return–beta relationship, 193	security characteristic line (SCL), 201
arbitrage, 213	factor portfolio, 216	security market line (SML), 195
arbitrage pricing theory (APT), 213	market portfolio, 191	
capital asset pricing model (CAPM), 190	multifactor models, 207	well-diversified portfolio, 213
	mutual fund theorem, 192	

PROBLEM SETS

 Select problems are available in McGraw-Hill Connect. Please see the packaging options section of the preface for more information.

Basic

1. Suppose investors believe that the standard deviation of the market-index portfolio has increased by 50%. What does the CAPM imply about the effect of this change on the required rate of return on Google's investment projects?

2. Consider the statement: "If we can identify a portfolio that beats the S&P 500 Index portfolio, then we should reject the single-index CAPM." Do you agree or disagree? Explain.

3. Which of the following statements is *true*? Explain.
   - *a.* It is possible that the APT is valid and the CAPM is not.
   - *b.* It is possible that the CAPM is valid and the APT is not.

Intermediate

4. What must be the beta of a portfolio with $E(r_P) = 20\%$, if $r_f = 5\%$ and $E(r_M) = 15\%$?

5. The market price of a security is $40. Its expected rate of return is 13%. The risk-free rate is 7%, and the market risk premium is 8%. What will the market price of the security be if its beta doubles (and all other variables remain unchanged)? Assume the stock is expected to pay a constant dividend in perpetuity.

6. You are a consultant to a large manufacturing corporation considering a project with the following net after-tax cash flows (in millions of dollars)

Years from Now	After-Tax CF
0	−20
1–9	10
10	20

The project's beta is 1.7. Assuming $r_f = 9\%$ and $E(r_M) = 19\%$, what is the net present value of the project? What is the highest possible beta estimate for the project before its NPV becomes negative?

7. Are the following statements *true* or *false*? Explain.
   a. Stocks with a beta of zero offer an expected rate of return of zero.
   b. The CAPM implies that investors require a higher return to hold highly volatile securities.
   c. You can construct a portfolio with a beta of .75 by investing .75 of the budget in T-bills and the remainder in the market portfolio.

8. Consider the following table, which gives a security analyst's expected return on two stocks for two particular market returns:

Market Return	Aggressive Stock	Defensive Stock
5%	2%	3.5%
20	32	14

   a. What are the betas of the two stocks?
   b. What is the expected rate of return on each stock if the market return is equally likely to be 5% or 20%?
   c. If the T-bill rate is 8%, and the market return is equally likely to be 5% or 20%, draw the SML for this economy.
   d. Plot the two securities on the SML graph. What are the alphas of each?
   e. What hurdle rate should be used by the management of the aggressive firm for a project with the risk characteristics of the defensive firm's stock?

If the simple CAPM is valid, which of the situations in Problems 9–15 below are possible? Explain. Consider each situation independently.

9.

Portfolio	Expected Return	Beta
A	20%	1.4
B	25	1.2

10.

Portfolio	Expected Return	Standard Deviation
A	30%	35%
B	40	25

11.

Portfolio	Expected Return	Standard Deviation
Risk-free	10%	0%
Market	18	24
A	16	12

12.

Portfolio	Expected Return	Standard Deviation
Risk-free	10%	0%
Market	18	24
A	20	22

13.

Portfolio	Expected Return	Beta
Risk-free	10%	0
Market	18	1.0
A	16	1.5

14.

Portfolio	Expected Return	Beta
Risk-free	10%	0
Market	18	1.0
A	16	.9

15.

Portfolio	Expected Return	Standard Deviation
Risk-free	10%	0%
Market	18	24
A	16	22

16. Go to **www.mhhe.com/bkm** and link to Chapter 7 materials, where you will find a spreadsheet with monthly returns for GM, Ford, and Toyota, the S&P 500, and Treasury bills.

    a. Estimate the index model for each firm over the full five-year period. Compare the betas of each firm.

    b. Now estimate the betas for each firm using only the first two years of the sample and then using only the last two years. How stable are the beta estimates obtained from these shorter subperiods?

eXcel

Please visit us at www.mhhe.com/bkm

In Problems 17–19 below, assume the risk-free rate is 8% and the expected rate of return on the market is 18%.

17. A share of stock is now selling for $100. It will pay a dividend of $9 per share at the end of the year. Its beta is 1.0. What do investors expect the stock to sell for at the end of the year?

18. I am buying a firm with an expected perpetual cash flow of $1,000 but am unsure of its risk. If I think the beta of the firm is zero, when the beta is really 1.0, how much *more* will I offer for the firm than it is truly worth?

19. A stock has an expected return of 6%. What is its beta?

20. Two investment advisers are comparing performance. One averaged a 19% return and the other a 16% return. However, the beta of the first adviser was 1.5, while that of the second was 1.0.

    a. Can you tell which adviser was a better selector of individual stocks (aside from the issue of general movements in the market)?

    b. If the T-bill rate were 6%, and the market return during the period were 14%, which adviser would be the superior stock selector?

    c. What if the T-bill rate were 3% and the market return 15%?

21. Suppose the yield on short-term government securities (perceived to be risk-free) is about 4%. Suppose also that the expected return required by the market for a portfolio with a beta of 1.0 is 12%. According to the capital asset pricing model:

 a. What is the expected return on the market portfolio?

 b. What would be the expected return on a zero-beta stock?

 c. Suppose you consider buying a share of stock at a price of $40. The stock is expected to pay a dividend of $3 next year and to sell then for $41. The stock risk has been evaluated at $\beta = -.5$. Is the stock overpriced or underpriced?

22. Based on current dividend yields and expected capital gains, the expected rates of return on portfolios A and B are 11% and 14%, respectively. The beta of A is .8 while that of B is 1.5. The T-bill rate is currently 6%, while the expected rate of return of the S&P 500 Index is 12%. The standard deviation of portfolio A is 10% annually, while that of B is 31%, and that of the index is 20%.

 a. If you currently hold a market index portfolio, would you choose to add either of these portfolios to your holdings? Explain.

 b. If instead you could invest *only* in bills and one of these portfolios, which would you choose?

23. Consider the following data for a one-factor economy. All portfolios are well diversified.

Portfolio	E(r)	Beta
A	10%	1.0
F	4	0

 Suppose another portfolio E is well diversified with a beta of 2/3 and expected return of 9%. Would an arbitrage opportunity exist? If so, what would the arbitrage strategy be?

24. Assume both portfolios A and B are well diversified, that $E(r_A) = 14\%$ and $E(r_B) = 14.8\%$. If the economy has only one factor, and $\beta_A = 1.0$ while $\beta_B = 1.1$, what must be the risk-free rate?

25. Assume a market index represents the common factor, and all stocks in the economy have a beta of 1.0. Firm-specific returns all have a standard deviation of 30%.

 Suppose an analyst studies 20 stocks and finds that one-half have an alpha of 3%, and one-half have an alpha of −3%. The analyst then buys $1 million of an equally weighted portfolio of the positive alpha stocks and sells short $1 million of an equally weighted portfolio of the negative alpha stocks.

 a. What is the expected profit (in dollars), and what is the standard deviation of the analyst's profit?

 b. How does your answer change if the analyst examines 50 stocks instead of 20? 100 stocks?

26. If the APT is to be a useful theory, the number of systematic factors in the economy must be small. Why?

27. The APT itself does not provide information on the factors that one might expect to determine risk premiums. How should researchers decide which factors to investigate? Is industrial production a reasonable factor to test for a risk premium? Why or why not?

28. Suppose two factors are identified for the U.S. economy: the growth rate of industrial production, IP, and the inflation rate, IR. IP is expected to be 4% and IR 6%. A stock with a beta of 1.0 on IP and .4 on IR currently is expected to provide a rate of return of 14%. If industrial production actually grows by 5%, while the inflation rate turns out to be 7%, what is your best guess for the rate of return on the stock?

29. Suppose there are two independent economic factors, M_1 and M_2. The risk-free rate is 7%, and all stocks have independent firm-specific components with a standard deviation of 50%. Portfolios A and B are both well diversified.

Portfolio	Beta on M_1	Beta on w_2	Expected Return (%)
A	1.8	2.1	40
B	2.0	−0.5	10

What is the expected return–beta relationship in this economy?

Challenge

30. As a finance intern at Pork Products, Jennifer Wainwright's assignment is to come up with fresh insights concerning the firm's cost of capital. She decides that this would be a good opportunity to try out the new material on the APT that she learned last semester. As such, she decides that three promising factors would be (i) the return on a broad-based index such as the S&P 500; (ii) the level of interest rates, as represented by the yield to maturity on 10-year Treasury bonds; and (iii) the price of hogs, which are particularly important to her firm. Her plan is to find the beta of Pork Products against each of these factors and to estimate the risk premium associated with exposure to each factor. Comment on Jennifer's choice of factors. Which are most promising with respect to the likely impact on her firm's cost of capital? Can you suggest improvements to her specification?

31. Suppose the market can be described by the following three sources of systematic risk. Each factor in the following table has a mean value of zero (so factor values represent realized surprises relative to prior expectations), and the risk premiums associated with each source of systematic risk are given in the last column.

Systematic Factor	Risk Premium
Industrial production, IP	6%
Interest rates, INT	2
Credit risk, CRED	4

The excess return, R, on a particular stock is described by the following equation that relates realized returns to surprises in the three systematic factors:

$$R = 6\% + 1.0 \text{ IP} + .5 \text{ INT} + .75 \text{ CRED} + e$$

Find the equilibrium expected excess return on this stock using the APT. Is the stock overpriced or underpriced?

CFA Problems

1. Which of the following statements about the security market line (SML) are *true*?
   a. The SML provides a benchmark for evaluating expected investment performance.
   b. The SML leads all investors to invest in the same portfolio of risky assets.
   c. The SML is a graphic representation of the relationship between expected return and beta.
   d. Properly valued assets plot exactly on the SML.

2. Karen Kay, a portfolio manager at Collins Asset Management, is using the capital asset pricing model for making recommendations to her clients. Her research department has developed the information shown in the following exhibit.

Forecasted Returns, Standard Deviations, and Betas		
	Forecasted Return	Standard Deviation	Beta
Stock X	14.0%	36%	0.8
Stock Y	17.0	25	1.5
Market index	14.0	15	1.0
Risk-free rate	5.0		

    a. Calculate expected return and alpha for each stock.

    b. Identify and justify which stock would be more appropriate for an investor who wants to

       i. Add this stock to a well-diversified equity portfolio.

      ii. Hold this stock as a single-stock portfolio.

3. Joan McKay is a portfolio manager for a bank trust department. McKay meets with two clients, Kevin Murray and Lisa York, to review their investment objectives. Each client expresses an interest in changing his or her individual investment objectives. Both clients currently hold well-diversified portfolios of risky assets.

    a. Murray wants to increase the expected return of his portfolio. State what action McKay should take to achieve Murray's objective. Justify your response in the context of the capital market line.

    b. York wants to reduce the risk exposure of her portfolio, but does not want to engage in borrowing or lending activities to do so. State what action McKay should take to achieve York's objective. Justify your response in the context of the security market line.

4. Jeffrey Bruner, CFA, uses the capital asset pricing model (CAPM) to help identify mispriced securities. A consultant suggests Bruner use arbitrage pricing theory (APT) instead. In comparing CAPM and APT, the consultant made the following arguments:

    a. Both the CAPM and APT require a mean-variance efficient market portfolio.

    b. The CAPM assumes that one specific factor explains security returns but APT does not.

State whether each of the consultant's arguments is correct or incorrect. Indicate, for each incorrect argument, why the argument is incorrect.

5. The security market line depicts:

    a. A security's expected return as a function of its systematic risk.

    b. The market portfolio as the optimal portfolio of risky securities.

    c. The relationship between a security's return and the return on an index.

    d. The complete portfolio as a combination of the market portfolio and the risk-free asset.

6. According to CAPM, the expected rate of return of a portfolio with a beta of 1.0 and an alpha of 0 is:

    a. Between r_M and r_f.

    b. The risk-free rate, r_f.

    c. $\beta\,(r_M - r_f)$.

    d. The expected return on the market, r_M.

The following table (for CFA Problems 7 and 8) shows risk and return measures for two portfolios.

Portfolio	Average Annual Rate of Return	Standard Deviation	Beta
R	11%	10%	0.5
S&P 500	14%	12%	1.0

7. When plotting portfolio *R* on the preceding table relative to the SML, portfolio *R* lies:

    a. On the SML.

    b. Below the SML.

    c. Above the SML.

    d. Insufficient data given.

8. When plotting portfolio *R* relative to the capital market line, portfolio *R* lies:

    a. On the CML.

    b. Below the CML.

    c. Above the CML.

    d. Insufficient data given.

9. Briefly explain whether investors should expect a higher return from holding portfolio *A* versus portfolio *B* under capital asset pricing theory (CAPM). Assume that both portfolios are fully diversified.

	Portfolio *A*	Portfolio *B*
Systematic risk (beta)	1.0	1.0
Specific risk for each individual security	High	Low

10. Assume that both *X* and *Y* are well-diversified portfolios and the risk-free rate is 8%.

Portfolio	Expected Return	Beta
X	16%	1.00
Y	12%	0.25

In this situation you could conclude that portfolios *X* and *Y:*
   a. Are in equilibrium.
   b. Offer an arbitrage opportunity.
   c. Are both underpriced.
   d. Are both fairly priced.

11. According to the theory of arbitrage:
   a. High-beta stocks are consistently overpriced.
   b. Low-beta stocks are consistently overpriced.
   c. Positive alpha investment opportunities will quickly disappear.
   d. Rational investors will pursue arbitrage consistent with their risk tolerance.

12. A zero-investment well-diversified portfolio with a positive alpha could arise if:
   a. The expected return of the portfolio equals zero.
   b. The capital market line is tangent to the opportunity set.
   c. The law of one price remains unviolated.
   d. A risk-free arbitrage opportunity exists.

13. An investor takes as large a position as possible when an equilibrium price relationship is violated. This is an example of:
   a. A dominance argument.
   b. The mean-variance efficient frontier.
   c. Arbitrage activity.
   d. The capital asset pricing model.

14. In contrast to the capital asset pricing model, arbitrage pricing theory:
   a. Requires that markets be in equilibrium.
   b. Uses risk premiums based on micro variables.
   c. Specifies the number and identifies specific factors that determine expected returns.
   d. Does not require the restrictive assumptions concerning the market portfolio.

Use data from the Standard & Poor's Market Insight Database at www.mhhe.com/edumarketinsight to answer the following questions.

1. In the previous chapter you used four years' data from Market Insight to calculate the beta of Alcoa. Now compute the alpha of the stock in two consecutive periods. Estimate the index model regression using the first two years of monthly data. (You can use four-week T-bill rates to calculate excess returns from the Federal Reserve Web site at **www.federalreserve.gov/releases/h15/data.htm**.) Now repeat the process using the last two years of monthly data. This will give you the alpha (intercept) and beta (slope) estimates for two consecutive time periods. How do the two alphas compare to the risk-free

rate and to each other? Select 11 other firms and repeat the regressions to find the alphas for the first two-year period and the last two-year period.

2. Given your results for Question 1, investigate the extent to which beta in one period predicts beta in future periods and whether alpha in one period predicts alpha in future periods. Regress the beta of each firm in the second period (Y) against the beta in the first period (X). (If you estimated regressions for a dozen firms in Question 1, you will have 12 observations in this regression.) Do the same for the alphas of each firm. Use the coefficients you found to forecast the betas of the 12 firms for the next two-year period.

3. Our expectation is that beta in the first period predicts beta in the next period, but that alpha in the first period has no power to predict alpha in the next period. (In other words, the regression coefficient on first-period beta will be statistically significant in explaining second-period beta, but the coefficient on alpha will not be.) Why does this prediction make sense? Is it borne out by the data?

4. From Market Insight, enter ticker symbol BMY for Bristol Myers Squibb. In the Excel Analytics section, click on Monthly Valuation Data. The report summarizes seven months of data related to stock market activity and contains several comparison reports to market indexes. Then repeat the procedure to obtain data for CQB (Chiquita Brands Intl.), GE (General Electric), ETFC (E Trade Financial Corp.), and MLP (Maui Land and Pineapple Company). After reviewing the reports, answer the following questions:

   a. Which of the stocks would you classify as defensive? Which would be classified as aggressive?

   b. Do the beta coefficients for the low-beta firms make sense given the industries in which these firms operate? Briefly explain.

   c. Describe the variations in the reported beta coefficients over the seven months of data. (Check the "% change" worksheet to see the percentage changes.) Which firm has experienced the largest changes from month to month?

5. From Market Insight, enter the ticker symbol ALL for Allstate Corp. In the S&P Stock Reports section open the Wall Street Consensus Report. What is the Wall Street Consensus Opinion for Allstate? How do the analysts' expectations for earnings compare to the firm's performance to date this year? Now open the Industry Outlook Report. What other firms are in Allstate's peer group? What are the firms' beta coefficients? Why might the betas vary among firms? Repeat the process for Monsanto (MON) and the firms in its peer group. Is there more or less variation among the betas in this industry relative to Allstate and its peers?

WEB *master*   ESTIMATING BETAS

A firm's beta can be estimated from the slope of the characteristic line. The first step is to plot the return on the firm's stock (y-axis) vs. the return on a broad market index (x-axis). Next, a regression line is estimated to find the slope.

1. Go to **finance.yahoo.com,** enter the symbol for a company of your choice, and click on "Get Quotes." On the left-side menu, click on "Historical Prices," then enter starting and ending dates that correspond to the most recent two years. Select the "Daily" option. Save the data to a spreadsheet.

2. Repeat the process to get comparable data for the S&P 500 Index (symbol ^GSPC). Download the data and copy it into the same spreadsheet as your firm's data with dates aligned.

3. Sort the data from earliest to latest. Calculate the return on the stock and the return on the index for each day using the adjusted closing prices.

4. Prepare an *xy* scatter plot with no line inserted. Be sure that the firm's returns represent the *y*-variable and the market's returns represent the *x*-variable.

5. Select one of the data points by pointing to it and clicking the left mouse button. While the point is selected, right-click to pull up a shortcut menu. Select "Add Trendline," choose the linear type, then click on the Options tab and select "Display equation on chart." When you click on "OK" the trendline and the equation appear. The trendline represents the regression equation. What is the firm's beta?

7.1. The CML would still represent efficient investments. We can characterize the entire population by two representative investors. One is the "uninformed" investor, who does not engage in security analysis and holds the market portfolio, while the other optimizes using the Markowitz algorithm with input from security analysis. The uninformed investor does not know what input the informed investor uses to make portfolio purchases. The uninformed investor knows, however, that if the other investor is informed, the market portfolio proportions will be optimal. Therefore, to depart from these proportions would constitute an uninformed bet, which will, on average, reduce the efficiency of diversification with no compensating improvement in expected returns.

7.2. Substituting the historical mean and standard deviation in Equation 7.1 yields a coefficient of risk aversion of

$$A^* = \frac{E(r_M) - r_f}{\sigma_M^2} = \frac{.075}{.20^2} = 1.88$$

This relationship also tells us that for the historical standard deviation and a coefficient of risk aversion of 3.5, the risk premium would be

$$E(r_M) - r_f = A^* \sigma_M^2 = 3.5 \times .20^2 = .14 = 14\%$$

7.3. $\beta_{Dell} = 1.25$, $\beta_{GE} = 1.15$. Therefore, given the investment proportions, the portfolio beta is

$$\beta_P = w_{Dell}\beta_{Dell} + w_{GE}\beta_{GE} = (.75 \times 1.25) + (.25 \times 1.15) = 1.225$$

and the risk premium of the portfolio will be

$$E(r_P) - r_f = \beta_P[E(r_M) - r_f] = 1.225 \times 8\% = 9.8\%$$

7.4. *a.* The alpha of a stock is its expected return in excess of that required by the CAPM.

$$\alpha = E(r) - \{r_f + \beta[E(r_M) - r_f]\}$$
$$\alpha_{XYZ} = 12 - [5 + 1.0(11 - 5)] = 1$$
$$\alpha_{ABC} = 13 - [5 + 1.5(11 - 5)] = -1\%$$

b. The project-specific required rate of return is determined by the project beta coupled with the market risk premium and the risk-free rate. The CAPM tells us that an acceptable expected rate of return for the project is

$$r_f + \beta[E(r_M) - r_f] = 8 + 1.3(16 - 8) = 18.4\%$$

which becomes the project's hurdle rate. If the IRR of the project is 19%, then it is desirable. Any project (of similar beta) with an IRR less than 18.4% should be rejected.

7.5. $E(r) = 4\% + 1.2 \times 4\% + .7 \times 2\% = 10.2\%$

7.6. Using Equation 7.11, the expected return is

$$4 + (0.2 \times 6) + (1.4 \times 8) = 16.4\%$$

8 Chapter

The Efficient Market Hypothesis

After Studying This Chapter You Should Be Able To:

- Demonstrate why security price movements should be essentially unpredictable in an efficient market.

- Cite evidence that supports and contradicts the efficient market hypothesis.

- Provide interpretations of various stock market "anomalies."

- Formulate investment strategies that make sense in informationally efficient markets.

One of the early applications of computers in economics in the 1950s was to analyze economic time series. Business cycle theorists felt that tracing the evolution of several economic variables over time would clarify and predict the progress of the economy through boom and bust periods. A natural candidate for analysis was the behavior of stock market prices over time. On the assumption that stock prices reflect the prospects of the firm, recurrent patterns of peaks and troughs in economic performance ought to show up in those prices.

When Maurice Kendall (1953) examined this proposition, however, he found to his great surprise that he could identify no predictable patterns in stock prices. Prices seemed to evolve randomly. They were as likely to go up as they were to go down on any particular day, regardless of past performance. The data provided no way to predict price movements.

At first blush, Kendall's results were disturbing to some financial economists. They seemed to imply that the stock market is dominated by erratic market psychology, or "animal spirits"—that it follows no logical rules. In short, the results appeared to confirm the irrationality of the market. On further reflection, however, economists came to reverse their interpretation of Kendall's study.

It soon became apparent that random price movements indicated a well-functioning or efficient market, not an irrational one. In this

chapter we explore the reasoning behind
what may seem a surprising conclusion. We
show how competition among analysts leads
naturally to market efficiency, and we examine

the implications of the efficient market hypothesis for investment policy. We also consider
empirical evidence that supports and contradicts the notion of market efficiency.

**Related Web sites
for this chapter
are available at
www.mhhe.com/bkm.**

8.1 | Random Walks and The Efficient Market Hypothesis

Suppose Kendall had discovered that stock prices are predictable. What a gold mine this would have been. If they could use Kendall's equations to predict stock prices, investors would reap unending profits simply by purchasing stocks that the computer model implied were about to increase in price and by selling those stocks about to fall in price.

A moment's reflection should be enough to convince yourself that this situation could not persist for long. For example, suppose that the model predicts with great confidence that XYZ stock price, currently at $100 per share, will rise dramatically in three days to $110. What would all investors with access to the model's prediction do today? Obviously, they would place a great wave of immediate buy orders to cash in on the forthcoming increase in stock price. No one holding XYZ, however, would be willing to sell. The net effect would be an *immediate* jump in the stock price to $110. The forecast of a future price increase will lead instead to an immediate price increase. In other words, the stock price will immediately reflect the "good news" implicit in the model's forecast.

This simple example illustrates why Kendall's attempt to find recurrent patterns in stock price movements was likely to fail. A forecast about favorable *future* performance leads instead to favorable *current* performance, as market participants all try to get in on the action before the price increase.

More generally, one might say that any information that could be used to predict stock performance should already be reflected in stock prices. As soon as there is any information indicating that a stock is underpriced and therefore offers a profit opportunity, investors flock to buy the stock and immediately bid up its price to a fair level, where only ordinary rates of return can be expected. These "ordinary rates" are simply rates of return commensurate with the risk of the stock.

However, if prices are bid immediately to fair levels, given all available information, it must be that they increase or decrease only in response to new information. New information, by definition, must be unpredictable; if it could be predicted, then the prediction would be part of today's information. Thus stock prices that change in response to new (unpredictable) information also must move unpredictably.

This is the essence of the argument that stock prices should follow a **random walk,** that is, that price changes should be random and unpredictable. Far from a proof of market irrationality, randomly evolving stock prices would be the necessary consequence of intelligent investors competing to discover relevant information on which to buy or sell stocks before the rest of the market becomes aware of that information.

random walk

The notion that stock price changes are random and unpredictable.

Don't confuse randomness in price *changes* with irrationality in the *level* of prices. If prices are determined rationally, then only new information will cause them to change. Therefore, a random walk would be the natural result of prices that always reflect all current knowledge. Indeed, if stock price movements were predictable, that would be damning evidence of stock market inefficiency, because the ability to predict prices would indicate that all available information was not already reflected in stock prices. Therefore, the notion that stocks already reflect all available information is referred to as the **efficient market hypothesis (EMH).**[1]

efficient market hypothesis

The hypothesis that prices of securities fully reflect available information about securities.

Figure 8.1 illustrates the response of stock prices to new information in an efficient market. The graph plots the price response of a sample of 194 firms that were targets of takeover attempts. In most takeovers, the acquiring firm pays a substantial premium over current market

---

[1]Market efficiency should not be confused with the idea of efficient portfolios introduced in Chapter 6. An informationally efficient *market* is one in which information is rapidly disseminated and reflected in prices. An efficient *portfolio* is one with the highest expected return for a given level of risk.

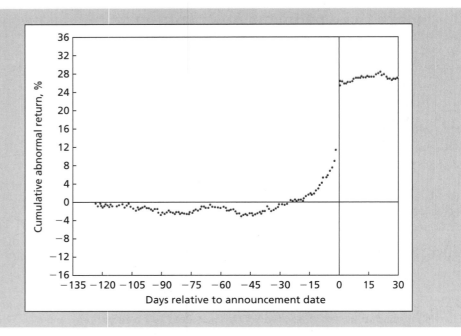

FIGURE 8.1

Cumulative abnormal returns
before takeover attempts:
Target companies

Source: Arthur Keown and
John Pinkerton, "Merger
Announcements and Insider
Trading Activity," *Journal
of Finance* 36 (September 1981).
Reprinted by permission of
the publisher, Blackwell
Publishing, Inc.

prices. Therefore, announcement of a takeover attempt should cause the stock price to jump. The figure shows that stock prices jump dramatically on the day the news becomes public. However, there is no further drift in prices *after* the announcement date, suggesting that prices reflect the new information, including the likely magnitude of the takeover premium, by the end of the trading day.

Even more dramatic evidence of rapid response to new information may be found in intraday prices. For example, Patel and Wolfson (1984) show that most of the stock price response to corporate dividend or earnings announcements occurs within 10 minutes of the announcement. A nice illustration of such rapid adjustment is provided in a study by Busse and Green (2002), who track minute-by-minute stock prices of firms that are featured on CNBC's "Morning" or "Midday Call" segments.[2] Minute 0 in Figure 8.2 is the time at which the stock

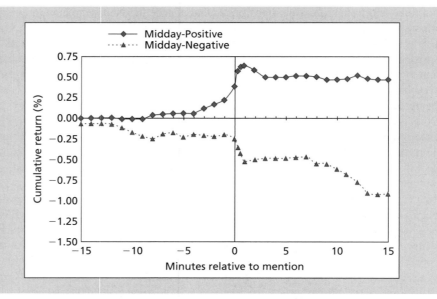

FIGURE 8.2

Stock price reaction to
CNBC reports. The figure
shows the reaction of stock
prices to on-air stock reports
during the "Midday Call" segment on CNBC. The chart
plots cumulative returns
beginning 15 minutes
before the stock report.

Source: Reprinted from
J. A. Busse and T. C. Green,
"Market Efficiency in Real Time,"
Journal of Financial Economics
65 (2002), p. 422. Copyright 2002
with permission from Elsevier
Science.

[2]You can find a nice intraday movie version of this figure at **www.bus.emory.edu/cgreen/docs/cnbc/cnbc.html**.

is mentioned on the midday show. The top line is the average price movement of stocks that receive positive reports, while the bottom line reports returns on stocks with negative reports. Notice that the top line levels off, indicating that the market has fully digested the news, within 5 minutes of the report. The bottom line levels off within about 12 minutes.

Competition as the Source of Efficiency

Why should we expect stock prices to reflect "all available information"? After all, if you are willing to spend time and money on gathering information, it might seem reasonable that you could turn up something that has been overlooked by the rest of the investment community. When information is costly to uncover and analyze, one would expect investment analysis calling for such expenditures to result in an increased expected return.

This point has been stressed by Grossman and Stiglitz (1980). They argued that investors will have an incentive to spend time and resources to analyze and uncover new information only if such activity is likely to generate higher investment returns. Thus, in market equilibrium, efficient information-gathering activity should be fruitful. Moreover, it would not be surprising to find that the degree of efficiency differs across various markets. For example, emerging markets that are less intensively analyzed than U.S. markets and in which accounting disclosure requirements are less rigorous may be less efficient than U.S. markets. Small stocks which receive relatively little coverage by Wall Street analysts may be less efficiently priced than large ones. Therefore, while we would not go so far as to say that you absolutely cannot come up with new information, it makes sense to consider and respect your competition.

EXAMPLE | 8.1

Rewards for Incremental Performance

Consider an investment management fund currently managing a $5 billion portfolio. Suppose that the fund manager can devise a research program that could increase the portfolio rate of return by one-tenth of 1% per year, a seemingly modest amount. This program would increase the dollar return to the portfolio by $5 billion × .001, or $5 million. Therefore, the fund would be willing to spend up to $5 million per year on research to increase stock returns by a mere tenth of 1% per year. With such large rewards for such small increases in investment performance, it should not be surprising that professional portfolio managers are willing to spend large sums on industry analysts, computer support, and research effort, and therefore that price changes are, generally speaking, difficult to predict.

With so many well-backed analysts willing to spend considerable resources on research, easy pickings in the market will be rare. Moreover, the incremental rates of return on research activity may be so small that only managers of the largest portfolios will find them worth pursuing.

Although it may not literally be true that "all" relevant information will be uncovered, it is virtually certain that there are many investigators hot on the trail of most leads that seem likely to improve investment performance. Competition among these many well-backed, highly paid, aggressive analysts ensures that, as a general rule, stock prices ought to reflect available information regarding their proper levels.

A concrete illustration of this point appears in the nearby box, which reports on hedge funds paying lobbying firms up to $20,000 per *month* for tips on upcoming legislation that may affect the prospects of particular firms. These "investments in information" can easily pay for themselves when applied to very large portfolios. The article also notes that both Congress and the SEC are uneasy about the ethics and legalities of such arrangements.

Versions of the Efficient Market Hypothesis

It is common to distinguish among three versions of the EMH: the weak, semistrong, and strong forms of the hypothesis. These versions differ by their notions of what is meant by the term "all available information."

The **weak-form** hypothesis asserts that stock prices already reflect all information that can be derived by examining market trading data such as the history of past prices, trading volume, or short interest. This version of the hypothesis implies that trend analysis is fruitless. Past stock price data are publicly available and virtually costless to obtain. The weak-form

weak-form EMH

The assertion that stock prices already reflect all information contained in the history of past trading.

HEDGE FUNDS HIRE LOBBYISTS TO GATHER TIPS IN WASHINGTON

As federal authorities try to crack down on illegal trading using secrets leaked from companies, some hedge-fund managers are tapping another source of information: the corridors of the Capitol.

Hedge funds are finding that Washington can be a gold mine of market-moving information, easily gathered by the politically connected. The funds are hiring lobbyists—not to influence government, but to tell them what it's going to do. Several lobbying firms are ramping up their "political-intelligence" units and charging hedge funds between $5,000 and $20,000 a month for tips and predictions.

The Securities and Exchange Commission is looking into whether laws are being broken somewhere in the transfer of information between Congress and Wall Street. It's not illegal for lawmakers to disclose information that is not publicly known about the workings of Congress, even if it could affect stock prices. It breaks congressional ethics rules only if they or their aides profit directly. But one question the SEC is trying to resolve is whether the passing of market-sensitive information by lobbyists to investors could violate insider-trading law.

The use of lobbyists as tipsters also is drawing attention from Congress. Democrats are considering requiring lobbyists to disclose their political-intelligence clients. Right now, lobbyists only have to disclose their work for clients seeking to influence government, while hedge funds and other clients seeking market-beating tips can stay in the shadows. Increasingly, lobbyists acting as advocates for a company on an issue may also have a client looking to trade on information about the same issue.

Employees of publicly traded companies are tightly bound by insider-trading laws, which also ban investors from trading public securities using material, nonpublic information that has been passed on improperly. But in most cases, members of Congress and their aides don't have a duty under the law to keep information private. They routinely exchange information about politics and policy with lobbyists—often not realizing that mere morsels are being sold to hedge funds who trade on the tidbits.

SOURCE: Abridged from *The Wall Street Journal,* December 8, 2006, p. A1. Reprinted by permission of *The Wall Street Journal,* Copyright © 2006 Dow Jones & Company, Inc. All Rights Reserved Worldwide.

hypothesis holds that if such data ever conveyed reliable signals about future performance, all investors already would have learned to exploit the signals. Ultimately, the signals lose their value as they become widely known because a buy signal, for instance, would result in an immediate price increase.

semistrong-form EMH

The assertion that stock prices already reflect all publicly available information.

The **semistrong-form** hypothesis states that all publicly available information regarding the prospects of a firm already must be reflected in the stock price. Such information includes, in addition to past prices, fundamental data on the firm's product line, quality of management, balance sheet composition, patents held, earning forecasts, and accounting practices. Again, if investors have access to such information from publicly available sources, one would expect it to be reflected in stock prices.

strong-form EMH

The assertion that stock prices reflect all relevant information, including inside information.

Finally, the **strong-form** version of the efficient market hypothesis states that stock prices reflect all information relevant to the firm, even including information available only to company insiders. This version of the hypothesis is quite extreme. Few would argue with the proposition that corporate officers have access to pertinent information long enough before public release to enable them to profit from trading on that information. Indeed, much of the activity of the Securities and Exchange Commission is directed toward preventing insiders from profiting by exploiting their privileged situation. Rule 10b-5 of the Security Exchange Act of 1934 sets limits on trading by corporate officers, directors, and substantial owners, requiring them to report trades to the SEC. These insiders, their relatives, and any associates who trade on information supplied by insiders are considered in violation of the law.

Defining insider trading is not always easy, however. After all, stock analysts are in the business of uncovering information not already widely known to market participants. As we saw in Chapter 3, the distinction between private and inside information is sometimes murky.

CONCEPT *check* **8.1**

a. Suppose you observed that high-level managers make superior returns on investments in their company's stock. Would this be a violation of weak-form market efficiency? Would it be a violation of strong-form market efficiency?

b. If the weak form of the efficient market hypothesis is valid, must the strong form also hold? Conversely, does strong-form efficiency imply weak-form efficiency?

8.2 | Implications of The EMH

Technical Analysis

Technical analysis is essentially the search for recurrent and predictable patterns in stock prices. Although technicians recognize the value of information regarding future economic prospects of the firm, they believe that such information is not necessary for a successful trading strategy. This is because whatever the fundamental reason for a change in stock price, if the stock price responds slowly enough, the analyst will be able to identify a trend that can be exploited during the adjustment period. The key to successful technical analysis is a sluggish response of stock prices to fundamental supply-and-demand factors. This prerequisite, of course, is diametrically opposed to the notion of an efficient market.

Technical analysts are sometimes called *chartists* because they study records or charts of past stock prices, hoping to find patterns they can exploit to make a profit. As an example of technical analysis, consider the *relative strength* approach. The chartist compares stock performance over a recent period to performance of the market or other stocks in the same industry. A simple version of relative strength takes the ratio of the stock price to a market indicator such as the S&P 500 Index. If the ratio increases over time, the stock is said to exhibit relative strength because its price performance is better than that of the broad market. Such strength presumably may continue for a long enough period of time to offer profit opportunities.

One of the most commonly heard components of technical analysis is the notion of **resistance levels** or **support levels.** These values are said to be price levels above which it is difficult for stock prices to rise, or below which it is unlikely for them to fall, and they are believed to be levels determined by market psychology.

technical analysis

Research on recurrent and predictable stock price patterns and on proxies for buy or sell pressure in the market.

resistance level

A price level above which it is supposedly unlikely for a stock or stock index to rise.

support level

A price level below which it is supposedly unlikely for a stock or stock index to fall.

Consider stock *XYZ*, which traded for several months at a price of $72, and then declined to $65. If the stock eventually begins to increase in price, $72 is considered a resistance level (according to this theory) because investors who bought originally at $72 will be eager to sell their shares as soon as they can break even on their investment. Therefore, at prices near $72 a wave of selling pressure would exist. Such activity imparts a type of "memory" to the market that allows past price history to influence current stock prospects.

EXAMPLE | 8.2

Resistance Levels

The efficient market hypothesis implies that technical analysis is without merit. The past history of prices and trading volume is publicly available at minimal cost. Therefore, any information that was ever available from analyzing past prices has already been reflected in stock prices. As investors compete to exploit their common knowledge of a stock's price history, they necessarily drive stock prices to levels where expected rates of return are exactly commensurate with risk. At those levels one cannot expect abnormal returns.

As an example of how this process works, consider what would happen if the market believed that a level of $72 truly were a resistance level for stock *XYZ* in Example 8.2. No one would be willing to purchase the stock at a price of $71.50, because it would have almost no room to increase in price, but ample room to fall. However, if no one would buy it at $71.50, then $71.50 would become a resistance level. But then, using a similar analysis, no one would buy it at $71, or $70, and so on. The notion of a resistance level is a logical conundrum. Its simple resolution is the recognition that if the stock is ever to sell at $71.50, investors *must* believe that the price can as easily increase as fall. The fact that investors are willing to purchase (or even hold) the stock at $71.50 is evidence of their belief that they can earn a fair expected rate of return at that price.

If everyone in the market believes in resistance levels, why do these beliefs not become self-fulfilling prophecies?

CONCEPT *check* **8.2**

An interesting question is whether a technical rule that seems to work will continue to work in the future once it becomes widely recognized. A clever analyst may occasionally uncover a profitable trading rule, but the real test of efficient markets is whether the rule itself becomes reflected in stock prices once its value is discovered. Once a useful technical rule (or price pattern) is discovered, it ought to be invalidated when the mass of traders attempts to exploit it. In this sense, price patterns ought to be *self-destructing*.

Thus the market dynamic is one of a continual search for profitable trading rules, followed by destruction by overuse of those rules found to be successful, followed by more search for yet-undiscovered rules. We return to the rationale for technical analysis as well as some of its methods in the next chapter.

Fundamental Analysis

fundamental analysis

Research on determinants of stock value, such as earnings and dividend prospects, expectations for future interest rates, and risk of the firm.

Fundamental analysis uses earnings and dividend prospects of the firm, expectations of future interest rates, and risk evaluation of the firm to determine proper stock prices. Ultimately, it represents an attempt to determine the present discounted value of all the payments a stockholder will receive from each share of stock. If that value exceeds the stock price, the fundamental analyst would recommend purchasing the stock.

Fundamental analysts usually start with a study of past earnings and an examination of company financial statements. They supplement this analysis with further detailed economic analysis, ordinarily including an evaluation of the quality of the firm's management, the firm's standing within its industry, and the prospects for the industry as a whole. The hope is to attain insight into future performance of the firm that is not yet recognized by the rest of the market. Chapters 12 through 14 provide a detailed discussion of the types of analyses that underlie fundamental analysis.

Once again, the efficient market hypothesis predicts that *most* fundamental analysis also is doomed to failure. If the analyst relies on publicly available earnings and industry information, his or her evaluation of the firm's prospects is not likely to be significantly more accurate than those of rival analysts. There are many well-informed, well-financed firms conducting such market research, and in the face of such competition it will be difficult to uncover data not also available to other analysts. Only analysts with a unique insight will be rewarded.

Fundamental analysis is much more difficult than merely identifying well-run firms with good prospects. Discovery of good firms does an investor no good in and of itself if the rest of the market also knows those firms are good. If the knowledge is already public, the investor will be forced to pay a high price for those firms and will not realize a superior rate of return.

The trick is not to identify firms that are good, but to find firms that are *better* than everyone else's estimate. Similarly, poorly run firms can be great bargains if they are not quite as bad as their stock prices suggest.

This is why fundamental analysis is difficult. It is not enough to do a good analysis of a firm; you can make money only if your analysis is better than that of your competitors because the market price will already reflect all commonly available information.

Active versus Passive Portfolio Management

By now it is apparent that casual efforts to pick stocks are not likely to pay off. Competition among investors ensures that any easily implemented stock evaluation technique will be used widely enough so that any insights derived will be reflected in stock prices. Only serious analysis and uncommon techniques are likely to generate the *differential* insight necessary to yield trading profits.

Moreover, these techniques are economically feasible only for managers of large portfolios. If you have only $100,000 to invest, even a 1% per year improvement in performance generates only $1,000 per year, hardly enough to justify herculean efforts. The billion-dollar manager, however, reaps extra income of $10 million annually from the same 1% increment.

If small investors are not in a favored position to conduct active portfolio management, what are their choices? The small investor probably is better off investing in mutual funds. By pooling resources in this way, small investors can gain from economies of scale.

More difficult decisions remain, though. Can investors be sure that even large mutual funds have the ability or resources to uncover mispriced stocks? Furthermore, will any mispricing be sufficiently large to repay the costs entailed in active portfolio management?

Proponents of the efficient market hypothesis believe that active management is largely wasted effort and unlikely to justify the expenses incurred. Therefore, they advocate a **passive investment strategy** that makes no attempt to outsmart the market. A passive strategy aims only at establishing a well-diversified portfolio of securities without attempting to find under- or overvalued stocks. Passive management is usually characterized by a buy-and-hold strategy. Because the efficient market theory indicates that stock prices are at fair levels, given all available information, it makes no sense to buy and sell securities frequently, which generates large brokerage fees without increasing expected performance.

One common strategy for passive management is to create an **index fund,** which is a fund designed to replicate the performance of a broad-based index of stocks. For example, Vanguard's 500 Index Fund holds stocks in direct proportion to their weight in the Standard & Poor's 500 stock price index. The performance of the 500 Index Fund therefore replicates the performance of the S&P 500. Investors in this fund obtain broad diversification with relatively low management fees. The fees can be kept to a minimum because Vanguard does not need to pay analysts to assess stock prospects and does not incur transaction costs from high portfolio turnover. Indeed, while the typical annual expense ratio for an actively managed equity fund is more than 1% of assets, the expense ratio of the 500 Index Fund is only .15%. Today, Vanguard's 500 Index Fund is among the largest equity mutual funds with about $75 billion of assets in May 2009, and about 10% of equity funds are indexed.

Indexing need not be limited to the S&P 500, however. For example, some of the funds offered by the Vanguard Group track the Wilshire 5000 Index, the Salomon Brothers Broad Investment Grade Bond Index, the MSCI index of small-capitalization U.S. companies, the European equity market, and the Pacific Basin equity market. Several other mutual fund complexes offer indexed portfolios, but Vanguard dominates the retail market for indexed products.

Exchange traded funds, or ETFs, are a close (and usually lower-expense) alternative to indexed mutual funds. As noted in Chapter 4, these are shares in diversified portfolios that can be bought or sold just like shares of individual stock. ETFs matching several broad stock market indexes such as the S&P 500 or Wilshire 5000 indexes and dozens of international and industry stock indexes are available to investors who want to hold a diversified sector of a market without attempting active security selection.

A hybrid strategy also is fairly common, where the fund maintains a *passive core,* which is an indexed position, and augments that position with one or more actively managed portfolios.

passive investment strategy

Buying a well-diversified portfolio without attempting to search out mispriced securities.

index fund

A mutual fund holding shares in proportion to their representation in a market index such as the S&P 500.

What would happen to market efficiency if *all* investors attempted to follow a passive strategy?

CONCEPT *check* **8.3**

The Role of Portfolio Management in an Efficient Market

If the market is efficient, why not throw darts at *The Wall Street Journal* instead of trying rationally to choose a stock portfolio? This is a tempting conclusion to draw from the notion that security prices are fairly set, but it is far too facile. There is a role for rational portfolio management, even in perfectly efficient markets.

You have learned that a basic principle in portfolio selection is diversification. Even if all stocks are priced fairly, each still poses firm-specific risk that can be eliminated through diversification. Therefore, rational security selection, even in an efficient market, calls for the selection of a well-diversified portfolio providing the systematic risk level that the investor wants.

Rational investment policy also requires that tax considerations be reflected in security choice. High-tax-bracket investors generally will not want the same securities that low-bracket investors find favorable. At an obvious level, high-bracket investors find it advantageous to buy tax-exempt municipal bonds despite their relatively low pretax yields, whereas those same bonds are unattractive to low-tax-bracket investors. At a more subtle level, high-bracket investors might want to tilt their portfolios in the direction of capital gains as opposed to interest income, because capital gains are taxed less heavily and because the option to defer the realization of capital gains income is more valuable the higher the current tax bracket. Hence these investors may prefer stocks that yield low dividends yet offer greater expected capital gain income. They also will be more attracted to investment opportunities for which returns are sensitive to tax benefits, such as real estate ventures.

A third argument for rational portfolio management relates to the particular risk profile of the investor. For example, a Toyota executive whose annual bonus depends on Toyota's profits generally should not invest additional amounts in auto stocks. To the extent that his or her compensation already depends on Toyota's well-being, the executive is already overinvested in Toyota and should not exacerbate the lack of diversification. This lesson was learned with considerable pain in September 2008 by Lehman Brothers employees who were famously invested in their own firm when the company failed. Roughly 30% of the shares in the firm were owned by its 24,000 employees, and their losses on those shares were around $10 billion.

Investors of varying ages also might warrant different portfolio policies with regard to risk bearing. For example, older investors who are essentially living off savings might choose to avoid long-term bonds whose market values fluctuate dramatically with changes in interest rates (discussed in Part Four). Because these investors are living off accumulated savings, they require conservation of principal. In contrast, younger investors might be more inclined toward long-term inflation-indexed bonds. The steady flow of real income over long periods of time that is locked in with these bonds can be more important than preservation of principal to those with long life expectancies.

In conclusion, there is a role for portfolio management even in an efficient market. Investors' optimal positions will vary according to factors such as age, tax bracket, risk aversion, and employment. The role of the portfolio manager in an efficient market is to tailor the portfolio to these needs, rather than to beat the market.

Resource Allocation

We've focused so far on the investments implications of the efficient market hypothesis. Deviations from efficiency may offer profit opportunities to better-informed traders at the expense of less-informed traders.

However, deviations from informational efficiency would also result in a large cost that will be borne by all citizens, namely, inefficient resource allocation. Recall that in a capitalist economy, investments in *real* assets such as plant, equipment, and know-how are guided in large part by the prices of financial assets. For example, if the value of telecommunication capacity reflected in stock market prices exceeds the cost of installing such capacity, managers might justifiably conclude that telecom investments seem to have positive net present value. In this manner, capital market prices guide allocation of real resources.

If markets were inefficient and securities commonly mispriced, then resources would be systematically misallocated. Corporations with overpriced securities will be able to obtain capital too cheaply and corporations with undervalued securities might forgo investment opportunities because the cost of raising capital will be too high. Therefore, inefficient capital markets would diminish one of the most potent benefits of a market economy. As an example of what can go wrong, consider the dot-com bubble of the late 1990s, which sent a strong but, as it turned out, wildly overoptimistic signal about prospects in Internet and telecommunication firms and ultimately led to substantial overinvestment in those industries.

Before writing off markets as a means to guide resource allocation, however, one has to be reasonable about what can be expected from market forecasts. In particular, you shouldn't confuse an efficient market, where all available information is reflected in prices, with a perfect foresight market. Even "all available information" is still far from complete information, and generally rational market forecasts will sometimes be wrong; sometimes, in fact, they will be very wrong.

8.3   Are Markets Efficient?

The Issues

Not surprisingly, the efficient market hypothesis does not exactly arouse enthusiasm in the community of professional portfolio managers. It implies that a great deal of the activity of portfolio managers—the search for undervalued securities—is at best wasted effort, and quite probably harmful to clients because it costs money and leads to imperfectly diversified portfolios. Consequently, the EMH has never been widely accepted on Wall Street, and debate continues today on the degree to which security analysis can improve investment performance. Before discussing empirical tests of the hypothesis, we want to note three factors that together imply that the debate probably never will be settled: the *magnitude issue,* the *selection bias issue,* and the *lucky event issue.*

The magnitude issue   We noted that an investment manager overseeing a $5 billion portfolio who can improve performance by only .1% per year will increase investment earnings by .001 × $5 billion = $5 million annually. This manager clearly would be worth her salary! Yet can we, as observers, statistically measure her contribution? Probably not: A .1% contribution would be swamped by the yearly volatility of the market. Remember, the annual standard deviation of the well-diversified S&P 500 Index has been around 20%. Against these fluctuations a small increase in performance would be hard to detect.

All might agree that stock prices are very close to fair values and that only managers of large portfolios can earn enough trading profits to make the exploitation of minor mispricing worth the effort. According to this view, the actions of intelligent investment managers are the driving force behind the constant evolution of market prices to fair levels. Rather than ask the qualitative question, Are markets efficient? we should instead ask a more quantitative question: How efficient are markets?

The selection bias issue   Suppose that you discover an investment scheme that could really make money. You have two choices: either publish your technique in *The Wall Street Journal* to win fleeting fame, or keep your technique secret and use it to earn millions of dollars. Most investors would choose the latter option, which presents us with a conundrum. Only investors who find that an investment scheme cannot generate abnormal returns will be willing to report their findings to the whole world. Hence opponents of the efficient markets view of the world always can use evidence that various techniques do not provide investment rewards as proof that the techniques that do work simply are not being reported to the public. This is a problem in *selection bias;* the outcomes we are able to observe have been preselected in favor of failed attempts. Therefore, we cannot fairly evaluate the true ability of portfolio managers to generate winning stock market strategies.

The lucky event issue   In virtually any month it seems we read an article about some investor or investment company with a fantastic investment performance over the recent past. Surely the superior records of such investors disprove the efficient market hypothesis.

Yet this conclusion is far from obvious. As an analogy to the investment game, consider a contest to flip the most number of heads out of 50 trials using a fair coin. The expected outcome for any person is, of course, 50% heads and 50% tails. If 10,000 people, however, compete in this contest, it would not be surprising if at least one or two contestants flipped more than 75% heads. In fact, elementary statistics tells us that the expected number of contestants flipping 75% or more heads would be two. It would be silly, though, to crown these people the "head-flipping champions of the world." Obviously, they are simply the contestants who happened to get lucky on the day of the event. (See the nearby box.)

The analogy to efficient markets is clear. Under the hypothesis that any stock is fairly priced given all available information, any bet on a stock is simply a coin toss. There is equal likelihood of winning or losing the bet. However, if many investors using a variety of schemes make fair bets, statistically speaking, *some* of those investors will be lucky and win a great

HOW TO GUARANTEE A SUCCESSFUL MARKET NEWSLETTER

Suppose you want to make your fortune publishing a market news-letter. You need first to convince potential subscribers that you have talent worth paying for. But what if you have no talent? The solution is simple: Start eight newsletters.

In year 1, let four of your newsletters predict an up-market and four a down-market. In year 2, let half of the originally optimistic group of newsletters continue to predict an up-market and the other half a down-market. Do the same for the originally pessimistic group. Continue in this manner to obtain the pattern of predictions in the table that follows (U = prediction of an up-market, D = prediction of a down-market).

After three years, no matter what has happened to the market, one of the newsletters would have had a perfect prediction record. This is because after three years there are $2^3 = 8$ outcomes for the market, and we have covered all eight possibilities with the eight newsletters. Now, we simply slough off the seven unsuccessful newsletters, and market the eighth newsletter based on its perfect track record. If we want to establish a newsletter with a perfect track record over a four-year period, we need $2^4 = 16$ newsletters. A five-year period requires 32 newsletters, and so on.

After the fact, the one newsletter that was always right will attract attention for your uncanny foresight and investors will rush to pay large fees for its advice. Your fortune is made, and you have never even researched the market!

WARNING: This scheme is illegal! The point, however, is that with hundreds of market newsletters, you can find one that has stumbled onto an apparently remarkable string of successful predic-tions without any real degree of skill. After the fact, *someone's* pre-diction history can seem to imply great forecasting skill. This person is the one we will read about in *The Wall Street Journal;* the others will be forgotten.

Newsletter Predictions								
Year	1	2	3	4	5	6	7	8
1	U	U	U	U	D	D	D	D
2	U	U	D	D	U	U	D	D
3	U	D	U	D	U	D	U	D

majority of the bets. For every big winner, there may be many big losers, but we never hear of these managers. The winners, though, turn up in *The Wall Street Journal* as the latest stock market gurus; then they can make a fortune publishing market newsletters.

Our point is that after the fact there will have been at least one successful investment scheme. A doubter will call the results luck, the successful investor will call it skill. The proper test would be to see whether the successful investors can repeat their performance in another period, yet this approach is rarely taken.

With these caveats in mind, we turn now to some of the empirical tests of the efficient market hypothesis.

CONCEPT *check* **8.4**

Legg Mason's Value Trust, managed by Bill Miller, outperformed the S&P 500 in each of the 15 years ending in 2005. Is Miller's performance sufficient to dissuade you from a belief in efficient markets? If not, would *any* performance record be sufficient to dissuade you? Now consider that in the next 3 years, the fund dramatically underperformed the S&P 500; by the end of 2008, its cumulative 18-year performance was barely different from the index. Does this affect your opinion?

Weak-Form Tests: Patterns in Stock Returns

Returns over short horizons Early tests of efficient markets were tests of the weak form. Could speculators find trends in past prices that would enable them to earn abnormal profits? This is essentially a test of the efficacy of technical analysis.

One way of discerning trends in stock prices is by measuring the *serial correlation* of stock market returns. Serial correlation refers to the tendency for stock returns to be related to past returns. Positive serial correlation means that positive returns tend to follow positive returns (a momentum type of property). Negative serial correlation means that positive returns tend to be followed by negative returns (a reversal or "correction" property). Both Conrad and Kaul (1988) and Lo and MacKinlay (1988) examine weekly returns of NYSE stocks and find positive serial correlation over short horizons. However, the correlation coefficients of weekly returns tend to be fairly small, at least for large stocks for which price data are the most reliably up-to-date. Thus, while these studies demonstrate weak price trends over short periods,[3] the evidence does not clearly suggest the existence of trading opportunities.

While broad market indexes demonstrate only weak serial correlation, there appears to be stronger momentum in performance across market sectors exhibiting the best and worst recent returns. In an investigation of intermediate-horizon stock price behavior (using 3- to 12-month holding periods), Jegadeesh and Titman (1993) found a **momentum effect** in which good or bad recent performance of particular stocks continues over time. They conclude that while the performance of individual stocks is highly unpredictable, *portfolios* of the best-performing stocks in the recent past appear to outperform other stocks with enough reliability to offer profit opportunities. Thus, it appears that there is evidence of short- to intermediate-horizon price momentum in both the aggregate market and cross-sectionally (i.e., across particular stocks).

Returns over long horizons

Although short- to intermediate-horizon returns suggest momentum in stock market prices, studies of long-horizon returns (i.e., returns over multiyear periods) by Fama and French (1988) and Poterba and Summers (1988) indicate pronounced *negative* long-term serial correlation in the performance of the aggregate market. The latter result has given rise to a "fads hypothesis," which asserts that the stock market might overreact to relevant news. Such overreaction leads to positive serial correlation (momentum) over short time horizons. Subsequent correction of the overreaction leads to poor performance following good performance and vice versa. The corrections mean that a run of positive returns eventually will tend to be followed by negative returns, leading to negative serial correlation over longer horizons. These episodes of apparent overshooting followed by correction give the stock market the appearance of fluctuating around its fair value.

These long-horizon results are dramatic, but the studies offer far from conclusive evidence regarding efficient markets. First, the study results need not be interpreted as evidence for stock market fads. An alternative interpretation of these results holds that they indicate only that the market risk premium varies over time. For example, when the risk premium and the required return on the market rises, stock prices will fall. When the market then rises (on average) at this higher rate of return, the data convey the impression of a stock price recovery. The apparent overshooting and correction is in fact no more than a rational response of market prices to changes in discount rates.

In addition to studies suggestive of overreaction in overall stock market returns over long horizons, many other studies suggest that over long horizons, extreme performance in particular securities also tends to reverse itself: The stocks that have performed best in the recent past seem to underperform the rest of the market in following periods, while the worst past performers tend to offer above-average future performance. De Bondt and Thaler (1985) and Chopra, Lakonishok, and Ritter (1992) find strong tendencies for poorly performing stocks in one period to experience sizable reversals over the subsequent period, while the best-performing stocks in a given period tend to follow with poor performance in the following period.

For example, the De Bondt and Thaler study found that if one were to rank-order the performance of stocks over a five-year period and then group stocks into portfolios based on investment performance, the base-period "loser" portfolio (defined as the 35 stocks with the worst investment performance) outperformed the "winner" portfolio (the top 35 stocks) by an average of 25% (cumulative return) in the following three-year period. This **reversal effect,** in which losers rebound and winners fade back, suggests that the stock market overreacts to relevant news. After the overreaction is recognized, extreme investment performance is reversed. This phenomenon would imply that a *contrarian* investment strategy—investing in recent losers and avoiding recent winners—should be profitable. Moreover, these returns seem pronounced enough to be exploited profitably.

momentum effect

The tendency of poorly performing stocks and well-performing stocks in one period to continue that abnormal performance in following periods.

reversal effect

The tendency of poorly performing stocks and well-performing stocks in one period to experience reversals in the following period.

---

[3]On the other hand, there is evidence that share prices of individual securities (as opposed to broad market indexes) are more prone to reversals than continuations at very short horizons. See, for example, B. Lehmann, "Fads, Martingales and Market Efficiency," *Quarterly Journal of Economics* 105 (February 1990), pp. 1–28; and N. Jegadeesh, "Evidence of Predictable Behavior of Security Returns," *Journal of Finance* 45 (September 1990), pp. 881–98. However, as Lehmann notes, this is probably best interpreted as due to liquidity problems after big movements in stock prices as market makers adjust their positions in the stock.

Thus it appears that there may be short-run momentum but long-run reversal patterns in price behavior both for the market as a whole and across sectors of the market. One interpretation of this pattern is that short-run overreaction (which causes momentum in prices) may lead to long-term reversals (when the market recognizes its past error).

Predictors of Broad Market Returns

Several studies have documented the ability of easily observed variables to predict market returns. For example, Fama and French (1988) showed that the return on the aggregate stock market tends to be higher when the dividend/price ratio, the dividend yield, is high. Campbell and Shiller (1988) found that the earnings yield can predict market returns. Keim and Stambaugh (1986) showed that bond market data such as the spread between yields on high- and low-grade corporate bonds also help predict broad market returns.

Again, the interpretation of these results is difficult. On the one hand, they may imply that stock returns can be predicted, in violation of the efficient market hypothesis. More probably, however, these variables are proxying for variation in the market risk premium. For example, given a level of dividends or earnings, stock prices will be lower and dividend and earnings yields will be higher when the risk premium (and therefore the expected market return) is higher. Thus a high dividend or earnings yield will be associated with higher market returns. This does not indicate a violation of market efficiency. The predictability of market returns is due to predictability in the risk premium, not in risk-adjusted abnormal returns.

Fama and French (1989) showed that the yield spread between high- and low-grade bonds has greater predictive power for returns on low-grade bonds than for returns on high-grade bonds, and greater predictive power for stock returns than for bond returns, suggesting that the predictability in returns is in fact a risk premium rather than evidence of market inefficiency. Similarly, the fact that the dividend yield on stocks helps to predict bond market returns suggests that the yield captures a risk premium common to both markets rather than mispricing in the equity market.

Semistrong Tests: Market Anomalies

Fundamental analysis uses a much wider range of information to create portfolios than does technical analysis. Investigations of the efficacy of fundamental analysis ask whether publicly available information beyond the trading history of a security can be used to improve investment performance, and therefore are tests of semistrong-form market efficiency. Surprisingly, several easily accessible statistics, for example a stock's price–earnings ratio or its market capitalization, seem to predict abnormal risk-adjusted returns. Findings such as these, which we will review in the following pages, are difficult to reconcile with the efficient market hypothesis, and therefore are often referred to as efficient market **anomalies.**

anomalies

Patterns of returns that seem to contradict the efficient market hypothesis.

A difficulty in interpreting these tests is that we usually need to adjust for portfolio risk before evaluating the success of an investment strategy. Many tests, for example, have used the CAPM to adjust for risk. However, we know that even if beta is a relevant descriptor of stock risk, the empirically measured quantitative trade-off between risk as measured by beta and expected return differs from the predictions of the CAPM. If we use the CAPM to adjust portfolio returns for risk, inappropriate adjustments may lead to the conclusion that various portfolio strategies can generate superior returns, when in fact it simply is the risk adjustment procedure that has failed.

Another way to put this is to note that tests of risk-adjusted returns are *joint tests* of the efficient market hypothesis *and* the risk adjustment procedure. If it appears that a portfolio strategy can generate superior returns, we must then choose between rejecting the EMH and rejecting the risk adjustment technique. Usually, the risk adjustment technique is based on more-questionable assumptions than is the EMH; by opting to reject the procedure, we are left with no conclusion about market efficiency.

P/E effect

Portfolios of low P/E stocks have exhibited higher average risk-adjusted returns than high P/E stocks.

An example of this issue is the discovery by Basu (1977, 1983) that portfolios of low price–earnings (P/E) ratio stocks have higher returns than do high P/E portfolios. The **P/E effect** holds up even if returns are adjusted for portfolio beta. Is this a confirmation that the market systematically misprices stocks according to P/E ratio? This would be an extremely

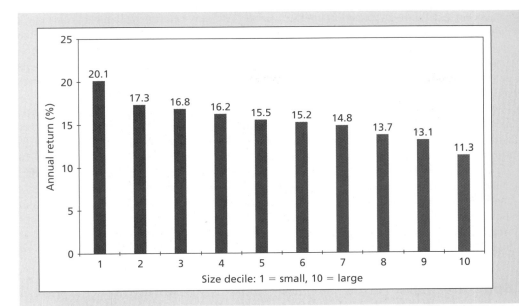

FIGURE 8.3

Average annual return for 10 size-based portfolios, 1926–2007

Source: Web site of Prof. Kenneth French, **http://mba.tuck. dartmouth.edu/pages/faculty/ ken.french/data_library.html.**

surprising and, to us, disturbing conclusion, because analysis of P/E ratios is such a simple procedure. Although it may be possible to earn superior returns by using hard work and much insight, it hardly seems plausible that such a simplistic technique is enough to generate abnormal returns.

Another interpretation of these results is that returns are not properly adjusted for risk. If two firms have the same expected earnings, the riskier stock will sell at a lower price and lower P/E ratio. Because of its higher risk, the low P/E stock also will have higher expected returns. Therefore, unless the CAPM beta fully adjusts for risk, P/E will act as a useful additional descriptor of risk, and will be associated with abnormal returns if the CAPM is used to establish benchmark performance.

The small-firm-in-January effect   The so-called size or **small-firm effect,** originally documented by Banz (1981), is illustrated in Figure 8.3. It shows the historical performance of portfolios formed by dividing the NYSE stocks into 10 portfolios each year according to firm size (i.e., the total value of outstanding equity). Average annual returns between 1926 and 2007 are consistently higher on the small-firm portfolios. The difference in average annual return between portfolio 10 (with the largest firms) and portfolio 1 (with the smallest firms) is 8.8%. Of course, the smaller-firm portfolios tend to be riskier. But even when returns are adjusted for risk using the CAPM, there is still a consistent premium for the smaller-sized portfolios.

Imagine earning a premium of this size on a billion-dollar portfolio. Yet it is remarkable that following a simple (even simplistic) rule such as "invest in low-capitalization stocks" should enable an investor to earn excess returns. After all, any investor can measure firm size at little cost. One would not expect such minimal effort to yield such large rewards.

Later studies (Keim, 1983; Reinganum, 1983; and Blume and Stambaugh, 1983) showed that the small-firm effect occurs virtually entirely in January, in fact, in the first 2 weeks of January. The size effect is in fact a "small-firm-in-January" effect.

The neglected-firm and liquidity effects   Arbel and Strebel (1983) gave another interpretation of the small-firm-in-January effect. Because small firms tend to be neglected by large institutional traders, information about smaller firms is less available. This information deficiency makes smaller firms riskier investments that command higher returns. "Brand-name" firms, after all, are subject to considerable monitoring from institutional investors, which promises high-quality information, and presumably investors do not purchase "generic" stocks without the prospect of greater returns.

small-firm effect

Stocks of small firms have earned abnormal returns, primarily in the month of January.

neglected-firm effect

The tendency of investments in stock of less-well-known firms to generate abnormal returns.

As evidence for the **neglected-firm effect,** Arbel (1985) divided firms into highly researched, moderately researched, and neglected groups based on the number of institutions holding the stock. The January effect was in fact largest for the neglected firms. An article by Merton (1987) shows that neglected firms might be expected to earn higher equilibrium returns as compensation for the risk associated with limited information. In this sense the neglected firm premium is not strictly a market inefficiency, but is a type of risk premium.

Work by Amihud and Mendelson (1986, 1991) on the effect of liquidity on stock returns might be related to both the small-firm and neglected-firm effects. They argue that investors will demand a rate-of-return premium to invest in less-liquid stocks that entail higher trading costs. Indeed, spreads for the least-liquid stocks can be more than 5% of stock value. In accord with their hypothesis, Amihud and Mendelson showed that these stocks show a strong tendency to exhibit abnormally high risk-adjusted rates of return. Because small and less-analyzed stocks as a rule are less liquid, the liquidity effect might be a partial explanation of their abnormal returns. However, this theory does not explain why the abnormal returns of small firms should be concentrated in January. In any case, exploiting these effects can be more difficult than it would appear. The high trading costs on small stocks can easily wipe out any apparent abnormal profit opportunity.

Book-to-market ratios   Fama and French (1992) showed that a powerful predictor of returns across securities is the ratio of the book value of the firm's equity to the market value of equity. Fama and French stratified firms into 10 groups according to book-to-market ratios and examined the average rate of return of each of the 10 groups. Figure 8.4 is an updated version of their results. The decile with the highest book-to-market ratio had an average annual return of 17.5%, while the lowest-ratio decile averaged only 11.2%. The dramatic dependence of returns on book-to-market ratio is independent of beta, suggesting either that high book-to-market ratio firms are relatively underpriced or that the book-to-market ratio is serving as a proxy for a risk factor that affects equilibrium expected returns.

book-to-market effect

The tendency for investments in shares of firms with high ratios of book value to market value to generate abnormal returns.

In fact, Fama and French found that after controlling for the size and **book-to-market effects,** beta seemed to have no power to explain average security returns.[4] This finding is an important challenge to the notion of rational markets, since it seems to imply that a factor that should affect returns—systematic risk—seems not to matter, while a factor that should not

FIGURE 8.4

Average annual return as a function of the book-to-market ratio, 1926–2007.

Source: Web site of Prof. Kenneth French, **http://mba.tuck. dartmouth.edu/pages/faculty/ ken. french/data_library.html.**

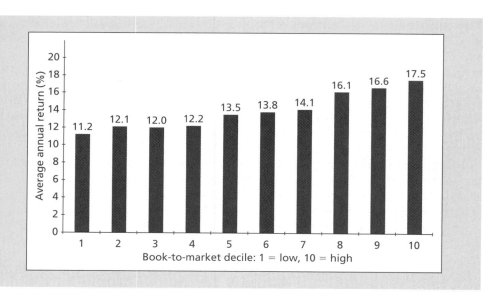

Book-to-market decile: 1 = low, 10 = high

[4]However, a study by S. P. Kothari, Jay Shanken, and Richard G. Sloan (1995) finds that when betas are estimated using annual rather than monthly returns, securities with high beta values do in fact have higher average returns. Moreover, the authors find a book-to-market effect that is attenuated compared to the results in Fama and French and furthermore is inconsistent across different samples of securities. They conclude that the empirical case for the importance of the book-to-market ratio may be somewhat weaker than the Fama and French study would suggest.

matter—the book-to-market ratio—seems capable of predicting future returns. We will return to the interpretation of this anomaly.

Post–earnings-announcement price drift

A fundamental principle of efficient markets is that any new information ought to be reflected in stock prices very rapidly. When good news is made public, for example, the stock price should jump immediately. A puzzling anomaly, therefore, is the apparently sluggish response of stock prices to firms' earnings announcements, as uncovered by Ball and Brown (1968). Their results were later confirmed and extended in many other papers.[5]

The "news content" of an earnings announcement can be evaluated by comparing the announcement of actual earnings to the value previously expected by market participants. The difference is the "earnings surprise." (Market expectations of earnings can be roughly measured by averaging the published earnings forecasts of Wall Street analysts or by applying trend analysis to past earnings.) Rendleman, Jones, and Latané (1982) provide an influential study of sluggish price response to earnings announcements. They calculate earnings surprises for a large sample of firms, rank the magnitude of the surprise, divide firms into 10 deciles based on the size of the surprise, and calculate abnormal returns for each decile. The abnormal return of each portfolio is the return adjusting for both the market return in that period and the portfolio beta. It measures return over and above what would be expected given market conditions in that period. Figure 8.5 plots cumulative abnormal returns by decile.

Their results are dramatic. The correlation between ranking by earnings surprise and abnormal returns across deciles is as predicted. There is a large abnormal return (a jump in cumulative abnormal return) on the earnings announcement day (time 0). The abnormal return is positive for positive-surprise firms and negative for negative-surprise firms.

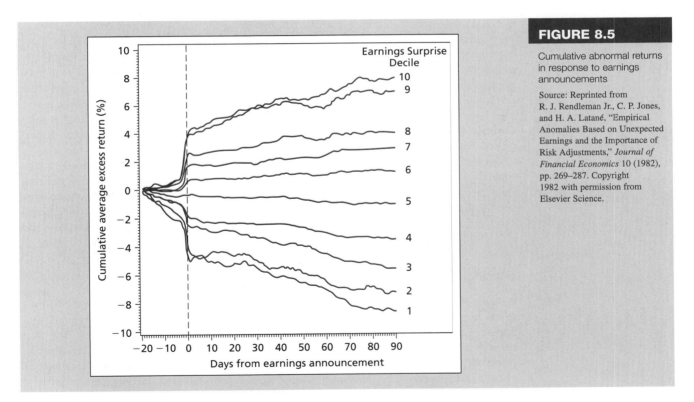

FIGURE 8.5

Cumulative abnormal returns in response to earnings announcements

Source: Reprinted from R. J. Rendleman Jr., C. P. Jones, and H. A. Latané, "Empirical Anomalies Based on Unexpected Earnings and the Importance of Risk Adjustments," *Journal of Financial Economics* 10 (1982), pp. 269–287. Copyright 1982 with permission from Elsevier Science.

[5]There is a voluminous literature on this phenomenon, often referred to as post–earnings-announcement price drift. For more recent papers that focus on why such drift may be observed, see V. Bernard and J. Thomas, "Evidence That Stock Prices Do Not Fully Reflect the Implications of Current Earnings for Future Earnings," *Journal of Accounting and Economics* 13 (1990), pp. 305–40, or R. H. Battalio and R. Mendenhall, "Earnings Expectation, Investor Trade Size, and Anomalous Returns around Earnings Announcements," *Journal of Financial Economics* 77 (2005), pp. 289–319.

The more remarkable, and interesting, result of the study concerns stock price movement *after* the announcement date. The cumulative abnormal returns of positive-surprise stocks continue to rise—in other words, exhibit momentum—even after the earnings information becomes public, while the negative-surprise firms continue to suffer negative abnormal returns. The market appears to adjust to the earnings information only gradually, resulting in a sustained period of abnormal returns.

Evidently, one could have earned abnormal profits simply by waiting for earnings announcements and purchasing a stock portfolio of positive-earnings-surprise companies. These are precisely the types of predictable continuing trends that ought to be impossible in an efficient market.

Bubbles and market efficiency   Every so often, it seems (at least in retrospect) that asset prices lose their grounding in reality. For example, in the tulip mania in seventeenth-century Holland, tulip prices peaked at several times the annual income of a skilled worker. This episode has become the symbol of a speculative "bubble" in which prices appear to depart from any semblance of intrinsic value. Less than a century later, the South Sea bubble in England became almost as famous. In this episode, the share price of the South Sea Company rose from £128 in January 1720 to £550 in May, and peaked at around £1,000 in August—just before the bubble burst and the share price collapsed to £150 in September, leading to widespread bankruptcies among those who had borrowed to buy shares on credit. In fact, the company was a major lender of money to investors willing to buy (and thus bid up) its shares. This sequence may sound familiar to anyone who lived through the dot-com boom and bust of 1995–2002[6] or, more recently, the financial turmoil of 2008, with origins widely attributed to a collapsing housing price bubble.

It is hard to defend the position that security prices in these instances represented rational, unbiased assessments of intrinsic value. But beware of jumping to the conclusion that prices may generally be thought of as arbitrary and obvious trading opportunities abundant. First, most bubbles become "obvious" only in retrospect. At the time, there is often a seemingly defensible rationale for the price run-up. In the dot-com boom, for example, many contemporary observers rationalized stock price gains as justified by the prospect of a new and more profitable economy, driven by technological advances. Even the irrationality of the tulip mania may have been overblown in its later retelling.[7] In addition, security valuation is intrinsically difficult. Given the considerable imprecision of estimates of intrinsic value, large bets on perceived mispricing may entail hubris.

Moreover, even if you suspect that prices are in fact "wrong," it can be difficult to take advantage of them. We explore these issues in more detail in the following chapter. For now, we can simply point out some impediments to making aggressive bets against an asset: the costs of short-selling overpriced securities as well as potential problems obtaining the securities to sell short and the possibility that, even if you are ultimately correct, the market may disagree and prices still can move dramatically against you in the short term, thus wiping out your capital.

Strong-Form Tests: Inside Information

It would not be surprising if insiders were able to make superior profits trading in their firm's stock. In other words, we do not expect markets to be strong-form efficient; we regulate and limit trades based on inside information. The ability of insiders to trade profitably in their own stock has been documented in studies by Jaffe (1974), Seyhun (1986), Givoly and Palmon (1985), and others. Jaffe's was one of the earlier studies that documented the tendency for stock prices to rise after insiders intensively bought shares and to fall after intensive insider sales.

---

[6]The dot-com boom gave rise to the term *irrational exuberance*. In this vein consider that one company, going public in the investment boom of 1720, described itself simply as "a company for carrying out an undertaking of great advantage, but nobody to know what it is."

[7]For interesting discussions of this possibility, see Peter Garber, *Famous First Bubbles: The Fundamentals of Early Manias* (Cambridge: MIT Press, 2000) and Anne Goldgar, *Tulipmania: Money, Honor, and Knowledge in the Dutch Golden Age* (Chicago: University of Chicago Press, 2007).

Can other investors benefit by following insiders' trades? The Securities and Exchange Commission requires all insiders to register their trading activity and it publishes these trades in an *Official Summary of Security Transactions and Holdings.* Since 2002, insiders must report large trades to the SEC within two business days. Once the *Official Summary* is published, the trades become public information. At that point, if markets are efficient, fully and immediately processing the information released in the *Official Summary* of trading, an investor should no longer be able to profit from following the pattern of those trades. Several Internet sites contain information on insider trading.

The study by Seyhun, which carefully tracked the public release dates of the *Official Summary,* found that following insider transactions would be to no avail. Although there is some tendency for stock prices to increase even after the *Official Summary* reports insider buying, the abnormal returns are not of sufficient magnitude to overcome transaction costs.

Interpreting the Evidence

How should we interpret the ever-growing anomalies literature? Does it imply that markets are grossly inefficient, allowing for simplistic trading rules to offer large profit opportunities? Or are there other, more-subtle interpretations?

Risk premiums or inefficiencies? The price-earnings, small-firm, market-to-book, momentum, and long-term reversal effects are currently among the most puzzling phenomena in empirical finance. There are several interpretations of these effects. First note that to some extent, some of these phenomena may be related. The feature that small firms, low-market-to-book firms, and recent "losers" seem to have in common is a stock price that has fallen considerably in recent months or years. Indeed, a firm can become a small firm or a low-market-to-book firm by suffering a sharp drop in price. These groups therefore may contain a relatively high proportion of distressed firms that have suffered recent difficulties.

Fama and French (1993) argue that these effects can be explained as manifestations of risk premiums. Using their three-factor model, they show that stocks with higher "betas" (also known as factor loadings) on size or market-to-book factors have higher average returns; they interpret these returns as evidence of a risk premium associated with the factor. This model does a much better job than the one-factor CAPM in explaining security returns. While size or book-to-market ratios per se are obviously not risk factors, they perhaps might act as proxies for more fundamental determinants of risk. Fama and French argue that these patterns of returns may therefore be consistent with an efficient market in which expected returns are consistent with risk. In this regard, it is worth noting that returns to "style factors," for example, the return on portfolios constructed based on the ratio of book-to-market value (specifically, the Fama-French high minus low book-to-market portfolio) or firm size (the return on the small minus big firm portfolio) do indeed seem to predict business cycles in many countries. Figure 8.6 shows that returns on these portfolios tend to have positive returns in years prior to rapid growth in gross domestic product.

The opposite interpretation is offered by Lakonishok, Shleifer, and Vishny (1995), who argue that these phenomena are evidence of inefficient markets, more specifically, of systematic errors in the forecasts of stock analysts. They believe that analysts extrapolate past performance too far into the future, and therefore overprice firms with recent good performance and underprice firms with recent poor performance. Ultimately, when market participants recognize their errors, prices reverse. This explanation is consistent with the reversal effect and also, to a degree, is consistent with the small-firm and book-to-market effects because firms with sharp price drops may tend to be small or have high book-to-market ratios.

If Lakonishok, Shleifer, and Vishney are correct, we ought to find that analysts systematically err when forecasting returns of recent "winner" versus "loser" firms. A study by La Porta (1996) is consistent with this pattern. He finds that equity of firms for which analysts predict low growth rates of earnings actually perform better than those with high expected earnings growth. Analysts seem overly pessimistic about firms with low growth prospects and overly optimistic about firms with high growth prospects. When these too-extreme expectations are "corrected," the low-expected-growth firms outperform high-expected-growth firms.

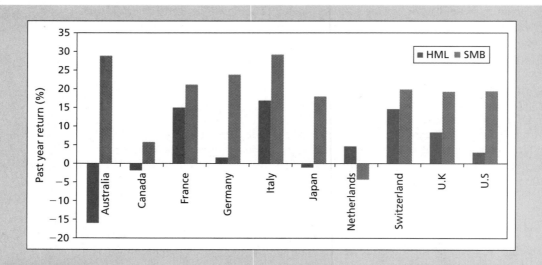

FIGURE 8.6

Return to style portfolio as a predictor of GDP growth. Average difference in the return on the style portfolio in years before good GDP growth versus in years before bad GDP growth. Positive value means the style portfolio does better in years prior to good macroeconomic performance. HML = high minus low portfolio, sorted on ratio of book-to-market value. SMB = small minus big portfolio, sorted on firm size.

Source: Reprinted from J. Liew and M. Vassalou, "Can Book-to-Market, Size, and Momentum Be Risk Factors That Predict Economic Growth?" *Journal of Financial Economics* 57 (2000), pp. 221–45. Copyright 2000 with permission from Elsevier Science.

Anomalies or data mining?   We have covered many of the so-called anomalies cited in the literature, but our list could go on and on. Some wonder whether these anomalies are really unexplained puzzles in financial markets or whether they instead are an artifact of data mining. After all, if one reruns the computer database of past returns over and over and examines stock returns along enough dimensions, simple chance will cause some criteria to *appear* to predict returns.

In this regard, it is noteworthy that some anomalies have not shown much staying power after being reported in the academic literature. For example, after the small-firm effect was published in the early 1980s, it promptly disappeared for much of the rest of the decade. Similarly, the book-to-market strategy, which commanded considerable attention in the early 1990s, was ineffective for the rest of that decade.

Still, even acknowledging the potential for data mining, a common thread seems to run through many of the anomalies we have considered, lending support to the notion that there is a real puzzle to explain. Value stocks—defined by low P/E ratio, high book-to-market ratio, or depressed prices relative to historic levels—seem to have provided higher average returns than "glamour" or growth stocks.

One way to address the problem of data mining is to find a data set that has not already been researched and see whether the relationship in question shows up in the new data. Such studies have revealed size, momentum, and book-to-market effects in other security markets around the world. While these phenomena may be a manifestation of a systematic risk premium, the precise nature of that risk is not fully understood.

8.4   Mutual Fund and Analyst Performance

We have documented some of the apparent chinks in the armor of efficient market proponents. For investors, the issue of market efficiency boils down to whether skilled investors can make consistent abnormal trading profits. The best test is to look at the performance of market professionals to see if they can generate performance superior to that of a passive index fund that buys and holds the market. We will look at two facets of professional performance: that of stock market analysts who recommend investment positions and that of mutual fund managers who actually manage portfolios.

Stock Market Analysts

Stock market analysts historically have worked for brokerage firms, which presents an immediate problem in interpreting the value of their advice: Analysts have tended to be overwhelmingly positive in their assessment of the prospects of firms.[8] For example, Barber, Lehavy, McNichols, and Trueman (2001) find that on a scale of 1 (strong buy) to 5 (strong sell), the average recommendation for 5,628 covered firms in 1996 was 2.04. As a result, one cannot take positive recommendations (e.g., to buy) at face value. Instead, we must look at either the relative strength of analyst recommendations compared to those for other firms or at the change in consensus recommendations.

Womack (1996) focuses on changes in analysts' recommendations and finds that positive changes are associated with increased stock prices of about 5%, and negative changes result in average price decreases of 11%. One might wonder whether these price changes reflect the market's recognition of analysts' superior information or insight about firms or, instead, simply result from new buy or sell pressure brought on by the recommendations themselves. Womack argues that price impact seems to be permanent and, therefore, consistent with the hypothesis that analysts do in fact reveal new information. Jegadeesh, Kim, Krische, and Lee (2004) also find that changes in consensus recommendations are associated with price changes, but that the *level* of consensus recommendations is an inconsistent predictor of future stock performance.

Barber, Lehavy, McNichols, and Trueman (2001) focus on the level of consensus recommendations and show that firms with the most-favorable recommendations outperform those with the least-favorable recommendations. While their results seem impressive, the authors note that portfolio strategies based on analyst consensus recommendations would result in extremely heavy trading activity with associated costs that probably would wipe out the potential profits from the strategy.

In sum, the literature suggests some value added by analysts, but some ambiguity remains. Are superior returns following analyst upgrades due to revelation of new information or due to changes in investor demand in response to the changed outlook? Also, are these results exploitable by investors who necessarily incur trading costs?

Mutual Fund Managers

As we pointed out in Chapter 4, casual evidence does not support the claim that professionally managed portfolios can consistently beat the market. Figure 4.3 in that chapter demonstrated that between 1972 and 2008 the returns of a passive portfolio indexed to the Wilshire 5000 typically would have been better than those of the average equity fund. On the other hand, there was some (admittedly inconsistent) evidence of persistence in performance, meaning that the better managers in one period tended to be better managers in following periods. Such a pattern would suggest that the better managers can with some consistency outperform their competitors, and it would be inconsistent with the notion that market prices already reflect all relevant information.

The analyses cited in Chapter 4 were based on total returns; they did not properly adjust returns for exposure to systematic risk factors. In this section we revisit the question of mutual fund performance, paying more attention to the benchmark against which performance ought to be evaluated.

As a first pass, we can examine the risk-adjusted returns (i.e., the alpha, or return in excess of required return based on beta and the market return in each period) of a large sample of mutual funds. But the market index may not be an adequate benchmark against which to

---

[8]This problem may be less severe in the future; as noted in Chapter 3, one recent reform intended to mitigate the conflict of interest in having brokerage firms that sell stocks also provide investment advice is to separate analyst coverage from the other activities of the firm.

TABLE 8.1

Performance of mutual funds based on three-index model

Type of Fund (Wiesenberger Classification)	Number of Funds	Alpha (%)	t-Statistic for Alpha
Equity funds			
Maximum capital gain	12	−4.59	−1.87
Growth	33	−1.55	−1.23
Growth and income	40	−0.68	−1.65
Balanced funds	31	−1.27	−2.73

Note: The three-index model calculates the alpha of each fund as the intercept of the following regression:

$$r - r_f = \alpha + \beta_M(r_M - r_f) + \beta_S(r_S - r_f) + \beta_D(r_D - r_f) + e$$

where r is the return on the fund, r_f is the risk-free rate, r_M is the return on the S&P 500 Index, r_s is the return on a non–S&P small-stock index, r_D is the return on a bond index, e is the fund's residual return, and the betas measure the sensitivity of fund returns to the various indexes.

Source: E. J. Elton, M. J. Gruber, S. Das, and M. Hlavka, "Efficiency with Costly Information: A Reinterpretation of Evidence from Managed Portfolios," *Review of Financial Studies* 6 (1993), pp. 1–22.

evaluate mutual fund returns. Because mutual funds tend to maintain considerable holdings in equity of small firms, whereas the S&P 500 is exclusively comprised of large firms, mutual funds as a whole will tend to outperform the S&P when small firms outperform large ones and underperform when small firms fare worse. Thus a better benchmark for the performance of funds would be an index that incorporates the stock market performance of smaller firms.

The importance of the benchmark can be illustrated by examining the returns on small stocks in various subperiods.[9] In the 20-year period between 1945 and 1964, a small-stock index underperformed the S&P 500 by about 4% per year (i.e., the alpha of the small-stock index after adjusting for systematic risk was −4%). In the following 20-year period between 1965 and 1984, small stocks outperformed the S&P 500 Index by 10%. Thus if one were to examine mutual fund returns in the earlier period, they would tend to look poor, not necessarily because fund managers were poor stock pickers, but simply because mutual funds as a group tended to hold more small stocks than were represented in the S&P 500. In the later period, funds would look better on a risk-adjusted basis relative to the S&P 500 because small stocks performed better. The "style choice," that is, the exposure to small stocks (which is an asset allocation decision) would dominate the evaluation of performance even though it has little to do with managers' stock-picking ability.[10]

Elton, Gruber, Das, and Hlavka (1993) attempted to control for the impact of non–S&P assets on mutual fund performance. They used a multifactor version of the index model of security returns and calculated fund alphas by using regressions that include as explanatory variables the excess returns of three benchmark portfolios rather than just one proxy for the market index. Their three factors are the excess return on the S&P 500 Index, the excess return on an equity index of non–S&P low capitalization (i.e., small) firms, and the excess return on a bond market index. Some of their results are presented in Table 8.1, which shows that average alphas are negative for each type of equity fund, although generally not of statistically significant magnitude. They concluded that after controlling for the relative performance of these three asset classes—large stocks, small stocks, and bonds—mutual fund managers as a group do not demonstrate an ability to beat passive index strategies that would simply mix

[9]This illustration and the statistics cited are based on E. J. Elton, M. J. Gruber, S. Das, and M. Hlavka, "Efficiency with Costly Information: A Reinterpretation of Evidence from Managed Portfolios," *Review of Financial Studies* 6 (1993), pp. 1–22, which is discussed shortly.

[10]Remember that the asset allocation decision is usually in the hands of the individual investor. Investors allocate their investment portfolios to funds in asset classes they desire to hold, and they can reasonably expect only that mutual fund portfolio managers will choose stocks advantageously *within* those asset classes.

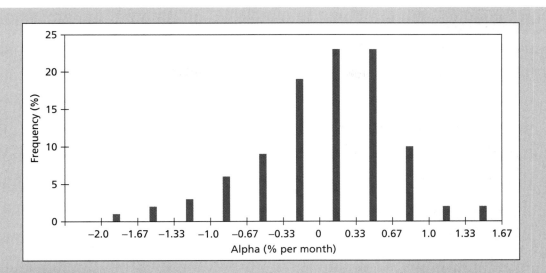

FIGURE 8.7

Mutual fund alphas computed using a four-factor model of expected return, 1993–2007. (The best and worst 2.5% of observations are excluded from this distribution.)

Source: Professor Richard Evans, University of Virginia, Darden School of Business.

index funds from among these asset classes. They also found that mutual fund performance is worse for firms that have higher expense ratios and higher turnover ratios. Thus it appears that funds with higher fees do not increase gross returns by enough to justify those fees.

The conventional performance benchmark today is a four-factor model, which employs the three Fama-French factors (the return on the market index, and returns to portfolios based on size and book-to-market ratio) augmented by a momentum factor (a portfolio constructed based on prior-year stock return). Alphas constructed using an expanded index model using these four factors control for a wide range of mutual fund–style choices that may affect average returns, for example, an inclination to growth versus value or small versus large capitalization stocks. Figure 8.7 shows a frequency distribution of four-factor alphas for U.S. domestic equity funds.[11] The results show that the distribution of alpha is roughly bell-shaped, with a slightly negative mean. On average, it does not appear that these funds outperform their style-adjusted benchmarks.

Carhart (1997) reexamined the issue of consistency in mutual fund performance—sometimes called the "hot hands" phenomenon—controlling for non–S&P factors in a manner similar to Elton, Gruber, Das, and Hlavka. Carhart used the four-factor extension described above and found that after controlling for these factors, there is some small persistence in relative performance across managers. However, much of that persistence seems due to expenses and transactions costs rather than gross investment returns. This last point is important; while there can be no consistently superior performers in a fully efficient market, there *can* be consistently inferior performers. Repeated weak performance would not be due to a tendency to pick bad stocks consistently (that would be impossible in an efficient market!) but could result from a consistently high expense ratio, high portfolio turnover, or higher-than-average transaction costs per trade. In this regard, it is interesting that in another study documenting apparent consistency across managers, Hendricks, Patel, and Zeckhauser (1993) also found the strongest consistency among the weakest performers.

Even allowing for expenses and turnover, some amount of performance persistence seems to be due to differences in investment strategy. Carhart found, however, that the evidence of

[11]We are grateful to Professor Richard Evans for this data.

FIGURE 8.8

Persistence of mutual fund
performance. Performance
over time of mutual fund
groups ranked by initial
year performance

Source: Mark M. Carhart,
"On Persistence in Mutual Fund
Performance," *Journal of Finance*
52 (March 1997), pp. 57–82.
Reprinted by permission of
the publisher, Blackwell
Publishing, Inc.

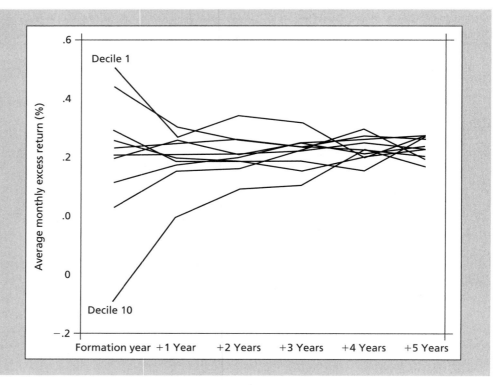

persistence is concentrated at the two extremes. Figure 8.8, from Carhart's study, documents performance persistence. Equity funds are ranked into 1 of 10 groups by performance in the formation year, and the performance of each group in the following years is plotted. It is clear that except for the best-performing top-decile group and the worst-performing 10th decile group, performance in future periods is almost independent of earlier-year returns. Carhart's results suggest that there may be a small group of exceptional managers who can with some consistency outperform a passive strategy, but that for the majority of managers over- or underperformance in any period is largely a matter of chance.

In contrast to the extensive studies of equity fund managers, there have been few studies of the performance of bond fund managers. Blake, Elton, and Gruber (1993) examined the performance of fixed-income mutual funds. They found that, on average, bond funds underperform passive fixed-income indexes by an amount roughly equal to expenses, and that there is no evidence that past performance can predict future performance. Their evidence is consistent with the hypothesis that bond managers operate in an efficient market in which performance before expenses is only as good as that of a passive index.

Thus the evidence on the risk-adjusted performance of professional managers is mixed at best. We conclude that the performance of professional managers is broadly consistent with market efficiency. The amounts by which professional managers as a group beat or are beaten by the market fall within the margin of statistical uncertainty. In any event, it is quite clear that performance superior to passive strategies is far from routine. Studies show either that most managers cannot outperform passive strategies or that if there is a margin of superiority, it is small.

On the other hand, a small number of investment superstars—Peter Lynch (formerly of Fidelity's Magellan Fund), Warren Buffett (of Berkshire Hathaway), John Templeton (of Templeton Funds), or George Soros among them—have compiled career records that show a consistency of superior performance hard to reconcile with absolutely efficient markets. In a careful statistical analysis of mutual fund "stars," Kosowski, Timmerman, Wermers, and White (2006) conclude that the stock-picking ability of a minority of managers is sufficient to cover their costs and that their superior performance tends to persist over time. However, Nobel Prize–winner Paul Samuelson (1989) points out that the records of the vast majority of professional money managers offer convincing evidence that there are no easy strategies to guarantee success in the securities markets.

Survivorship Bias in Mutual Fund Studies

In any period, some managers may be lucky, and others unlucky. We argued in Chapter 4 that a good way to separate skill from luck is to see whether the managers who perform well in one period tend to be above-average performers in subsequent periods. If they are, we should be more willing to ascribe their success to skill. Unfortunately, studies of mutual fund performance can be affected by *survivorship bias,* the tendency for less-successful funds to go out of business over time, thus leaving the sample. This can give rise to the appearance of persistence in performance, even if there is none in reality.

Define a "winner" fund as one in the top half of the distribution of returns in a given period and a "loser" fund as one in the bottom half of the sample. If performance is due solely to chance, the probability of being a winner or loser in the next period is the same regardless of first-period performance. A 2 × 2 tabulation of performance in two consecutive periods would look like this:

	Second Period	
First Period	**Winners**	**Losers**
Winners	.25	.25
Losers	.25	.25

For example, the first-period winners (50% of the sample) are equally likely to be winners or losers in the second period, so 25% of total outcomes fall in each cell in the first row.

But what happens if losing funds or managers are removed from the sample because they are shut down by their management companies? This can lead to the appearance of performance persistence. Brown, Goetzmann, Ibbotson, and Ross (1992) use a sample of mutual fund returns to simulate the potential import of survivorship bias. They simulate annual returns over a four-year period for 600 managers drawing from distributions constructed to mimic historical equity and fund returns in the United States, compute performance over two two-year periods, and construct 2 × 2 tables of winner/loser performance like the one above. Their results appear in Table 8.2. If all 600 managers remain in the simulated sample, the results

TABLE 8.2	**Second-Period Winners**	**Second-Period Losers**
Two-way table of managers classified by risk-adjusted returns over successive intervals	**A.** No cut-off (n = 600)	
	First-period winners — 150.09	149.51
	First-period losers — 149.51	150.09
	B. 5% cut-off (n = 494)	
	First-period winners — 127.49	119.51
	First-period losers — 119.51	127.49
	C. 10% cut-off (n = 398)	
	First-period winners — 106.58	92.42
	First-period losers — 92.42	106.58

Source: S. J. Brown, W. Goetzmann, R. G. Ibbotson, and S. A. Ross, "Survivorship Bias in Performance Studies," *Review of Financial Studies* 5 (1992), pp. 553–580.

look much like the ones above (see Panel A). But if the bottom 5% of first-period performers are removed from the sample each year (5% cut-off, Panel B), the diagonal terms are larger than the off-diagonal terms: winners seem more likely to remain winners, and losers to remain losers. If a higher fraction of poor performers are removed from the sample (Panel C), there is even greater appearance of performance persistence.

The appearance of persistence in the simulation is due to survivorship bias. Average alphas are constructed to be zero for all groups. These results serve as a warning that data sets used to assess performance of professional managers must be free of survivorship bias. Unfortunately, many are not.

So, Are Markets Efficient?

There is a telling joke about two economists walking down the street. They spot a $20 bill on the sidewalk. One starts to pick it up, but the other one says, "Don't bother; if the bill were real someone would have picked it up already."

The lesson is clear. An overly doctrinaire belief in efficient markets can paralyze the investor and make it appear that no research effort can be justified. This extreme view is probably unwarranted. There are enough anomalies in the empirical evidence to justify the search for underpriced securities that clearly goes on.

The bulk of the evidence, however, suggests that any supposedly superior investment strategy should be taken with many grains of salt. The market is competitive *enough* that only differentially superior information or insight will earn money; the easy pickings have been picked. In the end it is likely that the margin of superiority that any professional manager can add is so slight that the statistician will not easily be able to detect it.

We conclude that markets are very efficient, but that rewards to the especially diligent, intelligent, or creative may in fact be waiting.

SUMMARY

- Statistical research has shown that to a close approximation stock prices seem to follow a random walk with no discernible predictable patterns that investors can exploit. Such findings are now taken to be evidence of market efficiency, that is, evidence that market prices reflect all currently available information. Only new information will move stock prices, and this information is equally likely to be good news or bad news.
- Market participants distinguish among three forms of the efficient market hypothesis. The weak form asserts that all information to be derived from past trading data already is reflected in stock prices. The semistrong form claims that all publicly available information is already reflected. The strong form, which generally is acknowledged to be extreme, asserts that all information, including insider information, is reflected in prices.
- Technical analysis focuses on stock price patterns and on proxies for buy or sell pressure in the market. Fundamental analysis focuses on the determinants of the underlying value of the firm, such as current profitability and growth prospects. Because both types of analysis are based on public information, neither should generate excess profits if markets are operating efficiently.
- Proponents of the efficient market hypothesis often advocate passive as opposed to active investment strategies. The policy of passive investors is to buy and hold a broad-based market index. They expend resources neither on market research nor on frequent purchase and sale of stocks. Passive strategies may be tailored to meet individual investor requirements.
- Empirical studies of technical analysis do not generally support the hypothesis that such analysis can generate superior trading profits. One notable exception to this conclusion is the apparent success of momentum-based strategies over intermediate-term horizons.

- Several anomalies regarding fundamental analysis have been uncovered. These include the P/E effect, the small-firm-in-January effect, the neglected-firm effect, post–earnings-announcement price drift, and the book-to-market effect. Whether these anomalies represent market inefficiency or poorly understood risk premiums is still a matter of debate.
- By and large, the performance record of professionally managed funds lends little credence to claims that most professionals can consistently beat the market.

KEY TERMS

anomalies, 240
book-to-market effect, 242
efficient market
   hypothesis, 229
fundamental analysis, 234
index fund, 235
momentum effect, 239

neglected-firm effect, 242
passive investment
   strategy, 235
P/E effect, 240
random walk, 229
resistance level, 233
reversal effect, 239

semistrong-form
   EMH, 232
small-firm effect, 241
strong-form EMH, 232
support level, 233
technical analysis, 233
weak-form EMH, 231

PROBLEM SETS

Select problems are available in McGraw-Hill Connect. Please see the packaging options section of the preface for more information.

Basic

1. If markets are efficient, what should be the correlation coefficient between stock returns for two non-overlapping time periods?
2. "If all securities are fairly priced, all must offer equal expected rates of return." Comment.
3. If prices are as likely to increase as decrease, why do investors earn positive returns from the market on average?
4. A successful firm like Microsoft has consistently generated large profits for years. Is this a violation of the EMH?
5. At a cocktail party, your co-worker tells you that he has beaten the market for each of the last three years. Suppose you believe him. Does this shake your belief in efficient markets?
6. Which of the following statements are *true* if the efficient market hypothesis holds?
   a. It implies that future events can be forecast with perfect accuracy.
   b. It implies that prices reflect all available information.
   c. It implies that security prices change for no discernible reason.
   d. It implies that prices do not fluctuate.
7. In an efficient market, professional portfolio management can offer all of the following benefits *except*
   a. Low-cost diversification.
   b. A targeted risk level.
   c. Low-cost record keeping.
   d. A superior risk-return trade-off.
8. Which version of the efficient market hypothesis (weak, semistrong, or strong-form) focuses on the most inclusive set of information?
9. "Highly variable stock prices suggest that the market does not know how to price stocks." Respond.

Intermediate

10. Which of the following most appears to contradict the proposition that the stock market is *weakly* efficient? Explain.

a. Over 25% of mutual funds outperform the market on average.

b. Insiders earn abnormal trading profits.

c. Every January, the stock market earns abnormal returns.

11. Suppose that, after conducting an analysis of past stock prices, you come up with the following observations. Which would appear to *contradict* the *weak form* of the efficient market hypothesis? Explain.

a. The average rate of return is significantly greater than zero.

b. The correlation between the return during a given week and the return during the following week is zero.

c. One could have made superior returns by buying stock after a 10% rise in price and selling after a 10% fall.

d. One could have made higher-than-average capital gains by holding stocks with low dividend yields.

12. Which of the following observations would provide evidence *against* the *semistrong form* of the efficient market theory? Explain.

a. Mutual fund managers do not on average make superior returns.

b. You cannot make superior profits by buying (or selling) stocks after the announcement of an abnormal rise in dividends.

c. Low P/E stocks tend to have positive abnormal returns.

d. In any year approximately 50% of pension funds outperform the market.

13. Steady Growth Industries has never missed a dividend payment in its 94-year history. Does this make it more attractive to you as a possible purchase for your stock portfolio?

14. Suppose you find that prices of stocks before large dividend increases show on average consistently positive abnormal returns. Is this a violation of the EMH?

15. "If the business cycle is predictable, and a stock has a positive beta, the stock's returns also must be predictable." Respond.

16. Which of the following phenomena would be either consistent with or a violation of the efficient market hypothesis? Explain briefly.

a. Nearly half of all professionally managed mutual funds are able to outperform the S&P 500 in a typical year.

b. Money managers that outperform the market (on a risk-adjusted basis) in one year are likely to outperform in the following year.

c. Stock prices tend to be predictably more volatile in January than in other months.

d. Stock prices of companies that announce increased earnings in January tend to outperform the market in February.

e. Stocks that perform well in one week perform poorly in the following week.

17. Why are the following "effects" considered efficient market anomalies? Are there rational explanations for these effects?

a. P/E effect

b. Book-to-market effect

c. Momentum effect

d. Small-firm effect

18. Dollar-cost averaging means that you buy equal dollar amounts of a stock every period, for example, $500 per month. The strategy is based on the idea that when the stock price is low, your fixed monthly purchase will buy more shares, and when the price is high, fewer shares. Averaging over time, you will end up buying more shares when the stock is cheaper and fewer when it is relatively expensive. Therefore, by design, you will exhibit good market timing. Evaluate this strategy.

19. We know that the market should respond positively to good news and that good-news events such as the coming end of a recession can be predicted with at least some accuracy. Why, then, can we not predict that the market will go up as the economy recovers?

20. You know that firm XYZ is very poorly run. On a scale of 1 (worst) to 10 (best), you would give it a score of 3. The market consensus evaluation is that the management score is only 2. Should you buy or sell the stock?

21. Good News, Inc., just announced an increase in its annual earnings, yet its stock price fell. Is there a rational explanation for this phenomenon?

22. Shares of small firms with thinly traded stocks tend to show positive CAPM alphas. Is this a violation of the efficient market hypothesis?

Challenge

23. Examine the accompanying figure, which presents cumulative abnormal returns both before and after dates on which insiders buy or sell shares in their firms. How do you interpret this figure? What are we to make of the pattern of CARs before and after the event date?

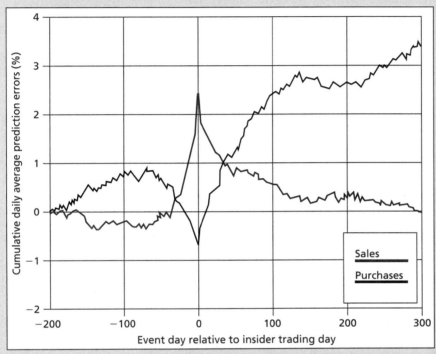

Source: Reprinted from Nejat H. Seyhun, "Insiders, Profits, Costs of Trading and Market Efficiency," *Journal of Financial Economics* 16 (1986). Copyright 1986 with permission from Elsevier Science.

24. Suppose that as the economy moves through a business cycle, risk premiums also change. For example, in a recession when people are concerned about their jobs, risk tolerance might be lower and risk premiums might be higher. In a booming economy, tolerance for risk might be higher and risk premiums lower.

    a. Would a predictably shifting risk premium such as described here be a violation of the efficient market hypothesis?

    b. How might a cycle of increasing and decreasing risk premiums create an appearance that stock prices "overreact," first falling excessively and then seeming to recover?

CFA Problems

1. The semistrong form of the efficient market hypothesis asserts that stock prices:
   a. Fully reflect all historical price information.
   b. Fully reflect all publicly available information.
   c. Fully reflect all relevant information including insider information.
   d. May be predictable.

2. Assume that a company announces an unexpectedly large cash dividend to its shareholders. In an efficient market *without* information leakage, one might expect:
   a. An abnormal price change at the announcement.
   b. An abnormal price increase before the announcement.
   c. An abnormal price decrease after the announcement.
   d. No abnormal price change before or after the announcement.

3. Which one of the following would provide evidence *against* the *semistrong form* of the efficient market theory?
   a. About 50% of pension funds outperform the market in any year.
   b. You cannot make abnormal profits by buying stocks after an announcement of strong earnings.
   c. Trend analysis is worthless in forecasting stock prices.
   d. Low P/E stocks tend to have positive abnormal returns over the long run.

4. According to the efficient market hypothesis:
   a. High-beta stocks are consistently overpriced.
   b. Low-beta stocks are consistently overpriced.
   c. Positive alphas on stocks will quickly disappear.
   d. Negative alpha stocks consistently yield low returns for arbitrageurs.

5. A "random walk" occurs when:
   a. Stock price changes are random but predictable.
   b. Stock prices respond slowly to both new and old information.
   c. Future price changes are uncorrelated with past price changes.
   d. Past information is useful in predicting future prices.

6. A market anomaly refers to:
   a. An exogenous shock to the market that is sharp but not persistent.
   b. A price or volume event that is inconsistent with historical price or volume trends.
   c. A trading or pricing structure that interferes with efficient buying and selling of securities.
   d. Price behavior that differs from the behavior predicted by the efficient market hypothesis.

7. Some scholars contend that professional managers are incapable of outperforming the market. Others come to an opposite conclusion. Compare and contrast the assumptions about the stock market that support (*a*) passive portfolio management and (*b*) active portfolio management.

8. You are a portfolio manager meeting a client. During the conversation that follows your formal review of her account, your client asks the following question:

   My grandson, who is studying investments, tells me that one of the best ways to make money in the stock market is to buy the stocks of small-capitalization firms late in December and to sell the stocks one month later. What is he talking about?

   a. Identify the apparent market anomalies that would justify the proposed strategy.
   b. Explain why you believe such a strategy might or might not work in the future.

9. a. Briefly explain the concept of the efficient market hypothesis (EMH) and each of its three forms—weak, semistrong, and strong—and briefly discuss the degree to which existing empirical evidence supports each of the three forms of the EMH.
   b. Briefly discuss the implications of the efficient market hypothesis for investment policy as it applies to:
      i. Technical analysis in the form of charting.
      ii. Fundamental analysis.
   c. Briefly explain the roles or responsibilities of portfolio managers in an efficient market environment.

10. Growth and value can be defined in several ways. "Growth" usually conveys the idea of a portfolio emphasizing or including only companies believed to possess above-average future rates of per-share earnings growth. Low current yield, high price-to-book

ratios, and high price-to-earnings ratios are typical characteristics of such portfolios. "Value" usually conveys the idea of portfolios emphasizing or including only issues currently showing low price-to-book ratios, low price-to-earnings ratios, above-average levels of dividend yield, and market prices believed to be below the issues' intrinsic values.

a. Identify and provide reasons why, over an extended period of time, value-stock investing might outperform growth-stock investing.

b. Explain why the outcome suggested in (a) should not be possible in a market widely regarded as being highly efficient.

11. Your investment client asks for information concerning the benefits of active portfolio management. She is particularly interested in the question of whether active managers can be expected to consistently exploit inefficiencies in the capital markets to produce above-average returns without assuming higher risk.

   The semistrong form of the efficient market hypothesis asserts that all publicly available information is rapidly and correctly reflected in securities prices. This implies that investors cannot expect to derive above-average profits from purchases made after information has become public because security prices already reflect the information's full effects.

a. Identify and explain two examples of empirical evidence that tend to support the EMH implication stated above.

b. Identify and explain two examples of empirical evidence that tend to refute the EMH implication stated above.

c. Discuss reasons why an investor might choose not to index even if the markets were, in fact, semistrong-form efficient.

Use data from the Standard & Poor's Market Insight Database at www.mhhe.com/edumarketinsight to answer the following questions.

STANDARD &POOR'S

1. Collect the following data for 25 firms from Market Insight.
   a. Book-to-market ratio.
   b. Price/EPS from operations ratio.
   c. Market capitalization (size).
   d. Price/Cash Flow ratio.
   e. Another criterion that interests you.

   You can find this information by choosing a company, then clicking on the *Financial Hlts.* link in the *Compustat Reports* section. Rank the firms based on each of the criteria separately and divide the firms into five groups based on their ranking for each criterion. Calculate the average rate of return for each group of firms.

   Do you confirm or reject any of the anomalies cited in this chapter? Can you uncover a new anomaly? Note: For your test to be valid, you must form your portfolios based on criteria observed at the *beginning* of the period when you form the stock groups. Why?

2. Use the price history from Market Insight to calculate the beta of each of the firms in the previous question. Use this beta, the T-bill rate, and the return on the S&P 500 to calculate the risk-adjusted abnormal return of each stock group. Does any anomaly uncovered in the previous question persist after controlling for risk?

3. Now form stock groups that use two criteria simultaneously. For example, form a portfolio of stocks that are both in the lowest quintile of price–earnings ratios and in the highest quintile of book-to-market ratio. Does selecting stocks based on more than one characteristic improve your ability to devise portfolios with abnormal returns? Repeat the analysis by forming groups that meet three criteria simultaneously. Does this yield any further improvement in abnormal returns?

SOLUTIONS TO CONCEPT *checks*

8.1. *a.* A high-level manager might well have private information about the firm. Her ability to trade profitably on that information is not surprising. This ability does not violate weak-form efficiency: The abnormal profits are not derived from an analysis of past price and trading data. If they were, this would indicate that there is valuable information that can be gleaned from such analysis. But this ability does violate strong-form efficiency. Apparently, there is some private information that is not already reflected in stock prices.

b. The information sets that pertain to the weak, semistrong, and strong form of the EMH can be described by the following illustration:

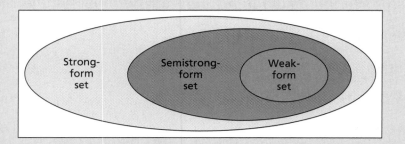

The weak-form information set includes only the history of prices and volumes. The semistrong-form set includes the weak form set *plus* all other publicly available information. In turn, the strong-form set includes the semistrong set *plus* insiders' information. It is illegal to act on this incremental information (insiders' private information). The direction of *valid* implication is

Strong-form EMH ⇒ Semistrong-form EMH ⇒ Weak-form EMH

The reverse direction implication is *not* valid. For example, stock prices may reflect all past price data (weak-form efficiency) but may not reflect relevant fundamental data (semistrong-form inefficiency).

8.2. The point we made in the preceding discussion is that the very fact that we observe stock prices near so-called resistance levels belies the assumption that the price can be a resistance level. If a stock is observed to sell *at any price*, then investors must believe that a fair rate of return can be earned if the stock is purchased at that price. It is logically impossible for a stock to have a resistance level *and* offer a fair rate of return at prices just below the resistance level. If we accept that prices are appropriate, we must reject any presumption concerning resistance levels.

8.3. If *everyone* follows a passive strategy, sooner or later prices will fail to reflect new information. At this point there are profit opportunities for active investors who uncover mispriced securities. As they buy and sell these assets, prices again will be driven to fair levels.

8.4. The answer depends on your prior beliefs about market efficiency. Miller's initial record was incredibly strong. On the other hand, with so many funds in existence, it is less surprising that *some* fund would appear to be consistently superior after the fact. Exceptional past performance of a small number of managers is possible by chance even in an efficient market. A better test is provided in "continuation studies." Are better performers in one period more likely to repeat that performance in later periods? Miller's record in the last three years fails the continuation or consistency criterion.

9 Chapter

Behavioral Finance and Technical Analysis

After Studying This Chapter You Should Be Able To:

- Demonstrate how the principles of behavioral finance can explain anomalies in stock market returns.

- Identify reasons why technical analysis may be profitable.

- Use the Dow theory to identify situations that technicians would characterize as buy or sell opportunities.

- Use indicators such as volume, put/call ratios, breadth, short interest, or confidence indexes to measure the "technical conditions" of the market.

The efficient market hypothesis makes two important predictions. First, it implies that security prices properly reflect whatever information is available to investors. A second implication follows immediately: Active traders will find it difficult to outperform passive strategies such as holding market indexes. To do so would require differential insight; this in a highly competitive market is very hard to come by.

Unfortunately, it is hard to devise measures of the "true" or intrinsic value of a security, and correspondingly difficult to test directly whether prices match those values. Therefore, most tests of market efficiency have focused on the performance of active trading strategies. These tests have been of two kinds. The anomalies literature has examined strategies that apparently *would* have provided superior risk-adjusted returns (e.g., investing in stocks with momentum or in value rather than glamour stocks). Other tests have looked at the results of *actual* investments by asking whether professional managers have been able to beat the market.

Neither class of tests has proven fully conclusive. The anomalies literature suggests that several strategies would have provided superior returns. But there are questions as to whether some of these apparent anomalies reflect risk premiums not captured by simple models of risk and return, or even if they merely reflect data mining. Moreover, the apparent inability of the typical money manager to turn these anomalies into superior returns on actual portfolios casts additional doubt on their "reality."

A relatively new school of thought dubbed *behavioral finance* argues that the sprawling literature on trading strategies has missed a larger and more important point by overlooking the first implication of efficient markets—the correctness of security prices. This may be the more important implication, since market economies rely on prices to allocate resources efficiently. The behavioral school argues that even if security prices are wrong, it still can be difficult to exploit them, and, therefore, that the failure to uncover obviously successful trading rules or traders cannot be taken as proof of market efficiency.

Whereas conventional theories presume that investors are rational, behavioral finance starts with the assumption that they might not be. We will examine some of the information-processing and behavioral irrationalities uncovered by psychologists in other contexts and show how these tendencies applied to financial markets might result in some of the anomalies discussed in the previous chapter. We then examine the limitations of strategies designed to take advantage of behaviorally induced mispricing. If the limits to such arbitrage activity are severe, mispricing can survive even if some rational investors attempt to exploit it. We turn next to technical analysis and show how behavioral models give some support to techniques that clearly would be useless in efficient markets. We close the chapter with a brief survey of some of these technical strategies.

Related Web sites for this chapter are available at www.mhhe.com/bkm.

9.1 | The Behavioral Critique

The premise of **behavioral finance** is that conventional financial theory ignores how real people make decisions and that people make a difference.[1] A growing number of economists have come to interpret the anomalies literature as consistent with several "irrationalities" that seem to characterize individuals making complicated decisions. These irrationalities fall into two broad categories: first, that investors do not always process information correctly and therefore infer incorrect probability distributions about future rates of return; and second, that even given a probability distribution of returns, they often make inconsistent or systematically suboptimal decisions.

Of course, the existence of irrational investors would not by itself be sufficient to render capital markets inefficient. If such irrationalities did affect prices, then sharp-eyed arbitrageurs taking advantage of profit opportunities might be expected to push prices back to their proper values. Thus, the second leg of the behavioral critique is that in practice the actions of such arbitrageurs are limited and therefore insufficient to force prices to match intrinsic value.

This leg of the argument is important. Virtually everyone agrees that if prices are right (i.e., price = intrinsic value), then there are no easy profit opportunities. But the converse is not necessarily true. If behaviorists are correct about limits to arbitrage activity, then the absence of profit opportunities does not necessarily imply that markets are efficient. We've noted that most tests of the efficient market hypothesis have focused on the existence of profit opportunities, often as reflected in the performance of money managers. But their failure to systematically outperform passive investment strategies need not imply that markets are in fact efficient.

We will start our summary of the behavioral critique with the first leg of the argument, surveying a sample of the informational processing errors uncovered by psychologists in other areas. We next examine a few of the behavioral irrationalities that seem to characterize

behavioral finance

Models of financial markets that emphasize potential implications of psychological factors affecting investor behavior.

[1]The discussion in this section is based on an excellent survey article: Nicholas Barberis and Richard Thaler, "A Survey of Behavioral Finance," in the *Handbook of the Economics of Finance*, eds. G. M. Constantinides, M. Harris, and R. Stulz (Amsterdam: Elsevier, 2003).

decision makers. Finally, we look at limits to arbitrage activity, and conclude with a tentative assessment of the import of the behavioral debate.

Information Processing

Errors in information processing can lead investors to misestimate the true probabilities of possible events or associated rates of return. Several such biases have been uncovered. Here are four of the more important ones.

Forecasting errors   A series of experiments by Kahneman and Tversky (1972, 1973) indicates that people give too much weight to recent experience compared to prior beliefs when making forecasts (sometimes dubbed a *memory bias*) and tend to make forecasts that are too extreme given the uncertainty inherent in their information. De Bondt and Thaler (1990) argue that the P/E effect can be explained by earnings expectations that are too extreme. In this view, when forecasts of a firm's future earnings are high, perhaps due to favorable recent performance, they tend to be *too* high relative to the objective prospects of the firm. This results in a high initial P/E (due to the optimism built into the stock price) and poor subsequent performance when investors recognize their error. Thus, high P/E firms tend to be poor investments.

Overconfidence   People tend to overestimate the precision of their beliefs or forecasts, and they tend to overestimate their abilities. In one famous survey, 90% of drivers in Sweden ranked themselves as better-than-average drivers. Such overconfidence may be responsible for the prevalence of active versus passive investment management—itself an anomaly to adherents of the efficient market hypothesis. Despite the growing popularity of indexing, only about 10% of the equity in the mutual fund industry is held in indexed accounts. The dominance of active management in the face of the typical underperformance of such strategies (consider the disappointing performance of actively managed mutual funds reviewed in Chapter 4 as well as in the previous chapter) is consistent with a tendency to overestimate ability.

An interesting example of overconfidence in financial markets is provided by Barber and Odean (2001), who compare trading activity and average returns in brokerage accounts of men and women. They find that men (in particular single men) trade far more actively than women, consistent with the greater overconfidence among men well-documented in the psychology literature. They also find that trading activity is highly predictive of poor investment performance. The top 20% of accounts ranked by portfolio turnover had average returns 7 percentage points lower than the 20% of the accounts with the lowest turnover rates. As they conclude, "trading [and by implication, overconfidence] is hazardous to your wealth."

conservatism bias

Investors are too slow (too conservative) in updating their beliefs in response to recent evidence.

Conservatism   A **conservatism bias** means that investors are too slow (too conservative) in updating their beliefs in response to new evidence. This means that they might initially underreact to news about a firm, so that prices will fully reflect new information only gradually. Such a bias would give rise to momentum in stock market returns.

representativeness bias

People are too prone to believe that a small sample is representative of a broad population and infer patterns too quickly.

Sample size neglect and representativeness   The notion of **representativeness bias** holds that people commonly do not take into account the size of a sample, apparently reasoning that a small sample is just as representative of a population as a large one. They may therefore infer a pattern too quickly based on a small sample and extrapolate apparent trends too far into the future. It is easy to see how such a pattern would be consistent with overreaction and correction anomalies. A short-lived run of good earnings reports or high stock returns would lead such investors to revise their assessments of likely future performance, and thus generate buying pressure that exaggerates the price run-up. Eventually, the gap between price and intrinsic value becomes glaring and the market corrects its initial error. Interestingly, stocks with the best recent performance suffer reversals precisely in the few days surrounding earnings announcements, suggesting that the correction occurs just as investors learn that their initial beliefs were too extreme (Chopra, Lakonishok, and Ritter, 1992).

Behavioral Biases

Even if information processing were perfect, many studies conclude that individuals would tend to make less-than-fully rational decisions using that information. These behavioral biases largely affect how investors frame questions of risk versus return, and therefore make risk-return trade-offs.

Framing   Decisions seem to be affected by how choices are **framed.** For example, an individual may reject a bet when it is posed in terms of the risk surrounding possible gains but may accept that same bet when described in terms of the risk surrounding potential losses. In other words, individuals may act risk averse in terms of gains but risk seeking in terms of losses. But in many cases, the choice of how to frame a risky venture—as involving gains or losses—can be arbitrary.

framing

Decisions are affected by how choices are posed, for example, as gains relative to a low baseline level or losses relative to a higher baseline.

EXAMPLE **9.1**

Framing

Consider a coin toss with a payoff of $50 for tails. Now consider a gift of $50 that is bundled with a bet that imposes a loss of $50 if that coin toss comes up heads. In both cases, you end up with zero for heads and $50 for tails. But the former description frames the coin toss as posing a risky gain while the latter frames the coin toss in terms of risky losses. The difference in framing can lead to different attitudes toward the bet.

Mental accounting   **Mental accounting** is a specific form of framing in which people segregate certain decisions. For example, an investor may take a lot of risk with one investment account, but establish a very conservative position with another account that is dedicated to her child's education. Rationally, it might be better to view both accounts as part of the investor's overall portfolio with the risk-return profiles of each integrated into a unified framework. Statman (1997) argues that mental accounting is consistent with some investors' irrational preference for stocks with high cash dividends (they feel free to spend dividend income, but would not "dip into capital" by selling a few shares of another stock with the same total rate of return) and with a tendency to ride losing stock positions for too long (since "behavioral investors" are reluctant to realize losses). In fact, investors are more likely to sell stocks with gains than those with losses, precisely contrary to a tax-minimization strategy (Shefrin and Statman, 1985; Odean, 1998).

mental accounting

A specific form of framing in which people segregate certain decisions.

Mental accounting effects also can help explain momentum in stock prices. The *house money effect* refers to gamblers' greater willingness to accept new bets if they currently are ahead. They think of (i.e., frame) the bet as being made with their "winnings account," that is, with the casino's and not with their own money, and thus are more willing to accept risk. Analogously, after a stock market run-up, individuals may view investments as largely funded out of a "capital gains account," become more tolerant of risk, discount future cash flows at a lower rate, and thus further push up prices.

Regret avoidance   Psychologists have found that individuals who make decisions that turn out badly have more regret (blame themselves more) when that decision was more unconventional. For example, buying a blue-chip portfolio that turns down is not as painful as experiencing the same losses on an unknown start-up firm. Any losses on the blue-chip stocks can be more easily attributed to bad luck rather than bad decision making and cause

regret avoidance

People blame themselves more for unconventional choices that turn out badly so they avoid regret by making conventional decisions.

less regret. De Bondt and Thaler (1987) argue that such **regret avoidance** is consistent with both the size and book-to-market effect. Higher book-to-market firms tend to have depressed stock prices. These firms are "out of favor" and more likely to be in a financially precarious position. Similarly, smaller, less-well-known firms are also less conventional investments. Such firms require more "courage" on the part of the investor, which increases the required rate of return. Mental accounting can add to this effect. If investors focus on the gains or losses of individual stocks, rather than on broad portfolios, they can become more risk averse concerning stocks with recent poor performance, discount their cash flows at a higher rate, and thereby create a value-stock risk premium.

CONCEPT *check* **9.2**   How might the P/E effect (discussed in the previous chapter) also be explained as a consequence of regret avoidance?

---

prospect theory

Behavioral theory that investor utility depends on gains or losses from starting position, rather than on their levels of wealth.

Prospect theory   **Prospect theory** modifies the analytic description of rational risk-averse investors found in standard financial theory.[2] Figure 9.1, Panel A, illustrates the conventional description of a risk-averse investor. Higher wealth provides higher satisfaction or "utility," but at a diminishing rate (the curve flattens as the individual becomes wealthier). This gives rise to risk aversion: A gain of $1,000 increases utility by less than a loss of $1,000 reduces it; therefore, investors will reject risky prospects that don't offer a risk premium.

Figure 9.1, Panel B, shows a competing description of preferences characterized by "loss aversion." Utility depends not on the *level* of wealth as in Panel A, but on *changes* in wealth from current levels. Moreover, to the left of zero (zero denotes no change from current wealth), the curve is convex rather than concave. This has several implications. Whereas many conventional utility functions imply that investors may become less risk averse as wealth increases, the function in Panel B always recenters on current wealth, thereby ruling out such decreases in risk aversion and possibly helping to explain high average historical equity risk premiums. Moreover, the convex curvature to the left of the origin in Panel B will induce investors to be risk seeking rather than risk averse when it comes to losses. Consistent with loss aversion, traders in the T-bond futures contract have been observed to assume significantly greater risk in afternoon sessions following morning sessions in which they have lost money (Coval and Shumway, 2005).

These are only a sample of many behavioral biases uncovered in the literature. Many have implications for investor behavior. The nearby box offers some good examples.

Limits to Arbitrage

Behavioral biases would not matter for stock pricing if rational arbitrageurs could fully exploit the mistakes of behavioral investors. Trades of profit-seeking investors would correct any misalignment of prices. However, behavioral advocates argue that in practice, several factors limit the ability to profit from mispricing.[3]

Fundamental risk   Suppose that a share of IBM is underpriced. Buying it may present a profit opportunity, but it is hardly risk-free, since the presumed market underpricing can get worse. While price eventually should converge to intrinsic value, this may not happen until after the trader's investment horizon. For example, the investor may be a mutual fund manager who may lose clients (not to mention a job!) if short-term performance is poor or

---

[2]Prospect theory originated with a highly influential paper about decision making under uncertainty by D. Kahneman and A. Tversky, "Prospect Theory: An Analysis of Decision under Risk," *Econometrica* 47 (1979), pp. 263–91.
[3]Some of the more influential references on limits to arbitrage are J. B. DeLong, A. Schleifer, L. Summers, and R. Waldmann, "Noise Trader Risk in Financial Markets," *Journal of Political Economy* 98 (August 1990), pp. 704–38; and A. Schleifer and R. Vishny, "The Limits of Arbitrage," *Journal of Finance* 52 (March 1997), pp. 35–55.

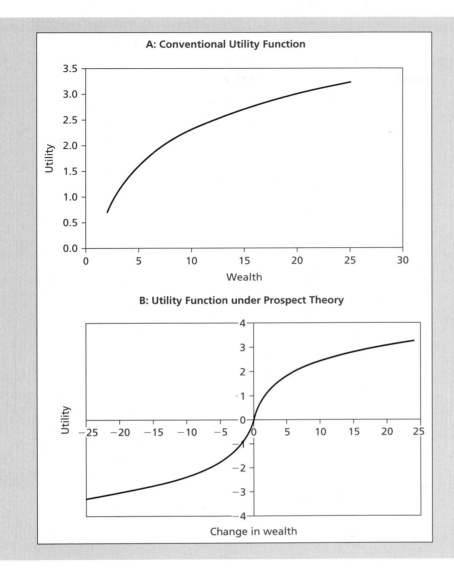

FIGURE 9.1

Prospect theory.
Panel A: A conventional utility
function is defined in terms
of wealth and is concave,
resulting in risk aversion.
Panel B: Under loss aversion,
the utility function is defined in
terms of changes from current
wealth. It is also convex to the
left of the origin, giving rise to
risk-seeking behavior in terms
of losses.

a trader who may run through her capital if the market turns against her, even temporarily. A comment often attributed to the famous economist John Maynard Keynes is that "markets can remain irrational longer than you can remain solvent." The *fundamental risk* incurred in exploiting apparent profit opportunities presumably will limit the activity of traders.

EXAMPLE 9.2

Fundamental Risk

In May 2009, the NASDAQ index fluctuated at a level around 1,700. From that perspective, the value the index had reached 8 years earlier, around 5,000, seemed obviously crazy. Surely some investors living through the Internet "bubble" of the late 1990s must have identified the index as grossly overvalued, suggesting a good selling opportunity. But this hardly would have been a risk-less arbitrage opportunity. Consider that NASDAQ may also have been overvalued in 1999 when it first crossed above 3,500 (more than double its value in 2008). An investor in 1999 who believed (as it turns out, quite correctly) that NASDAQ was overvalued at 3,500 and decided to sell it short would have suffered enormous losses as the index increased by another 1,500 points before finally peaking at 5,000. While the investor might have derived considerable satisfaction at eventually being proven right about the overpricing, by entering a year before the market "corrected," he might also have gone broke.

WHY IT'S SO TOUGH TO FIX YOUR PORTFOLIO

If your portfolio is out of whack, you could ask an investment adviser for help. But you might have better luck with your therapist.

It's a common dilemma: You know you have the wrong mix of investments, but you cannot bring yourself to fix the mess. Why is it so difficult to change? At issue are three mental mistakes.

CHASING WINNERS

Looking to lighten up on bonds and get back into stocks? Sure, you know stocks are a long-term investment and, sure, you know they are best bought when cheap.

Yet it's a lot easier to pull the trigger and buy stocks if the market has lately been scoring gains. "People are influenced by what has happened most recently, and then they extrapolate from that," says Meir Statman, a finance professor at Santa Clara University in California. "But often, they end up being optimistic and pessimistic at just the wrong time."

Consider some results from the UBS Index of Investor Optimism, a monthly poll conducted by UBS and the Gallup Organization. Each month, the poll asks investors what gain they expect from their portfolio during the next 12 months. Result? You guessed it: The answers rise and fall with the stock market.

For instance, during the bruising bear market, investors grew increasingly pessimistic, and at the market bottom they were looking for median portfolio gains of just 5%. But true to form, last year's rally brightened investors' spirits and by January they were expecting 10% returns.

GETTING EVEN

This year's choppy stock market hasn't scared off just bond investors. It has also made it difficult for stock investors to rejigger their portfolios.

Blame it on the old "get even, then get out" syndrome. With stocks treading water, many investors are reluctant to sell, because they are a long way from recovering their bear-market losses. To be sure, investors who bought near the peak are underwater, whether they sell or not. But selling losers is still agonizing, because it means admitting you made a mistake.

"If you're rational and you have a loss, you sell, take the tax loss and move on," Prof. Statman says. "But if you're a normal person, selling at a loss tears your heart out."

MUSTERING COURAGE

Whether you need to buy stocks or buy bonds, it takes confidence to act. And right now, investors just aren't confident. "There's this status-quo bias," says John Nofsinger, a finance professor at Washington State University in Pullman, Washington. "We're afraid to do anything, because we're afraid we'll regret it."

Once again, it's driven by recent market action. When markets are flying high, folks attribute their portfolio's gains to their own brilliance. That gives them the confidence to trade more and to take greater risks. Overreacting to short-term market results is, of course, a great way to lose a truckload of money. But with any luck, if you are aware of this pitfall, maybe you will avoid it.

Or maybe [this is] too optimistic. "You can tell somebody that investors have all these behavioral biases," says Terrance Odean, a finance professor at the University of California at Berkeley. "So what happens? The investor thinks, 'Oh, that sounds like my husband. I don't think many investors say, 'Oh, that sounds like me.'"

Implementation costs Exploiting overpricing can be particularly difficult. Short-selling a security entails costs: short-sellers may have to return the borrowed security on little notice, rendering the horizon of the short sale uncertain; other investors such as many pension or mutual fund managers face strict limits on their discretion to short securities. This can limit the ability of arbitrage activity to force prices to fair value.

Model risk One always has to worry that an apparent profit opportunity is more apparent than real. Perhaps you are using a faulty model to value the security, and the price actually is right. Mispricing may make a position a good bet, but it is still a risky one, which limits the extent to which it will be pursued.

Limits to Arbitrage and the Law of One Price

While one can debate the implications of much of the anomalies literature, surely the Law of One Price (positing that effectively identical assets should have identical prices) should be satisfied in rational markets. Yet there are several instances where the law seems to have been violated. These instances are good case studies of the limits to arbitrage.

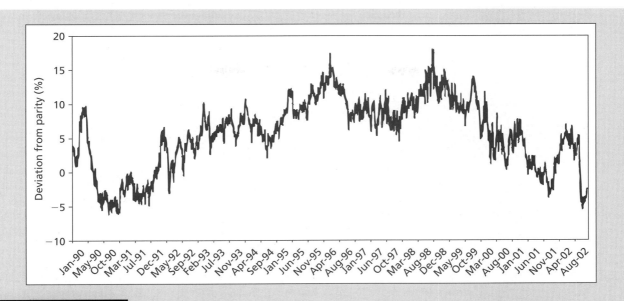

FIGURE 9.2

Pricing of Royal Dutch relative to Shell (*deviation from parity*)

Source: O. A. Lamont and R. H. Thaler, "Anomalies: The Law of One Price in Financial Markets," *Journal of Economic Perspectives* 17 (Fall 2003), pp. 191–202.

"Siamese twin" companies[4]   In 1907, Royal Dutch Petroleum and Shell Transport merged their operations into one firm. The two original companies, which continued to trade separately, agreed to split all profits from the joint company on a 60/40 basis. Shareholders of Royal Dutch receive 60% of the cash flow, and those of Shell receive 40%. One would therefore expect that Royal Dutch should sell for exactly 60/40 = 1.5 times the price of Shell. But this is not the case. Figure 9.2 shows that the relative value of the two firms has departed considerably from this "parity" ratio for extended periods of time.

Doesn't this mispricing give rise to an arbitrage opportunity? If Royal Dutch sells for more than 1.5 times Shell, why not buy relatively underpriced Shell and short-sell overpriced Royal? This seems like a reasonable strategy, but if you had followed it in February 1993 when Royal sold for about 10% more than its parity value, Figure 9.2 shows that you would have lost a lot of money as the premium widened to about 17% before finally reversing after 1999. As in Example 9.2, this opportunity posed fundamental risk.

Equity carve-outs   Several equity carve-outs also have violated the Law of One Price.[5] To illustrate, consider the case of 3Com, which in 1999 decided to spin off its Palm division. It first sold 5% of its stake in Palm in an IPO, announcing that it would distribute the remaining 95% of its Palm shares to 3Com shareholders six months later in a spinoff. Each 3Com shareholder would receive 1.5 shares of Palm in the spinoff.

Once Palm shares began trading, but prior to the spinoff, the share price of 3Com should have been *at least* 1.5 times that of Palm. After all, each share of 3Com entitled its owner to 1.5 shares of Palm *plus* an ownership stake in a profitable company. Instead, Palm shares at the IPO actually sold for *more* than the 3Com shares. The *stub value* of 3Com (i.e., the value of each 3Com share net of the value of the claim to Palm represented by that share) could be

---

[4]This discussion is based on K. A. Froot and E. M. Dabora, "How Are Stock Prices Affected by the Location of Trade?" *Journal of Financial Economics* 53 (1999), pp. 189–216.

[5]O. A. Lamont and R. H. Thaler, "Can the Market Add and Subtract? Mispricing in Tech Carve-outs," *Journal of Political Economy* 111 (2003), pp. 227–68.

computed as the price of 3Com minus 1.5 times the price of Palm. This calculation, however, implies that 3Com's stub value was negative, this despite the fact that it was a profitable company with cash assets alone of about $10 per share.

Again, an arbitrage strategy seems obvious. Why not buy 3Com and sell Palm? The limit to arbitrage in this case was the inability of investors to sell Palm short. Virtually all available shares in Palm were already borrowed and sold short, and the negative stub values persisted for more than two months.

Closed-end funds   We noted in Chapter 4 that closed-end funds often sell for substantial discounts or premiums from net asset value. This is "nearly" a violation of the Law of One Price, since one would expect the value of the fund to equal the value of the shares it holds. We say nearly, because in practice, there are a few wedges between the value of the closed-end fund and its underlying assets. One is expenses. The fund incurs expenses that ultimately are paid for by investors, and these will reduce share price. On the other hand, if managers can invest fund assets to generate positive risk-adjusted returns, share price might exceed net asset value.

Lee, Shleifer, and Thaler (1991) argue that the patterns of discounts and premiums on closed-end funds are driven by changes in investor sentiment. They note that discounts on various funds move together and are correlated with the return on small stocks, suggesting that all are affected by common variation in sentiment. One might consider buying funds selling at a discount from net asset value and selling those trading at a premium, but discounts and premiums can widen, subjecting this strategy too to fundamental risk. Pontiff (1996) demonstrates that deviations of price from net asset value in closed-end funds tend to be higher in funds that are more difficult to arbitrage, for example, those with more idiosyncratic volatility.

<table>
<tr><td>**CONCEPT**
c h e c k</td><td>**9.3**</td><td>Fundamental risk may be limited by a "deadline" that forces a convergence between price and intrinsic value. What do you think would happen to a closed-end fund's discount if the fund announced that it plans to liquidate in six months, at which time it will distribute NAV to its shareholders?</td></tr>
</table>

Closed-end fund discounts are a good example of so-called anomalies that also may have rational explanations. Ross (2002) demonstrates that they can be reconciled with rational investors even if expenses or fund abnormal returns are modest. He shows that if a fund has a dividend yield of δ, an alpha (risk-adjusted abnormal return) of α, and expense ratio of ε, then using the constant-growth dividend discount model (see Chapter 13), the premium of the fund over its net asset value will be

$$\frac{\text{Price} - \text{NAV}}{\text{NAV}} = \frac{\alpha - \varepsilon}{\delta + \varepsilon - \alpha}$$

If the fund manager's performance more than compensates for expenses (i.e., if $\alpha > \varepsilon$), the fund will sell at a premium to NAV; otherwise it will sell at a discount. For example, suppose $\alpha = .015$, the expense ratio is $\varepsilon = .0125$, and the dividend yield is $\delta = .02$. Then the premium will be .14, or 14%. But if the market turns sour on the manager and revises its estimate of α downward to .005, that premium quickly turns into a discount of 43%.

This analysis might explain why closed-end funds often are issued to the public at a premium; if investors do not expect α to exceed ε, they won't purchase shares in the fund. But the fact that most premiums eventually turn into discounts indicates how difficult it is for management to fulfill these expectations.[6]

---

[6]We might ask why this logic of discounts and premiums does not apply to open-end mutual funds since they incur similar expense ratios. Because investors in these funds can redeem shares for NAV, the shares cannot sell at a discount to NAV. Expenses in open-end funds reduce returns in each period rather than being capitalized into price and inducing a discount.

Bubbles and Behavioral Economics

In Example 9.2, we pointed out that the stock market run-up of the late 1990s, and even more spectacularly, the run-up of the technology-heavy NASDAQ market, seems in retrospect to have been an obvious bubble. In a six-year period beginning in 1995, the NASDAQ index increased by a factor of more than 6. Former Fed Chairman Alan Greenspan famously characterized the dot-com boom as an example of "irrational exuberance," and his assessment turned out to be correct: By October 2002, the index fell to less than one-fourth the peak value it had reached only two and a half years earlier. This episode seems to be a case in point for advocates of the behavioral school, exemplifying a market moved by irrational investor sentiment. Moreover, in accord with behavioral patterns, as the dot-com boom developed, it seemed to feed on itself, with investors increasingly confident of their investment prowess (overconfidence bias) and apparently willing to extrapolate short-term patterns into the distant future (representativeness bias).

On the other hand, bubbles are a lot easier to identify as such once they are over. While they are going on, it is not as clear that prices are irrationally exuberant, and, indeed, many financial commentators at the time justified the boom as consistent with glowing forecasts for the "new economy." A simple example shows how hard it can be to tie down the fair value of stock investments.[7]

EXAMPLE 9.3

A Stock Market Bubble?

In 2000, the dividends paid by the firms included in the S&P 500 totaled $154.6 million. If the discount rate for the index was 9.2% and the expected dividend growth rate was 8%, the value of these shares according to the constant-growth dividend discount model (see Chapter 13 for more on this model) would be

$$\text{Value} = \frac{\text{Dividend}}{\text{Discount rate} - \text{Growth rate}} = \frac{\$154.6}{.092 - .08} = \$12,883 \text{ million}$$

This was quite close to the actual total value of those firms at the time. But the estimate is highly sensitive to the input values, and even a small reassessment of their prospects would result in a big revision of price. Suppose the expected dividend growth rate fell to 7.4%. This would reduce the value of the index to

$$\text{Value} = \frac{\text{Dividend}}{\text{Discount rate} - \text{Growth rate}} = \frac{\$154.6}{.092 - .074} = \$8,589 \text{ million}$$

which was about the value to which the S&P 500 firms had fallen by October 2002. In light of this example, the run-up and crash of the 1990s seems easier to reconcile with rational behavior.

Still, other evidence seems to tag the dot-com boom as at least partially irrational. Consider, for example, the results of a study by Rau, Dimitrov, and Cooper (2001) documenting that firms adding ".com" to the end of their names during this period enjoyed a meaningful stock price increase. That doesn't sound like rational valuation to us.

Evaluating the Behavioral Critique

As investors, we are concerned with the existence of profit opportunities. The behavioral explanations of efficient market anomalies do not give guidance as to how to exploit any irrationality. For investors, the question is still whether there is money to be made from mispricing, and the behavioral literature is largely silent on this point.

However, as we have emphasized above, one of the important implications of the efficient market hypothesis is that security prices serve as reliable guides to the allocation of real

---

[7]The following example is taken from R. A. Brealey, S. C. Myers, and F. Allen, *Principles of Corporate Finance,* 9th ed. (Burr Ridge, IL: McGraw-Hill/Irwin, 2008).

capital. If prices are distorted, then capital markets will give misleading signals (and incentives) as to where the economy may best allocate resources. In this crucial dimension, the behavioral critique of the efficient market hypothesis is certainly important irrespective of any implication for investment strategies.

There is considerable debate among financial economists concerning the strength of the behavioral critique. Many believe that the behavioral approach is too unstructured, in effect allowing virtually any anomaly to be explained by some combination of irrationalities chosen from a laundry list of behavioral biases. While it is easy to "reverse engineer" a behavioral explanation for any particular anomaly, these critics would like to see a consistent or unified behavioral theory that can explain a *range* of anomalies.

More fundamentally, others are not convinced that the anomalies literature as a whole is a convincing indictment of the efficient market hypothesis. Fama (1998) reviews the anomalies literature and mounts a counterchallenge to the behavioral school. He notes that the anomalies are inconsistent in terms of their support for one type of irrationality versus another. For example, some papers document long-term corrections (consistent with overreaction) while others document long-term continuations of abnormal returns (consistent with underreaction). Moreover, the statistical significance of many of these results is less than meets the eye. Even small errors in choosing a benchmark against which to compare returns can cumulate to large apparent abnormalities in long-term returns. Therefore, many of the results in these studies are sensitive to small benchmarking errors, and Fama argues that seemingly minor changes in methodology can have big impacts on conclusions.

Behavioral finance is still in its infancy, however. Its critique of full rationality in investor decision making is well taken, but the extent to which limited rationality affects asset pricing is controversial. Whether or not investor irrationality affects asset prices, however, behavioral finance already makes important points about portfolio management. Investors who are aware of the potential pitfalls in information processing and decision making that seem to characterize their peers should be better able to avoid such errors. Ironically, the insights of behavioral finance may lead to some of the same policy conclusions embraced by efficient market advocates. For example, an easy way to avoid some behavioral minefields is to pursue passive, largely indexed, portfolio strategies. It seems that only rare individuals can consistently beat passive strategies; this conclusion may hold true whether your fellow investors are behavioral or rational.

9.2   Technical Analysis and Behavioral Finance

Technical analysis attempts to exploit recurring and predictable patterns in stock prices to generate superior investment performance. Technicians do not deny the value of fundamental information, but believe that prices only gradually close in on intrinsic value. As fundamentals shift, astute traders can exploit the adjustment to a new equilibrium.

For example, one of the best-documented behavioral tendencies is the *disposition effect,* which refers to the tendency of investors to hold on to losing investments. Behavioral investors seem reluctant to realize losses. Grinblatt and Han (2005) show that the disposition effect can lead to momentum in stock prices even if fundamental values follow a random walk. The fact that the demand of "disposition investors" for a company's shares depends on the price history of those shares means that prices close in on fundamental values only over time, consistent with the central motivation of technical analysis.

Behavioral biases may also be consistent with technical analysts' use of volume data. An important behavioral trait noted above is overconfidence, a systematic tendency to overestimate one's abilities. As traders become overconfident, they may trade more, inducing an association between trading volume and market returns (Gervais and Odean, 2001). Technical analysis thus uses volume data as well as price history to direct trading strategy.

Finally, technicians believe that market fundamentals can be perturbed by irrational or behavioral factors, sometimes labeled sentiment variables. More or less random price fluctuations will accompany any underlying price trend, creating opportunities to exploit corrections as these fluctuations dissipate.

Trends and Corrections

Much of technical analysis seeks to uncover trends in market prices. This is in effect a search for momentum. Momentum can be absolute, in which case one searches for upward price trends, or relative, in which case the analyst looks to invest in one sector over another (or even take on a long-short position in the two sectors). Relative strength statistics (see page 276) are designed to uncover these potential opportunities.

Dow theory The grandfather of trend analysis is the **Dow theory,** named after its creator, Charles Dow (who established *The Wall Street Journal*). Many of today's more technically sophisticated methods are essentially variants of Dow's approach.

Dow theory

A technique that attempts to discern long- and short-term trends in stock market prices.

The Dow theory posits three forces simultaneously affecting stock prices:

1. The *primary trend* is the long-term movement of prices, lasting from several months to several years.
2. *Secondary* or *intermediate trends* are caused by short-term deviations of prices from the underlying trend line. These deviations are eliminated via *corrections* when prices revert back to trend values.
3. *Tertiary* or *minor trends* are daily fluctuations of little importance.

Figure 9.3 represents these three components of stock price movements. In this figure, the primary trend is upward, but intermediate trends result in short-lived market declines lasting a few weeks. The intraday minor trends have no long-run impact on price.

Figure 9.4 depicts the course of the DJIA during 1988. The primary trend is upward, as evidenced by the fact that each market peak is higher than the previous peak (point *F* versus *D* versus *B*). Similarly, each low is higher than the previous low (*E* versus *C* versus *A*). This pattern of upward-moving "tops" and "bottoms" is one of the key ways to identify the underlying primary trend. Notice in Figure 9.4 that, despite the upward primary trend, intermediate trends still can lead to short periods of declining prices (points *B* through *C,* or *D* through *E*).

In evaluating the Dow theory, don't forget the lessons of the efficient market hypothesis. The Dow theory is based on a notion of predictably recurring price patterns. Yet the EMH holds that if any pattern is exploitable, many investors would attempt to profit from such predictability, which would ultimately move stock prices and cause the trading strategy to self-destruct. While Figure 9.4 certainly appears to describe a classic upward primary trend, one always must wonder whether we can see that trend only *after* the fact. Recognizing patterns as they emerge is far more difficult.

More recent variations on the Dow theory are the Elliott wave theory and the theory of Kondratieff waves. Like the Dow theory, the idea behind Elliott waves is that stock prices can be described by a set of wave patterns. Long-term and short-term wave cycles are superimposed and result in a complicated pattern of price movements, but by interpreting the cycles,

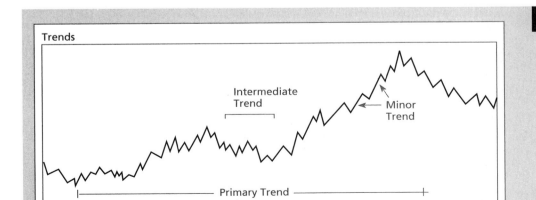

FIGURE 9.3

Dow theory trends

Source: From Melanie F. Bowman and Thom Hartle, "Dow Theory," *Technical Analysis of Stocks and Commodities,* September 1990, p.690.

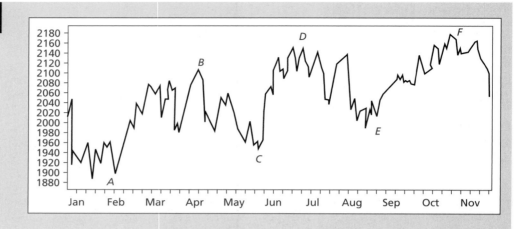

FIGURE 9.4

Dow Jones Industrial Average in 1988

Source: From Melanie F. Bowman and Thom Hartle, "Dow Theory" *Technical Analysis of Stocks and Commodities,* September 1990, p. 690.

FIGURE 9.5

Point and figure chart for Table 9.1

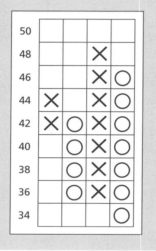

one can, according to the theory, predict broad movements. Similarly, Kondratieff waves are named after a Russian economist who asserted that the macroeconomy (and therefore the stock market) moves in broad waves lasting between 48 and 60 years. The Kondratieff waves are therefore analogous to Dow's primary trend, although they are of far longer duration. Kondratieff's assertion is hard to evaluate empirically, however, because cycles that last about 50 years provide only two independent data points per century, which is hardly enough data to test the predictive power of the theory.

Point and figure charts A variant on pure trend analysis is the *point and figure chart* depicted in Figure 9.5. This figure has no time dimension. It simply traces significant upward or downward movements in stock prices without regard to their timing. The data for Figure 9.5 come from Table 9.1.

Suppose, as in Table 9.1, that a stock's price is currently $40. If the price rises by at least $2, you put an X in the first column at $42 in Figure 9.5. Another increase of at least $2 calls for placement of another X in the first column, this time at the $44 level. If the stock then falls by at least $2, you start a new column and put an O next to $42. Each subsequent $2 price fall results in another O in the second column. When prices reverse yet again and head upward, you begin the third column with an X denoting each consecutive $2 price increase.

The single asterisks in Table 9.1 mark an event resulting in the placement of a new X or O in the chart. The daggers denote price movements that result in the start of a new column of Xs or Os.

Sell signals are generated when the stock price *penetrates* previous lows, and buy signals occur when previous high prices are penetrated. A *congestion area* is a horizontal band of Xs and Os created by several price reversals. These regions correspond to support and resistance levels and are indicated in Figure 9.6, which is an actual chart for Atlantic Richfield.

One can devise point and figure charts using price increments other than $2, but it is customary in setting up a chart to require reasonably substantial price changes before marking pluses or minuses.

CONCEPT
check   **9.4**   Draw a point and figure chart using the history in Table 9.1 with price increments of $3.

TABLE 9.1	Date	Price	Date	Price
Stock price history	January 2	$40	February 1	$40*
	January 3	40.50	February 2	41
	January 4	41	February 5	40.50
	January 5	42*	February 6	42*
	January 8	41.50	February 7	45*
	January 9	42.50	February 8	44.50
	January 10	43	February 9	46*
	January 11	43.75	February 12	47
	January 12	44*	February 13	48*
	January 15	45	February 14	47.50
	January 16	44	February 15	46†
	January 17	41.50†	February 16	45
	January 18	41	February 19	44*
	January 19	40*	February 20	42*
	January 22	39	February 21	41
	January 23	39.50	February 22	40*
	January 24	39.75	February 23	41
	January 25	38*	February 26	40.50
	January 26	35*	February 27	38*
	January 29	36†	February 28	39
	January 30	37	March 1	36*
	January 31	39*	March 2	34*

*Indicates an event that has resulted in a stock price increase or decrease of at least $2.
†Denotes a price movement that has resulted in either an upward or a downward reversal in the stock price.

Moving averages   The moving average of a stock index is the average level of the index over a given interval of time. For example, a 52-week moving average tracks the average index value over the most recent 52 weeks. Each week, the moving average is recomputed by dropping the oldest observation and adding the latest. Figure 9.7 is a moving average chart

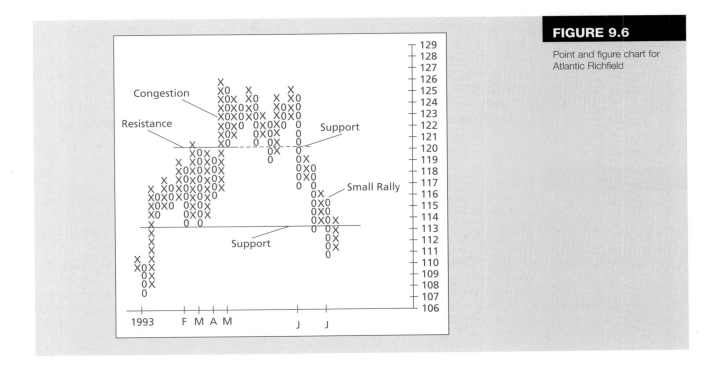

FIGURE 9.6

Point and figure chart for Atlantic Richfield

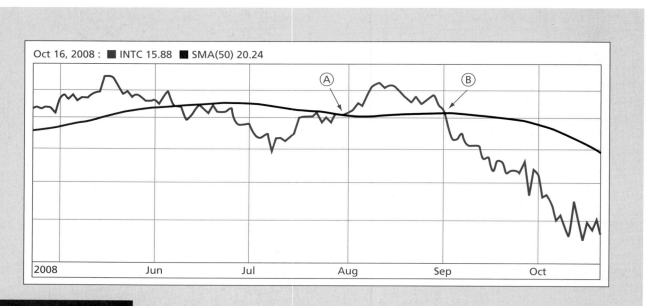

Oct 16, 2008 : ■ INTC 15.88 ■ SMA(50) 20.24

Ⓐ Ⓑ

| 2008 | Jun | Jul | Aug | Sep | Oct |

FIGURE 9.7

Share price and 50-day moving average for Intel

for Intel. Notice that the moving average plot (the colored curve) is a "smoothed" version of the original data series (dark curve).

After a period in which prices have generally been falling, the moving average will be above the current price (because the moving average "averages in" the older and higher prices). When prices have been rising, the moving average will be below the current price.

When the market price breaks through the moving average line from below, as at point A in Figure 9.7, it is taken as a bullish signal because it signifies a shift from a falling trend (with prices below the moving average) to a rising trend (with prices above the moving average). Conversely, when prices fall below the moving average as at point B, it's considered time to sell.

There is some variation in the length of the moving average considered most predictive of market movements. Two popular measures are 200-day and 53-week moving averages.

EXAMPLE 9.4

Moving Averages

Consider the price data in the following table. Each observation represents the closing level of the Dow Jones Industrial Average (DJIA) on the last trading day of the week. The five-week moving average for each week is the average of the DJIA over the previous five weeks. For example, the first entry, for week 5, is the average of the index value between weeks 1 and 5: 8,290, 8,380, 8,399, 8,379, and 8,450. The next entry is the average of the index values between weeks 2 and 6, and so on.

Figure 9.8 plots the level of the index and the five-week moving average. Notice that while the index itself moves up and down rather abruptly, the moving average is a relatively smooth series, since the impact of each week's price movement is averaged with that of the previous weeks. Week 16 is a bearish point according to the moving average rule. The price series crosses from above the moving average to below it, signifying the beginning of a downward trend in stock prices.

(continued)

EXAMPLE 9.4

Moving Averages (concluded)

Week	DJIA	5-Week Moving Average	Week	DJIA	5-Week Moving Average
1	8,290		11	8,590	8,555
2	8,380		12	8,652	8,586
3	8,399		13	8,625	8,598
4	8,379		14	8,657	8,624
5	8,450	8,380	15	8,699	8,645
6	8,513	8,424	16	8,647	8,656
7	8,500	8,448	17	8,610	8,648
8	8,565	8,481	18	8,595	8,642
9	8,524	8,510	19	8,499	8,610
10	8,597	8,540	20	8,466	8,563

Breadth   The **breadth** of the market is a measure of the extent to which movement in a market index is reflected widely in the price movements of all the stocks in the market. The most common measure of breadth is the spread between the number of stocks that advance and decline in price. If advances outnumber declines by a wide margin, then the market is viewed as being stronger because the rally is widespread. These breadth numbers are reported daily in *The Wall Street Journal* (see Figure 9.9).

Some analysts cumulate breadth data each day as in Table 9.2. The cumulative breadth for each day is obtained by adding that day's net advances (or declines) to the previous day's total. The direction of the cumulated series is then used to discern broad market trends. Analysts might use a moving average of cumulative breadth to gauge broad trends.

breadth

The extent to which movements in broad market indexes are reflected widely in movements of individual stock prices.

Relative strength   **Relative strength** measures the extent to which a security has outperformed or underperformed either the market as a whole or its particular industry. Relative strength is computed by calculating the ratio of the price of the security to a price index for the industry. For example, the relative strength of Toyota versus the auto industry would be measured by movements in the ratio of the price of Toyota divided by the level of an auto industry index. A rising ratio implies Toyota has been outperforming the rest of the industry. If relative strength can be assumed to persist over time, then this would be a signal to buy Toyota.

Similarly, the relative strength of an industry relative to the whole market can be computed by tracking the ratio of the industry price index to the market price index.

relative strength

Recent performance of a given stock or industry compared to that of a broader market index.

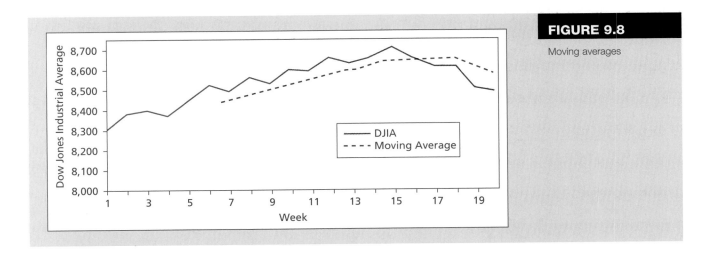

FIGURE 9.8

Moving averages

FIGURE 9.9

Market diary

Source: *The Wall Street Journal*, October 23, 2008. Reprinted by permission of Dow Jones & Company, Inc. Copyright © 2008 Dow Jones & Company, Inc. All Rights Reserved Worldwide.

Trading Diary: Volume, Advancers, Decliners

	NYSE	% chg from 65-day avg	Nasdaq	% chg from 65-day avg	AMEX	% chg from 65-day avg
Issues traded	3,259	−0.3	2,980	−1.0	1,218	−3.7
Advances	501	−65.7	420	−67.9	274	−48.1
Declines	2,712	56.1	2,448	55.0	878	33.6
Unchanged	46	−33.2	112	−9.4	66	−17.9
New highs	7	−74.2	2	−92.6	2	−84.3
New lows	543	44.7	290	53.0	130	−7.1
Adv. volume*	52,773,570	−91.9	328,339,215	−67.8	4,322,200	−70.7
Decl. volume*	1,463,015,266	89.5	2,251,271,900	76.6	25,221,127	43.1
Total volume*	1,517,045,236	6.0	2,589,426,876	11.6	30,493,827	−8.4
Closing tick	−833	...	−541	...	−244	...
Closing Arms (TRIN)†	5.12	...	1.18	...	1.82	...
Block trades*	p3,482	...	p6,534	...	p251	...

TABLE 9.2

Breadth

Day	Advances	Declines	Net Advances	Cumulative Breadth
1	1,802	1,748	54	54
2	1,917	1,640	277	331
3	1,703	1,772	−69	262
4	1,512	2,122	−610	−348
5	1,633	2,004	−371	−719

Note: The sum of advances plus declines varies across days because some stock prices are unchanged.

Sentiment Indicators

Trin statistic   Market volume is sometimes used to measure the strength of a market rise or fall. Increased investor participation in a market advance or retreat is viewed as a measure of the significance of the movement. Technicians consider market advances to be a more favorable omen of continued price increases when they are associated with increased trading volume. Similarly, market reversals are considered more bearish when associated with higher volume. The **trin statistic** is defined as

trin statistic

The ratio of average volume in declining issues to average volume in advancing issues.

$$\text{Trin} = \frac{\text{Volume declining/Number declining}}{\text{Volume advancing/Number advancing}}$$

Therefore, trin is the ratio of average trading volume in declining issues to average volume in advancing issues. Ratios above 1.0 are considered bearish because the falling stocks would then have higher average volume than the advancing stocks, indicating net selling pressure. *The Wall Street Journal* reports trin every day in the market diary section, as in Figure 9.9.

Note, however, that for every buyer, there must be a seller of stock. Rising volume in a rising market should not necessarily indicate a larger imbalance of buyers versus sellers. For example, a trin statistic above 1.0, which is considered bearish, could equally well be interpreted as indicating that there is more *buying* activity in declining issues.

Confidence index   *Barron's* computes a confidence index using data from the bond market. The presumption is that actions of bond traders reveal trends that will emerge soon in the stock market.

confidence index

Ratio of the yield of top-rated corporate bonds to the yield on intermediate-grade bonds.

The **confidence index** is the ratio of the average yield on 10 top-rated corporate bonds divided by the average yield on 10 intermediate-grade corporate bonds. The ratio will always be below 100% because higher rated bonds will offer lower promised yields to maturity. When bond traders are optimistic about the economy, however, they might require smaller default premiums on lower rated debt. Hence, the yield spread will narrow, and the confidence index will approach 100%. Therefore, higher values of the confidence index are bullish signals.

> Yields on lower-rated debt typically rise along with fears of recession. This reduces the confidence index. When these yields increase, should the stock market be expected to fall, or will it already have fallen?

CONCEPT *check* **9.5**

Short interest   **Short interest** is the total number of shares of stock currently sold short in the market. Some technicians interpret high levels of short interest as bullish, some as bearish. The bullish perspective is that, because all short sales must be covered (i.e., short-sellers eventually must purchase shares to return the ones they have borrowed), short interest represents latent future demand for the stocks. As short sales are covered, the demand created by the share purchase will force prices up.

short interest
The total number of shares currently sold-short in the market.

The bearish interpretation of short interest is based on the fact that short-sellers tend to be larger, more sophisticated investors. Accordingly, increased short interest reflects bearish sentiment by those investors "in the know," which would be a negative signal of the market's prospects.

Put/call ratio   Call options give investors the right to buy a stock at a fixed "exercise" price and therefore are a way of betting on stock price increases. Put options give the right to sell a stock at a fixed price and therefore are a way of betting on stock price decreases.[8] The ratio of outstanding put options to outstanding call options is called the **put/call ratio.** Because put options do well in falling markets while call options do well in rising markets, deviations of the ratio from historical norms are considered to be a signal of market sentiment and therefore predictive of market movements.

put/call ratio
Ratio of put options to call options outstanding on a stock.

Interestingly, however, a change in the ratio can be given a bullish or a bearish interpretation. Many technicians see an increase in the ratio as bearish, as it indicates growing interest in put options as a hedge against market declines. Thus, a rising ratio is taken as a sign of broad investor pessimism and a coming market decline. Contrarian investors, however, believe that a good time to buy is when the rest of the market is bearish because stock prices are then unduly depressed. Therefore, they would take an increase in the put/call ratio as a signal of a buy opportunity.

A Warning

The search for patterns in stock market prices is nearly irresistible, and the ability of the human eye to discern apparent patterns is remarkable. Unfortunately, it is possible to perceive patterns that really don't exist. Consider Figure 9.10, which presents simulated and actual values of the Dow Jones Industrial Average during 1956 taken from a famous study by Harry Roberts (1959). In Figure 9.10B, it appears as though the market presents a classic head-and-shoulders pattern where the middle hump (the head) is flanked by two shoulders. When the price index "pierces the right shoulder"—a technical trigger point—it is believed to be heading lower, and it is time to sell your stocks. Figure 9.10A also looks like a "typical" stock market pattern.

Can you tell which of the two graphs is constructed from the real value of the Dow and which from the simulated data? Figure 9.10A is based on the real data. The graph in Panel B was generated using "returns" created by a random-number generator. These returns *by construction* were patternless, but the simulated price path that is plotted appears to follow a pattern much like that of Panel A.

Figure 9.11 shows the weekly price *changes* behind the two panels in Figure 9.10. Here the randomness in both series—the stock price as well as the simulated sequence—is obvious.

A problem related to the tendency to perceive patterns where they don't exist is data mining. After the fact, you can always find patterns and trading rules that would have generated enormous profits. If you test enough rules, some will have worked in the past. Unfortunately, picking a theory that would have worked after the fact carries no guarantee of future success.

[8]Puts and calls were defined in Chapter 2, Section 2.5. They are discussed more fully in Chapter 15.

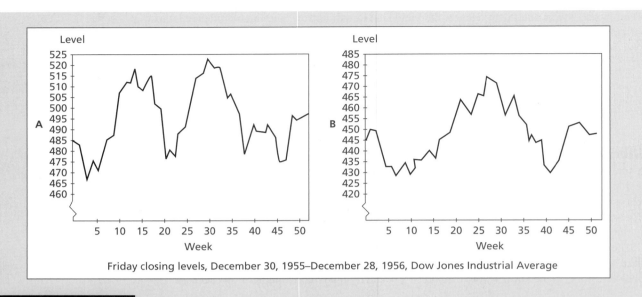

FIGURE 9.10

Actual and simulated levels for stock market prices of 52 weeks

Note: Friday closing levels, December 30, 1955–December 28, 1956, Dow Jones Industrial Average.
Source: Harry Roberts, "Stock Market 'Patterns' and Financial Analysis: Methodological Suggestions," *Journal of Finance*, March 1959, pp. 11–25. Reprinted by permission of the publisher, Blackwell Publishing, Inc.

In evaluating trading rules, you should always ask whether the rule would have seemed reasonable *before* you looked at the data. If not, you might be buying into the one arbitrary rule among many that happened to have worked in the recent past. The hard but crucial question is whether there is reason to believe that what worked in the past should continue to work in the future.

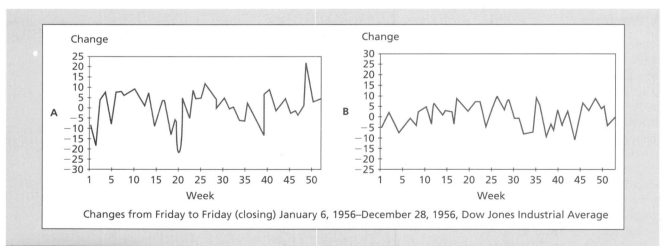

FIGURE 9.11

Actual and simulated changes in weekly stock prices for 52 weeks

Note: Changes from Friday to Friday (closing) January 6, 1956–December 28, 1956, Dow Jones Industrial Average.
Source: Harry Roberts, "Stock Market 'Patterns' and Financial Analysis: Methodological Suggestions," *Journal of Finance*, March 1959, pp. 11–25. Reprinted by permission of the publisher, Blackwell Publishing, Inc.

- Behavioral finance focuses on systematic irrationalities that characterize investor decision making. These "behavioral shortcomings" may be consistent with several efficient market anomalies.
- Among the information processing errors uncovered in the psychology literature are memory bias, overconfidence, conservatism, and representativeness. Behavioral tendencies include framing, mental accounting, regret avoidance, and loss aversion.
- Limits to arbitrage activity impede the ability of rational investors to exploit pricing errors induced by behavioral investors. For example, fundamental risk means that even if a security is mispriced, it still can be risky to attempt to exploit the mispricing. This limits the actions of arbitrageurs who take positions in mispriced securities. Other limits to arbitrage are implementation costs, model risk, and costs to short-selling. Occasional failures of the Law of One Price suggest that limits to arbitrage are sometimes severe.
- The various limits to arbitrage mean that even if prices do not equal intrinsic value, it still may be difficult to exploit the mispricing. As a result, the failure of traders to beat the market may not be proof that markets are in fact efficient, with prices equal to intrinsic value.
- Technical analysis is the search for recurring and predictable patterns in stock prices. It is based on the premise that prices only gradually close in on intrinsic value. As fundamentals shift, astute traders can exploit the adjustment to a new equilibrium.
- Technical analysis also uses volume data and sentiment indicators. These are broadly consistent with several behavioral models of investor activity.
- The Dow theory attempts to identify underlying trends in stock indexes. Moving averages, relative strength, and breadth are used in other trend-based strategies.
- Some sentiment indicators are the trin statistic, the confidence index, and the put/call ratio.

behavioral finance, 261	framing, 263	relative strength, 275
breadth, 275	mental accounting, 263	representativeness
confidence index, 276	prospect theory, 264	bias, 262
conservatism bias, 262	put/call ratio, 277	short interest, 277
Dow theory, 271	regret avoidance, 264	trin statistic, 276

Select problems are available in McGraw-Hill Connect. Please see the packaging options section of the preface for more information.

Basic

1. Match each example to one of the following behavioral characteristics.

a.	Investors are slow to update their beliefs when given new evidence.	i.	Disposition effect
b.	Investors are reluctant to bear losses due to their unconventional decisions.	ii.	Representativeness bias
c.	Investors exhibit less risk tolerance in their retirement accounts versus their other stock accounts.	iii.	Regret avoidance
d.	Investors are reluctant to sell stocks with "paper" losses.	iv.	Conservatism bias
e.	Investors disregard sample size when forming views about the future from the past.	v.	Mental accounting

2. After reading about three successful investors in *The Wall Street Journal* you decide that active investing will also provide you with superior trading results. What sort of behavioral tendency are you exhibiting?

3. What do we mean by fundamental risk, and why may such risk allow behavioral biases to persist for long periods of time?

4. What are the strong points of the behavioral critique of the efficient market hypothesis? What are some problems with the critique?

5. What are some possible investment implications of the behavioral critique?

6. Which one of the following would be a bullish signal to a technical analyst using moving average rules?
   a. A stock price crosses above its 52-week moving average.
   b. A stock price crosses below its 52-week moving average.
   c. The stock's moving average is increasing.
   d. The stock's moving average is decreasing.

Intermediate

7. What is meant by data mining, and why must technical analysts be careful not to engage in it?

8. Even if prices follow a random walk, they still may not be informationally efficient. Explain why this may be true, and why it matters for the efficient allocation of capital in our economy.

9. What is meant by "limits to arbitrage"? Give some examples of such limits.

10. Following a shock to a firm's intrinsic value, the share price will slowly but surely approach that new intrinsic value. Is this view characteristic of a technical analyst or a believer in efficient markets? Explain.

11. Use the data from *The Wall Street Journal* in Figure 9.9 to verify the trin ratio for the NYSE. Is the trin ratio bullish or bearish?

12. Calculate breadth for the NYSE using the data in Figure 9.9. Is the signal bullish or bearish?

13. Collect data on the DJIA for a period covering a few months. Try to identify primary trends. Can you tell whether the market currently is in an upward or downward trend?

14. Suppose Baa-rated bonds currently yield 7%, while Aa-rated bonds yield 5%. Now suppose that due to an increase in the expected inflation rate, the yields on both bonds increase by 1%. What would happen to the confidence index? Would this be interpreted as bullish or bearish by a technical analyst? Does this make sense to you?

15. Table 9.3 presents price data for Computers, Inc., and a computer industry index. Does Computers, Inc., show relative strength over this period?

16. Use the data in Table 9.3 to compute a five-day moving average for Computers, Inc. Can you identify any buy or sell signals?

17. Construct a point and figure chart for Computers, Inc., using again the data in Table 9.3. Use $2 increments for your chart. Do the buy or sell signals derived from your chart correspond to those derived from the moving average rule (see the previous problem)?

18. Yesterday, the Dow Jones industrials gained 54 points. However, 1,704 issues declined in price while 1,367 advanced. Why might a technical analyst be concerned even though the market index rose on this day?

19. Table 9.4 contains data on market advances and declines. Calculate cumulative breadth and decide whether this technical signal is bullish or bearish.

20. If the trading volume in advancing shares on day 1 in the previous problem was 1.1 billion shares, while the volume in declining issues was 0.9 billion shares, what was the trin statistic for that day? Was trin bullish or bearish?

21. Given the following data on bond yields, is the confidence index rising or falling? What might explain the pattern of yield changes?

TABLE 9.3
Computers, Inc., stock price history

Trading Day	Computers, Inc.	Industry Index	Trading Day	Computers, Inc.	Industry Index
1	19.63	50.0	21	19.63	54.1
2	20	50.1	22	21.50	54.0
3	20.50	50.5	23	22	53.9
4	22	50.4	24	23.13	53.7
5	21.13	51.0	25	24	54.8
6	22	50.7	26	25.25	54.5
7	21.88	50.5	27	26.25	54.6
8	22.50	51.1	28	27	54.1
9	23.13	51.5	29	27.50	54.2
10	23.88	51.7	30	28	54.8
11	24.50	51.4	31	28.50	54.2
12	23.25	51.7	32	28	54.8
13	22.13	52.2	33	27.50	54.9
14	22	52.0	34	29	55.2
15	20.63	53.1	35	29.25	55.7
16	20.25	53.5	36	29.50	56.1
17	19.75	53.9	37	30	56.7
18	18.75	53.6	38	28.50	56.7
19	17.50	52.9	39	27.75	56.5
20	19	53.4	40	28	56.1

	This Year	Last Year
Yield on top-rated corporate bonds	8%	8.5%
Yield on intermediate-grade corporate bonds	10.5	10

22. Go to **www.mhhe.com/bkm** and link to the material for Chapter 9, where you will find five years of weekly returns for the S&P 500.

   a. Set up a spreadsheet to calculate the 26-week moving average of the index. Set the value of the index at the beginning of the sample period equal to 100. The index value in each week is then updated by multiplying the previous week's level by (1 + rate of return over previous week).

   b. Identify every instance in which the index crosses through its moving average from below. In how many of the weeks following a cross-through does the index increase? Decrease?

eXcel

Please visit us at www.mhhe.com/bkm

TABLE 9.4
Market advances and declines

Day	Advances	Declines	Day	Advances	Declines
1	906	704	6	970	702
2	653	986	7	1002	609
3	721	789	8	903	722
4	503	968	9	850	748
5	497	1095	10	766	766

c. Identify every instance in which the index crosses through its moving average from above. In how many of the weeks following a cross-through does the index increase? Decrease?

d. How well does the moving average rule perform in identifying buy or sell opportunities?

23. Go to **www.mhhe.com/bkm** and link to the material for Chapter 9, where you will find five years of weekly returns for the S&P 500 and Fidelity's Select Banking Fund (ticker FSRBX).

a. Set up a spreadsheet to calculate the relative strength of the banking sector compared to the broad market. (*Hint:* as in the previous problem, set the initial value of the sector index and the S&P 500 Index equal to 100, and use each week's rate of return to update the level of each index.)

b. Identify every instance in which the relative strength ratio increases by at least 5% from its value five weeks earlier. In how many of the weeks immediately following a substantial increase in relative strength does the banking sector outperform the S&P 500? In how many of those weeks does the banking sector underperform the S&P 500?

c. Identify every instance in which the relative strength ratio decreases by at least 5% from its value five weeks earlier. In how many of the weeks immediately following a substantial decrease in relative strength does the banking sector underperform the S&P 500? In how many of those weeks does the banking sector outperform the S&P 500?

d. How well does the relative strength rule perform in identifying buy or sell opportunities?

Challenge

24. One apparent violation of the Law of One Price is the pervasive discrepancy between the prices and net asset values of closed-end mutual funds. Would you expect to observe greater discrepancies on diversified or less-diversified funds? Why?

CFA Problems

1. Don Sampson begins a meeting with his financial adviser by outlining his investment philosophy as shown below:

Statement Number	Statement
1	Investments should offer strong return potential but with very limited risk. I prefer to be conservative and to minimize losses, even if I miss out on substantial growth opportunities.
2	All nongovernmental investments should be in industry-leading and financially strong companies.
3	Income needs should be met entirely through interest income and cash dividends. All equity securities held should pay cash dividends.
4	Investment decisions should be based primarily on consensus forecasts of general economic conditions and company-specific growth.
5	If an investment falls below the purchase price, that security should be retained until it returns to its original cost. Conversely, I prefer to take quick profits on successful investments.
6	I will direct the purchase of investments, including derivative securities, periodically. These aggressive investments result from personal research and may not prove consistent with my investment policy. I have not kept records on the performance of similar past investments, but I have had some "big winners."

Select the statement from the table above that best illustrates each of the following behavioral finance concepts. Justify your selection.

i. Mental accounting.

ii. Overconfidence (illusion of control).

iii. Reference dependence (framing).

2. Monty Frost's tax-deferred retirement account is invested entirely in equity securities. Because the international portion of his portfolio has performed poorly in the past, he has reduced his international equity exposure to 2%. Frost's investment adviser has recommended an increased international equity exposure. Frost responds with the following comments:

   a. Based on past poor performance, I want to sell all my remaining international equity securities once their market prices rise to equal their original cost.

   b. Most diversified international portfolios have had disappointing results over the past five years. During that time, however, the market in Country XYZ has outperformed all other markets, even our own. If I do increase my international equity exposure, I would prefer that the entire exposure consist of securities from Country XYZ.

   c. International investments are inherently more risky. Therefore, I prefer to purchase any international equity securities in my "speculative" account, my best chance at becoming rich. I do not want them in my retirement account, which has to protect me from poverty in my old age.

   Frost's adviser is familiar with behavioral finance concepts but prefers a traditional or standard finance approach (modern portfolio theory) to investments.

   Indicate the behavioral finance concept that Frost most directly exhibits in each of his three comments. Explain how each of Frost's comments can be countered by using an argument from standard finance.

3. Louise and Christopher Maclin live in London, United Kingdom, and currently rent an apartment in the metropolitan area. During an initial discussion of the Maclins' financial plans, Christopher Maclin makes the following statements to the Maclins' financial adviser, Grant Webb:

   a. "I have used the Internet extensively to research the outlook for the housing market over the next five years, and I believe now is the best time to buy a house."

   b. "I do not want to sell any bond in my portfolio for a lower price than I paid for the bond."

   c. "I will not sell any of my company stock because I know my company and I believe it has excellent prospects for the future."

   For each statement (a)–(c) identify the behavioral finance concept most directly exhibited. Explain how each behavioral finance concept is affecting the Maclins' investment decision making.

4. During an interview with her investment adviser, a retired investor made the following two statements:

   a. "I have been very pleased with the returns I've earned on Petrie stock over the past two years and I am certain that it will be a superior performer in the future."

   b. "I am pleased with the returns from the Petrie stock because I have specific uses for that money. For that reason, I certainly want my retirement fund to continue owning the Petrie stock."

   Identify which principle of behavioral finance is most consistent with each of the investor's two statements.

5. Claire Pierce comments on her life circumstances and investment outlook:

   I must support my parents who live overseas on Pogo Island. The Pogo Island economy has grown rapidly over the past 2 years with minimal inflation, and consensus forecasts call for a continuation of these favorable trends for the foreseeable future. Economic growth has resulted from the export of a natural resource used in an exciting new technology application.

   I want to invest 10 percent of my portfolio in Pogo Island government bonds. I plan to purchase long-term bonds because my parents are likely to live more than 10 years. Experts uniformly do not foresee a resurgence of inflation on Pogo Island, so I am certain that the total returns produced by the bonds will cover my parents' spending needs for many years to come. There should be no exchange rate risk because the bonds are denominated in local currency. I want to buy the Pogo Island bonds, but am not willing to distort my portfolio's long-term asset allocation to do so. The overall mix of stocks, bonds, and other investments should not change. Therefore, I am considering selling one of my U.S. bond funds to raise cash to buy the Pogo Island bonds. One possibility is my High Yield Bond Fund, which has declined 5% in value year to date. I am not excited about this fund's prospects; in fact I think it is likely to decline more, but there is a small probability that it could recover very quickly. So I have decided instead to sell my Core Bond Fund that has appreciated 5% this year. I expect this investment to continue to deliver attractive returns, but there is a small chance this year's gains might disappear quickly.

Once that shift is accomplished, my investments will be in great shape. The sole exception is my Small Company Fund, which has performed poorly. I plan to sell this investment as soon as the price increases to my original cost.

Identify three behavioral finance concepts illustrated in Pierce's comments and describe each of the three concepts. Discuss how an investor practicing standard or traditional finance would challenge each of the three concepts.

STANDARD &POOR'S

Use data from the Standard & Poor's Market Insight Database at www.mhhe.com/edumarketinsight to answer the following questions.

1. Find the monthly closing prices for the most recent four years for Abercrombie & Fitch (ANF) from the Excel Analytics section of Market Insight. Also collect the closing level of the S&P 500 Index over the same period.
   a. Calculate the four-month moving average of both the stock and the S&P 500 over time. For each series, use Excel to plot the moving average against the actual level of the stock price or index. Examine the instances where the moving average and price series cross. Is the stock more or less likely to increase when the price crosses through the moving average? Does it matter whether the price crosses the moving average from above or below? How reliable would an investment rule based on moving averages be? Perform your analysis for both the stock price and the S&P 500.
   b. Calculate and plot the relative strength of the stock compared to the S&P 500 over the sample period. Find all instances in which relative strength of the stock increases by more than 10 percentage points (e.g., an increase in the relative strength index from .93 to 1.03) and all those instances in which relative strength of the stock decreases by more than 10 percentage points. Is the stock more or less likely to outperform the S&P in the following two months when relative strength has increased or to underperform when relative strength has decreased? In other words, does relative strength continue? How reliable would an investment rule based on relative strength be?

2. Go to the Market Insight database and click on the *Company* tab. Enter ticker symbol WMT for Wal-Mart Stores and click on *Go*.
   a. Select the *Charting by Profit* link on the menu. When the chart first appears you will need to reenter the WMT symbol in the box at the top left corner and click on *Go*. Click on the plus sign next to *Technical Studies,* then click on the plus sign next to *Moving Averages.* Double click on *Simple Moving Average* to see the Wal-Mart chart with a simple moving average. Do you see any patterns that might lead to a successful trading rule?
   b. Click on the plus sign next to *Support & Resistance.* Next, double click on *Projection Bands.* What observations do you have about how often the price has passed outside these bands and what tends to happen after the price crosses the band line?
   c. At the top of the graph locate the selection box next to the stock symbol. The default setting is Bar. Change this to Candle to see a Candle chart for Wal-Mart. Change the frequency (three boxes to the right of the stock symbol) from "D" (daily) to "W" (weekly) to get a better view of the candles. As you move the cursor along the plotted data look at the price information on top of the chart to see how the Candle chart was plotted.
   d. Explore some of the other graphs in the *Technical Studies* section. Do you have any favorites that you think might be particularly useful for making investment decisions?

SOLUTIONS TO CONCEPT *checks*

9.1. Conservatism implies that investors will at first respond too slowly to new information, leading to trends in prices. Representativeness can lead them to extrapolate trends too far into the future and overshoot intrinsic value. Eventually, when the pricing error is corrected, we observe a reversal.

9.2. Out-of-favor stocks will exhibit low prices relative to various proxies for intrinsic value such as earnings. Because of regret avoidance, these stocks will need to offer a more attractive rate of return to induce investors to hold them. Thus, low P/E stocks might on average offer higher rates of return.

9.3. At liquidation, price will equal NAV. This puts a limit on fundamental risk. Investors need only carry the position for a few months to profit from the elimination of the discount. Moreover, as the liquidation date approaches, the discount should dissipate. This greatly limits the risk that the discount can move against the investor. At the announcement of impending liquidation, the discount should immediately disappear, or at least shrink considerably.

9.4.

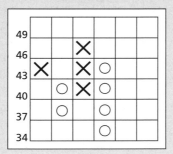

9.5. By the time the news of the recession affects bond yields, it also ought to affect stock prices. The market should fall *before* the confidence index signals that the time is ripe to sell.

PART 3

Debt Securities

Bond markets used to be a sedate arena for risk-averse investors who wanted worry-free investments with modest but stable returns. They are no longer so quiet. Annual trading in U.S. government bonds alone is about 10 times the total amount of national debt. The market in mortgage-backed securities alone is now about $3.8 trillion.

Higher trading activity is not the only reason these markets are more interesting than they once were. These markets are no longer free of risk. Interest rates in the last two decades have become more volatile than anyone in 1965 would have dreamed possible. Volatility means that investors have great opportunities for gain, but also for losses, and we have seen dramatic examples of both in recent years.

Long-Term Capital Management, at the time the world's most successful hedge fund, shocked Wall Street when it was felled by investment reversals in 1998, among them losses of more than $1 billion on its interest-rate positions. But those losses seem almost quaint when compared to the devastation suffered in the market meltdown of 2008–2009. The beginning of that period was signaled by revelation of losses of $1 billion on mortgage bonds held by two Bear Stearns hedge funds in 2007. Over the course of the next two years, hundreds of billions were lost by investors in other mortgage-backed bonds and those who sold insurance on those securities. Of course, in many of these instances, there were traders on the other side of the transaction who did quite well. The bearish bets made by hedge fund manager John Paulson in 2007 made his funds more than $15 billion.

The chapters in Part Three provide an introduction to debt markets and securities. We will show you how to value such securities and why their values change with interest rates. We will see what features determine the sensitivity of bond prices to interest rates, and how investors measure and manage interest rate risk.

Chapter 10

Bond Prices and Yields

After Studying This Chapter You Should Be Able To:

- Compute a bond's price given its yield to maturity, and compute its yield to maturity given its price.

- Calculate how bond prices will change over time for a given interest rate projection.

- Analyze how call, convertibility, and sinking fund provisions will affect a bond's equilibrium yield to maturity.

- Identify the determinants of bond safety and rating and how credit risk is reflected in bond yields and the prices of credit default swaps.

- Analyze the factors likely to affect the shape of the yield curve at any time.

In the previous chapters on risk and return relationships, we have treated securities at a high level of abstraction. We have assumed implicitly that a prior, detailed analysis of each security already has been performed and that its risk and return features have been assessed.

We turn now to specific analyses of particular security markets. We examine valuation principles, determinants of risk and return, and portfolio strategies commonly used within and across the various markets.

We begin by analyzing debt securities. A debt security is a claim on a specified periodic stream of income. Debt securities are often called *fixed-income securities,* because they promise either a fixed stream of income or a stream of income that is determined according to a specified formula. These securities have the advantage of being relatively easy to understand because the payment formulas are specified in advance. Uncertainty surrounding cash flows paid to the security holder is minimal as long as the issuer of the security is sufficiently creditworthy. That makes these securities a convenient starting point for our analysis of the universe of potential investment vehicles.

The bond is the basic debt security, and this chapter starts with an overview of bond markets, including Treasury, corporate, and international bonds. We turn next to bond pricing, showing how bond prices are set in accordance with market interest rates and why bond prices change with those rates. Given this background, we can compare the myriad measures of bond returns such as yield to maturity, yield to call, holding-period return, or realized compound rate of return. We show how bond prices evolve over time, discuss certain tax rules that apply to debt securities, and show how to calculate after-tax returns. Next, we consider the impact of default or credit risk on bond pricing and look at the determinants of credit risk and the default premium built into bond yields. Finally, we turn to the term structure of interest rates, the relationship between yield to maturity and time to maturity.

10.1 Bond Characteristics

bond

A security that obligates the issuer to make specified payments to the holder over a period of time.

A **bond** is a security that is issued in connection with a borrowing arrangement. The borrower issues (i.e., sells) a bond to the lender for some amount of cash; the bond is in essence the "IOU" of the borrower. The arrangement obligates the issuer to make specified payments to the bondholder on specified dates. A typical coupon bond obligates the issuer to make semiannual payments of interest, called *coupon payments,* to the bondholder for the life of the bond. These are called coupon payments because, in precomputer days, most bonds had coupons that investors would clip off and present to the issuer of the bond to claim the interest payment. When the bond matures, the issuer repays the debt by paying the bond's **par value** (or equivalently, its **face value**). The **coupon rate** of the bond determines the interest payment: The annual payment equals the coupon rate times the bond's par value. The coupon rate, maturity date, and par value of the bond are part of the *bond indenture,* which is the contract between the issuer and the bondholder.

face value, par value

The payment to the bondholder at the maturity of the bond.

coupon rate

A bond's annual interest payment per dollar of par value.

To illustrate, a bond with a par value of $1,000 and a coupon rate of 8% might be sold to a buyer for $1,000. The issuer then pays the bondholder 8% of $1,000, or $80 per year, for the stated life of the bond, say, 30 years. The $80 payment typically comes in two semiannual installments of $40 each. At the end of the 30-year life of the bond, the issuer also pays the $1,000 par value to the bondholder.

Bonds usually are issued with coupon rates set just high enough to induce investors to pay par value to buy the bond. Sometimes, however, **zero-coupon bonds** are issued that make no coupon payments. In this case, investors receive par value at the maturity date, but receive no interest payments until then: The bond has a coupon rate of zero. These bonds are issued at prices considerably below par value, and the investor's return comes solely from the difference between issue price and the payment of par value at maturity. We will return to these bonds below.

zero-coupon bond

A bond paying no coupons that sells at a discount and provides only a payment of par value at maturity.

Treasury Bonds and Notes

Figure 10.1 is an excerpt from the listing of Treasury issues from the *The Wall Street Journal Online.* Treasury notes are issued with original maturities between 1 and 10 years, while Treasury bonds are issued with maturities ranging from 10 to 30 years. Both bonds and notes may be purchased directly from the Treasury in denominations of only $100, but denominations of $1,000 are for more common. Both make semiannual coupon payments.

The highlighted issue in Figure 10.1 matures in January 2012. Its coupon rate is 1.125%. Par value is $1,000; thus, the bond pays interest of $11.25 per year in two semiannual payments of $5.625. Payments are made in January and July of each year. The bid and ask prices[1] are quoted in points plus fractions of $\frac{1}{32}$ of a point (the numbers after the colons are the fractions of a point). Although bonds are typically sold in denominations of $1,000 par value, the prices are quoted as a percentage of

---

[1]Recall that the bid price is the price at which you can sell the bond to a dealer. The ask price, which is slightly higher, is the price at which you can buy the bond from a dealer.

FIGURE 10.1

Prices and yields of U.S. Treasury bonds on January 15, 2009

Source: *The Wall Street Journal Online,* January 16, 2009. Reprinted by permission of *The Wall Street Journal* Copyright © 2009 Dow Jones & Company. All Rights Reserved Worldwide.

U.S. Treasury Quotes

Treasury note and bond data are representative over-the-counter quotations as of 3pm Eastern time. Figures after colons in bid and ask quotes represent 32nds; 101:26 means 101 26/32, or 101.8125% of face value; 99:01 means 99 1/32, or 99.03125% of face value. For notes and bonds callable prior to maturity, yields are computed to the earliest call date for issues quoted above par and to the maturity date for issues below par.

MATURITY	Coupon	BID	ASKED	CHG	ASK YLD	MATURITY	Coupon	BID	ASKED	CHG	ASK YLD
Apr 30 09	4.500	101:07	101:08	−1	0.12	Nov 15 12	4.000	111:07	111:08	−8	1.00
May 15 09	3.875	101:06	101:07	−1	0.14	Nov 30 12	3.375	108:31	109:00	−8	1.00
May 15 09	4.875	101:17	101:18	−1	0.12	Dec 31 12	3.625	110:02	110:04	−10	1.01
Nov 15 09	4.625	103:14	103:15	−1	0.44	May 15 16	7.250	134:07	134:09	+1	2.17
Nov 30 09	3.125	102:11	102:12	+1	0.41	Aug 15 16	4.875	120:02	120:04	+28	2.00
Dec 15 09	3.500	102:25	102:26	unch.	0.41	Nov 15 16	4.625	118:19	118:20	−8	2.04
Dec 31 09	3.250	102:22	102:23	−1	0.41	Nov 15 16	7.500	136:28	136:29	−13	2.32
Jan 15 10	3.625	103:09	103:10	+1	0.30	Feb 15 17	4.625	118:21	118:23	−7	2.09
Oct 31 11	4.625	110:12	110:14	+3	0.83	May 15 20	8.750	155:16	155:18	−2	2.95
Nov 15 11	1.750	102:06	102:08	unch.	0.95	Aug 15 20	8.750	155:27	155:29	−5	3.00
Nov 30 11	4.500	110:00	110:02	−1	0.94	Feb 15 21	7.875	148:17	148:19	+2	3.04
Dec 15 11	1.125	100:13	100:15	−1	0.96	Feb 15 37	4.750	134:25	134:28	+3	2.92
Dec 31 11	4.625	110:20	110:22	−1	0.95	May 15 37	5.000	139:26	139:28	+12	2.92
Jan 15 12	1.125	100:10	100:11	unch.	1.01	Feb 15 38	4.375	129:12	129:14	+13	2.87
Jan 31 12	4.750	111:07	111:09	+1	0.98	May 15 38	4.500	132:07	132.09	+17	2.87
Feb 15 12	4.875	111:22	111:24	+3	0.99						

par value. Therefore, the bid price of the bond is 100:10 = $100^{10}\!/_{32}$ = 100.313% of par value or $1,003.13, while the ask price is 100:11 = 100.344% of par, or $1,003.44.

The last column, labeled Ask Yld, is the bond's yield to maturity based on the ask price. The yield to maturity is often interpreted as a measure of the average rate of return to an investor who purchases the bond for the ask price and holds it until its maturity date. We will have much to say about yield to maturity below.

Accrued interest and quoted bond prices   The bond prices that you see quoted in the financial pages are not actually the prices that investors pay for the bond. This is because the quoted price does not include the interest that accrues between coupon payment dates.

If a bond is purchased between coupon payments, the buyer must pay the seller for accrued interest, the prorated share of the upcoming semiannual coupon. For example, if 30 days have passed since the last coupon payment, and there are 182 days in the semiannual coupon period, the seller is entitled to a payment of accrued interest of $^{30}\!/_{182}$ of the semiannual coupon. The sale, or *invoice price* of the bond, which is the amount the buyer actually pays, would equal the stated price plus the accrued interest.

In general, the formula for the amount of accrued interest between two dates is

$$\text{Accrued interest} = \frac{\text{Annual coupon payment}}{2} \times \frac{\text{Days since last coupon payment}}{\text{Days separating coupon payments}}$$

EXAMPLE   10.1

Accrued Interest

Suppose that the coupon rate is 8%. Then the semiannual coupon payment is $40. Because 30 days have passed since the last coupon payment, the accrued interest on the bond is $40 × $\left(^{30}\!/_{182}\right)$ = $6.59. If the quoted price of the bond is $990, then the invoice price will be $990 + $6.59 = $996.59.

The practice of quoting bond prices net of accrued interest explains why the price of a maturing bond is listed at $1,000 rather than $1,000 plus one coupon payment. A purchaser of an 8% coupon bond one day before the bond's maturity would receive $1,040 on the following day and so should be willing to pay a total price of $1,040 for the bond. In fact, $40 of that total payment constitutes the accrued interest for the preceding half-year period. The bond price is quoted net of accrued interest in the financial pages and thus appears as $1,000.[2]

[2]In contrast to bonds, stocks do not trade at flat prices with adjustments for "accrued dividends." Whoever owns the stock when it goes "ex-dividend" receives the entire dividend payment, and the stock price reflects the value of the upcoming dividend. The price therefore typically falls by about the amount of the dividend on the "ex day." There is no need to differentiate between reported and invoice prices for stocks.

FIGURE 10.2

Listing of corporate bonds

Source: *The Wall Street Journal Online,* January 21, 2009. Reprinted by permission of *The Wall Street Journal* Copyright © 2009 Dow Jones & Company, Inc. All Rights Reserved Worldwide.

ISSUER NAME	SYMBOL	COUPON	MATURITY	RATING MOODY'S/S&P/ FITCH	HIGH	LOW	LAST	CHANGE	YIELD %
BANK OF AMERICA	BAC.HDU	4.900%	May 2013	Aa3/A+/A+	99.627	96.059	97.659	−0.991	5.520
REGIONS BANK	RF.GO	3.250%	Dec 2011	Aaa/−/AAA	104.640	103.547	103.910	0.059	1.848
ABBOTT LABORATORIES	ABT.GO	5.875%	May 2016	A1/AA/A+	110.596	107.557	110.276	4.829	4.225
WELLS FARGO & CO	WFC.GDW	4.375%	Jan 2013	Aa3/AA/AA	101.394	97.830	99.616	−1.804	4.480
ALTRIA GP	MO.HC	9.700%	Nov 2018	Baa1/BBB/BBB+	114.761	107.500	113.307	−0.910	7.735
BANK OF AMERICA, N.A	BAC.HGS	1.700%	Dec 2010	Aaa/AAA/AAA	101.393	100.663	100.663	−0.123	1.349
GENERAL ELECTRIC CAPITAL	GE.HHG	6.875%	Jan 2039	Aaa/−/−	99.855	92.500	98.375	−0.875	7.005

Corporate Bonds

Like the government, corporations borrow money by issuing bonds. Figure 10.2 is a sample of corporate bond listings from *The Wall Street Journal Online,* which reports only the most actively traded corporate bonds. Although some bonds trade electronically on the NYSE Bonds platform, most bonds are traded over the counter in a network of bond dealers linked by a computer quotation system. In practice, the bond market can be quite "thin," in that there are few investors interested in trading a particular issue at any particular time.

The bond listings in Figure 10.2 include the coupon, maturity, price, and yield to maturity of each bond. The "rating" column is the estimation of bond safety given by the three major bond rating agencies, Moody's, Standard & Poor's, and Fitch. Bonds with A ratings are safer than those rated B or below. Notice that as a general rule, safer bonds with the higher ratings promise lower yields to maturity. We will return to this topic toward the end of the chapter.

callable bonds

Bonds that may be repurchased by the issuer at a specified call price during the call period.

Call provisions on corporate bonds While the Treasury no longer issues **callable bonds,** some corporate bonds are issued with call provisions, allowing the issuer to repurchase the bond at a specified *call price* before the maturity date. For example, if a company issues a bond with a high coupon rate when market interest rates are high, and interest rates later fall, the firm might like to retire the high-coupon debt and issue new bonds at a lower coupon rate to reduce interest payments. The proceeds from the new bond issue are used to pay for the repurchase of the existing higher coupon bonds at the call price. This is called *refunding.* Callable bonds typically come with a period of call protection, an initial time during which the bonds are not callable. Such bonds are referred to as *deferred* callable bonds.

The option to call the bond is valuable to the firm, allowing it to buy back the bonds and refinance at lower interest rates when market rates fall. Of course, the firm's benefit is the bondholder's burden. Holders of called bonds forfeit their bonds for the call price, thereby giving up the prospect of an attractive rate of interest on their original investment. To compensate investors for this risk, callable bonds are issued with higher coupons and promised yields to maturity than noncallable bonds.

CONCEPT *check* **10.1**

Suppose that Verizon issues two bonds with identical coupon rates and maturity dates. One bond is callable, however, while the other is not. Which bond will sell at a higher price?

convertible bond

A bond with an option allowing the bondholder to exchange the bond for a specified number of shares of common stock in the firm.

Convertible bonds **Convertible bonds** give bondholders an option to exchange each bond for a specified number of shares of common stock of the firm. The *conversion ratio* gives the number of shares for which each bond may be exchanged. Suppose a convertible bond is issued at par value of $1,000 and is convertible into 40 shares of a firm's stock. The current stock price is $20 per share, so the option to convert is not profitable now. Should the stock price later rise to $30, however, each bond may be converted profitably into $1,200 worth of stock. The *market conversion value* is the current value of the shares for which the bonds may be exchanged. At the $20 stock price, for example, the bond's conversion value is $800. The *conversion premium* is the excess of the bond price over its conversion value. If the bond were selling currently for $950, its premium would be $150.

Convertible bondholders benefit from price appreciation of the company's stock. Not surprisingly, this benefit comes at a price; convertible bonds offer lower coupon rates and stated or promised yields to maturity than nonconvertible bonds. At the same time, the actual return on the convertible bond may exceed the stated yield to maturity if the option to convert becomes profitable.

We discuss convertible and callable bonds further in Chapter 15.

Puttable bonds   While the callable bond gives the issuer the option to extend or retire the bond at the call date, the *extendable* or **put bond** gives this option to the bondholder. If the bond's coupon rate exceeds current market yields, for instance, the bondholder will choose to extend the bond's life. If the bond's coupon rate is too low, it will be optimal not to extend; the bondholder instead reclaims principal, which can be invested at current yields.

Floating-rate bonds   **Floating-rate bonds** make interest payments that are tied to some measure of current market rates. For example, the rate might be adjusted annually to the current T-bill rate plus 2%. If the one-year T-bill rate at the adjustment date is 4%, the bond's coupon rate over the next year would then be 6%. This arrangement means that the bond always pays approximately current market rates.

The major risk involved in floaters has to do with changing credit conditions. The yield spread is fixed over the life of the security, which may be many years. If the financial health of the firm deteriorates, then investors will demand a greater yield premium than is offered by the security. In this case, the price of the bond will fall. While the coupon rate on floaters adjusts to changes in the general level of market interest rates, it does not adjust to changes in the financial condition of the firm.

put bond

A bond that the holder may choose either to exchange for par value at some date or to extend for a given number of years.

floating-rate bonds

Bonds with coupon rates periodically reset according to a specified market rate.

Preferred Stock

Although preferred stock strictly speaking is considered to be equity, it often is included in the fixed-income universe. This is because, like bonds, preferred stock promises to pay a specified stream of dividends. However, unlike bonds, the failure to pay the promised dividend does not result in corporate bankruptcy. Instead, the dividends owed simply cumulate, and the common stockholders may not receive any dividends until the preferred stockholders have been paid in full. In the event of bankruptcy, the claim of preferred stockholders to the firm's assets has lower priority than that of bondholders, but higher priority than that of common stockholders.

Preferred stock commonly pays a fixed dividend. Therefore, it is in effect a perpetuity, providing a level cash flow indefinitely. More recently, however, adjustable or floating-rate preferred stock has become popular, in some years accounting for about half of new issues. Floating-rate preferred stock is much like floating-rate bonds. The dividend rate is linked to a measure of current market interest rates and is adjusted at regular intervals.

Unlike interest payments on bonds, dividends on preferred stock are not considered tax-deductible expenses to the firm. This reduces their attractiveness as a source of capital to issuing firms. On the other hand, there is an offsetting tax advantage to preferred stock. When one corporation buys the preferred stock of another corporation, it pays taxes on only 30% of the dividends received. For example, if the firm's tax bracket is 35%, and it receives $10,000 in preferred dividend payments, it will pay taxes on only $3,000 of that income: Total taxes owed on the income will be .35 × $3,000 = $1,050. The firm's effective tax rate on preferred dividends is therefore only .30 × 35% = 10.5%. Given this tax rule, it is not surprising that most preferred stock is held by corporations.

Preferred stock rarely gives its holders full voting privileges in the firm. However, if the preferred dividend is skipped, the preferred stockholders will then be provided some voting power.

Other Domestic Issuers

There are, of course, several issuers of bonds in addition to the Treasury and private corporations. For example, state and local governments issue municipal bonds. The outstanding feature of these is that interest payments are tax-free. We examined municipal bonds and the value of the tax exemption in Chapter 2.

Government agencies, such as the Federal Home Loan Bank Board, the Farm Credit agencies, and the mortgage pass-through agencies Ginnie Mae, Fannie Mae, and Freddie Mac also issue considerable amounts of bonds. These too were reviewed in Chapter 2.

International Bonds

International bonds are commonly divided into two categories: *foreign bonds* and *Eurobonds*. Foreign bonds are issued by a borrower from a country other than the one in which the bond is sold. The bond is denominated in the currency of the country in which it is marketed. For example, if a German firm sells a dollar-denominated bond in the U.S., the bond is considered a foreign bond. These bonds are given colorful names based on the countries in which they are marketed. For example, foreign bonds sold in the U.S. are called *Yankee bonds*. Like other bonds sold in the U.S., they are registered with the Securities and Exchange Commission. Yen-denominated bonds sold in Japan by non-Japanese issuers are called *Samurai bonds*. British pound-denominated foreign bonds sold in the U.K. are called *bulldog bonds*.

In contrast to foreign bonds, Eurobonds are bonds issued in the currency of one country but sold in other national markets. For example, the Eurodollar market refers to dollar-denominated bonds sold outside the U.S. (not just in Europe), although London is the largest market for Eurodollar bonds. Because the Eurodollar market falls outside of U.S. jurisdiction, these bonds are not regulated by U.S. federal agencies. Similarly, Euroyen bonds are yen-denominated bonds selling outside Japan, Eurosterling bonds are pound-denominated Eurobonds selling outside the U.K., and so on.

Innovation in the Bond Market

Issuers constantly develop innovative bonds with unusual features; these issues illustrate that bond design can be extremely flexible. Here are examples of some novel bonds. They should give you a sense of the potential variety in security design.

Inverse floaters   These are similar to the floating-rate bonds we described earlier, except that the coupon rate on these bonds *falls* when the general level of interest rates rises. Investors in these bonds suffer doubly when rates rise. Not only does the present value of each dollar of cash flow from the bond fall as the discount rate rises but the level of those cash flows falls as well. (Of course investors in these bonds benefit doubly when rates fall.)

Asset-backed bonds   Walt Disney has issued bonds with coupon rates tied to the financial performance of several of its films. Similarly, "David Bowie bonds" have been issued with payments that will be tied to royalties on some of his albums. These are examples of asset-backed securities. The income from a specified group of assets is used to service the debt. More conventional asset-backed securities are mortgage-backed securities or securities backed by auto or credit card loans, as we discussed in Chapter 2.

Pay-in-kind bonds   Issuers of pay-in-kind bonds may choose to pay interest either in cash or in additional bonds. If the issuer is short on cash, it will likely choose to pay with new bonds rather than scarce cash.

Catastrophe bonds   Oriental Land Co., which manages Tokyo Disneyland, issued a bond in 1999 with a final payment that depended on whether there had been an earthquake near the park. The Swiss firm Winterthur once issued a bond whose payments will be cut if a severe hailstorm in Switzerland results in extensive payouts on Winterthur policies.

TABLE 10.1
Principal and interest payments for a Treasury Inflation Protected Security

Time	Inflation in Year Just Ended	Par Value	Coupon Payment	+	Principal Repayment	=	Total Payment
0		$1,000.00					
1	2%	1,020.00	$40.80		0		$40.80
2	3	1,050.60	42.02		0		42.02
3	1	1,061.11	42.44		$1,061.11		1,103.55

These bonds are a way to transfer "catastrophe risk" from insurance companies to the capital markets. Investors in these bonds receive compensation in the form of higher coupon rates for taking on the risk. But in the event of a catastrophe, the bondholders will lose all or part of their investments. "Disaster" can be defined either by total insured losses or by criteria such as wind speed in a hurricane or Richter level in an earthquake. Issuance of catastrophe bonds has surged in recent years as insurers have sought ways to spread their risks across a wider spectrum of the capital market.

Indexed bonds Indexed bonds make payments that are tied to a general price index or the price of a particular commodity. For example, Mexico has issued bonds with payments that depend on the price of oil. Some bonds are indexed to the general price level. The United States Treasury started issuing such inflation-indexed bonds in January 1997. They are called Treasury Inflation Protected Securities (TIPS). By tying the par value of the bond to the general level of prices, coupon payments, as well as the final repayment of par value, on these bonds increase in direct proportion to the consumer price index. Therefore, the interest rate on these bonds is a risk-free real rate.

To illustrate how TIPS work, consider a newly issued bond with a three-year maturity, par value of $1,000, and a coupon rate of 4%. For simplicity, we will assume the bond makes annual coupon payments. Assume that inflation turns out to be 2%, 3%, and 1% in the next three years. Table 10.1 shows how the bond cash flows will be calculated. The first payment comes at the end of the first year, at $t = 1$. Because inflation over the year was 2%, the par value of the bond increases from $1,000 to $1,020; since the coupon rate is 4%, the coupon payment is 4% of this amount, or $40.80. Notice that principal value increases by the inflation rate, and because the coupon payments are 4% of principal, they too increase in proportion to the general price level. Therefore, the cash flows paid by the bond are fixed in *real* terms. When the bond matures, the investor receives a final coupon payment of $42.44 plus the (price-level-indexed) repayment of principal, $1,061.11.[3]

The *nominal* rate of return on the bond in the first year is

$$\text{Nominal return} = \frac{\text{Interest} + \text{Price appreciation}}{\text{Initial price}} = \frac{40.80 + 20}{1000} = 6.08\%$$

The real rate of return is precisely the 4% real yield on the bond:

$$\text{Real return} = \frac{1 + \text{Nominal return}}{1 + \text{Inflation}} - 1 = \frac{1.0608}{1.02} = .04, \text{ or } 4\%$$

One can show in a similar manner (see Problem 17 among the end-of-chapter questions) that the rate of return in each of the three years is 4% as long as the real yield on the bond remains

[3]By the way, total nominal income (i.e., coupon plus that year's increase in principal) is treated as taxable income in each year.

constant. If real yields do change, then there will be capital gains or losses on the bond. In early 2009, the real yield on TIPS bonds was about 2.2%.

10.2 Bond Pricing

Because a bond's coupon and principal repayments all occur months or years in the future, the price an investor would be willing to pay for a claim to those payments depends on the value of dollars to be received in the future compared to dollars in hand today. This "present value" calculation depends in turn on market interest rates. As we saw in Chapter 5, the nominal risk-free interest rate equals the sum of (1) a real risk-free rate of return and (2) a premium above the real rate to compensate for expected inflation. In addition, because most bonds are not riskless, the discount rate will embody an additional premium that reflects bond-specific characteristics such as default risk, liquidity, tax attributes, call risk, and so on.

We simplify for now by assuming there is one interest rate that is appropriate for discounting cash flows of any maturity, but we can relax this assumption easily. In practice, there may be different discount rates for cash flows accruing in different periods. For the time being, however, we ignore this refinement.

To value a security, we discount its expected cash flows by the appropriate discount rate. The cash flows from a bond consist of coupon payments until the maturity date plus the final payment of par value. Therefore

$$\text{Bond value} = \text{Present value of coupons} + \text{Present value of par value}$$

If we call the maturity date T and call the discount rate r, the bond value can be written as

$$\text{Bond value} = \sum_{t=1}^{T} \frac{\text{Coupon}}{(1 + r)^t} + \frac{\text{Par value}}{(1 + r)^T} \tag{10.1}$$

The summation sign in Equation 10.1 directs us to add the present value of each coupon payment; each coupon is discounted based on the time until it will be paid. The first term on the right-hand side of Equation 10.1 is the present value of an annuity. The second term is the present value of a single amount, the final payment of the bond's par value.

You may recall from an introductory finance class that the present value of a $1 annuity that lasts for T periods when the interest rate equals r is $\dfrac{1}{r}\left[1 - \dfrac{1}{(1 + r)^T}\right]$. We call this expression the T-period *annuity factor* for an interest rate of r.[4] Similarly, we call $\dfrac{1}{(1 + r)^T}$ the *PV factor,* that is, the present value of a single payment of $1 to be received in T periods. Therefore, we can write the price of the bond as

$$\text{Price} = \text{Coupon} \times \frac{1}{r}\left[1 - \frac{1}{(1 + r)^T}\right] + \text{Par value} \times \frac{1}{(1 + r)^T} \tag{10.2}$$
$$= \text{Coupon} \times \text{Annuity factor}(r, T) + \text{Par value} \times \text{PV factor}(r, T)$$

---

[4]Here is a quick derivation of the formula for the present value of an annuity. An annuity lasting T periods can be viewed as an equivalent to a perpetuity whose first payment comes at the end of the current period *less* another perpetuity whose first payment doesn't come until the end of period $T + 1$. The immediate perpetuity net of the delayed perpetuity provides exactly T payments. We know that the value of a $1 per period perpetuity is $1/$r$. Therefore, the present value of the delayed perpetuity is $1/$r$ discounted for T additional periods, or $\dfrac{1}{r} \times \dfrac{1}{(1 + r)^T}$. The present value of the annuity is the present value of the first perpetuity minus the present value of the delayed perpetuity, or $\dfrac{1}{r}\left[1 - \dfrac{1}{(1 + r)^T}\right]$.

EXAMPLE 10.2

Bond Pricing

We discussed earlier an 8% coupon, 30-year maturity bond with par value of $1,000 paying 60 semiannual coupon payments of $40 each. Suppose that the interest rate is 8% annually, or $r = 4\%$ per six-month period. Then the value of the bond can be written as

$$\text{Price} = \sum_{t=1}^{60} \frac{\$40}{(1.04)^t} + \frac{\$1,000}{(1.04)^{60}}$$

$$= \$40 \times \text{Annuity factor}(4\%, 60) + \$1,000 \times \text{PV factor}(4\%, 60)$$

It is easy to confirm that the present value of the bond's 60 semiannual coupon payments of $40 each is $904.94, and that the $1,000 final payment of par value has a present value of $95.06, for a total bond value of $1,000. You can calculate the value directly from Equation 10.2, perform these calculations on any financial calculator,[5] use a spreadsheet (see Spreadsheet 10.1 below), or a set of present value tables.

In this example, the coupon rate equals the market interest rate, and the bond price equals par value. If the interest rate were not equal to the bond's coupon rate, the bond would not sell at par value. For example, if the interest rate were to rise to 10% (5% per six months), the bond's price would fall by $189.29, to $810.71, as follows

$$\$40 \times \text{Annuity factor}(5\%, 60) + \$1,000 \times \text{PV factor}(5\%, 60)$$

$$= \$757.17 + \$53.54 = \$810.71$$

At a higher interest rate, the present value of the payments to be received by the bondholder is lower. Therefore, the bond price will fall as market interest rates rise. This illustrates a crucial general rule in bond valuation. When interest rates rise, bond prices must fall because the present value of the bond's payments is obtained by discounting at a higher interest rate.

Figure 10.3 shows the price of the 30-year, 8% coupon bond for a range of interest rates including 8%, at which the bond sells at par, and 10%, at which it sells for $810.71. The negative slope illustrates the inverse relationship between prices and yields. Note also from the figure (and from Table 10.2) that the shape of the curve implies that an increase in the interest rate results in a price decline that is smaller than the price gain resulting from a decrease of equal magnitude in the interest rate. This property of bond prices is called *convexity* because of the convex shape of the bond price curve. This curvature reflects the fact that progressive increases in the interest rate result in progressively smaller reductions in the bond price.[6] Therefore, the price curve becomes flatter at higher interest rates. We will return to the issue of convexity in the next chapter.

CONCEPT *check* **10.2**

Calculate the price of the bond for a market interest rate of 3% per half-year. Compare the capital gains for the interest rate decline to the losses incurred when the rate increases to 5%.

Corporate bonds typically are issued at par value. This means the underwriters of the bond issue (the firms that market the bonds to the public for the issuing corporation) must choose a coupon rate that very closely approximates market yields. In a primary issue of bonds, the underwriters attempt to sell the newly issued bonds directly to their customers. If the coupon rate is inadequate, investors will not pay par value for the bonds.

After the bonds are issued, bondholders may buy or sell bonds in secondary markets. In these markets, bond prices fluctuate inversely with the market interest rate.

---

[5]On your financial calculator, you would enter the following inputs: *n* (number of periods) = 60; FV (face or future value) = 1000; PMT (payment each period) = 40; *i* (per period interest rate) = 4%; then you would compute the price of the bond (COMP PV or CPT PV). You should find that the price is $1,000. Actually, most calculators will display the result as *minus* $1,000. This is because most (but not all) calculators treat the initial purchase price of the bond as a cash *outflow*. We will discuss financial calculators and spreadsheets more fully in a few pages.

[6]The progressively smaller impact of interest rate increases results from the fact that at higher rates the bond is worth less. Therefore, an additional increase in rates operates on a smaller initial base, resulting in a smaller price reduction.

FIGURE 10.3

The inverse relationship between bond prices and yields. Price of an 8% coupon bond with 30-year maturity making semiannual coupon payments.

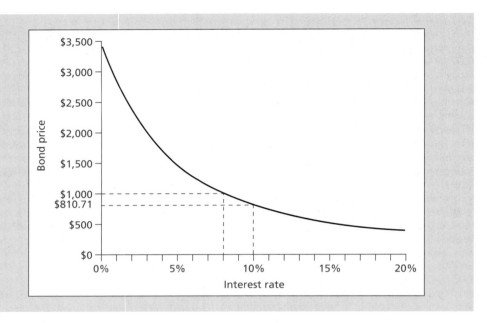

TABLE 10.2	Time to Maturity	Bond Price at Given Market Interest Rate				
Bond prices at different interest rates (8% coupon bond, coupons paid semiannually)		2%	4%	6%	8%	10%
	1 year	$1,059.11	$1,038.83	$1,019.13	$1,000.00	$981.41
	10 years	1,541.37	1,327.03	1,148.77	1,000.00	875.38
	20 years	1,985.04	1,547.11	1,231.15	1,000.00	828.41
	30 years	2,348.65	1,695.22	1,276.76	1,000.00	810.71

The inverse relationship between price and yield is a central feature of fixed-income securities. Interest rate fluctuations represent the main source of risk in the bond market, and we devote considerable attention in the next chapter to assessing the sensitivity of bond prices to market yields. For now, however, it is sufficient to highlight one key factor that determines that sensitivity, namely, the maturity of the bond.

As a general rule, keeping all other factors the same, the longer the maturity of the bond, the greater the sensitivity of its price to fluctuations in the interest rate. For example, consider Table 10.2, which presents the price of an 8% coupon bond at different market yields and times to maturity. For any departure of the interest rate from 8% (the rate at which the bond sells at par value), the change in the bond price is greater for longer times to maturity.

This makes sense. If you buy the bond at par with an 8% coupon rate, and market rates subsequently rise, then you suffer a loss: You have tied up your money earning 8% when alternative investments offer higher returns. This is reflected in a capital loss on the bond—a fall in its market price. The longer the period for which your money is tied up, the greater the loss and, correspondingly, the greater the drop in the bond price. In Table 10.2, the row for one-year maturity bonds shows little price sensitivity—that is, with only one year's earnings at stake, changes in interest rates are not too threatening. But for 30-year maturity bonds, interest rate swings have a large impact on bond prices. The force of discounting is greatest for the longest-term bonds.

This is why short-term Treasury securities such as T-bills are considered the safest. They are free not only of default risk but also largely of price risk attributable to interest rate volatility.

Bond Pricing between Coupon Dates

Equation 10.2 for bond prices assumes that the next coupon payment is in precisely one payment period, either a year for an annual payment bond or six months for a semiannual payment bond. But you probably want to be able to price bonds all 365 days of the year, not just on the one or two dates each year that it makes a coupon payment!

In principle, the fact that the bond is between coupon dates does not affect the pricing problem. The procedure is always the same: Compute the present value of each remaining payment and sum up. But if you are between coupon dates, there will be fractional periods remaining until each payment, and this does complicate the arithmetic computations.

Fortunately, bond pricing functions are included in many financial calculators and most spreadsheet programs such as Excel. The spreadsheets allow you to enter today's date as well as the maturity date of the bond, and so can provide prices for bonds at any date.

As we pointed out earlier, bond prices are typically quoted net of accrued interest. These prices, which appear in the financial press, are called *flat prices*. The actual *invoice price* that a buyer pays for the bond includes accrued interest. Thus,

$$\text{Invoice price} = \text{Flat price} + \text{Accrued interest}$$

When a bond pays its coupon, flat price equals invoice price, since at that moment accrued interest reverts to zero. However, this will be the exceptional case, not the rule.

Excel pricing functions provide the flat price of the bond. To find the invoice price, we need to add accrued interest. Excel also provides functions that count the days since the last coupon payment and thus can be used to compute accrued interest. Spreadsheet 10.1 illustrates how to use these functions. The spreadsheet provides examples using bonds that have just paid a coupon and so have zero accrued interest, as well as a bond that is between coupon dates.

Bond Pricing in Excel

Excel asks you to input both the date you buy the bond (called the *settlement date*) and the maturity date of the bond.

The Excel function for bond price is

=PRICE (settlement date, maturity date, annual coupon rate, yield to maturity,
    redemption value as percent of par value, number of coupon payments per year)

For the 1.125% coupon January 2012 maturity bond highlighted in Figure 10.1, we would enter the values in Spreadsheet 10.1. Alternatively, we could simply enter the following function in Excel:

=PRICE(DATE(2009,1,15), DATE(2012,1,15), .01125, .0101, 100, 2)

The DATE function in Excel, which we use for both the settlement and maturity date, uses the format DATE(year,month,day). The first date is January 15, 2009, when the bond may be purchased, and the second is January 15, 2012, when it matures. See Spreadsheet 10.1.

Notice that the coupon rate and yield to maturity are expressed as decimals, not percentages. In most cases, redemption value is 100 (i.e., 100% of par value), and the resulting price similarly is expressed as a percent of par value. Occasionally, however, you may encounter bonds that pay off at a premium or discount to par value. One example would be callable bonds, discussed shortly.

The value of the bond returned by the pricing function is 100.339 (cell B12), which nearly matches the price reported in *The Wall Street Journal*. (The yield to maturity is reported to only two decimal places, which induces some rounding error.) This bond has just paid a coupon. In other words, the settlement date is precisely at the beginning of the coupon period, so no adjustment for accrued interest is necessary.

To illustrate the procedure for bonds between coupon payments, let us apply the spreadsheet to the 4% coupon November 2012 bond which also appears in Figure 10.1. Using the entries in column D of the spreadsheet, we find in cell D12 that the (flat) price of the bond is 111.254, which matches the price given in *The Wall Street Journal*.

What about the bond's invoice price? Rows 12 through 16 make the necessary adjustments. The function described in cell C13 counts the days since the last coupon. This day count is based on the bond's settlement date, maturity date, coupon period (1 = annual; 2 = semiannual), and day count convention (choice 1 uses actual days). The function described in cell C14 counts the total days in each coupon payment period. Therefore, the entries for accrued interest in row 15 are the semiannual coupon multiplied by the fraction of a coupon period that has elapsed since the last payment. Finally, the invoice prices in row 16 are the sum of flat price (which matches the reported price in *The Wall Street Journal*) plus accrued interest.

As a final example, suppose you wish to find the price of the bond in Example 10.2. It is a 30-year maturity bond with a coupon rate of 8 percent (paid semiannually). The market interest rate given in the latter part of the example is 10%. However, you are not given a specific settlement or maturity date. You can still use the PRICE function to value the bond. Simply choose an *arbitrary* settlement date (January 1, 2000 is convenient) and let the maturity date be 30 years hence. The appropriate inputs appear in column F of the spreadsheet, with the resulting price, 81.071% of face value, appearing in cell F16.

SPREADSHEET 10.1

Valuing bonds using a spreadsheet

eXcel

Please visit us at www.mhhe.com/bkm

	A	B	C	D	E	F	G
1	1.125% coupon bond,			4% coupon bond,		8% coupon bond,	
2	maturing Jan 2012		Formula in column B	maturing Nov 2012		30-year maturity	
3							
4	Settlement date	1/15/2009	=DATE(2009,1,15)	1/15/2009		1/1/2000	
5	Maturity date	1/15/2012	=DATE(2012,1,15)	11/15/2012		1/1/2030	
6	Annual coupon rate	0.01125		0.04		0.08	
7	Yield to maturity	0.0101		0.0100		0.1	
8	Redemption value (% of face value)	100		100		100	
9	Coupon payments per year	2		2		2	
10							
11							
12	Flat price (% of par)	100.339	=PRICE(B4,B5,B6,B7,B8,B9)	111.254		81.071	
13	Days since last coupon	0	=COUPDAYBS(B4,B5,2,1)	61		0	
14	Days in coupon period	181	=COUPDAYS(B4,B5,2,1)	181		182	
15	Accrued interest	0	=(B13/B14)*B6*100/2	0.674		0	
16	Invoice price	100.339	=B12+B15	111.928		81.071	

10.3 Bond Yields

We have noted that the current yield of a bond measures only the cash income provided by the bond as a percentage of bond price and ignores any prospective capital gains or losses. We would like a measure of rate of return that accounts for both current income as well as the price increase or decrease over the bond's life. The yield to maturity is the standard measure of the total rate of return. However, it is far from perfect, and we will explore several variations of this measure.

Yield to Maturity

yield to maturity (YTM)

The discount rate that makes the present value of a bond's payments equal to its price.

In practice, an investor considering the purchase of a bond is not quoted a promised rate of return. Instead, the investor must use the bond price, maturity date, and coupon payments to infer the return offered by the bond over its life. The **yield to maturity** (YTM) is defined as the discount rate that makes the present value of a bond's payments equal to its price. This rate is often viewed as a measure of the average rate of return that will be earned on a bond if it is bought now and held until maturity. To calculate the yield to maturity, we solve the bond price equation for the interest rate given the bond's price.

For example, suppose an 8% coupon, 30-year bond is selling at $1,276.76. What average rate of return would be earned by an investor purchasing the bond at this price? We find the interest rate at which the present value of the remaining 60 semiannual payments equals the bond price. This is the rate consistent with the observed price of the bond. Therefore, we solve for r in the following equation

$$\$1,276.76 = \sum_{t=1}^{60} \frac{\$40}{(1+r)^t} + \frac{\$1,000}{(1+r)^{60}}$$

or, equivalently,

$$1,276.76 = 40 \times \text{Annuity factor}(r, 60) + 1,000 \times \text{PV factor}(r, 60)$$

These equations have only one unknown variable, the interest rate, r. You can use a financial calculator or spreadsheet to confirm that the solution is $r = .03$, or 3% per half-year.[7] This is the bond's yield to maturity.

The financial press reports yields on an annualized basis, and annualizes the bond's semiannual yield using simple interest techniques, resulting in an annual percentage rate or APR. Yields annualized using simple interest are also called *bond equivalent yields*. Therefore, the semiannual yield would be doubled and reported in the newspaper as a bond equivalent yield of 6%. The *effective* annual yield of the bond, however, accounts for compound interest. If one earns 3% interest every six months, then after one year, each dollar invested grows with interest to $\$1 \times (1.03)^2 = 1.0609$, and the effective annual interest rate on the bond is 6.09%.

The bond's yield to maturity is the internal rate of return on an investment in the bond. The yield to maturity can be interpreted as the compound rate of return over the life of the bond under the assumption that all bond coupons can be reinvested at that yield.[8] Yield to maturity therefore is widely accepted as a proxy for average return.

Yield to maturity can be difficult to calculate without a financial calculator or spreadsheet. However, it is easy to calculate with either. Financial calculators are designed with present value and future value formulas already programmed. The basic financial calculator uses five keys that correspond to the inputs for time value of money problems such as bond pricing:

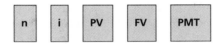

- n is the number of time periods. In the case of a bond, n equals the number of periods until the bond matures. If the bond makes semiannual payments, n is the number of half-year periods or, equivalently, the number of semiannual coupon payments. For example, if the bond has 10 years until maturity, you would enter 20 for n, since each payment period is one-half year.
- i is the interest rate per period, expressed as a percentage (not as a decimal, which is required by spreadsheet programs). For example, if the interest rate is 6%, you would enter 6, not .06.
- PV is the present value. Many calculators require that PV be entered as a negative number, in recognition of the fact that purchase of the bond is a cash *outflow,* while the receipt of coupon payments and face value are cash *inflows.*
- FV is the future value or face value of the bond. In general, FV is interpreted as a one-time future payment of a cash flow, which, for bonds, is the face (i.e., par) value.
- PMT is the amount of any recurring payment. For coupon bonds, PMT is the coupon payment; for zero-coupon bonds, PMT will be zero.

Given any four of these inputs, the calculator will solve for the fifth. We can illustrate with some examples.

---

[7]Without a financial calculator or spreadsheet, you still could solve the equation, but you would need to use a trial-and-error approach.
[8]If the reinvestment rate does not equal the bond's yield to maturity, the compound rate of return will differ from YTM. This is demonstrated below in Examples 10.5 and 10.6.

EXAMPLE 10.3

Bond Valuation Using a Financial Calculator

Consider the yield to maturity problem that we just solved. We would enter the following inputs (in any order):

n	60	The bond has a maturity of 30 years, so it makes 60 semiannual payments.
PMT	40	Each semiannual coupon payment is $40.
PV	(–)1,276.76	The bond can be purchased for $1,276.76, which on some calculators must be entered as a negative number as it is a cash outflow.
FV	1,000	The bond will provide a one-time cash flow of $1,000 when it matures.

Given these inputs, you now use the calculator to find the interest rate at which $1,276.76 actually equals the present value of the 60 payments of $40 each plus the one-time payment of $1,000 at maturity. On most calculators, you first punch the "compute" key (labeled *COMP* or *CPT*) and then enter *i* to have the interest rate computed. If you do so, you will find that *i* = 3, or 3% semiannually, as we claimed. (Notice that just as the cash flows are paid semiannually, the computed interest rate is a rate per semiannual time period.)

You can also find bond prices given a yield to maturity. For example, we saw in Example 10.2 that if the yield to maturity is 5% semiannually, the bond price will be $810.71. You can confirm this with the following inputs on your calculator:

$$n = 60; \ i = 5; \ FV = 1{,}000; \ PMT = 40$$

and then computing PV to find that PV = 810.71. Once again, your calculator may report the result as −810.71.

Excel also provides a function for yield to maturity. It is

= YIELD(settlement date, maturity date, annual coupon rate, bond price, redemption value as percent of par value, number of coupon payments per year)

The bond price used in the function should be the reported flat price, without accrued interest. For example, to find the yield to maturity of the bond in Example 10.3, we would use column E of Spreadsheet 10.2. If the coupons were paid only annually, we would change the entry for payments per year to 1 (see cell G9), and the yield would fall slightly to 5.99%.

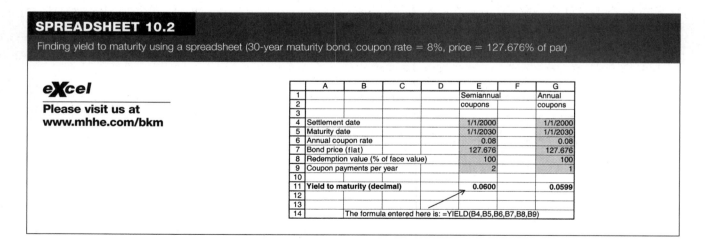

SPREADSHEET 10.2

Finding yield to maturity using a spreadsheet (30-year maturity bond, coupon rate = 8%, price = 127.676% of par)

eXcel

Please visit us at www.mhhe.com/bkm

	A	B	C	D	E	F	G
1					Semiannual		Annual
2					coupons		coupons
3							
4	Settlement date				1/1/2000		1/1/2000
5	Maturity date				1/1/2030		1/1/2030
6	Annual coupon rate				0.08		0.08
7	Bond price (flat)				127.676		127.676
8	Redemption value (% of face value)				100		100
9	Coupon payments per year				2		1
10							
11	Yield to maturity (decimal)				0.0600		0.0599
12							
13							
14		The formula entered here is: =YIELD(B4,B5,B6,B7,B8,B9)					

current yield

Annual coupon divided by bond price.

Yield to maturity differs from the **current yield** of a bond, which is the bond's annual coupon payment divided by the bond price. For example, for the 8%, 30-year bond currently selling at $1,276.76, the current yield would be $80/$1,276.76 = .0627, or 6.27% per year. In contrast, recall that the effective annual yield to maturity is 6.09%. For this bond, which is selling at a premium over par value ($1,276 rather than $1,000), the coupon rate (8%)

exceeds the current yield (6.27%), which exceeds the yield to maturity (6.09%). The coupon rate exceeds current yield because the coupon rate divides the coupon payments by par value ($1,000) rather than by the bond price ($1,276). In turn, the current yield exceeds yield to maturity because the yield to maturity accounts for the built-in capital loss on the bond; the bond bought today for $1,276 will eventually fall in value to $1,000 at maturity.

premium bonds

Bonds selling above par value.

This example illustrates a general rule: For **premium bonds** (bonds selling above par value), coupon rate is greater than current yield, which in turn is greater than yield to maturity. For **discount bonds** (bonds selling below par value), these relationships are reversed (see Concept Check 10.3).

discount bonds

Bonds selling below par value.

It is common to hear people talking loosely about the yield on a bond. In these cases, they almost always are referring to the yield to maturity.

> What will be the relationship among coupon rate, current yield, and yield to maturity for bonds selling at discounts from par? Illustrate using the 8% (semiannual payment) coupon bond assuming it is selling at a yield to maturity of 10%.
>
> **CONCEPT** *check* **10.3**

Yield to Call

Yield to maturity is calculated on the assumption that the bond will be held until maturity. What if the bond is callable, however, and may be retired prior to the maturity date? How should we measure average rate of return for bonds subject to a call provision?

Figure 10.4 illustrates the risk of call to the bondholder. The colored line is the value at various market interest rates of a "straight" (that is, noncallable) bond with par value of $1,000, an 8% coupon rate, and a 30-year time to maturity. If interest rates fall, the bond price, which equals the present value of the promised payments, can rise substantially. Now consider a bond that has the same coupon rate and maturity date but is callable at 110% of par value, or $1,100. When interest rates fall, the present value of the bond's *scheduled* payments rises, but the call provision allows the issuer to repurchase the bond at the call price. If the call price is less than the present value of the scheduled payments, the issuer can call the bond at the expense of the bondholder.

The dark line in Figure 10.4 is the value of the callable bond. At high market interest rates, the risk of call is negligible because the present value of scheduled payments is substantially less than the call price; therefore, the values of the straight and callable bonds converge. At lower rates, however, the values of the bonds begin to diverge, with the difference reflecting the value of the firm's option to reclaim the callable bond at the call price. At very low market rates the present value of schedule payments significantly exceeds the call price, so the bond is called. Its value at this point is simply the call price, $1,100.

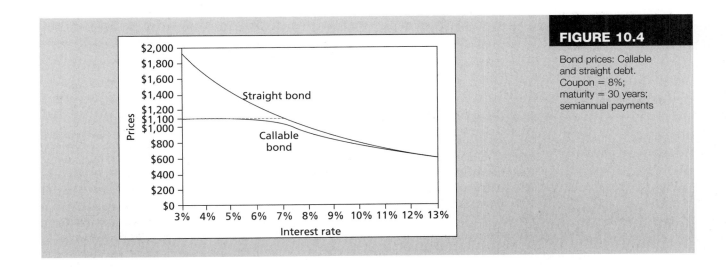

FIGURE 10.4

Bond prices: Callable and straight debt.
Coupon = 8%;
maturity = 30 years;
semiannual payments

This analysis suggests that bond market analysts might be more interested in a bond's yield to call rather than its yield to maturity, especially if the bond is likely to be called. The yield to call is calculated just like the yield to maturity, except that the time until call replaces time until maturity and the call price replaces the par value. This computation is sometimes called "yield to first call," as it assumes the issuer will call the bond as soon as it may do so.

EXAMPLE 10.4

Yield to Call

Suppose the 8% coupon, 30-year maturity bond sells for $1,150 and is callable in 10 years at a call price of $1,100. Its yield to maturity and yield to call would be calculated using the following inputs:

	Yield to Call	Yield to Maturity
Coupon payment	$40	$40
Number of semiannual periods	20 periods	60 periods
Final payment	$1,100	$1,000
Price	$1,150	$1,150

Yield to call is then 6.64%. To confirm this on your calculator, input $n = 20$; PV = (−)1150; FV = 1100; PMT = 40; compute i as 3.32%, or 6.64% bond equivalent yield. In contrast, yield to maturity is 6.82%. To confirm, input $n = 60$; PV = (−)1150; FV = 1000; PMT = 40; compute i as 3.41%, or 6.82% bond equivalent yield. In Excel, you can calculate yield to call as =YIELD (DATE(2000,01,01), DATE(2010,01,01), .08, 115, 110, 2). Notice that redemption value is 110, that is, 110% of par value.

We have noted that most callable bonds are issued with an initial period of call protection. In addition, an implicit form of call protection operates for bonds selling at deep discounts from their call prices. Even if interest rates fall a bit, deep-discount bonds still will sell below the call price and thus will not be subject to a call.

Premium bonds that might be selling near their call prices, however, are especially apt to be called if rates fall further. If interest rates fall, a callable premium bond is likely to provide a lower return than could be earned on a discount bond whose potential price appreciation is not limited by the likelihood of a call. Investors in premium bonds often are more interested in the bond's yield to call rather than yield to maturity as a consequence, because it may appear to them that the bond will be retired at the call date.

CONCEPT check 10.4

A 20-year maturity 9% coupon bond paying coupons semiannually is callable in five years at a call price of $1,050. The bond currently sells at a yield to maturity of 8% (bond equivalent yield). What is the yield to call?

Realized Compound Return versus Yield to Maturity

We have noted that yield to maturity will equal the rate of return realized over the life of the bond if all coupons are reinvested at an interest rate equal to the bond's yield to maturity. Consider for example, a two-year bond selling at par value paying a 10% coupon once a year. The yield to maturity is 10%. If the $100 coupon payment is reinvested at an interest rate of 10%, the $1,000 investment in the bond will grow after two years to $1,210, as illustrated in Figure 10.5, Panel A. The coupon paid in the first year is reinvested and grows with interest to a second-year value of $110, which, together with the second coupon payment and payment of par value in the second year, results in a total value of $1,210. To summarize, the initial value of the investment is $V_0 = \$1,000$. The final value in two years is $V_2 = \$1,210$. The compound rate of return, therefore, is calculated as follows.

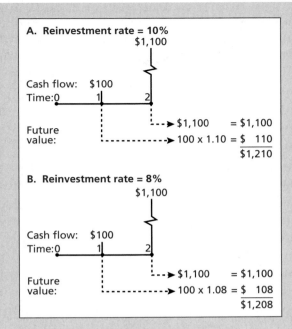

FIGURE 10.5

Growth of invested funds. In Panel A, interest payments are reinvested at 10%, the bond's yield to maturity. In Panel B, the reinvestment rate is only 8%.

$$V_0 (1 + r)^2 = V_2$$
$$\$1,000 (1 + r)^2 = \$1,210$$
$$r = .10 = 10\%$$

With a reinvestment rate equal to the 10% yield to maturity, the **realized compound return** equals yield to maturity.

But what if the reinvestment rate is not 10%? If the coupon can be invested at more than 10%, funds will grow to more than $1,210, and the realized compound return will exceed 10%. If the reinvestment rate is less than 10%, so will be the realized compound return. Consider the following example.

realized compound return

Compound rate of return on a bond with all coupons reinvested until maturity.

EXAMPLE 10.5

Realized Compound Return

If the interest rate earned on the first coupon is less than 10%, the final value of the investment will be less than $1,210, and the realized compound yield will be less than 10%. Suppose the interest rate at which the coupon can be invested equals 8%. The following calculations are illustrated in Panel B of Figure 10.5.

Future value of first coupon payment with interest earnings	$100 × 1.08 = $ 108
Cash payment in second year (final coupon plus par value)	1,100
Total value of investment with reinvested coupons	$1,208

The realized compound return is the compound rate of growth of invested funds, assuming that all coupon payments are reinvested. The investor purchased the bond for par at $1,000, and this investment grew to $1,208.

$$\$1,000(1 + r)^2 = \$1,208$$
$$r = .0991 = 9.91\%$$

Example 10.5 highlights the problem with conventional yield to maturity when reinvestment rates can change over time. However, in an economy with future interest rate uncertainty, the rates at which interim coupons will be reinvested are not yet known. Therefore, while realized compound return can be computed *after* the investment period ends, it cannot be

horizon analysis

Analysis of bond returns over multiyear horizon, based on forecasts of bond's yield to maturity and reinvestment rate of coupons.

computed in advance without a forecast of future reinvestment rates. This reduces much of the attraction of the realized return measure.

We also can calculate realized compound yield over holding periods greater than one period. This is called **horizon analysis** and is similar to the procedure in Example 10.5. The forecast of total return will depend on your forecasts of *both* the yield to maturity of the bond when you sell it *and* the rate at which you are able to reinvest coupon income. With a longer investment horizon, however, reinvested coupons will be a larger component of your final proceeds.

EXAMPLE 10.6	Suppose you buy a 30-year, 7.5% (annual payment) coupon bond for $980 (when its yield to maturity is 7.67%) and plan to hold it for 20 years. Your forecast is that the bond's yield to maturity will be 8% when it is sold and that the reinvestment rate on the coupons will be 6%. At the end of your investment horizon, the bond will have 10 years remaining until expiration, so the forecast sales price (using a yield to maturity of 8%) will be $966.45. The 20 coupon payments will grow with compound interest to $2,758.92. (This is the future value of a 20-year $75 annuity with an interest rate of 6%.)
Horizon Analysis	

Based on these forecasts, your $980 investment will grow in 20 years to $966.45 + $2,758.92 = $3,725.37. This corresponds to an annualized compound return of 6.90%:

$$\$980 \, (1+r)^{20} = \$3,725.37$$
$$r = .0690 = 6.90\%$$

Examples 10.5 and 10.6 demonstrate that as interest rates change, bond investors are actually subject to two sources of offsetting risk. On the one hand, when rates rise, bond prices fall, which reduces the value of the portfolio. On the other hand, reinvested coupon income will compound more rapidly at those higher rates. This **reinvestment rate risk** will offset the impact of price risk. In the next chapter, we will explore this trade-off in more detail and will discover that by carefully tailoring their bond portfolios, investors can precisely balance these two effects for any given investment horizon.

reinvestment rate risk

Uncertainty surrounding the cumulative future value of reinvested bond coupon payments.

10.4 Bond Prices Over Time

As we noted earlier, a bond will sell at par value when its coupon rate equals the market interest rate. In these circumstances, the investor receives fair compensation for the time value of money in the form of the recurring coupon payments. No further capital gain is necessary to provide fair compensation.

When the coupon rate is lower than the market interest rate, the coupon payments alone will not provide investors as high a return as they could earn elsewhere in the market. To receive a fair return on such an investment, investors also need to earn price appreciation on their bonds. The bonds, therefore, would have to sell below par value to provide a "built-in" capital gain on the investment.

EXAMPLE 10.7	To illustrate built-in capital gains or losses, suppose a bond was issued several years ago when the interest rate was 7%. The bond's annual coupon rate was thus set at 7%. (We will suppose for simplicity that the bond pays its coupon annually.) Now, with three years left in the bond's life, the interest rate is 8% per year. The bond's fair market price is the present value of the remaining annual coupons plus payment of par value. That present value is[9]
Fair Holding-Period Return	

$$\$70 \times \text{Annuity factor (8\%, 3)} + \$1,000 \times \text{PV factor (8\%, 3)} = \$974.23$$

which is less than par value.

In another year, after the next coupon is paid, the bond would sell at

$$\$70 \times \text{Annuity factor (8\%, 2)} + \$1,000 \times \text{PV factor (8\%, 2)} = \$982.17$$

thereby yielding a capital gain over the year of $7.94. If an investor had purchased the bond at $974.23, the total return over the year would equal the coupon payment plus capital gain, or $70 + $7.94 = $77.94. This represents a rate of return of $77.94/$974.23, or 8%, exactly the current rate of return available elsewhere in the market.

---

[9]Using a calculator, enter $n = 3$, $i = 8$, PMT = 70, FV = 1000, and compute PV.

CONCEPT *check* **10.5**

What will be the price of the bond in Example 10.7 in yet another year, when only one year remains until maturity? What is the rate of return to an investor who purchases the bond at $982.17 and sells it one year later?

When bond prices are set according to the present value formula, any discount from par value provides an anticipated capital gain that will augment a below-market coupon rate just enough to provide a fair total rate of return. Conversely, if the coupon rate exceeds the market interest rate, the interest income by itself is greater than that available elsewhere in the market. Investors will bid up the price of these bonds above their par values. As the bonds approach maturity, they will fall in value because fewer of these above-market coupon payments remain. The resulting capital losses offset the large coupon payments so that the bondholder again receives only a fair rate of return.

Problem 14 at the end of the chapter asks you to work through the case of the high coupon bond. Figure 10.6 traces out the price paths of high and low coupon bonds (net of accrued interest) as time to maturity approaches, at least for the case in which the market interest rate is constant. The low coupon bond enjoys capital gains, while the high coupon bond suffers capital losses.[10]

We use these examples to show that each bond offers investors the same total rate of return. Although the capital gain versus income components differ, the price of each bond is set to provide competitive rates, as we should expect in well-functioning capital markets. Security returns all should be comparable on an after-tax risk-adjusted basis. If they are not, investors will try to sell low-return securities, thereby driving down the prices until the total return at the now-lower price is competitive with other securities. Prices should continue to adjust until all securities are fairly priced in that expected returns are comparable (given appropriate risk and tax adjustments).

Yield to Maturity versus Holding-Period Return

In Example 10.7, the holding-period return and the yield to maturity were equal. The bond yield started and ended the year at 8%, and the bond's holding-period return also equaled 8%. This turns out to be a general result. When the yield to maturity is unchanged over the period, the rate of return on the bond will equal that yield. As we noted, this should not be surprising: The bond must offer a rate of return competitive with those available on other securities.

However, when yields fluctuate, so will a bond's rate of return. Unanticipated changes in market rates will result in unanticipated changes in bond returns, and after the fact, a bond's holding-period return can be better or worse than the yield at which it initially sells. An increase in the bond's yield to maturity acts to reduce its price, which means that the holding-period return will be less than the initial yield. Conversely, a decline in yield to maturity results in a holding-period return greater than the initial yield.

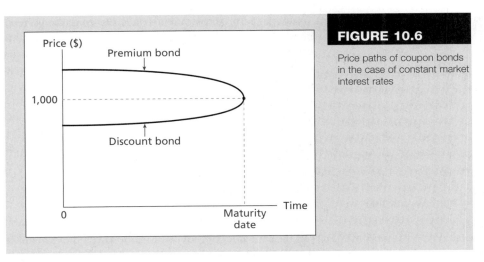

FIGURE 10.6

Price paths of coupon bonds in the case of constant market interest rates

---

[10]If interest rates are volatile, the price path will be "jumpy," vibrating around the price path in Figure 10.6 and reflecting capital gains or losses as interest rates fluctuate. Ultimately, however, the price must reach par value at the maturity date, so on average, the price of the premium bond will fall over time while that of the discount bond will rise.

Consider a 30-year bond paying an annual coupon of $80 and selling at par value of $1,000. The bond's initial yield to maturity is 8%. If the yield remains at 8% over the year, the bond price will remain at par, so the holding-period return also will be 8%. But if the yield falls below 8%, the bond price will increase. Suppose the yield falls and the price increases to $1,050. Then the holding-period return is greater than 8%:

$$\text{Holding-period return} = \frac{\$80 + (\$1,050 - \$1,000)}{\$1,000} = .13, \text{ or } 13\%$$

Show that if the yield to maturity increases, then holding-period return is *less* than that initial yield. For example, suppose in Example 10.8 that by the end of the first year, the bond's yield to maturity is 8.5%. Find the one-year holding-period return and compare it to the bond's initial 8% yield to maturity.

Here is another way to think about the difference between yield to maturity and holding-period return. Yield to maturity depends only on the bond's coupon, *current* price, and par value at maturity. All of these values are observable today, so yield to maturity can be easily calculated. Yield to maturity can be interpreted as a measure of the *average* rate of return if the investment in the bond is held until the bond matures. In contrast, holding-period return is the rate of return over a particular investment period and depends on the market price of the bond at the end of that holding period; of course this price is *not* known today. Since bond prices over the holding period will respond to unanticipated changes in interest rates, holding-period return can at most be forecast.

Zero-Coupon Bonds and Treasury STRIPS

Original issue discount bonds are less common than coupon bonds issued at par. These are bonds that are issued intentionally with low coupon rates that cause the bond to sell at a discount from par value. An extreme example of this type of bond is the *zero-coupon bond,* which carries no coupons and provides all its return in the form of price appreciation. Zeros provide only one cash flow to their owners, on the maturity date of the bond.

U.S. Treasury bills are examples of short-term zero-coupon instruments. If the bill has face value of $10,000, the Treasury issues or sells it for some amount less than $10,000, agreeing to repay $10,000 at maturity. All of the investor's return comes in the form of price appreciation.

Longer term zero-coupon bonds are commonly created from coupon-bearing notes and bonds. A broker that purchases a Treasury coupon bond may ask the Treasury to break down the cash flows into a series of independent securities, where each security is a claim to one of the payments of the original bond. For example, a 10-year coupon bond would be "stripped" of its 20 semiannual coupons and each coupon payment would be treated as a stand-alone zero-coupon bond. The maturities of these bonds would thus range from six months to 10 years. The final payment of principal would be treated as another stand-alone zero-coupon security. Each of the payments would then be treated as an independent security and assigned its own CUSIP number, the security identifier that allows for electronic trading over the Fedwire system. The payments are still considered obligations of the U.S. Treasury. The Treasury program under which coupon stripping is performed is called STRIPS (Separate Trading of Registered Interest and Principal of Securities), and these zero-coupon securities are called *Treasury strips.*

What should happen to prices of zeros as time passes? On their maturity dates, zeros must sell for par value. Before maturity, however, they should sell at discounts from par, because of the time value of money. As time passes, price should approach par value. In fact, if the interest rate is constant, a zero's price will increase at exactly the rate of interest.

To illustrate, consider a zero with 30 years until maturity, and suppose the market interest rate is 10% per year. The price of the bond today is $\$1,000/(1.10)^{30} = \$57.31$. Next year, with only 29 years until maturity, if the yield to maturity is still 10%, the price will be $1,000/(1.10)^{29} = \$63.04$, a 10% increase over its previous-year value. Because the par value of the bond is now discounted for one fewer year, its price has increased by the one-year discount factor.

Figure 10.7 presents the price path of a 30-year zero-coupon bond for an annual market interest rate of 10%. The bond's price rises exponentially, not linearly, until its maturity.

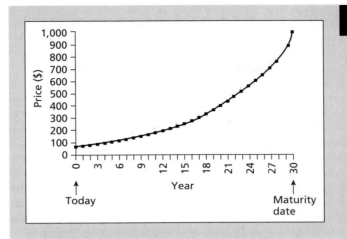

The price of a 30-year zero-coupon bond over time at a yield to maturity of 10%. Price equals $1000/(1.10)^T$ where T is time until maturity.

After-Tax Returns

The tax authorities recognize that the "built-in" price appreciation on original-issue discount (OID) bonds such as zero-coupon bonds represents an implicit interest payment to the holder of the security. The Internal Revenue Service (IRS), therefore, calculates a price appreciation schedule to impute taxable interest income for the built-in appreciation during a tax year, even if the asset is not sold or does not mature until a future year. Any additional gains or losses that arise from changes in market interest rates are treated as capital gains or losses if the OID bond is sold during the tax year.

EXAMPLE 10.9

Taxation of Original-Issue Discount Bonds

If the interest rate originally is 10%, the 30-year zero would be issued at a price of $1,000/(1.10)^{30} = \$57.31$. The following year, the IRS calculates what the bond price would be if its yield were still 10%. This is $1,000/(1.10)^{29} = \$63.04$. Therefore, the IRS imputes interest income of $63.04 − $57.31 = $5.73. This amount is subject to tax. Notice that the imputed interest income is based on a "constant yield method" that ignores any changes in market interest rates.

If interest rates actually fall, let's say to 9.9%, the bond price will be $1,000/(1.099)^{29} = \$64.72$. If the bond is sold, then the difference between $64.72 and $63.04 will be treated as capital gains income and taxed at the capital gains tax rate. If the bond is not sold, then the price difference is an unrealized capital gain and does not result in taxes in that year. In either case, the investor must pay taxes on the $5.73 of imputed interest at the ordinary income tax rate.

The procedure illustrated in Example 10.9 applies as well to the taxation of other original-issue discount bonds, even if they are not zero-coupon bonds. Consider, as another example, a 30-year maturity bond that is issued with a coupon rate of 4% and a yield to maturity of 8%. For simplicity, we will assume that the bond pays coupons once annually. Because of the low coupon rate, the bond will be issued at a price far below par value, specifically at a price of $549.69. (Confirm this for yourself.) If the bond's yield to maturity is still 8%, then its price in one year will rise to $553.66. (Confirm this also.) This would provide a pretax holding-period return of exactly 8%:

$$\text{HPR} = \frac{\$40 + (\$553.66 - \$549.69)}{\$549.69} = .08$$

The increase in the bond price based on a constant yield, however, is treated as interest income, so the investor is required to pay taxes on imputed interest income of $553.66 − $549.69 = $3.97, as well as on the explicit coupon income of $40. If the bond's yield actually changes during the year, the difference between the bond's price and the "constant yield value" of $553.66 would be treated as capital gains income if the bond were sold at year-end.

CONCEPT
check   **10.7**
Suppose that the yield to maturity of the 4% coupon, 30-year maturity bond falls to 7% by the end of the first year, and that the investor sells the bond after the first year. If the investor's federal plus state tax rate on interest income is 38% and the combined tax rate on capital gains is 20%, what is the investor's after-tax rate of return?

10.5 | Default Risk And Bond Pricing

Although bonds generally *promise* a fixed flow of income, that income stream is not riskless unless the investor can be sure the issuer will not default on the obligation. While U.S. government bonds may be treated as free of default risk, this is not true of corporate bonds. If the company goes bankrupt, the bondholders will not receive all the payments they have been promised. Therefore, the actual payments on these bonds are uncertain, for they depend to some degree on the ultimate financial status of the firm.

Bond default risk is measured by Moody's Investor Services, Standard & Poor's Corporation, and Fitch Investors Service, all of which provide financial information on firms as well as the credit risk of large corporate and municipal bond issues. International sovereign bonds, which also entail default risk, especially in emerging markets, also are commonly rated for default risk. Each rating firm assigns letter grades to reflect its assessment of bond safety. The top rating is AAA or Aaa. Moody's modifies each rating class with a 1, 2, or 3 suffix (e.g., Aaa1, Aaa2, Aaa3) to provide a finer gradation of ratings. The other agencies use a + or − modification.

investment grade bond

A bond rated BBB and above by Standard & Poor's, or Baa and above by Moody's.

Those rated BBB or above (S&P, Fitch) or Baa and above (Moody's) are considered **investment grade bonds,** while lower-rated bonds are classified as **speculative grade** or **junk bonds.** Certain regulated institutional investors such as insurance companies have not always been allowed to invest in speculative grade bonds.

Figure 10.8 provides the definitions of each bond rating classification.

speculative grade or junk bond

A bond rated BB or lower by Standard & Poor's, or Ba or lower by Moody's, or an unrated bond.

Junk Bonds

Junk bonds, also known as *high-yield bonds,* are nothing more than speculative grade (low-rated or unrated) bonds. Before 1977, almost all junk bonds were "fallen angels," that is, bonds issued by firms that originally had investment grade ratings but that had since been downgraded. In 1977, however, firms began to issue "original-issue junk."

Much of the credit for this innovation is given to Drexel Burnham Lambert, and especially its trader, Michael Milken. Drexel had long enjoyed a niche as a junk bond trader and had established a network of potential investors in junk bonds. Firms not able to muster an investment grade rating were happy to have Drexel (and other investment bankers) market their bonds directly to the public, as this opened up a new source of financing. Junk issues were a lower-cost financing alternative than borrowing from banks.

High-yield bonds gained considerable notoriety in the 1980s when they were used as financing vehicles in leveraged buyouts and hostile takeover attempts. Shortly thereafter, however, the legal difficulties of Drexel and Michael Milken in connection with Wall Street's insider trading scandals of the late 1980s tainted the junk bond market.

At the height of Drexel's difficulties, the high-yield bond market nearly dried up but eventually rebounded dramatically. However, it is worth noting that the average credit quality of newly issued high-yield debt today is higher than the average quality in the boom years of the 1980s.

Of course, in periods of financial stress, junk bonds are more vulnerable than investment grade bonds. During the credit crisis of 2008, prices on these bonds fell dramatically, and their yields to maturity rose equally dramatically. The spread between the Treasury bond yields on junk bonds widened from around 3% in early 2007 to an astonishing 15% by the start of 2009.

Bond Ratings				
	Very High Quality	**High Quality**	**Speculative**	**Very Poor**
Standard & Poor's	AAA AA	A BBB	BB B	CCC D
Moody's	Aaa Aa	A Baa	Ba B	Caa C

At times both Moody's and Standard & Poor's use adjustments to these ratings. S&P uses plus and minus signs: A+is the strongest A rating and A−the weakest. Moody's uses a 1, 2, or 3 designation, with 1 indicating the strongest.

Moody's	S&P	
Aaa	AAA	Debt rated Aaa and AAA has the highest rating. Capacity to pay interest and principal is extremely strong.
Aa	AA	Debt rated Aa and AA has a very strong capacity to pay interest and repay principal. Together with the highest rating, this group comprises the high-grade bond class.
A	A	Debt rated A has a strong capacity to pay interest and repay principal, although it is somewhat more susceptible to the adverse effects of changes in circumstances and economic conditions than debt in higher-rated categories.
Baa	BBB	Debt rated Baa and BBB is regarded as having an adequate capacity to pay interest and repay principal. Whereas it normally exhibits adequate protection parameters, adverse economic conditions or changing circumstances are more likely to lead to a weakened capacity to pay interest and repay principal for debt in this category than in higher-rated categories. These bonds are medium grade obligations.
Ba B Caa Ca	BB B CCC CC	Debt rated in these categories is regarded, on balance, as predominantly speculative with respect to capacity to pay interest and repay principal in accordance with the terms of the obligation. BB and Ba indicate the lowest degree of speculation, and CC and Ca the highest degree of speculation. Although such debt will likely have some quality and protective characteristics, these are outweighed by large uncertainties or major risk exposures to adverse conditions. Some issues may be in default.
C	C	This rating is reserved for income bonds on which no interest is being paid.
D	D	Debt rated D is in default, and payment of interest and/or repayment of principal is in arrears.

FIGURE 10.8

Definitions of each bond rating class

Sources: From Stephen A. Ross, Randolph W. Westerfield, and Jeffrey F. Jaffe, *Corporate Finance,* McGraw-Hill Publishing. Data from various editions of *Standard & Poor's Bond Guide* and *Moody's Bond Guide.*

Determinants of Bond Safety

Bond rating agencies base their quality ratings largely on an analysis of the level and trend of some of the issuer's financial ratios. The key ratios used to evaluate safety are:

1. *Coverage ratios.* Ratios of company earnings to fixed costs. For example, the *times-interest-earned ratio* is the ratio of earnings before interest payments and taxes to interest obligations. The *fixed-charge coverage ratio* includes lease payments and sinking fund payments with interest obligations to arrive at the ratio of earnings to all fixed cash obligations. Low or falling coverage ratios signal possible cash flow difficulties.

2. *Leverage ratio.* Debt-to-equity ratio. A too-high leverage ratio indicates excessive indebtedness, signaling the possibility the firm will be unable to earn enough to satisfy the obligations on its bonds.

TABLE 10.3
Financial ratios and default risk by rating class, long-term debt

	Three-Year (2002 to 2004) Medians						
	AAA	AA	A	BBB	BB	B	CCC
EBIT interest coverage multiple	23.8	19.5	8.0	4.7	2.5	1.2	0.4
EBITDA interest coverage multiple	25.5	24.6	10.2	6.5	3.5	1.9	0.9
Funds from operations/total debt (%)	203.3	79.9	48.0	35.9	22.4	11.5	5.0
Free operating cash flow/total debt (%)	127.6	44.5	25.0	17.3	8.3	2.8	(002.1)
Total debt/EBITDA multiple	0.4	0.9	1.6	2.2	3.5	5.3	7.9
Return on capital (%)	27.6	27.0	17.5	13.4	11.3	8.7	3.2
Total debt/total debt + equity (%)	12.4	28.3	37.5	42.5	53.7	75.9	113.5

Note: EBITDA is earnings before interest, taxes, depreciation, and amortization.

Source: *Corporate Rating Criteria*, Standard & Poor's, 2006. Reproduced by permission of Standard & Poor's, a division of The McGraw-Hill Companies, Inc.

3. *Liquidity ratios.* The two common liquidity ratios are the *current ratio* (current assets/current liabilities) and the *quick ratio* (current assets excluding inventories/current liabilities). These ratios measure the firm's ability to pay bills coming due with its most liquid assets.

4. *Profitability ratios.* Measures of rates of return on assets or equity. Profitability ratios are indicators of a firm's overall performance. The *return on assets* (earnings before interest and taxes divided by total assets) or return on equity (net income/equity) are the most popular of these measures. Firms with higher return on assets or equity should be better able to raise money in security markets because they offer prospects for better returns on the firm's investments.

5. *Cash flow-to-debt ratio.* This is the ratio of total cash flow to outstanding debt.

Standard & Poor's periodically computes median values of selected ratios for firms in several rating classes, which we present in Table 10.3. Of course, ratios must be evaluated in the context of industry standards, and analysts differ in the weights they place on particular ratios. Nevertheless, Table 10.3 demonstrates the tendency of ratios to improve along with the firm's rating class. And default rates vary dramatically with bond rating. Historically, only about 1% of bonds originally rated AA or better at issuance had defaulted after 15 years. That ratio is around 7.5% for BBB-rated bonds, and 40% for B-rated bonds. Credit risk clearly varies dramatically across rating classes.

Bond Indentures

indenture

The document defining the contract between the bond issuer and the bondholder.

In addition to specifying a payment schedule, the bond **indenture,** which is the contract between the issuer and the bondholder, also specifies a set of restrictions that protect the rights of the bondholders. Such restrictions include provisions relating to collateral, sinking funds, dividend policy, and further borrowing. The issuing firm agrees to these so-called protective covenants in order to market its bonds to investors concerned about the safety of the bond issue.

sinking fund

A bond indenture that calls for the issuer to periodically repurchase some proportion of the outstanding bonds prior to maturity.

Sinking funds Bonds call for the payment of par value at the end of the bond's life. This payment constitutes a large cash commitment for the issuer. To help ensure that the commitment does not create a cash flow crisis, the firm may agree to establish a **sinking fund** to spread the payment burden over several years. The fund may operate in one of two ways:

1. The firm may repurchase a fraction of the outstanding bonds in the open market each year.

2. The firm may purchase a fraction of outstanding bonds at a special call price associated with the sinking fund provision. The firm has an option to purchase the bonds at either the market price or the sinking fund price, whichever is lower. To allocate the burden of the sinking fund call fairly among bondholders, the bonds chosen for the call are selected at random based on serial number.[11]

The sinking fund call differs from a conventional call provision in two important ways. First, the firm can repurchase only a limited fraction of the bond issue at the sinking fund call price. At best, some indentures allow firms to use a *doubling option,* which allows repurchase of double the required number of bonds at the sinking fund call price. Second, while callable bonds generally have call prices above par value, the sinking fund call price usually is set at the bond's par value.

Although sinking funds ostensibly protect bondholders by making principal repayment more likely, they can hurt the investor. The firm will choose to buy back discount bonds (selling below par) at their market price, while exercising its option to buy back premium bonds (selling above par) at par. Therefore, if interest rates fall and bond prices rise, a firm will benefit from the sinking fund provision that enables it to repurchase its bonds at below-market prices. In these circumstances, the firm's gain is the bondholder's loss.

One bond issue that does not require a sinking fund is a *serial bond* issue in which the firm sells bonds with staggered maturity dates. As bonds mature sequentially, the principal repayment burden for the firm is spread over time just as it is with a sinking fund. Serial bonds do not include call provisions. Unlike sinking fund bonds, serial bonds do not confront security holders with the risk that a particular bond may be called for the sinking fund. The disadvantage of serial bonds, however, is that the bonds of each maturity date are different bonds, which reduces the liquidity of the issue. Trading these bonds, therefore, is more expensive.

Subordination of further debt   One of the factors determining bond safety is the total outstanding debt of the issuer. If you bought a bond today, you would be understandably distressed to see the firm tripling its outstanding debt tomorrow. Your bond would be riskier than it appeared when you bought it. To prevent firms from harming bondholders in this manner, **subordination clauses** restrict the amount of their additional borrowing. Additional debt might be required to be subordinated in priority to existing debt; that is, in the event of bankruptcy, *subordinated* or *junior* debtholders will not be paid unless and until the prior senior debt is fully paid off.

subordination clauses

Restrictions on additional borrowing that stipulate that senior bondholders will be paid first in the event of bankruptcy.

Dividend restrictions   Covenants also limit the dividends firms may pay. These limitations protect the bondholders because they force the firm to retain assets rather than pay them out to stockholders. A typical restriction disallows payments of dividends if cumulative dividends paid since the firm's inception exceed cumulative retained earnings plus proceeds from sales of stock.

Collateral   Some bonds are issued with specific collateral behind them. **Collateral** is a particular asset of the firm that the bondholders receive if the firm defaults. If the collateral is property, the bond is called a *mortgage bond.* If the collateral takes the form of other securities held by the firm, the bond is a *collateral trust bond.* In the case of equipment, the bond is known as an *equipment obligation bond.* This last form of collateral is used most commonly by firms such as railroads, where the equipment is fairly standard and can be easily sold to another firm should the firm default and the bondholders acquire the collateral.

collateral

A specific asset pledged against possible default on a bond.

Because of the collateral that backs them, collateralized bonds generally are considered safer. General **debenture** bonds by contrast do not provide for specific collateral; they are *unsecured,* and bond risk depends on the general earning power of the firm. If the firm defaults, debenture owners become general creditors of the firm. Because they are safer, collateralized bonds generally offer lower yields than general debentures.

debenture

A bond not backed by specific collateral.

---

[11]While it is uncommon, the sinking fund provision also may call for periodic payments to a trustee, with the payments invested so that the accumulated sum can be used for retirement of the entire issue at maturity.

FIGURE 10.9

Callable bond issued by Mobil

Source: *Moody's Industrial Manual*, Moody's Investor Services, 1997.

& Mobil Corp. debenture 8s, due 2032:
Rating — Aa2

AUTH — $250,000,000.
OUTSTG — Dec. 31, 1993, $250,000,000.
DATED — Oct. 30, 1991.
INTEREST — F&A 12.
TRUSTEE — Chemical Bank.
DENOMINATION — Fully registered, $1,000 and integral multiples thereof. Transferable and exchangeable without service charge.
CALLABLE — As a whole or in part, at any time, on or after Aug. 12, 2002, at the option of Co. on at least 30 but not more than 60 days' notice to each Aug. 11 as follows:

2003	105.007	2004	104.756	2005	104.506
2006	104.256	2007	104.005	2008	103.755
2009	103.505	2010	103.254	2011	103.004
2012	102.754	2013	102.503	2014	102.253
2015	102.003	2016	101.752	2017	101.502
2018	101.252	2019	101.001	2020	100.751
2021	100.501	2022	100.250		

and thereafter at 100 plus accrued interest.
SECURITY — Not secured. Ranks equally with all other unsecured and unsubordinated indebtedness of Co. Co. nor any Affiliate will not incurr any indebtedness; provided that Co. will not create as security for any indebtedness for borrowed money, any mortgage, pledge, security interest or lien on any stock or indebtedness is directly owned by Co., without effectively providing that the debt securities shall be secured equally and ratably with such indebtedness, so long as such indebtedness shall be so secured.
INDENTURE MODIFICATION — Indenture may be modified, except as provided with, consent of 66⅔% of debs. outstg.
RIGHTS ON DEFAULT — Trustee, or 25% of debs. outstg., may declare principal dua nad payable (30 days' grace for payment of interest).
LISTED — On New York Stock Exchange.
PURPOSE — Proceeds used for general corporate purposes.
OFFERED — ($250,000,000) at 99.51 plus accrued interest (proceeds to Co., 99.11) on Aug. 5, 1992 thru Merrill Lynch & Co., Donaldson, Lufkin & Jenerette Securities Corp., PaineWebber Inc., Prudential Securities Inc., Smith Barney, Harris Upham & Co. Inc. and associates.

Figure 10.9 shows the terms of a bond issued by Mobil as described in *Moody's Industrial Manual*. The terms of the bond are typical and illustrate many of the indenture provisions we have mentioned. The bond is registered and listed on the NYSE. It was issued in 1991, but it was not callable until 2002. Although the call price started at 105.007% of par value, it falls gradually until it reaches par after 2020.

Yield to Maturity and Default Risk

Because corporate bonds are subject to default risk, we must distinguish between the bond's promised yield to maturity and its expected yield. The promised or stated yield will be realized only if the firm meets the obligations of the bond issue. Therefore, the stated yield is the *maximum possible* yield to maturity of the bond. The expected yield to maturity must take into account the possibility of a default.

For example, in October 2008, as Ford Motor Company struggled, its 6.625% coupon bonds due in 2028 were rated CCC and were selling at about 33% of par value, resulting in a yield to maturity of about 20%. Investors did not really believe the expected rate of return on these bonds was 20%. They recognized the distinct possibility that bondholders would not receive all the payments promised in the bond contract and that the yield based on *expected* cash flows was far less than the yield based on *promised* cash flows.

EXAMPLE 10.10

Expected versus Promised Yield

Suppose a firm issued a 9% coupon bond 20 years ago. The bond now has 10 years left until its maturity date but the firm is having financial difficulties. Investors believe that the firm will be able to make good on the remaining interest payments but that at the maturity date, the firm will be forced into bankruptcy, and bondholders will receive only 70% of par value. The bond is selling at $750. Yield to maturity (YTM) would then be calculated using the following inputs:

	Expected YTM	Stated YTM
Coupon payment	$45	$45
Number of semiannual periods	20 periods	20 periods
Final payment	$700	$1,000
Price	$750	$750

The yield to maturity based on promised payments is 13.7%. Based on the expected payment of $700 at maturity, however, the yield would be only 11.6%. The stated yield to maturity is greater than the yield to maturity investors actually expect to receive.

Example 10.10 suggests that when a bond becomes more subject to default risk, its price will fall, and therefore its promised yield to maturity will rise. Therefore, the default premium,

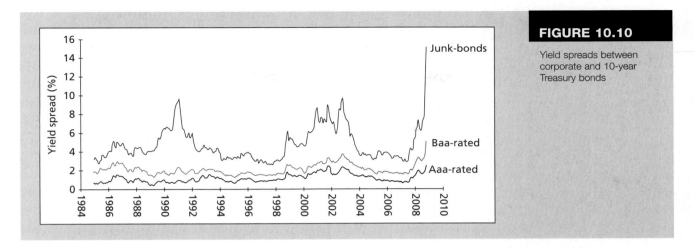

FIGURE 10.10

Yield spreads between corporate and 10-year Treasury bonds

the spread between the stated yield to maturity and that on otherwise comparable Treasury bonds, will rise. However, its expected yield to maturity, which ultimately is tied to the systematic risk of the bond, will be far less affected. Let's continue the example.

EXAMPLE | **10.11**

Default Risk and the Default Premium

Suppose that the condition of the firm in Example 10.10 deteriorates further, and investors now believe that the bond will pay off only 55% of face value at maturity. Investors now demand an expected yield to maturity of 12% (i.e., 6% semiannually), which is .4% higher than in Example 10.10. But the price of the bond will fall from $750 to $688 [$n = 20$; $i = 6$; FV = 550; PMT = $45]. At this price, the stated yield to maturity based on promised cash flows is 15.2%. While the expected yield to maturity has increased by .4%, the drop in price has caused the promised yield to maturity (and the default premium) to rise by 1.5%.

To compensate for the possibility of default, corporate bonds must offer a **default premium.** The default premium is the difference between the promised yield on a corporate bond and the yield of an otherwise identical government bond that is riskless in terms of default. If the firm remains solvent and actually pays the investor all of the promised cash flows, the investor will realize a higher yield to maturity than would be realized from the government bond. If, however, the firm goes bankrupt, the corporate bond is likely to provide a lower return than the government bond. The corporate bond has the potential for both better and worse performance than the default-free Treasury bond. In other words, it is riskier.

The pattern of default premiums offered on risky bonds is sometimes called the *risk structure of interest rates.* The greater the default risk, the higher the default premium. Figure 10.10 shows spreads between yields to maturity of bonds of different risk classes since 1984. You can see here clear evidence of default-risk premiums on promised yields. Note for example, the incredible run-up of credit spreads during the crisis of 2008–2009.

default premium

The increment to promised yield that compensates the investor for default risk.

Credit Default Swaps

A **credit default swap** (CDS) is in effect an insurance policy on the default risk of a corporate bond or loan. To illustrate, the annual premium in November 2008 on a five-year Citigroup CDS was about 2%, meaning that the CDS buyer would pay the seller an annual premium of $2 for each $100 of bond principal. The seller collects these annual payments for the term of the contract, but must compensate the buyer for loss of bond value in the event of a default.[12] That compensation can take two forms. The CDS buyer may deliver a defaulted bond to the

credit default swap

An insurance policy on the default risk of a corporate bond or loan.

---

[12]Actually, credit default swaps may pay off even short of an actual default. The contract specifies which particular "credit events" will trigger a payment. For example, restructuring (rewriting the terms of a firm's outstanding debt as an alternative to formal bankruptcy proceedings) may be defined as a triggering credit event.

FIGURE 10.11

Prices of credit default swaps
on several financial firms.

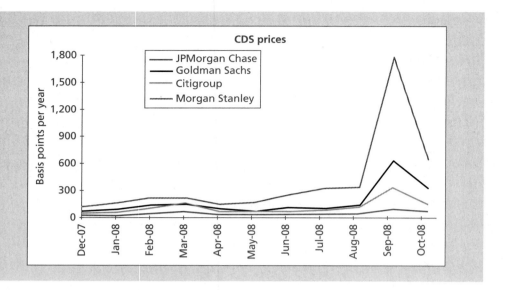

seller in return for the bond's par value. This is called *physical settlement*. Alternatively, the seller may pay the buyer the difference between the par value of the bond and its market price (even in a default, the bond will still sell at a positive price because there is some recovery of value to creditors in a bankruptcy). This is called *cash settlement*.

As originally envisioned, credit default swaps were designed to allow lenders to buy protection against losses on sizable loans. The natural buyers of CDSs would then be large bondholders or banks that had made large loans and wished to enhance the creditworthiness of those loans. Even if the borrowing firm had shaky credit standing, the "insured" debt would be as safe as the issuer of the CDS. An investor holding a bond with a BB rating could in principle raise the effective quality of the debt to AAA by buying a CDS on the issuer.

This insight suggests how CDS contracts should be priced. If a BB-rated bond bundled with insurance via a CDS is effectively equivalent to a AAA-rated bond, then the fair price of the swap ought to approximate the yield spread between AAA-rated and BB-rated bonds.[13] The risk structure of interest rates and CDS prices ought to be tightly aligned.

Figure 10.11 shows the sharp run-up in the prices of five-year CDSs on several financial firms in the months running up to the Lehman Brothers bankruptcy in September 2008. As perceived credit risk increased, so did the price of insuring their debt.

While CDSs were conceived as a form of bond insurance, it wasn't long before investors realized that they could be used to speculate on the financial health of particular companies. As Figure 10.11 makes clear, someone in August 2008 wishing to bet against the financial sector might have purchased CDS contracts on those firms and would have profited as CDS prices spiked in September. In fact, hedge fund manager John Paulson famously did just this. His bearish bets in 2007–2008 on commercial banks and Wall Street firms as well as on some riskier mortgage-backed securities made his funds more than $15 billion, bringing him a personal payoff of more than $3.7 billion.

In principle, with traders establishing CDS contracts purely to speculate on other firms, there can actually be more contracts outstanding than there are physical bonds to insure. As Lehman Brothers entered bankruptcy, about $400 billion of Lehman CDS contracts were outstanding, despite the fact that its total debt was only around $155 billion. However, while this apparent imbalance was widely noted at the time, it greatly overstated the true mismatch. That is because

---

[13]We say "approximately" because there are some differences between highly rated bonds and bonds synthetically enhanced with credit default swaps. For example, the term of the swap may not match the maturity of the bond. Tax treatment of coupon payments versus swap payments may differ, as may the liquidity of the bonds. Finally, some CDSs may entail one-time up-front payments as well as annual premiums.

CREDIT DEFAULT SWAPS, SYSTEMIC RISK, AND THE CREDIT CRISIS OF 2008

The credit crisis of 2008, when lending among banks and other financial institutions effectively seized up, was in large measure a crisis of transparency. The biggest problem was a widespread lack of confidence in the financial standing of counterparties to a trade. If one institution could not be confident that another would remain solvent, it would understandably be reluctant to offer it a loan. When doubt about the credit exposure of customers and trading partners spiked to levels not seen since the Great Depression, the market for loans dried up.

Credit default swaps were particularly cited for fostering doubts about counterparty reliability. By August 2008, $63 trillion of such swaps were reportedly outstanding. (By comparison, U.S. gross domestic product in 2008 was about $14 trillion.) As the subprime-mortgage market collapsed and the economy seemed sure to enter a recession, the potential obligations on these contracts ballooned to levels previously considered unimaginable and the ability of CDS sellers to honor their commitments was in doubt. For example, the huge insurance firm AIG alone had sold more than $400 billion of CDS contracts on subprime mortgages and other loans and was days from insolvency. But AIG's insolvency would have triggered the insolvency of other firms that had relied on its promise of protection against loan defaults. These in turn might have triggered further defaults. In the end, the government felt compelled to rescue AIG to prevent a chain reaction of insolvencies.

Counterparty risk and lax reporting requirements made it effectively impossible to tease out firms' exposures to credit risk. One problem was that CDS positions do not have to be accounted for on balance sheets. And the possibility of one default setting off a sequence of further defaults means that lenders may be exposed to the default of an institution with which it does not even directly trade. Such knock-on effects create *systemic risk*, in which the entire financial system can freeze up. With the ripple effects of bad debt extending in ever-widening circles, it can seem imprudent to lend to anyone.

The aftermath of the credit crisis of 2008 will inevitably bring new regulation and reforms. Among these will almost surely be the creation of a central clearing house for credit derivatives such as CDS contracts. Such a system would foster transparency of positions, allow netting of offsetting positions, and require daily recognition of gains or losses on positions through a margin or collateral account. If losses were to mount, positions would have to be unwound before growing to unsustainable levels. Allowing traders to accurately assess counterparty risk, and limiting such risk through margin accounts and the extra backup of the clearing house, would go a long way in limiting systemic risk.

---

many traders had offset CDS positions established at one date with opposite positions established at a later date. The widely cited $400 billion figure was the gross value of outstanding contracts and did not net out these offsetting positions. In the end, it seems that only about $7 billion needed to change hands to settle the CDS contracts.

Nevertheless, this episode highlighted the utter lack of transparency about firms' CDS obligations. Such uncertainty about firms' exposures to the credit risk of others gave rise to doubts about their own financial stability. The nearby box notes that this lack of transparency was a contributing factor in the credit meltdown of 2008.

10.6 | The Yield Curve

Return to Figure 10.1 again, and you will see that while yields to maturity on bonds of various maturities are reasonably similar, yields do differ. Bonds with shorter maturities generally offer lower yields to maturity than longer term bonds. The graphical relationship between the yield to maturity and the term to maturity is called the **yield curve**. The relationship also is called the **term structure of interest rates** because it relates yields to maturity to the term (maturity) of each bond. The yield curve is published regularly and may be found in *The Wall Street Journal* or on the Web at sites such as Yahoo! Finance. Four such sets of curves are reproduced in Figure 10.12. Figure 10.12 illustrates that a wide range of yield curves may be observed in practice. Panel A is an essentially flat yield curve. Panel B is an upward-sloping curve, and Panel C is a downward-sloping, or "inverted" yield curve. Finally the yield curve in Panel D is hump shaped, first rising and then falling. Rising yield curves are most commonly observed. We will see why momentarily.

Why should bonds of differing maturity offer different yields? The two most plausible possibilities have to do with expectations of future rates and risk premiums. We will consider each of these arguments in turn.

yield curve

A graph of yield to maturity as a function of term to maturity.

term structure of interest rates

The relationship between yields to maturity and terms to maturity across bonds.

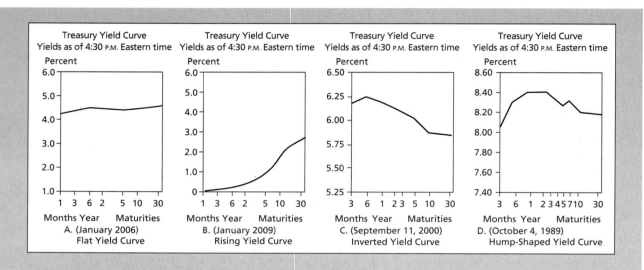

FIGURE 10.12

Treasury yield curves

The Expectations Theory

Suppose everyone in the market believes firmly that while the current one-year interest rate is 8%, the interest rate on one-year bonds next year will rise to 10%. What would this belief imply about the proper yield to maturity on two-year bonds issued today?

It is easy to see that an investor who buys the one-year bond and rolls the proceeds into another one-year bond in the following year will earn, on average, about 9% per year. This value is just the average of the 8% earned this year and the 10% expected for next year. More precisely, the investment will grow by a factor of 1.08 in the first year and 1.10 in the second year, for a total two-year growth factor of $1.08 \times 1.10 = 1.188$. This corresponds to an annual growth rate of 8.995% (because $1.08995^2 = 1.188$).

expectations hypothesis

The theory that yields to maturity are determined solely by expectations of future short-term interest rates.

For investments in two-year bonds to be competitive with the strategy of rolling over one-year bonds, these two-year bonds also must offer an average annual return of 8.995% over the two-year holding period. This is illustrated in Figure 10.13. The current short-term rate of 8% and the expected value of next year's short-term rate are depicted above the time line. The two-year rate that provides the same expected two-year total return is below the time line. In this example, therefore, the yield curve will be upward sloping; while one-year bonds offer an 8% yield to maturity, two-year bonds offer an 8.995% yield.

This notion is the essence of the **expectations hypothesis** of the yield curve, which asserts that the slope of the yield curve is attributable to expectations of changes in short-term rates. Relatively high yields on long-term bonds reflect expectations of future increases in rates, while relatively low yields on long-term bonds (a downward-sloping or inverted yield curve) reflect expectations of falling short-term rates.

One of the implications of the expectations hypothesis is that expected holding-period returns on bonds of all maturities ought to be about equal. Even if the yield curve is upward sloping

FIGURE 10.13

Returns to two two-year investment strategies

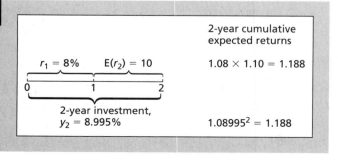

(so that two-year bonds offer higher yields to maturity than one-year bonds), this does not necessarily mean investors expect higher rates of return on the two-year bonds. As we've seen, the higher initial yield to maturity on the two-year bond is necessary to compensate investors for the fact that interest rates the next year will be even higher. Over the two-year period, and indeed over any holding period, this theory predicts that holding-period returns will be equalized across bonds of all maturities.

Suppose we buy the one-year zero-coupon bond with a current yield to maturity of 8%. If its face value is $1,000, its price will be $925.93, providing an 8% rate of return over the coming year. Suppose instead that we buy the two-year zero-coupon bond at its yield of 8.995%. Its price today is $1,000/(1.08995)^2 = $841.76. After a year passes, the zero will have a remaining maturity of only one year; based on the forecast that the one-year yield next year will be 10%, it then will sell for $1,000/1.10 = $909.09. The expected rate of return over the year is thus ($909.09 − $841.76)/$841.76 = .08, or 8%, precisely the same return provided by the one-year bond. This makes sense: If risk considerations are ignored when pricing the two bonds, they ought to provide equal expected rates of return.	**EXAMPLE 10.12** *Holding-Period Returns*

In fact, advocates of the expectations hypothesis commonly invert this analysis to *infer* the market's expectation of future short-term rates. They note that we do not directly observe the expectation of next year's rate, but we *can* observe yields on bonds of different maturities. Suppose, as in this example, we see that one-year bonds offer yields of 8% and two-year bonds offer yields of 8.995%. Each dollar invested in the two-year zero would grow after two years to $1 \times 1.08995^2 = $1.188. A dollar invested in the one-year zero would grow by a factor of 1.08 in the first year and, then, if reinvested or "rolled over" into another one-year zero in the second year, would grow by an additional factor of $1 + r_2$. Final proceeds would be $1 \times 1.08 \times (1 + r_2)$.

The final proceeds of the rollover strategy depend on the interest rate that actually transpires in year 2. However, we can solve for the second-year interest rate that makes the expected payoff of these two strategies equal. This "breakeven" value is called the **forward rate** for the second year, f_2, and is derived as follows:

forward rate

The inferred short-term rate of interest for a future period that makes the expected total return of a long-term bond equal to that of rolling over short-term bonds.

$$1.08995^2 = 1.08 \times (1 + f_2)$$

which implies that $f_2 = .10$, or 10%. Notice that the forward rate equals the market's expectation of the year-2 short rate. Hence, we conclude that when the expected total return of a long-term bond equals that of rolling over a short-term bond, the forward rate equals the expected short-term interest rate. This is why the theory is called the expectations hypothesis.

More generally, we obtain the forward rate by equating the return on an n-period zero-coupon bond with that of an $(n − 1)$-period zero-coupon bond rolled over into a one-year bond in year n:

$$(1 + y_n)^n = (1 + y_{n-1})^{n-1} (1 + f_n)$$

The actual total returns on the two n-year strategies will be equal if the short-term interest rate in year n turns out to equal f_n.

Suppose that two-year maturity bonds offer yields to maturity of 6%, and three-year bonds have yields of 7%. What is the forward rate for the third year? We could compare these two strategies as follows: 1. Buy a three-year bond. Total proceeds per dollar invested will be $$\$1 \times (1.07)^3 = \$1.2250$$	**EXAMPLE 10.13** *Forward Rates*

(continued)

EXAMPLE   10.13

*Forward Rates
(concluded)*

2. Buy a two-year bond. Reinvest all proceeds in a one-year bond in the third year, which will provide a return in that year of r_3. Total proceeds per dollar invested will be the result of two years' growth of invested funds at 6% plus the final year's growth at rate r_3:

$$\$1 \times (1.06)^2 \times (1 + r_3) = \$1.1236 \times (1 + r_3)$$

The forward rate is the rate in year 3 that makes the total return on these strategies equal:

$$1.2250 = 1.1236 \times (1 + f_3)$$

We conclude that the forward rate for the third year satisfies $(1 + f_3) = 1.0902$, so that f_3 is 9.02%.

While the expectations hypothesis gives us a tool to infer expectations of future market interest rates from the yield curve, it tells us nothing of what underlying considerations generated those expectations. Ultimately, interest rates reflect investors' expectations of the state of the macroeconomy. Not surprisingly, then, forward rates and the yield curve have proven themselves to be useful inputs for economic forecasts. The slope of the yield curve is one of the more important components of the index of leading economic indicators used to predict the course of economic activity. Inverted yield curves in particular, which imply falling interest rates, turn out to be among the best indicators of a coming recession.

The Liquidity Preference Theory

The expectations hypothesis starts from the assertion that bonds are priced so that "buy and hold" investments in long-term bonds provide the same returns as rolling over a series of short-term bonds. However, the risks of long- and short-term bonds are not equivalent.

We have seen that longer-term bonds are subject to greater interest rate risk than short-term bonds. As a result, investors in long-term bonds might require a risk premium to compensate them for this risk. In this case, the yield curve will be upward-sloping even in the absence of any expectations of future increases in rates. The source of the upward slope in the yield curve is investor demand for higher expected returns on assets that are perceived as riskier.

**liquidity preference
theory**

The theory that investors
demand a risk premium on
long-term bonds.

This viewpoint is called the **liquidity preference theory** of the term structure. Its name derives from the fact that shorter term bonds have more "liquidity" than longer term bonds, in the sense that they offer greater price certainty and trade in more active markets with lower bid-ask spreads. The preference of investors for greater liquidity makes them willing to hold these shorter term bonds even if they do not offer expected returns as high as those of longer term bonds.

liquidity premium

The extra expected return
demanded by investors as
compensation for the greater
risk of longer term bonds.

We can think of a **liquidity premium** as resulting from the extra compensation investors demand for holding longer term bonds with greater price risk. We measure it as the spread between the forward rate of interest and the expected short rate:

$$f_n = E(r_n) + \text{Liquidity premium}$$

In the absence of a liquidity premium, the forward rate would equal the expectation of the future short rate. But generally, we expect the forward rate to exceed that expectation to compensate investors for the lower liquidity of longer term bonds.

Advocates of the liquidity preference theory also note that issuers of bonds seem to prefer to issue long-term bonds. This allows them to lock in an interest rate on their borrowing for long periods and thus they may be willing to pay higher yields on these issues. In sum, borrowers demand higher rates on longer term bonds, and issuers are willing to pay higher rates on longer term bonds. The conjunction of these two preferences means longer term bonds typically should offer higher expected rates of return to investors than shorter term bonds. These expectations will show up in an upward-sloping yield curve.

According to the liquidity preference theory, forward rates of interest will exceed the market's expectations of future interest rates. Even if rates are expected to remain unchanged, the yield curve will slope upward because of the liquidity premium. That upward slope would be mistakenly attributed to expectations of rising rates if one were to use the pure expectations hypothesis to interpret the yield curve.

EXAMPLE 10.14

Liquidity Premia and the Yield Curve

Suppose that the short-term rate of interest is currently 8% and that investors expect it to remain at 8% next year. In the absence of a liquidity premium, with no expectation of a change in yields, the yield to maturity on two-year bonds also would be 8%, the yield curve would be flat, and the forward rate would be 8%. But what if investors demand a risk premium to invest in two-year rather than one-year bonds? If the liquidity premium is 1%, then the forward rate would be 8% + 1% = 9%, and the yield to maturity on the two-year bond would be determined by

$$(1 + y_2)^2 = 1.08 \times 1.09 = 1.1772$$

implying that $y_2 = .085 = 8.5\%$. Here, the yield curve is upward-sloping due solely to the liquidity premium embedded in the price of the longer term bond.

CONCEPT *check* **10.8**

Suppose that the expected value of the interest rate for year 3 remains at 8% but that the liquidity premium for that year is also 1%. What would be the yield to maturity on three-year zeros? What would this imply about the slope of the yield curve?

A Synthesis

Of course, we do not need to make an either/or choice between expectations and risk premiums. Both may influence the yield curve, and both should be considered in interpreting it.

Figure 10.14 shows two possible yield curves. In Figure 10.14A, rates are expected to rise over time. This fact, together with a liquidity premium, makes the yield curve steeply upward-sloping. In Figure 10.14B, rates are expected to fall, which by itself would make the yield curve slope downward. However, the liquidity premium lends something of an upward slope. The net effect of these two opposing factors is a "hump-shaped" curve.

These two examples make it clear that the combination of varying expectations and liquidity premiums can result in a wide array of yield-curve profiles. For example, an upward-sloping curve does not in and of itself imply expectations of higher future interest rates, because the

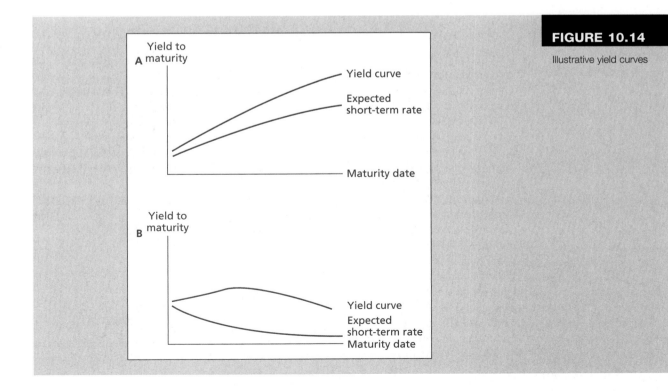

FIGURE 10.14

Illustrative yield curves

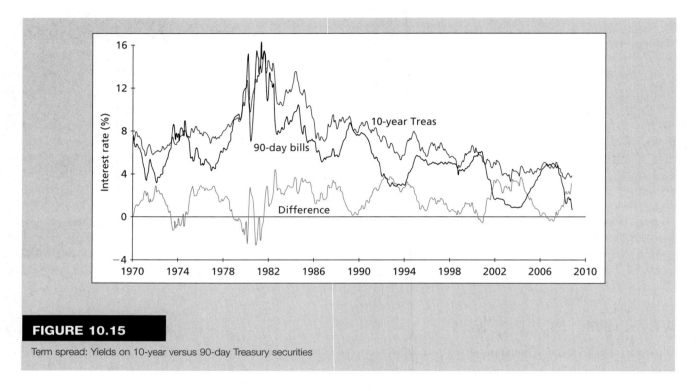

FIGURE 10.15

Term spread: Yields on 10-year versus 90-day Treasury securities

slope can result either from expectations or from risk premiums. A curve that is more steeply sloped than usual might signal expectations of higher rates, but even this inference is perilous.

Figure 10.15 presents yield spreads between 90-day T-bills and 10-year T-bonds since 1970. The figure shows that the yield curve is generally upward-sloping in that the longer-term bonds usually offer higher yields to maturity, despite the fact that rates could not have been expected to increase throughout the entire period. This tendency is the empirical basis for the liquidity premium doctrine that at least part of the upward slope in the yield curve must be due to a risk premium.

SUMMARY

- Debt securities are distinguished by their promise to pay a fixed or specified stream of income to their holders. The coupon bond is a typical debt security.
- Treasury notes and bonds have original maturities greater than one year. They are issued at or near par value, with their prices quoted net of accrued interest.
- Callable bonds should offer higher promised yields to maturity to compensate investors for the fact that they will not realize full capital gains should the interest rate fall and the bonds be called away from them at the stipulated call price. Bonds often are issued with a period of call protection. In addition, discount bonds selling significantly below their call price offer implicit call protection.
- Put bonds give the bondholder rather than the issuer the choice to terminate or extend the life of the bond.
- Convertible bonds may be exchanged, at the bondholder's discretion, for a specified number of shares of stock. Convertible bondholders "pay" for this option by accepting a lower coupon rate on the security.
- Floating-rate bonds pay a fixed premium over a referenced short-term interest rate. Risk is limited because the rate paid is tied to current market conditions.
- The yield to maturity is the single discount rate that equates the present value of a security's cash flows to its price. Bond prices and yields are inversely related. For premium bonds, the coupon rate is greater than the current yield, which is greater than the yield to maturity. These inequalities are reversed for discount bonds.

- The yield to maturity often is interpreted as an estimate of the average rate of return to an investor who purchases a bond and holds it until maturity. This interpretation is subject to error, however. Related measures are yield to call, realized compound yield, and expected (versus promised) yield to maturity.

- Treasury bills are U.S. government–issued zero-coupon bonds with original maturities of up to one year. Treasury STRIPS are longer term default-free zero-coupon bonds. Prices of zero-coupon bonds rise exponentially over time, providing a rate of appreciation equal to the interest rate. The IRS treats this price appreciation as imputed taxable interest income to the investor.

- When bonds are subject to potential default, the stated yield to maturity is the maximum possible yield to maturity that can be realized by the bondholder. In the event of default, however, that promised yield will not be realized. To compensate bond investors for default risk, bonds must offer default premiums, that is, promised yields in excess of those offered by default-free government securities. If the firm remains healthy, its bonds will provide higher returns than government bonds. Otherwise, the returns may be lower.

- Bond safety often is measured using financial ratio analysis. Bond indentures offer safeguards to protect the claims of bondholders. Common indentures specify sinking fund requirements, collateralization, dividend restrictions, and subordination of future debt.

- Credit default swaps provide insurance against the default of a bond or loan. The swap buyer pays an annual premium to the swap seller but collects a payment equal to lost value if the loan later goes into default.

- The term structure of interest rates is the relationship between time to maturity and term to maturity. The yield curve is a graphical depiction of the term structure. The forward rate is the break-even interest rate that would equate the total return on a rollover strategy to that of a longer-term zero-coupon bond.

- The expectations hypothesis holds that forward interest rates are unbiased forecasts of future interest rates. The liquidity preference theory, however, argues that long-term bonds will carry a risk premium known as a liquidity premium. A positive liquidity premium can cause the yield curve to slope upward even if no increase in short rates is anticipated.

KEY TERMS

bond, 288	floating-rate bonds, 291	realized compound
callable bonds, 290	forward rate, 317	return, 303
collateral, 311	horizon analysis, 304	reinvestment rate risk, 304
convertible bonds, 290	indenture, 310	sinking fund, 310
coupon rate, 288	investment grade	speculative grade or junk
credit default swap, 313	bonds, 308	bonds, 308
current yield, 300	liquidity preference	subordination clauses, 311
debenture, 311	theory, 318	term structure of interest
default premium, 313	liquidity premium, 318	rates, 315
discount bonds, 301	par value, 288	yield curve, 315
expectations hypothesis, 316	premium bonds, 301	yield to maturity, 298
face value, 288	put bond, 291	zero-coupon bond, 288

PROBLEM SETS

 Select problems are available in McGraw-Hill Connect. Please see the packaging options section of the preface for more information.

Basic

1. Define the following types of bonds:
   a. Catastrophe bond.
   b. Eurobond.
   c. Zero-coupon bond.

    d. Samurai bond.
    e. Junk bond.
    f. Convertible bond.
    g. Serial bond.
    h. Equipment obligation bond.
    i. Original issue discount bond.
    j. Indexed bond.

2. What is the option embedded in a callable bond? A puttable bond?

3. What would be the likely effect on the yield to maturity of a bond resulting from:
    a. An increase in the issuing firm's times interest-earned ratio?
    b. An increase in the issuing firm's debt-equity ratio?
    c. An increase in the issuing firm's quick ratio?

4. A coupon bond paying semiannual interest is reported as having an ask price of 117% of its $1,000 par value. If the last interest payment was made one month ago and the coupon rate is 6%, what is the invoice price of the bond?

5. A zero-coupon bond with face value $1,000 and maturity of five years sells for $746.22. What is its yield to maturity? What will happen to its yield to maturity if its price falls immediately to $730?

6. Why do bond prices go down when interest rates go up? Don't investors like high interest rates?

7. Two bonds have identical times to maturity and coupon rates. One is callable at 105, the other at 110. Which should have the higher yield to maturity? Why?

8. Consider a bond with a 10% coupon and with yield to maturity = 8%. If the bond's YTM remains constant, then in one year, will the bond price be higher, lower, or unchanged? Why?

9. A bond with an annual coupon rate of 4.8% sells for $970. What is the bond's current yield?

Intermediate

10. You buy an eight-year bond that has a 6% current yield and a 6% coupon (paid annually). In one year, promised yields to maturity have risen to 7%. What is your holding-period return?

11. The stated yield to maturity and realized compound yield to maturity of a (default-free) zero-coupon bond will always be equal. Why?

12. Which security has a higher *effective* annual interest rate?
    a. A three-month T-bill with face value of $100,000 currently selling at $97,645.
    b. A coupon bond selling at par and paying a 10% coupon semiannually.

13. Treasury bonds paying an 8% coupon rate with *semiannual* payments currently sell at par value. What coupon rate would they have to pay in order to sell at par if they paid their coupons *annually*?

14. Consider a bond paying a coupon rate of 10% per year semiannually when the market interest rate is only 4% per half-year. The bond has three years until maturity.
    a. Find the bond's price today and six months from now after the next coupon is paid.
    b. What is the total rate of return on the bond?

15. A 20-year maturity bond with par value $1,000 makes semiannual coupon payments at a coupon rate of 8%. Find the bond equivalent and effective annual yield to maturity of the bond if the bond price is:
    a. $950
    b. $1,000
    c. $1,050

16. Redo the previous problem using the same data, but now assume that the bond makes its coupon payments annually. Why are the yields you compute lower in this case?

17. Return to Table 10.1 and calculate both the real and nominal rates of return on the TIPS bond in the second and third years.

18. Fill in the table below for the following zero-coupon bonds, all of which have par values of $1,000.

Price	Maturity (years)	Yield to Maturity
$400	20	?
$500	20	?
$500	10	?
?	10	10%
?	10	8%
$400	?	8%

19. A bond has a par value of $1,000, a time to maturity of 10 years, and a coupon rate of 8% with interest paid annually. If the current market price is $800, what will be the approximate capital gain yield of this bond over the next year if its yield to maturity remains unchanged?

20. A bond with a coupon rate of 7% makes semiannual coupon payments on January 15 and July 15 of each year. *The Wall Street Journal* reports the ask price for the bond on January 30 at 100:02. What is the invoice price of the bond? The coupon period has 182 days.

21. A bond has a current yield of 9% and a yield to maturity of 10%. Is the bond selling above or below par value? Explain.

22. Is the coupon rate of the bond in the previous problem more or less than 9%?

23. Consider a bond with a settlement date of February 22, 2010, and a maturity date of March 15, 2018. The coupon rate is 5.5%. If the yield to maturity of the bond is 5.34% (bond equivalent yield, semiannual compounding), what is the list price of the bond on the settlement date? What is the accrued interest on the bond? What is the invoice price of the bond?

24. Now suppose the bond in the previous question is selling for 102. What is the bond's yield to maturity? What would the yield to maturity be at a price of 102 if the bond paid its coupons only once per year?

25. A 10-year bond of a firm in severe financial distress has a coupon rate of 14% and sells for $900. The firm is currently renegotiating the debt, and it appears that the lenders will allow the firm to reduce coupon payments on the bond to one-half the originally contracted amount. The firm can handle these lower payments. What are the stated and expected yields to maturity of the bonds? The bond makes its coupon payments annually.

26. A two-year bond with par value $1,000 making annual coupon payments of $100 is priced at $1,000. What is the yield to maturity of the bond? What will be the realized compound yield to maturity if the one-year interest rate next year turns out to be (*a*) 8%, (*b*) 10%, (*c*) 12%?

27. Suppose that today's date is April 15. A bond with a 10% coupon paid semiannually every January 15 and July 15 is listed in *The Wall Street Journal* as selling at an ask price of 101:04. If you buy the bond from a dealer today, what price will you pay for it?

28. Assume that two firms issue bonds with the following characteristics. Both bonds are issued at par.

Please visit us at
www.mhhe.com/bkm

Please visit us at
www.mhhe.com/bkm

	ABC Bonds	**XYZ Bonds**
Issue size	$1.2 billion	$150 million
Maturity	10 years*	20 years
Coupon	9%	10%
Collateral	First mortgage	General debenture
Callable	Not callable	In 10 years
Call price	None	110
Sinking fund	None	Starting in 5 years

*Bond is extendable at the discretion of the bondholder for an additional 10 years.

Ignoring credit quality, identify four features of these issues that might account for the lower coupon on the ABC debt. Explain.

29. A large corporation issued both fixed and floating-rate notes five years ago, with terms given in the following table:

	9% Coupon Notes	**Floating-Rate Note**
Issue size	$250 million	$280 million
Maturity	20 years	15 years
Current price (% of par)	93	98
Current coupon	9%	8%
Coupon adjusts	Fixed coupon	Every year
Coupon reset rule	—	1-year T-bill rate + 2%
Callable	10 years after issue	10 years after issue
Call price	106	102
Sinking fund	None	None
Yield to maturity	9.9%	—
Price range since issued	$85–$112	$97–$102

  a. Why is the price range greater for the 9% coupon bond than the floating-rate note?
  b. What factors could explain why the floating-rate note is not always sold at par value?
  c. Why is the call price for the floating-rate note not of great importance to investors?
  d. Is the probability of call for the fixed-rate note high or low?
  e. If the firm were to issue a fixed-rate note with a 15-year maturity, callable after 5 years at 106, what coupon rate would it need to offer to issue the bond at par value?
  f. Why is an entry for yield to maturity for the floating-rate note not appropriate?

30. A 30-year maturity, 8% coupon bond paying coupons semiannually is callable in five years at a call price of $1,100. The bond currently sells at a yield to maturity of 7% (3.5% per half-year).
  a. What is the yield to call?
  b. What is the yield to call if the call price is only $1,050?
  c. What is the yield to call if the call price is $1,100, but the bond can be called in two years instead of five years?

31. A newly issued 20-year maturity, zero-coupon bond is issued with a yield to maturity of 8% and face value $1,000. Find the imputed interest income in the first, second, and last year of the bond's life.

32. A newly issued 10-year maturity, 4% coupon bond making *annual* coupon payments is sold to the public at a price of $800. What will be an investor's taxable income from the bond over the coming year? The bond will not be sold at the end of the year. The bond is treated as an original-issue discount bond.

33. Masters Corp. issues two bonds with 20-year maturities. Both bonds are callable at $1,050. The first bond is issued at a deep discount with a coupon rate of 4% and a

price of $580 to yield 8.4%. The second bond is issued at par value with a coupon rate of 8.75%.
a. What is the yield to maturity of the par bond? Why is it higher than the yield of the discount bond?
b. If you expect rates to fall substantially in the next two years, which bond would you prefer to hold?
c. In what sense does the discount bond offer "implicit call protection"?

34. Under the expectations hypothesis, if the yield curve is upward-sloping, the market must expect an increase in short-term interest rates. True/false/uncertain? Why?

35. The yield curve is upward-sloping. Can you conclude that investors expect short-term interest rates to rise? Why or why not?

36. Assume you have a one-year investment horizon and are trying to choose among three bonds. All have the same degree of default risk and mature in 10 years. The first is a zero-coupon bond that pays $1,000 at maturity. The second has an 8% coupon rate and pays the $80 coupon once per year. The third has a 10% coupon rate and pays the $100 coupon once per year.
a. If all three bonds are now priced to yield 8% to maturity, what are their prices?
b. If you expect their yields to maturity to be 8% at the beginning of next year, what will their prices be then? What is your rate of return on each bond during the one-year holding period?

37. Under the liquidity preference theory, if inflation is expected to be falling over the next few years, long-term interest rates will be higher than short-term rates. True/false/uncertain? Why?

38. The current yield curve for default-free zero-coupon bonds is as follows:

Maturity (Years)	YTM
1	10%
2	11
3	12

a. What are the implied one-year forward rates?
b. Assume that the pure expectations hypothesis of the term structure is correct. If market expectations are accurate, what will the pure yield curve (that is, the yields to maturity on one- and two-year zero-coupon bonds) be next year?
c. If you purchase a two-year zero-coupon bond now, what is the expected total rate of return over the next year? What if you purchase a three-year zero-coupon bond? (*Hint:* Compute the current and expected future prices.) Ignore taxes.

39. The yield to maturity on one-year zero-coupon bonds is 8%. The yield to maturity on two-year zero-coupon bonds is 9%.
a. What is the forward rate of interest for the second year?
b. If you believe in the expectations hypothesis, what is your best guess as to the expected value of the short-term interest rate next year?
c. If you believe in the liquidity preference theory, is your best guess as to next year's short-term interest rate higher or lower than in (b)?

40. The following table contains spot rates and forward rates for three years. However, the labels got mixed up. Can you identify which row of the interest rates represents spot rates and which one the forward rates?

Year:	1	2	3
Spot rates or Forward rates?	10%	12%	14%
Spot rates or Forward rates?	10%	14.0364%	18.1078%

41. Consider the following $1,000 par value zero-coupon bonds:

Bond	Years until Maturity	Yield to Maturity
A	1	5%
B	2	6
C	3	6.5
D	4	7

According to the expectations hypothesis, what is the market's expectation of the one-year interest rate three years from now?

42. A newly issued bond pays its coupons once a year. Its coupon rate is 5%, its maturity is 20 years, and its yield to maturity is 8%.

a. Find the holding-period return for a one-year investment period if the bond is selling at a yield to maturity of 7% by the end of the year.

b. If you sell the bond after one year when its yield is 7%, what taxes will you owe if the tax rate on interest income is 40% and the tax rate on capital gains income is 30%? The bond is subject to original-issue discount (OID) tax treatment.

c. What is the after-tax holding-period return on the bond?

d. Find the realized compound yield *before taxes* for a two-year holding period, assuming that (i) you sell the bond after two years, (ii) the bond yield is 7% at the end of the second year, and (iii) the coupon can be reinvested for one year at a 3% interest rate.

e. Use the tax rates in part (b) to compute the *after-tax* two-year realized compound yield. Remember to take account of OID tax rules.

CFA Problems

1. The following multiple-choice problems are based on questions that appeared in past CFA examinations.

a. A bond with a call feature:
   (1) Is attractive because the immediate receipt of principal plus premium produces a high return.
   (2) Is more apt to be called when interest rates are high because the interest saving will be greater.
   (3) Will usually have a higher yield to maturity than a similar noncallable bond.
   (4) None of the above.

b. In which *one* of the following cases is the bond selling at a discount?
   (1) Coupon rate is greater than current yield, which is greater than yield to maturity.
   (2) Coupon rate, current yield, and yield to maturity are all the same.
   (3) Coupon rate is less than current yield, which is less than yield to maturity.
   (4) Coupon rate is less than current yield, which is greater than yield to maturity.

c. Consider a five-year bond with a 10% coupon selling at a yield to maturity of 8%. If interest rates remain constant, one year from now the price of this bond will be:
   (1) Higher
   (2) Lower
   (3) The same
   (4) Par

d. Which of the following statements is *true*?
   (1) The expectations hypothesis indicates a flat yield curve if anticipated future short-term rates exceed current short-term rates.
   (2) The basic conclusion of the expectations hypothesis is that the long-term rate is equal to the anticipated short-term rate.
   (3) The liquidity hypothesis indicates that, all other things being equal, longer maturities will have higher yields.

(4) The liquidity preference theory states that a rising yield curve necessarily implies that the market anticipates increases in interest rates.

2. On May 30, 2006, Janice Kerr is considering the newly issued 10-year AAA corporate bonds shown in the following exhibit:

Description	Coupon	Price	Callable	Call Price
Sentinal, due May 30, 2016	6.00%	100	Noncallable	NA
Colina, due May 30, 2016	6.20%	100	Currently callable	102

   a. Suppose that market interest rates decline by 100 basis points (i.e., 1%). Contrast the effect of this decline on the price of each bond.
   b. Should Kerr prefer the Colina over the Sentinal bond when rates are expected to rise or to fall?
   c. What would be the effect, if any, of an increase in the *volatility* of interest rates on the prices of each bond?

3. A convertible bond has the following features:

Coupon	5.25%
Maturity	June 15, 2017
Market price of bond	$77.50
Market price of underlying common stock	$28.00
Annual dividend	$1.20
Conversion ratio	20.83 shares

   Calculate the conversion premium for this bond.

4. *a.* Explain the impact on the offering yield of adding a call feature to a proposed bond issue.
   b. Explain the impact on the bond's expected life of adding a call feature to a proposed bond issue.
   c. Describe one advantage and one disadvantage of including callable bonds in a portfolio.

5. Bonds of Zello Corporation with a par value of $1,000 sell for $960, mature in five years, and have a 7% annual coupon rate paid semiannually.
   a. Calculate the:
      (1) Current yield.
      (2) Yield to maturity.
      (3) Horizon yield (also called realized compound return) for an investor with a three-year holding period and a reinvestment rate of 6% over the period. At the end of three years the 7% coupon bonds with two years remaining will sell to yield 7%.
   b. Cite *one* major shortcoming for *each* of the following fixed-income yield measures:
      (1) Current yield.
      (2) Yield to maturity.
      (3) Horizon yield (also called realized compound return).

Use data from the Standard & Poor's Market Insight Database at www.mhhe.com/edumarketinsight to answer the following question.

1. Use the *Financial Highlights* section of Market Insight to obtain Standard & Poor's bond rating of at least 10 firms in the database. Try to choose a sample with a wide range of bond ratings. Next use Market Insight's Annual Ratio Report to obtain, for each firm, the financial ratios tabulated in Table 10.3. What is the relationship between bond rating and these ratios? Can you tell from your sample which of these ratios are the more important determinants of bond rating?

WEB *master* DATA ON BOND ISSUES

The FINRA operates the TRACE (Trade Reporting and Compliance Engine) system, which reports over-the-counter secondary market trades of fixed income securities. Go to the FINRA home page at **www.finra.org** and click on the link for "Industry Professionals". Search (located at the top right) for the "TRACE Fact Book" and click the first link that appears. Find the detailed data tables and locate the table with information on issues, excluding convertible bonds (typically Table 1). For each of the last three years, calculate the following:

1. The percentage of bonds that were publicly traded and the percentage that were privately traded.

2. The percentage of bonds that were investment grade and the percentage that were high-yield.

3. The percentage of bonds that had fixed coupon rates and the percentage that had floating rates.

4. Do any patterns emerge over time?

5. Repeat the calculations using the information for convertible bond issues (typically in Table 2).

SOLUTIONS TO CONCEPT *checks*

10.1. The callable bond will sell at the *lower* price. Investors will not be willing to pay as much if they know that the firm retains a valuable option to reclaim the bond for the call price if interest rates fall.

10.2. At a semiannual interest rate of 3%, the bond is worth $40 \times$ Annuity factor(3%, 60) $+ \$1,000 \times$ PV factor(3%, 60) = \$1,276.76, which results in a capital gain of \$276.76. This exceeds the capital loss of \$189.29 (\$1,000 − \$810.71) when the interest rate increased to 5%.

10.3. Yield to maturity exceeds current yield, which exceeds coupon rate. Take as an example the 8% coupon bond with a yield to maturity of 10% per year (5% per half year). Its price is \$810.71, and therefore its current yield is 80/810.77 = 0.0987, or 9.87%, which is higher than the coupon rate but lower than the yield to maturity.

10.4. The current price of the bond can be derived from the yield to maturity. Using your calculator, set: $n = 40$ (semiannual periods); PMT = \$45 per period; FV = \$1,000; $i = 4\%$ per semiannual period. Calculate present value as \$1,098.96. Now we can calculate yield to call. The time to call is five years, or 10 semiannual periods. The price at which the bond will be called is \$1,050. To find yield to call, we set: $n = 10$ (semiannual periods); PMT = \$45 per period; FV = \$1,050; PV = \$1,098.96. Calculate the semiannual yield to call as 3.72%.

10.5. Price = \$70 $\times$ Annuity factor(8%, 1) + \$1,000 $\times$ PV factor(8%, 1) = \$990.74

$$\text{Rate of return to investor} = \frac{\$70 + (\$990.74 - \$982.17)}{\$982.17} = 0.080 = 8\%$$

10.6. By year-end, remaining maturity is 29 years. If the yield to maturity were still 8%, the bond would still sell at par and the holding-period return would be 8%. At a higher yield, price and return will be lower. Suppose the yield to maturity is 8.5%. With annual payments of \$80 and a face value of \$1,000, the price of the bond is \$946.70 ($n = 29$; $i = 8.5\%$; PMT = \$80; FV = \$1,000). The bond initially sold at \$1,000 when issued at the start of the year. The holding-period return is

$$\text{HPR} = \frac{80 + (946.70 - 1,000)}{1,000} = .0267 = 2.67\%$$

which is less than the initial yield to maturity of 8%.

10.7. At the lower yield, the bond price will be \$631.67 [$n = 29$, $i = 7\%$, FV = \$1,000, PMT = \$40]. Therefore, total after-tax income is

Coupon	$40 \times (1 - 0.38) =$	\$24.80
Imputed interest	$(\$553.66 - \$549.69) \times (1 - 0.38) =$	2.46
Capital gains	$(\$631.67 - \$553.66) \times (1 - 0.20) =$	62.41
Total income after taxes:		\$89.67

Rate of return = 89.67/549.69 = .163 = 16.3%

10.8. The yield to maturity on two-year bonds is 8.5%. The forward rate for the third year is $f_3 = 8\% + 1\% = 9\%$. We obtain the yield to maturity on three-year zeros from

$$(1 + y_3)^3 = (1 + y_2)^2 (1 + f_3) = 1.085^2 \times 1.09 = 1.2832$$

Therefore, $y_3 = .0867 = 8.67\%$. We note that the yield on one-year bonds is 8%, on two-year bonds is 8.5%, and on three-year bonds is 8.67%. The yield curve is upward-sloping due solely to the liquidity premium.

Chapter 11

Managing Bond Portfolios

After Studying This Chapter You Should Be Able To:

- Analyze the features of a bond that affect the sensitivity of its price to interest rates.

- Compute the duration of bonds.

- Formulate fixed-income immunization strategies for various investment horizons.

- Analyze the choices to be made in an actively managed bond portfolio.

In this chapter, we turn to various strategies that bond managers can pursue, making a distinction between passive and active strategies. A *passive investment strategy* takes market prices of securities as set fairly. Rather than attempting to beat the market by exploiting superior information or insight, passive managers act to maintain an appropriate risk-return balance given market opportunities. One special case of passive management is an immunization strategy that attempts to insulate the portfolio from interest rate risk.

An *active investment strategy* attempts to achieve returns that are more than commensurate with the risk borne. In the context of bond portfolios, this style of management can take two forms. Active managers either use interest rate forecasts to predict movements in the entire bond market, or they employ some form of intramarket analysis to identify particular sectors of the market (or particular securities) that are relatively mispriced.

Because interest rate risk is crucial to formulating both active and passive strategies, we begin our discussion with an analysis of the sensitivity of bond prices to interest rate fluctuations. This sensitivity is measured by the duration of the bond, and we devote considerable attention to what determines bond duration. We discuss several passive investment strategies, and show how duration-matching techniques can be used to immunize the holding-period return of a portfolio from interest rate risk. After examining the broad range of applications of the duration measure, we consider refinements in the way that interest rate sensitivity is measured, focusing on the concept of bond convexity. Duration is important in formulating active investment strategies as well, and we next explore several of these strategies. We conclude the chapter with a discussion of active fixed-income strategies. These include policies based on interest rate forecasting as well as intramarket analysis that seeks to identify relatively attractive sectors or securities within the fixed-income market.

11.1 Interest Rate Risk

You know already that there is an inverse relationship between bond prices and yields and that interest rates can fluctuate substantially. As interest rates rise and fall, bondholders experience capital losses and gains. It is these gains or losses that make fixed-income investments risky, even if the coupon and principal payments are guaranteed, as in the case of Treasury obligations.

Why do bond prices respond to interest rate fluctuations? In a competitive market, all securities must offer investors fair expected rates of return. If a bond is issued with an 8% coupon when competitive yields are 8%, then it will sell at par value. If the market rate rises to 9%, however, who would purchase an 8% coupon bond at par value? The bond price must fall until its expected return increases to the competitive level of 9%. Conversely, if the market rate falls to 7%, the 8% coupon on the bond is attractive compared to yields on alternative investments. Investors eager for that return will respond by bidding the bond price above its par value until the total rate of return falls to the market rate.

Interest Rate Sensitivity

The sensitivity of bond prices to changes in market interest rates is obviously of great concern to investors. To gain some insight into the determinants of interest rate risk, turn to Figure 11.1, which presents the percentage changes in price corresponding to changes in yield to maturity for four bonds that differ according to coupon rate, initial yield to maturity, and time to maturity. All four bonds illustrate that bond prices decrease when yields rise and that the price curve is convex, meaning that decreases in yields have bigger impacts on price than increases in yields of equal magnitude. We summarize these observations in the following two propositions:

1. *Bond prices and yields are inversely related: As yields increase, bond prices fall; as yields fall, bond prices rise.*
2. *An increase in a bond's yield to maturity results in a smaller price change than a decrease in yield of equal magnitude.*

Now compare the interest rate sensitivity of bonds A and B, which are identical except for maturity. Figure 11.1 shows that bond B, which has a longer maturity than bond A, exhibits greater sensitivity to interest rate changes. This illustrates another general property:

3. *Prices of long-term bonds tend to be more sensitive to interest rate changes than prices of short-term bonds.*

This is not surprising. If rates increase, for example, the bond is less valuable as its cash flows are discounted at a now-higher rate. The impact of the higher discount rate will be greater as that rate is applied to more-distant cash flows.

Notice that while bond B has six times the maturity of bond A, it has less than six times the interest rate sensitivity. Although interest rate sensitivity seems to increase with maturity, it does so less than proportionally as bond maturity increases. Therefore, our fourth property is that

4. *The sensitivity of bond prices to changes in yields increases at a decreasing rate as maturity increases. In other words, interest rate risk is less than proportional to bond maturity.*

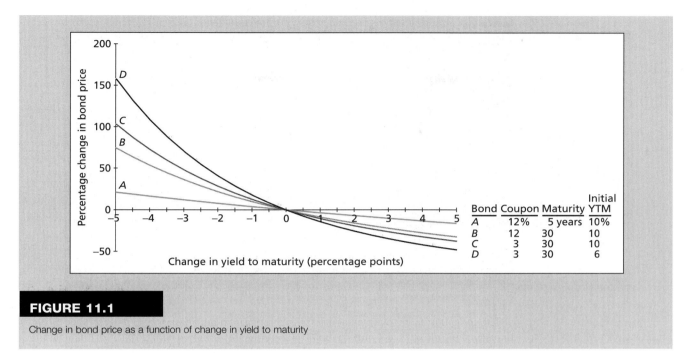

Bond	Coupon	Maturity	Initial YTM
A	12%	5 years	10%
B	12	30	10
C	3	30	10
D	3	30	6

FIGURE 11.1

Change in bond price as a function of change in yield to maturity

Bonds *B* and *C,* which are alike in all respects except for coupon rate, illustrate another point. The lower-coupon bond exhibits greater sensitivity to changes in interest rates. This turns out to be a general property of bond prices:

5. *Interest rate risk is inversely related to the bond's coupon rate. Prices of low-coupon bonds are more sensitive to changes in interest rates than prices of high-coupon bonds.*

Finally, bonds *C* and *D* are identical except for the yield to maturity at which the bonds currently sell. Yet bond *C,* with a higher yield to maturity, is less sensitive to changes in yields. This illustrates our final property:

6. *The sensitivity of a bond's price to a change in its yield is inversely related to the yield to maturity at which the bond currently is selling.*

The first five of these general properties were described by Malkiel (1962) and are sometimes known as Malkiel's bond-pricing relationships. The last property was demonstrated by Homer and Liebowitz (1972).

These six propositions confirm that maturity is a major determinant of interest rate risk. However, they also show that maturity alone is not sufficient to measure interest rate sensitivity. For example, bonds *B* and *C* in Figure 11.1 have the same maturity, but the higher coupon bond has less price sensitivity to interest rate changes. Obviously, we need to know more than a bond's maturity to quantify its interest rate risk.

To see why bond characteristics such as coupon rate or yield to maturity affect interest rate sensitivity, let's start with a simple numerical example.

Table 11.1 gives bond prices for 8% annual coupon bonds at different yields to maturity and times to maturity. (For simplicity, we assume coupons are paid once a year rather than semiannually.) The shortest term bond falls in value by less than 1% when the interest rate increases from 8% to 9%. The 10-year bond falls by 6.4% and the 20-year bond by more than 9%.

Let us now look at a similar computation using a zero-coupon bond rather than the 8% coupon bond. The results are shown in Table 11.2.

For maturities beyond one year, the price of the zero-coupon bond falls by a greater proportional amount than the price of the 8% coupon bond. The observation that long-term bonds

TABLE 11.1 Prices of 8% annual coupon bonds	Bond's Yield to Maturity	T = 1 Year	T = 10 Years	T = 20 Years
	8%	1,000.00	1,000.00	1,000.00
	9%	990.83	935.82	908.71
	Percent change in price*	−0.92%	−6.42%	−9.13%

*Equals value of bond at a 9% yield to maturity minus value of bond at (the original) 8% yield, divided by the value at 8% yield.

TABLE 11.2 Prices of zero-coupon bonds	Bond's Yield to Maturity	T = 1 Year	T = 10 Years	T = 20 Years
	8%	925.93	463.19	214.55
	9%	917.43	422.41	178.43
	Percent change in price*	−0.92%	−8.80%	−16.84%

*Equals value of bond at a 9% yield to maturity minus value of bond at (the original) 8% yield, divided by the value at 8% yield.

are more sensitive to interest rate movements than short-term bonds suggests that in some sense a zero-coupon bond represents a longer term investment than an equal-time-to-maturity coupon bond.

In fact, this insight about the effective maturity of a bond is a useful one that we can make mathematically precise. To start, note that the times to maturity of the two bonds in this example are not perfect measures of the long- or short-term nature of the bonds. The 8% bond makes many coupon payments, most of which come years before the bond's maturity date. Each payment may be considered to have its own "maturity date." In this sense, it is often useful to view a coupon bond as a "portfolio" of coupon payments. The *effective* maturity of the bond should be measured as some sort of average of the maturities of *all* the cash flows paid out by the bond. The zero-coupon bond, by contrast, makes only one payment at maturity. Its time to maturity is a well-defined concept.

A high-coupon rate bond has a higher fraction of its value tied to coupons rather than payment of par value, and so the portfolio is more heavily weighted toward the earlier, short-maturity payments, which give it lower "effective maturity." This explains Malkiel's fifth rule, that price sensitivity falls with coupon rate.

Similar logic explains our sixth rule, that price sensitivity falls with yield to maturity. A higher yield reduces the present value of all of the bond's payments, but more so for more distant payments. Therefore, at a higher yield, a higher fraction of the bond's value is due to its earlier payments, which have lower effective maturity and interest rate sensitivity. The overall sensitivity of the bond price to changes in yields is thus lower.

Duration

To deal with the concept of the "maturity" of a bond that makes many payments, we need a measure of the average maturity of the bond's promised cash flows to serve as a summary statistic of the effective maturity of the bond. This measure should also give us some information on the sensitivity of a bond to interest rate changes because we have noted that price sensitivity tends to increase with time to maturity.

Frederick Macaulay (1938) called the effective maturity concept the duration of the bond. **Macaulay's duration** equals the weighted average of the times to each coupon or principal payment made by the bond. The weight applied to each time to payment clearly should be related to the "importance" of that payment to the value of the bond. In fact, the weight for each payment time is the proportion of the total value of the bond accounted for by that payment, the present value of the payment divided by the bond price.

Macaulay's duration

A measure of the effective maturity of a bond, defined as the weighted average of the times until each payment, with weights proportional to the present value of the payment.

We define the weight, w_t, associated with the cash flow made at time t (denoted CF_t) as

$$w_t = \frac{CF_t/(1 + y)^t}{\text{Bond price}}$$

where y is the bond's yield to maturity. The numerator on the right-hand side of this equation is the present value of the cash flow occurring at time t, while the denominator is the present value of all the payments forthcoming from the bond. These weights sum to 1.0 because the sum of the cash flows discounted at the yield to maturity equals the bond price.

Using these values to calculate the weighted average of the times until the receipt of each of the bond's payments, we obtain Macaulay's formula for duration, denoted D.

$$D = \sum_{t=1}^{T} t \times w_t \qquad\qquad \textbf{(11.1)}$$

If we write out each term in the summation sign, we can express duration in the following equivalent equation

$$D = w_1 \quad + \quad 2w_2 \quad + \quad 3w_3 \quad + \quad 4w_4 \quad + \cdots + \; Tw_T$$

time until	weight of		time until	weight of
2nd cash flow	2nd CF		4th CF	4th CF

An example of how to apply Equation 11.1 appears in Spreadsheet 11.1, where we derive the durations of an 8% coupon and zero-coupon bond each with three years to maturity. We assume that the yield to maturity on each bond is 10%. The present value of each payment is

---

SPREADSHEET 11.1

Calculation of the duration of two bonds using Excel spreadsheet

eXcel

Please visit us at www.mhhe.com/bkm

	A	B	C	D	E	F
1	Interest rate:	10%				
2						
3		Time until			Payment		Column (B)
4		Payment			Discounted		x
5		(Years)		Payment	at 10%	Weight*	Column (E)
6	A. 8% coupon bond	1		80	72.727	0.0765	0.0765
7		2		80	66.116	0.0696	0.1392
8		3		1080	811.420	0.8539	2.5617
9	Sum:				950.263	1.0000	2.7774
10							
11	B. Zero-coupon bond	1		0	0.000	0.0000	0.0000
12		2		0	0.000	0.0000	0.0000
13		3		1000	751.315	1.0000	3.0000
14	Sum:				751.315	1.0000	3.0000
15							
16	*Weight = Present value of each payment (column D) divided by bond price						

	A	B	C	D	E	F
1	Interest rate:	0.1				
2						
3		Time until			Payment		Column (B)
4		Payment			Discounted		x
5		(Years)		Payment	at 10%	Weight	Column (E)
6	A. 8% coupon bond	1		80	=C6/(1+$B$1)^B6	=D6/D$9	=E6*B6
7		2		80	=C7/(1+$B$1)^B7	=D7/D$9	=E7*B7
8		3		1080	=C8/(1+$B$1)^B8	=D8/D$9	=E8*B8
9	Sum:				=SUM(D6:D8)	=D9/D$9	=SUM(F6:F8)
10							
11	B. Zero-coupon	1		0	=C11/(1+$B$1)^B11	=D11/D$14	=E11*B11
12		2		0	=C12/(1+$B$1)^B12	=D12/D$14	=E12*B12
13		3		1000	=C13/(1+$B$1)^B13	=D13/D$14	=E13*B13
14	Sum:				=SUM(D11:D13)	=D14/D$14	=SUM(F11:F13)

discounted at 10% for the number of years shown in column B. The weight associated with each payment time (column E) equals the present value of the payment (column D) divided by the bond price (the sum of the present values in column D).

The numbers in column F are the products of time to payment and payment weight. Each of these products corresponds to one of the terms in Equation 11.1. According to that equation, we can calculate the duration of each bond by adding the numbers in column F.

The duration of the zero-coupon bond is exactly equal to its time to maturity, three years. This makes sense for, with only one payment, the average time until payment must be the bond's maturity. The three-year coupon bond, in contrast, has a shorter duration of 2.7774 years.

While the top panel of the spreadsheet in Spreadsheet 11.1 presents numbers for our particular example, the bottom panel presents the formulas we actually entered in each cell. The inputs in the spreadsheet—specifying the cash flows the bond will pay—are given in columns B and C. In column D we calculate the present value of each cash flow using a discount rate of 10%, in column E we calculate the weights for Equation 11.1, and in column F we compute the product of time until payment and payment weight. Each of these terms corresponds to one of the terms in Equation 11.1. The sum of these terms, reported in cells F9 and F14, is therefore the duration of each bond. Using the spreadsheet, you can easily answer several "what if" questions such as the one in Concept Check 11.1.

CONCEPT check 11.1 Suppose the interest rate decreases to 9%. What will happen to the price and duration of each bond in Spreadsheet 11.1?

Duration is a key concept in bond portfolio management for at least three reasons. First, it is a simple summary measure of the effective average maturity of the portfolio. Second, it turns out to be an essential tool in immunizing portfolios from interest rate risk. We will explore this application in the next section. Third, duration is a measure of the interest rate sensitivity of a bond portfolio, which we explore here.

We have already noted that long-term bonds are more sensitive to interest rate movements than short-term bonds. The duration measure enables us to quantify this relationship. It turns out that, when interest rates change, the percentage change in a bond's price is proportional to its duration. Specifically, the proportional change in a bond's price can be related to the change in its yield to maturity, y, according to the rule

$$\frac{\Delta P}{P} = - D \times \left[\frac{\Delta(1 + y)}{1 + y} \right]$$ **(11.2)**

The proportional price change equals the proportional change in (1 plus the bond's yield) times the bond's duration. Therefore, bond price volatility is proportional to the bond's duration, and duration becomes a natural measure of interest rate exposure.[1] This relationship is key to interest rate risk management.

modified duration

Macaulay's duration divided by 1 + yield to maturity. Measures interest rate sensitivity of bond.

Practitioners commonly use Equation 11.2 in a slightly different form. They define **modified duration** as $D^* = D/(1 + y)$ and rewrite Equation 11.2 as

$$\frac{\Delta P}{P} = - D^* \Delta y$$ **(11.3)**

The percentage change in bond price is just the product of modified duration and the change in the bond's yield to maturity. Because the percentage change in the bond price is proportional to modified duration, modified duration is a natural measure of the bond's exposure to interest rate volatility.

[1]Actually, as we will see later, Equation 11.3 is only approximately valid for large changes in the bond's yield. The approximation becomes exact as one considers smaller, or localized, changes in yields.

A bond with maturity of 30 years has a coupon rate of 8% (paid annually) and a yield to maturity of 9%. Its price is $897.26, and its duration is 11.37 years. What will happen to the bond price if the bond's yield to maturity increases to 9.1%?

Equation 11.3 tells us that an increase of .1% in the bond's yield to maturity ($\Delta y = .001$ in decimal terms) will result in a price change of

$$\Delta P = -(D^* \Delta y) \times P$$
$$= -\frac{11.37}{1.09} \times .001 \times \$897.26 = -\$9.36$$

To confirm the relationship between duration and the sensitivity of bond price to interest rate changes, let's compare the price sensitivity of the three-year coupon bond in Spreadsheet 11.1, which has a duration of 2.7774 years, to the sensitivity of a zero-coupon bond with maturity and duration of 2.7774 years. Both should have equal interest rate exposure if duration is a useful measure of price sensitivity.

The three-year bond sells for $950.263 at the initial interest rate of 10%. If the bond's yield increases by 1 basis point (1/100 of a percent) to 10.01%, its price will fall to $950.0231, a percentage decline of .0252%. The zero-coupon bond has a maturity of 2.7774 years. At the initial interest rate of 10%, it sells at a price of $1,000/1.10^{2.7774} = \$767.425$. When the interest rate increases, its price falls to $1,000/1.1001^{2.7774} = \$767.2313$, for an identical .0252% capital loss. We conclude that equal-duration assets are equally sensitive to interest rate movements.

Incidentally, this example confirms the validity of Equation 11.2. The equation predicts that the proportional price change of the two bonds should have been $-2.7774 \times .0001/1.10 = .000252$, or .0252%, just as we found from direct computation.

a. In Concept Check 11.1, you calculated the price and duration of a three-year maturity, 8% coupon bond for an interest rate of 9%. Now suppose the interest rate increases to 9.05%. What is the new value of the bond and the percentage change in the bond's price?

b. Calculate the percentage change in the bond's price predicted by the duration formula in Equation 11.2 or 11.3. Compare this value to your answer for (a).

The equations for the durations of coupon bonds are somewhat tedious, and spreadsheets like Spreadsheet 11.1 are cumbersome to modify for different maturities and coupon rates. Fortunately, spreadsheet programs such as Excel come with built-in functions for duration. Moreover, these functions easily accommodate bonds that are between coupon payment dates. Spreadsheet 11.2 illustrates how to use Excel to compute duration. The spreadsheets use many of the same conventions as the bond pricing spreadsheets described in Chapter 10.

SPREADSHEET 11.2

Using Excel functions to compute duration

	A	B	C
1	Inputs		Formula in column B
2	Settlement date	1/1/2000	=DATE(2000,1,1)
3	Maturity date	1/1/2003	=DATE(2003,1,1)
4	Coupon rate	0.08	0.08
5	Yield to maturity	0.10	0.10
6	Coupons per year	1	1
7			
8	Outputs		
9	Macaulay duration	2.7774	=DURATION(B2,B3,B4,B5,B6)
10	Modified duration	2.5249	=MDURATION(B2,B3,B4,B5,B6)

eX**cel**

Please visit us at www.mhhe.com/bkm

We first use the spreadsheet to reconfirm the duration of the 8% coupon bond examined in Panel A of Spreadsheet 11.1. The settlement date (i.e., today's date) and maturity date are entered in cells B2 and B3 of Spreadsheet 11.2 using Excel's date function, DATE(year, month, day). For this three-year maturity bond, we don't have a specific settlement date. We arbitrarily set the settlement date to January 1, 2000, and use a maturity date precisely three years later. The coupon rate and yield to maturity are entered as decimals in cells B4 and B5, and the payment periods per year are entered in cell B6. Macaulay and modified duration appear in cells B9 and B10. Cell B9 shows that the duration of the bond is indeed 2.7774 years. The modified duration of the bond is 2.5249, which equals 2.7774/1.10.

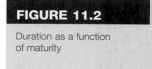

CONCEPT *check* **11.3**

Consider a 9% coupon, 8-year maturity bond with annual payments, selling at a yield to maturity of 10%. Use Spreadsheet 11.2 to confirm that the bond's duration is 5.97 years. What would its duration be if the bond paid its coupon semiannually? Why intuitively does duration fall?

What Determines Duration?

Malkiel's bond price relations, which we laid out in the previous section, characterize the determinants of interest rate sensitivity. Duration allows us to quantify that sensitivity, which greatly enhances our ability to formulate investment strategies. For example, if we wish to speculate on interest rates, duration tells us how strong a bet we are making. Conversely, if we wish to remain "neutral" on rates, and simply match the interest rate sensitivity of a chosen bond market index, duration allows us to measure that sensitivity and mimic it in our own portfolio. For these reasons, it is crucial to understand the determinants of duration and convenient to have formulas to calculate the duration of some commonly encountered securities. Therefore, in this section, we present several "rules" that summarize most of the important properties of duration. These rules are also illustrated in Figure 11.2, which contains plots of durations of bonds of various coupon rates, yields to maturity, and times to maturity.

We have already established:

Rule 1: The duration of a zero-coupon bond equals its time to maturity.

FIGURE 11.2

Duration as a function of maturity

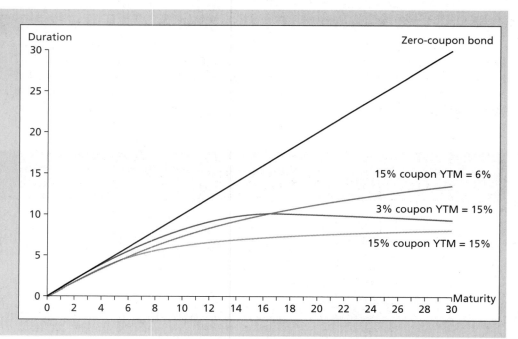

We also have seen that the three-year coupon bond has a lower duration than the three-year zero because coupons early in the bond's life reduce the bond's weighted average time until payments. This illustrates another general property:

Rule 2: With time to maturity and yield to maturity held constant, a bond's duration and interest rate sensitivity are higher when the coupon rate is lower.

This property corresponds to Malkiel's fifth bond-pricing relationship and is attributable to the impact of early coupons on the average maturity of a bond's payments. The lower these coupons, the less weight these early payments have on the weighted average maturity of all the bond's payments. In other words, a lower fraction of the total value of the bond is tied up in the (earlier) coupon payments whose values are relatively insensitive to yields rather than the (later and more yield-sensitive) repayment of par value. Compare the plots in Figure 11.2 of the durations of the 3% coupon and 15% coupon bonds, each with identical yields of 15%. The plot of the duration of the 15% coupon bond lies below the corresponding plot for the 3% coupon bond.

Rule 3: With the coupon rate held constant, a bond's duration and interest rate sensitivity generally increase with time to maturity. Duration always increases with maturity for bonds selling at par or at a premium to par.

This property of duration corresponds to Malkiel's third relationship and is fairly intuitive. What is surprising is that duration need not always increase with time to maturity. For some deep discount bonds, such as the 3% coupon bond selling to yield 15% in Figure 11.2, duration may eventually fall with increases in maturity. For virtually all traded bonds, however, it is safe to assume that duration increases with maturity.

Notice in Figure 11.2 that for the zero-coupon bond, maturity and duration are equal. For all the coupon bonds, however, duration increases by less than a year for each year's increase in maturity. The slope of the duration graph is less than 1.0, and duration is always less than maturity for positive-coupon bonds.

While long-maturity bonds generally will be high-duration bonds, duration is a better measure of the long-term nature of the bond because it also accounts for coupon payments. Maturity is an adequate measure only when the bond pays no coupons; then maturity and duration are equal.

Notice also in Figure 11.2 that the two 15% coupon bonds have different durations when they sell at different yields to maturity. The lower yield bond has longer duration. This makes sense, because at lower yields the more distant payments have relatively greater present values and thereby account for a greater share of the bond's total value. Thus, in the weighted-average calculation of duration, the distant payments receive greater weights, which results in a higher duration measure. This establishes

Rule 4: With other factors held constant, the duration and interest rate sensitivity of a coupon bond are higher when the bond's yield to maturity is lower.

As we noted above, the intuition for this rule is that while a higher yield reduces the present value of all of the bond's payments, it reduces the value of more distant payments by a greater proportional amount. Therefore, at higher yields a higher fraction of the total value of the bond lies in its earlier payments, thereby reducing effective maturity. Rule 4, which is the sixth bond-pricing relationship noted above, applies to coupon bonds. For zeros, duration equals time to maturity, regardless of the yield to maturity.

Finally, we present an algebraic rule for the duration of a perpetuity. This rule is derived from and is consistent with the formula for duration given in Equation 11.1, but it is far easier to use for infinitely lived bonds.

Rule 5: The duration of a level perpetuity is

$$\text{Duration of perpetuity} = \frac{1 + y}{y} \qquad \textbf{(11.4)}$$

TABLE 11.3	Years to Maturity	Coupon Rates (% per year)			
Durations of annual coupon bonds (initial bond yield = 8%)		6	8	10	12
	1	1.000	1.000	1.000	1.000
	5	4.439	4.312	4.204	4.110
	10	7.615	7.247	6.996	6.744
	20	11.231	10.604	10.182	9.880
	Infinite (perpetuity)	13.500	13.500	13.500	13.500

For example, at a 15% yield, the duration of a perpetuity that pays $100 once a year forever will equal 1.15/.15 = 7.67 years, while at an 8% yield, it will equal 1.08/.08 = 13.5 years.

Equation 11.4 makes it obvious that maturity and duration can differ substantially. The maturity of the perpetuity is infinite, while the duration of the instrument at a 15% yield is only 7.67 years. The present-value-weighted cash flows early on in the life of the perpetuity dominate the computation of duration. Notice from Figure 11.2 that as their maturities become ever longer, the durations of the two coupon bonds with yields of 15% both converge to the duration of the perpetuity with the same yield, 7.67 years.

CONCEPT
check **11.4**
Show that the duration of a perpetuity increases as the interest rate decreases, in accordance with Rule 4.

Durations can vary widely among traded bonds. Table 11.3 presents durations for several bonds, all paying annual coupons and yielding 8% per year. Duration decreases as coupon rates increase and increases with time to maturity. According to Table 11.3 and Equation 11.2, if the interest rate were to increase from 8% to 8.1%, the 6% coupon, 20-year bond would fall in value by about 1.04% (= − 11.231 × .1%/1.08) while the 10% coupon, one-year bond would fall by only .093% (= − 1 × .1%/1.08). Notice also from Table 11.3 that duration is independent of coupon rate only for perpetuities.

11.2 Passive Bond Management

Passive managers take bond prices as fairly set and seek to control only the risk of their fixed-income portfolios. Generally, there are two ways of viewing this risk, depending on the investor's circumstances. Some institutions, such as banks, are concerned with protecting the portfolio's current net worth or net market value against interest rate fluctuations. Risk-based capital guidelines for commercial banks and thrift institutions require the setting aside of additional capital as a buffer against potential losses in market value incurred from interest rate fluctuations. The amount of capital required is directly related to the losses that may be incurred under various changes in market interest rates. Other investors, such as pension funds, may have an investment goal to be reached after a given number of years. These investors are more concerned with protecting the future values of their portfolios.

What is common to the bank and pension fund, however, is interest rate risk. The net worth of the firm and its ability to meet future obligations fluctuate with interest rates. If they adjust the maturity structure of their portfolios, these institutions can shed their interest rate risk. **Immunization** and dedication techniques refer to strategies that investors use to shield their net worth from exposure to interest rate fluctuations.

immunization

A strategy to shield net worth from interest rate movements.

Immunization

Many banks and thrift institutions have a natural mismatch between the maturities of assets and liabilities. For example, bank liabilities are primarily the deposits owed to customers; these liabilities are short-term in nature and consequently of low duration. Assets largely

PENSION FUNDS LOSE GROUND DESPITE BROAD MARKET GAINS

The stock market had a banner year in 2003, with the S&P 500 providing a rate of return in excess of 25%. Not surprisingly, this performance showed up in the balance sheets of U.S. pension funds: Assets in these funds rose by more than $100 billion. Despite this apparent good news, pension funds actually *lost* ground in 2003, with the gap between assets and liabilities growing by about $45 billion.

How did this happen? Blame the decline in interest rates during the year that were in large part the force behind the stock market gains. As rates fell, the present value of pension obligations to retirees rose even faster than the value of the assets backing those promises. It turns out that the value of pension liabilities is more sensitive to interest rate changes than is the value of the typical assets held in those funds. So even though falling rates tend to pump up asset returns, they pump up liabilities even more so. In other words, the duration of fund investments tends to be shorter than the duration of its obligations. This duration mismatch makes funds vulnerable to interest rate declines.

Why don't funds better match asset and liability durations? One reason is that fund managers are often evaluated based on their performance relative to standard bond market indexes. Those indexes tend to have far shorter durations than pension fund liabilities. So to some extent, managers may be keeping their eyes on the wrong ball, one with the wrong interest rate sensitivity.

comprise commercial and consumer loans or mortgages. These assets are of longer duration than deposits, which means their values are correspondingly more sensitive than deposits to interest rate fluctuations. When interest rates increase unexpectedly, banks can suffer serious decreases in net worth—their assets fall in value by more than their liabilities.

Similarly, a pension fund may have a mismatch between the interest rate sensitivity of the assets held in the fund and the present value of its liabilities—the promise to make payments to retirees. The nearby box illustrates the dangers that pension funds face when they neglect the interest rate exposure of *both* assets and liabilities. It points out that when interest rates change, the present value of the fund's liabilities change. For example, in some recent years pension funds lost ground despite the fact that they enjoyed excellent investment returns. As interest rates fell, the value of their liabilities grew even faster than the value of their assets. The conclusion: Funds should match the interest rate exposure of assets and liabilities so that the value of assets will track the value of liabilities whether rates rise or fall. In other words, the financial manager might want to *immunize* the fund against interest rate volatility.

Pension funds are not alone in this concern. Any institution with a future fixed obligation might consider immunization a reasonable risk management policy. Insurance companies, for example, also pursue immunization strategies. In fact, the notion of immunization was introduced by F. M. Redington (1952), an actuary for a life insurance company. The idea is that duration-matched assets and liabilities let the asset portfolio meet the firm's obligations despite interest rate movements.

Consider, for example, an insurance company that issues a guaranteed investment contract, or GIC, for $10,000. (GICs are essentially zero-coupon bonds issued by the insurance company to its customers. They are popular products for individuals' retirement-savings accounts.) If the GIC has a five-year maturity and a guaranteed interest rate of 8%, the insurance company promises to pay $10,000 \times (1.08)^5 = \$14,693.28$ in five years.

Suppose that the insurance company chooses to fund its obligation with $10,000 of 8% *annual* coupon bonds, selling at par value, with six years to maturity. As long as the market interest rate stays at 8%, the company has fully funded the obligation, as the present value of the obligation exactly equals the value of the bonds.

Table 11.4A shows that if interest rates remain at 8%, the accumulated funds from the bond will grow to exactly the $14,693.28 obligation. Over the five-year period, the year-end coupon income of $800 is reinvested at the prevailing 8% market interest rate. At the end of the period, the bonds can be sold for $10,000; they still will sell at par value because the coupon rate still equals the market interest rate. Total income after five years from reinvested coupons and the sale of the bond is precisely $14,693.28.

If interest rates change, however, two offsetting influences will affect the ability of the fund to grow to the targeted value of $14,693.28. If interest rates rise, the fund will suffer a

TABLE 11.4	Payment Number	Years Remaining until Obligation	Accumulated Value of Invested Payment
Terminal value of a bond portfolio after five years (all proceeds reinvested)	**A. Rates remain at 8%**		
	1	4	$800 \times (1.08)^4 =$ 1,088.39
	2	3	$800 \times (1.08)^3 =$ 1,007.77
	3	2	$800 \times (1.08)^2 =$ 933.12
	4	1	$800 \times (1.08)^1 =$ 864.00
	5	0	$800 \times (1.08)^0 =$ 800.00
	Sale of bond	0	$10,800/1.08 =$ 10,000.00
			14,693.28
	B. Rates fall to 7%		
	1	4	$800 \times (1.07)^4 =$ 1,048.64
	2	3	$800 \times (1.07)^3 =$ 980.03
	3	2	$800 \times (1.07)^2 =$ 915.92
	4	1	$800 \times (1.07)^1 =$ 856.00
	5	0	$800 \times (1.07)^0 =$ 800.00
	Sale of bond	0	$10,800/1.07 =$ 10,093.46
			14,694.05
	C. Rates increase to 9%		
	1	4	$800 \times (1.09)^4 =$ 1,129.27
	2	3	$800 \times (1.09)^3 =$ 1,036.02
	3	2	$800 \times (1.09)^2 =$ 950.48
	4	1	$800 \times (1.09)^1 =$ 872.00
	5	0	$800 \times (1.09)^0 =$ 800.00
	Sale of bond	0	$10,800/1.09 =$ 9,908.26
			14,696.02

Note: The sale price of the bond portfolio equals the portfolio's final payment ($10,800) divided by $1 + r$, because the time to maturity of the bonds will be one year at the time of sale.

capital loss, impairing its ability to satisfy the obligation. The bonds will be worth less in five years than if interest rates had remained at 8%. However, at a higher interest rate, reinvested coupons will grow at a faster rate, offsetting the capital loss. In other words, fixed-income investors face two offsetting types of interest rate risk: *price risk* and *reinvestment rate risk*. Increases in interest rates cause capital losses but at the same time increase the rate at which reinvested income will grow. If the portfolio duration is chosen appropriately, these two effects will cancel out exactly. When the portfolio duration is set equal to the investor's horizon date, the accumulated value of the investment fund at the horizon date will be unaffected by interest rate fluctuations. *For a horizon equal to the portfolio's duration, price risk and reinvestment risk exactly cancel out.* The obligation is immunized.

In the example we are discussing, the duration of the six-year maturity bonds used to fund the GIC is five years. You can confirm this using either Spreadsheet 11.1 or 11.2. The duration of the (zero-coupon) GIC is also five years. Because the fully funded plan has equal duration for its assets and liabilities, the insurance company should be immunized against interest rate fluctuations. To confirm that this is the case, let us now investigate whether the bond can generate enough income to pay off the obligation five years from now regardless of interest rate movements.

Tables 11.4B and C consider two possible interest rate scenarios: Rates either fall to 7% or increase to 9%. In both cases, the annual coupon payments from the bond are reinvested at the new interest rate, which is assumed to change before the first coupon payment, and the bond is sold in year 5 to help satisfy the obligation of the GIC.

Table 11.4B shows that if interest rates fall to 7%, the total funds will accumulate to $14,694.05, providing a small surplus of $.77. If rates increase to 9% as in Table 11.4C, the fund accumulates to $14,696.02, providing a small surplus of $2.74.

Several points are worth highlighting. First, duration matching balances the difference between the accumulated value of the coupon payments (reinvestment rate risk) and the sale value of the bond (price risk). That is, when interest rates fall, the coupons grow less than in the base case, but the higher value of the bond offsets this. When interest rates rise, the value of the bond falls, but the coupons more than make up for this loss because they are reinvested at the higher rate. Figure 11.3 illustrates this case. The solid curve traces out the accumulated value of the bonds if interest rates remain at 8%. The dashed curve shows that value if interest rates happen to increase. The initial impact is a capital loss, but this loss eventually is offset by the now-faster growth rate of reinvested funds. At the five-year horizon date, equal to the bond's duration, the two effects just cancel, leaving the company able to satisfy its obligation with the accumulated proceeds from the bond.

We can also analyze immunization in terms of present as opposed to future values. Table 11.5A shows the initial balance sheet for the insurance company's GIC account. Both assets and the obligation have market values of $10,000, so that the plan is just fully funded. Table 11.5B and C show that whether the interest rate increases or decreases, the value of the bonds funding the GIC and the present value of the company's obligation change by virtually identical amounts. Regardless of the interest rate change, the plan remains fully funded, with the surplus in Table 11.5B and C just about zero. The duration-matching strategy has ensured that both assets and liabilities react equally to interest rate fluctuations.

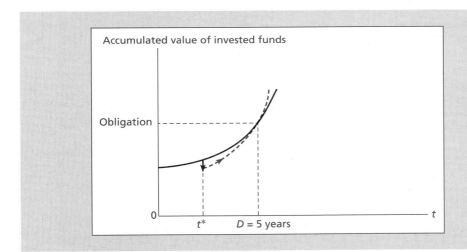

FIGURE 11.3

Growth of invested funds

Note: The solid curve represents the growth of portfolio value at the original interest rate. If interest rates increase at time t^* the portfolio value falls but increases thereafter at the faster rate represented by the broken curve. At time D (duration) the curves cross.

TABLE 11.5	**A. Interest rate = 8%**			
Market value balance sheets	**Assets**		**Liabilities**	
	Bonds	$10,000	Obligation	$10,000
	B. Interest rate = 7%			
	Assets		**Liabilities**	
	Bonds	$10,476.65	Obligation	$10,476.11
	C. Interest rate = 9%			
	Assets		**Liabilities**	
	Bonds	$9,551.41	Obligation	$9,549.62

Notes: Value of bonds = 800 × Annuity factor(r, 6) + 10,000 × PV factor(r, 6).

Value of obligation = $\dfrac{14,693.28}{(1 + r)^5}$ = 14,693.28 × PV factor(r, 5).

Figure 11.4 is a graph of the present values of the bond and the single-payment obligation as a function of the interest rate. At the current rate of 8%, the values are equal, and the obligation is fully funded by the bond. Moreover, the two present value curves are tangent at $y = 8\%$. As interest rates change, the change in value of both the asset and the obligation are equal, so the obligation remains fully funded. For greater changes in the interest rate, however, the present value curves diverge. This reflects the fact that the fund actually shows a small surplus at market interest rates other than 8%.

Why is there any surplus in the fund? After all, we claimed that a duration-matched asset and liability mix would make the investor indifferent to interest rate shifts. Actually, such a claim is valid for only *small* changes in the interest rate, because as bond yields change, so too does duration. (Recall Rule 4 for duration.) In fact, while the duration of the bond in this example is equal to five years at a yield to maturity of 8%, the duration rises to 5.02 years when the bond yield falls to 7% and drops to 4.97 years at $y = 9\%$. That is, the bond and the obligation were not duration-matched *across* the interest rate shift, so the position was not fully immunized.

rebalancing

Realigning the proportions of assets in a portfolio as needed.

This example demonstrates the need for **rebalancing** immunized portfolios. As interest rates and asset durations continually change, managers must rebalance, that is, change the composition of, the portfolio of fixed-income assets to realign its duration with the duration of the obligation. Moreover, even if interest rates do not change, asset durations *will* change solely because of the passage of time. Recall from Figure 11.2 that duration generally decreases less rapidly than maturity as time passes, so even if an obligation is immunized at the outset, the durations of the asset and liability will fall at different rates. Without portfolio rebalancing, durations will become unmatched and the goals of immunization will not be realized. Therefore, immunization is a passive strategy only in the sense that it does not involve attempts to identify undervalued securities. Immunization managers still actively update and monitor their positions.

EXAMPLE   11.2

Constructing an Immunized Portfolio

An insurance company must make a payment of $19,487 in seven years. The market interest rate is 10%, so the present value of the obligation is $10,000. The company's portfolio manager wishes to fund the obligation using three-year zero-coupon bonds and perpetuities paying annual coupons. (We focus on zeros and perpetuities to keep the algebra simple.) How can the manager immunize the obligation?

Immunization requires that the duration of the portfolio of assets equal the duration of the liability. We can proceed in four steps:

Step 1.   Calculate the duration of the liability. In this case, the liability duration is simple to compute. It is a single-payment obligation with duration of seven years.

Step 2.   Calculate the duration of the asset portfolio. The portfolio duration is the weighted average of duration of each component asset, with weights proportional to the funds placed in each asset. The duration of the zero-coupon bond is simply its maturity, three years. The duration of the perpetuity is $1.10/.10 = 11$ years. Therefore, if the fraction of the portfolio invested in the zero is called w, and the fraction invested in the perpetuity is $(1 - w)$, the portfolio duration will be

$$\text{Asset duration} = w \times 3 \text{ years} + (1 - w) \times 11 \text{ years}$$

Step 3.   Find the asset mix that sets the duration of assets equal to the seven-year duration of liabilities. This requires us to solve for w in the following equation

$$w \times 3 \text{ years} + (1 - w) \times 11 \text{ years} = 7 \text{ years}$$

This implies that $w = 1/2$. The manager should invest half the portfolio in the zero and half in the perpetuity. This will result in an asset duration of seven years.

Step 4.   Fully fund the obligation. Since the obligation has a present value of $10,000, and the fund will be invested equally in the zero and the perpetuity, the manager must purchase $5,000 of the zero-coupon bond and $5,000 of the perpetuity. Note that the *face value* of the zero will be $5,000 \times (1.10)^3 = \$6,655$.

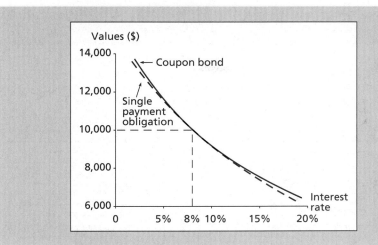

FIGURE 11.4

Immunization. The coupon bond fully funds the obligation at an interest rate of 8%. Moreover, the present value curves are tangent at 8%, so the obligation will remain fully funded even if rates change by a small amount.

Even if a position is immunized, however, the portfolio manager still cannot rest. This is because of the need for rebalancing in response to changes in interest rates. Moreover, even if rates do not change, the passage of time also will affect duration and require rebalancing. Let us continue Example 11.2 and see how the portfolio manager can maintain an immunized position.

Suppose that one year has passed, and the interest rate remains at 10%. The portfolio manager of Example 11.2 needs to reexamine her position. Is the position still fully funded? Is it still immunized? If not, what actions are required?

First, examine funding. The present value of the obligation will have grown to $11,000, as it is one year closer to maturity. The manager's funds also have grown to $11,000: The zero-coupon bonds have increased in value from $5,000 to $5,500 with the passage of time, while the perpetuity has paid its annual $500 coupons and remains worth $5,000. Therefore, the obligation is still fully funded.

The portfolio weights must be changed, however. The zero-coupon bond now will have a duration of two years, while the perpetuity duration remains at 11 years. The obligation is now due in six years. The weights must now satisfy the equation

$$w \times 2 + (1-w) \times 11 = 6$$

which implies that $w = 5/9$. To rebalance the portfolio and maintain the duration match, the manager now must invest a total of $11,000 \times 5/9 = $6,111.11 in the zero-coupon bond. This requires that the entire $500 coupon payment be invested in the zero, with an additional $111.11 of the perpetuity sold and invested in the zero-coupon bond.

EXAMPLE 11.3

Rebalancing

Of course, rebalancing the portfolio entails transaction costs as assets are bought or sold, so continuous rebalancing is not feasible. In practice, managers strike a compromise between the desire for perfect immunization, which requires continual rebalancing, and the need to control trading costs, which dictates less frequent rebalancing.

Look again at Example 11.3. What would have been the immunizing weights in the second year if the interest rate had fallen to 8%?

CONCEPT *check* **11.5**

Immunization

The Excel immunization model allows you to analyze any number of time-period or holding-period immunization examples. The model is built using the Excel-supplied formulas for bond duration, which allow the investigation of any maturity bond without building a table of cash flows.

	A	B	C	D	E	F	G	H
1			Holding Period Immunization					
2								
3	YTM	0.0800	Mar Price	1000.00				
4	Coupon R	0.0800						
5	Maturity	6			Duration	#NAME?		
6	Par Value	1000.00						
7	Holding P	5						
8	Duration	4.9927						
9								
10								
11	If Rates Increase by 200 basis points				If Rates Increase by 100 basis points			
12	Rate	0.1000			Rate	0.0900		
13	FV of CPS	488.41			FV of CPS	478.78		
14	SalesP	981.82			SalesP	990.83		
15	Total	1470.23			Total	1469.60		
16	IRR	0.0801			IRR	0.0800		
17								
18								
19								
20	If Rates Decrease by 200 basis points				If Rates Decrease by 100 basis points			
21	Rate	0.0600			Rate	0.0700		
22	FV of CPS	450.97			FV of CPS	460.06		
23	SalesP	1018.87			SalesP	1009.35		
24	Total	1469.84			Total	1469.40		
25	IRR	0.0801			IRR	0.0800		

Cash Flow Matching and Dedication

cash flow matching

Matching cash flows from a fixed-income portfolio with those of an obligation.

dedication strategy

Refers to multiperiod cash flow matching.

The problems associated with immunization seem to have a simple solution. Why not simply buy a zero-coupon bond that provides a payment in an amount exactly sufficient to cover the projected cash outlay? This is **cash flow matching,** which automatically immunizes a portfolio from interest rate movements because the cash flow from the bond and the obligation exactly offset each other.

Cash flow matching on a multiperiod basis is referred to as a **dedication strategy.** In this case, the manager selects either zero-coupon or coupon bonds that provide total cash flows that match a series of obligations in each period. The advantage of dedication is that it is a once-and-for-all approach to eliminating interest rate risk. Once the cash flows are matched, there is no need for rebalancing. The dedicated portfolio provides the cash necessary to pay the firm's liabilities regardless of the eventual path of interest rates.

Cash flow matching is not widely pursued, however, probably because of the constraints it imposes on bond selection. Immunization/dedication strategies are appealing to firms that do not wish to bet on general movements in interest rates, yet these firms may want to immunize using bonds they believe are undervalued. Cash flow matching places enough constraints on bond selection that it can make it impossible to pursue a dedication strategy using only "underpriced" bonds. Firms looking for underpriced bonds exchange exact and easy dedication for the possibility of achieving superior returns from their bond portfolios.

Sometimes, cash flow matching is not even possible. To cash flow match for a pension fund that is obligated to pay out a perpetual flow of income to current and future retirees, the pension fund would need to purchase fixed-income securities with maturities ranging up to hundreds of years. Such securities do not exist, making exact dedication infeasible. Immunization is easy, however. If the interest rate is 8%, for example, the duration of the pension fund obligation is $1.08/.08 = 13.5$ years (see Rule 5 above). Therefore, the fund can immunize its obligation by purchasing zero-coupon bonds with maturity of 13.5 years and a market value equal to that of the pension liabilities.

a. Suppose that this pension fund is obligated to pay out $800,000 per year in perpetuity. What should be the maturity and face value of the zero-coupon bond it purchases to immunize its obligation?
b. Now suppose the interest rate immediately increases to 8.1%. How should the fund rebalance in order to remain immunized against further interest rate shocks? Ignore transaction costs.

How would an increase in trading costs affect the attractiveness of dedication versus immunization?

11.3 Convexity

Duration clearly is a key tool in bond portfolio management. Yet, the duration rule for the impact of interest rates on bond prices is only an approximation. Equation 11.3, which we repeat here, states that the percentage change in the value of a bond approximately equals the product of modified duration times the change in the bond's yield:

$$\frac{\Delta P}{P} = -D^* \Delta y$$

This equation asserts that the percentage price change is directly proportional to the change in the bond's yield. If this were *exactly* so, however, a graph of the percentage change in bond price as a function of the change in its yield would plot as a straight line, with slope equal to $-D^*$. Yet we know from Figure 11.1, and more generally from Malkiel's five bond-pricing relationships (specifically relationship 2), that the relationship between bond prices and yields is *not* linear. The duration rule is a good approximation for small changes in bond yield, but it is less accurate for larger changes.

Figure 11.5 illustrates this point. Like Figure 11.1, this figure presents the percentage change in bond price in response to a change in the bond's yield to maturity. The curved

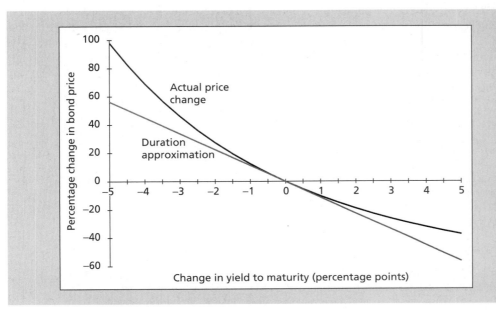

FIGURE 11.5

Bond price convexity. The percentage change in bond price is a convex function of the change in yield to maturity.

line is the percentage price change for a 30-year maturity, 8% coupon bond, selling at an initial yield to maturity of 8%. The straight line is the percentage price change predicted by the duration rule: The modified duration of the bond at its initial yield is 11.26 years, so the straight line is a plot of $-D^*\Delta y = -11.26 \times \Delta y$. Notice that the two plots are tangent at the initial yield. Thus, for small changes in the bond's yield to maturity, the duration rule is quite accurate. However, for larger changes in yield, there is progressively more "daylight" between the two plots, demonstrating that the duration rule becomes progressively less accurate.

Notice from Figure 11.5 that the duration approximation (the straight line) always understates the value of the bond; it underestimates the increase in bond price when the yield falls, and it overestimates the decline in price when the yield rises. This is due to the curvature of the true price-yield relationship. Curves with shapes such as that of the price-yield relationship are said to be convex, and the curvature of the price-yield curve is called the **convexity** of the bond.

convexity

The curvature of the price-yield relationship of a bond.

We can quantify convexity as the rate of change of the slope of the price-yield curve, expressed as a fraction of the bond price.[2] As a practical rule, you can view bonds with higher convexity as exhibiting higher curvature in the price-yield relationship. The convexity of noncallable bonds, such as that in Figure 11.5, is positive: The slope increases (i.e., becomes less negative) at higher yields.

Convexity allows us to improve the duration approximation for bond price changes. Accounting for convexity, Equation 11.3 can be modified as follows:[3]

$$\frac{\Delta P}{P} = -D^*\Delta y + \tfrac{1}{2} \times \text{Convexity} \times (\Delta y)^2 \qquad \text{(11.5)}$$

The first term on the right-hand side is the same as the duration rule, Equation 11.3. The second term is the modification for convexity. Notice that for a bond with positive convexity, the second term is positive, regardless of whether the yield rises or falls. This insight corresponds to the fact noted just above that the duration rule always underestimates the new value of a bond following a change in its yield. The more accurate Equation 11.5, which accounts for convexity, always predicts a higher bond price than Equation 11.3. Of course, if the change in yield is small, the convexity term, which is multiplied by $(\Delta y)^2$ in Equation 11.5, will be extremely small and will add little to the approximation. In this case, the linear approximation given by the duration rule will be sufficiently accurate. Thus, convexity is more important as a practical matter when potential interest rate changes are large.

Convexity is the reason that the immunization examples we considered above resulted in small errors. For example, if you turn back to Table 11.5 and Figure 11.4, you will see that the single payment obligation that was funded with a coupon bond of the same duration was well immunized for small changes in yields. However, for larger yield changes, the two pricing curves diverged a bit, implying that such changes in yields would result in small surpluses. This is due to the greater convexity of the coupon bond.

---

[2]If you have taken a calculus class, you will recognize that Equation 11.3 for modified duration can be written as $dP/P = -D^*dy$. Thus, $-D^* = 1/P \times dP/dy$ is the slope of the price-yield curve expressed as a fraction of the bond price. Similarly, the convexity of a bond equals the second derivative (the rate of change of the slope) of the price-yield curve divided by bond price: Convexity $= 1/P \times d^2P/dy^2$. The formula for the convexity of a bond with a maturity of n years making annual coupon payments is

$$\text{Convexity} = \frac{1}{P \times (1 + y)^2} \sum_{t=1}^{n} \left[\frac{CF_t}{(1 + y)^t}(t^2 + t) \right]$$

where CF_t is the cash flow paid to the bondholder at date t; CF_t represents either a coupon payment before maturity or final coupon plus par value at the maturity date.

[3]To use the convexity rule, you must express interest rates as decimals rather than percentages.

EXAMPLE   11.4

Convexity

The bond in Figure 11.5 has a 30-year maturity, an 8% coupon, and sells at an initial yield to maturity of 8%. Because the coupon rate equals yield to maturity, the bond sells at par value, or $1,000. The modified duration of the bond at its initial yield is 11.26 years, and its convexity is 212.4, which can be calculated using the formula in footnote 2. (You can find a spreadsheet to calculate the convexity of a 30-year bond at the book's Web site, **www.mhhe.com/bkm.** See also the nearby Excel Application.) If the bond's yield increases from 8% to 10%, the bond price will fall to $811.46, a decline of 18.85%. The duration rule, Equation 11.3, would predict a price decline of

$$\frac{\Delta P}{P} = -D^*\Delta y = -11.26 \times .02 = -.2252 = -22.52\%$$

which is considerably more than the bond price actually falls. The duration-with-convexity rule, Equation 11.5, is more accurate:

$$\frac{\Delta P}{P} = -D^*\Delta y + \frac{1}{2} \times \text{Convexity} \times (\Delta y)^2$$
$$= -11.26 \times .02 + \frac{1}{2} \times 212.4 \times (.02)^2 = -.1827 = -18.27\%$$

which is far closer to the exact change in bond price.

Notice that if the change in yield were smaller, say, .1%, convexity would matter less. The price of the bond actually would fall to $988.85, a decline of 1.115%. Without accounting for convexity, we would predict a price decline of

$$\frac{\Delta P}{P} = -D^*\Delta y = -11.26 \times .001 = -.01126 = -1.126\%$$

Accounting for convexity, we get almost the precisely correct answer:

$$\frac{\Delta P}{P} = -11.26 \times .001 + \frac{1}{2} \times 212.4 \times (.001)^2 = -.01115 = -1.115\%$$

Nevertheless, the duration rule is quite accurate in this case, even without accounting for convexity.

Why Do Investors Like Convexity?

Convexity is generally considered a desirable trait. Bonds with greater curvature gain more in price when yields fall than they lose when yields rise. For example, in Figure 11.6 bonds A and B have the same duration at the initial yield. The plots of their proportional price changes as a function of interest rate changes are tangent, meaning that their sensitivities to

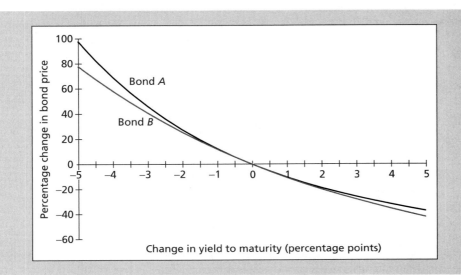

FIGURE 11.6

Convexity of two bonds. Bond A has greater convexity than bond B.

The Convexity spreadsheet allows you to calculate bond convexity. You can specify yield to maturity and coupon and allow for short maturities by setting later cash flows equal to zero and setting the last cash flow equal to principal plus final coupon payment.

	A	B	C	D	E	F	G	H
1					Chapter 11			
2					Convexity			
3								
4			Time (t)	Cash flow	PV(CF)	t + t^2	(t + t^2) x PV(CF)	
5								
6	Coupon	3	1	3	2.871	2	5.742	
7	YTM	0.045	2	3	2.747	6	16.483	
8	Maturity	10	3	3	2.629	12	31.547	
9	Price	$88.13	4	3	2.516	20	50.314	
10			5	3	2.407	30	72.221	
11			6	3	2.304	42	96.755	
12			7	3	2.204	56	123.451	
13			8	3	2.110	72	151.888	
14			9	3	2.019	90	181.684	
15			10	103	66.325	110	7295.701	
16								
17			Sum:		88.13092273		8025.785	
18								
19				Convexity:			83.392425	

changes in yields at that point are equal. However, bond *A* is more convex than bond *B*. It enjoys greater price increases and smaller price decreases when interest rates fluctuate by larger amounts. If interest rates are volatile, this is an attractive asymmetry that increases the expected return on the bond, since bond *A* will benefit more from rate decreases and suffer less from rate increases. Of course, if convexity is desirable, it will not be available for free: Investors will have to pay more and accept lower yields on bonds with greater convexity.

11.4 Active Bond Management

Sources of Potential Profit

Broadly speaking, there are two sources of potential value in active bond management. The first is interest rate forecasting, that is, anticipating movements across the entire spectrum of the fixed-income market. If interest rate declines are forecast, managers will increase portfolio duration; if increases seem likely, they will shorten duration. The second source of potential profit is identification of relative mispricing within the fixed-income market. An analyst might believe, for example, that the default premium on one bond is unnecessarily large and the bond is underpriced.

These techniques will generate abnormal returns only if the analyst's information or insight is superior to that of the market. There is no way of profiting from knowledge that rates are about to fall if everyone else in the market is onto this. In that case, the anticipated lower future rates are built into bond prices in the sense that long-duration bonds are already selling at higher prices that reflect the anticipated fall in future short rates. If the analyst does not have information before the market does, it will be too late to act on that information—prices will have responded already to the news. You know this from our discussion of market efficiency.

For now we simply repeat that valuable information is differential information. And it is worth noting that interest rate forecasters have a notoriously poor track record.

Homer and Leibowitz (1972) have developed a popular taxonomy of active bond portfolio strategies. They characterize portfolio rebalancing activities as one of four types of *bond swaps.* In the first two swaps, the investor typically believes the yield relationship between bonds or sectors is only temporarily out of alignment. Until the aberration is eliminated, gains can be realized on the underpriced bond during a period of realignment called the *workout period.*

1. The **substitution swap** is an exchange of one bond for a nearly identical substitute. The substituted bonds should be of essentially equal coupon, maturity, quality, call features, sinking fund provisions, and so on. A substitution swap would be motivated by a belief that the market has temporarily mispriced the two bonds, with a discrepancy representing a profit opportunity.

    An example of a substitution swap would be a sale of a 20-year maturity, 8% coupon Toyota bond that is priced to provide a yield to maturity of 8.05% coupled with a purchase of an 8% coupon Honda bond with the same time to maturity that yields 8.15%. If the bonds have about the same credit risk, there is no apparent reason for the Honda bonds to provide a higher yield. Therefore, the higher yield actually available in the market makes the Honda bond seem relatively attractive. Of course, the equality of credit risk is an important condition. If the Honda bond is in fact riskier, then its higher promised yield does not represent a bargain.

2. The **intermarket spread swap** is an exchange of two bonds from different sectors of the bond market. It is pursued when an investor believes the yield spread between two sectors of the bond market is temporarily out of line.

    For example, if the yield spread between 10-year Treasury bonds and 10-year Baa-rated corporate bonds is now 3%, and the historical spread has been only 2%, an investor might consider selling holdings of Treasury bonds and replacing them with corporates. If the yield spread eventually narrows, the Baa-rated corporate bonds will outperform the Treasury bonds.

    Of course, the investor must consider carefully whether there is a good reason that the yield spread seems out of alignment. For example, the default premium on corporate bonds might have increased because the market is expecting a severe recession. In this case, the wider spread would not represent attractive pricing of corporates relative to Treasuries, but would simply be an adjustment for a perceived increase in credit risk.

3. The **rate anticipation swap** is an exchange of bonds with different maturities. It is pegged to interest rate forecasting. Investors who believe rates will fall will swap into bonds of longer duration. For example, the investor might sell a five-year maturity Treasury bond, replacing it with a 25-year maturity Treasury bond. The new bond has the same lack of credit risk as the old one, but it has longer duration.

4. The **pure yield pickup swap** is an exchange of a shorter duration bond for a longer duration bond. This swap is pursued not in response to perceived mispricing but as a means of increasing return by holding higher yielding, longer maturity bonds. The investor is willing to bear the interest rate risk this strategy entails.

    A yield pickup swap can be illustrated using the Treasury bond listings in Figure 10.1 from the last chapter. You can see from that table that longer-term T-bonds offered higher yields to maturity than shorter ones. The investor who swaps the shorter term bond for the longer one will earn a higher rate of return as long as the yield curve does not shift upward during the holding period. Of course, if it does, the longer duration bond will suffer a greater capital loss.

We can add a fifth swap, called a **tax swap,** to this list. This simply refers to a swap to exploit some tax advantage. For example, an investor may swap from one bond that has decreased in price to another similar bond if realization of capital losses is advantageous for tax purposes.

Horizon Analysis

One form of interest rate forecasting, which we encountered in the last chapter, is called **horizon analysis.** The analyst selects a particular investment period and predicts bond yields

substitution swap
Exchange of one bond for a bond with similar attributes but more attractively priced.

intermarket spread swap
Switching from one segment of the bond market to another.

rate anticipation swap
A switch made in response to forecasts of interest rate changes.

pure yield pickup swap
Moving to higher yield bonds, usually with longer maturities.

tax swap
Swapping two similar bonds to receive a tax benefit.

horizon analysis
Forecast of bond returns based largely on a prediction of the yield curve at the end of the investment horizon.

at the end of that period. Given the predicted yield to maturity at the end of the investment period, the bond price can be calculated. The coupon income earned over the period is then added to the predicted capital gain or loss to obtain a forecast of the total return on the bond over the holding period.

EXAMPLE 11.5

Horizon Analysis

A 20-year maturity bond with a 10% coupon rate (paid annually) currently sells at a yield to maturity of 9%. A portfolio manager with a two-year horizon needs to forecast the total return on the bond over the coming two years. In two years, the bond will have an 18-year maturity. The analyst forecasts that two years from now, 18-year bonds will sell at yields to maturity of 8% and that coupon payments can be reinvested in short-term securities over the coming two years at a rate of 7%.

To calculate the two-year return on the bond, the analyst would perform the following calculations:

1. Current price = $100 × Annuity factor(9%, 20 years) + $1,000 × PV factor(9%, 20 years)
   = $1,091.29

2. Forecast price = $100 × Annuity factor(8%, 18 years) + $1,000 × PV factor(8%, 18 years)
   = $1,187.44

3. The future value of reinvested coupons will be ($100 × 1.07) + $100 = $207

4. The two-year return is $\dfrac{\$207 + (\$1,187.44 - \$1,091.29)}{\$1,091.29} = .278$, or 27.8%

The annualized rate of return over the two-year period would then be $(1.278)^{1/2} - 1 = .13$, or 13%.

CONCEPT
check **11.8**

What will be the rate of return in Example 11.5 if the manager forecasts that in two years the yield to maturity on 18-year maturity bonds will be 10% and that the reinvestment rate for coupons will be 8%?

An Example of a Fixed-Income Investment Strategy

To demonstrate a reasonable, active fixed-income portfolio strategy, we discuss here the policies of Sanford Bernstein & Co., as explained in a speech by its manager of fixed-income investments, Francis Trainer. The company believes big bets on general marketwide interest movements are unwise. Instead, it concentrates on exploiting numerous instances of perceived *relative* minor pricing misalignments *within* the fixed-income sector. The firm takes as a risk benchmark the Lehman Aggregate Bond Index, which includes the vast majority of publicly traded bonds with maturities greater than one year. Any deviation from this passive or neutral position must be justified by active analysis. Bernstein considers a neutral portfolio duration to be equal to that of the index.

The firm is willing to make only limited bets on interest rate movements. As Francis Trainer puts it in his speech:

> If we set duration of our portfolios at a level equal to the index and never allow them to vary, this would imply that we are perpetually neutral on the direction of interest rates. However, we believe the utilization of these forecasts will add value and, therefore, we incorporate our economic forecast into the bond management process by altering the durations of our portfolios.

> However, in order to prevent fixed-income performance from being dominated by the accuracy of just a single aspect of our research effort, we limit the degree to which we are willing to alter our interest rate exposure. Under the vast majority of circumstances, we will not permit the duration of our portfolios to differ from that of the [Lehman] Index by more than one year.

The company expends most of its effort in exploiting numerous but minor inefficiencies in bond prices that result from lack of attention by its competitors. Its analysts follow about 1,000 securities, attempting to "identify specific securities that are attractive or unattractive as well as identify trends in the richness or cheapness of industries and sectors." These two activities would be characterized as substitution swaps and intermarket spread swaps in the Homer–Leibowitz scheme.

Sanford Bernstein & Co. realizes that market opportunities will arise, if at all, only in sectors of the bond market that present the least competition from other analysts. For this reason, it tends to focus on relatively more complicated bond issues in the belief that extensive research efforts give the firm a comparative advantage in that sector. Finally, the company does not take unnecessary risks. If there do not appear to be enough seemingly attractive bonds, funds are placed in Treasury securities as a "neutral" parking space until new opportunities are identified.

To summarize the key features of this sort of strategy, we make the following observations:

1. A firm such as Bernstein has a respect for market prices. It believes that only minor mispricing usually can be detected. It works toward meaningful abnormal returns by combining numerous *small* profit opportunities, not by hoping for the success of one big bet.

2. To have value, information cannot already be reflected in market prices. A large research staff must focus on market niches that appear to be neglected by others.

3. Interest rate movements are extremely hard to predict, and attempts to time the market can wipe out all the profits of intramarket analysis.

SUMMARY

- Even default-free bonds such as Treasury issues are subject to interest rate risk. Longer term bonds generally are more sensitive to interest rate shifts than short-term bonds. A measure of the average life of a bond is Macaulay's duration, defined as the weighted average of the times until each payment made by the security, with weights proportional to the present value of the payment.
- Duration is a direct measure of the sensitivity of a bond's price to a change in its yield. The proportional change in a bond's price approximately equals the negative of duration times the proportional change in $1 + y$.
- Immunization strategies are characteristic of passive bond portfolio management. Such strategies attempt to render the individual or firm immune from movements in interest rates. This may take the form of immunizing net worth or, instead, immunizing the future accumulated value of a bond portfolio.
- Immunization of a fully funded plan is accomplished by matching the durations of assets and liabilities. To maintain an immunized position as time passes and interest rates change, the portfolio must be periodically rebalanced.
- Convexity refers to the curvature of a bond's price-yield relationship. Accounting for convexity can substantially improve on the accuracy of the duration approximation for bond-price sensitivity to changes in yields.
- A more direct form of immunization is dedication or cash flow matching. If a portfolio is perfectly matched in cash flow with projected liabilities, rebalancing will be unnecessary.
- Active bond management can be decomposed into interest rate forecasting techniques and intermarket spread analysis. One popular taxonomy classifies active strategies as substitution swaps, intermarket spread swaps, rate anticipation swaps, or pure yield pickup swaps.

KEY TERMS

cash flow matching, 344
convexity, 346
dedication strategy, 344
horizon analysis, 349
immunization, 338

intermarket spread
   swap, 349
Macaulay's duration, 332
modified duration, 334
pure yield pickup swap, 349

rate anticipation
   swap, 349
rebalancing, 342
substitution swap, 349
tax swap, 349

www.mhhe.com/bkm

PROBLEM SETS

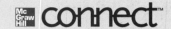

Select problems are available in McGraw-Hill Connect. Please see the packaging options section of the preface for more information.

Basic

1. How can a perpetuity, which has an infinite maturity, have a duration as short as 10 or 20 years?

2. You predict that interest rates are about to fall. Which bond will give you the highest capital gain?
   a. Low coupon, long maturity.
   b. High coupon, short maturity.
   c. High coupon, long maturity.
   d. Zero coupon, long maturity.

3. The historical yield spread between AAA bonds and Treasury bonds widened dramatically in 2008, If you believe the spread will soon return to more typical historical levels, what should you do? This would be an example of what sort of bond swap?

4. A bond currently sells for $1,050, which gives it a yield to maturity of 6%. Suppose that if the yield increases by 25 basis points, the price of the bond falls to $1,025. What is the duration of this bond?

5. Macaulay's duration is less than modified duration except for:
   a Zero-coupon bonds.
   b. Premium bonds.
   c. Bonds selling at par value.
   d. None of the above.

6. Is the decrease in a bond's price corresponding to an increase in its yield to maturity more or less than the price increase resulting from a decrease in yield of equal magnitude?

7. Short-term interest rates are more volatile than long-term rates. Despite this, the rates of return of long-term bonds are more volatile than returns on short-term securities. How can these two empirical observations be reconciled?

8. Find the duration of a 6% coupon bond making *annual* coupon payments if it has three years until maturity and a yield to maturity of 6%. What is the duration if the yield to maturity is 10%?

9. A nine-year bond has a yield of 10% and a duration of 7.194 years. If the bond's yield changes by 50 basis points, what is the percentage change in the bond's price?

Intermediate

10. A pension plan is obligated to make disbursements of $1 million, $2 million, and $1 million at the end of each of the next three years, respectively. Find the duration of the plan's obligations if the interest rate is 10% annually.

11. If the plan in the previous problem wants to fully fund and immunize its position, how much of its portfolio should it allocate to one-year zero-coupon bonds and perpetuities, respectively, if these are the only two assets funding the plan?

12. You own a fixed-income asset with a duration of five years. If the level of interest rates, which is currently 8%, goes down by 10 basis points, how much do you expect the price of the asset to go up (in percentage terms)?

13. Rank the interest rate sensitivity of the following pairs of bonds.
    a. Bond A is an 8% coupon, 20-year maturity bond selling at par value.
       Bond B is an 8% coupon, 20-year maturity bond selling below par value.
    b. Bond A is a 20-year, noncallable coupon bond with a coupon rate of 8%, selling at par.
       Bond B is a 20-year, callable bond with a coupon rate of 9%, also selling at par.

14. Long-term Treasury bonds currently are selling at yields to maturity of nearly 8%. You expect interest rates to fall. The rest of the market thinks that they will remain

unchanged over the coming year. In each question, choose the bond that will provide the higher capital gain if you are correct. Briefly explain your answer.

   a. (1) A Baa-rated bond with coupon rate 8% and time to maturity 20 years.

     (2) An Aaa-rated bond with coupon rate 8% and time to maturity 20 years.

   b. (1) An A-rated bond with coupon rate 4% and maturity 20 years, callable at 105.

     (2) An A-rated bond with coupon rate 8% and maturity 20 years, callable at 105.

   c. (1) A 6% coupon noncallable T-bond with maturity 20 years and YTM = 8%.

     (2) A 9% coupon noncallable T-bond with maturity 20 years and YTM = 8%.

15. You will be paying $10,000 a year in tuition expenses at the end of the next two years. Bonds currently yield 8%.

   a. What is the present value and duration of your obligation?

   b. What maturity zero-coupon bond would immunize your obligation?

   c. Suppose you buy a zero-coupon bond with value and duration equal to your obligation. Now suppose that rates immediately increase to 9%. What happens to your net position, that is, to the difference between the value of the bond and that of your tuition obligation? What if rates fall to 7%?

16. Pension funds pay lifetime annuities to recipients. If a firm remains in business indefinitely, the pension obligation will resemble a perpetuity. Suppose, therefore, that you are managing a pension fund with obligations to make perpetual payments of $2 million per year to beneficiaries. The yield to maturity on all bonds is 16%.

   a. If the duration of five-year maturity bonds with coupon rates of 12% (paid annually) is 4 years and the duration of 20-year maturity bonds with coupon rates of 6% (paid annually) is 11 years, how much of each of these coupon bonds (in market value) will you want to hold to both fully fund and immunize your obligation?

   b. What will be the *par value* of your holdings in the 20-year coupon bond?

17. You are managing a portfolio of $1 million. Your target duration is 10 years, and you can choose from two bonds: a zero-coupon bond with maturity 5 years, and a perpetuity, each currently yielding 5%.

   a. How much of each bond will you hold in your portfolio?

   b. How will these fractions change *next year* if target duration is now nine years?

18. Find the duration of a bond with settlement date May 27, 2010, and maturity date November 15, 2019. The coupon rate of the bond is 7%, and the bond pays coupons semiannually. The bond is selling at a yield to maturity of 8%. You can use Spreadsheet 11.2, available at **www.mhhe.com/bkm**; link to Chapter 11 material.

Please visit us at www.mhhe.com/bkm

19. What is the duration of the bond in the previous problem if coupons are paid annually? Explain why the duration changes in the direction it does.

Please visit us at www.mhhe.com/bkm

20. You manage a pension fund that will provide retired workers with lifetime annuities. You determine that the payouts of the fund are essentially going to resemble level perpetuities of $1 million per year. The interest rate is 10%. You plan to fully fund the obligation using 5-year and 20-year maturity zero-coupon bonds.

   a. How much *market value* of each of the zeros will be necessary to fund the plan if you desire an immunized position?

   b. What must be the *face value* of the two zeros to fund the plan?

21. Find the convexity of a 7-year maturity, 6% coupon bond selling at a yield to maturity of 8%. The bond pays its coupons annually. (*Hint:* You can use the spreadsheet from this chapter's Excel Application on Convexity, setting cash flows after year 7 equal to zero. The spreadsheet is available at **www.mhhe.com/bkm**; link to Chapter 11 material.)

Please visit us at www.mhhe.com/bkm

22. *a.* Use a spreadsheet to calculate the durations of the two bonds in Spreadsheet 11.1 if the interest rate increases to 12%. Why does the duration of the coupon bond fall while that of the zero remains unchanged? (*Hint:* Examine what happens to the weights computed in column E.)

   b. Use the same spreadsheet to calculate the duration of the coupon bond if the coupon were 12% instead of 8%. Explain why the duration is lower. (Again, start by looking at column E.)

Please visit us at www.mhhe.com/bkm

23. *a.* Footnote 2 in the chapter presents the formula for the convexity of a bond. Build a spreadsheet to calculate the convexity of the 8% coupon bond in Spreadsheet 11.1 at the initial yield to maturity of 10%.
    b. What is the convexity of the zero-coupon bond?

24. A 30-year maturity bond making annual coupon payments with a coupon rate of 12% has duration of 11.54 years and convexity of 192.4. The bond currently sells at a yield to maturity of 8%. Use a financial calculator or spreadsheet to find the price of the bond if its yield to maturity falls to 7% or rises to 9%. What prices for the bond at these new yields would be predicted by the duration rule and the duration-with-convexity rule? What is the percent error for each rule? What do you conclude about the accuracy of the two rules?

25. Currently, the term structure is as follows: one-year bonds yield 7%, two-year bonds yield 8%, three-year bonds and greater maturity bonds all yield 9%. You are choosing between one-, two-, and three-year maturity bonds all paying *annual* coupons of 8%, once a year. Which bond should you buy if you strongly believe that at year-end the yield curve will be flat at 9%?

26. A 30-year maturity bond has a 7% coupon rate, paid annually. It sells today for $867.42. A 20-year maturity bond has a 6.5% coupon rate, also paid annually. It sells today for $879.50. A bond market analyst forecasts that in five years, 25-year maturity bonds will sell at yields to maturity of 8% and that 15-year maturity bonds will sell at yields of 7.5%. Because the yield curve is upward-sloping, the analyst believes that coupons will be invested in short-term securities at a rate of 6%. Which bond offers the higher expected rate of return over the five-year period?

Challenge

27. A 12.75-year maturity zero-coupon bond selling at a yield to maturity of 8% (effective annual yield) has convexity of 150.3 and modified duration of 11.81 years. A 30-year maturity 6% coupon bond making annual coupon payments also selling at a yield to maturity of 8% has nearly identical modified duration—11.79 years—but considerably higher convexity of 231.2.
    a. Suppose the yield to maturity on both bonds increases to 9%. What will be the actual percentage capital loss on each bond? What percentage capital loss would be predicted by the duration-with-convexity rule?
    b. Repeat part (*a*), but this time assume the yield to maturity decreases to 7%.
    c. Compare the performance of the two bonds in the two scenarios, one involving an increase in rates, the other a decrease. Based on their comparative investment performance, explain the attraction of convexity.
    d. In view of your answer to (*c*), do you think it would be possible for two bonds with equal duration, but different convexity, to be priced initially at the same yield to maturity if the yields on both bonds always increased or decreased by equal amounts, as in this example? Would anyone be willing to buy the bond with lower convexity under these circumstances?

CFA Problems

1. Rank the following bonds in order of descending duration.

Bond	Coupon	Time to Maturity	Yield to Maturity
A	15%	20 years	10%
B	15	15	10
C	0	20	10
D	8	20	10
E	15	15	15

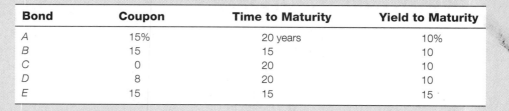

2. Philip Morris has issued bonds that pay annually with the following characteristics:

Coupon	Yield to Maturity	Maturity	Macaulay Duration
8%	8%	15 years	10 years

a. Calculate modified duration using the information above.
b. Explain why modified duration is a better measure than maturity when calculating the bond's sensitivity to changes in interest rates.
c. Identify the direction of change in modified duration if:
    i. The coupon of the bond were 4%, not 8%.
    ii. The maturity of the bond were 7 years, not 15 years.

3. As part of your analysis of debt issued by Monticello Corporation, you are asked to evaluate two specific bond issues, shown in the table below.

MONTICELLO CORPORATION BOND INFORMATION

	Bond A (callable)	Bond B (noncallable)
Maturity	2016	2016
Coupon	11.50%	7.25%
Current price	125.75	100.00
Yield to maturity	7.70%	7.25%
Modified duration to maturity	6.20	6.80
Call date	2010	—
Call price	105	—
Yield to call	5.10%	—
Modified duration to call	3.10	—

a. Using the duration and yield information in the table, compare the price and yield behavior of the two bonds under each of the following two scenarios:
    i. Strong economic recovery with rising inflation expectations.
    ii. Economic recession with reduced inflation expectations.
b. Using the information in the table, calculate the projected price change for bond B if the yield-to-maturity for this bond falls by 75 basis points.
c. Describe the shortcoming of analyzing bond A strictly to call or to maturity.

4. One common goal among fixed-income portfolio managers is to earn high incremental returns on corporate bonds versus government bonds of comparable durations. The approach of some corporate-bond portfolio managers is to find and purchase those corporate bonds having the largest initial spreads over comparable-duration government bonds. John Ames, HFS's fixed-income manager, believes that a more rigorous approach is required if incremental returns are to be maximized.

The following table presents data relating to one set of corporate/government spread relationships (in basis points, b.p.) present in the market at a given date:

CURRENT AND EXPECTED SPREADS AND DURATIONS OF HIGH-GRADE CORPORATE BONDS (ONE-YEAR HORIZON)

Bond Rating	Initial Spread over Governments	Expected Horizon Spread	Initial Duration	Expected Duration One Year from Now
Aaa	31 b.p.	31 b.p.	4 years	3.1 years
Aa	40	50	4	3.1

a. Recommend purchase of *either* Aaa *or* Aa bonds for a one-year investment horizon given a goal of maximizing incremental returns.
b. Ames chooses not to rely solely on initial spread relationships. His analytical framework considers a full range of other key variables likely to impact realized

incremental returns including: call provisions and potential changes in interest rates. Describe other variables that Ames should include in his analysis and explain how each of these could cause realized incremental returns to differ from those indicated by initial spread relationships.

5. Noah Kramer, a fixed-income portfolio manager based in the country of Sevista, is considering the purchase of a Sevista government bond. Kramer decides to evaluate two strategies for implementing his investment in Sevista bonds. Table 11.6 gives the details of the two strategies, and Table 11.7 contains the assumptions that apply to both strategies.

TABLE 11.6

Investment strategies (amounts are market value invested)

Strategy	5-Year Maturity (Modified Duration = 4.83 Years)	15-Year Maturity (Modified Duration = 14.35 Years)	25-Year Maturity (Modified Duration = 23.81 Years)
I	$5 million	0	$5 million
II	0	$10 million	0

TABLE 11.7

Investment strategy assumptions

Market Value of Bonds	$10 Million
Bond maturities	5 and 25 years or 15 years
Bond coupon rates	0.00%
Target modified duration	15 years

Before choosing one of the two bond investment strategies, Kramer wants to analyze how the market value of the bonds will change if an instantaneous interest rate shift occurs immediately after his investment. The details of the interest rate shift are shown in Table 11.8. Calculate, for the instantaneous interest rate shift shown in Table 11.8, the percent change in the market value of the bonds that will occur under each strategy.

TABLE 11.8

Instantaneous interest rate shift immediately after investment

Maturity	Interest Rate Change
5 year	Down 75 basis points
15	Up 25 bp
25	Up 50 bp

6. *a.* Janet Meer is a fixed-income portfolio manager. Noting that the current shape of the yield curve is flat, she considers the purchase of a newly issued, option-free corporate bond priced at par; the bond is described in Table 11.9. Calculate the duration of the bond.

TABLE 11.9

7% Option-free bond, maturity = 10 years

	Change in Yields	
	Up 10 Basis Points	Down 10 Basis Points
Price	99.29	100.71
Convexity	35.00	

b. Meer is also considering the purchase of a second newly issued, option-free corporate bond, which is described in Table 11.10. She wants to evaluate this second bond's price sensitivity to an instantaneous, downward parallel shift in the yield curve of 200 basis points. Estimate the total percentage price change for the bond if the yield curve experiences an instantaneous, downward parallel shift of 200 basis points.

TABLE 11.10 7.25% Option-free bond, maturity = 12 years	Original issue price	Par value, to yield 7.25%
	Modified duration (at original price)	7.90
	Convexity measure	41.55
	Convexity adjustment (yield change of 200 basis points)	1.66

7. Sandra Kapple presents Maria VanHusen with a description, given in the following exhibit, of the bond portfolio held by the Star Hospital Pension Plan. All securities in the bond portfolio are noncallable U.S. Treasury securities.

STAR HOSPITAL PENSION PLAN BOND PORTFOLIO

				Price if Yields Change		
Par Value (U.S. $)	Treasury Security	Market Value (U.S. $)	Current Price	Up 100 Basis Points	Down 100 Basis Points	Effective Duration
$48,000,000	2.375% due 2010	$48,667,680	$101.391	99.245	103.595	2.15
50,000,000	4.75% due 2035	50,000,000	100.000	86.372	116.887	
98,000,000	Total bond portfolio	98,667,680	—	—	—	

a. Calculate the effective duration of each of the following:
  i. The 4.75% Treasury security due 2035
  ii. The total bond portfolio
b. VanHusen remarks to Kapple, "If you changed the maturity structure of the bond portfolio to result in a portfolio duration of 5.25, the price sensitivity of that portfolio would be identical to the price sensitivity of a single, noncallable Treasury security that has a duration of 5.25." In what circumstance would VanHusen's remark be correct?

8. The ability to *immunize* a bond portfolio is very desirable for bond portfolio managers in some instances.
  a. Discuss the components of interest rate risk—that is, assuming a change in interest rates over time, explain the two risks faced by the holder of a bond.
  b. Define immunization and discuss why a bond manager would immunize his or her portfolio.
  c. Explain why a duration-matching strategy is a superior technique to a maturity-matching strategy for the minimization of interest rate risk.

9. You are the manager for the bond portfolio of a pension fund. The policies of the fund allow for the use of active strategies in managing the bond portfolio.

It appears that the economic cycle is beginning to mature, inflation is expected to accelerate, and, in an effort to contain the economic expansion, central bank policy is moving toward constraint. For each of the situations below, state which one of the two bonds you would prefer. Briefly justify your answer in each case.
  a. Government of Canada (Canadian pay), 4% due in 2014, and priced at 98.75 to yield 4.50% to maturity;
  or
  Government of Canada (Canadian pay), 4% due in 2024, and priced at 91.75 to yield 5.19% to maturity.

   b. Texas Power and Light Co., 5½% due in 2019, rated AAA, and priced at 85 to yield 8.1% to maturity;

   or

   Arizona Public Service Co., 5.45% due in 2019, rated A −, and priced at 80 to yield 9.1% to maturity.

   c. Commonwealth Edison, 2¾% due in 2018, rated Baa, and priced at 81 to yield 7.2% to maturity;

   or

   Commonwealth Edison, 9⅜% due in 2018, rated Baa, and priced at 114 to yield 7.2% to maturity.

   d. Shell Oil Co., 6¾% sinking fund debentures due in 2023, rated AAA (sinking fund begins in 2012 at par), and priced at 89 to yield 7.1% to maturity;

   or

   Warner-Lambert, 6⅞% sinking fund debentures due in 2023, rated AAA (sinking fund begins in 2016 at par), and priced at 95 to yield 7.0% to maturity.

   e. Bank of Montreal (Canadian pay), 4% certificates of deposit due in 2011, rated AAA, and priced at 100 to yield 4% to maturity;

   or

   Bank of Montreal (Canadian pay), floating-rate notes due in 2015, rated AAA. Coupon currently set at 3.7% and priced at 100 (coupon adjusted semiannually to 0.5% above the three-month Government of Canada Treasury bill rate).

10. a. Which set of conditions will result in a bond with the greatest price volatility?
    (1) A high coupon and a short maturity.
    (2) A high coupon and a long maturity.
    (3) A low coupon and a short maturity.
    (4) A low coupon and a long maturity.

    b. An investor who expects declining interest rates would be likely to purchase a bond that has a _____ coupon and a _____ term to maturity.
    (1) Low, long
    (2) High, short
    (3) High, long
    (4) Zero, long

    c. With a zero-coupon bond:
    (1) Duration equals the weighted average term to maturity.
    (2) Term to maturity equals duration.
    (3) Weighted average term to maturity equals the term to maturity.
    (4) All of the above.

    d. As compared with bonds selling at par, deep discount bonds will have:
    (1) Greater reinvestment risk.
    (2) Greater price volatility.
    (3) Less call protection.
    (4) None of the above.

11. A member of a firm's investment committee is very interested in learning about the management of fixed-income portfolios. He would like to know how fixed-income managers position portfolios to capitalize on their expectations concerning three factors which influence interest rates. Assuming that no investment policy limitations apply, formulate and describe a fixed-income portfolio management strategy for each of the following interest rate factors that could be used to exploit a portfolio manager's expectations about that factor. (*Note:* Three strategies are required, one for each of the listed factors.)

    a. Changes in the level of interest rates.
    b. Changes in yield spreads across/between sectors.
    c. Changes in yield spreads as to a particular instrument.

12. The following bond swaps could have been made in recent years as investors attempted to increase the total return on their portfolio.

   From the information presented below, identify possible reason(s) that investors may have made each swap.

Action		Call	Price	YTM (%)
a. Sell	Baa1 Electric Pwr. 1st mtg. 6⅜% due 2014	108.24	95	7.71
Buy	Baa1 Electric Pwr. 1st mtg. 2⅜% due 2015	105.20	79	7.39
b. Sell	Aaa Phone Co. notes 5½% due 2015	101.50	90	7.02
Buy	U.S. Treasury notes 6½% due 2015	NC	97.15	6.78
c. Sell	Aa1 Apex Bank zero coupon due 2017	NC	45	7.51
Buy	Aa1 Apex Bank float rate notes due 2030	103.90	90	—
d. Sell	A1 Commonwealth Oil & Gas 1st mtg. 6% due 2020	105.75	72	8.09
Buy	U.S. Treasury bond 5½% due 2026	NC	80.60	7.40
e. Sell	A1 Z mart convertible deb. 3% due 2020	103.90	62	6.92
Buy	A2 Lucky Ducks deb. 7¾% due 2026	109.86	75	10.43

Use data from the Standard & Poor's Market Insight Database at www.mhhe.com/edumarketinsight to answer the following questions.

STANDARD
&POOR'S

1. At the Market Insight *Company* page enter the stock ticker symbol HLT for Hilton Hotels Corporation and do the following:
   a. Review the recent Industry Outlook (in the S&P Stock Reports section) for the Hotels, Resorts, and Cruise Lines subindustry. What is the outlook for hotels? How might the outlook affect outstanding debt and the issuance of new debt?
   b. Review the variety of Hilton bonds and notes outstanding that are listed in the latest EDGAR 10K report for Hilton. Use the Edit, Find on This Page menu and search for the term "bond" to find the list about halfway through the document. How does the company's debt structure in the current year compare with its debt structure in the previous year? Based on the types and maturities of bonds outstanding, how much interest rate risk do the bondholders face?
   c. What percentage of the debt issues outstanding represents current liabilities? How did the percentage change during the past year?
   d. Go to **http://bonds.yahoo.com,** and search for the Hilton bonds. What are the current ratings and yields to maturity for Hilton's debt securities? Use the prices and the coupon rates shown to perform calculations to confirm the Current Yield shown for each bond.
   e. What type of investor would be interested in these bonds? For what kinds of portfolios would they be inappropriate?

2. Enter the stock symbol S to locate information for Sprint Nextel Corp. on Market Insight. Find the company's most recent annual Balance Sheet in the Excel Analytics section.
   a. Examine the company's assets and liabilities. What proportion of total assets are current assets? What proportion of total liabilities are current liabilities? Does it seem that there is a good match between the duration of the assets and the duration of the liabilities?
   b. Look at the Annual Statement of Cash Flows for Sprint Nextel, which is also found in the Excel Analytics section. Check the Financing Activities section to see if the company has issued new debt or reduced its debt outstanding. How much interest did the firm pay during the period?
   c. Repeat the exercise with several other companies of your choice. Try to pick companies in different industries. Do you notice any patterns that might be due to the industrial environments in which the firms operate?

WEB *master* BOND CALCULATIONS

Many bond calculators are offered on the Web. You can retrieve information about a particular bond issue, then calculate duration and convexity with the click of a button.

1. Select a bond from the most actively traded corporate bond list at **www.investinginbonds.com.** Go to the "Bond Markets and Prices" link, then select "Corporate Market At-a-Glance" to link to the most active list. Select a bond that has a maturity date a few years away and click on its CUSIP number to find further information.

2. Choose the most recent trading date listed and click on the "run calculations" link. The bond's characteristics are entered for you.

3. Confirm the amount of the accrued interest and the cash flow schedule listed.

4. Confirm the bond's duration by either performing the calculations in a spreadsheet or using Excel's DURATION function.

5. Based on the bond's current price, by what percent would the price change if the yield were to change by .5%?

6. Repeat the calculations by entering assumed prices of 90, 100, and 110, then answer the following questions:

   a. What are the duration and the convexity for the bond at the each of the prices?

   b. Is the bond price more or less sensitive to interest rates at higher prices relative to lower ones? How does convexity change as the price changes? Is the change in convexity symmetrical? That is, as the price decreases by $10 (from 100 to 90) and increases by $10 (from 100 to 110), are the changes in convexity equal but opposite in sign?

SOLUTIONS TO CONCEPT *checks*

11.1. Interest rate: 0.09

	(B) Time until Payment (years)	(C) Payment	(D) Payment Discounted at 9%	(E) Weight	Column (B) times Column (E)
A. 8% coupon bond	1	80	73.394	0.0753	0.0753
	2	80	67.334	0.0691	0.1382
	3	1080	833.958	0.8556	2.5668
Sum:			974.687	1.0000	2.7803
B. Zero-coupon bond	1	0	0.000	0.0000	0.0000
	2	0	0.000	0.0000	0.0000
	3	1000	772.183	1.0000	3.0000
Sum:			772.183	1.0000	3.0000

The duration of the 8% coupon bond rises to 2.7803 years. Price increases to $974.687. The duration of the zero-coupon bond is unchanged at 3 years, although its price also increases when the interest rate falls.

11.2. *a.* If the interest rate increases from 9% to 9.05%, the bond price falls from $974.687 to $973.445. The percentage change in price is −.127%.

   b. The duration formula would predict a price change of

$$-\frac{2.7802}{1.09} \times .0005 = -.00127 = -.127\%$$

which is the same answer that we obtained from direct computation in part (*a*).

11.3. Use Excel to confirm that DURATION(DATE(2000,1,1), DATE(2008,1,1), .09, .10, 1) = 5.97 years. If you change the last argument of the duration function from 1 to 2 (to allow for semi-annual coupons), you will find that DURATION(DATE(2000,1,1), DATE(2008,1,1), .09, .10, 2) = 5.80 years. Duration is lower when coupons are paid semiannually rather than annually because, on average, payments come earlier. Instead of waiting until year-end to receive the annual coupon, investors receive half the coupon midway through the year.

11.4. The duration of a level perpetuity is $(1 + y)/y$ or $1 + 1/y$, which clearly falls as y increases. Tabulating duration as a function of y we get:

y	D
.01 (i.e., 1%)	101 years
.02	51
.05	21
.10	11
.20	6
.25	5
.40	3.5

11.5. The perpetuity's duration now would be $1.08/.08 = 13.5$. We need to solve the following equation for w

$$w \times 2 + (1 - w) \times 13.5 = 6$$

Therefore, $w = .6522$.

11.6. *a.* The present value of the fund's obligation is $\$800,000/.08 = \$10$ million. The duration is 13.5 years. Therefore, the fund should invest $10 million in zeros with a 13.5-year maturity. The face value of the zeros will be $\$10,000,000 \times 1.08^{13.5} = \$28,263,159$.

b. When the interest rate increases to 8.1%, the present value of the fund's obligation drops to $800,000/.081 = \$9,876,543$. The value of the zero-coupon bond falls by roughly the same amount, to $\$28,263,159/1.081^{13.5} = \$9,875,835$. The duration of the perpetual obligation falls to $1.081/.081 = 13.346$ years. The fund should sell the zero it currently holds and purchase $9,876,543 in zero-coupon bonds with maturity of 13.346 years.

11.7. Dedication would be more attractive. Cash flow matching eliminates the need for rebalancing and, thus, saves transaction costs.

11.8. Current price $= \$1,091.29$

Forecast price $= \$100 \times$ Annuity factor $(10\%, 18$ years$) + \$1,000 \times$ PV factor$(10\%, 18$ years$) = \$1,000$

The future value of reinvested coupons will be $(\$100 \times 1.08) + \$100 = \$208$

The two-year return is $\dfrac{\$208 + (\$1,000 - \$1,091.29)}{\$1,091.29} = .107$, or 10.7%

The annualized rate of return over the two-year period would then be $(1.107)^{1/2} - 1 = .052$, or 5.2%.

PART 4

Security Analysis

Tell your friends or relatives that you are studying investments and they will ask you, "What stocks should I buy?" This is the question at the heart of security analysis. How do analysts choose the stocks and other securities to hold in their portfolios?

Security analysis requires a wide mix of skills. You need to be a decent economist with a good grasp of both macroeconomics and microeconomics, the former to help you form forecasts of the general direction of the market and the latter to help you assess the relative position of particular industries or firms. You need a good sense of demographic and social trends to help identify industries with bright prospects. You need to be a quick study of the ins and outs of particular industries to choose the firms that will succeed within each industry. You need a good accounting background to analyze the financial statements that firms provide to the public. You also need to have mastered corporate finance, since security analysis at its core is the ability to value a firm. In short, a good security analyst will be a generalist, with a grasp of the widest range of financial issues. This is where there is the biggest premium on "putting it all together."

The chapters in Part Four are an introduction to security analysis. We will provide you with a "top-down" approach to the subject, starting with an overview of international, macroeconomic, and industry issues, and only then progressing to the analysis of particular firms. These topics form the core of fundamental analysis. After reading these chapters, you will have a good sense of the various techniques used to analyze stocks and the stock market.

12

Macroeconomic and Industry Analysis

After Studying This Chapter You Should Be Able To:

- Predict the effect of monetary and fiscal policies on key macroeconomic variables such as gross domestic product, interest rates, and the inflation rate.

- Use leading, coincident, and lagging economic indicators to describe and predict the economy's path through the business cycle.

- Predict which industries will be more or less sensitive to business cycle fluctuations.

- Analyze the effect of industry life cycles and structure on industry earnings prospects over time.

To determine a proper price for a firm's stock, the security analyst must forecast the dividends and earnings that can be expected from the firm. This is the heart of **fundamental analysis,** that is, the analysis of determinants of value such as earnings prospects. Ultimately, the business success of the firm determines the dividends it can pay to shareholders and the price it will command in the stock market. Because the prospects of the firm are tied to those of the broader economy, however, valuation analyses must consider the business environment in which the firm operates. For some firms, macroeconomic and industry circumstances might have a greater influence on profits than the firm's relative performance within its industry. In other words, investors need to keep the big economic picture in mind.

Therefore, in analyzing a firm's prospects it often makes sense to start with the broad economic environment, examining the state of the aggregate economy and even the international economy. From there, one considers the implications of the outside environment on the industry in which the firm operates. Finally, the firm's position within the industry is examined.

This chapter examines the broadbased aspects of fundamental analysis — macroeconomic and industry analysis. The

fundamental analysis

The analysis of determinants of firm value, such as prospects for earnings and dividends.

363

following two chapters cover firm-specific analysis. We begin with a discussion of international factors relevant to firm performance and move on to an overview of the significance of the key variables usually used to summarize the state of the economy. We then discuss government macroeconomic policy and the determination of interest rates. We conclude the analysis of the macroeconomic environment with a discussion of business cycles. Next, we move to industry analysis, treating issues concerning the sensitivity of the firm to the business cycle, the typical life cycle of an industry, and strategic issues that affect industry performance.

12.1 | The Global Economy

A top-down analysis of a firm's prospects must start with the global economy. The international economy might affect a firm's export prospects, the price competition it faces from foreign competitors, or the profits it makes on investments abroad. Table 12.1 shows the importance of the global macroeconomy to firms' prospects. The effects of the subprime-mortgage and credit crises of 2008 were widespread and severe. Stock markets in virtually all countries were deeply affected, with average returns typically worse than −40%.

Despite the obvious importance of this global economic factor, there was also considerable variation in economic performance across countries. For example, while the economy of Japan grew by only .3%, Chinese output grew by 9.6%. Stock market returns also showed considerable dispersion. While the Russian market fell by 71.9% (with returns measured in U.S. dollars), the Swiss market fell by only 30.0%, a difference of 41.9%

These data illustrate that the national economic environment can be a crucial determinant of industry performance. It is far harder for businesses to succeed in a contracting economy than in an expanding one. This observation highlights the role of a big-picture macroeconomic analysis as a fundamental part of the investment process.

In addition, the global environment presents political risks of far greater magnitude than are typically encountered in U.S.-based investments. In the last decade, we have seen several instances where political developments had major impacts on economic prospects. For example, the biggest international economic story in late 1997 and 1998 was the turmoil in several Asian economies, notably Thailand, Indonesia, and South Korea. These episodes also highlighted the close interplay between politics and economics, as both currency and stock

TABLE 12.1 Economic performance, 2008	Stock Market Return (%)		Growth in GDP (%)
	In Local Currency	In U.S. Dollars	
Brazil	−42.0%	−57.0%	5.3%
Britain	−33.1	−51.1	0.3
Canada	−37.6	−49.6	0.6
China	−64.8	−62.5	9.6
France	−44.2	−45.7	0.9
Germany	−41.7	−43.2	1.4
India	−53.0	−61.7	6.2
Japan	−42.9	−29.2	0.3
Mexico	−24.2	−38.8	2.6
Russia	−66.6	−71.9	7.0
Singapore	−48.6	−48.6	2.2
Switzerland	−35.6	−30.0	1.8
Thailand	−47.9	−49.9	4.0
U.S.	−40.8	−40.8	1.3
Venezuela	−7.9	−59.1	4.2

Source: *The Economist*, January 3, 2009. © 2009 The Economist Newspaper Group, Inc. Reprinted with permission. Further reproduction is prohibited. **www.economist.com**.

values swung with enormous volatility in response to developments concerning the prospects for aid for these countries from the International Monetary Fund. In August 1998, the shock waves following Russia's devaluation of the ruble and default on some of its debt created havoc in world security markets, ultimately requiring a rescue of the giant hedge fund Long Term Capital Management to avoid further major disruptions. In the first decade of this century, stock prices have been highly sensitive to developments in Iraq and the security of energy supplies. Most recently, developments in the political response to the credit crisis have driven stock returns.

Other political issues that are less sensational but still extremely important to economic growth and investment returns include issues of protectionism and trade policy, the free flow of capital, and the status of a nation's workforce.

One obvious factor that affects the international competitiveness of a country's industries is the exchange rate between that country's currency and other currencies. The **exchange rate** is the rate at which domestic currency can be converted into foreign currency. For example, on January 1, 2009, it took about 91 Japanese yen to purchase one U.S. dollar. We would say that the exchange rate is ¥91 per dollar, or equivalently, $.0110 per yen.

exchange rate

The rate at which domestic currency can be converted into foreign currency.

As exchange rates fluctuate, the dollar value of goods priced in foreign currency similarly fluctuates. For example, in 1980, the dollar–yen exchange rate was about $.0045 per yen. Since the exchange rate in 2009 was $.0110 per yen, a U.S. citizen would have needed 2.44 times as many dollars in 2009 to buy a product selling for ¥10,000 as would have been required in 1980. If the Japanese producer were to maintain a fixed yen price for its product, the price expressed in U.S. dollars would more than double. This would make Japanese products more expensive to U.S. consumers, however, and result in lost sales. Obviously, appreciation of the yen creates a problem for Japanese producers such as automakers that must compete with U.S. producers.

Figure 12.1 shows the change in the purchasing power of the U.S. dollar relative to the purchasing power of several major currencies in the last decade. The ratio of purchasing powers is called the "real" or inflation-adjusted exchange rate. The change in the real exchange rate measures how much more or less expensive foreign goods have become to U.S. citizens, accounting for both exchange rate fluctuations and inflation differentials across countries. A positive value in Figure 12.1 means that the dollar has gained purchasing power relative to another currency; a negative number indicates a depreciating dollar. Therefore, the figure shows that goods priced in terms of euros or Canadian dollars became more expensive to U.S. consumers in the last 10 years but that goods priced in British pounds or yen became cheaper. Conversely, goods priced in U.S. dollars became more expensive to Japanese consumers, but more affordable to Canadian consumers.

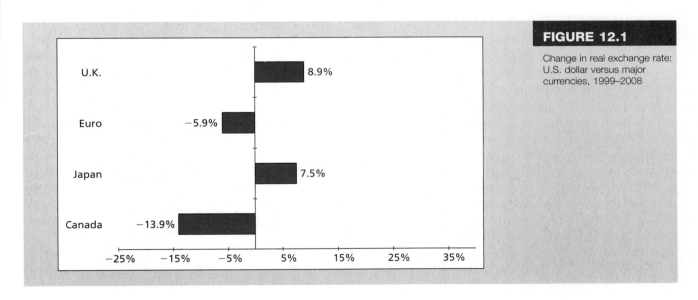

FIGURE 12.1

Change in real exchange rate: U.S. dollar versus major currencies, 1999–2008

12.2 | The Domestic Macroeconomy

The macroeconomy is the environment in which all firms operate. The importance of the macroeconomy in determining investment performance is illustrated in Figure 12.2, which compares the level of the S&P 500 stock price index to estimates of earnings per share of the S&P 500 companies. The graph shows that stock prices tend to rise along with earnings. While the exact ratio of stock price to earnings per share varies with factors such as interest rates, risk, inflation rates, and other variables, the graph does illustrate that, as a general rule, the ratio has tended to be in the range of 12 to 25. Given "normal" price-to-earnings ratios, we would expect the S&P 500 Index to fall within these boundaries. While the earnings-multiplier rule clearly is not perfect—note the dramatic increase in the P/E multiple in the 1990s—it also seems clear that the level of the broad market and aggregate earnings do trend together. Thus, the first step in forecasting the performance of the broad market is to assess the status of the economy as a whole.

The ability to forecast the macroeconomy can translate into spectacular investment performance. But it is not enough to forecast the macroeconomy well. One must forecast it *better* than one's competitors to earn abnormal profits. In this section, we will review some of the key economic statistics used to describe the state of the macroeconomy.

Gross Domestic Product

gross domestic product (GDP)

The market value of goods and services produced over a period of time.

Gross domestic product, or GDP, is the measure of the economy's total production of goods and services. Rapidly growing GDP indicates an expanding economy with ample opportunity for a firm to increase sales. Another popular measure of the economy's output is *industrial production.* This statistic provides a measure of economic activity more narrowly focused on the manufacturing side of the economy.

Employment

unemployment rate

The ratio of the number of people classified as unemployed to the total labor force.

The **unemployment rate** is the percentage of the total labor force (i.e., those who are either working or actively seeking employment) yet to find work. The unemployment rate measures the extent to which the economy is operating at full capacity. The unemployment rate is a statistic related to workers only, but further insight into the strength of the economy can be gleaned from the employment rate of other factors of production. For example, analysts also look at the factory *capacity utilization rate,* which is the ratio of actual output from factories to potential output.

FIGURE 12.2

S&P 500 Index versus earnings per share

Source: Authors' calculations using data from *The Economic Report of the President,* 2008.

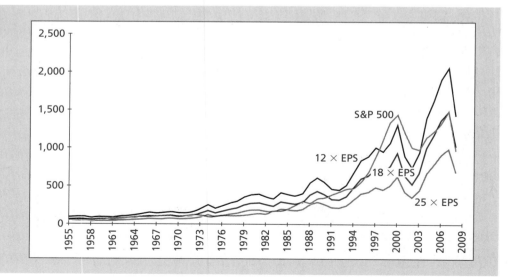

Inflation

Inflation is the rate at which the general level of prices is rising. High rates of inflation often are associated with "overheated" economies, that is, economies where the demand for goods and services is outstripping productive capacity, which leads to upward pressure on prices. Most governments walk a fine line in their economic policies. They hope to stimulate their economies enough to maintain nearly full employment, but not so much as to bring on inflationary pressures. The perceived trade-off between inflation and unemployment is at the heart of many macroeconomic policy disputes. There is considerable room for disagreement as to the relative costs of these policies as well as the economy's relative vulnerability to these pressures at any particular time.

inflation

The rate at which the general level of prices for goods and services is rising.

Interest Rates

High interest rates reduce the present value of future cash flows, thereby reducing the attractiveness of investment opportunities. For this reason, real interest rates are key determinants of business investment expenditures. Demand for housing and high-priced consumer durables such as automobiles, which are commonly financed, also is highly sensitive to interest rates because interest rates affect interest payments. In Section 12.3 we will examine the determinants of real interest rates.

Budget Deficit

The **budget deficit** of the federal government is the difference between government spending and revenues. Any budgetary shortfall must be offset by government borrowing. Large amounts of government borrowing can force up interest rates by increasing the total demand for credit in the economy. Economists generally believe excessive government borrowing will "crowd out" private borrowing and investing by forcing up interest rates and choking off business investment.

budget deficit

The amount by which government spending exceeds government revenues.

Sentiment

Consumers' and producers' optimism or pessimism concerning the economy are important determinants of economic performance. If consumers have confidence in their future income levels, for example, they will be more willing to spend on big-ticket items. Similarly, businesses will increase production and inventory levels if they anticipate higher demand for their products. In this way, beliefs influence how much consumption and investment will be pursued and affect the aggregate demand for goods and services.

> **CONCEPT** *check* **12.1**
>
> Consider an economy where the dominant industry is automobile production for domestic consumption as well as export. Now suppose the auto market is hurt by an increase in the length of time people use their cars before replacing them. Describe the probable effects of this change on (*a*) GDP, (*b*) unemployment, (*c*) the government budget deficit, and (*d*) interest rates.

12.3 Interest Rates

The level of interest rates is perhaps the most important macroeconomic factor to consider in one's investment analysis. Forecasts of interest rates directly affect the forecast of returns in the fixed-income market. If your expectation is that rates will increase by more than the consensus view, you will want to shy away from longer term fixed-income securities. Similarly, increases in interest rates tend to be bad news for the stock market. Unanticipated increases in rates generally are associated with stock market declines. Thus, a superior technique to forecast rates would be of immense value to an investor attempting to determine the best asset allocation for his or her portfolio.

Unfortunately, forecasting interest rates is one of the most notoriously difficult parts of applied macroeconomics. Nonetheless, we do have a good understanding of the fundamental factors that determine the level of interest rates:

1. The supply of funds from savers, primarily households.
2. The demand for funds from businesses to be used to finance physical investments in plant, equipment, and inventories.
3. The government's net supply and/or demand for funds as modified by actions of the Federal Reserve Bank.
4. The expected rate of inflation.

Although there are many different interest rates economywide (as many as there are types of securities), these rates tend to move together, so economists frequently talk as though there were a single representative rate. We can use this abstraction to gain some insights into determining the real rate of interest if we consider the supply and demand curves for funds.

Figure 12.3 shows a downward-sloping demand curve and an upward-sloping supply curve. On the horizontal axis, we measure the quantity of funds, and on the vertical axis, we measure the real rate of interest.

The supply curve slopes up from left to right because the higher the real interest rate, the greater the supply of household savings. The assumption is that at higher real interest rates, households will choose to postpone some current consumption and set aside or invest more of their disposable income for future use.

The demand curve slopes down from left to right because the lower the real interest rate, the more businesses will want to invest in physical capital. Assuming that businesses rank projects by the expected real return on invested capital, firms will undertake more projects the lower the real interest rate on the funds needed to finance those projects.

Equilibrium is at the point of intersection of the supply and demand curves, point *E* in Figure 12.3.

The government and the central bank (the Federal Reserve) can shift these supply and demand curves either to the right or to the left through fiscal and monetary policies. For example, consider an increase in the government's budget deficit. This increases the government's borrowing demand and shifts the demand curve to the right, which causes the equilibrium real interest rate to rise to point *E'*. That is, a forecast that indicates higher than previously expected government borrowing increases expectations of future interest rates. The Fed can offset such a rise through an increase in the money supply, which will increase the supply of loanable funds, and shift the supply curve to the right.

Thus, while the fundamental determinants of the real interest rate are the propensity of households to save and the expected productivity (or we could say profitability) of firms' investment in physical capital, the real rate can be affected as well by government fiscal and monetary policies.

The supply and demand framework illustrated in Figure 12.3 is a reasonable first approximation to the determination of the real interest rate. To obtain the *nominal* interest rate, one needs to add the expected inflation rate to the equilibrium real rate. As we discussed in Section 5.4, the inflation premium is necessary for investors to maintain a given real rate of return on their investments.

While monetary policy can clearly affect nominal interest rates, there is considerable controversy concerning its ability to affect real rates. There is widespread agreement that, in the long run, the ultimate impact of an increase in the money

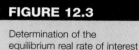

FIGURE 12.3

Determination of the equilibrium real rate of interest

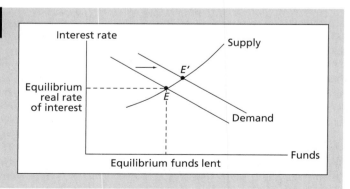

supply is an increase in prices with no permanent impact on real economic activity. A rapid rate of growth in the money supply, therefore, ultimately would result in a correspondingly high inflation rate and nominal interest rate, but it would have no sustained impact on the real interest rate. However, in the shorter run, changes in the money supply may well have an effect on the real interest rate.

12.4 Demand and Supply Shocks

A useful way to organize your analysis of the factors that might influence the macroeconomy is to classify any impact as a supply or demand shock. A **demand shock** is an event that affects the demand for goods and services in the economy. Examples of positive demand shocks are reductions in tax rates, increases in the money supply, increases in government spending, or increases in foreign export demand. A **supply shock** is an event that influences production capacity and costs. Examples of supply shocks are changes in the price of imported oil; freezes, floods, or droughts that might destroy large quantities of agricultural crops; changes in the educational level of an economy's workforce; or changes in the wage rates at which the labor force is willing to work.

demand shock

An event that affects the demand for goods and services in the economy.

supply shock

An event that influences production capacity and costs in the economy.

Demand shocks usually are characterized by aggregate output moving in the same direction as interest rates and inflation. For example, a big increase in government spending will tend to stimulate the economy and increase GDP. It also might increase interest rates by increasing the demand for borrowed funds by the government as well as by businesses that might desire to borrow to finance new ventures. Finally, it could increase the inflation rate if the demand for goods and services is raised to a level at or beyond the total productive capacity of the economy.

Supply shocks usually are characterized by aggregate output moving in the opposite direction of inflation and interest rates. For example, a big increase in the price of imported oil will be inflationary because costs of production will rise, which eventually will lead to increases in prices of finished goods. The increase in inflation rates over the near term can lead to higher nominal interest rates. Against this background, aggregate output will be falling. With raw materials more expensive, the productive capacity of the economy is reduced, as is the ability of individuals to purchase goods at now-higher prices. GDP, therefore, tends to fall.

How can we relate this framework to investment analysis? You want to identify the industries that will be most helped or hurt in any macroeconomic scenario you envision. For example, if you forecast a tightening of the money supply, you might want to avoid industries such as automobile producers that might be hurt by the likely increase in interest rates. We caution you again that these forecasts are no easy task. Macroeconomic predictions are notoriously unreliable. And again, you must be aware that in all likelihood your forecast will be made using only publicly available information. Any investment advantage you have will be a result only of better analysis—not better information.

12.5 Federal Government Policy

As the previous section would suggest, the government has two broad classes of macroeconomic tools—those that affect the demand for goods and services and those that affect their supply. For much of postwar history, demand-side policy has been of primary interest. The focus has been on government spending, tax levels, and monetary policy. Since the 1980s, however, increasing attention has also been focused on supply-side economics. Broadly interpreted, supply-side concerns have to do with enhancing the productive capacity of the economy, rather than increasing the demand for the goods and services the economy can produce. In practice, supply-side economists have focused on the appropriateness of the incentives to work, innovate, and take risks that result from our system of taxation. However, issues such as national policies on education, infrastructure (such as communication and transportation systems), and research and development also are properly regarded as part of supply-side macroeconomic policy.

Fiscal Policy

fiscal policy

The use of government spending and taxing for the specific purpose of stabilizing the economy.

Fiscal policy refers to the government's spending and tax actions and is part of "demand-side management." Fiscal policy is probably the most direct way either to stimulate or to slow the economy. Decreases in government spending directly deflate the demand for goods and services. Similarly, increases in tax rates immediately siphon income from consumers and result in fairly rapid decreases in consumption.

Ironically, although fiscal policy has the most immediate impact on the economy, the formulation and implementation of such policy is usually painfully slow and involved. This is because fiscal policy requires enormous amounts of compromise between the executive and legislative branches. Tax and spending policy must be initiated and voted on by Congress, which requires considerable political negotiations, and any legislation passed must be signed by the president, requiring more negotiation. Thus, while the impact of fiscal policy is relatively immediate, its formulation is so cumbersome that fiscal policy cannot in practice be used to fine-tune the economy.

Moreover, much of government spending, such as that for Medicare or Social Security, is nondiscretionary, meaning that it is determined by formula rather than policy and cannot be changed in response to economic conditions. This places even more rigidity into the formulation of fiscal policy.

A common way to summarize the net impact of government fiscal policy is to look at the government's budget deficit or surplus, which is simply the difference between revenues and expenditures. A large deficit means the government is spending considerably more than it is taking in by way of taxes. The net effect is to increase the demand for goods (via spending) by more than it reduces the demand for goods (via taxes), therefore, stimulating the economy.

Monetary Policy

monetary policy

Actions taken by the Board of Governors of the Federal Reserve System to influence the money supply or interest rates.

Monetary policy refers to the manipulation of the money supply to affect the macroeconomy and is the other main leg of demand-side policy. Monetary policy works largely through its impact on interest rates. Increases in the money supply lower short-term interest rates, ultimately encouraging investment and consumption demand. Over longer periods, however, most economists believe a higher money supply leads only to a higher price level and does not have a permanent effect on economic activity. Thus, the monetary authorities face a difficult balancing act. Expansionary monetary policy probably will lower interest rates and thereby stimulate investment and some consumption demand in the short run, but these circumstances ultimately will lead only to higher prices. The stimulation/inflation trade-off is implicit in all debate over proper monetary policy.

Fiscal policy is cumbersome to implement but has a fairly direct impact on the economy, while monetary policy is easily formulated and implemented but has a less immediate impact. Monetary policy is determined by the Board of Governors of the Federal Reserve System. Board members are appointed by the president for 14-year terms and are reasonably insulated from political pressure. The board is small enough and often sufficiently dominated by its chairperson that policy can be formulated and modulated relatively easily.

Implementation of monetary policy also is quite direct. The most widely used tool is the open market operation, in which the Fed buys or sells Treasury bonds for its own account. When the Fed buys securities, it simply writes a check, thereby increasing the money supply. (Unlike us, the Fed can pay for the securities without drawing down funds at a bank account.) Conversely, when the Fed sells a security, the money paid for it leaves the money supply. Open market operations occur daily, allowing the Fed to fine-tune its monetary policy.

Other tools at the Fed's disposal are the *discount rate,* which is the interest rate it charges banks on short-term loans, and the *reserve requirement,* which is the fraction of deposits that banks must hold as cash on hand or as deposits with the Fed. Reductions in the discount rate signal a more expansionary monetary policy. Lowering reserve requirements allows banks to

THE NEW OLD BIG THING IN ECONOMICS: J. M. KEYNES

The U.S. and dozens of other nations are returning to massive government spending as a recession fighter. Around the world, interest rates have been slashed and trillions of dollars have been committed to bailouts. But the global recession is deepening anyway. So policy makers are invoking the ideas of British economist John Maynard Keynes (pronounced "canes"), who argued in the 1930s that governments should fight the Great Depression with heavy spending. With consumer and business spending so weak, he argued, governments had to boost demand directly.

Keynesian policies fell out of favor in the 1970s, as government spending was blamed for helping to spur inflation around the world. But with the global economic turmoil being compared to the 1930s, government spending is once again back in vogue.

Critics argue that government deficits drive up interest rates and reduce investments in the private sector, which they say is more efficient at deploying capital. Still, with the U.S. economy facing 1930s-style threats, the Obama administration is looking back to the Great Depression for guidance. President Franklin Roosevelt's Works Progress Administration provided jobs to millions of Americans.

Keynesian fiscal stimulus remained popular globally into the 1960s, particularly in rebuilding Europe and Japan after the war. But limits of Keynes-inspired growth were reached in the following decades. Many countries mistimed their spending, pouring money into their economies and leading to economic overheating. Many nations also wasted their money: Japan became notorious for investing in little-used airports and bridges leading into sparsely populated islands. With the rise of Ronald Reagan and Britain's Margaret Thatcher, critics of stimulus policy came to the fore. The goal became to shrink government.

Monetary policy also began to play a bigger role, as central bankers drove up interest rates to bring down inflation. Recessions seemed to grow more distant and less painful. The era from the early 1980s until the recent crisis became known as "the Great Moderation," when economic activity and inflation became less volatile. But during this latest period of financial turmoil, monetary policy has been inadequate. The U.S. Federal Reserve lowered its interest-rate target to near zero last month, but the economy has continued to spiral downward.

So, nations are turning again to government stimulus spending to try knocking the economy back on track. Economists say that if governments can get money into the economy quickly, targeting projects that will have the biggest effect, and make sure the spending is temporary, they can avoid inflation and wasteful spending.

To ensure money is spent, the U.S. and other nations are focusing on infrastructure investment to create jobs. President-elect Barack Obama plans to use stimulus funds to repair schools, expand broadband Internet access, and put energy-efficient technologies in public buildings.

Inflation has quickly disappeared as a concern around the world. It's likely to reappear once growth perks up. That leaves a big test for the resurgence of fiscal stimulus: Once the economy revives, Mr. Keynes warned, the spending needs to be reversed and deficits cut. That's something nations have had a hard time doing.

SOURCE: Sudeep Reddy, "The New Old Big Thing in Economics: J. M. Keynes," *The Wall Street Journal,* January 8, 2009. Reprinted by permission of *The Wall Street Journal,* Copyright © 2009 Dow Jones & Company. All Rights Reserved Worldwide.

make more loans with each dollar of deposits and stimulates the economy by increasing the effective money supply.

While the discount rate is under the direct control of the Fed, it is changed relatively infrequently. The *federal funds rate* is by far the better guide to Federal Reserve policy. The federal funds rate is the interest rate at which banks make short-term, usually overnight, loans to each other. These loans occur because some banks need to borrow funds to meet reserve requirements, while other banks have excess funds. Unlike the discount rate, the fed funds rate is a market rate, meaning that it is determined by supply and demand rather than being set administratively. Nevertheless, the Federal Reserve Board targets the fed funds rate, expanding or contracting the money supply through open market operations as it nudges the fed funds to its targeted value. This is the benchmark short-term U.S. interest rate, and as such has considerable influence over other interest rates in the U.S. and the rest of the world.

Monetary policy affects the economy in a more roundabout way than fiscal policy. While fiscal policy directly stimulates or dampens the economy, monetary policy works largely through its impact on interest rates. Increases in the money supply lower interest rates, which stimulate investment demand. As the quantity of money in the economy increases, investors will find that their portfolios of assets include too much money. They will rebalance their portfolios by buying securities such as bonds, forcing bond prices up and interest rates down. In the longer run, individuals may increase their holdings of stocks as well and ultimately buy real assets, which stimulates consumption demand directly. The ultimate effect of monetary policy on investment and consumption demand, however, is less immediate than that of fiscal policy.

The nearby box focuses on the choices facing economic policy makers in early 2009, who were attempting to stave off or at least mitigate a developing recession. The box touches on many of the themes of economic policy, noting for example that with short-term interest rates near zero, monetary policy had already neared its limits, forcing governments to turn to fiscal policy. Indeed, at the time, the U.S. government alone was considering a $300 billion tax cut along with a massive increase in federal spending of around $375 billion on infrastructure projects. The article notes the danger that huge resulting federal deficits could increase interest rates and crowd out private investment and that, as the economy recovered, such deficits would need to be trimmed quickly to avoid the risk of reigniting inflation.

CONCEPT *check* **12.2**   Suppose the government wants to stimulate the economy without increasing interest rates. What combination of fiscal and monetary policy might accomplish this goal?

Supply-Side Policies

Fiscal and monetary policy are demand-oriented tools that affect the economy by stimulating the total demand for goods and services. The implicit belief is that the economy will not by itself arrive at a full-employment equilibrium and that macroeconomic policy can push the economy toward this goal. In contrast, supply-side policies treat the issue of the productive capacity of the economy. The goal is to create an environment in which workers and owners of capital have the maximum incentive and ability to produce and develop goods.

Supply-side economists also pay considerable attention to tax policy. While demand-siders look at the effect of taxes on consumption demand, supply-siders focus on incentives and marginal tax rates. They argue that lowering tax rates will elicit more investment and improve incentives to work, thereby enhancing economic growth. Some go so far as to claim that reductions in tax rates can lead to increases in tax revenues because the lower tax rates will cause the economy and the revenue tax base to grow by more than the tax rate is reduced.

CONCEPT *check* **12.3**   Large tax cuts in 2001 were followed by relatively rapid growth in GDP. How would demand-side and supply-side economists differ in their interpretations of this phenomenon?

12.6   Business Cycles

We've looked at the tools the government uses to fine-tune the economy, attempting to maintain low unemployment and low inflation. Despite these efforts, economies repeatedly seem to pass through good and bad times. One determinant of the broad asset allocation decision of many analysts is a forecast of whether the macroeconomy is improving or deteriorating. A forecast that differs from the market consensus can have a major impact on investment strategy.

The Business Cycle

business cycles

Recurring cycles of recession and recovery.

peak

The transition from the end of an expansion to the start of a contraction.

trough

The transition point between recession and recovery.

The economy recurrently experiences periods of expansion and contraction, although the length and depth of these cycles can be irregular. These recurring patterns of recession and recovery are called **business cycles.** Figure 12.4 presents graphs of several measures of production and output. The production series all show clear variation around a generally rising trend. The bottom graph of capacity utilization also evidences a clear cyclical (although irregular) pattern.

The transition points across cycles are called peaks and troughs, identified by the boundaries of the shaded areas of the graph. A **peak** is the transition from the end of an expansion to the start of a contraction. A **trough** occurs at the bottom of a recession just as the economy enters a recovery. The shaded areas in Figure 12.4 all represent periods of recession.

As the economy passes through different stages of the business cycle, the relative profitability of different industry groups might be expected to vary. For example, at a trough,

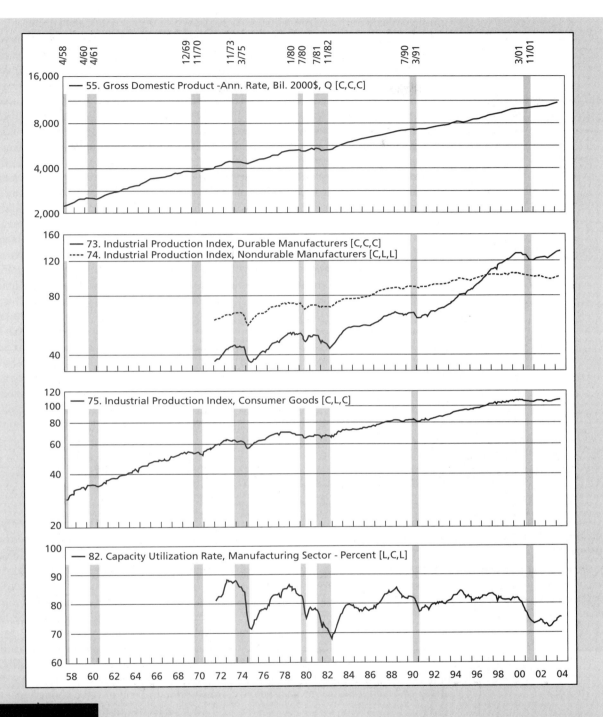

FIGURE 12.4

Cyclical indicators

Source: The Conference Board, *Business Cycle Indicators* 9, no 8 (August 2004), p. 10.

just before the economy begins to recover from a recession, one would expect that **cyclical industries,** those with above-average sensitivity to the state of the economy, would tend to outperform other industries. Examples of cyclical industries are producers of durable goods, such as automobiles or washing machines. Because purchases of these goods can be deferred

cyclical industries

Industries with above-average sensitivity to the state of the economy.

during a recession, sales are particularly sensitive to macroeconomic conditions. Other cyclical industries are producers of capital goods, that is, goods used by other firms to produce their own products. When demand is slack, few companies will be expanding and purchasing capital goods. Therefore, the capital goods industry bears the brunt of a slowdown but does well in an expansion.

defensive industries

Industries with below-average sensitivity to the state of the economy.

In contrast to cyclical firms, **defensive industries** have little sensitivity to the business cycle. These are industries that produce goods for which sales and profits are least sensitive to the state of the economy. Defensive industries include food producers and processors, pharmaceutical firms, and public utilities. These industries will outperform others when the economy enters a recession.

The cyclical/defensive classification corresponds well to the notion of systematic or market risk introduced in our discussion of portfolio theory. When perceptions about the health of the economy become more optimistic, for example, the prices of most stocks will increase as forecasts of profitability rise. Because the cyclical firms are most sensitive to such developments, their stock prices will rise the most. Thus, firms in cyclical industries will tend to have high-beta stocks. In general, then, stocks of cyclical firms will show the best results when economic news is positive, but they will also show the worst results when that news is bad. Conversely, defensive firms will have low betas and performance that is comparatively unaffected by overall market conditions.

If your assessments of the state of the business cycle were reliably more accurate than those of other investors, choosing between cyclical and defensive industries would be easy. You would choose cyclical industries when you were relatively more optimistic about the economy, and you would choose defensive firms when you were relatively more pessimistic. As we know from our discussion of efficient markets, however, attractive investment choices will rarely be obvious. It is usually not apparent that a recession or expansion has started or ended until several months after the fact. With hindsight, the transitions from expansion to recession and back might seem obvious, but it is often quite difficult to say whether the economy is heating up or slowing down at any moment.

Economic Indicators

leading economic indicators

Economic series that tend to rise or fall in advance of the rest of the economy.

Given the cyclical nature of the business cycle, it is not surprising that to some extent the cycle can be predicted. The Conference Board publishes a set of cyclical indicators to help forecast, measure, and interpret short-term fluctuations in economic activity. **Leading economic indicators** are those economic series that tend to rise or fall in advance of the rest of the economy. Coincident and lagging indicators, as their names suggest, move in tandem with or somewhat after the broad economy.

Ten series are grouped into a widely followed composite index of leading economic indicators. Similarly, four coincident and seven lagging indicators form separate indexes. The composition of these indexes appears in Table 12.2.

Figure 12.5 graphs these three series. The numbers on the charts near the turning points of each series indicate the length of the lead time or lag time (in months) from the turning point to the designated peak or trough of the corresponding business cycle. While the index of leading indicators consistently turns before the rest of the economy, the lead time is somewhat erratic. Moreover, the lead time for peaks is consistently longer than that for troughs.

The stock market price index is a leading indicator. This is as it should be, as stock prices are forward-looking predictors of future profitability. Unfortunately, this makes the series of leading indicators much less useful for investment policy—by the time the series predicts an upturn, the market has already made its move. While the business cycle may be somewhat predictable, the stock market may not be. This is just one more manifestation of the efficient market hypothesis.

TABLE 12.2
 	
Indexes of economic indicators
	A. Leading indicators
	  1. Average weekly hours of production workers (manufacturing).
	  2. Initial claims for unemployment insurance.
	  3. Manufacturers' new orders (consumer goods and materials industries).
	  4. Fraction of companies reporting slower deliveries.
	  5. New orders for nondefense capital goods.
	  6. New private housing units authorized by local building permits.
	  7. Yield curve: spread between 10-year T-bond yield and federal funds rate.
	  8. Stock prices, 500 common stocks.
	  9. Money supply (M2) growth rate.
	  10. Index of consumer expectations.
	B. Coincident indicators
	  1. Employees on nonagricultural payrolls.
	  2. Personal income less transfer payments.
	  3. Industrial production.
	  4. Manufacturing and trade sales.
	C. Lagging indicators
	  1. Average duration of unemployment.
	  2. Ratio of trade inventories to sales.
	  3. Change in index of labor cost per unit of output.
	  4. Average prime rate charged by banks.
	  5. Commercial and industrial loans outstanding.
	  6. Ratio of consumer installment credit outstanding to personal income.
	  7. Change in consumer price index for services.

Source: The Conference Board, *Business Cycle Indicators,* November 2008.

The money supply is another leading indicator. This makes sense in light of our earlier discussion concerning the lags surrounding the effects of monetary policy on the economy. An expansionary monetary policy can be observed fairly quickly, but it might not affect the economy for several months. Therefore, today's monetary policy might well predict future economic activity.

Other leading indicators focus directly on decisions made today that will affect production in the near future. For example, manufacturers' new orders for goods, contracts and orders for plant and equipment, and housing starts all signal a coming expansion in the economy.

A wide range of economic indicators are released to the public on a regular "economic calendar." Table 12.3 lists the public announcement dates and sources for about 20 statistics of interest. These announcements are reported in the financial press, for example, *The Wall Street Journal,* as they are released. They also are available at many sites on the Web, for example, at Yahoo!'s site. Figure 12.6 is an excerpt from a recent Economic Calendar page at Yahoo!. The page gives a list of the announcements released during the week of November 10, 2008. Notice that recent forecasts of each variable are provided along with the actual value of each statistic. This is useful, because in an efficient market, security prices will already reflect market expectations. The *new* information in the announcement will determine the market response.

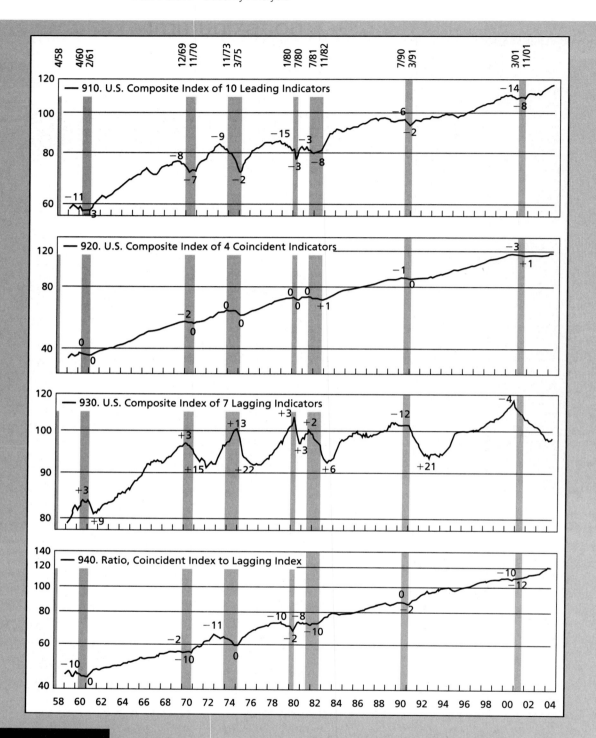

FIGURE 12.5

Indexes of leading, coincident, and lagging indicators

Source: The Conference Board, *Business Cycle Indicators,* August 2004, p. 3.

TABLE 12.3

Economic calendar

Statistic	Release Date*	Source	Web Site (www.)
Auto and truck sales	2nd of month	Commerce Department	commerce.gov
Business inventories	15th of month	Commerce Department	commerce.gov
Construction spending	1st business day of month	Commerce Department	commerce.gov
Consumer confidence	Last Tuesday of month	Conference Board	conference-board.org
Consumer credit	5th business day of month	Federal Reserve Board	federalreserve.gov
Consumer price index (CPI)	13th of month	Bureau of Labor Statistics	bls.gov
Durable goods orders	26th of month	Commerce Department	commerce.gov
Employment cost index	End of first month of quarter	Bureau of Labor Statistics	bls.gov
Employment record (unemployment, average workweek, nonfarm payrolls)	1st Friday of month	Bureau of Labor Statistics	bls.gov
Existing home sales	25th of month	National Association of Realtors	realtor.org
Factory orders	1st business day of month	Commerce Department	commerce.gov
Gross domestic product	3rd–4th week of month	Commerce Department	commerce.gov
Housing starts	16th of month	Commerce Department	commerce.gov
Industrial production	15th of month	Federal Reserve Board	federalreserve.gov
Initial claims for jobless benefits	Thursdays	Department of Labor	dol.gov
International trade balance	20th of month	Commerce Department	commerce.gov
Index of leading economic indicators	Beginning of month	Conference Board	conference-board.org
Money supply	Thursdays	Federal Reserve Board	federalreserve.gov
New home sales	Last business day of month	Commerce Department	commerce.gov
Producer price index	11th of month	Bureau of Labor Statistics	bls.gov
Productivity and costs	2nd month in quarter (approx. 7th day of month)	Bureau of Labor Statistics	bls.gov
Retail sales	13th of month	Commerce Department	commerce.gov
Survey of purchasing managers	1st business day of month	Institute for Supply Management	ism.ws

*Many of these release dates are approximate.

Last Week Next Week

Date	Time (ET)	Statistic	For	Actual	Briefing Forecast	Market Expects	Prior	Revised From
Nov 13	8:30 A.M.	Initial Claims	Nov 8	516K	475K	479K	484K	481K
Nov 13	8:30 A.M.	Trade Balance	Sep	−$56.5B	−$56.0B	−$57.0B	−$59.1B	–
Nov 13	2:00 P.M.	Treasury Budget	Oct	−$237.2B	NA	−$134.0B	−$55.6B	–
Nov 14	8:30 A.M.	Import Prices ex-oil	Oct	−0.9%	NA	NA	−0.9%	–
Nov 14	8:30 A.M.	Retail Sales	Oct	−2.8%	−1.9%	−2.1%	−1.3%	−1.2%
Nov 14	10:00 A.M.	Business Inventories	Sep	−0.2%	0.2%	−0.1%	0.2%	0.3%

FIGURE 12.6

Economic calendar at Yahoo!

Source: Yahoo! Briefing Economic Calendar, **biz.yahoo.com/c/e.html,** November 17, 2008. Reproduced with permission of Yahoo! Inc. © 2008 by Yahoo! Inc. Yahoo! and the Yahoo! logo are trademarks of Yahoo! Inc.

TABLE 12.4	
Useful economic indicators	
CEO polls **http://businessroundtable.org**	The business roundtable surveys CEOs about planned spending, a good measure of their optimism about the economy.
Temp jobs Search for "Temporary Help Services" at **www.bls.gov**	A useful leading indicator. Businesses often hire temporary workers as the economy first picks up, until it is clear that an upturn is going to be sustained. This series is available at the Bureau of Labor Statistics Web site.
Wal-Mart sales **www.walmartstores.com**	Wal-Mart sales are a good indicator of the retail sector. It publishes its same-store sales weekly.
Commercial and industrial loans **www.federalreserve.gov**	These loans are used by small and medium-sized firms. Information is published weekly by the Federal Reserve.
Semiconductors **www.semi.org**	The book-to-bill ratio (i.e., new sales versus actual shipments) indicates whether demand in the technology sector is increasing (ratio > 1) or falling. This ratio is published by Semiconductor Equipment and Materials International.
Commercial structures **www.bea.gov**	Investment in structures is an indicator of businesses' forecasts of demand for their products in the near future. This is one of the series compiled by the Bureau of Economic Analysis as part of its GDP series.

Other Indicators

You can find lots of important information about the state of the economy from sources other than the official components of the economic calendar or the components of business cycle indicators. Table 12.4, which is derived from some suggestions in *Inc.* magazine, contains a few.[1]

12.7 | Industry Analysis

Industry analysis is important for the same reason that macroeconomic analysis is: Just as it is difficult for an industry to perform well when the macroeconomy is ailing, it is unusual for a firm in a troubled industry to perform well. Similarly, just as we have seen that economic performance can vary widely across countries, performance also can vary widely across industries. Figure 12.7 illustrates the dispersion of industry performance. It shows return on equity for several major industry groups. ROE ranged from 10.2% for electric utilities to 36.8% for the cigarette industry.

Given this wide variation in profitability, it is not surprising that industry groups exhibit considerable dispersion in their stock market performance. Figure 12.8. presents the stock market performance of several industry-specific iShares during 2008. While this was a dismal year for virtually the entire economy, the spread in performance across industries is nevertheless remarkable, ranging from a 22.4% return for brewers to a 76.3% loss in automobiles. Recall that iShares are exchange-traded funds (see Chapter 4) that trade like stocks and thus allow even small investors to take a position in each traded industry. So this range of performance was very much available to virtually all investors in 2008. Alternatively, one can invest in mutual funds with an industry focus.

[1]Gene Sperling and Illustrations by Thomas Fuchs, "The Insider's Guide to Economic Forecasting," *Inc.*, August 2003, p. 96.

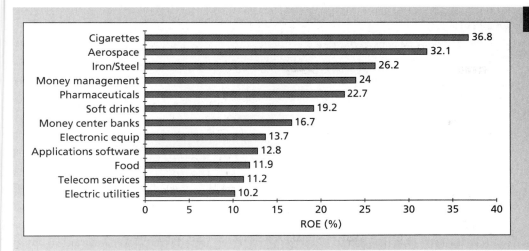

FIGURE 12.7

Return on equity, 2008

Source: Yahoo! Finance (**finance. yahoo.com**), November 17, 2008. Reproduced with permission of Yahoo! Inc. © 2000–2008 by Yahoo! Inc. Yahoo! and the Yahoo! logo are trademarks of Yahoo! Inc.

Defining an Industry

While we know what we mean by an industry, it can be difficult in practice to decide where to draw the line between one industry and another. Consider, for example, one of the industries depicted in Figure 12.7, application software firms. Even within this industry, there is substantial variation by focus and product line. Their differences may result in considerable dispersion in financial performance. Figure 12.9 shows ROE for a sample of the firms included in this industry, and performance did indeed wary widely: from 8.6% for Adobe to 54.1% for Microsoft.

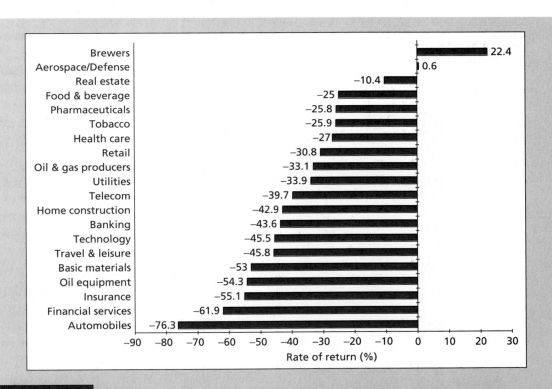

FIGURE 12.8

Industry stock price performance as measured by rate of return on Dow Jones Sector iShares, January–November 2008

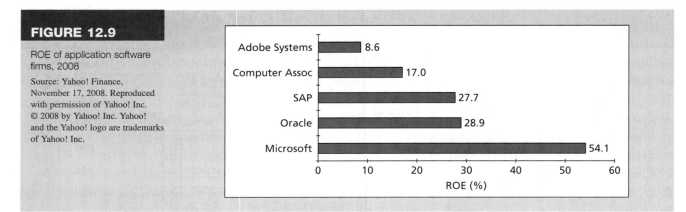

FIGURE 12.9

ROE of application software firms, 2008

Source: Yahoo! Finance, November 17, 2008. Reproduced with permission of Yahoo! Inc. © 2008 by Yahoo! Inc. Yahoo! and the Yahoo! logo are trademarks of Yahoo! Inc.

NAICS codes

Classification of firms into industry groups using numerical codes to identify industries.

A useful way to define industry groups in practice is given by the North American Industry Classification System, or **NAICS, codes.**[2] These are codes assigned to group firms for statistical analysis. The first two digits of the NAICS codes denote very broad industry classifications. For example, Table 12.5 shows that the codes for all construction firms start with 23. The next digits define the industry grouping more narrowly. For example, codes starting with 236 denote *building* construction, 2361 denotes *residential* construction, and 236115 denotes *single-family* construction. Firms with the same 4-digit NAICS codes are commonly taken to be in the same industry.

Industry classifications are never perfect. For example, both J.C. Penney and Neiman Marcus might be classified as department stores. Yet the former is a high-volume "value" store, while the latter is a high-margin elite retailer. Are they really in the same industry? Still, these classifications are a tremendous aid in conducting industry analysis since they provide a means of focusing on very broadly or fairly narrowly defined groups of firms.

Several other industry classifications are provided by other analysts, for example, Standard & Poor's reports on the performance of about 100 industry groups. S&P computes stock price indexes for each group, which is useful in assessing past investment performance. The *Value Line Investment Survey* reports on the conditions and prospects of about 1,700 firms, grouped

TABLE 12.5	NAICS Code	NAICS Title
Examples of NAICS industry codes	23	Construction
	236	Construction of Buildings
	2361	Residential Building Construction
	23611	Residential Building Construction
	236115	New Single-Family Housing Construction
	236116	New Multifamily Housing Construction
	236117	New Housing Operative Builders
	236118	Residential Remodelers
	2362	Nonresidential Building Construction
	23621	Industrial Building Construction
	236210	Industrial Building Construction
	23622	Commercial and Institutional Building Construction
	236220	Commercial and Institutional Building Construction

[2] These codes are used for firms operating inside the NAFTA (North American Free Trade Agreement) region, which includes the U.S., Mexico, and Canada. NAICS codes replaced the Standard Industry Classification or SIC codes previously used in the U.S.

into about 90 industries. Value Line's analysts prepare forecasts of the performance of industry groups as well as of each firm.

Sensitivity to the Business Cycle

Once the analyst forecasts the state of the macroeconomy, it is necessary to determine the implication of that forecast for specific industries. Not all industries are equally sensitive to the business cycle. For example, Figure 12.10 plots changes in retail sales (year over year) in two industries: jewelry and grocery stores. Clearly, sales of jewelry, which is a luxury good, fluctuate more widely than those of grocery stores. The downturn in jewelry sales in 2001 when the economy was in a recession is notable. In contrast, sales growth in the grocery industry is relatively stable, with no years in which sales decline. These patterns reflect the fact that jewelry is a discretionary good, whereas most grocery products are staples for which demand will not fall significantly even in hard times.

Three factors will determine the sensitivity of a firm's earnings to the business cycle. First is the sensitivity of sales. Necessities will show little sensitivity to business conditions. Examples of industries in this group are food, drugs, and medical services. Other industries with low sensitivity are those for which income is not a crucial determinant of demand. Tobacco products are examples of this type of industry. Another industry in this group is movies, because consumers tend to substitute movies for more expensive sources of entertainment when income levels are low. In contrast, firms in industries such as machine tools, steel, autos, and transportation are highly sensitive to the state of the economy.

The second factor determining business cycle sensitivity is operating leverage, which refers to the division between fixed and variable costs. (Fixed costs are those the firm incurs regardless of its production levels. Variable costs are those that rise or fall as the firm produces more or less product.) Firms with greater amounts of variable as opposed to fixed costs will be less sensitive to business conditions. This is because, in economic downturns, these firms can reduce costs as output falls in response to falling sales. Profits for firms with high fixed costs will swing more widely with sales because costs do not move to offset revenue variability. Firms with high fixed costs are said to have high operating leverage, as small swings in business conditions can have large impacts on profitability.

The third factor influencing business cycle sensitivity is financial leverage, which is the use of borrowing. Interest payments on debt must be paid regardless of sales. They are fixed costs that also increase the sensitivity of profits to business conditions. We will have more to say about financial leverage in Chapter 14.

Investors should not always prefer industries with lower sensitivity to the business cycle. Firms in sensitive industries will have high-beta stocks and are riskier. But while they swing lower in downturns, they also swing higher in upturns. As always, the issue you need to address is whether the expected return on the investment is fair compensation for the risks borne.

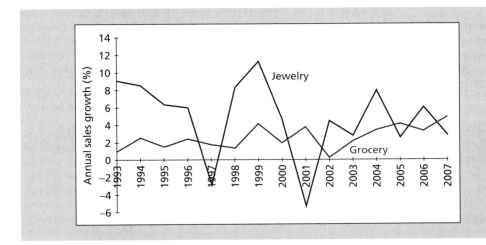

FIGURE 12.10

Industry cyclicality. Growth in sales, year over year, in two industries.

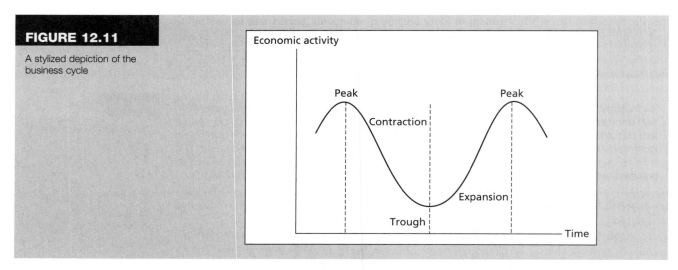

FIGURE 12.11

A stylized depiction of the business cycle

Sector Rotation

sector rotation

An investment strategy that entails shifting the portfolio into industry sectors that are expected to outperform others based on macroeconomic forecasts.

One way that many analysts think about the relationship between industry analysis and the business cycle is the notion of **sector rotation.** The idea is to shift the portfolio more heavily into industry or sector groups that are expected to outperform based on one's assessment of the state of the business cycle.

Figure 12.11 is a stylized depiction of the business cycle. Near the peak of the business cycle, the economy might be overheated with high inflation and interest rates and price pressures on basic commodities. This might be a good time to invest in firms engaged in natural resource extraction and processing such as minerals or petroleum.

Following a peak, when the economy enters a contraction or recession, one would expect defensive industries that are less sensitive to economic conditions, for example, pharmaceuticals, food, and other necessities, to be the best performers. At the height of the contraction, financial firms will be hurt by shrinking loan volume and higher default rates. Toward the end of the recession, however, contractions induce lower inflation and interest rates, which favor financial firms.

At the trough of a recession, the economy is poised for recovery and subsequent expansion. Firms might thus be spending on purchases of new equipment to meet anticipated increases in demand. This, then, would be a good time to invest in capital goods industries, such as equipment, transportation, or construction.

Finally, in an expansion, the economy is growing rapidly. Cyclical industries such as consumer durables and luxury items will be most profitable in this stage of the cycle. Banks might also do well in expansions, since loan volume will be high and default exposure low when the economy is growing rapidly.

Figure 12.12 illustrates sector rotation. When investors are relatively pessimistic about the economy, they will shift into noncyclical industries such as consumer staples or health care. When anticipating an expansion, they will prefer more cyclical industries such as materials and technology.

Let us emphasize again that sector rotation, like any other form of market timing, will be successful only if one anticipates the next stage of the business cycle better than other investors. The business cycle depicted in Figure 12.11 is highly stylized. In real life, it is never as clear how long each phase of the cycle will last, nor how extreme it will be. These forecasts are where analysts need to earn their keep.

CONCEPT
check   **12.4**

In which phase of the business cycle would you expect the following industries to enjoy their best performance?
(*a*) Newspapers   (*b*) Machine tools   (*c*) Beverages   (*d*) Timber.

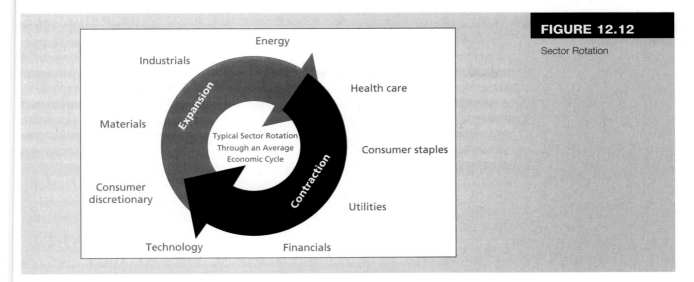

FIGURE 12.12

Sector Rotation

Industry Life Cycles

Examine the biotechnology industry and you will find many firms with high rates of investment, high rates of return on investment, and very low dividends as a percentage of profits. Do the same for the electric utility industry and you will find lower rates of return, lower investment rates, and higher dividend payout rates. Why should this be?

The biotech industry is still new. Recently available technologies have created opportunities for the highly profitable investment of resources. New products are protected by patents, and profit margins are high. With such lucrative investment opportunities, firms find it advantageous to put all profits back into the firm. The companies grow rapidly on average.

Eventually, however, growth must slow. The high profit rates will induce new firms to enter the industry. Increasing competition will hold down prices and profit margins. New technologies become proven and more predictable, risk levels fall, and entry becomes even easier. As internal investment opportunities become less attractive, a lower fraction of profits is reinvested in the firm. Cash dividends increase.

Ultimately, in a mature industry, we observe "cash cows," firms with stable dividends and cash flows and little risk. Their growth rates might be similar to that of the overall economy. Industries in early stages of their life cycles offer high-risk/high-potential-return investments. Mature industries offer lower risk, lower return combinations.

This analysis suggests that a typical **industry life cycle** might be described by four stages: a start-up stage characterized by extremely rapid growth; a consolidation stage characterized by growth that is less rapid but still faster than that of the general economy; a maturity stage characterized by growth no faster than the general economy; and a stage of relative decline, in which the industry grows less rapidly than the rest of the economy, or actually shrinks. This industry life cycle is illustrated in Figure 12.13. Let us turn to an elaboration of each of these stages.

industry life cycle

Stages through which firms typically pass as they mature.

Start-up stage The early stages of an industry are often characterized by a new technology or product, such as VCRs or personal computers in the 1980s, cell phones in the 1990s, or the new generation of smart phones being introduced today. At this stage, it is difficult to predict which firms will emerge as industry leaders. Some firms will turn out to be wildly successful, and others will fail altogether. Therefore, there is considerable risk in selecting one particular firm within the industry. For example, in the smart phone industry, there is still a battle among competing technologies, such as Google's G1 phone versus Apple's iPhone, and it is still difficult to predict which firms or technologies ultimately will dominate the market.

At the industry level, however, sales and earnings will grow at an extremely rapid rate since the new product has not yet saturated its market. For example, in 1990 very few households

FIGURE 12.13

The industry life cycle

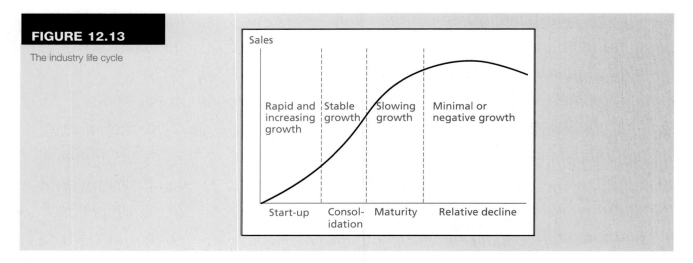

had cell phones. The potential market for the product therefore was huge. In contrast to this situation, consider the market for a mature product like refrigerators. Almost all households in the U.S. already have refrigerators, so the market for this good is primarily composed of households replacing old ones. Obviously, the growth rate in this market in the next decade will be far lower than for smart phones.

Consolidation stage   After a product becomes established, industry leaders begin to emerge. The survivors from the start-up stage are more stable, and market share is easier to predict. Therefore, the performance of the surviving firms will more closely track the performance of the overall industry. The industry still grows faster than the rest of the economy as the product penetrates the marketplace and becomes more commonly used.

Maturity stage   At this point, the product has reached its potential for use by consumers. Further growth might merely track growth in the general economy. The product has become far more standardized, and producers are forced to compete to a greater extent on the basis of price. This leads to narrower profit margins and further pressure on profits. Firms at this stage sometimes are characterized as "cash cows," firms with reasonably stable cash flow but offering little opportunity for profitable expansion. The cash flow is best "milked from" rather than reinvested in the company.

We pointed to VCRs as a start-up industry in the 1980s. By the mid-1990s it was a mature industry, with high market penetration, considerable price competition, low profit margins, and slowing sales. By the late 1990s, VCR sales were giving way to DVD players, which were in their own start-up phase. By today, one would have to judge DVDs as already having entered a maturity stage, with standardization, price competition, and considerable market penetration.

Relative decline   In this stage, the industry might grow at less than the rate of the overall economy, or it might even shrink. This could be due to obsolescence of the product, competition from new products, or competition from new low-cost suppliers, as illustrated by the steady displacement of VCRs by DVDs.

At which stage in the life cycle are investments in an industry most attractive? Conventional wisdom is that investors should seek firms in high-growth industries. This recipe for success is simplistic, however. If the security prices already reflect the likelihood for high growth, then it is too late to make money from that knowledge. Moreover, high growth and fat profits encourage competition from other producers. The exploitation of profit opportunities brings about new sources of supply that eventually reduce prices, profits, investment returns, and finally, growth. This is the dynamic behind the progression from one stage of the industry life cycle to another. The famous portfolio manager Peter Lynch makes this point in *One Up on Wall Street.* He says:

> Many people prefer to invest in a high-growth industry, where there's a lot of sound and fury. Not me. I prefer to invest in a low-growth industry. . . . In a low-growth industry, especially one that's boring and upsets people [such as funeral homes or the oil-drum retrieval business], there's no problem with competition. You don't have to protect your flanks from potential rivals . . . and this gives [the individual firm] the leeway to continue to grow. [page 131]

In fact, Lynch uses an industry classification system in a very similar spirit to the life-cycle approach we have described. He places firms in the following six groups:

1. *Slow Growers.* Large and aging companies that will grow only slightly faster than the broad economy. These firms have matured from their earlier fast-growth phase. They usually have steady cash flow and pay a generous dividend, indicating that the firm is generating more cash than can be profitably reinvested in the firm.
2. *Stalwarts.* Large, well-known firms like Coca-Cola or Colgate-Palmolive. They grow faster than the slow growers but are not in the very rapid growth start-up stage. They also tend to be in noncyclical industries that are relatively unaffected by recessions.
3. *Fast Growers.* Small and aggressive new firms with annual growth rates in the neighborhood of 20 to 25%. Company growth can be due to broad industry growth or to an increase in market share in a more mature industry.
4. *Cyclicals.* These are firms with sales and profits that regularly expand and contract along with the business cycle. Examples are auto companies, steel companies, or the construction industry.
5. *Turnarounds.* These are firms that are in bankruptcy or soon might be. If they can recover from what might appear to be imminent disaster, they can offer tremendous investment returns. A good example of this type of firm would be Chrysler in 1982, when it required a government guarantee on its debt to avoid bankruptcy. The stock price rose fifteenfold in the next five years.
6. *Asset Plays.* These are firms that have valuable assets not currently reflected in the stock price. For example, a company may own or be located on valuable real estate that is worth as much or more than the company's business enterprises. Sometimes the hidden asset can be tax-loss carryforwards. Other times the assets may be intangible. For example, a cable company might have a valuable list of cable subscribers. These assets do not immediately generate cash flow and so may be more easily overlooked by other analysts attempting to value the firm.

Industry Structure and Performance

The maturation of an industry involves regular changes in the firm's competitive environment. As a final topic, we examine the relationship between industry structure, competitive strategy, and profitability. Michael Porter (1980, 1985) has highlighted these five determinants of competition: threat of entry from new competitors, rivalry between existing competitors, price pressure from substitute products, the bargaining power of buyers, and the bargaining power of suppliers.

Threat of entry   New entrants to an industry put pressure on price and profits. Even if a firm has not yet entered an industry, the potential for it to do so places pressure on prices, since high prices and profit margins will encourage entry by new competitors. Therefore, barriers to entry can be a key determinant of industry profitability. Barriers can take many forms. For example, existing firms may already have secure distribution channels for their products based on long-standing relationships with customers or suppliers that would be costly for a new entrant to duplicate. Brand loyalty also makes it difficult for new entrants to penetrate a market and gives firms more pricing discretion. Proprietary knowledge or patent protection also may give firms advantages in serving a market. Finally, an existing firm's experience in a market may give it cost advantages due to the learning that takes place over time.

Rivalry between existing competitors   When there are several competitors in an industry, there will generally be more price competition and lower profit margins as competitors seek to expand their share of the market. Slow industry growth contributes to this competition since expansion must come at the expense of a rival's market share. High fixed costs also create pressure to reduce prices since fixed costs put greater pressure on firms to operate near full capacity. Industries producing relatively homogeneous goods also are subject to considerable price pressure since firms cannot compete on the basis of product differentiation.

Pressure from substitute products   Substitute products means that the industry faces competition from firms in related industries. For example, sugar producers compete with corn syrup producers. Wool producers compete with synthetic fiber producers. The availability of substitutes limits the prices that can be charged to customers.

Bargaining power of buyers   If a buyer purchases a large fraction of an industry's output, it will have considerable bargaining power and can demand price concessions. For example, auto producers can put pressure on suppliers of auto parts. This reduces the profitability of the auto parts industry.

Bargaining power of suppliers   If a supplier of a key input has monopolistic control over the product, it can demand higher prices for the good and squeeze profits out of the industry. One special case of this issue pertains to organized labor as a supplier of a key input to the production process. Labor unions engage in collective bargaining to increase the wages paid to workers. When the labor market is highly unionized, a significant share of the potential profits in the industry can be captured by the workforce.

   The key factor determining the bargaining power of suppliers is the availability of substitute products. If substitutes are available, the supplier has little clout and cannot extract higher prices.

SUMMARY

- Macroeconomic policy aims to maintain the economy near full employment without aggravating inflationary pressures. The proper trade-off between these two goals is a source of ongoing debate.
- The traditional tools of macropolicy are government spending and tax collection, which comprise fiscal policy, and manipulation of the money supply via monetary policy. Expansionary fiscal policy can stimulate the economy and increase GDP but tends to increase interest rates. Expansionary monetary policy works by lowering interest rates.
- The business cycle is the economy's recurring pattern of expansions and recessions. Leading economic indicators can be used to anticipate the evolution of the business cycle because their values tend to change before those of other key economic variables.
- Industries differ in their sensitivity to the business cycle. More sensitive industries tend to be those producing high-priced durable goods for which the consumer has considerable discretion as to the timing of purchase. Examples are automobiles or consumer durables. Other sensitive industries are those that produce capital equipment for other firms. Operating leverage and financial leverage increase sensitivity to the business cycle.

KEY TERMS

budget deficit, 367	fundamental analysis, 363	peak, 372
business cycles, 372	gross domestic product, 366	sector rotation, 382
cyclical industries, 373	industry life cycle, 383	NAICS codes, 380
defensive industries, 374	inflation, 367	supply shock, 369
demand shock, 369	leading economic	trough, 372
exchange rate, 365	indicators, 374	unemployment rate, 366
fiscal policy, 370	monetary policy, 370	

Select problems are available in McGraw-Hill's Connect. Please see the packaging options section of the preface for more information.

PROBLEM SETS

Basic

1. What are the differences between bottom-up and top-down approaches to security valuation? What are the advantages of a top-down approach?

2. Why does it make intuitive sense that the slope of the yield curve is considered a leading economic indicator?

3. Which one of the following firms would be described as having below-average sensitivity to the state of the economy?
   a. An asset play firm
   b. A cyclical firm
   c. A defensive firm
   d. A stalwart firm

4. The price of imported oil fell dramatically in late 2008. What sort of macroeconomic shock would this be considered?

5. How do each of the following affect the sensitivity of profits to the business cycle?
   a. Financial leverage
   b. Operating leverage

6. The present value of a firm's projected cash flows are $15 million. The break-up value of the firm if you were to sell the major assets and divisions separately would be $20 million. This is an example of what Peter Lynch would call a(n)
   a. Stalwart
   b. Slow-growth firm
   c. Turnaround
   d. Asset play

7. Define each of the following in the context of a business cycle.
   a. Peak
   b. Contraction
   c. Trough
   d. Expansion

8. What is typically true of corporate dividend payout rates in the early stages of an industry life cycle? Why does this make sense?

9. If the nominal interest rate is 5% and the inflation rate is 3%, then what is the real interest rate ?

10. FinanceCorp has fixed costs of $7 million and profits of $4 million. What is its degree of operating leverage (DOL)?

Intermediate

11. Choose an industry and identify the factors that will determine its performance in the next three years. What is your forecast for performance in that time period?

12. What monetary and fiscal policies might be prescribed for an economy in a deep recession?

13. If you believe the U.S. dollar is about to depreciate more dramatically than do other investors, what will be your stance on investments in U.S. auto producers?

14. Unlike other investors, you believe the Fed is going to dramatically loosen monetary policy. What would be your recommendations about investments in the following industries?
    a. Gold mining
    b. Construction

15. Consider two firms producing DVDs. One uses a highly automated robotics process, while the other uses human workers on an assembly line and pays overtime when there is heavy production demand.
    a. Which firm will have higher profits in a recession? In a boom?
    b. Which firm's stock will have a higher beta?

16. According to supply-side economists, what will be the long-run impact on prices of a reduction in income tax rates?

17. Here are four industries and four forecasts for the macroeconomy. Choose the industry that you would expect to perform best in each scenario.

    Industries: Housing construction, health care, gold mining, steel production.

    Economic Forecasts:

    Deep recession: Falling inflation, falling interest rates, falling GDP.

    Superheated economy: Rapidly rising GDP, increasing inflation and interest rates.

    Healthy expansion: Rising GDP, mild inflation, low unemployment.

    Stagflation: Falling GDP, high inflation.

18. For each pair of firms, choose the one that you think would be more sensitive to the business cycle.
    a. General Autos or General Pharmaceuticals.
    b. Friendly Airlines or Happy Cinemas.

19. In which stage of the industry life cycle would you place the following industries? (*Warning:* There is considerable room for disagreement concerning the "correct" answers to this question.)
    a. Oil well equipment.
    b. Computer hardware.
    c. Computer software.
    d. Genetic engineering.
    e. Railroads.

20. Why do you think the index of consumer expectations is a useful leading indicator of the macroeconomy? (See Table 12.2.)

21. Why do you think the change in the index of labor cost per unit of output is a useful lagging indicator of the macroeconomy? (See Table 12.2.)

22. You have $5,000 to invest for the next year and are considering three alternatives:
    a. A money market fund with an average maturity of 30 days offering a current annualized yield of 3%.
    b. A one-year savings deposit at a bank offering an interest rate of 4.5%.
    c. A 20-year U.S. Treasury bond offering a yield to maturity of 6% per year.

    What role does your forecast of future interest rates play in your decisions?

23. General Weedkillers dominates the chemical weed control market with its patented product Weed-ex. The patent is about to expire, however. What are your forecasts for changes in the industry? Specifically, what will happen to industry prices, sales, the profit prospects of General Weedkillers, and the profit prospects of its competitors? What stage of the industry life cycle do you think is relevant for the analysis of this market?

Challenge

24. OceanGate sells external hard drives for $200 each. Its total fixed costs are $30 million and its variable costs per unit are $140. The corporate tax rate is 30%. If the economy is strong, the firm will sell 2 million drives, but if there is a recession it will sell only half as many. What is the firm's degree of operating leverage? If the economy enters a recession, what will be the firm's after-tax profit?

CFA Problems

1. As a securities analyst you have been asked to review a valuation of a closely held business, Wigwam Autoparts Heaven, Inc. (WAH), prepared by the Red Rocks Group (RRG). You are to give an opinion on the valuation and to support your opinion by analyzing each part of the valuation. WAH's sole business is automotive parts

retailing. The RRG valuation includes a section called "Analysis of the Retail Auto Parts Industry," based completely on the data in Table 12.6 and the following additional information:

- WAH and its principal competitors each operated more than 150 stores at year-end 2008.
- The average number of stores operated per company engaged in the retail auto parts industry is 5.3.
- The major customer base for auto parts sold in retail stores consists of young owners of old vehicles. These owners do their own automotive maintenance out of economic necessity.

   a. One of RRG's conclusions is that the retail auto parts industry as a whole is in the maturity stage of the industry life cycle. Discuss three relevant items of data from Table 12.6 that support this conclusion.

   b. Another RRG conclusion is that WAH and its principal competitors are in the consolidation stage of their life cycle. Cite three items from Table 12.6 that suggest this conclusion. How can WAH be in a consolidation stage while its industry is in a maturity stage?

2. Universal Auto is a large multinational corporation headquartered in the United States. For segment reporting purposes, the company is engaged in two businesses: production of motor vehicles and information processing services.

   The motor vehicle business is by far the larger of Universal's two segments. It consists mainly of domestic United States passenger car production, but it also includes small truck manufacturing operations in the United States and passenger car production in other countries. This segment of Universal has had weak operating results for the past several years, including a large loss in 2010. Although the company does not reveal the operating results of its domestic passenger car segments, that part of Universal's

TABLE 12.6

Selected retail auto parts industry data

	2008	2007	2006	2005	2004	2003	2002	2001	2000	1999
Population 18–29 years old (percentage change)	−1.8%	−2.0%	−2.1%	−1.4%	−0.8%	−0.9%	−1.1%	−0.9%	−0.7%	−0.3%
Number of households with income more than $40,000 (percentage change)	6.0%	4.0%	8.0%	4.5%	2.7%	3.1%	1.6%	3.6%	4.2%	2.2%
Number of households with income less than $40,000 (percentage change)	3.0%	−1.0%	4.9%	2.3%	−1.4%	2.5%	1.4%	−1.3%	0.6%	0.1%
Number of cars 5–15 years old (percentage change)	0.9%	−1.3%	−6.0%	1.9%	3.3%	2.4%	−2.3%	−2.2%	−8.0%	1.6%
Automotive aftermarket industry retail sales (percentage change)	5.7%	1.9%	3.1%	3.7%	4.3%	2.6%	1.3%	0.2%	3.7%	2.4%
Consumer expenditures on automotive parts and accessories (percentage change)	2.4%	1.8%	2.1%	6.5%	3.6%	9.2%	1.3%	6.2%	6.7%	6.5%
Sales growth of retail auto parts companies with 100 or more stores	17.0%	16.0%	16.5%	14.0%	15.5%	16.8%	12.0%	15.7%	19.0%	16.0%
Market share of retail auto parts companies with 100 or more stores	19.0%	18.5%	18.3%	18.1%	17.0%	17.2%	17.0%	16.9%	15.0%	14.0%
Average operating margin of retail auto parts companies with 100 or more stores	12.0%	11.8%	11.2%	11.5%	10.6%	10.6%	10.0%	10.4%	9.8%	9.0%
Average operating margin of all retail auto parts companies	5.5%	5.7%	5.6%	5.8%	6.0%	6.5%	7.0%	7.2%	7.1%	7.2%

business is generally believed to be primarily responsible for the weak performance of its motor vehicle segment.

Idata, the information processing services segment of Universal, was started by Universal about 15 years ago. This business has shown strong, steady growth that has been entirely internal: No acquisitions have been made.

An excerpt from a research report on Universal prepared by Paul Adams, a CFA candidate, states: "Based on our assumption that Universal will be able to increase prices significantly on U.S. passenger cars in 2011, we project a multibillion dollar profit improvement . . ."

    a. Discuss the concept of an industrial life cycle by describing each of its four phases.

    b. Identify where each of Universal's two primary businesses—passenger cars and information processing—is in such a cycle.

    c. Discuss how product pricing should differ between Universal's two businesses, based on the location of each in the industrial life cycle.

3. Adams's research report (see the previous problem) continued as follows: "With a business expansion already underway, the expected profit surge should lead to a much higher price for Universal Auto stock. We strongly recommend purchase."

    a. Discuss the business cycle approach to investment timing. (Your answer should describe actions to be taken on both stocks and bonds at different points over a typical business cycle.)

    b. Assuming Adams's assertion is correct (that a business expansion is already under way), evaluate the timeliness of his recommendation to purchase Universal Auto, a cyclical stock, based on the business cycle approach to investment timing.

4. Janet Ludlow is preparing a report on U.S.-based manufacturers in the electric toothbrush industry and has gathered the information shown in Tables 12.7 and 12.8 on the next page. Ludlow's report concludes that the electric toothbrush industry is in the maturity (i.e., late) phase of its industry life cycle.

    a. Select and justify three factors from Table 12.7 that support Ludlow's conclusion.

    b. Select and justify three factors from Table 12.8 that refute Ludlow's conclusion.

TABLE 12.7

Ratios for electric toothbrush industry index and broad stock market index

Year	2005	2006	2007	2008	2009	2010
Return on equity						
Electric toothbrush industry index	12.5%	12.0%	15.4%	19.6%	21.6%	21.6%
Market index	10.2	12.4	14.6	19.9	20.4	21.2
Average P/E						
Electric toothbrush industry index	28.5×	23.2×	19.6×	18.7×	18.5×	16.2×
Market index	10.2	12.4	14.6	19.9	18.1	19.1
Dividend payout ratio						
Electric toothbrush industry index	8.8%	8.0%	12.1%	12.1%	14.3%	17.1%
Market index	39.2	40.1	38.6	43.7	41.8	39.1
Average dividend yield						
Electric toothbrush industry index	0.3%	0.3%	0.6%	0.7%	0.8%	1.0%
Market index	3.8	3.2	2.6	2.2	2.3	2.1

TABLE 12.8

Characteristics of the electric toothbrush manufacturing industry

- **Industry sales growth**—Industry sales have grown at 15–20% per year in recent years and are expected to grow at 10–15% per year over the next three years.
- **Non-U.S. markets**—Some U.S. manufacturers are attempting to enter fast-growing non-U.S. markets, which remain largely unexploited.
- **Mail order sales**—Some manufacturers have created a new niche in the industry by selling electric toothbrushes directly to customers through mail order. Sales for this industry segment are growing at 40% per year.
- **U.S. market penetration**—The current penetration rate in the United States is 60% of households and will be difficult to increase.
- **Price competition**—Manufacturers compete fiercely on the basis of price, and price wars within the industry are common.
- **Niche markets**—Some manufacturers are able to develop new, unexploited niche markets in the United States based on company reputation, quality, and service.
- **Industry consolidation**—Several manufacturers have recently merged, and it is expected that consolidation in the industry will increase.
- **New entrants**—New manufacturers continue to enter the market.

5. Dynamic Communication dominates a segment of the consumer electronics industry. A small competitor in that segment is Wade Goods & Co. Wade has just introduced a new product, the Carrycom, which will replace the existing Wade product line and could significantly affect the industry segment. Mike Brandreth is preparing an industry research update that focuses on Wade, including an analysis that makes extensive use of the five competitive forces identified by Michael Porter. Wade's president, Toby White, makes the following statements:

   - "Wade has an exclusive three-year production license for Carrycom technology from the patent owners of the new technology. This will provide us a window of opportunity to establish a leading position with this new product before competitors enter the market with similar products."

   - "A vital component in all existing competitive products is pari-copper, an enriched form of copper; production of pari-copper is limited and is effectively controlled by Dynamic. The Carrycom is manufactured with ordinary copper, thus overcoming the existing dependence on pari-copper. All other Carrycom components can be purchased from numerous sources."

   - "Existing products based on pari-copper are designed to work in a single geographic region that is predetermined during the manufacturing process. The Carrycom will be the only product on the market that can be reset by the user for use in different regions. We expect other products within our industry segment to incorporate this functionality at the end of our exclusive license period."

   - "The Carrycom and similar competitive products have recently added the function of automatic language conversion. This elevates these products to a superior position within the broader electronics market, ahead of personal digital assistants, personal computers, and other consumer electronics. We expect that the broader electronics market will not be able to integrate automatic language conversion for at least one year."

   - "We intend to replace Dynamic as the market leader within the next three years. We expect ordinary copper-based products with automatic language conversion to be the industry standard in three years. This will result in a number of similar products and limited pricing power after the three-year license expires."

   Brandreth has adequately researched two of Porter's competitive forces—the bargaining power of buyers and the bargaining power of suppliers—and now turns his attention to the remaining competitive forces needed to complete his analysis of Wade.

   Identify the three remaining competitive forces. Determine, with respect to each of the remaining competitive forces, whether Wade's position in the industry is likely to be strong or weak, both one year from now and five years from now.

6. The following questions have appeared on CFA examinations.
   a. Which one of the following statements *best* expresses the central idea of countercyclical fiscal policy?
      (1) Planned government deficits are appropriate during economic booms, and planned surpluses are appropriate during economic recessions.
      (2) The balanced budget approach is the proper criterion for determining annual budget policy.
      (3) Actual deficits should equal actual surpluses during a period of deflation.
      (4) Government deficits are planned during economic recessions, and surpluses are utilized to restrain inflationary booms.
   b. Based on historical data and assuming less-than-full employment, periods of sharp acceleration in the growth rate of the money supply tend to be associated *initially* with:
      (1) Periods of economic recession.
      (2) An increase in the velocity of money.
      (3) A rapid growth of gross domestic product.
      (4) Reductions in real gross domestic product.
   c. Which *one* of the following propositions would a strong proponent of supply-side economics be *most* likely to stress?
      (1) Higher marginal tax rates will lead to a reduction in the size of the budget deficit and lower interest rates because they expand government revenues.
      (2) Higher marginal tax rates promote economic inefficiency and thereby retard aggregate output because they encourage investors to undertake low productivity projects with substantial tax-shelter benefits.
      (3) Income redistribution payments will exert little impact on real aggregate supply because they do not consume resources directly.
      (4) A tax reduction will increase the disposable income of households. Thus, the primary impact of a tax reduction on aggregate supply will stem from the influence of the tax change on the size of the budget deficit or surplus.

STANDARD &POOR'S

Use data from the Standard & Poor's Market Insight Database at www.mhhe.com/edumarketinsight to answer the following questions.

1. Find the Industry Profiles from Market Insight for the Photographic Products and Pharmaceuticals industries. Compare the industries' price/book ratios to each other and to the composite ratio for the S&P 500. Do the differences make sense in light of their different stages in the industry life cycle?

2. Compare the price/earnings ratios for the two industries to each other and to the S&P 500 composite ratio. How do the ratios reflect the life cycle stages of the industries? Look at the one-year, three-year, and five-year industry total returns. Are the returns consistent with what you know about firm life cycles? To what extent do they reflect the general state of the economy during each period?

3. On the *Industry* tab of Market Insight, select the Publishing industry. Open the most recent S&P Industry Survey for Publishing, and then answer the following questions.
   a. What industries contribute the most advertising revenue to the publishing industry? How would the outlooks for these industries affect the performance of publishing companies?
   b. Look for the "Industry Trends" section of the report. What trends are noted? How might you expect these trends to affect the publishing industry's performance in the short term?
   c. Is this industry labor intensive? What demographic trends can you think of that might be important in this regard?
   d. Find the "Key Industry Statistics and Ratios" section of the report. Choose two of the features reported in this section and discuss how you think they will affect the industry.
   e. What suggestions does the survey have for evaluating the financial health and the prospects of a firm that specializes in magazines?

WEB *master*   LEADING ECONOMIC INDICATORS

This exercise will give you a chance to examine data on some of the leading economic indicators.

1. Download the data for new privately owned housing units authorized by building permits from **www.census.gov/const/www/C40/table1.html**. Choose the seasonally adjusted data for the United States in an Excel format. Graph the "Total" series.

2. Download the last five years of data for manufacturers' new orders of nondefense capital goods from the St. Louis Federal Reserve site at **research.stlouisfed.org/fred2/series/NEWORDER.** Graph the data.

3. Locate data for the average weekly hours of production workers in manufacturing, available at **www.bls.gov/lpc/lpcover.**

htm#Data. Select the historical time series link and then choose the Index data. Choose manufacturing as the sector and average weekly hours as the measure. Retrieve the report for the past five years. Use the options for a table format, non-HTML, and a space as a delimiter. This will give you both quarterly data and annual averages. When you copy the data into Excel you can use the Data, Text to Columns menu to put the data into a usable format. Create a graph of the data that shows the quarterly trend over the last five years.

4. The data series you retrieved are all leading economic indicators. Based on the tables and your graphs, what is your opinion of where the economy is heading in the near future?

12.1. The downturn in the auto industry will reduce the demand for the product in this economy. The economy will, at least in the short term, enter a recession. This would suggest that:

a. GDP will fall.

b. The unemployment rate will rise.

c. The government deficit will increase. Income tax receipts will fall, and government expenditures on social welfare programs probably will increase.

d. Interest rates should fall. The contraction in the economy will reduce the demand for credit. Moreover, the lower inflation rate will reduce nominal interest rates.

12.2. Expansionary fiscal policy coupled with expansionary monetary policy will stimulate the economy, with the loose monetary policy keeping down interest rates.

12.3. A traditional demand-side interpretation of the tax cuts is that the resulting increase in after-tax income increased consumption demand and stimulated the economy. A supply-side interpretation is that the reduction in marginal tax rates made it more attractive for businesses to invest and for individuals to work, thereby increasing economic output.

12.4. *a.* Newspapers will do best in an expansion when advertising volume is increasing.

b. Machine tools are a good investment at the trough of a recession, just as the economy is about to enter an expansion and firms may need to increase capacity.

c. Beverages are defensive investments, with demand that is relatively insensitive to the business cycle. Therefore, they are good investments if a recession is forecast.

d. Timber is a good investment at a peak period, when natural resource prices are high and the economy is operating at full capacity.

SOLUTIONS TO
CONCEPT
checks

13 Chapter

Equity Valuation

After Studying This Chapter You Should Be Able To:

- Calculate the intrinsic value of a firm using either a constant growth or multistage dividend discount model.

- Calculate the intrinsic value of a stock using a dividend discount model in conjunction with a price/earnings ratio.

- Assess the growth prospects of a firm from its P/E ratio.

- Value a firm using free cash flow models.

You saw in our discussion of market efficiency that finding undervalued securities is hardly easy. At the same time, there are enough chinks in the armor of the efficient market hypothesis that the search for such securities should not be dismissed out of hand. Moreover, it is the ongoing search for mispriced securities that maintains a nearly efficient market. Even infrequent discoveries of minor mispricing justify the salary of a stock market analyst.

This chapter describes the ways stock market analysts try to uncover mispriced securities. The models presented are those used by *fundamental analysts,* those analysts who use information concerning the current and prospective profitability of a company to assess its fair market value. Fundamental analysts are different from *technical analysts,* who largely use trend analysis to uncover trading opportunities.

We start with a discussion of alternative measures of the value of a company. From there, we progress to quantitative tools called dividend discount models that security analysts commonly use to measure the value of a firm as an ongoing concern. Next, we turn to price–earnings, or P/E, ratios, explaining why they are of such interest to analysts but also highlighting some of their shortcomings. We explain how P/E ratios are tied to dividend valuation models and, more generally, to the growth prospects of the firm.

We close the chapter with a discussion and extended example of free cash flow models used by analysts to value firms based on forecasts of the cash flows that will be generated from the firm's business endeavors. We apply the several valuation tools covered in the chapter to a real firm and find that there is some disparity in their conclusions—a conundrum that will confront any security analyst—and consider reasons for these discrepancies.

Related Web sites for this chapter are available at www.mhhe.com/bkm.

13.1 | Valuation By Comparables

The purpose of fundamental analysis is to identify stocks that are mispriced relative to some measure of "true" value that can be derived from observable financial data. Of course, true value can only be estimated. In practice, stock analysts use models to estimate the fundamental value of a corporation's stock from observable market data and from the financial statements of the firm and its competitors. These valuation models differ in the specific data they use and in the level of their theoretical sophistication. But at their heart, most of them use the notion of valuation by comparables: They look at the relationship between price and various determinants of value for similar firms, and then extrapolate that relationship to the firm in question.

The Internet makes it convenient to obtain relevant data. For U.S. companies, the Securities and Exchange Commission provides information available to the public at its EDGAR Web site **www.sec.gov/edgar.shtml**. The SEC requires all public companies (except foreign companies and companies with less than $10 million in assets and 500 shareholders) to file registration statements, periodic reports, and other forms electronically through EDGAR.

Many Web sites, such as **finance.yahoo.com**, also provide analysis and data derived from the EDGAR reports. Another source available to users of this text is Standard & Poor's Market Insight service, which includes COMPUSTAT. Table 13.1 shows an excerpt from Market Insight of financial highlights for Microsoft Corporation.

The price of a share of Microsoft common stock is shown as $17.66, and the total market value of all 8,889 million shares outstanding was $156,979 million. Under the heading "Valuation," Table 13.1 reports the ratios of Microsoft's stock price to four different items taken from its latest financial statements (each reported on a per-share basis): operating earnings, book value, sales revenue, and cash flow. Microsoft's price-to-earnings (P/E) ratio is 9.2, price-to-book value is 4.6, price-to-sales is 2.5, and price-to-cash-flow ratio is 8.0. Such comparative valuation ratios are used to assess the valuation of one firm versus others in the same industry; we will consider all of these ratios later in the chapter. In the column to the right in Table 13.1 are comparable ratios for the average firm in the PC software industry.

For example, an analyst might compare the P/E ratio for Microsoft, 9.2, to the industry average ratio of 15.3. By comparison with this standard, Microsoft appears to be priced significantly below industry norms.

The market price of a share of Microsoft stock was 4.6 times its book value at the end of December 2008. **Book value** is the net worth of a company as reported on its balance sheet. For the average firm in the PC software industry, the market-to-book ratio was 4.8. By comparison with this standard, Microsoft was valued pretty much in line with the rest of the industry, but its other valuation ratios are below industry benchmarks.

book value

The net worth of common equity according to a firm's balance sheet.

Limitations of Book Value

Shareholders in a firm are sometimes called "residual claimants," which means that the value of their stake is what is left over when the liabilities of the firm are subtracted from its assets. Shareholders' equity is this net worth. However, the values of both assets and liabilities recognized in financial statements are based on historical—not current—values. For example, the book value of an asset equals the *original* cost of acquisition less some adjustment for depreciation, even if the market price of that asset has changed over time. Moreover, depreciation allowances are used to allocate the original cost of the asset over several years, but do not reflect loss of actual value.

TABLE 13.1

Microsoft Corporation, financial highlights, year-end, 2008.*

Current Quarter Ended:	December 2008	Current Year Ended:	June 2008
Miscellaneous			
Current price	17.660000	Comn sharehldrs (actual)	145903
Comn shares outstdg (mil)	8889.000	Employees (actual)	91000
Market capitalization (mil)	156979.740	S&P issuer credit rating	AAA
Latest 12 Months	**Company**		**1 Yr Chng (%)**
Sales (mil)	61981.000		7.1
EBITDA (mil)	25877.000		5.0
Net income (mil)	17232.000		1.6
EPS from ops	1.91		6.7
Dividends/Share	0.460000		12.2
Valuation	**Company**		**Industry Avg**
Price/EPS from ops	9.2		15.3
Price/Book	4.6		4.8
Price/Sales	2.5		3.8
Price/Cash Flow	8.0		12.9
Profitability (%)			
Return on equity	50.0		30.8
Return on assets	26.2		15.9
Oper profit margin	37.9		32.7
Net profit margin	27.8		24.4
Financial Risk			

Note: **Additional information has been truncated intentionally.**

Source: Standard & Poor's Market Insight (**www.mhhe.com/edumarketinsight**), January 28, 2009. Access available through this text's Online Learning Center.

Whereas book values are based on original cost, market values measure *current* values of assets and liabilities. The market value of the shareholders' equity investment equals the difference between the current values of all assets and liabilities. (The stock price is just the market value of shareholders' equity divided by the number of outstanding shares.) We've emphasized that current values generally will not match historical ones. Equally or even more important, many assets, for example, the value of a good brand name or specialized expertise developed over many years, may not even be included on the financial statements but certainly influence market price. Market prices reflect the value of the firm as a going concern.

Can book value represent a "floor" for the stock's price, below which level the market price can never fall? Although Microsoft's book value per share is considerably less than its market price, other evidence disproves this notion. While it is not common, there are always some firms selling at a market price below book value. Typically, these are firms in considerable distress. For example, in early 2009, Citigroup was selling at only 20% of book value.

liquidation value

Net amount that can be realized by selling the assets of a firm and paying off the debt.

A better measure of a floor for the stock price is the firm's **liquidation value** per share. This represents the amount of money that could be realized by breaking up the firm, selling its assets, repaying its debt, and distributing the remainder to the shareholders. The reasoning behind this concept is that if the market price of equity drops below the liquidation value of the firm, the firm becomes attractive as a takeover target. A corporate raider would find it profitable to buy enough shares to gain control and then actually liquidate because the liquidation value exceeds the value of the business as a going concern.

replacement cost

Cost to replace a firm's assets.

Another balance sheet concept that is of interest in valuing a firm is the **replacement cost** of its assets less its liabilities. Some analysts believe the market value of the firm cannot get too far above its replacement cost for long because, if it did, competitors would try to replicate the firm. The competitive pressure of other similar firms entering the same industry would drive down the market value of all firms until they came into equality with replacement cost.

This idea is popular among economists, and the ratio of market price to replacement cost is known as **Tobin's q,** after the Nobel Prize–winning economist James Tobin. In the long run, according to this view, the ratio of market price to replacement cost will tend toward 1, but the evidence is that this ratio can differ significantly from 1 for very long periods of time.

Although focusing on the balance sheet can give some useful information about a firm's liquidation value or its replacement cost, the analyst usually must turn to the expected future cash flows for a better estimate of the firm's value as a going concern. We now examine the quantitative models that analysts use to value common stock in terms of the future earnings and dividends the firm will yield.

Tobin's q

Ratio of market value of the firm to replacement cost.

13.2 Intrinsic Value Versus Market Price

The most popular model for assessing the value of a firm as a going concern starts from the observation that the return on a stock investment comprises cash dividends and capital gains or losses. We begin by assuming a one-year holding period and supposing that ABC stock has an expected dividend per share, $E(D_1)$, of $4; that the current price of a share, P_0, is $48; and that the expected price at the end of a year, $E(P_1)$, is $52. For now, don't worry about how you derive your forecast of next year's price. At this point we ask only whether the stock seems attractively priced *today* given your forecast of *next year's* price.

The expected holding-period return is $E(D_1)$ plus the expected price appreciation, $E(P_1) - P_0$, all divided by the current price P_0.

$$\text{Expected HPR} = E(r) = \frac{E(D_1) + [E(P_1) - P_0]}{P_0}$$

$$= \frac{4 + (52 - 48)}{48} = .167 = 16.7\%$$

Note that $E(\ )$ denotes an expected future value. Thus, $E(P_1)$ represents the expectation today of the stock price one year from now. $E(r)$ is referred to as the stock's expected holding-period return. It is the sum of the expected dividend yield, $E(D_1)/P_0$, and the expected rate of price appreciation, the capital gains yield, $[E(P_1) - P_0]/P_0$.

But what is the required rate of return for ABC stock? The capital asset pricing model (CAPM) asserts that when stock market prices are at equilibrium levels, the rate of return that investors can expect to earn on a security is $r_f + \beta[E(r_M) - r_f]$. Thus, the CAPM may be viewed as providing the rate of return an investor can expect to earn on a security given its risk as measured by beta. This is the return that investors will require of any other investment with equivalent risk. We will denote this required rate of return as k. If a stock is priced "correctly," it will offer investors a "fair" return, i.e., its *expected* return will equal its *required* return. Of course, the goal of a security analyst is to find stocks that are mispriced. For example, an underpriced stock will provide an expected return greater than the required return.

Suppose that $r_f = 6\%$, $E(r_M) - r_f = 5\%$, and the beta of ABC is 1.2. Then the value of k is

$$k = 6\% + 1.2 \times 5\% = 12\%$$

The rate of return the investor expects exceeds the required rate based on ABC's risk by a margin of 4.7%. Naturally, the investor will want to include more of ABC stock in the portfolio than a passive strategy would dictate.

Another way to see this is to compare the intrinsic value of a share of stock to its market price. The **intrinsic value,** denoted V_0, of a share of stock is defined as the present value of all cash payments to the investor in the stock, including dividends as well as the proceeds from the ultimate sale of the stock, discounted at the appropriate risk-adjusted interest rate, k.

intrinsic value

The present value of a firm's expected future net cash flows discounted by the required rate of return.

Whenever the intrinsic value, or the investor's own estimate of what the stock is really worth, exceeds the market price, the stock is considered undervalued and a good investment. In the case of ABC, using a one-year investment horizon and a forecast that the stock can be sold at the end of the year at price $P_1 = \$52$, the intrinsic value is

$$V_0 = \frac{E(D_1) + E(P_1)}{1 + k} = \frac{\$4 + \$52}{1.12} = \$50$$

Equivalently, at a price of $50, the investor would derive a 12% rate of return—just equal to the required rate of return—on an investment in the stock. However, at the current price of $48, the stock is underpriced compared to intrinsic value. At this price, it provides better than a fair rate of return relative to its risk. In other words, using the terminology of the CAPM, it is a positive-alpha stock, and investors will want to buy more of it than they would following a passive strategy.

In contrast, if the intrinsic value turns out to be lower than the current market price, investors should buy less of it than under the passive strategy. It might even pay to go short on ABC stock, as we discussed in Chapter 3.

In market equilibrium, the current market price will reflect the intrinsic value estimates of all market participants. This means the individual investor whose V_0 estimate differs from the market price, P_0, in effect must disagree with some or all of the market consensus estimates of $E(D_1)$, $E(P_1)$, or k. A common term for the market consensus value of the required rate of return, k, is the **market capitalization rate,** which we use often throughout this chapter.

market capitalization rate

The market-consensus estimate of the appropriate discount rate for a firm's cash flows.

 **CONCEPT** *check* **13.1**

You expect the price of IBX stock to be $59.77 per share a year from now. Its current market price is $50, and you expect it to pay a dividend one year from now of $2.15 per share.

a.   What is the stock's expected dividend yield, rate of price appreciation, and expected holding-period return?

b.   If the stock has a beta of 1.15, the risk-free rate is 6% per year, and the expected rate of return on the market portfolio is 14% per year, what is the required rate of return on IBX stock?

c.   What is the intrinsic value of IBX stock, and how does it compare to the current market price?

13.3 Dividend Discount Models

Consider an investor who buys a share of Steady State Electronics stock, planning to hold it for one year. The intrinsic value of the share is the present value of the dividend to be received at the end of the first year, D_1, and the expected sales price P_1. We will henceforth use the simpler notation P_1 instead of $E(P_1)$ to avoid clutter. Keep in mind, though, that future prices and dividends are unknown, and we are dealing with expected values, not certain values. We've already established that

$$V_0 = \frac{D_1 + P_1}{1 + k} \tag{13.1}$$

While this year's dividend is fairly predictable given a company's history, you might ask how we can estimate P_1, the year-end price. According to Equation 13.1, V_1 (the year-end value) will be

$$V_1 = \frac{D_2 + P_2}{1 + k}$$

If we assume the stock will be selling for its intrinsic value next year, then $V_1 = P_1$, and we can substitute this value for P_1 into Equation 13.1 to find

$$V_0 = \frac{D_1}{1 + k} + \frac{D_2 + P_2}{(1 + k)^2}$$

This equation may be interpreted as the present value of dividends plus sales price for a two-year holding period. Of course, now we need to come up with a forecast of P_2. Continuing in the same way, we can replace P_2 by $(D_3 + P_3)/(1 + k)$, which relates P_0 to the value of dividends plus the expected sales price for a three-year holding period.

More generally, for a holding period of H years, we can write the stock value as the present value of dividends over the H years, plus the ultimate sales price, P_H.

$$V_0 = \frac{D_1}{1 + k} + \frac{D_2}{(1 + k)^2} + \cdots + \frac{D_H + P_H}{(1 + k)^H} \qquad \textbf{(13.2)}$$

Note the similarity between this formula and the bond valuation formula developed in Chapter 10. Each relates price to the present value of a stream of payments (coupons in the case of bonds, dividends in the case of stocks) and a final payment (the face value of the bond or the sales price of the stock). The key differences in the case of stocks are the uncertainty of dividends, the lack of a fixed maturity date, and the unknown sales price at the horizon date. Indeed, one can continue to substitute for price indefinitely to conclude

$$V_0 = \frac{D_1}{1 + k} + \frac{D_2}{(1 + k)^2} + \frac{D_3}{(1 + k)^3} + \cdots \qquad \textbf{(13.3)}$$

Equation 13.3 states the stock price should equal the present value of all expected future dividends into perpetuity. This formula is called the **dividend discount model (DDM)** of stock prices.

It is tempting, but incorrect, to conclude from Equation 13.3 that the DDM focuses exclusively on dividends and ignores capital gains as a motive for investing in stock. Indeed, we assume explicitly in Equation 13.1 that capital gains (as reflected in the expected sales price, P_1) are part of the stock's value. At the same time, the price at which you can sell a stock in the future depends on dividend forecasts at that time.

The reason only dividends appear in Equation 13.3 is not that investors ignore capital gains. It is instead that those capital gains will be determined by dividend forecasts at the time the stock is sold. That is why in Equation 13.2 we can write the stock price as the present value of dividends plus sales price for *any* horizon date. P_H is the present value at time H of all dividends expected to be paid after the horizon date. That value is then discounted back to today, time 0. The DDM asserts that stock prices are determined ultimately by the cash flows accruing to stockholders, and those are dividends.

dividend discount model (DDM)

A formula for the intrinsic value of a firm equal to the present value of all expected future dividends.

The Constant-Growth DDM

Equation 13.3 as it stands is still not very useful in valuing a stock because it requires dividend forecasts for every year into the indefinite future. To make the DDM practical, we need to introduce some simplifying assumptions. A useful and common first pass at the problem is to assume that dividends are trending upward at a stable growth rate that we will call g. Then if $g = .05$, and the most recently paid dividend was $D_0 = 3.81$, expected future dividends are

$$D_1 = D_0(1 + g) = 3.81 \times 1.05 = 4.00$$
$$D_2 = D_0(1 + g)^2 = 3.81 \times (1.05)^2 = 4.20$$
$$D_3 = D_0(1 + g)^3 = 3.81 \times (1.05)^3 = 4.41 \text{ etc.}$$

Using these dividend forecasts in Equation 13.3, we solve for intrinsic value as

$$V_0 = \frac{D_0(1 + g)}{1 + k} + \frac{D_0(1 + g)^2}{(1 + k)^2} + \frac{D_0(1 + g)^3}{(1 + k)^3} + \cdots$$

This equation can be simplified to

$$V_0 = \frac{D_0(1 + g)}{k - g} = \frac{D_1}{k - g} \qquad \text{(13.4)}$$

Note in Equation 13.4 that we divide D_1 (not D_0) by $k - g$ to calculate intrinsic value. If the market capitalization rate for Steady State is 12%, we can use Equation 13.4 to show that the intrinsic value of a share of Steady State stock is

$$\frac{\$4.00}{.12 - .05} = \$57.14$$

constant-growth DDM

A form of the dividend discount model that assumes dividends will grow at a constant rate.

Equation 13.4 is called the **constant-growth DDM** or the Gordon model, after Myron J. Gordon, who popularized the model. It should remind you of the formula for the present value of a perpetuity. If dividends were expected not to grow, then the dividend stream would be a simple perpetuity, and the valuation formula for such a nongrowth stock would be $P_0 = D_1/k$.[1] Equation 13.4 is a generalization of the perpetuity formula to cover the case of a *growing* perpetuity. As g increases, the stock price also rises.

EXAMPLE   13.1

Preferred Stock and the DDM

Preferred stock that pays a fixed dividend can be valued using the constant-growth dividend discount model. The constant growth rate of dividends is simply zero. For example, to value a preferred stock paying a fixed dividend of $2 per share when the discount rate is 8%, we compute

$$V_0 = \frac{\$2}{.08 - 0} = \$25$$

EXAMPLE   13.2

The Constant-Growth DDM

High Flyer Industries has just paid its annual dividend of $3 per share. The dividend is expected to grow at a constant rate of 8% indefinitely. The beta of High Flyer stock is 1.0, the risk-free rate is 6%, and the market risk premium is 8%. What is the intrinsic value of the stock? What would be your estimate of intrinsic value if you believed that the stock was riskier, with a beta of 1.25?

Because a $3 dividend has just been paid and the growth rate of dividends is 8%, the forecast for the year-end dividend is $3 × 1.08 = $3.24. The market capitalization rate is 6% + 1.0 × 8% = 14%. Therefore, the value of the stock is

$$V_0 = \frac{D_1}{k - g} = \frac{\$3.24}{.14 - .08} = \$54$$

If the stock is perceived to be riskier, its value must be lower. At the higher beta, the market capitalization rate is 6% + 1.25 × 8% = 16%, and the stock is worth only

$$\frac{\$3.24}{.16 - .08} = \$40.50$$

---

[1]Recall from introductory finance that the present value of a $1 per year perpetuity is $1/k$. For example, if $k = 10\%$, the value of the perpetuity is $1/.10 = $10. Notice that if $g = 0$ in Equation 13.4, the constant-growth DDM formula is the same as the perpetuity formula.

The constant-growth DDM is valid only when g is less than k. If dividends were expected to grow forever at a rate faster than k, the value of the stock would be infinite. If an analyst derives an estimate of g that is greater than k, that growth rate must be unsustainable in the long run. The appropriate valuation model to use in this case is a multistage DDM such as those discussed below.

The constant-growth DDM is so widely used by stock market analysts that it is worth exploring some of its implications and limitations. The constant growth rate DDM implies that a stock's value will be greater:

1. The larger its expected dividend per share.
2. The lower the market capitalization rate, k.
3. The higher the expected growth rate of dividends.

Another implication of the constant-growth model is that the stock price is expected to grow at the same rate as dividends. To see this, suppose Steady State stock is selling at its intrinsic value of $57.14, so that $V_0 = P_0$. Then

$$P_0 = \frac{D_1}{k - g}$$

Note that price is proportional to dividends. Therefore, next year, when the dividends paid to Steady State stockholders are expected to be higher by $g = 5\%$, price also should increase by 5%. To confirm this, note

$$D_2 = \$4(1.05) = \$4.20$$
$$P_1 = D_2/(k - g) = \$4.20/(.12 - .05) = \$60.00$$

which is 5% higher than the current price of $57.14. To generalize

$$P_1 = \frac{D_2}{k - g} = \frac{D_1(1 + g)}{k - g} = \frac{D_1}{k - g}(1 + g) = P_0(1 + g)$$

Therefore, the DDM implies that, in the case of constant expected growth of dividends, the expected rate of price appreciation in any year will equal that constant growth rate, g. Note that for a stock whose market price equals its intrinsic value ($V_0 = P_0$) the expected holding-period return will be

$$E(r) = \text{Dividend yield} + \text{Capital gains yield}$$
$$= \frac{D_1}{P_0} + \frac{P_1 - P_0}{P_0} = \frac{D_1}{P_0} + g \qquad \textbf{(13.5)}$$

This formula offers a means to infer the market capitalization rate of a stock, for if the stock is selling at its intrinsic value, then $E(r) = k$, implying that $k = D_1/P_0 + g$. By observing the dividend yield, D_1/P_0, and estimating the growth rate of dividends, we can compute k. This equation is known also as the *discounted cash flow (DCF) formula*.

This is an approach often used in rate hearings for regulated public utilities. The regulatory agency responsible for approving utility pricing decisions is mandated to allow the firms to charge just enough to cover costs plus a "fair" profit, that is, one that allows a competitive return on the investment the firm has made in its productive capacity. In turn, that return is taken to be the expected return investors require on the stock of the firm. The $D_1/P_0 + g$ formula provides a means to infer that required return.

EXAMPLE 13.3

The Constant-Growth Model

Suppose that Steady State Electronics wins a major contract for its revolutionary computer chip. The very profitable contract will enable it to increase the growth rate of dividends from 5% to 6% without reducing the current dividend from the projected value of $4.00 per share. What will happen to the stock price? What will happen to future expected rates of return on the stock?

The stock price ought to increase in response to the good news about the contract, and indeed it does. The stock price jumps from its original value of $57.14 to a postannouncement price of

$$\frac{D_1}{k-g} = \frac{\$4.00}{.12-.06} = \$66.67$$

Investors who are holding the stock when the good news about the contract is announced will receive a substantial windfall.

On the other hand, at the new price the expected rate of return on the stock is 12%, just as it was before the new contract was announced.

$$E(r) = \frac{D_1}{P_0} + g = \frac{\$4.00}{\$66.67} + .06 = .12, \text{ or } 12\%$$

This result makes sense, of course. Once the news about the contract is reflected in the stock price, the expected rate of return will be consistent with the risk of the stock. Since the risk of the stock has not changed, neither should the expected rate of return.

CONCEPT check 13.2

a. IBX's stock dividend at the end of this year is expected to be $2.15, and it is expected to grow at 11.2% per year forever. If the required rate of return on IBX stock is 15.2% per year, what is its intrinsic value?

b. If IBX's current market price is equal to this intrinsic value, what is next year's expected price?

c. If an investor were to buy IBX stock now and sell it after receiving the $2.15 dividend a year from now, what is the expected capital gain (i.e., price appreciation) in percentage terms? What is the dividend yield, and what would be the holding-period return?

Stock Prices and Investment Opportunities

Consider two companies, Cash Cow, Inc., and Growth Prospects, each with expected earnings in the coming year of $5 per share. Both companies could in principle pay out all of these earnings as dividends, maintaining a perpetual dividend flow of $5 per share. If the market capitalization rate were $k = 12.5\%$, both companies would then be valued at $D_1/k = \$5/.125 = \$40$ per share. Neither firm would grow in value, because with all earnings paid out as dividends, and no earnings reinvested in the firm, both companies' capital stock and earnings capacity would remain unchanged over time; earnings[2] and dividends would not grow.

Now suppose one of the firms, Growth Prospects, engages in projects that generate a return on investment of 15%, which is greater than the required rate of return, $k = 12.5\%$. It would be foolish for such a company to pay out all of its earnings as dividends. If Growth Prospects retains or plows back some of its earnings into its highly profitable projects, it can earn a 15% rate of return for its shareholders, whereas if it pays out all earnings as dividends, it forgoes the projects, leaving shareholders to invest the dividends in other opportunities at a fair market rate of only 12.5%. Suppose, therefore, Growth Prospects chooses a lower **dividend payout ratio** (the fraction of earnings paid out as dividends), reducing payout from 100% to 40%, and

dividend payout ratio

Percentage of earnings paid out as dividends.

---

[2]Actually, we are referring here to earnings net of the funds necessary to maintain the productivity of the firm's capital, that is, earnings net of "economic depreciation." In other words, the earnings figure should be interpreted as the maximum amount of money the firm could pay out each year in perpetuity without depleting its productive capacity. For this reason, the net earnings number may be quite different from the accounting earnings figure that the firm reports in its financial statements. We will explore this further in the next chapter.

FIGURE 13.1

Dividend growth for two
earnings reinvestment policies

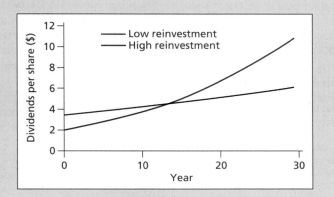

maintaining a **plowback ratio** (the fraction of earnings reinvested in the firm) of 60%. The
plowback ratio also is referred to as the **earnings retention ratio.**

The dividend of the company, therefore, will be only $2 (40% of $5 earnings) instead of $5.
Will the share price fall? No, it will rise! Although dividends initially fall under the earnings
reinvestment policy, subsequent growth in the assets of the firm because of reinvested profits
will generate growth in future dividends, which will be reflected in today's share price.

Figure 13.1 illustrates the dividend streams generated by Growth Prospects under two dividend policies. A low reinvestment rate plan allows the firm to pay higher initial dividends but
results in a lower dividend growth rate. Eventually, a high reinvestment rate plan will provide
higher dividends. If the dividend growth generated by the reinvested earnings is high enough,
the stock will be worth more under the high reinvestment strategy.

How much growth will be generated? Suppose Growth Prospects starts with plant and
equipment of $100 million and is all-equity-financed. With a return on investment or equity
(ROE) of 15%, total earnings are ROE × $100 million = .15 × $100 million = $15 million.
There are 3 million shares of stock outstanding, so earnings per share are $5, as posited above.
If 60% of the $15 million in this year's earnings is reinvested, then the value of the firm's capi-
tal stock will increase by .60 × $15 million = $9 million, or by 9%. The percentage increase
in the capital stock is the rate at which income was generated (ROE) times the plowback ratio
(the fraction of earnings reinvested in more capital), which we will denote as b.

Now endowed with 9% more capital, the company earns 9% more income and pays out 9%
higher dividends. The growth rate of the dividends, therefore, is[3]

$$g = \text{ROE} \times b = 15\% \times .60 = 9\%$$

If the stock price equals its intrinsic value, and this growth rate can be sustained (i.e., if the
ROE and payout ratios are consistent with the long-run capabilities of the firm), then the stock
should sell at

$$P_0 = \frac{D_1}{k - g} = \frac{\$2}{.125 - .09} = \$57.14$$

When Growth Prospects pursued a no-growth policy and paid out all earnings as dividends,
the stock price was only $40. Therefore, you can think of $40 as the value per share of the
assets the company already has in place.

---

[3]We can derive this relationship more generally by noting that with a fixed ROE, earnings (which equal ROE × Book
value) will grow at the same rate as the book value of the firm. Abstracting from net new capital raised by the firm,
the growth rate of book value equals reinvested earnings/book value. Therefore,

$$g = \frac{\text{Reinvested earnings}}{\text{Book value}} = \frac{\text{Reinvested earnings}}{\text{Total earnings}} \times \frac{\text{Total earnings}}{\text{Book value}} = b \times \text{ROE}$$

When Growth Prospects decided to reduce current dividends and reinvest some of its earnings in new investments, its stock price increased. The increase in the stock price reflects the fact that planned investments provide an expected rate of return greater than the required rate. In other words, the investment opportunities have positive net present value. The value of the firm rises by the NPV of these investment opportunities. This net present value is also called the **present value of growth opportunities**, or **PVGO**.

present value of growth opportunities (PVGO)

Net present value of a firm's future investments.

Therefore, we can think of the value of the firm as the sum of the value of assets already in place, or the no-growth value of the firm, plus the net present value of the future investments the firm will make, which is the PVGO. For Growth Prospects, PVGO = $17.14 per share:

$$\text{Price} = \text{No-growth value per share} + \text{PVGO}$$

$$P_0 = \frac{E_1}{k} + \text{PVGO}$$

$$\$57.14 = \$40 + \$17.14 \tag{13.6}$$

We know that in reality, dividend cuts almost always are accompanied by steep drops in stock prices. Does this contradict our analysis? Not necessarily: Dividend cuts are usually taken as bad news about the future prospects of the firm, and it is the *new information* about the firm—not the reduced dividend yield per se—that is responsible for the stock price decline.

In one well-known case, Florida Power & Light announced a cut in its dividend, not because of financial distress, but because it wanted to better position itself for a period of deregulation. At first, the stock market did not believe this rationale—the stock price dropped 14% on the day of the announcement. But within a month, the market became convinced that the firm had in fact made a strategic decision that would improve growth prospects, and the share price actually rose *above* its preannouncement value. Even including the initial price drop, the share price outperformed both the S&P 500 and the S&P utility index in the year following the dividend cut.

It is important to recognize that growth per se is not what investors desire. Growth enhances company value only if it is achieved by investment in projects with attractive profit opportunities (i.e., with ROE > k). To see why, let's now consider Growth Prospects' unfortunate sister company, Cash Cow. Cash Cow's ROE is only 12.5%, just equal to the required rate of return, k. Therefore, the NPV of its investment opportunities is zero. We've seen that following a zero-growth strategy with b = 0 and g = 0, the value of Cash Cow will be $E_1/k = \$5/.125 = \$40$ per share. Now suppose Cash Cow chooses a plowback ratio of b = .60, the same as Growth Prospects' plowback. Then g would be

$$g = \text{ROE} \times b = .125 \times .60 = .075$$

but the stock price is still

$$P_0 = \frac{D_1}{k - g} = \frac{\$2}{.125 - .075} = \$40$$

no different from the no-growth strategy.

In the case of Cash Cow, the dividend reduction that frees funds for reinvestment in the firm generates only enough growth to maintain the stock price at the current level. This is as it should be: If the firm's projects yield only what investors can earn on their own, then NPV is zero, and shareholders cannot be made better off by a high reinvestment rate policy. This demonstrates that "growth" is not the same as growth opportunities. To justify reinvestment, the firm must engage in projects with better prospective returns than those shareholders can find elsewhere. Notice also that the PVGO of Cash Cow is zero: $\text{PVGO} = P_0 - E_1/k = 40 - 40 = 0$. With ROE = k, there is no advantage to plowing funds back into the firm; this shows up as PVGO of zero. In fact, this is why firms with considerable cash flow, but limited investment prospects, are called "cash cows." The cash these firms generate is best taken out of or "milked from" the firm.

EXAMPLE 13.4

Growth Opportunities

Takeover Target is run by entrenched management that insists on reinvesting 60% of its earnings in projects that provide an ROE of 10%, despite the fact that the firm's capitalization rate is $k = 15\%$. The firm's year-end dividend will be $2 per share, paid out of earnings of $5 per share. At what price will the stock sell? What is the present value of growth opportunities? Why would such a firm be a takeover target for another firm?

Given current management's investment policy, the dividend growth rate will be

$$g = ROE \times b = 10\% \times .6 = 6\%$$

and the stock price should be

$$P_0 = \frac{\$2}{.15 - .06} = \$22.22$$

The present value of growth opportunities is

$$PVGO = \text{Price per share} - \text{No-growth value per share}$$
$$= \$22.22 - E_1/k = \$22.22 - \$5/.15 = -\$11.11$$

PVGO is *negative*. This is because the net present value of the firm's projects is negative: The rate of return on those assets is less than the opportunity cost of capital.

Such a firm would be subject to takeover, because another firm could buy the firm for the market price of $22.22 per share and increase the value of the firm by changing its investment policy. For example, if the new management simply paid out all earnings as dividends, the value of the firm would increase to its no-growth value, $E_1/k = \$5/.15 = \$33.33$.

CONCEPT check 13.3

a. Calculate the price of a firm with a plowback ratio of .60 if its ROE is 20%. Current earnings, E_1, will be $5 per share, and $k = 12.5\%$.
b. What if ROE is 10%, which is less than the market capitalization rate? Compare the firm's price in this instance to that of a firm with the same ROE and E_1, but a plowback ratio of $b = 0$.

Life Cycles and Multistage Growth Models

As useful as the constant-growth DDM formula is, you need to remember that it is based on a simplifying assumption, namely, that the dividend growth rate will be constant forever. In fact, firms typically pass through life cycles with very different dividend profiles in different phases. In early years, there are ample opportunities for profitable reinvestment in the company. Payout ratios are low, and growth is correspondingly rapid. In later years, the firm matures, production capacity is sufficient to meet market demand, competitors enter the market, and attractive opportunities for reinvestment may become harder to find. In this mature phase, the firm may choose to increase the dividend payout ratio, rather than retain earnings. The dividend level increases, but thereafter it grows at a slower rate because the company has fewer growth opportunities.

Table 13.2 illustrates this profile. It gives Value Line's forecasts of return on assets, dividend payout ratio, and three-year growth rate in earnings per share of a sample of the firms included in the computer software and services industry versus those of East Coast electric utilities. (We compare return on assets rather than return on equity because the latter is affected by leverage, which tends to be far greater in the electric utility industry than in the software industry. Return on assets measures operating income per dollar of total assets, regardless of whether the source of the capital supplied is debt or equity. We will return to this issue in the next chapter.)

Financial ratios in two industries

	Return on Assets (%)	Payout Ratio (%)	Growth Rate 2009–2012
Computer Software			
Adobe Systems	15.5%	0.0%	14.1%
Cognizant	19.0	0.0	20.8
Compuware	17.0	0.0	13.5
Intuit	20.5	0.0	11.0
Microsoft	34.5	26.0	14.8
Oracle	32.0	0.0	14.5
Red Hat	11.5	0.0	31.0
Parametric Tech	14.5	0.0	15.1
SAP	22.5	32.0	13.6
Median	19.0%	0.0%	14.5%
Electric Utilities			
Central Hudson G&E	5.0%	78.0%	3.2%
Central Vermont	5.0	56.0	1.0
Consolidated Edison	5.5	74.0	1.6
Duke Energy	5.5	73.0	3.7
Northeast Utilities	5.5	48.0	5.8
NStar	9.0	61.0	7.7
Pennsylvania Power	12.5	50.0	37.0
Public Services Enter.	11.5	43.0	6.0
United Illuminating	7.0	82.0	2.5
Median	5.5%	61.0%	3.7%

Source: From *Value Line Investment Survey,* November and December 2008. Reprinted with permission of Value Line Investment Survey © 2008 Value Line Publishing, Inc. All rights reserved.

By and large, software firms have attractive investment opportunities. The median return on assets of these firms is forecast to be 19%, and the firms have responded with quite high plowback ratios. Most of these firms pay no dividends at all. The high returns on assets and high plowback ratios result in rapid growth. The median growth rate of earnings per share in this group is projected at 14.5%.

In contrast, the electric utilities are more representative of mature firms. Their median return on assets is lower, 5.5%; dividend payout is higher, 61%; and average growth rate is lower, 3.7%.

We conclude that the higher payouts of the electric utilities reflect their more limited opportunities to reinvest earnings at attractive rates of return. Consistent with this analysis, Microsoft's announcement in 2004 that it would sharply increase its dividend and initiate multibillion dollar stock buybacks was widely seen as an indication that the firm was maturing into a lower-growth stage. It was generating far more cash than it had the opportunity to invest attractively, and so was paying out that cash to its shareholders.

To value companies with temporarily high growth, analysts use a multistage version of the dividend discount model. Dividends in the early high-growth period are forecast and their combined present value is calculated. Then, once the firm is projected to settle down to a steady growth phase, the constant-growth DDM is applied to value the remaining stream of dividends.

two-stage DDM

Dividend discount model in which dividend growth is assumed to level off only at some future date.

We can illustrate this with a real-life example using a **two-stage DDM.** Figure 13.2 is a *Value Line Investment Survey* report on Honda Motor Co. Some of Honda's relevant information of the end of 2008 is highlighted.

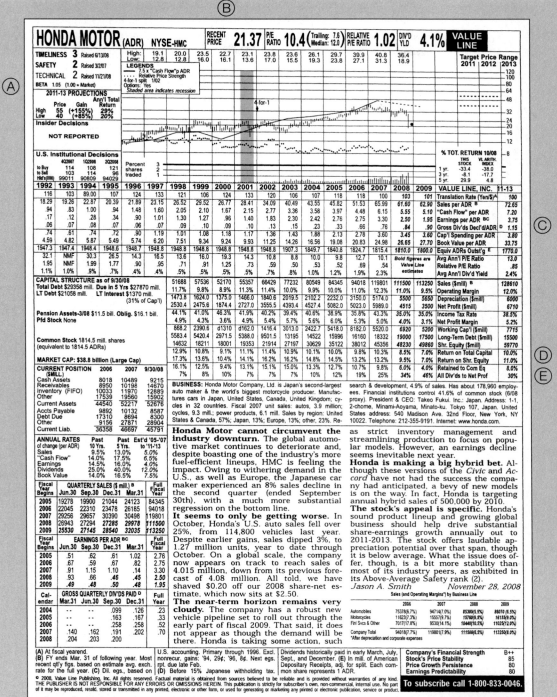

FIGURE 13.2

Value Line Investment Survey report on Honda Motor Co.

Source: *From Value Line Investment Survey*, November 28, 2008. Reprinted with permission of Value Line Investment Survey. © 2008 Value Line Publishing, Inc. All rights reserved.

Honda's beta appears at the circled A, its recent stock price at the B, the per-share dividend payments at the C, the ROE (referred to as "return on shareholder equity") at the D, and the dividend payout ratio (referred to as "all dividends to net profits") at the E.[4] The rows ending at C, D, and E are historical time series. The boldfaced italicized entries under 2009 are estimates for that year. Similarly, the entries in the far right column (labeled 11–13) are forecasts for some time between 2011 and 2013, which we will take to be 2012.

Value Line provides explicit dividend forecasts over the relative short term, with dividends rising from $.90 in 2009 to $1.15 in 2010. We can obtain dividend inputs for this initial period by using the explicit forecasts for 2009 and 2012 and linear interpolation for the years between:

2009	$ .90
2010	$ .98
2011	$1.06
2012	$1.15

Now let us assume the dividend growth rate will be steady beyond 2012. What is a good guess for that steady-state growth rate? Value Line forecasts a dividend payout ratio of .30 and an ROE of 11.0%, implying long-term growth will be

$$g = \text{ROE} \times b = 11.0\% \times (1 - .30) = 7.70\%$$

Our estimate of Honda's intrinsic value using an investment horizon of 2012 is therefore obtained from Equation 13.2, which we restate here:

$$V_{2008} = \frac{D_{2009}}{(1 + k)} + \frac{D_{2010}}{(1 + k)^2} + \frac{D_{2011}}{(1 + k)^3} + \frac{D_{2012} + P_{2012}}{(1 + k)^4}$$

$$= \frac{.90}{(1 + k)} + \frac{.98}{(1 + k)^2} + \frac{1.06}{(1 + k)^3} + \frac{1.15 + P_{2012}}{(1 + k)^4}$$

Here, P_{2012} represents the forecast price at which we can sell our shares of Honda at the end of 2012, when dividends enter their constant-growth phase. That price, according to the constant-growth DDM, should be

$$P_{2012} = \frac{D_{2013}}{k - g} = \frac{D_{2012}(1 + g)}{k - g} = \frac{1.15 \times 1.077}{k - .077}$$

The only variable remaining to be determined to calculate intrinsic value is the market capitalization rate, k.

One way to obtain k is from the CAPM. Observe from the Value Line data that Honda's beta is 1.05. The risk-free rate on longer term T-bonds in late 2008 was about 3.5%. Suppose that the market risk premium were forecast at 8%, roughly in line with its historical average. This would imply that the forecast for the market return was

$$\text{Risk-free rate} + \text{Market risk premium} = 3.5\% + 8\% = 11.5\%$$

Therefore, we can solve for the market capitalization rate for Honda as

$$k = r_f + \beta[E(r_M) - r_f]$$
$$= 3.5\% + 1.05\,(11.5 - 3.5) = 11.9\%$$

---

[4]Because Honda is a Japanese firm, Americans would hold its shares via ADRs, or American Depository Receipts. ADRs are not shares of the firm, but are *claims* to shares of the underlying foreign stock that are then traded in U.S. security markets. Value Line notes that each Honda ADR is a claim on one common share, but in other cases, each ADR may represent a claim to either multiple shares or even fractional shares.

Our forecast for the stock price in 2012 is thus

$$P_{2012} = \frac{\$1.15 \times 1.077}{.119 - .077} = \$29.49$$

and today's estimate of intrinsic value is

$$V_{2008} = \frac{.90}{1.119} + \frac{.98}{(1.119)^2} + \frac{1.06}{(1.119)^3} + \frac{1.15 + 29.49}{(1.119)^4} = \$21.88$$

We know from the Value Line report that Honda's actual price was $21.37 (at the circled B). Our intrinsic value analysis indicates Honda was underpriced by about 2.4%. Should we increase our holdings of Honda stock?

Perhaps. But before betting the farm, stop to consider how much confidence you should place in this estimate. We've had to guess at dividends in the near future, the ultimate growth rate of those dividends, and the appropriate discount rate. Moreover, we've assumed Honda will follow a relatively simple two-stage growth process. In practice, the growth of dividends can follow more complicated patterns. Even small errors in these approximations could upset a conclusion.

For example, we saw in Chapter 7 that betas are typically estimated with considerable imprecision. Suppose that Honda's beta is actually 1.10 rather than 1.05. Then its risk premium will be larger, and its market capitalization rate will be 12.3%. At this higher capitalization rate, the intrinsic value of the firm based on the two-stage model falls to $19.98, which is *less* than its recent stock price. Our conclusion regarding mispricing is reversed.

The exercise highlights the importance of assessing the sensitivity of your analysis to changes in underlying assumptions when you attempt to value stocks. Your estimates of stock values are no better than your assumptions. Sensitivity analysis will highlight the inputs that need to be most carefully examined. For example, we just found that even small changes in the estimated risk premium of the stock can result in big changes in intrinsic value. Similarly, small changes in the assumed growth rate change intrinsic value substantially. On the other hand, reasonable changes in the dividends forecast between 2009 and 2012 have a small impact on intrinsic value.

CONCEPT check 13.4

Confirm that the intrinsic value of Honda using the same data as in our example, but assuming its beta is 1.10, is $19.98. (*Hint:* First calculate the discount rate and stock price in 2012. Then calculate the present value of all interim dividends plus the present value of the 2012 sales price.)

Multistage Growth Models

The two-stage growth model that we just considered for Honda is a good start toward realism, but clearly we could do even better if our valuation model allowed for more flexible patterns of growth. Multistage growth models allow dividends per share to grow at several different rates as the firm matures. Many analysts use three-stage growth models. They may make year-by-year forecasts of dividends for the short term, a final period of sustainable growth, and a transition period in between, during which dividend growth rates taper off from the initial rate to the ultimate sustainable rate. These models are conceptually no harder to work with than a two-stage model, but they require many more calculations and can be tedious to do by hand. It is easy, however, to build an Excel spreadsheet for such a model.

Spreadsheet 13.1 is an example of such a model. Column B contains the inputs we have used so far for Honda. Column E contains dividend forecasts. In cells E2 through E5 we

SPREADSHEET 13.1

A three-stage growth model for Honda

*e**X**cel*

**Please visit us at
www.mhhe.com/bkm**

	A	B	C	D	E	F	G	H	I
1	Inputs			Year	Dividend	Div growth	Term value	Investor CF	
2	beta	1.05		2009	0.90			0.90	
3	mkt_prem	0.08		2010	0.98			0.98	
4	rf	0.035		2011	1.07			1.07	
5	k_equity	0.119		2012	1.15			1.15	
6	plowback	0.7		2013	1.25	0.0851		1.25	
7	ROE	0.11		2014	1.35	0.0843		1.35	
8	term_gwth	0.077		2015	1.47	0.0835		1.47	
9				2016	1.59	0.0827		1.59	
10				2017	1.72	0.0819		1.72	
11				2018	1.86	0.0811		1.86	
12	Value line			2019	2.01	0.0803		2.01	
13	forecasts of			2020	2.16	0.0794		2.16	
14	annual dividends			2021	2.34	0.0786		2.34	
15				2022	2.52	0.0778		2.52	
16				2023	2.71	0.0770		2.71	
17	Transitional period			2024	2.92	0.0770	74.86	77.78	
18	with slowing dividend								
19	growth							22.60	= PV of CF
20		Beginning of constant-			E17*(1+F17)/(B5−F17)				
21		growth period						NPV(B5,H2:H17)	

present the Value Line estimates for the next four years. Dividend growth in this period is about 8.51% annually. Rather than assume a sudden transition to constant dividend growth starting in 2012, we assume instead that the dividend growth rate in 2012 will be 8.51%, and that it will decline linearly through 2023 (see column F), finally reaching the constant terminal growth rate of 7.7% in 2023. Each dividend in the transition period is the previous year's dividend times that year's growth rate. Terminal value once the firm enters a constant-growth stage (cell G17) is computed from the constant-growth DDM. Finally, investor cash flow in each period (column H) equals dividends in each year plus the terminal value in 2024. The present value of these cash flows is computed in cell H19 as $22.60, a bit above the value we found in the two-stage model. We obtain a somewhat greater intrinsic value in this case because we assume that dividend growth only gradually declines to its steady-state value.

13.4 Price–Earnings Ratios

The Price–Earnings Ratio and Growth Opportunities

price–earnings multiple

The ratio of a stock's price to its earnings per share.

Much of the real-world discussion of stock market valuation concentrates on the firm's **price–earnings multiple,** the ratio of price per share to earnings per share, commonly called the P/E ratio. In fact, one common approach to valuing a firm is to use an earnings multiplier. The value of the stock is obtained by multiplying projected earnings per share by a forecast of the P/E ratio. This procedure seems simple, but its apparent simplicity is deceptive. First, forecasting earnings is challenging. As we saw in the previous chapter, earnings will depend on international, macroeconomic, and industry as well as firm-specific factors, many of which are highly unpredictable. Second, forecasting the P/E multiple is even more difficult. P/E ratios vary across industries and over time. Nevertheless, our discussion of stock valuation provides some insight into the factors that ought to determine a firm's P/E ratio.

Recall our discussion of growth opportunities, in which we compared two firms, Growth Prospects and Cash Cow, each of which had earnings per share of $5. Growth Prospects reinvested 60% of its earnings in prospects with an ROE of 15%, while Cash Cow paid out all of its earnings as dividends. Cash Cow had a price of $40, giving it a P/E multiple of

40/5 = 8.0, while Growth Prospects sold for $57.14, giving it a multiple of 57.14/5 = 11.4. This observation suggests the P/E ratio might serve as a useful indicator of expectations of growth opportunities. We can see this explicitly by rearranging Equation 13.6 to

$$\frac{P_0}{E_1} = \frac{1}{k}\left[1 + \frac{PVGO}{E_1/k}\right] \qquad \text{(13.7)}$$

When PVGO = 0, Equation 13.7 shows that $P_0 = E_1/k$. The stock is valued like a nongrowing perpetuity of EPS_1. The P/E ratio is just $1/k$. However, as PVGO becomes an increasingly dominant contributor to price, the P/E ratio can rise dramatically.

The ratio of PVGO to E/k has a simple interpretation. It is the ratio of the component of firm value reflecting growth opportunities to the component of value reflecting assets already in place (i.e., the no-growth value of the firm, E/k). When future growth opportunities dominate the estimate of total value, the firm will command a high price relative to current earnings. Thus, a high P/E multiple appears to indicate that a firm is endowed with ample growth opportunities.

EXAMPLE   13.5

P/E Ratios and Growth Opportunities

Return again to Takeover Target, the firm we first encountered in Example 13.4. Earnings are $5 per share and the capitalization rate is 15%, implying that the no-growth value of the firm is $E_1/k = \$5/.15 = \$33.33$. The stock price actually is $22.22, implying that the present value of growth opportunities equals −$11.11. This implies that the P/E ratio should be

$$\frac{P_0}{E_1} = \frac{1}{k}\left[1 + \frac{PVGO}{E/k}\right] = \frac{1}{.15}\left[1 + \frac{-\$11.11}{\$33.3}\right] = 4.44$$

In fact, the stock price is $22.22 and earnings are $5 per share, so the P/E ratio is $22.22/$5 = 4.44.

Let's see if P/E multiples do vary with growth prospects. Between 1992 and 2008, for example, McDonald's P/E ratio averaged about 19.05 while Consolidated Edison's average P/E was only 12.8. These numbers do not necessarily imply that McDonald's was overpriced compared to Con Ed. If investors believed McDonald's would grow faster than Con Ed, the higher price per dollar would be justified. That is, investors might well pay a higher price per dollar of *current earnings* if they expect that earnings stream to grow more rapidly. In fact McDonald's growth rate has been consistent with its higher P/E multiple. In this period, its earnings per share grew more than fivefold, while Con Ed's earnings grew by only 20%. Figure 13.4 (on page 416) shows the EPS history of the two companies.

Clearly, it is the differences in expected growth opportunities that justify particular differentials in P/E ratios across firms. The P/E ratio is in large part a reflection of the market's optimism concerning a firm's growth prospects. In their use of a P/E ratio, analysts must decide whether they are more or less optimistic than the market. If they are more optimistic, they will recommend buying the stock.

There is a way to make these insights more precise. Look again at the constant-growth DDM formula, $P_0 = D_1/(k - g)$. Now recall that dividends equal the earnings that are *not* reinvested in the firm: $D_1 = E_1(1 - b)$. Recall also that $g = ROE \times b$. Hence, substituting for D_1 and g, we find that

$$P_0 = \frac{E_1(1 - b)}{k - (ROE \times b)}$$

implying that the P/E ratio for a firm growing at a long-run sustainable pace is

$$\frac{P_0}{E_1} = \frac{1 - b}{k - (ROE \times b)} \qquad \text{(13.8)}$$

TABLE 13.3		Plowback Ratio (b)			
		0	**.25**	**.50**	**.75**
Effect of ROE and plowback on growth and the P/E ratio		**A. Growth rate, g**			
	ROE				
	10%	0%	2.5%	5.0%	7.5%
	12	0	3.0	6.0	9.0
	14	0	3.5	7.0	10.5
		B. P/E ratio			
	ROE				
	10%	8.33	7.89	7.14	5.56
	12	8.33	8.33	8.33	8.33
	14	8.33	8.82	10.00	16.67

Note: Assumption: $k = 12\%$ per year.

It is easy to verify that the P/E ratio increases with ROE. This makes sense, because high ROE projects give the firm good opportunities for growth.[5] We also can verify that the P/E ratio increases for higher plowback, b, as long as ROE exceeds k. This too makes sense. When a firm has good investment opportunities, the market will reward it with a higher P/E multiple if it exploits those opportunities more aggressively by plowing back more earnings into those opportunities.

Remember, however, that growth is not desirable for its own sake. Examine Table 13.3, where we use Equation 13.8 to compute both growth rates and P/E ratios for different combinations of ROE and b. While growth always increases with the plowback ratio (move across the rows in Panel A of Table 13.3), the P/E ratio does not (move across the rows in Panel B). In the top row of Table 13.3B, the P/E falls as the plowback rate increases. In the middle row, it is unaffected by plowback. In the third row, it increases.

This pattern has a simple interpretation. When the expected ROE is less than the required return, k, investors prefer that the firm pay out earnings as dividends rather than reinvest earnings in the firm at an inadequate rate of return. That is, for ROE lower than k, the value of the firm falls as plowback increases. Conversely, when ROE exceeds k, the firm offers superior investment opportunities, so the value of the firm is enhanced as those opportunities are more fully exploited by increasing the plowback ratio.

Finally, where ROE just equals k, the firm offers "break-even" investment opportunities with a fair rate of return. In this case, investors are indifferent between reinvestment of earnings in the firm or elsewhere at the market capitalization rate, because the rate of return in either case is 12%. Therefore, the stock price is unaffected by the plowback ratio.

One way to summarize these relationships is to say the higher the plowback ratio, the higher the growth rate, but a higher plowback ratio does not necessarily mean a higher P/E ratio. A higher plowback ratio increases P/E only if investments undertaken by the firm offer an expected rate of return higher than the market capitalization rate. Otherwise, higher plowback hurts investors because it means more money is sunk into prospects with inadequate rates of return.

Notwithstanding these fine points, P/E ratios commonly are taken as proxies for the expected growth in dividends or earnings. In fact, a common Wall Street rule of thumb is that the growth rate ought to be roughly equal to the P/E ratio. In other words, the ratio of P/E to g, often called the **PEG ratio**, should be about 1.0. Peter Lynch, the famous portfolio manager, puts it this way in his book *One Up on Wall Street:*

PEG ratio

Ratio of P/E multiple to earnings growth rate.

> The P/E ratio of any company that's fairly priced will equal its growth rate. I'm talking here about growth rate of earnings. . . . If the P/E ratio of Coca-Cola is 15, you'd expect the company to be

---

[5]Note that Equation 13.8 is a simple rearrangement of the DDM formula, with ROE $\times$ $b = g$. Because that formula requires that $g < k$, Equation 13.8 is valid only when ROE $\times$ $b < k$.

growing at about 15% per year, etc. But if the P/E ratio is less than the growth rate, you may have found yourself a bargain.

Let's try his rule of thumb.

Assume:

$$r_f = 8\% \text{ (about the value when Peter Lynch was writing)}$$
$$r_M - r_f = 8\% \text{ (about the historical average market risk premium)}$$
$$b = .4 \text{ (a typical value for the plowback ratio in the U.S.)}$$

Therefore, $r_M = r_f + $ Market risk premium $= 8\% + 8\% = 16\%$, and $k = 16\%$ for an average ($\beta = 1$) company. If we also accept as reasonable that ROE $= 16\%$ (the same value as the expected return on the stock) we conclude that

$$g = \text{ROE} \times b = 16\% \times .4 = 6.4\%$$

and

$$\text{P/E} = \frac{1 - .4}{.16 - .064} = 6.26$$

Thus the P/E ratio and g are about equal using these assumptions, consistent with the rule of thumb. However, note that this rule of thumb, like almost all others, will not work in all circumstances. For example, the value of r_f today is more like 3.5%, so a comparable forecast of r_M today would be:

$$r_f + \text{Market risk premium} = 3.5\% + 8\% = 11.5\%$$

If we continue to focus on a firm with $\beta = 1$, and ROE still is about the same as k, then

$$g = 11.5\% \times .4 = 4.6\%$$

while

$$\text{P/E} = \frac{1 - .4}{.115 - .046} = 8.70$$

The P/E ratio and g now diverge and the PEG ratio is now 8.70/4.6 = 1.9. Nevertheless, lower-than-average PEG ratios are still widely seen as signalling potential underpricing.

Whatever its shortcomings, the PEG ratio is widely followed. The PEG ratio for the S&P over the last 20 years typically has fluctuated within the range between 1.0 and 1.5.

ABC stock has an expected ROE of 12% per year, expected earnings per share of $2, and expected dividends of $1.50 per share. Its market capitalization rate is 10% per year.
a. What are its expected growth rate, its price, and its P/E ratio?
b. If the plowback rate were .4, what would be the firm's expected dividend per share, growth rate, price, P/E, and PEG ratio?

The importance of growth opportunities is nowhere more evident than in the Internet boom of the late 1990s. Many companies that had yet to turn a profit were valued by the market at billions of dollars. The value of these companies was *exclusively* growth opportunities. For example, the online auction firm eBay had 1998 profits of $2.4 million, far less than the $45 million profit earned by the traditional auctioneer Sotheby's; yet eBay's market value was more than 10 times greater: $22 billion versus $1.9 billion. As it turns out, the market was quite right to value eBay so much more aggressively than Sotheby's. By 2006, its net income was over $1 billion, more than 15 times that of Sotheby's and, despite setbacks since than, its income in 2007 and 2008 was still far greater than Sotheby's.

On the MARKET FRONT

FINDING GEMS IN MARKET DEBRIS—PRICE DECLINES LEAVE MANY STOCKS AT HISTORICALLY LOW VALUATIONS

The news for investors continues to be uniformly grim, but among individual stocks, a growing number of long-term opportunities may be beckoning. Of course, for many names—especially financials, housing and automotive stocks—there is good reason for prices to be as low as they are.

But even outside those parts of the market hardest hit by the credit crunch and the deepening economic slump, price declines have many individual stocks trading at historically low valuations. The percentage of stocks trading with a trailing one-year price/earnings ratio below 10 is at 61%, the highest level since the early 1980s.

"Bear markets give you an opportunity to buy best-of-breed companies without paying a premium," says Neil Hokanson, president of Hokanson Associates, investment advisors in Solana Beach, Calif. Part of the challenge is that valuation has two elements: the price and the fundamentals of a company. If earnings and sales continue to decline, what looked cheap can swiftly prove to be expensive. In addition, valuations could be low for years if the market goes into a prolonged malaise.

Already, the prices on many stocks suggest investors expect earnings to fall nearly by half from their recent peak. The earnings outlook "is a huge shadow of uncertainty," says J.P. Morgan stock strategist Thomas Lee. "We don't know how deep or how long this recession will be and it's tough to know where the earnings will bottom."

Paul Sutherland, chief investment officer at FIM Group in Traverse City, Mich., says he is now buying a few blue-chips he "never thought would become cheap enough to own." Among them is General Electric Corp. He acknowledges concerns about the company's big finance unit, GE Capital. But fears about that business are "making it a buying opportunity," he says.

Mr. Sutherland also likes DuPont Co. because of its strong dividend yield, numerous patents, and focus on forward-looking businesses, including renewable energy. Yet DuPont's shares are down 29% from the 2002 market lows. For both trailing and the next 12 months its P/E is under 9.

SOURCE: Tom Lauricella and Annelena Lobb, *"Finding Gems in Market Debris—Price Declines Leave Many Stocks at Historically Low Valuations,"* The Wall Street Journal, November 17, 2008. Reprinted by permission of The Wall Street Journal, Copyright © 2008 Dow Jones & Company, Inc. All Rights Reserved Worldwide.

Of course, when company valuation is determined primarily by growth opportunities, those values can be very sensitive to reassessments of such prospects. When the market became more skeptical of the business prospects of most Internet retailers at the close of the 1990s, that is, as it revised the estimates of growth opportunities downward, their stock prices plummeted.

As perceptions of future prospects wax and wane, share price can swing wildly. Growth prospects are intrinsically difficult to tie down; ultimately, however, those prospects drive the value of the most dynamic firms in the economy.

The nearby box is an example of a valuation analysis based on the P/E ratio. The article points out that in late 2008, P/E ratios based on trailing (last year's) earnings are lower than they have been in years, making many stocks appear attractive. The problem, of course, is that earnings for the coming year are expected to be depressed by the ongoing economic crisis. Against that backdrop, the case for bargain valuations is far less compelling.

P/E Ratios and Stock Risk

One important implication of any stock valuation model is that (holding all else equal) riskier stocks will have lower P/E multiples. We can see this quite easily in the context of the constant-growth model by examining the formula for the P/E ratio (Equation 13.8):

$$\frac{P}{E} = \frac{1 - b}{k - g}$$

Riskier firms will have higher required rates of return (i.e., higher values of k). Therefore, their P/E multiples will be lower. This is true even outside the context of the constant-growth model. For *any* expected earnings and dividend stream, the present value of those cash flows will be lower when the stream is perceived to be riskier. Hence the stock price and the ratio of price to earnings will be lower.

Of course, if you scan *The Wall Street Journal,* you will observe many small, risky, start-up companies with very high P/E multiples. This does not contradict our claim that P/E multiples should fall with risk: Instead, it is evidence of the market's expectations of high growth

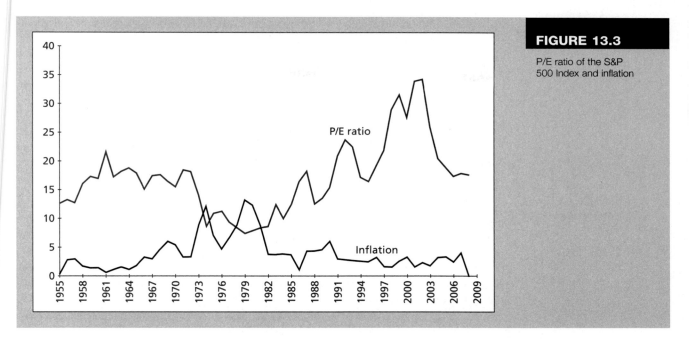

FIGURE 13.3

P/E ratio of the S&P 500 Index and inflation

rates for those companies. This is why we said that high risk firms will have lower P/E ratios *holding all else equal.* Given a growth projection, the P/E multiple will be lower when risk is perceived to be higher.

Pitfalls in P/E Analysis

No description of P/E analysis is complete without mentioning some of its pitfalls. First, consider that the denominator in the P/E ratio is accounting earnings, which are influenced by somewhat arbitrary accounting rules such as the use of historical cost in depreciation and inventory valuation. In times of high inflation, historic cost depreciation and inventory costs will tend to underrepresent true economic values because the replacement cost of both goods and capital equipment will rise with the general level of prices. As Figure 13.3 demonstrates, P/E ratios fell dramatically in the 1970s when inflation spiked. This reflected the market's assessment that earnings in these periods are of "lower quality," artificially distorted by inflation, and warranting lower P/E ratios.

Earnings management is the practice of using flexibility in accounting rules to improve the apparent profitability of the firm. We will have much to say on this topic in the next chapter on interpreting financial statements. A version of earnings management that became common in recent years was the reporting of "pro forma earnings" measures. These measures are sometimes called *operating earnings,* a term with no precise generally accepted definition.

Pro forma earnings are calculated ignoring certain expenses, for example, restructuring charges, stock-option expenses, or write-downs of assets from continuing operations. Firms argue that ignoring these expenses gives a clearer picture of the underlying profitability of the firm.

But when there is too much leeway for choosing what to exclude it becomes hard for investors or analysts to interpret the numbers or to compare them across firms. The lack of standards gives firms considerable leeway to manage earnings.

Even GAAP allows firms considerable discretion to manage earnings. For example, in the late 1990s, Kellogg took restructuring charges, which are supposed to be one-time events, nine quarters in a row. Were these really one-time events, or were they more appropriately treated as ordinary expenses? Given the available leeway in reporting earnings, the justified P/E multiple becomes difficult to gauge.

Another confounding factor in the use of P/E ratios is related to the business cycle. We were careful in deriving the DDM to define earnings as being net of *economic* depreciation, that is, the maximum flow of income that the firm could pay out without depleting its productive

earnings management
The practice of using flexibility in accounting rules to improve the apparent profitability of the firm.

capacity. And reported earnings, as we note above, are computed in accordance with generally accepted accounting principles and need not correspond to economic earnings. Beyond this, however, notions of a normal or justified P/E ratio, as in Equation 13.7 or 13.8, assume implicitly that earnings rise at a constant rate, or, put another way, on a smooth trend line. In contrast, reported earnings can fluctuate dramatically around a trend line over the course of the business cycle.

Another way to make this point is to note that the "normal" P/E ratio predicted by Equation 13.8 is the ratio of today's price to the trend value of future earnings, E_1. The P/E ratio reported in the financial pages of the newspaper, by contrast, is the ratio of price to the most recent *past* accounting earnings. Current accounting earnings can differ considerably from future economic earnings. Because ownership of stock conveys the right to future as well as current earnings, the ratio of price to most recent earnings can vary substantially over the business cycle, as accounting earnings and the trend value of economic earnings diverge by greater and lesser amounts.

As an example, Figure 13.4 graphs the earnings per share of McDonald's and Consolidated Edison since 1992. Note that McDonald's EPS fluctuate around its trend line more than Con Ed's. This reflects the company's higher sensitivity to macroeconomic conditions. Value Line estimates its beta at .80. Con Ed, by contrast, shows much less variation in earnings per share around a smoother and flatter trend line. Its beta was only .65.

Because the market values the entire stream of future dividends generated by the company, when earnings are temporarily depressed, the P/E ratio should tend to be high—that is, the denominator of the ratio responds more sensitively to the business cycle than the numerator. This pattern is borne out well.

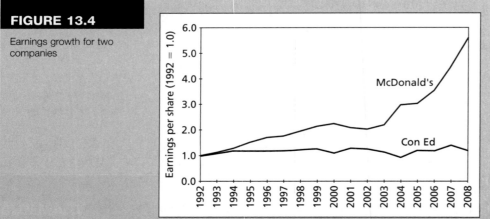

FIGURE 13.4

Earnings growth for two companies

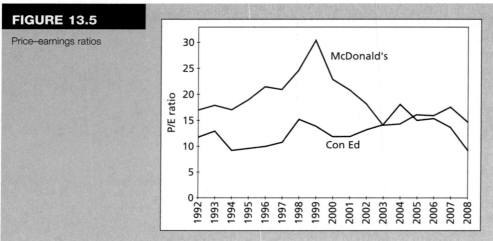

FIGURE 13.5

Price–earnings ratios

Figure 13.5 graphs the P/E ratios of the two firms. McDonald's has greater earnings volatility and more variability in its P/E ratio. Its clearly higher average growth rate shows up in its generally higher P/E ratio. The only period in which Con Ed's ratio exceeded McDonald's was in 2003–2005, a period when Con Ed's earnings temporarily dipped below their trend line and McDonald's earnings rose faster than their trend. The market seems to have recognized that these were both temporary conditions; prices did not respond dramatically to these fluctuations in earnings, so Con Ed's P/E ratio rose and McDonald's fell.

This example shows why analysts must be careful in using P/E ratios. There is no way to say a P/E ratio is overly high or low without referring to

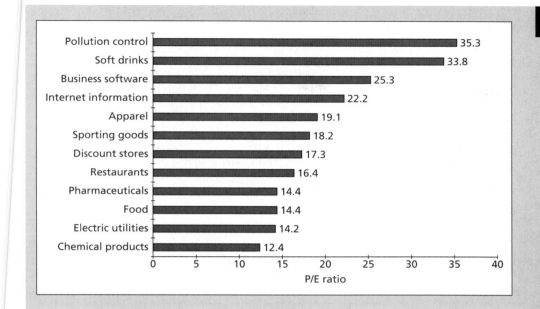

FIGURE 13.6

P/E ratios

Source: Yahoo! Finance, February 2, 2009. Reproduced with permission of Yahoo! Inc. © 2008 by Yahoo! Inc. Yahoo! and the Yahoo! logo are trademarks of Yahoo! Inc.

the company's long-run growth prospects, as well as to current earnings per share relative to the long-run trend line.

Nevertheless, Figures 13.4 and 13.5 demonstrate a clear relationship between P/E ratios and growth. Despite short-run fluctuations, McDonald's EPS clearly trended upward over the period. Its compound rate of growth in the 1992–2008 period was 11.4%. Con Edison's earnings grew far less rapidly, with a compound growth rate of 1.1%. The growth prospects of McDonald's are reflected in its consistently higher P/E multiple.

This analysis suggests that P/E ratios should vary across industries and, in fact, they do. Figure 13.6 shows P/E ratios for a sample of industries. Notice that the industries with the highest multiples—business software, soft drinks, and pollution control—have attractive investment opportunities, whereas the industries with the lowest multiples—electric utilities and chemical products—are in more mature industries with limited growth prospects. The relationship between P/E and growth is not perfect, which is not surprising in light of the pitfalls discussed in this section, but as a general rule, the P/E multiple tracks growth opportunities.

Combining P/E Analysis and the DDM

Some analysts use P/E ratios in conjunction with earnings forecasts to estimate the price of stock at an investor's horizon date. The Honda analysis in Figure 13.2 shows that Value Line forecasted a P/E ratio for 2012 of 13. EPS for 2012 were forecast at $3.75, implying a price in 2012 of 13 × $3.75 = $48.75. Given an estimate of $48.75 for the 2012 sales price, we would compute Honda's intrinsic value as

$$V_{2008} = \frac{.90}{(1.119)} + \frac{.98}{(1.119)^2} + \frac{1.06}{(1.119)^3} + \frac{1.15 + \$48.75}{(1.119)^4} = \$34.17$$

Other Comparative Valuation Ratios

The price–earnings ratio is an example of a comparative valuation ratio. Such ratios are used to assess the valuation of one firm versus another based on a fundamental indicator such as earnings. For example, an analyst might compare the P/E ratios of two firms in the same industry to test whether the market is valuing one firm "more aggressively" than the other. Other such comparative ratios are commonly used.

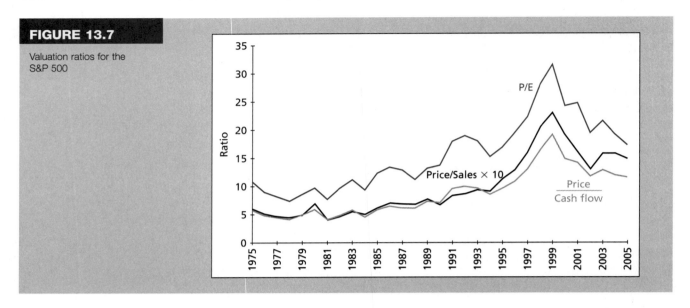

FIGURE 13.7

Valuation ratios for the
S&P 500

Price-to-book ratio   This is the ratio of price per share divided by book value per share. As we noted earlier in this chapter, some analysts view book value as a useful measure of fundamental value and therefore treat the ratio of price-to-book value as an indicator of how aggressively the market values the firm.

Price-to-cash-flow ratio   Earnings as reported on the income statement can be affected by the company's choice of accounting practices and thus are commonly viewed as subject to some imprecision and even manipulation. In contrast, cash flow—which tracks cash actually flowing into or out of the firm—is less affected by accounting decisions. As a result, some analysts prefer to use the ratio of price to cash flow per share rather than price to earnings per share. Some analysts use operating cash flow when calculating this ratio; others prefer free cash flow, that is, operating cash flow net of new investment.

Price-to-sales ratio   Many start-up firms have no earnings. As a result, the P/E ratio for these firms is meaningless. The price-to-sales ratio (the ratio of stock price to the annual sales per share) is sometimes taken as a valuation benchmark for these firms. Of course, price-to-sales ratios can vary markedly across industries, since profit margins vary widely.

Be creative   Sometimes a standard valuation ratio will simply not be available, and you will have to devise your own. In the 1990s, some analysts valued retail Internet firms based on the number of Web hits their sites received. In retrospect, they valued these firms using too generous "price-to-hits" ratios. Nevertheless, in a new investment environment, these analysts used the information available to them to devise the best valuation tools they could.

Figure 13.7 presents the behavior of these valuation measures for the S&P 500. While the levels of these ratios differ considerably, for the most part they track each other fairly closely, with upturns and downturns at the same times.

13.5 Free Cash Flow Valuation Approaches

An alternative approach to the dividend discount model values the firm using free cash flow, that is, cash flow available to the firm or the equityholders net of capital expenditures. This approach is particularly useful for firms that pay no dividends, for which the dividend discount model would be difficult to implement. But free cash flow models are valid for any firm, and can provide useful insights about firm value beyond the DDM.

One approach is to discount the *free cash flow* for the *firm* (FCFF) at the weighted-average cost of capital to obtain the value of the firm, and then subtract the then-existing value of debt to find the value of equity. Another is to focus from the start on the free cash flow to *equity-holders* (FCFE), discounting those directly at the cost of equity to obtain the market value of equity.

The free cash flow to the firm is given as follows:

$$\text{FCFF} = \text{EBIT}(1 - t_c) + \text{Depreciation} - \text{Capital expenditures} - \text{Increase in NWC} \qquad \textbf{(13.9)}$$

where

EBIT = earnings before interest and taxes

t_c = the corporate tax rate

NWC = net working capital

This is the cash flow that accrues from the firm's operations, net of investments in capital and net working capital. It includes cash flows available to both debt- and equityholders.[6]

Alternatively, we can focus on cash flow available to equityholders. This will differ from free cash flow to the firm by after-tax interest expenditures, as well as by cash flow associated with net issuance or repurchase of debt (i.e., principal repayments minus proceeds from issuance of new debt).

$$\text{FCFE} = \text{FCFF} - \text{Interest expense} \times (1 - t_c) + \text{Increases in net debt} \qquad \textbf{(13.10)}$$

The free cash flow to the firm approach discounts year-by-year cash flows plus some estimate of terminal value, P_T. In Equation 13.11, we use the constant-growth model to estimate terminal value. The appropriate discount rate is the weighted average cost of capital.

$$\text{Firm value} = \sum_{t=1}^{T} \frac{1 + \text{FCFF}_t}{(1 + \text{WACC})^t} + \frac{P_T}{(1 + \text{WACC})^T} \qquad \textbf{(13.11)}$$

where

$$P_T = \frac{\text{FCFF}_{T+1}}{\text{WACC} - g}$$

To find equity value, we subtract the existing market value of debt from the derived value of the firm.

Alternatively, we can discount free cash flows to *equity* (FCFE) at the cost of *equity, k_E,*

$$\text{Market value of equity} = \sum_{t=1}^{T} \frac{\text{FCFE}_t}{(1 + k_E)^t} + \frac{P_T}{(1 + k_E)^T} \qquad \textbf{(13.12)}$$

where

$$P_T = \frac{\text{FCFE}_{T+1}}{k_E - g}$$

As in the dividend discount model, free cash flow models use a terminal value to avoid adding the present values of an infinite sum of cash flows. That terminal value may simply be the present value of a constant-growth perpetuity (as in the formulas above) or it may be based on a multiple of EBIT, book value, earnings, or free cash flow. As a general rule, estimates of intrinsic value depend critically on terminal value.

---

[6]This is firm cash flow assuming all-equity financing. Any tax advantage to debt financing is recognized by using an after-tax cost of debt in the computation of weighted average cost of capital. This issue is discussed in any introductory corporate finance text.

Spreadsheet 13.2 presents a free cash flow valuation of Honda using the data supplied by Value Line in Figure 13.2. We start with the free cash flow to the firm approach given in Equation 13.9. Panel A of the spreadsheet lays out values supplied by Value Line. (Entries for middle years are interpolated from beginning and final values.) Panel B calculates free cash flow. The sum of after-tax profits in row 11 plus after-tax interest payments in row 12 [that is, interest expense $\times (1 - t_c)$] equals EBIT$(1 - t_c)$. In row 13 we subtract the change in net working capital, in row 14 we add back depreciation, and in row 15 we subtract capital expenditures. The result in row 17 is the free cash flow to the firm, FCFF, for each year between 2009 and 2012.

To find the present value of these cash flows, we will discount at WACC, which is calculated in panel C. WACC is the weighted average of the after-tax cost of debt and the cost of equity in each year. When computing WACC, we must account for the change in leverage forecasted by Value Line. To compute the cost of equity, we will use the CAPM as in our earlier (dividend discount model) valuation exercise, but account for the fact that equity beta will decline each year as the firm reduces leverage.[7]

SPREADSHEET 13.2

Free cash flow valuation of Honda Motor

eXcel

Please visit us at www.mhhe.com/bkm

	A	B	C	D	E	F	G	H	I	J	K	L	M
1		2007	2008	2009	2010	2011	2012						
2	A. Value Line data												
3	P/E	10.10	10.68	11.26	11.84	12.42	13.00						
4	Cap spending/shr		3.45	3.60	3.67	3.73	3.80						
5	LT debt		19000	17500	16833	16167	15500						
6	Shares		1810	1800	1790	1780	1770						
7	EPS		2.50	1.95	2.55	3.15	3.75						
8	Working capital		6920	5200	6038	6877	7715						
9													
10	B. Cash flow calculations												
11	Profits (after tax)		4515.0	3500.0	4570.0	5640.0	6710.0						
12	Interest (after tax)		701.1	645.8	621.2	596.6	572.0	= r_debt * (1-tax) * LT Debt					
13	Chg working cap			−1720.0	838.3	838.3	838.3						
14	Depreciation			5500.0	5650.0	5833.3	6000.0						
15	Cap spending			6480.0	6562.0	6644.0	6726.0						
16								Terminal value					
17	FCFF			4885.8	3440.8	4587.6	5717.6	85382.0					
18	FCFE			2740.0	2153.0	3324.3	4479.0	72233.6	assumes fixed debt ratio after 2012				
19													
20	C. Discount rate calculations												
21	Current beta	1.05							from Value Line				
22	Unlevered beta	0.845							current beta /[1+(1-tax)*debt/equity)]				
23	terminal growth	0.03											
24	tax_rate	0.385							from Value Line				
25	r_debt	0.060							YTM in 2008 on A-rated LT debt				
26	risk-free rate	0.035											
27	market risk prem	0.08											
28	MV equity		48220	39410	54109	70049	87230		Row 3 × Row 11				
29	Debt/Value		0.28	0.31	0.24	0.19	0.15		Row 5/(Row 5+Row 28)				
30	Levered beta		1.050	1.076	1.007	0.965	0.938		unlevered beta × [1+(1-tax)*debt/equity]				
31	k_equity		0.119	0.121	0.116	0.112	0.110	0.110	from CAPM and levered beta				
32	WACC		0.096	0.095	0.097	0.098	0.099	0.099	(1-t)*r_debt*D/V+k_equity*(1-D/V)				
33	PV factor for FCFF		1.000	0.913	0.832	0.758	0.690	0.690	Discount each year at WACC				
34	PV factor for FCFE		1.000	0.892	0.800	0.719	0.648	0.648	Discount each year at k_equity				
35													
36	D. Present values									Intrinsic val	Equity val	Intrin/share	
37	PV(FCFF)			4461	2864	3478	3944	58896		73643	54643	30.19	
38	PV(FCFE)			2444	1722	2390	2901	46784		56241	56241	31.07	

[7]Call β_L the firm's equity beta at the initial level of leverage as provided by Value Line. Equity betas reflect both business risk and financial risk. When a firm changes its capital structure (debt/equity mix), it changes financial risk, and therefore equity beta changes. How should we recognize the change in financial risk? As you may remember from an introductory corporate finance class, you must first unleverage beta. This leaves us a beta that reflects only business risk. We use the following formula to find unleveraged beta, β_U, (where D/E is the firm's current debt-equity ratio):

$$\beta_U = \frac{\beta_L}{1 + (D/E)(1 - t_c)}$$

Then, we re-leverage beta in any particular year using the forecast capital structure (which reintroduces the financial risk associated with that year's capital structure):

$$\beta_L = \beta_U [1 + (D/E)(1 - t_c)]$$

A reasonable approximation to Honda's cost of debt, which was rated A in 2008, is the yield to maturity on comparably rated long-term debt, approximately 6% (cell B25). Honda's debt-to-value ratio is computed in row 29 (assuming that its debt is selling near par value), and WACC is computed in row 32. WACC increases slightly over time as the debt-to-value ratio steadily declines between 2009 and 2012. The present value factor for cash flows accruing in each year is the previous year's factor divided by $(1 + \text{WACC})$ for that year. The present value of each cash flow (row 37) is the free cash flow times the cumulative discount factor.

The terminal value of the firm (cell H17) is computed from the constant-growth model as $\text{FCFF}_{2012} \times (1 + g)/(\text{WACC}_{2012} - g)$, where g (cell B23) is the assumed value for the steady growth rate.[8] We assume in the spreadsheet that $g = .03$, roughly the long-run growth rate of the broad economy.[9] Terminal value is also discounted back to 2008 (cell H37), and the intrinsic value of the firm is thus found as the sum of discounted free cash flows between 2009 and 2012 plus the discounted terminal value. Finally, the value of debt in 2008 is subtracted from firm value to arrive at the intrinsic value of equity in 2008 (cell K37), and value per share is calculated in cell L37 as equity value divided by number of shares in 2008.

The free cash flow to equity approach yields a similar intrinsic value for the stock. FCFE (row 18) is obtained from FCFF by subtracting after-tax interest expense and net debt repurchases. The cash flows are then discounted at the equity rate. Like WACC, the cost of equity changes each period as leverage changes. The present value factor for equity cash flows is presented in row 34. Equity value is reported in cell J38, which is put on a per share basis in cell L38.

Spreadsheet 13.2 is available at the Online Learning Center, **www.mhhe.com/bkm.**

Comparing the Valuation Models

In principle, the free cash flow approach is fully consistent with the dividend discount model and should provide the same estimate of intrinsic value if one can extrapolate to a period in which the firm begins to pay dividends growing at a constant rate. This was demonstrated in two famous papers by Modigliani and Miller (1958, 1961). However, in practice, you will find that values from these models may differ, sometimes substantially. This is due to the fact that in practice, analysts are always forced to make simplifying assumptions. For example, how long will it take the firm to enter a constant-growth stage? How should depreciation best be treated? What is the best estimate of ROE? Answers to questions like these can have a big impact on value, and it is not always easy to maintain consistent assumptions across the models.

We have now valued Honda using several approaches, with estimates of intrinsic value as follows:

Model	Intrinsic Value
Two-stage dividend discount model	$21.88
DDM with earnings multiple terminal value	34.17
Three-stage DDM	22.60
Free cash flow to the firm	30.19
Free cash flow to equity	31.07
Market price in 2008	21.37

---

[8]Over the 2008–2012 period, Value Line predicts that Honda will retire a considerable fraction of its outstanding debt. The implied debt repurchases are a use of cash and reduce the cash flow available to equity. Such repurchases cannot be sustained indefinitely, however, for debt outstanding would soon be run down to zero. Therefore, in our estimate of terminal value, we compute the final cash flow assuming that by 2012 Honda will begin *issuing* enough debt to maintain its debt-to-value ratio unchanged. This approach is consistent with the assumption of constant growth and constant discount rates after 2012.

[9]In the long run a firm can't grow forever at a rate higher than the aggregate economy. So by the time we assert that growth is in a stable stage, it seems reasonable that the growth rate should not be significantly greater than that of the overall economy (although it can be less if the firm is in a declining industry).

What should we make of these differences? The two-stage dividend discount model is the most conservative of the estimates, probably because it assumes that Honda's dividend growth rate will fall to its terminal value after only three years. In contrast, the three-stage DDM allows growth to taper off over a longer period. But both these estimates are exceedingly close to the actual market price. In contrast, both free cash flow models result in value estimates $10 higher than the actual stock price. The DDM with a terminal value provided by the earnings multiple is even higher. Perhaps the assumed terminal growth rate used in our valuation exercise is unrealistically high, or perhaps the stock is indeed underpriced compared to intrinsic value.

This valuation exercise shows that finding bargains is not as easy as it seems. While these models are easy to apply, establishing proper inputs is more of a challenge. This should not be surprising. In even a moderately efficient market, finding profit opportunities will be more involved than analyzing Value Line data for a few hours. The models are extremely useful to analysts, however. They provide ballpark estimates of intrinsic value. More than that, they force rigorous thought about underlying assumptions and highlight the variables with the greatest impact on value and the greatest payoff to further analysis.

13.6 The Aggregate Stock Market

The most popular approach to forecasting the overall stock market is the earnings multiplier approach applied at the aggregate level. The first step is to forecast corporate profits for the coming period. Then we derive an estimate of the earnings multiplier, the aggregate P/E ratio, based on a forecast of long-term interest rates. The product of the two forecasts is the estimate of the end-of-period level of the market.

The forecast of the P/E ratio of the market is sometimes derived from a graph similar to that in Figure 13.8, which plots the *earnings yield* (earnings per share divided by price per share, the reciprocal of the P/E ratio) of the S&P 500 and the yield to maturity on 10-year Treasury bonds. The figure shows that both yields rose dramatically in the 1970s. In the case of Treasury bonds, this was because of an increase in the inflationary expectations built into interest rates. The earnings yield on the S&P 500, however, probably rose because of inflationary distortions that artificially increased reported earnings. We have already seen that P/E ratios tend to fall when inflation rates increase. When inflation moderated in the 1980s, both Treasury and earnings yields fell. For most of the last 30 years, the earnings yield has been within about one percentage point of the T-bond rate, although the spread widened considerably in 2008 as Treasury yields plummeted.

FIGURE 13.8

Earnings yield of S&P 500 versus 10-year Treasury bond yield

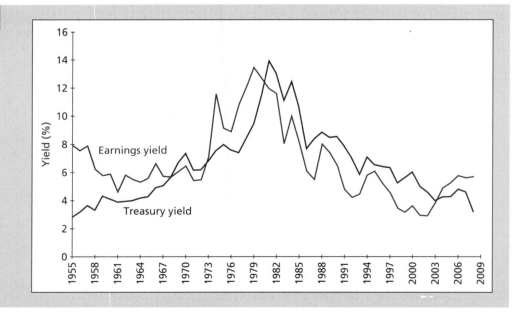

One might use this relationship and the current yield on 10-year Treasury bonds to forecast the earnings yield on the S&P 500. Given that earnings yield, a forecast of earnings could be used to predict the level of the S&P in some future period. Let's consider a simple example of this procedure.

<table>
<tr><td>At the beginning of 2009, the S&P 500 was at 900. The forecast for 12-month forward earnings per share for the S&P 500 portfolio was about $55. The long-term Treasury bond yield at this time was about 3.2%. As a first approach, we might posit that the spread between the earnings yield and the Treasury yield, which was around 2.5% at the start of 2009, will remain at that level by the end of the year. Given the Treasury yield of 3.2%, this would imply an earnings yield for the S&P of 5.7% and a P/E ratio of 1/.057 = 17.54. Our forecast for the level of the S&P Index would then be 17.54 × 55 = 965. This would imply a one-year capital gain on the index of 65/900 = 7.2%.

Of course, there is uncertainty regarding all three inputs into this analysis: the actual earnings on the S&P 500 stocks, the level of Treasury yields at year-end, and the spread between the Treasury yield and the earnings yield. One would wish to perform sensitivity or scenario analysis to examine the impact of changes in all of these variables. To illustrate, consider Table 13.4, which shows a simple scenario analysis treating possible effects of variation in the Treasury bond yield. The scenario analysis shows that the forecast level of the stock market varies inversely and with dramatic sensitivity to interest rate changes.</td><td>**EXAMPLE 13.7**

Forecasting the Aggregate Stock Market</td></tr>
</table>

Some analysts use an aggregate version of the dividend discount model rather than an earnings multiplier approach. All of these models, however, rely heavily on forecasts of such macroeconomic variables as GDP, interest rates, and the rate of inflation, which are difficult to predict accurately.

Because stock prices reflect expectations of future dividends, which are tied to the economic fortunes of firms, it is not surprising that the performance of a broad-based stock index like the S&P 500 is taken as a leading economic indicator, that is, a predictor of the performance of the aggregate economy. Stock prices are viewed as embodying consensus forecasts of economic activity and are assumed to move up or down in anticipation of movements in the economy. The government's index of leading economic indicators, which is taken to predict the progress of the business cycle, is made up in part of recent stock market performance. However, the predictive value of the market is far from perfect. A well-known joke, often attributed to Paul Samuelson, is that the market has forecast eight of the last five recessions.

TABLE 13.4 S&P 500 index forecasts under various scenarios		**Most Likely Scenario**	**Pessimistic Scenario**	**Optimistic Scenario**
	Treasury bond yield	3.20%	3.70%	2.70%
	Earnings yield	5.70%	6.20%	5.20%
	Resulting P/E ratio	17.5	16.1	19.2
	EPS forecast	55	55	55
	Forecast for S&P 500	965	887	1058

Note: The forecast for the earnings yield on the S&P 500 equals the Treasury bond yield plus 2.5%. The P/E ratio is the reciprocal of the forecasted earnings yield.

SUMMARY

- One approach to firm valuation is to focus on the firm's book value, either as it appears on the balance sheet or adjusted to reflect the current replacement cost of assets or the liquidation value. Another approach is to focus on the present value of expected future dividends.
- The dividend discount model holds that the price of a share of stock should equal the present value of all future dividends per share, discounted at an interest rate commensurate with the risk of the stock.

- The constant-growth version of the DDM asserts that, if dividends are expected to grow at a constant rate forever, then the intrinsic value of the stock is determined by the formula

$$V_0 = \frac{D_1}{k - g}$$

- This version of the DDM is simplistic in its assumption of a constant value of g. There are more sophisticated multistage versions of the model for more complex environments. When the constant-growth assumption is reasonably satisfied, however, the formula can be inverted to infer the market capitalization rate for the stock:

$$k = \frac{D_1}{P_0} + g$$

- Stock market analysts devote considerable attention to a company's price–earnings ratio. The P/E ratio is a useful measure of the market's assessment of the firm's growth opportunities. Firms with no growth opportunities should have a P/E ratio that is just the reciprocal of the capitalization rate, k. As growth opportunities become a progressively more important component of the total value of the firm, the P/E ratio will increase.
- Many analysts form their estimates of a stock's value by multiplying their forecast of next year's EPS by a predicted P/E multiple. Some analysts mix the P/E approach with the dividend discount model. They use an earnings multiplier to forecast the terminal value of shares at a future date and add the present value of that terminal value with the present value of all interim dividend payments.
- The free cash flow approach is the one used most in corporate finance. The analyst first estimates the value of the firm as the present value of expected future free cash flows to the entire firm and then subtracts the value of all claims other than equity. Alternatively, the free cash flows to equity can be discounted at a discount rate appropriate to the risk of the stock.
- The models presented in this chapter can be used to explain or to forecast the behavior of the aggregate stock market. The key macroeconomic variables that determine the level of stock prices in the aggregate are interest rates and corporate profits.

KEY TERMS

book value, 395
constant-growth
  DDM, 400
dividend discount model
  (DDM), 399
dividend payout
  ratio, 402
earnings management, 415

earnings retention
  ratio, 403
intrinsic value, 397
liquidation value, 396
market capitalization
  rate, 398
PEG ratio, 412
plowback ratio, 403

present value of growth
  opportunities
  (PVGO), 404
price–earnings
  multiple, 410
replacement cost, 396
Tobin's q, 397
two-stage DDM, 406

PROBLEM SETS

Select problems are available in McGraw-Hill's connect. Please see the packaging options section of the preface for more information.

Basic

1. In what circumstances would you choose to use a dividend discount model rather than a free cash flow model to value a firm?

2. In what circumstances is it most important to use multistage dividend discount models rather than constant-growth models?

3. If a security is underpriced (i.e., intrinsic value > price), then what is the relationship between its market capitalization rate and its expected rate of return?

4. A firm has current assets that could be sold for their book value of $10 million. The book value of its fixed assets is $60 million, but they could be sold for $90 million today. The firm has total debt with a book value of $40 million but interest rate declines have caused the market value of the debt to increase to $50 million. What is this firm's market-to-book ratio?

5. The market capitalization rate for Admiral Motors Company is 8%. Its expected ROE is 10% and its expected EPS is $5.00. If the firm's plowback ratio is 60%, what will be its P/E ratio?

6. Miltmar Corporation will pay a year-end dividend of $4, and dividends thereafter are expected to grow at the constant rate of 4% per year. The risk-free rate is 4%, and the expected return on the market portfolio is 12%. The stock has a beta of .75. What is the intrinsic value of the stock?

7. Sisters Corp expects to earn $6 per share next year. The firm's ROE is 15% and its plowback ratio is 60%. If the firm's market capitalization rate is 10%, what is the present value of its growth opportunities?

8. Eagle Products' EBIT is $300, its tax rate is 35%, depreciation is $20, capital expenditures are $60, and the planned increase in net working capital is $30. What is the free cash flow to the firm?

9. FinCorp's free cash flow to the firm is reported as $205 million. The firm's interest expense is $22 million. Assume the tax rate is 35% and the net debt of the firm increases by $3 million. What is the market value of equity if the FCFE is projected to grow at 3% indefinitely and the cost of equity is 12%?

10. A common stock pays an annual dividend per share of $2.10. The risk-free rate is 7% and the risk premium for this stock is 4%. If the annual dividend is expected to remain at $2.10, what is the value of the stock?

11. The risk-free rate of return is 5%, the required rate of return on the market is 10%, and High-Flyer stock has a beta coefficient of 1.5. If the dividend per share expected during the coming year, D_1, is $2.50 and $g = 4\%$, at what price should a share sell?

Intermediate

12. Explain why the following statements are true/false/uncertain.
    a. With all else held constant, a firm will have a higher P/E if its beta is higher.
    b. P/E will tend to be higher when ROE is higher (assuming plowback is positive).
    c. P/E will tend to be higher when the plowback rate is higher.

13. a. Computer stocks currently provide an expected rate of return of 16%. MBI, a large computer company, will pay a year-end dividend of $2 per share. If the stock is selling at $50 per share, what must be the market's expectation of the growth rate of MBI dividends?
    b. If dividend growth forecasts for MBI are revised downward to 5% per year, what will happen to the price of MBI stock? What (qualitatively) will happen to the company's price–earnings ratio?

14. Even Better Products has come out with a new and improved product. As a result, the firm projects an ROE of 20%, and it will maintain a plowback ratio of .30. Its earnings this year will be $2 per share. Investors expect a 12% rate of return on the stock.
    a. At what price and P/E ratio would you expect the firm to sell?
    b. What is the present value of growth opportunities?
    c. What would be the P/E ratio and the present value of growth opportunities if the firm planned to reinvest only 20% of its earnings?

15. *a.* MF Corp. has an ROE of 16% and a plowback ratio of 50%. If the coming year's earnings are expected to be $2 per share, at what price will the stock sell? The market capitalization rate is 12%.

    b. What price do you expect MF shares to sell for in three years?

16. The market consensus is that Analog Electronic Corporation has an ROE = 9% and a beta of 1.25. It plans to maintain indefinitely its traditional plowback ratio of 2/3. This year's earnings were $3 per share. The annual dividend was just paid. The consensus estimate of the coming year's market return is 14%, and T-bills currently offer a 6% return.

    a. Find the price at which Analog stock should sell.

    b. Calculate the P/E ratio.

    c. Calculate the present value of growth opportunities.

    d. Suppose your research convinces you Analog will announce momentarily that it will immediately reduce its plowback ratio to 1/3. Find the intrinsic value of the stock. The market is still unaware of this decision. Explain why V_0 no longer equals P_0 and why V_0 is greater or less than P_0.

17. The FI Corporation's dividends per share are expected to grow indefinitely by 5% per year.

    a. If this year's year-end dividend is $8 and the market capitalization rate is 10% per year, what must the current stock price be according to the DDM?

    b. If the expected earnings per share are $12, what is the implied value of the ROE on future investment opportunities?

    c. How much is the market paying per share for growth opportunities (that is, for an ROE on future investments that exceeds the market capitalization rate)?

18. The stock of Nogro Corporation is currently selling for $10 per share. Earnings per share in the coming year are expected to be $2. The company has a policy of paying out 50% of its earnings each year in dividends. The rest is retained and invested in projects that earn a 20% rate of return per year. This situation is expected to continue indefinitely.

    a. Assuming the current market price of the stock reflects its intrinsic value as computed using the constant-growth DDM, what rate of return do Nogro's investors require?

    b. By how much does its value exceed what it would be if all earnings were paid as dividends and nothing were reinvested?

    c. If Nogro were to cut its dividend payout ratio to 25%, what would happen to its stock price? What if Nogro eliminated the dividend?

19. The risk-free rate of return is 8%, the expected rate of return on the market portfolio is 15%, and the stock of Xyrong Corporation has a beta coefficient of 1.2. Xyrong pays out 40% of its earnings in dividends, and the latest earnings announced were $10 per share. Dividends were just paid and are expected to be paid annually. You expect that Xyrong will earn an ROE of 20% per year on all reinvested earnings forever.

    a. What is the intrinsic value of a share of Xyrong stock?

    b. If the market price of a share is currently $100, and you expect the market price to be equal to the intrinsic value one year from now, what is your expected one-year holding-period return on Xyrong stock?

20. The MoMi Corporation's cash flow from operations before interest and taxes was $2 million in the year just ended, and it expects that this will grow by 5% per year forever. To make this happen, the firm will have to invest an amount equal to 20% of pretax cash flow each year. The tax rate is 35%. Depreciation was $200,000 in the year just ended and is expected to grow at the same rate as the operating cash flow. The appropriate market capitalization rate for the unleveraged cash flow is 12% per year, and the firm currently has debt of $4 million outstanding. Use the free cash flow approach to value the firm's equity.

21. Recalculate the intrinsic value of Honda using the three-stage growth model of Spreadsheet 13.1 (available at **www.mhhe.com/bkm;** link to Chapter 13 material). Treat each of the following scenarios independently.

a. ROE in the constant-growth period will be 10%.

b. Honda's actual beta is 1.15.

c. The market risk premium is 8.5%.

22. Recalculate the intrinsic value of Honda shares using the free cash flow model of Spreadsheet 13.2 (available at **www.mhhe.com/bkm;** link to Chapter 13 material). Treat each scenario independently.

a. Honda's P/E ratio starting in 2012 will be 12.5.

b. Honda's unlevered beta is .9.

c. The market risk premium is 8.5%.

Challenge

23. Chiptech, Inc., is an established computer chip firm with several profitable existing products as well as some promising new products in development. The company earned $1 a share last year, and just paid out a dividend of $.50 per share. Investors believe the company plans to maintain its dividend payout ratio at 50%. ROE equals 20%. Everyone in the market expects this situation to persist indefinitely.

a. What is the market price of Chiptech stock? The required return for the computer chip industry is 15%, and the company has just gone ex-dividend (i.e., the next dividend will be paid a year from now, at $t = 1$).

b. Suppose you discover that Chiptech's competitor has developed a new chip that will eliminate Chiptech's current technological advantage in this market. This new product, which will be ready to come to the market in two years, will force Chiptech to reduce the prices of its chips to remain competitive. This will decrease ROE to 15%, and, because of falling demand for its product, Chiptech will decrease the plowback ratio to .40. The plowback ratio will be decreased at the end of the second year, at $t = 2$: The annual year-end dividend for the second year (paid at $t = 2$) will be 60% of that year's earnings. What is your estimate of Chiptech's intrinsic value per share? (*Hint:* Carefully prepare a table of Chiptech's earnings and dividends for each of the next three years. Pay close attention to the change in the payout ratio in $t = 2$.)

c. No one else in the market perceives the threat to Chiptech's market. In fact, you are confident that no one else will become aware of the change in Chiptech's competitive status until the competitor firm publicly announces its discovery near the end of year 2. What will be the rate of return on Chiptech stock in the coming year (i.e., between $t = 0$ and $t = 1$)? In the second year (between $t = 1$ and $t = 2$)? The third year (between $t = 2$ and $t = 3$)? (*Hint:* Pay attention to when the *market* catches on to the new situation. A table of dividends and market prices over time might help.)

CFA Problems

1. Which of the following assumptions does the constant-growth dividend discount model require?

a. Dividends grow at a constant rate.

b. ROE and the plowback rate are constant.

c. The required rate of return is less than the dividend growth rate.

2. At Litchfield Chemical Corp. (LCC), a director of the company said that the use of dividend discount models by investors is "proof" that the higher the dividend, the higher the stock price.

a. Using a constant-growth dividend discount model as a basis of reference, evaluate the director's statement.

b. Explain how an increase in dividend payout would affect each of the following (holding all other factors constant):

  i. Sustainable growth rate.

  ii. Growth in book value.

3. Phoebe Black's investment club wants to buy the stock of either NewSoft, Inc, or Capital Corp. In this connection, Black prepared the following table. You have been asked to help her interpret the data, based on your forecast for a healthy economy and a strong stock market over the next 12 months.

	NewSoft, Inc.	Capital Corp.	S&P 500 Index
Current price	$30	$32	
Industry	Computer software	Capital goods	
P/E ratio (current)	25	14	16
P/E ratio (5-year average)	27	16	16
Price/book ratio (current)	10	3	3
Price/book ratio (5-year average)	12	4	2
Beta	1.5	1.1	1.0
Dividend yield	.3%	2.7%	2.8%

 a. Newsoft's shares have higher price–earnings (P/E) and price–book value (P/B) ratios than those of Capital Corp. (The price–book ratio is the ratio of market value to book value.) Briefly discuss why the disparity in ratios may not indicate that NewSoft's shares are overvalued relative to the shares of Capital Corp. Answer the question in terms of the two ratios, and assume that there have been no extraordinary events affecting either company.

 b. Using a constant-growth dividend discount model, Black estimated the value of NewSoft to be $28 per share and the value of Capital Corp. to be $34 per share. Briefly discuss weaknesses of this dividend discount model and explain why this model may be less suitable for valuing NewSoft than for valuing Capital Corp.

 c. Recommend and justify a more appropriate dividend discount model for valuing NewSoft's common stock.

4. Peninsular Research is initiating coverage of a mature manufacturing industry. John Jones, CFA, head of the research department, gathered the following fundamental industry and market data to help in his analysis:

Forecast industry earnings retention rate	40%
Forecast industry return on equity	25%
Industry beta	1.2
Government bond yield	6%
Equity risk premium	5%

 a. Compute the price-to-earnings (P_0/E_1) ratio for the industry based on this fundamental data.

 b. Jones wants to analyze how fundamental P/E ratios might differ among countries. He gathered the following economic and market data:

Fundamental Factors	Country A	Country B
Forecast growth in real GDP	5%	2%
Government bond yield	10%	6%
Equity risk premium	5%	4%

Determine whether each of these fundamental factors would cause P/E ratios to be generally higher for Country A or higher for Country B.

5. Janet Ludlow's firm requires all its analysts to use a two-stage DDM and the CAPM to value stocks. Using these measures, Ludlow has valued QuickBrush Company at $63 per share. She now must value SmileWhite Corporation.

a. Calculate the required rate of return for SmileWhite using the information in the following table:

	December 2007	
	QuickBrush	**SmileWhite**
Beta	1.35	1.15
Market price	$45.00	$30.00
Intrinsic value	$63.00	?

Note: Risk-free rate = 4.50%; expected market return = 14.50%.

b. Ludlow estimates the following EPS and dividend growth rates for SmileWhite:

First three years:	12% per year
Years thereafter:	9% per year

Estimate the intrinsic value of SmileWhite using the table above, and the two-stage DDM. Dividends per share in 2007 were $1.72.

c. Recommend QuickBrush or SmileWhite stock for purchase by comparing each company's intrinsic value with its current market price.

d. Describe *one* strength of the two-stage DDM in comparison with the constant-growth DDM. Describe *one* weakness inherent in all DDMs.

6. Rio National Corp. is a U.S.-based company and the largest competitor in its industry. Tables 13.5–13.8 present financial statements and related information for the company. Table 13.9 presents relevant industry and market data.

The portfolio manager of a large mutual fund comments to one of the fund's analysts, Katrina Shaar: "We have been considering the purchase of Rio National Corp. equity shares, so I would like you to analyze the value of the company. To begin, based on

TABLE 13.5		**2009**	**2008**
Rio National Corp. Summary year-end balance sheets (U.S. $ millions)	Cash	$ 13.00	$ 5.87
	Accounts receivable	30.00	27.00
	Inventory	209.06	189.06
	Current assets	$252.06	$221.93
	Gross fixed assets	474.47	409.47
	Accumulated depreciation	(154.17)	(90.00)
	Net fixed assets	320.30	319.47
	Total assets	$572.36	$541.40
	Accounts payable	$ 25.05	$ 26.05
	Notes payable	0.00	0.00
	Current portion of long-term debt	0.00	0.00
	Current liabilities	$ 25.05	$ 26.05
	Long-term debt	240.00	245.00
	Total liabilities	$265.05	$271.05
	Common stock	160.00	150.00
	Retained earnings	147.31	120.35
	Total shareholders' equity	$307.31	$270.35
	Total liabilities and shareholders' equity	$572.36	$541.40

TABLE 13.6 Rio National Corp. Summary income statement for the year ended December 31, 2009 (U.S. $ millions)	Revenue	$300.80
	Total operating expenses	(173.74)
	Operating profit	127.06
	Gain on sale	4.00
	Earnings before interest, taxes, depreciation & amortization (EBITDA)	131.06
	Depreciation and amortization	(71.17)
	Earnings before interest & taxes (EBIT)	59.89
	Interest	(16.80)
	Income tax expense	(12.93)
	Net income	$ 30.16

TABLE 13.7

Rio National Corp. Supplemental notes for 2009

Note 1: Rio National had $75 million in capital expenditures during the year.

Note 2: A piece of equipment that was originally purchased for $10 million was sold for $7 million at year-end, when it had a net book value of $3 million. Equipment sales are unusual for Rio National.

Note 3: The decrease in long-term debt represents an unscheduled principal repayment; there was no new borrowing during the year.

Note 4: On 1 January 2009, the company received cash from issuing 400,000 shares of common equity at a price of $25.00 per share.

Note 5: A new appraisal during the year increased the estimated market value of land held for investment by $2 million, which was not recognized in 2009 income.

TABLE 13.8 Rio National Corp. Common equity data for 2009	Dividends paid (U.S. $ millions)	$3.20
	Weighted average shares outstanding during 2009	16,000,000
	Dividend per share	$0.20
	Earnings per share	$1.89
	Beta	1.80

Note: The dividend payout ratio is expected to be constant.

TABLE 13.9 Industry and market data December 31, 2009	Risk-free rate of return	4.00%
	Expected rate of return on market index	9.00%
	Median industry price/earnings (P/E) ratio	19.90
	Expected industry earnings growth rate	12.00%

Rio National's past performance, you can assume that the company will grow at the same rate as the industry."

a. Calculate the value of a share of Rio National equity on December 31, 2009, using the constant growth model and the capital asset pricing model.

b. Calculate the sustainable growth rate of Rio National on December 31, 2009. Use 2009 beginning-of-year balance sheet values.

7. While valuing the equity of Rio National Corp. (from the previous problem), Katrina Shaar is considering the use of either free cash flow to the firm (FCFF) or free cash flow to equity (FCFE) in her valuation process.

a. State two adjustments that Shaar should make to FCFF to obtain free cash flow to equity.

b. Shaar decides to calculate Rio National's FCFE for the year 2009, starting with net income. Determine for each of the five supplemental notes given in Table 13.7 whether an adjustment should be made to net income to calculate Rio National's free cash flow to equity for the year 2009, and the dollar amount of any adjustment.

c. Calculate Rio National's free cash flow to equity for the year 2009.

8. Shaar (from the previous problem) has revised slightly her estimated earnings growth rate for Rio National and, using normalized (underlying trend) EPS, which is adjusted for temporary impacts on earnings, now wants to compare the current value of Rio National's equity to that of the industry, on a growth-adjusted basis. Selected information about Rio National and the industry is given in Table 13.10.

TABLE 13.10	**Rio National**	
Rio National Corp. vs. industry	Estimated earnings growth rate	11.00%
	Current share price	$25.00
	Normalized (underlying trend) EPS for 2009	$ 1.71
	Weighted-average shares outstanding during 2009	16,000,000
	Industry	
	Estimated earnings growth rate	12.00%
	Median price/earnings (P/E) ratio	19.90

Compared to the industry, is Rio National's equity overvalued or undervalued on a P/E-to-growth (PEG) basis, using normalized (underlying) earnings per share. Assume that the risk of Rio National is similar to the risk of the industry.

9. Helen Morgan, CFA, has been asked to use the DDM to determine the value of Sundanci, Inc. Morgan anticipates that Sundanci's earnings and dividends will grow at 32% for two years and 13% thereafter.

Calculate the current value of a share of Sundanci stock by using a two-stage dividend discount model and the data from Tables 13.11 and 13.12.

TABLE 13.11	**Income Statement**	**2009**	**2010**
Sundanci actual 2009 and forecast 2010 financial statements for fiscal years ending May 31 ($ million, except per-share data)	Revenue	$ 474	$ 598
	Depreciation	20	23
	Other operating costs	368	460
	Income before taxes	86	115
	Taxes	26	35
	Net income	60	80
	Dividends	18	24
	Earnings per share	$0.714	$0.952
	Dividend per share	$0.214	$0.286
	Common shares outstanding (millions)	84.0	84.0
	Balance Sheet	**2009**	**2010**
	Current assets	$ 201	$ 326
	Net property, plant, and equipment	474	489
	Total assets	675	815
	Current liabilities	57	141
	Long-term debt	0	0
	Total liabilities	57	141
	Shareholders' equity	618	674
	Total liabilities and equity	675	815
	Capital expenditures	34	38

TABLE 13.12 Selected financial information	Required rate of return on equity	14%
	Growth rate of industry	13%
	Industry P/E ratio	26

10. To continue with Sundanci, Abbey Naylor, CFA, has been directed to determine the value of Sundanci's stock using the Free Cash Flow to Equity (FCFE) model. Naylor believes that Sundanci's FCFE will grow at 27% for two years and 13% thereafter. Capital expenditures, depreciation, and working capital are all expected to increase proportionately with FCFE.

    a. Calculate the amount of FCFE per share for the year 2010, using the data from Table 13.11.

    b. Calculate the current value of a share of Sundanci stock based on the two-stage FCFE model.

    c. i. Describe one limitation of the two-stage DDM model that is addressed by using the two-stage FCFE model.

        ii. Describe one limitation of the two-stage DDM model that is *not* addressed by using the two-stage FCFE model.

11. Christie Johnson, CFA, has been assigned to analyze Sundanci using the constant-dividend-growth price/earnings (P/E) ratio model. Johnson assumes that Sundanci's earnings and dividends will grow at a constant rate of 13%.

    a. Calculate the P/E ratio based on information in Tables 13.11 and 13.12 and on Johnson's assumptions for Sundanci.

    b. Identify, within the context of the constant dividend growth model, how each of the following factors would affect the P/E ratio.
    • Risk (beta) of Sundanci.
    • Estimated growth rate of earnings and dividends.
    • Market risk premium.

STANDARD &POOR'S

Use data from the Standard & Poor's Market Insight Database at www.mhhe.com/edumarketinsight to answer the following questions.

1. Click on the Market Insight Company tab, then the Population tab, and scroll through the list to find 10 firms that interest you. Click on a firm's name and its symbol will automatically be entered. Click on Go, then on the Financial Highlights link in the Compustat Reports section.

    a. For each firm, find the return on equity (ROE), the number of shares outstanding, the dividends per share, and the net income. Record them in a spreadsheet.

    b. Calculate the total amount of dividends paid (dividends per share × number of shares outstanding), the dividend payout ratio (total dividends paid/net income), and the plowback ratio (1 − dividend payout ratio).

    c. Compute the sustainable growth rate, $g = b \times$ ROE, where b equals the plowback ratio.

    d. Compare the growth rates (g) with the P/E ratios of the firms by plotting the P/Es against the growth rates in a scatter diagram. Is there a relationship between the two?

    e. Find the price-to-book, price-to-sales, and price-to-cash-flow ratios for your sample of firms. Use a line chart to plot these three ratios on the same set of axes. What relationships do you see among the three series?

    f. For each firm, compare the five-year growth rate of earnings per share with the growth rate you calculated above. Is the actual rate of earnings growth correlated with the sustainable growth rate you calculated?

2. Use the data from Market Insight to estimate the intrinsic values of three firms from your sample. Use the firms' betas from the S&P Stock Report section. Make reasonable judgments about the market risk premium and the risk-free rate or find estimates from the Internet.

    a. What is the required return on each firm based on the CAPM?

    b. Look in the Valuation Data section of the Excel Analytics menu. Find the forecasted price for next year. Use the forecasted price, information about dividends (collected in the previous problem), and the CAPM required return to calculate the intrinsic value of the stock today. How does this compare to the stock's current market price?

   c. Try using a two-stage growth model, making reasonable assumptions about how future growth rates will differ from current growth rates. Compare the intrinsic values derived from the two-stage model to the intrinsic values you found assuming a constant-growth rate. Which estimate seems more reasonable for each firm?

3. On the Market Insight home page, click on the Industry tab and select the Restaurants category. In the Compustat Reports section, click on the Constituents link to get a list of companies in this industry. Choose five of the firms listed and follow the links to get to the Financial Highlights for each firm.

   a. Perform a "Valuation by Comparables" analysis by looking at the Price/Earnings, Price/Book Value, Price/Sales, and Price/Cash Flow ratios of the firms relative to each other and to the industry average. Which of the firms seem to be overvalued? Which seem to be undervalued? Can you think of reasons for any apparent mispricings?

   b. Calculate the firms' dividend payout ratios (total dividends paid/net income) and their sustainable growth rates ($g = b \times$ ROE). What impact does the growth rate seem to have on firm value?

WEB *master* STOCK VALUATION

The actually expected return on a stock based on estimates of future dividends and future price can be compared to the "required" or equilibrium return given its risk. If the expected return is greater than the required return, the stock may be an attractive investment.

1. First calculate the expected holding-period return (HPR) on Target Corporation's stock based on its current price, its expected price, and its expected dividend.

   a. Go to **moneycentral.msn.com/investor/home.asp** and link to the Stock Research Wizard. Enter TGT to find information about Target Corporation. Find the average estimated target price for the next fiscal year.

   b. Click on the "Company Report" link and collect information about today's price and the dividend rate. Calculate the company's expected dividend in dollars for the next fiscal year.

   c. Use these inputs to calculate Target's expected HPR for the next year.

2. Calculate the required return based on the Capital Asset Pricing Model (CAPM).

   a. Use a risk-free rate from **moneycentral.msn.com/investor/market/treasuries.aspx.**

   b. Use the beta coefficient shown in Target's Company Report.

   c. Calculate the historical return on a broad-based market index of your choice. You may use any time period that you deem appropriate. Your goal is to derive an estimate of the expected return on the market index for the coming year.

   d. Use the data you've collected as inputs for the CAPM to find the required rate of return for Target Corporation.

3. Compare the expected HPR you calculated in Part 1 to the required CAPM return you calculated in Part 2. What is your best judgment about the stock's current status—do you think it is selling at an appropriate price?

SOLUTIONS TO CONCEPT *checks*

13.1. *a.* Dividend yield = \$2.15/\$50 = 4.3%

      Capital gains yield = (59.77 − 50)/50 = 19.54%

      Total return = 4.3% + 19.54% = 23.84%

   b. k = 6% + 1.15(14% − 6%) = 15.2%

   c. V_0 = (\$2.15 + \$59.77)/1.152 = \$53.75, which exceeds the market price. This would indicate a "buy" opportunity.

13.2. *a.* $D_1/(k − g)$ = \$2.15/(.152 − .112) = \$53.75

   b. $P_1 = P_0(1 + g)$ = \$53.75(1.112) = \$59.77

   c. The expected capital gain equals \$59.77 − \$53.75 = \$6.02, for a percentage gain of 11.2%. The dividend yield is D_1/P_0 = 2.15/53.75 = 4%, for a holding-period return of 4% + 11.2% = 15.2%.

13.3. *a.* g = ROE $\times b$ = .20 $\times$ .60 = .12

      P_0 = 2/(.125 − .12) = 400

   b. When the firm invests in projects with ROE less than k, its stock price falls. If b = .60, then g = 10% $\times$ .60 = 6% and P_0 = \$2/(.125 − .06) = \$30.77. In contrast, if b = 0, then P_0 = \$5/.125 = \$40

13.4. Because $\beta = 1.10$, $k = 3.5\% + 1.1 \times 8\% = 12.3\%$

$$V_{2008} = \frac{.90}{1.123} + \frac{.98}{(1.123)^2} + \frac{1.06}{(1.123)^3} + \frac{1.15 + P_{2012}}{(1.123)^4}$$

Now compute the sales price in 2012 using the constant-growth dividend discount model.

$$P_{2012} = \frac{1.15 \times (1 + g)}{k - g} = \frac{1.15 \times 1.077}{.123 - 0.77} = \$26.93$$

Therefore, $V_{2008} = \$19.98$

13.5. *a.* ROE = 12%

$b = \$.50/\$2.00 = .25$

$g = \text{ROE} \times b = 12\% \times .25 = 3\%$

$P_0 = D_1/(k - g) = \$1.50/(.10 - .03) = \$21.43$

$P_0/E_1 = 21.43/\$2.00 = 10.71$

b. If $b = .4$, then $.4 \times \$2 = \$.80$ would be reinvested and the remainder of earnings, or \$1.20, would be paid as dividends.

$g = 12\% \times .4 = 4.8\%$

$P_0 = D_1/(k - g) = \$1.20/(.10 - .048) = \$23.08$

$P_0/E_1 = \$23.08/\$2.00 = 11.54$

PEG = 11.54/4.8 = 2.4

Chapter 14

Financial Statement Analysis

After Studying This Chapter You Should Be Able To:

- Use a firm's income statement, balance sheet, and statement of cash flows to calculate standard financial ratios.

- Calculate the impact of taxes and leverage on a firm's return on equity using ratio decomposition analysis.

- Measure a firm's operating efficiency by using various asset utilization ratios.

- Identify likely sources of biases in conventional accounting data.

In the previous chapter, we explored equity valuation techniques. These techniques take as inputs the firm's dividends and earnings prospects. While the valuation analyst is interested in economic earnings streams, only financial accounting data are readily available. What can we learn from a company's accounting data that can help us estimate the intrinsic value of its common stock?

In this chapter, we show how investors can use financial data as inputs into stock valuation analysis. We start by reviewing the basic sources of such data: the income statement, the balance sheet, and the statement of cash flows. We next discuss the difference between economic and accounting earnings.

While economic earnings are more important for issues of valuation, whatever their shortcomings, accounting data still are useful in assessing the economic prospects of the firm. We show how analysts use financial ratios to explore the sources of a firm's profitability and evaluate the "quality" of its earnings in a systematic fashion. We also examine the impact of debt policy on various financial ratios. Finally, we conclude with a discussion of the challenges you will encounter when using financial statement analysis as a tool in uncovering mispriced securities. Some of these issues arise from differences in firms' accounting procedures. Others are due to inflation-induced distortions in accounting numbers.

Related Web sites for this chapter are available at www.mhhe.com/bkm.

14.1 The Major Financial Statements

The Income Statement

income statement

A financial statement showing a firm's revenues and expenses during a specified period.

The **income statement** is a summary of the profitability of the firm over a period of time, such as a year. It presents revenues generated during the operating period, the expenses incurred during that same period, and the company's net earnings or profits, which are simply the difference between revenues and expenses.

It is useful to distinguish among four broad classes of expenses: cost of goods sold, which is the direct cost attributable to producing the product sold by the firm; general and administrative expenses, which correspond to overhead expenses, salaries, advertising, and other costs of operating the firm that are not directly attributable to production; interest expense on the firm's debt; and taxes on earnings owed to federal and local governments.

Table 14.1 presents a 2008 income statement for Hewlett-Packard. At the top are the company's revenues. Next come operating expenses, the costs incurred in the course of generating these revenues, including a depreciation allowance. The difference between operating revenues and operating costs is called operating income. Income (or expenses) from other, primarily nonrecurring, sources is then added to obtain earnings before interest and taxes (EBIT), which is what the firm would have earned if not for obligations to its creditors and the tax authorities. EBIT is a measure of the profitability of the firm's operations abstracting from any interest burden attributable to debt financing. The income statement then goes on to subtract net interest expense from EBIT to arrive at taxable income. Finally, the income tax due the government is subtracted to arrive at net income, the "bottom line" of the income statement.

Analysts also commonly prepare a *common-size income statement,* in which all items on the income statement are expressed as a fraction of total revenue. This makes it easier to compare firms of different sizes. The right-hand column of Table 14.1 is HP's common-size income statement.

TABLE 14.1 Consolidated Statement of Income for Hewlett-Packard, 2008	**$ Million**	**Percent of Revenue**
Operating revenues		
Net sales	$118,364	100.0%
Operating Expenses		
Cost of goods sold	$ 86,236	72.9
Selling, general and administrative expenses	13,104	11.1
Research and development expenses	3,543	3.0
Depreciation	3,356	2.8
Operating income	12,125	10.2
Other income (expense)	(1,323)	−1.1
EBIT	$ 10,802	9.1
Interest expense	329	0.3
Taxable income	$ 10,473	8.8
Taxes	2,144	1.8
Net income	$ 8,329	7.0
Allocation of net income		
Dividends	796	0.7
Addition to retained earnings	7,533	6.4

Note: Sums subject to rounding error.

Source: Hewlett-Packard Annual Report.

The Balance Sheet

While the income statement provides a measure of profitability over a period of time, the **balance sheet** provides a "snapshot" of the financial condition of the firm at a particular time. The balance sheet is a list of the firm's assets and liabilities at that moment. The difference in assets and liabilities is the net worth of the firm, also called *stockholders' equity* or, equivalently, *shareholders' equity*. Like income statements, balance sheets are reasonably standardized in presentation. Table 14.2 is HP's balance sheet for year-end 2008.

The first section of the balance sheet gives a listing of the assets of the firm. Current assets are presented first. These are cash and other items such as accounts receivable or inventories that will be converted into cash within one year. Next comes a listing of long-term or "fixed" assets. Tangible fixed assets are items such as buildings, equipment, or vehicles. HP also has several intangible assets such as a respected brand name and expertise. But accountants generally are reluctant to include these assets on the balance sheet, as they are so hard to value. However, when one firm purchases another for a premium over its book value, that difference is called "goodwill" and is listed on the balance sheet as an intangible fixed asset. HP has unusually high goodwill because of its acquisition of Compaq Computer in 2002.[1]

The liability and shareholders' equity section is arranged similarly. Listed first are short-term or "current" liabilities, such as accounts payable, accrued taxes, and debts that are due within one year. Long-term debt and other liabilities due in more than a year follow. The difference between total assets and total liabilities is shareholders' equity. This is the net worth or book value of the firm. Shareholders' equity is divided into par value of stock, capital surplus (additional paid-in capital), and retained earnings, although this division is usually unimportant. Briefly, par value plus capital surplus represents the proceeds realized from the sale of stock to the public, while retained earnings represent the buildup of equity from profits plowed back into the firm. Even if the firm issues no new equity, book value will increase each year due to reinvested earnings.

The first panel in the balance sheet in Table 14.2 presents the dollar value of each asset. To make it easier to compare firms of different sizes, analysts often present each item on the balance sheet as a percentage of total assets. This is called a *common-size balance sheet* and is presented in panel B.

balance sheet

An accounting statement of a firm's financial position at a specified time.

The Statement of Cash Flows

The income statement and balance sheets are based on accrual methods of accounting, which means revenues and expenses are recognized at the time of a sale even if no cash has yet been exchanged. In contrast, the **statement of cash flows** recognizes only transactions in which cash changes hands. For example, if goods are sold now, with payment due in 60 days, the income statement will treat the revenue as generated when the sale occurs, and the balance sheet will be immediately augmented by accounts receivable, but the statement of cash flows will not recognize the transaction until the bill is paid and the cash is in hand.

Table 14.3 is the 2008 statement of cash flows for HP. The first entry listed under cash flows from operations is net income. The following entries modify that figure for components of income that have been recognized but for which cash has not yet changed hands. For example, HP's accounts receivable increased by $3,168 million in 2008. This portion of its income was claimed on the income statement, but the cash had not yet been collected. Increases in accounts receivable reduce the cash flows realized from operations in this period. Similarly, increases in accounts payable mean expenses have been incurred, but cash has not yet left the firm. Any payment delay increases the company's net cash flows in this period.

Another major difference between the income statement and the statement of cash flows involves depreciation, which accounts for a substantial addition in the adjustment section of the statement of cash flows in Table 14.3. The income statement attempts to "smooth" large

statement of cash flows

A financial statement showing a firm's cash receipts and cash payments during a specified period.

---

[1]Firms are required to test their goodwill assets for "impairment" each year. If it becomes apparent that the value of the acquired firm is less than its purchase price, that amount must be charged off as an expense. AOL Time Warner set a record when it recognized an impairment of $99 billion in 2002 following the January 2001 merger of Time Warner with AOL.

TABLE 14.2

Consolidated Balance Sheet for Hewlett-Packard, 2008

Panel A: (millions of dollars)

Assets	2008	2007
Current assets		
Cash and marketable securities	$ 10,246	11,445
Receivables	29,359	26,191
Inventories	7,879	8,033
Other current assets	4,244	1,733
Total current assets	$ 51,728	47,402
Fixed assets		
Tangible fixed assets		
Property, plant, and equipment	$ 10,838	7,798
Long-term investments	2,722	2,778
Total tangible fixed assets	$ 13,560	10,576
Intangible fixed assets		
Goodwill	$ 32,335	21,773
Other intangible assets	7,962	4,079
Total intangible fixed assets	$ 40,297	25,852
Total fixed assets	$ 53,857	36,428
Other assets	7,746	4,869
Total assets	$113,331	88,699

Liabilities and shareholders' equity	2008	2007
Current liabilities		
Debt due for repayment	$ 10,176	$ 3,186
Accounts payable	32,317	25,822
Other current liabilities	10,446	10,252
Total current liabilities	$ 52,939	$39,260
Long-term debt	7,676	4,997
Deferred liabilities	6,314	2,459
Other long-term liabilities	7,460	3,457
Total liabilities	$ 74,389	$50,173
Shareholders' equity		
Common stock and other paid-in capital	$ 13,971	$21,088
Retained earnings	24,971	17,438
Total shareholders' equity	$ 38,942	38,526
Total liabilities and shareholders' equity	$113,331	$88,699

(continued)

Panel B (Common size, percentage of total assets)

Assets	2008	2007
Current assets		
Cash and marketable securities	9.0%	12.9%
Receivables	25.9	29.5
Inventories	7.0	9.1
Other current assets	3.7	2.0
Total current assets	45.6%	53.4%
Fixed assets		
Tangible fixed assets		
Property, plant, and equipment	9.6%	8.8%
Less accumulated depreciation	2.4	3.1
Net tangible fixed assets	12.0%	11.9%
Intangible fixed assets		
Goodwill	28.5%	24.5
Other intangible assets	7.0	4.6
Total intangible fixed assets	35.6%	29.1%
Total fixed assets	47.5	41.1%
Other assets	6.8	5.5
Total assets	100.0%	100.0%

Liabilities and shareholders' equity	2008	2007
Current liabilities		
Debt due for repayment	9.0%	3.6%
Accounts payable	28.5	29.1
Other current liabilities	9.2	11.6
Total current liabilities	46.7%	44.3%
Long-term debt	6.8	5.6
Deferred liabilities	5.6	2.8
Other long-term liabilities	6.6	3.9
Total liabilities	65.6%	56.6%
Shareholders' equity		
Common stock and other paid-in capital	22.0%	23.8%
Retained earnings	12.3	19.7
Total shareholders' equity	34.4%	43.4%
Total liabilities and shareholders' equity	100.0%	100.0%

Note: Column sums subject to rounding error.

Source: Hewlett-Packard Annual Report.

TABLE 14.3		$ Million
Statement of Cash Flows for Hewlett-Packard, 2008	**Cash provided by operations**	
	Net income	$ 8,329
	Adjustments to net income	
	Depreciation	3,356
	Changes in working capital	
	Decrease (increase) in receivables	(3,168)
	Decrease (increase) in inventories	154
	Decrease (increase) in other current assets	(2,511)
	Increase (decrease) in accounts payable	6,495
	Increase (decrease) in other current liabilities	194
	Total adjustments	$ 4,520
	Cash provided by operations	12,849
	Cash flows from investments	
	Gross investment in tangible fixed assets	$ (6,340)
	Investments in tangible fixed assets	(14,445)
	Investment in other assets	(2,877)
	Cash provided by (used for) investments	$ (23,662)
	Cash provided by (used for) financing activities	
	Additions to (reductions in) long-term debt	$ 2,679
	Additions to (reductions in) short-term debt	6,990
	Additions to (reductions in) deferred and other long-term liabilities	7,858
	Net issues (repurchases of) shares	(7,117)
	Dividends	(796)
	Cash provided by (used for) financing activities	$ 9,614
	Net increase in cash	$ (1,199)

Source: Data from Tables 14.1 and 14.2.

capital expenditures over time. The depreciation expense on the income statement does this by recognizing capital expenditures over a period of many years rather than at the specific time of purchase. In contrast, the statement of cash flows recognizes the cash implication of a capital expenditure when it occurs. Therefore, it adds back the depreciation "expense" that was used to compute net income; instead it acknowledges a capital expenditure when it is paid. It does so by reporting cash flows separately for operations, investing, and financing activities. This way, any large cash flows, such as those for big investments, can be recognized without affecting the measure of cash flow provided by operations.

The second section of the statement of cash flows is the accounting of cash flows from investing activities. For example, HP used $6,340 million of cash investing in tangible fixed assets. These entries are investments in the assets necessary for the firm to maintain or enhance its productive capacity.

Finally, the last section of the statement lists the cash flows realized from financing activities. Issuance of securities contributes positive cash flows, while redemption of outstanding securities uses cash. For example, HP expended $7,117 million to repurchase shares of its stock in 2008, which was a major use of cash. Its dividend payments, $796 million, also used cash. In total, HP's financing activities in 2008 provided $9,614 million of cash.

To summarize, HP's operations generated a cash flow of $12,849 million. The company laid out $23,662 million to pay for new investments. But it raised $9,614 million through its financing activities. HP's cash holdings therefore changed by $12,849 − $23,662 + $9,614 = −$1,199 million. This is reported on the last line of Table 14.3.

The statement of cash flows provides important evidence on the well-being of a firm. If a company cannot pay its dividends and maintain the productivity of its capital stock out of cash flow from operations, for example, and it must resort to borrowing to meet these demands, this is a serious warning that the firm cannot maintain payout at its current level in the long run. The statement of cash flows will reveal this developing problem when it shows that cash flow from operations is inadequate and that borrowing is being used to maintain dividend payments at unsustainable levels.

14.2 Accounting versus Economic Earnings

We've seen that stock valuation models require a measure of **economic earnings**—the sustainable cash flow that can be paid out to stockholders without impairing the productive capacity of the firm. In contrast, **accounting earnings** are affected by several conventions regarding the valuation of assets such as inventories (e.g., LIFO versus FIFO treatment) and by the way some expenditures such as capital investments are recognized over time (as depreciation expenses). We will discuss problems with some of these accounting conventions in greater detail later in the chapter. In addition to these accounting issues, as the firm makes its way through the business cycle, its earnings will rise above or fall below the trend line that might more accurately reflect sustainable economic earnings. This introduces an added complication in interpreting net income figures. One might wonder how closely accounting earnings approximate economic earnings and, correspondingly, how useful accounting data might be to investors attempting to value the firm.

In fact, the net income figure on the firm's income statement does convey considerable information concerning a firm's products. We see this in the fact that stock prices tend to increase when firms announce earnings greater than market analysts or investors had anticipated.

economic earnings

The real flow of cash that a firm could pay out without impairing its productive capacity.

accounting earnings

Earnings of a firm as reported on its income statement.

14.3 Profitability Measures

Profitability measures focus on the firm's earnings. To facilitate comparisons across firms, total earnings are expressed on a per-dollar-invested basis. So return on equity (ROE), which measures profitability for contributors of equity capital, is defined as (after-tax) profits divided by the book value of equity. Similarly, return on assets (ROA), which measures profitability for all contributors of capital, is defined as earnings before interest and taxes divided by total assets. Not surprisingly, ROA and ROE are linked, but as we will see shortly, the relationship between them is affected by the firm's financial policies.

Past versus Future ROE

We noted in Chapter 13 that **return on equity (ROE)** is one of the two basic factors in determining a firm's growth rate of earnings. Sometimes it is reasonable to assume that future ROE will approximate its past value, but a high ROE in the past does not necessarily imply a firm's future ROE will be high. A declining ROE, on the other hand, is evidence that the firm's new investments have offered a lower ROE than its past investments. The vital point for a security analyst is not to accept historical values as indicators of future values. Data from the recent past may provide information regarding future performance, but the analyst should always keep an eye on the future. Expectations of *future* dividends and earnings determine the intrinsic value of the company's stock.

return on equity (ROE)

The ratio of net profits to common equity.

Financial Leverage and ROE

An analyst interpreting the past behavior of a firm's ROE or forecasting its future value must pay careful attention to the firm's debt–equity mix and to the interest rate on its debt. An example will show why. Suppose Nodett is a firm that is all-equity financed and has total assets of $100 million. Assume it pays corporate taxes at the rate of 40% of taxable earnings.

Table 14.4 shows the behavior of sales, earnings before interest and taxes, and net profits under three scenarios representing phases of the business cycle. It also shows the behavior of two of the most commonly used profitability measures: operating **return on assets (ROA)**, which equals EBIT/total assets, and ROE, which equals net profits/equity.

return on assets (ROA)

Earnings before interest and taxes divided by total assets.

TABLE 14.4

Nodett's profitability over the business cycle

Scenario	Sales ($ millions)	EBIT ($ millions)	ROA (% per year)	Net Profit ($ millions)	ROE (% per year)
Bad year	$ 80	$ 5	5%	$3	3%
Normal year	100	10	10	6	6
Good year	120	15	15	9	9

TABLE 14.5

Impact of financial leverage on ROE

		Nodett		Somdett	
Scenario	EBIT ($ millions)	Net Profit ($ millions)	ROE (%)	Net Profit* ($ millions)	ROE† (%)
Bad year	$ 5	$3	3%	$1.08	1.8%
Normal year	10	6	6	4.08	6.8
Good year	15	9	9	7.08	11.8

*Somdett's after-tax profits equal 0.6(EBIT − $3.2 million).
†Somdett's equity is only $60 million.

Somdett is an otherwise identical firm to Nodett, but $40 million of its $100 million of assets are financed with debt bearing an interest rate of 8%. It pays annual interest expenses of $3.2 million. Table 14.5 shows how Somdett's ROE differs from Nodett's.

Note that annual sales, EBIT, and therefore ROA for both firms are the same in each of the three scenarios, that is, business risk for the two companies is identical. It is their financial risk that differs. Although Nodett and Somdett have the same ROA in each scenario, Somdett's ROE exceeds that of Nodett in normal and good years and is lower in bad years.

We can summarize the exact relationship among ROE, ROA, and leverage in the following equation[2]

$$ROE = (1 - \text{Tax rate})\left[ROA + (ROA - \text{Interest rate})\frac{\text{Debt}}{\text{Equity}}\right] \quad \text{(14.1)}$$

The relationship has the following implications. If there is no debt or if the firm's ROA equals the interest rate on its debt, its ROE will simply equal (1 − tax rate) times ROA. If its ROA exceeds the interest rate, then its ROE will exceed (1 − tax rate) times ROA by an amount that will be greater the higher the debt/equity ratio.

---

[2] The derivation of Equation 14.1 is as follows:

$$ROE = \frac{\text{Net profit}}{\text{Equity}} = \frac{\text{EBIT} - \text{Interest} - \text{Taxes}}{\text{Equity}} = \frac{(1 - \text{Tax rate})(\text{EBIT} - \text{Interest})}{\text{Equity}}$$

$$= (1 - \text{Tax rate})\frac{(ROA \times \text{Assets} - \text{Interest rate} \times \text{Debt})}{\text{Equity}}$$

$$= (1 - \text{Tax rate})\left[ROA \times \frac{(\text{Equity} + \text{Debt})}{\text{Equity}} - \text{Interest rate} \times \frac{\text{Debt}}{\text{Equity}}\right]$$

$$= (1 - \text{Tax rate})\left[ROA + (ROA - \text{Interest rate})\frac{\text{Debt}}{\text{Equity}}\right]$$

This result makes sense: If ROA exceeds the borrowing rate, the firm earns more on its money than it pays out to creditors. The surplus earnings are available to the firm's owners, the equityholders, which raises ROE. If, on the other hand, ROA is less than the interest rate paid on debt, then ROE will decline by an amount that depends on the debt/equity ratio.

EXAMPLE 14.1

Leverage and ROE

To illustrate the application of Equation 14.1, we can use the numerical example in Table 14.5. In a normal year, Nodett has an ROE of 6%, which is (1 − tax rate), or .6, times its ROA of 10%. However, Somdett, which borrows at an interest rate of 8% and maintains a debt/equity ratio of ⅔, has an ROE of 6.8%. The calculation using Equation 14.1 is

$$ROE = .6[10\% + (10\% - 8\%)\tfrac{2}{3}]$$
$$= .6(10\% + \tfrac{4}{3}\%) = 6.8\%$$

The important point is that increased debt will make a positive contribution to a firm's ROE only if the firm's ROA exceeds the interest rate on the debt.

Notice that financial leverage increases the risk of the equityholder returns. Table 14.5 shows that ROE on Somdett is worse than that of Nodett in bad years. Conversely, in good years, Somdett outperforms Nodett because the excess of ROA over ROE provides additional funds for equityholders. The presence of debt makes Somdett's ROE more sensitive to the business cycle than Nodett's. Even though the two companies have equal business risk (reflected in their identical EBIT in all three scenarios), Somdett's stockholders carry greater financial risk than Nodett's because all of the firm's business risk is absorbed by a smaller base of equity investors.

Even if financial leverage increases the expected ROE of Somdett relative to Nodett (as it seems to in Table 14.5), this does not imply that Somdett's share price will be higher. Financial leverage increases the risk of the firm's equity as surely as it raises the expected ROE, and the higher discount rate will offset the higher expected earnings.

CONCEPT check 14.1

Mordett is a company with the same assets as Nodett and Somdett but a debt/equity ratio of 1.0 and an interest rate of 9%. What would its net profit and ROE be in a bad year, a normal year, and a good year?

Ratio Analysis

Decomposition of ROE

To understand the factors affecting a firm's ROE, including its trend over time and its performance relative to competitors, analysts often "decompose" ROE into the product of a series of ratios. Each component ratio is in itself meaningful, and the process serves to focus the analyst's attention on the separate factors influencing performance. This kind of decomposition of ROE is often called the **DuPont system.**

One useful decomposition of ROE is

$$ROE = \underbrace{\frac{\text{Net profit}}{\text{Pretax profit}}}_{(1)} \times \underbrace{\frac{\text{Pretax profit}}{\text{EBIT}}}_{(2)} \times \underbrace{\frac{\text{EBIT}}{\text{Sales}}}_{(3)} \times \underbrace{\frac{\text{Sales}}{\text{Assets}}}_{(4)} \times \underbrace{\frac{\text{Assets}}{\text{Equity}}}_{(5)} \quad \textbf{(14.2)}$$

Table 14.6 shows all these ratios for Nodett and Somdett under the three different economic scenarios. Let us first focus on factors 3 and 4. Notice that their product gives us the firm's ROA = EBIT/Assets.

Factor 3 is known as the firm's operating **profit margin,** or **return on sales,** which equals operating profit per dollar of sales. In an average year, Nodett's margin is .10, or 10%; in a bad year, it is .0625, or 6.25%; and in a good year, it is .125, or 12.5%.

DuPont system

Decomposition of profitability measures into component ratios.

profit margin or return on sales

The ratio of operating profits per dollar of sales (EBIT divided by sales).

TABLE 14.6
Ratio decomposition analysis for Nodett and Somdett

	ROE	(1) Net Profit / Pretax Profit	(2) Pretax Profit / EBIT	(3) EBIT / Sales (Margin)	(4) Sales / Assets (Turnover)	(5) Assets / Equity	(6) Compound Leverage Factor (2) × (5)
Bad year							
Nodett	.030	.6	1.000	.0625	0.800	1.000	1.000
Somdett	.018	.6	0.360	.0625	0.800	1.667	0.600
Normal year							
Nodett	.060	.6	1.000	.100	1.000	1.000	1.000
Somdett	.068	.6	0.680	.100	1.000	1.667	1.134
Good year							
Nodett	.090	.6	1.000	.125	1.200	1.000	1.000
Somdett	.118	.6	0.787	.125	1.200	1.667	1.311

total asset turnover (ATO)

The annual sales generated by each dollar of assets (sales/assets).

Factor 4, the ratio of sales to total assets, is known as **total asset turnover (ATO).** It indicates the efficiency of the firm's use of assets in the sense that it measures the annual sales generated by each dollar of assets. In a normal year, Nodett's ATO is 1.0 per year, meaning that sales of $1 per year were generated per dollar of assets. In a bad year, this ratio declines to .8 per year, and in a good year, it rises to 1.2 per year.

Comparing Nodett and Somdett, we see that factors 3 and 4 do not depend on a firm's financial leverage. The firms' ratios are equal to each other in all three scenarios.

Similarly, factor 1, the ratio of net income after taxes to pretax profit, is the same for both firms. We call this the tax-burden ratio. Its value reflects both the government's tax code and the policies pursued by the firm in trying to minimize its tax burden. In our example, it does not change over the business cycle, remaining a constant .6.

While factors 1, 3, and 4 are not affected by a firm's capital structure, factors 2 and 5 are. Factor 2 is the ratio of pretax profits to EBIT. The firm's pretax profits will be greatest when there are no interest payments to be made to debtholders. In fact, another way to express this ratio is

$$\frac{\text{Pretax profits}}{\text{EBIT}} = \frac{\text{EBIT} - \text{Interest expense}}{\text{EBIT}}$$

We will call this factor the *interest-burden (IB) ratio.* It takes on its highest possible value, 1, for Nodett, which has no financial leverage. The higher the degree of financial leverage, the lower the IB ratio. Nodett's IB ratio does not vary over the business cycle. It is fixed at 1.0, reflecting the total absence of interest payments. For Somdett, however, because interest expense is fixed in a dollar amount while EBIT varies, the IB ratio varies from a low of .36 in a bad year to a high of .787 in a good year.

interest coverage ratio or times interest earned

A financial leverage measure arrived at by dividing earnings before interest and taxes by interest expense.

A closely related statistic to the interest burden ratio is the **interest coverage ratio,** or **times interest earned.** The ratio is defined as

$$\text{Interest coverage} = \frac{\text{EBIT}}{\text{Interest expense}}$$

A high coverage ratio indicates that the likelihood of bankruptcy is low because annual earnings are significantly greater than annual interest obligations. It is widely used by both lenders and borrowers in determining the firm's debt capacity and is a major determinant of the firm's bond rating.

TABLE 14.7		Margin	×	ATO	=	ROA
Differences between profit margin and asset turnover across industries	Supermarket chain	2%		5.0		10%
	Utility	20%		0.5		10%

Factor 5, the ratio of assets to equity, is a measure of the firm's degree of financial leverage. It is called the **leverage ratio** and is equal to 1 plus the debt/equity ratio.[3] In our numerical example in Table 14.6, Nodett has a leverage ratio of 1, while Somdett's is 1.667.

leverage ratio
Measure of debt to total capitalization of a firm.

From our discussion of Equation 14.1, we know that financial leverage helps boost ROE only if ROA is greater than the interest rate on the firm's debt. How is this fact reflected in the ratios of Table 14.6?

The answer is that to measure the full impact of leverage in this framework, the analyst must take the product of the IB and leverage ratios (that is, factors 2 and 5, shown in Table 14.6 as column 6). For Nodett, factor 6, which we call the compound leverage factor, remains a constant 1.0 under all three scenarios. But for Somdett, we see that the compound leverage factor is greater than 1 in normal years (1.134) and in good years (1.311), indicating the positive contribution of financial leverage to ROE. It is less than 1 in bad years, reflecting the fact that when ROA falls below the interest rate, ROE falls with increased use of debt.

We can summarize all of these relationships as follows:

$$ROE = Tax\ burden \times Interest\ burden \times Margin \times Turnover \times Leverage$$

Because

$$ROA = Margin \times Turnover \qquad (14.3)$$

and

$$Compound\ leverage\ factor = Interest\ burden \times Leverage$$

we can decompose ROE equivalently as follows:

$$ROE = Tax\ burden \times ROA \times Compound\ leverage\ factor$$

Table 14.6 for Nodett and Somdett compares firms with the same profit margin and turnover but different degrees of financial leverage. Note, however, that comparison of profit margin and turnover usually is meaningful only in evaluating firms in the same industry. Cross-industry comparisons of these two ratios are often meaningless and can even be misleading.

EXAMPLE   14.2

Margin vs. Turnover

Consider two firms with the same ROA of 10% per year. The first is a discount supermarket chain and the second is a gas and electric utility.

As Table 14.7 shows, the supermarket chain has a "low" profit margin of 2% and achieves a 10% ROA by "turning over" its assets five times per year. The capital-intensive utility, on the other hand, has a "low" asset turnover ratio (ATO) of only .5 times per year and achieves its 10% ROA through its higher, 20%, profit margin. The point here is that a "low" margin or ATO ratio need not indicate a troubled firm. Each ratio must be interpreted in light of industry norms.

Even within an industry, margin and ATO sometimes can differ markedly among firms pursuing different marketing strategies. In the retailing industry, for example, Neiman-Marcus pursues a high-margin, low-turnover policy compared to Wal-Mart, which pursues a low-margin, high-turnover policy.

[3] $\dfrac{Assets}{Equity} = \dfrac{Equity + Debt}{Equity} = 1 + \dfrac{Debt}{Equity}$

Do a ratio decomposition analysis for the Mordett corporation of Concept Check 1, preparing a table similar to Table 14.6.

Turnover and Other Asset Utilization Ratios

It is often helpful in understanding a firm's ratio of sales to assets to compute comparable efficiency-of-utilization, or turnover, ratios for subcategories of assets. For example, fixed-asset turnover would be

$$\frac{\text{Sales}}{\text{Fixed assets}}$$

This ratio measures sales per dollar of the firm's money tied up in fixed assets.

To illustrate how you can compute this and other ratios from a firm's financial statements, consider Growth Industries, Inc. (GI). GI's income statement and opening and closing balance sheets for the years 2008, 2009, and 2010 appear in Table 14.8.

GI's total asset turnover in 2010 was .303, which was below the industry average of .4. To understand better why GI underperformed, we compute asset utilization ratios separately for fixed assets, inventories, and accounts receivable.

GI's sales in 2010 were $144 million. Its only fixed assets were plant and equipment, which were $216 million at the beginning of the year and $259.2 million at year's end. Average fixed assets for the year were, therefore, $237.6 million [($216 million + $259.2 million)/2]. GI's fixed-asset turnover for 2010 was $144 million per year/$237.6 million = .606 per year. In other words, for every dollar of fixed assets, there was $.606 in sales during the year 2008.

Comparable figures for the fixed-asset turnover ratio for 2008 and 2009 and the 2010 industry average are

2008	2009	2010	2010 Industry Average
.606	.606	.606	.700

GI's fixed-asset turnover has been stable over time and below the industry average.

Notice that when a financial ratio includes one item from the income statement, which covers a period of time, and another from the balance sheet, which is a "snapshot" at a particular time, common practice is to take the average of the beginning and end-of-year balance sheet figures. Thus, in computing the fixed-asset turnover ratio you divide sales (from the income statement) by average fixed assets (from the balance sheet).

inventory turnover ratio

Cost of goods sold divided by average inventory.

Another widely followed turnover ratio is the **inventory turnover ratio,** which is the ratio of cost of goods sold per dollar of inventory. It is usually expressed as cost of goods sold (instead of sales revenue) divided by average inventory. It measures the speed with which inventory is turned over.

In 2008, GI's cost of goods sold (less depreciation) was $40 million, and its average inventory was $82.5 million [($75 million + $90 million)/2]. Its inventory turnover was .485 per year ($40 million/$82.5 million). In 2008 and 2009, inventory turnover remained the same and continued below the industry average of .5 per year. In other words, GI was burdened with a higher level of inventories per dollar of sales than its competitors. This higher investment in working capital in turn resulted in a higher level of assets per dollar of sales or profits, and a lower ROA than its competitors.

average collection period, or days receivables

Accounts receivable per dollar of daily sales.

Another measure of efficiency is the ratio of accounts receivable to sales. The accounts receivable ratio usually is computed as average accounts receivable/sales × 365. The result is a number called the **average collection period,** or **days receivables,** which equals the total credit extended to customers per dollar of daily sales. It is the number of days' worth of sales tied up in accounts receivable. You can also think of it as the average lag between the date of sale and the date payment is received.

TABLE 14.8

Growth Industries financial statements ($thousands)

	2007	2008	2009	2010
Income statements				
Sales revenue		$100,000	$120,000	$144,000
Cost of goods sold (including depreciation)		55,000	66,000	79,200
Depreciation		15,000	18,000	21,600
Selling and administrative expenses		15,000	18,000	21,600
Operating income		30,000	36,000	43,200
Interest expense		10,500	19,095	34,391
Taxable income		19,500	16,905	8,809
Income tax (40% rate)		7,800	6,762	3,524
Net income		11,700	10,143	5,285
Balance sheets (end of year)				
Cash and marketable securities	$ 50,000	$ 60,000	$ 72,000	$ 86,400
Accounts receivable	25,000	30,000	36,000	43,200
Inventories	75,000	90,000	108,000	129,600
Net plant and equipment	150,000	180,000	216,000	259,200
Total assets	$300,000	$360,000	$432,000	$518,400
Accounts payable	$ 30,000	$ 36,000	$ 43,200	$ 51,840
Short-term debt	45,000	87,300	141,957	214,432
Long-term debt (8% bonds maturing in 2022)	75,000	75,000	75,000	75,000
Total liabilities	$150,000	$198,300	$260,157	$341,272
Shareholders' equity (1 million shares outstanding)	$150,000	$161,700	$171,843	$177,128
Other data				
Market price per common share at year-end		$ 93.60	$ 61.00	$ 21.00

For GI in 2010, this number was 100.4 days:

$$\frac{(\$36 \text{ million} + \$43.2 \text{ million})/2}{\$144 \text{ million}} \times 365 = 100.4 \text{ days}$$

The industry average was 60 days. This statistic tells us that GI's average receivables per dollar of sales exceeds that of its competitors. Again, this implies a higher required investment in working capital, and ultimately a lower ROA.

In summary, use of these ratios lets us see that GI's poor total asset turnover relative to the industry is in part caused by lower than average fixed-asset turnover and inventory turnover, and higher than average days receivables. This suggests GI may be having problems with excess plant capacity along with poor inventory and receivables management practices.

Liquidity Ratios

Liquidity and interest coverage ratios are of great importance in evaluating the riskiness of a firm's securities. They aid in assessing the financial strength of the firm.

Liquidity ratios include the current ratio, quick ratio, and cash ratio.

1. **Current ratio:** current assets/current liabilities. This ratio measures the ability of the firm to pay off its current liabilities by liquidating its current assets (that is, turning them into cash). It indicates the firm's ability to avoid insolvency in the short run. GI's current ratio in 2008, for example, was (60 + 30 + 90)/(36 + 87.3) = 1.46. In other years, it was

current ratio

Current assets/current liabilities.

2008	2009	2010	2010 Industry Average
1.46	1.17	0.97	2.0

This represents an unfavorable time trend and poor standing relative to the industry. This troublesome pattern is not surprising given the working capital burden resulting from GI's subpar performance with respect to receivables and inventory management.

quick ratio, or acid test ratio

A measure of liquidity similar to the current ratio except for exclusion of inventories.

2. **Quick ratio:** (cash + marketable securities + receivables)/current liabilities. This ratio is also called the **acid test ratio.** It has the same denominator as the current ratio, but its numerator includes only cash, cash equivalents such as marketable securities, and receivables. The quick ratio is a better measure of liquidity than the current ratio for firms whose inventory is not readily convertible into cash. GI's quick ratio shows the same disturbing trends as its current ratio:

2008	2009	2010	2010 Industry Average
0.73	0.58	0.49	1.0

cash ratio

Another liquidity measure. Ratio of cash and marketable securities to current liabilities.

3. **Cash ratio.** A company's receivables are less liquid than its holdings of cash and marketable securities. Therefore, in addition to the quick ratio, analysts also compute a firm's cash ratio, defined as

$$\text{Cash ratio} = \frac{\text{Cash + Marketable securities}}{\text{Current liabilities}}$$

GI's cash ratios are

2008	2009	2010	2010 Industry Average
.487	.389	.324	.70

GI's liquidity ratios have fallen dramatically over this three-year period, and by 2010, they are far below the industry average. The decline in the liquidity ratios combined with the decline in coverage ratio (you can confirm that times interest earned also has fallen over this period) suggest that its credit rating has been declining as well and, no doubt, GI is considered a relatively poor credit risk in 2010.

Market Price Ratios

There are two important market price ratios: the market-to-book-value ratio and the price–earnings ratio.

market-to-book-value ratio

Market price of a share divided by book value per share.

The **market-to-book-value ratio** (P/B) equals the market price of a share of the firm's common stock divided by its *book value,* that is, shareholders' equity per share. Analysts sometimes consider the stock of a firm with a low market-to-book value to be a "safer" investment, seeing the book value as a "floor" supporting the market price.

Analysts presumably view book value as the level below which market price will not fall because the firm always has the option to liquidate, or sell, its assets for their book values. However, this view is questionable. In fact, some firms do sometimes sell for less than book value. For example, in February 2009, shares in both Bank of America and Citigroup sold for less than 25% of book value per share. Nevertheless, a low market-to-book-value ratio is seen by some as providing a "margin of safety," and some analysts will screen out or reject high P/B firms in their stock selection process.

In fact, a better interpretation of the price-to-book ratio is as a measure of growth opportunities. Recall from the previous chapter that we may view the two components of firm value as assets in place and growth opportunities. As the next example illustrates, firms with greater growth opportunities will tend to exhibit higher multiples of market price to book value.

EXAMPLE 14.3

Price-to-Book and Growth Options

Consider two firms, both of which have book value per share of $10, a market capitalization rate of 15%, and a plowback ratio of .60.

Bright Prospects has an ROE of 20%, which is well in excess of the market capitalization rate; this ROE implies that the firm is endowed with ample growth opportunities. With ROE = .20, Bright Prospects will earn .20 × 10 = $2 per share this year. With its plowback ratio of .60, it pays out a dividend of $D_1 = (1 − .6) × $2 = $.80$, has a growth rate of $g = b × ROE = .60 × .20 = .12$, and a stock price of $D_1/(k − g) = $.80/(.15 − .12) = 26.67. Its P/B ratio is 26.67/10 = 2.667.

In contrast, Past Glory has an ROE of only 15%, just equal to the market capitalization rate. It therefore will earn .15 × 10 = $1.50 per share this year and will pay a dividend of $D_1 = .4 × $1.50 = $.60$. Its growth rate is $g = b × ROE = .60 × .15 = .09$, and its stock price is $D_1/(k − g) = $.60/(.15 − .09) = 10. Its P/B ratio is $10/$10 = 1.0. Not surprisingly, a firm that earns just the required rate of return on its investments will sell for book value, and no more.

We conclude that the price-to-book value ratio is determined in large part by growth prospects.

Another measure used to place firms along a growth versus value spectrum is the **price–earnings ratio (P/E).** In fact, we saw in the last chapter that the ratio of the present value of growth options to the value of assets in place largely determines the P/E multiple. While low P/E stocks allow you to pay less per dollar of *current* earnings, the high P/E stock may still be a better bargain if its earnings are expected to grow quickly enough.[4]

price–earnings ratio

The ratio of a stock's price to its earnings per share. Also referred to as the P/E multiple.

Many analysts nevertheless believe that low P/E stocks are more attractive than high P/E stocks. And in fact, low P/E stocks have generally been positive-alpha investments using the CAPM as a benchmark. But an efficient market adherent would discount this track record, arguing that such a simplistic rule could not really generate abnormal returns and that the CAPM may not be a good benchmark for returns in this case.

In any event, the important points to remember are that ownership of the stock conveys the right to future as well as current earnings and, therefore that a high P/E ratio may best be interpreted as a signal that the market views the firm as enjoying attractive growth opportunities.

Before leaving the P/B and P/E ratios, it is worth pointing out the relationship among these ratios and ROE.

$$\text{ROE} = \frac{\text{Earnings}}{\text{Book value}} = \frac{\text{Market price}}{\text{Book value}} \div \frac{\text{Market price}}{\text{Earnings}} \qquad \textbf{(14.4)}$$

$$= \text{P/B ratio} \div \text{P/E ratio}$$

Rearranging terms, we find that a firm's **earnings yield,** the ratio of earnings to price, equals ROE divided by the market-to-book-value ratio:

earnings yield

The ratio of earnings to price, E/P.

$$\frac{E}{P} = \frac{\text{ROE}}{\text{P/B}}$$

Thus, a company with a high ROE can have a relatively low earnings yield because its P/B ratio is high.

Wall Street often distinguishes between "good firms" and "good investments." A good firm may be highly profitable, with a correspondingly high ROE. But if its stock price is bid up to a level commensurate with this ROE, its P/B ratio will be above 1 and the earnings yield to stockholders will be less than ROE, as Equation 14.4 demonstrates. The high ROE does not by itself imply that the stock is a good investment. Conversely, troubled firms with low ROEs can be good investments if their prices are low enough.

Table 14.9 summarizes the ratios reviewed in this section.

---

[4]Remember, though, P/E ratios reported in the financial pages are based on *past* earnings, while price is determined by the firm's prospects of *future* earnings. Therefore, reported P/E ratios may reflect variation in current earnings around a trend line.

CONCEPT
check   **14.3**   What were GI's ROE, P/E, and P/B ratios in the year 2010? How do they compare to these
industry average ratios: ROE = 8.64%, P/E = 8, and P/B = .69. How does GI's earnings yield
in 2010 compare to the industry average?

TABLE 14.9
Summary of key financial ratios

Leverage ratios:

Interest burden

$$\frac{\text{EBIT} - \text{Interest expense}}{\text{EBIT}}$$

Interest coverage (Times interest earned)

$$\frac{\text{EBIT}}{\text{Interest expense}}$$

Leverage

$$\frac{\text{Assets}}{\text{Equity}} = 1 + \frac{\text{Debt}}{\text{Equity}}$$

Compound leverage factor

Interest burden $\times$ Leverage

Asset utilization:

Total asset turnover

$$\frac{\text{Sales}}{\text{Average total assets}}$$

Fixed asset turnover

$$\frac{\text{Sales}}{\text{Average fixed assets}}$$

Inventory turnover

$$\frac{\text{Cost of goods sold}}{\text{Average inventories}}$$

Days receivables

$$\frac{\text{Average accounts receivables}}{\text{Annual sales}} \times 365$$

Liquidity:

Current ratio

$$\frac{\text{Current assets}}{\text{Current liabilities}}$$

Quick ratio

$$\frac{\text{Cash} + \text{Marketable securities} + \text{Receivables}}{\text{Current liabilities}}$$

Cash ratio

$$\frac{\text{Cash} + \text{Marketable securities}}{\text{Current liabilities}}$$

Profitability ratios:

Return on assets

$$\frac{\text{EBIT}}{\text{Average total assets}}$$

Return on equity

$$\frac{\text{Net income}}{\text{Average stockholder's equity}}$$

Return on sales (Profit margin)

$$\frac{\text{EBIT}}{\text{Sales}}$$

Market price ratios:

Market-to-book

$$\frac{\text{Price per share}}{\text{Book value per share}}$$

Price–earnings ratio

$$\frac{\text{Price per share}}{\text{Earnings per share}}$$

Earnings yield

$$\frac{\text{Earnings per share}}{\text{Price per share}}$$

Choosing a Benchmark

We have discussed how to calculate the principal financial ratios. To evaluate the performance of a given firm, however, you need a benchmark to which you can compare its ratios. One obvious benchmark is the ratio for the same company in earlier years. For example, Figure 14.1 shows Hewlett-Packard's return on assets, profit margin, and asset turnover ratio for the last few years. You can see there that most of the variation in HP's return on assets has been driven by the considerable variation in its asset turnover ratio. In contrast, its profit margin has been relatively stable.

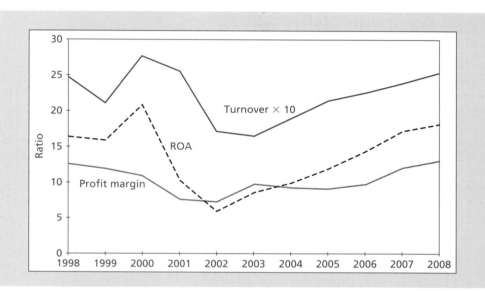

FIGURE 14.1

DuPont decomposition for Hewlett-Packard

TABLE 14.10

Financial Ratios for Major Industry Groups

	LT Debt Assets	Interest Coverage	Current Ratio	Quick Ratio	Asset Turnover	Profit Margin (%)	Return on Assets (%)	Return on Equity (%)	Payout Ratio
All manufacturing	.19	4.08	1.31	0.91	0.95	6.73	6.39	16.97	.36
Food products	.23	4.14	1.26	0.76	1.21	6.55	7.92	16.88	.31
Clothing	.23	5.68	1.29	0.41	1.76	4.78	8.43	13.92	.15
Printing/publishing	.38	1.99	1.33	1.01	1.39	5.58	7.75	11.97	.35
Chemicals	.20	4.00	1.28	0.94	0.59	11.27	6.71	18.21	.29
Drugs	.16	6.51	1.39	1.12	0.43	18.99	8.23	19.67	.22
Machinery	.17	4.88	1.20	0.77	0.92	8.20	7.51	16.72	.22
Electrical	.13	4.98	1.10	0.70	0.70	9.01	6.34	14.27	.66
Motor vehicles	.26	−1.12	0.97	0.68	0.96	−3.13	−3.00	−19.54	−.40
Computer and Electronic	.14	2.04	1.61	1.31	0.61	3.07	1.87	5.00	.56

Source: U.S. Department of Commerce, *Quarterly Financial Report for Manufacturing, Mining and Trade Corporations,* third quarter 2008. **www.census.gov/csd/qfr/qfr08q3.pdf.**

It is also helpful to compare financial ratios to those of other firms in the same industry. Financial ratios for industries are published by the U.S. Department of Commerce, Dun & Bradstreet, the Risk Management Association, and others, and many ratios are available on the Web, for example, on the Yahoo! Finance site. Standard & Poor's Market Insight is a good source of ratios and is available to users of this text at **www.mhhe.com/edumarketinsight**.

Table 14.10 presents ratios for a sample of major industry groups to give you a feel for some of the differences across industries. You should note that while some ratios such as asset turnover or total debt ratio tend to be relatively stable, others such as return on assets or equity are more sensitive to current business conditions. Notice for example the negative profitability measures for the motor vehicle industry.

14.5 Economic Value Added

economic value added, or residual income

A measure of the dollar value of a firm's return in excess of its opportunity cost.

One common use of financial ratios is to evaluate the performance of the firm. While it is common to use profitability to measure that performance, profitability is really not enough. A firm should be viewed as successful only if the return on its projects is better than the rate investors could expect to earn for themselves (on a risk-adjusted basis) in the capital market. Plowing back funds into the firm increases share value only if the firm earns a higher rate of return on the reinvested funds than the opportunity cost of capital, that is, the market capitalization rate. To account for this opportunity cost, we might measure the success of the firm using the *difference* between the return on assets, ROA, and the opportunity cost of capital. **Economic value added** (EVA) is the spread between ROA and the cost of capital multiplied by the capital invested in the firm. It therefore measures the dollar value of the firm's return in excess of its opportunity cost. Another term for EVA (the term coined by Stern Stewart, a consulting firm that has promoted the concept) is **residual income.**

EXAMPLE 14.4

Economic Value Added

In 2008, Wal-Mart had a weighted-average cost of capital of 5.7% (based on its cost of debt, its capital structure, its equity beta, and estimates derived from the CAPM for the cost of equity). Wal-Mart's return on assets was 8.8%, fully 3.1% greater than the opportunity cost of capital on its investments in plant, equipment, and know-how. In other words, each dollar invested by Wal-Mart earned about 3.1 cents more than the return that investors could have anticipated by investing in equivalent-risk stocks. Wal-Mart earned this superior rate of return on a capital base of $111.40 billion. Its economic value added, that is, its return in excess of opportunity cost was therefore $(.088 - .057) \times \$111.40 = \$3.46$ billion.

Table 14.11 shows EVA for a small sample of firms.[5] The EVA leader in this sample was Wal-Mart. Notice that its EVA was greater than GlaxoSmithKline's, despite a considerably

TABLE 14.11		**EVA** ($ billion)	**Capital** ($ billion)	**ROA (%)**	**Cost of Capital (%)**
Economic Value Added, 2008	Wal-Mart	3.46	111.40	8.8	5.7
	GlaxoSmithKline	2.62	31.04	14.9	6.5
	Genentech	1.87	18.38	15.6	5.4
	Procter & Gamble	1.36	102.85	7.5	6.2
	Intel	0.83	42.61	11.4	9.4
	Amazon	−0.25	9.21	6.6	9.4
	AT&T	−1.90	169.84	5.3	6.4

Source: Authors' calculations using data from **finance.yahoo.com**.

[5]Actual EVA estimates reported by Stern Stewart differ from the values in Table 14.11 because of adjustments to the accounting data involving issues such as treatment of research and development expenses, taxes, advertising expenses, and depreciation. The estimates in Table 14.11 are designed to show the logic behind EVA but must be taken as imprecise.

smaller margin between ROA and the cost of capital. This is because Wal-Mart applied its margin to a much larger capital base. At the other extreme, AT&T earned less than its opportunity cost on a very large capital base, which resulted in a large negative EVA.

Notice that even the EVA "losers" in Table 14.11 had positive profits. For example, by conventional standards, Amazon was solidly profitable in 2008, with an ROA of 6.6%. But by virtue of its high business risk, its cost of capital was higher, at 9.4%. By this standard, Amazon did not cover its opportunity cost of capital, and its EVA in 2008 was negative. EVA treats the opportunity cost of capital as a real cost that, like other costs, should be deducted from revenues to arrive at a more meaningful "bottom line." A firm that is earning profits but is not covering its opportunity cost might be able to redeploy its capital to better uses. Therefore, a growing number of firms now calculate EVA and tie managers' compensation to it.

14.6 An Illustration of Financial Statement Analysis

In her 2010 annual report to the shareholders of Growth Industries, Inc., the president wrote: "2010 was another successful year for Growth Industries. As in 2009, sales, assets, and operating income all continued to grow at a rate of 20%."

Is she right?

We can evaluate her statement by conducting a full-scale ratio analysis of Growth Industries. Our purpose is to assess GI's performance in the recent past, to evaluate its future prospects, and to determine whether its market price reflects its intrinsic value.

Table 14.12 shows some key financial ratios we can compute from GI's financial statements. The president is certainly right about the growth in sales, assets, and operating income. Inspection of GI's key financial ratios, however, contradicts her first sentence: 2010 was not another successful year for GI—it appears to have been another miserable one.

ROE has been declining steadily from 7.51% in 2008 to 3.03% in 2010. A comparison of GI's 2010 ROE to the 2010 industry average of 8.64% makes the deteriorating time trend especially alarming. The low and falling market-to-book-value ratio and the falling price–earnings ratio indicate that investors are less and less optimistic about the firm's future profitability.

The fact that ROA has not been declining, however, tells us that the source of the declining time trend in GI's ROE must be due to financial leverage. And in fact, as GI's leverage ratio climbed from 2.117 in 2008 to 2.723 in 2010, its interest-burden ratio worsened from .650 to .204—with the net result that the compound leverage factor fell from 1.376 to .556.

The rapid increase in short-term debt from year to year and the concurrent increase in interest expense make it clear that, to finance its 20% growth rate in sales, GI has incurred sizable amounts of short-term debt at high interest rates. The firm is paying rates of interest greater

TABLE 14.12

Key financial ratios of Growth Industries, Inc.

Year	ROE	(1) Net Profit Pretax Profit	(2) Pretax Profit EBIT	(3) EBIT Sales (Margin)	(4) Sales Assets (Turnover)	(5) Assets Equity	(6) Compound Leverage Factor (2) × (5)	(7) ROA (3) × (4)	P/E	P/B
2008	7.51%	.6	.650	30%	.303	2.117	1.376	9.09%	8	.58
2009	6.08	.6	.470	30	.303	2.375	1.116	9.09	6	.35
2010	3.03	.6	.204	30	.303	2.723	0.556	9.09	4	.12
Industry average	8.64	.6	.800	30	.400	1.500	1.200	12.00	8	.69

than the ROA it is earning on the investment financed with the new borrowing. As the firm has expanded, its situation has become ever more precarious.

In 2010, for example, the average interest rate on short-term debt was 20% versus an ROA of 9.09%. (You can calculate the interest rate on GI's short-term debt using the data in Table 14.8 as follows. The balance sheet shows us that the coupon rate on its long-term debt was 8% and its par value was $75 million. Therefore the interest paid on the long-term debt was .08 × $75 million = $6 million. Total interest paid in 2009 was $34,391,000, so the interest paid on the short-term debt must have been $34,391,000 − $6,000,000 = $28,391,000. This is 20% of GI's short-term debt at the start of the year.)

GI's problems become clear when we examine its statement of cash flows in Table 14.13. The statement is derived from the income statement and balance sheet data in Table 14.8. GI's cash flow from operations is falling steadily, from $12,700,000 in 2008 to $6,725,000 in 2010. The firm's investment in plant and equipment, by contrast, has increased greatly. Net plant and equipment (i.e., net of depreciation) rose from $150,000,000 in 2007 to $259,200,000 in 2010. This near doubling of capital assets makes the decrease in cash flow from operations all the more troubling.

The source of the difficulty is GI's enormous amount of short-term borrowing. In a sense, the company is being run as a pyramid scheme. It borrows more and more each year to maintain its 20% growth rate in assets and income. However, the new assets are not generating enough cash flow to support the extra interest burden of the debt, as the falling cash flow from operations indicates. Eventually, when the firm loses its ability to borrow further, its growth will be at an end.

At this point, GI stock might be an attractive investment. Its market price is only 12% of its book value, and with a P/E ratio of 4, its earnings yield is 25% per year. GI is a likely candidate for a takeover by another firm that might replace GI's management and build shareholder value through a radical change in policy.

TABLE 14.13		**2008**	**2009**	**2010**
Growth Industries statement of cash flows ($ thousands)	**Cash flow from operating activities**			
	Net income	$ 11,700	$ 10,143	$ 5,285
	+ Depreciation	15,000	18,000	21,600
	+ Decrease (increase) in accounts receivable	(5,000)	(6,000)	(7,200)
	+ Decrease (increase) in inventories	(15,000)	(18,000)	(21,600)
	+ Increase in accounts payable	6,000	7,200	8,640
		$ 12,700	$ 11,343	$ 6,725
	Cash flow from investing activities			
	Investment in plant and equipment*	$(45,000)	$(54,000)	$(64,800)
	Cash flow from financing activities			
	Dividends paid†	$ 0	$ 0	$ 0
	Short-term debt issued	42,300	54,657	72,475
	Change in cash and marketable securities‡	$ 10,000	$ 12,000	$ 14,400

*Gross investment equals increase in net plant and equipment plus depreciation.

†We can conclude that no dividends are paid because stockholders' equity increases each year by the full amount of net income, implying a plowback ratio of 1.0.

‡Equals cash flow from operations plus cash flow from investment activities plus cash flow from financing activities. Note that this equals the yearly change in cash and marketable securities on the balance sheet.

You have the following information for IBX Corporation for the years 2008 and 2011 (all figures are in $millions):

	2011	2008
Net income	$ 253.7	$ 239.0
Pretax income	411.9	375.6
EBIT	517.6	403.1
Average assets	4,857.9	3,459.7
Sales	6,679.3	4,537.0
Shareholders' equity	2,233.3	2,347.3

What is the trend in IBX's ROE, and how can you account for it in terms of tax burden, margin, turnover, and financial leverage?

14.7 Comparability Problems

Financial statement analysis gives us a good amount of ammunition for evaluating a company's performance and future prospects. But comparing financial results of different companies is not so simple. There is more than one acceptable way to represent various items of revenue and expense according to generally accepted accounting principles (GAAP). This means two firms may have exactly the same economic income yet very different accounting incomes.

Furthermore, interpreting a single firm's performance over time is complicated when inflation distorts the dollar measuring rod. Comparability problems are especially acute in this case because the impact of inflation on reported results often depends on the particular method the firm adopts to account for inventories and depreciation. The security analyst must adjust the earnings and the financial ratio figures to a uniform standard before attempting to compare financial results across firms and over time.

Comparability problems can arise out of the flexibility of GAAP guidelines in accounting for inventories and depreciation and in adjusting for the effects of inflation. Other important potential sources of noncomparability include the capitalization of leases and other expenses, the treatment of pension costs, and allowances for reserves.

Inventory Valuation

There are two commonly used ways to value inventories: **LIFO** (last-in, first-out) and **FIFO** (first-in, first-out). We can explain the difference using a numerical example.

Suppose Generic Products, Inc. (GPI), has a constant inventory of 1 million units of generic goods. The inventory turns over once per year, meaning the ratio of cost of goods sold to inventory is 1.

The LIFO system calls for valuing the million units used up during the year at the current cost of production, so that the last goods produced are considered the first ones to be sold. They are valued at today's cost. The FIFO system assumes that the units used up or sold are the ones that were added to inventory first, and goods sold should be valued at original cost.

If the price of generic goods were constant, at the level of $1, say, the book value of inventory and the cost of goods sold would be the same, $1 million under both systems. But suppose the price of generic goods rises by 10 cents per unit during the year as a result of inflation.

LIFO accounting would result in a cost of goods sold of $1.1 million, while the end-of-year balance sheet value of the 1 million units in inventory remains $1 million. The balance sheet value of inventories is given as the cost of the goods still in inventory. Under LIFO, the last goods produced are assumed to be sold at the current cost of $1.10; the goods remaining

LIFO

The last-in first-out accounting method of valuing inventories.

FIFO

The first-in first-out accounting method of valuing inventories.

are the previously produced goods, at a cost of only $1. You can see that, although LIFO accounting accurately measures the cost of goods sold today, it understates the current value of the remaining inventory in an inflationary environment.

In contrast, under FIFO accounting, the cost of goods sold would be $1 million, and the end-of-year balance sheet value of the inventory is $1.1 million. The result is that the LIFO firm has both a lower reported profit and a lower balance sheet value of inventories than the FIFO firm.

LIFO is preferred over FIFO in computing economics earnings (that is, real sustainable cash flow), because it uses up-to-date prices to evaluate the cost of goods sold. However, LIFO accounting induces balance sheet distortions when it values investment in inventories at original cost. This practice results in an upward bias in ROE because the investment base on which return is earned is undervalued.

Depreciation

Another source of problems is the measurement of depreciation, which is a key factor in computing true earnings. The accounting and economic measures of depreciation can differ markedly. According to the *economic* definition, depreciation is the amount of a firm's operating cash flow that must be reinvested in the firm to sustain its real cash flow at the current level.

The *accounting* measurement is quite different. Accounting depreciation is the amount of the original acquisition cost of an asset that is allocated to each accounting period over an arbitrarily specified life of the asset. This is the figure reported in financial statements.

Assume, for example, that a firm buys machines with a useful economic life of 20 years at $100,000 apiece. In its financial statements, however, the firm can depreciate the machines over 10 years using the straight-line method, for $10,000 per year in depreciation. Thus, after 10 years, a machine will be fully depreciated on the books, even though it remains a productive asset that will not need replacement for another 10 years.

In computing accounting earnings, this firm will overestimate depreciation in the first 10 years of the machine's economic life and underestimate it in the last 10 years. This will cause reported earnings to be understated compared with economic earnings in the first 10 years and overstated in the last 10 years.

Depreciation comparability problems add one more wrinkle. A firm can use different depreciation methods for tax purposes than for other reporting purposes. Most firms use accelerated depreciation methods for tax purposes and straight-line depreciation in published financial statements. There also are differences across firms in their estimates of the depreciable life of plant, equipment, and other depreciable assets.

Another complication arises from inflation. Because conventional depreciation is based on historical costs rather than on the current replacement cost of assets, measured depreciation in periods of inflation is understated relative to replacement cost, and *real* economic income (sustainable cash flow) is correspondingly overstated.

For example, suppose Generic Products, Inc., has a machine with a three-year useful life that originally cost $3 million. Annual straight-line depreciation is $1 million, regardless of what happens to the replacement cost of the machine. Suppose inflation in the first year turns out to be 10%. Then the true annual depreciation expense is $1.1 million in current terms, while conventionally measured depreciation remains fixed at $1 million per year. Accounting income therefore overstates *real* economic income.

Inflation and Interest Expense

While inflation can cause distortions in the measurement of a firm's inventory and depreciation costs, it has perhaps an even greater effect on the calculation of *real* interest expense. Nominal interest rates include an inflation premium that compensates the lender for inflation-induced erosion in the real value of principal. From the perspective of both lender and borrower, therefore, part of what is conventionally measured as interest expense should be treated more properly as repayment of principal.

Suppose Generic Products has debt outstanding with a face value of $10 million at an interest rate of 10% per year. Interest expense as conventionally measured is $1 million per year. However, suppose inflation during the year is 6%, so that the real interest rate is 4%. Then $.6 million of what appears as interest expense on the income statement is really an inflation premium, or compensation for the anticipated reduction in the real value of the $10 million principal; only $.4 million is *real* interest expense. The $.6 million reduction in the purchasing power of the outstanding principal may be thought of as repayment of principal, rather than as an interest expense. Real income of the firm is, therefore, understated by $.6 million.

Mismeasurement of real interest means that inflation results in an underestimate of real income. The effects of inflation on the reported values of inventories and depreciation that we have discussed work in the opposite direction.

CONCEPT *check* **14.5**

In a period of rapid inflation, companies ABC and XYZ have the same *reported* earnings. ABC uses LIFO inventory accounting, has relatively fewer depreciable assets, and has more debt than XYZ. XYZ uses FIFO inventory accounting. Which company has the higher *real* income and why?

Fair Value Accounting

Many major assets and liabilities do not have easily observable values. For example, we cannot simply look up the values of employee stock options, health care benefits for retired employees, or buildings and other real estate. More recently, even values of financial securities such as subprime-mortgage pools and derivative contracts backed by these pools have come into question as trading in these instruments dried up. Without well-functioning markets, estimating (much less observing) market values is prone to substantial error. While the true financial status of a firm may depend critically on these values, which can swing widely over time, common practice has been to simply value them at historic cost. Proponents of **fair value accounting** also known as **mark-to-market accounting** argue that financial statements would give a truer picture of the firm if they better reflected the current market values of all assets and liabilities.

The Financial Accounting Standards Board's Statement No. 157 places assets in one of three "buckets." Level 1 assets are traded in active markets and therefore should be valued at their market price. Level 2 assets are not actively traded, but their values still may be estimated using observable market data on similar assets. Level 3 assets can be valued only with inputs that are difficult to observe. Level 2 and 3 assets may be valued using pricing models, for example, based on a theoretical price derived from a computer model. Rather than mark to market, these values are often called "mark to model," although they are also disparagingly known as mark-to-make-believe, as the estimates are so prone to manipulation by creative use of model inputs.

Critics of fair value accounting argue that it relies too heavily on estimates. Such estimates potentially introduce considerable noise in firms' accounts and can induce great profit volatility as fluctuations in asset valuations are recognized. Even worse, subjective valuations may offer management a tempting tool to manipulate earnings or the apparent financial condition of the firm at opportune times. For example, Bergstresser, Desai, and Rauh (2006) find that firms make more aggressive assumptions about returns on defined benefit pension plans (which lowers the computed present value of pension obligations) during periods in which executives are actively exercising their stock options.

A contentious debate over the application of fair value accounting to troubled financial institutions erupted in 2008. Some feel that mark-to-market accounting exacerbated the financial meltdown; others that a failure to mark would be tantamount to willfully ignoring reality and abdicating the responsibility to redress problems at nearly or already insolvent banks. The nearby box discusses the debate.

fair value or mark-to-market accounting

Use of current market values rather than historic cost in the firm's financial statements.

MARK-TO-MARKET ACCOUNTING: CURE OR DISEASE?

As banks and other institutions holding mortgage-backed securities revalued their portfolios throughout 2008, their net worth fell along with the value of those securities. The losses on these securities were painful enough but, in addition, they led to knock-on effects that only increased the banks' woes. For example, banks are required to maintain adequate levels of capital relative to assets. If capital reserves decline, a bank may be forced to shrink until its remaining capital is once again adequate compared to its asset base. But such shrinkage may require the bank to cut back on its lending, which restricts its customers' access to credit. It may also have to sell some of its assets; and if many banks attempt to shrink their portfolios at once, waves of forced sales may put further pressure on prices, resulting in additional write-downs and reductions to capital in a self-feeding cycle. Critics of mark-to-market accounting therefore conclude that it has acted to exacerbate the problems of an already reeling economy.

Advocates of fair value accounting contend that the critics confuse the message with the messenger. Mark-to-market accounting makes transparent losses that have already been incurred, but it does not cause those losses. But the critics retort that when markets are faltering, market prices may be unreliable. If trading activity has largely broken down, and assets can be sold only at fire-sale prices, then those prices may no longer be indicative of fundamental value. Markets cannot be efficient if they are not even functioning. In the turmoil surrounding the defaulted mortgages weighing down bank portfolios, one of the early proposals of then–Treasury Secretary Henry Paulson was for the government to buy bad assets at "hold to maturity" prices based on estimates of intrinsic value in a normally functioning market. Variants of that proposal are still under consideration. In the same spirit, in April 2009, FASB granted financial firms more leeway to put off write-downs on assets deemed to be only "temporarily impaired."

Waiving write-down requirements may best be viewed as thinly veiled regulatory forbearance. Regulators know that losses have been incurred and that capital has been impaired. But by allowing firms to carry assets on their books at model rather than market prices, the unpleasant implications of that fact for capital adequacy may be politely ignored for a time. Even so, if the goal is to avoid forced sales in a distressed market, transparency may nevertheless be the best policy. Better to acknowledge losses and explicitly modify capital regulations to help institutions recover their footing in a difficult economy, than to deal with losses by ignoring them. After all, why bother preparing financial statements if they are allowed to obscure the true condition of the firm?

Before abandoning fair value accounting, it would be prudent to consider the alternative. Traditional historic-cost accounting, which would allow firms to carry assets on the books at their original purchase price, has even less to recommend it. It would leave investors without an accurate sense of the condition of shaky institutions, and by the same token lessen the pressure on those firms to get their houses in order. Dealing with losses must surely first require acknowledging them.

Quality of Earnings and Accounting Practices

Many firms make accounting choices that present their financial statements in the best possible light. The different choices that firms can make give rise to the comparability problems we have discussed. As a result, earnings statements for different companies may be more or less rosy presentations of true "economic earnings"—sustainable cash flow that can be paid to shareholders without impairing the firm's productive capacity. Analysts commonly evaluate the **quality of earnings** reported by a firm. This concept refers to the realism and conservatism of the earnings number, in other words, the extent to which we might expect the reported level of earnings to be sustained.

quality of earnings

The realism and sustainability of reported earnings.

Examples of the accounting choices that influence quality of earnings are:

- *Allowance for bad debt.* Most firms sell goods using trade credit and must make an allowance for bad debt. An unrealistically low allowance reduces the quality of reported earnings. Look for a rising average collection period on accounts receivable as evidence of potential problems with future collections.

- *Nonrecurring items.* Some items that affect earnings should not be expected to recur regularly. These include asset sales, effects of accounting changes, effects of exchange rate movements, or unusual investment income. For example, in 2003, which was a banner year for equity returns, some firms enjoyed large investment returns on securities held. These contributed to that year's earnings, but should not be expected to repeat regularly. They would be considered a "low-quality" component of earnings. Similarly gains in corporate pension plans can generate large, but one-time, contributions to reported earnings.

- *Earnings smoothing.* In 2003, Freddie Mac was the subject of a major accounting scandal, with the disclosure that it had improperly reclassified mortgages held in its portfolio in an attempt to *reduce* its current earnings. Similarly, in the 1990s, W. R. Grace chose to offset high earnings in one of its subsidiaries by setting aside extra reserves. Why would these firms take such actions? Because later, if earnings turned down, they could "release" earnings by reversing these transactions, and thereby create the appearance of steady earnings growth. Wall Street likes strong, steady earnings growth, but these firms planned to provide such growth only cosmetically, through earnings management.

- *Revenue recognition.* Under GAAP accounting, a firm is allowed to recognize a sale before it is paid. This is why firms have accounts receivable. But sometimes it can be hard to know when to recognize sales. For example, suppose a computer firm signs a contract to provide products and services over a five-year period. Should the revenue be booked immediately or spread out over five years? A more extreme version of this problem is called "channel stuffing," in which firms "sell" large quantities of goods to customers, but give them the right to later either refuse delivery or return the product. The revenue from the "sale" is booked now, but the likely returns are not recognized until they occur (in a future accounting period). According to the SEC, Sunbeam, which filed for bankruptcy in 2001, generated $60 million in fraudulent profits in 1999 using this technique. If you see accounts receivable increasing far faster than sales, or becoming a larger percentage of total assets, beware of these practices. Given the wide latitude firms have in how they recognize revenue, many analysts choose instead to concentrate on cash flow, which is far harder for a company to manipulate.

- *Off-balance-sheet assets and liabilities.* Suppose that one firm guarantees the outstanding debt of another firm, perhaps a firm in which it has an ownership stake. That obligation ought to be disclosed as a *contingent liability,* since it may require payments down the road. But these obligations may not be reported as part of the firm's outstanding debt. Similarly, leasing may be used to manage off-balance-sheet assets and liabilities. Airlines, for example, may show no aircraft on their balance sheets but have long-term leases that are virtually equivalent to debt-financed ownership. However, if the leases are treated as operating rather than capital leases, they may appear only as footnotes to the financial statements.

International Accounting Conventions

The examples cited above illustrate some of the problems that analysts can encounter when attempting to interpret financial data. Even greater problems arise in the interpretation of the financial statements of foreign firms. This is because these firms do not follow GAAP guidelines. Accounting practices in various countries differ to greater or lesser extents from U.S. standards. Here are some of the major issues that you should be aware of when using the financial statements of foreign firms.

Reserving practices   Many countries allow firms considerably more discretion in setting aside reserves for future contingencies than is typical in the United States. Because additions to reserves result in a charge against income, reported earnings are far more subject to managerial discretion than in the United States.

Depreciation   In the United States, firms typically maintain separate sets of accounts for tax and reporting purposes. For example, accelerated depreciation is used for tax purposes, while straight-line depreciation is used for reporting purposes. In contrast, most other countries do not allow dual sets of accounts, and most firms in foreign countries use accelerated depreciation to minimize taxes despite the fact that it results in lower reported earnings. This makes reported earnings of foreign firms lower than they would be if the firms were allowed to follow the U.S. practice.

Intangibles   Treatment of intangibles can vary widely. Are they amortized or expensed? If amortized, over what period? Such issues can have a large impact on reported profits.

FIGURE 14.2

Adjusted versus reported
price–earnings ratios

Source: Lawrence S. Speidell
and Vinod Bavishi, "GAAP
Arbitrage: Valuation Opportunities
in International Accounting
Standards," *Financial Analysts
Journal,* November–December
1992, pp. 58–66. Copyright
1992. Association for Investment
Management and Research.
Reproduced and republished from
Financial Analysts Journal with
permission from the Association
for Investment Management and
Research. All Rights Reserved.

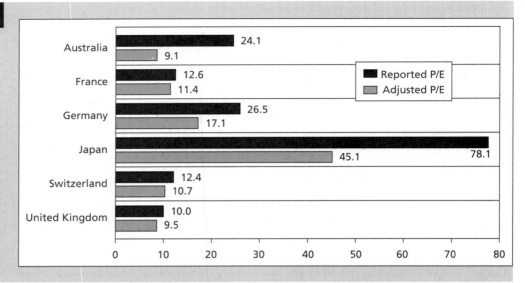

The effect of different country practices can be substantial. Figure 14.2, compares average P/E ratios for several countries as reported and restated on a common basis. While P/E multiples have changed considerably since this study was published, these results illustrate how different accounting rules can have a big impact on these ratios.

Such differences in international accounting standards have become more of a problem as the drive to globally integrate capital markets progresses. For example, many foreign firms would like to list their shares on the New York Stock Exchange in order to more easily tap the U.S. equity markets, and the NYSE would like to have those firms listed. But the Securities and Exchange Commission (SEC) until recently has not allowed such shares to be listed unless the firms prepared their financial statements in accordance with U.S. GAAP standards. This has limited the listing of non-U.S. companies dramatically.

**international financial
reporting standards**

A principles-based set of
accounting rules adopted by
around 100 countries around
the world including the
European Union.

In contrast, the European Union has moved to institute common **international financial reporting standards** (IFRS) across the EU. IFRS seem on their way to becoming global standards, even outside the European Union. By 2008, over 100 countries had adopted them, and they were making inroads even in the United States. In November 2007, the SEC began allowing foreign firms to issue securities in the U.S. if their financial statements were prepared using IFRS. The SEC noted that the goal of its new ruling is to encourage the development of IFRS as a uniform global standard to enhance consistency and comparability. In 2008, the SEC went even further when it proposed allowing large U.S. multinational firms to report earnings using IFRS rather than GAAP starting in 2010, with all U.S. firms to follow by 2014.

The major difference between IFRS and GAAP has to do with "principles"-versus "rules"-based standards. U.S. rules are detailed, explicit, and lengthy. European rules are more flexible, but firms must be prepared to demonstrate that they have conformed to general principles meant to ensure that financial accounts faithfully reflect the actual status of the firm.

14.8 Value Investing: The Graham Technique

No presentation of fundamental security analysis would be complete without a discussion of the ideas of Benjamin Graham, the greatest of the investment "gurus." Until the evolution of modern portfolio theory in the latter half of the twentieth century, Graham was the single most important thinker, writer, and teacher in the field of investment analysis. His influence on investment professionals remains very strong.

Graham's magnum opus is *Security Analysis,* written with Columbia Professor David Dodd in 1934. Its message is similar to the ideas presented in this chapter. Graham believed careful analysis of a firm's financial statements could turn up bargain stocks. Over the years, he developed many different rules for determining the most important financial ratios and the critical values for judging a stock to be undervalued. Through many editions, his book has had a profound influence on investment professionals. It has been so influential and successful, in fact, that widespread adoption of Graham's techniques has led to elimination of the very bargains they are designed to identify.

In a 1976 seminar Graham said[6]

> I am no longer an advocate of elaborate techniques of security analysis in order to find superior value opportunities. This was a rewarding activity, say, forty years ago, when our textbook "Graham and Dodd" was first published; but the situation has changed a good deal since then. In the old days any well-trained security analyst could do a good professional job of selecting undervalued issues through detailed studies; but in the light of the enormous amount of research now being carried on, I doubt whether in most cases such extensive efforts will generate sufficiently superior selections to justify their cost. To that very limited extent I'm on the side of the "efficient market" school of thought now generally accepted by the professors.

Nonetheless, in that same seminar, Graham suggested a simplified approach to identifying bargain stocks:

> My first, more limited, technique confines itself to the purchase of common stocks at less than their working-capital value, or net current-asset value, giving no weight to the plant and other fixed assets, and deducting all liabilities in full from the current assets. We used this approach extensively in managing investment funds, and over a thirty-odd-year period we must have earned an average of some 20% per year from this source. For awhile, however, after the mid-1950s, this brand of buying opportunity became very scarce because of the pervasive bull market. But it has returned in quantity since the 1973–1974 decline. In January 1976 we counted over 100 such issues in the Standard & Poor's *Stock Guide*—about 10% of the total. I consider it a foolproof method of systematic investment—once again, not on the basis of individual results but in terms of the expectable group outcome.

There are two convenient sources of information for those interested in trying out the Graham technique. Both Standard & Poor's *Outlook* and *The Value Line Investment Survey* carry lists of stocks selling below net working capital value.

[6]As cited by John Train in *Money Masters* (New York: Harper & Row, Publishers, Inc., 1987).

SUMMARY

- The primary focus of the security analyst should be the firm's real economic earnings rather than its reported earnings. Accounting earnings as reported in financial statements can be a biased estimate of real economic earnings, although empirical studies reveal that reported earnings convey considerable information concerning a firm's prospects.
- A firm's ROE is a key determinant of the growth rate of its earnings. ROE is affected profoundly by the firm's degree of financial leverage. An increase in a firm's debt/equity ratio will raise its ROE and hence its growth rate only if the interest rate on the debt is less than the firm's return on assets.
- It is often helpful to the analyst to decompose a firm's ROE ratio into the product of several accounting ratios and to analyze their separate behavior over time and across companies within an industry. A useful breakdown is

$$\text{ROE} = \frac{\text{Net profits}}{\text{Pretax profits}} \times \frac{\text{Pre-tax profits}}{\text{EBIT}} \times \frac{\text{EBIT}}{\text{Sales}} \times \frac{\text{Sales}}{\text{Assets}} \times \frac{\text{Assets}}{\text{Equity}}$$

- Other accounting ratios that have a bearing on a firm's profitability and/or risk are fixed-asset turnover, inventory turnover, days receivable, and the current, quick, and interest coverage ratios.
- Two ratios that make use of the market price of the firm's common stock in addition to its financial statements are the ratios of market-to-book value and price to earnings. Analysts sometimes take low values for these ratios as a margin of safety or a sign that the stock is a bargain.
- A major problem in the use of data obtained from a firm's financial statements is comparability. Firms have a great deal of latitude in how they choose to compute various items of revenue and expense. It is, therefore, necessary for the security analyst to adjust accounting earnings and financial ratios to a uniform standard before attempting to compare financial results across firms.
- Comparability problems can be acute in a period of inflation. Inflation can create distortions in accounting for inventories, depreciation, and interest expense.

KEY TERMS

accounting earnings, 441	FIFO, 455	price–earnings ratio, 449
acid test ratio, 448	income statement, 436	profit margin, 443
average collection period, 446	interest coverage ratio, 444	quality of earnings, 458
balance sheet, 437	international financial reporting standards, 460	quick ratio, 448
cash ratio, 448		residual income, 452
current ratio, 447	inventory turnover ratio, 446	return on assets, 441
days receivables, 446	leverage ratio, 445	return on equity, 441
DuPont system, 443	LIFO, 455	return on sales, 443
earnings yield, 449	mark-to-market accounting, 457	statement of cash flows, 437
economic earnings, 441		
economic value added, 452	market-to-book-value ratio, 448	times interest earned, 444
fair value accounting, 457		total asset turnover, 444

PROBLEM SETS

Select problems are available in McGraw-Hill Connect. Please see the packaging options section of the preface for more information.

Basic

1. Use the following financial statements of Heifer Sports Inc in Table 14.14 to find Heifer's
   a. Inventory turnover ratio in 2009.
   b. Debtequity ratio in 2009.
   c. Cash flow from operating activities in 2009.
   d. Average collection period.
   e. Asset turnover ratio.
   f. Interest coverage ratio.
   g. Operating profit margin.
   h. Return on equity.
   i. P/E ratio.
   j. Compound leverage ratio.
   k. Net cash provided by operating activities.

TABLE 14.14	Income Statement	2009	
Heifer Sports Financial Statements	Sales	$5,500,000	
	Cost of goods sold	2,850,000	
	Depreciation	280,000	
	Selling & administrative expenses	1,500,000	
	EBIT	870,000	
	Interest expense	130,000	
	Taxable income	740,000	
	Taxes	330,000	
	Net income	$ 410,000	
	Balance Sheet, year-end	**2009**	**2008**
	Assets		
	Cash	$ 50,000	$ 40,000
	Accounts receivable	660,000	690,000
	Inventory	490,000	480,000
	Total current assets	$1,200,000	$1,210,000
	Fixed assets	3,100,000	2,800,000
	Total assets	$4,300,000	$4,010,000
	Liabilities and shareholders' equity		
	Accounts payable	$ 340,000	$ 450,000
	Short-term debt	480,000	550,000
	Total current liabilities	$ 820,000	$1,000,000
	Long-term bonds	2,520,000	2,200,000
	Total liabilities	$3,340,000	$3,200,000
	Common stock	$ 310,000	$ 310,000
	Retained earnings	650,000	500,000
	Total shareholders' equity	$ 960,000	810,000
	Total liabilities and shareholders' equity	$4,300,000	$4,010,000

2. Use the following cash flow data for Rocket Transport to find Rocket's
   a. Net cash provided by or used in investing activities.
   b. Net cash provided by or used in financing activities.
   c. Net increase or decrease in cash for the year.

Cash dividend	$ 80,000
Purchase of bus	$ 33,000
Interest paid on debt	$ 25,000
Sales of old equipment	$ 72,000
Repurchase of stock	$ 55,000
Cash payments to suppliers	$ 95,000
Cash collections from customers	$300,000

3. The Crusty Pie Co., which specializes in apple turnovers, has a return on sales higher than the industry average, yet its ROA is the same as the industry average. How can you explain this?

4. The ABC Corporation has a profit margin on sales below the industry average, yet its ROA is above the industry average. What does this imply about its asset turnover?

5. A company's current ratio is 2.0. If the company uses cash to retire notes payable due within one year, would this transaction increase or decrease the current ratio? What about the asset turnover ratio?

6. Cash flow from investing activities *excludes:*
   a. Cash paid for acquisitions.
   b. Cash received from the sale of fixed assets.
   c. Inventory increases due to a new (internally developed) product line.
   d. All of the above.

7. Cash flow from operating activities *includes:*
   a. Inventory increases resulting from acquisitions.
   b. Inventory changes due to changing exchange rates.
   c. Interest paid to bondholders.
   d. Dividends paid to stockholders.

Intermediate

8. Use the DuPont system and the following data to find return on equity.
   - Leverage ratio   2.2
   - Total asset turnover   2.0
   - Net profit margin   5.5%
   - Dividend payout ratio   31.8%

   What is the company's return on equity?

9. A firm has an ROE of 3%, a debt/equity ratio of .5, a tax rate of 35%, and pays an interest rate of 6% on its debt. What is its operating ROA?

10. A firm has a tax burden ratio of .75, a leverage ratio of 1.25, an interest burden of .6, and a return on sales of 10%. The firm generates $2.40 in sales per dollar of assets. What is the firm's ROE?

11. An analyst gathers the following information about Meyer, Inc.:
   - Meyer has 1,000 shares of 8% cumulative preferred stock outstanding, with a par value of $100, and liquidation value of $110.
   - Meyer has 20,000 shares of common stock outstanding, with a par value of $20.
   - Meyer had retained earnings at the beginning of the year of $5,000,000.
   - Net income for the year was $70,000.
   - This year, for the first time in its history, Meyer paid no dividends on preferred or common stock.

   What is the book value per share of Meyer's common stock?

CFA Problems

1. Jones Group has been generating stable after-tax return on equity (ROE) despite declining operating income. Explain how it might be able to maintain its stable after-tax ROE.

2. Which of the following *best* explains a ratio of "net sales to average net fixed assets" that *exceeds* the industry average?
   a. The firm added to its plant and equipment in the past few years.
   b. The firm makes less efficient use of its assets than other firms.
   c. The firm has a lot of old plant and equipment.
   d. The firm uses straight-line depreciation.

3. The information in the following table comes from the 2007 financial statements of QuickBrush Company and SmileWhite Corporation:

NOTES TO THE 2007 FINANCIAL STATEMENTS		
	QuickBrush	**SmileWhite**
Goodwill	The company amortizes goodwill over 20 years.	The company amortizes goodwill over 5 years.
Property, plant, and equipment	The company uses a straight-line depreciation method over the economic lives of the assets, which range from 5 to 20 years for buildings.	The company uses an accelerated depreciation method over the economic lives of the assets, which range from 5 to 20 years for buildings.
Accounts receivable	The company uses a bad debt allowance of 2% of accounts receivable.	The company uses a bad debt allowance of 5% of accounts receivable.

Determine which company has the higher quality of earnings by discussing *each* of the *three* notes.

4. The cash flow data of Palomba Pizza Stores for the year ended December 31, 2009, are as follows:

Cash payment of dividends	$ 35,000
Purchase of land	14,000
Cash payments for interest	10,000
Cash payments for salaries	45,000
Sale of equipment	38,000
Retirement of common stock	25,000
Purchase of equipment	30,000
Cash payments to suppliers	85,000
Cash collections from customers	250,000
Cash at beginning of year	50,000

    a. Prepare a statement of cash flows for Palomba showing:
- Net cash provided by operating activities.
- Net cash provided by or used in investing activities.
- Net cash provided by or used in financing activities.

    b. Discuss, from an analyst's viewpoint, the purpose of classifying cash flows into the three categories listed above.

5. The financial statements for Chicago Refrigerator Inc. (see Tables 14.5 and 14.6) are to be used to compute the ratios *a* through *h* for 2009.
    a. Quick ratio.
    b. Return on assets.
    c. Return on common shareholders' equity.
    d. Earnings per share of common stock.
    e. Profit margin.
    f. Times interest earned.
    g. Inventory turnover.
    h. Leverage ratio.

6. Janet Ludlow is a recently hired analyst. After describing the electric toothbrush industry, her first report focuses on two companies, QuickBrush Company and SmileWhite Corporation, and concludes:

QuickBrush is a more profitable company than SmileWhite, as indicated by the 40% sales growth and substantially higher margins it has produced over the last few years. SmileWhite's sales and earnings are growing at a 10% rate and produce much lower margins. We do not think

TABLE 14.15

Chicago Refrigerator Inc. balance sheet, as of December 31 ($ thousands)

	2008	2009
Assets		
Current assets		
Cash	$ 683	$ 325
Accounts receivable	1,490	3,599
Inventories	1,415	2,423
Prepaid expenses	15	13
Total current assets	$3,603	$6,360
Property, plant, equipment, net	1,066	1,541
Other	123	157
Total assets	$4,792	$8,058
Liabilities		
Current liabilities		
Notes payable to bank	$ —	$ 875
Current portion of long-term debt	38	115
Accounts payable	485	933
Estimated income tax	588	472
Accrued expenses	576	586
Customer advance payment	34	963
Total current liabilities	$1,721	$3,945
Long-term debt	122	179
Other liabilities	81	131
Total liabilities	$1,924	$4,255
Shareholders' equity		
Common stock, $1 par value 1,000,000 shares authorized; 550,000 and 829,000 outstanding, respectively	$ 550	$ 829
Preferred stock, Series A 10%; $25.00 par value; 25,000 authorized; 20,000 and 18,000 outstanding, respectively	500	450
Additional paid-in capital	450	575
Retained earnings	1,368	1,949
Total shareholders' equity	$2,868	$3,803
Total liabilities and shareholders' equity	$4,792	$8,058

TABLE 14.16

Chicago Refrigerator Inc. income statement, years ending December 31 ($ thousands)

	2008	2009
Net sales	$7,570	$12,065
Other income, net	261	345
Total revenues	$7,831	$12,410
Cost of goods sold	$4,850	$ 8,048
General administrative and marketing expenses	1,531	2,025
Interest expense	22	78
Total costs and expenses	$6,403	$10,151
Net income before tax	$1,428	$ 2,259
Income tax	628	994
Net income	$ 800	$ 1,265

SmileWhite is capable of growing faster than its recent growth rate of 10% whereas QuickBrush can sustain a 30% long-term growth rate.

a. Criticize Ludlow's analysis and conclusion that QuickBrush is more profitable, as defined by return on equity (ROE), than SmileWhite and that it has a higher sustainable growth rate. Use only the information provided in Tables 14.17 and 14.18. Support your criticism by calculating and analyzing:
- The five components that determine ROE.
- The two ratios that determine sustainable growth: ROE and plowback.

b. Explain how QuickBrush has produced an average annual earnings per share (EPS) growth rate of 40% over the last two years with an ROE that has been declining. Use only the information provided in Table 14.17.

TABLE 14.17
Quickbrush Company financial statements: Yearly data ($000 except per share data)

Income Statement	December 2007	December 2008	December 2009
Revenue	$3,480	$5,400	$7,760
Cost of goods sold	2,700	4,270	6,050
Selling, general, and admin. expense	500	690	1,000
Depreciation and amortization	30	40	50
Operating income (EBIT)	$ 250	$ 400	$ 660
Interest expense	0	0	0
Income before taxes	$ 250	$ 400	$ 660
Income taxes	60	110	215
Income after taxes	$ 190	$ 290	$ 445
Diluted EPS	$ 0.60	$ 0.84	$ 1.18
Average shares outstanding (000)	317	346	376

Financial Statistics	December 2007	December 2008	December 2009	3-Year Average
COGS as % of sales	77.59%	79.07%	77.96%	78.24%
General & admin. as % of sales	14.37	12.78	12.89	13.16
Operating margin (%)	7.18	7.41	8.51	
Pretax income/EBIT (%)	100.00	100.00	100.00	
Tax rate (%)	24.00	27.50	32.58	

Balance Sheet	December 2007	December 2008	December 2009
Cash and cash equivalents	$ 460	$ 50	$ 480
Accounts receivable	540	720	950
Inventories	300	430	590
Net property, plant, and equipment	760	1,830	3,450
Total assets	$2,060	$3,030	$5,470
Current liabilities	$ 860	$1,110	$1,750
Total liabilities	$ 860	$1,110	$1,750
Stockholders' equity	1,200	1,920	3,720
Total liabilities and equity	$2,060	$3,030	$5,470
Market price per share	$21.00	$30.00	$45.00
Book value per share	$ 3.79	$ 5.55	$ 9.89
Annual dividend per share	$ 0.00	$ 0.00	$ 0.00

TABLE 14.18

Smilewhite Corporation financial statements: Yearly data ($000 except per share data)

Income Statement	December 2007	December 2008	December 2009
Revenue	$104,000	$110,400	$119,200
Cost of goods sold	72,800	75,100	79,300
Selling, general, and admin. expense	20,300	22,800	23,900
Depreciation and amortization	4,200	5,600	8,300
Operating income (EBIT)	$ 6,700	$ 6,900	$ 7,700
Interest expense	600	350	350
Income before taxes	$ 6,100	$ 6,550	$ 7,350
Income taxes	2,100	2,200	2,500
Income after taxes	$ 4,000	$ 4,350	$ 4,850
Diluted EPS	$ 2.16	$ 2.35	$ 2.62
Average shares outstanding (000)	1,850	1,850	1,850

Financial Statistics	December 2007	December 2008	December 2009	3-Year Average
COGS as % of sales	70.00%	68.00%	66.53%	68.10%
General & admin. as % of sales	19.52	20.64	20.05	20.08
Operating margin (%)	6.44	6.25	6.46	
Pretax income/EBIT (%)	91.04	94.93	95.45	
Tax rate (%)	34.43	33.59	34.01	

Balance Sheet	December 2007	December 2008	December 2009
Cash and cash equivalents	$ 7,900	$ 3,300	$ 1,700
Accounts receivable	7,500	8,000	9,000
Inventories	6,300	6,300	5,900
Net property, plant, and equipment	12,000	14,500	17,000
Total assets	$ 33,700	$ 32,100	$ 33,600
Current liabilities	$ 6,200	$ 7,800	$ 6,600
Long-term debt	9,000	4,300	4,300
Total liabilities	$ 15,200	$ 12,100	$ 10,900
Stockholders' equity	18,500	20,000	22,700
Total liabilities and equity	$ 33,700	$ 32,100	$ 33,600
Market price per share	$ 23.00	$ 26.00	$ 30.00
Book value per share	$ 10.00	$ 10.81	$ 12.27
Annual dividend per share	$ 1.42	$ 1.53	$ 1.72

7. Scott Kelly is reviewing MasterToy's financial statements in order to estimate its sustainable growth rate. Using the information presented in Table 14.19
   a. Identify and calculate the components of the DuPont formula.
   b. Calculate the ROE for 2009 using the components of the DuPont formula.
   c. Calculate the sustainable growth rate for 2009 from the firm's ROE and plowback ratios.

8. The DuPont formula defines the net return on shareholders' equity as a function of the following components:
   • Operating margin
   • Asset turnover

TABLE 14.19		**2008**	**2009**
Mastertoy, Inc.: Actual 2008 and estimated 2009 financial statements for fiscal year ending December 31 ($ millions, except per-share data)	**Income Statement**		
	Revenue	$4,750	$5,140
	Cost of goods sold	2,400	2,540
	Selling, general, and administrative	1,400	1,550
	Depreciation	180	210
	Goodwill amortization	10	10
	Operating income	$ 760	$ 830
	Interest expense	20	25
	Income before taxes	$ 740	$ 805
	Income taxes	265	295
	Net income	$ 475	$ 510
	Earnings per share	$ 1.79	$ 1.96
	Average shares outstanding (millions)	265	260
	Balance Sheet		
	Cash	$ 400	$ 400
	Accounts receivable	680	700
	Inventories	570	600
	Net property, plant, and equipment	800	870
	Intangibles	500	530
	Total assets	$2,950	$3,100
	Current liabilities	$ 550	$ 600
	Long-term debt	300	300
	Total liabilities	$ 850	$ 900
	Stockholders' equity	2,100	2,200
	Total liabilities and equity	$2,950	$3,100
	Book value per share	$ 7.92	$ 8.46
	Annual dividend per share	0.55	0.60

TABLE 14.20		**2006**	**2009**
Income statements and balance sheets	**Income statement data**		
	Revenues	$542	$979
	Operating income	38	76
	Depreciation and amortization	3	9
	Interest expense	3	0
	Pretax income	32	67
	Income taxes	13	37
	Net income after tax	$ 19	$ 30
	Balance sheet data		
	Fixed assets	$ 41	$ 70
	Total assets	245	291
	Working capital	123	157
	Total debt	16	0
	Total shareholders' equity	$159	$220

- Interest burden
- Financial leverage
- Income tax rate

Using *only* the data in Table 14.20:

a. Calculate each of the five components listed above for 2006 and 2009, and calculate the return on equity (ROE) for 2006 and 2009, using all of the five components.

b. Briefly discuss the impact of the changes in asset turnover and financial leverage on the change in ROE from 2006 to 2009.

STANDARD &POOR'S

Use data from the Standard & Poor's Market Insight Database at www.mhhe.com/edumarketinsight to answer the following questions.

1. Use Market Insight to find information about Vulcan Materials Company (VMC), Southwest Airlines (LUV), Honda Motor Company (HMC), Nordstrom, Inc. (JWN), and Abbott Laboratories (ABT). Use the Excel Analytics section to find the most recent Income Statement and Balance Sheet.

   a. Calculate the Operating Profit Margin (Operating Profit/Sales) and the Asset Turnover (Sales/Assets) for each firm.

   b. Calculate the Return on Assets directly (ROA = Operating Profit/Total Assets) and then confirm it by calculating ROA = Operating Margin × Asset Turnover.

   c. In what industries do these firms operate? Do the ratios make sense when you consider the industry types?

   d. For the firms that have relatively low ROAs, does the source of the problem seem to be the Operating Profit Margin, the Asset Turnover, or both?

   e. Calculate the return on equity (ROE = Net Income/Equity) for each firm. For the two firms with the lowest ROEs, perform a DuPont analysis to isolate the source(s) of the problem.

2. Select the Industry tab and choose the Home Furnishing industry. In the Compustat Reports section, click on the link to get a list of the subindustry constituents. Pick two companies from the list and do the following for each firm.

   a. Retrieve the latest annual Balance Sheet from the Excel Analytics section. Save it to your computer so you will be able to manipulate it and do calculations. Insert a column to the right of the last fiscal year's numbers. Calculate the common-size percentages for the Balance Sheet in the new column.

   b. Compare the firms' investments in accounts receivable, inventory, and net plant, property, and equipment. Which firm has more invested in these items on a percentage basis?

   c. Compare the firms' investments in current liabilities and long-term liabilities. Does one firm have a significantly higher burden in either of these areas?

   d. Analyze the firms' capital structures by examining the debt ratios and the percentages of preferred and common equity. How much do the firms' capital structures differ from each other?

3. Enter the Market Insight database and link to Company, then Population. Select a company of interest to you and link to its Annual Cash Flow Statement in the Excel Analytics section. Answer the following questions about the firm's cash flow activities.

   a. Did the firm have positive or negative cash flow from operations?

   b. Did the firm invest in or sell off long-term investments?

   c. What were the major sources of financing for the firm?

   d. What was the net change in cash?

   e. Did exchange rates have any effect on the firm's cash flows?

   Now follow the link to the Annual Ratio Report and answer these questions:

   f. How liquid is the firm?

   g. How well is the firm using its assets?

   h. How effectively is the firm using leverage?

   i. Is the firm profitable?

WEB *master* FINANCIAL STATEMENT ANALYSIS

Use the **moneycentral.msn.com/investor** site to research the stocks of Kraft Foods (KFT) and Sara Lee (SLE). Look in the financial results area to find the key ratios for each firm. Copy the indicated ratios into a spreadsheet and produce the charts described below.

1. Plot the following ratios for both firms and the industry on one column chart: five-year annual average sales growth rate, five-year annual average net income growth rate. Which firm is growing faster? How do the firms' growth rates compare to the industry's growth rates?

2. Plot the net profit margins for both firms and the industry on another column chart. How do the firms' profit margins compare to each other and to the industry average?

3. Plot the firms' and the industry's current and quick ratios on a third chart. Analyze the firms' liquidity status.

4. Look at the firms' return on equity ratios, both the ones for the current year and the five-year averages. Compare them to each other and to the industry average to see how the firm's investments are faring.

5. Record the receivables turnover, inventory turnover, and total asset turnover ratios for the firms and for the industry. How efficiently are the managers using these assets?

6. Click on the Research Wizard on the left-side menu and select the Comparison submenu to compare Kraft and Sara Lee. What items do you see that have not been previously considered but might be important in judging the financial health of the firms?

7. If you want to add one of the stocks to your portfolio, which one would you choose?

SOLUTIONS TO CONCEPT *checks*

14.1. A debt/equity ratio of 1 implies that Mordett will have $50 million of debt and $50 million of equity. Interest expense will be .09 × $50 million, or $4.5 million per year. Mordett's net profits and ROE over the business cycle will therefore be

Scenario	EBIT	Nodett			Mordett	
		Net Profits	ROE		Net Profits*	ROE†
Bad year	$ 5M	$3M	3%		$0.3M	0.6%
Normal year	10	6	6		3.3	6.6
Good year	15	9	9		6.3	12.6%

*Mordett's after-tax profits are given by: 0.6(EBIT − $4.5 million).
†Mordett's equity is only $50 million.

14.2. Ratio decomposition analysis for Mordett Corporation:

Year	ROE	(1) Net Profit / Pretax Profit	(2) Pretax Profit / EBIT	(3) EBIT / Sales (Margin)	(4) Sales / Assets (Turnover)	(5) Assets / Equity	(6) Compound Leverage Factor (2) × (5)
a. Bad year							
Nodett	.030	.6	1.000	.0625	0.800	1.000	1.000
Somdett	.018	.6	0.360	.0625	0.800	1.667	0.600
Mordett	.006	.6	0.100	.0625	0.800	2.000	0.200
b. Normal year							
Nodett	.060	.6	1.000	.100	1.000	1.000	1.000
Somdett	.068	.6	0.680	.100	1.000	1.667	1.134
Mordett	.066	.6	0.550	.100	1.000	2.000	1.100
c. Good year							
Nodett	.090	.6	1.000	.125	1.200	1.000	1.000
Somdett	.118	.6	0.787	.125	1.200	1.667	1.311
Mordett	.126	.6	0.700	.125	1.200	2.000	1.400

14.3. GI's ROE in 2010 was 3.03%, computed as follows:

$$ROE = \frac{\$5,285}{.5(\$171,843 + \$177,128)} = .0303, \text{ or } 3.03\%$$

Its P/E ratio was $21/$5.285 = 4.0 and its P/B ratio was $21/$177 = .12. Its earnings yield was 25% compared with an industry average of 12.5%.

Note that in our calculations the earnings yield does not equal ROE/(P/B) because we have computed ROE with *average* shareholders' equity in the denominator and P/B with *end*-of-year shareholders' equity in the denominator.

14.4. IBX Ratio Analysis

Year	ROE	(1) Net Profit / Pretax Profit	(2) Pretax Profit / EBIT	(3) EBIT / Sales (Margin)	(4) Sales / Assets (Turnover)	(5) Assets / Equity	(6) Compound Leverage Factor (2) × (5)	(7) ROA (3) × (4)
2011	11.4%	0.616	0.796	7.75%	1.375	2.175	1.731	10.65%
2008	10.2	0.636	0.932	8.88	1.311	1.474	1.374	11.65

ROE increased despite a decline in operating margin and a decline in the tax burden ratio because of increased leverage and turnover. Note that ROA declined from 11.65% in 2008 to 1.65% in 2011.

14.5. LIFO accounting results in lower reported earnings than does FIFO. Fewer assets to depreciate result in lower reported earnings because there is less bias associated with the use of historic cost. More debt results in lower reported earnings because the inflation premium in the interest rate is treated as part of interest.

Derivative Markets

Horror stories about large losses incurred by high-flying traders in derivatives markets such as those for futures and options periodically become a staple of the evening news. Indeed, there were some amazing losses to report in the last decade: several totaling hundreds of millions of dollars, and a few amounting to more than a billion dollars. Among the most notorious of these were the loss of $7.2 billion in equity futures contracts by Société Générale in January 2008 and the loss of more than $100 billion on positions in credit derivatives by American International Group that a resulted in massive government bailout in September 2008. In the wake of these debacles, some venerable institutions have gone under, notable among them Barings Bank, which once helped the U.S. finance the Louisiana Purchase and the British Empire finance the Napoleonic Wars.

These stories, while important, fascinating, and even occasionally scandalous, often miss the point. Derivatives, when misused, can indeed provide a quick path to insolvency. Used properly, however, they are potent tools for risk management and control. In fact, you will discover in these chapters that one firm was sued for *failing* to use derivatives to hedge price risk. One headline in *The Wall Street Journal* on hedging applications using derivatives was entitled "Index Options Touted as Providing Peace of Mind." Hardly material for bankruptcy court or the *National Enquirer*.

Derivatives provide a means to control risk that is qualitatively different from the techniques traditionally considered in portfolio theory. In contrast to the mean-variance analysis we discussed in Parts Two and Three, derivatives allow investors to change the *shape* of the probability distribution of investment returns. An entirely new approach to risk management follows from this insight.

The following chapters will explore how derivatives can be used as parts of a well-designed portfolio strategy. We will examine some popular portfolio strategies utilizing these securities and take a look at how derivatives are valued.

Chapter

Options Markets

After Studying This Chapter You Should Be Able To:

- Calculate the profit to various option positions as a function of ultimate security prices.

- Formulate option strategies to modify portfolio risk-return attributes.

- Identify embedded options in various securities and determine how option characteristics affect the prices of those securities.

Derivative securities, or simply *derivatives,* play a large and increasingly important role in financial markets. These are securities whose prices are determined by, or "derive from," the prices of other securities. These assets also are called *contingent claims* because their payoffs are contingent on the prices of other securities.

Options and futures contracts are both derivative securities. We will see that their payoffs depend on the value of other securities. Swap contracts, which we will discuss in Chapter 17, also are derivatives. Because the value of derivatives depends on the value of other securities, they can be powerful tools for both hedging and speculation. We will investigate these applications in the next three chapters, beginning in this chapter with options.

Trading of standardized options on a national exchange started in 1973 when the Chicago Board Options Exchange (CBOE) began listing call options. These contracts were almost immediately a great success, crowding out the previously existing over-the-counter trading in stock options.

Options contracts now are traded on several exchanges. They are written on common stock, stock indexes, foreign exchange, agricultural commodities, precious metals, and interest rates. In addition, the over-the-counter market also has enjoyed a tremendous resurgence in recent years as its trading in custom-tailored options has exploded. Popular and potent for modifying portfolio characteristics, options have become essential tools that every portfolio manager must understand.

This chapter is an introduction to options markets. It explains how puts and calls work and examines their investment characteristics. Popular option strategies are considered next. Finally, we will examine a range of securities with embedded options such as callable or convertible bonds.

15.1 The Option Contract

A **call option** gives its holder the right to purchase an asset for a specified price, called the **exercise** or **strike price,** on or before some specified expiration date. For example, a March call option on IBM stock with exercise price $100 entitles its owner to purchase IBM stock for a price of $100 at any time up to and including the expiration date in March. The holder of the call is not required to exercise the option. The holder will choose to exercise only if the market value of the asset to be purchased exceeds the exercise price. When the market price does exceed the exercise price, the option holder may "call away" the asset for the exercise price. Otherwise, the option may be left unexercised. If it is not exercised before the expiration date of the contract, a call option simply expires and no longer has value. Therefore, if the stock price is greater than the exercise price on the expiration date, the value of the call option will equal the difference between the stock price and the exercise price; but if the stock price is less than the exercise price at expiration, the call will be worthless. The *net profit* on the call is the value of the option minus the price originally paid to purchase it.

The purchase price of the option is called the **premium.** It represents the compensation the purchaser of the call must pay for the ability to exercise the option if exercise becomes profitable. Sellers of call options, who are said to *write* calls, receive premium income now as payment against the possibility they will be required at some later date to deliver the asset in return for an exercise price lower than the market value of the asset. If the option is left to expire worthless because the market price of the asset remains below the exercise price, then the writer of the call clears a profit equal to the premium income derived from the sale of the option. But if the call is exercised, the profit to the option writer is the premium income derived when the option was initially sold *minus* the difference between the value of the stock that must be delivered and the exercise price that is paid for those shares. If that difference is larger than the initial premium, the writer will incur a loss.

call option

The right to buy an asset at a specified exercise price on or before a specified expiration date.

exercise or strike price

Price set for calling (buying) an asset or putting (selling) an asset.

premium

Purchase price of an option.

EXAMPLE 15.1

Profits and Losses on a Call Option

Consider the March 2009 expiration call option on a share of IBM with an exercise price of $100 that was selling on February 6, 2009, for $2.80. Exchange-traded options expire on the third Friday of the expiration month, which for this option was March 20. Until the expiration date, the purchaser of the calls may buy shares of IBM for $100. On February 6, IBM sells for $96.14. Because the stock price is currently less than $100 a share, it clearly would not make sense at the moment to exercise the option to buy at $100. Indeed, if IBM remains below $100 by the expiration date, the call will be left to expire worthless. On the other hand, if IBM is selling above $100 at expiration, the call holder will find it optimal to exercise. For example, if IBM sells for $102 on March 20, the option will be exercised, as it will give its holder the right to pay $100 for a stock worth $102. The value of the option on the expiration date would then be

Value at expiration = Stock price − Exercise price = $102 − $100 = $2

Despite the $2 payoff at expiration, the call holder still realizes a loss of $.80 on the investment because the initial purchase price was $2.80:

Profit = Final value − Original investment = $2.00 − $2.80 = −$.80

Nevertheless, exercise of the call is optimal at expiration if the stock price exceeds the exercise price because the exercise proceeds will offset at least part of the cost of the option. The investor in the call will clear a profit if IBM is selling above $102.80 at the expiration date. At that stock price, the proceeds from exercise will just cover the original cost of the call.

put option

The right to sell an asset at a specified exercise price on or before a specified expiration date.

A **put option** gives its holder the right to *sell* an asset for a specified exercise or strike price on or before some expiration date. A March put on IBM with exercise price $100 entitles its owner to sell IBM stock to the put writer at a price of $100 at any time before expiration in March, even if the market price of IBM is less than $100. While profits on call options increase when the asset increases in value, profits on put options increase when the asset value falls. A put will be exercised only if the exercise price is greater than the price of the underlying asset, that is, only if its holder can deliver for the exercise price an asset with market value less than the exercise price. (One doesn't need to own the shares of IBM to exercise the IBM put option. Upon exercise, the investor's broker purchases the necessary shares of IBM at the market price and immediately delivers or "puts them" to an option writer for the exercise price. The owner of the put profits by the difference between the exercise price and market price.)

EXAMPLE 15.2

Profits and Losses on a Put Option

Now consider the March 2009 expiration put option on IBM with an exercise price of $100, selling on February 6, 2009, for $6.47. It entitled its owner to sell a share of IBM for $100 at any time until March 20. If the holder of the put buys a share of IBM and immediately exercises the right to sell at $100, net proceeds will be $100 − $96.14 = $3.86. Obviously, an investor who pays $6.47 for the put has no intention of exercising it immediately. If, on the other hand, IBM sells for $92 at expiration, the put turns out to be a profitable investment. Its value at expiration would be

Value at expiration = Exercise price − Stock price = $100 − $92 = $8

and the investor's profit would be $8.00 − $6.47 = $1.53. This is a holding-period return of $1.53/$6.47 = .236 or 23.6%—over only 42 days! Apparently, put option sellers on February 6 (who are on the other side of the transaction) did not consider this outcome very likely.

in the money

An option where exercise would be profitable.

out of the money

An option where exercise would not be profitable.

at the money

An option where the exercise price and asset price are equal.

An option is described as **in the money** when its exercise would produce a positive payoff for its holder. An option is **out of the money** when exercise would be unprofitable. Therefore, a call option is in the money when the exercise price is below the asset value. It is out of the money when the exercise price exceeds the asset value; no one would exercise the right to purchase for the exercise price an asset worth less than that price. Conversely, put options are in the money when the exercise price exceeds the asset's value, because delivery of the lower valued asset in exchange for the exercise price is profitable for the holder. Options are **at the money** when the exercise price and asset price are equal.

Options Trading

Some options trade on over-the-counter (OTC) markets. The OTC market offers the advantage that the terms of the option contract—the exercise price, expiration date, and number of shares committed—can be tailored to the needs of the traders. The costs of establishing an OTC option contract, however, are relatively high. Today, most option trading occurs on organized exchanges.

Options contracts traded on exchanges are standardized by allowable expiration dates and exercise prices for each listed option. Each stock option contract provides for the right to buy or sell 100 shares of stock (except when stock splits occur after the contract is listed and the contract is adjusted for the terms of the split).

Standardization of the terms of listed option contracts means all market participants trade in a limited and uniform set of securities. This increases the depth of trading in any particular option, which lowers trading costs and results in a more competitive market. Exchanges, therefore, offer two important benefits: ease of trading, which flows from a central marketplace where buyers and sellers or their representatives congregate, and a liquid secondary market where buyers and sellers of options can transact quickly and cheaply.

Until recently, most options trading in the U.S. took place on the Chicago Board Options Exchange. However, by 2003 the International Securities Exchange, an electronic exchange based in New York, had displaced the CBOE as the largest options market. Options trading in Europe is uniformly transacted in electronic exchanges.

IBM (IBM)								Underlying stock price: 96.14
			Call				**Put**	
Expiration	**Strike**	**Last**	**Volume**	**Open Interest**	**Last**	**Volume**	**Open Interest**
Feb	90	6.83	2501	17389	0.80	2504	9336
Mar	90	8.70	699	6764	2.60	1491	5072
Apr	90	9.96	101	8095	3.70	568	11298
Jul	90	13.44	994	5638	7.03	176	4066
Feb	95	3.20	6342	14541	2.25	2981	2749
Mar	95	5.30	1182	5319	4.28	918	3701
Apr	95	6.75	561	20533	5.63	779	8058
Jul	95	9.80	141	4628	9.00	81	620
Feb	100	1.00	7929	12437	4.90	782	599
Mar	100	2.80	3946	10965	6.47	1206	238
Apr	100	4.10	1517	8839	7.83	90	2385
Jul	100	7.35	115	4039	11.66	25	461

FIGURE 15.1

Options on IBM,
February 6, 2009

Source: *The Wall Street Journal Online,* February 7, 2009.
Reprinted by permission of *The Wall Street Journal,* Copyright © 2009 Dow Jones & Company, Inc. All Rights Reserved Worldwide.

Figure 15.1 is a reproduction of listed stock option quotations for IBM from *The Wall Street Journal Online.* The last recorded price on the New York Stock Exchange for IBM stock was $96.14 per share.[1] Options are reported at exercise prices of $90 through $100, in $5 increments. These values also are called the *strike prices.*

The exercise or strike prices bracket the stock price. While exercise prices generally are set at five-point intervals for stocks, larger intervals may be set for stocks selling above $100, and intervals of $2.50 may be used for stocks selling below $30.[2] If the stock price moves outside the range of exercise prices of the existing set of options, new options with appropriate exercise prices may be offered. Therefore, at any time, both in-the-money and out-of-the-money options will be listed, as in this example.

Figure 15.1 shows both call and put options listed for each exercise price and expiration date. The three sets of columns for each option report closing price, trading volume in contracts (each contract is for 100 shares of stock), and open interest (number of outstanding contracts).

When we compare the prices of call options with the same expiration date but different exercise prices in Figure 15.1, we see that the value of the call is lower when the exercise price is higher. This makes sense, for the right to purchase a share at a given exercise price is not as valuable when the purchase price is higher. Thus, the February expiration IBM call option with strike price $95 sells for only $3.20, while the $90 exercise price February call sells for $6.83. Conversely, put options are worth *more* when the exercise price is higher: You would rather have the right to sell IBM shares for $95 than for $90, and this is reflected in the prices of the puts. The February expiration put option with strike price $95 sells for $2.25, while the $90 exercise price February put sells for only $.80.

Not infrequently, you will find some options that go an entire day without trading. A lack of trading would be denoted by three dots in the volume and price columns in Figure 15.1. Because trading is infrequent, it is not unusual to find option prices that appear out of line with other prices. You might see, for example, two calls with different exercise prices that seem to sell for the same price. This discrepancy arises because the last trades for these options may have occurred at different times during the day. At any moment, the call with the lower exercise

[1]Occasionally, this price may not match the closing price listed for the stock on the stock market page. This is because some NYSE stocks also trade on exchanges that close after the NYSE, and the stock pages may reflect the more recent closing price. The options exchanges, however, close with the NYSE, so the closing NYSE stock price is appropriate for comparison with the closing option price.

[2]If a stock splits, the terms of the option—such as the exercise price—are adjusted to offset the impact of the split. Therefore, stock splits will also result in exercise prices that are not multiples of $5.

price must be worth more, and the put less, than an otherwise-identical call or put with a higher exercise price.

Expirations of most exchange-traded options tend to be fairly short, ranging up to only several months. For larger firms and several stock indexes, however, longer-term options are traded with expirations ranging up to three years. These options are called LEAPS (for Long-term Equity AnticiPation Securities).

a. What will be the proceeds and net profits to an investor who purchases the March 2009 expiration IBM calls with exercise price $95 if the stock price at option expiration is $85? What if the stock price at expiration is $105?

b. Now answer part (a) for an investor who purchases a March expiration IBM put option with exercise price $95.

American and European Options

American option

Can be exercised on or before its expiration.

European option

Can be exercised only at expiration.

An **American option** allows its holder to exercise the right to purchase (if a call) or sell (if a put) the underlying asset on or *before* the expiration date. **European options** allow for exercise of the option only on the expiration date. American-style options, because they allow more leeway than their European-style counterparts, generally will be more valuable. Most traded options in the U.S. are American-style. Foreign currency options and some stock index options are notable exceptions to this rule, however.

The Option Clearing Corporation

The Option Clearing Corporation (OCC), the clearinghouse for options trading, is jointly owned by the exchanges on which stock options are traded. The OCC places itself between options traders, becoming the effective buyer of the option from the writer and the effective writer of the option to the buyer. All individuals, therefore, deal only with the OCC, which effectively guarantees contract performance.

When an option holder exercises an option, the OCC arranges for a member firm with clients who have written that option to make good on the option obligation. The member firm selects from among its clients who have written that option to fulfill the contract. The selected client must deliver 100 shares of stock at a price equal to the exercise price for each call option contract written or must purchase 100 shares at the exercise price for each put option contract written.

Because the OCC guarantees contract performance, option writers are required to post margin to guarantee that they can fulfill their contract obligations. The margin required is determined in part by the amount by which the option is in the money, because that value is an indicator of the potential obligation of the option writer upon exercise of the option. When the required margin exceeds the posted margin, the writer will receive a margin call. The *holder* of the option need not post margin because the holder will exercise the option only if it is profitable to do so. After purchasing the option, no further money is at risk.

Margin requirements also depend on whether the underlying asset is held in portfolio. For example, a call option writer owning the stock against which the option is written can satisfy the margin requirement simply by allowing a broker to hold that stock in the brokerage account. The stock is then guaranteed to be available for delivery should the call option be exercised. If the underlying security is not owned, however, the margin requirement is determined by the value of the underlying security as well as by the amount by which the option is in or out of the money. Out-of-the-money options require less margin from the writer, for expected payouts are lower.

Other Listed Options

Options on assets other than stocks also are widely traded. These include options on market indexes and industry indexes, on foreign currency, and even on the futures prices of agricultural products, gold, silver, fixed-income securities, and stock indexes. We will discuss these in turn.

Index options An index option is a call or put based on a stock market index such as the S&P 500 or the New York Stock Exchange index. Index options are traded on several broad-based indexes as well as on several industry-specific indexes. We discussed many of these indexes in Chapter 2.

The construction of the indexes can vary across contracts or exchanges. For example, the S&P 100 Index is a value-weighted average of the 100 stocks in the Standard & Poor's 100 stock group. The weights are proportional to the market value of outstanding equity for each stock. The Dow Jones Industrial Average, by contrast, is a price-weighted average of 30 stocks.

Options contracts on many foreign stock indexes also trade. For example, options on the Nikkei Stock Index of Japanese stocks trade on the Chicago Mercantile Exchange. Options on European indexes such as the Financial Times Share Exchange (FTSE 100) and the Eurotrak index also trade. The Chicago Board Options Exchange as well as the American exchange list options on industry indexes such as the high-tech, pharmaceutical, or banking industries.

In contrast to stock options, index options do not require that the call writer actually "deliver the index" upon exercise or that the put writer "purchase the index." Instead, a cash settlement procedure is used. The payoff that would accrue upon exercise of the option is calculated, and the option writer simply pays that amount to the option holder. The payoff is equal to the difference between the exercise price of the option and the value of the index. For example, if the S&P index is at 880 when a call option on the index with exercise price 870 is exercised, the holder of the call receives a cash payment equal to the difference, $880 - 870$, times the contract multiplier of $100, or $1,000 per contract.

Options on the major indices, that is, the S&P 100 contract, often called the OEX after its ticker symbol, the S&P 500 Index (the SPX), and the Dow Jones Industrials (the DJX), are by far the most actively traded contracts on the CBOE. Together, these contracts dominate CBOE volume.

Futures options Futures options give their holders the right to buy or sell a specified futures contract, using as a futures price the exercise price of the option. Although the delivery process is slightly complicated, the terms of futures options contracts are designed in effect to allow the option to be written on the futures price itself. The option holder receives upon exercise net proceeds equal to the difference between the current futures price on the specified asset and the exercise price of the option. Thus, if the futures price is, say, $37, and the call has an exercise price of $35, the holder who exercises the call option on the futures gets a payoff of $2.

Foreign currency options A currency option offers the right to buy or sell a quantity of foreign currency for a specified amount of domestic currency. Currency option contracts call for purchase or sale of the currency in exchange for a specified number of U.S. dollars. Contracts are quoted in cents or fractions of a cent per unit of foreign currency.

There is an important difference between currency options and currency *futures* options. The former provide payoffs that depend on the difference between the exercise price and the exchange rate at expiration. The latter are foreign exchange futures options that provide payoffs that depend on the difference between the exercise price and the exchange rate *futures price* at expiration. Because exchange rates and exchange rate futures prices generally are not equal, the options and futures-options contracts will have different values, even with identical expiration dates and exercise prices. Today, trading volume in currency futures options dominates by far trading in currency options.

Interest rate options Options also are traded on Treasury notes and bonds, Treasury bills, certificates of deposit, GNMA pass-through certificates, and yields on Treasury securities of various maturities. Options on several interest rate futures also are traded. Among them are contracts on Treasury bond, Treasury note, municipal bond, LIBOR, Eurodollar, and British and euro-denominated interest rates.

15.2 | Values of Options at Expiration

Call Options

Recall that a call option gives the right to purchase a security at the exercise price. If you hold a call option on Fin Corp stock with an exercise price of $80, and Fin Corp is now selling at $90, you can exercise your option to purchase the stock at $80 and simultaneously sell the shares at the market price of $90, clearing $10 per share. Yet if the shares sell below $80, you can sit on the option and do nothing, realizing no further gain or loss. The value of the call option at expiration equals

$$\text{Payoff to call holder at expiration} = S_T - X \text{ if } S_T > X$$
$$0 \text{ if } S_T \leq X$$

where S_T is the value of the stock at the expiration date, and X is the exercise price. This formula emphasizes the option property because the payoff cannot be negative. That is, the option is exercised only if S_T exceeds X. If S_T is less than X, exercise does not occur, and the option expires with zero value. The loss to the option holder in this case equals the price originally paid. More generally, the *profit* to the option holder is the payoff to the option minus the original purchase price.

The value at expiration of the call with exercise price $80 is given by the following schedule.

Stock price	$60	$70	$80	$90	$100
Option value	0	0	0	10	20

For stock prices at or below $80, the option expires worthless. Above $80, the option is worth the excess of the stock price over $80. The option's value increases by one dollar for each dollar increase in the stock price. This relationship can be depicted graphically, as in Figure 15.2.

The solid line in Figure 15.2 depicts the value of the call at expiration. The net *profit* to the holder of the call equals the gross payoff less the initial investment in the call. Suppose the call cost $14. Then the profit to the call holder would be as given in the dashed (bottom) line of Figure 15.2. At option expiration, the investor has suffered a loss of $14 if the stock price is less than or equal to $80.

Profits do not become positive unless the stock price at expiration exceeds $94. The break-even point is $94, because at that price the payoff to the call, $S_T - X = \$94 - \$80 = \$14$, equals the cost paid to acquire the call. Hence, the call holder shows a profit only if the stock price is higher.

Conversely, the writer of the call incurs losses if the stock price is high. In that scenario, the writer will receive a call and will be obligated to deliver a stock worth S_T for only X dollars.

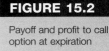

FIGURE 15.2

Payoff and profit to call option at expiration

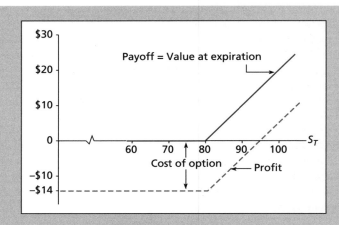

$$\text{Payoff to call writer} = -(S_T - X) \text{ if } S_T > X$$
$$0 \text{ if } S_T \leq X$$

The call writer, who is exposed to losses if the stock price increases, is willing to bear this risk in return for the option premium.

Figure 15.3 depicts the payoff and profit diagrams for the call writer. These are the mirror images of the corresponding diagrams for call holders. The break-even point for the option writer also is $94. The (negative) payoff at that point just offsets the premium originally received when the option was written.

Put Options

A put option conveys the right to sell an asset at the exercise price. In this case, the holder will not exercise the option unless the asset price is *less* than the exercise price. For example, if Fin Corp shares were to fall to $70, a put option with exercise price $80 could be exercised to give a $10 payoff to its holder. The holder would purchase a share for $70 and simultaneously deliver it to the put option writer for the exercise price of $80.

The value of a put option at expiration is

$$\text{Payoff to put holder} = 0 \qquad \text{if } S_T \geq X$$
$$X - S_T \text{ if } S_T < X$$

The solid line in Figure 15.4 illustrates the payoff at expiration to the holder of a put option on Fin Corp stock with an exercise price of $80. If the stock price at option expiration is above $80, the put has no value, as the right to sell the shares at $80 would not be exercised. Below a price of $80, the put value at expiration increases by $1 for each dollar the stock price falls. The dashed line in Figure 15.4 is a graph of the put option owner's profit at expiration, net of the initial cost of the put.

Writing puts *naked* (i.e., writing a put without an offsetting short position in the stock for hedging purposes) exposes the writer to losses if the market falls. Writing naked out-of-the-money puts was once considered an attractive way to generate income, as it was believed that as long as the market did not fall sharply before the option expiration, the option premium could be collected without the put holder ever exercising the option against the writer. Because only sharp drops in the market could result in losses to the writer of the put, the strategy was not viewed as overly risky. However, the nearby box notes that in the wake of the market crash of October 1987, such put writers suffered huge losses. Participants now perceive much greater risk to this strategy.

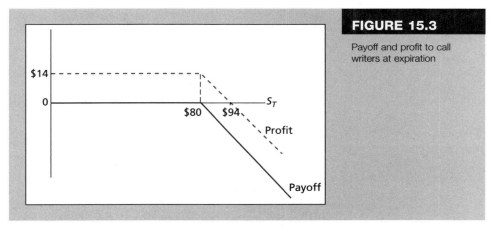

FIGURE 15.3

Payoff and profit to call writers at expiration

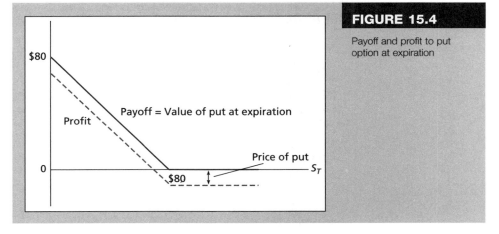

FIGURE 15.4

Payoff and profit to put option at expiration

On the MARKET FRONT

THE BLACK HOLE: PUTS AND THE MARKET CRASH

THEIR SALES OF "NAKED PUTS" QUICKLY COME TO GRIEF, DAMAGE SUITS ARE FILED

When Robert O'Connor got involved in stock-index options, he hoped his trading profits would help put his children through college. His broker, Mr. O'Connor explains, "said we would make about $1,000 a month, and if our losses got to $2,000 to $3,000, he would close out the account."

Instead, Mr. O'Connor, the 46-year-old owner of a small medical X-ray printing concern in Grand Rapids, Michigan, got caught in one of the worst investor blowouts in history. In a few minutes on October 19, he lost everything in his account plus an *additional* $91,000—a total loss of 175% of his original investment.

SCENE OF DISASTER

For Mr. O'Connor and hundreds of other investors, a little-known corner of the Chicago Board Options Exchange was the "black hole" of Black Monday's market crash. In a strategy marketed by brokers nationwide as a sure thing, these customers had sunk hundreds of millions of dollars into "naked puts"—unhedged, highly leveraged bets that the stock market was in no danger of plunging. Most of these naked puts seem to have been options on the Standard & Poor's 100 stock index, which are traded on the CBOE. When stocks crashed, many traders with unhedged positions got margin calls for several times their original investment.

THE "PUT" STRATEGY

The losses were especially sharp in "naked, out-of-the-money puts." A seller of puts agrees to buy stock or stock-index contracts at a set price before the put expires. These contracts are usually sold "out of the money"—priced at a level below current market prices that makes it unprofitable to exercise the option so long as the market rises or stays flat. The seller pockets a small amount per contract.

But if the market plunges, as it did October 19, the option swings into the money. The seller, in effect, has to pay pre-plunge stock prices to make good on his contract—and he takes a big loss.

"You have to recognize that there is unlimited potential for disaster" in selling naked options, says Peter Thayer, executive vice president of Gateway Investment Advisors Inc., a Cincinnati-based investment firm that trades options to hedge its stock portfolios. Last September, Gateway bought out-of-the-money put options on the S&P 100 stock index on the CBOE at $2 to $3 a contract as "insurance" against a plunging market. By October 20, the day after the crash, the value of those contracts had soared to $130. Although Gateway profited handsomely, the parties on the other side of the trade were clobbered.

FIRM SUED

Brokers who were pushing naked options assumed that the stock market wouldn't plunge into uncharted territory. Frank VanderHoff, one of the two main brokers who put 50 to 70 H.B. Shaine clients into stock-index options, says he told clients that the strategy's risk was "moderate barring a nuclear attack or a crash like 1929." It wasn't speculative. The market could go up or down, but not *substantially* up or down. If the crash had only been as bad as '29, he adds, "we would have made it."

SOURCE: Abridged from *The Wall Street Journal,* December 2, 1987. Reprinted by permission of *The Wall Street Journal,* © 1987 Dow Jones & Company, Inc. All Rights Reserved Worldwide.

CONCEPT check 15.2

Consider these four option strategies: (i) buy a call; (ii) write a call; (iii) buy a put; (iv) write a put.

a. For each strategy, plot both the payoff and profit diagrams as a function of the final stock price.

b. Why might one characterize both buying calls and writing puts as "bullish" strategies? What is the difference between them?

c. Why might one characterize both buying puts and writing calls as "bearish" strategies? What is the difference between them?

Options versus Stock Investments

Purchasing call options is a bullish strategy; that is, the calls provide profits when stock prices increase. Purchasing puts, in contrast, is a bearish strategy. Symmetrically, writing calls is bearish, while writing puts is bullish. Because option values depend on the price of the underlying stock, the purchase of options may be viewed as a substitute for direct purchase or sale of a stock. Why might an option strategy be preferable to direct stock transactions? We can begin to answer this question by comparing the values of option versus stock positions in Fin Corp.

Suppose you believe the stock will increase in value from its current level, which we assume is $90. You know your analysis could be incorrect, however, and that the share price also could fall. Suppose a six-month maturity call option with exercise price of $90 sells for $10, and the semiannual interest rate is 2%. Consider the following three strategies for investing a sum of $9,000. Suppose the firm will not pay any dividends until after the options expire.

Strategy *A:* Invest entirely in stock. Buy 100 shares, each selling for $90.

Strategy *B:* Invest entirely in at-the-money call options. Buy 900 calls, each selling for $10. (This would require 9 contracts, each for 100 shares.)

Strategy *C:* Purchase 100 call options for $1,000. Invest the remaining $8,000 in six-month T-bills, to earn 2% interest.

Let us trace the possible values of these three portfolios when the options expire in six months as a function of the stock price at that time.

	Stock Price					
Portfolio	**$85**	**$90**	**$95**	**$100**	**$105**	**$110**
A: 100 shares stock	$8,500	$9,000	$9,500	$10,000	$10,500	$11,000
B: 900 call options	0	0	4,500	9,000	13,500	18,000
C: 100 calls plus $8,000 in T-bills	8,160	8,160	8,660	9,160	9,660	10,160

Portfolio *A* will be worth 100 times the share price. Portfolio *B* is worthless unless the shares sell for more than the exercise price of the call. Once that point is reached, the portfolio is worth 900 times the excess of the stock price over the exercise price. Finally, portfolio *C* is worth $8,160 from the investment in T-bills ($8,000 × 1.02 = $8,160) plus any profits from the 100 call options. Remember that each of these portfolios involves the same $9,000 initial investment. The rates of return on these three portfolios are as follows:

	Stock Price					
Portfolio	**$85**	**$90**	**$95**	**$100**	**$105**	**$110**
A: 100 shares stock	−5.56%	0.0%	5.56%	11.11%	16.67%	22.22%
B: 900 call options	−100.0	−100.0	−50.00	0.0	50.0	100.0
C: 100 calls plus $8,000 in T-bills	−9.33	−9.33	−3.78	1.78	7.33	12.89

These rates of return are graphed in Figure 15.5.

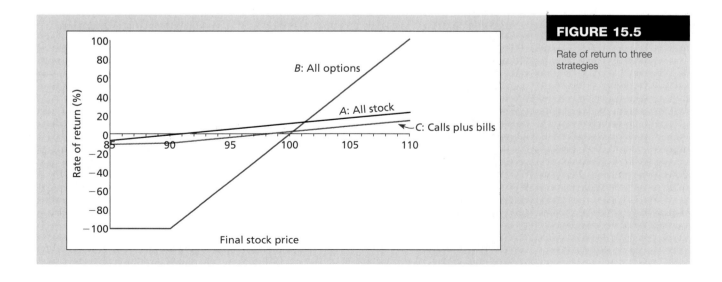

FIGURE 15.5

Rate of return to three strategies

An Excel model based on the Fin Corp example discussed in the text is shown below. The model allows you to use any variety of options, stock, and lending or borrowing with a set investment amount and demonstrates the investment flexibility of options.

	A	B	C	D	E	F	G	H
1	Current stock price	90						
2	Exercise price	90						
3	Interest rate	0.02						
4	Investment budget	9000						
5	Call price	10						
6								
7			Dollar value of portfolio as a function of Fin Corp price					
8	**Portfolio**		$85	$90	$95	$100	$105	$110
9	Portfolio A: All stock		$8,500	$9,000	$9,500	$10,000	$10,500	$11,000
10	Portfolio B: All call options		0	0	4,500	9,000	13,500	18,000
11	Portfolio C: Call plus bills		8,160	8,160	8,660	9,160	9,660	10,160
12								
13								
14			Rate of return as a function of Fin Corp price					
15	**Portfolio**		$85	$90	$95	$100	$105	$110
16	Portfolio A: All stock		-5.6%	0.00%	5.6%	11.1%	16.7%	22.2%
17	Portfolio B: All call options		-100.0%	-100.0%	-50.0%	0.0%	50.0%	100.0%
18	Portfolio C: Call plus bills		-9.33%	-9.33%	-3.78%	1.78%	7.33%	12.89%

Comparing the returns of portfolios *B* and *C* to those of the simple investment in stock represented by portfolio *A,* we see that options offer two interesting features. First, an option offers leverage. Compare the returns of portfolios *B* and *A.* When the stock fares poorly, ending anywhere below $90, the value of portfolio *B* falls precipitously to zero—a rate of return of negative 100%. Conversely, modest increases in the rate of return on the stock result in disproportionate increases in the option rate of return. For example, a 4.8% increase in the stock price from $105 to $110 would increase the rate of return on the call from 50% to 100%. In this sense, calls are a levered investment on the stock. Their values respond more than proportionately to changes in the stock value.

Figure 15.5 vividly illustrates this point. For stock prices above $90, the slope of the all-option portfolio is far steeper than that of the all-stock portfolio, reflecting its greater proportional sensitivity to the value of the underlying security. The leverage factor is the reason that investors (illegally) exploiting inside information commonly choose options as their investment vehicle.

The potential insurance value of options is the second interesting feature, as portfolio *C* shows. The T-bill plus option portfolio cannot be worth less than $8,160 after six months, as the option can always be left to expire worthless. The worst possible rate of return on portfolio *C* is −9.33%, compared to a (theoretically) worst possible rate of return on the stock of −100% if the company were to go bankrupt. Of course, this insurance comes at a price: When the share price increases, portfolio *C* does not perform as well as portfolio *A,* the all-stock portfolio. For stock prices above $90, portfolio *C* underperforms portfolio *A* by about 9.33 percentage points.

This simple example makes an important point. While options can be used by speculators as effectively leveraged stock positions, as in portfolio *B,* they also can be used by investors who desire to tailor their risk exposures in creative ways, as in portfolio *C.* For example, the call plus T-bills strategy of portfolio *C* provides a rate of return profile quite unlike that of the stock alone. The absolute limitation on downside risk is a novel and attractive feature of this strategy. In the next section we will discuss several option strategies that provide other novel risk profiles that might be attractive to hedgers and other investors.

Option Strategies

An unlimited variety of payoff patterns can be achieved by combining puts and calls with various exercise prices. Below we explain the motivation and structure of some of the more popular ones.

Protective put　Imagine you would like to invest in a stock, but you are unwilling to bear potential losses beyond some given level. Investing in the stock alone seems risky to you because in principle you could lose all the money you invest. You might consider instead investing in stock and purchasing a put option on the stock.

　　Table 15.1 shows the total value of your portfolio at option expiration. Whatever happens to the stock price, you are guaranteed a payoff equal to the put option's exercise price because the put gives you the right to sell the share for the exercise price even if the stock price is below that value.

　　Figure 15.6 illustrates the payoff and profit to this **protective put** strategy. The solid line in Figure 15.6C is the total payoff. The dashed line is displaced downward by the cost of establishing the position, $S_0 + P$. Notice that potential losses are limited.

protective put

An asset combined with a put option that guarantees minimum proceeds equal to the put's exercise price.

EXAMPLE 15.3

Protective Put

Suppose the strike price is $X = \$90$ and the stock is selling for $87 at option expiration. Then the value of your total portfolio is $90: The stock is worth $87 and the value of the expiring put option is

$$X - S_T = \$90 - \$87 = \$3$$

Another way to look at it is that you are holding the stock and a put contract giving you the right to sell the stock for $90. Even if $S < \$90$, you can still sell the stock for $90 by exercising the put. On the other hand, if the stock price is above $90, say, $94, then the right to sell a share at $90 is worthless. You allow the put to expire unexercised, ending up with a share of stock worth $S_T = \$94$.

　　It is instructive to compare the profit on the protective put strategy with that of the stock investment. For simplicity, consider an at-the-money protective put, so that $X = S_0$. Figure 15.7 compares the profits for the two strategies. The profit on the stock is zero if the stock price remains unchanged, and $S_T = S_0$. It rises or falls by $1 for every dollar swing in the ultimate stock price. The profit on the protective put is negative and equal to the cost of the put if S_T is below S_0. The profit on the protective put increases one for one with increases in the stock price once the stock price exceeds X.

　　Figure 15.7 makes it clear that the protective put offers some insurance against stock price declines in that it limits losses. As we shall see in the next chapter, protective put strategies are the conceptual basis for the portfolio insurance industry. The cost of the protection is that, in the case of stock price increases, your profit is reduced by the cost of the put, which turned out to be unneeded.

　　This example also shows that despite the common perception that "derivatives mean risk," derivative securities can be used effectively for **risk management.** In fact, such risk management is becoming accepted as part of the fiduciary responsibility of financial managers. Indeed, in a highly cited court case, *Brane* v. *Roth,* a company's board of directors was successfully sued for failing to use derivatives to hedge the price risk of grain held in storage. Such hedging might have been accomplished using protective puts. Some observers believe that this case will ultimately lead to a broad legal obligation for firms to use derivatives and other techniques to manage risk.

risk management

Strategies to limit the risk of a portfolio.

　　The claim that derivatives are best viewed as risk management tools may seem surprising in light of the credit crisis of the last few years. The crisis was immediately precipitated when the highly risky positions that many financial institutions had established in credit derivatives blew up in 2007–2008, resulting in large losses and grave threats to their solvency. Still, the same characteristics that make derivatives potent tools to increase risk also make them highly

TABLE 15.1		$S_T \leq X$	$S_T > X$
Payoff to protective put strategy	Stock	S_T	S_T
	Put	$X - S_T$	0
	Total	X	S_T

FIGURE 15.6

Value of a protective put position at expiration

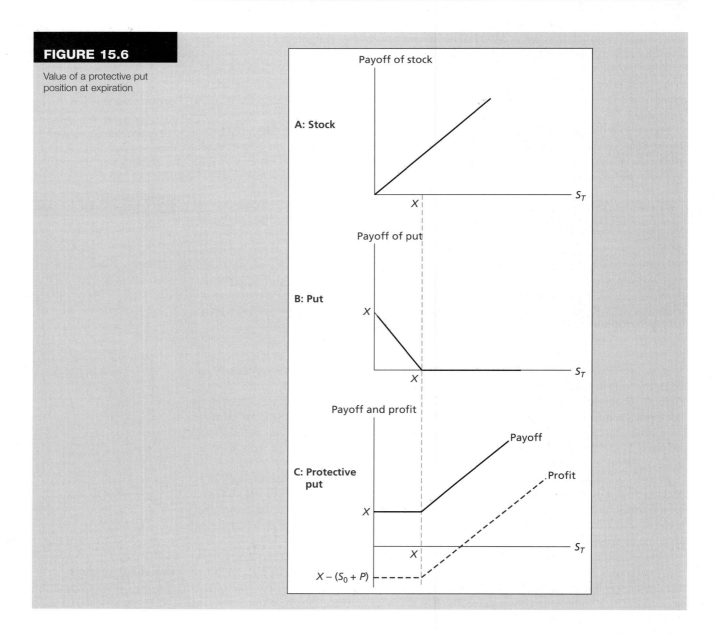

effective in managing risk, at least when used properly. Derivatives have aptly been compared to power tools: very useful in skilled hands but also very dangerous when not handled with care. The nearby box makes the case for derivatives as central to risk management.

covered call

Writing a call on an asset together with buying the asset.

Covered calls   A **covered call** position is the purchase of a share of stock with the simultaneous sale of a call on that stock. The written option is "covered" because the potential obligation to deliver the stock is covered by the stock held in the portfolio. Writing an option without an offsetting stock position is called by contrast *naked option writing*. The payoff to

THE CASE FOR DERIVATIVES

They've been dubbed financial weapons of mass destruction, attacked for causing the financial turmoil sweeping the nation and identified as the kryptonite that brought down the global economy. Yet few Main Streeters really know what derivatives are—namely, financial contracts between a buyer and a seller that derive value from an underlying asset, such as a mortgage or a stock. There seems to be near consensus that derivatives were a source of undue risk.

And then there's Robert Shiller. The Yale economist believes just the opposite is true. A champion of financial innovation and an expert in management of risk, Shiller contends that derivatives, far from being a problem, are actually the solution. Derivatives, Shiller says, are merely a risk-management tool the same way insurance is. "You pay a premium and if an event happens, you get a payment." That tool can be used well or, as happened recently, used badly. Shiller warns that banishing the tool gets us nowhere.

For all the trillions in derivative trading, there were very few traders. Almost all the subprime mortgages that were bundled and turned into derivatives were sold by a handful of Wall Street institutions, working with a small number of large institutional buyers. It was a huge but illiquid and opaque market.

Meanwhile, the system was built on the myriad decisions of individual homeowners and lenders around the world. None of them, however, could hedge their bets the way large institutions can. Those buying a condo in Miami had no way to protect themselves if the market went down.

Derivatives, according to Shiller, could be used by homeowners—and, by extension, lenders—to insure themselves against falling prices. In Shiller's scenario, you would be able to go to your broker and buy a new type of financial instrument, perhaps a derivative that is inversely related to a regional home-price index. If the value of houses in your area declined, the financial instrument would increase in value, offsetting the loss. Lenders could do the same thing, which would help them hedge against foreclosures. The idea is to make the housing market more liquid. More buyers and sellers means that markets stay liquid and functional even under pressure.

Some critics dismiss Shiller's basic premise that more derivatives would make the housing market more liquid and more stable. They point out that futures contracts haven't made equity markets or commodity markets immune from massive moves up and down. They add that a ballooning world of home-based derivatives wouldn't lead to homeowners' insurance: it would lead to a new playground for speculators.

In essence, Shiller is laying the intellectual groundwork for the next financial revolution. We are now suffering through the first major crisis of the Information Age economy. Shiller's answers may be counterintuitive, but no more so than those of doctors and scientists who centuries ago recognized that the cure for infectious diseases was not flight or quarantine, but purposely infecting more people through vaccinations. "We've had a major glitch in derivatives and securitization," says Shiller. "The Titanic sank almost a century ago, but we didn't stop sailing across the Atlantic."

Of course, people did think twice about getting on a ship, at least for a while. But if we listen only to our fears, we lose the very dynamism that has propelled us this far. That is the nub of Shiller's call for more derivatives and more innovation. Shiller's appeal is a tough sell at a time when derivatives have produced so much havoc. But he reminds us that the tools that got us here are not to blame; they can be used badly and they can be used well. And trying to stem the ineffable tide of human creativity is a fool's errand.

SOURCE: Zachary Karabell, "The Case for Derivatives," *Newsweek*, February 2, 2009.

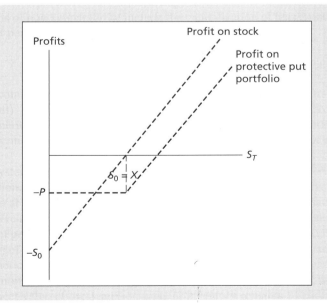

FIGURE 15.7

Protective put versus stock investment (at-the-money put option)

a covered call, presented in Table 15.2, equals the stock value minus the payoff of the call. The call payoff is subtracted because the covered call position involves issuing a call to another investor who can choose to exercise it to profit at your expense.

The solid line in Figure 15.8C illustrates the payoff pattern. You see that the total position is worth S_T when the stock price at time T is below X and rises to a maximum of X when S_T exceeds X. In essence, the sale of the call option means the call writer has sold the claim to any stock value above X in return for the initial premium (the call price). Therefore, at

TABLE 15.2		$S_T \leq X$	$S_T > X$
Payoff to a covered call	Payoff of stock	S_T	S_T
	−Payoff of call	−0	$-(S_T - X)$
	Total	S_T	X

FIGURE 15.8

Value of a covered call position at expiration

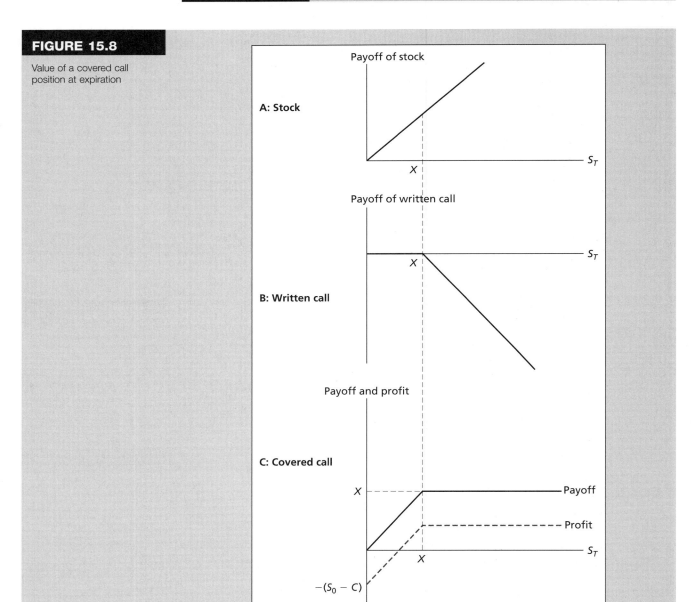

Using spreadsheets to analyze combinations of options is very helpful. Once the basic models are built, it is easy to extend the analysis to different bundles of options. The Excel model "Spreads and Straddles" shown below can be used to evaluate the profitability of different strategies.

	A	B	C	D	E	F	G	H	I	J	K	L
1						Spreads and Straddles						
2												
3	Stock Prices											
4	Beginning Market Price	116.5										
5	Ending Market Price	130						X 110 Straddle			X 120 Straddle	
6							Ending	Profit		Ending	Profit	
7	Buying Options:						Stock Price	-15.40		Stock Price	-24.00	
8	Call Options Strike	Price	Payoff	Profit	Return %		50	24.60		50	36.00	
9	110	22.80	20.00	-2.80	-12.28%		60	14.60		60	26.00	
10	120	16.80	10.00	-6.80	-40.48%		70	4.60		70	16.00	
11	130	13.60	0.00	-13.60	-100.00%		80	-5.40		80	6.00	
12	140	10.30	0.00	-10.30	-100.00%		90	-15.40		90	-4.00	
13							100	-25.40		100	-14.00	
14	Put Options Strike	Price	Payoff	Profit	Return %		110	-35.40		110	-24.00	
15	110	12.60	0.00	-12.60	-100.00%		120	-25.40		120	-34.00	
16	120	17.20	0.00	-17.20	-100.00%		130	-15.40		130	-24.00	
17	130	23.60	0.00	-23.60	-100.00%		140	-5.40		140	-14.00	
18	140	30.50	10.00	-20.50	-67.21%		150	4.60		150	-4.00	
19							160	14.60		160	6.00	
20	Straddle	Price	Payoff	Profit	Return %		170	24.60		170	16.00	
21	110	35.40	20.00	-15.40	-43.50%		180	34.60		180	26.00	
22	120	34.00	10.00	-24.00	-70.59%		190	44.60		190	36.00	
23	130	37.20	0.00	-37.20	-100.00%		200	54.60		200	46.00	
24	140	40.80	10.00	-30.80	-75.49%		210	64.60		210	56.00	
25												

expiration, the position is worth at most X. The dashed line of Figure 15.8C is the net profit to the covered call.

Writing covered call options has been a popular investment strategy among institutional investors. Consider the managers of a fund invested largely in stocks. They might find it appealing to write calls on some or all of the stock in order to boost income by the premiums collected. Although they thereby forfeit potential capital gains should the stock price rise above the exercise price, if they view X as the price at which they plan to sell the stock anyway, then the call may be viewed as enforcing a kind of "sell discipline." The written call guarantees the stock sale will occur as planned.

EXAMPLE 15.4

Covered Call

Assume a pension fund holds 1,000 shares of GXX stock, with a current price of $130 per share. Suppose the portfolio manager intends to sell all 1,000 shares if the share price hits $140, and a call expiring in 90 days with an exercise price of $140 currently sells for $5. By writing 10 GXX call contracts (100 shares each) the fund can pick up $5,000 in extra income. The fund would lose its share of profits from any movement of GXX stock above $140 per share, but given that it would have sold its shares at $140, it would not have realized those profits anyway.

Straddle A long **straddle** is established by buying both a call and a put on a stock, each with the same exercise price, X, and the same expiration date, T. Straddles are useful strategies for investors who believe a stock will move a lot in price but are uncertain about the direction of the move. For example, suppose you believe an important court case that will make or break a company is about to be settled, and the market is not yet aware of the situation. The stock will either double in value if the case is settled favorably or will drop by half if the settlement goes against the company. The straddle position will do well regardless of the outcome because its value is highest when the stock price makes extreme upward or downward moves from X.

straddle

A combination of a call and a put, each with the same exercise price and expiration date.

The worst-case scenario for a straddle is no movement in the stock price. If S_T equals X, both the call and the put expire worthless, and the investor's outlay for the purchase of both options is lost. Straddle positions basically are bets on volatility. An investor who establishes a straddle must view the stock as more volatile than the market does. Conversely, investors who *write* straddles—selling both a call and a put—must believe the market is less volatile. They accept the option premiums now, hoping the stock price will not change much before option expiration.

The payoff to a straddle is presented in Table 15.3. The solid line of Figure 15.9C illustrates this payoff. Notice that the portfolio payoff is always positive, except at the one point where the portfolio has zero value, $S_T = X$. You might wonder why all investors don't pursue such a no-lose strategy. To see why, remember that the straddle requires that both the put and

TABLE 15.3		$S_T \leq X$	$S_T > X$
Payoff to a straddle	Payoff of call	0	$S_T - X$
	+Payoff of put	$+(X - S_T)$	$+0$
	Total	$X - S_T$	$S_T - X$

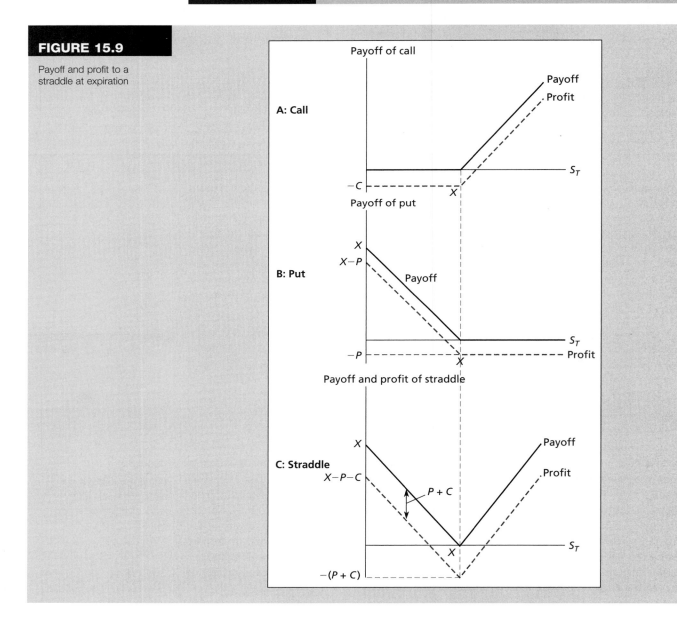

FIGURE 15.9

Payoff and profit to a straddle at expiration

the call be purchased. The value of the portfolio at expiration, while never negative, still must exceed the initial cash outlay for a straddle investor to clear a profit.

The dashed line of Figure 15.9C is the profit to the straddle. The profit line lies below the payoff line by the cost of purchasing the straddle, $P + C$. It is clear from the diagram that the straddle position generates a loss unless the stock price deviates substantially from X. The stock price must depart from X by the total amount expended to purchase the call *and* the put in order for the purchaser of the straddle to clear a profit.

Strips and *straps* are variations of straddles. A strip is two puts and one call on a security with the same exercise price and expiration date. A strap is two calls and one put.

Spreads   A **spread** is a combination of two or more call options (or two or more puts) on the same stock with differing exercise prices or times to expiration. Some options are bought, while others are sold, or written. A *money spread* involves the purchase of one option and the simultaneous sale of another with a different exercise price. A *time spread* refers to the sale and purchase of options with differing expiration dates.

Consider a money spread in which one call option is bought at an exercise price X_1, while another call with identical expiration date, but higher exercise price, X_2, is written. The payoff to this position will be the difference in the value of the call held and the value of the call written, as in Table 15.4.

There are now three instead of two outcomes to distinguish: the lowest-price region, where S_T is below both exercise prices; a middle region, where S_T is between the two exercise prices; and a high-price region, where S_T exceeds both exercise prices. Figure 15.10 illustrates the payoff and profit to this strategy, which is called a *bullish spread* because the payoff either increases or is unaffected by stock price increases. Holders of bullish spreads benefit from stock price increases.

One motivation for a bullish spread might be that the investor thinks one option is over-priced relative to another. For example, an investor who believes an $X = \$50$ call is cheap compared to an $X = \$55$ call might establish the spread, even without a strong desire to take a bullish position in the stock.

spread
A combination of two or more call options or put options on the same asset with differing exercise prices or times to expiration.

Collars   A **collar** is an options strategy that brackets the value of a portfolio between two bounds. Suppose that an investor currently is holding a large position in Eagle Corp., which is currently selling at $70 per share. A lower bound of $60 can be placed on the value of the portfolio by buying a protective put with exercise price $60. This protection, however, requires that the investor pay the put premium. To raise the money to pay for the put, the investor might write a call option, say, with exercise price $80. The call might sell for roughly the same price as the put, meaning that the net outlay for the two options positions is approximately zero. Writing the call limits the portfolio's upside potential. Even if the stock price moves above $80, the investor will do no better than $80, because at a higher price the stock will be called away. Thus the investor obtains the downside protection represented by the exercise price of the put by selling her claim to any upside potential beyond the exercise price of the call.

collar
An options strategy that brackets the value of a port-folio between two bounds.

A collar would be appropriate for an investor who has a target wealth goal in mind but is unwilling to risk losses beyond a certain level. Suppose you are contemplating buying a house for $160,000, for example. You might set this figure as your goal. Your current wealth may be $140,000, and you are unwilling to risk losing more than $20,000. A collar established by (1) purchasing 2,000 shares of stock currently selling at $70 per share, (2) purchasing 2,000 put options (20 option contracts) with exercise price $60, and (3) writing 2,000 calls with exercise price $80 would give you a good chance to realize the $20,000 capital gain without risking a loss of more than $20,000.

TABLE 15.4		$S_T \leq X_1$	$X_1 < S_T \leq X_2$	$S_T > X_2$
Payoff to a bullish spread	Payoff of first call, exercise price = X_1	0	$S_T - X_1$	$S_T - X_1$
	$-$ Payoff of second call; exercise price = X_2	-0	-0	$-(S_T - X_2)$
	Total	0	$S_T - X_1$	$X_2 - X_1$

FIGURE 15.10

Value of a bullish spread position at expiration

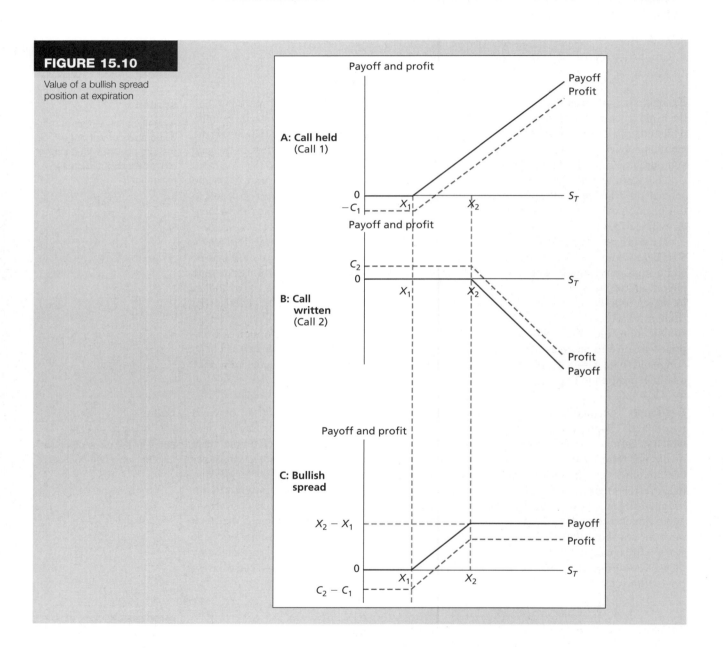

15.3 | Optionlike Securities

Suppose you never intend to trade an option directly. Why do you need to appreciate the properties of options in formulating an investment plan? Many financial instruments and agreements have features that convey implicit or explicit options to one or more parties. If you are to value and use these securities correctly, you must understand these embedded option attributes.

Callable Bonds

You know from Chapter 10 that many corporate bonds are issued with call provisions entitling the issuer to buy bonds back from bondholders at some time in the future at a specified call price. A call provision conveys a call option to the issuer, where the exercise price is equal to the price at which the bond can be repurchased. A callable bond arrangement is essentially a sale of a *straight bond* (a bond with no option features such as callability or convertibility) to the investor and the concurrent sale of a call option by the investor to the bond-issuing firm.

Investors must receive some compensation for offering this implicit call option. If the callable bond were issued with the same coupon rate as a straight bond, we would expect it to sell at a discount to the straight bond equal to the value of the call. To sell callable bonds at par, firms must issue them with coupon rates higher than the coupons on straight debt. The higher coupons are the investor's compensation for the call option retained by the issuer. Coupon rates usually are selected so that the newly issued bond will sell at par value.

Figure 15.11 illustrates this optionlike property. The horizontal axis is the value of a straight bond with otherwise identical terms as the callable bond. The dashed 45-degree line represents the value of straight debt. The solid line is the value of the callable bond, and the dotted line is the value of the call option retained by the firm. A callable bond's potential for capital gains is limited by the firm's option to repurchase at the call price.

How is a callable bond similar to a covered call strategy on a straight bond?	**CONCEPT** *check* **15.5**

The option inherent in callable bonds actually is more complex than an ordinary call option because usually it may be exercised only after some initial period of call protection. The price at which the bond is callable may change over time also. Unlike exchange-listed options, these features are defined in the initial bond covenants and will depend on the needs of the issuing firm and its perception of the market's tastes.

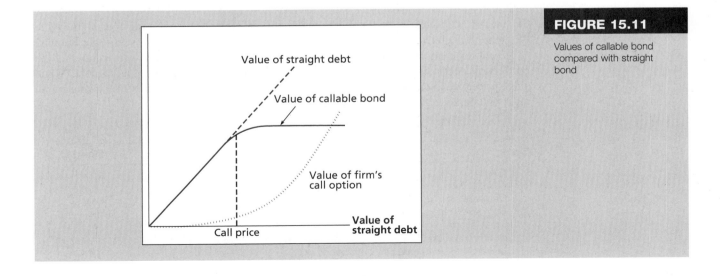

FIGURE 15.11

Values of callable bond compared with straight bond

CONCEPT
check   **15.6**
Suppose the period of call protection is extended. How will this affect the coupon rate the company needs to offer to enable it to sell the bonds at par value?

Convertible Securities

Convertible bonds and convertible preferred stock convey options to the holder of the security rather than to the issuing firm. A convertible security typically gives its holder the right to exchange each bond or share of preferred stock for a fixed number of shares of common stock, regardless of the market prices of the securities at the time.

CONCEPT
check   **15.7**
Should a convertible bond issued at par value have a higher or lower coupon rate than a nonconvertible bond issued at par?

For example, a bond with a conversion ratio of 10 allows its holder to convert one bond of par value $1,000 into 10 shares of common stock. Alternatively, we say the conversion price in this case is $100: To receive 10 shares of stock, the investor sacrifices bonds with face value $1,000 or $100 of face value per share. If the present value of the bond's scheduled payments is less than 10 times the value of one share of stock, it may pay to convert; that is, the conversion option is in the money. A bond worth $950 with a conversion ratio of 10 could be converted profitably if the stock were selling above $95, as the value of the 10 shares received for each bond surrendered would exceed $950. Most convertible bonds are issued "deep out of the money." That is, the issuer sets the conversion ratio so that conversion will not be profitable unless there is a substantial increase in stock prices and/or decrease in bond prices from the time of issue.

A bond's conversion value equals the value it would have if you converted it into stock immediately. Clearly, a bond must sell for at least its conversion value. If it did not, you could purchase the bond, convert it immediately, and clear a riskless profit. This condition could never persist, for all investors would pursue such a strategy and quickly bid up the price of the bond.

The straight bond value or "bond floor" is the value the bond would have if it were not convertible into stock. The bond must sell for more than its straight bond value because a convertible bond has more value; it is in fact a straight bond plus a valuable call option. Therefore, the convertible bond has two lower bounds on its market price: the conversion value and the straight bond value.

Figure 15.12 illustrates the optionlike properties of the convertible bond. Figure 15.12A shows the value of the straight debt as a function of the stock price of the issuing firm. For healthy firms, the straight debt value is almost independent of the value of the stock because default risk is small. However, if the firm is close to bankruptcy (stock prices are low), default risk increases, and the straight bond value falls. Panel B shows the conversion value of the bond. Panel C compares the value of the convertible bond to these two lower bounds.

When stock prices are low, the straight bond value is the effective lower bound, and the conversion option is nearly irrelevant. The convertible will trade like straight debt. When stock prices are high, the bond's price is determined by its conversion value. With conversion all but guaranteed, the bond is essentially equity in disguise.

We can illustrate with two examples.

	Bond *A*	Bond *B*
Annual coupon	$80	$80
Maturity date	10 years	10 years
Quality rating	Baa	Baa
Conversion ratio	20	25
Stock price	$30	$50
Conversion value	$600	$1,250
Market yield on 10-year Baa-rated bonds	8.5%	8.5%
Value as straight debt	$967	$967
Actual bond price	$972	$1,255
Reported yield to maturity	8.42%	4.76%

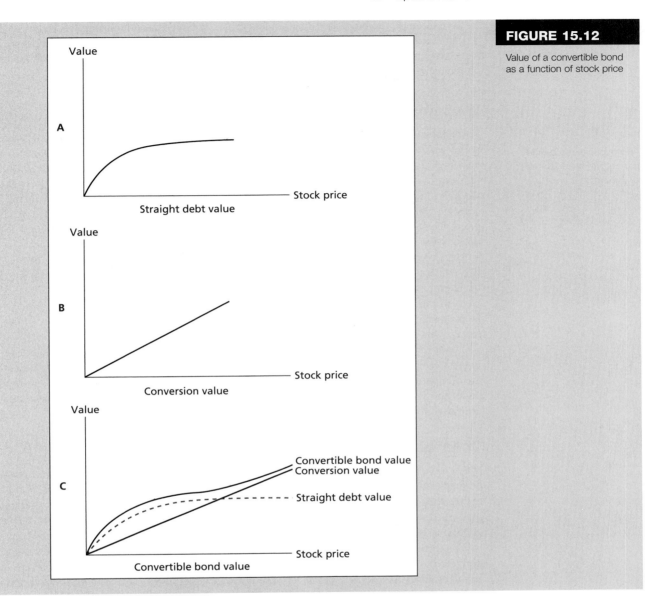

FIGURE 15.12

Value of a convertible bond as a function of stock price

Bond *A* has a conversion value of only $600. Its value as straight debt, in contrast, is $967. This is the present value of the coupon and principal payments at a market rate for straight debt of 8.5%. The bond's price is $972, so the premium over straight bond value is only $5, reflecting the low probability of conversion. Its reported yield to maturity based on scheduled coupon payments and the market price of $972 is 8.42%, close to that of straight debt.

The conversion option on bond *B* is in the money. Conversion value is $1,250, and the bond's price, $1,255, reflects its value as equity (plus $5 for the protection the bond offers against stock price declines). The bond's reported yield is 4.76%, far below the comparable yield on straight debt. The big yield sacrifice is attributable to the far greater value of the conversion option.

In theory, we could value convertible bonds by treating them as straight debt plus call options. In practice, however, this approach is often impractical for several reasons:

1. The conversion price frequently increases over time, which means the exercise price for the option changes.

2. Stocks may pay several dividends over the life of the bond, further complicating the option value analysis.

3. Most convertibles also are callable at the discretion of the firm. In essence, both the investor and the issuer hold options on each other. If the issuer exercises its call option

to repurchase the bond, the bondholders typically have a month during which they still can convert. When issuers use a call option, knowing that bondholders will choose to convert, the issuer is said to have *forced a conversion.* These conditions together mean the actual maturity of the bond is indeterminate.

Warrants

Warrants are essentially call options issued by a firm. One important difference between calls and warrants is that exercise of a warrant requires the firm to issue a new share of stock to satisfy its obligation—the total number of shares outstanding increases. Exercise of a call option requires only that the writer of the call deliver an already-issued share of stock to discharge the obligation. In this case, the number of shares outstanding remains fixed. Also unlike call options, warrants result in a cash flow to the firm when the warrant holder pays the exercise price. These differences mean warrant values will differ somewhat from the values of call options with identical terms.

Like convertible debt, warrant terms may be tailored to meet the needs of the firm. Also like convertible debt, warrants generally are protected against stock splits and dividends in that the exercise price and the number of warrants held are adjusted to offset the effects of the split.

Warrants often are issued in conjunction with another security. Bonds, for example, may be packaged together with a warrant "sweetener," frequently a warrant that may be sold separately. This is called a *detachable warrant.*

Issues of warrants and convertible securities create the potential for an increase in outstanding shares of stock if exercise occurs. Exercise obviously would affect financial statistics that are computed on a per-share basis, so annual reports must provide earnings per share figures under the assumption that all convertible securities and warrants are exercised. These figures are called *fully diluted earnings per share.*[3]

Collateralized Loans

Many loan arrangements require that the borrower put up collateral to guarantee the loan will be paid back. In the event of default, the lender takes possession of the collateral. A nonrecourse loan gives the lender no recourse beyond the right to the collateral. That is, the lender may not sue the borrower for further payment if the collateral turns out not to be valuable enough to repay the loan.[4]

This arrangement gives an implicit call option to the borrower. Assume the borrower is obligated to pay back L dollars at the maturity of the loan. The collateral will be worth S_T dollars at maturity. (Its value today is S_0.) The borrower has the option to wait until loan maturity and repay the loan only if the collateral is worth more than the L dollars necessary to satisfy the loan. If the collateral is worth less than L, the borrower can default on the loan, discharging the obligation by forfeiting the collateral, which is worth only S_T.

Another way of describing such a loan is to view the borrower as turning over collateral to the lender but retaining the right to reclaim it by paying off the loan. The transfer of the collateral with the right to reclaim it is equivalent to a payment of S_0 dollars, less a simultaneous recovery of a sum that resembles a call option with exercise price L. In effect, the borrower turns over collateral, but keeps an option to "repurchase" it for L dollars at the maturity of the loan if L turns out to be less than S_T. This is a call option.

A third way to look at a collaterized loan is to assume the borrower will repay the L dollars with certainty but also retain the option to sell the collateral to the lender for L dollars, even if S_T is less than L. In this case, the sale of the collateral would generate the cash necessary

---

[3]We should note that the exercise of a convertible bond need not reduce earnings per share (EPS). Diluted EPS will be less than undiluted EPS only if interest saved (per share) on the converted bonds is less than the prior EPS.
[4]In reality, of course, defaulting on a loan is not so simple. Losses of reputation are involved as well as considerations of ethical behavior. This is a description of a pure nonrecourse loan where both parties agree from the outset that only the collateral backs the loan and that default is not to be taken as a sign of bad faith if the collateral is insufficient to repay the loan.

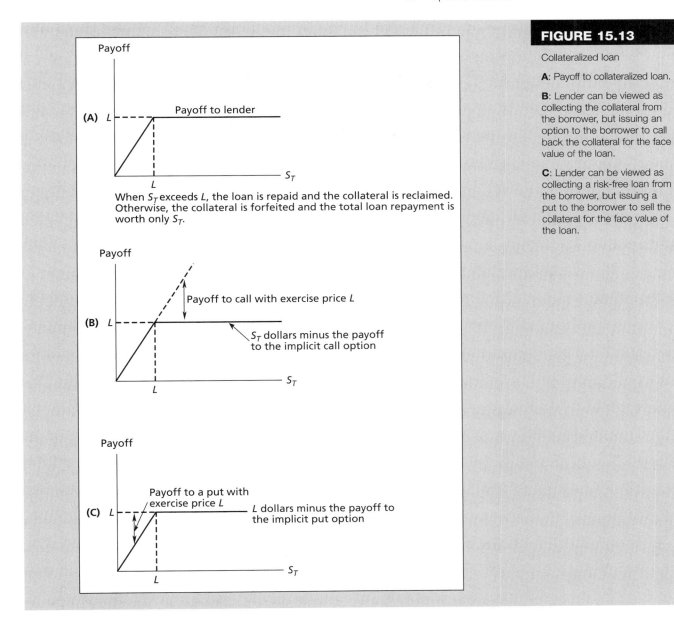

FIGURE 15.13

Collateralized loan

A: Payoff to collateralized loan.

B: Lender can be viewed as collecting the collateral from the borrower, but issuing an option to the borrower to call back the collateral for the face value of the loan.

C: Lender can be viewed as collecting a risk-free loan from the borrower, but issuing a put to the borrower to sell the collateral for the face value of the loan.

to satisfy the loan. The ability to "sell" the collateral for a price of L dollars represents a put option, which guarantees the borrower can raise enough money to satisfy the loan simply by turning over the collateral.

Figure 15.13 illustrates these interpretations. Figure 15.13A is the value of the payment to be received by the lender, which equals the minimum of S_T or L. Panel B shows that this amount can be expressed as S_T minus the payoff of the call implicitly written by the lender and held by the borrower. Panel C shows it also can be viewed as a receipt of L dollars minus the proceeds of a put option.

Leveraged Equity and Risky Debt

Investors holding stock in incorporated firms are protected by limited liability, which means that if the firm cannot pay its debts, the firm's creditors may attach only the firm's assets and may not sue the corporation's equityholders for further payment. In effect, any time the corporation borrows money, the maximum possible collateral for the loan is the total of the firm's assets. If the firm declares bankruptcy, we can interpret this as an admission that the assets of the firm are insufficient to satisfy the claims against it. The corporation may discharge its obligations by transferring ownership of the firm's assets to the creditors.

Just as is true for nonrecourse collateralized loans, the required payment to the creditors represents the exercise price of the implicit option, while the value of the firm is the underlying asset. The equityholders have a put option to transfer their ownership claims on the firm to the creditors in return for the face value of the firm's debt.

Alternatively, we may view the equityholders as retaining a call option. They have, in effect, already transferred their ownership claim to the firm to the creditors but have retained the right to reacquire the ownership claim by paying off the loan. Hence, the equityholders have the option to "buy back" the firm for a specified price, or they have a call option.

The significance of this observation is that analysts can value corporate bonds using option-pricing techniques. The default premium required of risky debt in principle can be estimated using option valuation models. We will consider some of these models in the next chapter.

15.4 | Exotic Options

Investors clearly value the portfolio strategies made possible by trading options; this is reflected in the heavy trading volume in these markets and their tremendous success. Success breeds imitation, and in recent years we have witnessed tremendous innovation in the range of option instruments available to investors. Part of this innovation has occurred in the market for customized options, which now trade in active over-the-counter markets. Many of these options have terms that would have been highly unusual even a few years ago; they therefore are called "exotic options." In this section, we will survey some of the more interesting variants of these new instruments.

Asian Options

You already have been introduced to American and European options. *Asian options* are options with payoffs that depend on the average (rather than final) price of the underlying asset during at least some portion of the life of the option. For example, an Asian call option may have a payoff equal to the average stock price over the last three months minus the exercise price, if that value is positive, or zero. These options may be of interest to firms that wish to hedge a profit stream that depends on the average price of a commodity over some period of time.

Barrier Options

Barrier options have payoffs that depend not only on some asset price at option expiration but also on whether the underlying asset price has crossed through some "barrier." For example, a *down-and-out option* is one type of barrier option that automatically expires worthless if and when the stock price falls below some barrier price. Similarly, *down-and-in options* will not provide a payoff unless the stock price *does* fall below some barrier at least once during the life of the option. These options also are referred to as knock-out and knock-in options.

Lookback Options

Lookback options have payoffs that depend in part on the minimum or maximum price of the underlying asset during the life of the option. For example, a lookback call option might provide a payoff equal to the maximum stock price during the life of the option minus the exercise price, as opposed to the *closing* stock price minus the exercise price. Such an option provides (at a price, of course) a form of perfect market timing, providing the call holder with a payoff equal to the one that would accrue if the asset were purchased for X dollars and later sold at what turns out to be its highest price.

Currency-Translated Options

Currency-translated options have either asset or exercise prices denominated in a foreign currency. A good example of such an option is the *quanto,* which allows an investor to fix in advance the exchange rate at which an investment in a foreign currency can be converted back into dollars. The right to translate a fixed amount of foreign currency into dollars at a given exchange rate is a simple foreign exchange option. Quantos are more interesting, however, because the amount of currency that will be translated into dollars depends on the investment performance of the foreign security. Therefore, a quanto in effect provides a *random number* of options.

Digital Options

Digital options, also called *binary* or "bet" options, have fixed payoffs that depend on whether a condition is satisfied by the price of the underlying asset. For example, a binary call option might pay off a fixed amount of $100 if the stock price at expiration exceeds the exercise price.

- A call option is the right to buy an asset at an agreed-upon exercise price. A put option is the right to sell an asset at a given exercise price.
- American-style options allow exercise on or before the exercise date. European-style options allow exercise only on the expiration date. Most traded options are American in nature.
- Options are traded on stocks, stock indexes, foreign currencies, fixed-income securities, and several futures contracts.
- Options can be used either to lever up an investor's exposure to an asset price or to provide insurance against volatility of asset prices. Popular option strategies include covered calls, protective puts, straddles, and spreads.
- Many commonly traded securities embody option characteristics. Examples of these securities are callable bonds, convertible bonds, and warrants. Other arrangements, such as collateralized loans and limited-liability borrowing, can be analyzed as conveying implicit options to one or more parties.

American option, 478	exercise price, 475	risk management, 485
at the money, 476	in the money, 476	spread, 491
call option, 475	out of the money, 476	straddle, 489
collar, 491	premium, 475	strike price, 475
covered call, 486	protective put, 485	warrant, 496
European option, 478	put option, 476	

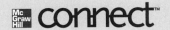 Select problems are available in McGraw-Hill Connect. Please see the packaging options section of the preface for more information.

Basic

1. We said that options can be used either to scale up or reduce overall portfolio risk. What are some examples of risk-increasing and risk-reducing options strategies? Explain each.
2. Why do you think the most actively traded options tend to be the ones that are near the money?
3. The following price quotations are for exchange-listed options on Primo Corporation common stock.

Company	Strike	Expiration	Call	Put
Primo 61.12	55	Feb	7.25	.48

www.mhhe.com/bkm

With transaction costs ignored, how much would a buyer have to pay for one call option contract?

4. Turn back to Figure 15.1, which lists the prices of various IBM options. Use the data in the figure to calculate the payoff and the profits for investments in each of the following July expiration options, assuming that the stock price on the expiration date is $95.
   a. Call option, $X = 90$
   b. Put option, $X = 90$
   c. Call option, $X = 95$
   d. Put option, $X = 95$
   e. Call option, $X = 100$
   f. Put option, $X = 100$

5. You purchase one IBM March 100 put contract for a premium of $6.47. what is your maximum possible profit? (See Figure 15.1.)

6. An investor buys a call at a price of $4.50 with an exercise price of $40. At what stock price will the investor break even on the purchase of the call?

7. You establish a straddle on Intel using September call and put options with a strike price of $50. The call premium is $4.25 and the put premium is $5.00.
   a. What is the most you can lose on this position?
   b. What will be your profit or loss if Intel is selling for $58 in September?
   c. At what stock prices will you break even on the straddle?

8. The following diagram shows the value of a put option at expiration:

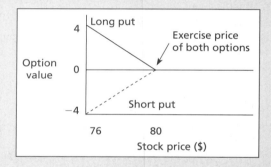

Ignoring transaction costs, which of the following statements about the value of the put option at expiration is *true*?
   a. The value of the short position in the put is $4 if the stock price is $76.
   b. The value of the long position in the put is −$4 if the stock price is $76.
   c. The long put has value when the stock price is below the $80 exercise price.
   d. The value of the short position in the put is zero for stock prices equaling or exceeding $76.

Intermediate

9. Imagine that you are holding 5,000 shares of stock, currently selling at $40 per share. You are ready to sell the shares, but would prefer to put off the sale until next year due to tax reasons. If you continue to hold the shares until January, however, you face the risk that the stock will drop in value before year-end. You decide to use a collar to limit downside risk without laying out a good deal of additional funds. January call options with a strike price of $45 are selling at $2, and January puts with a strike price of $35 are selling at $3. what will be the value of your portfolio in January (net of the proceeds from the options) if the stock price ends up at: (a) $30? (b) $40? (c) $50? Compare these proceeds to what you would realize if you simply continued to hold the shares.

10. Suppose you think Wal-Mart stock is going to appreciate substantially in value in the next year. Say the stock's current price, S_0, is $100, and the call option expiring in one year has an exercise price, X, of $100 and is selling at a price, C, of $10. With $10,000 to invest, you are considering three alternatives:
    a. Invest all $10,000 in the stock, buying 100 shares.
    b. Invest all $10,000 in 1,000 options (10 contracts).
    c. Buy 100 options (one contract) for $1,000 and invest the remaining $9,000 in a money market fund paying 4% interest annually.

    What is your rate of return for each alternative for four stock prices one year from now? Summarize your results in the table and diagram below.

RATE OF RETURN ON INVESTMENT

	Price of Stock 1 Year from Now			
	$80	**$100**	**$110**	**$120**
a. All stocks (100 shares)				
b. All options (1,000 shares)				
c. Bills + 100 options				

11. The common stock of the P.U.T.T. Corporation has been trading in a narrow price range for the past month, and you are convinced it is going to break far out of that range in the next three months. You do not know whether it will go up or down, however. The current price of the stock is $100 per share, the price of a three-month call option with an exercise price of $100 is $10, and a put with the same expiration date and exercise price costs $7.
    a. What would be a simple options strategy to exploit your conviction about the stock price's future movements?
    b. How far would the price have to move in either direction for you to make a profit on your initial investment?

12. The common stock of the C.A.L.L. Corporation has been trading in a narrow range around $50 per share for months, and you believe it is going to stay in that range for the next three months. The price of a three-month put option with an exercise price of $50 is $4, and a call with the same expiration date and exercise price sells for $7.
    a. What would be a simple options strategy using a put and a call to exploit your conviction about the stock price's future movement?
    b. What is the most money you can make on this position? How far can the stock price move in either direction before you lose money?
    c. How can you create a position involving a put, a call, and riskless lending that would have the same payoff structure as the stock at expiration? The stock will pay no dividends in the next three months. What is the net cost of establishing that position now?

13. Joseph Jones, a manager at Computer Science, Inc. (CSI), received 10,000 shares of company stock as part of his compensation package. The stock currently sells at $40 a share. Joseph would like to defer selling the stock until the next tax year. In January, however, he will need to sell all his holdings to provide for a down payment on his new house. Joseph is worried about the price risk involved in keeping his shares. At current prices, he would receive $40,000 for the stock. If the value of his stock holdings falls below $35,000, his ability to come up with the necessary down payment would be

jeopardized. On the other hand, if the stock value rises to $45,000, he would be able to maintain a small cash reserve even after making the down payment. Joseph considers three investment strategies:

a. Strategy A is to write January call options on the CSI shares with strike price $45. These calls are currently selling for $3 each.

b. Strategy B is to buy January put options on CSI with strike price $35. These options also sell for $3 each.

c. Strategy C is to establish a zero-cost collar by writing the January calls and buying the January puts.

Evaluate each of these strategies with respect to Joseph's investment goals. What are the advantages and disadvantages of each? Which would you recommend?

14. a. A butterfly spread is the purchase of one call at exercise price X_1, the sale of two calls at exercise price X_2, and the purchase of one call at exercise price X_3. X_1 is less than X_2, and X_2 is less than X_3 by equal amounts, and all calls have the same expiration date. Graph the payoff diagram to this strategy.

b. A vertical combination is the purchase of a call with exercise price X_2 and a put with exercise price X_1, with X_2 greater than X_1. Graph the payoff to this strategy.

15. A bearish spread is the purchase of a call with exercise price X_2 and the sale of a call with exercise price X_1, with X_2 greater than X_1. Graph the payoff to this strategy and compare it to Figure 15.10.

16. You are attempting to formulate an investment strategy. On the one hand, you think there is great upward potential in the stock market and would like to participate in the upward move if it materializes. However, you are not able to afford substantial stock market losses and so cannot run the risk of a stock market collapse, which you recognize is also possible. Your investment adviser suggests a protective put position: Buy shares in a market index stock fund *and* put options on those shares with three-months until expiration and exercise price of $1,040. The stock index is currently at $1,200. However, your uncle suggests you instead buy a three-month call option on the index fund with exercise price $1,120 and buy three-month T-bills with face value $1,120.

a. On the same graph, draw the *payoffs* to each of these strategies as a function of the stock fund value in three months. (*Hint*: Think of the options as being on one "share" of the stock index fund, with the current price of each share of the index equal to $1,200.)

b. Which portfolio must require a greater initial outlay to establish? (*Hint*: Does either portfolio provide a final payoff that is always at least as great as the payoff of the other portfolio?)

c. Suppose the market prices of the securities are as follows.

Stock fund	$1,200
T-bill (face value $1,120)	1,080
Call (exercise price $1,120)	160
Put (exercise price $1,040)	8

Make a table of profits realized for each portfolio for the following values of the stock price in three months: $S_T = \$0, \$1,040, \$1,120, \$1,200,$ and $\$1,280$. Graph the profits to each portfolio as a function of S_T on a single graph.

d. Which strategy is riskier? Which should have a higher beta?

Please visit us at www.mhhe.com/bkm

17. Use the spreadsheet from the Excel Application boxes on spreads and straddles (available at **www.mhhe.com/bkm;** link to Chapter 15 material) to answer these questions.

a. Plot the payoff and profit diagrams to a straddle position with an exercise (strike) price of $130. Assume the options are priced as they are in the Excel Application.

b. Plot the payoff and profit diagrams to a spread position with exercise (strike) prices of $120 and $130. Assume the options are priced as they are in the Excel Application.

18. In what ways is owning a corporate bond similar to writing a put option? A call option?

19. An executive compensation scheme might provide a manager a bonus of $1,000 for every dollar by which the company's stock price exceeds some cutoff level. In what way is this arrangement equivalent to issuing the manager call options on the firm's stock?

20. Consider the following options portfolio. You write a July 2009 expiration call option on IBM with exercise price $100. You also write a July expiration IBM put option with exercise price $95.
    a. Graph the payoff of this portfolio at option expiration as a function of IBM's stock price at that time.
    b. What will be the profit/loss on this position if IBM is selling at $97 on the option expiration date? What if IBM is selling at $105? Use *The Wall Street Journal* listing from Figure 15.1 to answer this question.
    c. At what two stock prices will you just break even on your investment?
    d. What kind of "bet" is this investor making; that is, what must this investor believe about IBM's stock price in order to justify this position?

21. Consider the following portfolio. You *write* a put option with exercise price $90 and *buy* a put with the same expiration date with exercise price $95.
    a. Plot the value of the portfolio at the expiration date of the options.
    b. On the same graph, plot the profit of the portfolio. Which option must cost more?

22. A put option with strike price $60 trading on the Acme options exchange sells for $2. To your amazement, a put on the firm with the same expiration selling on the Apex options exchange but with strike price $62 also sells for $2. If you plan to hold the options position until expiration, devise a zero-net-investment arbitrage strategy to exploit the pricing anomaly. Draw the profit diagram at expiration for your position.

23. You buy a share of stock, write a one-year call option with $X = \$10$, and buy a one-year put option with $X = \$10$. Your net outlay to establish the entire portfolio is $9.50. What must be the risk-free interest rate? The stock pays no dividends.

24. Joe Finance has just purchased a stock index fund, currently selling at $1,200 per share. To protect against losses, Joe plans to purchase an at-the-money European put option on the fund for $60, with exercise price $1,200, and three-month time to expiration. Sally Calm, Joe's financial adviser, points out that Joe is spending a lot of money on the put. She notes that three-month puts with strike prices of $1,170 cost only $45, and suggests that Joe use the cheaper put.
    a. Analyze Joe's and Sally's strategies by drawing the *profit* diagrams for the stock-plus-put positions for various values of the stock fund in three months.
    b. When does Sally's strategy do better? When does it do worse?
    c. Which strategy entails greater systematic risk?

25. You write a call option with $X = \$50$ and buy a call with $X = \$60$. The options are on the same stock and have the same expiration date. One of the calls sells for $3; the other sells for $9.
    a. Draw the *payoff* graph for this strategy at the option expiration date.
    b. Draw the *profit* graph for this strategy.
    c. What is the break-even point for this strategy? Is the investor bullish or bearish on the stock?

26. Devise a portfolio using only call options and shares of stock with the following value (payoff) at the option expiration date. If the stock price is currently $53, what kind of bet is the investor making?

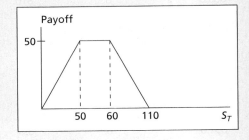

Challenge

27. The agricultural price support system guarantees farmers a minimum price for their output. Describe the program provisions as an option. What is the asset? The exercise price?

28. Use the put-call parity relationship to demonstrate that an at-the-money call option on a nondividend-paying stock must cost more than an at-the-money put option. Show that the put and call will be equally costly if $S = (1 + r)^T$.

CFA Problems

1. Which one of the following statements about the value of a call option at expiration is *false*?
   a. A short position in a call option will result in a loss if the stock price exceeds the exercise price.
   b. The value of a long position equals zero or the stock price minus the exercise price, whichever is higher.
   c. The value of a long position equals zero or the exercise price minus the stock price, whichever is higher.
   d. A short position in a call option has a zero value for all stock prices equal to or less than the exercise price.

2. Donna Donie, CFA, has a client who believes the common stock price of TRT Materials (currently $58 per share) could move substantially in either direction in reaction to an expected court decision involving the company. The client currently owns no TRT shares, but asks Donie for advice about implementing a strangle strategy to capitalize on the possible stock price movement. A strangle is a portfolio of a put and a call with different exercise prices but the same expiration date. Donie gathers the following TRT option price data:

Characteristic	Call Option	Put Option
Price	$ 5	$ 4
Strike Price	$60	$55
Time to expiration	90 days from now	90 days from now

   a. Recommend whether Donie should choose a long strangle strategy or a short strangle strategy to achieve the client's objective.
   b. Calculate, at expiration for the appropriate strangle strategy in part (*a*), the
      i. Maximum possible loss per share.
      ii. Maximum possible gain per share.
      iii. Break-even stock price(s).

3. A member of an investment committee, interested in learning more about fixed-income investment procedures, recalls that a fixed-income manager recently stated that derivative instruments could be used to control portfolio duration, saying "a futures-like position can be created in a portfolio by using put and call options on Treasury bonds."
   a. Identify the options market exposure or exposures that create a "futures-like position" similar to being long Treasury bond futures. Explain why the position you created is similar to being long Treasury bond futures.
   b. Explain in which direction and why the exposure(s) you identified in part (*a*) would affect portfolio duration.
   c. Assume that a pension plan's investment policy requires the fixed-income manager to hold portfolio duration within a narrow range. Identify and briefly explain circumstances or transactions in which the use of Treasury bond futures would be helpful in managing a fixed-income portfolio when duration is constrained.

4. Suresh Singh, CFA, is analyzing a convertible bond. The characteristics of the bond and the underlying common stock are given in the following exhibit:

Convertible Bond Characteristics	
Par value	$1,000
Annual coupon rate (annual pay)	6.5%
Conversion ratio	22
Market price	105% of par value
Straight value	99% of par value
Underlying Stock Characteristics	
Current market price	$40 per share
Annual cash dividend	$1.20 per share

Compute the bond's
a. Conversion value.
b. Market conversion price.

5. Rich McDonald, CFA, is evaluating his investment alternatives in Ytel Incorporated by analyzing a Ytel convertible bond and Ytel common equity. Characteristics of the two securities are given in the following exhibit:

Characteristics	Convertible Bond	Common Equity
Par value	$1,000	—
Coupon (annual payment)	4%	—
Current market price	$980	$35 per share
Straight bond value	$925	—
Conversion ratio	25	—
Conversion option	At any time	—
Dividend	—	$0
Expected market price in 1 year	$1,125	$45 per share

a. Calculate, based on the exhibit, the
   i. Current market conversion price for the Ytel convertible bond.
   ii. Expected one-year rate of return for the Ytel convertible bond.
   iii. Expected one-year rate of return for the Ytel common equity.

One year has passed and Ytel's common equity price has increased to $51 per share. Also, over the year, the yield to maturity on Ytel's nonconvertible bonds of the same maturity increased, while credit spreads remained unchanged.

b. Name the two components of the convertible bond's value. Indicate whether the value of each component should decrease, stay the same, or increase in response to the
   i. Increase in Ytel's common equity price.
   ii. Increase in bond yield.

Use data from the Standard & Poor's Market Insight Database at www.mhhe.com/edumarketinsight to answer the following questions.

STANDARD
&POOR'S

1. On the Market Insight Company page, enter stock symbol GE for General Electric. Go to the S&P Stock Reports section for GE.
   a. Scroll down to Key Stock Statistics and locate the 52-week range for GE.
   b. Now go to Yahoo! Finance (**finance.yahoo.com**) and enter stock symbol GE. At what price did GE last trade?
   c. Click on the link to Options on the left side of the Yahoo! Finance screen. Choose an expiration date three months in the future, and then choose one of the call options listed by selecting an exercise (strike) price. What is the last price (premium) shown for the call option?

d. Is the call option in the money?

e. Draw a graph that shows the payoff and the profit to the holder of this call option over a range of prices, including the prices you found in the 52-week range of the S&P Stock Report.

f. Repeat the steps for a put option on GE with the same expiration date and the same strike price.

2. Select 10 firms that interest you from the Market Insight population. For each firm, open the Stock Report. From the first page of the report, note the stock's current price, target price, and the S&P Recommendation. On the basis of this information, if you had to choose between buying a put option or a call option on the stock, which would you choose? Under the lower right corner of the Price Performance chart, check to see if there are options available on the stock and, if so, where they trade.

WEB *master*   OPTIONS AND STRADDLES

Go to **www.nasdaq.com** and select IBM in the quote section. Once you have the information quote, request the information on options. You will be able to access the prices for the calls and puts that are closest to the money. For example, if the price of IBM is $96.72, you will use the options with the $95 exercise price. Use near-term options. For example, in February, you would select April and July expirations.

1. What are the prices for the put and call with the nearest expiration date?

2. What would be the cost of a straddle using these options?

3. At expiration, what would be the break-even stock prices for the straddle?

4. What would be the percentage increase or decrease in the stock price required to break even?

5. What are the prices for the put and call with a later expiration date?

6. What would be the cost of a straddle using the later expiration date? At expiration, what would be the break-even stock prices for the straddle?

7. What would be the percentage increase or decrease in the stock price required to break even?

15.1. a. Proceeds $= S_T - X = S_T - \$95$ if this value is positive; otherwise, the call expires worthless.
Profit = Proceeds − Price of call option = Proceeds − $5.30.

	$S_T = \$85$	$S_T = \$105$
Proceeds	$0	$10
Profits	−5.30	4.70

b. Proceeds $= X - S_T = \$95 - S_T$ if this value is positive; otherwise, the put expires worthless.
Profit = Proceeds − Price of put option = Proceeds − $4.28.

	$S_T = \$85$	$S_T = \$105$
Proceeds	$10	$0
Profits	5.72	−4.28

15.2. a.

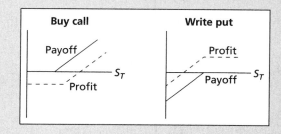

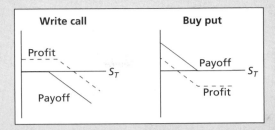

b. The payoffs and profits to both buying calls and writing puts generally are higher when the stock price is higher. In this sense, both positions are bullish. Both involve potentially taking delivery of the stock. However, the call holder will *choose* to take delivery when the stock price is high, while the put writer *is obligated* to take delivery when the stock price is low.

c. The payoffs and profits to both writing calls and buying puts generally are higher when the stock price is lower. In this sense, both positions are bearish. Both involve potentially making delivery of the stock. However, the put holder will *choose* to make delivery when the stock price is low, while the call writer *is obligated* to make delivery when the stock price is high.

15.3.

PAYOFF TO A STRIP

	$S_T \leq X$	$S_T > X$
2 Puts	$2(X - S_T)$	0
1 Call	0	$S_T - X$

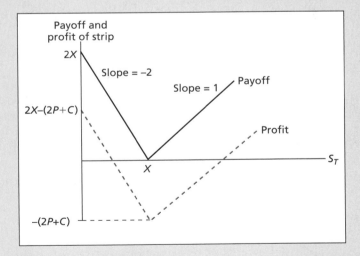

PAYOFF TO A STRAP

	$S_T \leq X$	$S_T > X$
1 Put	$X - S_T$	0
2 Calls	0	$2(S_T - X)$

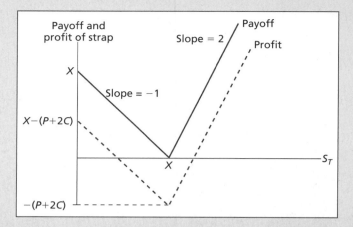

15.4. The payoff table on a per share basis is as follows:

	$S_T < 60$	$60 < S_T < 80$	$S_T > 80$
Buy put ($X = 60$)	$60 - S_T$	0	0
Share	S_T	S_T	S_T
Write call ($X = 80$)	0	0	$-(S_T - 80)$
Total	60	S_T	80

The graph of the payoff follows. If you multiply the per share values by 2,000, you will see that the collar provides a minimum payoff of $120,000 (representing a maximum loss of $20,000) and a maximum payoff of $160,000 (which is the cost of the house).

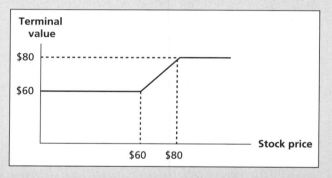

15.5. The covered call strategy would consist of a straight bond with a call written on the bond. The payoff value of the covered call position at option expiration as a function of the value of the straight bond is given in the following figure, and is virtually identical to the value of the callable bond in Figure 15.11.

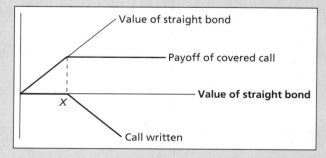

15.6. The call option is less valuable as call protection is expanded. Therefore, the coupon rate need not be as high.

15.7. Lower. Investors will accept a lower coupon rate in return for the conversion option.

Chapter 16

Option Valuation

After Studying This Chapter You Should Be Able To:

- Identify the features of an option that affect its market value.

- Compute an option value in a two-scenario model of the economy.

- Compute the Black-Scholes value and implied volatility of an option.

- Compute the proper relationship between call and put prices.

- Compute the hedge ratio of an option.

- Formulate a portfolio insurance plan using option hedge ratios.

In the previous chapter, we examined option markets and strategies. We ended by noting that many securities contain embedded options that affect both their values and their risk-return characteristics. In this chapter, we turn our attention to option valuation issues. Understanding most of these models requires considerable mathematical and statistical background. Still, many of their ideas and insights can be demonstrated in simple examples, and we will concentrate on these.

We start with a discussion of the factors that ought to affect option prices. After this qualitative discussion, we present a simple "two-state" quantitative option valuation model and show how we can generalize it into a useful and accurate pricing tool. Next, we move on to one particular option valuation formula, the famous Black-Scholes model. Option-pricing models allow us to "back out" market estimates of stock-price volatility, and we will examine these estimates of implied volatility.

Next we turn to some of the more important applications of option pricing theory in risk management. Finally, we take a brief look at some of the empirical evidence on option pricing and the implications of that evidence concerning the limitations of the Black-Scholes model.

Related Web sites for this chapter are available at www.mhhe.com/bkm.

16.1 Option Valuation: Introduction

Intrinsic and Time Values

Consider a call option that is out of the money at the moment, with the stock price below the exercise price. This does not mean the option is valueless. Even though immediate exercise would be unprofitable, the call retains a positive value because there is always a chance the stock price will increase sufficiently by the expiration date to allow for profitable exercise. If not, the worst that can happen is that the option will expire with zero value.

intrinsic value

Stock price minus exercise price, or the profit that could be attained by immediate exercise of an in-the-money call option.

The value $S_0 - X$ is sometimes called the **intrinsic value** of an in-the-money call option because it gives the payoff that could be obtained by immediate exercise. Intrinsic value is set equal to zero for out-of-the-money or at-the-money options. The difference between the actual call price and the intrinsic value is commonly called the **time value** of the option.

Time value is an unfortunate choice of terminology because it may confuse the option's time value with the time value of money. Time value in the options context simply refers to the difference between the option's price and the value the option would have if it were expiring immediately. It is the part of the option's value that may be attributed to the fact that it still has positive time to expiration.

time value

Difference between an option's price and its intrinsic value.

Most of an option's time value typically is a type of "volatility value." As long as the option holder can choose not to exercise, the payoff cannot be worse than zero. Even if a call option is out of the money now, it still will sell for a positive price because it offers the potential for a profit if the stock price increases, while imposing no risk of additional loss should the stock price fall. The volatility value lies in the right *not* to exercise the option if that action would be unprofitable. The option to exercise, as opposed to the obligation to exercise, provides insurance against poor stock price performance.

As the stock price increases substantially, it becomes more likely that the call option will be exercised by expiration. In this case, with exercise all but assured, the volatility value becomes minimal. As the stock price gets ever larger, the option value approaches the "adjusted" intrinsic value—the stock price minus the present value of the exercise price, $S_0 - PV(X)$.

Why should this be? If you *know* the option will be exercised and the stock purchased for X dollars, it is as though you own the stock already. The stock certificate might as well be sitting in your safe-deposit box now, as it will be there in only a few months. You just haven't paid for it yet. The present value of your obligation is the present value of X, so the present value of the net payoff of the call option is $S_0 - PV(X)$.[1]

Figure 16.1 illustrates the call option valuation function. The value curve shows that when the stock price is low, the option is nearly worthless because there is almost no chance that it will be exercised. When the stock price is very high, the option value approaches adjusted intrinsic value. In the midrange case, where the option is approximately at the money, the option curve diverges from the straight lines corresponding to adjusted intrinsic value. This is because, while exercise today would have a negligible (or negative) payoff, the volatility value of the option is quite high in this region. The option always increases in value with the stock price. The slope is greatest, however, when the option is deep in the money. In this case, exercise is all but assured, and the option increases in price one-for-one with the stock price.

Determinants of Option Values

We can identify at least six factors that should affect the value of a call option: the stock price, the exercise price, the volatility of the stock price, the time to expiration, the interest rate, and the dividend rate of the stock. The call option should increase in value with the stock price and decrease in value with the exercise price because the payoff to a call, if exercised, equals

---

[1]This discussion presumes the stock pays no dividends until after option expiration. If the stock does pay dividends before expiration, then there *is* a reason you would care about getting the stock now rather than at expiration—getting it now entitles you to the interim dividend payments. In this case, the adjusted intrinsic value of the option must subtract the value of the dividends the stock will pay out before the call is exercised. Adjusted intrinsic value would more generally be defined as $S_0 - PV(X) - PV(D)$, where D represents dividends to be paid before option expiration.

$S_T - X$. The magnitude of the expected payoff from the call increases with the difference $S_0 - X$.

Call option value also increases with the volatility of the underlying stock price. To see why, consider circumstances where possible stock prices at expiration may range from $10 to $50 compared to a situation where stock prices may range only from $20 to $40. In both cases, the expected, or average, stock price will be $30. Suppose the exercise price on a call option is also $30. What are the option payoffs?

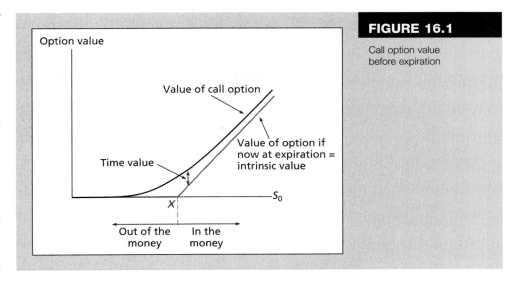

FIGURE 16.1

Call option value before expiration

High-Volatility Scenario

Stock price	$10	$20	$30	$40	$50
Option payoff	0	0	0	10	20

Low-Volatility Scenario

Stock price	$20	$25	$30	$35	$40
Option payoff	0	0	0	5	10

If each outcome is equally likely, with probability .2, the expected payoff to the option under high-volatility conditions will be $6, but under the low-volatility conditions, the expected payoff to the call option is half as much, only $3.

Despite the fact that the average stock price in each scenario is $30, the average option payoff is greater in the high-volatility scenario. The source of this extra value is the limited loss an option holder can suffer, or the volatility value of the call. No matter how far below $30 the stock price drops, the option holder will get zero. Obviously, extremely poor stock price performance is no worse for the call option holder than moderately poor performance.

In the case of good stock performance, however, the call option will expire in the money, and it will be more profitable the higher the stock price. Thus, extremely good stock outcomes can improve the option payoff without limit, but extremely poor outcomes cannot worsen the payoff below zero. This asymmetry means volatility in the underlying stock price increases the expected payoff to the option, thereby enhancing its value.[2]

Should a put option increase in value with the volatility of the stock?

CONCEPT **16.1**
check

---

[2]You should be careful interpreting the relationship between volatility and option value. Neither the focus of this analysis on total (as opposed to systematic) volatility, nor the conclusion that options buyers seem to like volatility, contradicts modern portfolio theory. In conventional discounted cash flow analysis, we find the discount rate appropriate for a *given* distribution of future cash flows. Greater risk implies a higher discount rate and lower present value. Here, however, the cash flow from the *option* depends on the volatility of the *stock*. The option value increases not because traders like risk but because the expected cash flow to the option holder increases along with the volatility of the underlying asset.

TABLE 16.1	If This Variable Increases	The Value of a Call Option
Determinants of call option values	Stock price, S	Increases
	Exercise price, X	Decreases
	Volatility, σ	Increases
	Time to expiration, T	Increases
	Interest rate, r_f	Increases
	Dividend payouts	Decreases

Similarly, longer time to expiration increases the value of a call option. For more distant expiration dates, there is more time for unpredictable future events to affect prices, and the range of likely stock prices increases. This has an effect similar to that of increased volatility. Moreover, as time to expiration lengthens, the present value of the exercise price falls, thereby benefiting the call option holder and increasing the option value. As a corollary to this issue, call option values are higher when interest rates rise (holding the stock price constant), because higher interest rates also reduce the present value of the exercise price.

Finally, the dividend payout policy of the firm affects option values. A high dividend payout policy puts a drag on the rate of growth of the stock price. For any expected total rate of return on the stock, a higher dividend yield must imply a lower expected rate of capital gain. This drag on stock appreciation decreases the potential payoff from the call option, thereby lowering the call value. Table 16.1 summarizes these relationships.

CONCEPT check 16.2

Prepare a table like Table 16.1 for the determinants of put option values. How should put values respond to increases in S, X, T, σ, r_f, and dividend payout?

16.2 Binomial Option Pricing

Two-State Option Pricing

A complete understanding of commonly used option valuation formulas is difficult without a substantial mathematics background. Nevertheless, we can develop valuable insight into option valuation by considering a simple special case. Assume a stock price can take only two possible values at option expiration: The stock will either increase to a given higher price or decrease to a given lower price. Although this may seem an extreme simplification, it allows us to come closer to understanding more complicated and realistic models. Moreover, we can extend this approach to describe far more reasonable specifications of stock price behavior. In fact, several major financial firms employ variants of this simple model to value options and securities with optionlike features.

Suppose the stock now sells at $100, and the price will either increase by a factor of $u = 1.2$ to $120 ($u$ stands for "up") or fall by a factor of $d = .9$ to $90 ($d$ stands for "down") by year-end. A call option on the stock might specify an exercise price of $110 and a time to expiration of one year. The interest rate is 10%. At year-end, the payoff to the holder of the call option will be either zero, if the stock falls, or $10, if the stock price goes to $120.

These possibilities are illustrated by the following "value trees":

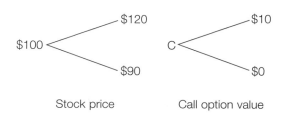

Stock price   Call option value

Compare this payoff to that of a portfolio consisting of one share of the stock and borrowing of $81.82 at the interest rate of 10%. The payoff of this portfolio also depends on the stock price at year-end.

	$90	$120
Value of stock at year-end	$90	$120
− Repayment of loan with interest	−90	−90
Total	$ 0	$ 30

We know the cash outlay to establish the portfolio is $18.18: $100 for the stock, less the $81.82 proceeds from borrowing. Therefore, the portfolio's value tree is

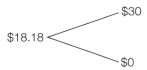

The payoff of this portfolio is exactly three times that of the call option for either value of the stock price. In other words, three call options will exactly replicate the payoff to the portfolio; it follows that three call options should have the same price as the cost of establishing the portfolio. Hence, the three calls should sell for the same price as the "replicating portfolio." Therefore

$$3C = \$18.18$$

or each call should sell at $C = \$6.06$. Thus, given the stock price, exercise price, interest rate, and volatility of the stock price (as represented by the magnitude of the up or down movements), we can derive the fair value for the call option.

This valuation approach relies heavily on the notion of *replication*. With only two possible end-of-year values of the stock, the payoffs to the levered stock portfolio replicate the payoffs to three call options and so need to command the same market price. This notion of replication is behind most option-pricing formulas. For more complex price distributions for stocks, the replication technique is correspondingly more complex, but the principles remain the same.

One way to view the role of replication is to note that, using the numbers assumed for this example, a portfolio made up of one share of stock and three call options written is perfectly hedged. Its year-end value is independent of the ultimate stock price:

	$90	$120
Stock value	$90	$120
− Obligations from 3 calls written	−0	−30
Net payoff	$90	$ 90

The investor has formed a riskless portfolio with a payout of $90. Its value must be the present value of $90, or $90/1.10 = $81.82. The value of the portfolio, which equals $100 from the stock held long, minus $3C$ from the three calls written, should equal $81.82. Hence, $\$100 - 3C = \$81.82$, or $C = \$6.06$.

The ability to create a perfect hedge is the key to this argument. The hedge locks in the end-of-year payout, which therefore can be discounted using the *risk-free* interest rate. To find the value of the option in terms of the value of the stock, we do not need to know the option's or the stock's beta or expected rate of return. The perfect hedging, or replication, approach enables us to express the value of the option in terms of the current value of the stock without this information. With a hedged position, the final stock price does not affect the investor's payoff, so the stock's risk and return parameters have no bearing.

The hedge ratio of this example is one share of stock to three calls, or one-third. For every call option written, one-third share of stock must be held in the portfolio to hedge away risk. This ratio has an easy interpretation in this context: It is the ratio of the range of the values of the option to those of the stock across the two possible outcomes. The stock, which originally sells for $S_0 = \$100$, will be worth either $d \times \$100 = \$90$ or $u \times \$100 = \$120$, for a range of $30. If the stock price increases, the call will be worth $C_u = \$10$, whereas if the stock price decreases, the call will be worth $C_d = 0$, for a range of $10. The ratio of ranges, $10/$30, is one-third, which is the hedge ratio we have established.

The hedge ratio equals the ratio of ranges because the option and stock are perfectly correlated in this two-state example. When the returns of the option and stock are perfectly correlated, a perfect hedge requires that the option and stock be held in a fraction determined only by relative volatility.

We can generalize the hedge ratio for other two-state option problems as

$$H = \frac{C_u - C_d}{uS_0 - dS_0}$$

where C_u or C_d refers to the call option's value when the stock goes up or down, respectively, and uS_0 and dS_0 are the stock prices in the two states. The hedge ratio, H, is the ratio of the swings in the possible end-of-period values of the option and the stock. If the investor writes one option and holds H shares of stock, the value of the portfolio will be unaffected by the stock price. In this case, option pricing is easy: Simply set the value of the hedged portfolio equal to the present value of the known payoff.

Using our example, the option-pricing technique would proceed as follows:

1. Given the possible end-of-year stock prices, $uS_0 = \$120$ and $dS_0 = \$90$, and the exercise price of $110, calculate that $C_u = \$10$ and $C_d = \$0$. The stock price range is $30, while the option price range is $10.
2. Find that the hedge ratio is $10/$30 $= \frac{1}{3}$.
3. Find that a portfolio made up of $\frac{1}{3}$ share with one written option would have an end-of-year value of $30 with certainty.
4. Show that the present value of $30 with a one-year interest rate of 10% is $27.27.
5. Set the value of the hedged position equal to the present value of the certain payoff:

$$\frac{1}{3}S_0 - C_0 = \$27.27$$
$$\$33.33 - C_0 = \$27.27$$

6. Solve for the call's value, $C_0 = \$6.06$.

What if the option were overpriced, perhaps selling for $6.50? Then you can make arbitrage profits. Here is how.

		Cash Flow in 1 Year for Each Possible Stock Price	
	Initial Cash Flow	$S_1 = \$90$	$S_1 = \$120$
1. Write 3 options.	$ 19.50	$ 0	$-30
2. Purchase 1 share.	-100	90	120
3. Borrow $80.50 at 10% interest; repay in 1 year.	80.50	-88.55	-88.55
Total	$ 0	$ 1.45	$ 1.45

Although the net initial investment is zero, the payoff in one year is positive and risk-less. If the option were underpriced, one would simply reverse this arbitrage strategy: Buy the option, and sell the stock short to eliminate price risk. Note, by the way, that the present value of the profit to the above arbitrage strategy equals three times the amount by which the option is overpriced. The present value of the risk-free profit of $1.45 at an 10% interest rate is $1.32. With three options written in the strategy above, this translates to a profit of $.44 per option, exactly the amount by which the option was overpriced: $6.50 versus the "fair value" of $6.06.

Suppose the call option had been underpriced, selling at $5.50. Formulate the arbitrage strategy to exploit the mispricing, and show that it provides a riskless cash flow in one year of $.6167 per option purchased. Compare the present value of this cash flow to the option mispricing.

Generalizing the Two-State Approach

Although the two-state stock price model seems simplistic, we can generalize it to incorporate more realistic assumptions. To start, suppose we were to break up the year into two six-month segments and then assert that over each half-year segment the stock price could take on two values. Here we will say it can increase 10% (i.e., $u = 1.10$) or decrease 5% (i.e., $d = .95$). A stock initially selling at $100 could follow the following possible paths over the course of the year:

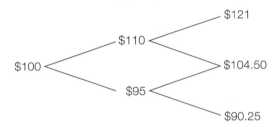

The midrange value of $104.50 can be attained by two paths: an increase of 10% followed by a decrease of 5%, or a decrease of 5% followed by an increase of 10%.

There are now three possible end-of-year values for the stock and three for the option:

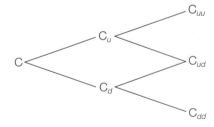

Using methods similar to those we followed above, we could value C_u from knowledge of C_{uu} and C_{ud}, then value C_d from knowledge of C_{du} and C_{dd}, and finally value C from knowledge of C_u and C_d. And there is no reason to stop at six-month intervals. We could next break the year into 4 three-month units, or 12 one-month units, or 365 one-day units, each of which would be posited to have a two-state process. Although the calculations become quite numerous and correspondingly tedious, they are easy to program into a computer, and such computer programs are used widely by participants in the options market.

EXAMPLE 16.1

Binomial Option Pricing

Suppose that the risk-free interest rate is 5% per six-month period and we wish to value a call option with exercise price $110 on the stock described in the two-period price tree just above. We start by finding the value of C_u. From this point, the call can rise to an expiration-date value of $C_{uu} = \$11$ (since at this point the stock price is $u \times u \times S_0 = \$121$) or fall to a final value of $C_{ud} = 0$ (since at this point the stock price is $u \times d \times S_0 = \$104.50$, which is less than the $110 exercise price). Therefore, the hedge ratio at this point is

$$H = \frac{C_{uu} - C_{ud}}{uuS_0 - udS_0} = \frac{\$11 - 0}{\$121 - \$104.5} = \frac{2}{3}$$

Thus, the following portfolio will be worth $209 at option expiration regardless of the ultimate stock price:

	$udS_0 = \$104.50$	$uuS_0 = \$121$
Buy 2 shares at price $uS_0 = \$110$	$209	$242
Write 3 calls at price C_u	0	−33
Total	$209	$209

The portfolio must have a current market value equal to the present value of $209:

$$2 \times \$110 - 3C_u = \$209/1.05 = \$199.047$$

Solve to find that $C_u = \$6.984$.

Next we find the value of C_d. It is easy to see that this value must be zero. If we reach this point (corresponding to a stock price of $95), the stock price at option expiration will be either $104.50 or $90.25; in both cases, the option will expire out of the money. (More formally, we could note that with $C_{ud} = C_{dd} = 0$, the hedge ratio is zero, and a portfolio of *zero* shares will replicate the payoff of the call!)

Finally, we solve for C by using the values of C_u and C_d. The following Concept Check leads you through the calculations that show the option value to be $4.434.

CONCEPT
check
16.4

Show that the initial value of the call option in Example 16.1 is $4.434.
a.   Confirm that the spread in option values is $C_u - C_d = \$6.984$.
b.   Confirm that the spread in stock values is $uS_0 - dS_0 = \$15$.
c.   Confirm that the hedge ratio is .4656 shares purchased for each call written.
d.   Demonstrate that the value in one period of a portfolio comprising .4656 shares and one call written is riskless.
e.   Calculate the present value of this payoff.
f.   Solve for the option value.

As we break the year into progressively finer subintervals, the range of possible year-end stock prices expands and, in fact, will ultimately take on a familiar bell-shaped distribution. This can be seen from an analysis of the event tree for the stock for a period with three subintervals.

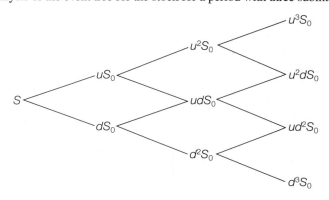

First, notice that as the number of subintervals increases, the number of possible stock prices also increases. Second, notice that extreme events such as u^3S_0 or d^3S_0 are relatively rare, as they require either three consecutive increases or decreases in the three subintervals. More moderate, or midrange, results such as u^2dS_0 can be arrived at by more than one path; any combination of two price increases and one decrease will result in stock price u^2dS_0. Thus, the midrange values will be more likely. The probability of each outcome is described by the binomial distribution, and this multiperiod approach to option pricing is called the **binomial model**.

For example, using an initial stock price of $100, equal probability of stock price increases or decreases, and three intervals for which the possible price increase is 5% and the decrease is 3%, we can obtain the probability distribution of stock prices from the following calculations. There are eight possible combinations for the stock price movement in the three periods: *uuu, uud, udu, duu, udd, dud, ddu, ddd.* Each has a probability of ⅛. Therefore, the probability distribution of stock prices at the end of the last interval would be as follows.

binomial model

An option valuation model predicated on the assumption that stock prices can move to only two values over any short time period.

Event	Probability	Final Stock Price	
3 up movements	⅛	$100 × 1.05³	= $115.76
2 up and 1 down	⅜	$100 × 1.05² × .97	= $106.94
1 up and 2 down	⅜	$100 × 1.05 × .97²	= $ 98.79
3 down movements	⅛	$100 × .97³	= $ 91.27

The midrange values are three times as likely to occur as the extreme values. Figure 16.2A is a graph of the frequency distribution for this example. The graph begins to exhibit the appearance of the familiar bell-shaped curve. In fact, as the number of intervals increases, as in Figure 16.2B, the frequency distribution progressively approaches the lognormal distribution rather than the normal distribution.[3]

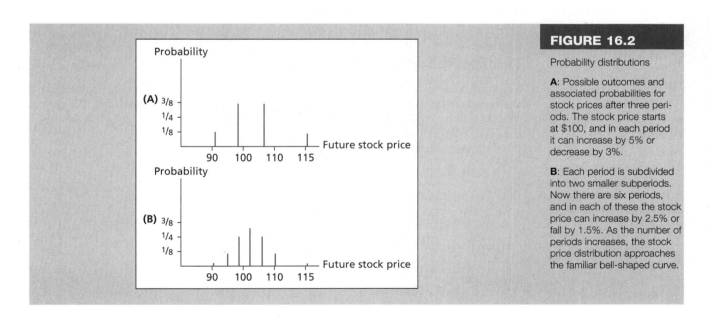

FIGURE 16.2

Probability distributions

A: Possible outcomes and associated probabilities for stock prices after three periods. The stock price starts at $100, and in each period it can increase by 5% or decrease by 3%.

B: Each period is subdivided into two smaller subperiods. Now there are six periods, and in each of these the stock price can increase by 2.5% or fall by 1.5%. As the number of periods increases, the stock price distribution approaches the familiar bell-shaped curve.

[3]Actually, more complex considerations enter here. The limit of this process is lognormal only if we assume also that stock prices move continuously, by which we mean that over small time intervals only small price movements can occur. This rules out rare events such as sudden, extreme price moves in response to dramatic information (like a takeover attempt). For a treatment of this type of "jump process," see John C. Cox and Stephen A. Ross, "The Valuation of Options for Alternative Stochastic Processes," *Journal of Financial Economics* 3 (January–March 1976), pp. 145–66; or Robert C. Merton, "Option Pricing When Underlying Stock Returns Are Discontinuous," *Journal of Financial Economics* 3 (January–March 1976), pp. 125–44.

Suppose we were to continue subdividing the interval in which stock prices are posited to move up or down. Eventually, each node of the event tree would correspond to an infinitesimally small time interval. The possible stock price movement within that time interval would be correspondingly small. As those many intervals passed, the end-of-period stock price would more and more closely resemble a lognormal distribution. Thus, the apparent oversimplification of the two-state model can be overcome by progressively subdividing any period into many subperiods.

At any node, one still could set up a portfolio that would be perfectly hedged over the next tiny time interval. Then, at the end of that interval, on reaching the next node, a new hedge ratio could be computed and the portfolio composition could be revised to remain hedged over the coming small interval. By continuously revising the hedge position, the portfolio would remain hedged and would earn a riskless rate of return over each interval. This is called *dynamic hedging,* the continued updating of the hedge ratio as time passes. As the dynamic hedge becomes ever finer, the resulting option valuation procedure becomes more precise.

CONCEPT *check* **16.5** Would you expect the hedge ratio to be higher or lower when the call option is more in the money?

16.3 Black-Scholes Option Valuation

While the binomial model we have described is extremely flexible, it requires a computer to be useful in actual trading. An option pricing *formula* would be far easier to use than the tedious algorithm involved in the binomial model. It turns out that such a formula can be derived if one is willing to make just two more assumptions: that both the risk-free interest rate and stock price volatility are constant over the life of the option. In this case, as the time to expiration is divided into ever more subperiods, the distribution of the stock price at expiration progressively approaches the lognormal distribution, as suggested by Figure 16.2. When the stock price distribution is actually lognormal, we can derive an exact option-pricing formula.

The Black-Scholes Formula

Black-Scholes pricing formula

A formula to value an option that uses the stock price, the risk-free interest rate, the time to expiration, and the standard deviation of the stock return.

Financial economists searched for years for a workable option-pricing model before Black and Scholes (1973) and Merton (1973) derived a formula for the value of a call option. Now widely used by options market participants, the **Black-Scholes pricing formula** for a European-style call option is

$$C_0 = S_0 e^{-\delta T} N(d_1) - X e^{-rT} N(d_2) \qquad \textbf{(16.1)}$$

where

$$d_1 = \frac{\ln(S_0/X) + (r - \delta + \sigma^2/2)T}{\sigma\sqrt{T}}$$

$$d_2 = d_1 - \sigma\sqrt{T}$$

and where

C_0 = Current call option value.

S_0 = Current stock price.

$N(d)$ = The probability that a random draw from a standard normal distribution will be less than d. This equals the area under the normal curve up to d, as in the shaded area of Figure 16.3. In Excel, this function is called NORMSDIST( ).

X = Exercise price.

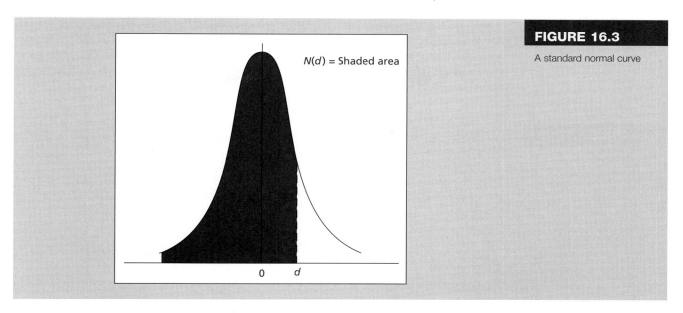

FIGURE 16.3

A standard normal curve

$N(d)$ = Shaded area

0   d

e = The base of the natural log function, approximately 2.71828. In Excel, e^x can be evaluated using the function EXP(x).

δ = Annual dividend yield of underlying stock. (We assume for simplicity that the stock pays a continuous income flow, rather than discrete periodic payments, such as quarterly dividends.)

r = Risk-free interest rate, expressed as a decimal (the annualized continuously compounded rate[4] on a safe asset with the same maturity as the expiration date of the option, which is to be distinguished from r_f, the discrete period interest rate).

T = Time remaining until expiration of option (in years).

ln = Natural logarithm function. In Excel, ln(x) can be calculated as LN(x).

σ = Standard deviation of the annualized continuously compounded rate of return of the stock, expressed as a decimal, not a percent.

Notice a surprising feature of Equation 16.1: The option value does not depend on the expected rate of return on the stock. In a sense, this information is already built into the formula with inclusion of the stock price, which itself depends on the stock's risk and return characteristics. This version of the Black-Scholes formula is predicated on the assumption that the underlying asset has a constant dividend (or income) yield.

Although you may find the Black-Scholes formula intimidating, we can explain it at a somewhat intuitive level. Consider a nondividend-paying stock, for which $\delta = 0$. Then $S_0 e^{-\delta T} = S_0$.

The trick is to view the $N(d)$ terms (loosely) as risk-adjusted probabilities that the call option will expire in the money. First, look at Equation 16.1 assuming both $N(d)$ terms are close to 1.0; that is, when there is a very high probability that the option will be exercised. Then the call option value is equal to $S_0 - Xe^{-rT}$, which is what we called earlier the adjusted intrinsic value, $S_0 - PV(X)$. This makes sense; if exercise is certain, we have a claim on a stock with current value S_0 and an obligation with present value PV(X), or with continuous compounding, Xe^{-rT}.

Now look at Equation 16.1, assuming the $N(d)$ terms are close to zero, meaning the option almost certainly will not be exercised. Then the equation confirms that the call is worth nothing. For middle-range values of $N(d)$ between 0 and 1, Equation 16.1 tells us that the call value can be viewed as the present value of the call's potential payoff adjusting for the probability of in-the-money expiration.

---

[4]See Chapter 5, Section 5.1, for a review of continuous compounding.

How do the $N(d)$ terms serve as risk-adjusted probabilities? This question quickly leads us into advanced statistics. Notice, however, that d_1 and d_2 both increase as the stock price increases. Therefore, $N(d_1)$ and $N(d_2)$ also increase with higher stock prices. This is the property we would desire of our "probabilities." For higher stock prices relative to exercise prices, future exercise is more likely.

EXAMPLE 16.2

Black-Scholes Call Option Valuation

You can use the Black-Scholes formula fairly easily. Suppose you want to value a call option under the following circumstances:

Stock price	$S_0 = 100$
Exercise price	$X = 95$
Interest rate	$r = .10$
Dividend yield	$\delta = 0$
Time to expiration	$T = .25$ (one-quarter year)
Standard deviation	$\sigma = .50$

First calculate

$$d_1 = \frac{\ln(100/95) + (.10 - 0 + .5^2/2).25}{.5\sqrt{0.25}} = .43$$

$$d_2 = .43 - .5\sqrt{.25} = .18$$

Next find $N(d_1)$ and $N(d_2)$. The normal distribution function is tabulated and may be found in many statistics textbooks. A table of $N(d)$ is provided as Table 16.2. The normal distributionfunction $N(d)$ is also provided in any spreadsheet program. In Microsoft Excel, for example, the function name is NORMSDIST. Using either Excel or Table 16.2 (using interpolation for .43), we find that

$$N(.43) = .6664$$
$$N(.18) = .5714$$

Finally, remember that with $\delta = 0$, $S_0 e^{-\delta T} = S_0$. Thus, the value of the call option is

$$C = 100 \times .6664 - 95e^{-0.10 \times 0.25} \times .5714$$
$$= 66.64 - 52.94 = \$13.70$$

CONCEPT check 16.6

Calculate the call option value if the standard deviation on the stock is .6 instead of .5. Confirm that the option is worth more using this higher volatility.

What if the option price in Example 16.2 were $15 rather than $13.70? Is the option mispriced? Maybe, but before betting your career on that, you may want to reconsider the valuation analysis. First, like all models, the Black-Scholes formula is based on some simplifying abstractions that make the formula only approximately valid.

Some of the important assumptions underlying the formula are the following:

1. The stock will pay a constant, continuous dividend yield until the option expiration date.
2. Both the interest rate, r, and variance rate, σ^2, of the stock are constant (or in slightly more general versions of the formula, both are *known* functions of time—any changes are perfectly predictable).
3. Stock prices are continuous, meaning that sudden extreme jumps, such as those in the aftermath of an announcement of a takeover attempt, are ruled out.

TABLE 16.2	d	N(d)	d	N(d)	d	N(d)
Cumulative normal distribution	−3.00	0.0013	−1.36	0.0869	−0.32	0.3745
	−2.95	0.0016	−1.34	0.0901	−0.30	0.3821
	−2.90	0.0019	−1.32	0.0934	−0.28	0.3897
	−2.85	0.0022	−1.30	0.0968	−0.26	0.3974
	−2.80	0.0026	−1.28	0.1003	−0.24	0.4052
	−2.75	0.0030	−1.26	0.1038	−0.22	0.4129
	−2.70	0.0035	−1.24	0.1075	−0.20	0.4207
	−2.65	0.0040	−1.22	0.1112	−0.18	0.4286
	−2.60	0.0047	−1.20	0.1151	−0.16	0.4365
	−2.55	0.0054	−1.18	0.1190	−0.14	0.4443
	−2.50	0.0062	−1.16	0.1230	−0.12	0.4523
	−2.45	0.0071	−1.14	0.1271	−0.10	0.4602
	−2.40	0.0082	−1.12	0.1314	−0.08	0.4681
	−2.35	0.0094	−1.10	0.1357	−0.06	0.4761
	−2.30	0.0107	−1.08	0.1401	−0.04	0.4841
	−2.25	0.0122	−1.06	0.1446	−0.02	0.4920
	−2.20	0.0139	−1.04	0.1492	0.00	0.5000
	−2.15	0.0158	−1.02	0.1539	0.02	0.5080
	−2.10	0.0179	−1.00	0.1587	0.04	0.5160
	−2.05	0.0202	−0.98	0.1635	0.06	0.5239
	−2.00	0.0228	−0.96	0.1685	0.08	0.5319
	−1.98	0.0239	−0.94	0.1736	0.10	0.5398
	−1.96	0.0250	−0.92	0.1788	0.12	0.5478
	−1.94	0.0262	−0.90	0.1841	0.14	0.5557
	−1.92	0.0274	−0.88	0.1894	0.16	0.5636
	−1.90	0.0287	−0.86	0.1949	0.18	0.5714
	−1.88	0.0301	−0.84	0.2005	0.20	0.5793
	−1.86	0.0314	−0.82	0.2061	0.22	0.5871
	−1.84	0.0329	−0.80	0.2119	0.24	0.5948
	−1.82	0.0344	−0.78	0.2177	0.26	0.6026
	−1.80	0.0359	−0.76	0.2236	0.28	0.6103
	−1.78	0.0375	−0.74	0.2297	0.30	0.6179
	−1.76	0.0392	−0.72	0.2358	0.32	0.6255
	−1.74	0.0409	−0.70	0.2420	0.34	0.6331
	−1.72	0.0427	−0.68	0.2483	0.36	0.6406
	−1.70	0.0446	−0.66	0.2546	0.38	0.6480
	−1.68	0.0465	−0.64	0.2611	0.40	0.6554
	−1.66	0.0485	−0.62	0.2676	0.42	0.6628
	−1.64	0.0505	−0.60	0.2743	0.44	0.6700
	−1.62	0.0526	−0.58	0.2810	0.46	0.6773
	−1.60	0.0548	−0.56	0.2877	0.48	0.6844
	−1.58	0.0571	−0.54	0.2946	0.50	0.6915
	−1.56	0.0594	−0.52	0.3015	0.52	0.6985
	−1.54	0.0618	−0.50	0.3085	0.54	0.7054
	−1.52	0.0643	−0.48	0.3156	0.56	0.7123
	−1.50	0.0668	−0.46	0.3228	0.58	0.7191
	−1.48	0.0694	−0.44	0.3300	0.60	0.7258
	−1.46	0.0721	−0.42	0.3373	0.62	0.7324
	−1.44	0.0749	−0.40	0.3446	0.64	0.7389
	−1.42	0.0778	−0.38	0.3520	0.66	0.7454
	−1.40	0.0808	−0.36	0.3594	0.68	0.7518
	−1.38	0.0838	−0.34	0.3669	0.70	0.7580

(continued)

TABLE 16.2	d	N(d)	d	N(d)	d	N(d)
(concluded)	0.72	0.7642	1.30	0.9032	1.88	0.9699
	0.74	0.7704	1.32	0.9066	1.90	0.9713
	0.76	0.7764	1.34	0.9099	1.92	0.9726
	0.78	0.7823	1.36	0.9131	1.94	0.9738
	0.80	0.7882	1.38	0.9162	1.96	0.9750
	0.82	0.7939	1.40	0.9192	1.98	0.9761
	0.84	0.7996	1.42	0.9222	2.00	0.9772
	0.86	0.8051	1.44	0.9251	2.05	0.9798
	0.88	0.8106	1.46	0.9279	2.10	0.9821
	0.90	0.8159	1.48	0.9306	2.15	0.9842
	0.92	0.8212	1.50	0.9332	2.20	0.9861
	0.94	0.8264	1.52	0.9357	2.25	0.9878
	0.96	0.8315	1.54	0.9382	2.30	0.9893
	0.98	0.8365	1.56	0.9406	2.35	0.9906
	1.00	0.8414	1.58	0.9429	2.40	0.9918
	1.02	0.8461	1.60	0.9452	2.45	0.9929
	1.04	0.8508	1.62	0.9474	2.50	0.9938
	1.06	0.8554	1.64	0.9495	2.55	0.9946
	1.08	0.8599	1.66	0.9515	2.60	0.9953
	1.10	0.8643	1.68	0.9535	2.65	0.9960
	1.12	0.8686	1.70	0.9554	2.70	0.9965
	1.14	0.8729	1.72	0.9573	2.75	0.9970
	1.16	0.8770	1.74	0.9591	2.80	0.9974
	1.18	0.8810	1.76	0.9608	2.85	0.9978
	1.20	0.8849	1.78	0.9625	2.90	0.9981
	1.22	0.8888	1.80	0.9641	2.95	0.9984
	1.24	0.8925	1.82	0.9656	3.00	0.9986
	1.26	0.8962	1.84	0.9671	3.05	0.9989
	1.28	0.8997	1.86	0.9686		

Variants of the Black-Scholes formula have been developed to deal with many of these limitations.

Second, even within the context of the Black-Scholes model, you must be sure of the accuracy of the parameters used in the formula. Four of these—S_0, X, T, and r—are straightforward. The stock price, exercise price, and time to expiration are readily determined. The interest rate used is the money market rate for a maturity equal to that of the option, and the dividend yield is usually reasonably stable, at least over short horizons.

The last input, though, the standard deviation of the stock return, is not directly observable. It must be estimated from historical data, from scenario analysis, or from the prices of other options, as we will describe momentarily. Because the standard deviation must be estimated, it is always possible that discrepancies between an option price and its Black-Scholes value are simply artifacts of error in the estimation of the stock's volatility.

In fact, market participants often give the option valuation problem a different twist. Rather than calculating a Black-Scholes option value for a given stock standard deviation, they ask instead: What standard deviation would be necessary for the option price that I actually observe to be consistent with the Black-Scholes formula? This is called the **implied volatility** of the option, the volatility level for the stock that the option price implies. Investors can then judge whether they think the actual stock standard deviation exceeds the implied volatility. If it does, the option is considered a good buy; if actual volatility seems greater than the implied volatility, the option's fair price would exceed the observed price.

implied volatility

The standard deviation of stock returns that is consistent with an option's market value.

SPREADSHEET 16.1

Spreadsheet to calculate Black-Scholes call-option values

	A	B	C	D	E	F	G	H	I	J
1	INPUTS			OUTPUTS			FORMULA FOR OUTPUT IN COLUMN E			
2	Standard deviation (annual)	.2783		d1	0.0029		(LN(B5/B6)+(B4-B7+.5*B2^2)*B3)/(B2*SQRT(B3))			
3	Expiration (in years)	.5		d2	-0.1939		E2-B2*SQRT(B3)			
4	Risk-free rate (annual)	.06		N(d1)	0.5012		NORMSDIST(E2)			
5	Stock price	100		N(d2)	0.4231		NORMSDIST(E3)			
6	Exercise price	105		B/S call value	7.0000		B5*EXP(-B7*B3)*E4-B6*EXP(-B4*B3)*E5			
7	Dividend yield (annual)	0		B/S put value	8.8967		B6*EXP(-B4*B3)*(1-E5)-B5*EXP(-B7*B3)*(1-E4)			

eXcel

Please visit us at
www.mhhe.com/bkm

Another variation is to compare two options on the same stock with equal expiration dates but different exercise prices. The option with the higher implied volatility would be considered relatively expensive because a higher standard deviation is required to justify its price. The analyst might consider buying the option with the lower implied volatility and writing the option with the higher implied volatility.

The Black-Scholes call-option valuation formula, as well as implied volatilities, are easily calculated using an Excel spreadsheet, as in Spreadsheet 16.1. The model inputs are provided in column B, and the outputs are given in column E. The formulas for d_1 and d_2 are provided in the spreadsheet, and the Excel formula NORMSDIST(d_1) is used to calculate $N(d_1)$. Cell E6 contains the Black-Scholes call option formula.

To compute an implied volatility, we can use the Goal Seek command from the Tools menu in Excel. (See Figure 16.4 for an illustration.) Goal Seek asks us to change the value of one cell to make the value of another cell (called the target cell) equal to a specific value. For example, if we observe a call option selling for $7 with other inputs as given in the spreadsheet, we can use Goal Seek to change the value in cell B2 (the standard deviation of the stock) to set the option value in cell E6 equal to $7. The target cell, E6, is the call price, and the spreadsheet manipulates cell B2. When you click "OK," the spreadsheet finds that a standard

	A	B	C	D	E	F	G	H	I	J	K
1	INPUTS			OUTPUTS			FORMULA FOR OUTPUT IN COLUMN E				
2	Standard deviation (annual)	.2783		d1	0.0029		(LN(B5/B6)+(B4-B7+.5*B2^2)*B3)/(B2*SQRT(B3))				
3	Expiration (in years)	.5		d2	-0.1939		E2-B2*SQRT(B3)				
4	Risk-free rate (annual)	.06		N(d1)	0.5012		NORMSDIST(E2)				
5	Stock price	100		N(d2)	0.4231		NORMSDIST(E3)				
6	Exercise price	105		B/S call value	7.0000		B5*EXP(-B7*B3)*E4-B6*EXP(-B4*B3)*E5				
7	Dividend yield (annual)	0		B/S put value	8.8968		B6*EXP(-B4*B3)*(1-E5)-B5*EXP(-B7*B3)*(1-E4)				
8											
9											
10											
11				**Goal Seek**							
12											
13				Set cell:	$E$6						
14				To value:	7						
15				By changing cell:	$B$2						
16					OK	Cancel					
17											

FIGURE 16.4

Using Goal Seek to find implied volatility

FIGURE 16.5

Implied volatility of the
S&P 500 (VIX index),
expressed as an annualized
standard deviation.

Source: Chicago Board
Options Exchange

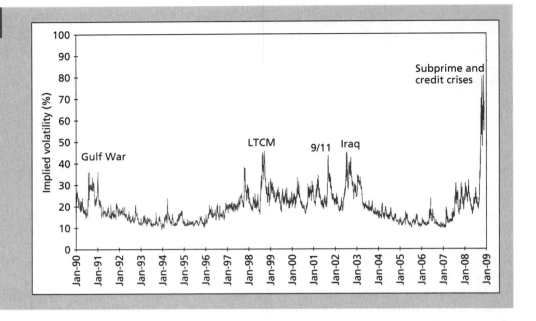

deviation equal to .2783 is consistent with a call price of $7; therefore, 27.83% would be the call's implied volatility if it were selling at $7.

CONCEPT *check* **16.7**

Consider the call option in Example 16.2. If it sells for $15 rather than the value of $13.70 found in the example, is its implied volatility more or less than .5? Use Spreadsheet 16.1 (available at the Online Learning Center) to find its implied volatility at this price.

The Chicago Board Options Exchange regularly computes the implied volatility of major stock indexes. Figure 16.5 is a graph of the implied (30-day) volatility of the S&P 500. During periods of turmoil, implied volatility can spike quickly. Notice the peaks in January 1991 (Gulf War), in August 1998 (collapse of Long-Term Capital Management), on September 11, 2001, in 2002 (buildup to invasion of Iraq) and most dramatically, during the credit crisis of 2008. Because implied volatility correlates with crisis, it is sometimes called an "investor fear gauge."

In March 2004, a futures contract on the 30-day implied volatility of the S&P 500 began trading on the CBOE Futures Exchange. The payoff of the contract depends on market implied volatility at the expiration of the contract. The ticker symbol of the contract is VIX.

Figure 16.5 also reveals an awkward empirical fact. While the Black-Scholes formula is derived assuming that stock volatility is constant, the time series of implied volatilities consistent with that formula is in fact far from constant. This contradiction reminds us that the Black-Scholes model (like all models) is a simplification that does not capture all aspects of real markets. In this particular context, extensions of the pricing model that allow stock volatility to evolve randomly over time would be desirable, and in fact, many extensions of the model along these lines have been suggested.[5]

The fact that volatility changes unpredictably means that it can be difficult to choose the proper volatility input to use in any option-pricing model. A considerable amount of recent research has been devoted to techniques to predict changes in volatility. These techniques, which go by the name ARCH and stochastic volatility models, posit that changes in volatility are partially predictable and that by analyzing recent levels and trends in volatility, one can improve predictions of future volatility.[6]

[5]Influential articles on this topic are Hull and White (1987), Wiggins (1987), and Heston (1993). For a more recent review, see Ghysels, Harvey, and Renault (1996).

[6]For an introduction to these models see Alexander (2001).

The Put-Call Parity Relationship

So far, we have focused on the pricing of call options. In many important cases, put prices can be derived simply from the prices of calls. This is because prices of European put and call options are linked together in an equation known as the put-call parity relationship. Therefore, once you know the value of a call, put pricing is easy.

To derive the parity relationship, suppose you buy a call option and write a put option, each with the same exercise price, X, and the same expiration date, T. At expiration, the payoff on your investment will equal the payoff to the call, minus the payoff that must be made on the put. The payoff for each option will depend on whether the ultimate stock price, S_T, exceeds the exercise price at contract expiration.

	$S_T \leq X$	$S_T > X$
Payoff of call held	0	$S_T - X$
− Payoff of put written	$-(X - S_T)$	0
Total	$S_T - X$	$S_T - X$

Figure 16.6 illustrates this payoff pattern. Compare the payoff to that of a portfolio made up of the stock plus a borrowing position, where the money to be paid back will grow, with interest, to X dollars at the maturity of the loan. Such a position is a *levered* equity position in which $PV(X) = Xe^{-rT}$ dollars is borrowed today (so that X will be repaid at maturity), and S_0 dollars is invested in the stock. The total payoff of the levered equity position is $S_T - X$, the same as that of the option strategy. Thus, the long call–short put position replicates the levered equity position. Again, we see that option trading provides leverage.

Because the option portfolio has a payoff identical to that of the levered equity position, the costs of establishing them must be equal. The net cash outlay necessary to establish the option position is $C - P$: The call is purchased for C, while the written put generates income of P. Likewise, the levered equity position requires a net cash outlay of $S_0 - Xe^{-rT}$, the cost of the stock less the proceeds from borrowing. Equating these costs, we conclude

$$C - P = S_0 - Xe^{-rT} \quad \textbf{(16.2)}$$

Equation 16.2 is called the **put-call parity relationship** because it represents the proper relationship between put and call prices. If the parity relationship is ever violated, an arbitrage opportunity arises.

put-call parity relationship

An equation representing the proper relationship between put and call prices.

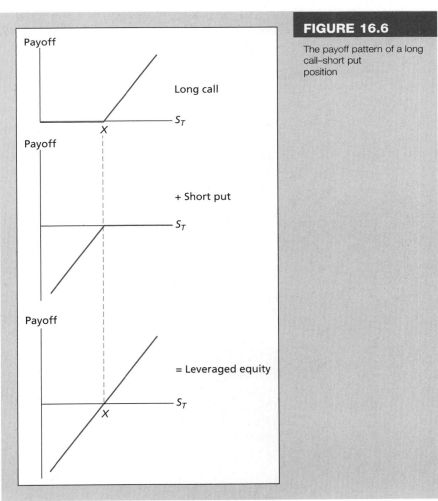

FIGURE 16.6

The payoff pattern of a long call–short put position

EXAMPLE 16.3	Suppose you observe the following data for a certain stock.

Put-Call Parity

Stock price	$110
Call price (six-month maturity, $X = \$105$)	14
Put price (six-month maturity, $X = \$105$)	5
Risk-free interest rate	5% continuously compounded rate

We use these data in the put-call parity relationship to see if parity is violated.

$$C - P \overset{?}{=} S_0 - Xe^{-rT}$$

$$14 - 5 \overset{?}{=} 110 - 105e^{-.05 \times 5}$$

$$9 \overset{?}{=} 7.59$$

This result, a violation of parity (9 does not equal 7.59) indicates mispricing and leads to an arbitrage opportunity. You can buy the relatively cheap portfolio (the stock plus borrowing position represented on the right-hand side of Equation 16.2) and sell the relatively expensive portfolio (the long call–short put position corresponding to the left-hand side, that is, write a call and buy a put).

Let's examine the payoff to this strategy. In six months, the stock will be worth S_T. You borrowed the present value of the exercise price, $105, and must pay back the loan with interest, resulting in a cash outflow of $105. The written call will result in a cash outflow of $S_T - \$105$ if S_T exceeds $105. The purchased put pays off $105 - S_T$ if the stock price is below $105.

Table 16.3 summarizes the outcome. The immediate cash inflow is $1.41, precisely equal to the mispricing of the option. In six months, the various positions provide exactly offsetting cash flows: The $1.41 inflow is realized risklessly without any offsetting outflows. This is an arbitrage opportunity that investors will pursue on a large scale until buying and selling pressure restores the parity condition expressed in Equation 16.2.

Equation 16.2 actually applies only to options on stocks that pay no dividends before the expiration date of the option. It also applies only to European options, as the cash flow streams from the two portfolios represented by the two sides of Equation 16.2 will match only if each position is held until expiration. If a call and a put may be optimally exercised at different times before their common expiration date, then the equality of payoffs cannot be assured, or even expected, and the portfolios will have different values.

The extension of the parity condition for European call options on dividend-paying stocks is, however, straightforward. Problem 26 at the end of the chapter leads you through the extension of the parity relationship. The more general formulation of the put-call parity condition is

$$P = C - S_0 + \text{PV}(X) + \text{PV (dividends)} \tag{16.3}$$

where PV(dividends) is the present value of the dividends that will be paid by the stock during the life of the option. If the stock does not pay dividends, Equation 16.3 becomes identical to Equation 16.2.

TABLE 16.3		Immediate	Cash Flow in Six Months	
Arbitrage Strategy	**Position**	**Cash Flow**	**$S_T < 105$**	**$S_T \geq 105$**
	Buy stock	−110	S_T	S_T
	Borrow $Xe^{-rT} = \$102.41$	+102.41	−105	−105
	Sell call	+14	0	$-(S_T - 105)$
	Buy put	−5	$105 - S_T$	0
	Total	1.41	0	0

Notice that this generalization would apply as well to European options on assets other than stocks. Instead of using dividend income in Equation 16.3, we would let any income paid out by the underlying asset play the role of the stock dividends. For example, European put and call options on bonds would satisfy the same parity relationship, except that the bond's coupon income would replace the stock's dividend payments in the parity formula.

Let's see how well parity works using real data on the IBM options in Figure 15.1 from the previous chapter. The March expiration call with exercise price $100 and time to expiration of 42 days cost $2.80 while the corresponding put option cost $6.47. IBM was selling for $96.14, and the annualized short-term interest rate on this date was .2%. No dividends will be paid between the date of the listing, February 6, and the option expiration date. According to parity, we should find that

$$P \quad = \quad C \quad + \quad PV(X) \quad - \quad S_0 \quad + \quad PV(\text{dividends})$$

$$\$6.47 \quad \overset{?}{=} \quad \$2.80 \quad + \quad \frac{100}{(1.002)^{42/365}} \quad - \quad \$96.14 \quad + \quad 0$$

$$\$6.47 \quad \overset{?}{=} \quad \$2.80 \quad + \quad \$99.97 - \$96.14$$

$$\$6.47 \quad \overset{?}{=} \quad \$6.63$$

So, parity is violated by about $.16 per share. Is this a big enough difference to exploit? Probably not. You have to weigh the potential profit against the trading costs of the call, put, and stock. More important, given the fact that options may trade relatively infrequently, this deviation from parity might not be "real" but may instead be attributable to "stale" (i.e., out-of-date) price quotes at which you cannot actually trade.

Put Option Valuation

As we saw in Equation 16.3, we can use the put-call parity relationship to value put options once we know the call option value. Sometimes, however, it is easier to work with a put option valuation formula directly. The Black-Scholes formula for the value of a European put option[7]

$$P = Xe^{-rT}[1 - N(d_2)] - S_0 e^{-\delta T}[1 - N(d_1)] \tag{16.4}$$

Using data from the Black-Scholes call option in Example 16.2 we find that a European put option on that stock with identical exercise price and time to expiration is worth

$$\$95e^{-.10\times.25}(1-.5714) - \$100(1-.6664) = \$6.35$$

Notice that this value is consistent with put-call parity:

$$P = C + PV(X) - S_0 + PV(\text{Div}) = 13.70 + 95e^{-.10\times.25} - 100 + 0 = 6.35$$

As we noted traders can do, we might then compare this formula value to the actual put price as one step in formulating a trading strategy.

EXAMPLE   16.4

Black-Scholes Put Option Valuation

Equation 16.4 is valid for European puts. Most listed put options are American-style, however, and offer the opportunity of early exercise. Because an American option allows its owner to exercise at any time before the expiration date, it must be worth at least as much as the corresponding European option. However, while Equation 16.4 describes only the lower bound on the true value of the American put, in many applications the approximation is very accurate.

---

[7]This formula is consistent with the put-call parity relationship, and in fact can be derived from it. If you want to try to do so, remember to take present values using continuous compounding, and note that when a stock pays a continuous flow of income in the form of a constant dividend yield, δ, the present value of that dividend flow is $S_0(1 - e^{-\delta T})$. (Notice that $e^{-\delta T}$ approximately equals $1 - \delta T$, so the value of the dividend flow is approximately $\delta T S_0$.)

16.4 Using the Black-Scholes Formula

Hedge Ratios and the Black-Scholes Formula

hedge ratio or delta

The number of shares of stock required to hedge the price risk of holding one option.

In the last chapter, we considered two investments in FinCorp stock: 100 shares or 900 call options. We saw that the call option position was more sensitive to swings in the stock price than the all-stock position. To analyze the overall exposure to a stock price more precisely, however, it is necessary to quantify these relative sensitivities. A tool that enables us to summarize the overall exposure of portfolios of options with various exercise prices and times to expiration is the hedge ratio. An option's **hedge ratio** is the change in the price of an option for a $1 increase in the stock price. A call option, therefore, has a positive hedge ratio, and a put option has a negative hedge ratio. The hedge ratio is commonly called the option's **delta.**

If you were to graph the option value as a function of the stock value as we have done for a call option in Figure 16.7, the hedge ratio is simply the slope of the value function evaluated at the current stock price. For example, suppose the slope of the curve at $S_0 = \$120$ equals .60. As the stock increases in value by $1, the option increases by approximately $.60, as the figure shows.

For every call option written, .60 shares of stock would be needed to hedge the investor's portfolio. For example, if one writes 10 options and holds six shares of stock, according to the hedge ratio of .6, a $1 increase in stock price will result in a gain of $6 on the stock holdings, while the loss on the 10 options written will be $10 \times \$.60$, an equivalent $6. The stock price movement leaves total wealth unaltered, which is what a hedged position is intended to do. The investor holding both the stock and options in proportions dictated by their relative price movements hedges the portfolio.

Black-Scholes hedge ratios are particularly easy to compute. The hedge ratio for a call is $N(d_1)$, while the hedge ratio for a put is $N(d_1) - 1$. We defined $N(d_1)$ as part of the Black-Scholes formula in Equation 16.1. Recall that $N(d)$ stands for the area under the standard normal curve up to d. Therefore, the call option hedge ratio must be positive and less than 1.0, while the put option hedge ratio is negative and of smaller absolute value than 1.0.

Figure 16.7 verifies the insight that the slope of the call option valuation function is less than 1.0, approaching 1.0 only as the stock price becomes extremely large. This tells us that option values change less than one-for-one with changes in stock prices. Why should this be? Suppose an option is so far in the money that you are absolutely certain it will be exercised. In that case, every $1 increase in the stock price would increase the option value by $1. But if there is a reasonable chance the call option will expire out of the money, even after a moderate stock price gain, a $1 increase in the stock price will not necessarily increase the ultimate payoff to the call; therefore, the call price will not respond by a full $1.

FIGURE 16.7

Call option value and hedge ratio

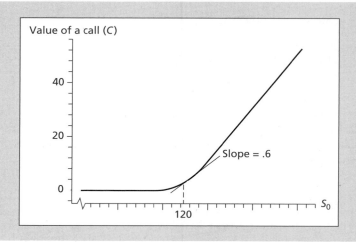

The fact that hedge ratios are less than 1.0 does not contradict our earlier observation that options offer leverage and are sensitive to stock price movements. Although *dollar* movements in option prices are slighter than dollar movements in the stock price, the *rate of return* volatility of options remains greater than stock return volatility because options sell at lower prices. In our example, with the stock selling at $120, and a hedge ratio of .6, an option with exercise price $120 may sell for $5. If the stock price increases to $121, the call price would be expected to increase by only $.60, to $5.60. The percentage increase in the option value is $.60/$5.00 = 12%, however, while the percentage stock price increase is only $1/$120 = .83%. The ratio of the percent changes is 12%/.83% = 14.4. For every 1% increase in the stock price, the option price increases by 14.4%. This ratio, the percent change in option price per percent change in stock price, is called the **option elasticity.**

The hedge ratio is an essential tool in portfolio management and control. An example will show why.

option elasticity

The percentage increase in an option's value given a 1% increase in the value of the underlying security.

EXAMPLE 16.5

Portfolio Hedge Ratios

Consider two portfolios, one holding 750 IBM calls and 200 shares of IBM and the other holding 800 shares of IBM. Which portfolio has greater dollar exposure to IBM price movements? You can answer this question easily using the hedge ratio.

Each option changes in value by H dollars for each dollar change in stock price, where H stands for the hedge ratio. Thus, if H equals .6, the 750 options are equivalent to 450 shares ($= .6 \times 750$) in terms of the response of their market value to IBM stock price movements. The first portfolio has less dollar sensitivity to stock price change because the 450 share-equivalents of the options plus the 200 shares actually held are less than the 800 shares held in the second portfolio.

This is not to say, however, that the first portfolio is less sensitive to the stock's rate of return. As we noted in discussing option elasticities, the first portfolio may be of lower total value than the second, so despite its lower sensitivity in terms of total market value, it might have greater rate of return sensitivity. Because a call option has a lower market value than the stock, its price changes more than proportionally with stock price changes, even though its hedge ratio is less than 1.0.

CONCEPT *check* **16.8**

What is the elasticity of a put option currently selling for $4 with exercise price $120, and hedge ratio $-.4$ if the stock price is currently $122?

Portfolio Insurance

In Chapter 15, we showed that protective put strategies offer a sort of insurance policy on an asset. The protective put has proven to be extremely popular with investors. Even if the asset price falls, the put conveys the right to sell the asset for the exercise price, which is a way to lock in a minimum portfolio value. With an at-the-money put ($X = S_0$), the maximum loss that can be realized is the cost of the put. The asset can be sold for X, which equals its original price, so even if the asset price falls, the investor's net loss over the period is just the cost of the put. If the asset value increases, however, upside potential is unlimited. Figure 16.8 graphs the profit or loss on a protective put position as a function of the change in the value of the underlying asset.

While the protective put is a simple and convenient way to achieve **portfolio insurance,** that is, to limit the worst-case portfolio rate of return, there are practical difficulties in trying to insure a portfolio of stocks. First, unless the investor's portfolio corresponds to a standard market index for which puts are traded, a put option on the portfolio will not be available for purchase. And if index puts are used to protect a nonindexed portfolio, tracking error can result. For example, if the portfolio falls in value while the market index rises, the put will fail to provide the intended protection. Tracking error limits the investor's freedom to pursue active stock selection because such error will be greater as the managed portfolio departs more substantially from the market index.

Moreover, the desired horizon of the insurance program must match the maturity of a traded put option in order to establish the appropriate protective put position. Today, long-term index

portfolio insurance

Portfolio strategies that limit investment losses while maintaining upside potential.

FIGURE 16.8

Profit on a protective put strategy

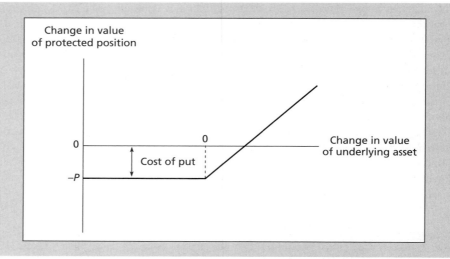

options called LEAPS (for Long-Term Equity AnticiPation Securities) trade on the Chicago Board Options Exchange with expirations of several years. However, in the mid-1980s, while most investors pursuing insurance programs had horizons of several years, actively traded puts were limited to expirations of less than a year. Rolling over a sequence of short-term puts, which might be viewed as a response to this problem, introduces new risks because the prices at which successive puts will be available in the future are not known today.

Providers of portfolio insurance with horizons of several years, therefore, cannot rely on the simple expedient of purchasing protective puts for their clients' portfolios. Instead, they follow trading strategies that replicate the payoffs to the protective put position.

Here is the general idea. Even if a put option on the desired portfolio with the desired expiration date does not exist, a theoretical option-pricing model (such as the Black-Scholes model) can be used to determine how that option's price *would* respond to the portfolio's value if the option did trade. For example, if stock prices were to fall, the put option would increase in value. The option model could quantify this relationship. The net exposure of the (hypothetical) protective put portfolio to swings in stock prices is the sum of the exposures of the two components of the portfolio: the stock and the put. The net exposure of the portfolio equals the equity exposure less the (offsetting) put option exposure.

We can create "synthetic" protective put positions by holding a quantity of stocks with the same net exposure to market swings as the hypothetical protective put position. The key to this strategy is the option delta, or hedge ratio, that is, the change in the price of the protective put option per change in the value of the underlying stock portfolio.

EXAMPLE 16.6

*Synthetic
Protective Puts*

Suppose a portfolio is currently valued at $100 million. An at-the-money put option on the portfolio might have a hedge ratio or delta of −.6, meaning the option's value swings $.60 for every dollar change in portfolio value, but in an opposite direction. Suppose the stock portfolio falls in value by 2%. The profit on a hypothetical protective put position (if the put existed) would be as follows (in millions of dollars):

Loss on stocks:	2% of $100 = $2.00
+ Gain on put:	.6 × $2.00 = 1.20
Net loss	$0.80

(continued)

We create the synthetic option position by selling a proportion of shares equal to the put option's delta (i.e., selling 60% of the shares) and placing the proceeds in risk-free T-bills. The rationale is that the hypothetical put option would have offset 60% of any change in the stock portfolio's value, so one must reduce portfolio risk directly by selling 60% of the equity and putting the proceeds into a risk-free asset. Total return on a synthetic protective put position with $60 million in risk-free investments such as T-bills and $40 million in equity is

Loss on stocks:	2% of $40 = $.80
+ Loss on bills:	0
Net loss	$.80

The synthetic and actual protective put positions have equal returns. We conclude that if you sell a proportion of shares equal to the put option's delta and place the proceeds in cash equivalents, your exposure to the stock market will equal that of the desired protective put position.

The difficulty with synthetic positions is that deltas constantly change. Figure 16.9 shows that as the stock price falls, the absolute value of the appropriate hedge ratio increases. Therefore, market declines require extra hedging, that is, additional conversion of equity into cash. This constant updating of the hedge ratio is called **dynamic hedging**, as discussed in Section 16.2. Another term for such hedging is *delta hedging,* because the option delta is used to determine the number of shares that need to be bought or sold.

Dynamic hedging is one reason portfolio insurance has been said to contribute to market volatility. Market declines trigger additional sales of stock as portfolio insurers strive to increase their hedging. These additional sales are seen as reinforcing or exaggerating market downturns.

In practice, portfolio insurers do not actually buy or sell stocks directly when they update their hedge positions. Instead, they minimize trading costs by buying or selling stock index futures as a substitute for sale of the stocks themselves. As you will see in the next chapter, stock prices and index future prices usually are very tightly linked by cross-market arbitrageurs so that futures transactions can be used as reliable proxies for stock transactions. Instead of selling equities based on the put option's delta, insurers will sell an equivalent number of futures contracts.[8]

Several portfolio insurers suffered great setbacks during the market "crash" of October 19, 1987, when the Dow Jones Industrial Average fell more than 20%. A description of what

dynamic hedging

Constant updating of hedge positions as market conditions change.

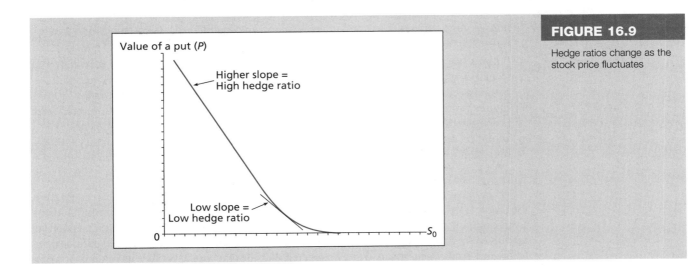

FIGURE 16.9

Hedge ratios change as the stock price fluctuates

[8]Notice, however, that the use of index futures reintroduces the problem of tracking error between the portfolio and the market index.

J. P. MORGAN ROLLS DICE ON MICROSOFT OPTIONS

Microsoft, in a shift that could be copied throughout the technology business, said yesterday that it plans to stop issuing stock options to its employees, and instead will provide them with restricted stock.

The deal could portend a seismic shift for Microsoft's Silicon Valley rivals, and it could well have effects on Wall Street. Though details of the plan still aren't clear, J. P. Morgan effectively plans to buy the options from Microsoft employees who opt for restricted stock instead. Employee stock options are granted as a form of compensation and allow employees the right to exchange the options for shares of company stock.

The price offered to employees for the options presumably will be lower than the current value, giving J. P. Morgan a chance to make a profit on the deal. Rather than holding the options, and thus betting Microsoft's stock will rise, people familiar with the bank's strategy say J. P. Morgan probably will match each option it buys from the company's employees with a separate trade in the stock market that both hedges the bet and gives itself a margin of profit.

For Wall Street's so-called rocket scientists who do complicated financial transactions such as this one, the strategy behind J. P. Morgan's deal with Microsoft isn't particularly unique or sophisticated. They add that the bank has several ways to deal with the millions of Microsoft options that could come its way.

The bank, for instance, could hedge the options by shorting, or betting against, Microsoft stock. Microsoft has the largest market capitalization of any stock in the market, and its shares are among the most liquid, meaning it would be easy to hedge the risk of holding those options.

J. P. Morgan also could sell the options to investors, much as they would do with a syndicated loan, thereby spreading the risk. During a conference call with investors, [Microsoft Chief Executive Steve] Ballmer said employees could sell their options to "a third party or set of third parties," adding that the company was still working out the details with J. P. Morgan and the SEC.

SOURCE: Excerpt from *The Wall Street Journal*, July 9, 2003. Reprinted by permission of *The Wall Street Journal*, Copyright © 2003 Dow Jones & Company, Inc. All Rights Reserved Worldwide.

happened then should help you appreciate the complexities of applying a seemingly straightforward hedging concept.

1. Market volatility at the crash was much greater than ever encountered before. Put option deltas computed from historical experience were too low; insurers underhedged, held too much equity, and suffered excessive losses.

2. Prices moved so fast that insurers could not keep up with the necessary rebalancing. They were "chasing deltas" that kept getting away from them. The futures market saw a "gap" opening, where the opening price was nearly 10% below the previous day's close. Prices dropped before insurers could update their hedge ratios.

3. Execution problems were severe. First, current market prices were unavailable, with trade execution and the price quotation system hours behind, which made computation of correct hedge ratios impossible. Moreover, trading in stocks and stock futures ceased during some periods. The continuous rebalancing capability that is essential for a viable insurance program vanished during the precipitous market collapse.

4. Futures prices traded at steep discounts to their proper levels compared to reported stock prices, thereby making the sale of futures (as a proxy for equity sales) to increase hedging seem expensive. While you will see in the next chapter that stock index futures prices normally exceed the value of the stock index, on October 19, futures sold far below the stock index level. When some insurers gambled that the futures price would recover to its usual premium over the stock index and chose to defer sales, they remained underhedged. As the market fell farther, their portfolios experienced substantial losses.

While most observers believe that the portfolio insurance industry will never recover from the market crash, dynamic hedges are still widely used by large firms to hedge potential losses from options positions. For example, the nearby box notes that when Microsoft ended its employee stock option program and J. P. Morgan purchased many already-issued options from Microsoft employees, it was widely expected that Morgan would protect its options position by selling shares in Microsoft in accord with a delta hedging strategy.

16.5 | Empirical Evidence

There have been an enormous number of empirical tests of the Black-Scholes option-pricing model. For the most part, the results of the studies have been positive in that the Black-Scholes model generates option values quite close to the actual prices at which options trade. At the same time, some smaller but regular empirical failures of the model have been noted.

Whaley (1982) examines the performance of the Black-Scholes formula relative to that of more complicated option formulas that allow for early exercise. His findings indicate that formulas that allow for the possibility of early exercise do better at pricing than the Black-Scholes formula. The Black-Scholes formula seems to perform worst for options on stocks with high dividend payouts. The true American call option formula, on the other hand, seems to fare equally well in the prediction of option prices on stocks with high or low dividend payouts.

Rubinstein (1994) has emphasized a more serious problem with the Black-Scholes model. If the model were accurate, the implied volatility of all options on a particular stock with the same expiration date would be equal—after all, the underlying asset and expiration date are the same for each option, so the volatility inferred from each also ought to be the same. But in fact, when one actually plots implied volatility as a function of exercise price, the typical results appear as in Figure 16.10, which treats S&P 500 Index options as the underlying asset. Implied volatility steadily falls as the exercise price rises. Clearly, the Black-Scholes model is missing something.

Rubinstein suggests that the problem with the model has to do with fears of a market crash like that of October 1987. The idea is that deep out-of-the-money puts would be nearly worthless if stock prices evolve smoothly, since the probability of the stock falling by a large amount (and the put option thereby moving into the money) in a short time would be very small. But a possibility of a sudden large downward jump that could move the puts into the money, as in a market crash, would impart greater value to these options. Thus, the market might price these options as though there is a bigger chance of a large drop in the stock price than would be suggested by the Black-Scholes assumptions. The result of the higher option price is a greater implied volatility derived from the Black-Scholes model.

Interestingly, Rubinstein points out that prior to the 1987 market crash, plots of implied volatility like the one in Figure 16.10 were relatively flat, consistent with the notion that the market was then less attuned to fears of a crash. However, postcrash plots have been consistently downward-sloping, exhibiting a shape often called the *option smirk*. When we use

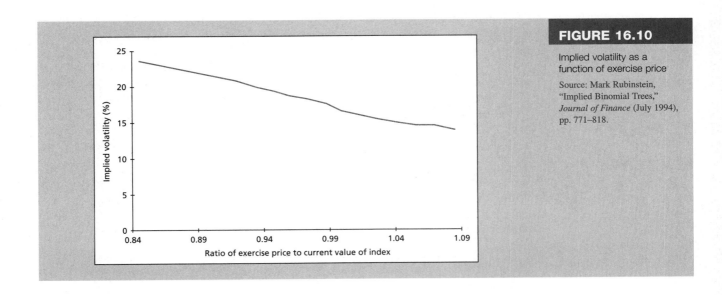

FIGURE 16.10

Implied volatility as a function of exercise price

Source: Mark Rubinstein, "Implied Binomial Trees," *Journal of Finance* (July 1994), pp. 771–818.

option-pricing models that allow for more general stock price distributions, including jumps and random changes in volatility, they generate downward-sloping implied volatility curves similar to the one observed in Figure 16.10.[9]

SUMMARY

- Option values may be viewed as the sum of intrinsic value plus time or "volatility" value. The volatility value is the right to choose not to exercise if the stock price moves against the holder. Thus, option holders cannot lose more than the cost of the option regardless of stock price performance.
- Call options are more valuable when the exercise price is lower, when the stock price is higher, when the interest rate is higher, when the time to expiration is greater, when the stock's volatility is greater, and when dividends are lower.
- Options may be priced relative to the underlying stock price using a simple two-period, two-state pricing model. As the number of periods increases, the model can approximate more realistic stock price distributions. The Black-Scholes formula may be seen as a limiting case of the binomial option model, as the holding period is divided into progressively smaller subperiods.
- The put-call parity theorem relates the prices of put and call options. If the relationship is violated, arbitrage opportunities will result. Specifically, the relationship that must be satisfied is

$$P = C - S_0 + PV(X) + PV(\text{dividends})$$

where X is the exercise price of both the call and the put options, and $PV(X)$ is the present value of the claim to X dollars to be paid at the expiration date of the options.
- The implied volatility of an option is the standard deviation of stock returns consistent with an option's market price. It can be backed out of an option-pricing model by finding the stock volatility that makes the option's value equal to its observed price.
- The hedge ratio is the number of shares of stock required to hedge the price risk involved in writing one option. Hedge ratios are near zero for deep out-of-the-money call options and approach 1.0 for deep in-the-money calls.
- Although hedge ratios are less than 1.0, call options have elasticities greater than 1.0. The rate of return on a call (as opposed to the dollar return) responds more than one-for-one with stock price movements.
- Portfolio insurance can be obtained by purchasing a protective put option on an equity position. When the appropriate put is not traded, portfolio insurance entails a dynamic hedge strategy where a fraction of the equity portfolio equal to the desired put option's delta is sold, with proceeds placed in risk-free securities.
- Empirically, implied volatilities derived from the Black-Scholes formula tend to be lower on options with higher exercise prices. This may be evidence that the option prices reflect the possibility of a sudden dramatic decline in stock prices. Such "crashes" are inconsistent with the Black-Scholes assumptions.

KEY TERMS

binomial model, 517	hedge ratio, 528	put-call parity
Black-Scholes pricing	implied volatility, 522	relationship, 525
formula, 518	intrinsic value, 510	time value, 510
delta, 528	option elasticity, 529	
dynamic hedging, 531	portfolio insurance, 529	

[9]For an extensive discussion of these more general models, see R. L. McDonald, *Derivatives Markets*, 2nd ed. (Boston: Pearson Education, Addison-Wesley, 2006).

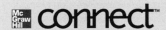 Select problems are available in McGraw-Hill Connect. Please see the packaging options section of the preface for more information.

PROBLEM SETS

Basic

1. A call option with a strike price of $50 on a stock selling at $55 costs $6.50. What are the call option's intrinsic and time values?

2. A put option on a stock with a current price of $33 has an exercise price of $35. The price of the corresponding call option is $2.25. According to put-call parity, if the effective annual risk-free rate of interest is 4% and there are three months until expiration, what should be the value of the put?

3. A call option on Jupiter Motors stock with an exercise price of $75 and one-year expiration is selling at $3. A put option on Jupiter stock with an exercise price of $75 and one-year expiration is selling at $2.50. If the risk-free rate is 8% and Jupiter pays no dividends, what should the stock price be?

4. We showed in the text that the value of a call option increases with the volatility of the stock. Is this also true of put option values? Use the put-call parity relationship as well as a numerical example to prove your answer.

Intermediate

5. In each of the following questions, you are asked to compare two options with parameters as given. The risk-free interest rate for *all* cases should be assumed to be 6%. Assume the stocks on which these options are written pay no dividends.

   a.

Put	T	X	σ	Price of Option
A	.5	50	.20	10
B	.5	50	.25	10

   Which put option is written on the stock with the lower price?
   (1) A
   (2) B
   (3) Not enough information

   b.

Put	T	X	σ	Price of Option
A	.5	50	.2	10
B	.5	50	.2	12

   Which put option must be written on the stock with the lower price?
   (1) A
   (2) B
   (3) Not enough information

   c.

Call	S	X	σ	Price of Option
A	50	50	.20	12
B	55	50	.20	10

Which call option must have the lower time to expiration?

(1) A

(2) B

(3) Not enough information

d.

Call	T	X	S	Price of Option
A	.5	50	55	10
B	.5	50	55	12

Which call option is written on the stock with higher volatility?

(1) A

(2) B

(3) Not enough information

e.

Call	T	X	S	Price of Option
A	.5	50	55	10
B	.5	55	55	7

Which call option is written on the stock with higher volatility?

(1) A

(2) B

(3) Not enough information

6. Reconsider the determination of the hedge ratio in the two-state model (Section 16.2), where we showed that one-third share of stock would hedge one option. What would be the hedge ratio for each of the following exercise prices: $120, $110, $100, $90? What do you conclude about the hedge ratio as the option becomes progressively more in the money?

7. Show that Black-Scholes call option hedge ratios increase as the stock price increases. Consider a one-year option with exercise price $50 on a stock with annual standard deviation 20%. The T-bill rate is 3% per year. Find $N(d_1)$ for stock prices $45, $50, and $55.

8. We will derive a two-state put option value in this problem. Data: $S_0 = 100$; $X = 110$; $1 + r = 1.10$. The two possibilities for S_T are 130 and 80.

   a. Show that the range of S is 50 while that of P is 30 across the two states. What is the hedge ratio of the put?

   b. Form a portfolio of three shares of stock and five puts. What is the (nonrandom) pay-off to this portfolio? What is the present value of the portfolio?

   c. Given that the stock currently is selling at 100, show that the value of the put must be 10.91.

9. Calculate the value of a *call* option on the stock in the previous problem with an exercise price of 110. Verify that the put-call parity relationship is satisfied by your answers to both Problems 8 and 9. (Do not use continuous compounding to calculate the present value of X in this example, because the interest rate is quoted as an effective per period rate.)

Please visit us at
www.mhhe.com/bkm

10. Use the Black-Scholes formula to find the value of a call option on the following stock:

   Time to expiration = 6 months

   Standard deviation = 50% per year

   Exercise price   = $50

   Stock price   = $50

   Interest rate   = 3%

11. Find the Black-Scholes value of a put option on the stock in the previous problem with the same exercise price and expiration as the call option.

12. Recalculate the value of the option in Problem 10, successively substituting one of the changes below while keeping the other parameters as in Problem 10:
    a. Time to expiration = 3 months
    b. Standard deviation = 25% per year
    c. Exercise price   = $55
    d. Stock price   = $55
    e. Interest rate   = 5%

    Consider each scenario independently. Confirm that the option value changes in accordance with the prediction of Table 16.1.

13. What would be the Excel formula in Spreadsheet 16.1 for the Black-Scholes value of a straddle position?

14. Would you expect a $1 increase in a call option's exercise price to lead to a decrease in the option's value of more or less than $1?

15. All else being equal, is a put option on a high beta stock worth more than one on a low beta stock? The firms have identical firm-specific risk.

16. All else being equal, is a call option on a stock with a lot of firm-specific risk worth more than one on a stock with little firm-specific risk? The betas of the stocks are equal.

17. All else being equal, will a call option with a high exercise price have a higher or lower hedge ratio than one with a low exercise price?

18. Should the rate of return of a call option on a long-term Treasury bond be more or less sensitive to changes in interest rates than the rate of return of the underlying bond?

19. If the stock price falls and the call price rises, then what has happened to the call option's implied volatility?

20. If the time to expiration falls and the put price rises, then what has happened to the put option's implied volatility?

21. According to the Black-Scholes formula, what will be the value of the hedge ratio of a call option as the stock price becomes infinitely large? Explain briefly.

22. According to the Black-Scholes formula, what will be the value of the hedge ratio of a put option for a very small exercise price?

23. The hedge ratio of an at-the-money call option on IBM is .4. The hedge ratio of an at-the-money put option is −.6. What is the hedge ratio of an at-the-money straddle position on IBM?

24. Consider a six-month expiration European call option with exercise price $105. The underlying stock sells for $100 a share, and pays no dividends. The risk-free rate is 5%. What is the implied volatility of the option if the option currently sells for $8? Use Spreadsheet 16.1 (available at **www.mhhe.com/bkm;** link to Chapter 16 material) to answer this question.

    a. Go to the Tools menu of the spreadsheet and select Goal Seek. The dialog box will ask you for three pieces of information. In that dialog box, you should *set cell E6 to value 8 by changing cell* B2. In other words, you ask the spreadsheet to find the value of standard deviation (which appears in cell B2) that forces the value of the option (in cell E6) equal to $8. Then click OK, and you should find that the call is now worth $8, and the entry for standard deviation has been changed to a level consistent with this value. This is the call's implied standard deviation at a price of $8.
    b. What happens to implied volatility if the option is selling at $9? Why?
    c. What happens to implied volatility if the option price is unchanged at $8, but option expiration is lower, say, only four months? Why?
    d. What happens to implied volatility if the option price is unchanged at $8, but the exercise price is lower, say, only $100? Why?
    e. What happens to implied volatility if the option price is unchanged at $8, but the stock price is lower, say, only $98? Why?

25. These three put options all are written on the same stock. One has a delta of $-.9$, one a delta of $-.5$, and one a delta of $-.1$. Assign deltas to the three puts by filling in the table below.

Put	X	Delta
A	10	
B	20	
C	30	

26. In this problem, we derive the put-call parity relationship for European options on stocks that pay dividends before option expiration. For simplicity, assume that the stock makes one dividend payment of D per share at the expiration date of the option.
    a. What is the value of the stock-plus-put position on the expiration date of the option?
    b. Now consider a portfolio consisting of a call option and a zero-coupon bond with the same expiration date as the option and with face value $(X + D)$. What is the value of this portfolio on the option expiration date? You should find that its value equals that of the stock-plus-put portfolio, regardless of the stock price.
    c. What is the cost of establishing the two portfolios in parts (a) and (b)? Equate the cost of these portfolios, and you will derive the put-call parity relationship, Equation 16.3.

27. A collar is established by buying a share of stock for $50, buying a six-month put option with exercise price $45, and writing a six-month call option with exercise price $55. Based on the volatility of the stock, you calculate that for an exercise price of $45 and maturity of six months, $N(d_1) = .60$, whereas for the exercise price of $55, $N(d_1) = .35$.
    a. What will be the gain or loss on the collar if the stock price increases by $1?
    b. What happens to the delta of the portfolio if the stock price becomes very large? Very small?

28. You are *very* bullish (optimistic) on stock EFG, much more so than the rest of the market. In each question, choose the portfolio strategy that will give you the biggest dollar profit if your bullish forecast turns out to be correct. Explain your answer.
    a. *Choice A:* $100,000 invested in calls with $X = 50$.
       Choice B: $100,000 invested in EFG stock.
    b. *Choice A:* 10 call options contracts (for 100 shares each), with $X = 50$.
       Choice B: 1,000 shares of EFG stock.

29. You are attempting to value a call option with an exercise price of $100 and one year to expiration. The underlying stock pays no dividends, its current price is $100, and you believe it has a 50% chance of increasing to $120 and a 50% chance of decreasing to $80. The risk-free rate of interest is 10%. Calculate the call option's value using the two-state stock price model.

30. Consider an increase in the volatility of the stock in the previous problem. Suppose that if the stock increases in price, it will increase to $130, and that if it falls, it will fall to $70. Show that the value of the call option is higher than the value derived using the original assumptions.

31. Return to Example 16.1. Use the binomial model to value a one-year European put option with exercise price $110 on the stock in that example. Does your solution for the put price satisfy put-call parity?

Challenge

32. Imagine you are a provider of portfolio insurance. You are establishing a four-year program. The portfolio you manage is currently worth $100 million, and you promise to provide a minimum return of 0%. The equity portfolio has a standard deviation of 25% per year, and T-bills pay 5% per year. Assume for simplicity that the portfolio pays no dividends (or that all dividends are reinvested).

   a. What fraction of the portfolio should be placed in bills? What fraction in equity?

   b. What should the manager do if the stock portfolio falls by 3% on the first day of trading?

33. You would like to be holding a protective put position on the stock of XYZ Co. to lock in a guaranteed minimum value of $100 at year-end. XYZ currently sells for $100. Over the next year, the stock price will either increase by 10% or decrease by 10%. The T-bill rate is 5%. Unfortunately, no put options are traded on XYZ Co.

   a. Suppose the desired put option were traded. How much would it cost to purchase?

   b. What would have been the cost of the protective put portfolio?

   c. What portfolio position in stock and T-bills will ensure you a payoff equal to the payoff that would be provided by a protective put with $X = \$100$? Show that the payoff to this portfolio and the cost of establishing the portfolio matches that of the desired protective put.

CFA Problems

1. Ken Webster manages a $200 million equity portfolio benchmarked to the S&P 500 Index. Webster believes the market is overvalued when measured by several traditional fundamental/economic indicators. He is therefore concerned about potential losses but recognizes that the S&P 500 Index could nevertheless move above its current 883 level.

    Webster is considering the following *option collar* strategy:

    • Protection for the portfolio can be attained by purchasing an S&P 500 Index put with a strike price of 880 (just out of the money).

    • The put can be financed by selling two 900 calls (further out-of-the-money) for every put purchased.

    • Because the combined delta of the two calls (see following table) is less than 1 (that is, $2 \times .36 = .72$) the options will not lose more than the underlying portfolio will gain if the market advances.

    The information in the following table describes the two options used to create the collar.

Characteristics	900 Call	880 Put
Option price	$ 8.60	$ 16.10
Option implied volatility	20%	22%
Option's delta	0.36	−0.44
Contracts needed for collar	602	301

Notes:

Ignore transaction costs.

S&P 500 historical 30-day volatility = 21%.

Time to option expiration 30 days.

   a. Describe the potential returns of the combined portfolio (the underlying portfolio plus the option collar) if after 30 days the S&P 500 Index has:

     i. risen approximately 5% to 927.

     ii. remained at 883 (no change).

     iii. declined by approximately 5% to 841.

     (No calculations are necessary.)

   b. Discuss the effect on the hedge ratio (delta) of *each* option as the S&P 500 approaches the level for *each* of the potential outcomes listed in part (*a*).

    c. Evaluate the pricing of each of the following in relation to the volatility data provided:
- i. the put
- ii. the call

2. Michael Weber, CFA, is analyzing several aspects of option valuation, including the determinants of the value of an option, the characteristics of various models used to value options, and the potential for divergence of calculated option values from observed market prices.
   - *a.* What is the expected effect on the value of a call option on common stock if (i) the volatility of the underlying stock price decreases; (ii) The time to expiration of the option increases.
   - *b.* Using the Black-Scholes option-pricing model, Weber calculates the price of a three-month call option and notices the option's calculated value is different from its market price. With respect to Weber's use of the Black-Scholes option-pricing model (i) discuss why the calculated value of an out-of-the-money European option may differ from its market price; (ii) discuss why the calculated value of an American option may differ from its market price.

3. A stock index is currently trading at 50. Paul Tripp, CFA, wants to value two-year index options using the binomial model. In any year, the stock will either increase in value by 20% or fall in value by 20%. The annual risk-free interest rate is 6%. No dividends are paid on any of the underlying securities in the index.
   - *a.* Construct a two-period binomial tree for the value of the stock index.
   - *b.* Calculate the value of a European call option on the index with an exercise price of 60.
   - *c.* Calculate the value of a European put option on the index with an exercise price of 60.
   - *d.* Confirm that your solutions for the values of the call and the put satisfy put-call parity.

STANDARD &POOR'S

Use data from the Standard & Poor's Market Insight Database at www.mhhe.com/edumarketinsight to answer the following questions.

Go to the Market Insight page. Click on the Company tab and enter KO for Coca-Cola Company. Find the company's report in the S&P Stock Reports section.

a. What is Coca-Cola's current price? What is its 12-month target price? What is the S&P buy/hold/sell recommendation? Based on this information, would it make more sense to buy a call option or a put option on Coca-Cola?

b. What is Coca-Cola volatility rating? You can find this in the Quantitative Evaluations section. How would this affect the value of the company's options? Relate your answer to the Black-Scholes model.

c. On the Market Insight main page enter stock symbol PEP for Pepsico, Inc. Find the company's current price, 12-month target price, S&P buy/hold/sell recommendation, and volatility rating by looking at its S&P Stock Report. Based on this information, would it make more sense to buy a call option or a put option on Pepsico?

d. Now find similar information for Genzyme Corporation (GENZ) and Cephalon, Inc. (CEPH). Would you recommend the purchase of a call option or a put option on these stocks?

e. Can you see a general pattern for the soft-drink industry, represented by KO and PEP vs. the biotechnology industry, represented by GENZ and CEPH, with respect to

- volatility
- buy/hold/sell recommendation
- expected price increases or decreases?

f. Suppose you believe that the volatility of KO is going to increase from currently anticipated levels. Would its call options be overpriced or underpriced? What about its put options?

g. Could you take positions in both puts and calls on KO in such a manner as to speculate on your volatility beliefs without taking a stance on whether the stock price is going to increase or decrease? Would you buy or write each type of option?

h. How would your relative positions in puts and calls be related to the delta of each option?

WEB *master* IMPLIED VOLATILITY

Calculating implied volatility can be difficult if you don't have a spreadsheet handy. Fortunately, many tools are available to perform the calculation; **www.numa.com** and **www.math.columbia.edu/~smirnov/options13.html** contain options calculators that also compute implied volatility.

Using daily price data, calculate the annualized standard deviation of the daily percentage change in a stock price. For the same stock, use **www.numa.com** or **www.math.columbia.edu/~smirnov/options13.html** to find the implied volatility. Option price data can be retrieved from **www.cboe.com**.

Recalculate the standard deviation using three months, six months, and nine months of daily data. Which of the calculations most closely approximates implied volatility? What time frame does the market seem to use for assessing stock price volatility?

16.1. Yes. Consider the same scenarios as for the call.

Stock price	$10	$20	$30	$40	$50
Put payoff	20	10	0	0	0
Stock price	20	25	30	35	40
Put payoff	10	5	0	0	0

The low volatility scenario yields a lower expected payoff.

16.2.

If This Variable Increases . . .	The Value of a Put Option
S	Decreases
X	Increases
σ	Increases
T	Increases/Uncertain*
r_f	Decreases
Dividend payouts	Increases

*For American puts, increase in time to expiration *must* increase value. One can always choose to exercise early if this is optimal; the longer expiration date simply expands the range of alternatives open to the option holder, thereby making the option more valuable. For a European put, where early exercise is not allowed, longer time to expiration can have an indeterminate effect. Longer maturity increases volatility value since the final stock price is more uncertain, but it reduces the present value of the exercise price that will be received if the put is exercised. The net effect on put value is ambiguous.

www.mhhe.com/bkm

16.3. Because the option now is underpriced, we want to reverse our previous strategy.

	Initial Cash Flow	Cash Flow in 1 Year for Each Possible Stock Price	
		$S = \$90$	$S = \$120$
Buy 3 options	$\$-16.50$	$\$\ 0$	$\$\ \ 30$
Short-sell 1 share; re-pay in 1 year	100	-90	-120
Lend $83.50 at 10% interest rate	-83.50	91.85	91.85
Total	$\$\ \ \ 0$	$\$\ \ 1.85$	$\$\ \ \ \ 1.85$

The riskless cash flow in one year per option is $\$1.85/3 = \$.6167$, and the present value is $\$.6167/1.10 = \$.56$, precisely the amount by which the option is underpriced.

16.4. *a.* $C_u - C_d = \$6.984 - 0 = \$6.984$

b. $uS_0 - dS_0 = \$110 - \$95 = \$15$

c. $6.984/15 = .4656$

d.

Action Today (time 0)	Value in Next Period as Function of Stock Price	
	$dS_0 = \$95$	$uS_0 = \$110$
Buy .4656 shares at price $S_0 = \$100$	$\$44.232$	$\$51.216$
Write 1 call at price C_0	0	-6.984
Total	$\$44.232$	$\$44.232$

The portfolio must have a market value equal to the present value of $44.232.

e. $\$44.232/1.05 = \$42.126$

f. $.4656 \times \$100 - C_0 = \$42.126$

$C_0 = \$46.56 - \$42.126 = \$4.434$

16.5. Higher. For deep out-of-the-money options, an increase in the stock price still leaves the option unlikely to be exercised. Its value increases only fractionally. For deep in-the-money options, exercise is likely, and option holders benefit by a full dollar for each dollar increase in the stock, as though they already own the stock.

16.6. Because $\sigma = .6$, $\sigma^2 = .36$.

$$d_1 = \frac{\ln(100/95) + (0.10 + 0.36/2)0.25}{0.6\sqrt{0.25}} = .4043$$

$$d_2 = d_1 - .6\sqrt{0.25} = .1043$$

Using Table 16.2 and interpolation, or a spreadsheet function,

$$N(d_1) = .6570$$

$$N(d_2) = .5415$$

$$C = 100 \times .6570 - 95e^{-0.10 \times 0.25} \times .5415 = 15.53$$

16.7. Implied volatility exceeds .5. Given a standard deviation of .5, the option value is $13.70. A higher volatility is needed to justify the actual $15 price. Using Spreadsheet 16.1 and Goal Seek, we find the implied volatility is .5714, or 57.14%.

16.8. A $1 increase in stock price is a percentage increase of $1/122 = .82\%$. The put option will fall by $(.4 \times \$1) = \$.40$, a percentage decrease of $\$.40/\$4 = 10\%$. Elasticity is $-10/.82 = -12.2$.

Chapter 17

Futures Markets and Risk Management

After Studying This Chapter You Should Be Able To:

- Calculate the profit on futures positions as a function of current and eventual futures prices.

- Formulate futures market strategies for hedging or speculative purposes.

- Compute the futures price appropriate to a given price on the underlying asset.

- Design arbitrage strategies to exploit futures market mispricing.

- Determine how swaps can be used to mitigate interest rate risk.

Futures and forward contracts are like options in that they specify the purchase or sale of some underlying security at some future date. The key difference is that the holder of an option to buy is not compelled to buy and will not do so if the trade is unprofitable. A futures or forward contract, however, carries the obligation to go through with the agreed-upon transaction.

A forward contract is not an investment in the strict sense that funds are paid for an asset. It is only a commitment today to transact in the future. Forward arrangements are part of our study of investments, however, because they offer a powerful means to hedge other investments and generally modify portfolio characteristics.

Forward markets for future delivery of various commodities go back at least to ancient Greece. Organized *futures markets,* though, are a relatively modern development, dating only to the 19th century. Futures markets replace informal forward contracts with highly standardized, exchange-traded securities.

While futures markets have their roots in agricultural products and commodities, the markets today are dominated by trading in financial futures such as those on stock indices, interest-rate-dependent securities such as government bonds, and foreign exchange. The markets themselves also have changed. An ever-greater proportion of futures trading is conducted electronically, and this trend seems sure to continue.

Related Web sites
for this chapter
are available at
www.mhhe.com/bkm.

This chapter describes the workings of futures markets and the mechanics of trading in these markets. We show how futures contracts are useful investment vehicles for both hedgers and speculators and how the futures price relates to the spot price of an asset. Next, we take a look at some specific financial futures contracts—those written on stock indexes, foreign exchange, and fixed-income securities. Finally, we show how swap contracts, an extension of forward contracts, may be used in portfolio management.

17.1 | The Futures Contract

To see how futures and forwards work and how they might be useful, consider the portfolio diversification problem facing a farmer growing a single crop, let us say wheat. The entire planting season's revenue depends critically on the highly volatile crop price. The farmer can't easily diversify his position because virtually his entire wealth is tied up in the crop.

The miller who must purchase wheat for processing faces a portfolio problem that is the mirror image of the farmer's. He is subject to profit uncertainty because of the unpredictable future cost of the wheat.

forward contract

An arrangement calling for future delivery of an asset at an agreed-upon price.

Both parties can reduce this source of risk if they enter into a **forward contract** calling for the farmer to deliver the wheat when harvested at a price agreed upon now, regardless of the market price at harvest time. No money need change hands at this time. A forward contract is simply a deferred-delivery sale of some asset with the sales price agreed upon now. All that is required is that each party be willing to lock in the ultimate price to be paid or received for delivery of the commodity. A forward contract protects each party from future price fluctuations.

Futures markets formalize and standardize forward contracting. Buyers and sellers do not have to rely on a chance matching of their interests; they can trade in a centralized futures market. The futures exchange also standardizes the types of contracts that may be traded: It establishes contract size, the acceptable grade of commodity, contract delivery dates, and so forth. While standardization eliminates much of the flexibility available in informal forward contracting, it has the offsetting advantage of liquidity because many traders will concentrate on the same small set of contracts. Futures contracts also differ from forward contracts in that they call for a daily settling up of any gains or losses on the contract. In contrast, in the case of forward contracts, no money changes hands until the delivery date.

In a centralized market, buyers and sellers can trade through brokers without personally searching for trading partners. The standardization of contracts and the depth of trading in each contract allows futures positions to be liquidated easily through a broker rather than personally renegotiated with the other party to the contract. Because the exchange guarantees the performance of each party to the contract, costly credit checks on other traders are not necessary. Instead, each trader simply posts a good faith deposit, called the *margin,* in order to guarantee contract performance.

The Basics of Futures Contracts

futures price

The agreed-upon price to be paid on a futures contract at maturity.

The futures contract calls for delivery of a commodity at a specified delivery or maturity date, for an agreed-upon price, called the **futures price,** to be paid at contract maturity. The contract specifies precise requirements for the commodity. For agricultural commodities, the exchange sets allowable grades (e.g., No. 2 hard winter wheat or No. 1 soft red wheat). The place or means of delivery of the commodity is specified as well. Delivery of agricultural commodities is made by transfer of warehouse receipts issued by approved warehouses. In the case of financial futures, delivery may be made by wire transfer; in the case of index futures, delivery may be accomplished by a cash settlement procedure such as those used for index options. (Although the futures contract technically calls for delivery of an asset, delivery rarely occurs. Instead, parties to the contract much more commonly close out their positions before contract maturity, taking gains or losses in cash. We will show you how this is done later in the chapter.)

Because the futures exchange specifies all the terms of the contract, the traders need bargain only over the futures price. The trader taking the **long position** commits to purchasing the commodity on the delivery date. The trader who takes the **short position** commits to delivering the commodity at contract maturity. The trader in the long position is said to "buy" a contract; the short-side trader "sells" a contract. The words *buy* and *sell* are figurative only, because a contract is not really bought or sold like a stock or bond; it is entered into by mutual agreement. At the time the contract is entered into, no money changes hands.

Figure 17.1 shows prices for a sample of futures contracts as they appear in *The Wall Street Journal*. The boldface heading lists in each case the commodity, the exchange where the futures contract is traded in parentheses, the contract size, and the pricing unit. For example, the first contract listed under "Agriculture Futures" is for corn, traded on the Chicago Board of Trade (CBT). Each contract calls for delivery of 5,000 bushels, and prices in the entry are quoted in cents per bushel.

The next several rows detail price data for contracts expiring on various dates. The March 2009 maturity corn contract, for example, opened during the day at a futures price of 349 cents per bushel. The highest futures price during the day was 356.25, the lowest was 348.50, and the settlement price (a representative trading price during the last few minutes of trading) was 353.25. The settlement price increased by 4 cents from the previous trading day. Finally, open interest, or the number of outstanding contracts, was 169,716. Similar information is given for each maturity date.

The trader holding the long position, that is, the person who will purchase the good, profits from price increases. Suppose that when the contract matures in March, the price of corn turns out to be 358.25 cents per bushel. The long position trader who entered the contract at the futures price of 353.25 cents on February 19 (the date of the *Wall Street Journal* listing) earns a profit of 5 cents per bushel: The eventual price is 5 cents higher than the originally agreed-upon futures price. As each contract calls for delivery of 5,000 bushels (ignoring brokerage fees), the profit to the long position equals $5,000 \times \$.05 = \$250$ per contract. Conversely, the short position loses 5 cents per bushel. The short position's loss equals the long position's gain.

To summarize, at maturity

$$\text{Profit to long} = \text{Spot price at maturity} - \text{Original futures price}$$
$$\text{Profit to short} = \text{Original futures price} - \text{Spot price at maturity}$$

where the spot price is the actual market price of the commodity at the time of the delivery.

The futures contract is, therefore, a *zero sum game,* with losses and gains to all positions netting out to zero. Every long position is offset by a short position. The aggregate profits to futures trading, summing over all investors, also must be zero, as is the net exposure to changes in the commodity price.

Figure 17.2, Panel A, is a plot of the profits realized by an investor who enters the long side of a futures contract as a function of the price of the asset on the maturity date. Notice that profit is zero when the ultimate spot price, P_T, equals the initial futures price, F_0. Profit per unit of the underlying asset rises or falls one-for-one with changes in the final spot price. Unlike the payoff of a call option, the payoff of the long futures position can be negative: This will be the case if the spot price falls below the original futures price. Unlike the holder of a call, who has an *option* to buy, the long futures position trader cannot simply walk away from the contract. Also unlike options, in the case of futures there is no need to distinguish gross payoffs from net profits. This is because the futures contract is not purchased; it is simply a contract that is agreed to by two parties. The futures price adjusts to make the present value of either side of the contract equal to zero.

long position

The futures trader who commits to purchasing the asset.

short position

The futures trader who commits to delivering the asset.

Futures Contracts

Metal & Petroleum Futures

	Open	Contract High hi lo	Low	Settle	Chg	Open interest
Copper-High (CMX)-25,000 lbs.; cents per lb.						
Feb	148.50	148.50	146.10	**146.80**	3.45	358
May	145.55	151.00	145.40	**148.80**	3.35	42,130
Gold (CMX)-100 troy oz.; $ per troy oz.						
Feb	982.70	986.20	972.00	**976.10**	−1.60	2,307
April	987.00	987.90	969.50	**976.50**	−1.70	239,594
June	987.50	989.30	972.70	**978.70**	−1.70	50,431
Aug	984.50	990.80	976.40	**980.80**	−1.60	12,950
Dec	992.50	995.30	980.00	**984.90**	−1.70	18,528
Dec'10	1002.30	1005.00	997.30	**998.30**	−1.80	9,156
Platinum (NYM)-50 troy oz.; $ per troy oz.						
April	1105.00	1113.80	1066.10	**1076.50**	−22.40	19,427
July	1100.00	1100.00	1072.30	**1080.50**	−22.40	957
Silver (CMX)-5,000 troy oz.; cnts per troy oz.						
Feb	1430.5	1430.5 ▲	1388.5	**1393.3**	−35.5	40
March	1431.5	1437.0	1385.0	**1393.5**	−35.5	37,483
Crude Oil, Light Sweet (NYM)-1,000 bbls.; $ per bbl.						
March	34.75	39.85	34.59	**39.48**	4.86	49,455
April	37.54	40.27 ▼	37.12	**40.18**	2.77	309,540
May	39.80	42.60 ▼	39.42	**42.51**	2.79	130,756
June	41.17	44.04 ▼	40.85	**43.97**	2.82	145,651
Dec	46.96	49.60	46.14	**49.54**	2.81	97,062
Dec'10	53.50	56.40	52.90	**56.59**	2.93	70,861
Heating Oil No. 2 (NYM)-42,000 gal.; $ per gal.						
March	1.1600	1.2110	1.1433	**1.2045**	.0576	31,371
April	1.1500	1.2075 ▼	1.1359	**1.2005**	.0591	52,767
Gasoline-NY RBOB (NYM)-42,000 gal.; $ per gal.						
March	1.0662	1.1057	1.0310	**1.0986**	.0334	28,588
April	1.1492	1.2050	1.1202	**1.1990**	.0493	61,452
Natural Gas (NYM)-10,000 MMBtu.; $ per MMBtu.						
March	4.228	4.280 ▼	4.001	**4.078**	−.136	64,788
April	4.251	4.301 ▼	4.016	**4.111**	−.127	137,589
May	4.364	4.380 ▼	4.110	**4.198**	−.129	74,656
June	4.494	4.500 ▼	4.240	**4.328**	−.126	43,518
July	4.611	4.615 ▼	4.381	**4.466**	−.119	37,537
Oct	4.805	4.805	4.620	**4.691**	−.118	38,500

Agriculture Futures

	Open	Contract High hi lo	Low	Settle	Chg	Open interest
Corn (CBT)-5,000 bu.; cents per bu.						
March	349.00	356.25	348.50	**353.25**	4.00	169,716
May	357.50	364.75	357.00	**362.00**	4.00	231,940
Ethanol (CBT)-29,000 gal.; $ per gal.						
March	1.55	1.55	1.54	**1.55**	.01	262
April	1.55	1.55	1.54	**1.55**	.01	575
Oats (CBT)-5,000 bu.; cents per bu.						
March	175.75	175.75	168.50	**171.50**	...	2,903
May	182.25	183.25	177.25	**180.00**	...	7,430
Soybeans (CBT)-5,000 bu.; cents per bu.						
March	885.50	902.00	881.25	**884.50**	−3.00	72,753
May	884.75	901.50	882.75	**886.00**	−.50	121,870
Rough Rice (CBT)-2,000 cwt.; cents per cwt.						
March	1215.00	1244.50	1203.00	**1229.00**	13.50	2,274
May	1214.00	1247.00	1207.00	**1230.00**	9.50	2,597
Wheat (CBT)-5,000 bu.; cents per bu.						
March	511.00	523.25	510.75	**519.50**	8.75	55,504
May	522.00	535.00	522.00	**531.00**	8.00	104,313
Cattle-Feeder (CME)-50,000 lbs.; cents per lb.						
March	88.750	90.800	88.525	**90.625**	1.600	7,243
April	89.875	92.100	89.725	**91.875**	1.350	7,293

Interest Rate Futures

	Open	Contract High hi lo	Low	Settle	Chg	Open interest
Treasury Bonds (CBT)-$100,000; pts 32nds of 100%						
March	128-065	128-175	126-030	**126-085**	−2-12.5	694,355
June	126-310	127-090	124-275	**125-010**	−2-11.5	57,034
Treasury Notes (CBT)-$100,000; pts 32nds of 100%						
March	123-115	123-205	122-080	**122-170**	−1-04.5	956,440
June	121-210	121-230	120-120	**120-200**	−1-04.5	93,153
5 Yr. Treasury Notes (CBT)-$100,000; pts 32nds of 100%						
March	118-125	118-180	117-277	**118-017**	−14.0	910,179
June	117-022	117-050	116-225	**116-267**	−15.2	122,310
2 Yr. Treasury Notes (CBT)-$200,000; pts 32nds of 100%						
March	108-262	108-297	108-245	**108-250**	−2.5	483,006
June	108-150	108-150	108-112	**108-115**	−2.7	19,957
30 Day Federal Funds (CBT)-$5,000,000; 100 - daily avg.						
Feb	99.768	99.783	99.768	**99.770**	.002	70,189
May	99.710	99.750	99.710	**99.730**	.015	51,667
1 Month Libor (CME)-$3,000,000; pts of 100%						
March	99.4300	99.4750	99.4250	**99.4700**	.0350	5,948
April	99.3650	99.3725	99.3600	**99.3600**	.0350	1,740
Eurodollar (CME)-$1,000,000; pts of 100%						
March	98.6875	98.7500	98.6600	**98.7250**	.0425	1,255,769
June	98.7150	98.7550	98.6500	**98.7300**	.0450	1,012,130
Sept	98.6750	98.6850	98.5750	**98.6500**	.0200	898,158
Dec	98.5250	98.5350	98.4200	**98.4800**	−.0100	776,849

Currency Futures

	Open	Contract High hi lo	Low	Settle	Chg	Open interest
Japanese Yen (CME)-¥12,500,000; $ per 100¥						
March	1.0680	1.0722	1.0588	**1.0596**	−.0077	100,394
June	1.0690	1.0742	1.0615	**1.0621**	−.0080	5,710
Canadian Dollar (CME)-CAD 100,000; $ per CAD						
March	.7936	.8020	.7919	**.7964**	.0020	65,677
June	.7940	.8022	.7930	**.7969**	.0021	3,767
British Pound (CME)-£62,500; $ per £						
March	1.4240	1.4451	1.4215	**1.4299**	.0082	80,024
June	1.4270	1.4443	1.4242	**1.4294**	.0081	4,122
Swiss Franc (CME)-CHF 125,000; $ per CHF						
March	.8506	.8548	.8479	**.8527**	.0024	34,494
June	.8530	.8567	.8508	**.8547**	.0021	457
Australian Dollar (CME)-AUD 100,000; $ per AUD						
March	.6375	.6512	.6362	**.6442**	.0065	48,240
June	.6378	.6478	.6372	**.6414**	.0065	865
Mexican Peso (CME)-MXN 500,000; $ per 10MXN						
March	.67925	.68700	.67375	**.67850**	−.00075	44,565
June	.67350	.67350 ▼	.66425	**.66750**	−.00075	265
Euro (CME)-€125,000; $ per €						
March	1.2545	1.2757	1.2534	**1.2681**	.0132	152,001
June	1.2560	1.2753	1.2539	**1.2679**	.0131	2,947

Index Futures

	Open	Contract High hi lo	Low	Settle	Chg	Open interest
DJ Industrial Average (CBT)-$10 x index						
March	7500	7617 ▼	7430	**7462**	−21	22,401
June	7465	7564	7455	**7421**	−22	51
S&P 500 Index (CME)-$250 x index						
March	780.00	796.50	775.00	**779.40**	−0.10	568,602
June	791.00	792.80	772.50	**776.20**	−0.10	25,891
Nasdaq 100 (CME)-$100 x index						
March	1176.50	1202.00	1164.00	**1170.50**	−9.50	30,990
June	1168.50	1168.50	1168.50	**1170.50**	−9.25	141

FIGURE 17.1

Futures listings for February 19, 2009.

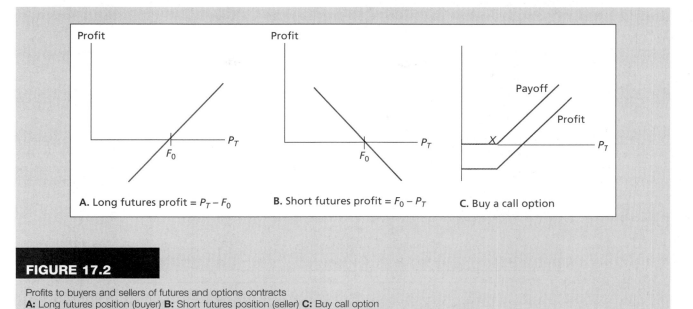

FIGURE 17.2

Profits to buyers and sellers of futures and options contracts
A: Long futures position (buyer) **B:** Short futures position (seller) **C:** Buy call option

The distinction between futures and options is highlighted by comparing Panel A of Figure 17.2 to the payoff and profit diagrams for an investor in a call option with exercise price, X, chosen equal to the futures price F_0 (see Panel C). The futures investor is exposed to considerable losses if the asset price falls. In contrast, the investor in the call cannot lose more than the cost of the option.

Figure 17.2, Panel B, is a plot of the profits realized by an investor who enters the short side of a futures contract. It is the mirror image of the profit diagram for the long position.

> **CONCEPT** **17.1**
> *check*
>
> a. Compare the profit diagram in Figure 17.2B to the payoff diagram for a long position in a put option. Assume the exercise price of the option equals the initial futures price.
> b. Compare the profit diagram in Figure 17.2B to the payoff diagram for an investor who writes a call option.

Existing Contracts

Futures and forward contracts are traded on a wide variety of goods in four broad categories: agricultural commodities, metals and minerals (including energy commodities), foreign currencies, and financial futures (fixed-income securities and stock market indexes). In addition to indexes on broad stock indexes, one can now trade so-called **single stock futures** on individual stocks and narrowly based indexes. OneChicago (a joint venture of the Chicago Board Options Exchange, Chicago Mercantile Exchange, and Chicago Board of Trade) has operated an entirely electronic market in single stock futures since 2002. The exchange maintains futures markets in actively traded stocks with the most liquidity. However, trading volume in this market has to date been disappointing.

Innovation in financial futures has been rapid and is ongoing. Table 17.1 offers a sample of contracts trading in 2009. Contracts now trade on items that would not have been considered possible only a few years ago. For example, there are now electricity as well as weather futures and options contracts. Weather derivatives (which trade on the Chicago Mercantile Exchange) have payoffs that depend on average weather conditions, for example, the number of degree-days by which the temperature in a region exceeds or falls short of 65 degrees Fahrenheit. The potential use of these derivatives in managing the risk surrounding electricity or oil and natural gas use should be evident.

single stock futures

A futures contract on the shares of an individual company.

PREDICTION MARKETS

If you find S&P 500 or T-bond contracts a bit dry, perhaps you'd be interested in futures contracts with payoffs that depend on the winner of a presidential election, or the severity of the next influenza season, or the host city of the 2016 Olympics. You can now find "futures markets" in these events and many others.

Intrade (**www.intrade.com**) and Iowa Electronic Markets (**www.biz.uiowa.edu/iem**), for example, maintain presidential futures markets. Contracts pay off $1 if the candidate you "purchase" wins the election. The contract price for each candidate therefore may be viewed as the probability of that candidate's success, at least according to the consensus view of the participants in the market. So, during the 2008 presidential primary races, if you had wished to bet on a Hillary Clinton victory, you could have purchased a Clinton contract. Each Clinton contract would have paid $1 if she had won the Democratic nomination and nothing if she lost. If you thought the probability of her victory in the primaries was 55%, you would have been prepared to pay up to $.55 for the contract. Alternatively, if you had wanted to bet against her, you could have sold a Clinton contract.

The accompanying figure shows prices of the three major Democratic contenders (Hillary Clinton, Barack Obama, and John Edwards) through the end of February 2008. Notice the dramatic increase in the Obama contract price after his January win in the Iowa caucuses, the equally dramatic decrease the next week when Clinton won the New Hampshire primary, and substantial run-up in Obama's price throughout February as he went on to win a lengthy succession of state primaries.

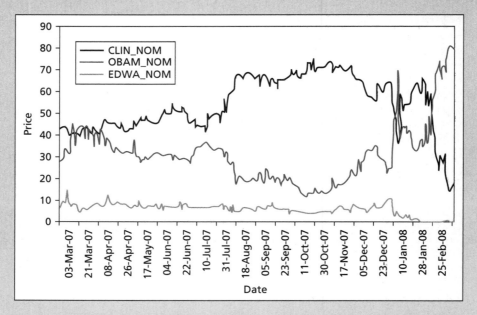

Prediction markets for the 2008 Democratic nomination

Source: Iowa Electronic Markets, February 2008.

While Table 17.1 includes many contracts, the large and ever-growing array of markets makes this list necessarily incomplete. The nearby box discusses some comparatively fanciful futures markets in which payoffs may be tied to the winner of presidential elections, the box office receipts of a particular movie, or anything else in which participants are willing to take positions.

Outside the futures markets, a well-developed network of banks and brokers has established a forward market in foreign exchange. This forward market is not a formal exchange in the sense that the exchange specifies the terms of the traded contract. Instead, participants in a forward contract may negotiate for delivery of any quantity of goods at any time, whereas, in the formal futures markets, contract size and delivery dates are set by the exchange. In forward arrangements, banks and brokers simply negotiate contracts for clients (or themselves) as needed.

TABLE 17.1 Sample of futures contracts				
Foreign Currencies	**Agricultural**	**Metals and Energy**	**Interest Rate Futures**	**Equity Indexes**
British pound	Corn	Copper	Eurodollars	Dow Jones Industrials
Canadian dollar	Oats	Aluminum	Euroyen	S&P Midcap 400
Japanese yen	Soybeans	Gold	Euro-denominated	NASDAQ 100
Euro	Soybean meal	Platinum	bond	NYSE index
Swiss franc	Soybean oil	Palladium	Euroswiss	Russell 2000 index
Australian dollar	Wheat	Silver	Sterling	Nikkei 225 (Japanese)
Mexican peso	Barley	Crude oil	British gov't bond	FTSE index (British)
Brazilian real	Flaxseed	Heating oil	German gov't bond	CAC index (French)
New Zealand dollar	Canola	Gas oil	Italian gov't bond	DAX index (German)
	Rye	Natural gas	Canadian gov't bond	All ordinary (Australian)
	Cattle	Gasoline	Treasury bonds	Toronto 35 (Canadian)
	Milk	Propane	Treasury notes	Titans 30 (Italian)
	Hogs	Commodity	Treasury bills	Dow Jones Euro STOXX 50
	Pork bellies	index	LIBOR	Industry indexes, e.g.,
	Cocoa	Electricity	EURIBOR	banking
	Coffee	Weather	Municipal bond index	natural resources
	Cotton		Federal funds rate	chemical
	Orange juice		Bankers' acceptance	health care
	Sugar		S&P 500 Index	technology
	Lumber		Interest rate swaps	retail
	Rice			utilities
				telecom

17.2 | Mechanics of Trading In Futures Markets

The Clearinghouse and Open Interest

Until about 10 years ago, most futures trades in the United States occurred among floor traders in the "trading pit" for each contract. Participants there use voice or hand signals to signify their desire to buy or sell and locate a trader willing to accept the opposite side of a trade. Today, however, trading is increasingly done over electronic networks, particularly for financial futures.

The impetus for this shift originated in Europe, where electronic trading is the norm. Eurex, which is jointly owned by the Deutsche Börse and Swiss exchange, is currently the world's largest futures and options exchange. It operates a fully electronic trading and clearing platform, and in 2004, received clearance from regulators to list contracts in the U.S. In response, the Chicago Board of Trade adopted an electronic platform provided by Eurex's European rival Euronext.liffe,[1] and the great majority of the CBOT's Treasury contracts are now traded electronically. The Chicago Mercantile Exchange maintains another electronic trading system called Globex. These electronic exchanges enable trading around the clock. The CBOT and CME agreed in 2007 to merge into one combined company, named the CME Group, intending to ultimately move all electronic trading from both exchanges onto CME Globex. It seems inevitable that electronic trading will continue to displace floor trading.

---

[1] Euronext.liffe is the international derivatives market of Euronext. It resulted from Euronext's purchase of LIFFE (the London International Financial Futures and Options Exchange) and a merger with the Lisbon exchange in 2002. Euronext was itself the result of a 2000 merger of the exchanges of Amsterdam, Brussels, and Paris.

clearinghouse

Established by exchanges to facilitate trading. The clearinghouse may interpose itself as an intermediary between two traders.

Once a trade is agreed to, the **clearinghouse** enters the picture. Rather than having the long and short traders hold contracts with each other, the clearinghouse becomes the seller of the contract for the long position and the buyer of the contract for the short position. The clearinghouse is obligated to deliver the commodity to the long position and to pay for delivery from the short; consequently, the clearinghouse's position nets to zero. This arrangement makes the clearinghouse the trading partner of each trader, both long and short. The clearinghouse, bound to perform on its side of each contract, is the only party that can be hurt by the failure of any trader to observe the obligations of the futures contract. This arrangement is necessary because a futures contract calls for future performance, which cannot be as easily guaranteed as an immediate stock transaction.

Figure 17.3 illustrates the role of the clearinghouse. Panel A shows what would happen in the absence of the clearinghouse. The trader in the long position would be obligated to pay the futures price to the short position trader, and the trader in the short position would be obligated to deliver the commodity. Panel B shows how the clearinghouse becomes an intermediary, acting as the trading partner for each side of the contract. The clearinghouse's position is neutral, as it takes a long and a short position for each transaction.

The clearinghouse makes it possible for traders to liquidate positions easily. If you are currently long in a contract and want to undo your position, you simply instruct your broker to enter the short side of a contract to close out your position. This is called a *reversing trade*. The exchange nets out your long and short positions, reducing your net position to zero. Your zero net position with the clearinghouse eliminates the need to fulfill at maturity either the original long or reversing short position.

The *open interest* on the contract is the number of contracts outstanding. (Long and short positions are not counted separately, meaning that open interest can be defined as either the number of long or short contracts outstanding.) The clearinghouse's position nets out to zero, and so it is not counted in the computation of open interest. When contracts begin trading, open interest is zero. As time passes, open interest increases as progressively more contracts are entered.

There are many apocryphal stories about futures traders who wake up to discover a small mountain of wheat or corn on their front lawn. But the truth is that futures contracts rarely result in actual delivery of the underlying asset. Traders establish long or short positions in contracts that will benefit from a rise or fall in the futures price and almost always close out those positions before the contract expires. The fraction of contracts that result in actual delivery is estimated to range from less than 1% to 3%, depending on the commodity and activity in the contract. In the unusual case of actual deliveries of commodities, they occur via regular channels of supply, usually via warehouse receipts.

You can see the typical pattern of open interest in Figure 17.1. In the gold contract, for example, the February delivery contracts are close to maturity and open interest is small; most

FIGURE 17.3
A: Trading without the clearinghouse
B: Trading with a clearinghouse

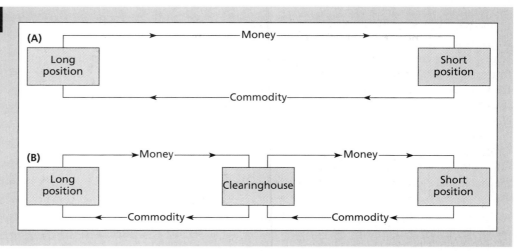

contracts have been reversed already. The next few maturities have significantly greater open interest. Finally, the most distant maturity contracts have less open interest, as they have been available only recently and few participants have yet traded. For other contracts such as most of the interest rate futures, for which the nearest maturity is still more than a month away, open interest is highest in the nearest contract.

Marking to Market and the Margin Account

The total profit or loss realized by the long trader who buys a contract at time 0 and closes, or reverses, it at time t is just the change in the futures price over the period, $F_t - F_0$. Symmetrically, the short trader earns $F_0 - F_t$.

The process by which profits or losses accrue to traders is called **marking to market.** At initial execution of a trade, each trader establishes a margin account. The margin is a security account consisting of cash or near-cash securities, such as Treasury bills, that ensures the trader will be able to satisfy the obligations of the futures contract. Because both parties to the futures contract are exposed to losses, both must post margin. To illustrate, return to the March corn contract listed in Figure 17.1. If the initial required margin on corn, for example, is 10%, the trader must post $1,766.25 per contract for the margin account. This is 10% of the value of the contract ($3.5325 per bushel × 5,000 bushels per contract).

marking to market
The daily settlement of obligations on futures positions.

Because the initial margin may be satisfied by posting interest-earning securities, the requirement does not impose a significant opportunity cost of funds on the trader. The initial margin is usually set between 5% and 15% of the total value of the contract. Contracts written on assets with more volatile prices require higher margins.

On any day that futures contracts trade, futures prices may rise or fall. Instead of waiting until the maturity date for traders to realize all gains and losses, the clearinghouse requires all positions to recognize profits as they accrue daily. If the futures price of corn rises from 353.25 to 355.25 cents per bushel, for example, the clearinghouse credits the margin account of the long position for 5,000 bushels times 2 cents per bushel, or $100 per contract. Conversely, for the short position, the clearinghouse takes this amount from the margin account for each contract held. Therefore, as futures prices change, proceeds accrue to the trader's account immediately.

Marking to market is the major way in which futures and forward contracts differ, besides contract standardization. Futures follow this pay- (or receive-) as-you-go method. Forward contracts are simply held until maturity, and no funds are transferred until that date, although the contracts may be traded.

What must be the net inflow or outlay from marking to market for the clearinghouse?

CONCEPT
check **17.2**

If a trader accrues sustained losses from daily marking to market, the margin account may fall below a critical value called the **maintenance margin.** If the value of the account falls below this value, the trader receives a margin call. Margins and margin calls safeguard the position of the clearinghouse. Positions are closed out before the margin account is exhausted—the trader's losses are covered, and the clearinghouse is not put at risk.

maintenance margin
An established value below which a trader's margin may not fall. Reaching the maintenance margin triggers a margin call.

Suppose the maintenance margin is 5% while the initial margin was 10% of the value of the corn, or $1,766.25. Then a margin call will go out when the original margin account has fallen about in half, or by $883. Each 1 cent decline in the corn price results in a $50 loss to the long position. Therefore, the futures price need fall only by 18 cents to trigger a margin call. Either new funds must be transferred into the margin account or the broker will close out enough of the trader's account to reestablish the required margin for the position.

EXAMPLE 17.1

Maintenance Margin

It is important to note that the futures price on the delivery date will equal the spot price of the commodity on that date. As a maturing contract calls for immediately delivery, the futures price on that day must equal the spot price—the cost of the commodity from the two competing sources is equalized in a competitive market.[2] You may obtain delivery of the commodity either by purchasing it directly in the spot market or by entering the long side of a maturing futures contract.

A commodity available from two sources (the spot and futures markets) must be priced identically, or else investors will rush to purchase it from the cheap source in order to sell it in the high-priced market. Such arbitrage activity could not persist without prices adjusting to eliminate the arbitrage opportunity. Therefore, the futures price and the spot price must converge at maturity. This is called the **convergence property.**

convergence property

The convergence of futures prices and spot prices at the maturity of the futures contract.

For an investor who establishes a long position in a contract now (time 0) and holds that position until maturity (time T), the sum of all daily settlements will equal $F_T - F_0$, where F_T stands for the futures price at contract maturity. Because of convergence, however, the futures price at maturity, F_T, equals the spot price, P_T, so total futures profits also may be expressed as $P_T - F_0$. Thus, we see that profits on a futures contract held to maturity perfectly track changes in the value of the underlying asset.

EXAMPLE 17.2

Marking to Market and Futures Contract Profits

Assume the current futures price for silver for delivery five days from today is $12.10 per ounce. Suppose that over the next five days, the futures price evolves as follows:

Day	Futures Price
0 (today)	$12.10
1	12.20
2	12.25
3	12.18
4	12.18
5 (delivery)	12.21

The spot price of silver on the delivery date is $12.21: The convergence property implies that the price of silver in the spot market must equal the futures price on the delivery day.

The daily mark-to-market settlements for each contract held by the long positions will be as follows:

Day	Profit (loss) per Ounce	× 5,000 Ounces/Contract = Daily Proceeds
1	$12.20 − $12.10 = $ .10	$500
2	12.25 − 12.20 = .05	250
3	12.18 − 12.25 = −.07	−350
4	12.18 − 12.18 = 0	0
5	12.21 − 12.18 = .03	150
		Sum = $550

The profit on day 1 is the increase in the futures price from the previous day, or ($12.20 − $12.10) per ounce. Because each silver contract on the Commodity Exchange calls for purchase and delivery of 5,000 ounces, the profit per contract is 5,000 times $.10, or $500. On day 3, when the futures price falls, the long position's margin account will be debited by $350. By day 5, the sum of all daily proceeds is $550. This is exactly equal to 5,000 times the difference between the final futures price of $12.21 and the original futures price of $12.10. Thus, the sum of all the daily proceeds (per ounce of silver held long) equals $P_T - F_0$.

---

[2]Small differences between the spot and futures prices at maturity may persist because of transportation costs, but this is a minor factor.

Cash versus Actual Delivery

Most futures markets call for delivery of an actual commodity, such as a particular grade of wheat or a specified amount of foreign currency, if the contract is not reversed before maturity. For agricultural commodities, where quality of the delivered good may vary, the exchange sets quality standards as part of the futures contract. In some cases, contracts may be settled with higher or lower grade commodities. In these cases, a premium or discount is applied to the delivered commodity to adjust for the quality differences.

Some futures contracts call for **cash settlement.** An example is a stock index futures contract where the underlying asset is an index such as the Standard & Poor's 500 Index. Delivery of every stock in the index clearly would be impractical. Hence, the contract calls for "delivery" of a cash amount equal to the value that the index attains on the maturity date of the contract. The sum of all the daily settlements from marking to market results in the long position realizing total profits or losses of $S_T - F_0$, where S_T is the value of the stock index on the maturity date T, and F_0 is the original futures price. Cash settlement closely mimics actual delivery, except the cash value of the asset rather than the asset itself is delivered by the short position in exchange for the futures price.

More concretely, the S&P 500 Index contract calls for delivery of $250 times the value of the index. At maturity, the index might list at 800, a market value-weighted index of the prices of all 500 stocks in the index. The cash settlement contract would then call for delivery of 250×800, or $200,000 cash in return for $250 times the futures price. This yields exactly the same profit as would result from directly purchasing 250 units of the index for $200,000 and then delivering it for $250 times the original futures price.

cash settlement

The cash value of the underlying asset (rather than the asset itself) is delivered to satisfy the contract.

Regulations

Futures markets are regulated by the Commodity Futures Trading Commission (CFTC), a federal agency. The CFTC sets capital requirements for member firms of the futures exchanges, authorizes trading in new contracts, and oversees maintenance of daily trading records.

The futures exchange may set limits on the amount by which futures prices may change from one day to the next. For example, if the price limit on silver contracts is $1, and silver futures close today at $12.10 per ounce, trades in silver tomorrow may vary only between $13.10 and $11.10 per ounce. The exchange may increase or reduce these price limits in response to perceived changes in the price volatility of the contract. Price limits often are eliminated as contracts approach maturity, usually in the last month of trading.

Price limits traditionally are viewed as a means to limit violent price fluctuations. This reasoning seems dubious. Suppose an international monetary crisis overnight drives up the spot price of silver to $17.00. No one would sell silver futures at prices for future delivery as low as $12.10. Instead, the futures price would rise each day by the $1 limit, although the quoted price would represent only an unfilled bid order—no contracts would trade at the low quoted price. After several days of limit moves of $1 per day, the futures price would finally reach its equilibrium level, and trading would occur again. This process means no one could unload a position until the price reached its equilibrium level. This example shows that price limits offer no real protection against fluctuations in equilibrium prices.

Taxation

Because of the mark-to-market procedure, investors do not have control over the tax year in which they realize gains or losses. Instead, price changes are realized gradually, with each daily settlement. Therefore, taxes are paid at year-end on cumulated profits or losses regardless of whether the position has been closed out.

17.3 Futures Market Strategies

Hedging and Speculation

Hedging and speculating are two polar uses of futures markets. A speculator uses a futures contract to profit from movements in futures prices, a hedger to protect against price movements.

If speculators believe prices will increase, they will take a long position for expected profits. Conversely, they exploit expected price declines by taking a short position.

EXAMPLE 17.3

Speculating with Oil Futures

Suppose you believe that crude oil prices are going to increase. You might purchase crude oil futures, the listings for which appear in Figure 17.1. Each contract calls for delivery of 1,000 barrels of oil. The current futures price for delivery in March (the first listed contract) is $39.48 per barrel. For every dollar increase in the price of crude, the long position gains $1,000 and the short position loses that amount.

Conversely, suppose you think that prices are heading lower. If crude oil prices fall, then the short side gains $1,000 for every dollar that prices decline.

If crude oil is selling for $41.48 at the contract maturity date, the long side will profit by $2,000 per contract purchased. The short side will lose an identical amount on each contract sold. On the other hand, if oil has fallen to $37.48, the long side will lose, and the short side will gain, $2,000 per contract.

Why would a speculator buy a futures contract? Why not buy the underlying asset directly? One reason lies in transaction costs, which are far smaller in futures markets.

Another reason is the leverage futures trading provides. Recall that futures contracts require traders to post margin considerably less than the value of the asset underlying the contract. Therefore, they allow speculators to achieve much greater leverage than is available from direct trading in a commodity.

EXAMPLE 17.4

Futures and Leverage

Suppose the initial margin requirement for the oil contract is 10%. At a current futures price of $39.48, and contract size of 1,000 barrels, this would require margin of $.10 \times 39.48 \times 1,000 = $3,948. A $2 jump in oil prices represents an increase of 5.066%, and results in a $2,000 gain on the contract for the long position. This is a percentage gain of 50.66% in the $3,948 posted as margin, precisely 10 times the percentage increase in the oil price. The 10-to-1 ratio of percentage changes reflects the leverage inherent in the futures position, since the contract was established with an initial margin of one-tenth the value of the underlying asset.

Hedgers, by contrast, use futures to insulate themselves against price movements. A firm planning to sell oil, for example, might anticipate a period of market volatility and wish to protect its revenue against price fluctuations. To hedge the total revenue derived from the sale, the firm enters a short position in oil futures. As the following example illustrates, this locks in its total proceeds (i.e., revenue from the sale of the oil plus proceeds from its futures position).

EXAMPLE 17.5

Hedging with Oil Futures

Consider an oil distributor planning to sell 100,000 barrels of oil in March that wishes to hedge against a possible decline in oil prices. Because each contract calls for delivery of 1,000 barrels, it would sell 100 contracts. Any decrease in prices would then generate a profit on the contracts that would offset the lower sales revenue from the oil.

To illustrate, continue to use the oil futures listing in Figure 17.1, and suppose that the only three possible prices for oil in April are $37.48, $39.48, and $41.48 per barrel. The revenue from the oil sale will be 100,000 times the price per barrel. The profit on each contract sold will be 1,000 times any decline in the futures price. At maturity, the convergence property ensures that the final futures price will equal the spot price of oil. Therefore, the profit on the 100 contracts sold will equal 100,000 $\times$ ($F_0 - P_T$), where P_T is the oil price on the delivery date, and F_0 is the original futures price, $39.48.

(continued)

Now consider the firm's overall position. The total revenue in March can be computed as follows:

	Oil Price in March, P_T		
	$37.48	**$39.48**	**$41.48**
Revenue from oil sale: $100,000 \times P_T$	$3,748,000	$3,948,000	$4,148,000
+ Profit on futures: $100,000 \times (F_0 - P_T)$	200,000	0	−200,000
Total Proceeds	$3,948,000	$3,948,000	$3,948,000

The revenue from the oil sale plus the proceeds from the contracts equals the current futures price, $39.48 per barrel. The variation in the price of the oil is precisely offset by the profits or losses on the futures position. For example, if oil falls to $37.48 a barrel, the short futures position generates $200,000 profit, just enough to bring total revenues to $3,948,000. The total is the same as if one were to arrange today to sell the oil in March at the futures price.

Figure 17.4 illustrates the nature of the hedge in Example 17.5. The upward-sloping line is the revenue from the sale of oil. The downward-sloping line is the profit on the futures contract. The horizontal line is the sum of sales revenue plus futures profits. This line is flat, as the hedged position is independent of oil prices.

To generalize Example 17.5, note that oil will sell for P_T per barrel at the maturity of the contract. The profit per barrel on the futures will be $F_0 - P_T$. Therefore, total revenue is $P_T + (F_0 - P_T) = F_0$, which is independent of the eventual oil price.

The utility in this example engaged in a *short hedge,* taking a short futures position to offset risk in the sales price of a particular asset. A *long hedge* is the analogous hedge for someone who wishes to eliminate the risk of an uncertain purchase price. For example, suppose a power supplier planning to purchase oil is afraid that prices might rise by the time of the purchase. As the following Concept Check illustrates, the supplier might *buy* oil futures to lock in the net purchase price at the time of the transaction.

> **CONCEPT** *check* **17.3**
>
> Suppose as in Example 17.5 that oil will be selling in March for $37.48, $39.48, or $41.48 per barrel. Consider a firm that plans to buy 100,000 barrels of oil in March. Show that if the firm buys 100 oil contracts, its net expenditures will be hedged and equal to $3,948,000.

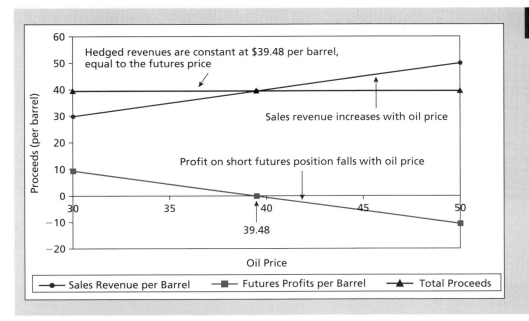

FIGURE 17.4

Hedging revenues using futures, Example 17.5 (Futures price = $39.48)

Exact futures hedging may be impossible for some goods because the necessary futures contract is not traded. For example, a portfolio manager might want to hedge the value of a diversified, actively managed portfolio for a period of time. However, futures contracts are listed only on indexed portfolios. Nevertheless, because returns on the manager's diversified portfolio will have a high correlation with returns on broad-based indexed portfolios, an effective hedge may be established by selling index futures contracts. Hedging a position using futures on another asset is called *cross-hedging*.

What are the sources of risk to an investor who uses stock index futures to hedge an actively managed stock portfolio?

Basis Risk and Hedging

basis

The difference between the futures price and the spot price.

The **basis** is the difference between the futures price and the spot price.[3] As we have noted, on the maturity date of a contract, the basis must be zero: The convergence property implies that $F_T - P_T = 0$. Before maturity, however, the futures price for later delivery may differ substantially from the current spot price.

For example, in Example 17.5, we discussed the case of a short hedger who manages risk by entering a short position to deliver oil in the future. If the asset and futures contract are held until maturity, the hedger bears no risk. Risk is eliminated because the futures price and spot price at contract maturity must be equal: Gains and losses on the futures and the underlying asset will exactly cancel. If the contract and asset are to be liquidated early, before contract maturity, however, the hedger bears **basis risk,** because the futures price and spot price need not move in perfect lockstep at all times before the delivery date. In this case, gains and losses on the contract and the asset may not exactly offset each other.

basis risk

Risk attributable to uncertain movements in the spread between a futures price and a spot price.

Some speculators try to profit from movements in the basis. Rather than betting on the direction of the futures or spot prices per se, they bet on the changes in the difference between the two. A long spot–short futures position will profit when the basis narrows.

EXAMPLE   17.6

Speculating on the Basis

Consider an investor holding 100 ounces of gold, who is short one gold futures contract. Suppose that gold today sells for $991 an ounce, and the futures price for June delivery is $996 an ounce. Therefore, the basis is currently $5. Tomorrow, the spot price might increase to $994, while the futures price increases to $998.50, so the basis narrows to $4.50. The investor's gains and losses are as follows:

Gain on holdings of gold (per ounce): $994 − $991 = $3.00
Loss on gold futures position (per ounce): $998.50 − $996 = $2.50

The investor gains $3 per ounce on the gold holdings, but loses $2.50 an ounce on the short futures position. The net gain is the decrease in the basis, or $.50 an ounce.

spread (futures)

Taking a long position in a futures contract of one maturity and a short position in a contract of a different maturity, both on the same commodity.

A related strategy is a **spread** position, where the investor takes a long position in a futures contract of one maturity and a short position in a contract on the same commodity, but with a different maturity. Profits accrue if the difference in futures prices between the two contracts changes in the hoped-for direction; that is, if the futures price on the contract held long increases by more (or decreases by less) than the futures price on the contract held short. Like basis strategies, spread positions aim to exploit movements in relative price structures rather than to profit from movements in the general level of prices.

---

[3]Usage of the word *basis* is somewhat loose. It sometimes is used to refer to the futures-spot difference, $F - P$, and other times it is used to refer to the spot-futures difference, $P - F$. We will consistently call the basis $F - P$.

Consider an investor who holds a September maturity contract long and a June contract short. If the September futures price increases by 5 cents while the June futures price increases by 4 cents, the net gain will be 5 cents − 4 cents, or 1 cent.

EXAMPLE 17.7

Speculating on the Spread

17.4 The Determination of Futures Prices

Spot-Futures Parity

There are at least two ways to obtain an asset at some date in the future. One way is to purchase the asset now and store it until the targeted date. The other way is to take a long futures position that calls for purchase of the asset on the date in question. As each strategy leads to an equivalent result, namely, the ultimate acquisition of the asset, you would expect the market-determined cost of pursuing these strategies to be equal. There should be a predictable relationship between the current price of the asset, including the costs of holding and storing it, and the futures price.

To make the discussion more concrete, consider a futures contract on gold. This is a particularly simple case: Explicit storage costs for gold are minimal, gold provides no income flow for its owners (in contrast to stocks or bonds that make dividend or coupon payments), and gold is not subject to the seasonal price patterns that characterize most agricultural commodities. Instead, in market equilibrium, the price of gold will be at a level such that the expected rate of capital gains will equal the fair expected rate of return given gold's investment risk. Two strategies that will assure possession of the gold at some future date T are:

Strategy A: Buy the gold now, paying the current or "spot" price, S_0, and hold it until time T, when its spot price will be S_T.

Strategy B: Initiate a long futures position, and invest enough money now in order to pay the futures price when the contract matures.

Strategy B will require an immediate investment of the *present value* of the futures price in a riskless security such as Treasury bills, that is, an investment of $F_0/(1 + r_f)^T$ dollars, where r_f is the interest rate on T-bills. Examine the cash flow streams of the following two strategies.[4]

	Action	**Initial Cash Flow**	**Cash Flow at Time T**
Strategy A:	Buy gold	$-S_0$	S_T
Strategy B:	Enter long position	0	$S_T - F_0$
	Invest $F_0/(1 + r_f)^T$ in bills	$-F_0/(1 + r_f)^T$	F_0
	Total for strategy B	$-F_0/(1 + r_f)^T$	S_T

The initial cash flow of strategy A is negative, reflecting the cash outflow necessary to purchase the gold at the current spot price, S_0. At time T, the gold will be worth S_T.

Strategy B involves an initial investment equal to the present value of the futures price that will be paid at the maturity of the futures contract. By time T, the investment will grow to F_0. In addition, the profits to the long position at time T will be $S_T - F_0$. The sum of the two components of strategy B will be S_T dollars, exactly enough to purchase the gold at time T regardless of its price at that time.

---

[4]We ignore the margin requirement on the futures contract and treat the cash flow involved in establishing the futures position as zero for the two reasons mentioned above: First, the margin is small relative to the amount of gold controlled by one contract; and second, and more important, the margin requirement may be satisfied with interest-bearing securities. For example, the investor merely needs to transfer Treasury bills already owned into the brokerage account. There is no time-value-of-money cost.

Each strategy results in an identical value of S_T dollars at T. Therefore, the cost, or initial cash outflow, required by these strategies also must be equal; it follows that

$$F_0/(1 + r_f)^T = S_0$$

or

$$F_0 = S_0(1 + r_f)^T \qquad \text{(17.1)}$$

This gives us a relationship between the current price and the futures price of the gold. The interest rate in this case may be viewed as the "cost of carrying" the gold from the present to time T. The cost in this case represents the time-value-of-money opportunity cost—instead of investing in the gold, you could have invested risklessly in Treasury bills to earn interest income.

EXAMPLE   17.8

Futures Pricing

Suppose that gold currently sells for $900 an ounce. If the risk-free interest rate is .5% per month, a six-month maturity futures contract should have a futures price of

$$F_0 = S_0(1+r_f)^T = \$900(1.005)^6 = \$927.34$$

If the contract has a 12-month maturity, the futures price should be

$$F_0 = \$900(1.005)^{12} = \$955.51$$

If Equation 17.1 does not hold, investors can earn arbitrage profits. For example, suppose the six-month maturity futures price in Example 17.8 were $928 rather than the "appropriate" value of $927.34 that we just derived. An investor could realize arbitrage profits by pursuing a strategy involving a long position in strategy A (buy the gold) and a short position in strategy B (sell the futures contract and borrow enough to pay for the gold purchase).

Action	Initial Cash Flow	Cash Flow at Time T (6 months)
Borrow $900, repay with interest at time T	+$900	$-\$900(1.005)^6 = -\$927.34$
Buy gold for $900	−900	S_T
Enter short futures position ($F_0 = \$928$)	0	$928 - S_T$
Total	$ 0	$.66

The net initial investment of this strategy is zero. Moreover, its cash flow at time T is positive and riskless: The total payoff at time T will be $.66 regardless of the price of gold. (The profit is equal to the mispricing of the futures contract, $928 rather than $927.34.) Risk has been eliminated because profits and losses on the futures and gold positions exactly offset each other. The portfolio is perfectly hedged.

Such a strategy produces an arbitrage profit—a riskless profit requiring no initial net investment. If such an opportunity existed, all market participants would rush to take advantage of it. The results? The price of gold would be bid up, and/or the futures price offered down, until Equation 17.1 is satisfied. A similar analysis applies to the possibility that F_0 is less than $927.34. In this case, you simply reverse the above strategy to earn riskless profits. We conclude, therefore, that in a well-functioning market in which arbitrage opportunities are competed away, $F_0 = S_0(1 + r_f)^T$.

CONCEPT
check **17.5**

Return to the arbitrage strategy just laid out. What would be the three steps of the strategy if F_0 were too low, say, $927? Work out the cash flows of the strategy now and at time T in a table like the one above.

The Parity spreadsheet allows you to calculate futures prices corresponding to a spot price for different maturities, interest rates, and income yields. You can use the spreadsheet to see how prices of more distant contracts will fluctuate with spot prices and the cost of carry.

You can learn more about this spreadsheet by using the version available on our Web site at **www.mhhe.com/bkm.**

eXcel

Please visit us at www.mhhe.com/bkm

	A	B	C	D	E
1					
2		**Spot-Futures Parity and Time Spreads**			
3					
4	Spot price	100			
5	Income yield (%)	2		Futures prices versus maturity	
6	Interest rate (%)	4.5			
7	Today's date	5/14/09		Spot price	100.00
8	Maturity date 1	11/17/09		Futures 1	101.26
9	Maturity date 2	1/2/10		Futures 2	101.58
10	Maturity date 3	6/7/10		Futures 3	102.66
11					
12	Time to maturity 1	0.51			
13	Time to maturity 2	0.63			
14	Time to maturity 3	1.06			

The arbitrage strategy can be represented more generally as follows:

Action	Initial Cash Flow	Cash Flow at Time T
1. Borrow S_0	$+S_0$	$-S_0(1 + r_f)^T$
2. Buy gold for S_0	$-S_0$	S_T
3. Enter short futures position	0	$F_0 - S_T$
Total	0	$F_0 - S_0(1 + r_f)^T$

The initial cash flow is zero by construction: The money necessary to purchase the gold in step 2 is borrowed in step 1, and the futures position in step 3, which is used to hedge the value of the gold, does not require an initial outlay. Moreover, the total cash flow to the strategy at time T is riskless because it involves only terms that are already known when the contract is entered. This situation could not persist, as all investors would try to cash in on the arbitrage opportunity. Ultimately prices would change until the time T cash flow was reduced to zero, at which point F_0 would equal $S_0(1 + r_f)^T$. This result is called the **spot-futures parity theorem** or **cost-of-carry relationship**; it gives the normal or theoretically correct relationship between spot and futures prices.

We can easily extend the parity theorem to the case where the underlying asset provides a flow of income to its owner. For example, consider a futures contract on a stock index such as the S&P 500. In this case, the underlying asset (i.e., the stock portfolio indexed to the S&P 500 index), pays a dividend yield to the investor. If we denote the dividend yield as d, then the net cost of carry is only $r_f - d$; the forgone interest earnings on the wealth tied up in the stock is offset by the flow of dividends from the stock. The net opportunity cost of holding the stock is the forgone interest less the dividends received. Therefore, in the dividend-paying case, the spot-futures parity relationship is[5]

$$F_0 = S_0(1 + r_f - d)^T \qquad (17.2)$$

spot-futures parity theorem, or cost-of-carry relationship

Describes the theoretically correct relationship between spot and futures prices. Violation of the parity relationship gives rise to arbitrage opportunities.

[5]This relationship is only approximate in that it assumes the dividend is paid just before the maturity of the contract.

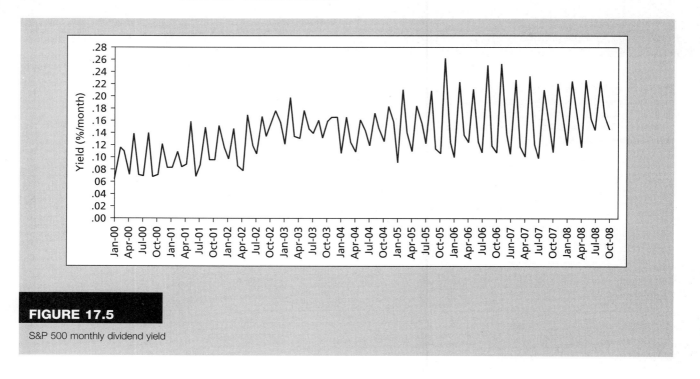

FIGURE 17.5

S&P 500 monthly dividend yield

where d is the dividend yield on the stock. Problem 10 at the end of the chapter leads you through a derivation of this result.

Although dividends of individual securities may fluctuate unpredictably, the annualized dividend yield of a broad-based index such as the S&P 500 is fairly stable, recently in the neighborhood of about 2% per year. The yield is seasonal, however, with regular peaks and troughs, so the dividend yield for the relevant months must be the one used. Figure 17.5 illustrates the yield pattern for the S&P 500. Some months, such as January or April, have consistently low yields, while others, such as May, have consistently high ones.

The arbitrage strategy just described should convince you that these parity relationships are more than just theoretical results. Any violations of the parity relationship give rise to arbitrage opportunities that can provide large profits to traders. We will see shortly that index arbitrage in the stock market is a tool used to exploit violations of the parity relationship for stock index futures contracts.

EXAMPLE   17.9

Stock Index Futures Pricing

Suppose that the risk-free interest rate is .3% per month, the dividend yield on the stock index is 0.2% per month, and the stock index is currently at 800. The net cost of carry is therefore .3% − .2% = .1% per month. Given this, a three-month contract should have a futures price of $800(1.001)^3 =$ 802.40, while a six-month contract should have a futures price of $800(1.001)^6 =$ 804.81. If the index rises to 810, both futures prices will rise commensurately: The three-month futures price will rise to $810(1.001)^3 =$ 812.43, while the six-month futures price will rise to $810(1.001)^6 =$ 814.87.

Spreads

Just as we can predict the relationship between spot and futures prices, there are similar ways to determine the proper relationships among futures prices for contracts of different maturity dates. Equation 17.2 shows that the futures price is in part determined by time to maturity. If $r_f < d$, as was true of S&P 500 stock index futures in early 2009, then the futures price will be lower on longer-maturity contracts. You can easily verify this by examining Figure 17.1, which includes *Wall Street Journal* listings of several stock index futures contracts. For futures on assets like gold, which pay no "dividend yield," we can set $d = 0$ and conclude that F must increase as time to maturity increases.

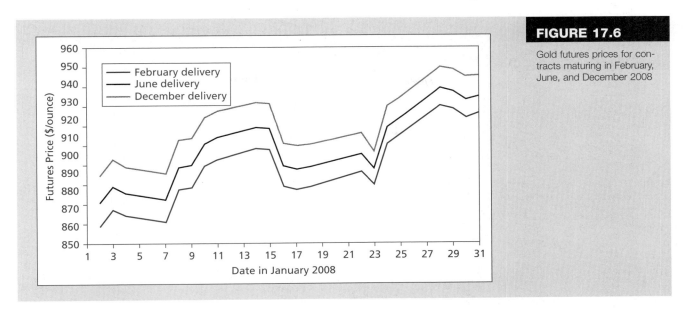

FIGURE 17.6

Gold futures prices for contracts maturing in February, June, and December 2008

Equation 17.2 shows that futures prices should all move together. It is not surprising that futures prices for different maturity dates move in unison, for all are linked to the same spot price through the parity relationship. Figure 17.6 plots futures prices on gold for three maturity dates. It is apparent that the prices move in virtual lockstep and that the more distant delivery dates command higher futures prices, as Equation 17.2 predicts should be the case for gold, for which $d = 0$.

17.5 Financial Futures

Although futures markets have their origins in agricultural commodities, today's market is dominated by contracts on financial assets. We review the most important of these contracts in this section: stock index contracts, foreign exchange contracts, and interest-rate contracts.

Stock Index Futures

Futures trade actively on stock market indexes such as the Standard & Poor's 500. In contrast to most futures contracts, which call for delivery of a specified asset, these contracts are settled by a cash amount equal to the value of the stock index in question on the contract maturity date times a multiplier that scales the size of the contract. This cash settlement duplicates the profits that would arise with actual delivery.

There are several stock index futures contracts currently traded. Table 17.2 lists some contracts on major indexes, showing under contract size the multiplier used to calculate contract settlements. An S&P 500 contract with an initial futures price of 800 and a final index value of 810, for example, would result in a profit for the long side of $250 \times (810 - 800) = \$2,500$. The S&P contract by far dominates the market in stock index futures.[6]

The broad-based U.S. stock market indexes are all highly correlated. Table 17.3 presents a correlation matrix for four U.S. indexes. Notice that the correlations among the Dow Jones Industrial Average, the New York Stock Exchange Index, and the S&P 500 are all well above .9. The NASDAQ Composite Index, which is dominated by technology firms, and the Russell 2000 Index of smaller capitalization firms have smaller correlations with the large-cap indexes and with each other, but for the most part even these are above .8.

---

[6]We should point out that while the multipliers on these contracts may make the resulting positions too large for many small investors, there are effectively equivalent futures contracts with only one-half the multiplier called *E-Minis* that are traded on the Chicago Mercantile Exchange's Globex electronic exchange. The exchange offers E-Mini contracts in several stock indexes as well as foreign currencies.

TABLE 17.2

Stock index futures

Contract	Underlying Market Index	Contract Size	Exchange
S&P 500	Standard & Poor's 500 Index. A value-weighted arithmetic average of 500 stocks.	$250 times the S&P 500 Index.	Chicago Mercantile Exchange
Dow Jones Industrials (DJIA)	Price-weighted arithmetic average of 30 blue-chip stocks.	$10 times the Dow Jones Industrial Average	Chicago Board of Trade
S&P Midcap	Index of 400 firms of midrange market value.	$500 times index.	Chicago Mercantile Exchange
NASDAQ 100	Value-weighted arithmetic average of 100 of the largest over-the-counter stocks.	$100 times the OTC index.	Chicago Mercantile Exchange
Russell 2000	Index of 2,000 smaller firms.	$500 times the index.	Chicago Mercantile Exchange
Nikkei	Nikkei 225 stock average.	$5 times the Nikkei index.	Chicago Mercantile Exchange
FTSE 100	Financial Times-Stock Exchange Index of 100 U.K. firms.	£ 10 times the FTSE Index.	London International Financial Futures Exchange
CAC 40	Index of 40 of the largest French firms.	10 euros times the index.	Euronext Paris
DAX 30	Index of 30 of the largest German firms.	25 euros times the index.	Eurex
DJ Euro STOXX 50	Value-weighted index of 50 large stocks in Eurozone.	10 euros times the index.	Eurex

TABLE 17.3

Correlations among major U.S. stock market indexes

	DJIA	NYSE	NASDAQ	S&P 500	Russell 2000
DJIA	1.000				
NYSE	0.931	1.000			
NASDAQ	0.839	0.825	1.000		
S&P 500	0.957	0.973	0.899	1.000	
Russell 2000	0.758	0.837	0.855	0.822	1.000

Source: Authors' calculations.

Creating Synthetic Stock Positions

One reason stock index futures are so popular is that they can substitute for holdings in the underlying stocks themselves. Index futures let investors participate in broad market movements without actually buying or selling large numbers of stocks.

Because of this, we say futures represent "synthetic" holdings of the market position. Instead of holding the market directly, the investor takes a long futures position in the index. Such a strategy is attractive because the transaction costs involved in establishing and liquidating futures positions are much lower than what would be required to take actual spot positions. Investors who wish to buy and sell market positions frequently find it much cheaper and easier to play the futures market. Market timers who speculate on broad market moves rather than individual securities are large players in stock index futures for this reason.

One way to market time is to shift between Treasury bills and broad-based stock market holdings. Timers attempt to shift from bills into the market before market upturns and to shift back into bills to avoid market downturns, thereby profiting from broad market movements. Market timing of this sort, however, can result in huge trading costs with the frequent purchase and sale of many stocks. An attractive alternative is to invest in Treasury bills and hold varying amounts of market index futures contracts.

The strategy works like this. When timers are bullish, they will establish many long futures positions that they can liquidate quickly and cheaply when expectations turn bearish. Rather than shifting back and forth between T-bills and stocks, traders buy and hold T-bills and adjust only the futures position. (Recall strategies A and B of the preceding section where we showed that a T-bill plus futures position resulted in a payoff equal to the stock price.) This strategy minimizes transaction costs. An advantage of this technique for timing is that investors can implicitly buy or sell the market index in its entirety, whereas market timing in the spot market would require the simultaneous purchase or sale of all the stocks in the index. This is technically difficult to coordinate and can lead to slippage in the execution of a timing strategy.

The nearby box illustrates that it is now commonplace for money managers to use futures contracts to create synthetic equity positions in stock markets. Futures positions can be particularly helpful in establishing synthetic positions in foreign equities, where trading costs tend to be greater and markets tend to be less liquid.

Index Arbitrage

Whenever the actual futures price differs from its parity value, there is an opportunity for profit. This is why the parity relationships are so important. One of the most notable developments in trading activity has been the advent of **index arbitrage,** an investment strategy that exploits divergences between the actual futures price on a stock market index and its theoretically correct parity value.

index arbitrage
Strategy that exploits divergences between actual futures prices and their theoretically correct parity values to make a riskless profit.

In principle, index arbitrage is simple. If the futures price is too high, short the futures contract and buy the stocks in the index. If it is too low, go long in futures and short the stocks. You can perfectly hedge your position and should earn arbitrage profits equal to the mispricing of the contract.

In practice, however, index arbitrage can be difficult to implement. The problem lies in buying the stocks in the index. Selling or purchasing shares in all 500 stocks in the S&P 500 is difficult for two reasons. The first is transaction costs, which may outweigh any profits to be made from the arbitrage. Second, it is extremely difficult to buy or sell the stock of 500 different firms simultaneously—and any lags in the execution of such a strategy can destroy the effectiveness of a plan to exploit short-lived price discrepancies.

Arbitrageurs need to trade an entire portfolio of stocks quickly and simultaneously if they hope to exploit temporary disparities between the futures price and its corresponding stock index. For this they need a coordinated trading program; hence the term **program trading,** which refers to coordinated purchases or sales of entire portfolios of stocks. Such strategies can be executed using electronic trading, which enables traders to send coordinated buy or sell programs to the floor of the stock exchange over computer lines. (See Chapter 3 for a discussion of electronic trading.) Program trading commonly accounts for more than 30% of NYSE daily volume.

program trading
Coordinated buy orders and sell orders of entire portfolios, usually with the aid of computers, often to achieve index arbitrage objectives.

Foreign Exchange Futures

Exchange rates between currencies vary continually and often substantially. This variability can be a source of concern for anyone involved in international business. A U.S. exporter who sells goods in England, for example, will be paid in British pounds, and the dollar value of those pounds depends on the exchange rate at the time payment is made. Until that date, the U.S. exporter is exposed to foreign exchange rate risk. This risk can be hedged through currency futures or forward markets. For example, if you know you will receive £100,000 in 60 days, you can sell those pounds forward today in the forward market and lock in an exchange rate equal to today's forward price.

GOT A BUNDLE TO INVEST FAST? THINK INDEX FUTURES

As investors go increasingly global and market turbulence grows, stock-index futures are emerging as the favorite way for nimble money managers to deploy their funds.

What's the big appeal? Speed, ease, and cheapness. For most major markets, stock futures not only boast greater liquidity but also offer lower transaction costs than traditional trading methods.

"When I decide it's time to move into France, Germany, or Britain, I don't necessarily want to wait around until I find exactly the right stocks," says Fabrizio Pierallini, manager of New York-based Vontobel Ltd.'s Euro Pacific Fund.

Mr. Pierallini says he later finetunes his market picks by gradually shifting out of futures into favorite stocks. To the extent Mr. Pierallini's stocks outperform the market, futures provide a means to preserve those gains, even while hedging against market declines.

For instance, by selling futures equal to the value of the underlying portfolio, a manager can almost completely insulate a portfolio from market moves. Say a manager succeeds in outperforming the market, but still loses 3% while the market as a whole falls 10%. Hedging with futures would capture that margin of outperformance, transforming the loss into a profit of roughly 7%. Demand for such protection helped account for stock futures' surging popularity in last year's difficult markets, Goldman said in its report.

Among futures-intensive strategies is "global tactical asset allocation," which involves trading whole markets worldwide as traditional managers might trade stocks. The growing popularity of such asset-allocation strategies has given futures a big boost in recent years.

When it comes to investing overseas, futures are often the only vehicle that makes sense from a cost standpoint. Abroad, transaction taxes and sky-high commissions can wipe out more than 1% of the money deployed on each trade. By contrast, a comparable trade in futures costs as little as 0.05%.

SOURCE: Excerpted from Suzanne McGee, *The Wall Street Journal*, February 21, 1995. Reprinted by permission of *The Wall Street Journal*, Copyright © 1995 Dow Jones & Company, Inc. All Rights Reserved Worldwide.

The forward market in foreign exchange is relatively informal. It is simply a network of banks and brokers that allows customers to enter forward contracts to purchase or sell currency in the future at a currently agreed-upon rate of exchange. The bank market in currencies is among the largest in the world, and most large traders with sufficient creditworthiness execute their trades here rather than in futures markets. Contracts in these markets are not standardized in a formal market setting. Instead, each is negotiated separately. Moreover, there is no marking to market as would occur in futures markets. Forward contracts call for execution only at the maturity date.

For currency futures, however, there are formal markets established by the Chicago Mercantile Exchange (International Monetary Market), the London International Financial Futures Exchange, and other exchanges. Here, contracts are standardized by size, and daily marking to market is observed. Moreover, there are standard clearing arrangements that allow traders to enter or reverse positions easily.

Figure 17.7 reproduces a *Wall Street Journal* listing of foreign exchange spot and forward rates. The listing gives the number of U.S. dollars required to purchase a unit of foreign currency and then the amount of foreign currency needed to purchase $1.

The forward quotations in Figure 17.7 always apply to rolling delivery in 30, 90, or 180 days. Thus, tomorrow's forward listings will apply to a maturity date one day later than today's listing. In contrast, foreign exchange futures contracts mature at specified dates in March, June, September, and December (see Figure 17.1); these four maturity days are the only dates each year when futures contracts settle.

Interest Rate Futures

The major U.S. interest rate contracts currently traded are on Eurodollars, Treasury bills, Treasury notes, and Treasury bonds. The range of these securities provides an opportunity to hedge against interest rate risk in a wide spectrum of maturities from very short (T-bills) to long term (T-bonds). In addition, futures contracts tied to interest rates in Europe (euro-denominated), Japan, the United Kingdom, and several other countries actively trade. Figure 17.1 shows listings of some of these contracts.

The Treasury contracts call for delivery of a Treasury bond, bill, or note. Should interest rates rise, the market value of the security at delivery will be less than the original futures

FIGURE 17.7

Spot and forward prices in foreign exchange

Source: From *The Wall Street Journal*, February 20, 2009. Reprinted by permission of *The Wall Street Journal*, Copyright © 2009 Dow Jones & Company, Inc. All Rights Reserved Worldwide.

Currencies

February 19, 2009

U.S.-dollar foreign-exchange rates in late New York trading

Country/currency	Thurs in US$	Thurs per US$	US$ vs, YTD chg (%)	Country/currency	Thurs in US$	Thurs per US$	US$ vs, YTD chg (%)
Americas				**Europe**			
Argentina peso*	.2832	3.5311	2.2	**Czech Rep.** koruna**	.04378	22.842	18.8
Brazil real	.4224	2.3674	2.3	**Denmark** krone	.1699	5.8858	10.5
Canada dollar	.7943	1.2590	3.5	**Euro area** euro	1.2656	.7901	10.4
1-mos forward	.7941	1.2593	3.5	**Hungary** forint	.004169	239.87	26.2
3-mos forward	.7944	1.2588	3.5	**Norway** krone	.1451	6.8918	-0.9
6-mos forward	.7951	1.2577	3.5	**Poland** zloty	.2640	3.7879	27.6
Chile peso	.001644	608.27	-4.7	**Russia** ruble‡	.02773	36.062	18.1
Colombia peso	.0003914	2554.93	13.6	**Sweden** krona	.1145	8.7336	11.6
Ecuador US dollar	1	1	unch	**Switzerland** franc	.8508	1.1754	10.1
Mexico peso*	.0679	14.7297	7.3	1-mos forward	.8512	1.1748	10.1
Peru new sol	.3082	3.245	3.5	3-mos forward	.8525	1.1730	10.0
Uruguay peso†	.04280	23.36	-4.2	6-mos forward	.8548	1.1699	10.1
Venezuela b. fuerte	.465701	2.1473	unch	**Turkey** lira**	.5890	1.6977	10.2
Asia-Pacific				**UK pound**	1.4282	.7002	2.2
Australian dollar	.6428	1.5557	10.7	1-mos forward	1.4278	.7004	2.1
China yuan	.1463	6.8355	0.2	3-mos forward	1.4275	.7005	2.1
Hong Kong dollar	.1290	7.7548	0.1	6-mos forward	1.4270	.7008	2.1
India rupee	.02025	49.383	1.6	**Middle East/Africa**			
Indonesia rupiah	.0000835	11976	9.8				
Japan yen	.010602	94.32	4.0	**Bahrain** dinar	2.6529	.3769	unch
1-mos forward	.010607	94.28	4.0	**Egypt** pound*	.1792	5.5813	1.5
3-mos forward	.010624	94.13	4.0	**Israel** shekel	.2415	4.1408	9.6
6-mos forward	.010652	93.88	3.9	**Jordan** dinar	1.4104	.7090	0.1
Malaysia ringgit§	.2733	3.6590	6.0	**Kuwait** dinar	3.4215	.2923	5.8
New Zealand dollar	.5113	1.9558	14.7	**Lebanon** pound	.0006660	1501.50	-0.4
Pakistan rupee	.01253	79.809	0.9	**Saudi Arabia** riyal	.2666	3.7509	-0.1
Philippines peso	.0209	47.893	0.9	**South Africa** rand	.0991	10.0908	7.4
Singapore dollar	.6548	1.5272	6.6	**UAE** dirham	.2723	3.6724	unch
South Korea won	.0006748	1481.92	17.3				
Taiwan dollar	.02891	34.590	5.5	**SDR**††	1.4781	.6765	4.2
Thailand baht	.02814	35.537	2.2				
Vietnam dong	.00005720	17484	unch				

*Floating rate †Financial §Government rate ‡Russian Central Bank rate **Rebased as of Jan 1, 2005 ††Special Drawing Rights (SDR); from the International Monetary Fund; based on exchange rates for U.S., British and Japanese currencies.

Note: Based on trading among banks of $1 million and more, as quoted at 4 p.m. ET by Reuters.

price, and the deliverer will profit. Hence, the short position in the interest rate futures contract gains when interest rates rise and bond prices fall.

Similarly, Treasury bond futures can be useful hedging vehicles for bond dealers or underwriters. Consider, for example, these problems:

1. A fixed-income manager holds a bond portfolio on which considerable capital gains have been earned. She foresees an increase in interest rates but is reluctant to sell her portfolio and replace it with a lower duration mix of bonds because such rebalancing would result in large trading costs as well as realization of capital gains for tax purposes. Still, she would like to hedge her exposure to interest rate increases.

2. A corporation plans to issue bonds to the public. It believes that now is a good time to act, but it cannot issue the bonds for another three months because of the lags inherent in SEC registration. It would like to hedge the uncertainty surrounding the yield at which it eventually will be able to sell the bonds.

3. A pension fund will receive a large cash inflow next month that it plans to invest in long-term bonds. It is concerned that interest rates may fall by the time it can make the investment and would like to lock in the yield currently available on long-term issues.

In each of these cases, the investment manager wishes to hedge interest rate changes. To illustrate the procedures that might be followed, we will focus on the first example, and suppose that the portfolio manager has a $10 million bond portfolio with a modified duration of

9 years.[7] If, as feared, market interest rates increase and the bond portfolio's yield also rises, say by 10 basis points (.10%), the fund will suffer a capital loss. Recall from Chapter 11 that the capital loss in percentage terms will be the product of modified duration, D^*, and the change in the portfolio yield. Therefore, the loss will be

$$D^* \times \Delta y = 9 \times .10\% = .9\%$$

or $90,000. This establishes that the sensitivity of the value of the unprotected portfolio to changes in market yields is $9,000 per 1 basis point change in the yield. Market practitioners call this ratio the **price value of a basis point,** or PVBP. The PVBP represents the sensitivity of the dollar value of the portfolio to changes in interest rates. Here, we've shown that

price value of a basis point

The change in the value of an asset due to a 1 basis point change in its yield to maturity.

$$\text{PVBP} = \frac{\text{Change in portfolio value}}{\text{Predicted change in yield}} = \frac{\$90,000}{10 \text{ basis points}} = \$9,000 \text{ per basis point}$$

One way to hedge this risk is to take an offsetting position in an interest rate futures contract. The Treasury bond contract is the most widely traded contract. The bond nominally calls for delivery of $100,000 par value T-bonds with 6% coupons and 20-year maturity. In practice, the contract delivery terms are fairly complicated because many bonds with different coupon rates and maturities may be substituted to settle the contract. However, we will assume that the bond to be delivered on the contract already is known and has a modified duration of 10 years. Finally, suppose that the futures price currently is $90 per $100 par value. Because the contract requires delivery of $100,000 par value of bonds, the contract multiplier is $1,000.

Given these data, we can calculate the PVBP for the futures contract. If the yield on the delivery bond increases by 10 basis points, the bond value will fall by $D^* \times .1\% = 10 \times .1\% = 1\%$. The futures price also will decline 1% from 90 to 89.10.[8] Because the contract multiplier is $1,000, the gain on each short contract will be $1,000 \times .90 = \$900$. Therefore, the PVBP for one futures contract is $900/10-basis-point change, or $90 for a change in yield of 1 basis point.

Now we can easily calculate the hedge ratio as follows:

$$H = \frac{\text{PVBP of portfolio}}{\text{PVBP of hedge vehicle}} = \frac{\$90,000}{\$90 \text{ per contract}} = 100 \text{ contracts}$$

Therefore, 100 T-bond futures contracts will serve to offset the portfolio's exposure to interest rate fluctuations.

CONCEPT check 17.6

Suppose the bond portfolio is twice as large, $20 million, but that its modified duration is only 4.5 years. Show that the proper hedge position in T-bond futures is the same as the value just calculated, 100 contracts.

Although the hedge ratio is easy to compute, the hedging problem in practice is more difficult. For example, we assumed in our example that the yields on the T-bond contract and the bond portfolio would move perfectly in unison. Although interest rates on various fixed-income instruments do tend to vary in tandem, there is considerable slippage across sectors of the fixed-income market.

cross-hedging

Hedging a position in one asset by establishing an offsetting position in a related, but different, asset.

This problem highlights the fact that most hedging activity is in fact **cross-hedging,** meaning that the hedge vehicle is a different asset from the one to be hedged. To the extent that there is slippage between prices or yields of the two assets, the hedge will not be perfect. Nevertheless, even cross-hedges can eliminate a large fraction of the total risk of the unprotected portfolio.

[7]Recall that modified duration, D^*, is related to duration, D, by the formula $D^* = D/(1 + y)$, where y is the bond's yield to maturity. If the bond pays coupons semiannually, then y should be measured as a semiannual yield. For simplicity, we will assume annual coupon payments, and treat y as the effective annual yield to maturity.
[8]This assumes the futures price will be exactly proportional to the bond price, which ought to be nearly true.

17.6 | Swaps

Swaps are multiperiod extensions of forward contracts. For example, rather than agreeing to exchange British pounds for U.S. dollars at an agreed-upon forward price at one single date, a **foreign exchange swap** would call for an exchange of currencies on several future dates. For example, the parties might exchange $1.8 million for £ 1 million in each of the next five years. Similarly, **interest rate swaps** call for the exchange of a series of cash flows proportional to a given interest rate for a corresponding series of cash flows proportional to a floating interest rate.[9] For example, one party might exchange a variable cash flow equal to $1 million times a short-term interest rate for $1 million times a fixed interest rate of 8% for each of the next seven years.

The swap market is a huge component of the derivatives market, with well over $200 trillion in swap agreements outstanding. We will illustrate how these contracts work using a simple interest rate swap as an example.

foreign exchange swap

An agreement to exchange a sequence of payments denominated in one currency for payments in another currency at an exchange rate agreed to today.

interest rate swaps

Contracts between two parties to trade cash flows corresponding to different interest rates.

	EXAMPLE 17.10

Interest Rate Swap

Consider the manager of a large portfolio that currently includes $100 million par value of long-term bonds paying an average coupon rate of 7%. The manager believes that interest rates are about to rise. As a result, he would like to sell the bonds and replace them with either short-term or floating-rate issues. However, it would be exceedingly expensive in terms of transaction costs to replace the portfolio every time the forecast for interest rates is updated. A cheaper and more flexible way to modify the portfolio is for the managers to "swap" the $7 million a year in interest income the portfolio currently generates for an amount of money that is tied to the short-term interest rate. That way, if rates do rise, so will the portfolio's interest income.

A swap dealer might advertise its willingness to exchange, or "swap," a cash flow based on the six-month LIBOR rate for one based on a fixed rate of 7%. (The LIBOR, or London InterBank Offered Rate, is the interest rate at which banks borrow from each other in the Eurodollar market. It is the most commonly used short-term interest rate in the swap market.) The portfolio manager would then enter into a swap agreement with the dealer to *pay* 7% on **notional principal** of $100 million and *receive* payment of the LIBOR rate on that amount of notional principal.[10] In other words, the manager swaps a payment of .07 × $100 million for a payment of LIBOR × $100 million. The manager's *net* cash flow from the swap agreement is therefore (LIBOR −.07) × $100 million. Note that the swap arrangement does not mean that a loan has been made. The participants have agreed only to exchange a fixed cash flow for a variable one.

Now consider the net cash flow to the manager's portfolio in three interest rate scenarios:

notional principal

Principal amount used to calculate swap payments.

	LIBOR Rate		
	6.5%	**7.0%**	**7.5%**
Interest income from bond portfolio (= 7% of $100 million bond portfolio)	$7,000,000	$7,000,000	$7,000,000
Cash flow from swap [= (LIBOR − 7%) × notional principal of $100 million]	(500,000)	0	500,000
Total (= LIBOR × $100 million)	$6,500,000	$7,000,000	$7,500,000

Notice that the total income on the overall position—bonds plus swap agreement—is now equal to the LIBOR rate in each scenario times $100 million. The manager has, in effect, converted a fixed-rate bond portfolio into a synthetic floating-rate portfolio.

---

[9]Interest rate swaps have nothing to do with the Homer-Liebowitz bond swap taxonomy described in Chapter 11.

[10]The participants to the swap do not loan each other money. They agree only to exchange a fixed cash flow for a variable cash flow that depends on the short-term interest rate. This is why the principal is described as *notional*. The notional principal is simply a way to describe the size of the swap agreement. In this example, the parties to the swap exchange a 7% fixed rate for the LIBOR rate; the difference between LIBOR and 7% is multiplied by notional principal to determine the cash flow exchanged by the parties.

Swaps and Balance Sheet Restructuring

Example 17.10 illustrates why interest rate swaps have tremendous appeal to fixed-income managers. These contracts provide a means to quickly, cheaply, and anonymously restructure the balance sheet. Suppose a corporation that has issued fixed-rate debt believes that interest rates are likely to fall; it might prefer to have issued floating-rate debt. In principle, it could issue floating-rate debt and use the proceeds to buy back the outstanding fixed-rate debt. In practice, however, this would be enormously expensive in terms of transaction costs. Instead, the firm can convert the outstanding fixed-rate debt into synthetic floating-rate debt by entering a swap to receive a fixed interest rate (offsetting its fixed-rate coupon obligation) and pay a floating rate.

Conversely, a bank that pays current market interest rates to its depositors, and thus is exposed to increases in rates, might wish to convert some of its financing to a fixed-rate basis. It would enter a swap to receive a floating rate and pay a fixed rate on some amount of notional principal. This swap position, added to its floating-rate deposit liability, would result in a net liability of a fixed stream of cash. The bank might then be able to invest in long-term fixed-rate loans without encountering interest rate risk.

As a final example, consider a fixed-income portfolio manager. Swaps enable the manager to switch back and forth between a fixed- or floating-rate profile quickly and cheaply as forecast for interest rate changes. A manager who holds a fixed-rate portfolio can transform it into a synthetic floating-rate portfolio by entering a pay fixed–receive floating swap and can later transform it back by entering the opposite side of a similar swap.

The Swap Dealer

What about the swap dealer? Why is the dealer, which is typically a financial intermediary such as a bank, willing to take on the opposite side of the swaps desired by these participants in these hypothetical swaps?

Consider a dealer who takes on one side of a swap, let's say paying LIBOR and receiving a fixed rate. The dealer will search for another trader in the swap market who wishes to receive a fixed rate and pay LIBOR. For example, company A may have issued a 7% coupon fixed-rate bond that it wishes to convert into synthetic floating-rate debt, while company B may have issued a floating-rate bond tied to LIBOR that it wishes to convert into synthetic fixed-rate debt. The dealer will enter a swap with company A in which it pays a fixed rate and receives LIBOR, and will enter another swap with company B in which it pays LIBOR and receives a fixed rate. When the two swaps are combined, the dealer's position is effectively neutral on interest rates, paying LIBOR on one swap and receiving it on another. Similarly, the dealer pays a fixed rate on one swap and receives it on another. The dealer becomes little more than an intermediary, funneling payments from one party to the other.[11] The dealer finds this activity profitable because it will charge a bid–asked spread on the transaction.

This rearrangement is illustrated in Figure 17.8. Company A has issued 7% fixed-rate debt (the leftmost arrow in the figure) but enters a swap to pay the dealer LIBOR and receive a 6.95% fixed rate. Therefore, the company's net payment is 7% + (LIBOR − 6.95%) = LIBOR + .05%. It has thus transformed its fixed-rate debt into synthetic floating-rate debt. Conversely, company B has issued floating-rate debt paying LIBOR (the rightmost arrow), but enters a swap to pay a 7.05% fixed rate in return for LIBOR. Therefore, its net payment is LIBOR + (7.05% − LIBOR) = 7.05%. It has thus transformed its floating-rate debt into synthetic fixed-rate debt. The bid–asked spread, the source of the dealer's profit, in the example illustrated in Figure 17.8 is .10% of notional principal each year.

---

[11]Actually, things are a bit more complicated. The dealer is more than just an intermediary because it bears the credit risk that one or the other of the parties to the swap might default on the obligation. Referring to Figure 17.8, if firm A defaults on its obligation, for example, the swap dealer still must maintain its commitment to firm B. In this sense, the dealer does more than simply pass through cash flows to the other swap participants.

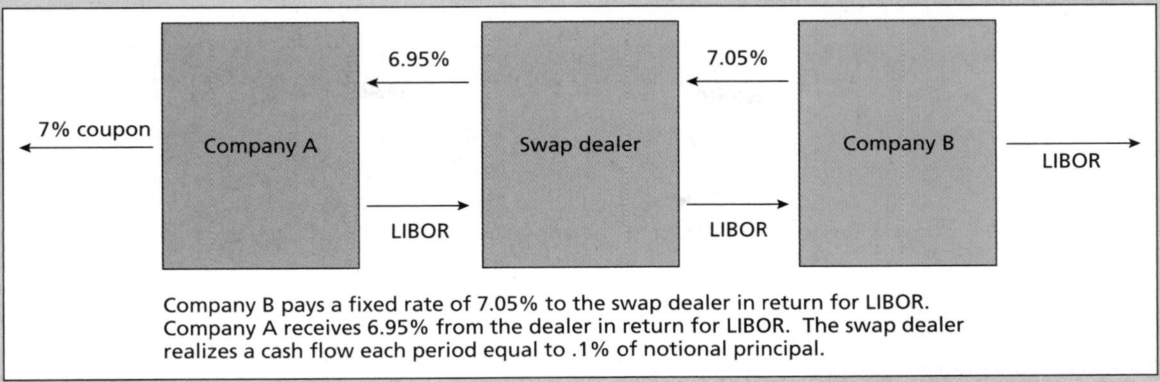

Company B pays a fixed rate of 7.05% to the swap dealer in return for LIBOR. Company A receives 6.95% from the dealer in return for LIBOR. The swap dealer realizes a cash flow each period equal to .1% of notional principal.

FIGURE 17.8

Interest rate swap

A pension fund holds a portfolio of money market securities that the manager believes are paying excellent yields compared to other comparable-risk short-term securities. However, the manager believes that interest rates are about to fall. What type of swap will allow the fund to continue to hold its portfolio of short-term securities while at the same time benefiting from a decline in rates?

SUMMARY

- Forward contracts are arrangements that call for the future delivery of an asset at a currently agreed-upon price. The long trader is obligated to purchase the good, and the short trader is obligated to deliver it. If the price at the maturity of the contract exceeds the forward price, the long side benefits by virtue of acquiring the good at the contract price.
- A futures contract is similar to a forward contract, differing most importantly in the aspects of standardization and marking to market, which is the process by which gains and losses on futures contract positions are settled daily. In contrast, forward contracts call for no cash transfers until contract maturity.
- Futures contracts are traded on organized exchanges that standardize the size of the contract, the grade of the deliverable asset, the delivery date, and the delivery location. Traders negotiate only the contract price. This standardization creates increased liquidity in the marketplace and means buyers and sellers can easily find many traders for a desired purchase or sale.
- The clearinghouse acts as an intermediary between each pair of traders, acting as the short position for each long, and as the long position for each short, so traders need not be concerned about the performance of the trader on the opposite side of the contract. Traders are required to post margins in order to guarantee their own performance on the contracts.
- The gain or loss to the long side for a futures contract held between time 0 and t is $F_t - F_0$. Because $F_T = P_T$ at maturity, the long's profit if the contract is held until maturity is $P_T - F_0$, where P_T is the spot price at time T and F_0 is the original futures price. The gain or loss to the short position is $F_0 - P_T$.

www.mhhe.com/bkm

- Futures contracts may be used for hedging or speculating. Speculators use the contracts to take a stand on the ultimate price of an asset. Short hedgers take short positions in contracts to offset any gains or losses on the value of an asset already held in inventory. Long hedgers take long positions in futures contracts to offset gains or losses in the purchase price of a good.

- The spot-futures parity relationship states that the equilibrium futures price on an asset providing no service or payments (such as dividends) is $F_0 = P_0(1 + r_f)^T$. If the futures price deviates from this value, then market participants can earn arbitrage profits.

- If the asset provides services or payments with yield d, the parity relationship becomes $F_0 = P_0 (1 + r_f - d)^T$. This model is also called the cost-of-carry model, because it states that the futures price must exceed the spot price by the net cost of carrying the asset until maturity date T.

- Futures contracts calling for cash settlement are traded on various stock market indexes. The contracts may be mixed with Treasury bills to construct artificial equity positions, which makes them potentially valuable tools for market timers. Market index contracts also are used by arbitrageurs who attempt to profit from violations of the parity relationship.

- Interest rate futures allow for hedging against interest rate fluctuations in several different markets. The most actively traded contract is for Treasury bonds.

- The interest rate swap market is a major component of the fixed-income market. In these arrangements, parties trade the cash flows of different securities without actually exchanging any securities directly. This is a useful tool to manage the interest-rate exposure of a portfolio.

KEY TERMS

basis, 556	forward contract, 544	price value of a basis
basis risk, 556	futures price, 544	point, 566
cash settlement, 553	index arbitrage, 563	program trading, 563
clearinghouse, 550	interest rate swaps, 567	short position, 545
convergence property, 552	long position, 545	single stock
cost-of-carry	maintenance	futures, 547
relationship, 559	margin, 551	spot-futures parity
cross-hedging, 566	marking to market, 551	theorem, 559
foreign exchange swap, 567	notional principal, 567	spread, 556

PROBLEM SETS

Select problems are available in McGraw-Hill Connect. Please see the packaging options section of the preface for more information.

Basic

1. On January 1, you sold one March maturity S&P 500 Index futures contract at a futures price of 800. If the futures price is 850 on February 1, what is your profit? The contract multiplier is $250.

2. The current level of the S&P 500 is 800. The dividend yield on the S&P 500 is 2%. The risk-free interest rate is 1%. What should a futures contract with a one-year maturity be selling for?

3. A one-year gold futures contract is selling for $941. Spot gold prices are $900 and the one-year risk-free rate is 4%. What arbitrage opportunity is available to investors? What strategy should they use, and what will be the profits on the strategy?

4. You purchase a Treasury-bond futures contract with an initial margin requirement of 15% and a futures price of $115,098. The contract is traded on a $100,000 underlying par value bond. If the futures price falls to $108,000, what will be the percentage loss on your position?

5. *a.* Turn to Figure 17.1 and locate the contract on the Standard & Poor's 500 Index. If the margin requirement is 10% of the futures price times the multiplier of $250, how much must you deposit with your broker to trade the March contract?

   b. If the March futures price were to increase to 790, what percentage return would you earn on your net investment if you entered the long side of the contract at the price shown in the figure?

   c. If the March futures price falls by 1%, what is the percentage gain or loss on your net investment?

6. Why might individuals purchase futures contracts rather than the underlying asset?

7. What is the difference in cash flow between short-selling an asset and entering a short futures position?

Intermediate

8. Suppose the value of the S&P 500 Stock Index is currently $800. If the one-year T-bill rate is 3% and the expected dividend yield on the S&P 500 is 2%, what should the one-year maturity futures price be?

9. It is now January. The current interest rate is 4%. The June futures price for gold is $946.30, while the December futures price is $952. Is there an arbitrage opportunity here? If so, how would you exploit it?

10. Consider a stock that will pay a dividend of D dollars in one year, which is when a futures contract matures. Consider the following strategy: Buy the stock, short a futures contract on the stock, and borrow S_0 dollars, where S_0 is the current price of the stock.

    a. What are the cash flows now and in one year? (*Hint:* Remember the dividend the stock will pay.)

    b. Show that the equilibrium futures price must be $F_0 = S_0(1 + r) - D$ to avoid arbitrage.

    c. Call the dividend yield $d = D/S_0$, and conclude that $F_0 = S_0(1 + r - d)$.

11. *a.* A single-stock futures contract on a nondividend-paying stock with current price $150 has a maturity of one year. If the T-bill rate is 3%, what should the futures price be?

    b. What should the futures price be if the maturity of the contract is three years?

    c. What if the interest rate is 5% and the maturity of the contract is three years?

12. The Excel Application box in the chapter (available at **www.mhhe.com/bkm;** link to Chapter 17 material) shows how to use the spot-futures parity relationship to find a "term structure of futures prices," that is, futures prices for various maturity dates.

    a. Suppose that today is January 1, 2010. Assume the interest rate is 3% per year and a stock index currently at 800 pays a dividend yield of 2%. Find the futures price for contract maturity dates of February 14, 2010, May 21, 2010, and November 18, 2010.

    b. What happens to the term structure of futures prices if the dividend yield is higher than the risk-free rate? For example, what if the interest rate is only 1%?

**Please visit us at
www.mhhe.com/bkm**

13. One Chicago has just introduced a new single-stock futures contract on the stock of Brandex, a company that currently pays no dividends. Each contract calls for delivery of 1,000 shares of stock in one year. The T-bill rate is 6% per year.

    a. If Brandex stock now sells at $120 per share, what should the futures price be?

    b. If the Brandex stock price drops by 3%, what will be the change in the futures price and the change in the investor's margin account?

    c. If the margin on the contract is $12,000, what is the percentage return on the investor's position?

14. The multiplier for a futures contract on the stock market index is $250. The maturity of the contract is one year, the current level of the index is 800, and the risk-free interest rate is .5% per month. The dividend yield on the index is .2% per month. Suppose that after one month, the stock index is at 810.

    a. Find the cash flow from the mark-to-market proceeds on the contract. Assume that the parity condition always holds exactly.

    b. Find the one-month holding-period return if the initial margin on the contract is $10,000.

15. Suppose the S&P 500 Index portfolio pays a dividend yield of 2% annually. The index currently is 800. The T-bill rate is 3%, and the S&P futures price for delivery in one year is $833. Construct an arbitrage strategy to exploit the mispricing and show that your profits one year hence will equal the mispricing in the futures market.

16. *a.* How should the parity condition (Equation 17.2) for stocks be modified for futures contracts on Treasury bonds? What should play the role of the dividend yield in that equation?

    b. In an environment with an upward-sloping yield curve, should T-bond futures prices on more distant contracts be higher or lower than those on near-term contracts?

    c. Confirm your intuition by examining Figure 17.1.

17. Desert Trading Company has issued $100 million worth of long-term bonds at a fixed rate of 7%. The firm then enters into an interest rate swap where it pays LIBOR and receives a fixed 6% on notional principal of $100 million. What is the firm's overall cost of funds?

18. What type of interest rate swap would be appropriate for a speculator who believes interest rates soon will fall?

19. The margin requirement on the S&P 500 futures contract is 10%, and the stock index is currently 800. Each contract has a multiplier of $250. How much margin must be put up for each contract sold? If the futures price falls by 1% to 792, what will happen to the margin account of an investor who holds one contract? What will be the investor's percentage return based on the amount put up as margin?

20. The multiplier for a futures contract on a certain stock market index is $250. The maturity of the contract is one year, the current level of the index is 800, and the risk-free interest rate is .2% per *month*. The dividend yield on the index is .1% per month. Suppose that *after one month,* the stock index is at 820.

    a. Find the cash flow from the mark-to-market proceeds on the contract. Assume that the parity condition always holds exactly.

    b. Find the holding-period return if the initial margin on the contract is $10,000.

21. You are a corporate treasurer who will purchase $1 million of bonds for the sinking fund in three months. You believe rates soon will fall and would like to repurchase the company's sinking fund bonds, which currently are selling below par, in advance of requirements. Unfortunately, you must obtain approval from the board of directors for such a purchase, and this can take up to two months. What action can you take in the futures market to hedge any adverse movements in bond yields and prices until you actually can buy the bonds? Will you be long or short? Why?

22. A manager is holding a $1 million bond portfolio with a modified duration of eight years. She would like to hedge the risk of the portfolio by short-selling Treasury bonds. The modified duration of T-bonds is 10 years. How many dollars' worth of T-bonds should she sell to minimize the risk of her position?

23. A corporation plans to issue $10 million of 10-year bonds in three months. At current yields the bonds would have modified duration of eight years. The T-note futures contract is selling at $F_0 = 100$ and has modified duration of six years. How can the firm use this futures contract to hedge the risk surrounding the yield at which it will be able to sell its bonds? Both the bond and the contract are at par value.

Challenge

24. The S&P 500 Index is currently at 800. You manage a $4 million indexed equity portfolio. The S&P 500 futures contract has a multiplier of $250.

    a. If you are temporarily bearish on the stock market, how many contracts should you sell to fully eliminate your exposure over the next six months?

b. If T-bills pay 2% per six months and the semiannual dividend yield is 1%, what is the parity value of the futures price? Show that if the contract is fairly priced, the total risk-free proceeds on the hedged strategy in part (*a*) provide a return equal to the T-bill rate.

c. How would your hedging strategy change if, instead of holding an indexed portfolio, you hold a portfolio of only one stock with a beta of .6? How many contracts would you now choose to sell? Would your hedged position be riskless? What would be the beta of the hedged position?

25. A corporation has issued a $10 million issue of floating-rate bonds on which it pays an interest rate 1% over the LIBOR rate. The bonds are selling at par value. The firm is worried that rates are about to rise, and it would like to lock in a fixed interest rate on its borrowings. The firm sees that dealers in the swap market are offering swaps of LIBOR for 7%. What swap arrangement will convert the firm's borrowings to a synthetic fixed-rate loan? What interest rate will it pay on that synthetic fixed-rate loan?

26. The one-year futures price on a particular stock-index portfolio is 406, the stock index currently is 400, the one-year risk-free interest rate is 3%, and the year-end dividend that will be paid on a $400 investment in the index portfolio is $5.

a. By how much is the contract mispriced?

b. Formulate a zero-net-investment arbitrage portfolio and show that you can lock in riskless profits equal to the futures mispricing.

c. Now assume (as is true for small investors) that if you short sell the stocks in the market index, the proceeds of the short sale are kept with the broker, and you do not receive any interest income on the funds. Is there still an arbitrage opportunity (assuming you don't already own the shares in the index)? Explain.

d. Given the short-sale rules, what is the no-arbitrage *band* for the stock-futures price relationship? That is, given a stock index of 400, how high and how low can the futures price be without giving rise to arbitrage opportunities?

CFA Problems

1. The open interest on a futures contract at any given time is the total number of outstanding
   a. Contracts.
   b. Unhedged positions.
   c. Clearinghouse positions.
   d. Long and short positions.

2. In futures trading, the minimum level to which an equity position may fall before requiring additional margin is *most accurately* termed the
   a. Initial margin.
   b. Variation margin.
   c. Cash flow margin.
   d. Maintenance margin.

3. A silver futures contract requires the seller to deliver 5,000 Troy ounces of silver. Jerry Harris sells one July silver futures contract at a price of $14 per ounce, posting a $4,000 initial margin. If the required maintenance margin is $2,500, what is the *first* price per ounce at which Harris would receive a maintenance margin call?

4. In each of the following cases, discuss how you, as a portfolio manager, could use financial futures to protect a portfolio.
   a. You own a large position in a relatively illiquid bond that you want to sell.
   b. You have a large gain on one of your long Treasuries and want to sell it, but you would like to defer the gain until the next accounting period, which begins in four weeks.
   c. You will receive a large contribution next month that you hope to invest in long-term corporate bonds on a yield basis as favorable as is now available.

5. Futures contracts and options contracts can be used to modify risk. Identify the fundamental distinction between a futures contract and an option contract, and briefly explain the difference in the manner that futures and options modify portfolio risk.

6. Joan Tam, CFA, believes she has identified an arbitrage opportunity for a commodity as indicated by the information given in the following exhibit.

Commodity Price and Interest Rate Information	
Spot price for commodity	$120
Futures price for commodity expiring in one year	$125
Interest rate for one year	8%

   a. Describe the transactions necessary to take advantage of this specific arbitrage opportunity.
   b. Calculate the arbitrage profit.

7. Several Investment Committee members have asked about interest rate swap agreements and how they are used in the management of domestic fixed-income portfolios.
   a. Define an interest rate swap and briefly describe the obligation of each party involved.
   b. Cite and explain two examples of how interest rate swaps could be used by a fixed-income portfolio manager to control risk or improve return.

8. Janice Delsing, a U.S.-based portfolio manager, manages an $800 million portfolio ($600 million in stocks and $200 million in bonds). In reaction to anticipated short-term market events, Delsing wishes to adjust the allocation to 50 percent stocks and 50 percent bonds through the use of futures. Her position will be held only until "the time is right to restore the original asset allocation." Delsing determines a financial futures-based asset allocation strategy is appropriate. The stock futures index multiplier is $250 and the denomination of the bond futures contract is $100,000. Other information relevant to a futures-based strategy is given in the following exhibit.

Information for Futures-Based Strategy	
Bond portfolio modified duration	5 years
Bond portfolio yield to maturity	7%
Price value of basis point (PVBP) of bond futures	$97.85
Stock index futures price	1378
Stock portfolio beta	1.0

   a. Describe the financial futures-based strategy needed and explain how the strategy allows Delsing to implement her allocation adjustment. No calculations are necessary.
   b. Compute the number of each of the following needed to implement Delsing's asset allocation strategy:
      i. Bond futures contracts
      ii. Stock index futures contracts

9. Maria VanHusen, CFA, suggests that forward contracts on fixed income securities can be used to protect the value of the Star Hospital Pension Plan's bond portfolio against the possibility of rising interest rates. VanHusen prepares the following example to illustrate how such protection would work:
   • A 10-year bond with a face value of $1,000 is issued today at par value. The bond pays an annual coupon.
   • An investor intends to buy this bond today and sell it in six months.
   • The six-month risk-free interest rate today is 5% (annualized).
   • A six-month forward contract on this bond is available, with a forward price of $1,024.70.
   • In six months, the price of the bond, including accrued interest, is forecast to fall to $978.40 as a result of a rise in interest rates.

a. Should the investor buy or sell the forward contract to protect the value of the bond against rising interest rates during the holding period?
b. Calculate the value of the forward contract for the investor at the maturity of the forward contract if VanHusen's bond-price forecast turns out to be accurate.
c. Calculate the change in value of the combined portfolio (the underlying bond and the appropriate forward contract position) six months after contract initiation.

WEB *master*   PROFIT OR LOSS ON A SPREAD POSITION

1. Suppose that you want to create a spread position using S&P 500 futures contracts. Go to **www.cmegroup.com** and listed under Equity Index Products, select the S&P 500. Click on "Contract Specifications" at the top of product listing. Review the contract's specifications. Click on the "Product Calendar" link to see the contracts that are available for trading. Note the code for one contract that expires in approximately three months and the code for another that expires in approximately nine months.

2. Assume that you bought the three month contract and sold the nine month contract about two months ago. The Wall Street Journal provides a comprehensive list of current and historical prices at **online.wsj.com/mdc/page/marketsdata.html.** Specifically, navigate to the "Commodities & Futures" tab and

then the Complete US Index listing. Once you locate the S&P 500 Comp, click on the Chart icon to the left of the contract contained in your strategy. From here you can move your mouse over any day and retrieve the closing price on that day. Choose a trading date that occurred two months ago and note the price. Find the closing prices for the two contracts that you selected.

3. Return to the CME listings and find the closing prices of the two contracts on today's date. Assume that you close your positions in both contracts.

4. Using the beginning and ending prices for the futures contracts that you bought and sold, calculate the return you earned on the spread position during the two-month period, before commissions.

17.1. a. The payoff on the put looks like that on the short futures contract when the asset price falls below X or F_0, but when the asset price rises above F_0, the futures payoff turns negative whereas the value of the put cannot fall below zero. The put (which must be purchased) gives you upside potential if the asset price falls but limits downside risk, whereas the futures gives you both upside and downside exposure.

b. The payoff on the written call looks like that on the short futures contract when the asset price rises above F_0, but when the asset price falls, the futures payoff is positive, whereas the payoff on the written call is never positive. The written call gives you downside exposure, but your upside potential is limited to the premium you received for the option.

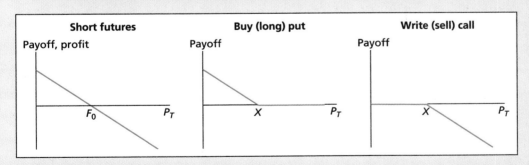

17.2. The clearinghouse has a zero net position in all contracts. Its long and short positions are offsetting, so that net cash flow from marking to market must be zero.

17.3.

	Oil Price in March, P_T		
	$37.48	**$39.48**	**$41.48**
Cash flow to purchase oil: $-100{,}000 \times P_T$	−$3,748,000	−$3,948,000	−$4,148,000
+ Profit on long futures: $100{,}000 \times (P_T - F_0)$	−200,000	0	+200,000
Total cash flow	−$3,948,000	−$3,948,000	−$3,948,000

17.4. The risk would be that the index and the portfolio do not move perfectly together. Thus, risk involving the spread between the futures price and the portfolio value could persist even if the index futures price were set perfectly relative to index itself.

17.5.

Action	Initial Cash Flow	Time-T Cash Flow
Lend $900	−$900	$900(1.005)^6 = $927.34
Sell gold short	+900	$-S_T$
Long futures	0	$S_T - $927
Total	$0	$.34 risklessly

17.6. The price value of a basis point is still $9,000, as a one-basis-point change in the interest rate reduces the value of the $20 million portfolio by .01% × 4.5 = .045%. Therefore, the number of futures needed to hedge the interest rate risk is the same as for a portfolio half the size with double the modified duration.

17.7. The manager would like to hold on to the money market securities because of their attractive relative pricing compared to other short-term assets. However, there is an expectation that rates will fall. The manager can hold this *particular* portfolio of short-term assets and still benefit from the drop in interest rates by entering a swap to pay a short-term interest rate and receive a fixed interest rate. The resulting synthetic fixed-rate portfolio will increase in value if rates do fall.

PART 6

Active Investment Management

Passive investment, or indexing, is the preferred strategy for those who believe markets are essentially efficient. While administration of passive portfolios requires an efficient organizational and trading structure, there is obviously less need for knowledge of security analysis or portfolio strategy if one is limited to managing index portfolios. In contrast, active managers take it on faith that markets are not always efficient and that, at least occasionally, bargains may be found in security markets. Active managers must apply asset valuation and portfolio theory to best establish their positions.

Chapter 18 begins this part of the text by discussing the theory of active portfolio management in imperfectly efficient markets. Effective exploitation of security mispricing calls for balancing investment in underpriced securities with diversification concerns. How should this balance be struck? The answer is inseparable from the quandary of how to assess the performance of an active portfolio. Accordingly, Chapter 18 begins with methods of performance evaluation and proceeds to suggest techniques to achieve the goal of superior performance.

Investing across borders is conceptually a simple extension of portfolio diversification. This pursuit confronts the effects of political risk and uncertain exchange rates on future performance, however. These issues, unique to international investing, are addressed in Chapter 19.

Chapter 20 covers hedge funds, probably the most active of active managers. It also focuses on some of the special problems encountered in evaluation of hedge fund performance.

Investments originate with a savings plan that diverts funds from consumption to investment. Taxes and inflation complicate the relationship between how much you save and what you will be able to achieve with your accumulating investment fund. Chapter 21 introduces a framework and tools that can be used to formulate a comprehensive household savings/investment plan.

Professional management of active investment begins with a contractual relationship between a client and portfolio manager. The economic needs of clients must be articulated and their objectives translated into an operational financial plan. For this purpose, the CFA Institute has laid out a broad framework for active investment management. Chapter 22 familiarizes you with this framework.

Chapters in This Part:

Chapter

Portfolio Performance Evaluation

After Studying This Chapter You Should Be Able To:

- Compute risk-adjusted rates of return, and use these measures to evaluate investment performance.

- Determine which risk-adjusted performance measure is appropriate in a variety of investment contexts.

- Apply style analysis to assess portfolio strategy.

- Decompose portfolio returns into components attributable to asset allocation choices versus security selection choices.

- Assess the value of market timing ability.

In previous chapters, we derived predictions for expected return as a function of risk. In this chapter, we ask how we can evaluate the performance of a portfolio manager given the risk of his or her portfolio. Difficulties in adjusting average returns for risk present a host of issues because the proper measure of risk may not be obvious and risk levels may change along with portfolio composition.

We begin with conventional approaches to risk adjustment. These use the risk measures developed in Part Two of the text to compare investment results. We show the problems with these approaches when you try to apply them in a real and complex world. Finally, we examine evaluation procedures used in the field. We show how overall investment results are decomposed and attributed to the underlying asset allocation and security selection decisions of the portfolio manager.

Even if you largely accept the efficient market hypothesis, we will see that there are reasons to consider active portfolio management. We consider the objective of active management and analyze two forms: market timing based solely on macroeconomic factors, and security selection that includes microeconomic forecasting.

Related Web sites for this chapter are available at www.mhhe.com/bkm.

18.1 | Risk-Adjusted Returns

Investment Clients, Service Providers, and Objectives of Performance Evaluation

Individual households as well as institutional money managers must decide whether to use passive or active portfolio management. **Passive management** involves (1) capital allocation between **cash** (i.e., almost-risk-free vehicles such as money market funds), and the investor's optimal risky portfolio (i.e., a portfolio constructed from one or more index funds or ETFs), and (2) asset allocation, the weighting of the index funds or ETFs within the risky portion of the complete portfolio.

Still, the concept of passive management is not completely unambiguous. At one extreme, passive investors will commit to capital and asset allocation weights, and change them only infrequently in response to significant changes in circumstances or risk tolerance. At the other extreme, they will regularly adjust portfolio weights based on estimates of the risk of the index fund(s), derived for example from VIX contracts (the volatility indexes traded on the CBOE, discussed in Chapter 16) or from other sources.

Alternatively, households and institutional endowments may choose **active management,** in which case they usually become clients of professional portfolio managers.[1] The dividing line between passive and active management is the forecasting of future rates of return on asset classes and/or individual assets. Such forecasting is more difficult than estimation of risk by an order of magnitude. The reason for this is quite subtle and is lost on many professional as well as novice investors. Competition among the vast number of investors means that security prices generally reflect publicly available information. Thus, successful forecasting of future prices and rates of return requires differential *private* information. To estimate risk, on the other hand, investors can freely and quite easily use publicly available information, making these estimates a commodity. Accordingly, we call active managers those who forecast returns in conjunction with risk to construct optimal portfolios. A few professionals restrict their activity to **market timing** (switching between risky portfolios and cash), some concentrate on asset allocation only, and most engage in both asset allocation and security selection.[2]

Both clients and professionals are interested in performance evaluation. Clients need to know whether their chosen professionals produce adequate net-of-fee returns. Professionals need to shore up their methodology and maintain qualified staff with adequate compensation to compete in the market for these services. Lapses in performance can cost them dearly as evidence shows that funds under management flow quickly from underachievers to superperformers.

Performance evaluation of a portfolio is complicated because of the great volatility of asset returns. A portfolio's average return over an evaluation period is inadequate to measure performance. To begin with, the average return realized over any particular period may not represent the *expected* return. Surely, luck (either good or bad) should not be allowed to dominate the evaluation process. Even when the average return does approximate expected return, it still would be invalid as a measure of performance because it ignores risk—we expect higher risk investments to outperform lower risk ones in average to boom markets, and to underperform in bear markets. Hence, we must estimate portfolio risk to determine the adequacy of the average return. Since volatility generates statistical errors in estimates of both expected return and risk, we must remain skeptical of the evaluation process.

Comparison Groups

The simplest and most popular way to adjust returns for portfolio risk is to compare rates of return with those of other investment funds with similar risk characteristics. For example, high-yield bond portfolios are grouped into one "universe," growth stock equity funds are

---

passive management

Holding a well-diversified portfolio without attempting to search out security mispricing.

cash

Shorthand for virtually risk-free money market securities.

active management

Attempts to achieve portfolio returns more than commensurate with risk, whether by forecasting broad markets or by identifying mispriced securities.

market timing

A strategy that moves funds between the risky portfolio and cash, based on forecasts of relative performance.

---

[1]Households and institutional endowments that conduct active management in-house become their own clients. The adage that a lawyer who represents himself has a fool for a client doesn't necessarily apply here.

[2]Many professional managers are prohibited from extensive market timing by a prospectus or contract that fixes a range of allowed weights in cash instruments.

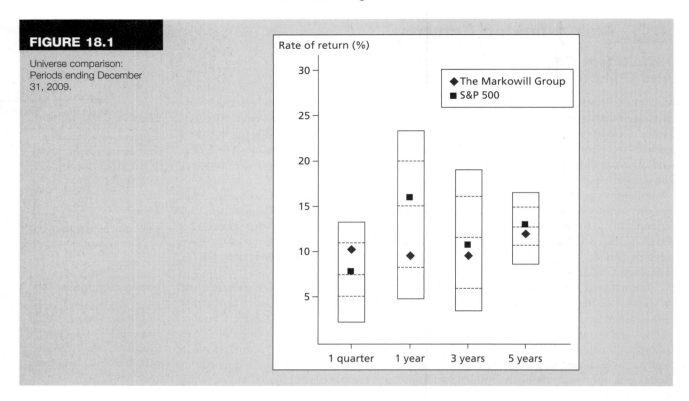

FIGURE 18.1

Universe comparison: Periods ending December 31, 2009.

comparison universe

The set of portfolio managers with similar investment styles that is used in assessing the relative performance of an individual portfolio manager.

grouped into another universe, and so on. Then the average returns of each fund within the universe are ordered, and each portfolio manager receives a percentile ranking depending on relative performance within the **comparison universe,** the collection of funds to which performance is compared. For example, the manager with the ninth-best performance in a universe of 100 funds would be the 90th percentile manager: Her performance was better than 90% of all competing funds over the evaluation period.

These relative rankings usually are displayed in a chart like that shown in Figure 18.1. The chart summarizes performance rankings over four periods: one quarter, one year, three years, and five years. The top and bottom lines of each box are drawn at the rate of return of the 95th and 5th percentile managers. The three dotted lines correspond to the rates of return of the 75th, 50th (median), and 25th percentile managers. The diamond is drawn at the average return of a particular fund, the Markowill Group, and the square is drawn at the average return of a benchmark index such as the S&P 500. This format provides an easy-to-read representation of the performance of the fund relative to the comparison universe.

This comparison with other managers of similar investment groups is a useful first step in evaluating performance. Even so, such rankings can be misleading. Consider that within a particular universe some managers may concentrate on particular subgroups, so that portfolio characteristics are not truly comparable. For example, within the equity universe, one manager may concentrate on high-beta stocks. Similarly, within fixed-income universes, interest rate risk can vary across managers. These considerations suggest that we need a more precise means for risk adjustment.

Basic Performance-Evaluation Statistics

Performance evaluation relies on the index model discussed in Sections 6.5 and 7.2 and on the CAPM of Section 7.1. The single-index model equation applied to a portfolio P is

$$R_{Pt} = \beta_P R_{Mt} + \alpha_P + e_{Pt}$$

(18.1)

where $R_{Pt} (= r_{Pt} - r_{ft})$ is portfolio P's excess return over cash equivalents during period t, r_{ft} is the return on cash, and R_{Mt} is the excess return on the market-index portfolio, M. The beta of portfolio P, β_P, is its sensitivity to the index portfolio, hence its measure of systematic risk, and $\beta_P R_{Mt}$ is the component of return that is driven by the market index. The extramarket or nonsystematic component of P's returns, $\alpha_P + e_{Pt}$, includes the portfolio alpha plus zero-mean noise, e, called the residual, which is uncorrelated with R_M. Thus, the expected return of the portfolio for some evaluation period is

$$E(R_P) = \beta_P E(R_M) + \alpha_P \qquad \textbf{(18.2)}$$

We measure *expected* returns over the period (unfortunately, with sampling error) by *average* return.

The CAPM hypothesis is that the market portfolio is mean-variance efficient. The index model uses an index portfolio, M, to proxy for the theoretical market portfolio, and hence it is the benchmark passive strategy against which competing portfolios are measured. The CAPM hypothesis is that the alpha of all securities and competing portfolios is zero. A professional who strives to outperform the index, however, must produce a positive alpha; the validity of the CAPM doesn't preclude some professionals from doing so, as long as the totality of investments that exhibit positive alpha is not large relative to aggregate wealth in the economy.

What about portfolio risk? As noted above, beta measures *systematic* risk since the variance of the market-driven return component is

$$\text{Var}(\beta_P R_{Mt}) = \beta_P^2 \sigma_M^2 \qquad \textbf{(18.3)}$$

and the term σ_M^2 is the same for all portfolios. The extramarket component of return contributes the quantity $\text{Var}(e_P)$ to portfolio variance. The standard deviation of the residual return e, which we will denote here as σ_e, is called residual risk or residual SD. The variance of the return on P is thus the sum of the variances (since the systematic and residual components are uncorrelated):

$$\sigma_P^2 = \beta_P^2 \sigma_M^2 + \sigma_e^2 \qquad \textbf{(18.4)}$$

We may now prepare the statistics that are used for performance evaluation of a portfolio P from a sample of observations over an interval of T periods (usually months). The procedure includes the following steps:

1. Obtain the time series of R_{Pt} for portfolio P, and R_{Mt} for the benchmark M.
2. Compute the arithmetic averages of the series $\overline{R}_P$, $\overline{R}_M$. These are taken as estimates of the expected returns of portfolios P and M for the evaluation period.
3. Compute the standard deviations of returns for portfolios P and M, σ_P and σ_M. These serve as estimates of the total risk of P and M.
4. Run a regression of R_{Pt} on R_{Mt} to obtain estimates of P's beta, alpha, residual SD, and correlation with the benchmark. Check the significance statistics to see that the sample is reasonable. In particular, if the beta coefficient estimate is not significant, the sample may be insufficient for the performance-evaluation statistics discussed below.
5. Use Equation 18.2 to compute P's alpha as $\alpha_P = \overline{R}_P - \beta_P \overline{R}_M$.
6. Use Equation 18.4 to compute the residual SD as $\sigma_e = \text{SQRT}(\sigma_P^2 - \beta_P^2 \sigma_M^2)$.

Table 18.1 presents performance-evaluation statistics for two professionally managed portfolios, P and Q, the benchmark portfolio, M, and cash. Notice that P is an aggressive portfolio with a beta of 1.25. Q might be a hedge fund, not completely market-neutral (which would entail a beta of zero), but still with a defensive beta of .5. Thus, Q's standard deviation is relatively low (18%), and most of that volatility reflects its residual SD (15.44%).

TABLE 18.1

Performance of two managed portfolios, P and Q, the benchmark portfolio, M, and cash equivalents

	Portfolio P	Portfolio Q	Benchmark	Cash
Average return	13.6	9.5	10.4	4
Average excess return (%)	9.60	5.50	6.37	0
Standard deviation (%)	24.1	18.0	18.5	0
Beta (pure number)	1.25	0.50	1.0	0
Alpha (%)	1.6	2.3	0	0
Residual SD(%)	6.79	15.44	0	0
Correlation with benchmark	0.96	0.51	1	0
Sharpe measure	0.398	0.306	0.344	0
M-square	1.00	(0.72)	0	0
Treynor measure	7.68	11.00	6	0
Information ratio	0.24	0.15	0	0

Performance Evaluation of Entire-Wealth Portfolios Using the Sharpe Measure and M²

Sharpe measure

Reward-to-volatility ratio; ratio of portfolio excess return to standard deviation.

Consider a small charity, The Diabetes Foundation, whose board has decided to invest the entire risk-bound portion of its endowment in one of the three portfolios of Table 18.1. In this case, the total risk of the chosen portfolio, as measured by its standard deviation, will be the source of all of the endowment's risk. Accordingly, the familiar **Sharpe ratio,**

$$S = \frac{\bar{R}}{\sigma} \tag{18.5}$$

which measures reward (incremental expected return over cash) to total volatility (SD), must determine the choice. Table 18.1 shows that the Sharpe ratio of portfolio P (.398) is larger than that of either Q (.306) or M (.344); hence P would be the charity's choice. Notice that P's average return is sufficiently large to compensate for the fact that it has the largest SD of the three portfolios; conversely, although Q is the least volatile, its Sharpe ratio is the lowest.

The Sharpe ratio has a clear interpretation, namely, the incremental return an investor may expect for every increase of 1% of standard deviation. It is the slope of the capital allocation line supported by that portfolio. But should investors consider the difference in Sharpe measures between portfolio P and the benchmark portfolio M (.398 − .344 = .054) large? That is harder to interpret and leads us to a variant on the Sharpe measure.

We can more easily interpret magnitudes with the following calculation: Suppose the foundation wished to limit its risk to match that of the benchmark, with SD = 18.5%. Since P's SD is 24.1%, the foundation could invest a proportion 18.5/24.1 = .7676 in P and .2324 in risk-free cash to obtain the same standard deviation as M. The average excess return would then be 7.37% (you should verify this), which is 1% greater than the 6.37% returned by M. Put differently, portfolio P provides a 1% incremental return over the benchmark when a position in bills is used to match its volatility to the benchmark. This volatility-matched return differential is therefore a natural performance measure, and is sometimes called **M-square or M²** after Leah and Franco Modigliani.[3] (The square in this case is not a mathematical operation, but is simply a nod to the two Modiglianis after whom the measure is named.) Mathematically, M² is simply a variant of the Sharpe ratio, specifically, the difference between the Sharpe ratio of P and the benchmark M, multiplied by the standard deviation of M:

M-square (M²)

Return difference between a managed portfolio leveraged to match the volatility of a passive index and the return on that index.

$$M^2 = (S_P - S_M)\sigma_M \tag{18.6}$$

Here, M² = (.398 − .344)18.5 = 1.0%.

---

[3]The M-square measure was developed independently by Graham and Harvey (1997) and by Modigliani and Modigliani (1997).

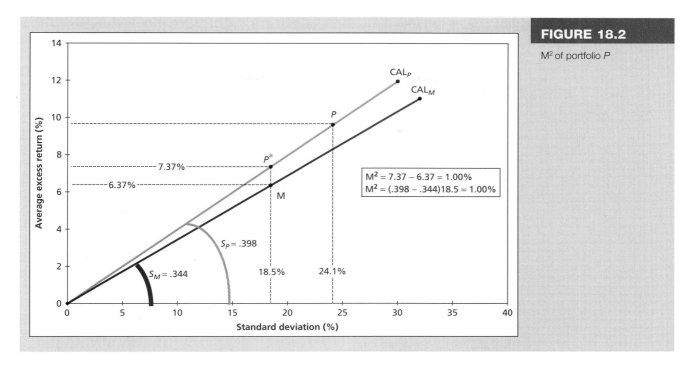

FIGURE 18.2

M^2 of portfolio P

Figure 18.2 illustrates the logic behind the measure. The focal point is portfolio P^*. Its excess return ($R_{P*} = 7.37\%$) can be arrived at in two ways: (1) Start at portfolio P (with standard deviation σ_P) and slide down CAL_P by mixing P with T-bills. You will arrive at P^* with a standard deviation that matches the benchmark, σ_M, if the portfolio weights you use are $w_P = \sigma_M/\sigma_P$ and $w_{\text{bills}} = 1 - \sigma_M/\sigma_P$. For example, if portfolio P has double the standard deviation of M, then half the weight is on P and half is on bills, and this mixture matches the standard deviation of the benchmark. The vertical distance from P^* to M, $R_{P*} - R_M$, is the M^2 measure. It is the difference in expected return of the two positions with matched standard deviations. (2) Alternatively, use the slope of CAL_P (i.e., the Sharpe measure S_P) to find that $R_{P*} = S_P \times \sigma_M$, and the slope of CAL_M to find that $R_M = S_M \times \sigma_M$. The difference between these expected returns is $R_{P*} - R_M = (S_P - S_M)\sigma_M$. Notice that while the M^2 of P is positive, the M^2 of Q is negative, $-.72\%$, because its Sharpe ratio is less than that of the benchmark.

Performance Evaluation of Fund of Funds Using the Treynor Measure

We have used the Sharpe measure, or its variant M-square, to choose between an actively managed portfolio competing with a passive benchmark as the sole risky position for an endowment. But some funds are so large that they might engage *several* managers to run risky component portfolios. For example, CalPERS (the California Public Employee Retirement System) is a large pension fund with around $180 billion to invest in early 2009. Like many large plans, it uses a **fund of funds** approach, allocating the endowment among a number of professional managers (funds) based in part on performance. This requires a different performance measure.

To see why, suppose CalPERS considers two managers, and it so happens that both establish portfolios with average returns, beta, and residual standard deviation equal to those of portfolio P in Table 18.1. The average excess return of the fund-of-funds portfolio will be the same as that of portfolio P, 9.6%. Since beta is the same, 1.25, the systematic variance will be the same as well: $1.25^2 \times 18.5^2 = 534.77$. But the residual variance will be partly diversified away because residual returns are not perfectly correlated. Assume for the sake of illustration that the residual returns for the two funds are in fact uncorrelated. In

fund of funds

Mutual funds or hedge funds that invest in other funds.

that case, if CalPERS mixes the two funds with weights of one-half in each, the resulting residual variance will be only one-half the value of the two component portfolios: instead of 6.79^2, it will be only $6.79^2/2 = 23.02$. Thus the total variance of the fund-of-two-funds will be $534.77 + 23.02 = 557.79$, implying a standard deviation of 23.62%, slightly lower than that of P, which has a standard deviation of 24.1%. If we continue to increase the number of managers, the residual risk will fall further as a result of greater diversification. With a large number of managers and uncorrelated residual returns, the standard deviation of residual risk will eventually near zero. In the end, we will be left with only the systematic variance of 534.77 or, equivalently, a standard deviation of 23.61. At that point, the Sharpe ratio will be $9.6/23.61 = .4064$, slightly better than that of portfolio P with a Sharpe ratio of .4.

Suppose now that CalPERS chose among managers who established portfolios like Q in Table 18.1. Allocating the fund to many such managers, this fund-of-funds portfolio also would be left only with its systematic standard deviation of $.5 \times 18.5 = 9.25\%$. A fund of funds that mimics portfolio Q would have a Sharpe measure of $5.5/9.25 = .595$, and $M^2 = (.595 - .344)18.5 = 4.6\%$, far better than P or the fund of funds composed of P look-alikes. The Sharpe measure (which is higher for portfolio P) clearly would fail to properly rank component portfolios for a fund of funds. Another performance measure is called for this case.

This exercise suggests that for a fund of funds, where residual risk can be largely diversified away, we should compare average excess return to nondiversifiable or *systematic*, rather than total risk. Since beta measures systematic risk, Treynor (1965) proposed the following measure, since named after him:

$$T = \frac{\overline{R}}{\beta} \tag{18.7}$$

Treynor measure

Ratio of portfolio excess return to beta.

As Table 18.1 demonstrates, the **Treynor measure** can differ from Sharpe's, suggesting that the proper performance measure depends on the role of the risky position in the investor's overall portfolio.

Performance Evaluation of a Portfolio Added to the Benchmark using the Information Ratio

Now we consider yet another scenario, one in which an endowment considers adding a position in an actively managed portfolio to an already existing passive portfolio. The Central State University endowment has so far been a passive investor. Presented with a positive alpha achieved by the managers of P and Q the board decides that given the limited size of the endowment, it can justify adding a position in just one of the portfolios. Which should it choose? To answer, we must choose the portfolio which, when combined with the benchmark, generates an efficient frontier with the better optimized portfolio, that is, with the higher Sharpe ratio. In Section 6.5 we saw that the key to this problem is the **information ratio**.

information ratio

Ratio of alpha to the standard deviation of diversifiable risk.

We can calculate the Sharpe ratio of the optimized portfolio from the Sharpe ratio of benchmark portfolio M, and the information ratio of the added portfolio using Equation 6.17, which we repeat here:

$$S_O = \text{SQRT}\left[S_M^2 + \left(\frac{\alpha_P}{\sigma_P} \right)^2 \right] \tag{18.8}$$

where $\frac{\alpha_P}{\sigma_P}$ is the information ratio of portfolio P. Table 18.1 indicates that the information ratio of P, .24, is higher than that of Q, .15. Equation 18.8 tells us that the Sharpe ratio of the optimized portfolio using P will be .42, but only .38 using Q—still better than the benchmark's .34. Once again, we see that the role of the evaluated portfolio in the investor's complete portfolio determines the choice of performance measure and that a different measure can lead to different judgment of superiority. The following table summarizes our conclusions:

Performance Measure	Definition	Application
Sharpe	$$\frac{\text{Excess return}}{\text{Standard deviation}}$$	When choosing among portfolios competing as the optimal risky position
Treynor	$$\frac{\text{Excess return}}{\text{Beta}}$$	When ranking many portfolios that will be mixed to form the optimal risky portfolio
Information ratio	$$\frac{\text{alpha}}{\text{residual standard deviation}}$$	When evaluating a portfolio to be mixed with a position in the passive benchmark portfolio

The Relation of Alpha to Performance Measures

Alpha, also known as **Jensen's measure** after Michael Jensen, who first proposed it, appears everywhere in performance evaluation; why then, did we not present it as a performance measure? To answer, we must see its relation in the three performance measures.

Jensen measure

The alpha of an investment.

The relation of Jensen's measure to the Sharpe and Treynor measures can be gleaned from Equation 18.2. Substituting the right-hand side of the equation for the average excess return and employing some manipulation, we find that the Sharpe measure is

$$S_P = \frac{\beta_P \overline{R}_M}{\sigma_P} + \frac{\alpha_P}{\sigma_P} \qquad \beta_P = \rho \frac{\sigma_P}{\sigma_M}$$

$$S_P = S_M \rho + \frac{\alpha_P}{\sigma_P} \tag{18.9}$$

$$S_P - S_M = S_M(\rho - 1) + \frac{\alpha_P}{\sigma_P}$$

where ρ is the correlation between the excess return of P and the benchmark. First, observe that alpha alone does not determine which portfolio has a larger Sharpe ratio. The standard deviation of P and its correlation with the benchmark are also important. Thus positive alpha is *not* a sufficient condition for a managed portfolio to offer a higher Sharpe measure than the passive benchmark.

While it is not sufficient, a positive alpha is *necessary* to obtain a higher Sharpe ratio than the benchmark's S_M, because $S_M(\rho - 1)$ is negative. Superior performance in this context is a stiff challenge because, to achieve a positive alpha, it is necessary to construct a portfolio that is different from the benchmark. But this, in turn, will increase residual risk (which lowers the correlation coefficient) and offset the improvement in alpha. Notice that portfolio Q has a larger alpha, 2.3%, than P, 1.6%. Moreover, its ratio of alpha to standard deviation ($2.3/18 = .128$) is far greater than P's ($1.6/24.1 = .066$). Despite all this, Q's Sharpe ratio is smaller because its correlation coefficient with M is low (.51) compared with P's (.96).

The Treynor measure, which measures performance of a portfolio within a fund of funds, also is related to the portfolio alpha via Equation 18.2 as follows:

$$T_P = \frac{\overline{R}_P}{\beta_P} = \frac{\beta_P \overline{R}_M + \alpha_P}{\beta_P} = \overline{R}_M + \frac{\alpha_P}{\beta_P}$$

$$\beta_M = 1 \qquad T_M = \overline{R}_M \tag{18.10}$$

$$T_P - T_M = \frac{\alpha_P}{\beta_P}$$

$\overline{R}_M$ is common to all portfolios; therefore, the relative rank of T_P is determined by the ratio $\frac{\alpha_P}{\beta_P}$.

Thus here, too, a positive alpha is necessary but not sufficient to rank alternative active portfolios; we also need to know beta.

Finally, a positive alpha is neither necessary (at least when short sales are allowed[4]) nor sufficient for the square of the information ratio, $\frac{\alpha_P}{\sigma_{eP}}$, to be positive.[5] The absolute value of alpha also is not sufficient to rank portfolios because it does not guarantee that the squared ratio of alpha to residual SD is higher than that of another portfolio with a smaller absolute alpha value.

CONCEPT check 18.1	Consider the following data for a particular sample period when returns were high:

	Portfolio *P*	Market *M*
Average return	35%	28%
Beta	1.2	1.0
Standard deviation	42%	30%

Calculate alpha and the three performance measures for portfolio *P* and the market. The T-bill rate during the period was 6%. By which measures did portfolio *P* outperform the market?

Alpha Capture and Alpha Transport

In the next chapter, we will see that many hedge funds seek positions with positive alpha, but zero beta. They may wish to speculate on a portfolio that appears underpriced, but without taking a stance on the direction of the broad market. Even if they are right about the portfolio being *relatively* underpriced, they still might lose money investing in it, if it falls along with the broad market. The solution is to hedge out the market exposure of the portfolio by selling either the stock index or stock index futures. This long stock–short index strategy provides a *market neutral* position in the portfolio. It captures alpha without the systematic risk of the portfolio. Then, you can establish any desired sensitivity to particular market sectors using index products such as ETFs.

alpha transfer/alpha transport

Investing in one market where you find positive alpha opportunities, but using index products both to hedge broad exposure to that market and to establish exposure to a different market.

This procedure is called **alpha transfer** or **alpha transport**, because you transfer alpha from the sector where you find it to the market sector in which you establish exposure. Finding alpha requires skill. By contrast, beta, or market exposure, is a "commodity product" that can be supplied cheaply through index funds.

Suppose the excess return on an actively managed portfolio is

$$R_{Pt} = \alpha_P + \beta_P R_{Mt} + e_{Pt}$$

To hedge out the market exposure, you can sell (or short sell) β_P dollars of the index for every dollar invested in the portfolio, investing the proceeds of the sale in T-bills. The excess return on this market-hedged, zero-beta position, call it portfolio *Z*, is:

$$
\begin{aligned}
R_{Zt} = &\ \alpha_P + \beta_P R_{Mt} + e_{Pt} && \text{[the excess return per dollar invested in } P] \\
&- \beta_P R_{Mt} && \text{[the excess return on the } \beta \text{ dollars sold in } M] \\
&+ 0 && \text{[the excess return on bills is zero]}
\end{aligned}
$$

Adding up terms, we see that the short position in *M* has indeed eliminated market exposure:

$$R_{Zt} = \alpha_P + e_{Pt} \qquad \bar{R}_Z = \alpha_P \tag{18.11}$$

Because its beta is zero, the correlation of *Z* with the benchmark *M* is also zero.

Notice that portfolio *Z* requires a short position in *M* when β_P is positive (the typical case) or leverage when it is negative. Hence, many institutions may be prohibited from creating such portfolios.

[4]When short sales are allowed and a portfolio alpha is negative, you can sell it short and turn the alpha to positive. When short sales are not allowed, then a positive alpha is required to raise the Sharpe ratio of the optimized portfolio of *P* and *M*.

[5]Recall that the information ratio is squared in Equation 18.6 for the Sharpe ratio of the optimized portfolio.

The construction of portfolio Z is also called **alpha capture;** it distills from the portfolio all systematic risk. Applying Equation 18.9 for this special zero-beta portfolio (with $\rho = 0$) we find that portfolio Z's Sharpe ratio simplifies to P's information ratio:

alpha capture
construction of a positive-alpha portfolio with all systematic risk hedged away.

$$\rho = 0 \qquad \alpha_Z = \alpha_P \qquad \sigma_Z = \sigma_{eZ} = \sigma_{eP}$$

$$S_Z = \rho S_M + \frac{\alpha_Z}{\sigma_Z} = \frac{\alpha_P}{\sigma_{eP}} = \text{portfolio } P\text{'s information ratio} \qquad \textbf{(18.12)}$$

We conclude that when short positions and leverage are allowed, a nonzero alpha is a necessary and sufficient condition for improved Sharpe and information ratios.[6] Otherwise, a positive alpha is necessary but not sufficient for an improved Sharpe measure.

Since Z has a zero beta, its Treynor measure is undefined, and we cannot tell whether combining it with the fund will improve its Sharpe ratio. This would depend on the fund's alpha and residual SD.

An important issue that is often lost when evaluating alpha is its statistical significance. After all, even if the true alpha is zero, you expect to estimate a positive alpha in roughly 50% of the evaluated portfolios (and a negative alpha in the other 50%). Given capital market volatility, it is fair to expect that even truly nonzero alphas often would be statistically insignificant. However, another indication of a nonzero alpha would be persistence over time. Take a look at Figure 8.8 of Chapter 8. The graph suggests that persistence of alpha is mostly found for negative-alpha portfolios, and little is evident in portfolios of positive alpha.

Performance Evaluation with a Multi-Index Model

The Fama-French (FF) three-factor model discussed in Section 7.4 has almost completely replaced the single-index model in academic performance evaluation, and has been gaining "market share" in the investment services industry[7]. Evidence in favor of augmenting the market index with the size (SMB) and value (HML) portfolios is compelling. How should this affect performance evaluation?

Expanding Equation 18.1 to include the size and value factors, we have[8],

$$R_{Pt} = \beta_P R_{Mt} + \beta_{SMB} r_{SMBt} + \beta_{HML} r_{HMLt} + \alpha_P + e_{Pt} \qquad \textbf{(18.13)}$$

and

$$\overline{R}_{Pt} = \beta_P \overline{R}_{Mt} + \beta_{SMB} \overline{r}_{SMBt} + \beta_{HML} \overline{r}_{HMLt} + \alpha_P \qquad \textbf{(18.14)}$$

A multi-index model is called for when it better explains asset returns. An indication that the expanded model is preferred to the single-index specification is that passive investments (e.g., a market index portfolio) will appear to have a zero alpha when evaluated using the multi-index model but not using the single-index one. A successful multi-index model also suggests that an efficient passive investment will include positions in all factors, that is, holding the single index alone is not efficient. Moreover, when a multi-index model dominates the single index one, then using a single index in performance evaluation will yield misleading results, that is, apparent nonzero alpha values even in the absence of superior performance.

Recent research by Cremers, Petajisto, and Zitzewitz (2008) shows that indexes such as the S&P 500 and Russell 2000 demonstrate significant nonzero alphas when evaluated using the FF model even when a momentum factor is added. The problem in finding adequate passive benchmarks tells us that performance evaluation is really (after more than 40 years) still in its infancy and our inferences should elicit some healthy skepticism.

---

[6]If a security or portfolio has a negative alpha, we could apply this analysis in an analogous manner, but starting instead with a short position in the overpriced security.

[7]The three FF factors (market, SMB, and HML) sometimes are augmented by a momentum portfolio (long in recent losers and short in recent gainers), and/or by a liquidity portfolio (long in liquid and short in illiquid stocks).

[8]Notice that we replace uppercase R (which usually denotes an excess return relative to the risk-free rate) with lowercase r for the SMB and HML factors because these portfolios already are excess returns, for example, small stock returns over large stock returns. These are zero-net-investment portfolios (for example, long small stocks and short large stocks), and thus have an opportunity cost of zero rather than r_f.

Performance Measures

The Excel model "Performance Measures" calculates all of the performance measures discussed in this chapter. The model available on our Web site is built to allow you to compare eight different portfolios and to rank them on all measures discussed in this chapter.

**Please visit us at
www.mhhe.com/bkm**

	A	B	C	D	E	F	G	H	I	J	K
1					Performance Measurement						
2											
3											
4											
5		Average	Standard	Beta	Unsystematic	Sharpe	Treynor	Jensen	M^2	T^2	Appraisal
6	Fund	Return	Deviation	Coefficient	Risk	Ratio	Measure	Alpha	Measure	Measure	Ratio
7	Alpha	.2800	.2700	1.7000	.0500	0.8148	.1294	-.0180	-.0015	-.0106	-0.3600
8	Omega	.3100	.2600	1.6200	.0600	0.9615	.1543	.0232	.0235	.0143	0.3867
9	Omicron	.2200	.2100	0.8500	.0200	0.7619	.1882	.0410	-.0105	.0482	2.0500
10	Millennium	.4000	.3300	2.5000	.2700	1.0303	.1360	-.0100	.0352	-.0040	-0.0370
11	Big Value	.1500	.1300	0.9000	.0300	0.6923	.1000	-.0360	-.0223	-.0400	-1.2000
12	Momentum Watcher	.2900	.2400	1.4000	.1600	0.9583	.1643	.0340	.0229	.0243	0.2125
13	Big Potential	.1500	.1100	0.5500	.0150	0.8182	.1636	.0130	-.0009	.0236	0.8667
14	S&P Index Return	.2000	.1700	1.0000	.0000	0.8235	.1400	.0000	.0000	.0000	0.0000
15	T-Bill Return	.06		0							
16											
17	Ranking by Sharpe										
18		Return	S.D.	Beta	Unsy. Risk	Sharpe	Treynor	Jensen	M^2	T^2	Appraisal
19	Millennium	.4000	.3300	2.5000	.2700	1.0303	.1360	-.0100	.0352	-.0040	-0.0370
20	Omega	.3000	.2600	1.6200	.0600	0.9615	.1543	.0232	.0235	.0143	0.3867
21	Momentum Watcher	.2900	.2400	1.4000	.1600	0.9583	.1643	.0340	.0229	.0243	0.2125
22	S&P Index Return	.2000	.1700	1.0000	.0000	0.8235	.1400	.0000	.0000	.0000	0.0000
23	Big Potential	.1500	.1100	0.5500	.0150	0.8182	.1636	.0130	-.0009	.0236	0.8667
24	Alpha	.2800	.2700	1.7000	.0500	0.8148	.1294	-.0180	-.0015	-.0106	-0.3600
25	Omicron	.2200	.2100	0.8500	.0200	0.7619	.1882	.0410	-.0105	.0482	2.0500
26	Big Value	.1500	.1300	0.9000	.0300	0.6923	.1000	-.0360	-.0223	-.0400	-1.2000
27											
28	Ranking by Treynor										
29		Return	S.D.	Beta	Unsy. Risk	Sharpe	Treynor	Jensen	M^2	T^2	Appraisal
30	Omicron	.2200	.2100	0.8500	.0200	0.7619	.1882	.0410	-.0105	.0482	2.0500
31	Momentum Watcher	.2900	.2400	1.4000	.1600	0.9583	.1643	.0340	.0229	.0243	0.2125
32	Big Potential	.1500	.1100	0.5500	.0150	0.8182	.1636	.0130	-.0009	.0236	0.8667
33	Omega	.3100	.2600	1.6200	.0600	0.9615	.1543	.0232	.0235	.0143	0.3867
34	S&P Index Return	.2000	.1700	1.0000	.0000	0.8235	.1400	.0000	.0000	.0000	0.0000
35	Millennium	.4000	.3300	2.5000	.2700	1.0303	.1360	-.0100	.0352	-.0040	-0.0370
36	Alpha	.2800	.2700	1.7000	.0500	0.8148	.1294	-.0180	-.0015	-.0106	-0.3600

18.2 Style Analysis

Style analysis was introduced by Nobel Laureate William Sharpe (1992). The popularity of the concept was aided by a widely-cited study (Brinson et al, 1991) concluding that 91.5% of the variation in returns of 82 mutual funds could be explained by the funds' asset allocation to bills, bonds, and stocks. Later studies that considered asset allocation across a broader range of asset classes found that as much as 97% of fund returns can be explained by asset allocation alone.

Sharpe considered 12 asset class (style) portfolios. His idea was to regress fund returns on indexes representing a range of asset classes. The regression coefficient on each index would then measure the implicit allocation to that "style." Because funds are barred from short positions, the regression coefficients are constrained to be either zero or positive and to sum to 100%, so as to represent a complete asset allocation. The R-square of the regression would then measure the percentage of return variability due to style choice rather than security selection.

To illustrate the approach, consider Sharpe's study of the monthly returns on Fidelity's Magellan Fund over the period January 1985 through December 1989, shown in Table 18.2. While there are 12 asset classes, each one represented by a stock index, the regression coefficients are positive for only four of them. We can conclude that the fund returns are well

TABLE 18.2		Regression Coefficient*
Sharpe's style portfolios for the Magellan fund	Bills	0
	Intermediate bonds	0
	Long-term bonds	0
	Corporate bonds	0
	Mortgages	0
	Value stocks	0
	Growth stocks	47
	Medium-cap stocks	31
	Small stocks	18
	Foreign stocks	0
	European stocks	4
	Japanese stocks	0
	Total	100.00
	R-squared	97.3%

*Regressions are constrained to have nonnegative coefficients and to have coefficients that sum to 100%.

Source: William F. Sharpe, "Asset Allocation: Management Style and Performance Evaluation," *Journal of Portfolio Management*, Winter 1992, pp. 7–19. Copyrighted material is reprinted with permission from Institutional Investor.

explained by only four style portfolios. Moreover, these four style portfolios alone explain 97.3% of the variance of returns.

The proportion of return variability *not* explained by asset allocation can be attributed to security selection within asset classes. For Magellan, this was $100 - 97.3 = 2.7\%$. To evaluate the average contribution of stock selection to fund performance we track the residuals from the regression, displayed in Figure 18.3. The figure plots the cumulative effect of these residuals; the steady upward trend confirms Magellan's success at stock selection in this period. Notice that the plot in Figure 18.3 is far smoother than the plot in Figure 18.4, which shows Magellan's performance compared to a standard benchmark, the S&P 500. This reflects the fact that the regression-weighted index portfolio tracks Magellan's overall style much better than the S&P 500. The performance spread is much noisier using the S&P as the benchmark.

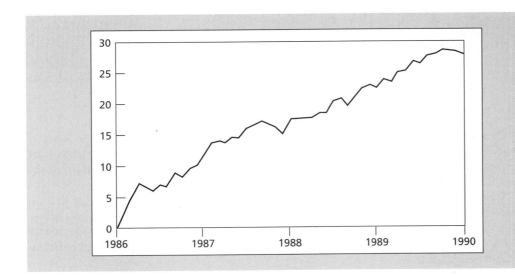

FIGURE 18.3

Fidelity Magellan Fund cumulative return difference: Fund versus style benchmark

Source: William F. Sharpe, "Asset Allocation: Management Style and Performance Evaluation," *Journal of Portfolio Management*, Winter 1992, pp. 7–19. Copyrighted material is reprinted with permission from Institutional Investor.

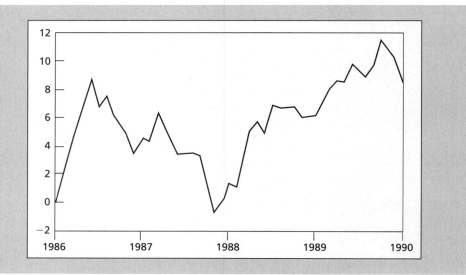

FIGURE 18.4

Fidelity Magellan Fund cumulative return difference: Fund versus S&P 500

Source: William F. Sharpe, "Asset Allocation: Management Style and Performance Evaluation," *Journal of Portfolio Management,* Winter 1992, pp. 7–19. Copyrighted material is reprinted with permission from Institutional Investor.

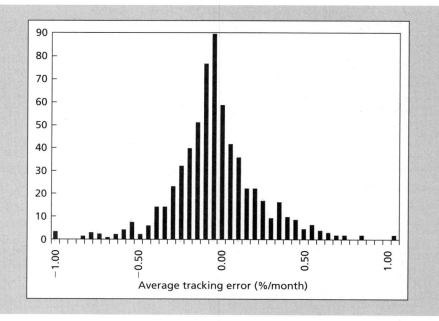

FIGURE 18.5

Average tracking error, 636 mutual funds, 1985–1989

Source: William F. Sharpe, "Asset Allocation: Management Style and Performance Evaluation," *Journal of Portfolio Management,* Winter 1992, pp. 7–19. Copyrighted material is reprinted with permission from Institutional Investor.

Of course, Magellan's consistently positive residual returns (reflected in the steadily increasing plot of cumulative return difference) is hardly common. Figure 18.5 shows the frequency distribution of average residuals across 636 mutual funds. The distribution has the familiar bell shape with a slightly negative mean of $-.074\%$ per month.

Style analysis has become very popular in the investment management industry and has spawned quite a few variations on Sharpe's methodology. Many portfolio managers utilize Web sites that help investors identify their style and stock selection performance. The nearby box shows that style analysis is at the heart of recent debates about the investment performance of hedge funds.

WHAT'S IT ALL ABOUT, ALPHA?

Too many notes. That's what Emperor Joseph II famously said to Mozart on seeing his opera "The Marriage of Figaro." But surely to think of a musical work as just a series of notes is to miss the magic.

Could the same be said about fund management? It is the fashion these days to separate beta (the systematic return delivered by the market) from alpha (the manager's skill). Investors are happy to pay high fees for the skill, but regard the market return as a commodity. Distinguishing the two is, however, sometimes difficult.

A fund manager might beat the market because of luck or recklessness, rather than skill, for example. Suppose he has packed his portfolio with oil stocks and then profits when the price of crude rises. More generally, alpha skeptics often attribute abnormal returns to "style bias," such as the manager who favors stocks with an energy focus. Popular style biases are often based on factors that seem to have predicted past alpha, such as firm size. But should the skeptics be biased against style bias? After all, the only portfolio utterly free of bias would be one that included the entire market.

Academics have entered this debate, trying to pin down the factors that drive a fund's performance. Bill Fung and Narayan Naik of London Business School have come up with a seven-factor model which, they say, can explain the bulk of hedge-fund performance. After allowing for these factors, the average fund of hedge funds has not produced any alpha in the past decade, except during the dot-com bubble. This approach suggests the whole idea of alpha might be an illusion.

However, it is also possible to take the opposite tack. This type of analysis gives managers no credit for choosing the systematic factors—the betas—that drive their portfolios. Yes, these betas could often have been bought for very low fees. But would an investor have been able to put them together in the right combination?

It is as if a diner in Gordon Ramsay's restaurants were brave enough to tell the irascible chef: "This meal was delicious. But chemical analysis shows it is 65% chicken, 20% carrot, 10% flour and 5% milk. I could have bought those ingredients for £1.50. Why should I pay £20?" The chef's reply, shorn of its expletives, might be: "The secret is in the mixing." This debate matters because people are now trying to replicate the performance of hedge funds with cloned portfolios.

There are two potential criticisms of the cloned approach. One is that it will simply reproduce all the systematic returns that hedge funds generate and none of their idiosyncratic magic. However, this "magic" is hard to pin down, and even if it does exist, it may be worth no more than the fees hedge funds charge.

The second criticism is that the clones will always be a step behind the smart money. You cannot clone a hedge fund until you know where it has been. But by then it may have moved on.

Mozart might have sympathized. His operas were more than the sum of his notes. But even if the great composer had no peers, he has had plenty of imitators.

SOURCE: *The Economist,* March 22, 2007.

18.3   Morningstar's Risk-Adjusted Rating

The commercial success of Morningstar, Inc., the premier source of information on mutual funds, has made its *Risk Adjusted Rating* (RAR) among the most widely used performance measures. The Morningstar five-star rating is coveted by the managers of the thousands of funds covered by the service.

Morningstar calculates a number of RAR performance measures that are similar, although not identical, to the standard mean-variance measures (see Chapter 4 for a more detailed discussion). The most distinct measure, the Morningstar Star Rating, is based on comparison of each fund to a peer group. The peer group for each fund is selected on the basis of the fund's investment universe (e.g., international, growth versus value, fixed-income, and so on) as well as portfolio characteristics such as average price-to-book value, price–earnings ratio, and market capitalization.

Morningstar computes fund returns (adjusted for loads) as well as a risk measure based on fund performance in its worst years. The risk-adjusted performance is ranked across funds in a style group and stars are awarded based on the following table:

Percentile	Stars
0–10	1
10–32.5	2
32.5–67.5	3
67.5–90	4
90–100	5

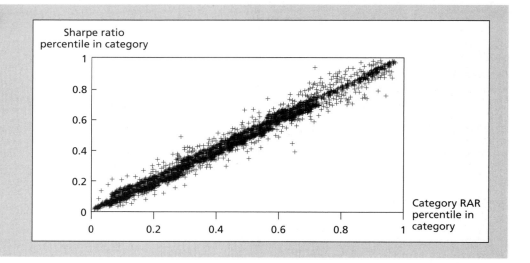

FIGURE 18.6

Rankings based on Morningstar's category RARs and excess return Sharpe ratios

Source: William F. Sharpe (1997), "Morningstar Performance Measures," **www.stanford .edu/~wfsharpe.**

The Morningstar RAR method produces results that are similar but not identical to that of the mean/variance-based Sharpe ratios. Figure 18.6 demonstrates the fit between ranking by RAR and by Sharpe ratios from the performance of 1,286 diversified equity funds over the period 1994–1996. Sharpe notes that this period is characterized by high returns that contribute to a good fit.

18.4   Risk Adjustments with Changing Portfolio Composition

One potential problem with risk-adjustment techniques is that they all assume that portfolio risk, whether it is measured by standard deviation or beta, is constant over the relevant time period. This isn't necessarily so. If a manager attempts to increase portfolio beta when she thinks the market is about to go up and to decrease beta when she is pessimistic, both the standard deviation and the beta of the portfolio will change over time. This can wreak havoc with our performance measures.

EXAMPLE 18.1

Risk Measurement with Changing Portfolio Composition

Suppose the Sharpe measure of the passive strategy (investing in a market index fund) is .4. A portfolio manager is in search of a better, active strategy. Over an initial period of, say, four quarters, he executes a low-risk or defensive strategy with an annualized mean excess return of 1% and a standard deviation of 2%. This makes for a Sharpe measure of .5, which beats the passive strategy.

Over the next period of another four quarters, this manager finds that a high-risk strategy is optimal, with an annual mean excess return of 9% and standard deviation of 18%. Here again the Sharpe measure is .5. Over the two years, our manager maintains a better-than-passive Sharpe measure.

Figure 18.7 shows a pattern of (annualized) quarterly returns that is consistent with our description of the manager's strategy over two years. In the first four quarters, the excess returns are −1%, 3%, −1%, and 3%, making for an average of 1% and standard deviation of 2%. In the next four quarters, the excess returns are −9%, 27%, −9%, and 27%, making for an average of 9% and standard deviation of 18%. Thus, *each* year exhibits a Sharpe measure of .5.

But if we take the eight-quarter sequence as a single measurement period, instead of two independent periods, and measure the portfolio's mean and standard deviation over that full period, we get an average excess return of 5% and standard deviation of 13.42%, resulting in a Sharpe measure of only .37, apparently inferior to the passive strategy!

What went wrong in Example 18.1? Sharpe's measure does not recognize the shift in the mean from the first four quarters to the next as a result of a strategy change. Instead, the difference in mean returns in the two years adds to the *appearance* of volatility in portfolio returns. The change in mean returns across time periods contributed to the variability of returns over the same period. But in this case, variability per se should not be interpreted as volatility or riskiness in returns. Part of the variability in returns is due to intentional choices that shift the expected or mean return. This part should not be ascribed to uncertainty in returns. Unfortunately, an outside observer might not realize that policy changes within the

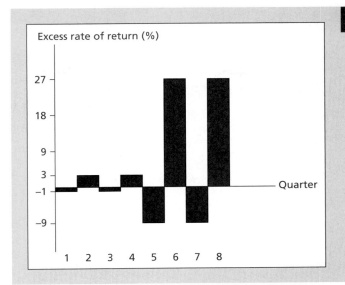

FIGURE 18.7

Portfolio returns. In the first four quarters, the firm follows a low-risk, low-return policy. In the next four quarters, it shifts to a high-risk, high-return policy.

sample period are the source of some of the return variability. Therefore, the active strategy with shifting means appears riskier than it really is, which biases the estimate of the Sharpe measure downward.

When assessing the performance of actively managed portfolios, therefore, it is crucial to keep track of portfolio composition and changes in portfolio mean return and risk. We will see another example of this problem when we turn to market timing.

Another warning: When we address the performance of mutual funds selected *because* they have been successful, we need to be highly cautious in evaluating their track records. In particular, we need to recognize that even if all managers were equally skilled, a few "winners" would emerge by sheer chance each period. With thousands of funds in operation, the best-performing funds will have been wildly successful, even if these results reflect luck rather than skill. The nearby box addresses this issue.

18.5 Performance Attribution Procedures

Rather than focus on risk-adjusted returns, practitioners often want simply to ascertain which decisions resulted in superior or inferior performance. Superior investment performance depends on an ability to be in the "right" securities at the right time. Such timing and selection ability may be considered broadly, such as being in equities as opposed to fixed-income securities when the stock market is performing well. Or it may be defined at a more detailed level, such as choosing the relatively better-performing stocks within a particular industry.

Portfolio managers constantly make both broad-brush asset market allocation decisions as well as more detailed sector and security allocation decisions within markets. Performance attribution studies attempt to decompose overall performance into discrete components that may be identified with a particular level of the portfolio selection process.

Attribution analysis starts from the broadest asset allocation choices and progressively focuses on ever-finer details of portfolio choice. The difference between a managed portfolio's performance and that of a benchmark portfolio then may be expressed as the sum of the contributions to performance of a series of decisions made at the various levels of the portfolio construction process. For example, one common attribution system decomposes performance into three components: (1) broad asset market allocation choices *across* equity, fixed-income, and money markets; (2) industry (sector) choice *within* each market; and (3) security choice *within* each sector.

To illustrate this method, consider the attribution results for a hypothetical portfolio. The portfolio invests in stocks, bonds, and money market securities. An attribution analysis appears in Tables 18.3 through 18.6. The portfolio return over the month is 5.34%.

On the MARKET FRONT

THE MAGELLAN FUND AND MARKET EFFICIENCY: ASSESSING THE PERFORMANCE OF MONEY MANAGERS

Fidelity's Magellan Fund outperformed the S&P 500 in eleven of the thirteen years ending in 1989. Is such performance consistent with the efficient market hypothesis? Casual statistical analysis would suggest not.

If outperforming the market were like flipping a fair coin, as would be the case if all securities were fairly priced, then the odds of an arbitrarily selected manager producing eleven out of thirteen winning years would be only about 0.95%, or 1 in 105. The Magellan Fund, however, is not a randomly selected fund. Instead, it is the fund that emerged after a thirteen-year "contest" as a clear winner. Given that we have chosen to focus on the winner of a money management contest, should we be surprised to find performance far above the mean? Clearly not.

Once we select a fund precisely because it has outperformed all other funds, the proper benchmark for predicted performance is no longer a standard index such as the S&P 500. The benchmark must be the expected performance of the best-performing fund out of a sample of randomly selected funds.

Consider as an analogy a coin flipping contest. If fifty contestants were to flip a coin thirteen times, and the winner were to flip eleven heads out of thirteen, we would not consider that evidence that the winner's coin was biased. Instead, we would recognize that with fifty contestants, the probability is greater than 40% that the individual who emerges as the winner would in fact flip heads eleven or more times. (In contrast, a coin chosen at random that resulted in eleven out of thirteen heads would be highly suspect!)

How then ought we evaluate the performance of those managers who show up in the financial press as (recently) superior performers? We know that after the fact some managers will have been lucky. When is the performance of a manager so good that even after accounting for selection bias—the selection of the ex post winner—we still cannot account for such performance by chance?

SELECTION BIAS AND PERFORMANCE BENCHMARKS

Consider this experiment. Allow fifty money managers to flip a coin thirteen times, and record the maximum number of heads realized by any of the contestants. (If markets are efficient, the coin will have the same probability of turning up heads as that of a money manager beating the market.) Now repeat the contest, and again record the winning number of heads. Repeat this experiment 10,000 times. When we are done, we can compute the frequency distribution of the winning number of heads over the 10,000 trials.

Table 1 (column 1) presents the results of such an experiment simulated on a computer. The table shows that in 9.2% of the contests, the winning number of heads was nine; in 47.4% of the trials ten heads would be enough to emerge as the best manager. Interestingly, in 43.3% of the trials, the winning number of heads was eleven or better out of thirteen.

SOURCE: Alan J. Marcus, "The Magellan Fund and Market Efficiency." *The Journal of Portfolio Management*, Fall 1990, pp. 85–86. Copyrighted material is reprinted with permission from Institutional Investor.

TABLE 1

PROBABILITY DISTRIBUTION OF NUMBER OF SUCCESSFUL YEARS OUT OF THIRTEEN FOR THE BEST-PERFORMING MONEY MANAGER

Winning Years	Managers in Contest			
	50	100	250	500
8	0.1%	0	0	0
9	9.2	0.9	0	0
10	47.4	31.9	5.7	0.2
11	34.8	51.3	59.7	42.3
12	7.7	14.6	31.8	51.5
13	0.8	1.2	2.8	5.9
Mean winning years of best performer	10.43	10.83	11.32	11.63

Viewed in this context, the performance of Magellan is still impressive but somewhat less surprising. The simulation shows that out of a sample of 50 managers, chance alone would provide a 43.3% probability that *someone* would beat the market at least eleven out of thirteen years. Averaging over all 10,000 trials, the mean number of winning years necessary to emerge as most reliable manager over the thirteen-year contest was 10.43.

Therefore, once we recognize that Magellan is not a fund chosen at random, but a fund that came to our attention precisely because it turned out to perform so well, the frequency with which it beat the market is no longer high enough to be considered a violation of market efficiency. Indeed, using the conventional 5% confidence level, we could not reject the hypothesis that the consistency of its performance was due to chance.

The other columns in Table 1 present the frequency distributions of the winning number of successful coin flips (analogously, the number of years in which the best-performing manager beats an efficient market) for other possible sample sizes. Not surprisingly, as the pool of managers increases, the predicted best performance steadily gets better. By providing as a benchmark the probability distribution of the best performance, rather than the average performance, the table tells us how many grains of salt to add to reports of the latest investment guru.

The first step is to establish a benchmark level of performance against which performance ought to be compared. This benchmark is called the **bogey.** It is designed to measure the returns the portfolio manager would earn if she were to follow a completely passive strategy. "Passive" in this context has two attributes. First, it means the allocation of funds across broad asset classes is set in accord with a notion of "usual" or neutral allocation across sectors. This would be considered a passive asset market allocation. Second, it means that, within each asset class, the portfolio manager holds an indexed portfolio, for example, the S&P 500 Index for the equity sector. The passive strategy used as a performance benchmark rules out both asset allocation and security selection decisions. Any departure of the manager's return from the passive benchmark must be due to either asset allocation bets (departures from the neutral allocation across markets) or security selection bets (departures from the passive index within asset classes).

While we've already discussed in earlier chapters the justification for indexing within sectors, it is worth briefly explaining the determination of the neutral allocation of funds across the broad asset classes. Weights that are designated as "neutral" will depend on the risk tolerance of the investor and must be determined in consultation with the client. For example, risk-tolerant clients may place a large fraction of their portfolio in the equity market, perhaps directing the fund manager to set neutral weights of 75% equity, 15% bonds, and 10% cash equivalents. Any deviation from these weights must be justified by a belief that one or another market will either over- or underperform its usual risk-return profile. In contrast, more risk-averse clients may set neutral weights of 45%/35%/20% for the three markets. Therefore, their portfolios in normal circumstances will be exposed to less risk than that of the risk-tolerant clients. Only intentional bets on market performance will result in departures from this profile.

In Table 18.3, the neutral weights have been set at 60% equity, 30% fixed-income, and 10% cash equivalents (money market securities). The bogey portfolio, comprising investments in each index with the 60/30/10 weights, returned 3.97%. The managed portfolio's measure of performance is positive and equal to its actual return less the return of the bogey: $5.34 - 3.97 = 1.37\%$. The next step is to allocate the 1.37% excess return to the separate decisions that contributed to it.

bogey

The rate of return an investment manager is compared to for performance evaluation.

Asset Allocation Decisions

The managed portfolio is actually invested in the equity, fixed-income, and money markets with weights of 70%, 7%, and 23%, respectively. The portfolio's performance could be due to the departure of this weighting scheme from the benchmark 60/30/10 weights and/or to superior or inferior results *within* each of the three broad markets.

TABLE 18.3

Performance of the managed portfolio

Bogey Performance and Excess Return		
Component	**Benchmark Weight**	**Return of Index during Month (%)**
Equity (S&P 500)	.60	5.81
Bonds (Lehman Bros. Index)	.30	1.45
Cash (money market)	.10	0.48
Bogey = (.60 × 5.81) + (.30 × 1.45) + (.10 × .48) = 3.97%		
Return of managed portfolio		5.34%
−Return of bogey portfolio		3.97
Excess return of managed portfolio		1.37%

TABLE 18.4

Performance attribution

A. Contribution of Asset Allocation to Performance

Market	(1) Actual Weight in Market	(2) Benchmark Weight in Market	(3) Excess Weight	(4) Index Return (%)	(5) = (3) × (4) Contribution to Performance (%)
Equity	.70	.60	.10	5.81	.5810
Fixed-income	.07	.30	−.23	1.45	−.3335
Cash	.23	.10	.13	0.48	.0624
Contribution of asset allocation					.3099

B. Contribution of Selection to Total Performance

Market	(1) Portfolio Performance (%)	(2) Index Performance (%)	(3) Excess Performance (%)	(4) Portfolio Weight	(5) = (3) × (4) Contribution (%)
Equity	7.28	5.81	1.47	.70	1.03
Fixed-income	1.89	1.45	0.44	.07	0.03
Contribution of selection within markets					1.06

To isolate the effect of the manager's asset allocation choice, we measure the performance of a hypothetical portfolio that would have been invested in the *indexes* for each market with weights 70/7/23. This return measures the effect of the shift away from the benchmark 60/30/10 weights without allowing for any effects attributable to active management of the securities selected within each market.

Superior performance relative to the bogey is achieved by overweighting investments in markets that turn out to perform better than the bogey and by underweighting those in poorly performing markets. The contribution of asset allocation to superior performance equals the sum over all markets of the excess weight in each market times the return of the market index.

Table 18.4A demonstrates that asset allocation contributed 31 basis points to the portfolio's overall excess return of 137 basis points. The major factor contributing to superior performance in this month is the heavy weighting of the equity market in a month when the equity market has an excellent return of 5.81%.

Sector and Security Selection Decisions

If .31% of the excess performance can be attributed to advantageous asset allocation across markets, the remaining 1.06% then must be attributable to sector selection and security selection within each market. Table 18.4B details the contribution of the managed portfolio's sector and security selection to total performance.

Panel B shows that the equity component of the managed portfolio has a return of 7.28% versus a return of 5.81% for the S&P 500. The fixed-income return is 1.89% versus 1.45% for the Lehman Brothers Index. The superior performance in both equity and fixed-income markets weighted by the portfolio proportions invested in each market sums to the 1.06% contribution to performance attributable to sector and security selection.

Table 18.5 documents the sources of the equity market performance by each sector within the market. The first three columns detail the allocation of funds within the equity market

TABLE 18.5

Sector allocation within the equity market

	(1)	(2)	(3)	(4)	(5) = (3) × (4)
	Beginning of Month Weights				**Contribution**
Sector	**Portfolio**	**S&P 500**	**Difference in Weights**	**Sector Return (%)**	**of Sector Allocation (%)**
Basic materials	0.0196	0.083	−.0634	6.9	−0.437
Business services	0.0784	0.041	.0374	7.0	0.262
Capital goods	0.0187	0.078	−.0593	4.1	−0.243
Consumer cyclical	0.0847	0.125	−.0403	8.8	−0.355
Consumer noncyclical	0.4037	0.204	.1997	10.0	1.997
Credit sensitive	0.2401	0.218	.0221	5.0	0.111
Energy	0.1353	0.142	−.0067	2.6	−0.017
Technology	0.0195	0.109	−.0895	0.3	−0.027
Total	1.0000	1.000	.0000		1.290

compared to their representation in the S&P 500. Column (4) shows the rate of return of each sector, and column (5) equals the product of the difference in the sector weight and the sector's performance.

Note that good performance derives from overweighting well-performing sectors such as consumer noncyclicals, as well as underweighting poorly performing sectors such as technology. The excess return of the equity component of the portfolio attributable to sector allocation alone is 1.29%. As the equity component of the portfolio outperformed the S&P 500 by 1.47%, we conclude that the effect of security selection within sectors must have contributed an additional 1.47 − 1.29, or .18%, to the performance of the equity component of the portfolio.

A similar sector analysis can be applied to the fixed-income portion of the portfolio, but we do not show those results here.

Summing Up Component Contributions

In this particular month, all facets of the portfolio selection process were successful. Table 18.6 details the contribution of each aspect of performance. Asset allocation across the major security markets contributes 31 basis points. Sector and security allocation within

TABLE 18.6

Portfolio attribution: summary

		Contribution (basis points)
1. Asset allocation		31.0
2. Selection		
a. Equity excess return		
i. Sector allocation	129	
ii. Security selection	18	
	147 × .70 (portfolio weight) =	102.9
b. Fixed-income excess return	44 × .07 (portfolio weight) =	3.1
Total excess return of portfolio		137.0

Performance Attribution

The Excel model "Performance Attribution" that is available on our Web site is built on the example that appears in Section 18.5. The model allows you to specify different allocations and to analyze the contribution sectors and weightings for different performances.

eXcel

Please visit us at www.mhhe.com/bkm

	A	B	C	D	E	F
1			Chapter 18			
2			Performance Attribution			
3	Solution to Question					
4	Bogey Portfolio		Weight	Return on	Portfolio	
5	Component	Index	Benchmark	Index	Return	
6	Equity	S&P500	0.6	5.8100%	3.4860%	
7	Bonds	Lehman Index	0.3	1.4500%	0.4350%	
8	Cash	Money Market	0.1	0.4800%	0.0480%	
9						
10	Return on Bogey				3.9690%	
11						
12						
13	Managed Portfolio	Portfolio	Actual	Portfolio		
14	Component	Weight	Return	Return		
15	Equity	.75	6.5000%	4.8750%		
16	Bonds	.12	1.2500%	0.1500%		
17	Cash	.13	0.4800%	0.0624%		
18						
19	Return on Managed			5.0874%		
20						
21	Excess Return			1.1184%		
22						
23						
24			Contribution of Asset Allocation			
25		Actual Weight	Benchmark	Excess	Market	Performance
26	Market	in Portfolio	Weight	Weight	Return	Contribution
27	Equity	.75	.6	.15	5.8100%	.8715%
28	Fixed Income	.12	.3	-.18	1.4500%	-.2610%
29	Cash	.13	.1	.03	0.4800%	.0144%
30	Contribution of					
31	Asset Allocation					.6249%

those markets contributes 106 basis points, for total excess portfolio performance of 137 basis points.

The sector and security allocation of 106 basis points can be partitioned further. Sector allocation within the equity market results in excess performance of 129 basis points, and security selection within sectors contributes 18 basis points. (The total equity excess performance of 147 basis points is multiplied by the 70% weight in equity to obtain the contribution to portfolio performance.) Similar partitioning could be done for the fixed-income sector.

CONCEPT
check **18.2**

a. Suppose the benchmark weights had been set at 70% equity, 25% fixed-income, and 5% cash equivalents. What then would be the contributions of the manager's asset allocation choices?

b. Suppose the S&P 500 return had been 5%. Recompute the contribution of the manager's security selection choices.

18.6 Market Timing

market timing

A strategy that moves funds between the risky portfolio and cash, based on forecasts of relative performance.

Pure **market timing** involves switching funds between the risky portfolio and cash in response to forecasts of relative performance. To evaluate the potential of a pure market-timing strategy, consider the fortunes of three families of investors who had $1 to invest on December 1, 1926. Their heirs counted their blessings 82 years later, in 2008. The investment history of the families included the Great Depression, a major bear market in 2008 (when the S&P 500 lost

TABLE 18.7

Performance of cash, stocks, and perfect-timing strategies

I. Family fund as of the end of 2008

	Family/Strategy		
	A. Cash	**B. Stocks**	**C. Perfect Timing**
Final proceeds	$20	$1,626	$36,699,302,473

II. Annualized monthly rate of return statistics (%)

Geometric average	3.71	9.44	34.54
Arithmetic average	3.71	11.48	35.44
Minimum monthly rate*	−0.03	−28.73	−0.03
Maximum monthly rate**	1.52	41.65	41.65
Average excess return	0.00	7.77	31.73
Standard deviation	3.54	19.38	12.44

*Occurred in September 1931.

**Occurred in April 1933.

Both extreme values occurred during the Great Depression.

39%), and seven other recessions in-between. The families differed wildly in their investment strategy:

1. Family A invested solely in a money market or cash equivalents.
2. Family B invested solely in stocks (the S&P 500 portfolio), reinvesting all dividends.
3. Family C switched, *every month,* 100% of its funds between stocks and cash, based on its forecast of which sector would do better next month.

While the strategies of families A and B are straightforward, that of family C is worth pondering. Try asking friends: "What would it take to be a perfect market timer?" Many would venture that to accomplish perfect timing, the timer would need to be able to forecast the rate of return on stocks at the start of every month. But actually, you wouldn't need the precise rate of return: "all" the perfect timer would have to know is whether stocks will outperform cash! You might think that such elementary knowledge wouldn't be worth all that much. But examine Table 18.7, computed from the actual return history on cash and stocks.

The first panel of Table 18.7 provides the punch line: After 82 years, $1 returned $20 to the cash fund of family A, and most of those nominal profits were undone by inflation over the period. Despite the Great Depression and recessions of varying severity, the stock fund of family B outdid the cash fund by a factor of more than 80, ending up with $1,626. But the gains to the perfect-timing family C would have been otherworldly indeed (as was the family's power of prediction); the timing fund starting with $1 would have ended with $36.7 *billion,* giving Bill Gates and Warren Buffet a good run for the title of world's richest person.

CONCEPT *check* **18.3**

Use annual rates of return from the Online Learning Center (**www.mhhe.com/bkm**) to replicate Table 18.7 for a market timer who can perfectly forecast only a year, rather than every month. Why is the performance of the annual timer not as good as that of the monthly timer?

These results have some lessons for us. The first has to do with the power of compounding. This effect is particularly important as ever more funds under management represent pension savings. The horizons of pension investments may not be as long as 82 years, but they are measured in decades, making compounding an important factor.

The second is a huge difference between the end value of the all-safe asset strategy ($20) and of the all-equity strategy ($1,626). Why would anyone invest in safe assets? By now you know the reason: risk. The annual standard deviation of the equity strategy was 19.38%. The significantly higher standard deviation of the rate of return on the equity portfolio is commensurate with its significantly higher average return. The higher average excess return reflects the risk premium.

Is the return premium on the perfect-timing strategy also a risk premium? It can't be: Because the perfect timer never does worse than either bills or the market, the extra return cannot be compensation for the possibility of poor returns; instead it is attributable to superior analysis. The value of superior information is reflected in the tremendous ending value of the portfolio. This value does not reflect compensation for risk.

To see why, consider how you might choose between two hypothetical strategies. Strategy 1 offers a sure rate of return of 5%; strategy 2 offers an uncertain return that is given by 5% *plus* a random number that is zero with a probability of .5 and 5% with a probability of .5. The results for each strategy are

	Strategy 1 (%)	Strategy 2 (%)
Expected return	5	7.5
Standard deviation	0	2.5
Highest return	5	10.0
Lowest return	5	5.0

Clearly, strategy 2 dominates strategy 1, as its rate of return is *at least* equal to that of strategy 1 and sometimes greater. No matter how risk averse you are, you will always prefer strategy 2 to strategy 1, even though strategy 2 has a significant standard deviation. Compared to strategy 1, strategy 2 provides only good surprises, so the standard deviation in this case cannot be a measure of risk.

You can look at these strategies as analogous to the case of the perfect timer compared with either an all-equity or all-cash strategy. In every period, the perfect timer obtains at least as good a return, in some cases better. Therefore, the timer's standard deviation is a misleading measure of risk when you compare perfect timing to an all-equity or all-cash strategy.

Valuing Market Timing as an Option

Merton (1981) shows that the key to analyzing the pattern of returns of a perfect market timer is to compare the returns of a perfect foresight investor with those of another investor who holds a call option on the equity portfolio. Investing 100% in T-bills plus holding a call option on the equity portfolio will yield returns identical to those of the portfolio of the perfect timer who invests 100% in either the safe asset or the equity portfolio, whichever will yield the higher return. The perfect timer's return is shown in Figure 18.8. The rate of return is bounded from below by the risk-free rate, r_f.

To see how the value of information can be treated as an option, suppose the market index currently is at S_0 and a call option on the index has exercise price of $X = S_0(1 + r_f)$. If the market outperforms bills over the coming period, S_T will exceed X; it will be less than X otherwise. Now look at the payoff to a portfolio consisting of this option and S_0 dollars invested in bills.

	Payoff to Portfolio	
Outcome:	$S_T \leq X$	$S_T > X$
Bills	$S_0(1 + r_f)$	$S_0(1 + r_f)$
Option	0	$S_T - X$
Total	$S_0(1 + r_f)$	S_T

The portfolio returns the risk-free rate when the market is bearish (that is, when the market return is less than the risk-free rate) and pays the market return when the market is bullish and beats bills. This represents perfect market timing. Consequently, the value of perfect-timing ability is equivalent to the value of the call option, for a call enables the investor to earn the market return only when it exceeds r_f.

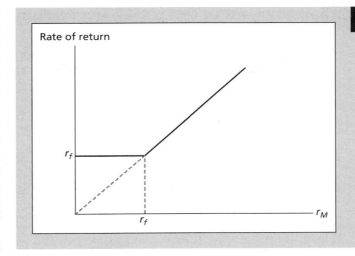

FIGURE 18.8

Rate of return of a perfect market timer

Valuation of the call option embedded in market timing is relatively straightforward using the Black-Scholes formula. Set $S_0 = \$1$ (to find the value of the call per dollar invested in the market), use an exercise price of $X = (1 + r_f)$ (the current risk-free rate, in early 2009, is about .12%), and a volatility of $\sigma = 18\%$ (about the historical annual standard deviation of the S&P 500). For a once-a-month timer, $T = \frac{1}{12}$. According to the Black-Scholes formula, the call option conveyed by market timing ability is worth 2.1% of assets, and this is the monthly fee one could presumably charge for such services. Annualized, that fee is about 28%, similar to the excess return of the market timer in Table 18.7. Less frequent timing would be worth less (see Concept Check 18.3). If one could time the market only on an annual basis, then $T = 1$ and the value of perfect timing would be about 7.2% per year.

The Value of Imperfect Forecasting

But managers are not perfect forecasters. While managers who are right most of the time presumably do very well, "right most of the time" does not mean merely the *percentage* of the time a manager is right. For example, a Tucson, Arizona, weather forecaster who *always* predicts "no rain" may be right 90% of the time, but this "stopped clock" strategy does not require any forecasting ability.

Neither is the overall proportion of correct forecasts an appropriate measure of market forecasting ability. If the market is up two days out of three, and a forecaster always predicts a market advance, the two-thirds success rate is not a measure of forecasting ability. We need to examine the proportion of bull markets ($r_M > r_f$) correctly forecast *and* the proportion of bear markets ($r_M < r_f$) correctly forecast.

If we call P_1 the proportion of the correct forecasts of bull markets and P_2 the proportion for bear markets, then $P_1 + P_2 - 1$ is the correct measure of timing ability. For example, a forecaster who always guesses correctly will have $P_1 = P_2 = 1$ and will show ability of 1 (100%). An analyst who always bets on a bear market will mispredict all bull markets ($P_1 = 0$), will correctly "predict" all bear markets ($P_2 = 1$), and will end up with timing ability of $P_1 + P_2 - 1 = 0$. If C denotes the (call option) value of a perfect market timer, then $(P_1 + P_2 - 1)C$ measures the value of imperfect forecasting ability.

The incredible potential payoff to accurate timing versus the relative scarcity of billionaires suggests that market timing is far from a trivial exercise and that very imperfect timing is the most that we can hope for.

What is the market timing score of someone who flips a fair coin to predict the market?

CONCEPT *check* **18.4**

Measurement of Market Timing Performance

In its pure form, market timing involves shifting funds between a market index portfolio and cash equivalents, such as T-bills or a money market fund, depending on whether the market as a whole is expected to outperform cash. In practice, most managers do not shift fully between cash and the market. How might we measure partial shifts into the market when it is expected to perform well?

To simplify, suppose the investor holds only the market index portfolio and T-bills. If the weight on the market were constant, say, .6, then the portfolio beta would also be constant, and the portfolio characteristic line would plot as a straight line with a slope .6, as in Figure 18.9A. If, however, the investor could correctly time the market and shift funds into it in periods when the market does well, the characteristic line would plot as in Figure 18.9B. The idea is that if the timer can predict bull and bear markets, more will be shifted into the market when the market is about to go up. The portfolio beta and the slope of the characteristic line will be higher when r_M is higher, resulting in the curved line that appears in Figure 18.9B.

Treynor and Mazuy (1966) tested to see whether portfolio betas did in fact increase prior to market advances, but they found little evidence of timing ability. A similar test was implemented by Henriksson (1984). His examination of market timing ability for 116 funds in 1968–1980 found that, on average, portfolio betas actually *fell* slightly during the market advances, although in most cases the response of portfolio betas to the market was not statistically significant. Eleven funds had statistically positive values of market timing, while eight had significantly negative values. Overall, 62% of the funds had negative point estimates of timing ability.

In sum, empirical tests to date show little evidence of market timing ability. Perhaps this should be expected; given the tremendous values to be reaped by a successful market timer, it would be surprising to uncover clear-cut evidence of such skills in nearly efficient markets.

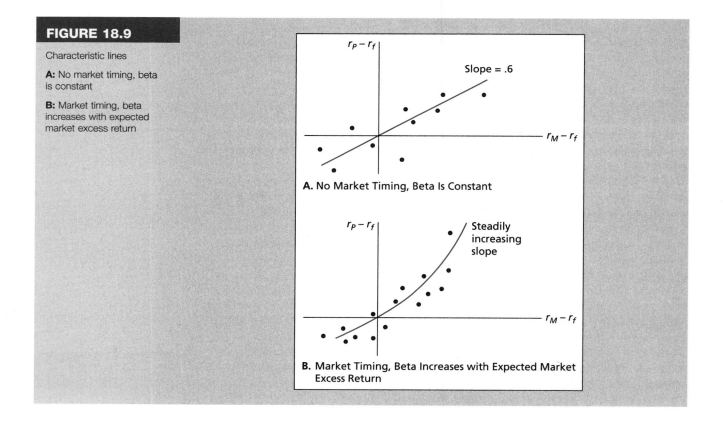

FIGURE 18.9

Characteristic lines

A: No market timing, beta is constant

B: Market timing, beta increases with expected market excess return

A. No Market Timing, Beta Is Constant

B. Market Timing, Beta Increases with Expected Market Excess Return

SUMMARY

- The appropriate performance measure depends on the investment context. The Sharpe measure is most appropriate when the portfolio represents the entire investment fund. The Treynor measure is appropriate when the portfolio is to be mixed with several other assets, allowing for diversification of firm-specific risk outside of each portfolio. The information ratio may be used when evaluating a portfolio to be mixed with the passive index portfolio.

- The shifting mean and variance of actively managed portfolios make it harder to assess performance. A typical example is the attempt of portfolio managers to time the market, resulting in ever-changing portfolio betas and standard deviations.

- Common attribution procedures partition performance improvements to asset allocation, sector selection, and security selection. Performance is assessed by calculating departures of portfolio composition from a benchmark or neutral portfolio.

- Active management has two components: market timing (or, more generally, asset allocation) and security analysis.

- The value of perfect market-timing ability is enormous. The rate of return to a perfect market timer will be uncertain, but the risk cannot be measured by standard deviation, because perfect timing dominates a passive strategy, providing only "good" surprises.

- Perfect-timing ability is equivalent to having a call option on the market portfolio. The value of that option can be determined using valuation techniques such as the Black-Scholes formula.

- The value of *imperfect* market timing depends on the sum of the probabilities of the true outcome conditional on the forecast: $P_1 + P_2 - 1$. If perfect timing is equivalent to call option C, then imperfect timing can be valued by: $(P_1 + P_2 - 1)C$.

KEY TERMS

active management, 579	cash, 579	M-square (M²), 582
alpha capture, 587	comparison universe, 580	market timing, 579
alpha transfer or	fund of funds, 583	passive management, 579
alpha transport, 586	information ratio, 584	Sharpe measure, 582
bogey, 595	Jensen measure, 585	Treynor measure, 584

PROBLEM SETS

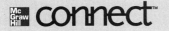

Select problems are available in McGraw-Hill Connect. Please see the packaging options section of the preface for more information.

Basic

1. The finance committee of an endowment has decided to shift part of its investment in an index fund to one of two professionally managed portfolios. Upon examination of past performance, a committee member proposes to choose the portfolio that achieved a greater alpha value.
   a. Do you agree? Why or why not?
   b. Could a positive alpha be associated with inferior performance? Explain.

2. The board of a large pension fund noticed that the alpha value of the portfolio of one of its contract managers has recently increased. Should the fund increase the allocation to this portfolio?

3. Could portfolio A show a higher Sharpe ratio than that of B and at the same time a lower M² measure? Explain.

4. Two portfolio managers use different procedures to estimate alpha. One uses a single-index model regression, the other the Fama-French model. Other things equal, would you prefer the portfolio with the larger alpha based on the index model or the FF model?

Intermediate

5. Based on current dividend yields and expected capital gains, the expected rates of return on portfolios A and B are 11% and 14%, respectively. The beta of A is .8 while that of

B is 1.5. The T-bill rate is currently 6%, while the expected rate of return of the S&P 500 index is 12%. The standard deviation of portfolio *A* is 10% annually, while that of *B* is 31%, and that of the index is 20%.

    a. If you currently hold a market index portfolio, would you choose to add either of these portfolios to your holdings? Explain.

    b. If instead you could invest *only* in bills and *one* of these portfolios, which would you choose?

6. Evaluate the timing and selection abilities of the four managers whose performances are plotted in the following four scatter diagrams.

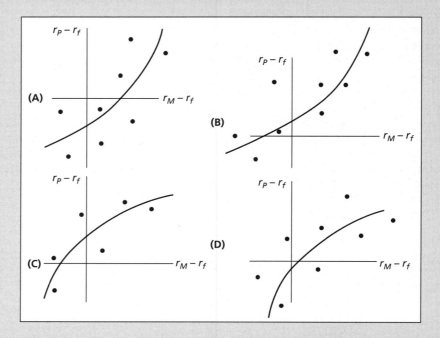

7. Consider the following information regarding the performance of a money manager in a recent month. The table presents the actual return of each sector of the manager's portfolio in column (1), the fraction of the portfolio allocated to each sector in column (2), the benchmark or neutral sector allocations in column (3), and the returns of sector indexes in column (4).

	(1) **Actual Return**	(2) **Actual Weight**	(3) **Benchmark Weight**	(4) **Index Return**
Equity	2.0%	0.70	0.60	2.5% (S&P 500)
Bonds	1.0	0.20	0.30	1.2 (Aggregate Bond index)
Cash	0.5	0.10	0.10	0.5

    a. What was the manager's return in the month? What was her over- or underperformance?

    b. What was the contribution of security selection to relative performance?

    c. What was the contribution of asset allocation to relative performance? Confirm that the sum of selection and allocation contributions equals her total "excess" return relative to the bogey.

8. Conventional wisdom says one should measure a manager's investment performance over an entire market cycle. What arguments support this contention? What arguments contradict it?

9. Does the use of universes of managers with similar investment styles to evaluate relative investment performance overcome the statistical problems associated with instability of beta or total variability?

10. During a particular year, the T-bill rate was 6%, the market return was 14%, and a portfolio manager with beta of .5 realized a return of 10%. Evaluate the manager based on the portfolio alpha.

11. Go to **www.mhhe.com/bkm** and link to the material for Chapter 18, where you will find five years of monthly returns for two mutual funds, Vanguard's U.S. Growth Fund and U.S. Value Fund, as well as corresponding returns for the S&P 500 and the Treasury bill rate.

    a. Set up a spreadsheet to calculate each fund's excess rate of return over T-bills in each month.

    b. Calculate the standard deviation of each fund over the five-year period.

    c. What was the beta of each fund over the five-year period? (You may wish to review the spreadsheets from Chapters 5 and 6 on the Index model.)

    d. What were the Sharpe, Jensen, and Treynor measures for each fund?

Challenge

12. Historical data suggest the standard deviation of an all-equity strategy is about 5.5% per month. Suppose the risk-free rate is now 1% per month and market volatility is at its historical level. What would be a fair monthly fee to a perfect market timer, according to the Black-Scholes formula?

13. A fund manager scrutinizing the record of two market timers comes up with this information:

Number of months that $r_M > r_f$	135
Correctly predicted by timer A 78	
Correctly predicted by timer B 86	
Number of months that $r_M < r_f$	92
Correctly predicted by timer A 57	
Correctly predicted by timer B 50	

    a. What are the conditional probabilities, P_1 and P_2, and the total ability parameters for timers A and B?

    b. Using the data given in this problem, and the historical data in the previous problem, what is a fair monthly fee for the two timers?

CFA Problems

1. A plan sponsor with a portfolio manager who invests in small-capitalization, high-growth stocks should have the plan sponsor's performance measured against which *one* of the following?

    a. S&P 500 Index.

    b. Wilshire 5000 Index.

    c. Dow Jones Industrial Average.

    d. Russell 2000 Index.

2. Assume you purchased a rental property for $50,000 and sold it one year later for $55,000 (there was no mortgage on the property). At the time of the sale, you paid $2,000 in commissions and $600 in taxes. If you received $6,000 in rental income (all of it received at the end of the year), what annual rate of return did you earn?

3. A two-year investment of $2,000 results in a return of $150 at the end of the first year and a return of $150 at the end of the second year, in addition to the return of the original investment. What is the internal rate of return on the investment?

4. The chairman provides you with the following data, covering one year, concerning the portfolios of two of the fund's equity managers (manager *A* and manager *B*). Although

the portfolios consist primarily of common stocks, cash reserves are included in the calculation of both portfolio betas and performance. By way of perspective, selected data for the financial markets are included in the following table.

	Total Return	Beta
Manager A	24.0%	1.0
Manager B	30.0	1.5
S&P 500	21.0	
Lehman Bond Index	31.0	
91-day Treasury bills	12.0	

a. Calculate and compare the risk-adjusted performance of the two managers relative to each other and to the S&P 500.

b. Explain *two* reasons the conclusions drawn from this calculation may be misleading.

5. Carl Karl, a portfolio manager for the Alpine Trust Company, has been responsible since 2015 for the City of Alpine's Employee Retirement Plan, a municipal pension fund. Alpine is a growing community, and city services and employee payrolls have expanded in each of the past 10 years. Contributions to the plan in fiscal 2020 exceeded benefit payments by a three-to-one ratio.

The plan's Board of Trustees directed Karl five years ago to invest for total return over the long term. However, as trustees of this highly visible public fund, they cautioned him that volatile or erratic results could cause them embarrassment. They also noted a state statute that mandated that not more than 25% of the plan's assets (at cost) be invested in common stocks.

At the annual meeting of the trustees in November 2020, Karl presented the following portfolio and performance report to the Board.

ALPINE EMPLOYEE RETIREMENT PLAN

Asset Mix as of 9/30/20	At Cost (millions)		At Market (millions)	
Fixed-income assets:				
Short-term securities	$ 4.5	11.0%	$ 4.5	11.4%
Long-term bonds and mortgages	26.5	64.7	23.5	59.5
Common stocks	10.0	24.3	11.5	29.1
	$41.0	100.0%	$39.5	100.0%

INVESTMENT PERFORMANCE

	Annual Rates of Return for Periods Ending 9/30/20	
	5 Years	1 Year
Total Alpine Fund:		
Time-weighted	8.2%	5.2%
Dollar-weighted (Internal)	7.7%	4.8%
Assumed actuarial return	6.0%	6.0%
U.S. Treasury bills	7.5%	11.3%
Large sample of pension funds	10.1%	14.3%
(average 60% equities, 40% fixed income)		
Common stocks—Alpine Fund	13.3%	14.3%
Average portfolio beta coefficient	0.90	0.89
Standard & Poor's 500 Stock Index	13.8%	21.1%
Fixed-income securities—Alpine Fund	6.7%	1.0%
Salomon Brothers' Bond Index	4.0%	−11.4%

Karl was proud of his performance and was chagrined when a trustee made the following critical observations:

a. "Our one-year results were terrible, and it's what you've done for us lately that counts most."

b. "Our total fund performance was clearly inferior compared to the large sample of other pension funds for the last five years. What else could this reflect except poor management judgment?"

c. "Our common stock performance was especially poor for the five-year period."

d. "Why bother to compare your returns to the return from Treasury bills and the actuarial assumption rate? What your competition could have earned for us or how we would have fared if invested in a passive index (which doesn't charge a fee) are the only relevant measures of performance."

e. "Who cares about time-weighted return? If it can't pay pensions, what good is it!"

Appraise the merits of each of these statements and give counterarguments that Mr. Karl can use.

6. A portfolio manager summarizes the input from the macro and micro forecasts in the following table:

MICRO FORECASTS

Asset	Expected Return (%)	Beta	Residual Standard Deviation (%)
Stock A	20	1.3	58
Stock B	18	1.8	71
Stock C	17	0.7	60
Stock D	12	1.0	55

MACRO FORECASTS

Asset	Expected Return (%)	Standard Deviation (%)
T-bills	8	0
Passive equity portfolio	16	23

a. Calculate expected excess returns, alpha values, and residual variances for these stocks.

b. Construct the optimal risky portfolio.

c. What is Sharpe's measure for the optimal portfolio and how much of it is contributed by the active portfolio? What is the M^2?

18.1. Sharpe: $(\bar{r} - \bar{r}_f)/\sigma$

$S_P = (35 - 6)/42 = .69$

$S_M = (28 - 6)/30 = .733$

Jensen (or alpha): $\bar{r} - [\bar{r}_f + \beta(\bar{r}_M - \bar{r}_f)]$

$\alpha_P = 35 - [6 + 1.2(28 - 6)] = 2.6\%$

$\alpha_M = 0$

Treynor: $(\bar{r} - \bar{r}_f)/\beta$

$T_P = (35 - 6)/1.2 = 24.2$

$T_M = (28 - 6)/1.0 = 22$

18.2. Performance attribution

First compute the new bogey performance as

$(.70 \times 5.81) + (.25 \times 1.45) + (.05 \times .48) = 4.45\%$

a. Contribution of asset allocation to performance

Market	(1) Actual Weight in Market	(2) Benchmark Weight in Market	(3) Excess Weight	(4) Index Return (%)	(5) = (3) × (4) Contribution to Performance (%)
Equity	.70	.70	.00	5.81	.000
Fixed-income	.07	.25	−.18	1.45	−.261
Cash	.23	.05	.18	0.48	.086
Contribution of asset allocation					−.175

b. Contribution of selection to total performance

Market	(1) Portfolio Performance (%)	(2) Index Performance (%)	(3) Excess Performance (%)	(4) Portfolio Weight	(5) = (3) × (4) Contribution (%)
Equity	7.28	5.00	2.28	0.70	1.60
Fixed-income	1.89	1.45	0.44	0.07	0.03
Contribution of selection within markets					1.63

18.3. Import the series of annual returns on T-bills and large stocks (S&P 500).

a. Compute the return to the perfect timer. You can use the Excel function = max(stock return, bill return) to select the greater of the two returns each year.

b. Use Excel functions to estimate average and SD.

c. Generate the wealth index series. Set the wealth index at the end of 1925 to 1.0. Because the rates of return are expressed in percentages, the index value at the end of 1926 = 1 + rate(1926)/100. For the following years, index = previous index*(1 + this year's return/100).

d. The wealth index for 2008 is the terminal value of the fund per $1 invested at the beginning of 1926.

e. The geometric average equals: Terminal value^(1/82) − 1. Notice that this calculation results in a return expressed as a decimal, not percent.

f. The performance of the annual timer is not as good as the monthly timer. The annual timer may switch funds between the market and T-bills only once per year. He cannot advantageously move funds between the market and bills across months *within* each year. Someone who can time perfectly will always be better off when allowed to make more frequent allocation choices.

18.4. The timer will guess bear or bull markets randomly. One-half of all bull markets will be preceded by a correct forecast, and, similarly, one-half of all bear markets will be preceded by a correct forecast. Hence, $P_1 + P_2 - 1 = \frac{1}{2} + \frac{1}{2} - 1 = 0$.

Chapter

Globalization and International Investing

After Studying This Chapter You Should Be Able To:

- Demonstrate the advantages of international diversification.

- Formulate hedge strategies to offset the currency risk involved in international investments.

- Understand international investment strategies.

- Decompose investment returns into contributing factors such as country, currency, and stock selection.

The S&P 500 market-index is widely used in practice as "the" risky market portfolio. This may be justified on the grounds that an S&P 500 Index fund or ETF is the simplest acceptable passive portfolio of U.S. equities, and thus can be viewed as an appropriate benchmark. But the S&P index does not cover all U.S. equity, and even the broadest U.S. equities index makes up only about 40% of world equity market value. In this chapter, we look beyond domestic markets to survey issues of extended diversification.

In one sense, international investing may be viewed as no more than a straightforward generalization of our earlier treatment of portfolio selection with a larger menu of assets from which to construct a portfolio. One faces similar issues of diversification, security analysis, security selection, and asset allocation. On the other hand, international investments pose some problems not encountered in domestic markets. Among these are the presence of exchange rate risk, restrictions on capital flows across national boundaries, an added dimension of political risk and country-specific regulations, and differing accounting practices in different countries.

We begin by looking at market capitalization of stock exchanges around the world and its relation to the home country GDP. Next, we examine exchange rate risk and how such risk can be mitigated by using foreign exchange futures and forward contracts. We also introduce political and country-specific risk that must be considered in the overall risk assessment of international investments. We then examine correlation across country portfolios with and without hedging foreign exchange risk.

Based on these insights, we assess the efficacy of investing globally in the context of equilibrium in international capital markets. Finally, we show how performance attribution procedures can be adapted to an international setting.

Related Web sites for this chapter are available at www.mhhe.com/bkm.

19.1 Global Markets for Equities

Developed Countries

To appreciate the myopia of an exclusive investment focus on U.S. stocks and bonds, consider the data in Table 19.1. The World Bank listed 65 developed countries in 2007, many of them with very small exchanges. Our list includes 25 countries with the largest equity capitalization, the smallest of which is New Zealand with a capitalization of $44 billion in 2007.[1] These countries made up 85% of the World gross domestic product in 2007.

The first six columns of Table 19.1 show market capitalization over the years 2002–2007. The first line shows capitalization for all world exchanges, showing total capitalization of corporate equity in 2007 as $48.3 trillion, of which U.S. stock exchanges made up $15.9 trillion, or 32.9%.[2] The year-to-year changes in the figures in these columns demonstrate the volatility of these markets.

The next three columns of Table 19.1 show country equity capitalization as a percentage of the world's in 2002 and 2007, as well as the growth in capitalization over those five years. The weights of the five largest countries behind the U.S. (Japan, U.K., France, Germany, and Canada) added up to 29.5% in 2007, so that in the universe of these six countries alone, the weight of the U.S. was only 53% [= 32.9/(32.9 + 29.5)] in 2007. Clearly, U.S. stocks may not comprise an adequately diversified portfolio of equities.

The last three columns of Table 19.1 show GDP, per capita GDP, and the equity capitalization as a percentage of GDP for the year 2007. As we would expect, per capita GDP in developed countries is not as variable across countries as total GDP, which is determined in part by total population. But market capitalization as a percentage of GDP is quite variable, suggesting widespread differences in economic structure even across developed countries. We return to this issue in the next section.

Emerging Markets

For a passive strategy, one could argue that a portfolio of equities of just the six countries with the largest capitalization would make up 62.5% (in 2007) of the world portfolio and may be sufficiently diversified. However, this argument will not hold for active portfolios that seek to tilt investments toward promising assets. Active portfolios will naturally include many stocks or indexes of emerging markets.

Table 19.2 makes the point. Surely, active portfolio managers must prudently scour stocks in markets such as China, Brazil, or Thailand. Table 19.2 shows data from the 20 largest emerging markets, the most notable of which is China, which grew by more than 3,000% between 2002 and 2007. But managers also would not want to have missed other markets that exhibited marked, if not dramatic, growth over the same years.

---

[1]GDPs for 2008 were not available as of the writing of this edition; therefore we match the available 2007 GDP data with 2007 market capitalization figures. New Zealand's capitalization stood at $22 billion as of January 1, 2009. Other excluded developed countries had smaller capitalizations, for example, Hungary with $19 billion.

[2]Although U.S. capitalization fell to $9.6 trillion as of 2009, stock market valuations in other countries fell as well, so the U.S. share of World equity remained at 34.4%.

TABLE 19.1

Market capitalization of stock exchanges in developed countries

Name	Market Capitalization Billions of U.S. Dollars						Percent of World		Growth (%)	GDP	GDP per Capita	Market Capitalization as % of GDP
	2002	2003	2004	2005	2006	2007	2002	2007	2002–2007	2007	2007	2007
World	**$20,025**	**$27,084**	**$31,701**	**$35,525**	**$43,104**	**$48,333**	**100%**	**100%**	**141.4%**	**54,585**	**8,219**	**89%**
U.S.	9,172	12,023	13,345	13,934	15,606	15,921	45.8	32.9	73.6	13,808	45,725	115
Japan	2,076	2,934	3,486	4,420	4,505	4,280	10.4	8.9	106.1	4,382	34,296	98
U.K.	1,796	2,363	2,730	2,925	3,692	3,723	9.0	7.7	107.4	2,804	46,099	133
France	911	1,238	1,436	1,667	2,313	2,572	4.6	5.3	182.2	2,594	42,034	99
Germany	633	990	1,117	1,219	1,599	2,020	3.2	4.2	218.9	3,321	40,400	61
Canada	488	750	960	1,206	1,339	1,669	2.4	3.5	242.3	1,436	43,674	116
Hong Kong	402	593	706	778	1,120	1,669	2.0	3.5	314.9	207	29,753	806
Switzerland	543	710	812	921	1,193	1,251	2.7	2.6	130.2	427	58,513	293
Australia	360	540	641	721	933	1,188	1.8	2.5	229.8	909	43,163	131
Italy	463	600	778	786	1,020	1,070	2.3	2.2	131.3	2,105	35,745	51
Spain	312	479	635	651	926	1,017	1.6	2.1	225.6	1,440	32,090	71
Korea	200	265	356	549	655	865	1.0	1.8	332.5	970	20,015	89
Netherlands	437	539	612	543	725	777	2.2	1.6	77.8	777	46,774	100
Sweden	170	267	343	366	510	499	0.8	1.0	194.0	455	49,603	110
Singapore	92	133	154	183	314	412	0.5	0.9	345.9	161	35,163	255
Belgium	127	171	269	270	335	359	0.6	0.7	183.9	453	42,618	79
Finland	133	161	174	198	252	341	0.7	0.7	156.9	246	46,856	139
Norway	65	92	137	193	267	340	0.3	0.7	422.6	389	83,485	87
Denmark	72	110	143	163	201	231	0.4	0.5	220.5	312	57,137	74
Greece	52	83	105	124	174	228	0.3	0.5	334.9	314	28,152	73
Austria	31	54	87	133	173	203	0.2	0.4	547.0	371	44,852	55
Israel	33	54	67	85	109	156	0.2	0.3	371.2	164	23,579	95
Portugal	46	62	74	71	106	136	0.2	0.3	193.2	223	21,082	61
Ireland	53	76	106	111	157	136	0.3	0.3	158.4	261	60,209	52
New Zealand	21	31	40	39	41	44	0.1	0.1	112.5	129	30,390	34
Other	1,336	1,767	2,388	3,220	4,780	7,225	6.7	14.9	440.7	15,926		

TABLE 19.2

Market capitalization of stock exchanges in emerging markets

	Market Capitalization Billions of U.S. Dollars						Percent of World		Growth (%)	GDP	GDP per Capita	Market Capitalization as % of GDP
	2002	2003	2004	2005	2006	2007	2002	2007	2002–2007	2007	2007	2007
India	$101	$220	$301	$408	$605	$1,285	0.5%	2.7%	1174.8%	1,101	942	117%
Russia	101	172	221	458	892	1,167	0.5	2.4	1051.6	1,290	9,075	91
Brazil	111	216	323	407	604	1,136	0.6	2.4	920.1	1,314	6,938	86
China	20	48	59	163	421	637	0.1	1.3	3137.3	3,280	2,483	19
Taiwan	190	281	332	351	437	488	0.9	1.0	157.0	383	16,697	127
South Africa	102	149	225	284	333	394	0.5	0.8	286.1	283	5,916	139
Mexico	99	124	171	238	346	356	0.5	0.7	260.5	1,023	9,717	35
Malaysia	94	116	137	142	183	249	0.5	0.5	166.4	187	6,956	133
Turkey	29	59	83	128	135	241	0.1	0.5	734.8	659	9,569	37
Chile	43	74	94	111	145	180	0.2	0.4	318.9	164	9,884	110
Indonesia	24	43	64	70	120	178	0.1	0.4	639.6	433	1,925	41
Poland	27	34	63	77	125	169	0.1	0.3	521.9	422	11,072	40
Thailand	33	86	86	97	107	154	0.2	0.3	367.5	245	3,732	63
Philippines	16	21	26	41	60	91	0.1	0.2	476.2	144	1,626	63
Czech Rep.	12	17	30	38	50	77	0.1	0.2	532.1	175	16,956	44
Peru	8	13	15	19	55	60	0.0	0.1	622.3	107	3,826	56
Colombia	6	10	20	42	42	54	0.0	0.1	729.4	203	4,264	27
Hungary	13	17	28	33	42	46	0.1	0.1	252.9	138	13,745	33
Argentina	7	20	21	24	30	36	0.0	0.1	387.0	260	6,609	14
Venezuela	3	3	6	5	8	12	0.0	0.0	279.9	228	8,282	5

Source: Market capitalzation: Datastream; GDP and per capita GDP: IMF.

These 20 emerging markets make up 22% of the world GDP and, together with the 25 developed markets in Table 19.1, make up 95% of the world GDP. Per capita GDP in these emerging markets was quite variable, ranging from $942 (India) to 16,956 (Czech Republic); still, no active manager would want to ignore India in an international portfolio. Market capitalization as a percent of GDP, which ranges from 5% (Venezuela) to 139% (South Africa), suggests that these financial markets are expected to show significant growth over the coming years, even absent spectacular growth in GDP.

The growth of capitalization in emerging markets over this period was much more volatile than growth in developed countries, suggesting that both risk and rewards in this segment of the globe may be substantial.

Market Capitalization and GDP

The contemporary view of economic development (rigorously stated in de Soto, 2000) holds that an important requirement for economic advancement is a developed code of business laws, institutions, and regulations that allows citizens to legally own, capitalize, and trade capital assets. As a corollary, we expect that development of equity markets will serve as catalysts for enrichment of the population, that is, that countries with larger relative capitalization of equities will tend to be richer.

Figure 19.1 is a simple (perhaps simplistic, since other relevant explanatory variables are omitted) rendition of the argument that a developed market for corporate equity contributes to the enrichment of the population. The R-square of the regression line shown in Figure 19.1, Panel A (for 2003), is 28% and the slope coefficient is .66, suggesting that an increase of 1% in the ratio of market capitalization to GDP is associated with an increase in per capita GDP of .66%. It is remarkable that of all the developed countries, only Hong Kong lies below the regression line; in contrast, most of the low-income emerging markets lie below the line. Countries like Venezuela and Norway that lie above the line, that is, exhibit higher per capita GDP than predicted by the regression, enjoy oil wealth that contributes to population income. Countries below the line, such as Indonesia, Philippines, Colombia, and Peru, suffered from deterioration of the business environment due to political strife and/or government policies that restricted the private sector.

It is interesting to look at the corresponding plot in Panel B for 2007 (and it will be even more interesting to do so for 2008, after the large decline of world equities). It is evident that per capita income has generally increased, as has total equity capitalization. More dramatic is the bunching of all countries toward the regression line, reducing the slope (to .46 from .66), and suggesting that there is less to achieve in this direction. Most striking is the continued delineation between developed and emerging countries; Hong Kong remains the only crossover developed economy in 2007.

Home-Country Bias

One would expect that most investors, particularly institutional and professional investors, would be aware of the opportunities offered by international investing. Yet in practice, investor portfolios notoriously overweight home-country stocks compared to a neutral indexing strategy and underweight, or even completely ignore, foreign equities. This has come to be known as the *home-country bias*. Despite a continuous increase in cross-border investing, home-country bias still pervades investor portfolios. We return to this issue in Section 19.3.

19.2 Risk Factors in International Investing

Opportunities in international investments do not come free of risk or of the cost of specialized analysis. The risk factors that are unique to international investments are exchange rate risk and country-specific risk, discussed in the next two sections.

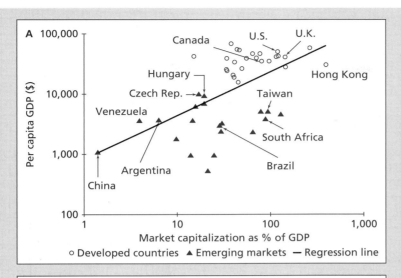

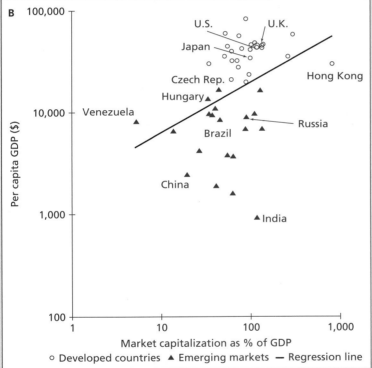

FIGURE 19.1

Per capita GDP and market capitalization as percent of GDP.

A: log scale, 2003 data.

B: log scale, 2007 data.

Exchange Rate Risk

It is best to begin with a simple example.

EXAMPLE 19.1

Exchange Rate Risk

Consider an investment in risk-free British government bills paying 10% annual interest in British pounds. While these U.K. bills would be the risk-free asset to a British investor, this is not the case for a U.S. investor. Suppose, for example, the current exchange rate is $2 per pound, and the U.S. investor starts with $20,000. That amount can be exchanged for £10,000 and invested at a riskless 10% rate in the United Kingdom to provide £11,000 in one year.

What happens if the dollar–pound exchange rate varies over the year? Say that during the year, the pound depreciates relative to the dollar, so that by year-end only $1.80 is required to purchase £1. The £11,000 can be exchanged at the year-end exchange rate for only $19,800 (=£11,000 × $1.80/£), resulting in a loss of $200 relative to the initial $20,000 investment. Despite the positive 10% pound-denominated return, the dollar-denominated return is negative 1%.

We can generalize from Example 19.1. The $20,000 is exchanged for $20,000/$E_0$ pounds, where E_0 denotes the original exchange rate ($2/£). The U.K. investment grows to $(20,000/E_0)[1 + r_f(\text{UK})]$ British pounds, where $r_f(\text{UK})$ is the risk-free rate in the United Kingdom. The pound proceeds ultimately are converted back to dollars at the subsequent exchange rate E_1, for total dollar proceeds of $20,000(E_1/E_0)[1 + r_f(\text{UK})]$. The dollar-denominated return on the investment in British bills, therefore, is

$$1 + r(\text{US}) = [1 + r_f(\text{UK})]E_1/E_0 \qquad \textbf{(19.1)}$$

We see in Equation 19.1 that the dollar-denominated return for a U.S. investor equals the pound-denominated return times the exchange rate "return." For a U.S. investor, the investment in British bills is a combination of a safe investment in the United Kingdom and a risky investment in the performance of the pound relative to the dollar. Here, the pound fared poorly, falling from a value of $2.00 to only $1.80. The loss on the pound more than offsets the earnings on the British bill.

Figure 19.2 illustrates this point. It presents rates of returns on stock market indexes in several countries for 2007. The dark boxes depict returns in local currencies, while the light boxes depict returns in dollars, adjusted for exchange rate movements. It's clear that exchange rate fluctuations over this period had large effects on dollar-denominated returns in several countries.

CONCEPT check **19.1**	Using the data in Example 19.1, calculate the rate of return in dollars to a U.S. investor holding the British bill if the year-end exchange rate is: (a) $E_1 = \$2.00/£$; (b) $E_1 = \$2.20/£$.

FIGURE 19.2

Stock market returns in U.S. dollars and local currencies for 2007

Source: Datastream.

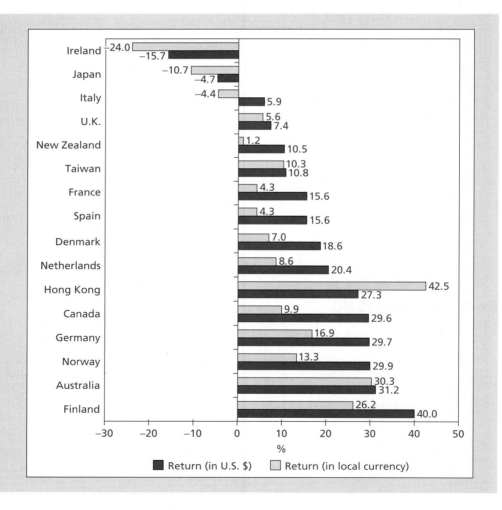

TABLE 19.3

Rates of change in the U.S. dollar against major world currencies, 2003–2007 (monthly data)

A. Standard deviation (annualized)

Country Currency	Euro (€)	U.K. (£)	Japan (¥)	Australia ($A)	Canada ($C)
Standard deviation	7.77	9.97	7.66	8.26	7.74

B. Correlation matrix

	Euro (€)	U.K. (£)	Japan (¥)	Australia ($A)	Canada ($C)
Euro (€)	1.00				
U.K. (£)	−0.60	1.00			
Japan (¥)	−0.46	0.28	1.00		
Australia ($A)	−0.39	0.59	0.16	1.00	
Canada ($C)	−0.75	0.62	0.38	0.31	1.00

C. Average Annual Returns from Rolling Over One-Month LIBOR Rates

Country	Currency	Return in Local Currency	Expected Appreciation in Local Currency Relative to U.S.$	Actual Gains from Exchange Rates	Average Annual Return in U.S. $	Surprise Gain/Loss Relative to U.S.	Standard Deviation of Average Annual Return
U.S.	U.S.$	3.75			3.75		
Europe	(€)	2.80	0.95	−6.09	−3.29	−7.04	3.69
U.K.	(£)	4.95	−1.20	9.87	14.83	11.08	3.46
Japan	(¥)	0.24	3.51	1.48	1.73	−2.02	4.46
Australia	A$	5.79	−2.04	10.14	15.93	12.18	3.48
Canada	C$	3.41	0.34	4.56	7.98	4.23	3.42

Source: Exchange rates: Datastream; LIBOR rates: **www.economagic.com**.

Pure **exchange rate risk** is the risk borne by investments in foreign safe assets. The investor in U.K. bills of Example 19.1 bears only the risk of the U.K./U.S. exchange rate. We can assess the magnitude of exchange rate risk by examination of historical rates of change in various exchange rates and their correlations.

Table 19.3A shows historical exchange rate risk measured by the standard deviation of monthly percent changes in the exchange rates of major currencies against the U.S. dollar over the period 2003–2007. The data show that currency risk is quite high. The annualized standard deviation of the percent changes in the exchange rate ranged from 7.66% (Japanese yen) to 9.97% (U.K. pound). The standard deviation of returns on U.S. large stocks for the same period was 8.7%, low by historical standards. Hence, exchange rate risk was of the same order of magnitude as the volatility on stocks. Clearly, an active investor who believes that Japanese stocks are underpriced, but has no information about any mispricing of the Japanese yen, should consider hedging the yen risk exposure when tilting the portfolio toward Japanese stocks. Exchange rate risk of the major currencies seems quite stable over time. For example, a study by Solnik (1999) for the period 1971–1998 finds similar standard deviations, ranging from 4.8% (Canadian dollar) to 12.0% (Japanese yen).

In the context of international portfolios, exchange rate risk may be mostly diversifiable. This is evident from the low correlation coefficients in Table 19.3B. (This observation will be reinforced when we compare the risk of hedged and unhedged country portfolios in a later section.) Thus, passive investors with well-diversified international portfolios need not be concerned with hedging exposure to foreign currencies.

exchange rate risk

The uncertainty in asset returns due to movements in the exchange rates between the U.S. dollar and foreign currency.

The effect of exchange rate fluctuations also shows up in Table 19.3C, which presents the returns on money market investments in different countries. While these investments are virtually risk-free in local currency, they are risky in dollar terms because of exchange rate risk. International investment flows by currency speculators should equalize the expected dollar returns in various currencies, adjusted for risk. Moreover, exchange-rate risk is largely diversifiable, as Table 19.3B shows, and hence we would expect similar dollar returns from cash investments in major currencies.

We can illustrate exchange rate risk using a yen-denominated investment during this period. The low yen-denominated LIBOR rate, .24%, compared to the U.S. dollar LIBOR rate, 3.75%, suggests that investors expected the yen to appreciate against the dollar by around 3.51%, the interest rate differential across the two countries. But those expectations were not fully realized; in fact, the yen actually appreciated against the dollar at an annual rate of only 1.48%, leading to an annual dollar-denominated return on a yen investment of 1.73% (the total return derived from the .24% yen interest rate together with the realized exchange rate appreciation of 1.48%). However, deviations between prior expectations and actual returns of this magnitude are not shocking. The standard deviation of the average annual return on a five-year investment (assuming no serial correlation in returns) equals the annual standard deviation divided by $\sqrt{5}$, which amounts to 3.42% for the yen. Thus, the shortfall of 2.02% (the difference in the U.S. LIBOR return minus the yen LIBOR return converted into dollars) is less than one standard deviation.

Investors can hedge exchange rate risk using a forward or futures contract in foreign exchange. Recall that such contracts entail delivery or acceptance of one currency for another at a stipulated exchange rate. To illustrate, recall Example 19.1. In this case, to hedge her exposure to the British pound, the U.S. investor would agree to deliver pounds for dollars at a fixed exchange rate, thereby eliminating the future risk involved with conversion of the pound investment back into dollars.

EXAMPLE   **19.2**

Hedging Exchange Rate Risk

If the futures exchange rate in Example 19.1 had been $F_0 = \$1.93/£$ when the investment was made, the U.S. investor could have assured a riskless dollar-denominated return by locking in the year-end exchange rate at $\$1.93/£$. In this case, the riskless U.S. return would have been 6.15%:

$$[1 + r_f(\text{UK})]F_0/E_0$$
$$= (1.10)\,1.93/2.00$$
$$= 1.0615$$

Here are the steps to lock in the dollar-denominated returns. The futures contract entered in the second step exactly offsets the exchange rate risk incurred in step 1.

Initial Transaction	End-of-Year Proceeds in Dollars
Exchange $20,000 for £10,000 and invest at 10% in the United Kingdom.	£11,000 × E_1
Enter a contract to deliver £11,000 for dollars at the (forward) exchange rate $1.93/£.	£11,000 (1.93 − E_1)
Total	£11,000 × $1.93/£ = $21,230

You may have noticed that the futures hedge in Example 19.2 is the same type of hedging strategy at the heart of the spot-futures parity relationship discussed in Chapter 17. In both instances, futures markets are used to eliminate the risk of holding another asset. The U.S. investor can lock in a riskless dollar-denominated return either by investing in the United Kingdom and hedging exchange rate risk or by investing in riskless U.S. assets. Because the returns on two riskless strategies must provide equal returns, we conclude that

$$[1 + r_f(\text{UK})]F_0/E_0 = 1 + r_f(\text{US})$$

or

$$\frac{F_0}{E_0} = \frac{1 + r_f(\text{US})}{1 + r_f(\text{UK})} \qquad \text{(19.2)}$$

This relationship is called the **interest rate parity relationship** or **covered interest arbitrage relationship.**

Consider the intuition behind this result. If $r_f(\text{US})$ is greater than $r_f(\text{UK})$, money invested in the United States will grow at a faster rate than money invested in the United Kingdom. If this is so, why wouldn't all investors decide to invest their money in the United States? One important reason is that the dollar may be depreciating relative to the pound. Although dollar investments in the United States grow faster than pound investments in the United Kingdom, each dollar is worth progressively fewer pounds as time passes. Such an effect will exactly offset the advantage of the higher U.S. interest rate.

To complete the argument, we need only determine how a depreciating dollar will be reflected in Equation 19.2. If the dollar is depreciating, meaning that progressively more dollars are required to purchase each pound, then the forward exchange rate, F_0 (which equals the dollars required to purchase one pound for delivery in the future), must exceed E_0, the current exchange rate.

That is exactly what Equation 19.2 tells us: When $r_f(\text{US})$ exceeds $r_f(\text{UK})$, F_0 must exceed E_0. The depreciation of the dollar embodied in the ratio of F_0 to E_0 exactly compensates for the difference in interest rates available in the two countries. Of course, the argument also works in reverse: If $r_f(\text{US})$ is less than $r_f(\text{UK})$, then F_0 will be less than E_0.

interest rate parity relationship, or covered interest arbitrage relationship

The spot-futures exchange rate relationship that precludes arbitrage opportunities.

EXAMPLE   19.3

Covered Interest Arbitrage

What if the interest rate parity relationship were violated? Suppose $r_f(\text{US})$ is 6.15%, but the futures price is \$1.90/£ instead of \$1.93/£. You could adopt the following strategy to reap arbitrage profits. In this example, let E_1 denote the exchange rate that will prevail in one year. E_1 is, of course, a random variable from the perspective of today's investors.

Action	Initial Cash Flow (in \$)	Cash Flow in One Year (in \$)
1. Borrow 1 British pound in London. Repay in one year.	\$ 2.00	$-E_1(1.10)$
2. Convert the pound to \$2 and lend in the United States.	\$−2.00	$2.00(1.0615)$
3. Enter a contract to purchase 1.10 pounds at a (futures) price of $F_0 = \$1.90/£$	0	$1.10(E_1 - 1.90)$
Total	\$ 0	\$.033

In step 1, you borrow one pound in the United Kingdom (worth \$2 at the current exchange rate) and, after one year, repay the pound borrowed with interest. Because the loan is made in the United Kingdom at the U.K. interest rate, you would repay 1.10 pounds, which would be worth $E_1(1.10)$ dollars. The U.S. loan in step 2 is made at the U.S. interest rate of 6.15%. The futures position in step 3 results in receipt of 1.10 pounds, for which you would first pay F_0 (i.e., 1.90) dollars each and then convert into dollars at exchange rate E_1.

The exchange rate risk here is exactly offset between the pound obligation in step 1 and the futures position in step 3. The profit from the strategy is, therefore, riskless and requires no net investment. This is an arbitrage opportunity.

CONCEPT *check* **19.2**

What are the arbitrage strategy and associated profits if the initial future price is $F_0 = \$1.95/\text{pound}$?

Ample empirical evidence bears out this theoretical relationship. For example, on April 3, 2009, the interest rate on one-year U.S. Treasury securities was .58%, while the rate in Germany was .78%. The spot exchange rate was \$1.3488/€. Substituting these values into Equation 19.2, we find that interest rate parity implies that the forward exchange rate for delivery in one year should have been $1.3488 \times 1.0058/1.0078 = \$1.3461/€$. The actual forward rate was \$1.3473/€, which was so close to the parity value that transaction costs would have prevented arbitrageurs from profiting from the discrepancy.

Direct versus indirect quotes   The exchange rate in Example 19.1 is expressed as dollars per pound. This is an example of what is termed a *direct* exchange rate quote. The euro–dollar exchange rate is also typically expressed as a direct quote. In contrast, exchange rates for other currencies such as the Japanese yen or Swiss franc are typically expressed as *indirect* quotes, that is, as units of foreign currency per dollar, for example, 120 yen per dollar. For currencies expressed as indirect quotes, depreciation of the dollar would result in a *decrease* in the quoted exchange rate (\$1 buys fewer yen); in contrast, dollar depreciation versus the pound would show up as a *higher* exchange rate (more dollars are required to buy £1). When the exchange rate is quoted as foreign currency per dollar, the domestic and foreign exchange rates in Equation 19.2 must be switched: In this case the equation becomes

$$F_0(\text{foreign currency/\$}) = \frac{1 + r_f(\text{foreign})}{1 + r_f(\text{U.S.})} \times E_0(\text{foreign currency/\$})$$

For example, if the interest rate in the U.S. is higher than in Japan, the dollar will sell in the forward market at a lower price than in the spot market.

Imperfect Exchange Rate Risk Hedging

Unfortunately, perfect exchange rate hedging usually is not so easy. In Example 19.2, we knew exactly how many pounds to sell in the forward or futures market because the pound-denominated proceeds in the United Kingdom were riskless. If the U.K. investment had not been in bills, but instead had been in risky U.K. equity, we would know neither the ultimate value in pounds of our U.K. investment nor how many pounds to sell forward. That is, the hedging opportunity offered by foreign exchange forward contracts would be imperfect.

To summarize, the generalization of Equation 19.1 is that

$$1 + r(\text{US}) = [1 + r(\text{foreign})]E_1/E_0 \qquad \textbf{(19.3)}$$

where $r(\text{foreign})$ is the possibly risky return earned in the currency of the foreign investment. You can set up a perfect hedge only in the special case that $r(\text{foreign})$ is itself a known number. In that case, you know you must sell in the forward or futures market an amount of foreign currency equal to $[1 + r(\text{foreign})]$ for each unit of that currency you purchase today.

CONCEPT *check* **19.3**   How many pounds would the investor in Example 19.2 need to sell forward to hedge exchange rate risk if: (a) $r(\text{UK}) = 20\%$; and (b) $r(\text{UK}) = 30\%$?

Country-Specific Risk

In principle, security analysis at the macroeconomic, industry, and firm-specific level is similar in all countries. Such analysis aims to provide estimates of expected returns and risk of individual assets and portfolios. However, to achieve the same quality of information about assets in a foreign country is by nature more difficult and hence more expensive. Moreover, the risk of coming by false or misleading information is greater.

Consider two investors: an American wishing to invest in Indonesian stocks and an Indonesian wishing to invest in U.S. stocks. While each would have to consider macroeconomic analysis of the foreign country, the task would be much more difficult for the American investor. The

TABLE 19.4

Composite risk ratings for July 2008 versus August 2007

Rank in July 2008	Country	Composite Risk Rating July 2008	July 2008 versus August 2007	Rank in August 2007
	Very low risk			
1	Norway	91.8	−0.5	1
11	Canada	85.0	1.25	17
22	Japan	81.8	−2	17
	Low risk			
35	United Kingdom	78.8	−2	29
36	China	78.5	−0.75	35
46	United States	76.5	2.75	57
70	Argentina	71.5	−3	52
	Moderate risk			
82	Indonesia	69.0	−0.5	83
94	India	67.3	−3	79
114	Turkey	63.5	−1.5	108
	High risk			
128	Lebanon	58.5	0.25	129
135	Iraq	53.0	4.25	137
	Very high risk			
140	Somalia	39.3	−0.5	140

Source: *International Country Risk Guide,* July 2008, Table 1.

reason is not that investment in Indonesia is necessarily riskier than investment in the U.S. You can easily find many U.S. stocks that are, in the final analysis, riskier than a number of Indonesian stocks. The difference lies in the fact that U.S. financial markets are more transparent than those of Indonesia.

In the past, when international investing was novel, the added risk was referred to as **political risk** and its assessment was an art. As cross-border investment has increased and more resources have been utilized, the quality of related analysis has improved. A leading organization in the field (which is quite competitive) is the PRS Group (Political Risk Services) and the presentation here follows the PRS methodology.[3]

PRS's country risk analysis results in a country composite risk rating on a scale of 0 (most risky) to 100 (least risky). Countries are then ranked by the composite risk measure and divided into five categories: very low risk (100–80), low risk (79.9–70), moderate risk (69.9–60), high risk (59.9–50), and very high risk (less than 50). To illustrate, Table 19.4 shows the placement of countries in the July 2008 issue of the PRS *International Country Risk Guide.* It is not surprising to find Norway at the top of the very-low-risk list, and small emerging markets at the bottom, with Somalia (ranked 140) closing the list. What may be surprising is the fairly mediocre ranking of the U.S. (ranked 46), comparable to China (36) and the U.K. (35), all three appearing in the low-risk category.

The composite risk rating is a weighted average of three measures: political risk, financial risk, and economic risk. Political risk is measured on a scale of 100–0, while financial and economic risk are measured on a scale of 50–0. The three measures are added and divided by two to obtain the composite rating. The variables used by PRS to determine the composite risk rating from the three measures are shown in Table 19.5.

political risk

Possibility of expropriation of assets, changes in tax policy, restrictions on the exchange of foreign currency for domestic currency, or other changes in the business climate of a country.

[3]You can find more information on the Web site: **www.prsgroup.com**. We are grateful to the PRS Group for supplying us data and guidance.

TABLE 19.5

Variables used in PRS's political risk score

Political Risk Variables	Financial Risk Variables	Economic Risk Variables
Government stability	Foreign debt (% of GDP)	GDP per capita
Socioeconomic conditions	Foreign debt service (% of GDP)	Real annual GDP growth
Investment profile	Current account (% of exports)	Annual inflation rate
Internal conflicts	Net liquidity in months of imports	Budget balance (% of GDP)
External conflicts	Exchange rate stability	Current account balance (% GDP)
Corruption		
Military in politics		
Religious tensions		
Law and order		
Ethnic tensions		
Democratic accountability		
Bureaucracy quality		

Table 19.6 shows the three risk measures for five of the countries in Table 19.4, in order of the July 2008 ranking of the composite risk ratings. The table shows that by political risk, the United States ranked second among these five countries. But in the financial risk measure, the U.S. ranked *last* among the five. The surprisingly poor performance of the U.S. in this dimension was probably due to its exceedingly large government and balance-of-trade deficits, which put considerable pressure on its exchange rate. Exchange rate stability, foreign trade imbalance, and foreign indebtedness all enter PRS's computation of financial risk. The financial crisis that began in August of 2008 was a striking vindication of PRS's judgment; our initial surprise at the rank of the U.S. arose from a failure to carefully consider the underpinnings of their methodology.

Country risk is captured in greater depth by scenario analysis for the composite measure and each of its components. Table 19.7 (A and B) shows one- and five-year worst case and best case scenarios for the composite ratings and for the political risk measure. Risk stability is based on the difference in the rating between the best and worst case scenarios and is quite large in most cases. The worst case scenario can move a country to a higher risk category. For example, Table 19.7B shows that in the worst-case five-year scenario, India was particularly vulnerable to deterioration in the political environment.

Finally, Table 19.8 shows ratings of political risk by each of its 12 components. Corruption (variable F) in Japan is rated worse than in the U.S. but better than in China and India. In democratic accountability (variable K), China ranked worst, and the United States, Canada, and India best, while China ranked best in government stability (variable A).

TABLE 19.6

Current risk ratings and composite risk forecasts

	Composite Ratings		Current Ratings		
Country	Year Ago August 2007	Current July 2008	Political Risk July 2008	Financial Risk July 2008	Economic Risk July 2008
Canada	83.75	**85**	86	42	42
Japan	83.75	**81.75**	77.5	46	40
China	80.5	**78.5**	67.5	48	41.5
United States	73.5	**76.5**	81	32	40
India	71	**67.25**	60.5	43.5	30.5

Source: *International Country Risk Guide,* July 2008, Table 2B.

TABLE 19.7

Composite and political risk forecasts

A. Composite risk forecasts

Country	Current Rating July 2008	One Year Ahead			Five Years Ahead		
		Worst Case	Best Case	Risk Stability	Worst Case	Best Case	Risk Stability
Canada	85.0	80.8	87.8	7.0	78.0	90.8	12.8
Japan	81.8	78.3	85.0	6.8	75.5	89.0	13.5
China	78.5	72.3	80.3	8.0	63.3	83.3	20.0
United States	76.5	74.8	82.0	7.3	71.0	84.3	13.3
India	67.3	63.8	71.3	7.5	61.8	76.3	14.5

B. Political Risk Forecasts

Country	Current Rating July 2008	One Year Ahead			Five Years Ahead		
		Worst Case	Best Case	Risk Stability	Worst Case	Best Case	Risk Stability
Canada	86.0	83.5	88.5	5.0	83.0	92.5	9.5
Japan	77.5	75.0	83.0	8.0	74.0	89.0	15.0
China	67.5	63.5	70.5	7.0	60.5	77.0	16.5
United States	81.0	79.0	87.0	8.0	77.0	87.5	10.5
India	60.5	59.0	65.5	6.5	61.0	72.5	11.5

Sources: **A:** *International Country Risk Guide,* July 2008, Table 2C; **B:** *International Country Risk Guide,* July 2008, Table 3C.

TABLE 19.8

Political risk points by component, July 2008

This table lists the total points for each of the following political risk components out of the maximum points indicated. The final column in the table shows the overall political risk rating (the sum of the points awarded to each component).

A	Government Stability	12	G	Military in Politics		6
B	Socioeconomic Conditions	12	H	Religious Tensions		6
C	Investment Profile	12	I	Law and Order		6
D	Internal Conflict	12	J	Ethnic Tensions		6
E	External Conflict	12	K	Democratic Accountability		6
F	Corruption	6	L	Bureaucracy Quality		4

Country	A	B	C	D	E	F	G	H	I	J	K	L	Political Risk Rating July 2008
Canada	8.0	8.5	11.5	10.5	11.0	5.0	6.0	6.0	6.0	3.5	6.0	4.0	86.0
Japan	5.0	8.0	11.5	10.5	9.5	3.0	5.0	5.5	5.0	5.5	5.0	4.0	77.5
China	10.5	7.5	7.0	9.5	10.0	2.5	3.0	5.0	4.5	4.5	1.5	2.0	67.5
United States	7.5	8.0	12.0	10.5	9.5	4.0	4.0	5.5	5.0	5.0	6.0	4.0	81.0
India	6.0	5.0	8.5	6.5	10.0	2.5	4.0	2.5	4.0	2.5	6.0	3.0	60.5

Source: *International Country Risk Guide,* July 2008, Table 3B.

Each monthly issue of the *International Country Risk Guide* of the PRS Group includes great detail and holds some 250 pages. Other organizations compete in supplying such evaluations. The result is that today's investor can become well equipped to properly assess the risk involved in international investing.

19.3 International Investing: Risk, Return, and Benefits from Diversification

U.S. investors have several avenues through which they can invest internationally. The most obvious method, which is available in practice primarily to larger institutional investors, is to purchase securities directly in the capital markets of other countries. However, even small investors now can take advantage of several investment vehicles with an international focus.

Shares of several foreign firms are traded in U.S. markets in the form of American depository receipts, or ADRs. A U.S. financial institution such as a bank will purchase shares of a foreign firm in that firm's country, then issue claims to those shares in the United States. Each ADR is then a claim on a given number of the shares of stock held by the bank. In this way, the stock of foreign companies can be traded on U.S. stock exchanges. Trading foreign stocks with ADRs is therefore as easy as trading U.S. stocks.

There is also a wide array of mutual funds and exchange-traded funds with an international focus. Single-country funds invest in the shares of only one country. In addition to single-country funds, there are several open-end mutual and exchange-traded funds with an international focus. For example, Fidelity offers funds with investments concentrated overseas, generally in Europe, in the Pacific Basin, and in developing economies in its emerging opportunities fund. Vanguard, consistent with its indexing philosophy, offers separate index funds for Europe, the Pacific Basin, and emerging markets. The nearby box discusses a wide range of single-country exchange-traded index funds.

U.S. investors also can trade derivative securities based on prices in foreign security markets. For example, they can trade options and futures on the Nikkei stock index of 225 stocks on the Tokyo stock exchange, or on FTSE (Financial Times Share Exchange) indexes of U.K. and European stocks.

Risk and Return: Summary Statistics

Illustrations for most of our discussions in the remaining part of this chapter derive from a database of country market-index returns. We use 10 years of monthly returns over 1999–2008 for 48 non-U.S. country market-indexes as well as the U.S. S&P 500. This relatively short period begins at the tail end of the high-tech bubble (the late 1990s), contains a mild recession (which was still quite disastrous for stocks in 2001), and ends with a severe recession that hammered world equities in 2008.

Analysis of risky assets typically focuses on *excess* returns over the risk-free rate. This alone adds a perplexing aspect to international investing, since the appropriate risk-free rate varies around the globe. Rates of return on identical indexes (as well as individual assets) will generate different excess returns when safe bonds are denominated in different currencies. Although our perspective is U.S.-based, our methodology would serve investors in any country, yet the numbers may be different when applied to risk-free rates denominated in other currencies.

As we shall see, the tumultuous period we analyze produced negative average excess returns for stock indexes of quite a few markets, and lower-than-historical averages for almost all. This fact alone conveys an important lesson. It provides an extreme example of the general observation that realized returns are very noisy reflections of investor expectations and cannot provide accurate forecasts of future returns. Past returns do, however, provide an indication of risk, at least for the near future. While the near-efficient market hypothesis applies *to expected returns* (to wit: future returns cannot be forecast from past returns), it does *not* apply to forecasting risk. Thus our exercise will allow us to demonstrate the distinction between what you can and cannot learn from historical returns that evidently departed from prior expectations.

LOW-COST FOREIGN INDEX FUNDS CALLED WEBS ELIMINATE SOME OF THE GUESSWORK AND COSTS OF INVESTING ABROAD

With foreign markets generally stronger this year, a new way to invest abroad has appeared at a good time. WEBS, an acronym for World Equity Benchmark Shares, represents an investment in a portfolio of publicly traded foreign stocks in a selected country. Each WEBS Index Series seeks to generate investment results that generally correspond to the price and yield performance of a specific Morgan Stanley Capital International (MSCI) index.

You sell these shares rather than redeeming them, but there the similarity to closed-end country funds ends. WEBS are equity securities, not mutual funds. WEBS shares trade continuously on a secondary market, the Amex, during regular Amex trading hours, like any other publicly traded U.S. stock listed on the exchange. In contrast, mutual fund shares do not trade in the secondary market, and are normally bought and sold from the issuing mutual fund at prices determined only at the end of the day. The new funds create and redeem shares in large blocks as needed, thus preventing the big premiums or discounts to net asset value typical of closed-end country funds. As index portfolios, WEBS are passively managed, so their expenses run much lower than for current open- or closed-end country funds.

WEBS shares offer U.S. investors portfolio exposure to country-specific equity markets, in a single, listed security you can easily buy, sell, or short on the Amex. Unlike American Depository Receipts (ADRs) that give you an investment in just one company, WEBS shares enable you to gain exposure to a broad portfolio of a desired foreign country's stocks. You gain broad exposure in the country or countries of your choice without the complications usually associated with buying, owning, or monitoring direct investments in foreign countries. You also have the conveniences of trading on a major U.S. exchange and dealing in U.S. dollars.

Some investors may prefer the active management, diversity, and flexibility of open-end international equity index funds as a way to limit currency and political risks of investing in foreign markets. As conventional open-end funds, however, the international funds are sometimes forced by net redemptions to sell stocks at inopportune times, which can be a particular problem in foreign markets with highly volatile stocks.

You pay brokerage commissions on the purchase and sale of WEBS, but since their portfolios are passively managed, their management and administrative fees are relatively low and they eliminate most of the transaction charges typical of managed funds.

FOREIGN INDEX BASKETS

WEBS	Ticker Symbol	WEBS	Ticker Symbol
Australia	EWA	Malaysia	EWM
Austria	EWO	Mexico	EWW
Belgium	EWK	Netherlands	EWN
Canada	EWC	Singapore	EWS
France	EWQ	Spain	EWP
Germany	EWG	Sweden	EWD
Hong Kong	EWH	Switzerland	EWL
Italy	EWI	U.K.	EWU
Japan	EWJ		

SOURCES: Modified from *The Outlook,* May 22, 1996, published by Standard and Poor's; and Amex Web site, **www.amex.com,** February 2000. Reprinted by permission of Standard & Poor's, a division of The McGraw-Hill Companies, Inc.

While active-strategy managers engage in individual-market asset allocation and security selection, we will restrict our international diversification to country market-index portfolios, keeping us on the side of an enhanced passive strategy. Nevertheless, our analysis illustrates the essential features of extended active management as well.

We begin with an investigation of the characteristics of individual markets, and then proceed to analyze the benefits of diversification, using portfolios constructed from these individual markets. Table 19.9A shows the market capitalization of 49 country indexes as of the end of 2008. The country indexes are sorted by capitalization, developed versus emerging status, and geographical blocks, with one exception: China is placed in the "large markets" block, as befits a market that has become one of the driving forces of the world economy.

Table 19.9A highlights the fact that the case for international diversification has become compelling. Notice that the large-markets (excluding U.S.) portfolio is larger than that of the U.S., and that U.S. capitalization accounts for only 34% of the aggregate capitalization of the 49 countries. Table 19.9B presents summary return statistics for the country indexes, as well as seven internationally diversified portfolios formed from developed and emerging markets. We begin by comparing developed to emerging markets.

Are Investments in Emerging Markets Riskier?

In Figure 19.3, developed countries and emerging markets are separately ordered from lowest to highest standard deviation. The standard deviations of investments in emerging markets

TABLE 19.9A

Market capitalization of 49 market-index portfoilos (January 1, 2009) and their weights in investable portfolios and World portfolio

	Capitalization ($ million)	Portfolio Average ($ million)	Portfolio Weights	
			Investable	World
Developed markets				
USA	**9,607,520**	**9,607,520**	0.98	**0.3438**
Large six (non-U.S.) markets				
Japan	3,086,949		0.32	0.1105
U.K.	1,837,139		0.19	0.0657
China*	1,458,973		0.15	0.0522
France	1,408,104		0.14	0.0504
Germany	1,094,608		0.11	0.0392
canada	892,731		0.09	0.0319
Total	**9,778,504**	**1,629,751**	1.00	**0.3499**
EU developed markets				
Spain	649,335		0.27	0.0232
Italy	524,341		0.22	0.0188
Netherlands	304,398		0.13	0.0109
Sweden	234,707		0.10	0.0084
Belgium	155,596		0.06	0.0056
Finland	147,816		0.06	0.0053
Denmark	115,306		0.05	0.0041
Greece	79,927		0.03	0.0029
Austria	76,588		0.03	0.0027
Portugal	65,231		0.03	0.0023
Ireland	44,589		0.02	0.0016
Total	**2,397,834**	**217,985**	1.00	**0.0858**
Australia + Far East				
Hong Kong	853,144		0.41	0.0305
Australia	597,142		0.29	0.0214
Korea	389,862		0.19	0.0140
Singapore	221,542		0.11	0.0079
New Zealand	22,373		0.01	0.0008
Total Aus + FE	**2,084,063**	**416,813**	1.00	**0.0746**
Europe developed (excluding EU) markets				
Switzerland	849,570		0.78	0.0304
Norway	125,959		0.11	0.0045
Israel	88,644		0.08	0.0032
Luxemburg	31,144		0.03	0.0011
Total	**1,095,317**	**273,829**	1.00	**0.0392**
Emerging Markets				
Far East + South Africa				
India	513,549		0.37	0.0184
Taiwan	270,574		0.20	0.0097
South Africa	224,532		0.16	0.0080
Malaysia	151,319		0.11	0.0054
Indonesia	81,514		0.06	0.0029

(continued)

TABLE 19.9A

(concluded)

	Capitalization ($ million)	Portfolio Average ($ million)	Portfolio Weights	
			Investable	World
Thailand	80,551		0.06	0.0029
Philippines	45,120		0.03	0.0016
Pakistan	15,966		0.01	0.0006
Sri Lanka	3,369		0.00	0.0001
Total	**1,386,494**	154,055	1.00	**0.0496**
Latin America				
Brazil	519,671		0.51	0.0186
Mexico	212,190		0.21	0.0076
Chile	113,009		0.11	0.0040
Colombia	81,695		0.08	0.0029
Peru	40,052		0.04	0.0014
Argentina	35,902		0.04	0.0013
Venezuela	8,960		0.01	0.0003
Total	**1,011,479**	144,497	1.00	**0.0362**
Emerging Europe				
Russia	331,182		0.57	0.0119
Turkey	105,843		0.18	0.0038
Poland	77,120		0.13	0.0028
Czech	43,517		0.07	0.0016
Hungary	18,693		0.03	0.0007
Cyprus	7,124		0.01	0.0003
Total	**583,479**	97,247	1.00	**0.0209**
Total for all 13 Portfolios	**27,944,690**	558,894		**1.0000**

*China is still usually classified as "emerging," but given its size and importance, we place it with the large developed markets.

Source: Datastream.

are charted with those in developed countries. The graphs clearly show that investment in emerging markets is generally riskier than in developed countries, at least as measured by total volatility of returns. Still, you can find emerging markets that appear safer than some developed countries.

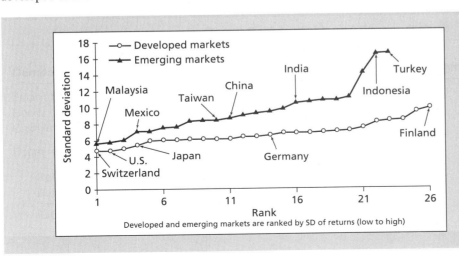

FIGURE 19.3

Monthly standard deviation of excess returns in developed and emerging markets (1999–2008)

TABLE 19.9B

Monthly return and performance statistics for index portfolios, 1999–2008 (Returns in U.S. Dollars, Percent)

	Monghly Excess Return		Regression on U.S. Returns				Performance	
	Av. Return	SD	Correlation	Beta	Alpha	Resid SD	Info ratio	Sharpe
Developed markets								
USA	−0.47	4.81	1	1	0	0	0	−0.10
Large markets								
Japan	−0.37	5.48	0.51	0.58	−0.09	4.70	−0.02	−0.07
U.K.	−0.35	5.02	0.86	0.89	0.07	2.60	0.03	−0.07
China	−0.11	8.67	0.16	0.30	0.03	8.55	0.00	−0.01
France	0.07	6.15	0.83	1.06	0.56	3.44	0.16	0.01
Germany	−0.04	6.61	0.84	1.15	0.49	3.62	0.14	−0.01
Canada	0.35	6.20	0.81	1.05	0.83	3.64	0.23	0.06
Large-market portfolio	**−0.16**	**4.71**	**0.79**	**0.77**	**0.20**	**2.90**	**0.07**	**−0.03**
Other EU developed								
Spain	0.20	5.98	0.78	0.97	0.65	3.75	0.17	0.03
Italy	−0.13	6.18	0.72	0.93	0.30	4.26	0.07	−0.02
Netherlands	−0.36	7.02	0.82	1.20	0.20	4.02	0.05	−0.05
Sweden	−0.10	8.15	0.82	1.39	0.55	4.66	0.12	−0.01
Belgium	−0.20	6.87	0.71	1.01	0.27	4.84	0.06	−0.03
Finland	−0.11	9.90	0.69	1.41	0.55	7.19	0.08	−0.01
Denmark	0.32	6.39	0.77	1.02	0.80	4.10	0.20	0.05
Greece	−0.48	8.34	0.56	0.97	−0.03	6.92	0.00	−0.06
Austria	0.29	6.94	0.64	0.92	0.72	5.36	0.13	0.04
Portugal	−0.03	6.10	0.62	0.79	0.34	4.79	0.07	−0.01
Ireland	−0.48	6.89	0.71	1.02	−0.01	4.85	0.00	−0.07
EU-dev portfolio	**−0.05**	**6.08**	**0.84**	**1.06**	**0.44**	**3.33**	**0.13**	**−0.01**
Australia + Far East								
Hong Kong	0.08	6.40	0.70	0.93	0.51	4.58	0.11	0.01
Australia	0.23	6.13	0.78	0.99	0.70	3.84	0.18	0.04
Korea	0.04	9.44	0.71	1.39	0.68	6.69	0.10	0.00
Singapore	−0.12	6.85	0.69	0.99	0.34	4.94	0.07	−0.02
New Zealand	0.26	6.11	0.64	0.81	0.64	4.72	0.13	0.04
Aust + FE portfolio	**0.10**	**6.21**	**0.80**	**1.04**	**0.58**	**3.68**	**0.16**	**0.02**
Other Europe (Excluding-EU) Developed								
Switzerland	0.10	4.77	0.75	0.75	0.45	3.14	0.14	0.02
Norway	0.31	8.42	0.72	1.26	0.90	5.84	0.15	0.04
Israel	0.33	7.48	0.55	0.86	0.73	6.23	0.12	0.04
Luxemburg	0.14	7.08	0.58	0.85	0.54	5.78	0.09	0.02
Europe-dev portfolio	**0.14**	**4.95**	**0.79**	**0.82**	**0.52**	**3.01**	**0.17**	**0.03**
Emerging Markets Far East + South Africa								
India	0.74	10.50	0.57	1.24	1.32	8.66	0.15	0.07
Taiwan	−0.71	8.40	0.55	0.97	−0.26	7.00	−0.04	−0.08
South Africa	0.58	8.31	0.63	1.08	1.09	6.49	0.17	0.07
Malaysia	0.20	5.68	0.43	0.51	0.44	5.11	0.09	0.03
Indonesia	−0.61	16.42	0.22	0.76	−0.26	16.01	−0.02	−0.04
Thailand	−0.15	9.80	0.55	1.11	0.37	8.20	0.05	−0.02
Philippines	−0.56	7.15	0.43	0.64	−0.26	6.45	−0.04	−0.08

(continued)

TABLE 19.9B

(concluded)

	Monthly Excess Return		Regression on U.S. Returns				Performance	
	Average	SD	Correlation	Beta	Alpha	Resid SD	Info ratio	Sharpe
Pakistan	0.59	10.78	0.11	0.25	0.71	10.71	0.07	0.06
Sri Lanka	0.42	7.52	0.18	0.27	0.55	7.40	0.07	0.06
EM FE SA portfolio	**0.20**	**7.10**	**0.69**	**1.01**	**0.67**	**5.17**	**0.13**	**0.03**
Latin America								
Brazil	1.02	10.65	0.74	1.63	1.79	7.20	0.25	0.10
Mexico	0.58	7.10	0.77	1.13	1.11	4.55	0.24	0.08
Chile	0.43	5.87	0.65	0.79	0.80	4.46	0.18	0.07
Colombia	1.15	8.36	0.43	0.74	1.50	7.57	0.20	0.14
Peru	0.74	6.12	0.32	0.40	0.93	5.81	0.16	0.12
Argentina	−0.54	8.99	0.41	0.77	−0.18	8.20	−0.02	−0.06
Venezuela	0.14	11.11	0.14	0.33	0.29	11.00	0.03	0.01
EM-LA portfolio	**0.80**	**7.83**	**0.78**	**1.27**	**1.39**	**4.90**	**0.28**	**0.10**
Europe								
Russia	1.27	10.76	0.58	1.29	1.87	8.78	0.21	0.12
Turkey	0.11	16.57	0.62	2.13	1.11	13.04	0.08	0.01
Poland	0.25	9.42	0.59	1.16	0.79	7.59	0.10	0.03
Czech	1.56	7.59	0.50	0.79	1.92	6.57	0.29	0.20
Hungary	0.26	9.22	0.61	1.18	0.81	7.27	0.11	0.03
Cyprus	−0.13	14.18	0.43	1.28	0.47	12.79	0.04	−0.01
EM Europe portfolio	**0.90**	**9.54**	**0.70**	**1.38**	**1.54**	**6.84**	**0.23**	**0.09**
World minus U.S.	**0.01**	**5.19**	**0.84**	**0.91**	**0.44**	**2.79**	**0.30**	**0.00**
World portfolio	**−0.15**	**4.88**	**0.93**	**0.94**	**0.29**	**1.84**	**0.16**	**−0.03**

It is evident that standard deviations of developed market portfolios are more uniform than those of emerging markets. However, if one considers adding an investment in a country index to an indexed U.S. portfolio, the more relevant risk measure is the country's beta against the U.S. Figure 19.4 therefore ranks and charts the betas of country returns (in U.S. dollars) against the U.S. index. Here we see that a significant number of emerging markets would reduce the risk of an international portfolio composed only of developed markets.

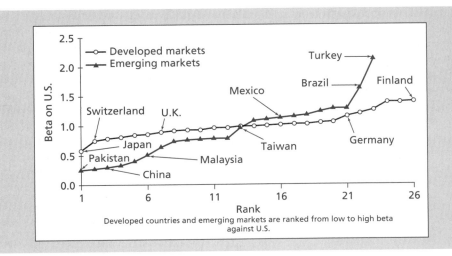

FIGURE 19.4

Beta on U.S. of Developed and Emerging Markets 1999–2008

FIGURE 19.5

Average dollar-denominated excess returns of developed and emerging markets 1999–2008

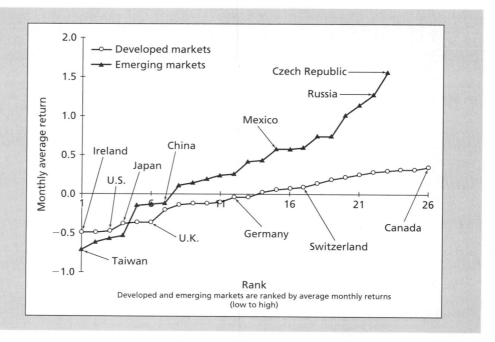

Are Average Returns Higher in Emerging Markets?

Figure 19.5 repeats the previous exercise for average returns. The graph shows that emerging markets generally provided higher average returns over the period 1999–2008 than developed markets. The fact that a number of markets averaged a lower rate than the risk-free alternative for the period (with some average returns even negative) is proof positive that realized returns may fall short of expectations even over fairly long periods. Beyond that, we see that countries with relatively low betas (e.g., Pakistan) earned higher returns than countries with relatively high betas, even the highest-beta country, Turkey.

We shouldn't be too surprised by these results. Remember again that the SD of an average estimated over 120 months (absent serial correlation, which indeed is absent from the data) is given by: SD(10-year average) = SD(1-month average)/$\sqrt{120}$. Thus, the SD of the 10-year average monthly return for Pakistan would be about .98%, and that of Turkey about 1.51%. An outcome of one SD in opposite directions for these two portfolios would span a distance of about 2.5%. The conclusion is one we've noted before: We cannot read too much into realized averages even over periods as long as 10 years.

Given this imprecision, the question to be asked is: "Can we learn anything from these data about the risk-return trade-off in international investing?" Here, the answer is more encouraging. Table 19.10 presents several statistics on risk and return for our sample of 49 countries. The first row presents average monthly returns, standard deviation of monthly returns, beta against the U.S. index, and total capitalization for the U.S. stock market. The second row presents the averages of these statistics for the sample of 49 country markets, and the third row presents the cross-country standard deviation of each statistic. Finally, the last row contains regression estimates of the average monthly return for each country as a function of that country's standard deviation, beta against the U.S., and logarithm of market capitalization.[4] There is considerable noise in the relationship: The correlation coefficient between actual average monthly returns and the prediction of the regression equation is low (.18), and the coefficients are not statistically significant. This might have been expected from a turbulent period such as 1999–2008. The results are nevertheless economically interesting. The coefficient on

---

[4]We focus on the logarithm of market size. Using the logarithm of a variable (here, market capitalization), implies that the percent change (not the dollar change) in capitalization affects a "dependent" variable (here, average monthly returns).

TABLE 19.10

Cross-section country-return statistics and coefficients of regression of monthly returns on SD, beta, and ln (capitalization)

| | Average Monthly Return | SD of Monthly Return | Beta on U.S. | Capitalization | |
				Log of Capitalization	($ Billion)
U.S.	−.47	4.81	1	16.08	9,607,520
Simple average of all countries	.14	8.06	.96	11.97	570,300
Standard deviation across countries	.49	2.60	.35	1.62	1,437,774
Regression coefficients explaining monthly returns*		−0.02	.15	−0.06	

*Correlation coefficient between predicted and actual average monthly returns = .18; Intercept = .88; n = 49.

beta is .15, implying that the risk premium attributable to the average beta on the U.S. alone, .96, would raise a country excess monthly return by .96 × .15 = .14, or 1.7% annually.

The coefficient on size is −.06, consistent with empirical findings of a "size effect" around the world, which conclude that market capitalization is an important variable that predicts lower average returns. Cross-country returns also suggest that investors bid up security prices in markets with better transparency, regulation, and business-law enforcement; they apparently are willing to accept lower risk premiums in these "high-quality" markets. Since transparency, regulation, and law enforcement are all empirically associated with high market capitalization, we can expect the latter to be associated with negative average returns. Indeed, the −.06 regression coefficient on market capitalization implies that a one-standard-deviation increase in capitalization is associated with a decrease in average return of .1% per month.

Finally, the coefficient on standard deviation is also negative, −.02. On its face, the inverse relation between returns and volatility is surprising. It may indicate that once we control for systematic risk, total variability does not add to expected return. Additionally, the correlation coefficient between country capitalization and return standard deviation is quite high, .38, suggesting difficulty in separating the two effects. Perhaps lower standard deviations are also associated with some of the same "market quality" indicators that drive up values and drive down expected returns. We will revisit this issue when we observe performance of various portfolios of country indexes.

Is Exchange Rate Risk Important in International Portfolios?

Table 19.3 revealed that changes in exchange rates are not highly correlated across countries. This suggests that when international portfolios are well diversified, the exchange rate component of overall risk will be effectively diminished. Another feature that would render exchange rate risk diversifiable is low correlation between changes in exchange rates and country stock returns in local currencies.

In Figures 19.6–19.8 we compare results for SD, beta coefficients, and correlation with U.S. stock returns using dollar and local-currency returns. These graphs show that local currency SDs (Figure 19.6) are nearly identical to SDs of dollar-denominated returns, indicating little presence of exchange rate risk. Beta coefficients (Figure 19.7) are also only very slightly lower for local currency returns.

These results are consistent with the almost identical correlations of country returns with U.S. returns in U.S. dollars and in local currency returns as documented in Figure 19.8.

Hedging currency risk when investing internationally is often undertaken to reduce overall portfolio risk. However, the decision of whether to hedge foreign currencies in an internationally diversified portfolio can also be made as part of active management. If a portfolio manager believes the U.S. dollar is, say, overvalued against a given currency, then hedging the exposure to that currency would, if correct, enhance the portfolio return in U.S dollars. The potential

632

FIGURE 19.6

Standard deviation of investments across the globe in U.S. dollars vs. local currency, 1999–2008

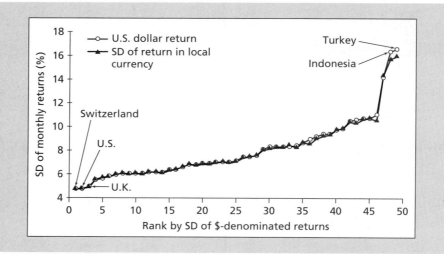

FIGURE 19.7

Beta against U.S. measuring returns in U.S. dollars vs. local currency, 1999–2008

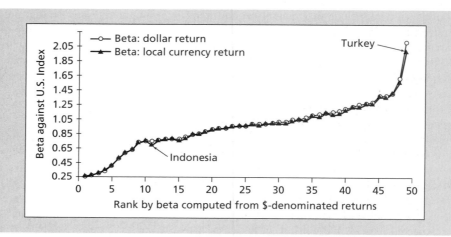

FIGURE 19.8

Correlation of returns with U.S. market, measuring returns in U.S. dollars and in local currency, 1999–2008

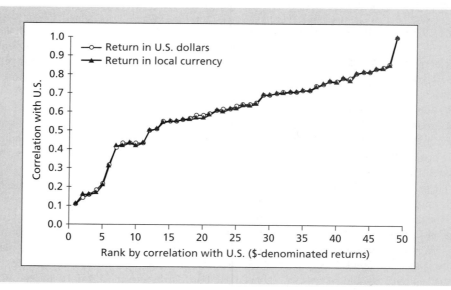

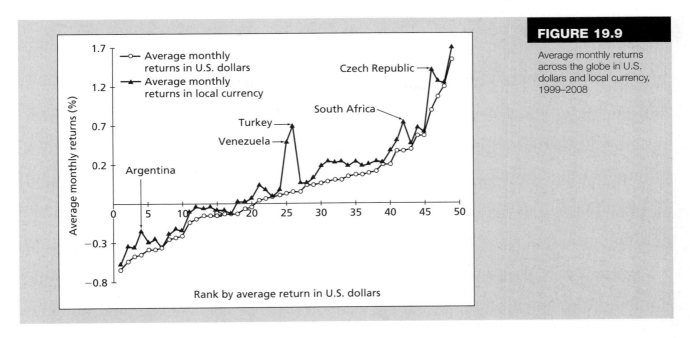

FIGURE 19.9

Average monthly returns across the globe in U.S. dollars and local currency, 1999–2008

gain from this decision depends on the weight of that currency in the overall portfolio. Such a decision applied to investments in only one country would have a small effect on overall risk. But what if the manager estimates that the dollar is generally overvalued against most or all currencies? In this case, hedging the entire exposure would constitute a bet with significant effect on total risk. At the same time, if the decision is correct, such a large position can provide handsome gains.

Figure 19.9 suggests that in 1999 the dollar was indeed overvalued, as over the following 10 years, almost all hedged country returns (that is, returns in local currency) outperformed unhedged returns (returns in U.S. dollars), in many instances by a wide margin. This widespread oversight highlights how difficult it is to forecast currency returns.

Benefits from International Diversification

Table 19.11 presents correlations between returns on stock and long-term bond portfolios in various countries. Panel A shows correlation of returns in U.S. dollars, that is, returns to a U.S. investor when currency risk is not hedged. Panel B shows correlation of returns in local currencies, that is, returns to a U.S. investor when the exchange risk is hedged. As noted earlier, the correlation coefficients of the hedged (local currency) and unhedged (U.S. dollar) returns are very similar, suggesting that hedging currencies is not a significant issue in diversifying internationally.

The correlation coefficients between a stock index of one country and bond portfolios of another are very low, implying that income portfolios that are balanced between stocks and bonds would greatly benefit from international diversification. The correlation among unhedged stock portfolios of the countries in Table 19.11A is much higher, in the range of .40 (Japan–Germany) to .94 (France–Germany). These correlation coefficients are much higher than conventional wisdom; they suggest that cross-border correlation of stock indexes has been increasing. For another, independent example, Table 19.12 shows the correlation of various country indexes with U.S. stocks using monthly excess returns over the period 1970–1989, next to the same coefficients estimated over 1999–2008. The marked increase in correlation with 17 stock indexes and the world portfolio is uniform.

These results raise the question of whether the increase in correlation is an artifact of the sample period or a result of globalization and increased capital market integration that would be expected to increase cross-border correlation. The fact that we find the increase in correlation

TABLE 19.11

Correlations for asset returns; unhedged and hedged currencies

A. Correlation of Monthly Asset Return 1999–2003 in $U.S. (unhedged currencies)

	Stocks							Bonds						
	U.S.	Germany	U.K.	Japan	Australia	Canada	France	U.S.	Germany	U.K.	Japan	Australia	Canada	France
Stocks														
U.S.	1.00													
Germany	0.77	1.00												
U.K.	0.84	0.85	1.00											
Japan	0.54	0.40	0.52	1.00										
Australia	0.76	0.72	0.77	0.53	1.00									
Canada	0.82	0.77	0.77	0.55	0.75	1.00								
France	0.75	0.94	0.88	0.46	0.69	0.78	1.00							
Bonds														
U.S.	−0.10	−0.07	−0.12	0.07	−0.19	0.00	−0.03	1.00						
Germany	−0.27	−0.20	−0.29	−0.27	−0.26	−0.19	−0.20	0.66	1.00					
U.K.	−0.19	−0.09	−0.19	−0.09	−0.25	−0.10	−0.09	0.80	0.85	1.00				
Japan	−0.08	−0.13	−0.06	0.01	−0.11	−0.05	−0.07	0.75	0.40	0.56	1.00			
Australia	−0.22	−0.09	−0.19	−0.10	−0.29	0.00	−0.09	0.78	0.71	0.81	0.51	1.00		
Canada	−0.17	−0.13	−0.21	−0.10	−0.23	−0.05	−0.11	0.88	0.77	0.77	0.55	0.80	1.00	
France	−0.28	−0.20	−0.30	−0.28	−0.25	−0.18	−0.21	0.66	0.99	0.83	0.39	0.68	0.77	1.00

B. Correlation of Monthly Asset Return 1999–2003 in $U.S. (hedged currencies)

	Stocks							Bonds						
	U.S.	Germany	U.K.	Japan	Australia	Canada	France	U.S.	Germany	U.K.	Japan	Australia	Canada	France
Stocks														
U.S.	1.00													
Germany	0.79	1.00												
U.K.	0.84	0.82	1.00											
Japan	0.55	0.46	0.46	1.00										
Australia	0.74	0.74	0.75	0.48	1.00									
Canada	0.79	0.75	0.74	0.52	0.69	1.00								
France	0.79	0.95	0.86	0.51	0.71	0.78	1.00							
Bonds														
U.S.	−0.10	0.00	−0.08	0.00	−0.04	0.07	0.05	1.00						
Germany	−0.25	−0.17	−0.23	−0.31	−0.16	−0.11	−0.15	0.75	1.00					
U.K.	−0.18	−0.09	−0.16	−0.16	−0.14	−0.01	−0.06	0.87	0.89	1.00				
Japan	−0.06	0.00	0.02	0.01	0.04	0.04	0.07	0.76	0.47	0.61	1.00			
Australia	−0.16	−0.05	−0.14	−0.13	−0.13	0.08	−0.01	0.88	0.83	0.91	0.58	1.00		
Canada	−0.15	−0.07	−0.11	−0.14	−0.08	0.01	−0.02	0.91	0.87	0.86	0.59	0.87	1.00	
France	−0.25	−0.16	−0.22	−0.30	−0.14	−0.10	−0.15	0.74	0.99	0.87	0.47	0.80	0.87	1.00

DANCING IN STEP

Individual stock markets are increasingly being driven by global rather than local factors. But why do national markets not have minds of their own? They did have once.

Traditionally, one way that investors sought to reduce risk was by diversifying overseas: when American shares slumped, the loss there would be offset by a gain in, say, European shares. That, at any rate, was the theory. In recent years, however, stock markets seem to have moved more closely in step with one another. The correlation between changes in American and European share prices has risen from 0.4 in the mid-1990s to 0.8 last year.

The health of a market's home economy may matter less than it used to for a number of reasons. First, the scrapping of controls on capital (combined with more efficient trading systems) has increased cross-border trading of shares, creating something closer to a global equity market. Second, it has become increasingly common for big companies to be listed on more than one market. Third, as a result of the wave of cross-border mergers and acquisitions, overseas profits

account for a bigger slice of many companies' overall profits—high-tech firms are especially global in their reach. And finally, the Internet has made it easier for investors to get information on foreign firms. So firms in the same industry, but in different economies, are valued on a similar basis.

By breaking down movements in share prices into global effects, country-specific effects, and firm-specific effects, a new study by economists at the IMF tries to find out what percentage of a stock's performance is due to global rather than country factors. The model distinguishes between two kinds of global factors: the global business cycle and global-industry effects, which similarly influence firms in the same sector but in different countries.

The study finds that there has indeed been a big increase in the importance of global factors—of both kinds—in explaining movements in share prices since the mid-1990s.

SOURCE: Abridged from *The Economist,* March 22, 2001. Copyright © 2001 The Economist Newspaper Group, Inc. Reprinted with permission. Further reproduction prohibited. **www.economist.com.**

across the board suggests that globalization and market integration are the more plausible cause, as discussed in the nearby box. Recent research indicates that industry factors provide the largest impetus to the increase in cross-country correlation. This suggests that as countries diversify their industry mix, their correlations with other country stock indexes will increase. As a result, investors who diversify across industries within a particular country may find smaller benefits from international diversification.

TABLE 19.12	Monthly Excess Return in U.S. Dollars	
Correlation of U.S. equity returns with country equity returns	**1999—2008**	**1970—1989**
World	.93	.86
United Kingdom	.86	.49
Canada	.81	.72
Sweden	.82	.38
Germany	.84	.33
Australia	.78	.47
France	.83	.42
Netherlands	.82	.56
Hong Kong	.70	.29
Denmark	.77	.33
Spain	.78	.25
Norway	.72	.44
Switzerland	.75	.49
Italy	.72	.22
Japan	.51	.27
Belgium	.71	.41
Austria	.64	.12

Source: 1999–2008: Authors' calculations using data from Datastream; 1970–1989: Campbell R. Harvey, "The World Price of Covariance Risk," *Journal of Finance* 46 (March 1991), issue 1, pp. 111–158.

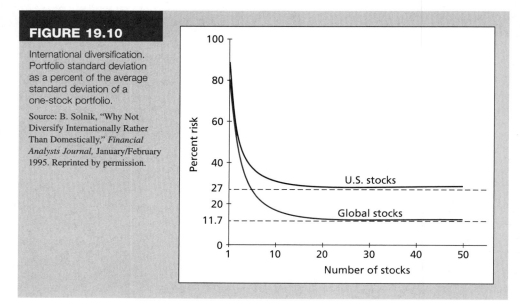

The observed high correlation across markets brings into question the conventional wisdom of large diversification benefits from international investing. This conventional wisdom is depicted in Figure 19.10, which is based on data for the period 1961–1975. Figure 19.10 suggests that international diversification can reduce the standard deviation of a domestic portfolio by as much as half (from about 27% to about 12%). This improvement may well be exaggerated if correlation across markets has markedly increased as data from recent years suggest.

Misleading Representation of Diversification Benefits

The baseline technique for constructing efficient portfolios is the efficient frontier. A useful efficient frontier is constructed from *expected* returns and an estimate of the covariance matrix of returns. This frontier, combined with cash assets, generates the capital allocation line—the set of efficient complete portfolios, as elaborated in Chapters 6 and 7. The benefit from this efficient diversification is reflected in the curvature of the efficient frontier. Other things equal, the lower the covariance across stocks, the greater the curvature of the efficient frontier and the greater the risk reduction for any desired *expected* return. So far, so good. But suppose we replace *expected* returns with *realized* average returns from a sample period to construct an efficient frontier; what is the possible use of this graph?

The ex-post efficient frontier (derived from realized returns) describes the portfolio choices of only one investor—the clairvoyant who actually expected the precise averages of realized returns on all assets and estimated a covariance matrix that materialized, precisely, in the actual realizations of the sample period returns on all assets. Obviously, we are talking about a slim to empty set of investors. For all other, less-than-clairvoyant investors such a frontier may have value only for purposes of performance evaluation.

In the world of volatile stocks, some stocks are bound to realize large, *unexpected* average returns. This will be reflected in ex-post efficient frontiers of enormous "potential." They will, however, suggest exaggerated diversification benefits. Such (elusive) potential was enumerated in Chapter 18 on performance evaluation. It has no use as a tool to discuss the potential for future investments for real-life investors.

Realistic Benefits from International Diversification

While recent realized returns can be highly misleading estimates of expected future returns, they are more useful for measuring prospective risk. There are two compelling reasons for this. First, market efficiency (or even near efficiency) implies that stock price movements will be impossible to predict with any accuracy, but no such implication applies to risk measures. Second, it is a statistical fact that errors in estimates of standard deviation and correlation from realized data are of a lower order of magnitude than estimates of expected returns. For these reasons, using risk estimates from realized returns does not exaggerate as much the potential benefits from diversification.

Figure 19.11 shows the efficient frontier using realized average monthly returns on the stock indexes of the 25 developed countries, with and without short sales. Even when the

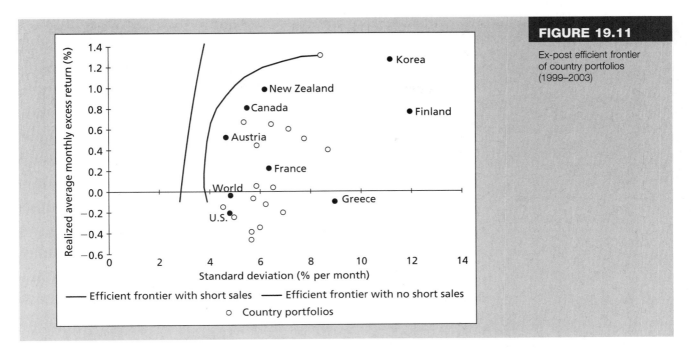

FIGURE 19.11

Ex-post efficient frontier
of country portfolios
(1999–2003)

(ex-post) efficient frontier is constrained to preclude short sales, it greatly exaggerates the benefits from diversification. Unfortunately, such misleading efficient frontiers are presented in many articles and texts on the benefits of diversification.

A more reasonable description of diversification is achievable only when we input reasonable equilibrium expected returns. Absent superior information, such expected returns are best based on appropriate risk measures of the assets. The capital asset pricing model (CAPM) suggests using the beta of the stock against the world portfolio. To generate expected excess returns (over the risk-free rate) for all assets, we specify the expected excess return on the world portfolio. We obtain the expected excess return on each asset by multiplying the beta of the asset by the world portfolio expected excess return. This procedure presupposes that the world portfolio will lie on the efficient frontier, at the point of tangency with the world capital market line. The curvature of the efficient frontier will not be affected by the estimate of the world portfolio excess return. A higher estimate will shift the curve upward. The capital market line will have a steeper slope.

We perform this procedure with risk measures estimated from actual returns, and further impose the likely applicable constraint on short sales. We use the betas to compute the expected return on individual markets, assuming the expected excess return on the world portfolio is either .3% or .6% per month. These excess returns are in the range of averages realized over the period 1999–2003, and in line with the average return over the previous 50 years. Varying this estimate would not qualitatively affect the results shown in Figures 19.12A and 19.12B. The figures reveal quite modest benefits for U.S. investors from international diversification using only developed markets. Incorporating emerging markets would slightly increase these benefits.

Are Benefits from International Diversification Preserved in Bear Markets?

Some studies (e.g., Longin and Solnik, 1995, or Jacquier and Marcus, 2001) suggest that correlation in country portfolio returns increases during periods of turbulence in capital markets. If so, benefits from diversification would be lost exactly when they are needed the most. For example, a study by Roll (1988) of the crash of October 1987 shows that all 23 country indexes studied declined over the crash period of October 12–26. This correlation is reflected in the highly synchronized movements of regional indexes depicted in Figure 19.13A. Roll

FIGURE 19.12

Efficient frontier of country portfolios.

A: World expected excess return = .3% per month
B: World expected excess return = .6% per month

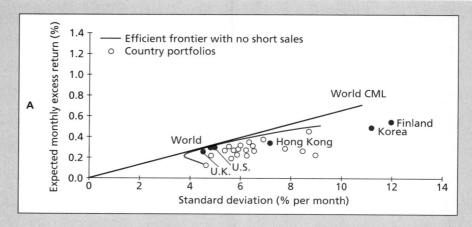

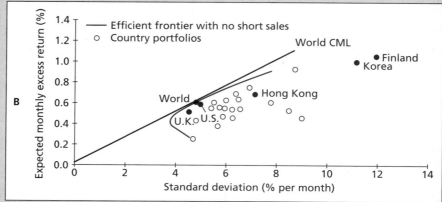

FIGURE 19.13A

Regional indexes around the crash, October 14–October 26, 1987

Source: From Richard Roll, "The International Crash of October 1987," *Financial Analysts Journal*, September–October 1988. Copyright 1998, CFA Institute. Reproduced and republished from *Financial Analysts Journal* with permission from the CFA Institute. All Rights Reserved.

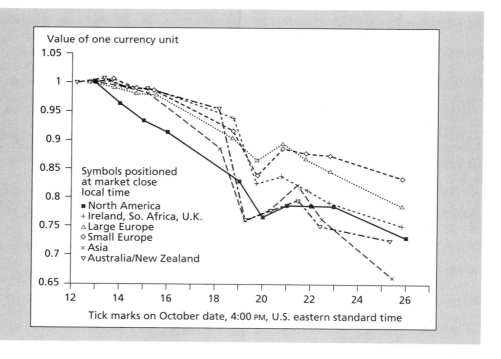

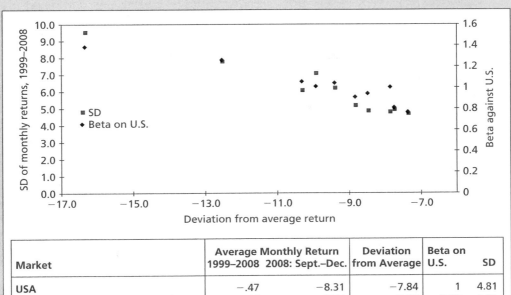

Market	Average Monthly Return 1999–2008	2008: Sept.–Dec.	Deviation from Average	Beta on U.S.	SD
USA	−.47	−8.31	−7.84	1	4.81
World largest six (non–U.S.) markets	−.16	−7.51	−7.35	0.77	4.71
EU developed markets	−.05	−10.34	−10.29	1.06	6.08
Other Europe developed markets	.14	−7.59	−7.73	0.82	4.95
Australia + Far East	.10	−9.29	−9.38	1.04	6.21
Emerging Far East + South Africa	.20	−9.70	−9.90	1.01	7.10
Emerging Latin America	.80	−11.72	−12.52	1.27	7.83
Emerging markets in Europe	.90	−15.43	−16.32	1.38	9.54
World minus U.S. (48 countries by cap)	.01	−8.79	−8.81	0.91	5.19
World portfolio (by country cap)	−.15	−8.60	−8.45	0.94	4.88

FIGURE 19.13B

Beta and SD of portfolios against deviation of monthly return over Sept–Dec. 2008 from average over 1999–2008

Source: Authors' Calculations.

found that the beta of a country index on the world index (estimated prior to the crash) was the best predictor of that index's response to the October crash of the U.S. stock market. This suggests a common factor underlying the movement of stocks around the world. This model predicts that a macroeconomic shock would affect all countries and that diversification can mitigate only country-specific events.

The 2008 crash of stock markets around the world allows us to test Roll's prediction. The data in Figure 19.13B include average monthly rates of return for both the 10-year period 1999–2008 and the crisis period corresponding to the last four months of 2008, as well as the beta on the U.S. market and monthly standard deviation for several portfolios. The graph shows that both beta against the U.S. and the country-index standard deviation explain the difference between crisis period returns and overall period averages. Market behavior during the 1987 crisis, that is, larger correlations in extreme bad times, repeated itself in the crisis of 2008, vindicating Roll's prediction.

19.4 How to Go about International Diversification and the Benefit We Can Expect

So far, we have dissected our sample of recent returns for 1999–2008 for clues about the benefits from international diversification. But all of this tells us little about how a U.S. investor might actually implement this diversification. We begin with the case of a passive investor.

As noted earlier, scholars have indirectly questioned passive as well as active investors for their apparently home country–biased portfolios. A certain degree of home bias may be justified on theoretical grounds. Investor consumption consists in large part of goods and services produced in the home country, and prices of these goods and services are correlated with home-country stock prices. To illustrate, consider an investor who lives in Silicon Valley. Prices of homes and other big-ticket items will be correlated with the success of local corporations. These prices therefore can be partially hedged by investing in the equity of local firms.[5] Moreover, "keeping up with the Joneses" of Silicon Valley also calls for tilting your portfolio toward local investment opportunities to keep your wealth aligned with that of your neighbors'.

On top of these considerations, moving from a U.S.-only to a World portfolio would actually have increased standard deviation of monthly returns over 1999–2008 from 4.81% to 4.86%! This surprising result is due to the fact that the U.S. ranked second lowest in standard deviation, and correlations across countries are quite high. This means that in this period a completely passive investment, that is, investing in all countries by capitalization shares, would not have lowered risk at all. We have already seen that hedging currencies would not have changed the picture in a material way. Most importantly, recent crises suggest that risk reduction (if any) by international diversification breaks down when the U.S. stock market crashes. We are faced with the conclusion that reducing risk through international diversification requires further analytical work.

Nevertheless, we still expect the World portfolio to be reasonably efficient despite its higher standard deviation. Recall that we hardly expect minimum-variance portfolios to be the efficient choice. Despite their low variance, their expected returns also would be lower. A capitalization-weighted portfolio of all World stocks may not be on the (unobserved) efficient frontier, but it may be close enough to outperform the minimum-variance portfolio. In the end, however, a World capitalization-weighted portfolio may be too cumbersome for a passive investor to hold. A practical solution would be a simple low-variance portfolio that combines the U.S. with other markets to improve the diversification provided by the U.S. index alone.

Choosing a Practical Internationally Diversified Portfolio

Figure 19.14 presents a set of alternative strategies from which investors can choose the most practical, yet promising solution. The lowest-variance alternatives are achieved by diversifying into all countries. Checking first the (impractical) solution of allowing short sales, the minimum-variance portfolio provides a monthly standard deviation as low as 1.9%, considerably below the 4.81% standard deviation for the U.S.-only portfolio. For a more practical solution we repeat this calculation with a no-short-sales constraint that eliminates 39 foreign markets from the list. We end up with a portfolio of 10 countries with a standard deviation of 3.44%, still a large improvement over the U.S.-only portfolio. However, most investors would reject this portfolio since the position in the U.S. index is only 2%, while those of Malaysia and Sri Lanka are 18% and 13%, respectively.

The two remaining alternatives shown in Figure 19.14 diversify the U.S. portfolio using (1) index portfolios of large markets (44%) and Australia plus the Far East (18%), or (2) just two large markets, Japan (31%) and China (16%). As it often happens, the more attractive second alternative (with a larger position in the U.S. and a smaller number of foreign indexes involved) also has a larger standard deviation of 4.46%, not a great improvement over the U.S.-only solution. These results suggest that passive international diversification is a lot less effective than it is often made out to be.

Active Management and International Diversification

As we mentioned at the outset, the great potential of adding foreign stocks and bonds to the investable universe is obvious. The likelihood of identifying a diversified set of mispriced securities directly increases with the number of analyzed securities.

[5]For a formal analysis of this idea, see DeMarzo (2005).

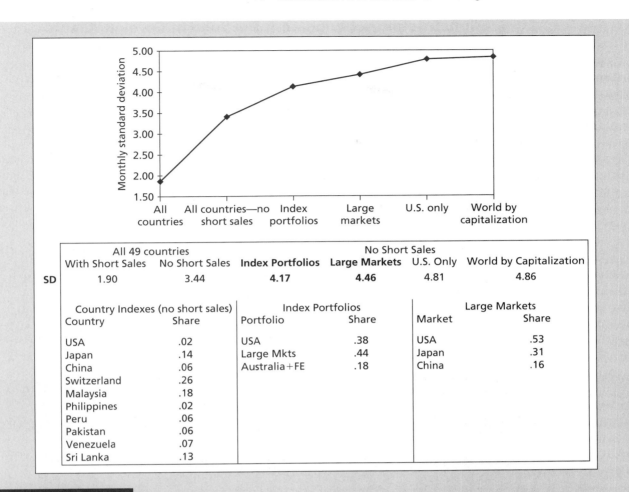

FIGURE 19.14

Portfolio standard deviation; countries ordered by beta and by market capitalization, indexes ordered by market capitalization

The hierarchy of active management entails two levels. At the ground level, security selection and asset allocation (plus currency hedging as deemed optimal) within each market would lead to a country portfolio superior to the passive index. At the next level, an international portfolio would optimize allocation across country portfolios. Take a second look at Table 19.9B, and observe the large values of alpha and information ratios. Analysis leading to even very noisy forecasts of these values would result in a portfolio of greatly superior performance.

19.5   International Investing and Performance Attribution

The benefits from international diversification may be modest for passive investors but for active managers international investing offers greater opportunities. International investing calls for specialization in additional fields of analysis: currency, country and worldwide industry, as well as a greater universe for stock selection.

Constructing a Benchmark Portfolio of Foreign Assets

European, Australian, Far East (EAFE) index

A widely used index of non-U.S. stocks computed by Morgan Stanley.

Active international investing, as well as passive, requires a benchmark portfolio (the bogey). One widely used index of non-U.S. stocks is the **European, Australian, Far East (EAFE) index** computed by Morgan Stanley. Additional indexes of world equity performance are published by Capital International Indices, Salomon Brothers, Credit Suisse First Boston, and Goldman Sachs. Portfolios designed to mirror or even replicate the country, currency, and company representation of these indexes would be the obvious generalization of the purely domestic passive equity strategy.

An issue that sometimes arises in the international context is the appropriateness of market-capitalization weighting schemes in the construction of international indexes. Capitalization weighting is far and away the most common approach. However, some argue that it might not be the best weighting scheme in an international context. This is in part because different countries have differing proportions of their corporate sector organized as publicly traded firms.

Table 19.13 shows 1998 and 2007 data for market capitalization weights versus GDP weights for countries in the EAFE index. These data reveal substantial disparities between the relative sizes of market capitalization and GDP. Since market capitalization is a stock figure (the value of equity at one point in time), while GDP is a flow figure (production of goods and services during the entire year), we expect capitalization to be more volatile and the relative shares to be more variable over time. Some discrepancies are persistent, however.

TABLE 19.13

Weighting schemes for EAFE countries

| Country | 2007 | | 1998 | |
	% of EAFE Market Capitalization	% of EAFE GDP	% of EAFE Market Capitalization	% of EAFE GDP
Japan	16.1	14.6	26.8%	29.1%
United Kingdom	14.0	9.4	22.4	10.5
France	9.7	8.7	7.2	10.7
Germany	7.6	11.1	8.9	15.8
Switzerland	4.7	1.4	6.0	1.9
Italy	4.0	7.0	3.9	8.8
Netherlands	2.9	2.6	5.9	2.9
Hong Kong	6.3	0.7	4.0	1.2
Australia	4.5	3.0	2.9	2.7
Spain	3.8	4.8	2.7	4.3
Sweden	1.9	1.5	2.4	1.8
Finland	1.3	0.8	0.7	1.0
Belgium	1.3	1.5	1.4	1.8
Singapore	1.5	0.5	1.1	0.6
Denmark	0.9	1.0	0.9	1.3
Norway	1.3	1.3	0.6	1.1
Ireland	0.5	0.9	0.5	0.6
Greece	0.9	1.0	0.3	0.9
Portugal	0.5	0.7	0.6	0.8
Austria	0.8	1.2	0.4	1.6
New Zealand	0.2	0.4	0.4	0.4

Source: Datastream database.

MSCI ANNOUNCES SOME LONG-AWAITED INDEX CHANGES

Old-fashioned investors may be inclined to grumble as they assess the impact of the decision by Morgan Stanley Capital International (MSCI, a leading provider of equity indices) to overhaul the way it treats the companies it tracks. The share prices of some will rise, and others will fall, not because of any change in the companies' profitability, but thanks simply to a new weighting methodology.

MSCI has decided to weight companies in its indices according to the number of shares that are freely tradable rather than their total market capitalization. It will also increase the share of each market that it covers, from 60% of the market's capitalization to 85% of a free-float adjusted capitalization, meaning that more and smaller companies will go in. Because a lot of money now simply mimics the shares held in various MSCI indices, a group of "index-tracker" fund managers will now be obliged to buy and sell the same shares at much the same time. Billions of dollars could shift between and within markets.

In MSCI's new world, the stockmarkets of Britain and America gain, largely at the expense of Japan, France and Germany, where more substantial chunks of companies tend to be held by governments, founding families or other companies. Emerging markets will be hit as well: the total value of the Emerging Markets Free Index, which represents 26 emerging markets, will fall by two-fifths, from $950 billion to $560 billion.

MSCI is the last big index provider to have made a shift to weighting according to free-float, after its main rivals, FTSE International, Standard & Poor's and Dow Jones. The aim is to tie a company's weight directly to the number of shares that investors can buy. Under the old system, the prices of some shares were pushed up because investors could not buy enough of them to reach the required index weight.

SOURCE: Excerpted from "Shares Indices Reweighted: Flotsam and Jetsam: MSCI Announces Some Long-awaited Index Changes," *The Economist,* May 26, 2001. © 2001 The Economist Newspaper Group, Inc. Reprinted with permission. Further reproduction is prohibited. **www.economist.com.**

For example, Hong Kong's share of capitalization is about eight times its share of GDP, while Germany's share of capitalization is much less than its share of GDP. These disparities indicate that a greater proportion of economic activity is conducted by publicly traded firms in Hong Kong than in Germany.

Some argue that it would be more appropriate to weight international indexes by GDP rather than market capitalization. The justification for this view is that an internationally diversified portfolio should purchase shares in proportion to the broad asset base of each country, and GDP might be a better measure of the importance of a country in the international economy than the value of its outstanding stocks. Others have even suggested weights proportional to the import share of various countries. The argument is that investors who wish to hedge the price of imported goods might choose to hold securities in foreign firms in proportion to the goods imported from those countries. The nearby box discusses recent changes in the most popular international stock indexes, those of MSCI.

Performance Attribution

We can measure the contribution of each of these factors following a manner similar to the performance attribution techniques introduced in Chapter 18.

1. **Currency selection** measures the contribution to total portfolio performance attributable to exchange rate fluctuations relative to the investor's benchmark currency, which we will take to be the U.S. dollar. We might use a benchmark like the EAFE index to compare a portfolio's currency selection for a particular period to a passive benchmark. EAFE currency selection would be computed as the weighted average of the currency appreciation of the currencies represented in the EAFE portfolio using as weights the fraction of the EAFE portfolio invested in each currency.

2. **Country selection** measures the contribution to performance attributable to investing in the better-performing stock markets of the world. It can be measured as the weighted

currency selection

Asset allocation in which the investor chooses among investments denominated in different currencies.

country selection

Asset allocation in which the investor chooses among investments in different countries.

average of the equity *index* returns of each country using as weights the share of the manager's portfolio in each country. We use index returns to abstract from the effect of security selection within countries. To measure a manager's contribution relative to a passive strategy, we might compare country selection to the weighted average across countries of equity index returns using as weights the share of the EAFE portfolio in each country.

stock selection

Choice of specific stocks within a country's equity market.

cash/bond selection

Choice between money market versus longer term bonds.

3. **Stock selection** ability may, as in Chapter 18, be measured as the weighted average of equity returns *in excess of the equity index* in each country. Here, we would use local currency returns and use as weights the investments in each country.

4. **Cash/bond selection** may be measured as the excess return derived from weighting bonds and bills differently from some benchmark weights.

Table 19.14 gives an example of how to measure the contribution of the decisions an international portfolio manager might make.

CONCEPT
check   **19.4**

Using the data in Table 19.15, compute the manager's country and currency selection if portfolio weights had been 40% in Europe, 20% in Australia, and 40% in the Far East.

TABLE 19.14

Example of performance attribution: international

	EAFE Weight	Return on Equity Index	Currency Appreciation $E_1/E_0 - 1$	Manager's Weight	Manager's Return
Europe	.30	10%	10%	.35	8%
Australia	.10	5	−10	.10	7
Far East	.60	15	30	.55	18

Overall performance (dollar return = return on index + currency appreciation)

EAFE: .30(10 + 10) + .10(5 − 10) + .60(15 + 30) = 32.5%
Manager: .35(8 + 10) + .10(7 − 10) + .55(18 + 30) = 32.4%
Loss of .10% relative to EAFE

Currency selection

EAFE: (.30 × 10%) + (.10 × (−10%)) + (.60 × 30%) = 20% appreciation
Manager: (.35 × 10%) + (.10 × (−10%)) + (.55 × 30%) = 19% appreciation
Loss of 1% relative to EAFE

Country selection

EAFE: (.30 × 10%) + (.10 × 5%) + (.60 × 15%) = 12.5%
Manager: (.35 × 10%) + (.10 × 5%) + (.55 × 15%) = 12.25%
Loss of 0.25% relative to EAFE

Stock selection

                (8% − 10%) × 0.35 + (7% − 5%) × .10 + (18% − 15%) × .55 = 1.15%
Contribution of 1.15% relative to EAFE

Sum of attributions (equal to overall performance)

Currency (−1%) + country (−.25%) + selection (1.15%) = −.10%

This Excel model provides an efficient frontier analysis similar to that in Chapter 6. In Chapter 6 the frontier was based on individual securities, whereas this model examines the returns on international exchange-traded funds. Using the model with this return data enables us to analyze the benefits of international diversification.

Please visit us at www.mhhe.com/bkm

	A	B	C	D	E	F	G	H	I
58		Bordered Covariance Matrix for Target Return Portfolio							
59		EWD	EWH	EWI	EWJ	EWL	EWP	EWW	SP 500
60	Weights	.00	.00	0.08	0.38	0.02	.00	.00	0.52
61	.0000	.00	.00	0.00	0.00	0.00	.00	.00	0.00
62	.0000	.00	.00	0.00	0.00	0.00	.00	.00	0.00
63	.0826	.00	.00	4.63	3.21	0.55	.00	.00	7.69
64	.3805	.00	.00	3.21	98.41	1.82	.00	.00	53.79
65	.0171	.00	.00	0.55	1.82	0.14	.00	.00	2.09
66	.0000	.00	.00	0.00	0.00	0.00	.00	.00	0.00
67	.0000	.00	.00	0.00	0.00	0.00	.00	.00	0.00
68	.5198	.00	.00	7.69	53.79	2.09	.00	.00	79.90

SUMMARY

- U.S. assets are only a part of the world portfolio. International capital markets offer important opportunities for portfolio diversification with enhanced risk-return characteristics.
- Exchange rate risk imparts an extra source of uncertainty to investments denominated in foreign currencies. Much of that risk can be hedged in foreign exchange futures or forward markets, but a perfect hedge is not feasible unless the foreign currency rate of return is known.
- Several world market indexes can form a basis for passive international investing. Active international management can be partitioned into currency selection, country selection, stock selection, and cash/bond selection.

KEY TERMS

cash/bond selection, 644
country selection, 643
covered interest arbitrage
  relationship, 619

currency selection, 643
European, Australian, Far
  East (EAFE) index, 642
exchange rate risk, 617

interest rate parity
  relationship, 619
political risk, 621
stock selection, 644

PROBLEM SETS

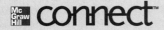

Select problems are available in McGraw-Hill Connect. Please see the packaging options section of the preface for more information.

Basic

For Questions 1–4, answer True or False. Explain your answer.

1. Due to currency risk, dollar-denominated returns of international portfolios will have a higher standard deviation than local currency–denominated returns.
2. The principle of diversification assures us that diversifying a U.S. portfolio internationally will reduce standard deviation.
3. For a passive investor, the minimum-variance portfolio of country indexes is optimal.
4. A currency-hedged foreign-stock portfolio return is the weighted average of the foreign stock returns *in local currency*.

www.mhhe.com/bkm

Intermediate

5. Suppose a U.S. investor wishes to invest in a British firm currently selling for £40 per share. The investor has $10,000 to invest, and the current exchange rate is $2/£.
   a. How many shares can the investor purchase?
   b. Fill in the table below for rates of return after one year in each of the nine scenarios (three possible prices per share in pounds times three possible exchange rates).

Price per Share (£)	Pound-Denominated Return (%)	Dollar-Denominated Return for Year-End Exchange Rate		
		$1.80/£	$2/£	$2.20/£
£35				
£40				
£45				

   c. When is the dollar-denominated return equal to the pound-denominated return?

6. If each of the nine outcomes in Problem 5 is equally likely, find the standard deviation of both the pound- and dollar-denominated rates of return.

7. Now suppose the investor in Problem 5 also sells forward £5,000 at a forward exchange rate of $2.10/£.
   a. Recalculate the dollar-denominated returns for each scenario.
   b. What happens to the standard deviation of the dollar-denominated return? Compare it to both its old value and the standard deviation of the pound-denominated return.

8. Calculate the contribution to total performance from currency, country, and stock selection for the manager in the following table. All exchange rates are expressed as units of foreign currency that can be purchased with one U.S. dollar.

	EAFE Weight	Return on Equity Index	E_1/E_0	Manager's Weight	Manager's Return
Europe	.30	20%	0.9	.35	18%
Australia	.10	15	1.0	.15	20
Far East	.60	25	1.1	.50	20

9. If the current exchange rate is $1.75/£, the one-year forward exchange rate is $1.85/£, and the interest rate on British government bills is 8% per year, what risk-free dollar-denominated return can be locked in by investing in the British bills?

10. If you were to invest $10,000 in the British bills of Problem 5, how would you lock in the dollar-denominated return?

11. Suppose that the spot price of the euro is currently $1.30. The one-year futures price is $1.35. Is the U.S. interest rate higher than the euro rate?

12. a. Suppose the spot price of the British pound is currently $1.50. If the risk-free interest rate on one-year government bonds is 4% in the United States and 3% in the United Kingdom, what must the forward price of the pound be for delivery one year from now?
    b. How could an investor make risk-free arbitrage profits if the forward price were higher than the price you gave in answer to (a)? Give a numerical example.

13. Consider the following information:
    $r_{US} = 5\%$
    $r_{UK} = 7\%$

$E_0 = 2.0$ dollars per pound

$F_0 = \$1.97/\pounds$ (one-year delivery)

where the interest rates are annual yields on U.S. or U.K. bills. Given this information,

a. Where would you lend?

b. Where would you borrow?

c. How could you arbitrage?

Challenge

14. Suppose you forecast the information ratios of the seven international portfolios (as shown in Table 19.9B). Construct the optimal portfolio of the U.S. index with the seven portfolios and assess its performance.

CFA Problems

1. Renée Michaels, CFA, plans to invest $1 million in U.S. government cash equivalents for the next 90 days. Michaels's client has authorized her to use non-U.S. government cash equivalents, but only if the currency risk is hedged to U.S. dollars by using forward currency contracts.

   a. Calculate the U.S. dollar value of the hedged investment at the end of 90 days for each of the two cash equivalents in the table below. Show all calculations.

   b. Briefly explain the theory that best accounts for your results.

   c. Based upon this theory, estimate the implied interest rate for a 90-day U.S. government cash equivalent.

Interest Rates 90-Day Cash Equivalents	
Japanese government	7.6%
Swiss government	8.6

Exchange Rates: Currency Units per U.S. Dollar		
	Spot	90-Day Forward
Japanese yen	133.05	133.47
Swiss franc	1.5260	1.5348

2. John Irish, CFA, is an independent investment adviser who is assisting Alfred Darwin, the head of the Investment Committee of General Technology Corporation, to establish a new pension fund. Darwin asks Irish about international equities and whether the Investment Committee should consider them as an additional asset for the pension fund.

   a. Explain the rationale for including international equities in General's equity portfolio. Identify and describe three relevant considerations in formulating your answer.

   b. List three possible arguments against international equity investment and briefly discuss the significance of each.

   c. To illustrate several aspects of the performance of international securities over time, Irish shows Darwin the accompanying graph of investment results experienced by a U.S. pension fund in the recent past. Compare the performance of the U.S.-dollar and non-U.S.-dollar equity and fixed-income asset categories, and explain the significance of the result of the account performance index relative to the results of the four individual asset class indexes.

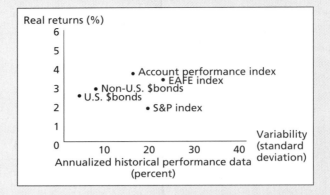

3. You are a U.S. investor considering purchase of one of the following securities. Assume that the currency risk of the Canadian government bond will be hedged, and the six-month discount on Canadian dollar forward contracts is −.75% versus the U.S. dollar.

Bond	Maturity	Coupon	Price
U.S. government	6 months	6.50%	100.00
Canadian government	6 months	7.50%	100.00

Calculate the expected price change required in the Canadian government bond that would result in the two bonds having equal total returns in U.S. dollars over a six-month horizon. Assume that the yield on the U.S. bond is expected to remain unchanged.

4. After much research on the developing economy and capital markets of the country of Otunia, your firm, GAC, has decided to include an investment in the Otunia stock market in its Emerging Markets Commingled Fund. However, GAC has not yet decided whether to invest actively or by indexing. Your opinion on the active versus indexing decision has been solicited. The following is a summary of the research findings:

Otunia's economy is fairly well diversified across agricultural and natural resources, manufacturing (both consumer and durable goods), and a growing finance sector. Transaction costs in securities markets are relatively large in Otunia because of high commissions and government "stamp taxes" on securities trades. Accounting standards and disclosure regulations are quite detailed, resulting in wide public availability of reliable information about companies' financial performance.

Capital flows into and out of Otunia, and foreign ownership of Otunia securities is strictly regulated by an agency of the national government. The settlement procedures under these ownership rules often cause long delays in settling trades made by nonresidents. Senior finance officials in the government are working to deregulate capital flows and foreign ownership, but GAC's political consultant believes that isolationist sentiment may prevent much real progress in the short run.

a. Briefly discuss aspects of the Otunia environment that favor investing actively, and aspects that favor indexing.

b. Recommend whether GAC should invest in Otunia actively or by indexing. Justify your recommendation based on the factors identified in part (*a*).

WEB *master* INTEREST RATE PARITY

A common misconception is that investors can earn excess returns by investing in foreign bonds with higher interest rates than are available in the U.S. Interest rate parity implies that any such interest rate differentials will be offset by premiums or discounts in the forward or futures market for foreign currency.

Interest rates on government bonds in the U.S., U.K., Japan, Germany, Brazil, and Australia can be found at **www.bloomberg.com/markets/rates/index.html.**

Spot exchange rates on international currencies can be found at **www.bloomberg.com/markets/currencies/fxc.html.**

Forward exchange rates on currency futures contracts can be found at **www.cmegroup.com/trading/fx/index.html.**

1. Select one of these countries and record the yield on a short-term government security from the Bloomberg Web site. Also

make note of the U.S. Treasury yield on an instrument with the same maturity.

2. Record the spot exchange rate from the Bloomberg site and the futures contract exchange rate from the CME Web site for the date closest to the maturity of the investment you chose in the previous step.

3. Calculate the rate of return available on the foreign government security, converting the foreign currency transactions into dollars at the current and forward exchange rates.

4. How well does interest rate parity seem to hold? Are there bargains to be found in other currencies? What factors might account for interest-rate parity violation?

SOLUTIONS TO CONCEPT *checks*

19.1. $1 + r(\text{US}) = [(1 + r_f(\text{UK}))] \times (E_1/E_0)$

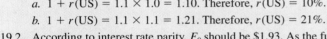

   a. $1 + r(\text{US}) = 1.1 \times 1.0 = 1.10$. Therefore, $r(\text{US}) = 10\%$.

   b. $1 + r(\text{US}) = 1.1 \times 1.1 = 1.21$. Therefore, $r(\text{US}) = 21\%$.

19.2. According to interest rate parity, F_0 should be $1.93. As the futures price is too high, we should reverse the arbitrage strategy just considered.

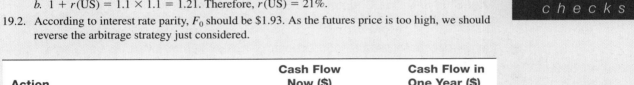

Action	Cash Flow Now ($)	Cash Flow in One Year ($)
Borrow $2 in the United States.	$ 2.00	$-2.00(1.0615)
Convert the borrowed dollars to pounds, and lend in the United Kingdom at a 10% interest rate.	-2.00	$1.10E_1$
Enter a contract to sell 1.10 pounds at a futures price of $1.95/£.	0.00	$1.10(1.95 - E_1)$
Total	$ 0.00	$ 0.022

19.3. You must sell forward the number of pounds you will end up with at the end of the year. This value cannot be known with certainty, however, unless the rate of return of the pound-denominated investment is known.

   a. $10{,}000 \times 1.20 = 12{,}000$ pounds

   b. $10{,}000 \times 1.30 = 13{,}000$ pounds

19.4. *Country selection:*

$$(.40 \times 10\%) + (.20 \times 5\%) + (.40 \times 15\%) = 11\%$$

This is a loss of 1.5% (11% versus 12.5%) relative to the EAFE passive benchmark.

Currency selection:

$$(.40 \times 10\%) + (.20 \times (-10\%)) + (.40 \times 30\%) = 14\%$$

This is a loss of 6% (14% versus 20%) relative to the EAFE benchmark.

Hedge Funds

After Studying This Chapter, You Should Be Able To:

● Identify directional versus nondirectional or market-neutral investment strategies.

● Formulate "pure plays" on seemingly misaligned security prices, and identify the risks that are hedged in these strategies as well as the risks that remain.

● Cite the various difficulties entailed in evaluating hedge fund investment performance.

● Interpret incentive fees charged by hedge funds as implicit options and value them using option-pricing methods.

While mutual funds are still the dominant form of investing in securities markets for most individuals, hedge funds enjoyed far greater growth rates in the last decade. Assets under hedge fund management increased from around $200 billion in 1997 to nearly $2 trillion before declining asset values and hefty withdrawals during the market downturn of 2008 reduced that value to below $1.6 trillion in the latter part of the year. Like mutual funds, hedge funds allow private investors to pool assets to be invested by a fund manager. Unlike mutual funds, however, they are commonly organized as private partnerships and thus not subject to many SEC regulations. They typically are open only to wealthy or institutional investors.

Hedge funds touch on virtually every issue discussed in the earlier chapters of the text, including liquidity, security analysis, market efficiency, portfolio analysis, hedging, and option pricing. For example, these funds often bet on relative mispricing of specific securities, but hedge broad market exposure. This sort of pure "alpha-seeking" behavior requires a procedure for optimally mixing a hedge fund position with a more traditional portfolio. Other funds engage in aggressive market timing; their risk profiles can shift rapidly and substantially, raising difficult questions for performance evaluation. Many hedge funds take extensive derivatives positions. Even those funds that do not trade derivatives charge incentive fees that resemble the payoff to a call option; an option-pricing background therefore is necessary to interpret both hedge fund strategies and costs. In short, hedge funds raise the full range of issues that one might confront in active portfolio management.

We begin with a survey of various hedge fund orientations. We devote considerable attention to the classic "market-neutral" or hedged strategies that historically gave hedge funds their name. We move on to evidence on hedge fund performance, and the difficulties in evaluating that performance. Finally, we consider the implications of their unusual fee structure for investors in and managers of such funds.

Related Web sites for this chapter are available at www.mhhe.com/bkm.

20.1 | Hedge Funds versus Mutual Funds

Like mutual funds, the basic idea behind **hedge funds** is investment pooling. Investors buy shares in these funds, which then invest the pooled assets on their behalf. The net asset value of each share represents the value of the investor's stake in the portfolio. In this regard, hedge funds operate much like mutual funds. However, there are important differences between the two.

hedge fund

A private investment pool, open to wealthy or institutional investors, that is largely exempt from SEC regulation and therefore can pursue more speculative policies than mutual funds.

Transparency   Mutual funds are subject to the Securities Act of 1933 and the Investment Company Act of 1940 (designed to protect unsophisticated investors), which require transparency and predictability of strategy. They periodically must provide the public with information on portfolio composition. In contrast, hedge funds usually are set up as limited liability partnerships, and provide minimal information about portfolio composition and strategy to their investors only.

Investors   Hedge funds traditionally have no more than 100 "sophisticated" investors, in practice usually defined by minimum net worth and income requirements. They do not advertise to the general public, although the recent trend is to market as well to ever-smaller and less sophisticated investors. Minimum investments for some new funds are as low as $25,000, compared to traditional $250,000–$1 million minimums.

Investment Strategies   Mutual funds lay out their general investment approach (e.g., large, value stock orientation versus small-cap growth orientation) in their prospectus. They face pressure to avoid *style drift* (departures from their stated investment orientation), especially given the importance of retirement funds such as 401(k) plans to the industry, and the demand of such plans for predictable strategies. Most mutual funds promise to limit their use of short-selling and leverage, and their use of derivatives is highly restricted. In recent years, some so-called 130/30 funds have opened, primarily for institutional clients, with prospectuses that explicitly allow for more active short-selling and derivatives positions, but even these have less flexibility than hedge funds.[1] In contrast, hedge funds may effectively partake in any investment strategy and may act opportunistically as conditions evolve. For this reason, it would be a mistake to view hedge funds as anything remotely like a uniform asset class. Hedge funds by design are empowered to invest in a wide range of investments, with various funds focusing on derivatives, distressed firms, currency speculation, convertible bonds, emerging markets, merger arbitrage, and so on. Other funds may jump from one asset class to another as perceived investment opportunities shift.

Liquidity   Hedge funds often impose **lock-up periods,** that is, periods as long as several years in which investments cannot be withdrawn. Many also employ redemption notices that require investors to provide notice weeks or months in advance of their desire to redeem funds. These restrictions limit the liquidity of investors but in turn enable the funds to invest in illiquid assets where returns may be higher, without worrying about meeting unanticipated demands for redemptions.

lock-up period

Period in which investors cannot redeem investments in the hedge fund.

[1]These are funds that may sell short up to 30% of the value of their portfolios, using the proceeds of the sale to increase their positions in invested assets. So for every $100 in net assets, the fund could sell short $30, investing the proceeds to increase its long positions to $130. This gives rise to the 130/30 moniker.

Compensation Structure   Hedge funds also differ from mutual funds in their fee structure. Whereas mutual funds assess management fees equal to a fixed percentage of assets, for example, between .5% and 1.5% annually for typical equity funds, hedge funds charge a management fee, usually between 1% and 2% of assets, *plus* a substantial *incentive fee* equal to a fraction of any investment profits beyond some benchmark. The incentive fee typically is 20%, but is sometimes higher. The threshold return to earn the incentive fee is often a money market rate such as LIBOR. Indeed, some observers only half-jokingly characterize hedge funds as "a compensation scheme masquerading as an asset class."

20.2 | Hedge Fund Strategies

directional strategy

Speculation that one market sector will outperform other sectors.

nondirectional strategy

A position designed to exploit temporary misalignments in relative pricing. Typically involves a long position in one security hedged with a short position in a related security.

Table 20.1 presents a list of most of the common investment themes found in the hedge fund industry. The list contains a wide diversity of styles and suggests how hard it can be to speak generically about hedge funds as a group. We can, however, divide hedge fund strategies into two general categories: directional and nondirectional.

Directional and Nondirectional Strategies

Directional strategies are easy to understand. They are simply bets that one sector or another will outperform other sectors of the market.

In contrast, **nondirectional strategies** are usually designed to exploit temporary misalignments in security valuations. For example, if the yield on mortgage-backed securities seems abnormally high compared to that on Treasury bonds, the hedge fund would buy mortgage–backed

---

TABLE 20.1

Hedge fund styles

Convertible arbitrage	Hedged investing in convertible securities, typically long convertible bonds and short stock.
Dedicated short bias	Net short position, usually in equities, as opposed to pure short exposure.
Emerging markets	Goal is to exploit market inefficiencies in emerging markets. Typically long-only because short-selling is not feasible in many of these markets.
Equity market neutral	Commonly uses long-short hedges. Typically controls for industry, sector, size, and other exposures, and establishes market-neutral positions designed to exploit some market inefficiency. Commonly involves leverage.
Event driven	Attempts to profit from situations such as mergers, acquisitions, restructuring, bankruptcy, or reorganization.
Fixed-income arbitrage	Attempts to profit from price anomalies in related interest-rate securities. Includes interest rate swap arbitrage, U.S. versus non-U.S. government bond arbitrage, yield-curve arbitrage, and mortgage-backed arbitrage.
Global macro	Involves long and short positions in capital or derivative markets across the world. Portfolio positions reflect views on broad market conditions and major economic trends.
Long-Short equity hedge	Equity-oriented positions on either side of the market (i.e., long or short), depending on outlook. *Not* meant to be market neutral. May establish a concentrated focus regionally (e.g., U.S. or Europe) or on a specific sector (e.g., tech or health care stocks). Derivatives may be used to hedge positions.
Managed futures	Uses financial, currency, or commodity futures. May make use of technical trading rules or a less structured judgmental approach.
Multistrategy	Opportunistic choice of strategy depending on outlook.
Fund of funds	Fund allocates its cash to several other hedge funds to be managed.

CS/TASS (Credit Suisse/Tremont Advisors Shareholder Services) maintains one of the most comprehensive databases on hedge fund performance. It categorizes hedge funds into these 11 different investment styles.

and short sell Treasury securities. Notice that the fund is *not* betting on broad movements in the entire bond market: it buys one type of bond and sells another. By taking a long mortgage–short Treasury position, the fund hedges its interest rate exposure, while making a bet on the *relative* valuation across the two sectors. The idea is that when yield spreads converge back to their "normal" relationship, the fund will profit from the realignment regardless of the general trend in the level of interest rates. In this respect, it strives to be **market neutral,** or hedged with respect to the direction of interest rates, which gives rise to the term "hedge fund."

Nondirectional strategies are sometimes further divided into *convergence* or *relative value* positions. The difference between convergence and relative value is a time horizon at which one can say with confidence that any mispricing ought to be resolved. An example of a convergence strategy would entail mispricing of a futures contract that must be corrected by the time the contract matures. In contrast, the mortgage versus Treasury spread we just discussed would be a relative value strategy, because there is no obvious horizon during which the yield spread would "correct" from unusual levels.

market neutral

A strategy designed to exploit relative mispricing within a market, but which is hedged to avoid taking a stance on the direction of the board market.

EXAMPLE 20.1

Market-Neutral Positions

We can illustrate a market-neutral position with a strategy used extensively by several hedge funds, which have observed that newly issued or "on-the-run" 30-year Treasury bonds regularly sell at higher prices (lower yields) than 29½-year bonds with almost identical duration. The yield spread presumably is a premium due to the greater liquidity of the on-the-run bonds. Hedge funds, which have relatively low liquidity needs, therefore buy the 29½-year bond and sell the 30-year bond. This is a hedged, or market-neutral, position that will generate a profit whenever the yields on the two bonds converge, as typically happens when the 30-year bonds age, are no longer the most liquid on-the-run bond, and are no longer priced at a premium.

Notice that this strategy should generate profits regardless of the general direction of interest rates. The long-short position will return a profit as long as the 30-year bonds underperform the 29½-year bonds, as they should when the liquidity premium dissipates. Because the pricing discrepancies between these two securities almost necessarily *must* disappear at a given date, this strategy is an example of convergence arbitrage. While the convergence date in this application is not quite as definite as the maturity of a futures contract, one can be sure that the currently on-the-run T-bonds will lose that status by the time the Treasury next issues 30-year bonds.

Long-short positions such as in Example 20.1 are characteristic of hedged strategies. They are designed to *isolate* a bet on some mispricing without taking on market exposure. Profits are made regardless of broad market movements once prices "converge" or return to their "proper" levels. Hence, use of short positions and derivatives are part and parcel of the industry.

A more complex long-short strategy is *convertible bond arbitrage,* one of the more prominent sectors of the hedge-fund universe. Noting that a convertible bond may be viewed as a straight bond plus a call option on the underlying stock, the market-neutral strategy in this case involves a position in the bond offset by an opposite position in the stock. For example, if the convertible is viewed as underpriced, the fund will buy it, and offset its resultant exposure to declines in the stock price by shorting the stock.

Although these market-neutral positions are hedged, we emphasize that they are *not* risk-free arbitrage strategies. Rather they should be viewed as **pure plays,** that is, bets on *particular* (perceived) mispricing between two sectors or securities, with extraneous sources of risk such as general market exposure hedged away. Moreover, because the funds often operate with considerable leverage, returns can be quite volatile.

pure plays

Bets on particular mispricing across two or more securities, with extraneous sources of risk such as general market exposure hedged away.

CONCEPT *check* **20.1**

Classify each of the following strategies as directional or nondirectional.

a. The fund buys shares in the India Investment Fund, a closed-end fund that is selling at a discount to net asset value, and sells the MSCI India Index Swap.

b. The fund buys shares in Petrie Stores and sells Toys "R" Us, which is a major component of Petrie's balance sheet.

c. The fund buys shares in Generic Pharmaceuticals, betting that it will be acquired at a premium by Pfizer.

Statistical Arbitrage

statistical arbitrage

Use of quantitative system to uncover many perceived misalignments in relative pricing and ensure profit by averaging over all of these small bets.

Statistical arbitrage is a version of a market-neutral strategy, but one that merits its own discussion. It differs from pure arbitrage in that it does not seek out risk-free positions based on unambiguous mispricing (such as index arbitrage). Instead, it uses quantitative and often automated trading systems that seek out many temporary and modest misalignments in prices among securities. By taking relatively small positions in many of these opportunities, the law of averages would make the probability of profiting from the collection of ostensibly positive-value bets very high, ideally almost a "statistical certainty." Of course, this strategy presumes that the fund's modeling techniques can actually identify reliable, if small, market inefficiencies. The law of averages will work for the fund only if the expected return is positive!

Statistical arbitrage often involves trading in hundreds of securities a day with holding periods that can be measured in minutes or less. Such rapid and heavy trading requires extensive use of quantitative tools such as automated trading and mathematical algorithms to identify profit opportunities and efficient diversification across positions. These strategies try to profit from the smallest of perceived mispricing opportunities, and require the fastest trading technology and the lowest possible trading costs. They would not be possible without the electronic communication networks discussed in Chapter 3.

pairs trading

Stocks are paired up based on underlying similarities, and long-short positions are established to exploit any relative mispricing between each pair.

A particular form of statistical arbitrage is **pairs trading,** in which stocks are paired up based on an analysis of either fundamental similarities or market exposures (betas). The general approach is to pair up similar companies whose returns are highly correlated but where one company seems to be priced more aggressively than the other.[2] Market-neutral positions can be formed by buying the relatively cheap firm and selling the expensive one. Many such pairs comprise the hedge fund's overall portfolio. Each pair may have an uncertain outcome, but with many such matched pairs, the presumption is that the large number of long-short bets will provide a very high probability of a positive abnormal return. More general versions of pairs trading allow for positions in clusters of stocks that may be relatively mispriced.

data mining

Sorting through large amounts of historical data to uncover systematic patterns that can be exploited.

Statistical arbitrage is commonly associated with **data mining,** which refers to sorting through huge amounts of historical data to uncover systematic patterns in returns that can be exploited by traders. The risk of data mining, and statistical arbitrage in general, is that historical relationships may break down when fundamental economic conditions change or, indeed, that the apparent patterns in the data may be due to pure chance. Enough analysis applied to enough data is sure to produce apparent patterns that do not reflect real relationships that can be counted on to persist in the future.

20.3 Portable Alpha

portable alpha or **alpha transfer**

A strategy in which you invest in positive alpha positions, then hedge the systematic risk of that investment, and finally, establish market exposure where you want it using passive indexes.

An important implication of the market-neutral pure play is the notion of **portable alpha.** Suppose that you wish to speculate on a stock that you think is underpriced, but you think that the market is about to fall. Even if you are right about the stock being *relatively* underpriced, it still might decline in response to declines in the broad market. You would like to separate the stock-specific bet from the implicit asset allocation bet on market performance that arises because the stock's beta is positive. The solution is to buy the stock and eliminate the resultant market exposure by selling enough index futures to drive beta to zero. This long stock–short futures strategy gives you a pure play or, equivalently, a *market-neutral* position on the stock.

More generally, you might wish to separate asset allocation from security selection. The idea is to invest wherever you can "find alpha." You would then hedge the systematic risk of that investment to isolate its alpha from the asset market where it was found. Finally, you establish exposure to desired market sectors by using passive products such as indexed mutual funds or ETFs. In other words, you have created portable alpha that can be mixed with an exposure to whatever

---

[2]Rules for deciding relative "aggressiveness" of pricing may vary. In one approach, a computer scans for stocks whose prices historically have tracked very closely but have recently diverged. If the differential in cumulative return typically dissipates, the fund will buy the recently underperforming stock and sell the outperforming one. In other variants, pricing aggressiveness may be determined by evaluating the stocks based on the ratio of price to some measure of intrinsic value.

sector of the market you choose. This procedure is also called **alpha transfer,** because you transfer alpha from the sector where you find it to the asset class in which you ultimately establish exposure. Finding alpha requires skill. By contrast, beta, or market exposure, is a "commodity" that can be supplied cheaply through index funds or ETFs, and offers little value added.

An Example of a Pure Play

Suppose you manage a $1 million portfolio. You believe that the alpha of the portfolio is positive, $\alpha > 0$, but also that the market is about to fall, that is, that $r_M < 0$. You would therefore try to establish a pure play on the perceived mispricing.

The return on portfolio over the next month may be described by Equation 20.1, which states that the portfolio return will equal its "fair" CAPM return (the first two terms on the right-hand side), plus firm-specific risk reflected in the "residual," e, plus an alpha that reflects perceived mispricing:

$$r_{\text{portfolio}} = r_f + \beta(r_M - r_f) + e + \alpha \qquad \text{(20.1)}$$

To be concrete, suppose that $\beta = 1.20$, $\alpha = .02$, $r_f = .01$, the current value of the S&P 500 Index is $S_0 = 800$, and, for simplicity, that the portfolio pays no dividends. You want to capture the positive alpha of 2% per month, but you don't want the positive beta that the stock entails because you are worried about a market decline. So you choose to hedge your exposure by selling S&P 500 futures contracts.

Because the S&P contracts have a multiplier of $250, and the portfolio has a beta of 1.20, your stock position can be hedged for one month by selling five futures contracts[3]:

$$\text{Hedge ratio} = \frac{\$1,000,000}{800 \times \$250} \times 1.20 = 6 \text{ contracts}$$

The dollar value of your portfolio after one month will be

$$
\begin{aligned}
\$1,000,000 \times (1 + r_{\text{portfolio}}) &= \$1,000,000 \,[1 + .01 + 1.20\,(r_M - .01) + .02 + e] \\
&= \$1,018,000 + \$1,200,000 \times r_M + \$1,000,000 \times e
\end{aligned}
$$

The dollar proceeds from your futures position will be:

$6 \times \$250 \times (F_0 - F_1)$	Mark-to-market on 6 contracts sold
$= \$1,500 \times [S_0(1.01) - S_1]$	Substitute for futures prices, F_0, from parity relationship
$= \$1,500 \times S_0[1.01 - (1 + r_M)]$	Because $S_1 = S_0(1 + r_M)$ when no dividends are paid
$= \$1,500 \times [S_0(.01 - r_M)]$	Simplify
$= \$12,000 - \$1,200,000 \times r_M$	Because $S_0 = 800$

The total value of the stock plus futures position at month's end will be the sum of the portfolio value plus the futures proceeds, which equals

$$\text{Hedged proceeds} = \$1,030,000 + \$1,200,000 \times e \qquad \text{(20.2)}$$

Notice that the dollar exposure to the market from your futures position precisely offsets your exposure from the stock portfolio. In other words, you have reduced beta to zero. Your investment is $1 million, so your total monthly rate of return is 3% plus the remaining nonsystematic risk (the second term of Equation 20.2). The fair or equilibrium expected rate of return on such a zero-beta position is the risk-free rate, 1%, so you have preserved your alpha of 2%, while eliminating the market exposure of the stock portfolio.

[3]We simplify here by assuming that the maturity of the futures contract precisely equals the hedging horizon, in this case, one month. If the contract maturity were longer, one would have to slightly reduce the hedge ratio in a process called "tailing the hedge."

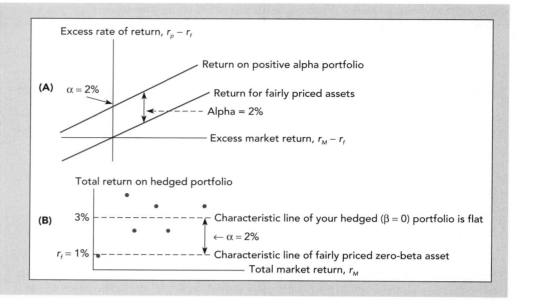

FIGURE 20.1

A pure play.
Panel A: unhedged position.
Panel B: hedged position.

This is an idealized example of a pure play. In particular, it simplifies by assuming a known and fixed portfolio beta, but it illustrates that the goal is to speculate on the stock while hedging out the undesired market exposure. Once this is accomplished, you can establish any desired exposure to other sources of systematic risk by buying indexes or entering index futures contracts in those markets. Thus, you have made alpha portable.

Figure 20.1 is a graphical analysis of this pure play. Panel A shows the excess returns to betting on a positive-alpha stock portfolio "naked," that is, unhedged. Your *expected* return is better than an equilibrium return given your risk, but because of your market exposure you still can lose if the market declines. Panel B shows the characteristic line for the position with systematic risk hedged out. There is no market exposure.

A warning: Even market-neutral positions are still bets, and they can go wrong. This is not true arbitrage because your profits still depend on whether your analysis (your perceived alpha) is correct. Moreover, you can be done in by simple bad luck, that is, your analysis may be correct but a bad realization of idiosyncratic risk (negative values of e in Equation 20.1 or 20.2) can still result in losses.

CONCEPT *check* **20.2**

What would be the dollar value and rate of return on the market-neutral position if the value of the residual turns out to be −4%? If the market return in that month is 5%, where would the plot of the strategy return lie in each panel of Figure 20.1?

EXAMPLE 20.2

The Risks of Pure Plays

An apparently market-neutral bet misfired badly in 1998. While the 30- versus 29½-year maturity T-bond strategy (see Example 20.1) worked well over several years, it backfired badly when Russia defaulted on its debt, triggering massive investment demand for the safest, most liquid assets that drove up the price of the 30-year Treasury relative to its 29½-year counterpart. The big losses that ensued illustrate that even the safest bet—one based on convergence arbitrage—carries risks. Although the T-bond spread had to converge eventually, and in fact it did several weeks later, Long Term Capital Management (LTCM) and other hedge funds suffered large losses on their positions when the spread widened temporarily. The ultimate convergence came too late for LTCM, which was also facing massive losses on its other positions and had to be bailed out.[4]

[4]This timing problem is a common one for active managers. We saw other examples of this issue when we discussed limits to arbitrage in Chapter 9. More generally, when security analysts think they have found a mispriced stock, they usually acknowledge that it is hard to know how long it will take for price to converge to intrinsic value.

Even market-neutral bets can result in considerable volatility because most hedge funds use considerable leverage. Most incidents of relative mispricing are fairly minor, and the hedged nature of long-short strategies makes overall volatility low. The hedge funds respond by scaling up their bets. This amplifies gains when their bets work out, but also amplifies losses. In the end, the volatility of the funds is not small.

20.4 Style Analysis for Hedge Funds

While the classic hedge fund strategy may have focused on market-neutral opportunities, as the market has evolved, the freedom to use derivatives contracts and short positions means that hedge funds can in effect follow any investment strategy. While many hedge funds pursue market-neutral strategies, a quick glance at the range of investment styles in Table 20.1 should convince you that many, if not most, funds pursue directional strategies. In these cases, the fund makes an outright bet, for example, on currency movements, the outcome of a takeover attempt, or the performance of an investment sector. These funds are most certainly not hedged, despite their name.

In Chapter 18, we introduced you to style analysis, which uses regression analysis to measure the exposure of a portfolio to various factors or asset classes. The analysis thus measures the implicit asset class exposure of a portfolio. The betas on a series of factors measure the fund's exposure to each source of systematic risk. A market-neutral fund will have no sensitivity to an index for that market. In contrast, directional funds will exhibit significant betas, often called *loadings* in this context, on whatever factors the fund tends to bet on. Observers attempting to measure investment style can use these factor loadings to impute exposures to a range of variables.

We present a simple style analysis for the hedge fund indexes in Table 20.2. The four systematic factors we consider are

- *Interest rates*—the return on long-term U.S. Treasury bonds.
- *Equity markets*—the return on the S&P 500.
- *Credit conditions*—the difference in the return on Baa-rated bonds over Treasury bonds.
- *Foreign exchange*—the percentage change in the value of the U.S. dollar against a basket of foreign currencies.

The returns on hedge fund index i in month t may be statistically described by

$$R_{it} = \alpha_i + \beta_{i1} \text{Factor1}_t + \cdots + \beta_{i4} \text{Factor4}_t + e_{it} \qquad \textbf{(20.3)}$$

The betas (equivalently, factor loadings) measure the sensitivity to each factor. As usual, the residual, e_{it}, measures "nonsystematic" risk that is uncorrelated with the set of explanatory factors, and the intercept, α_i, measures average performance of fund i net of the impact of these systematic factors.

Table 20.2 presents factor exposure estimates for 13 hedge fund indexes. The results confirm that most funds are in fact directional with very clear exposures to one or more of the four factors. Moreover, the estimated factor betas seem reasonable in terms of the funds' stated style. For example:

- The equity market neutral funds have uniformly low and statistically insignificant factor betas, as one would expect of a market-neutral posture.
- Dedicated short bias funds exhibit substantial negative betas on the S&P index.
- Distressed firm funds have significant exposure to credit conditions (more positive credit spreads in this table indicate better economic conditions) as well as to the S&P 500. This exposure arises because restructuring activities often depend on access to borrowing, and successful restructuring depends on the state of the economy.
- Global macro funds show negative exposure to a stronger U.S. dollar, which would make the dollar value of foreign investments less valuable.

We conclude that, by and large, most hedge funds are making very explicit directional bets on a wide array of economic factors.

TABLE 20.2

Style analysis for a sample of hedge fund indexes

Funds Group*	Alpha	S&P 500	Long T-bond	Credit Conditions	U.S. Dollar
All funds	0.0052	0.2718	0.0189	0.1755	−0.1897
	3.3487	5.0113	0.3064	2.0462	−2.1270
Market neutral	0.0014	0.1677	−0.0163	0.3308	−0.5097
	0.1990	0.6917	−0.0589	0.8631	−1.2790
Short bias	0.0058	−0.9723	0.1310	0.3890	−0.2630
	1.3381	−6.3684	0.7527	1.6113	−1.0476
Event driven	0.0071	0.2335	0.0000	0.2056	−0.1165
	5.1155	4.7858	−0.0002	2.6642	0.1520
Risk arbitrage	0.0034	0.1498	0.0130	−0.0006	−0.2130
	3.0678	3.8620	0.0442	−0.0097	−3.3394
Distressed	0.0068	0.2080	0.0032	0.2521	−0.1156
	5.7697	4.9985	0.0679	3.8318	−1.6901
Emerging markets	0.0082	0.3750	0.2624	0.4551	−0.2169
	2.8867	3.7452	2.2995	2.8748	−1.3173
Fixed Income arb	0.0018	0.1719	0.2284	0.5703	−0.1714
	1.0149	2.8139	3.2806	5.9032	−1.7063
Convertible arb	0.0005	0.2477	0.2109	0.5021	−0.0972
	0.2197	3.1066	2.3214	3.9825	−0.7414
Global macro	0.0079	0.0746	0.0593	0.1492	−0.2539
	3.5217	0.9437	0.6587	1.1938	−1.9533
Long-short equity	0.0053	0.4442	−0.0070	0.0672	−0.1471
	2.5693	6.1425	−0.0850	0.5874	−1.2372
Managed futures	0.0041	0.2565	−0.2991	−0.5223	−0.2703
	0.8853	1.5944	−1.6310	−2.0528	−1.0217
Multistrategy	0.0075	0.2566	−0.0048	0.1781	−0.1172
	4.2180	4.1284	−0.0684	1.8116	−1.1471

*Fund definitions given in Table 20.1.

Note: Top line of each entry is the estimate of the factor beta. Lower line is the *t*-statistic for that estimate.

Source: Authors' calculations. Hedge fund returns are on indexes computed by Credit Suisse/Tremont Index, LLC, available at **www.hedgeindex.com**.

CONCEPT *check* **20.3**   Analyze the betas of the fixed-income arbitrage index in Table 20.2. Based on these results, are these funds typically market neutral? If not, do their factor exposures make sense in terms of the markets in which they operate?

20.5 Performance Measurement for Hedge Funds

Hasanhodzic and Lo (2007) calculate both style-adjusted alphas and Sharpe ratios for a large sample of hedge funds, and find that average performance measures appear considerably higher than those of a passive index such as the S&P 500. What might be the source of such seemingly impressive performance?

One possibility, of course, is the obvious one: these results may reflect a high degree of skill among hedge fund managers. Another possibility is that funds maintain some exposure to omitted risk factors that convey a positive risk premium, but given the extensive list of included factors, this seems unlikely. However, there are several other factors that make hedge fund performance difficult to evaluate, and these are worth considering.

Liquidity and Hedge Fund Performance

Another explanation for these attractive performance measures is liquidity. Recall that one of the more important extensions of the CAPM is a version that allows for the possibility of a return premium for investors willing to hold less liquid assets. Hedge funds tend to hold more illiquid assets than other institutional investors such as mutual funds. They can do so because of restrictions such as the lock-up provisions that commit investors to keep their investment in the fund for some period of time. Therefore, it is important to control for liquidity when evaluating performance. If it is ignored, what may be no more than compensation for illiquidity may appear to be true alpha, that is, risk-adjusted abnormal returns.

Aragon (2007) demonstrates that hedge funds with lock-up restrictions do tend to hold less liquid portfolios. Moreover, once he controlled for lock-ups or other share restrictions (such as redemption notice periods), the apparently positive average alpha of those funds turned insignificant. Aragon's work suggests that the typical "alpha" exhibited by hedge funds may be better interpreted as an equilibrium liquidity premium rather than a sign of stock-picking ability, in other words as a "fair" reward for providing liquidity to other investors.

Whereas Aragon focuses on the average level of liquidity, Sadka (2008) addresses the liquidity *risk* of hedge funds. He shows that exposure to unexpected declines in market liquidity is an important determinant of hedge fund returns, and that the spread in average returns across the funds with the highest and lowest liquidity exposure may be as much as 8%. Hedge fund performance may therefore reflect significant compensation for liquidity risk.

One symptom of illiquid assets is serial correlation in returns. Positive serial correlation means that positive returns are more likely to be followed by positive than by negative returns. Such a pattern is often taken as an indicator of less liquid markets for the following reason. When accurate and timely prices are not available because an asset is not actively traded, the hedge fund must estimate its value to calculate net asset value and rates of return. But such procedures are at best imperfect and, as demonstrated by Getmansky, Lo, and Makarov (2004), tend to result in serial correlation in prices as firms either smooth out their value estimates or only gradually mark prices to true market values. Positive serial correlation is therefore often interpreted as evidence of liquidity problems; in nearly efficient markets with frictionless trading, we would expect serial correlation or other predictable patterns in prices to be minimal. Most mutual funds show almost no evidence of such correlation in their returns and the serial correlation of the S&P 500 is just about zero.

Hasanhodzic and Lo (2007) find that hedge fund returns in fact exhibit significant serial correlation. This symptom of smoothed prices has two important implications. First, it lends further support to the hypothesis that hedge funds are holding less liquid assets and that their apparent alphas may in fact be liquidity premiums. Second, it implies that their performance measures are upward-biased, because any smoothing in the estimates of portfolio value will reduce total volatility (increasing the Sharpe ratio) as well as covariances and therefore betas with systematic factors (increasing risk-adjusted alphas). In fact, Figure 20.2 shows that the serial correlations exhibited by hedge funds are highly associated with their apparent Sharpe ratios.

Returns can be even more difficult to interpret if a hedge fund takes advantage of illiquid markets to manipulate returns by purposely misvaluing illiquid assets. In this regard, it is worth noting a *Santa effect:* hedge funds report average returns in December that are substantially greater than their average returns in other months (Agarwal, Daniel, and Naik, 2007). The pattern is stronger for funds that are near or beyond the threshold return at which performance incentive fees kick in and suggests that illiquid assets are more generously valued in December, when annual performance relative to benchmarks is being calculated. In fact, it seems that the December spike in returns is stronger for lower-liquidity funds. If funds take advantage of illiquid markets to manage returns, then accurate performance measurement becomes almost impossible.

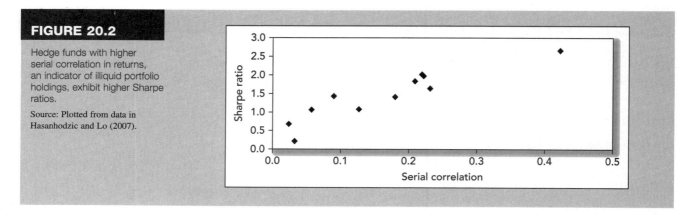

FIGURE 20.2

Hedge funds with higher serial correlation in returns, an indicator of illiquid portfolio holdings, exhibit higher Sharpe ratios.

Source: Plotted from data in Hasanhodzic and Lo (2007).

backfill bias

Bias in the average returns of a sample of funds induced by including past returns on funds that entered the sample only if they happened to be successful.

survivorship bias

Bias in the average returns of a sample of funds induced by excluding past returns on funds that left the sample because they happened to be unsuccessful.

Hedge Fund Performance and Survivorship Bias

We already know that survivorship bias (when only successful funds remain in a database) can affect the estimated performance of a sample of mutual funds. The same problems, as well as related ones, apply to hedge funds. **Backfill bias** arises because hedge funds report returns to database publishers only if they choose to. Funds started with seed capital will open to the public and therefore enter standard databases only if their past performance is deemed sufficiently successful to attract clients. Therefore, the prior performance of funds that are eventually included in the sample may not be representative of typical performance. **Survivorship bias** arises when unsuccessful funds that cease operation stop reporting returns and leave a database, leaving behind only the successful funds. Malkiel and Saha (2005) find that attrition rates for hedge funds are far higher than for mutual funds—in fact, commonly more than double the attrition rate of mutual funds—making this an important issue to address. Estimates of survivorship bias in various studies are typically substantial, in the range of 2–4%.[5]

Hedge Fund Performance and Changing Factor Loadings

In Chapter 18, we pointed out that an important assumption underlying conventional performance evaluation is that the portfolio manager maintains a reasonably stable risk profile over time. But hedge funds are designed to be opportunistic and have considerable flexibility to change that profile. This too can make performance evaluation tricky. If risk is not constant, then estimated alphas will be biased if we use a standard, linear index model. And if the risk profile changes in systematic manner with the expected return on the market, performance evaluation is even more difficult.

To see why, look at Figure 20.3, which illustrates the characteristic line of a perfect market timer (see Chapter 18, Section 18.6) who engages in no security selection but moves funds from T-bills into the market portfolio only when the market will outperform bills. The characteristic line is nonlinear, with a slope of 0 when the market's excess return is negative, and a slope of 1 when it is positive. But a naïve attempt to estimate a regression equation from this pattern would result in a fitted line with a slope between 0 and 1, and a positive alpha. Neither statistic accurately describes the fund.

As we noted in Chapter 18, and as is evident from Figure 20.3, an ability to conduct perfect market timing is much like obtaining a call option on the underlying portfolio without having to pay for it. Similar nonlinearities would arise if the fund actually buys or writes options. Figure 20.4, Panel A, illustrates the case of a fund that holds a stock portfolio and writes put options on it, and Panel B illustrates the case of a fund that holds a stock portfolio

[5]For example, Malkiel and Saha (2005) estimate the bias at 4.4%, Amin and Kat (2003) find a bias of about 2%, and Fung and Hsieh (2000) find a bias of about 3.6%.

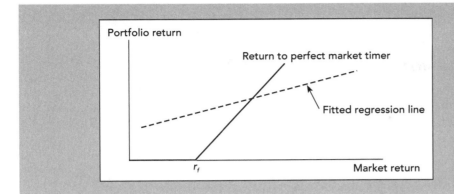

FIGURE 20.3

Characteristic line of a perfect market timer. The true characteristic line is kinked, with a shape like that of a call option. Fitting a straight line to the relationship will result in misestimated slope and intercept.

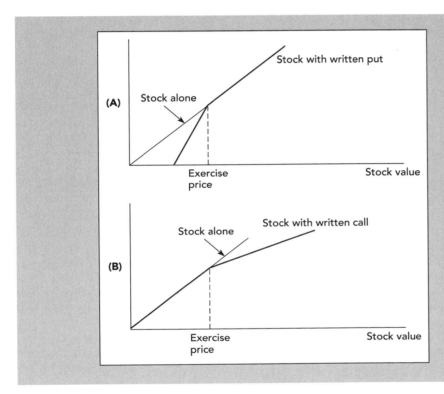

FIGURE 20.4

Characteristic lines of stock portfolio with written options.
Panel A: Buy stock, write put. Here, the fund writes fewer puts than the number of shares it holds.
Panel B: Buy stock, write calls. Here, the fund writes fewer calls than the number of shares it holds.

and writes call options. In both cases, the characteristic line is steeper when portfolio returns are poor—in other words, the fund has greater sensitivity to the market when it is falling than when it is rising. This is the opposite profile that would arise from timing ability, which is much like acquiring rather than writing options, and therefore would give the fund greater sensitivity to market advances.[6]

Figure 20.5 presents evidence on these sorts of nonlinearities. A nonlinear regression line is fitted to the scatter diagram of returns on hedge funds plotted against returns on the S&P 500. The fitted lines in each panel suggest that these funds have higher down-market betas (higher slopes) than up-market betas.[7]

---

[6]But the fund that writes options would at least receive fair compensation for the unattractive shape of its characteristic line in the form of the premium received when it writes the options.

[7]Not all the hedge fund categories exhibited this sort of pattern. Many showed effectively symmetric up- and down-market betas. However, Panel A shows that the asymmetry affect hedge funds taken as group. Panels B and C are for the two sectors with the most prominent asymmetries.

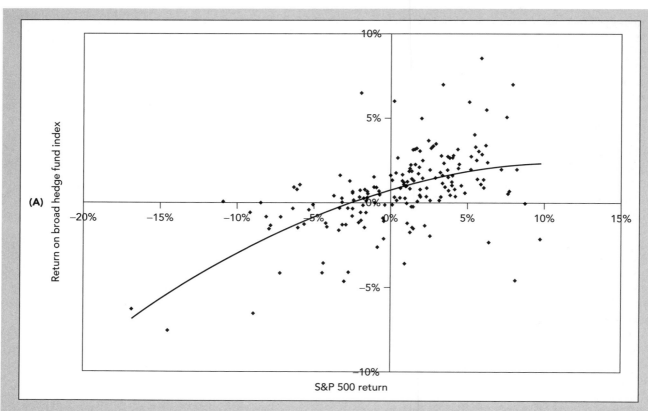

(A)

Return on broad hedge fund index

S&P 500 return

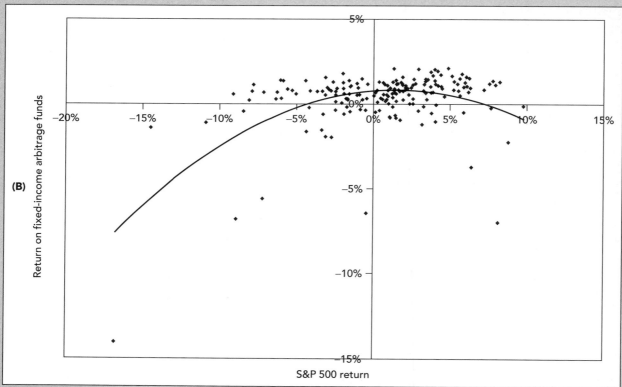

(B)

Return on fixed-income arbitrage funds

S&P 500 return

FIGURE 20.5

Return on hedge fund indexes versus return on S&P 500, 1993–2008

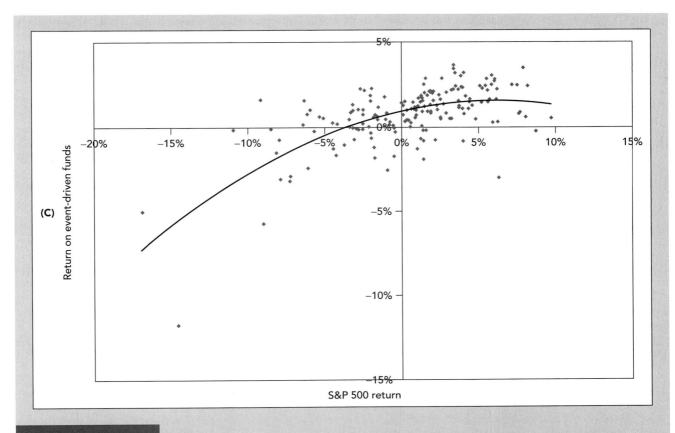

FIGURE 20.5

Return on hedge fund indexes versus return on S&P 500, 1993–2008

Source: Constructed from data downloaded from **www.hedgeindex.com** and **finance.yahoo.com**.

This is precisely what investors presumably do *not* want: higher market sensitivity when the market is weak. This is evidence that these funds may be *writing* options, either explicitly or implicitly through dynamic trading strategies (see Chapter 16, Section 16.4, for a discussion of such dynamic strategies).

Tail Events and Hedge Fund Performance

Imagine a hedge fund whose entire investment strategy is to hold an S&P 500 Index fund and write deep out-of-the-money put options on the index. Clearly the fund manager brings no skill to his job. But if you knew only his investment results over limited periods, and not his underlying strategy, you might be fooled into thinking that he is extremely talented. For if the put options are written sufficiently out-of-the-money, they will only rarely end up imposing a loss, and such a strategy can appear over long periods—even over many years—to be consistently profitable. In most periods, the strategy brings in a modest premium from the written puts and therefore outperforms the S&P 500, yielding the impression of consistently superior performance. The huge loss that might be incurred in an extreme market decline might not be experienced even over periods as long as years. Every so often, such as in the market crash of October 1987, the strategy may lose multiples of its entire gain over the last decade. But if you are lucky enough to avoid these rare but extreme *tail events* (so named because they fall in the far-left tail of the probability distribution), the strategy might appear to be gilded.

The evidence in Figure 20.5 indicating that hedge funds are at least implicitly option writers should make us nervous about taking their measured performance at face value. The problem in interpreting strategies with exposure to extreme tail events (such as short options positions) is that these events by definition occur very infrequently, so it can take *decades* of results to fully appreciate their true risk and reward attributes. Nassim Taleb (2004, 2007) who is a hedge fund operator himself, makes the case that many hedge funds are analogous to our hypothetical manager, racking up fame and fortune through strategies that make money *most* of the time, but expose investors to rare but extreme losses.

Taleb uses the metaphor of the black swan to discuss the importance of highly improbable, but highly impactful, events. Until the discovery of Australia, Europeans believed that all swans were white: They had never encountered swans that were not white. In their experience, the black swan was outside the realm of reasonable possibility, in statistical jargon, an extreme outlier relative to their sample of observations. Taleb argues that the world is filled with black swans, deeply important developments that simply could not have been predicted from the range of accumulated experience to date. While we can't predict which black swans to expect, we nevertheless know that some black swan may be making an appearance at any moment. The October 1987 crash, when the market fell by more than 20% in one day, or the credit crisis of 2008 might be viewed as black swans—events that had never taken place before, ones that most market observers would have dismissed as impossible and certainly not worth modeling, but with high impact. These sorts of events seemingly come out of the blue, and they caution us to show great humility when we use past experience to evaluate the future risk of our actions. With this in mind, consider again the example of Long Term Capital Management.

EXAMPLE   20.3

Tail Events and Long Term Capital Management

In the late 1990s, Long Term Capital Management was widely viewed as the most successful hedge fund in history. It had consistently provided double-digit returns to its investors, and it had earned hundreds of millions of dollars in incentive fees for its managers. The firm used sophisticated computer models to estimate correlations across assets and believed that its capital was almost 10 times the annual standard deviation of its portfolio returns, presumably enough to withstand any "possible" shock to capital (at least, assuming normal distributions!). But in the summer of 1998, things went badly. On August 17, 1998, Russia defaulted on its sovereign debt and threw capital markets into chaos. LTCM's *one-day* loss on August 21 was $550 million (approximately nine times its estimated *monthly* standard deviation). Total losses in August were about $1.3 billion, despite the fact that LTCM believed that the great majority of its positions were market-neutral relative-value trades. Losses accrued on virtually all of its positions, flying in the face of the presumed diversification of the overall portfolio.

How did this happen? The answer lies in the massive flight to quality and, even more so, to liquidity that was set off by the Russian default. LTCM was typically a seller of liquidity (holding less liquid assets, selling more liquid assets with lower yields, and earning the yield spread) and suffered huge losses. This was a different type of shock from those that appeared in its historical sample/modeling period. In the liquidity crisis that engulfed asset markets, the unexpected commonality of liquidity risk across ostensibly uncorrelated asset classes became obvious. Losses that seemed statistically impossible on past experience had in fact come to pass; LTCM fell victim to a black swan.

---

incentive fee

A fee charged by hedge funds equal to a share of any investment returns beyond a stipulated benchmark performance.

20.6   Fee Structure in Hedge Funds

The typical hedge fund fee structure is a management fee of 1% to 2% of assets plus an **incentive fee** equal to 20% of investment profits beyond a stipulated benchmark performance, annually. Incentive fees are effectively call options on the portfolio with a strike price equal to current portfolio value times $1 +$ benchmark return. The manager gets the fee if the portfolio value rises sufficiently, but loses nothing if it falls. Figure 20.6 illustrates the incentive fee for a fund with a 20% incentive fee and a hurdle rate equal to the money market rate, r_f. The current value of the portfolio is denoted S_0 and the year-end value is S_T. The incentive fee is equivalent to .20 call options on the portfolio with exercise price $S_0(1 + r_f)$.

FIGURE 20.6

Incentive fees as a call option. The current value of the portfolio is denoted S_0 and its year-end value is S_T. The incentive fee is equivalent to .20 call options on the portfolio with exercise price $S_0(1 + r_f)$.

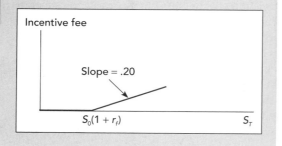

Incentive fee

Slope = .20

$S_0(1 + r_f)$ S_T

EXAMPLE | **20.4**

Black-Scholes Valuation of Incentive Fees

Suppose the standard deviation of a hedge fund's annual rate of return is 30% and the incentive fee is 20% of any investment return over the risk-free money market rate. If the portfolio currently has a net asset value of $100 per share, and the effective annual risk-free rate is 5% (or 4.88% expressed as a continuously compounded rate), then the implicit exercise price on the incentive fee is $105. The Black-Scholes value of a call option with $S_0 = 100$, $X = 105$, $\sigma = .30$, $r = .0488$, $T = 1$ year is $11.92, just a shade below 12% of net asset value. Because the incentive fee is worth 20% of the call option, its value is just about 2.4% of net asset value. Together with a typical management fee of 2% of net asset value, the investor in the fund pays fees with a total value of 4.4%.

The major complication to this description of the typical compensation structure is the **high water mark.** If a fund experiences losses, it may not be able to charge an incentive fee unless and until it recovers to its previous higher value. With large losses, this may be difficult. High water marks therefore give managers an incentive to shut down funds that have performed poorly, and likely are a cause of the high attrition rate for funds noted above.

One of the fastest-growing sectors in the hedge fund universe has been in **funds of funds.** These are hedge funds that invest in one or more other hedge funds. By 2008, these funds were responsible for almost half of assets invested in the hedge fund industry.

Funds of funds are also called *feeder funds*, because they feed assets from the original investor to the ultimate hedge fund. They market themselves as providing investors the capability to diversify across funds, and also as providing the due diligence involved in screening funds for investment worthiness. In principle, this can be a valuable service because many hedge funds are opaque and feeder funds may have greater insight than typical outsiders. However, when Bernard Madoff was arrested in December 2008 after admitting to a $60 billion Ponzi scheme, it emerged that many large feeder funds were among his biggest clients, and that their "due diligence" may have been, to put it mildly, lacking. At the head of the list was Fairfield Greenwich Advisors, with exposure reported at $7.5 billion, but several other feeder funds and asset management firms around the world were also on the hook for amounts greater than $1 billion, among them Tremont Group Holdings, Banco Santander (a Spanish bank, one of the largest in the euro area), Ascot Partners, and Access International Advisors. In the end, it appears that some funds had in effect become little more than marketing agents for Madoff. The nearby box presents further discussion of the Madoff affair.

Optionality can have a big impact on expected fees in funds of funds. This is because the fund of funds pays an incentive fee to each underlying fund that outperforms its benchmark, even if the aggregate performance of the fund of funds is poor. In this case, diversification can hurt you (Brown, Goetzmann, and Liang, 2004)!

high water mark

The previous value of a portfolio that must be re-attained before a hedge fund can charge incentive fees.

funds of funds

Hedge funds that invest in several other hedge funds.

EXAMPLE | **20.5**

Incentive Fees in Funds of Funds

Suppose a fund of funds is established with $1 million invested in each of three hedge funds. For simplicity, we will ignore the asset-value-based portion of fees (the management fee) and focus only on the incentive fee. Suppose that the hurdle rate for the incentive fee is a zero return, so each fund charges an incentive fee of 20% of total return. The following table shows the performance of each underlying fund over a year, the gross rate of return, and the return realized by the fund of funds net of the incentive fee. Funds 1 and 2 have positive returns, and therefore earn an incentive fee, but Fund 3 has terrible performance, so its incentive fee is zero.

	Fund 1	Fund 2	Fund 3	Fund of Funds
Start of year (millions)	$1.00	$1.00	$1.00	$3.00
End of year (millions)	$1.20	$1.40	$0.25	$2.85
Gross rate of return	20%	40%	−75%	−5%
Incentive fee (millions)	$0.04	$0.08	$0.00	$0.12
End of year, net of fee	$1.16	$1.32	$.25	$2.73
Net rate of return	16%	32%	−75%	−9%

Even though the return on the aggregate portfolio of the fund of funds is *negative* 5%, it still pays incentive fees of $.12 for every $3 invested, which amounts to 4% of net asset value. As demonstrated in the last column, this reduces the rate of return earned by the fund of funds from −5% to −9%.

THE BERNARD MADOFF SCANDAL

On December 13, 2008, Bernard Madoff reportedly confessed to his two sons that he had for years been operating a Ponzi scheme, one that had reached a staggering $60 billion. A Ponzi scheme is an investment fraud in which a manager collects funds from clients, claims to invest those funds on their behalf, reports extremely favorable investment returns, but in fact uses the funds for his own purposes. (The schemes are named after Charles Ponzi, whose success with this scheme in the early 1900s made him notorious throughout the United States.) Early investors who ask to redeem their investments are paid back with the funds coming in from new investors rather than with true earnings. The scheme can continue as long as new investors provide enough funds to cover the redemption requests of the earlier ones—and these inflows are attracted both by the superior returns "earned" by early investors as well as their apparent ability to redeem funds as requested.

As a highly respected member of the Wall Street establishment, Madoff was in a perfect position to perpetrate such a fraud. He was a pioneer in electronic trading and had served as chairman of the NASDAQ stock market. Aside from its trading operations, Bernard L. Madoff Investment Securities LLC also acted as a money manager, and it claimed to achieve highly consistent annual returns, between 10% and 12% in good markets as well as bad. Its strategy was supposedly based on option hedging strategies, but Madoff was never precise about his approach. Still, his stature on Wall Street and the prestige of his client list seemed to testify to his legitimacy. Moreover, he played hard-to-get with new investors, and it appeared that one needed connections to join the fund, which only increased its appeal. The scheme seems to have operated for decades, but in the 2008 stock market downturn several large clients requested redemptions totaling around $7 billion. With far less than $1 billion of assets left in the firm, the scheme collapsed.

Not everyone was fooled and, in retrospect, several red flags should have aroused suspicion. For example, some institutional investors shied away from the fund, objecting to its unusual opacity. Given the magnitude of the assets supposedly under management, the option hedging trades purportedly at the heart of Madoff's investment strategy should have dominated options market trading volume, yet there was no evidence of their execution. Moreover, Madoff's auditor, a small firm with only three employees (including only one active accountant!), seemed grossly inadequate to audit such a large and complex operation. In addition, Madoff's fee structure was highly unusual. Rather than acting as a hedge fund that would charge a percentage of assets plus incentive fees, he claimed to profit instead through trading commissions on the account—if true, this would have been a colossal price break to clients. Finally, rather than placing assets under management with a custodial bank as most funds do, Madoff claimed to keep the funds in house, which meant that no one could independently verify their existence. In 2000, the SEC received a letter from an industry professional named Harry Markopolos concluding that "Madoff Securities is the world's largest Ponzi scheme," but Madoff continued to operate unimpeded.

Several questions remain unanswered. Did Madoff act alone as he claims, or did he have help from others? How much money was actually lost? Some of the "lost" funds represented fictitious earnings on invested money, and some was returned to early investors. Where did the money go? Was it lost to bad trades, or was it skimmed off to support Madoff's lifestyle? And why didn't the red flags and early warnings prompt a more aggressive response from regulators?

The idea behind funds of funds is to spread risk across several different funds. However, investors need to be aware that these funds of funds operate with considerable leverage, on top of the leverage of the primary funds in which they invest, which can make returns highly volatile. Moreover, if the various hedge funds in which these funds of funds invest have similar investment styles, the diversification benefits of spreading investments across several funds may be illusory—but the extra layer of steep management fees paid to the manager of the fund of funds certainly is not.[8]

[8]One small silver lining: While funds of funds pay incentive fees to each of the underlying funds, the incentive fees they charge their own investors tend to be lower, typically around 10% rather than 20%.

SUMMARY

- Like mutual funds, hedge funds pool the assets of several clients and manage the pooled assets on their behalf. However, hedge funds differ from mutual funds with respect to disclosure, investor base, flexibility and predictability of investment orientation, regulation, and fee structure.
- Directional funds take a stance on the performance of broad market sectors. Nondirectional funds establish market-neutral positions on relative mispricing. However, even these hedged positions still present idiosyncratic risk.
- Statistical arbitrage is the use of quantitative systems to uncover many perceived misalignments in relative pricing and ensure profits by averaging over all of these small bets. It often uses data-mining methods to uncover past patterns that form the basis for the established investment positions.

- Portable alpha is a strategy in which one invests in positive-alpha positions, then hedges the systematic risk of that investment, and, finally, establishes market exposure where desired by using passive indexes or futures contracts.
- Performance evaluation of hedge funds is complicated by survivorship bias, by the potential instability of risk attributes, by the existence of liquidity premiums, and by unreliable market valuations of infrequently traded assets. Performance evaluation is particularly difficult when the fund engages in option positions. Tail events make it hard to assess the true performance of positions involving options without extremely long histories of returns.
- Hedge funds typically charge investors both a management fee and an incentive fee equal to a percentage of profits beyond some threshold value. The incentive fee is akin to a call option on the portfolio. Funds of hedge funds pay the incentive fee to each underlying fund that beats its hurdle rate, even if the overall performance of the portfolio is poor.

KEY TERMS

alpha transfer, 654–655
backfill bias, 660
data mining, 654
directional strategy, 652
funds of funds, 665
hedge fund, 651

high water mark, 665
incentive fee, 664
lock-up period, 651
market neutral, 653
nondirectional
    strategy, 652

pairs trading, 654
portable alpha, 654
pure plays, 653
statistical arbitrage, 654
survivorship bias, 660

PROBLEM SETS

 Select problems are available in McGraw-Hill Connect. Please see the packaging options section of the preface for more information.

Basic

1. Would a market-neutral hedge fund be a good candidate for an investor's entire retirement portfolio? If not, would there be a role for the hedge fund in the overall portfolio of such an investor?

2. A fund manages a $1.2 billion equity portfolio with a beta of .6. If the S&P contract multiplier is $250 and the index is currently at 800, how many contracts should the fund sell to make its overall position market neutral?

3. A hedge fund charges an incentive fee of 20% of any investment returns above the T-bill rate, which currently is 2%. In the first year, the fund suffers a loss of 8%. What rate of return must it earn in the second year to be eligible for an incentive fee?

4. How might the incentive fee of a hedge fund affect the manager's proclivity to take on high-risk assets in the portfolio?

5. Why is it harder to assess the performance of a hedge fund portfolio manager than that of a typical mutual fund manager?

6. Is statistical arbitrage true arbitrage? Explain.

Intermediate

7. A hedge fund with $1 billion of assets charges a management fee of 2% and an incentive fee of 20% of returns over a money market rate, which currently is 5%. Calculate total fees, both in dollars and as a percent of assets under management, for portfolio returns of:
   a. −5%
   b. 0
   c. 5%
   d. 10%

8. A hedge fund with net asset value of $62 per share currently has a high water mark of $66. Is the value of its incentive fee more or less than it would be if the high water mark were $67?

9. Reconsider the hedge fund in the previous problem. Suppose it is January 1, the standard deviation of the fund's annual returns is 50%, and the risk-free rate is 4%. The fund has an incentive fee of 20%, but its current high water mark is $66, and net asset value is $62.
    a. What is the value of the annual incentive fee according to the Black-Scholes formula?
    b. What would the annual incentive fee be worth if the fund had no high water mark and it earned its incentive fee on its total return?
    c. What would the annual incentive fee be worth if the fund had no high water mark and it earned its incentive fee on its return in excess of the risk-free rate? (Treat the risk-free rate as a continuously compounded value to maintain consistency with the Black-Scholes formula.)
    d. Recalculate the incentive fee value for part (b) now assuming that an increase in fund leverage increases volatility to 60%.

**Please visit us at
www.mhhe.com/bkm**

10. Go to the Online Learning Center at **www.mhhe.com/bkm,** link to Chapter 20, and find there a spreadsheet containing monthly values of the S&P 500 Index. Suppose that in each month you had written an out-of-the-money put option on one unit of the index with an exercise price 5% lower than the current value of the index.
    a. What would have been the average value of your gross monthly payouts on the puts over the 10-year period October 1977–September 1987? The standard deviation?
    b. Now extend your sample by one month to include October 1987, and recalculate the average payout and standard deviation of the put-writing strategy. What do you conclude about tail risk in naked put writing?

**Please visit us at
www.mhhe.com/bkm**

11. Suppose a hedge fund follows the following strategy. Each month it holds $100 million of an S&P 500 Index fund and writes out-of-the-money put options on $100 million of the index with exercise price 5% lower than the current value of the index. Suppose the premium it receives for writing each put is $.25 million, roughly in line with the actual value of the puts.
    a. Calculate the Sharpe ratio the fund would have realized in the period October 1982–September 1987. Compare its Sharpe ratio to that of the S&P 500. Use the data from the previous problem available at the Online Learning Center, and assume the monthly risk-free interest rate over this period was .7%.
    b. Now calculate the Sharpe ratio the fund would have realized if we extend the sample period by one month to include October 1987. What do you conclude about performance evaluation and tail risk for funds pursuing optionlike strategies?

12. The following is part of the computer output from a regression of monthly returns on Waterworks stock against the S&P 500 Index. A hedge fund manager believes that Waterworks is underpriced, with an alpha of 2% over the coming month.

Beta	R-square	Standard Deviation of Residuals
.75	.65	.06 (i.e., 6% monthly)

    a. If he holds a $3 million portfolio of Waterworks stock, and wishes to hedge market exposure for the next month using one-month maturity S&P 500 futures contracts, how many contracts should he enter? Should he buy or sell contracts? The S&P 500 currently is at 1,000 and the contract multiplier is $250.
    b. What is the standard deviation of the monthly return of the hedged portfolio?
    c. Assuming that monthly returns are approximately normally distributed, what is the probability that this market-neutral strategy will lose money over the next month? Assume the risk-free rate is .5% per month.

Challenge

13. Return to the previous problem.
    a. Suppose you hold an equally weighted portfolio of 100 stocks with the same alpha, beta, and residual standard deviation as Waterworks. Assume the residual returns (the

e terms in Equations 20.1 and 20.2) on each of these stocks are independent of each other. What is the residual standard deviation of the portfolio?

b. Recalculate the probability of a loss on a market-neutral strategy involving equally weighted, market-hedged positions in the 100 stocks over the next month.

14. Return again to the previous problem. Now suppose that the manager misestimates the beta of Waterworks stock, believing it to be .50 instead of .75. The standard deviation of the monthly market rate of return is 5%.

   a. What is the standard deviation of the (now improperly) hedged portfolio?

   b. What is the probability of incurring a loss over the next month if the monthly market return has an expected value of 1% and a standard deviation of 5%? Compare your answer to the probability you found in Problem 12.

   c. What would be the probability of a loss using the data in the previous problem if the manager similarly misestimated beta as .50 instead of .75? Compare your answer to the probability you found in the previous problem.

   d. Why does the misestimation of beta matter so much more for the 100-stock portfolio than it does for the 1-stock portfolio?

15. Here are data on three hedge funds. Each fund charges its investors an incentive fee of 20% of total returns. Suppose initially that a fund of funds (FF) manager buys equal amounts of each of these funds and also charges its investors a 20% incentive fee. For simplicity, assume also that management fees other than incentive fees are zero for all funds.

	Hedge Fund 1	Hedge Fund 2	Hedge Fund 3
Start of year value (millions)	$100	$100	$100
Gross portfolio rate of return	20%	10%	30%

   a. Compute the rate of return after incentive fees to an investor in the fund of funds.

   b. Suppose that instead of buying shares in each of the three hedge funds, a stand-alone (SA) hedge fund purchases the same *portfolio* as the three underlying funds. The total value and composition of the SA fund is therefore identical to the one that would result from aggregating the three hedge funds. Consider an investor in the SA fund. After paying 20% incentive fees, what would be the value of the investor's portfolio at the end of the year?

   c. Confirm that the investor's rate of return in SA is higher than in FF by an amount equal to the extra layer of fees charged by the fund of funds.

   d. Now suppose that the return on the portfolio held by hedge fund 3 were −30% rather than +30%. Recalculate your answers to parts (*a*) and (*b*). Will either FF or SA charge an incentive fee in this scenario? Why then does the investor in FF still do worse than the investor in SA?

WEB *master* HEDGE FUND STYLES AND RESULTS

Log on to **www.hedgeindex.com,** a site run by Credit Suisse/Tremont, which maintains the TASS Hedge Funds Data Base of the performance of more than 2,000 hedge funds and produces indexes of investment performance for several hedge fund classes. Click the Downloads tab (free registration is required for access to this part of the Web site). From the Downloads page, you can access historical rates of return on each of the hedge fund subclasses (e.g., market neutral, event-driven, dedicated short bias, and so on).

1. Download the most recent five years of monthly returns for each subclass and download returns on the S&P 500 for the same period from **finance.yahoo.com.**

2. Calculate the beta of the equity-market-neutral and dedicated short bias funds. Do the results seem reasonable in terms of the orientation of these funds?

3. Look at the year-by-year performance of each hedge fund class. How does the variability of performance results in different years compare to that of the S&P 500?

20.1. *a.* Nondirectional. The shares in the fund and the short position in the index swap constitute a hedged position. The hedge fund is betting that the discount on the closed-end fund will shrink and that it will profit regardless of the general movements in the Indian market.

b. Nondirectional. The value of both positions is driven by the value of Toys "R" Us. The hedge fund is betting that the market is undervaluing Petri relative to Toys "R" Us, and that as the *relative* values of the two positions come back into alignment, it will profit regardless of the movements in the underlying shares.

c. Directional. This is an outright bet on the price that Generic Pharmaceuticals will eventually command at the conclusion of the predicted takeover attempt.

20.2. The expected rate of return on the position (in the absence of any knowledge about idiosyncratic risk reflected in the residual) is 3%. If the residual turns out to be -4%, then the position will lose 1% of its value over the month and fall to \$990,000. The excess return on the market in this month over T-bills would be $5\% - 1\% = 4\%$, while the excess return on the hedged strategy would be $-1\% - 1\% = -2\%$, so the strategy would plot in Panel A as the point $(4\%, -2\%)$. In Panel B, which plots *total* returns on the market and the hedge position, the strategy would plot as the point $(5\%, -1\%)$.

20.3. Fixed-income arbitrage portfolios show positive exposure to the long bond and to the credit spread. This pattern suggests that these are *not* hedged arbitrage portfolios, but in fact are directional portfolios.

Chapter 21

Taxes, Inflation, and Investment Strategy

After Studying This Chapter You Should Be Able To:

- Analyze lifetime savings plans.

- Account for inflation in formulating savings and investment plans.

- Account for taxes in formulating savings and investment plans.

- Understand tax shelters.

- Design your own savings plan.

A good deal of investment management in practice revolves around the individual's need to devise and manage a lifetime savings and investment plan. This forces one to confront many real-world complications such as taxes and tax shelters, Social Security, insurance, and inflation. Our major objective in this chapter is to introduce the *principles* of managing personal savings in a complex environment in which taxes and inflation interact, rather than to provide a detailed analysis of the (ever-changing) tax code.

Retirement, purchase of a home, and financing the education of children are the major objectives of saving in most households. Inflation and taxes make the task of gearing investment to accomplish these objectives complex. The long-term nature of savings intertwines the power of compounding with inflation and tax effects. Only the most experienced investors tend to fully integrate these issues into their investment strategies. Appropriate investment strategy also must address adequate insurance coverage for contingencies such as death, disability, and property damage.

We introduce some of these issues by starting with one of the long-term goals: formulating a retirement plan. We investigate the effect of inflation on the savings plan and examine how tax shelters may be integrated into one's strategy. (Readers in other countries will find it easy to adapt the analysis to the tax code of their own country.) Next we incorporate Social Security and show how to generalize the savings plan to meet other objectives such as owning a home and financing children's education. Finally, we discuss uncertainty about longevity and other contingencies. Understanding the spreadsheets we develop along the way will enable you to devise savings/investment plans for yourself and other households and adapt them to an ever-changing environment.

21.1 | Saving For the Long Run

Our objective in this chapter is to quantify the essentials of savings/investment plans and adapt them to environments in which investors confront both inflation and taxes. In the next chapter we will describe the framework that the CFA Institute has established to help financial advisers communicate with and involve client households in structuring their savings/investment plans.[1] As a first step, we set up a spreadsheet for a simple retirement plan, ignoring for the moment saving for other objectives.

Before we dive in, a brief word on what we mean by saving. Economists think of saving as a way to smooth out the lifetime consumption stream; you save when you have high earnings in order to support consumption in low-income years. In a "global" sense, the concept implies that you save for retirement so that consumption during the retirement years will not be too low relative to consumption during the saving years. In a "local" sense, smoothing consumption implies that you might finance a large purchase such as a car, rather than buy it for cash. Clearly, local consumption smoothing is of second-order importance, that is, how you purchase durable goods has little effect on the overall savings plan, except, perhaps, for very large expenditures such as buying a home or sending children to college. We begin therefore with a savings plan that ignores even large expenditures and later discuss how to augment the plan to account for these needs.

A Hypothetical Household

Imagine you are now 30 years old and have already completed your formal education, accumulated some work experience, and settled down to plan the rest of your economic life. Your plan is to retire at age 65 with a remaining life expectancy of an additional 25 years. Later on, we will further assume that you have two small children and plan to finance their college education.

For starters, we assume you intend to obtain a (level) annuity for your 25-year retirement period; we postpone discussion of planning for the uncertain time of death. (You may well live to over 100 years; what then?) Suppose your gross income this year was $50,000, and you expect annual income to increase at a rate of 7% per year. In this section, we assume that you ignore the impact of inflation and taxes. You intend to steadily save 15% of income and invest in safe government bonds that will yield 6% over the entire period. Proceeds from your investments will be automatically reinvested at the same 6% until retirement. Upon retirement, your funds in the retirement account will be used to purchase a 25-year annuity (using the same 6% interest rate) to finance a steady consumption annuity. Let's examine the consequences of this framework.

The Retirement Annuity

retirement annuity

Stream of cash flows available for consumption during one's retirement years.

We can easily obtain your **retirement annuity** from Spreadsheet 21.1, where we have hidden the lines for ages 32–34, 36–44, 46–54, and 56–64. You can obtain all the spreadsheets in this chapter from the Web page for the text: **www.mhhe.com/bkm**.

[1]Even if you do not read Chapter 22 carefully, you may want to skim through it to get an idea of how financial planners articulate a saver's objectives, constraints, and investment policy.

SPREADSHEET 21.1

The savings plan

	A	B	C	D	E
1	Retirement Years	Income Growth	Savings Rate	ROR	
2	25	.07	.15	.06	
3	Age	Income	Savings	Cumulative Savings	Consumption
4	30	50,000	7,500	7,500	42,500
5	31	53,500	8,025	15,975	45,475
9	35	70,128	10,519	61,658	59,608
19	45	137,952	20,693	308,859	117,259
29	55	271,372	40,706	943,477	230,666
39	65	533,829	80,074	2,457,518	453,755
40	Total	7,445,673	1,116,851	Retirement Annuity	192,244

	A	B	C	D	E
1	Retirement Years	Income Growth	Savings Rate	ROR	
2	25	.07	.15	.06	
3	Age	Income	Savings	Cumulative Savings	Consumption
4	30	50000	=B4*$C$2	=C4	=B4-C4
5	31	=B4*(1+$B$2)	=B5*$C$2	=D4*(1+$D$2)+C5	=B5-C5
39	65	=B38*(1+$B$2)	=B39*$C$2	=D38*(1+$D$2)+C39	=B39-C39
40	Total	=SUM(B4:B39)	=SUM(C4:C39)	Retirement Annuity	=PMT($D$2,$A$2,-$D$39,0,0)

eXcel

Please visit us at www.mhhe.com/bkm

Let's first see how this spreadsheet was constructed. To view the formulas of all cells in an Excel spreadsheet, choose "Preferences" and select the box "Formulas" in the "View" tab. The formula view of Spreadsheet 21.1 is also shown in the lower panel (numbers are user inputs).

Inputs in row 2 include: retirement years (cell A2 = 25); income growth rate (cell B2 = .07); age (column A); and income at age 30 (B4 = 50,000). Column B computes income in future years using the growth rate in cell B2; column C computes annual savings by applying the savings rate (cell C2) to income; and column E computes consumption as the difference between income and savings: column B − column C. Cumulative savings appear in column D. To obtain the value in D6, for example, multiply cell D5 by 1 plus the assumed rate of return in cell D2 (the ROR) and then add current savings from column C. Finally, C40 shows the sum of dollars saved over the lifetime, and E40 converts cumulative savings (including interest) at age 65 to a 25-year annuity using the financial function PMT from Excel's function menu. Excel provides a function to solve for annuity levels given the values of the interest rate, the number of periods, the present value of the savings account, and the future value of the account: PMT(rate, nper, PV, FV).

We observe that your retirement fund will accumulate approximately $2.5 million (cell D39) by age 65. This hefty sum shows the power of compounding, since your contributions to the savings account were only $1.1 million (C40). This fund will yield an annuity of $192,244 per year (E40) for your 25-year retirement, which seems quite attractive, except that the standard of living you'll have to get accustomed to in your retirement years is much lower than your consumption at age 65 (E39). In fact, if you unhide the hidden lines, you'll see that upon retirement, you'll have to make do with what you used to consume at age 51. This may not worry you much since, with your children having flown the coop and the mortgage paid up, you may be able to maintain the luxury to which you recently became accustomed. But your projected well-being is deceptive: Get ready to account for inflation and taxes.

If you project an ROR of only 5%, what savings rate would you need to provide the same retirement annuity?

CONCEPT *check* **21.1**

21.2 Accounting For Inflation

Inflation puts a damper on your plans in two ways: First, it erodes the purchasing power of the cumulative dollars you have so far saved. Second, the *real* dollars you earn on your portfolio each year depend on the *real* interest rate, which is approximately equal to the nominal rate minus inflation. Since an appropriate savings plan must generate a decent *real* annuity, we must recast the entire plan in real dollars. We will assume your income still is forecast to grow at a 7% rate, but now you recognize that part of income growth is due to inflation, which is running at 3% per year.

A Real Savings Plan

To convert nominal dollars to real dollars we need to calculate the price level in future years relative to today's prices. The "deflator" (or relative price level) for a given year is that year's price level divided by today's. It equals the dollars needed at that future date to provide the same purchasing power as $1 today (at age 30). For an inflation rate of $i = 3\%$, the deflator for age 35 is $(1 + i)^5$, or in Excel notation, $(1 + i)\char`^5 = 1.03\char`^5 = 1.16$. By age 65, the deflator is 2.81. Thus, even with a moderate rate of inflation (3% is below the historical average, nominal dollars will lose a lot of purchasing power over long horizons. We also can compute the *real* rate of return (rROR) from the nominal ROR of 6%: rROR $= (ROR - i)/(1 + i) = 3/1.03 = 2.91\%$.

real consumption

Nominal consumption divided by the price deflator.

Spreadsheet 21.2, with the formula view below it, is the reworked Spreadsheet 21.1 adjusted for inflation. In addition to the rate of inflation (cell C2) and the real rate of return (F2), the major addition to this sheet is the price level deflator (column C). Instead of nominal consumption, we present **real consumption** (column F), calculated by dividing nominal consumption (column B − column D) by the price deflator, column C.

The numbers have changed considerably. Gone is the luxurious retirement we anticipated earlier. At age 65 and beyond, with a real annuity of $49,668, you will have to revert to a standard of living equal to that you attained at age 34; this is less than a third of your real consumption in your last working year, at age 65. The reason is that the retirement fund of $2.5 million (E39) is worth only $873,631 in today's purchasing power (E39/C39). Such is the effect of inflation. If you wish to do better than that, you must save more.

In our initial plan (Spreadsheet 21.1), we envisioned consuming a level, nominal annuity for the retirement years. This is an inappropriate goal once we account for inflation, since it would imply a declining standard of living starting at age 65. Its purchasing power at age 65 in terms of current dollars would be $68,320 (i.e., $192,244/1.03^{35}$), and at age 90 only $32,630. (Check this!)

It is tempting to contemplate solving the problem of an inadequate retirement annuity by increasing the assumed rate of return on investments. However, this can only be accomplished

---

SPREADSHEET 21.2

A real retirement plan

Please visit us at
www.mhhe.com/bkm

	A	B	C	D	E	F
1	Retirement Years	Income Growth	Rate of Inflation	Savings Rate	ROR	rROR
2	25	.07	.03	.15	.06	.0291
3	Age	Income	Deflator	Saving	Cumulative Savings	rConsumption
4	30	50,000	1.00	7,500	7,500	42,500
5	31	53,500	1.03	8,025	15,975	44,150
9	35	70,128	1.16	10,519	61,658	51,419
19	45	137,952	1.56	20,693	308,859	75,264
29	55	271,372	2.09	40,706	943,477	110,167
39	65	533,829	2.81	80,074	2,457,518	161,257
40	Total	7,445,673		1,116,851	Real Annuity	49,668

	A	B	C	D	E	F
1	Retirement Years	Income Growth	Rate of Inflation	Savings Rate	ROR	rROR
2	25	.07	.03	.15	.06	=(E2-C2)/(1+C2)
3	Age	Income	Deflator	Savings	Cumulative Savings	rConsumption
4	30	50000	1	=B4*$D$2	=D4	=(B4-D4)/C4
5	31	=B4*(1+$B$2)	=C4*(1+$C$2)	=B5*$D$2	=E4*(1+$E$2)+D5	=(B5-D5)/C5
39	65	=B38*(1+$B$2)	=C38*(1+$C$2)	=B39*$D$2	=E38*(1+$E$2)+D39	=(B39-D39)/C39
40	Total	=SUM(B4:B39)		=SUM(D4:D39)	Real Annuity	=PMT($F$2,$A$2,-$E$39/$C$39,0,0)

by putting your savings at risk. Much of this text elaborates on how to do so efficiently; yet it also emphasizes that while taking on risk will give you an *expectation* for a better retirement, it implies as well a nonzero probability of doing a lot worse. At the age of 30, you should be able to tolerate some risk to the retirement annuity for the simple reason that if things go wrong, you can change course, increase your savings rate, and work harder. As you get older, this option progressively fades, and increasing risk becomes less of a viable option. If you do choose to increase risk, you can set a "safety-first target" (i.e., a minimum acceptable goal) for the retirement annuity and continuously monitor your risky portfolio. If the portfolio does poorly and approaches the safety-first target, you progressively shift into risk-free bonds— you may recognize this strategy as a version of dynamic hedging.

The difficulty with this strategy is twofold: First, it requires monitoring, which is time-consuming and may be nerve-racking as well. Second, when decision time comes, it may be psychologically hard to withdraw. By shifting out of the risky portfolio if and when your portfolio is hammered, you give up any hope of recovery. This is hard to do and many investors fail the test. For these investors, therefore, the right approach is to stick with the safe, lower ROR and make the effort to balance standard of living before and after retirement. Avoiding sleepless nights is ample reward.

Therefore, the only variable we leave under your control in this spreadsheet is the rate of saving. To improve retirement lifestyle relative to the preretirement years, without jeopardizing its safety, you will have to reduce consumption during the saving years—there is no free lunch.

> If you project a rate of inflation of 4%, what nominal ROR on investments would you need to maintain the same real retirement annuity as in Spreadsheet 21.2?
>
> **CONCEPT** *check* **21.2**

An Alternative Savings Plan

In Spreadsheet 21.2, we saved a constant fraction of income. But since real income grows over time (nominal income grows at 7% while inflation is only 3%), we might consider deferring our savings toward future years when real income is higher. By applying a higher savings rate to future (higher) real income, we can afford to reduce the current savings rate. In Spreadsheet 21.3, we use a base savings rate of 10% (lower than the savings rate in the previous spreadsheet), but we increase it by 3% per year. Saving in each year therefore equals a fixed savings rate times annual income (column B), times the exponential growing factor 1.03^t. By saving a larger fraction of income in later years, when real income is larger, you create a smoother profile of real consumption.

Spreadsheet 21.3 shows that with an *initial* savings rate of 10%, compared with the unchanging 15% rate in the previous spreadsheet, you can achieve a retirement annuity of $59,918, larger than the $49,668 annuity in the previous plan.

Notice that real consumption in the early years is greater than with the previous plan. What you have done is to postpone saving until your income is higher. At first blush, this plan is preferable: It allows for a more comfortable consumption of 90% of income at the outset, a consistent increase in standard of living during your earning years, all without significantly affecting the retirement annuity. But this program has one serious downside: By postponing the bulk of your savings to a later age, you come to depend on your health, longevity, and, more ominously (*and without possibility of insurance*), on a successful future career. Put differently, this plan achieves comfort by increasing risk, making this choice a matter of risk tolerance.

> Suppose you like the plan of tilting savings toward later years, but worry about the increased risk of postponing the bulk of your savings to later years. Is there anything you can do to mitigate the risk?
>
> **CONCEPT** *check* **21.3**

SPREADSHEET 21.3

Backloading the real savings plan

Please visit us at www.mhhe.com/bkm

	A	B	C	D	E	F
1	Retirement Years	Income Growth	Rate of Inflation	Savings Rate	ROR	rROR
2	25	.07	.03	.1	.06	.0291
3	Age	Income	Deflator	Savings	Cumulative Savings	rConsumption
4	30	50,000	1.00	5,000	5,000	45,000
5	31	53,500	1.03	5,511	10,811	46,592
9	35	70,128	1.16	8,130	44,351	53,480
19	45	137,952	1.56	21,492	260,927	74,751
29	55	271,372	2.09	56,819	947,114	102,471
39	65	533,829	2.81	150,212	2,964,669	136,331
40	Total	7,445,673		1,572,466	Real Annuity	59,918

	A	B	C	D	E	F
1	Retirement Years	Income Growth	Rate of Inflation	Savings Rate	ROR	rROR
2	25	.07	.03	.1	.06	=(E2-C2)/(1+C2)
3	Age	Income	Deflator	Savings	Cumulative Savings	rConsumption
4	30	50000	1	=B4*C4*$D$2	=D4	=(B4-D4)/C4
5	31	=B4*(1+$B$2)	=C4*(1+$C$2)	=B5*C5*$D$2	=E4*(1+$E$2)+D5	=(B5-D5)/C5
39	65	=B38*(1+$B$2)	=C38*(1+$C$2)	=B39*C39*$D$2	=E38*(1+$E$2)+D39	=(B39-D39)/C39
40	Total	=SUM(B4:B39)		=SUM(D4:D39)	Real Annuity	=PMT($F$2,$A$2,-$E$39/$C$39,0,0)

21.3 Accounting for Taxes

flat tax

A tax code that taxes all income above some exemption at a fixed rate.

To initiate a discussion of taxes, let's assume that you are subject to a **flat tax** rate of 25% on taxable income less one exemption of $15,000. This is similar to several proposals for a simplified U.S. tax code that have been floated by one presidential candidate or another prior to elections—at least when you add state taxes to the proposed flat rate. An important feature of this (and the existing) tax code is that the tax rate is levied on nominal income and applies as well to investment income. (The tax on investment income is sometimes characterized as double taxation—you pay taxes when you earn income and then you pay taxes again when your savings earn interest.) Some relief from the effect of taxing nominal dollars both in this proposal and the current U.S. code is provided by raising the exemption, annually, by the rate of inflation. To adapt our spreadsheet to this simple tax code, we must add columns for taxes and after-tax income. The tax-adjusted plan is shown in Spreadsheet 21.4. It adapts the savings plan of Spreadsheet 21.2, that is, saving 15% of nominal income.

The top panel of the sheet deals with the earning years. Column D adjusts the exemption (D2) by the price level (column C). Column E applies the tax rate (cell E2) to taxable income (column B − column D). The savings rate (F2) is applied to after-tax income (column B − column E), allowing us to calculate cumulative savings (column G) and real consumption (column H). The formula view shows the detailed construction.

As you might have expected, real consumption is lower in the presence of taxes, as are savings and the retirement fund. The retirement fund provides for a real, before-tax annuity of only $37,882, compared with $49,668 absent taxes in Spreadsheet 21.2.

The bottom panel of the sheet shows the further reduction in real consumption due to taxes paid during the retirement years. While you do not pay taxes on the cumulative savings in the retirement plan (you did that already as the savings accrued interest), you do pay taxes on interest earned by the fund while you are drawing it down. These taxes are quite significant and further deplete the fund and its net-of-tax earning power. For this reason, your consumption annuity is lower in the early years when your fund has not yet been depleted and taxable interest income is higher.

In the end, despite a handsome income that grows at a real rate of almost 4%, an aggressive savings rate of 15%, a modest rate of inflation, and a realistic tax, you will be able to achieve only a modest (but at least low-risk) real retirement income. This is a reality with which most people must struggle. Whether to sacrifice more of today's standard of living

SPREADSHEET 21.4

Saving with a simple tax code

	A	B	C	D	E	F	G	H
1	Retirement Years	Income Growth	Rate of Inflation	Exemption Now	Tax Rate	Savings Rate	ROR	rROR
2	25	.07	.03	15000	.25	.15	.06	.0291
3	Age	Income	Deflator	Exemption	Taxes	Savings	Cumulative Savings	rConsumption
4	30	50,000	1.00	15,000	8,750	6,188	6,188	35,063
5	31	53,500	1.03	15,450	9,605	6,584	13,143	36,224
9	35	70,128	1.16	17,389	13,775	8,453	50,188	41,319
19	45	137,952	1.56	23,370	31,892	15,909	245,334	57,864
29	55	271,372	2.09	31,407	69,943	30,214	733,467	81,773
39	65	533,829	2.81	42,208	148,611	57,783	1,874,346	116,365
40	Total				1,884,163	834,226	Real Annuity=	37,882
41	**RETIREMENT**							
42	Age	Nom Withdraw	Deflator	Exemption	Taxes		Funds Left	rConsumption
43	66	109,792	2.90	43,474	17,247		1,877,014	31,931
47	70	123,572	3.26	48,931	15,743		1,853,382	33,056
52	75	143,254	3.78	56,724	12,200		1,721,015	34,656
57	80	166,071	4.38	65,759	6,047		1,422,954	36,503
62	85	192,521	5.08	76,232	0		883,895	37,882
67	90	223,185	5.89	88,374	0		0	37,882
68	Total	4,002,944			203,199			

eXcel

Please visit us at www.mhhe.com/bkm

	A	B	C	D	E	F	G	H
1	Retirement Years	Income Growth	Rate of Inflation	Exemption Now	Tax Rate	Savings Rate	ROR	rROR
2	25	.07	.03	15000	.25	.15	.06	=(G2-C2)/(1+C2)
3	Age	Income	Deflator	Exemption	Taxes	Savings	Cumulative Savings	rConsumption
4	30	50000	1	=$D$2*C4	=(B4-D4)*$E$2	=(B4-E4)*$F$2	=F4	=(B4-E4-F4)/C4
5	31	=B4*(1+$B$2)	=C4*(1+$C$2)	=$D$2*C5	=(B5-D5+G4*$G$2)*$E$2	=(B5-E5)*$F$2	=G4*(1+$G$2)+F5	=(B5-E5-F5)/C5
39	65	=B38*(1+$B$2)	=C38*(1+$C$2)	=$D$2*C39	=(B39-D39+G38*$G$2)*$E$2	=(B39-E39)*$F$2	=G38*(1+$G$2)+F39	=(B39-E39-F39)/C39
40	Total				=SUM(E4:E39)	=SUM(F4:F39)	Real Annuity	=PMT($H$2,$A$2,-$G$39/$C$39,0,0)
41	**RETIREMENT**							
42	Age	Nom Withdraw	Deflator	Exemption	Taxes		Funds Left	rConsumption
43	66	=$H$40*C43	=C39*(1+$C$2)	=$D$2*C43	=MAX(0,(G39*$G$2-D43)*$E$2)		=G39*(1+$G$2)-B43	=(B43-E43)/C43
44	67	=$H$40*C44	=C43*(1+$C$2)	=$D$2*C44	=MAX(0,(G43*$G$2-D44)*$E$2)		=G43*(1+$G$2)-B44	=(B44-E44)/C44
67	90	=$H$40*C67	=C66*(1+$C$2)	=$D$2*C67	=MAX(0,(G66*$G$2-D67)*$E$2)		=G66*(1+$G$2)-B67	=(B67-E67)/C67
68	Total	=SUM(B43:B67)			=SUM(E43:E67)			

through an increased rate of saving, or take some risk in the form of saving a real annuity and/or invest in a risky portfolio with a higher expected return, is a question of preference and risk tolerance.

One often hears complaints about the double taxation resulting from taxing income earned on savings from dollars on which taxes were already paid. It is interesting to see what effective tax rate is imposed on your lifetime earnings by double taxation. To do so, we use Spreadsheet 21.4 to set up your lifetime earnings, exemptions, and taxes:

Income		
(1) Lifetime labor income		$7,445,673
Total exemptions during working years	949,139	
(2) Lifetime taxable labor income		6,496,534
Taxes		
During labor years	1,884,163	
During retirement	203,199	
(3) Lifetime taxes		2,087,362
Lifetime average tax rate = (3)/(1)		28%
Lifetime tax rate on taxable income = (3)/(2)		32%

Thus, double taxation is equivalent to raising the tax rate on taxable income to 32%. It creates a lifetime *average* tax rate (28%) that is higher than the prescribed *marginal* rate of 25%.

Would a 1% increase in the exemption compensate you for a 1% increase in the tax rate? **CONCEPT** *check* **21.4**

21.4 | The Economics of Tax Shelters

tax shelters

Means by which to postpone payment of tax liabilities for as long as possible.

Tax shelters range from the simple to the mind-bogglingly complex, yet they all have one common objective: to postpone payment of tax liabilities for as long as possible. We know already that this isn't small fry. Postponement implies a smaller present value of tax payment, and a tax paid with a long delay can have present value near zero. However, delay is necessarily beneficial only when the tax rate doesn't increase over time. If the tax rate on retirement income is higher than during earning years, the value of a tax deferral may be questionable; if the tax rate will decline, deferral is even more preferable.

A Benchmark Tax Shelter

Postponing tax payments is the only attainable (legal) objective since, whenever you have taxable income, a tax liability is created that can (almost) never be erased.[2] For this reason, a benchmark tax shelter *postpones all* taxes on savings and the income on those savings. In this case, taxes on your entire savings account will be paid during retirement, as you draw down the retirement fund. This sort of shelter is actually equivalent to the tax treatment of Individual Retirement Accounts (IRAs) which we discuss later, so we will describe this structure as having an "IRA style."

To examine the impact of an IRA-style structure (assuming you could shelter all your savings) in a situation comparable to the nonsheltered flat-tax case, we maintain the same consumption level as in Spreadsheet 21.4 (flat tax with no shelter), but now input the new, sheltered savings plan in Spreadsheet 21.5. This focuses the entire effect of the tax shelter onto retirement consumption.

SPREADSHEET 21.5

Saving with a flat tax and an IRA-style tax shelter

Please visit us at www.mhhe.com/bkm

	A	B	C	D	E	F	G	H
1	Retirement Years	Income Growth	Rate of Inflation	Exemption Now	Tax Rate	Savings Rate	ROR	rROR
2	25	.07	.03	15000	.25	.15	.06	.0291
3	Age	Income	Deflator	Exemption	Taxes	Savings	Cumulative Savings	rConsumption
4	30	50,000	1.00	15,000	5,016	9,922	9,922	35,063
5	31	53,500	1.03	15,450	5,465	10,724	21,242	36,224
9	35	70,128	1.16	17,389	7,628	14,600	83,620	41,319
19	45	137,952	1.56	23,370	16,695	31,106	438,234	57,864
29	55	271,372	2.09	31,407	34,952	65,205	1,393,559	81,773
39	65	533,829	2.81	42,208	71,307	135,087	3,762,956	116,365
40	**Total**					944,536	1,773,854	**Real Annuity**	76,052
41	**RETIREMENT**							
42	Age	Nom Withdraw	Deflator	Exemption	Taxes		Funds Left	rConsumption
43	66	220,420	2.90	43,474	44,236		3,768,313	60,789
47	70	248,085	3.26	48,931	49,789		3,720,867	60,789
52	75	287,598	3.78	56,724	57,719		3,455,127	60,789
57	80	333,405	4.38	65,759	66,912		2,856,737	60,789
62	85	386,508	5.08	76,232	77,569		1,774,517	60,789
67	90	448,068	5.89	88,374	89,924		0	60,789
68	**Total**		8,036,350			1,612,828		

	A	B	C	D	E	F	G	H
1	Retirement Years	Income Growth	Rate of Inflation	Exemption Now	Tax Rate	Savings Rate	ROR	rROR
2	25	.07	.03	15000	.25	.15	.06	=(G2-C2)/(1+C2)
3	Age	Income	Deflator	Exemption	Taxes	Savings	Cumulative Savings	rConsumption
4	30	50000	1	=$D$2*C4	=(H4*C4-D4)*$E$2	=B4-E4-H4*C4	=F4	35062.5
5	31	=B4*(1+$B$2)	=C4*(1+$C$2)	=$D$2*C5	=(H5*C5-D5)*$E$2	=B5-E5-H5*C5	=G4*(1+$G$2)+F5	36223.7712378641
39	65	=B38*(1+$B$2)	=C38*(1+$C$2)	=$D$2*C39	=(H39*C39-D39)*$E$2	=B39-E39-H39*C39	=G38*(1+$G$2)+F39	116364.980523664
40	**Total**				=SUM(E4:E39)	=SUM(F4:F39)	**Real Annuity**	=PMT($H$2,$A$2,-$G$39/$C$39,0,0)
41	**RETIREMENT**							
42	Age	Nom Withdraw	Deflator	Exemption	Taxes		Funds Left	rConsumption
43	66	=$H$40*C43	=C39*(1+$C$2)	=$D$2*C43	=MAX(0,(B43-D43)*$E$2)		=G39*(1+$G$2)-B43	=(B43-E43)/C43
44	67	=$H$40*C44	=C43*(1+$C$2)	=$D$2*C44	=MAX(0,(B44-D44)*$E$2)		=G43*(1+$G$2)-B44	=(B44-E44)/C44
67	90	=$H$40*C67	=C66*(1+$C$2)	=$D$2*C67	=MAX(0,(B67-D67)*$E$2)		=G66*(1+$G$2)-B67	=(B67-E67)/C67
68	**Total**	=SUM(B43:B67)			=SUM(E43:E67)			

---

[2]Bankruptcy or death can erase some tax liabilities, though. We will avoid dealing with these unhappy outcomes.

In this sheet, we input desired real consumption (column H, copied from Spreadsheet 21.4). Taxes (column E) are then calculated by applying the tax rate (E2) to nominal consumption less the exemption (H × C − D). Thus, savings are the residual from nominal income (B) minus taxes (E), minus nominal consumption (H × C). The retirement panel shows that you pay taxes on all withdrawals—all funds in the retirement account are subject to tax.

The results are interesting. Total lifetime taxes paid with the IRA tax shelter amount to $2.5 million, a lot more than $2.1 million absent the shelter. The reason is that the tax shelter allows for larger savings that increase lifetime income to $3.7 million compared with only $1.9 million absent the shelter. Since in this comparison income and consumption during the earnings years are as before, the entire net gain from the shelter is pushed to the retirement years. Thus, the real annuity (annual consumption) during retirement increases from $37,882 to $76,052.

With the IRA-style tax shelter, all your taxes are due during retirement. Is the trade-off between exemption and tax rate different from the circumstance where you have no shelter?	**CONCEPT** *check* **21.5**

The Effect of the Progressive Nature of the Tax Code

Because of the exemption, the flat tax is somewhat progressive: Taxes are an increasing fraction of income. For very high incomes, the marginal tax rate (25%) is only slightly higher than the average rate. With income of $50,000 at the outset, the average tax rate is 17.5% (.25 × 35,000/50,000), and grows steadily over time. In general, with a flat tax, the ratio of the average to marginal rate equals the ratio of taxable to gross income. This ratio becomes .89 at age 45, at which point the average tax rate is above 22%. The current U.S. tax code, with multiple income brackets, is much more progressive than our assumed structure.

In Spreadsheet 21.6 we work with a more **progressive tax** structure that is closer to the U.S. Federal tax code augmented with an average state tax. Our hypothetical tax schedule is described in Table 21.1.

progressive tax

Taxes are an increasing fraction of income.

We have seen that taxes on income during the earning period have a greater effect because of the time value of money; early tax payments (during earning years) have a larger effect than later payments during retirement years. In a progressive tax environment, this effect is magnified if your retirement income (withdrawal from the retirement fund) is lower than income during the earning years. This has been the case in all the alternatives that we have analyzed so far.

SPREADSHEET 21.6

Saving with a progressive tax

	A	B	C	D	E	F	G	H
1	Retirement Years	Income Growth	Rate of Inflation	Exemption Now	Tax rates in	Savings Rate	ROR	rROR
2	25	.07	.03	10000	Table 21.1	.15	.06	.0291
3	Age	Income	Deflator	Exemption	Taxes	Savings	Cumulative Savings	rConsumption
4	30	50,000	1.00	10,000	8,000	6,300	6,300	35,700
5	31	53,500	1.03	10,300	8,716	6,718	13,396	36,958
9	35	70,128	1.16	11,593	12,489	8,646	51,310	42,262
19	45	137,952	1.56	15,580	32,866	15,763	248,018	57,333
29	55	271,372	2.09	20,938	76,587	29,218	731,514	79,076
39	65	533,829	2.81	28,139	186,335	52,124	1,833,644	104,970
40	Total		Total	632,759	2,116,533	799,371	Real Annuity	37,059
41	RETIREMENT							
42	Age	Nom Withdraw	Deflator	Exemption	Taxes		Fund Left	rConsumption
43	66	107,408	2.90	28,983	16,207		1,836,254	31,467
47	70	120,889	3.26	32,620	15,371		1,813,134	32,347
52	75	140,143	3.78	37,816	13,083		1,683,643	33,599
57	80	162,464	4.38	43,839	8,831		1,392,054	35,045
62	85	188,341	5.08	50,821	1,757		864,701	36,714
67	90	218,338	5.89	58,916	0		0	37,059
68	Total	3,916,018			227,675			

Please visit us at www.mhhe.com/bkm

TABLE 21.1	Taxable Income* Over	But Not Over	The Tax Is	of the Amount Over
Income tax schedule used for the progressive tax	$ 0	$ 50,000	$ 0 + 20%	$ 0
	50,000	150,000	10,000 + 30	50,000
	150,000	...	40,000 + 40	150,000

*Current exemption with this code is assumed to be $10,000, that is, taxable income = income − 10,000. The exemption and tax brackets are continuously adjusted for inflation.

Spreadsheet 21.6, which continues to maintain the same income and consumption during the earning years, differs from Spreadsheet 21.4 only in that column E replaces the flat tax with the schedule of Table 21.1. Surprisingly, the effect on consumption in both earning and retirement years is small. This is due to two offsetting effects. The higher tax rate applied to the high incomes of the later earning years increases the tax bite. At the same time, the lower income and corresponding lower tax bracket during both early earning and retirement years dampen that effect. The bottom line is that a roughly middle–class life cycle of earnings mitigates the difference between flat and progressive tax schedules. This is an important point in favor of a flat tax that is simpler and reduces the incentive to devote resources to avoiding taxation.

Spreadsheet 21.7 augments the progressive tax code with our benchmark (IRA-style) tax shelter that allows you to pay taxes on consumption (minus an exemption) and accumulate tax liability to be paid during your retirement years. The construction of this spreadsheet is identical to Spreadsheet 21.5, with the only difference being the tax structure built into column E. We copied the real preretirement consumption stream from Spreadsheet 21.6 to focus the effect of the tax shelter on the standard of living during the retirement years. Spreadsheet 21.7 shows that the lower tax bracket during the retirement years allows you to pay lower taxes over the life of the plan and significantly increases retirement consumption. The use of the IRA-style tax shelter increases the retirement annuity by an average of $32,000 a year, a better improvement than we obtained from the shelter with the flat tax.

The effectiveness of the shelter also has a sort of hedge quality. If you become fortunate and strike it rich, the tax shelter will be less effective, since your tax bracket will be higher at retirement. However, mediocre or worse outcomes will result in low marginal rates upon retirement, making the shelter more effective and the tax bite lower.

SPREADSHEET 21.7

The benchmark (IRA) tax shelter with a progressive tax code

Please visit us at
www.mhhe.com/bkm

	A	B	C	D	E	F	G	H
1	Retirement Years	Income Growth	Rate of Inflation	Exemption Now	Tax rates in	Savings Rate	ROR	rROR
2	25	.07	.03	10000	Table 21.1	.15	.06	.0291
3	Age	Income	Deflator	Exemption	Taxes	Savings	Cumulative Savings	rConsumption
4	30	50,000	1.00	10,000	5,140	9,160	9,160	35,700
5	31	53,500	1.03	10,300	5,553	9,880	19,590	36,958
9	35	70,128	1.16	11,593	7,480	13,654	77,112	42,262
19	45	137,952	1.56	15,580	14,749	33,880	434,916	57,333
29	55	271,372	2.09	20,938	32,920	72,885	1,455,451	79,076
39	65	533,829	2.81	28,139	66,100	172,359	4,125,524	104,970
40	Total			632,759	879,430	2,036,474	Real Annuity	83,380
41	RETIREMENT							
42	Age	Nom Withdraw	Deflator	Exemption	Taxes		Funds Left	rConsumption
43	66	241,658	2.90	28,983	49,311		4,131,398	66,366
47	70	271,988	3.26	32,620	55,500		4,079,381	66,366
52	75	315,309	3.78	37,816	64,340		3,788,036	66,366
57	80	365,529	4.38	43,839	74,588		3,131,989	66,366
62	85	423,749	5.08	50,821	86,467		1,945,496	66,366
67	90	491,241	5.89	58,916	100,239		0	66,366
68	Total	8,810,670	Total		1,797,848			

21.5 A Menu of Tax Shelters

Individual Retirement Accounts

Individual Retirement Accounts (IRAs) were set up by Congress to increase the incentives to save for retirement. The limited scope of these accounts is an important feature. Currently, annual contributions are limited to $5,000. Workers 50 years of age and up can increase annual contributions by up to another $1,000. IRAs are somewhat illiquid (as are most shelters), in that there is a 10% penalty on withdrawals prior to age 59½. However, allowances for early withdrawal with no penalty for qualified reasons such as (one-time) purchase of a home or higher education expenses substantially mitigate the problem.

There are two types of IRAs to choose from; the better alternative is not easy to determine.

Traditional IRA   Contributions to **traditional IRA** accounts are tax deductible, as are the earnings in the account until retirement. In principle, if you were able to contribute all your savings to a traditional IRA, your savings plan would be identical to our benchmark tax shelter (Spreadsheets 21.5 and 21.7), with the effectiveness of tax mitigation depending on your marginal tax rate upon retirement.

Roth IRA   A **Roth IRA** is a variation on the traditional IRA tax shelter, with both a drawback and an advantage. Contributions to Roth IRAs are *not* tax deductible. However, earnings on the accumulating funds in the Roth account are tax-free, and unlike a traditional IRA, no taxes are paid upon withdrawals of savings during retirement. The trade-off is not easy to evaluate. To gain insight and illustrate how to analyze the trade-off, we contrast Roth with traditional IRAs under the currently more realistic, progressive tax code.

traditional IRA

Contributions to the account and investment earnings are tax sheltered until retirement.

Roth IRA

Contributions are not tax sheltered, but investment earnings are tax free.

Roth IRA with the Progressive Tax Code

As we have noted, a traditional IRA is identical to the benchmark tax shelter set up under two alternative tax codes in Spreadsheets 21.5 and 21.7. We saw that, as a general rule, the effectiveness of a tax shelter depends on the progressivity of the tax code: Lower tax rates during retirement favor the postponement of tax obligations until one's retirement years. However, with a Roth IRA, you pay no taxes at all on withdrawals during the retirement phase. In this case, therefore, the effectiveness of the shelter does not depend on the tax rates during the retirement years. The question for any investor is whether this advantage is sufficient to compensate for the nondeductibility of contributions, which is the primary advantage of the traditional IRA.

To evaluate the trade-off, Spreadsheet 21.8 modifies Spreadsheet 21.7 (progressive tax) to conform to the features of a Roth IRA, that is, we eliminate deductibility of contributions and taxes during the retirement phase. We keep consumption during the earning years the same as they were in the benchmark (traditional IRA) tax shelter to compare the standard of living in retirement afforded by a Roth IRA tax shelter.

Table 21.2 demonstrates the difference between the two types of shelters. In both cases, lifetime income and real consumption during the earning years, as well as the progressive tax scheme, are identical. The only difference is which IRA plan you choose, traditional or Roth. Hence the first line of Table 21.2, lifetime labor income, is fixed at $7.4 million. But the shelter works differently in each case. The traditional IRA shelters more income during the earning years, resulting in total taxes of only $879,430, compared with $1.75 million under the Roth IRA. In the retirement years, however, the Roth IRA plan entails no taxes, while the traditional IRA results in taxes of just under $1.8 million. Lifetime taxes are $2.7 million

SPREADSHEET 21.8

Roth IRA with a progressive tax

eXcel

Please visit us at
www.mhhe.com/bkm

	A	B	C	D	E	F	G	H
3	Retirement Years	Income Growth	Rate of Inflation	Exemption Now	Tax Rates in	Savings Rate	ROR	rROR
4	25	.07	.03	10000	Table 21.1	.15	.06	.0291
5	Age	Income	Deflator	Exemption	Taxes	Savings	Cumulative Savings	rConsumption
6	30	50,000	1.00	10,000	8,000	6,300	6,300	35,700
7	31	53,500	1.03	10,300	8,640	6,793	13,471	36,958
11	35	70,128	1.16	11,593	11,764	9,370	52,995	42,262
21	45	137,952	1.56	15,580	28,922	19,707	278,528	57,333
31	55	271,372	2.09	20,938	64,661	41,143	883,393	79,076
41	65	533,829	2.81	28,139	145,999	92,460	2,432,049	104,970
42	**Total**	7,445,673		632,759	1,752,425	1,163,478	**Real Annuity**	49,153
43	**RETIREMENT**							
44	Age	Nom Withdraw	Deflator	Exemption	Taxes		Funds Left	rConsumption
45	66	142,460	2.90	28,983	0		2,435,512	49,153
49	70	160,340	3.26	32,620	0		2,404,847	49,153
54	75	185,879	3.78	37,816	0		2,233,096	49,153
59	80	215,484	4.38	43,839	0		1,846,348	49,153
64	85	249,805	5.08	50,821	0		1,146,895	49,153
69	90	289,593	5.89	58,916	0		0	49,153
70	**Total**	5,194,003			0			

using the traditional IRA compared with only $1.75 million for the Roth IRA. Despite this, the larger accumulation in the traditional IRA saving account results in a larger retirement fund ($4.1 million compared with $2.4 million) and a larger real after-tax retirement annuity of $66,366. The bottom line is that the traditional IRA is more effective for the middle-income family we examine here.

The explanation of why the traditional IRA is better for a middle-income family also indicates when the Roth IRA may be preferred. If earnings are sharply back-loaded, that is, most of your earnings are close to retirement, then tax-free accumulation of investment income is less important, and the Roth IRA may dominate. This can happen if you start with fewer years to retirement and your income grows faster. Without changing the number of years to retirement, you would need to change nominal income growth in both spreadsheets from 7% to an extreme 40% for the Roth IRA to dominate. (The Web site **www.quicken.com** allows you to make the comparison for your own circumstances.)

Notice in Table 21.2 that the lifetime average tax rate for saving with traditional IRAs is 35.96%. This is a result of large accumulation of earnings on savings that are taxed on retirement and shows the importance of early accumulation. Despite the higher lifetime taxes, this tax shelter ends up with larger after-tax real consumption during retirement. The lifetime-average tax rate is not a good measure of the effect of taxes on lifetime consumption, because it does not fully account for the timing of tax collections. In the circumstances we postulated (a long period with middle-class earnings levels) the tax savings with Roth trumps the traditional IRA.

TABLE 21.2

Traditional vs. Roth IRA tax shelters under a progressive tax code

	Traditional IRA	Roth IRA
Lifetime labor income	**$7,445,673**	**$7,445,673**
Taxes ($)		
Earning years	$ 879,430	$ 1,752,425
Retirement years	1,797,848	0
Total paid over lifetime	**2,677,278**	**1,752,425**
Lifetime average tax rate (%)	35.96%	23.54%
Retirement annuity:		
Before-tax	$ 83,380	$ 49,153
After-tax	66,366	49,153

401k and 403b Plans

Under the Employee Retirement Income Security Act of 1974 (ERISA), an employer manages one of two types of pension plans for its employees. One is a *defined benefit* plan, where the employer is required to endow the pension fund with enough assets to finance a stipulated or "defined" package of benefits to retirees. Here, the *employer* bears the risk of the rate of return on the pension fund investments, since the employees are entitled to a defined benefit regardless of investment performance. Employees do, however, bear the risk of employer bankruptcy, which may be significant. The federal Pension Benefit Guarantee Corporation (PBGC), set up to insure the pension benefits of employees against the failure of their employers, will in most cases replace the fund's retirement package with a substantially inferior one in the event of a bankruptcy.

The more common pension plan is a *defined contribution* plan. Here, employers offer one or more investment options to their employees. Often, those options are administered by a mutual fund complex such as Fidelity or Vanguard, and employees contribute a limited, tax–deductible fraction of their wages to their own individual account. Employees may allocate their contributions across any one of several funds offered in the retirement plan, and it is common for employers to match a portion of the employee's contribution. The investment returns of the employee are applied to his individual account, and thus the *employees* bear the fund's investment risk[3]. Upon retirement, retirees withdraw these funds to finance their retirement consumption. Defined contribution funds are named after named the relevant sections of the U.S. tax code, 401k in the corporate sector and 403b in the public and nonprofit sectors. The two are quite similar and the discussion of 401k plans applies to 403b plans as well.

401k plans have two distinct features. First and foremost, your employer may match your contribution to various degrees, up to a certain level. This means that if you elect not to participate in the plan, you forgo part of your potential employment compensation. Needless to say, regardless of tax considerations, any employee should contribute to the plan at least as much as the employer will match, except for extreme circumstances of cash needs. While some employees may face cash constraints and think they would be better off skipping contributions, in many circumstances, they would be better off borrowing to bridge the liquidity shortfall while continuing to contribute up to the level matched by the employer.

The second feature of the plan is akin to a traditional IRA in tax treatment and similar in other restrictions. Contributions to 401k plans are restricted (details can be found on many Web sites, e.g., **www.morningstar.com**), but the limits on contributions generally exceed the level matched by the employer. Hence you must decide how much of your salary to contribute beyond the level matched by your employer. You can incorporate 401k plans, like the traditional IRA, in your savings-plan spreadsheet, review the trade-off, and make an informed decision on how much to save.

401k plans

Defined contribution pension plans wherein the employer matches the employee's contribution up to a set percentage.

Risky Investments and Capital Gains as Tax Shelters

So far we have limited our discussion to safe investments that yield a sure 6%. This number, coupled with the inflation assumption (3%), determined the results of various savings rules given the appropriate tax configuration. Clearly, the 6% return and 3% inflation assumptions are not hard numbers and you must consider the implications of other possible scenarios over the life of the savings plan. The spreadsheets we developed make scenario analysis quite easy. Once you set up a spreadsheet with a contemplated savings plan, you simply vary the inputs for ROR (the nominal rate of return) and inflation and record the implications for each

---

[3]Employees bear no bankruptcy risk in these plans, since they are the owners of the individual accounts; even if the employer were to go bankrupt, creditors could not seize any of the assets.

scenario. The probabilities of possible deviations from the expected numbers and your risk tolerance will dictate which savings plan provides you with sufficient security of obtaining your goals. This sensitivity analysis will be even more important when you consider risky investments.

The tax shelters we described allow you to invest in a broad array of securities and mutual funds, and you can invest your nonsheltered savings in any asset. Which portfolio to choose is a matter of risk versus return. That said, taxes lend importance to the otherwise largely irrelevant aspect of cash dividends and interest income versus capital gains.

According to current U.S. tax law, there are two applicable capital gains rates for most investments: 15% if your marginal tax rate is higher than 25%, and 5%[4] if you are in a lower tax bracket. More important, you pay the applicable rate only when you sell the security. Thus, investing in nondividend-paying securities is an implicit partial tax shelter with no restrictions on contributions or withdrawals. Because this investment is not tax deductible, it is similar to a Roth IRA, but somewhat inferior in that you do pay a tax on withdrawal, however low. Still, such investments can be more effective than traditional IRA and 401k plans, as we discussed earlier. Since annual contributions to all IRAs and 401k plans are quite limited, investment in a low- or no-dividend portfolio may be the efficient shelter for many investors who wish to exceed the contribution limit. Another advantage of such portfolios is that you can sell securities that have lost value to realize capital losses and thereby reduce your tax bill in any given year. This virtue of risky securities is called the *tax-timing option.* Managing a portfolio with efficient utilization of the tax-timing option requires expert attention, however, and may not be appropriate for many savers.

The average dividend yield on the S&P 500 stocks is on the order of 2%, and other indexes (such as NASDAQ) bear an even lower yield. This means that you can easily construct a well-diversified portfolio with a very low dividend yield. Such a portfolio allows you to utilize the tax advantage of capital gains versus dividends. Spreadsheet 21.9 adapts Spreadsheet 21.6 (progressive tax with no shelter) to a no-dividend portfolio of stocks, maintaining the same preretirement consumption stream, holding the ROR at 6%, and assuming 15% capital gains tax. Real retirement consumption, averaging $45,105, is almost identical to that supported by a Roth IRA (Spreadsheet 21.8).[5]

SPREADSHEET 21.9

Saving with no-dividend stocks under a progressive tax

Please visit us at
www.mhhe.com/bkm

	A	B	C	D	E	F	G	H
3	Retirement Years	Income Growth	Rate of Inflation	Exemption Now	Tax rates in	Savings Rate	ROR	rROR
4	25	.07	.03	10000	Table 21.1	.15	.06	.0291
5	Age	Income	Deflator	Exemption	Taxes	Savings	Cumulative Savings	rConsumption
6	30	50,000	1.00	10,000	8,000	6,300	6,300	35,700
7	31	53,500	1.03	10,300	8,640	6,793	13,471	36,958
11	35	70,128	1.16	11,593	11,764	9,370	52,995	42,262
21	45	137,952	1.56	15,580	28,922	19,707	278,528	57,333
31	55	271,372	2.09	20,938	64,661	41,143	883,393	79,076
41	65	533,829	2.81	28,139	145,999	92,460	2,432,049	104,970
42	Total				1,752,425	1,163,478	Real Annuity	49,153
43	RETIREMENT				Tax Rate	Capital Gains		.15
44	Age	Nom Withdraw	Deflator	Cum Cap Gains	on Exemption	Taxes	Funds Left	rConsumption
45	66	142,460	2.90	1,340,186	28,983	6,799	2,435,512	46,808
49	70	160,340	3.26	1,561,124	32,620	10,178	2,404,847	46,033
54	75	185,879	3.78	1,660,844	37,816	14,598	2,233,096	45,293
59	80	215,484	4.38	1,503,386	43,839	19,338	1,846,348	44,742
64	85	249,805	5.08	995,489	50,821	24,535	1,146,895	44,326
69	90	289,593	5.89	1,500	58,916	30,626	0	43,955
70	Total				1,056,691	445,850		

---

[4]The rate goes up to 10% if you hold the security for less than five years.

[5]In Spreadsheet 21.9 we did not take full advantage of the tax code. You can defer capital gains longer by specifying the particular shares you sell so that you sell first new shares with little capital gains and old shares last.

TABLE 21.3 Investing Roth IRA contributions in stocks and bonds	Phase	Asset	Stocks Inside; Bonds Outside	Stocks Outside; Bonds Inside
	Savings	Bonds	Taxed upon accrual	No taxes
		Stocks	No taxes	Taxes deferred
	Withdrawal*	Bonds	No taxes	No taxes
				Taxed at capital gains rate
		Stocks	No taxes	

*Since the retirement annuity is similar in both IRAs, taxes on this annuity are ignored.

Sheltered versus Unsheltered Savings

Suppose your desired level of savings is double the amount allowed in IRAs and 401k (or 403b) plans. At the same time you wish to invest equal amounts in stocks and bonds. Where should you keep the stocks and where the bonds? You will be surprised to know how many investors make the costly mistake of holding the stocks in a tax-protected account and the bonds in an unsheltered account. This is a mistake because most of the return from bonds is in the form of taxable interest payments, while stocks by their nature already provide some tax shelter.

Recall that tax shelters enhance the retirement annuity with two elements: (1) tax deferral on contributions and (2) tax deferral on income earned on savings. The effectiveness of each element depends on the tax rate on withdrawals. Of the two types of tax shelters we analyzed, traditional IRA and 401k (or 403b) plans contain both elements, while a Roth IRA provides only the second, but with the advantage that the tax rate on withdrawals is zero. Therefore, we need to analyze the stock–bond shelter question separately for each type of retirement plan. Table 21.3 shows the hierarchy of this analysis when a Roth IRA is used. The difference is apparent by comparing the taxes in each column. With stocks inside and bonds outside the shelter you pay taxes early and at the ordinary income rate. When you remove stocks from and move bonds into the shelter you pay taxes later at the lower capital gains rate.

When you use either a traditional IRA or 401k plan, contributions are tax deferred regardless of whether you purchase stocks or bonds, so we need to compare only taxes on income from savings and withdrawal. Table 21.4 shows the trade-off for a traditional IRA or 401k plan.

The advantage ends up being the same as with the Roth IRA. By removing stocks from and moving bonds into the shelter you gain the deferral on the bond interest during the savings phase. During the retirement phase you gain the difference between the ordinary income and the capital gains rate on the gains from the stocks.

Does the rationale of sheltering bonds rather than stocks apply to preferred stocks?   **CONCEPT** *check* **21.8**

TABLE 21.4 Investing traditional IRA or 401k contributions in stocks and bonds	Phase	Asset	Stocks Inside; Bonds Outside	Stocks Outside; Bonds Inside
	Savings	Bonds	Taxed on accrual	Taxes deferred
		Stocks	Tax deferred	Taxes deferred
	Withdrawal*	Bonds	No taxes	Taxed at marginal rate
		Stocks	Taxed at marginal rate	Taxed at capital gains rate

*Since the retirement annuity is similar in both IRAs, taxes on this annuity are ignored.

21.6 | Social Security

Social Security

Federally mandated pension plan established to provide minimum retirement benefits to all workers.

Social Security (SS) is a cross between a pension and an insurance plan. It is quite regressive in the way it is financed, in that employees pay a proportional (currently 7.65%) tax on gross wages, with no exemption but with an income cap ($106,800 in 2009). Employers match employees' contributions and pay SS directly.[6]

On the other hand, SS is progressive in the way it allocates benefits; low-income individuals receive a relatively larger share of preretirement income upon retirement. Of the SS tax of 7.65%, 6.2% goes toward retirement benefits and 1.45% toward retirement health care services provided by Medicare. Thus, combining your payments with your employer's, the real retirement annuity is financed by $2 \times 6.2 = 12.4\%$ of your income (up to the aforementioned cap); we do not examine the Medicare component of SS in this chapter.

SS payments are made throughout one's entire working life; however, only 35 years of contributions count for the determination of benefits. Benefits are in the form of a lifetime real annuity based on a retirement age of 67, although you can retire earlier (as of age 62) or later (up to age 70) and draw a smaller or larger annuity, respectively[7]. One reason SS is projected to face fiscal difficulties in future years is the increased longevity of the population. The current plan to mitigate this problem is to gradually increase the retirement age.

Calculation of benefits for individuals retiring in a given year is done in four steps:

1. The series of your taxed annual earnings (using the cap) is compiled. The status of this series is shown in your annual SS statement.
2. An indexing factor series is compiled for all past years. This series is used to account for population earnings growth during your lifetime contributions.
3. The indexing factors are applied to your recorded earnings to arrive at the Average Indexed Monthly Earnings (AIME).
4. Your AIME is used to determine the Primary Insurance Amount (PIA), which is your monthly retirement annuity.

All this sounds more difficult than it really is, so let's describe steps 2 through 4 in detail.

The Indexing Factor Series

Suppose your first wage on which you paid the SS tax was earned 40 years ago. To arrive at today's value of this wage, we must calculate its future value over the 40 years, that is, FV = wage $\times (1 + g)^{40}$. The SS administration refers to this as the "near-current level" indexed earnings for that year, and the FV factor, $(1 + g)^{40}$, is the index for that year. This calculation is made for each year, resulting in a series of near-current (indexed) earnings which, when summed, is the value today of the entire stream of lifetime taxed earnings.

A major issue is the rate to be used in producing the index factor for each year. The SS administration uses the growth in the average wage index (AWI) of the U.S. population in that year. While the AWI adjustment will generally track inflation, it will increase real retiree income in good times when the AWI leads inflation, and vice versa. This procedure allows SS recipients to share in the general economic advances (or declines) experienced by the rest of society. Another, less compelling nuance, results in an incentive to retire early: the index factor is set to 1.0 for the year in which an SS contributor reaches age 60 and beyond, impounding zero growth for near-retirement years. For years prior to age 60, the index factor increases by the growth rate of AWI in that year.

To illustrate, in 2007 the index factor for 1972 (35 years earlier) was 5.6639, indicating that the average wage grew over the years 1972–2007 at an annual rate of 5.08% ($1.0508^{35} = 5.6639$). By comparison, the CPI grew over the same years at a rate of 4.62%,

---

[6]Absent the SS tax, it is reasonable to assume that the amount contributed by employers would be added to your pretax income, hence your actual contribution is really 15.3%. For this reason, self-employed individuals are required to contribute 15.3% to SS.

[7]Retirement age for individuals born before 1960 is 66. For a complete listing of retirement ages, go to **www.socialsecurity.gov**.

and T-bills returned 5.92% annually. Thus, the growth rate used for the period was just shy of fully accounting for the time value of money.[8] Wage growth was not constant over these years. For example, it was as high as 10.07% in 1980–1981 and as low as .86% in 1992–1993.

The Average Indexed Monthly Earnings (AIME)

The series of a retiree's lifetime indexed contributions (there may be zeros in the series for periods when the retiree was unemployed) is used to determine the base for the retirement annuity. The 35 highest indexed contributions are identified, summed, and then divided by $35 \times 12 = 420$ to achieve your Average Indexed Monthly Income (AIME). If you worked less than 35 years, all your indexed earnings will be summed, but your AIME might be low since you still divide the sum by 420. If you worked more than 35 years, only the 35 highest indexed wages will be used to compute the average. Unless late-year earnings are high, another incentive to retire early is in force.

The Primary Insurance Amount (PIA)

In this stage of the calculation of monthly SS benefits, low-income workers (with a low AIME) are favored to increase income equality. The exact formula may change from one year to the next, but the example of four representative individuals who attained age 62 in 2005 demonstrates the principle.[9] The AIME of these individuals relative to the average in the population and their Primary Insurance Amount (PIA) are calculated in Table 21.5.

Table 21.5 presents the value of SS to U.S. employees who attained age 62 in 2005. The first part of the table shows how SS calculates the real annuity to be paid to retirees.[10] The results differ for the four representative individuals. One measure of this differential is the *income replacement rate* (i.e., retirement income as a percent of working income) provided to the four

TABLE 21.5

Calculation of the retirement annuity of representative retirees who retire in 2009 at age 66

AIME Rank	Low	Average	High	Maximum
% of average wage	50	100	150	Max*
AIME ($ month)	1,375	2,750	4,125	6,600
PIA formula**				
90% of the first $627	564	564	564	564
32% of AIME over $627 through $3779	239	679	1,009	1,009
15% of AIME over $3779	0	0	52	423
Total 5 PIA ($/month)	804	1,244	1,625	1,996
Real retirement annuity = PIA × 12 + COLA***	11,224	17,370	22,694	27,879
Income replacement (%)	58.4%	45.2%	39.4%	NA*
IRR**** assuming longevity = 82 (male); inflation = 3%	6.87	5.86	5.30	4.21
IRR**** assuming longevity = 85 (female); inflation = 3%	7.29	6.33	5.81	4.80
Longevity implied by SS (years) for IRR = 6%	13	18	22	32

*Income is above the maximum taxable and income replacement cannot be calculated.

**2005 PIA parameters (bend points) are used. The year of eligiblity; that is, the year in which a worker attains age 62.

***Cost-of-living adjustments, or COLAs, for 2005 through 2008.

****Internal rate of return.

[8]We use a wage growth rate of 7% in our exercises, assuming our readers are well educated and can expect a higher than average growth. Special attention must be given to this and other input if you advise other people.
[9]The Exact formula for 2009 can be found at **www.ssa.gov/OACT/anypia/index.html**.
[10]The annuity of special-circumstance low-income retirees is supplemented.

income brackets in Table 21.5. Low-income retirees have a replacement rate of 58.4%, 1.5 times that of the high-wage employees (39.4%).

The net after-tax benefits may be reduced if the individual has other sources of income, because a portion of the retirement annuity is subject to income tax. Currently, retired households with combined taxable income over $32,000 pay taxes on a portion of the SS benefits. At income of $44,000, 50% of the SS annuity is subject to tax, but the proportion rises at higher income levels. You can find current numbers and some useful calculators at **www.ssa. gov.** This Web site also allows you to project Social Security benefits at various levels of sophistication.

When evaluating the attractiveness of SS as an investment for current retirees (the bottom part of Table 21.5), we must consider current **longevity** figures. For a male, current remaining life expectancy at age 65 is roughly an additional 17 years, and for a female 20 years. Using these figures, the current PIA provides male retirees an internal rate of return on SS contributions in the range of 6.87–4.21%, and female retirees 7.29–4.80%.[11] These IRRs are obtained by taking 12.4% (the combined SS tax) of the series of 35 annual earnings of the four employees as cash outflows. The series of annuity payments (17 years for males and 20 for females), assuming inflation at 3%, is used to compute cash inflows.

To examine SS performance another way, the last line in the table shows the longevity (number of annual payments) required to achieve an IRR of 6%. Except for the highest income bracket, all have life expectancy greater than this threshold. Why are these numbers so attractive, when SS is so often criticized for poor investment performance? The reason benefits are so generous is that the PIA formula sets a high replacement rate relative to the SS tax rate, the proportion of income taxed. Taking history as a guide, to achieve an IRR equal to the rate of inflation plus the historical average real rate on a safe investment such as T-bills (with a historical real rate of .66%), the formula would need to incorporate a lower replacement rate. With a future rate of inflation of 3%, this would imply a nominal IRR of 3.7%. Is the ROR assumed in our spreadsheets (6%) the right one to use, or is the expected IRR based on past real rates the correct one to use? In short, we simply don't know. But averaging across the population, SS may well be a fair pension plan, taking into consideration its role in promoting equality of income.

The solvency of SS is threatened by two factors: population longevity and a below-replacement growth of the U.S. population. Over the next 35 years, longevity is expected to increase by almost two years, increasing steady-state expenditures by more than 10%. To keep a level population (ignoring immigration) requires an average of 2.1 children per female, yet the current average of 2.0 is expected to decline further.[12] The projected large deficit, beginning in 2016, requires reform of SS. Increasing the retirement age to account for increased longevity does not constitute a reduction in the plan's IRR and therefore seems a reasonable solution to deficits arising from this factor. Eliminating the deficit resulting from population decline is more difficult. It is projected that doing so by increasing the SS tax may require an increase in the combined SS tax of as much as 10% within your working years. Such a simple solution is considered politically difficult. Another possiblity is changes in benefits.

The idea of privatizing a portion of SS so that investors will be able to choose portfolios with risk levels according to their personal risk tolerance faded in the early 2000s. The big strike against this option is that many individuals and even some finance professionals wrongly believe that a long-term investment in stocks is not all that risky. We believe that with appropriate risk adjustment, future retirees will find it difficult to beat the SS plan and should be made fully aware of this fact.[13]

longevity

Remaining life expectancy.

---

[11]However, income is correlated with longevity and with durability of marriage. This means that wealthy retirees and their spouses draw longer annuities than the poor. It is suggested that this difference may as much as completely offset the progressivity built into the PIA schedule.

[12]Fertility rates in Europe, Japan, and (until recently) in China are even lower, exacerbating the problems of their Social Security systems.

[13]Here, again, we collide with those who consider stocks to be low-risk investments in the long run (some of them esteemed colleagues). One cannot overestimate the misleading nature of this assessment (see Chapter 6, Section 6.6). Perhaps the extremely negative returns in 2008 have driven this point home.

21.7 Children's Education and Large Purchases

Sending a child to a private college can cost a family in excess of $40,000 a year, in current dollars, for four years. Even a state college can cost in excess of $25,000 a year. Many families will send two or more children to college within a few years, creating a need to finance large expenditures within a few years. Other large expenditures such as a second home (we deal with the primary residence in the next section) or an expensive vehicle present similar problems on a smaller scale.

The question is whether planned, large outflows during the working years require a major innovation to our planning tools. The answer is no. All you need to do is add a column to your spreadsheet for extra-consumption expenditures that come out of savings. As long as cumulative savings do not turn negative as the outflows take place, the only effect to consider is the reduction in the retirement annuity that results from these expenditures. To respond to a lower-than-desired retirement annuity you have four options: (1) increase the savings rate, (2) live with a smaller retirement annuity, (3) do away with or reduce the magnitude of the expenditure item, or (4) increase expected ROR by taking on more risk. Recall though, that in Section 21.2, we suggested option 4 isn't viable for many investors.

The situation is a little more complicated when the extra-consumption expenditures create negative cumulative savings in the retirement plan. In principle, one can simply borrow to finance these expenditures with debt (as is common for large purchases such as automobiles). Again, the primary variable of interest is the retirement annuity. The problem, however, is that if you arrive at a negative savings level quite late in your savings plan, you will be betting the farm on the success of the plan in later years. Recalling, again, the discussion of Section 21.2, pushing risk into later years, other things equal, is more dangerous since you will have little time to recover from any setback.

An illuminating example requires adding only one column to Spreadsheet 21.2, as shown in Spreadsheet 21.10. Column G adds the extra-consumption expenditures. We use as input (cell G2) the current cost of one college year per child—$40,000. We assume your first child will be college-bound when you are 48 years old and the second when you are 50. The expenditures in column G are inflated by the price level in column C and subtracted from cumulative savings in column E.

SPREADSHEET 21.10

Financing children's education

	A	B	C	D	E	F	G
1	Retirement Years	Income Growth	Rate of Inflation	Savings Rate	ROR	rROR	Extra-Cons
2	25	.07	.03	.15	.06	.0291	40,000
3	Age	Income	Deflator	Savings	Cumulative Savings	rConsumption	Expenditures
4	30	50,000	1.00	7,500	7,500	42,500	0
5	31	53,500	1.03	8,025	15,975	44,150	0
9	35	70,128	1.16	10,519	61,658	51,419	0
19	45	137,952	1.56	20,693	308,859	75,264	0
22	48	168,997	1.70	25,349	375,099	84,378	68,097
23	49	180,826	1.75	27,124	354,588	87,654	70,140
24	50	193,484	1.81	29,023	260,397	91,058	144,489
25	51	207,028	1.86	31,054	158,252	94,595	148,824
26	52	221,520	1.92	33,228	124,331	98,268	76,644
27	53	237,026	1.97	35,554	88,401	102,084	78,943
28	54	253,618	2.03	38,043	131,748	106,049	0
29	55	271,372	2.09	40,706	180,359	110,167	0
39	65	533,829	2.81	80,074	1,090,888	161,257	0
40	Total			1,116,851	**Real Annuity**	22,048	

e**X**cel

Please visit us at
www.mhhe.com/bkm

The real retirement annuity prior to this extra-consumption expenditure was $49,688, but "after-children" only $22,048, less than half. The expenditure of $320,000 in today's dollars costs you total lifetime real consumption of 25 × ($49,688 − $22,048) = $690,514 because of the loss of interest on the funds that would have been saved. If you change the input in G2 to $25,000 (reflecting the cost of a public college), the retirement annuity falls to $32,405, a loss of "only" 35% in the standard of living.

CONCEPT *check* **21.10**   What if anything should you do about the risk of a rapid increase in college tuition?

21.8 Home Ownership: The Rent-versus-Buy Decision

Most people dream of owning a home and for good reason. In addition to the natural desire for roots that goes with owning your home, this investment is an important hedge for most families. Dwelling is the largest long-term consumption item and fluctuations in the cost of dwelling are responsible for the largest consumption risk they face. Dwelling costs, in turn, are subject to general price inflation, as well as to significant fluctuations specific to geographic location. This combination makes it difficult to hedge the risk with investments in securities.[14] In addition, the law favors home ownership in a number of ways, chief of which is tax deductibility of mortgage interest.

Common (though not necessarily correct) belief is that the mortgage tax break is the major reason for investing in rather than renting a home. In competitive markets, though, rents will reflect the mortgage tax-deduction that applies to rental residence as well. Moreover, homes are illiquid assets and transaction costs in buying/selling a house are high. Therefore, purchasing a home that isn't expected to be a long-term residence for the owner may well be a speculative investment with inferior expected returns. The right time for investing in your home is when you are ready to settle someplace for the long haul. Speculative investments in real estate ought to be made in a portfolio context through instruments such as Real Estate Investment Trusts (REITs), although the experience of 2007–2010 should give you pause.

With all this in mind, it is evident that investment in a home enters the savings plan in two ways. First, during the working years the cash down payment and mortgage payments should be treated just like any other large, extra-consumption expenditure as discussed earlier. Second, home ownership affects your retirement plan because if you own your home free and clear by the time you retire, you will need a smaller annuity to get by; moreover, the value of the house is part of retirement wealth.

CONCEPT *check* **21.11**   Should you have any preference for fixed- versus variable-rate mortgages?

21.9 Uncertain Longevity and Other Contingencies

Perhaps the most daunting uncertainty in our life is the time it will end. Most people consider this uncertainty a blessing, yet, blessing or curse, this uncertainty has economic implications. Old age is hard enough without worrying about expenses. Yet the amount of money you may need is at least linear in longevity, if not exponential. Not knowing how much you will need, plus a healthy degree of risk aversion, would require us to save a lot more than necessary just to insure against the fortune of longevity.

---

[14]A recent innovation allows hedging of home prices in some localities with futures contracts written on the Case-Shiller housing price indexes.

One solution to this problem is to invest in a life annuity to supplement Social Security benefits, your base life annuity. When you own a **life annuity** (an annuity that pays you income until you die), the provider takes on the risk of the time of death. To survive, the provider must be sure to earn a rate of return commensurate with the risk. Except for wars and natural disasters, however, an individual's time of death is a unique, nonsystematic risk.[15] It would appear, then, that the cost of a life annuity should be a simple calculation of interest rates applied to life expectancy from mortality tables. Unfortunately, adverse selection comes in the way.

Adverse selection is the tendency for any proposed contract (deal) to attract the type of party who would make the contract (deal) a losing proposition to the offering party. A good example of adverse selection arises in health care. Suppose that Blue Cross offers health coverage where you choose your doctor and Blue Cross pays 80% of the costs. Suppose another HMO covers 100% of the cost and charges only a nominal fee per treatment. If HMOs were to price the services on the basis of a survey of the average health care needs in the population at large, they would be in for an unpleasant surprise. People who need frequent and expensive care would prefer the HMO over Blue Cross. The adverse selection in this case is that high-need individuals will choose the plan that provides more complete coverage. The individuals that the HMO most wants *not* to insure are most likely to sign up for coverage. Hence, to stay in business HMOs must expect their patients to have greater than average needs, and price the policy on this basis.

Providers of life annuities can expect a good dose of adverse selection as well, as people with the longest life expectancies will be their most enthusiastic customers. Therefore, it is advantageous to acquire these annuities at a younger age, before either individuals or insurers learn much about their particular life expectancies. The SS trust does not face adverse selection since virtually the entire population is forced into the purchase, allowing it to be a fair deal on both sides.

Unfortunately we also must consider untimely death or disability. These require an appropriate amount of life and disability insurance, particularly in the early stage of the life cycle. The appropriate coverage should be thought of in the context of a retirement annuity. Coverage should replace at least the most essential part of the retirement annuity.

Finally, there is the need to hedge labor income. Since you cannot insure wages, the least you can do is maintain a portfolio that is uncorrelated with your labor income. As Enron, Lehman Brothers, and other recent bankruptcies have demonstrated, too many are unaware of the perils of having their pension income tied to their career, employment, and compensation. Investing a significant fraction of your portfolio in the industry you work in, not to mention the company you work for, is akin to a "Texas hedge": betting on the horse you own.

life annuity

An annuity that pays you income until you die.

adverse selection

The tendency for any proposed deal to attract the type of party who would make the deal a losing proposition to the offering party.

Insurance companies offer life insurance on your children. Does it make economic sense to buy such insurance?

CONCEPT *check* **21.12**

21.10 | Matrimony, Bequest, and Intergenerational Transfers

In the context of a retirement plan, we think of risk in terms of safety first. The imperative to avoid disastrous outcomes makes mean-variance analysis inadequate. We have already touched on this issue earlier, in the context of (1) raising the ROR with risky investments, (2) avoiding savings plans that rely too heavily on savings in later years, and (3) acquiring life insurance and including life annuities in the savings portfolio.

One sort of insurance the market cannot supply is wage insurance. If we could obtain wage insurance, a savings plan would be a lot easier to formulate. **Moral hazard** is the

moral hazard

The phenomenon whereby a party to a contract has an incentive to change behavior in a way that makes the contract less attractive to the other party.

---

[15]For this reason, life insurance policies include fine print excluding payment in case of events such as wars, epidemics, and famine.

reason for this void in the marketplace. Moral hazard is the phenomenon whereby a party to a contract (deal) has an incentive to change behavior in a way that makes the deal less attractive to the other party.[16] For example, a person who buys wage insurance would then have an incentive to consume leisure at the expense of work effort. Moral hazard is also why insuring items for more than their market or intrinsic value is prohibited. If your warehouse were insured for lots more than its value, you might have less incentive to prevent fires, an obvious moral hazard.

In contrast, marriage provides a form of co-insurance that extends also to the issue of longevity. A married couple has a greater probability that at least one will survive to an older age, giving greater incentive to save for a longer life. Put differently, saving for a longer life has a smaller probability of going to waste. A study by Kotlikoff and Spivack (1981) simulated reasonable individual preferences to show that a marriage contract increases the dollar value of lifetime savings by as much as 25%. Old sages who have been preaching the virtue of matrimony for millennia must have known more about economics than we give them credit for.

Bequest is another motive for saving. There is something special about bequest that differentiates it from other "expense" items. When you save for members of the next generation (or beyond), you double the planning horizon, and by considering later generations as well, you can make it effectively infinite. This has implications for the composition of the savings portfolio. For example, the conventional wisdom that, as you grow older, you should gradually shift out of stocks and into bonds is not as true when bequest is an important factor in the savings plan.[17]

Having discussed marriage co-insurance and bequest, we cannot fail to mention that despite the virtues of saving for the longest term, many individuals overshoot the mark. When a person saves for old age and passes on before taking full advantage of the nest egg, the estate is called an "involuntary, intergenerational transfer." Data show that such transfers are widespread. Kotlikoff and Summers (1981) estimate that about 75% of wealth left behind is actually involuntary transfer. This suggests that people make too little use of the market for life annuities. Hopefully you will not be one of them, both because you will live to a healthy old age and because you'll have a ball spending your never-expiring annuity.

---

[16]Moral hazard and adverse selection can reinforce each other. Restaurants that offer an all-you-can-eat meal attract big eaters (adverse selection) and induce "normal" eaters to overeat (moral hazard).

[17]A recent innovation that caters to those who wish to reduce retirement risk as they grow older is a Target Date Retirement Fund (TDRF). Asset allocation in this sort of fund is linked to your planned retirement date. As time passes and you approach retirement, the fund gradually shifts your asset allocation from risky to risk-free investments, usually ending risk-free upon your retirement date.

SUMMARY

- The major objective of a savings plan is to provide for adequate retirement income.
- Even moderate inflation will affect the purchasing power of the retirement annuity. Therefore, the plan must be cast in terms of real consumption and retirement income.
- From a standpoint of smoothing consumption, it is advantageous to save a fixed or rising fraction of real income. However, postponement of savings to later years increases the risk of the retirement fund.
- The IRA-style tax shelter, akin to a consumption tax, defers taxes on both contributions and earnings on savings.
- The progressive tax code sharpens the importance of taxes during the retirement years. High tax rates during retirement reduce the effectiveness of the tax shelter.
- A Roth IRA tax shelter does not shield contributions but eliminates taxes during retirement. Savers who anticipate high retirement income (and taxes) must examine whether this shelter is more beneficial than a traditional IRA account.
- 401k plans are similar to traditional IRAs and allow matched contributions by employers. This benefit should not be forgone.

www.mhhe.com/bkm

- Capital gains can be postponed and later taxed at a lower rate. Therefore, investment in low-dividend stocks is a natural tax shelter. Investments in interest-bearing securities should be sheltered first.
- Social Security benefits are an important component of retirement income.
- Savings plans should be augmented for large expenditures such as children's education.
- Home ownership should be viewed as a hedge against rental cost.
- Uncertain longevity and other contingencies should be handled via life annuities and appropriate insurance coverage.

KEY TERMS

401k plans, 683	moral hazard, 691	Social Security, 686
adverse selection, 691	progressive tax, 679	tax shelters, 678
flat tax, 676	real consumption, 674	traditional IRA, 681
life annuity, 691	retirement annuity, 672	
longevity, 688	Roth IRA, 681	

PROBLEM SETS

 Select problems are available in McGraw-Hill Connect. Please see the packaging options section of the preface for more information.

Basic

1. A ship owner is attempting to insure an old vessel for twice its current market value. Is this an adverse selection or moral hazard issue?

2. The same ship owner advertises a tariff whereby the freight charged for all cargo will be same. What kind of good can the ship owner except to attract?

3. What type of investors would be interested in a target date retirement fund? Why?

4. What is the insurance aspect of the Social Security annuity?

5 Why does a progressive tax code produce a retirement annuity for a middle-class household that is similar to that which would follow from a flat tax?

Intermediate

6. With no taxes or inflation (Spreadsheet 21.1), what would be your retirement annuity if you increase the savings rate by 1%?

7. With a 3% inflation (Spreadsheet 21.2), by how much would your retirement annuity grow if you increase the savings rate by 1%? Is the benefit greater in the face of inflation?

8. What savings rate from real income (Spreadsheet 21.3) will produce the same retirement annuity as a 15% savings rate from nominal income?

9. Under the flat tax (Spreadsheet 21.4), will a 1% increase in ROR offset a 1% increase in the tax rate?

10. With an IRA tax shelter (Spreadsheet 21.5), compare the effect on real consumption during retirement of a 1% increase in the rate of inflation to a 1% increase in the tax rate.

11. With a progressive tax (Spreadsheet 21.6), compare the effects of an increase of 1% in the lowest tax bracket to an increase of 1% in the highest tax bracket.

12. Verify that the IRA tax shelter with a progressive tax (Spreadsheet 21.7) acts as a hedge. Compare the effect of a decline of 2% in the ROR to an increase of 2% in ROR.

13. What is the trade-off between ROR and the rate of inflation with a Roth IRA under a progressive tax (Spreadsheet 21.8)?

14. Suppose you could defer capital gains tax to the last year of your retirement (Spreadsheet 21.9). Would it be worthwhile given the progressivity of the tax code?

15. Project your Social Security benefits with the parameters of Section 21.6.

16. Using Spreadsheet 21.10, assess the present value of a 1% increase in college tuition as a fraction of the present value of labor income.

e*X*cel

Please visit us at www.mhhe.com/bkm

Problems 6–16 can be completed using Excel.

17. Give another example of adverse selection.

18. In addition to expected longevity, what traits might affect an individual's demand for a life annuity?

19. Give another example of a moral hazard problem.

WEB *master* RETIREMENT PLANNING

Visit the AARP's Financial Planning and Retirement Web site at **www.aarpmagazine.org/www.aarp.org/money/ financial_planning.** Locate the Retirement Roadmap link in the Retirement Planning section. Click on the link and take the interactive survey to see how your expectations for retirement match your financial capacity.

Return to the Financial Planning and Retirement page and follow the link to the Retirement Planning Calculator. The calculator allows you to enter information about your retirement plans, your current level of assets, expected benefits from other sources, and your spouse's financial data and needs. Use the AARP Retirement Planning Calculator to enter your specific data and assumptions. Take advantage of the "Estimate" features offered to get a better idea of realistic inputs.

1. On the Results page, do you have a projected excess of funds or a shortfall of funds at the end of the retirement period? Can you meet your goals by following your current financial path? What suggestion(s) does the simulator make to help you achieve your goals?

2. Look at the list of parameters toward the bottom of the page. Which one would be the easiest for you to change to make your goals attainable? Some people might choose to work longer, some to leave a smaller estate, etc. Choose the combination of factors that would work best for you, then click on the Recalculate button to see the new results. Repeat if necessary. Can you come up with a plan that offers you a combination of factors that offers you an acceptable level of comfort?

SOLUTIONS TO CONCEPT *checks*

21.1. When ROR falls by 1% to 5%, the retirement annuity falls from $192,244 to $149,855 (i.e., by 22.45%). To restore this annuity, the savings rate must rise by 4.24 percentage points to 19.24%. With this savings rate, the entire loss of 1% in ROR falls on consumption during the earning years.

21.2. Intuition suggests you need to keep the real rate (2.91%) constant, that is, increase the nominal rate to 7% (confirm this). However, this will not be sufficient because the nominal income growth of 7% (column B) has a lower real growth when inflation is higher. Result: You must increase the real ROR to compensate for a lower growth in real income, ending with a nominal rate of 7.67%.

21.3. There are two components to the risk of relying on future labor income: disability/death and career failure/unemployment. You can insure the first component, but not the second.

21.4. With before-tax income held constant, your after-tax income will remain unchanged if your average tax rate, and hence total tax liability, is unchanged:

$$\text{Total tax} = (\text{Income} - \text{Exemption}) \times \text{Tax rate, or } T = (I - E) \times t$$

A 1% increase in the tax rate will increase T by $.01(I - E)$. A 1% increase in the exemption will decrease T by $.01 \times E \times t$. Realistically, $I - E$ will be greater than $E \times t$ and hence you will be worse off with the increase in exemption and tax rate.

21.5. The qualitative result is the same. However, with no shelter you are worse off early and hence lose also the earning power of the additional tax bills.

21.6. No, an increase in the low-bracket tax rate applies to your entire taxable income, while an increase in the high-bracket tax rate applies only to a fraction of your taxable income.

21.7. No, in your hypothetical case, the Roth IRA tax shelter produces less taxes yet a smaller real retirement annuity. The reason is the timing of the taxes. The timing issue does not affect the stream of tax revenues to the IRS because at any point in time, taxpayers are distributed over all ages. In this case, the IRS can replace all Roth IRAs with traditional IRAs and lower the tax rates. The IRS will collect similar revenue each year, and retirees will enjoy higher real retirement annuities.

21.8. No, in terms of cash income, preferred stocks are more similar to bonds.

21.9.   Your projected retirement fund is risky because of uncertainty about future labor income and future real returns on savings. The projected Social Security real annuity is risky because of political uncertainty about future benefits. It's hard to judge which risk is greater.

21.10. You need an investment that pays more when tuition is higher. Several states now offer "tuition futures" contracts that allow you to lock in the price of future tuition expenditures.

21.11. A fixed-rate mortgage is the lower risk, higher expected cost option. Homeowners with greater risk tolerance might opt for a variable-rate mortgage which is expected to average a lower rate over the life of the mortgage.

21.12. In the old days, children were more than a bundle of joy; they also provided a hedge for old-age income. Under such circumstance, insuring children would make economic sense. These days, children may well be a financial net expenditure, ruling out insurance on economic grounds. Other nonfinancial considerations are a matter of individual preference.

22 Chapter

Investors and the Investment Process

After Studying This Chapter You Should Be Able To:

- Specify investment objectives of individual and institutional investors.

- Identify constraints on individual and institutional investors.

- Compare and contrast major types of investment policies.

Translating the aspirations and circumstances of diverse households into appropriate investment decisions is a daunting task. The task is equally difficult for institutions, most of which have many stakeholders and often are regulated by various authorities. The investment process is not easily reduced to a simple or mechanical algorithm.

While many principles of investments are quite general and apply to virtually all investors, some issues are peculiar to the specific investor. For example, tax bracket, age, risk tolerance, wealth, job prospects, and uncertainties make each investor's circumstances somewhat unique. In this chapter we focus on the process by which investors systematically review their particular objectives, constraints, and circumstances. Along the way, we survey some of the major classes of institutional investors and examine the special issues they must confront.

There is of course no unique "correct" investment process. However, some approaches are better than others, and it can be helpful to take one high-quality approach as a useful case study. For this reason, we will examine the systematic approach suggested by the CFA Institute. Among other things, the Institute administers examinations to certify investment professionals as CFAs, or Chartered Financial Analysts. Therefore, the approach we outline is also one that a highly respected professional group endorses through the curriculum that it requires investment practitioners to master. The nearby box describes how to become a CFA Charterholder.

The basic framework involves dividing the investment process into four stages: specifying objectives, specifying constraints, formulating policy, and monitoring and updating the portfolio as needed. We will treat each of these activities in turn. We start with a description of the major types of investors, both individual and institutional, as well as their special objectives. We turn next to the constraints or circumstances peculiar to each investor class, and we consider some of the investment policies that each can choose.

Related Web sites for this chapter are available at www.mhhe.com/bkm.

22.1 | The Investment Management Process

The CFA Institute divides the process of investment management into three main elements that constitute a dynamic feedback loop: planning, execution, and feedback. Figure 22.1 and Table 22.1 describe the steps in that process. As shorthand, you might think of *planning* as focused largely on establishing all the inputs necessary for decision making. These include data about the client as well as the capital market, resulting in very broad policy guidelines (the strategic asset allocation). *Execution* fleshes out the details of optimal asset allocation and security selection. Finally, *feedback* is the process of adapting to changes in expectations and objectives as well as to changes in portfolio composition that result from changes in market prices.

The result of this analysis can be summarized in an *investment policy statement* (IPS) addressing the topics specified in Table 22.2. In the next sections we elaborate on the steps leading to such an IPS. We start with the planning phase, the top panel of Table 22.1.

Table 22.1 indicates that the management planning process starts off by analyzing one's investment clients—in particular, by considering the objectives and constraints that govern their decisions. Portfolio objectives center on the risk-return trade-off between the expected return the investors want (their return requirements in the first column of Table 22.3) and how much risk they are willing to assume (their risk tolerance). Investment managers must know the level of risk that can be tolerated in the pursuit of higher expected return. All investors also must deal with various constraints on their choice that derive from considerations such as liquidity needs, regulations, or tax concerns. The second column of Table 22.3 lists some of the more important constraints.

In the next sections, we explore some of these objectives and constraints.

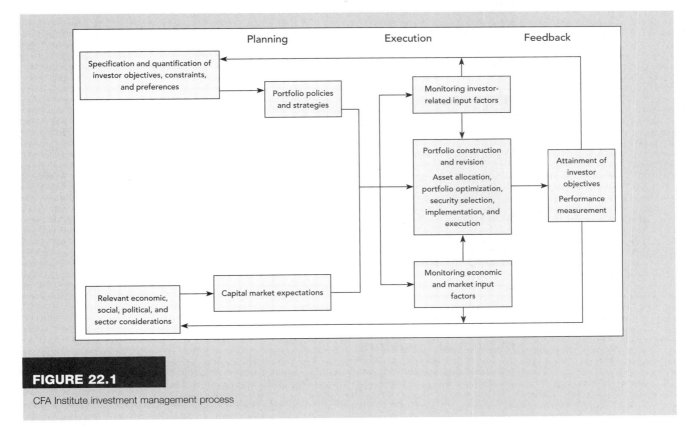

FIGURE 22.1

CFA Institute investment management process

TABLE 22.1	I. Planning
Components of the investment management process	A. Identifying and specifying the investor's objectives and constraints
	B. Creating the *investment policy statement* [See Table 22.2.]
	C. Forming capital market expectations
	D. Creating the strategic asset allocation (Target minimum and maximum class weights.)
	II. Execution: Portfolio construction and revision
	A. Asset allocation (including tactical) and portfolio optimization (Combine assets to meet risk and return objectives.)
	B. Security selection
	C. Implementation and execution
	III. Feedback
	A. Monitoring (investor, economic, and market input factors)
	B. Rebalancing
	C. Performance evaluation

Source: John L. Maginn, Donald L. Tuttle, Dennis W. McLeavey, and Jerald E. Pinto, "The Portfolio Management Process and the Investment Policy Statement," in *Managing Investment Portfolios: A Dynamic Process, 3rd ed*, (CFA Institute, 2007) and correspondence with Tom Robinson, head of educational content.

TABLE 22.2	1. Brief client description.
Components of the investment policy statement	2. Purpose of establishing policies and guidelines.
	3. Duties and investment responsibilities of parties involved.
	4. Statement of investment goals, objectives, and constraints.
	5. Schedule for review of investment performance and the IPS.
	6. Performance measures and benchmarks.
	7. Any considerations in developing strategic asset allocation.
	8. Investment strategies and investment styles.
	9. Guidelines for rebalancing.

TABLE 22.3	Objectives	Constraints
Determination of portfolio policies	Return requirements	Liquidity
	Risk tolerance	Horizon
		Regulations
		Taxes
		Unique needs, such as:
		Ethical concerns
		Specific hedging needs
		Age
		Wealth

22.2 Investor Objectives

Individual Investors

The basic factors affecting an individual investor's objectives usually arise from that investor's stage in the life cycle. The first significant investment decision for most individuals concerns education, which is an investment in "human capital." The major asset most people have

HOW TO BECOME A CHARTERED FINANCIAL ANALYST

The CFA Institute is a nonprofit international organization with a mission of serving investors by educating investment professionals and setting high standards for ethical practice. The Institute also has established a *Code of Ethics and Standards of Professional Conduct* that lays out guidelines of practice for investment professionals.

The CFA Institute was established in January 1990 through the combination of the previously existing Financial Analysts Federation and the Institute of Chartered Financial Analysts. The CFA Institute administers the program through which an investment professional can be designated as a Chartered Financial Analyst (CFA). This designation has become a progressively more important requirement for a career in institutional money management. About 88,000 investment professionals were members of the CFA Institute in 2007, and the Institute was affiliated with 134 professional societies in 55 countries.

To become a CFA, you must pass a series of three annual examinations that demonstrate knowledge of:

- Valuation principles for fixed-income, equity, and derivative securities.
- Financial statement analysis and corporate finance.
- Industry and company analysis.
- Microeconomic and macroeconomic theory.
- Quantitative methods.
- Principles of portfolio construction and management.
- Capital market theory.
- Financial markets and instruments.
- The CFA Institute Code of Ethics and Standards of Professional Conduct.

Beyond these exams, the candidate must have three years of work experience in money management and must be a member of a local Society of the Financial Analysts Federation.

For more information, you can visit the CFA Institute Web site at **www.cfainstitute.org.**

---

during their early working years is the earning power derived from their skills. For these people, the financial risk due to illness or injury is far greater than that associated with the rate of return on their portfolios of financial assets. At this point in the life cycle, the most important financial decisions concern insurance against the possibility of disability or death.

As one ages and accumulates savings to provide for consumption during retirement, the composition of wealth shifts from human capital toward financial capital. At this point, portfolio choices become progressively more important. In middle age, most investors will be willing to take on a meaningful amount of portfolio risk to increase their expected rates of return. As retirement draws near, however, risk tolerance seems to diminish.

Questionnaire results suggest that attitudes shift away from risk tolerance and toward risk aversion as investors near retirement age. (See, for example, the questionnaire in the nearby box.) With age, individuals lose the potential to recover from a disastrous investment performance. When they are young, investors can respond to a loss by working harder and saving more of their income. But as retirement approaches, investors realize there will be less time to recover, hence the shift to safe assets.

The task of life-cycle financial planning is a formidable one for most people. It is not surprising that a whole industry has sprung up to provide personal financial advice.

Professional Investors

Professional investors provide investment management services for a fee. Some are employed directly by wealthy individual investors. Most professional investors, however, either pool many individual investor funds and manage them or serve institutional investors.

Personal trusts   A **personal trust** is established when an individual confers legal title to property to another person or institution, who then manages that property for one or more beneficiaries. The holder of the title is called the *trustee*. The trustee is usually a bank, a lawyer, or an investment professional. Investment of a trust is subject to state trust laws and *prudent investor rules* that limit the types of allowable trust investment.

The objectives of personal trusts normally are more limited in scope than those of the individual investor. Because of their fiduciary responsibility, personal trust managers typically are

personal trust

An interest in an asset held by a trustee for the benefit of another person.

TIME FOR INVESTING'S FOUR-LETTER WORD

What four-letter word should pop into mind when the stock market takes a harrowing nose dive?

No, not those. R-I-S-K.

Risk is the potential for realizing low returns or even losing money, possibly preventing you from meeting important objectives, like sending your kids to the college of their choice or having the retirement lifestyle you crave.

Assessing your risk tolerance, however, can be tricky. You must consider not only how much risk you can *afford* to take but also how much risk you can *stand* to take. Determining how much risk you can stand—your temperamental tolerance for risk—is more difficult. It isn't quantifiable.

To that end, many financial advisers, brokerage firms, and mutual-fund companies have created risk quizzes to help people determine whether they are conservative, moderate, or aggressive investors. Some firms that offer such quizzes include Merrill Lynch, T. Rowe Price Associates Inc., Baltimore, Zurich Group Inc.'s Scudder Kemper Investments Inc., New York, and Vanguard Group in Malvern, Pa.

Typically, risk questionnaires include 7 to 10 questions about a person's investing experience, financial security, and tendency to make risky or conservative choices.

The benefit of the questionnaires is that they are an objective resource people can use to get at least a rough idea of their risk tolerance. "It's impossible for someone to assess their risk tolerance alone," says Mr. Bernstein. "I may say I don't like risk, yet will take more risk than the average person."

Many experts warn, however, that the questionnaires should be used simply as a first step to assessing risk tolerance. The second step, many experts agree, is to ask yourself some difficult questions, such as: How much can you stand to lose over the long term?

"Most people can stand to lose a heck of a lot temporarily," says Mr. Schatsky. The real acid test, he says, is how much of your portfolio's value you can stand to lose over months or years.

As it turns out, most people rank as middle-of-the-road risk-takers, say several advisers. "Only about 10% to 15% of my clients are aggressive," says Mr. Roge.

WHAT'S YOUR RISK TOLERANCE?

Circle the letter that corresponds to your answer.

1. Just 60 days after you put money into an investment, its price falls 20 percent. Assuming none of the fundamentals have changed, what would you do?
   a. Sell to avoid further worry and try something else
   b. Do nothing and wait for the investment to come back
   c. Buy more. It was a good investment before; now it's a cheap investment, too

2. Now look at the previous question another way. Your investment fell 20 percent, but it's part of a portfolio being used to meet investment goals with three different time horizons.

2A. What would you do if the goal were five years away?
   a. Sell
   b. Do nothing
   c. Buy more

2B. What would you do if the goal were 15 years away?
   a. Sell
   b. Do nothing
   c. Buy more

---

expected to invest with more risk aversion than individual investors. Certain asset classes, such as options and futures contracts, for example, and some strategies, such as short-selling or buying on margin are ruled out. Short sales and margin purchases were discussed in Chapter 3.

mutual fund

A firm pooling and managing funds of investors.

Mutual funds Mutual funds are firms that manage pools of individual investor money. They invest in accordance with their objectives and issue shares that entitle investors to a pro rata portion of the income generated by the funds.

The return requirement and risk tolerance for mutual funds are highly variable because funds segment the investor market. Various funds appeal to distinct investor groups and will adopt a return requirement and risk tolerance that fit an entire spectrum of market niches. For example, "income" funds cater to the conservative investor, while "high-growth" funds seek out the more risk-tolerant ones. Tax-free bond funds segment the market by tax bracket.

A mutual fund's objectives are spelled out in its prospectus. We discussed mutual funds in detail in Chapter 4.

Pension funds There are two basic types of pension plans: *defined contribution* and *defined benefit*. Defined contribution plans are in effect savings accounts established by the firm for its employees. The employer contributes funds to the plan, but the employee bears all the risk of the fund's investment performance. These plans are called defined contribution because the firm's only obligation is to make the stipulated contributions to the employee's retirement account. The employee is responsible for directing the management of the assets,

2C. What would you do if the goal were 30 years away?

    a. Sell

    b. Do nothing

    c. Buy more

3. The price of your retirement investment jumps 25% a month after you buy it. Again, the fundamentals haven't changed. After you finish gloating, what do you do?

    a. Sell it and lock in your gains

    b. Stay put and hope for more gain

    c. Buy more: It could go higher

4. You're investing for retirement, which is 15 years away. Which would you rather do?

    a. Invest in a money-market fund or guaranteed investment contract, giving up the possibility of major gains, but virtually assuring the safety of your principal

    b. Invest in a 50-50 mix of bond funds and stock funds, in hopes of getting some growth, but also giving yourself some protection in the form of steady income

    c. Invest in aggressive growth mutual funds whose value will probably fluctuate significantly during the year, but have the potential for impressive gains over five or 10 years

5. You just won a big prize! But which one? It's up to you.

    a. $2,000 in cash

    b. A 50% chance to win $5,000

    c. A 20% chance to win $15,000

6. A good investment opportunity just came along. But you have to borrow money to get in. Would you take out a loan?

    a. Definitely not

    b. Perhaps

    c. Yes

7. Your company is selling stock to its employees. In three years, management plans to take the company public. Until then, you won't be able to sell your shares and you will get no dividends. But your investment could multiply as much as 10 times when the company goes public. How much money would you invest?

    a. None

    b. Two months' salary

    c. Four months' salary

SCORING YOUR RISK TOLERANCE

To score the quiz, add up the number of answers you gave in each category *a–c,* then multiply as shown to find your score:

(*a*) answers _____ × 1 = _____ points

(*b*) answers _____ × 2 = _____ points

(*c*) answers _____ × 3 = _____ points

YOUR SCORE _____ points

If you scored . . .	You may be a:
9–14 points	Conservative investor
15–21 points	Moderate investor
22–27 points	Aggressive investor

usually by selecting among several investment funds in which the assets can be placed. Investment earnings in these retirement plans are not taxed until the funds are withdrawn, usually after retirement.

In defined benefit plans, by contrast, the employer has an obligation to provide a specified annual retirement benefit. That benefit is defined by a formula that typically takes into account years of service and the level of salary or wages. For example, the employer may pay the retired employee a yearly amount equal to 2% of the employee's final annual salary for each year of service. A 30-year employee would then receive an annual benefit equal to 60% of his or her final salary. The payments are an obligation of the employer, and the assets in the pension fund provide collateral for the promised benefits. If the investment performance of the assets is poor, the firm is obligated to make up the shortfall by contributing additional assets to the fund. In contrast to defined contribution plans, the risk surrounding investment performance in defined benefit plans is borne by the firm.

A pension actuary makes an assumption about the rate of return that will be earned on the plan's assets and uses this assumed rate to compute the amount the firm must contribute regularly to fund the plan's liabilities. For example, if the actuary assumes a rate of return of 10%, then the firm must contribute $385.54 now to fund $1,000 of pension liabilities that will arise in 10 years, because $385.54 \times 1.10^{10} = \$1,000$.

If a pension fund's *actual* rate of return exceeds the actuarial *assumed* rate, then the firm's shareholders reap an unanticipated gain, because the excess return can be used to reduce future contributions. If the plan's actual rate of return falls short of the assumed rate, however, the firm will have to increase future contributions. Because the sponsoring firm's shareholders bear the risk in a defined benefit pension plan, the objective of the plan will be consistent with the objective of the firm's shareholders.

Many pension plans view their assumed actuarial rate of return as their target rate of return and have little tolerance for earning less than that. Hence, they will take only as much risk as necessary to earn the actuarial rate.

Life Insurance Companies

Life insurance companies generally invest so as to hedge their liabilities, which are defined by the policies they write. The company can reduce its risk by investing in assets that will return more in the event the insurance policy coverage becomes more expensive.

For example, if the company writes a policy that pays a death benefit linked to the consumer price index, then the company is subject to inflation risk. It might search for assets expected to return more when the rate of inflation rises, thus hedging the price-index linkage of the policy.

There are as many objectives as there are distinct types of insurance policies. Until the 1970s, only two types of life insurance policies were available for individuals: whole-life and term.

A *whole-life insurance policy* combines a death benefit with a kind of savings plan that provides for a gradual buildup of cash value that the policyholder can withdraw later in life, usually at age 65. *Term insurance,* on the other hand, provides death benefits only, with no buildup of cash value.

The interest rate embedded in the schedule of cash value accumulation promised under the whole-life policy is a fixed rate. One way life insurance companies try to hedge this liability is by investing in long-term bonds. Often the insured individual has the right to borrow at a prespecified fixed interest rate against the cash value of the policy.

During the high-interest-rate years of the 1970s and early 1980s, many older whole-life policies allowed policyholders to borrow at rates as low as 4 or 5% per year; some holders borrowed heavily against the cash value to invest in assets paying double-digit yields. Other actual and potential policyholders abandoned whole-life policies and took out term insurance, which accounted for more than half the volume of new sales of individual life policies.

In response to these developments, the insurance industry came up with two new policy types: variable life and universal life. A *variable life policy* entitles the insured to a fixed death benefit plus a cash value that can be invested in the policyholder's choice of mutual funds. A *universal life policy* allows policyholders to increase or reduce either the insurance premium (the annual fee paid on the policy) or the death benefit (the cash amount paid to beneficiaries in the event of death) according to their changing needs. Furthermore, the interest rate on the cash value component changes with market interest rates. The great advantage of variable and universal life insurance policies is that earnings on the cash value are not taxed until the money is withdrawn.

Non-Life-Insurance Companies

Non-life-insurance companies such as property and casualty insurers have investable funds primarily because they pay claims *after* they collect policy premiums. Typically, they are conservative in their attitude toward risk.

A common thread in the objectives of pension plans and insurance companies is the need to hedge predictable long-term liabilities. Investment strategies typically call for hedging these liabilities with bonds of various maturities.

Banks

Most bank investments are loans to businesses and consumers, and most of their liabilities are accounts of depositors. As investors, banks try to match the risk of assets to liabilities while earning a profitable spread between the lending and borrowing rates

Most liabilities of banks and thrift institutions are checking accounts, time or savings deposits, and certificates of deposit (CDs). Checking account funds may be withdrawn at any time, so they are of the shortest maturity. Time or savings deposits are of various maturities. Some time deposits may extend as long as seven years, but, on average, they are of fairly short maturity. CDs are bonds of various maturities that the bank issues to investors. While the range of maturities is from 90 days to 10 years, the average is about one year.

Traditionally, a large part of the loan portfolio of savings and loan (S&L) institutions was in collateralized real estate loans, better known as mortgages. Typically, mortgages are of 15 to 30 years, significantly longer than the maturity of the average liability. Thus, profits are exposed to interest rate risk. When rates rise, thrifts have to pay higher rates to depositors, while the income from their longer term investments is relatively fixed.

Banks earn profit from the interest rate spread between loans extended (the bank's assets) and deposits and CDs (the bank's liabilities), as well as from fees for services. Managing bank assets calls for balancing the loan portfolio with the portfolio of deposits and CDs. A bank can increase the interest rate spread by lending to riskier borrowers and by increasing the proportion of longer term loans. Both policies threaten bank solvency though, so their deployment must match the risk tolerance of the bank shareholders. In addition, bank capital regulations now are risk-based, so higher-risk strategies will elicit higher capital requirements as well as the possibility of greater regulatory interference in the bank's affairs.

As we noted in Chapter 2, most long-term fixed-rate mortgages today are securitized into pass-through certificates and held as securities in the portfolios of mutual funds, pension funds, and other institutional investors. Mortgage originators typically sell a portion of the mortgages they originate to pass-through agencies like Fannie Mae or Freddie Mac rather than holding them in a portfolio. They earn their profits on mortgage origination and servicing fees. The trend away from maintaining portfolio holdings of long-term mortgages also has reduced interest rate risk.

Endowment Funds

Endowment funds are held by organizations chartered to use their money for specific nonprofit purposes. They are financed by gifts from one or more sponsors and are typically managed by educational, cultural, and charitable organizations or by independent foundations established solely to carry out the fund's specific purposes. Generally, the investment objectives of an endowment fund are to produce a steady flow of income subject to only a moderate degree of risk. Trustees of an endowment fund, however, can specify other objectives as circumstances dictate.

endowment funds

Portfolios operated for the benefit of a nonprofit entity.

Describe several distinguishing characteristics of endowment funds that differentiate them from pension funds.

CONCEPT *check* **22.1**

Table 22.4 summarizes the objectives governing these classes of investors.

TABLE 22.4
Matrix of objectives

Type of Investor	Return Requirement	Risk Tolerance
Individual and personal trusts	Life cycle (education, children, retirement)	Life cycle (younger are more risk tolerant)
Mutual funds	Variable	Variable
Pension funds	Assumed actuarial rate	Depends on proximity of payouts
Endowment funds	Determined by current income needs and need for asset growth to maintain real value	Generally conservative
Life insurance companies	Should exceed new money rate by sufficient margin to meet expenses and profit objectives; also actuarial rates important	Conservative
Non-life-insurance companies	No minimum	Conservative
Banks	Interest spread	Variable

22.3 | Investor Constraints

Even with identical attitudes toward risk, different households and institutions might choose different investment portfolios because of their differing circumstances. These circumstances include tax status, requirements for liquidity or a flow of income from the portfolio, or various regulatory restrictions. These circumstances impose *constraints* on investor choice. Together, objectives and constraints determine appropriate investment policy.

As noted, constraints usually have to do with investor circumstances. For example, if a family has children about to enter college, there will be a high demand for liquidity since cash will be needed to pay tuition bills. Other times, however, constraints are imposed externally. For example, banks and trusts are subject to legal limitations on the types of assets they may hold in their portfolios. Finally, some constraints are self-imposed. For example, "social investing" means that investors will not hold shares of firms involved in ethically objectionable activities. Some criteria that have been used to judge firms as ineligible for a portfolio are: involvement in countries with human rights abuses; production of tobacco or alcohol; participation in polluting activities.

Five common types of constraints are described below.

Liquidity

liquidity

Liquidity refers to the speed and ease with which an asset can be converted to cash.

Liquidity is the speed and ease with which an asset can be sold and still fetch a fair price. It is a relationship between the time dimension (how long it will take to sell) and the price dimension (the discount from fair market price) of an investment asset.

When an actual concrete measure of liquidity is necessary, one thinks of the discount when an immediate sale is unavoidable.[1] Cash and money market instruments such as Treasury bills and commercial paper, where the bid–ask spread is a small fraction of 1%, are the most liquid assets, and real estate is among the least liquid. Office buildings and manufacturing structures in extreme cases can suffer a 50% liquidity discount.

Both individual and institutional investors must consider how likely they are to require cash at short notice. From this likelihood, they establish the minimum level of liquid assets they need in the investment portfolio.

Investment Horizon

investment horizon

The planned liquidation date.

This is the *planned* liquidation date of the investment. Examples of an individual's **investment horizon** could be the time to fund a college education or the retirement date for a wage earner. For a university or hospital endowment, an investment horizon could relate to the time to fund a major construction project. Horizon dates must be considered when investors choose between assets of various maturities. For example, the maturity date of a bond might make it a more attractive investment if it coincides with a date on which cash is needed.

Regulations

prudent investor rule

The fiduciary responsibility of a professional investor.

Only professional and institutional investors are constrained by regulations. First and foremost is the **prudent investor rule.** That is, professional investors who manage other people's money have a fiduciary responsibility to restrict investment to assets that would have been approved by a prudent investor. The law is purposefully nonspecific. Every professional investor must stand ready to defend an investment policy in a court of law, and interpretation may differ according to the standards of the times.

Also, specific regulations apply to various institutional investors. For instance, U.S. mutual funds may not hold more than 5% of the shares of any publicly traded corporation.

---

[1]In many cases, it is impossible to know the liquidity of an asset with certainty until it is put up for sale. In more developed markets, however, the liquidity of the traded assets can be observed from the bid–ask spread that is, the difference between the "bid" quote (the lower price available when someone wishes to sell an asset) and the "ask" quote (the higher price a buyer would have to pay to acquire the asset).

Sometimes, "self-imposed" regulations also affect the investment choice. We have noted several times, for example, that mutual funds describe their investment policies in a prospectus. These policy guidelines amount to constraints on the ability to choose portfolios freely.

Tax Considerations

Tax consequences are central to investment decisions. The performance of any investment strategy should be measured by its rate of return *after* taxes. For household and institutional investors who face significant tax rates, tax sheltering and deferral of tax obligations may be pivotal in their investment strategy.

Unique Needs

Virtually every investor faces special circumstances. Imagine husband-and-wife aeronautical engineers holding high-paying jobs in the same aerospace corporation. The entire human capital of that household is tied to a single player in a rather cyclical industry. This couple would need to hedge the risk of a deterioration in the economic well-being of the aerospace industry.

Similar issues would confront an executive on Wall Street who owns an apartment near work. Because the value of the home in that part of Manhattan probably depends on the vitality of the securities industry, the individual is doubly exposed to the vagaries of the stock market. Because both job and home already depend on the fortunes of Wall Street, the purchase of a typical diversified stock portfolio would actually increase the exposure to the stock market.

These examples illustrate that the job is often the primary "investment" of an individual, and the unique risk profile that results from employment can play a big role in determining a suitable investment portfolio.

Other unique needs of individuals often center around their stage in the life cycle, as discussed above. Retirement, housing, and children's education constitute three major demands for funds, and investment policy will depend in part on the proximity of these expenditures.

Institutional investors also face unique needs. For example, pension funds will differ in their investment policy, depending on the average age of plan participants. Another example of a unique need for an institutional investor would be a university whose trustees allow the administration to use only cash income from the endowment fund. This constraint would translate into a preference for high-dividend-paying assets.

Table 22.5 presents a matrix of constraints for various investors. As you would expect, liquidity and tax constraints for individuals are variable because of wealth and age differentials.

A particular constraint for mutual funds arises from investor response to the fund's performance. When a mutual fund earns an unsatisfactory rate of return, investors often redeem their shares—they withdraw money from the fund. The mutual fund then contracts. The reverse happens when a mutual fund earns an unusually high return: It can become popular with investors overnight, and its asset base will grow dramatically.

TABLE 22.5
Matrix of constraints

Type of Investor	Liquidity	Horizon	Regulatory	Taxes
Individuals and personal trusts	Variable	Life cycle	Prudent investor laws (for trusts)	Variable
Mutual funds	Low	Short	Little	None
Pension funds	Young, low; mature, high	Long	ERISA	None
Endowment funds	Little	Long	Little	None
Life insurance companies	Low	Long	Complex	Yes
Non-life-insurance companies	High	Short	Little	Yes
Banks	Low	Short	Changing	Yes

Pension funds are heavily regulated by the Employee Retirement Income Security Act of 1974 (ERISA). This law revolutionized savings for retirement in the United States and remains a major piece of social legislation. Thus, for pension funds, regulatory constraints are relatively important. Also, mature pension funds are required to pay out more than young funds and hence need more liquidity.

Endowment funds, on the other hand, usually do not need to liquidate assets, or even use dividend income, to finance payouts. Contributions are expected to exceed payouts and increase the real value of the endowment fund, so liquidity is not an overriding concern.

Life insurance companies are subject to complex regulation. The corporate tax rate, which today is 35% for large firms, also applies to insurance company investment income, so taxes are an important concern.

Property and casualty insurance, like term life insurance, is written on a short-term basis. Most policies must be renewed annually, which means property and casualty insurance companies are subject to short-term horizon constraints.

The short horizon constraint for banks comes from the interest rate risk component of the interest rate spread (i.e., the risk of interest rate increases that banks face when financing long-term assets with short-term liabilities).

CONCEPT *check* **22.2**	*a.*	Think about the financial circumstances of your closest relative in your parents' generation (for example, your parents' household if you are fortunate enough to have them around). Write down the objectives and constraints for their investment decisions.
	b.	Now consider the financial situation of your closest friend or relative who is in his or her 30s. Write down the objectives and constraints that would fit his or her investment decision.
	c.	How much of the difference between the two statements is due to the age of the investors?

22.4 Investment Policies

Once objectives and constraints are determined, an investment policy that suits the investor can be formulated. That policy must reflect an appropriate risk-return profile as well as needs for liquidity, income generation, and tax positioning. Institutional investors such as pension plans and endowments often must issue formal statements of their investment policy. These policy statements should be based on, and often make explicit, the objectives and constraints of the investment fund. The following is an example of a portion of a policy statement for a defined benefit pension plan.

> The Plan should emphasize production of adequate levels of real return as its primary return objective, giving special attention to the inflation-related aspects of the plan. To the extent consistent with appropriate control of portfolio risk, investment action should seek to maintain or increases the surplus of plan assets relative to benefit liabilities over time. Five-year periods, updated annually, shall be employed in planning for investment decision making; the plan's actuary shall update the benefit liabilities breakdown by country every three years.
>
> The orientation of investment planning shall be long term in nature. In addition, minimal liquidity reserves shall be maintained so long as annual company funding contributions and investment income exceed annual benefit payments to retirees and the operating expenses of the plan. The plan's actuary shall update plan cash flow projections annually. Plan administration shall ensure compliance with all laws and regulations related to maintenance of the plan's tax-exempt status and will all requirements of the Employee Retirement Income Security Act (ERISA).

The most important portfolio decision an investor makes is the proportion of the total investment fund allocated to risky as opposed to safe assets such as money market securities, usually called cash equivalents or simply cash. This choice is the most fundamental means of controlling investment risk.

It follows that the first decision an investor must make is the asset allocation decision. Asset allocation refers to the allocation of the portfolio across major asset categories such as:

1. Money market assets (cash equivalents).
2. Fixed-income securities (primarily bonds).
3. Stocks.
4. Non-U.S. stocks and bonds.
5. Real estate.
6. Precious metals and other commodities.

Only after the broad asset classes to be held in the portfolio are determined can one sensibly choose the specific securities to purchase.

Investors who have relatively high degrees of risk tolerance will choose asset allocations more concentrated in higher-risk investment classes, such as equity, to obtain higher expected rates of return. More conservative investors will choose asset allocations with a greater weight in bonds and cash equivalents.

Asset allocation also will depend on expectations for capital market performance in the coming period. (Look back at Figure 22.1 and Table 22.1, and you will see that the CFA Institute classifies this part of the planning process as the formation of "capital market expectations.") Given the risk-return positioning of the investor and the set of expectations, an optimal asset mix may be formed (see step II, Execution, in Table 22.1).

Top-Down Policies for Institutional Investors

Individual investors need not concern themselves with organizational efficiency. But professional investors with large amounts to invest must structure asset allocation activities to decentralize some of the decision making.

A common feature of large organizations is the investment committee and the asset universe. The investment committee includes top management officers, senior portfolio managers, and senior security analysts. The committee determines investment policies and verifies that portfolio managers and security analysts are operating within the bounds of specified policies. A major responsibility of the investment committee is to translate the objectives and constraints of the company into an **asset universe,** an approved list of assets for each of the company's portfolios.

Thus, the investment committee has responsibility for broad asset allocation. While the investment manager might have some leeway to tilt the portfolio toward or away from one or another asset class, the investment committee establishes the benchmark allocation that largely determines the risk characteristics of the portfolio. The task of choosing specific securities from the approved universe is more fully delegated to the investment manager.

asset universe
Approved list of assets in which a portfolio manager may invest.

Figure 22.2 illustrates the stages of the portfolio choice process for Palatial Investments, a hypothetical firm that invests internationally. The first two stages are asset allocation choices. The broadest choice is in the weighting of the portfolio between U.S. and Japanese securities. Palatial has chosen a weight of 75% in the United States and 25% in Japan. The allocation of the portfolio across asset classes may now be determined. For example, 15% of the U.S. portfolio is invested in cash equivalents, 40% in fixed income, and 45% in equity. The asset-class weights are, in general, a policy decision of the investment committee, although the investment manager might have some authority to alter the asset allocation to limited degrees based on her expectations concerning the investment performance of various asset classes. Finally, security selection within each country is determined by the portfolio manager from the approved universe. For example, 45% of funds held in the U.S. equity market will be placed in IBM, 35% in GE, and 20% in ExxonMobil. (We show only three securities in the figure because of space limitations. Obviously a $1 billion fund will hold securities of many more firms.)

These ever-finer decisions determine the proportion of each individual security in the overall portfolio. As an example, consider the determination of the proportion of Palatial's portfolio invested in ExxonMobil, 6.75%. This fraction results from the following decisions.

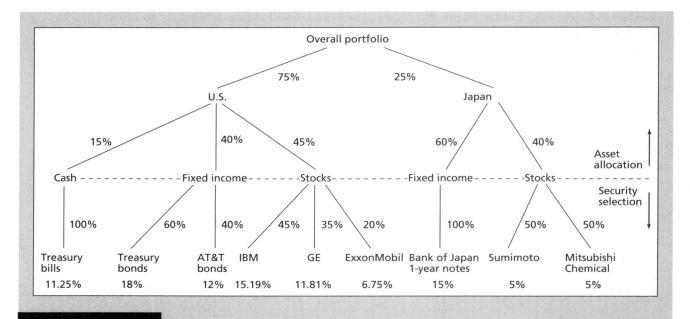

FIGURE 22.2

Asset allocation and security selection for Palatial Investments

First, the United States receives a weight of 75% of the overall portfolio, and equities comprise 45% of the U.S. component of the portfolio. These are asset allocation choices. ExxonMobil comprises 20% of the U.S. equity component of the portfolio. This is a security selection choice. Therefore, ExxonMobil's weight in the overall portfolio is $.75 \times .45 \times .20 = .0675$, or 6.75%. If the entire portfolio is $1 billion, $67,500,000 will be invested in ExxonMobil. If ExxonMobil is selling for $75 a share, 900,000 shares must be purchased. The bottom line in Figure 22.2 shows the percentage of the overall portfolio held in each asset.

This example illustrates a top-down approach that is consistent with the needs of large organizations. The top managers set the overall policy of the portfolio by specifying asset allocation guidelines. Lower-level portfolio managers fill in the details with their security selection decisions.

Active versus Passive Policies

One choice that must be confronted by all investors, individual as well as institutional, is the degree to which the portfolio will be actively versus passively managed. Recall that passive management is based on the belief that security prices usually are at close to "fair" levels. Instead of spending time and other resources attempting to "beat the market," that is, to find mispriced securities with unusually attractive risk-return characteristics, the investor simply assumes that she will be fairly compensated for the risk she is willing to take on and selects a portfolio consistent with her risk tolerance.[2]

Passive management styles can be applied to both the security selection and the asset allocation decisions. With regard to asset allocation, passive management simply means that the manager does not depart from his or her "normal" asset-class weightings in response to changing expectations about the performance of different markets. Those "normal" weights are based on the investor's risk and return objectives, as discussed earlier. For example, Vanguard has recommended an asset allocation for a 45-year-old investor of 65% equity, 20% bonds,

---

[2]We discussed arguments for passive management in previous chapters. Here, we simply present an overview of the issues.

and 15% cash equivalents. A purely passive manager would not depart from these weights in response to forecasts of market performances. The weighting scheme would be adjusted only in response to changes in risk tolerance as age and wealth change over time.

Next consider passive security selection. Imagine that you must choose a portfolio of stocks without access to any special information about security values. This would be the case if you believed that anything you know about a stock is already known by the rest of the investors in the market and therefore is already reflected in the stock price. If you cannot predict which stocks will be winners, you should broadly diversify your portfolio to avoid putting all your eggs in one basket. A natural course of action for such an investor would be to choose a portfolio with "a little bit of everything."

This reasoning leads one to look for a portfolio that is invested across the entire security market. We saw in Chapter 4 that some mutual fund operators have established index funds that follow just such a strategy. These funds hold each stock or bond in proportion to its representation in a particular index, such as the Standard & Poor's 500 stock price index or the Barclay's Capital (formerly the Lehman Brothers) bond index. Holding an indexed portfolio represents purely passive security selection since the investor's return simply duplicates the return of the overall market without making a bet on one or another stock or sector of the market.

In contrast to passive strategies, active management assumes an ability to outguess the other investors in the market and to identify either securities or asset classes that will shine in the near future. Active security selection for institutional investors typically requires two layers: security analysis and portfolio choice. Security analysts specialize in particular industries and companies and prepare assessments of their particular market niches. The portfolio managers then sift through the reports of many analysts. They use forecasts of market conditions to make asset allocation decisions and use the security analysts' recommendations to choose the particular securities to include within each asset class.

The choice between active and passive strategies need not be all-or-nothing. One can pursue both active security selection and passive asset allocation, for example. In this case, the manager would maintain fixed asset allocation targets but would actively choose the securities within each asset class. Or one could pursue active asset allocation and passive security selection. In this case, the manager might actively shift the allocation between equity and bond components of the portfolio but hold indexed portfolios within each sector. Another mixed approach is called a *passive core* strategy. In this case, the manager indexes *part* of the portfolio, the passive core, and actively manages the rest of the portfolio.

Is active or passive management the better approach? It might seem at first blush that active managers have the edge because active management is necessary to achieve outstanding performance. But remember that active managers start out with some disadvantages as well. They incur significant costs when preparing their analyses of markets and securities and incur heavier trading costs from the more rapid turnover of their portfolios. If they don't uncover information or insights currently unavailable to other investors (not a trivial task in a nearly efficient market), then all of this costly activity will be wasted, and they will underperform a passive strategy. In fact, low-cost passive strategies have performed surprisingly well in the last few decades, as we saw in Chapters 4 and 8.

Classify the following statements according to where each fits in the objective-constraints-policies framework.

CONCEPT *check* **22.3**

a. Invest 5% in bonds and 95% in stocks.
b. Do not invest more than 10% of the budget in any one security.
c. Shoot for an average rate of return of 11%.
d. Make sure there is $95,000 in cash in the account on December 31, 2025.
e. If the market is bearish, reduce the investment in stocks to 80%.
f. As of next year, we will be in a higher tax bracket.
g. Our new president believes pension plans should take no risk whatsoever with the pension fund.
h. Our acquisition plan will require large sums of cash to be available at any time.

22.5 Monitoring and Revising Investment Portfolios

Choosing the investment portfolio requires the investor to set objectives, acknowledge constraints, determine asset-class proportions, and perform security analysis. Is the process ever finished and behind us? By the time we have completed all of these steps, many of the inputs we have used will be out of date. Moreover, our circumstances as well as our objectives change over time. Therefore, the investment process requires that we continually monitor and update our portfolios. This is the task of rebalancing, part of the feedback process described earlier in Table 22.1 and Figure 22.1.

Moreover, even if our circumstances do not change, our portfolios necessarily will. For example, suppose you currently hold 1,000 shares of ExxonMobil, selling at $75 a share, and 1,000 shares of Microsoft, selling at $25 a share. If the price of ExxonMobil falls to $60 a share, while that of Microsoft rises to $30 a share, the fractions of your portfolio allocated to each security change without your taking any direct action. The value of your investment in ExxonMobil is now lower, and the value of the Microsoft investment is higher. Unless you are happy with this reallocation of investment proportions, you will need to take some action to restore the portfolio weights to desired levels.

Asset allocation also will change over time, as the investment performance of different asset classes diverges. If the stock market outperforms the bond market, the proportion of your portfolio invested in stocks will increase, while the proportion invested in bonds will decrease. If you are uncomfortable with this shift in the asset mix, you must rebalance the portfolio by selling some of the stocks and purchasing bonds.

Therefore, investing is a *dynamic process,* meaning that you must continually update and reevaluate your decisions over time.

SUMMARY

- The CFA Institute has developed a systematic framework for the translation of investor goals to investment strategy. Its three main parts are: objectives, constraints, and policy. Investor objectives include the return requirement and risk tolerance, reflecting the overriding concern of investment with the risk-return trade-off. Investor constraints include liquidity requirements, investment horizon, regulatory concerns, tax obligations, and the unique needs of various investors. Investment policies specify the portfolio manager's asset allocation and security selection decisions.

- Major institutional investors include pension funds, mutual funds, life insurance companies, non-life-insurance companies, banks, and endowment funds. For individual investors, life-cycle concerns are the most important factor in setting objectives, constraints, and policies.

- Major asset classes include: cash (money market assets), fixed-income securities (bonds), stocks, real estate, precious metals, and collectibles. Asset allocation refers to the decision made as to the investment proportion to be allocated to each asset class. An active asset allocation strategy calls for the production of frequent market forecasts and the adjustment of asset allocation according to these forecasts.

- Active security selection requires security analysis and portfolio choice. Analysis of individual securities is required to choose securities that will make up a coherent portfolio and outperform a passive benchmark.

- Perhaps the most important feature of the investment process is that it is dynamic. Portfolios must be continually monitored and updated. The frequency and timing of various decisions are in themselves important decisions. Successful investment management requires management of these dynamic aspects.

www.mhhe.com/bkm

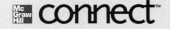   Select problems are available in McGraw-Hill   **PROBLEM SETS**
Connect. Please see the packaging options section
of the preface for more information.

Intermediate

1. You are P. J. Walter, CFA, a managing partner of a prestigious investment counseling
   firm that specializes in individual rather than institutional accounts. The firm has developed a national reputation for its ability to blend modern portfolio theory and traditional
   portfolio methods. You have written a number of articles on portfolio management. You
   are an authority on the subject of establishing investment policies and programs for
   individual clients, tailored to their particular circumstances and needs.

   Dr. and Mrs. A. J. Mason have been referred to your firm and to you in particular.
   At your first meeting on June 2, 2006, Dr. Mason explained that he is an electrical engineer and long-time professor at the Essex Institute. He is also an inventor, and, after 30
   years of teaching, the rights to one of his patented inventions, the "inverse thermothrocle
   valve," have just been acquired by a new electronics company, ACS, Inc.

   In anticipation of the potential value of his invention, Dr. Mason had followed his
   accountant's advice and established a private corporation, wholly owned by the Masons,
   to hold the title to the inverse thermothrocle valve patent. It was this corporation that
   ACS acquired from the Masons for $1 million in cash, payable at the closing on June 7,
   2006. In addition, ACS has agreed to pay royalties to Dr. Mason or his heirs based on
   its sales of systems that utilize the inverse thermothrocle valve.

   Since ACS has no operating record, it is difficult for either the company or Dr. Mason
   to forecast future sales and royalties. While all parties are optimistic about prospects for
   success, they are also mindful of the risks associated with any new firm, especially those
   exposed to the technological obsolescence of the electronics industry. The management
   of ACS has indicated to Dr. Mason that he might expect royalties of as much as $100,000
   in the first year of production and maximum royalties of as much as $500,000 annually
   thereafter.

   During your counseling meeting, Mrs. Mason expressed concern for the proper
   investment of the $1,000,000 initial payment. She pointed out that Dr. Mason has
   invested all of their savings in his inventions. Thus, they will have only their Social
   Security retirement benefits and a small pension from the Essex Institute to provide
   for their retirement. Dr. Mason will be 65 in 2010. His salary from the Essex Institute
   is $55,000 per year. Additionally, he expects to continue earning $10,000–$25,000
   annually from consulting and speaking engagements.

   The Masons have two daughters and a son, all of whom are married and have
   families of their own. Dr. and Mrs. Mason are interested in helping with the education
   of their grandchildren and have provided in their wills for their estate to be divided
   among their children and grandchildren.

   In the event that the royalty payments from ACS meet the projections cited above,
   Mrs. Mason is interested in providing a scholarship fund in the name of Dr. Mason for
   the benefit of enterprising young engineers attending the Essex Institute. The scholarship fund ranks third behind the provision for the Masons' retirement and for the
   education of their grandchildren.

   In your discussions with Dr. and Mrs. Mason, you have stressed the importance of
   identifying investment objectives and constraints and having an appropriate investment

policy. Identify and describe an appropriate set of investment objectives and investment constraints for Dr. and Mrs. Mason, and prepare a comprehensive investment policy statement based on these investment objectives and constraints.

2. You are being interviewed for a job as a portfolio manager at an investment counseling partnership. As part of the interview, you are asked to demonstrate your ability to develop investment portfolio policy statements for the clients listed below:
   a. A pension fund that is described as a mature defined-benefit plan; with the workforce having an average age of 54; no unfunded pension liabilities; and wage cost increases forecast at 5% annually.
   b. A university endowment fund that is described as conservative; with investment returns being utilized along with gifts and donations received to meet current expenses, the spending rate is 5% per year; and inflation in costs is expected at 3% annually.
   c. A life insurance company that is described as specializing in annuities; policy premium rates are based on a minimum annual accumulation rate of 7% in the first year of the policy and a 4% minimum annual accumulation rate in the next five years.

   List and discuss separately for *each* client described above the objectives and constraints that will determine the portfolio policy you would recommend for that client.

CFA Problems

1. Your client says, "With the unrealized gains in my portfolio, I have almost saved enough money for my daughter to go to college in eight years, but educational costs keep going up." Based on this statement alone, which one of the following appears to be least important to your client's investment policy?
   a. Time horizon.
   b. Purchasing power risk.
   c. Liquidity.
   d. Taxes.

2. The aspect least likely to be included in the portfolio management process is
   a. Identifying an investor's objectives, constraints, and preferences.
   b. Organizing the management process itself.
   c. Implementing strategies regarding the choice of assets to be used.
   d. Monitoring market conditions, relative values, and investor circumstances.

3. A clearly written investment policy statement is critical for
   a. Mutual funds
   b. Individuals
   c. Pension funds
   d. All investors

4. The investment policy statement of an institution must be concerned with all of the following *except:*
   a. Its obligations to its clients.
   b. The level of the market.
   c. Legal regulations.
   d. Taxation.

5. Under the provisions of a typical corporate defined-benefit pension plan, the employer is responsible for:
   a. Paying benefits to retired employees.
   b. Investing in conservative fixed-income assets.
   c. Counseling employees in the selection of asset classes.
   d. Maintaining an actuarially determined, fully funded pension plan.

6. Which of the following statements reflects the importance of the asset allocation decision to the investment process? The asset allocation decision:
   a. Helps the investor decide on realistic investment goals.
   b. Identifies the specific securities to include in a portfolio.

    c. Determines most of the portfolio's returns and volatility over time.

    d. Creates a standard by which to establish an appropriate investment time horizon.

7. You are a portfolio manager and senior executive vice president of Advisory Securities Selection, Inc. Your firm has been invited to meet with the trustees of the Wood Museum Endowment Funds. Wood Museum is a privately endowed charitable institution that is dependent on the investment return from a $25 million endowment fund to balance the budget. The treasurer of the museum has recently completed the budget that indicates a need for cash flow of $3 million in 2009, $3.2 million in 2010, and $3.5 million in 2011 from the endowment fund to balance the budget in those years. Currently, the entire endowment portfolio is invested in Treasury bills and money market funds because the trustees fear a financial crisis. The trustees do not anticipate any further capital contributions to the fund.

    The trustees are all successful businesspeople, and they have been critical of the fund's previous investment advisers because they did not follow a logical decision-making process. In fact, several previous managers have been dismissed because of their inability to communicate with the trustees and their preoccupation with the fund's relative performance rather than the cash flow needs.

    Advisory Securities Selection, Inc., has been contacted by the trustees because of its reputation for understanding and relating to the client's needs. The trustees have asked you, as a prospective portfolio manager for the Wood Museum Endowment Fund, to prepare a written report in response to the following questions. Your report will be circulated to the trustees before the initial interview on June 15, 2009.

    Explain in detail how each of the following relates to the determination of either investor objectives or investor constraints that can be used to determine the portfolio policies for this three-year period for the Wood Museum Endowment Fund.

    a. Liquidity requirements.

    b. Return requirements.

    c. Risk tolerance.

    d. Time horizon.

    e. Tax considerations.

    f. Regulatory and legal considerations.

    g. Unique needs and circumstances.

8. Mrs. Mary Atkins, age 66, has been your firm's client for five years, since the death of her husband, Dr. Charles Atkins. Dr. Atkins had built a successful newspaper business that he sold two years before his death to Merit Enterprises, a publishing and broadcasting conglomerate, in exchange for Merit common stock. The Atkinses have no children, and their wills provide that upon their deaths the remaining assets shall be used to create a fund for the benefit of Good Samaritan Hospital, to be called the Atkins Endowment Fund.

    Good Samaritan is a 180-bed, not-for-profit hospital with an annual operating budget of $12.5 million. In the past, the hospital's operating revenues have often been sufficient to meet operating expenses and occasionally even generate a small surplus. In recent years, however, rising costs and declining occupancy rates have caused Good Samaritan to run a deficit. The operating deficit has averaged $300,000 to $400,000 annually over the last several years. Existing endowment assets (that is, excluding the Atkins's estate) of $7.5 million currently generate approximately $375,000 of annual income, up from less than $200,000 five years ago. This increased income has been the result of somewhat higher interest rates, as well as a shift in asset mix toward more bonds. To offset operating deficits, the Good Samaritan Board of Governors has determined that the endowment's current income should be increased to approximately 6% of total assets (up from 5% currently). The hospital has not received any significant additions to its endowment assets in the past five years.

    Identify and describe an appropriate set of investment objectives and constraints for the Atkins Endowment Fund to be created after Mrs. Atkins's death.

9. Several discussion meetings have provided the following information about one of your firm's new advisory clients, a charitable endowment fund recently created by means of a one-time $10 million gift:

Objectives

Return requirement. Planning is based on a minimum total return of 8% per year, including an initial current income component of $500,000 (5% on beginning capital). Realizing this current income target is the endowment fund's primary return goal. (See "unique needs" below.)

Constraints

Time horizon. Perpetuity, except for requirement to make an $8,500,000 cash distribution on June 30, 2010. (See "unique needs.")

Liquidity needs. None of a day-to-day nature until 2010. Income is distributed annually after year-end. (See "unique needs.")

Tax considerations. None; this endowment fund is exempt from taxes.

Legal and regulatory considerations. Minimal, but the prudent investor rule applies to all investment actions.

Unique needs, circumstances, and preferences. The endowment fund must pay out to another tax-exempt entity the sum of $8,500,000 in cash on June 30, 2010. The assets remaining after this distribution will be retained by the fund in perpetuity. The endowment fund has adopted a "spending rule" requiring a first-year current income payout of $500,000; thereafter, the annual payout is to rise by 3% in real terms. Until 2010, annual income in excess of that required by the spending rule is to be reinvested. After 2010, the spending rate will be reset at 5% of the then-existing capital.

With this information and information found in this chapter, do the following:

a. Formulate an appropriate investment policy statement for the endowment fund.

b. Identify and briefly explain three major ways in which your firm's initial asset allocation decisions for the endowment fund will be affected by the circumstances of the account.

10. You have been named as investment adviser to a foundation established by Dr. Walter Jones with an original contribution consisting entirely of the common stock of Jomedco, Inc. Founded by Dr. Jones, Jomedco manufactures and markets medical devices invented by the doctor and collects royalties on other patented innovations.

All of the shares that made up the initial contribution to the foundation were sold at a public offering of Jomedco common stock, and the $5 million proceeds will be delivered to the foundation within the next week. At the same time, Mrs. Jones will receive $5 million in proceeds from the sale of her stock in Jomedco.

Dr. Jones's purpose in establishing the Jones Foundation was to "offset the effect of inflation on medical school tuition for the maximum number of worthy students."

You are preparing for a meeting with the foundation trustees to discuss investment policy and asset allocation.

a. Define and give examples that show the differences between an investment objective, an investment constraint, and investment policy.

b. Identify and describe an appropriate set of investment objectives and investment constraints for the Jones Foundation.

c. Based on the investment objectives and investment constraints identified in part *b,* prepare a comprehensive investment policy statement for the Jones Foundation to be recommended for adoption by the trustees.

WEB *master*   PERSONAL DIVERSIFICATION

The proper asset allocation for an investor planning for retirement changes dramatically over time. Investors who do NOT frequently update their asset allocation could be caught in a tragic investment scenario that significantly delays retirement. This is exactly what occurred in 2008, when investors planning for retirement realized they had not reallocated their portfolios away from stocks and into fixed income securities over the years, as they should have.

    Go to **money.cnn.com/retirement** and under the Retirement tab, select Retirement Calculators. Click the last calculator on the list, defined as "Get the right asset allocation." Calculate an asset allocation for the following two scenarios.

A. Need the money: 20+ years
    How much risk: As much as possible
    How flexible: If I miss my goal . . . OK.
    During market sell offs: See an opportunity to buy

B. Need the money: 3–5 years
    How much risk: Not much at all
    How flexible: I can't afford to miss my target
    During market sell offs: Do nothing

1. What is the ratio of stock to bonds in each scenario? Notice the dramatic shift from risky assets to safe assets. How would this change impact in investor during the stock market crash of 2008?

2. Explain the impact on an investor planning to retire in 3–5 years if the investor had maintained asset allocation A and not asset allocation B during the 2008 stock market crash.

3. How frequently do you think investors should examine their asset allocation? What else should investors review on a periodic basis in addition to asset allocation?

22.1. A convenient and effective way to organize the answer to this question is to cast it in the context of the investment policy statement framework.

    Risk: Endowment funds have no "safety nets" such as pension funds enjoy in the event of difficulty, either in the form of corporate assets to fall back on or a call on public assistance, such as from the Pension Benefit Guaranty Corporation. Moreover, endowment fund cash flows may be highly erratic due to the uncertain timing of income from gifts and/or bequests, while pension fund cash flows tend to be very predictable and steady. These differences suggest the typical endowment fund will adopt a more conservative risk-bearing posture than will the typical pension fund, both as to asset-class exposures and to the type of security content of such exposures.

    Return: Because investment-related spending usually is limited to "income yield," endowment funds often focus their return goals on the matter of current spendable income; pension funds, on the other hand, tend to adopt total return approaches, at least until a plan matures. Although inflation protection should be of great importance to both types of funds, endowment funds appear to be less concerned with real return production than are pension funds, perhaps because of their common emphasis on "income now" in setting return goals.

    Time horizon: Theoretically, an endowment fund is a perpetuity while a pension fund may well have a finite life span. Therefore, an endowment fund should operate with a very long-term view of investment. However, such funds in practice tend to adopt shorter horizons than are typical of pension funds (just as they typically assume less risk). Their tendency to emphasize income production in the near term is the probable reason for this common occurrence.

    Liquidity: Endowment funds, particularly those that use gifts and bequests to supplement their investment income, often have fairly large liquidity reserves—both to protect against fluctuations in their cash flows and reflecting their generally conservative outlooks—while, except for very mature plans, pension funds tend to require minimum liquidity reserves. Endowment funds also frequently maintain substantial liquid holdings to provide for known future cash payout requirements, such as for new buildings.

    Taxes: Here, although differing in detail, the situations of the two forms of institutions are very much the same. In the United States, tax considerations are normally of minimal importance in both cases.

    Regulatory/Legal: Endowment fund investment is carried out under state governance, while pension fund investment, in the United States, is carried out under federal law, specifically under ERISA. The difference is significant. Endowment funds operate under the prudent investor rule, whereby each investment must be judged on its own merits apart from any other portfolio holdings, while pension plans operate under a broader context for investment—each security being judged in terms of the portfolio as a whole—and an ERISA-mandated diversification requirement that often leads to wider asset-class exposures.

Unique circumstances: Endowment funds often are faced with unique situations that sometimes affect pension fund management, including the scrutiny of such special-interest groups as trustees, alumni, faculty, student organizations, local community pressure groups, etc., each with separate and often incompatible constraints and goals that may need to be accommodated in policy setting and/or in investment content. Similarly, endowment funds may be subjected to severe "social pressures" that, as in the case of tobacco firm divestment, can have an important investment impact by restricting the available universe of investment securities, mandating participation or nonparticipation in certain industries, sectors, or countries, or otherwise changing investment action from what it would otherwise have been. In pension fund investment, ERISA mandates that no other interests be put ahead of the interests of the beneficiaries in determining investment actions.

22.2. Identify the elements that are life-cycle driven in the two schemes of objectives and constraints.

22.3. *a.* Policy, asset allocation.

b. Constraint, regulation.

c. Objective, return requirement.

d. Constraint, horizon.

e. Policy, market timing.

f. Constraint, taxes.

g. Objectives, risk tolerance.

h. Constraint, liquidity.

Appendix A

References

Affleck-Graves, John, and Richard R. Mendenhall. "The Relation between the Value Line Enigma and Post-Earnings-Announcement Drift." *Journal of Financial Economics* 31 (February 1992), pp. 75–96.

Agarwal, Vikas; Naveen D. Daniel; and Narayan Y. Naik. "Why Is Santa So Kind to Hedge Funds? The December Return Puzzle!" March 29, 2007, **http://ssrn. com/abstract = 891169.**

Alexander, C. *Market Models.* Chichester, England: Wiley, 2001.

Alexander, Sidney. "Price Movements in Speculative Markets: Trends or Random Walks, No. 2." In *The Random Character of Stock Market Prices,* ed. Paul Cootner. Cambridge, MA: MIT Press, 1964.

Amihud, Yakov, and Haim Mendelson. "Asset Pricing and the Bid-Ask Spread." *Journal of Financial Economics* 17 (December 1986), pp. 223–50.

———. "Liquidity, Asset Prices, and Financial Policy." *Financial Analysts Journal* 47 (November/ December 1991), pp. 56–66.

Amin, G., and H. Kat. "Stocks, Bonds and Hedge Funds: Not a Free Lunch!" *Journal of Portfolio Management* 29 (Summer 2003), pp. 113–20.

Aragon, George O. "Share Restrictions and Asset Pricing: Evidence from the Hedge Fund Industry." *Journal of Financial Economics* 83 (2007), pp. 33–58.

Arbel, Avner. "Generic Stocks: An Old Product in a New Package." *Journal of Portfolio Management,* Summer 1985, pp. 4–13.

Arbel, Avner, and Paul J. Strebel. "Pay Attention to Neglected Firms." *Journal of Portfolio Management,* Winter 1983, pp. 37–42.

Arnott, Robert. "Orthodoxy Overwrought." *Institutional Investor,* December 18, 2006.

Asness, Cliff. "The Value of Fundamental Indexing." *Institutional Investor,* October 16, 2006, pp. 94–99.

Ball, R., and P. Brown. "An Empirical Evaluation of Accounting Income Numbers." *Journal of Accounting Research* 9 (1968), pp. 159–78.

Banz, Rolf. "The Relationship between Return and Market Value of Common Stocks." *Journal of Financial Economics* 9 (March 1981), pp. 3–18.

Barber, B.; R. Lehavy; M. McNichols; and B. Trueman. "Can Investors Profit from the Prophets? Security Analysts Recommendations and Stock Returns." *Journal of Finance* 56 (April 2001), pp. 531–63.

Barber, Brad, and Terrance Odean. "Trading Is Hazardous to Your Wealth: The Common Stock Investment Performance of Individual Investors." *Journal of Finance* 55 (2000), pp. 773–806.

———. "Boys Will Be Boys: Gender, Overconfidence, and Common Stock Investment." *Quarterly Journal of Economics* 16 (2001), pp. 262–92.

Barberis, Nicholas, and Richard Thaler. "A Survey of Behavioral Finance." In *The Handbook of the Economics of Finance,* ed. G. M. Constantinides, M. Harris, and R. Stulz. Amsterdam: Elsevier, 2003.

Basu, Sanjoy. "The Investment Performance of Common Stocks in Relation to Their Price-Earnings Ratios: A Test of the Efficient Market Hypothesis." *Journal of Finance* 32 (June 1977), pp. 663–82.

———. "The Relationship between Earnings Yield, Market Value, and Return for NYSE Common Stocks: Further Evidence." *Journal of Financial Economics* 12 (June 1983), pp. 129–56.

Battalio, R. H., and R. Mendenhall. "Earnings Expectation, Investor Trade Size, and Anomalous Returns around Earnings Announcements." *Journal of Financial Economics* 77 (2005), pp. 289–319.

Benveniste, Lawrence, and William Wilhelm. "Initial Public Offerings: Going by the Book." *Journal of Applied Corporate Finance* 10 (March 1997), pp. 98–108.

Bergstresser, D.; M. Desai; and J. Rauh. "Earnings Manipulation, Pension Assumptions, and Managerial Investment Decisions." *Quarterly Journal of Economics* 121 (2006), pp. 157–95.

Bernard, Victor L., and Jacob K. Thomas. "Post-Earnings-Announcement Drift: Delayed Price Response or Risk Premium?" *Journal of Accounting Research* 27 (1989), pp. 1–36.

Bernard, V., and J. Thomas. "Evidence That Stock Prices Do Not Fully Reflect the Implications of Current Earnings for Future Earnings." *Journal of Accounting and Economics* 13 (1990), pp. 305–40.

Bernhard, Arnold. *Value Line Methods of Evaluating Common Stocks.* New York: Arnold Bernhard, 1979.

Black, Fischer. "Yes, Virginia, There Is Hope: Tests of the Value Line Ranking System." Graduate School of Business, University of Chicago, 1971.

Black, Fischer; Michael C. Jensen; and Myron Scholes. "The Capital Asset Pricing Model: Some Empirical Tests." *Studies in the Theory of Capital Markets,* ed. Michael C. Jensen. New York: Praeger, 1972.

Black, Fischer, and Myron Scholes. "The Pricing of Options and Corporate Liabilities." *Journal of Political Economy* 81 (May–June 1973), pp. 637–59.

"*From Black-Scholes to Black Holes: New Frontiers in Options.*" *RISK Magazine.* London, 1992.

Blake, Christopher; Edwin J. Elton; and Martin J. Gruber. "The Performance of Bond Mutual Funds." *Journal of Business* 66 (July 1993), pp. 371–404.

717

Blume, Marshall E., and Robert F. Stambaugh. "Biases in Computed Returns: An Application to the Size Effect." *Journal of Finance Economics,* 1983, pp. 387–404.

Bogle, John C. "Investing in the 1990s: Remembrance of Things Past, and Things Yet to Come." *Journal of Portfolio Management,* Spring 1991, pp. 5–14.

———. *Bogle on Mutual Funds.* Burr Ridge, IL: Irwin, 1994.

Brav, Alon; Christopher Geczy; and Paul A. Gompers. "Is the Abnormal Return Following Equity Issuances Anomalous?" *Journal of Financial Economics* 56 (2000), pp. 209–49.

Brennan, Michael. "Taxes, Market Valuation and Corporate Financial Policy." *National Tax Journal,* 1970.

Brinson, G.; C. R. Hood; and G. Beebower. "Determinants of Portfolio Performance." *Financial Analysts Journal,* July–August 1986.

Brinson, Gary; Brian Singer; and Gilbert Beebower. "Determinants of Portfolio Performance." *Financial Analysts Journal,* May/June 1991.

Brock, William; Josef Lakonishok; and Blake LeBaron. "Simple Technical Trading Rules and the Stochastic Properties of Stock Returns." *Journal of Finance* 47 (December 1992), pp. 1731–64.

Brown, David, and Robert H. Jennings. "On Technical Analysis." *Review of Financial Studies* 2 (1989), pp. 527–52.

Brown, Lawrence D., and Michael Rozeff. "The Superiority of Analysts' Forecasts as Measures of Expectations: Evidence from Earnings." *Journal of Finance,* March 1978.

Brown. S. J.; W. Goetzmann; R. G. Ibbotson; and S. A. Ross. "Survivorship Bias in Performance Studies." *Review of Financial Studies* 5 (1992).

Brown, S. J.; W. N. Goetzmann; and B. Liang. "Fees on Fees in Funds of Funds." *Journal of Investment Management* 2 (2004), pp. 39–56.

Busse, J. A., and T. C. Green. "Market Efficiency in Real Time." *Journal of Financial Economics* 65 (2002), pp. 415–37.

Campbell, John Y., and Robert Shiller. "Stock Prices, Earnings and Expected Dividends." *Journal of Finance* 43 (July 1988), pp. 661–76.

Carhart, Mark. "On Persistence in Mutual Fund Performance." *Journal of Finance* 52 (1997), pp. 57–82.

Chen, Nai-fu; Richard Roll; and Stephen Ross. "Economic Forces and the Stock Market." *Journal of Business* 59 (1986), pp. 383–403.

Chopra, Navin; Josef Lakonishok; and Jay R. Ritter. "Measuring Abnormal Performance: Do Stocks Overreact?" *Journal of Financial Economics* 31 (1992), pp. 235–68.

Clarke, Roger, and Mark P. Kritzman. *Currency Management: Concepts and Practices.* Charlottesville: Research Foundation of the Institute of Chartered Financial Analysts, 1996.

Clayman, Michelle. "In Search of Excellence: The Investor's Viewpoint." *Financial Analysts Journal,* May–June 1987.

Connolly, Robert. "An Examination of the Robustness of the Weekend Effect." *Journal of Financial and Quantitative Analysis* 24 (June 1989), pp. 133–69.

Conrad, Jennifer, and Gautam Kaul. "Time-Variation in Expected Returns." *Journal of Business* 61 (October 1988), pp. 409–25.

Copeland, Thomas E., and David Mayers. "The Value Line Enigma (1965–1978): A Case Study of Performance Evaluation Issues." *Journal of Financial Economics,* November 1982.

Coval, Joshua D., and Tyler Shumway. "Do Behavioral Biases Affect Prices?" *Journal of Finance* 60 (February 2005), pp. 1–34.

Cremers, Martijn; Antti Petajisto; and Eric Zitzewitz. "Should Benchmark Indices Have Alpha? Revisiting Performance Evaluation." 2008, available at **http://ssrn.com/abstract=1108856.**

Davis, James L.; Eugene F. Fama; and Kenneth R. French. "Characteristics, Covariances, and Average Returns, 1929 to 1997." *Journal of Finance* 55 (2000), pp. 389–406.

De Bondt, W.F.M., and R. H. Thaler. "Does the Stock Market Overreact?" *Journal of Finance* 40 (1985), pp. 793–805.

———. "Further Evidence on Investor Overreaction and Stock Market Seasonality." *Journal of Finance* 42 (1987), pp. 557–81.

———. "Do Security Analysts Overreact?" *American Economic Review* 80 (1990), pp. 52–57.

———. "Financial Decision Making in Markets and Firms." In *Handbooks in Operations Research and Management Science, Vol. 9: Finance,* ed. R. A. Jarrow, V. Maksimovic, and W. T. Ziemba. Amsterdam: Elsevier, 1995.

DeLong, J. Bradford; Andrei Schleifer; Lawrence Summers; and Robert Waldmann. "Noise Trader Risk in Financial Markets." *Journal of Political Economy* 98 (August 1990), pp. 704–38.

DeMarzo, Peter M.; Ron Kaniel; and Ilan Kremer. "Diversification as a Public Good: Community Effects in Portfolio Choice." *Journal of Finance* 59 (August 2004), pp. 1677–1716.

de Soto, Hernando. *The Mystery of Capital: Why Capitalism Triumphs in the West and Fails Everywhere Else.* New York: Basic Books, 2000.

Dimson, E.; P. R. Marsh; and M. Staunton. *Millennium Book II: 101 Years of Investment Returns.* London: ABN-Amro and London Business School, 2001.

Douglas, George W. "Risk in Equity Markets: An Empirical Appraisal of Market Efficiency." *Yale Economic Essays* IX (Spring 1969).

Dunn, Patricia, and Rolf D. Theisen. "How Consistently Do Active Managers Win?" *Journal of Portfolio Management* 9 (Summer 1983), pp. 47–53.

Elton, E. J.; M. J. Gruber; S. Das; and M. Hlavka. "Efficiency with Costly Information: A Reinterpretation of Evidence from Managed Portfolios." *Review of Financial Studies* 6 (1993), pp. 1–22.

Errunza, Vihang, and Etienne Losq. "International Asset Pricing under Mild Segmentation: Theory and Test." *Journal of Finance* 40 (March 1985), pp. 105–24.

Fama, Eugene. "The Behavior of Stock Market Prices." *Journal of Business* 38 (January 1965), pp. 34–105.

———. "Market Efficiencies, Long-Term Returns, and Behavioral Finance." *Journal of Financial Economics* 49 (September 1998), pp. 283–306.

Fama, Eugene, and Marshall Blume. "Filter Rules and Stock Market Trading Profits." *Journal of Business* 39 (Supplement, January 1966), pp. 226–41.

Fama, Eugene F., and Kenneth R. French. "Permanent and Temporary Components of Stock Prices." *Journal of Political Economy* 96 (1988), pp. 246–73.

———. "Dividend Yields and Expected Stock Returns." *Journal of Financial Economics* 22 (October 1988), pp. 3–25.

———. "Business Conditions and Expected Returns on Stocks and Bonds." *Journal of Financial Economics* 25 (November 1989), pp. 3–22.

————. "The Cross Section of Expected Stock Returns." *Journal of Finance* 47 (June 1992), pp. 427–65.

————. "Common Risk Factors in the Returns on Stocks and Bonds." *Journal of Financial Economics* 33 (1993), pp. 3–56.

————. "Multifactor Explanations of Asset Pricing Anomalies." *Journal of Finance* 51 (1996), pp. 55–84.

————. "The Equity Premium." *Journal of Finance* 57 (April 2002), pp. 637–60.

Fama, Eugene, and James MacBeth. "Risk, Return and Equilibrium: Empirical Tests." *Journal of Political Economy* 81 (March 1973).

Fisher, Irving. *The Theory of Interest: As Determined by Impatience to Spend Income and Opportunity to Invest It.* New York: Augustus M. Kelley, 1965, originally published in 1930.

Flannery, Mark J., and Christopher M. James. "The Effect of Interest Rate Changes on the Common Stock Returns of Financial Institutions." *Journal of Finance* 39 (September 1984), pp. 1141–54.

Foster, George; Chris Olsen; and Terry Shevlin. "Earnings Releases, Anomalies, and the Behavior of Security Returns." *The Accounting Review* 59 (October 1984).

French, Kenneth. "Stock Returns and the Weekend Effect." *Journal of Financial Economics* 8 (March 1980), pp. 55–69.

Froot, K. A., and E. M. Dabora. "How Are Stock Prices Affected by the Location of Trade?" *Journal of Financial Economics* 53 (1999), pp. 189–216.

Fung, William, and David Hsieh. "Empirical Characteristics of Dynamic Trading Strategies: The Case of Hedge Funds." *Review of Financial Studies* 10 (1997), pp. 275–302.

Fung, William, and David Hsieh. "Performance Characteristics of Hedge Funds and CTA Funds: Natural versus Spurious Biases." *Journal of Financial and Quantitative Analysis* 35(2000), pp. 291–307.

Gervais, S., and T. Odean. "Learning to Be Overconfident." *Review of Financial Studies* 14 (2001), pp. 1–27.

Geske, Robert, and Richard Roll. "On Valuing American Call Options with the Black-Scholes European Formula." *Journal of Finance* 39 (June 1984), pp. 443–56.

Getmansky, Mila; Andrew W. Lo; and Igor Makarov. "An Econometric Model of Serial Correlation and Illiquidity in Hedge Fund Returns." *Journal of Financial Economics* 74 (2004), pp. 529–609.

Ghysels, E.; A. Harvey; and E. Renault. "Stochastic Volatility." In *Statistical Methods in Finance,* ed. C. Rao and G. Maddala. Amsterdam: Elsevier Science, North-Holland Series in Statistics and Probability, 1996.

Gibbons, Michael, and Patrick Hess. "Day of the Week Effects and Asset Returns." *Journal of Business* 54 (October 1981), pp. 579–98.

Givoly, Dan, and Dan Palmon. "Insider Trading and Exploitation of Inside Information: Some Empirical Evidence." *Journal of Business* 58 (1985), pp. 69–87.

Goetzmann, William N., and Roger G. Ibbotson. "Do Winners Repeat?" *Journal of Portfolio Management,* Winter 1994, pp. 9–18.

Graham, J. R., and C. R. Harvey. "Expectations of Equity Risk Premia, Volatility and Asymmetry from a Corporate Finance Perspective." 2001, available at SSRN, **http://ssrn.com/abstract=292623.**

————. "Grading the Performance of Market Timing Newsletters." *Financial Analysts Journal* 53 (November/December 1997), pp. 54–66.

Grieves, Robin, and Alan J. Marcus. "Riding the Yield Curve: Reprise." *Journal of Portfolio Management,* Winter 1992.

Grinblatt, Mark, and Bing Han. "Prospect Theory, Mental Accounting, and Momentum." *Journal of Financial Economics* 78 (November 2005), pp. 311–39.

Grinblatt, Mark, and Sheridan Titman. "Mutual Fund Performance: An Analysis of Quarterly Portfolio Holdings." *Journal of Business* 62 (1989), pp. 393–416.

Grossman, Sanford J., and Joseph E. Stiglitz. "On the Impossibility of Informationally Efficient Markets." *American Economic Review* 70 (June 1980), pp. 393–408.

Hasanhodzic, Jasmina, and Andrew W. Lo. "Can Hedge Fund Returns Be Replicated?: The Linear Case." *Journal of Investment Management* 5 (2007), pp. 5–45.

Haugen, Robert A. *The New Finance: The Case Against Efficient Markets.* Englewood Cliffs, NJ: Prentice Hall, 1995.

Hendricks, Darryll; Jayendu Patel; and Richard Zeckhauser. "Hot Hands in Mutual Funds: Short-Run Persistence of Relative Performance, 1974–1988." *Journal of Finance* 43 (March 1993), pp. 93–130.

Henriksson, Roy D. "Market Timing and Mutual Fund Performance: An Empirical Investigation." *Journal of Business* 57 (January 1984).

Heston, S. L. "A Closed-Form Solution for Options with Stochastic Volatility with Applications to Bonds and Currency Options." *Review of Financial Studies* 6 (1993), pp. 327–43.

Hirshleifer, David. "Investor Psychology and Asset Pricing." *Journal of Finance* 56 (August 2001), pp. 1533–97.

Homer, Sidney, and Martin L. Leibowitz. *Inside the Yield Book: New Tools for Bond Market Strategy.* Englewood Cliffs, NJ: Prentice Hall, 1972.

Hull, J. C., and A. White. "The Pricing of Options on Assets with Stochastic Volatilities." *Journal of Finance* 42 (1987), pp. 281–300.

Ibbotson, Roger G. "Price Performance of Common Stock New Issues." *Journal of Financial Economics* 2 (September 1975).

Ibbotson, Roger; Richard C. Carr; and Anthony W. Robinson. "International Equity and Bond Returns." *Financial Analysts Journal,* July–August 1982.

Ibbotson, R. G., and L. B. Siegel. "The World Market Wealth Portfolio." *Journal of Portfolio Management,* Winter 1983.

Ibbotson, R. G.; L. B. Siegel; and K. Love. "World Wealth: Market Values and Returns." *Journal of Portfolio Management,* Fall 1985.

Jacquier, Eric, and Alan Marcus. "Asset Allocation Models and Market Volatility." *Financial Analysts Journal* 57 (March/April 2001), pp. 16–30.

Jaffe, Jeffrey F. "Special Information and Insider Trading." *Journal of Business* 47 (July 1974), pp. 410–28.

————. "Gold and Gold Stocks as Investments for Institutional Portfolios." *Financial Analysts Journal* 45 (March–April 1989), pp. 53–59.

Jagannathan, R.; E. R. McGrattan; and A. Scherbina. "The Declining U.S. Equity Premium." *Federal Reserve Bank of Minneapolis Quarterly Review* 24 (Fall 2000), pp. 3–19.

Jagannathan, Ravi, and Zhenyu Wang. "The Conditional CAPM and the Cross-Section of Expected Returns." *Staff Report 208,* Federal Reserve Bank of Minneapolis, 1996.

Jegadeesh, Narasimhan. "Evidence of Predictable Behavior of Security Returns." *Journal of Finance* 45 (September 1990), pp. 881–98.

Jegadeesh, N.; J. Kim; S. D. Krische; and C. M. Lee. "Analyzing the Analysts: When Do Recommendations Add Value?" *Journal of Finance* 59 (June 2004), pp. 1083–1124.

Jegadeesh, Narasimhan, and Sheridan Titman. "Returns to Buying Winners and Selling Losers: Implications for Stock Market Efficiency." *Journal of Finance* 48 (March 1993), pp. 65–91.

Jensen, Michael C. "The Performance of Mutual Funds in the Period 1945–1964." *Journal of Finance,* May 1968.

———. "Risk, the Pricing of Capital Assets, and the Evaluation of Investment Portfolios." *Journal of Business* 42 (April 1969), pp. 167–247.

Kahneman, D., and A. Tversky. "Subjective Probability: A Judgment of Representativeness." *Cognitive Psychology* 3 (1972), pp. 430–54.

———. "On the Psychology of Prediction." *Psychology Review* 80 (1973), pp. 237–51.

Keim, Donald B. "Size Related Anomalies and Stock Return Seasonality: Further Empirical Evidence." *Journal of Financial Economics* 12 (June 1983), pp. 13–32.

Keim, Donald B., and Robert F. Stambaugh. "Predicting Returns in the Stock and Bond Markets." *Journal of Financial Economics* 17 (1986), pp. 357–90.

Kendall, Maurice. "The Analysis of Economic Time Series, Part I: Prices." *Journal of the Royal Statistical Society* 96 (1953), pp. 11–25.

Kopcke, Richard W., and Geoffrey R. H. Woglom. "Regulation Q and Savings Bank Solvency—The Connecticut Experience." In *The Regulation of Financial Institutions,* Federal Reserve Bank of Boston Conference Series, No. 21, 1979.

Kosowski, R.; A. Timmermann; R. Wermers; and H. White. "Can Mutual Fund 'Stars' Really Pick Stocks? New Evidence from a Bootstrap Analysis." *Journal of Finance* 61 (December 2006), pp. 2551–95.

Kothari, S. P.; Jay Shanken; and Richard G. Sloan. "Another Look at the Cross-Section of Expected Stock Returns." *Journal of Finance* 50 (March 1995), pp. 185–224.

Kotlikoff, Laurence J., and Avia Spivack. "The Family as an Incomplete Annuities Market." *Journal of Political Economy* 89, no. 2 (April 1981), pp. 372–91.

Kotlikoff, Laurence J., and Lawrence H. Summers. "The Role of Intergenerational Transfers in Aggregate Capital Accumulation." *The Journal of Political Economy* 89, no. 4 (August 1981), pp. 706–32.

Lakonishok, Josef; Andrei Shleifer; and Robert W. Vishny. "Contrarian Investment, Extrapolation, and Risk." *Journal of Finance* 50 (1995), pp. 1541–78.

Lamont, O. A., and R. H. Thaler. "Can the Market Add and Subtract? Mispricing in Tech Carve-outs." *Journal of Political Economy* 111 (2003), pp. 227–68.

La Porta, Raphael. "Expectations and the Cross-Section of Stock Returns." *Journal of Finance* 51 (December 1996), pp. 1715–42.

Latane, H. A., and C. P. Jones. "Standardized Unexpected Earnings—1971–1977." *Journal of Finance,* June 1979.

Lease, R.; W. Lewellen; and G. Schlarbaum. "Market Segmentation: Evidence on the Individual Investor." *Financial Analysts Journal* 32 (1976), pp. 53–60.

Lee, C. M.; A. Shleifer; and R. H. Thaler. "Investor Sentiment and the Closed-End Fund Puzzle." *Journal of Finance* 46 (March 1991), pp. 75–109.

Lehmann, Bruce. "Fads, Martingales and Market Efficiency." *Quarterly Journal of Economics* 105 (February 1990), pp. 1–28.

Levy, Robert A. "The Predictive Significance of Five-Point Chart Patterns." *Journal of Business* 44 (July 1971), pp. 316–23.

Liebowitz, Martin L., and Alfred Weinberger. "Contingent Immunization—Part I: Risk Control Procedure." *Financial Analysts Journal* 38 (November–December 1982).

Lo, Andrew W., and Craig MacKinlay. "Stock Market Prices Do Not Follow Random Walks: Evidence from a Simple Specification Test." *Review of Financial Studies* 1 (Spring 1988), pp. 41–66.

Loeb, T. F. "Trading Cost: The Critical Link between Investment Information and Results." *Financial Analysts Journal,* May–June 1983.

Longin, F., and B. Solnik. "Is the Correlation in International Equity Returns Constant: 1960–1990?" *Journal of International Money and Finance* 14 (1995), pp. 3–26.

Lynch, Peter, with John Rothchild. *One Up on Wall Street.* New York: Penguin Books, 1989.

Macaulay, Frederick. *Some Theoretical Problems Suggested by the Movements of Interest Rates, Bond Yields, and Stock Prices in the United States since 1856.* New York: National Bureau of Economic Research, 1938.

Malkiel, Burton G. "Expectations, Bond Prices, and the Term Structure of Interest Rates." *Quarterly Journal of Economics* 76 (May 1962), pp. 197–218.

———. "Returns from Investing in Equity Mutual Funds: 1971–1991." *Journal of Finance* 50 (June 1995), pp. 549–72.

Malkiel, Burton G., and Atanu Saha. "Hedge Funds: Risk and Return." *Financial Analysts Journal* 61 (2005), pp. 80–88.

Marcus, Alan J. "The Magellan Fund and Market Efficiency." *Journal of Portfolio Management* 17 (Fall 1990), pp. 85–88.

Mayers, David. "Nonmarketable Assets and Capital Market Equilibrium under Uncertainty." In *Studies in the Theory of Capital Markets,* ed. M. C. Jensen. New York: Praeger, 1972.

McDonald, Robert L. *Derivative Markets,* 2nd ed. Boston: Addison-Wesley, 2005.

Merton, Robert C. "Theory of Rational Option Pricing." *Bell Journal of Economics and Management Science* 4 (Spring 1973), pp. 141–83.

———. "On Market Timing and Investment Performance: An Equilibrium Theory of Value for Market Forecasts." *Journal of Business* 54 (July 1981).

———. "A Simple Model of Capital Market Equilibrium with Incomplete Information." *Journal of Finance* 42 (1987), pp. 483–510.

Miller, Merton H., and Myron Scholes. "Rate of Return in Relation to Risk: A Re-examination of Some Recent Findings." In *Studies in the Theory of Capital Markets,* ed. Michael C. Jensen. New York: Praeger, 1972.

Modigliani, Franco, and M. Miller. "The Cost of Capital, Corporation Finance, and the Theory of Investment." *American Economic Review,* June 1958.

———. "Dividend Policy, Growth, and the Valuation of Shares." *Journal of Business,* October 1961.

Modigliani, Franco, and Leah Modigliani. "Risk-Adjusted Performance." *Journal of Portfolio Management,* Winter 1997, pp. 45–54.

Morrell, John A. "Introduction to International Equity Diversification." In *International Investing for U.S. Pension Funds,* Institute for Fiduciary Education, London/Venice, May 6–13, 1989.

Niederhoffer, Victor, and Patrick Regan. "Earnings Changes, Analysts' Forecasts, and Stock Prices." *Financial Analysts Journal,* May–June 1972.

Norby, W. C. "Applications of Inflation-Adjusted Accounting Data." *Financial Analysts Journal,* March–April 1983.

Odean, T. "Are Investors Reluctant to Realize Their Losses?" *Journal of Finance* 53 (1998), pp. 1775–98.

Patel, J. M., and M. A. Wolfson. "The Intraday Speed of Adjustment of Stock Prices to Earnings and Dividend Announcements." *Journal of Financial Economics* 13 (June 1984), pp. 223–52.

Perold, André. "Fundamentally Flawed Indexing." HBS mimeo, January 2007.

Perry, Kevin, and Robert A. Taggart. "The Growing Role of Junk Bonds in Corporate Finance." *Continental Bank Journal of Applied Corporate Finance* 1 (Spring 1988).

Pontiff, Jeffrey. "Closed-End Fund Premia and Returns Implications for Financial Market Equilibrium." *Journal of Financial Economics* 37 (1995), pp. 341–70.

———. "Costly Arbitrage: Evidence from Closed-End Funds." *Quarterly Journal of Economics* 111 (November 1996), pp. 1135–51.

Porter, Michael E. *Competitive Advantage: Creating and Sustaining Superior Performance.* New York: Free Press, 1985.

———. *Competitive Strategy: Techniques for Analyzing Industries and Competitors.* New York: Free Press, 1980.

Poterba, James M., and Lawrence Summers. "Mean Reversion in Stock Market Prices: Evidence and Implications." *Journal of Financial Economics* 22 (1988), pp. 27–59.

Rau, P. R.; O. Dimitrov; and M. Cooper. "A Rose.com by Any Other Name." *Journal of Finance* 56 (2001), pp. 2371–88.

Ready, Mark J. "Profits from Technical Trading Rules." *Financial Management* 31 (Autumn 2002), pp. 43–62.

Redington, F. M. "Review of the Principle of Life-Office Valuations." *Journal of the Institute of Actuaries* 78 (1952), pp. 286–340.

Reinganum, Marc R. "The Anatomy of a Stock Market Winner." *Financial Analysts Journal,* March–April 1988, pp. 272–84.

———. "The Anomalous Stock Market Behavior of Small Firms in January: Empirical Tests for Tax-Loss Effects." *Journal of Financial Economics* 12 (June 1983), pp. 89–104.

Rendleman, Richard J., Jr.; Charles P. Jones; and Henry A. Latané. "Empirical Anomalies Based on Unexpected Earnings and the Importance of Risk Adjustments." *Journal of Financial Economics* 10 (November 1982), pp. 269–87.

Ritter, Jay R. "The Buying and Selling Behavior of Individual Investors at the Turn of the Year." *Journal of Finance* 43 (July 1988), pp. 701–17.

Roberts, Harry. "Stock Market 'Patterns' and Financial Analysis: Methodological Suggestions." *Journal of Finance* 14 (March 1959), pp. 11–25.

Roll, Richard. "A Critique of the Capital Asset Theory Tests: Part I: On Past and Potential Testability of the Theory." *Journal of Financial Economics* 4 (1977).

———. "The International Crash of October 1987." *Financial Analysts Journal,* September–October 1988.

Ross, Stephen A. "Neoclassical Finance, Alternative Finance and the Closed End Fund Puzzle." *European Financial Management* 8 (2002), pp. 129–37, **ssrn.com/abstract = 313444.**

———. "Return, Risk and Arbitrage." In *Risk and Return in Finance,* ed. I. Friend and J. Bicksler. Cambridge, MA: Ballinger, 1976.

Rubinstein, Mark. "Implied Binomial Trees." *Journal of Finance* 49 (July 1994), pp. 771–818.

Sadka, Ronnie. "Liquidity Risk and the Cross-Section of Hedge-Fund Returns." Working paper, Boston College, December 2008.

Samuelson, Paul. "The Judgment of Economic Science on Rational Portfolio Management." *Journal of Portfolio Management* 16 (Fall 1989), pp. 4–12.

Schleifer, Andrei. *Inefficient Markets.* New York: Oxford University Press, 2000.

Schleifer, Andrei, and Robert Vishny. "Equilibrium Short Horizons of Investors and Firms." *American Economic Review* 80 (May 1990), pp. 148–53.

———. "The Limits of Arbitrage." *Journal of Finance* 52 (March 1997), pp. 35–55.

Seyhun, H. Nejat. "Insiders' Profits, Costs of Trading and Market Efficiency." *Journal of Financial Economics* 16 (1986), pp. 189–212.

Sharpe, William F. "Asset Allocation: Management Style and Performance Evaluation." *Journal of Portfolio Management,* Winter 1992, pp. 7–19.

———. "Mutual Fund Performance." *Journal of Business* 39 (January 1966).

———. "A Simplified Model for Portfolio Analysis." *Management Science* IX (January 1963), pp. 277–93.

Shefrin, Hersh. *Beyond Greed and Fear.* Boston: Harvard Business School Press, 2002.

Shefrin, Hersh, and Meir Statman. "The Disposition to Sell Winners Too Early and Ride Losers Too Long: Theory and Evidence." *Journal of Finance* 40 (July 1985), pp. 777–90.

Shiller, Robert. "Do Stock Prices Move Too Much to Be Justified by Subsequent Changes in Dividends?" *American Economic Review* 71 (June 1981).

Solnik, B. *International Investing,* 4th ed. Reading, MA: Addison-Wesley, 1999.

Solnik, Bruno, and A. De Freitas. "International Factors of Stock Price Behavior." CESA Working Paper, February 1986 (cited in Bruno Solnik, *International Investments.* Reading, MA: Addison-Wesley, 1988).

Speidell, Lawrence S., and Vinod Bavishi. "GAAP Arbitrage: Valuation Opportunities in International Accounting Standards." *Financial Analysts Journal,* November–December 1992, pp. 58–66.

Statman, Meir. "Behavioral Finance." *Contemporary Finance Digest* 1 (Winter 1997), pp. 5–22.

Stickel, Scott E. "The Effect of Value Line Investment Survey Rank Changes on Common Stock Prices." *Journal of Financial Economics* 14 (1986), pp. 121–44.

Taleb, Nassim N. *Fooled by Randomness: The Hidden Role of Chance in Life and in the Markets.* New York: TEXERE (Thomson), 2004).

Taleb, Nassim N. *The Black Swan: The Impact of the Highly Improbable.* New York: Random House, 2007.

Thaler, Richard H. *The Winner's Curse.* Princeton, NJ: Princeton University Press, 1992.

———. *Advances in Behavioral Finance.* New York: Russell Sage Foundation, 1993.

Thompson, Rex. "The Information Content of Discounts and Premiums on Closed-End Fund Shares." *Journal of Financial Economics* 6 (1978), pp. 151–86.

Tobin, James. "Liquidity Preference as Behavior toward Risk." *Review of Economic Studies* XXVI (February 1958), pp. 65–86.

Treynor, Jack L. "How to Rate Management Investment Funds." *Harvard Business Review* 43 (January–February 1966).

Treynor, Jack L., and Kay Mazuy. "Can Mutual Funds Outguess the Market?" *Harvard Business Review* 43 (July–August 1966).

Treynor, Jack, and Fischer Black. "How to Use Security Analysis to Improve Portfolio Selection." *Journal of Business* 46 (January 1973).

Trippi, Robert R., and Duane Desieno. "Trading Equity Index Futures with Neural Networks." *Journal of Portfolio Management* 19 (Fall 1992).

Trippi, Robert R.; Duane Desieno; and Efraim Turban, eds. *Neural Networks in Finance and Investing.* Chicago: Probus, 1993.

Wallace, A. "Is Beta Dead?" *Institutional Investor* 14 (July 1980), pp. 22–30.

Whaley, Robert E. "Valuation of American Call Options on Dividend-Paying Stocks: Empirical Tests." *Journal of Financial Economics* 10 (1982), pp. 29–58.

Wiggins, J. B. "Option Values under Stochastic Volatilities." *Journal of Financial Economics* 19 (1987), pp. 351–72.

Womack, K. L. "Do Brokerage Analysts' Recommendations Have Investment Value?" *Journal of Finance* 51 (March 1996), pp. 137–67.

References To CFA Questions

Each end-of-chapter CFA question is reprinted with permission from the CFA Institute, Charlottesville, Virginia.[1] Following is a list of the CFA questions in the end-of-chapter material and the exams/study guides from which they were taken and updated.

Chapter 2

CFA 1. 1986 Level II CFA Study Guide, © 1986.

Chapter 3

CFA 1–3. 1986 Level I CFA Study Guide, © 1986.

Chapter 5

CFA 1–3. 1998 Level I CFA Study Guide, © 1998.

CFA 4–6. 1991 Level I CFA Study Guide, © 1991.

CFA 7–11. 1993 Level I CFA Study Guide, © 1993.

Chapter 6

CFA 1. 1998 Level I CFA Study Guide, © 1998.

CFA 2. 2001 Level III CFA Study Guide, © 2001.

CFA 3. 2001 Level II CFA Study Guide, © 2001.

CFA 4–6. 1982 Level III CFA Study Guide, © 1982.

CFA 7. 2000 Level II CFA Study Guide, © 2000.

Chapter 7

CFA 1. 1998 Level I CFA Study Guide, © 1998.

[1] The CFA Institute does not endorse, promote, review, or warrant the accuracy of the product or services offered by The McGraw-Hill Companies.

CFA 2. 2000 Level II CFA Study Guide, © 2000.

CFA 3. 2002 Level II CFA Study Guide, © 2002.

CFA 4. 2001 Level II CFA Study Guide, © 2001.

CFA 5–14. Various CFA exams.

Chapter 8

CFA 1–5. 1993 Level I CFA Study Guide, © 1993.

CFA 6. 1998 Level I CFA Study Guide, © 1998.

CFA 7. 1981 Level I CFA Study Guide, © 1981.

CFA 8. 1989 Level III CFA Study Guide, © 1989.

CFA 9. 1996 Level III CFA Study Guide, © 1996.

CFA 10. 1996 Level III CFA Study Guide, © 1996.

CFA 11. 1996 Level III CFA Study Guide, © 1996.

Chapter 9

CFA 1. 2000 Level III CFA Study Guide, © 2000.

CFA 2. 2001 Level III CFA Study Guide, © 2001.

CFA 3. 2004 Level III CFA Study Guide, © 2004.

CFA 4. 2003 Level III CFA Study Guide, © 2003.

CFA 5. 2002 Level III CFA Study Guide, © 2002.

Chapter 10

CFA 1. From various CFA exams.

CFA 2. 1999 Level II CFA Study Guide, © 1999.

CFA 3. 1992 Level II CFA Study Guide, © 1992.

CFA 4. 1993 Level I CFA Study Guide, © 1993.

CFA 5. 1994 Level I CFA Study Guide, © 1994.

Chapter 11

CFA 1. 1985 Level I CFA Study Guide, © 1985.

CFA 2. 1985 Level I CFA Study Guide, © 1985.

CFA 3. 1992 Level II CFA Study Guide, © 1992.

CFA 4. 1983 Level III CFA Study Guide, © 1983.

CFA 5. 2001 Level II CFA Study Guide, © 2001.

CFA 6. 2003 Level II CFA Study Guide, © 2003.

CFA 7. 2004 Level II CFA Study Guide, © 2004.

CFA 8–9. 1983 Level III CFA Study Guide, © 1983.

CFA 10. From various CFA exams.

CFA 11–12. 1983 Level III CFA Study Guide, © 1983.

Chapter 12

CFA 1. 1995 Level II CFA Study Guide, © 1995.

CFA 2. 1993 Level II CFA Study Guide, © 1993.

CFA 3. 1993 Level II CFA Study Guide, © 1993.

CFA 4. 1998 Level II CFA Study Guide, © 1998.

CFA 5. 2004 Level II CFA Study Guide, © 2004.

CFA 6. From various CFA exams.

Chapter 13

CFA 1. 1998 Level I CFA Study Guide, © 1998.

CFA 2. 1995 Level II CFA Study Guide, © 1995.

CFA 3. 1987 Level I CFA Study Guide, © 1987.

CFA 4. 2001 Level II CFA Study Guide, © 2001.

CFA 5. 1994 Level II CFA Study Guide, © 1994.

CFA 6. 2003 Level I CFA Study Guide, © 2003.

CFA 7. 2003 Level I CFA Study Guide, © 2003.

CFA 8. 2003 Level II CFA Study Guide, © 2003.

CFA 9. 2001 Level II CFA Study Guide, © 2001.

CFA 10. 2001 Level II CFA Study Guide, © 2001.

CFA 11. 2001 Level II CFA Study Guide, © 2001.

Chapter 14

CFA 1. 2002 Level II CFA Study Guide, © 2002.

CFA 2. 1988 Level I CFA Study Guide, © 1988.

CFA 3. 1998 Level II CFA Study Guide, © 1998.

CFA 4. 1992 Level I CFA Study Guide, © 1992.

CFA 5. 1987 Level I CFA Study Guide, © 1987.

CFA 6. 1998 Level II CFA Study Guide, © 1998.

CFA 7. 1999 Level II CFA Study Guide, © 1999.

CFA 8. 1998 Level II CFA Study Guide, © 1998.

Chapter 15

CFA 1. 1984 Level III CFA Study Guide, © 1984.

CFA 2. 2000 Level II CFA Study Guide, © 2000.

CFA 3. 1984 Level III CFA Study Guide, © 1984.

CFA 4. 2001 Level II CFA Study Guide, © 2001.

CFA 5. 2002 Level II CFA Study Guide, © 2002.

Chapter 16

CFA 1. 2000 Level I CFA Study Guide, © 2000.

CFA 2. 2000 Level I CFA Study Guide, © 2000.

CFA 3. 2000 Level II CFA Study Guide, © 2000.

Chapter 17

CFA 1–3. 1998 Level I CFA Study Guide, © 1998.

CFA 4. 1982 Level III CFA Study Guide, © 1982.

CFA 5. 1986 Level III CFA Study Guide, © 1986.

CFA 6. 2000 Level II CFA Study Guide, © 2000.

CFA 7. 1993 Level I CFA Study Guide, © 1993.

CFA 8. 2000 Level III Study Guide, © 2000.

CFA 9. 2004 Level II CFA Study Guide, © 2004.

Chapter 18

CFA 1–3. From various CFA exams.

CFA 4. 1981 Level I Study Guide, © 1981.

CFA 5. 1981 Level I Study Guide, © 1981.

CFA 6. 2000 Level I Study Guide, © 2000.

Chapter 19

CFA 1. 1986 Level III Study Guide, © 1986.

CFA 2. 1986 Level III Study Guide, © 1986.

CFA 3. 1991 Level II Study Guide, © 1991.

CFA 4. 1998 Level II Study Guide, © 1998.

Chapter 22

CFA 1. 1988 Level I CFA Study Guide, © 1988.

CFA 2. 1988 Level I CFA Study Guide, © 1988.

CFA 3. From various CFA exams.

CFA 4. From various CFA exams.

CFA 5. 1981 Level II CFA Study Guide, © 1981.

CFA 6. 1985 Level III CFA Study Guide, © 1985.

CFA 7. 1988 Level I CFA Study Guide, © 1988.

CFA 8. 1982 Level III CFA Study Guide, © 1982.

CFA 9–10. From various CFA exams.

Entries in **bold** indicate a definition on that page. Page numbers with an *f* indicate material found in figures; an *n*, notes; a *t*, tables.

Useful Formulas

Measures of Risk

Variance of returns: $\sigma^2 = \sum_s p(s)[r(s) - E(r)]^2$

Standard deviation: $\sigma = \sqrt{\sigma^2}$

Covariance between
returns: $\mathrm{Cov}(r_i, r_j) = \sum_s p(s)[r_i(s) - E(r_i)]\,[r_j(s) - E(r_j)]$

Beta of security i: $\beta_i = \dfrac{\mathrm{Cov}(r_i, r_M)}{\mathrm{Var}(r_M)}$

Portfolio Theory

Expected rate of return on a portfolio
with weights w_i in each security: $E(r_p) = \sum_{i=1}^{n} w_i E(r_i)$

Variance of portfolio rate of return: $\sigma_p^2 = \sum_{j=1}^{n} \sum_{i=1}^{n} w_j w_i \,\mathrm{Cov}(r_i, r_j)$

Market Equilibrium

The security market line: $E(r_i) = r_f + \beta_i[E(r_M) - r_f]$

Fixed-Income Analysis

Present value of $1:

Discrete period compounding: $PV = 1/(1 + r)^T$

Continuous compounding: $PV = e^{-rT}$

Forward rate of interest for period T: $f_T = \dfrac{(1 + y_T)^T}{(1 + y_{T-1})^{T-1}} - 1$

Real interest rate: $r = \dfrac{1 + R}{1 + i} - 1$

where R is the nominal interest rate
and i is the inflation rate

Duration of a security: $D = \sum_{t=1}^{T} t \times \dfrac{CF_t}{(1 + y)^t} / \text{Price}$

Modified duration: $D^* = D/(1 + y)$

Useful Formulas

Measures of Risk

Variance of returns: $\sigma^2 = \sum_s p(s)[r(s) - E(r)]^2$

Standard deviation: $\sigma = \sqrt{\sigma^2}$

Covariance between returns: $\text{Cov}(r_i, r_j) = \sum_s p(s)[r_i(s) - E(r_i)]\,[r_j(s) - E(r_j)]$

Beta of security i: $\beta_i = \dfrac{\text{Cov}(r_i, r_M)}{\text{Var}(r_M)}$

Portfolio Theory

Expected rate of return on a portfolio with weights w_i in each security: $E(r_p) = \sum_{i=1}^{n} w_i E(r_i)$

Variance of portfolio rate of return: $\sigma_p^2 = \sum_{j=1}^{n} \sum_{i=1}^{n} w_j w_i \, \text{Cov}(r_i, r_j)$

Market Equilibrium

The security market line: $E(r_i) = r_f + \beta_i[E(r_M) - r_f]$

Fixed-Income Analysis

Present value of $1:

Discrete period compounding: $PV = 1/(1 + r)^T$

Continuous compounding: $PV = e^{-rT}$

Forward rate of interest for period T: $f_T = \dfrac{(1 + y_T)^T}{(1 + y_{T-1})^{T-1}} - 1$

Real interest rate: $r = \dfrac{1 + R}{1 + i} - 1$

where R is the nominal interest rate and i is the inflation rate

Duration of a security: $D = \sum_{t=1}^{T} t \times \dfrac{CF_t}{(1 + y)^t} \Big/ \text{Price}$

Modified duration: $D^* = D/(1 + y)$